A Review of the Events of 1972

The 1973 World Book Year Book

The Annual Supplement to The World Book Encyclopedia

Field Enterprises Educational Corporation

Chicago London Paris Rome Stuttgart Sydney Tokyo Toronto

Staff

Editorial Director
William H. Nault

Editorial Staff

Executive Editor
Wayne Wille

Managing Editor
Paul C. Tullier

Chief Copy Editor
Joseph P. Spohn

Senior Editors
Allan Davidson, Ed Nelson,
Darlene R. Stille,
Foster P. Stockwell, Lillian Zahrt

Assistant Copy Editor
Helen Howell Dixon

Index Editor
Pamela Williams

Editorial Assistants
Irene Laura, Andrea Wallis

Executive Editor,
The World Book Encyclopedia
A. Richard Harmet

Art Staff

Executive Art Director
Gordon J. Kwiatkowski

Senior Art Director
Clifford L. Birklund

Art Director
for Year Book
Robert Schemmel

Senior Artist
Gumé Nuñez

Artists
Roberta Dimmer,
Norton Rock, Wilma Stevens

Cartographic Designer
Leon Bishop

Photography Director
Fred C. Eckhardt, Jr.

Assistant Photography Director
Ann Eriksen

Senior Photographs Editors
Marilyn Gartman
John Marshall

Art Production Director
Barbara J. McDonald

Art Quality Control
Alfred J. Mozdzen

Research and Services

Director of Educational Services
John Sternig

Director of Editorial Services
Carl A. Tamminen

Head, Editorial Research
Jo Ann McDonald

Head, Cartographic Services
Joseph J. Stack

Cartographer
H. George Stoll

Cartographic Designer
Mary Jo Schrader

Cartographic Researcher
Maria Stewart

Manufacturing Staff

Executive Director
Philip B. Hall

Production Manager
Joseph C. LaCount

Assistant Production Manager
Patrick Kelly

Manager, Research
and Development
Henry Koval

Manager, Pre-Press
John Babrick

Assistant Manager, Pre-Press
Marguerite DuMais

Printed in the United States of America
ISBN 0-7166-0473-6
Library of Congress Catalog Card Number: 62-4818

Preface

The making of a YEAR BOOK is comparable to putting together the intricate mechanisms of a watch. Unless each part fits precisely, it will not perform the function for which it was created.

The two-part, 44-page section entitled "Traditional Africa in a Modern World" that begins on page 94 is this edition's equivalent of a complex timepiece. The first part is a Trans-Vision® unit tracing Africa's past; the second part is a Special Report that deals with its present and future.

Work actually began on the section in May, 1971, when we decided that one of the most timely things we could do in the 1973 edition would be provide insights into an area that is one of the most important–but least known–in the world. As we do with all such projects, we turned to acknowledged experts to help prepare the section. We wanted to ensure that it not only would be factually accurate, but would address itself to significant matters. Two noted scholars joined us for the Trans-Vision®. One was Kenneth Onwuka Dike, professor of history at Harvard University and former vice-chancellor of the University of Ibadan in Nigeria. The other was Donald E. Vermeer, associate professor of geography and anthropology at Louisiana State University. Each visited our editorial offices several times for all-day work sessions. Visits were made to them. Letters and telephone calls added to the flow of information. When we decided to include an essay on how modern historians look at Africa, Professor Dike suggested just the person to write it. He was Sylvanus J. S. Cookey, then at the University of California, Los Angeles, and now chairman of the African Studies Committee at the State University of New York at Binghamton.

Consultants Dike, at left, and Vermeer

Finally, to complete the section, we asked Philip D. Curtin, a historian at the University of Wisconsin and one of the United States most eminent Africanists, to write the Special Report. The teamwork between these four scholars and our editors, artists, and cartographers has resulted in a section of which all of us are proud. We believe that you, too, will find it interesting, educational, and provocative.

WAYNE WILLE

Contents

A chronology of the most important events of 1972 appears on pages 8 to 14. A preview of 1973 is given on pages 627 and 628.

Contributors

Abrams, Edward, Ph.D.; Director of Technical Development, Chemetron Corporation. [CHEMICAL INDUSTRY]

Alexiou, Arthur G., M.S., E.E.; Program Director, Office of Sea Grant Programs, National Science Foundation. [OCEAN]

Anderson, Joseph P., M.S., LL.D.; Consultant, National Association of Social Workers. [MEDICARE; Social Organizations]

Arnold, Rus, Photojournalism Editor, *Writer's Digest.* [PHOTOGRAPHY]

Banovetz, James M., Ph.D.; Professor of Political Science and Director, Center for Governmental Studies, Northern Illinois University. [CITY; City Articles; HOUSING]

Bautz, Laura P., Ph.D.; Assistant Professor of Astronomy, Northwestern University. [ASTRONOMY]

Bazell, Robert J., B.A., C. Phil.; News Writer, *New York Post.* [SCIENCE AND RESEARCH]

Beaumont, Lynn, Travel and Public Relations Consultant. [FAIRS AND EXPOSITIONS; TRAVEL]

Beckwith, David C., J.D.; Correspondent, *Time* Magazine. [COURTS AND LAWS]

Benson, Barbara N., A.B., M.S.; Graduate Assistant, Southern Illinois University. [BOTANY; ZOOLOGY]

Berger, Ivan, Electronics Editor, *Popular Mechanics* Magazine. [ELECTRONICS]

Berkwitt, George J., B.S.J.; Senior Editor, *Dun's Review* Magazine. [MANUFACTURING]

Bornstein, Leon, B.A., M.A.; Labor Economist, U.S. Dept. of Labor. [LABOR]

Boyum, Joy Gould, Ph.D.; Associate Professor of English, New York University. [MOTION PICTURES]

Bradley, Van Allen, B.J.; former Literary Editor, *Chicago Daily News.* [LITERATURE]

Bradsher, Henry S., A.B., B.J.; Correspondent, *The Washington Star.* [KOREA, NORTH; KOREA, SOUTH; PHILIPPINES]

Brown, Kenneth, European Journalist. [Western Europe Articles]

Brown, Madison B., M.D.; Acting President, American Hospital Association. [HOSPITALS]

Burger, Warren E., LL.B.; Chief Justice of the United States. [Special Report Essay: TOWARD SPEEDIER JUSTICE]

Cain, Charles C., III, B.A.; Automotive Writer, Associated Press. [AUTOMOBILE]

Carroll, Paul, M.A.; Professor of English; Chairman, Program for Writers, University of Illinois at Chicago Circle. [POETRY]

Collins, William G., B.S., M.A.; Research Meteorologist, National Meteorological Center. [WEATHER]

Cook, Robert C.; Population Consultant, National Parks Association. [POPULATION, WORLD]

Cookey, Sylvanus J. S., Ph.D.; Chairman, African Studies Committee, State University of New York at Binghamton; formerly Lecturer in History, University of California, Los Angeles. [Trans-Vision® Essay: THE STUDY OF AFRICA'S HISTORY]

Cromie, William J., B.S.; Vice-President and Editor, Universal Science News, Inc. [ASTRONAUTS]

Csida, June Bundy; Former Radio-TV Editor, *Billboard* Magazine. [RADIO; TELEVISION; Special Report: THE SECOND FEMINIST REVOLT]

Curtin, Philip D., Ph.D.; Professor of History and African Studies, University of Wisconsin. [Special Report: AFRICA: OLD AND NEW]

Cuscaden, Rob; Author; Architecture Critic, *Chicago Sun-Times.* [ARCHITECTURE]

Cviic, Chris, B.A., B.Sc.; Editorial Staff, *The Economist.* [Eastern Europe Articles]

Dale, Edwin L., Jr., B.A.; Reporter, *The New York Times,* Washington Bureau. [INTERNATIONAL TRADE AND FINANCE]

Davies, Richard P., B.S.; Medical Writer. [HEALTH AND DISEASE; MEDICINE; MENTAL HEALTH]

Delaune, Lynn de Grummond, M.A.; Assistant Professor, College of William and Mary; Author. [LITERATURE FOR CHILDREN]

Dewald, William G., Ph.D.; Professor of Economics, Ohio State University. [Finance Articles]

Dike, Kenneth O., Ph.D.; Professor of History, Harvard University. [Consultant, Africa Trans-Vision®]

Evans, Earl A., Jr., Ph.D.; Professor and Chairman, Department of Biochemistry, University of Chicago. [BIOCHEMISTRY; BIOLOGY]

Farr, David M. L., D.Phil.; Professor of History, Carleton University, Ottawa. [CANADA; MICHENER, ROLAND; TRUDEAU, PIERRE ELLIOTT]

Feather, Leonard; Author, *The Encyclopedia of Jazz in the Sixties.* [MUSIC, POPULAR; RECORDINGS]

Flynn, Betty, B.A.; UN Correspondent, *Chicago Daily News.* [UNITED NATIONS]

French, Charles E., Ph.D.; Head, Agricultural Economics Department, Purdue University. [AGRICULTURE]

Gayn, Mark, B.S.; Asia Bureau Chief, *The Toronto Star;* Author. [BANGLADESH; CHINA; INDIA; PAKISTAN]

Goldner, Nancy, B.A.; Critic, *Dance News* and *Christian Science Monitor.* [DANCING]

Goldstein, Jane, B.A.; U.S. Representative, International Racing Bureau. [HORSE RACING]

Goy, Robert W., Ph.D.; Director, Wisconsin Regional Primate Research Center. [PSYCHOLOGY]

Grasso, Thomas X., M.A.; Associate Professor and Chairman, Department of Geosciences, Monroe Community College. [GEOLOGY]

Griffin, Alice, Ph.D.; Professor of English, Lehman College, City University of New York. [THEATER]

Havighurst, Robert J., Ph.D.; Professor of Education and Human Development, University of Chicago. [OLD AGE]

Healey, Gerald B.; Midwest Editor, *Editor & Publisher* Magazine. [NEWSPAPERS]

Hechinger, Fred M., B.A.; Education Editor, *The New York Times.* [EDUCATION]

Holmes, Jay E., B.A.; Program Manager, Research Utilization, National Science Foundation. [SPACE EXPLORATION]

Jacobi, Peter P., B.S.J., M.S.J.; Professor and Associate Dean, Medill School of Journalism, Northwestern University. [MUSIC, CLASSICAL]

Jessup, Mary E., B.A.; former News Editor, *Civil Engineering* Magazine. [DRUGS; Engineering Articles; PETROLEUM AND GAS]

Joseph, Lou, B.A.; Assistant Director, Bureau of Public Information, American Dental Association. [DENTISTRY]

Kind, Joshua B., Ph.D.; Associate Professor of Art History, Northern Illinois University; Author, *Rouault;* Midwest Correspondent, *Art News.* [VISUAL ARTS]

Koenig, Louis W., Ph.D., L.H.D.; Professor of Government, New York University; Author: *The Life and Times of William Jennings Bryan.* [CIVIL RIGHTS]

Lach, Alma, Diplome de Cordon Bleu; Author, *Cooking à la Cordon Bleu.* [FOOD]

Levy, Emanuel, B.A.; Editor, *Insurance Advocate.* [INSURANCE]

Lewis, Ralph H., M.A.; Chief, Branch of Museum Operations, National Park Service. [MUSEUMS]

Litsky, Frank, B.S.; Assistant Sports Editor, *The New York Times.* [Sports Articles]

Livingston, Kathryn Zahony, B.A.; Feature Editor, *Town and Country.* [FASHION]

Maki, John M., Ph.D.; Vice-Dean, College of Arts and Sciences, University of Massachusetts. [JAPAN]

Malia, Thomas M., Ph.B.; Executive Editor, *Telecommunications Reports.* [COMMUNICATIONS]

Marty, Martin E., Ph.D.; Associate Editor, *The Christian Century.* [PROTESTANT; RELIGION; Special Report: ECUMENISM IN THE '70s]

McGaffin, William, B.A., B.Sc.; Washington Correspondent, *Chicago Daily News.* [Political and Government Articles]

Montmeat, John K., B.S.; Marketing Manager, Magazine Publishers Association. [MAGAZINES]

Morton, Elizabeth H., LL.D.; Former Editor in Chief, Canadian Library Association. [CANADIAN LIBRARY ASSOCIATION; CANADIAN LITERATURE]

Mullen, Frances A., Ph.D.; Consultant on Education of the Handicapped. [CHILD WELFARE]

Nelson, Larry L., Ph.D.; Executive Vice-President, Snyder Associates, Inc. [AGRICULTURE]

Newman, Andrew L., M.A.; Deputy Director of Information, U.S. Department of the Interior. [Conservation Articles]

Norman, Lloyd H., B.S.; Military Affairs Correspondent, *Newsweek* Magazine. [ARMED FORCES OF THE WORLD; ESPIONAGE; NATIONAL DEFENSE]

O'Connor, James J., E. E.; Editor in Chief, *Power* Magazine. [ENERGY]

O'Leary, Theodore M., B.A.; Regional Correspondent, *Sports Illustrated* Magazine. [BRIDGE, CONTRACT; CHESS; COIN COLLECTING; GAMES, MODELS, AND TOYS; HOBBIES; PET; STAMP COLLECTING]

Petacque, Art; Investigative Reporter covering crime and government, *Chicago Sun-Times.* [CRIME]

Plog, Fred, Ph.D.; Assistant Professor, Department of Anthropology, University of California, Los Angeles. [ANTHROPOLOGY; ARCHAEOLOGY]

Pyle, Howard; President, National Safety Council. [SAFETY]

Rabb, George B., Ph.D.; Associate Director, Research and Education, Chicago Zoological Park. [ZOOS AND AQUARIUMS]

Reed, Michael, B.S.; Managing Editor, WORLD BOOK SCIENCE YEAR. [Biographies; CELEBRATIONS]

Rogers, Morris E., B.S.; Chicago Area Editor, *Drovers Journal.* [INTERNATIONAL LIVE STOCK EXPOSITION]

Rowen, Joseph R., A.B.; Vice-President, National Retail Merchants Association. [RETAILING]

Rowse, Arthur E., I.A., M.B.A.; President, Consumer News, Inc. [ADVERTISING; CONSUMER AFFAIRS]

Samson, Jack, B.A.; Editor, *Field & Stream.* [HUNTING AND FISHING]

Schaefle, Kenneth E., M.B.A.; President, The Communication Center, Inc. [AVIATION; TRANSIT; TRANSPORTATION]

Schmemann, The Reverend Alexander, S.T.D., D.D., LL.D., Th.D.; Dean, St. Vladimir's Orthodox Theological Seminary, New York. [EASTERN ORTHODOX CHURCHES]

Schubert, Helen C., B.S.; Home Furnishings Writer. [INTERIOR DESIGN]

Scott, George, B.A.; Author; Journalist; Broadcaster; Staff Member, *The Economist.* [CYPRUS; GREAT BRITAIN; IRELAND; MALTA; NORTHERN IRELAND]

Shaw, Robert J., B.S.B.A.; Editor, *Library Technology Reports,* American Library Association. [LIBRARY]

Shearer, Warren W., Ph.D.; former Chairman, Department of Economics, Wabash College. [ECONOMY, THE]

Sheerin, John B., C.S.P., A.B., M.A., LL.D., J.D.; Editor, *Catholic World.* [ROMAN CATHOLIC CHURCH]

Shepherd, George W., Ph.D.; Professor, Graduate School of International Studies, University of Denver. [Africa Articles]

Shulvass, Moses A., Rabbi, M.A., Ph.D.; Professor of Jewish History, Spertus College of Judaica. [JEWS]

Smith, Henry H., Ph.D.; Director, Bureau of the Census, U.S. Department of Commerce. [CENSUS]

Snow, Richard E., Ph.D.; Associate Professor of Education, Stanford University. [Special Report: ALWAYS TESTING]

Soper, Mary Webster, B.A.; Editor, *Noticias* Magazine. [LATIN AMERICA; Latin America Articles]

Spencer, William, Ph.D.; Professor of History, Florida State University; Author, *Land and People of Algeria.* [Middle East Articles; North Africa Articles]

Stalker, John N., Ph.D.; Professor of History, University of Hawaii. [ASIA; Asia Articles]

Star, Jack, former Midwest Editor, *Look* Magazine. [Special Report: YOUR DAY (OR YEARS) IN COURT]

Steffek, Edwin F., B.S.; Editor, *Horticulture* Magazine. [GARDENING]

Struever, Stuart, Ph.D.; Professor of Anthropology, Northwestern University. [Special Report: A NEW LOOK AT EARLY MAN IN NORTH AMERICA]

Swanson, Curtis E., B.A.; Manager, Public Relations, American Library Association. [AMERICAN LIBRARY ASSOCIATION]

Thompson, Carol L., M.A.; Editor, *Current History* Magazine. [U.S. Government Articles]

Trombley, William, M.S.; Education Writer, The *Los Angeles Times.* [Special Report: THE PRESCOTT EXPERIMENT]

Vermeer, Donald E., Ph.D.; Associate Professor of Geography and Anthropology, Louisiana State University. [Consultant, Africa Trans-Vision®]

von Smolinski, Alfred W., Ph.D.; Assistant Professor of Chemistry, University of Illinois at the Medical Center. [CHEMISTRY]

Weber, Robert H., B.A., M.A.; Director of Publications, Council of State Governments. [STATE GOVERNMENT]

White, Thomas O., Ph.D.; Physicist, National Accelerator Laboratory, Batavia, Ill. [PHYSICS]

Contributors not listed on these pages are members of the WORLD BOOK YEAR BOOK editorial staff.

Chronology 1972

January

Sun	Mon	Tue	Wed	Thu	Fri	Sat
						1
2	3	4	5	6	7	8
9	10	11	12	13	14	15
16	17	18	19	20	21	22
23	24	25	26	27	28	29
30	31					

1 **The Federation of Arab Republics** flag is raised simultaneously in ceremonies held in Cairo, Egypt; Damascus, Syria; and Tripoli, Libya.

7 **President Nixon officially announces** his candidacy for a second presidential term.
Lewis F. Powell, Jr., and William H. Rehnquist are sworn in as the 99th and 100th members of the Supreme Court of the United States.

10 **Sheik Mujibur Rahman** takes over as leader of the new nation of Bangladesh.

13 **Prime Minister Kofi A. Busia** of Ghana is overthrown by Ghanaian army officers in a bloodless coup d'état.

15 **Princess Margrethe is proclaimed** Queen Margrethe II following the death of her father King Frederik IX; she becomes the first reigning queen in the history of Denmark.
Malta cancels deadline for the evacuation of all British forces from the island.

17 **Canadian air traffic controllers strike** closes 116 airports and forces the rerouting of international flights.
United States seizes Russian fishing vessels in the Bering Sea; the commander of the Russian fishing fleet and two shipmasters are charged with violating U.S. fishing regulations.
Black Rhodesians riot in protest against Great Britain's independence agreement with the all-white government of Rhodesia.
Longshoremen strike closes West Coast ports; Taft-Hartley injunction had opened the ports on Oct. 16, 1971, after a 100-day strike.

18 **The 92nd Congress reconvenes** for its second session.

20 **President Nixon** delivers his State of the Union message to Congress.

22 **Signing the Treaty of Brussels,** Denmark, Great Britain, Ireland, and Norway agree to join the European Community (Common Market) subject to ratification by their parliaments and electorates.
India creates three new states and two union territories in the northeastern region, increasing the number of states to 21 and union territories to 9.

24 **Sheik Khalid bin Mohammed al-Qasimi,** ruler of the state of Sharja in the Union of Arab Emirates, is assassinated in an attempted coup.

25 **President Nixon's peace proposal** offers a total cease-fire in Indochina, withdrawal of all U.S. and allied forces within six months of Hanoi's acceptance, and a new presidential election for South Vietnam.

27 **Maurice H. Stans resigns** as U.S. secretary of commerce.
Air traffic controllers end strike in Canada and submit to binding arbitration.

30 **President Philibert Tsiranana** of Malagasy Republic, running unopposed, is re-elected.
Violent clash in Londonderry, Northern Ireland, between British soldiers and Roman Catholics, who were taking part in a civil rights demonstration, leaves 13 dead.

February

Sun	Mon	Tue	Wed	Thu	Fri	Sat
		1	2	3	4	5
6	7	8	9	10	11	12
13	14	15	16	17	18	19
20	21	22	23	24	25	26
27	28	29				

2 **Rioters burn British Embassy** in Dublin, Ireland, during protest over the Londonderry killings.

3 **Winter Olympic Games open** in Sapporo, Japan; about 1,300 athletes from 35 countries compete in the 11th Winter Games.

4 **The last members** of Thailand's 12,000-man force in South Vietnam are withdrawn.
The UN Security Council concludes a special eight-day session in Addis Ababa, Ethiopia; it is the first session held outside New York City in 20 years and the first ever held in Africa.

5 **United States gets Greek home-port** facilities for the Sixth Fleet at Piraeus in pact announced jointly by the United States and Greece.

6 **More than 30,000 Irish demonstrators** join civil rights march at Newry, Northern Ireland, in defiance of a ban.

7 **Keith J. Holyoake** resigns as prime minister of New Zealand after nearly 12 years in office; he is succeeded by Deputy Prime Minister John Marshall of the ruling National Party.

8 **West Coast dock strike** negotiators reach a tentative agreement.

9 **British coal strike,** the first nationwide shut-down in 46 years, enters its sixth week; the government bans use of electricity for advertising and display in an effort to conserve power.

15 **Attorney General John N. Mitchell resigns** (as of March 1) to head President Nixon's campaign for re-election.
President José María Velasco Ibarra of Ecuador is overthrown in a bloodless coup.

21 **President Nixon arrives in Peking** for talks with Chinese leaders, including Mao Tse-tung and Chou En-lai. He becomes the first U.S. President to visit China while in office.

22 **Sheik Ahmed bin Ali al-Thani,** ruler of the Persian Gulf emirate of Qatar, is deposed in a bloodless coup and replaced by his cousin, Sheik Khalifa bin Hammad al-Thani.
Attempted coup led by disgruntled members of the armed forces fails in Congo (Brazzaville).

25 **Colonel Arturo Armando Molina** is proclaimed president-elect of El Salvador after all candidates fail to gain an absolute majority in the February 20 elections.

26 **After only nine days in office,** Prime Minister Giulio Andreotti and his Cabinet resign, ending Italy's 34th government since World War II.

27 **Communiqué on U.S.-China talks** reveals that President Nixon pledged to remove all U.S. troops from Taiwan, the Nationalist Chinese base of President Chiang Kai-shek. Nixon and Premier Chou En-lai of China also pledged a new era of peaceful coexistence, increased trade, and scientific, sports, and cultural exchanges.

28 **President Nixon returns to United States** and describes his visit to China as the trip that "changed the world."

March

Sun	Mon	Tue	Wed	Thu	Fri	Sat
			1	2	3	4
5	6	7	8	9	10	11
12	13	14	15	16	17	18
19	20	21	22	23	24	25
26	27	28	29	30	31	

2 **Russia and Bangladesh sign** agreements providing aid for the new Asian nation.
United States launches *Pioneer 10* from Cape Kennedy, Fla., on an unmanned flight that will take it past the planet Jupiter in December, 1973, and then out of the solar system.

7 **Syria forms a five-party** national front in a major government shakeup.

10-12 **National black political convention,** first in U.S. history, is held in Gary, Ind., with about 3,300 voting delegates and 5,000 observers attending.

12 **Last Indian troops** leave Bangladesh.
The Congress Party of Prime Minister Indira Gandhi wins control in 14 of India's 17 states in Indian state elections.

13 **United States and Chinese envoys** meet in Paris for the first time since President Nixon's trip to China.
Great Britain and China establish full diplomatic relations after Britain acknowledges that Taiwan is a "province" of China.

15 **Jordan's King Hussein I** proposes a new Arab state composed of two semiautonomous regions—Jordan and the West Bank region now occupied by Israel.

16 **Israel rejects Jordan plan** for a semiautonomous Palestinian state.
The first U.S. draft call for 1972 takes men with lottery numbers from 1 to 15.

18 **China explodes nuclear device** in the atmosphere.

19 **A 25-year mutual defense pact** is signed by Prime Minister Indira Gandhi of India and Sheik Mujibur Rahman of Bangladesh.

21 **Chiang Kai-shek is re-elected** to his fifth six-year term as president of Taiwan.

22 **Senate approves women's rights** amendment to the U.S. Constitution;
Hawaii becomes the first state to ratify the amendment.

23 **United States halts Paris peace talks** until North Vietnamese Communists show willingness for serious discussion on issues defined in advance.

24 **Britain suspends home rule** in Northern Ireland and takes over Ulster government.

26 **Britain and Malta sign pact** allowing British forces to continue using military bases on Malta.

28 **Ulster Parliament closes** as 100,000 Protestants demonstrate in Belfast following suspension of provincial government by Britain.

30 **North Vietnamese attack** across the Demilitarized Zone in the biggest offensive since 1968; the United States calls the drive an invasion of South Vietnam.

April

Sun	Mon	Tue	Wed	Thu	Fri	Sat
						1
2	3	4	5	6	7	8
9	10	11	12	13	14	15
16	17	18	19	20	21	22
23	24	25	26	27	28	29
30						

1 **Major-league players strike** against baseball club owners in a pension dispute; it is the first strike in 102 years of organized baseball.

3 **U.S. Secretary of the Navy** John H. Chafee resigns.

4 **United States recognizes Bangladesh**; Secretary of State William P. Rogers says the United States will open an embassy there.

5 **Colombian university students** boycott classes to express solidarity with striking teachers, after violent disturbances in Bogotá.

6 **United States resumes massive bombing** of North Vietnam after a 3½-year pause; U.S. naval vessels also bombard targets in North Vietnam.
Egypt breaks relations with Jordan over King Hussein's proposal for a federated state of Jordanians and Palestinians.

10 **About 70 nations sign treaty** prohibiting the stockpiling of biological weapons at ceremonies in Washington, London, and Moscow.

14 **The Pakistani National Assembly** approves an interim Constitution and sets April 21 as the end of martial law in the nation.

15 **President Nixon concludes** Canada visit; he and Prime Minister Pierre Elliott Trudeau pledge joint efforts to combat pollution in the Great Lakes.
The Uruguayan Congress declares a 30-day "state of internal war" in an effort to eliminate leftist Tupamaro guerrillas.

16 ***Apollo 16* astronauts** lift off from Cape Kennedy, Florida, on the first manned mission to the mountains of the moon.

18 **Bangladesh joins** the Commonwealth of Nations.

20 **General Ne Win resigns** as army chief of staff to become prime minister of Burma's first civilian government in 10 years.

22 **Quebec teachers and civil servants** return to their jobs after the Canadian government passes legislation ending an 11-day strike over salary increases.

27 ***Apollo 16* splashes down** safely in the Pacific Ocean; astronauts John W. Young and Charles M. Duke, Jr., spent a record 20 hours 14 minutes walking, working, and driving on the moon.

May

Sun	Mon	Tue	Wed	Thu	Fri	Sat
	1	2	3	4	5	6
7	8	9	10	11	12	13
14	15	16	17	18	19	20
21	22	23	24	25	26	27
28	29	30	31			

2 **J. Edgar Hoover,** the first and only director of the Federal Bureau of Investigation (FBI) in its 48-year history, dies in Washington, D.C.
L. Patrick Gray III is named acting director.

7-8 **National elections in Italy** give ruling Christian Democratic Party predominant position in Parliament.

8 **President Nixon** orders the mining of Haiphong and other harbors in North Vietnam.

9 **United States and Brazil sign treaty** regulating operations of U.S. shrimp boats within the 200-mile offshore limit set by Brazil.

10 **President Nguyen Van Thieu** declares martial law in South Vietnam, the first time since the Tet offensive in 1968 that such a law has been imposed.
Ireland's voters approve overwhelmingly membership in the European Community (Common Market).

11 **Uganda reopens border with Sudan** after 17 years.
FBI will recruit women as special agents, acting director L. Patrick Gray III announces.

15 **Burundi's President** Michel Micombero announces government forces defeated rebels seeking to overthrow his government after three weeks of fighting.
Governor George C. Wallace of Alabama is shot and seriously wounded while campaigning for Democratic nomination for President in Laurel, Md. His assailant, Arthur H. Bremer, was arrested.
The United States formally returns Okinawa and other Ryukyu Islands to Japan, ending 27 years of American rule.

16 **John B. Connally resigns** as secretary of the treasury; George P. Shultz is named to succeed him.

17 **West German Bundestag** (Parliament) approves nonaggression treaties with Russia and Poland.

18 **Malagasy Republic President** Philibert Tsiranana yields full power to General Gabriel Ramanantsoa, army chief of staff, after several weeks of antigovernment violence by students and workers.

19 **A bomb explodes** in the Pentagon, causing damage estimated at $75,000.

20 **Chiang Kai-shek is sworn** in for his fifth term as president of Taiwan.

21 **Michelangelo's *Pietà,*** one of the world's sculptural masterpieces, is severely damaged in St. Peter's Basilica in the Vatican by Laszlo Toth, a Hungarian-born emigré.

22 **Ceylon is proclaimed** the independent Socialist Republic of Sri Lanka under a new Constitution, ending its status as a British dominion. Sirimavo Bandaranaike is sworn in as the republic's first prime minister.

President Nixon arrives in Moscow, the first U.S. President to visit the Russian capital. Mr. Nixon subsequently signs accords covering space, health, and environmental cooperation.

26 **President Nixon** and Russian party leader Leonid I. Brezhnev sign agreements that for the first time put limits on strategic weapons.

30 **Three Japanese terrorists** attack the Lod International Airport near Tel Aviv, Israel, killing 28 persons and wounding 76 others. The Japanese were reportedly recruited by a Palestinian commando group.

27-28 **Council of Ministers** of the Southeast Asia Treaty Organization hold their annual meeting in Canberra, Australia.

28 **General Frederick C. Weyland** succeeds General Creighton W. Abrams as U.S. commander in South Vietnam following Abrams' appointment as Army chief of staff.

June

Sun	Mon	Tue	Wed	Thu	Fri	Sat
				1	2	3
4	5	6	7	8	9	10
11	12	13	14	15	16	17
18	19	20	21	22	23	24
25	26	27	28	29	30	

1 **Chile recognizes** North Korea and North Vietnam, becoming the first South American country to establish diplomatic relations with both.

3 **The 3,000-ton frigate** *Nilgiri,* first warship built in India, is launched in Bombay.

Four-power Berlin accord, intended to ease tensions in that divided city, is signed by Great Britain, France, Russia, and the United States.

4 **Lon Nol is elected** to a five-year term as president of Cambodia.

5 **UN Conference on Human Environment** convenes in Stockholm, Sweden. About 1,200 delegates from 114 nations and about 400 international agencies attend the meetings.

12-15 **Organization of African Unity** annual meeting convenes in Rabat, Morocco, and is attended by representatives from 40 African nations, including 23 heads of state.

17 **Police arrest five men** at 2 A.M. in Democratic National Committee headquarters in Washington, D.C. The men, who had electronic surveillance equipment with them, were charged with second-degree burglary.

19 **One-day work stoppage** is carried out by airline pilots throughout the world to stress the need for more effective international sanctions against aircraft hijacking.

25 **Ex-President Juan D. Perón,** former dictator of Argentina now living in exile in Spain, is nominated for president by the Justicialista Party at its convention in Buenos Aires.

26 **The government of South Africa** announces it plans to give self-rule to Ovamboland, the most populous tribal area within the controversial territory of Namibia (South West Africa).

A new coalition government, headed by Prime Minister Giulio Andreotti, is sworn in.

July

Sun	Mon	Tue	Wed	Thu	Fri	Sat
						1
2	3	4	5	6	7	8
9	10	11	12	13	14	15
16	17	18	19	20	21	22
23	24	25	26	27	28	29
30	31					

3 **Marshal Lon Nol** swears himself in as first president of Cambodia.

India and Pakistan sign accord ending a diplomatic impasse that separated the two countries after their war in December, 1971.

4 **North and South Korea** agree to hold negotiations designed to reunite the divided country.

5 **A special session** of the Japanese Diet (Parliament) confirms the election of Kakuei Tanaka to succeed Eisaku Sato as prime minister.

6 **Premier Fidel Castro** ends a tour of 10 nations in Africa and Europe after an unprecedented two-month absence from Cuba.

10-13 **Senator George S. McGovern** (D., S.Dak.) wins the Democratic nomination for President at the party's convention in Miami Beach, Fla. He selects Senator Thomas F. Eagleton (D., Mo.) as his running mate.

13 **Paris peace talks** resume after a 10-week suspension.

16 **The Ghanaian government** announces it has thwarted a plot to restore exiled former Prime Minister Kofi Busia to power.

18 **President Anwar al-Sadat** orders Russian military advisers and experts to leave Egypt and declares that all Russian bases and equipment in the country will be under the sole control of Egyptian forces.

24 **Crown Prince** Jigme Singhi Wangchuk is crowned king of Bhutan, succeeding his father Jigme Dorji Wangchuk, who died two days earlier while visiting Nairobi, Kenya.

August

Sun	Mon	Tue	Wed	Thu	Fri	Sat
		1	2	3	4	5
6	7	8	9	10	11	12
13	14	15	16	17	18	19
20	21	22	23	24	25	26
27	28	29	30	31		

1 **Senator Eagleton formally withdraws** as Democratic Party vice-presidential candidate after disclosing he was hospitalized three times during the 1960s for nervous exhaustion.

2 **Egypt and Libya** agree to establish a unified political leadership by Sept. 1, 1973, thus creating the largest state in Africa.

4 **Representative John G. Schmitz** (R., Calif.), is nominated for President by the American Party at its convention in Louisville, Ky.

Jury convicts Arthur H. Bremer of attempting to assassinate Governor George C. Wallace; he is sentenced to 63 years in prison, including three 10-year sentences for assault with intent to murder the three other persons he shot on May 15.

5 **A decree restricting** South Vietnam's newspapers is announced by President Nguyen Van Thieu; newsmen and diplomatic observers regard it as an attempt to muzzle criticism of the Thieu regime.

Uganda's President Idi Amin Dada gives Asians with British passports three months to settle their affairs and emigrate to other countries.

6 **Egypt and Russia** announce that the withdrawal of Russian military advisers, pilots, and missile crews from Egypt has been completed.

Panama voters elect a new 505-member Assembly of Community Representatives in the first election held since General Omar Torrijos Herrera seized power in 1968.

8 **The Democratic National Committee** certifies presidential candidate George McGovern's choice of Sargent Shriver as his vice-presidential running mate to replace Senator Thomas F. Eagleton.

President Kristjan Eldjarn of Iceland is re-elected for a new term.

9 **President Américo Deus Rodrigues Thomaz** is sworn in for a third term as Portugal's chief executive following an uncontested election held July 25.

11 **India's second** atomic power plant begins operating. The 400-megawatt facility, built with Canadian aid, was located in Rajasthan State.

11-15 **UN Secretary-General** Kurt Waldheim visits China and confers with Premier Chou En-lai and other officials. It marks the first trip to mainland China by a UN secretary-general since a visit by Dag Hammarskjöld in 1954.

21 **A British dock strike** that tied up Britain's ports for more than three weeks ends as nearly 42,000 dockworkers return to work. Between 500 and 600 ships had been tied up in British ports during the strike.

Violent protests over acute food shortages prompt Chile's President Salvador Allende Gossens to declare a state of emergency in Santiago province.

21-23 **The Republican Party renominates** President Richard M. Nixon and Vice-President Spiro T. Agnew at its convention in Miami Beach, Fla.

22 **The Thieu government** issues a decree abolishing popular democratic elections in South Vietnam's 10,775 hamlets; the new statute makes all hamlet and village posts appointive positions.

25 **China casts its first veto** in the UN Security Council to bar Bangladesh from UN membership.

30 **Red Cross delegates** from North and South Korea meet for the first time in formal session in Pyongyang and agree to push efforts to reunite families separated in the two areas, "thus laying a stepping stone for unification of the fatherland."

September

Sun	Mon	Tue	Wed	Thu	Fri	Sat
					1	2
3	4	5	6	7	8	9
10	11	12	13	14	15	16
17	18	19	20	21	22	23
24	25	26	27	28	29	30

1 **President Nixon meets** Japanese Prime Minister Kakuei Tanaka in Hawaii; they agree on short-term measures designed to cut a U.S. trade deficit with Japan.

4 **Kalevi Sorsa** is sworn in as prime minister of a four-party coalition cabinet in Finland.

5 **Arab terrorists,** members of the Black September organization, slip into the Olympic Village in Munich, West Germany, kill two members of the Israeli Olympic team, and seize nine others as hostages. Later that same day, the hostages are killed at a military airport during a shoot-out between the terrorists and West German police and soldiers.

8 **Israeli aircraft attack** Arab guerrilla bases and naval installations in Lebanon and Syria in retaliation for the slaying of 11 Israeli Olympic athletes in Munich.

14 **West Germany and Poland agree** to establish diplomatic relations and open embassies in their respective capitals.

19 **The 27th session of the UN** General Assembly convenes in New York City under the gavel of its new president, Stanislaw Trepczynski of Poland, who was elected on September 12.

20 **An attempted invasion** by about 1,000 guerrilla troops based in Tanzania is thwarted by government forces in Uganda.

21 **Large-scale maneuvers** by the North Atlantic Treaty Organization (NATO) end in Norway; they featured 65,000 men, 350 ships, and about 700 aircraft from 12 nations and are believed to be the largest NATO maneuvers ever held.

23 **President Ferdinand E. Marcos** declares a state of martial law throughout the Philippines because of terrorist activities.

24-25 **Norwegian voters,** in a national referendum, reject entry into the European Community with 53.6 per cent of the electorate opposed and 46.4 per cent in favor.

26 **Heavy border fighting** erupts between the military forces of the two Yemens.

29 **Chinese and Japanese leaders,** meeting in Peking, end the legal state of war that has existed for 35 years and agree to establish diplomatic relations.

October

Sun	Mon	Tue	Wed	Thu	Fri	Sat
1	2	3	4	5	6	7
8	9	10	11	12	13	14
15	16	17	18	19	20	21
22	23	24	25	26	27	28
29	30	31				

2 **Danish voters approve** membership in the European Community.

3 **Anker Jorgensen,** a member of Parliament since 1964, succeeds Jens Otto Krag as prime minister of Denmark. Krag had resigned for personal reasons.

5 **Uganda and Tanzania** sign an agreement ending hostilities that erupted in September when Tanzania-based guerrillas attempted to invade Uganda.

6 **Poland and France** sign a 10-year treaty of friendship and cooperation.

7 **Prime Minister Trygve Bratteli** of Norway and his Labor government resign after referendum rejects membership in the European Community. Lars Korvald is asked by King Olav V to form a new government.

12 **General Gabriel Ramanantsoa** takes full control of the Malagasy Republic government and replaces President Philibert Tsiranana.

17 **President Chung Hee Park** suspends the Constitution and proclaims martial law throughout South Korea.

18 **Months of negotiations end** as the United States and Russia reach agreement on a three-year trade pact; the Russians agree to settle their lend-lease debts of World War II.

26 **Army forces in Dahomey** oust the ruling Presidential Council and dissolve the National Consultative Assembly.

Presidential Adviser Henry A. Kissinger announces that "peace is at hand" in Indochina after weeks of intensive secret talks with representatives of both North and South Vietnam.

President Justin Ahomadegbe of Dahomey is ousted and replaced by an 11-man military junta.

30 **In the closest federal election** in Canadian history, the opposition Progressive Conservative Party led by Robert L. Stanfield captures 107 seats to 109 won by Prime Minister Pierre Elliott Trudeau and the Liberal Party.

November

Sun	Mon	Tue	Wed	Thu	Fri	Sat
			1	2	3	4
5	6	7	8	9	10	11
12	13	14	15	16	17	18
19	20	21	22	23	24	25
26	27	28	29	30		

2 **Koca Popovic,** a major Serbian political figure in Yugoslavia's government, resigns from the federal presidency in protest against President Tito's antinationalism policy.
Australia's Parliament is formally dissolved pending elections scheduled for December.
5 **A series of strikes** in 21 provinces of Chile end after President Salvador Allende Gossens agrees to meet labor demands.
6 **East and West Germany** reach agreement on a treaty preparing the way for diplomatic relations between the two countries as well as their eventual admission to UN membership.
7 **President Nixon,** in a landslide victory, wins re-election to a second term; he carries 49 of the 50 states. Spiro T. Agnew continues as Vice-President.
Rafael Hernández Colón, in an unexpected political upset, wins the race for governor of Puerto Rico over Luis A. Ferré, who had sought re-election.
8 **Pakistan formally withdraws** as a member of the Southeast Asia Treaty Organization.
13 **Japanese Prime Minister** Kakuei Tanaka dissolves the House of Representatives and announces elections will be held in December.
17 **Ex-President Juan D. Perón,** after spending 17 years in exile, returns to Argentina in anticipation of presidential elections scheduled for 1973.
19 **West German Chancellor** Willy Brandt and his coalition government, in a national test of the voters' confidence, win an unexpectedly large margin of seats in the Bundestag.
28 **President Nixon** nominates Elliott L. Richardson as secretary of defense; he names Caspar W. Weinberger as his choice for secretary of health, education, and welfare.
29 **President Nixon** names Peter J. Brennan as his next secretary of labor.
The Netherlands' Catholic Party, the largest in the minority coalition government, suffers a major defeat by losing 7 of its 35 seats in Parliament.

December

Sun	Mon	Tue	Wed	Thu	Fri	Sat
					1	2
3	4	5	6	7	8	9
10	11	12	13	14	15	16
17	18	19	20	21	22	23
24	25	26	27	28	29	30
31						

5 **President Nixon announces** that James T. Lynn is his nominee for secretary of housing and urban development.
Edward Gough Whitlam, head of the Labor Party, is sworn in as prime minister of Australia; he succeeds William McMahon.
6 **Frederick B. Dent** is named President Nixon's choice for secretary of commerce; he will replace Peter G. Peterson.
7 ***Apollo 17,*** the last planned U.S. flight to the moon, lifts off from Cape Kennedy, Fla., at 12:33 A.M.
India and Pakistan sign accords ending their bitter dispute over a cease-fire line in Kashmir.
President Nixon names Claude S. Brinegar as his second-term secretary of labor.
Voters in Ireland, in a national referendum, overwhelmingly support a measure abolishing "the special position" occupied by the Roman Catholic Church in the Constitution.
8 **Florida becomes the first state** to reinstitute the death penalty; executions had been halted as a result of a ruling by the U.S. Supreme Court.
President Nixon's announcement that Richard G. Kleindienst will remain as attorney general completes the President's second-term Cabinet.
10 **Japanese Prime Minister Kakuei Tanaka** and his Liberal-Democratic Party are returned to power through a solid victory in nationwide elections.
11 **Two U.S. astronauts,** Eugene A. Cernan and Harrison H. Schmitt, land on the moon.
14 **Willy Brandt is inaugurated** for a second term as chancellor of the Federal Republic of (West) Germany.
18 **President Nixon** orders resumption of full-scale bombing of North Vietnam "until such time as a settlement is arrived at."
19 **The *Apollo 17* astronauts** splash down safely in the Pacific Ocean, completing man's ninth mission to the moon since 1968.
26 **Harry S. Truman,** 33rd President of the United States, dies.
30 **A halt to the bombing** of North Vietnam is ordered by President Nixon, who announces that Henry A. Kissinger will resume negotiations for a Vietnam settlement in Paris on Jan. 8, 1973.

Section One

The Year In Focus

THE YEAR BOOK Board of Editors analyzes some significant developments of 1972 and considers their impact on contemporary affairs. The Related Articles list following each report directs the reader to THE YEAR BOOK's additional coverage of related subjects.

Focus on The World

Alastair Buchan

In 1972, the shape of a new structure of world politics began to come into focus, with the United States, China, and Russia as the world's Big Three

Ten years ago, world politics were still dominated by the interaction of two hostile superpowers, the United States and Russia. At that time, these two nations possessed virtually a monopoly of nuclear weapons, generated nearly three-fourths of the world's wealth, and were each the center of a tightly knit system of alliances. Then, gradually, the international system started to become more multipolar in character, with the Sino-Soviet rift of the early 1960s, the development of the European Community (Common Market), and the rise of Japan to become the world's third economic giant. But the imminence of change was partly obscured through much of the 1960s by other developments: the Cultural Revolution in China, France's exclusion of Great Britain from the European Community, the Russian invasion of Czechoslovakia in 1968, and America's preoccupation with Vietnam.

The signs that a major realignment of world politics was impending began to accumulate after 1969–when China clearly identified Russia as a more serious adversary than the United States, President Richard M. Nixon announced a policy of withdrawal of U.S. troops from Vietnam, the United States and Russia embarked on serious negotiations on strategic arms limitations, and France began to withdraw its objections to the British entry into Europe. In 1970, the tide was partly reversed by the extension of the Vietnam War into Cambodia and by a serious flare-up in the Middle East. But in 1971, the process of change accelerated with the exploratory visit to Peking, China, by Henry A. Kissinger, the President's assistant for national security affairs, and the admission of China to the United Nations in October.

If 1971 was the year in which the end of the postwar bipolar world became readily apparent, 1972 was the year in which the outlines of a new structure of world politics began to emerge. This was partly as a consequence of American initiatives and a redefinition of the U.S. role in world affairs as one large power among several, rather than as the central pillar of world order, and partly as a consequence of the ramifications of China-Russia hostility.

The President's visit to China made Russia more ready to sign some agreements

In 1971, President Nixon had announced that he would visit both China and Russia in 1972, and on February 21 he arrived in Peking. His reception there was at first muted. Then, later the first day, he had an unscheduled hour-long meeting with Chairman Mao Tse-tung, and after it the warmth of the Chinese welcome rose perceptibly. In various official speeches, the President and Premier Chou En-lai spoke of the long-standing friendship of the American and Chinese people, and at the end of the visit a communiqué was issued that dealt primarily with the problem of Taiwan.

In one section of the communiqué, the United States said it "would progressively withdraw its forces and military installations in Taiwan as tension in the area diminishes, with complete withdrawal as an ultimate objective." It also spoke of new Sino-American scientific, technological, and cultural exchanges, and declared–without mentioning formal diplomatic recognition–that the two countries would stay in touch through various channels. In other sections of the communiqué, the Chinese stressed their desire for the reunification of both Korea and Vietnam and their opposition to Japanese militarism. The United States, by contrast, declared its interest in self-determination "for each country of Indochina," its support for South Korea, and its friendship for Japan. The United States also said it "acknowledges that all Chinese on either side of the Taiwan Strait maintain there is but one China, and that Taiwan is part of China." That statement represented a considerable American political concession to Peking. On his return to Washington, President Nixon spoke of his visit as "a week that had changed the world." But it was clear that the evolution of entirely normal relations between China and the United States would still be a matter of some years.

Leaders Nixon and Brezhnev

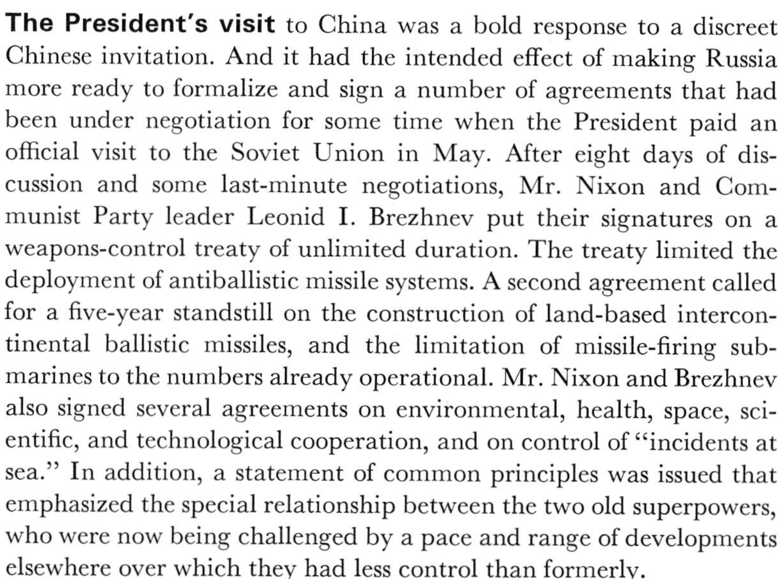

The President's visit to China was a bold response to a discreet Chinese invitation. And it had the intended effect of making Russia more ready to formalize and sign a number of agreements that had been under negotiation for some time when the President paid an official visit to the Soviet Union in May. After eight days of discussion and some last-minute negotiations, Mr. Nixon and Communist Party leader Leonid I. Brezhnev put their signatures on a weapons-control treaty of unlimited duration. The treaty limited the deployment of antiballistic missile systems. A second agreement called for a five-year standstill on the construction of land-based intercontinental ballistic missiles, and the limitation of missile-firing submarines to the numbers already operational. Mr. Nixon and Brezhnev also signed several agreements on environmental, health, space, scientific, and technological cooperation, and on control of "incidents at sea." In addition, a statement of common principles was issued that emphasized the special relationship between the two old superpowers, who were now being challenged by a pace and range of developments elsewhere over which they had less control than formerly.

But these two summit meetings–and the new triangular relationship between the United States, Russia, and China that they formalized–left a good deal of unfinished business in the relations of the great powers. One irritant was their differing perspectives on developments in the Indian subcontinent of Asia during the latter months of 1971 when the Awami League in East Pakistan successfully revolted against the parent regime in the West with the active aid of Indian troops. Russia fully supported the intervention of its ally India, and recognized the new independent state of Bangladesh in January, 1972. The United States withheld recognition of Bangladesh for several months. China not only refused to recognize Bangladesh, but in August it used its first veto as a member of the United Nations Security Council to prevent Bangladesh's entry into the United Nations.

Japan was left hanging in the air by the fast changes in Big Three relations

An important country also left hanging in the air by the swift evolution in the relations of the new Big Three was Japan, which had not been privy to the change of American policy toward China, and which feels closely affected by the possibility of a change in the status of Taiwan. The government of Prime Minister Eisaku Sato came under increasing criticism from both the left and the center of the Japanese political spectrum for not having defined Japanese interests more closely and asserted them more positively. In June, Sato tendered his resignation. He was succeeded by Kakuei Tanaka, a man with a reputation for flexibility. In late September, Prime Minister Tanaka paid an official visit to Peking, from which emerged a nine-point agreement whereby Japan recognized the People's Republic as the sole government of China (Japan had voted against Chinese admission to the United Nations just a year earlier), and stated that it regarded Taiwan as an inalienable part of China. In this, Japan–as the United States had done–made a considerable political concession to Peking. For its part, China renounced any claim to indemnities for damage during Japan's 14-year (1931 to 1945) war with China, and the two countries agreed to resume normal diplomatic relations.

Leaders Tanaka and Chou

As with the United States, so with Japan. The opening of relations with Peking led to a more mellow attitude toward Japan on the part of Russia. This included hints of Soviet adherence to a peace treaty with Japan (which, unlike the other World War II belligerents, Russia failed to sign in 1951), and of the return to Japan of some if not all of the Kuril Islands, which Russia occupied at the end of the war. The new pattern of great power relations in East Asia also had its influence upon the hostility between North and South Korea, which entered into diplomatic conversations in July.

But an equally dramatic development in the politics of Asia was the possibility of final settlement of the war in Vietnam. The year opened with gloom in Washington, D.C., because the Paris peace talks had been stalled for nearly four years, Laos appeared to be on the verge of collapse, and Cambodia was in the grip of civil war. On March 30, North Vietnamese forces launched a major offensive across the demilitarized zone, meeting only rather shaky resistance from the South Vietnamese Army. On May 8, President Nixon decided to mine Haiphong harbor and blockade the ports of North Vietnam. This came as a shock to world opinion, but–though it brought a condemnation from Russia–it did not disturb President Nixon's negotiations in Moscow two weeks later. By summer, it was clear that North Vietnam was beginning to feel the strain both of the blockade and of declining Russian diplomatic support.

In Europe also, there was change and movement during the year

The Paris peace negotiations disappeared from sight behind a pall of obscurity as Kissinger commuted almost fortnightly across the Atlantic for talks with the North Vietnamese negotiators. In early October, they appeared to withdraw their long-standing demand that a political settlement for the whole of Vietnam must be arrived at before a cease-fire could be discussed. At the same time, the United States conceded that a cease-fire could occur before the withdrawal of all North Vietnamese forces from the South. Thereafter it became possible to discuss–despite the reluctance of President Nguyen Van Thieu of South Vietnam–the outlines of an agreement that would provide for the following: a cease-fire with all forces in Vietnam remaining where they were at the time; the withdrawal of the remaining American support forces from the country 60 days after the cease-fire; the return of prisoners; the creation of a National Council of Reconciliation (not, in U.S. eyes, the same thing as a coalition government in Saigon) as well as international machinery to supervise both the cease-fire and free elections in South Vietnam; and, finally, the convening of a peace conference on the future of all of Indochina. But as the year closed, it became clear that the principles of such an agreement were by no means finalized, and the President found it necessary to continue exerting pressure on North Vietnam by bombing as well as using diplomatic pressure on the South.

Kissinger in Paris

In Europe also there was change and movement, partly as a consequence of growing Russian preoccupation with the containment of China. Negotiations between East Germany and West Germany continued virtually all year, leading to an agreement on traffic in the spring and to a much more important treaty of mutual recognition in November. The wide margin of victory for Chancellor Willy Brandt and his coalition government in the West German general elections later that month showed popular approval for his policy of reconciliation with the East and made certain that the treaty would be ratified. Russia joined with the other three allied powers of World War II–France, Great Britain, and the United States–in reasserting their residual rights in the event that a single German state should ever be reconstituted.

Russia's main attention in Europe, however, was focused on the diplomatic preparations in Helsinki, Finland, for the 1973 Conference on European Security and Cooperation, which will be attended by 32 European countries plus Canada and the United States. For the East European countries, the objective in this conference is improved technological cooperation with the West. For the West European and North American countries, it is greater freedom of movement across the old Iron Curtain. But for Russia, which originally proposed the conference, the prime objective is full international acceptance of a politically divided Europe. At the same time, Russia acknowledged that it could not neglect its special relationship with the United States. It did so by embarking in late autumn on a new round of bilateral negotiations on strategic arms limitation whose goal is an actual reduction of missiles, rather than merely a standstill.

U.S. relations with Japan and the community were a concern

But the year witnessed other European developments that raised questions about the future of unity and cooperation among the Western powers themselves. One was the consummation of earlier decisions by the six members of the original European Community to enlarge their membership to include Great Britain, Ireland, and Denmark. (Norway, which was also an applicant, found its status clouded because of a national referendum on September 25 that voted against market membership.) When the prime ministers of the nine countries met in Paris in October, they decided to give priority to the creation of a full monetary union by the end of the 1970s, rather than to the development of more comprehensive political institutions, largely because they envisage difficult economic and monetary negotiations with the United States and Japan over the next few years. By the same token, the U.S. government showed its disapproval of the community's decision to create a preferential trading area out of the Mediterranean countries. The United States believes this would undermine such existing arrangements as the General Agreement on Tariffs and Trade.

Both the Communist powers and the allies of the United States welcomed the re-election of President Nixon as providing continuity in American foreign policy during a period of rapid change in the structure and focus of international politics. The principal achievement of his first Administration was to lay the foundations of a new tripolar political balance between the United States, China, and Russia that permits greater flexibility in the conduct of U.S. foreign policy. But by the end of 1972, it was clear that one of the prime concerns of Mr. Nixon's second Administration would be the development of a second relationship of compromise and balance between the United States, Japan, and the European Community. Their trade and investment patterns are now to a certain extent competitive, and each has its own priorities in dealing with Eastern Europe, Russia, and China. Yet none of the three power centers of "the West" wishes to relinquish the security that alliances with each other have provided and still provide.

Germans at treaty signing

Related Articles

For further information on international relations in 1972, see the articles on the various nations in Section Three, and also the following:

Africa
Asia
Europe
International Trade and Finance
Latin America
Middle East
Pacific Islands
United Nations

Focus on The Nation

James Reston

President Nixon's landslide victory at the polls in November dramatized the enduring principle of moderation in the United States political life

The main event in the United States in 1972 was the re-election of President Richard M. Nixon, and it dramatized the enduring principle of moderation in American political life. From the beginning of the 20th century, now approaching its last quarter, the American people have generally tended to support the progressive forces of change and reform, but whenever any minority has seemed to be pulling them too far to the left or the right, they have invariably moved back toward the center.

When the conservative forces seemed to be putting their selfish interests ahead of the general welfare during the period of industrial and continental expansion at the beginning of the century, President Theodore Roosevelt and later President Woodrow Wilson took over the direction of the nation in the name of progressive reform.

When Wilson took the country into World War I and then led a world crusade for self-determination and world organization, the majority rebelled against such dramatic change and, for the decade of the 1920s, turned the White House back to the conservative leadership of Presidents Warren G. Harding, Calvin Coolidge, and Herbert C. Hoover.

Again there was a reaction. The surge of reform was re-established by Presidents Franklin D. Roosevelt and Harry S. Truman, only to be slowed down again in the 1950s under President Dwight D. Eisenhower, and revived again by Presidents Lyndon B. Johnson and John F. Kennedy, and challenged once more by President Nixon.

It would be wrong to think of this historic pattern as alternating phases of action and reaction, of progressive policies being abandoned or reversed by conservative policies. Rather, they are periods of consolidation, of moving from one plateau upward to another, then pausing there before moving up again in another period of lively innovation.

In the election of 1972, the Democratic Party's presidential nominee, Senator George S. McGovern of South Dakota, based his campaign on the assumption that the time had come for another period of dramatic change and reform. It was time, he felt, not for a steady withdrawal from the war in Vietnam, but for an immediate cease-fire; not for modifications in the existing tax structure, but for a redistribution of the nation's wealth; not for minor cuts in defense expenditures, but for major reductions; not for a pause in the social gains for the poor and the sick, but for another dramatic attack on poverty.

Mr. Nixon's win was strictly a personal, not a party, victory

The response of the American voters to this appeal was both interesting and traditional. Only antiwar, pro-Kennedy Massachusetts and predominantly black District of Columbia voted for McGovern. The other 49 states voted for the President. Mr. Nixon got 520 electoral votes–a total exceeded only by Franklin D. Roosevelt, who got 523 in 1936. The President won 60.7 per cent of the popular vote, second only to Lyndon B. Johnson's 61.09 per cent in 1964.

Mr. Nixon not only carried the normally Republican rural and suburban areas, but also won all the big normally Democratic states and even some of the big Democratic cities such as Cleveland, and almost carried New York City. The "new coalition" Senator McGovern had hoped to lead in a new surge of progressive reform was overwhelmed in the Nixon avalanche. The President won the votes of almost half the newly enfranchised 18- to 21-year-old voters and carried a majority of the votes of Roman Catholics, which no other Republican nominee had done in recent history. In addition, he took 60 per cent of the blue-collar workers, slightly over half the labor voters, and a large minority of Jewish voters.

In short, the Republican President smashed the old Roosevelt coalition of the blue-collar workers, the ethnics, and the South, but it was strictly a presidential and a personal victory and not a party victory. For the Democrats picked up 2 additional seats in the Senate, gained 1 more governorship, and lost only 14 seats in the House of Representatives–thus leaving both houses of Congress and a large majority of the state governorships in the hands of the Democratic Party.

Election result

What the voters seemed to be saying was what they have said on several occasions since the beginning of the century: We want balance and moderation. We want change, but not radical change. We want Nixon and not McGovern, but we also want a Democratic majority on Capitol Hill to watch and balance the power of the Republicans in the White House.

In many ways, the election was more significant as an indicator of the mood of the American people about the balance of social power in America than as a measure of the balance of political power. In his struggle to win the Democratic nomination, Senator McGovern had identified himself as the champion of the very poor, the blacks, and the young intellectuals who were crying for a reordering of American society–for less military arms and more social and economic equality.

This was an effective appeal 40 years before when Franklin Roosevelt broke the control of the Republican Party during the days of the Great Depression of the 1930s. But by 1972, while there were still many Americans living under the so-called poverty level, a majority of Americans were living in comparatively comfortable circumstances.

In 1972, more than half the families in the United States had an annual income of over $10,000, partly due to the large increase in the number of working mothers, and 1 out of every 4 American families had an annual income of over $15,000. Thus, the electorate as a whole was totally different, and the appeals of the past did not work for McGovern as they had for Roosevelt.

McGovern seemed to want to move too far and too fast to the left

More than that, the election indicated that there was a powerful reaction among many middle-class voters against what they saw as increasingly large government welfare payments to citizens able but unwilling to take available jobs. And a reaction as well against politicians like McGovern who seemed to favor busing schoolchildren from one area to another to create racial balance in the public schools, and who had the support of social innovators who favored legalizing marijuana and abortion, and wanted to grant amnesty to men who had dodged the military draft or deserted from the military services during the Vietnam War.

Just as Senator Barry Goldwater, the Republican Party's presidential nominee in 1964, was overwhelmingly defeated because he seemed to be going too far and too fast to the right, so McGovern was overwhelmingly defeated because he seemed to want to go too far and too fast to the left. What Senator McGovern asked the voters to do, after a generation of war and unprecedented change, was to accept more and even faster change, and they rejected his appeal. President Nixon judged the popular mood more accurately: He was for slower change, for stern attitudes and policies against permissiveness and crime, and this combination of pragmatism and security carried the day on November 7.

Mr. Nixon also gained more popular support in 1972 because of his bold innovations and his experience in the field of foreign relations. He took advantage of the hostility between China and Russia to visit the capitals of both these Communist countries, to parley with both without offending either. He broke the long hostility, including his own, toward Peking, and he entered into new arms and trade agreements with Moscow. It was generally recognized as a formidable achievement.

McGovern concedes

Meanwhile, he did not allow these accommodations with China and Russia to keep him from launching a bold naval and aerial blockade of Communist North Vietnam after that country had staged a massive military offensive against South Vietnam. And this resulted, just before the election, in an offer by North Vietnam to reach a compromise cease-fire in the Indochina war on terms that were acceptable to the President and even to most of his antiwar critics.

At home in 1972, the President had serious economic problems. He came to the end of his first four years in the White House with a deficit of over $90 billion, an unfavorable trade balance, and an alarming rate of inflation. But again in this field, though he was obliged to devalue the dollar in relation to other world currencies, he showed the same capacity for bold action, even though this meant reversing policies he had favored in the past. Thus, he adopted price and wage controls, which did not solve but at least eased the inflationary pressures, cut the rate of unemployment to 5.5 per cent, and contributed to a strong revival in the economy by the end of the year.

He wanted new men, looking for new ideas, in his last four years

One effect of all this, however, was to bring him up to his inauguration for a second term, not only with a powerful Democratic majority in the Congress, but also with an aggrieved and powerful Negro minority that felt he was more interested in comforting the comfortable and reassuring the powerful big business forces of the nation than in relieving the plight of the very poor. He encouraged these grievances, perhaps unintentionally, by proclaiming that the average American is "just like a child in the family," who may be made "soft" by too much generosity. Government social programs, he observed vaguely, may "make him completely dependent and pamper him and cater to him too much." Thus, he went into his second term with a promise to maintain a strong and expensive defense budget, and to approve no appropriations that would lead to an increase in taxes in the coming years of his Administration.

Nevertheless, the President acted briskly as soon as the election was over to change his Administration and indicate that he was going into his last four years in office with new men, looking for new ideas, and new beginnings. He reshuffled his Cabinet, cut down the size (though not the principal characters) in the White House staff, and indicated a willingness to have the Cabinet keep in closer touch with the leaders of the Democratic Congress on legislation for the next four years.

Black political convention

This, however, was not likely to avoid a fairly stormy passage. "The suggestion has been made," he said after the election, "that, not facing the problem of re-election, I will now be more free to advocate some massive new social programs. Nothing could be further from the truth." His attitude was that "the nation has enough on its plate." But the attitude of many powerful Democrats in Congress was that millions of Americans did not have enough on their plates to maintain a decent standard of living and that a just, let alone a compassionate, government should think about them before calling for even higher military budgets and more military aid to foreign governments.

Another controversy faced the President in his second term over his promise to continue appointing more conservative judges to the Supreme Court of the United States. Already in his first term he had appointed four new justices, changing the balance of power on criminal and some social issues, and the likelihood was that he would have the opportunity to appoint another judge—if not two or more—to the high bench before his retirement in 1977.

With the Vietnam War coming to an end at the close of 1972, President Nixon planned new initiatives in the field of foreign affairs. He started the second phase of his talks with Russia to control the race in strategic arms. He invited Secretary Leonid I. Brezhnev of the Russian Communist Party to visit the United States in the spring of 1973, and he planned trips to both Japan and Western Europe to try to strengthen relations with America's allies there who have felt somewhat undervalued during Washington's preoccupation with the war in Vietnam.

He had won big, but winning and governing aren't the same thing

Also, "The Middle East will have a very high priority," the President said about his second term, "because it can explode at any time." This is likely to cause him increasing difficulty in the coming years. He wishes to maintain close relations with Israel, but, at the same time, the United States faces an increasing energy crisis in the coming generation and will probably have to rely increasingly on the Arab states of the Middle East for essential supplies of oil.

Hard as these problems may be, however, Mr. Nixon went into his last four years with more support than at any other time in his long and remarkable political career. Though the Democrats control the Congress, they were deeply divided and feebly led at the start of 1973. And even before the end of 1972, the maneuvering for succession to the presidency had started in both parties, with Vice-President Spiro T. Agnew the favorite in the Republican Party, followed by Senator Charles H. Percy of Illinois and Secretary of Health, Education, and Welfare Elliot L. Richardson of Massachusetts (who was to become secretary of defense in 1973), and with Senator Edward M. Kennedy of Massachusetts the leading contender for the Democrats.

The main question at the start of the second term, however, was fairly simple: Could Mr. Nixon count on the people who elected him to help him govern effectively in the coming four years? He had put together what he called a "new majority" and had won overwhelmingly, but it was, paradoxically, a vote against Senator McGovern and almost an unpopular landslide for Mr. Nixon. As even his closest supporters observed, winning and governing are not the same thing, and this was the President's problem as he took the oath of office on Jan. 20, 1973, for the second time.

Vice-President Agnew

Related Articles

For further information on national affairs in 1972, see also Section One, Focus on The Economy; and the following articles in Section Three:

American Party
Civil Rights
Congress of the United States
Courts and Laws
Democratic Party
Economy, The
Elections
Labor
National Defense
Nixon, Richard M.
President of the U.S.
Republican Party
Taxation
U.S. Government

Focus on The Economy

Sylvia Porter

At home and in the international monetary sphere, the United States did pretty well in 1972—but not well enough—and some profound questions have appeared

In the economic sphere at home, the United States did a lot of things right in 1972. As a result, its economy expanded throughout the year in a broad, solid, accelerating upturn to the highest peaks ever achieved by any nation.

But the United States in 1972 did not win the crucial battle against inflation. All we were able to do was to slow inflation from an intolerable annual "galloping" rate of more than 6 per cent to a still clearly unacceptable annual "jogging" rate of 3.5 per cent. This is *all* we managed–despite price-wage controls, despite a gratifying rise in output-per-hour (productivity) of both manpower and machines, despite the absence of pressures and the lack of shortages.

Nor did the United States win the equally crucial battle against unemployment. All we were able to do was to lower unemployment from an intolerable rate of more than 6 per cent to a still clearly unacceptable rate of well over 5 per cent. This is *all* we managed–despite the sustained economic advance, despite a substantial rise in total employment, despite some attempts to help the jobless by means of direct training-retraining programs.

Beyond dispute, the U.S. economy in 1972 was in far, far better shape than it was before President Richard M. Nixon dramatically repudiated his own initial do-nothing wage-price policies on Aug. 15, 1971, and adopted bold programs to restimulate business activity while restraining the price-wage leapfrog. Overall, our economy responded in virtually textbook fashion to the classic antirecession weapons. The federal budget was deeply in the red all year and thereby poured billions of dollars into the economic stream to create paychecks and profits and to encourage borrowing for purposes ranging from buying a car to building a giant factory. The Federal Reserve System pursued an expansionist monetary policy all year and thereby poured billions of dollars into the banking system to create the credit

JOBS
Information
CENTER
MONEY SALE!
Anniversary
we're selling
$10,000 cash
at a 20% discount
LOWER
FOOD
PRICES
WE NEVER CLOSE! OPEN 2

to fill the demands of business and individual borrowers. Tax incentives were voted by Congress and thereby spurred the economy in general and the automobile industry in particular.

These tools worked as the textbooks say they should work. The recession of 1969-1970–deliberately engineered by the Nixon Administration to curb inflation–passed into history in 1971. As 1972 progressed, the pace of expansion quickened. The Dow Jones average of industrial stocks finally cracked the magic milestone of 1,000, other records tumbled with monotony, and the upswing was maintained by a series of rotating booms–a most noteworthy feature of the expansion.

The dollar's loss in buying power averaged about 3.2 per cent in 1972

First came the boom in housing, which fanned out to spur thousands of other industries and services connected with housing. Then came the upturn in business spending for new plants and equipment, which also fanned out to stimulate the wide range of industries and services connected with the building of new plants and equipment. Next came the increase in consumer spending, which brightened the entire economy. And then, it was the turn of inventory accumulation by businessmen to feed the advance. It was a magnificent performance.

But inflation failed to respond as hoped, and as 1973 began, there appeared to be emerging in the nation a resignation to an annual rate of inflation in the 3 to 3.5 per cent range in the years ahead. That would be 3 or 3.5 per cent a year–year after year after year–with the cost of living increases built into the country's economic structure and compounded.

What would that mean to you? Before I get to that, let me underline this vital point: We turned in a much better record of controlling inflation in 1972 than any other major country. The dollar's loss in purchasing power in 1972 averaged only 3.2 per cent, impressively below the rate for the currencies of other prime industrial nations and comparing with an average loss of 6.1 per cent for Europe's currencies.

Consumer spending

Nevertheless, despite our superior achievement, as our advance gained momentum, a revival of demand-pull inflation (surging demands for goods and services pulling up prices) was admittedly a mounting danger. To illustrate: In the price-wage freeze of August-November, 1971, the annual rate of price rise was a mere "creep" of 1.9 per cent. In the first quarter of 1972, it was back above 3 per cent. In the latter part of the year, it was back up to 3.5 per cent.

Is the implication that America's historic experiment with price-wage controls in 1972–the first ever imposed in the United States in a period of decelerating war, of high unemployment, and of surpluses of goods–was a failure? No. In 1972, the experiment turned out surprisingly, even remarkably, well. More specifically, the 12 months of trial underlined at least these four key points:

- The experiment defied the cliché that price-wage controls cannot work in the United States in any other atmosphere than wartime urgency and great patriotism.
- The controls demonstrated that, if limited in application to the big powers in the market place, they can win acceptance and still have

an impact. Let's be honest. The Nixon Administration was utterly unprepared for its own decision in mid-1971 to adopt controls. There was no machinery ready to administer or to police restraints. Businessmen would never have been so sympathetic had the curbs been more onerous. Union leaders would have used the breakdown in the Pay Board in early 1972 to tear the wage curbs apart had they not been able to obtain pay increases exceeding average price increases.

■ The psychological lift of the controls was not a "thing" you could put your hands on, but you could still "feel" it. In 1971, the country was pleading for White House leadership to stop the leapfrogging of prices and wages. And the relief when the President responded was unmistakable.

■ And the controls dramatized the genius of "Nixonomics"–an economics strategy that covers the entire waterfront, that can be reversed over a weekend, and that is geared not to fundamental theories, but rather to policies that will turn failures into triumphs or will just "work." Do not forget that 1971-1972's controls were ordered by a President who entered the White House in 1969 with a solemn pledge never to interfere with private price-wage decisions.

The overall rate of unemployment hid higher rates for blacks, the young, and others

But after giving all this credit where credit is due, we must come back to the pivotal point that there is an inherent bias toward ever-higher prices in our land and in the world of the late 20th century. And now, there's hardly a word among informed economists of a return to the "creeping" rate of 1.5 to 2 per cent–the rate that prevailed in the pre-Vietnam era and that was the equivalent of price stability in an economy as dynamic as ours. Instead, more and more businessmen and investors are "building" into their projections an inflation "factor" of 3 to 3.5 per cent a year.

At that annual inflation rate year after year, prices would double and triple in a quarter-century or so. Well before this century ends, a 3 per cent rate would have cut the dollar's buying power in half.

Unemployment also proved a lot stickier than anticipated in 1972–and hidden behind the overall rate were disgracefully higher jobless rates for the young, the unskilled, blacks, women, and such very highly skilled professionals as engineers, scientists, and technicians. And here also as 1973 began, there appeared to be emerging in Washington a tolerance of an unemployment rate in the 5 per cent range for prolonged periods. The reasoning was that the business upturn has slashed the jobless rate among married men–the key group of breadwinners–to 2.75 per cent, satisfactorily low and hard to criticize. The steep jobless rates among teen-agers, blacks, and women were unfortunate, but dismissed as simply not that important.

In sum, the judgment on the domestic economy: good, but clearly not yet good enough. And the questions: Dare we accept inflation-unemployment rates near these levels? What are the economic-social implications of "jogging" inflation as a way of life? Will this prospect tend to turn our country toward the left or the right? Are we facing these profound questions? Have we begun even to explore them?

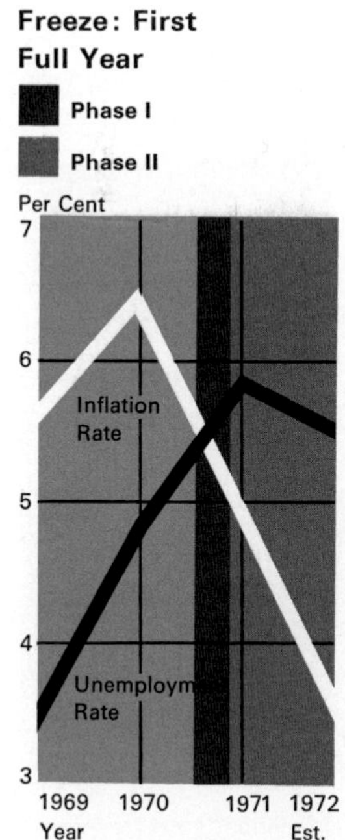

Meanwhile, in the sphere of international monetary reform and global trade, the United States did a lot more things right in 1972–with the result that as 1973 started, the world was firmly on the way to creating a reformed currency system that can finance an ever-increasing volume of trade and sustain world prosperity. Formal negotiations on monetary reform have just begun. It will be several years–1974 at the earliest–before the nations can sign a detailed agreement.

As 1973 began, the world was on its way to creating a new monetary system

While the currency reform negotiations are going on, however, and while the emphasis, as always, will be on the differences among the nations (and particularly, the differences between the position of the United States and those of other individual governments), a focus on 1972 promises that there will be no catastrophic breakdown in trade and communications. The basis for this optimism lies in what did not occur this past year. Consider:

After Aug. 15, 1971–when President Nixon, by a stroke of the pen and a few sentences on a nationwide television broadcast, buried the 27-year-old Bretton Woods monetary system–the network of currency relationships did not break down, the nations did continue to talk and seek areas in which they might cooperate for their mutual salvation. The so-called Smithsonian Agreement of Dec. 18, 1971, represented the first realignment of currencies ever negotiated over a conference table–instead of in response to the ruthless, cruel disciplines of the open market. That was a sign of cooperation not to be lost in signs of noncooperation.

Although there were many warnings and forecasts of a dangerous shrinkage of trade following the floating of currencies after August 15, the shrinkage did not take place. Instead, trade continued to expand.

Although there were also widespread predictions that investments would dry up in a phase of uncertainty about how much each currency was worth in terms of other currencies, the drying up did not develop. Instead, investments continued to grow.

Common Market leaders

The complaints of the smaller nations that they were being ignored were heeded–and, to the surprise of nearly everyone, the group of 10 wealthiest nations appointed to negotiate a new monetary system became a group of 20 big and small countries to hammer out the details. The nations controlled their "dirty floating"–their intervention in the money markets to influence the rates of their own currencies in favor of themselves. And–don't downgrade this–they made an effort to give the appearance of cooperation. Other Free World nations faced up to the fact that if they undercut the U.S. dollar, they simultaneously undercut the billions of U.S. dollars they held.

And even at the very start of bargaining among the nations, there was consensus that at the core of whatever monetary system ultimately replaces the Bretton Woods Agreement will be Special Drawing Rights (SDR). This is the so-called Paper Gold–created by the International Monetary Fund (IMF) in 1969, first issued in 1970, and outstanding at the end of 1972 in a total of $9.3 billion.

In itself, this consensus is of shining significance, for the SDR is a new form of world "money" without precedent in all history. It doesn't actually exist except as a bookkeeping entry on the books of the IMF as member-nations settle their accounts with each other.

Still, SDR's are far more than bookkeeping entries. They are a claim against the assets of each member-nation of the IMF and they are, therefore, backed by the credit and faith of all the nations now belonging to the IMF. We are moving toward creation of a single world currency. We are preparing to make another giant–almost miraculous–leap away from the tyranny of gold and the weaknesses of a single nation's paper money and toward a truly international unit.

How much is the United States willing to give up control over its own economy?

None of this is intended to shrug off the complexity of the problems. You can, in fact, easily get utterly discouraged when you realize that the fundamental issue involved in these currency negotiations is national sovereignty–the "gut" of all gut issues, indeed. Yet maybe just because so much is at stake is why the odds are so heavily on a reformed, workable monetary system. To put it succinctly, the alternatives are too unspeakable to contemplate.

And while all these events and nonevents occupied world headlines, Europe continued to mold itself into a Common Market (European Community), soon to include Great Britain and to total nine nations. Tortuous though the Common Market's progress may be, the trend in Europe is toward unity, common purpose, and increasing power. At a meeting in Paris in October, the political leaders of the enlarged European Community agreed to establish a monetary cooperation fund, to act as a unit and with a single voice in international monetary talks. The European Community moves on. The United States and Russia made exciting progress toward trade with each other, and the United States made a breakthrough in trade with China as well.

In sum, the judgment: good, but in the international monetary sphere too, clearly not yet good enough. And the questions:

Since the gut issue in monetary reform is national sovereignty, how much are we in the United States willing to relinquish our control over our own economy? How much are we willing to submit to strict international rules governing our behavior in the economic-financial sphere? If the rules dictated monetary-fiscal policies threatening a recession in our economy, would we "play"? Or would we pick up our marbles and go home?

Are we facing these profound questions? Have we begun even to explore them?

Related Articles

For further information on the 1972 year in economics, see the following articles in Section Three:

Agriculture
Banks and Banking
Economy, The
International Trade and Finance
Labor
Manufacturing
Money
Stocks and Bonds

A controversial study—*The Limits to Growth*—stirred passions by suggesting that present trends could lead to the collapse of civilization in a century

The almost explosive attention that has been given to problems of the human environment in recent years was highlighted in 1972 by two greatly different but equally significant events. The first was the United Nations Conference on the Human Environment, which attracted hundreds of national representatives to Stockholm, Sweden, to discuss the environmental consequences of man's actions. The second was the appearance of a remarkable and highly publicized book, *The Limits to Growth*, the product of an interdisciplinary team of Massachusetts Institute of Technology (M.I.T.) scholars headed by Dennis L. Meadows.

The project that led to the book was conceived by the so-called Club of Rome, an informal organization of some 75 scientists, businessmen, and politicians who share a common concern about the future of man. The group, which was formed in 1968 by Aurelio Peccei, an Italian industrialist, settled on the systems dynamics group at M.I.T. as being the best able to undertake a mathematical analysis of worldwide trends of population, food, resources, industrialization, and the environment. The result was a mathematical model of the human condition today.

For their model, the authors necessarily make a number of simplifying assumptions, for the real world is enormously complex. The description of even the simplest of ecological systems involves the use of fairly complex mathematics. For example, rabbits placed in a fenced-in field of alfalfa will quickly multiply and reach the maximum number that can be supported by the rate of alfalfa growth. Actually, not knowing, when they breed, what the alfalfa conditions will be like when they give birth to young, the rabbit population will eventually exceed that which can be supported on a continuing basis. With a scarcity of food, the death rate of the rabbits will eventually increase, and the population will fall. With fewer rabbits present, the alfalfa will then grow more rapidly. In short, the rabbit population will oscillate about an average level determined by the average rate of growth of the alfalfa.

Focus on Science

Harrison Brown

The rabbit-alfalfa system comes close to being the simplest that can be imagined, and yet in a very real sense it is complex. Were we to introduce predators into the system, foxes for example, it would become considerably more complex. And, depending upon such factors as gestation periods and sizes of litters, the oscillations could result in the stabilization of the rabbit population at a new level—or they could result in extinction of the rabbits.

The forecast of the future was based largely on past behavior

The real world, of course, is enormously more complex than one composed solely of alfalfa, rabbits, and foxes. There are thousands of variables, all interacting with each other. Of these variables, the M.I.T. group considered the most important to be human population growth, the food supply, the availability of mineral resources, industrialization, capital, and the pollution of the environment. They constructed about 100 relationships between these factors and then asked the computer to solve the equations. The results suggest that if present trends are allowed to run their course, civilization may collapse within a century.

The results of the M.I.T. study have aroused strong passions. Some groups have urged that economic growth, including population growth, be halted. Others have condemned the study, pointing to its simplified assumptions and emphasizing in particular the failure of the authors to take technological innovation adequately into account. The editors of the prestigious scientific journals *Science* and *Nature* have criticized the study, as have scores of well-known economists. On the other hand, the study has been defended by numerous respected members of the scientific community.

The authors agree that their study has oversimplified the real world. At the same time, they suggest that their simplified model probably comes closer to describing the real world than do the models that most people carry in their heads, either consciously or unconsciously. They point to the fact that their model reproduces the basic behavior of the major variables for a period of 70 years starting in 1900, and they emphasize that their forecast of the future is based largely upon this past behavior.

Family planning in India

Defenders of the study contend that useful insights can be obtained from such a simplified model, and they stress that the general behavior of the model is surprisingly unaffected by drastic changes in assumptions. If one is a technological optimist, for example, and assumes there is an unlimited availability of energy, the ultimate world crisis is eventually caused by pollution. On the other hand, if one assumes the existence of effective pollution controls, the crisis is ultimately brought about by an inadequate food supply.

The authors of *The Limits to Growth* attempt to view human actions and needs as parts of a continuum. Yet, during the past quarter-century we have seen the splitting of humanity into two separate and distinct cultures: the rich and the poor. The culture of the rich is made up of about 1 billion persons, who have a per capita gross national product (GNP) of about $2,800. But the larger of the cultures is that of the poor. It is made up of about 2.6 billion persons with a per capita

GNP of about $215–or some 13 times less per person than in the rich countries. The economies of the two groups are growing at about the same rate. But the rate of population growth in the poor countries is high and still growing, while that of the rich countries is low and decreasing. As a result, the per capita GNP of the rich countries is growing much faster than that of the poor countries. Between 1961 and 1971, the GNP of both the rich and the poor countries increased by about 60 per cent in constant dollars. But during the same period, the per capita GNP in the poor countries increased only 26 per cent, while that in the rich countries increased by 42 per cent. Thus, in large part because of population growth, the gap between the rich and the poor is growing.

The gap between the rich and the poor is growing wider

Were the present rates to continue, 130 years would be required for the poor countries to reach the level of affluence that the rich countries enjoy today. By that time, the population of the poor countries would be a staggering 130 billion persons. The population of the rich countries would not be much larger than it is today, and their per capita GNP would approach the fantastic level of $1 million.

Clearly, continuation of the present trends leads us to an impossible situation. Long before another 130 years have passed something must change–virtually everyone agrees that this is so. But what will change? By how much? When? Under what circumstances? Here there is little agreement, much controversy, and a lively display of strong emotions.

Can population growth rates be reduced in time to avoid the catastrophe suggested by *The Limits to Growth*? Here the major problem is presented by the poor countries, for the evidence suggests that the rich countries are not far away in time from "zero population growth." In spite of the fact that the average rate of growth of population in the poor countries is still increasing, there is some evidence that birth rates are decreasing in China, Taiwan, South Korea, and Hong Kong. Some experts say that this may portend a general decrease of birth rates in the poor countries. Others maintain, however, that it is doubtful that a rapid decline in birth rates will take place unless the rate of economic growth is substantially accelerated.

Crop-dusting in America

Can food production keep pace with the present rapid rate of population growth? From the technological point of view alone, this is a possibility–for a time. The Green Revolution is destined to spread over large areas of Africa, Asia, and Latin America. But in order for there to be a Green Revolution, large quantities of fertilizers and pesticides must be available, and their use in the necessary quantities can give rise to a multitude of serious environmental problems. Also, the production, distribution, and application of the fertilizers and pesticides requires the building of industries and transportation systems. This, in turn, requires capital, which often is not available.

Can the rich countries decrease their levels of pollution and the magnitude of their assault upon the environment? Noting that pollution increases with affluence, some persons suggest that the rich countries should stop growing economically. Others maintain that this is not possible in the foreseeable future, but they point to the fact that, in principle, most pollution could be eliminated by applying technology properly. Still others contend that the elimination of pollution necessitates the expenditure of large quantities of energy—and that waste heat itself is a form of pollution.

It is not at all certain that the forecasts made in the study are warranted

Will our nonrenewable resources be adequate to meet humanity's growing needs? Some experts point to the decreasing availability of high-grade ores. Others point to the fact that if enough energy is available, we can get all of the materials we need from low-grade ores and that, indeed, we could even meet our needs by processing ordinary rock if we had to.

Is there enough energy to meet the growing needs? Some point to the fact that supplies of oil and natural gas are limited and unevenly distributed around the world. Others point to vast reserves of coal. Still others point to the technical difficulties of burning coal without polluting the atmosphere with irritating and dangerous sulfur oxides. Others maintain that we could shift entirely to a nuclear economy. Still others maintain that we don't know how to do this safely.

Is our increasing consumption of energy leading us into a dangerous situation with respect to climate? Some point to the large quantities of particulate matter that are placed in the air by coal-fired power plants and to the vast quantities of carbon dioxide that result from the combustion of fossil fuels. They also point to the possibility that these substances might be changing the radiation balance of the earth in harmful ways. Others suggest that if this problem becomes serious, we can shift to nuclear power. Still others point out that our vast outpouring of waste heat into the atmosphere and oceans could conceivably trigger a major change in atmospheric circulation patterns, which, in turn, might adversely affect the climate.

Nuclear power station

Clearly, our ignorance of these various factors and of the ways in which they interact with each other is enormous. It is by no means certain that the conclusions reached in *The Limits to Growth* are warranted. Nor does the evidence warrant an unequivocal condemnation of the study. More facts and better theories are badly needed.

Let us assume, nevertheless, that the M.I.T. study correctly describes the interactions between such factors as population growth, resources, food, economic development, and environment. The authors go further, however, and assume for the purpose of forecasting that these factors will continue to interact in the future as they have in the past. This is not necessarily true, for man has it within his power to modify the picture. Indeed, one can imagine a sequence of events that could result in a noncatastrophic, peaceful resolution of these problems.

It is quite possible that concerted efforts could lower the birth rates and thus the rates of population growth in the poor countries. Such efforts, properly combined with substantially increased programs of technical and capital assistance from the rich countries, might accelerate dramatically the rates of economic growth of the poorer countries.

The rates of economic growth—and thus of increasing resource demand and pollution of the richest of the rich countries—could be decelerated without lowering standards of living. Most affluent societies are extremely wasteful, and much of that waste could be eliminated by building machines and other objects that will last longer, by effective recycling of materials, by improved design of buildings, and by creating more efficient transportation systems. Life styles in the rich countries could be altered so that people would live closer to their work, would use bicycles rather than automobiles, and would throw fewer things away. Such steps could have profound effects upon the course of human history. They would not in themselves be total solutions, but they would buy time during which man could learn more about these problems and devise new technological and social means for overcoming them.

It is essential that we try to learn much more about the system in which we live

In the meantime, it is essential that we attempt to learn as much as we can about the system in which we live so that we can more precisely anticipate problems and more effectively devise solutions. The M.I.T. study, inadequate as it is, will hopefully stimulate a wide variety of similar studies aimed at achieving a better understanding of the real world.

Fortunately, concern about these problems is spreading throughout the world. Russia and the United States have signed an agreement for scientific cooperation on environmental problems. An international agreement was reached in 1972 to establish the International Institute for Applied Systems Analysis in Vienna, Austria. There, scientists from 14 nations will work on the development of analytical tools that can be used to study the complex interactions between man and nature.

It is also essential that a global monitoring system be developed to detect critical changes in the levels of atmospheric and ocean pollution and follow climatic changes so that situations endangering man can be anticipated. With this in mind, the International Council of Scientific Unions established the Special Committee on Problems of the Environment, which is now attempting to specify the details of a global monitoring network. Hopefully, the combination of growing concern and increasing actions will lead not only to a better understanding of the predicament of mankind, but also to the solution of these extremely complex and difficult problems that must be solved if civilization is to survive.

City cyclist

Related Articles

For further information on science and technology in 1972, see the articles on the various sciences in Section Three.

Focus on Education

Lawrence A. Cremin

While efforts to equalize educational opportunity continued in 1972, there was growing skepticism over whether education even contributes to equality

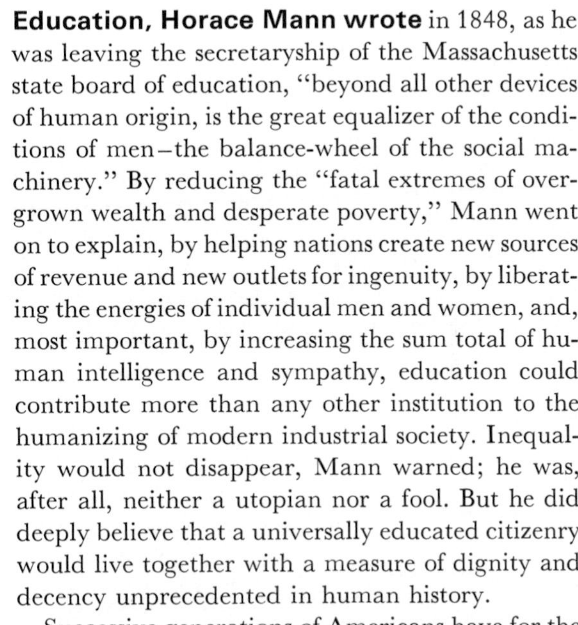

Education, Horace Mann wrote in 1848, as he was leaving the secretaryship of the Massachusetts state board of education, "beyond all other devices of human origin, is the great equalizer of the conditions of men–the balance-wheel of the social machinery." By reducing the "fatal extremes of overgrown wealth and desperate poverty," Mann went on to explain, by helping nations create new sources of revenue and new outlets for ingenuity, by liberating the energies of individual men and women, and, most important, by increasing the sum total of human intelligence and sympathy, education could contribute more than any other institution to the humanizing of modern industrial society. Inequality would not disappear, Mann warned; he was, after all, neither a utopian nor a fool. But he did deeply believe that a universally educated citizenry would live together with a measure of dignity and decency unprecedented in human history.

Successive generations of Americans have for the most part shared Mann's vision. More than any other people, Americans have tried to reconcile the competing claims of liberty, equality, and fraternity through their schools. And it has been taken as a matter of national faith that education has been the "great equalizer of the conditions of men–the balance-wheel of the social machinery." Yet 1972 witnessed a sharpening debate over that faith, as continued efforts toward greater equalization of educational opportunity confronted growing skepticism over whether education really contributes to equality in the first place.

The drive toward equalization was clearly behind a continuing attempt to reform the methods of financing American schools, which had already achieved a major victory during the summer of 1971. On August 30 of that year, the California Supreme Court ruled in *Serrano v. Priest* that the state's system of school support, based as it was on local property taxes, violated the equal protection provisions of the California Constitution and the U.S. Constitution. Having declared the arrangement illegal, the court directed the California legislature to devise a new system that would be more equitable. Of course, the final arbiter of what the U.S. Constitution means is not any state court but rather the Supreme Court of the United States; and at the end of 1971, it seemed only a matter of time before the *Serrano* decision would be appealed and its doctrine reviewed by the highest court in the land.

The argument was that students were due equal opportunities for schooling

The state of California decided not to appeal; but another opportunity presented itself on Dec. 23, 1971, when a federal district court in San Antonio, Tex., ruled in the case of *Rodriguez v. San Antonio Independent School District* that the Texas system of supporting public schools violated the 14th Amendment of the U.S. Constitution because it "discriminated on the basis of wealth by permitting citizens of affluent districts to provide a higher quality education for their children, while paying lower taxes." The state of Texas did decide to appeal, and the U.S. Supreme Court agreed to review the decision. The case was actually argued on Oct. 12, 1972, though by the year's end the court had not yet handed down a decision. What was clear, however, was that whichever way the court ruled, the issue of inequality in educational financing within the several states and between one state and another had already been sufficiently dramatized that corrective action would be attempted. At least four states–California, Colorado, Michigan, and Oregon–had November referendums proposing to abolish the property tax as a first step toward reform, though, interestingly, all four propositions failed to pass. There was widespread discussion in state legislatures over how to change educational tax structures. And, in Washington, D.C., there was considerable talk of a value-added tax–a tax on the increasing value or price of a product at various stages of manufacture, processing, or distribution–as the basis for a radically expanded program of federal school support.

Antibusing protesters

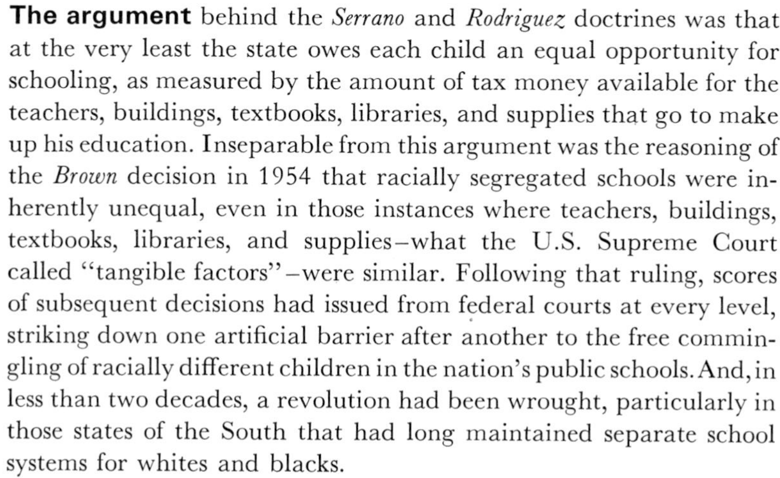

The argument behind the *Serrano* and *Rodriguez* doctrines was that at the very least the state owes each child an equal opportunity for schooling, as measured by the amount of tax money available for the teachers, buildings, textbooks, libraries, and supplies that go to make up his education. Inseparable from this argument was the reasoning of the *Brown* decision in 1954 that racially segregated schools were inherently unequal, even in those instances where teachers, buildings, textbooks, libraries, and supplies–what the U.S. Supreme Court called "tangible factors"–were similar. Following that ruling, scores of subsequent decisions had issued from federal courts at every level, striking down one artificial barrier after another to the free commingling of racially different children in the nation's public schools. And, in less than two decades, a revolution had been wrought, particularly in those states of the South that had long maintained separate school systems for whites and blacks.

But, as the *Brown* decision had been applied in the Northern cities, where racially segregated neighborhoods had led to *de facto* (actual) as contrasted with *de jure* (legal) segregation in the schools, the question soon arose as to how far it would require not merely the redrawing of school district boundaries, but also the combining of urban and suburban school districts and the extensive transportation of large numbers of students from one district to another. If racially segregated schools were inherently unequal, despite equality of "tangible factors," to what extent did provision of equal educational opportunity, as defined in the *Brown* decision, require racial integration? The issue exploded into the headlines in 1971 and 1972 in such widely separated cities as San Francisco, Detroit, and New York, and actually became a major issue in the presidential campaign of 1972. By the year's end, the President, the Congress, and the Supreme Court were all deeply involved in efforts to develop just and reasonable policies, but no one could predict what those policies would be or how much political conflict they would ultimately occasion.

Some argued that achieving equal attainment might require unequal school resources

The *Serrano, Rodriguez,* and *Brown* doctrines, taken together, held that educational equality in 1972 meant the availability of equal school facilities and services and of racially mixed classrooms, where the social composition of the population permitted it. Few would deny that extensive political, economic, and social reforms would be needed if such equality were to be achieved in the near future. Yet even as political coalitions were being organized to attempt those reforms in the courts, in Congress, and in the various state legislatures, other voices were arguing with increasing vigor that the whole effort was misdirected to begin with, since equality of educational opportunity, particularly as defined in the *Serrano* and *Rodriguez* doctrines, produced, not greater equality of educational and social attainment, but rather less. Boys and girls come to school with very different abilities to profit from its instruction, the argument ran, depending in large measure on the social, racial, ethnic, and religious backgrounds of their families. Once they are in school, existing gaps in educational attainment, deriving from differences in family training, simply widen. Seen in this way, equality of educational opportunity, as manifested in equal facilities and equal services, yields unequal educational attainment, and no amount of financial equalizing can reverse that tendency. What is needed, the argument concluded, is greater equality of educational attainment, and this actually requires considerable inequality of educational resources, with more going to poor and minority-group children, who are ill-equipped to profit from the schools.

Classroom scene

The argument, a novel one in the history of American educational discussion, stemmed from an immensely influential study carried out by sociologist James S. Coleman in 1965, under a little-noticed provision of the Civil Rights Act of 1964 requiring a survey "concerning the lack of availability of equal educational opportunity for individuals by reason of race, color, religion, or national origin" in public schools at all levels. What the Congress, the U.S. Office of Education (which sponsored the survey), and Coleman himself doubtless expected to find were gross disparities in the educational resources of white and black schools; and the anticipation, of course, was that the data would become the basis of new federal attempts to remove the disparities.

What Coleman found, however, was that by 1965 the differences in "tangible factors" between white and black schools had narrowed significantly. Nevertheless, differences in the academic achievement of white and black children, which were already evident in the first grade, seemed only to mount as the children progressed. Finding that most of the disparities in achievement appeared within particular schools rather than between one school and another, Coleman concluded that the differences attributable to family background and training within the first five or six years accounted for much more of the variation in student achievement than did schooling itself.

The debate over public policy was profoundly shaped by the shift in focus

Coleman's massive report was largely statistical, and embodied no policy recommendations. But the very nature of his inquiry and findings occasioned a fundamental change in the concept of educational equality, from a concern for equal educational *resources* to a concern for equal educational *achievement*. Coleman saw the creation of racially integrated classrooms as one important way of moving toward opportunity for equal educational achievement–but only one among many. For his view in its very nature took discussion beyond the confines of the school to the many agencies that educate–family, church, library, museum, youth group, playground, and television station. And it prodded educators to consider how all these agencies might play a role in correcting for the accident of birth into a particular home or social environment.

The shift in focus, from equality of educational resources to equality of educational achievement, profoundly influenced the debate over public policy. For those who tended to accept Coleman's reinterpretation of equal education found themselves increasingly resistant to spending and equalization programs of the traditional variety. Thus, for example, Daniel P. Moynihan of Harvard University, who had been counselor to the President during the early years of the first Nixon Administration, argued in the autumn of 1972 that increased expenditures for education along time-honored lines, even following the *Serrano* and *Rodriguez* principle of equalization within states, would probably have no substantial influence on educational achievement. Indeed, Moynihan continued, attempts to equalize educational expenditures within states would probably see considerable sums taken from schools attended by the lowest-income and the highest-income students and given to schools attended by middle-income students. And, in any case, increases in educational expenditures would almost certainly be absorbed in higher salaries for the very same teachers now in the schools. The only effective answer to educational inequality, Moynihan concluded, was a series of radically new special programs directed to the problems of the poor, which would affect such critical educational factors as the child's relationships with his family, his playmates, and his teachers.

James S. Coleman

The debate was already heated by the autumn of 1972, when the appearance of a massive study, entitled *Inequality*, by Christopher Jencks and his associates at Harvard University's Graduate School of

Education, fanned the fires. Purporting to be an assessment of the effects of family and schooling on social and economic success in America, the study concluded: (1) that educational opportunity is very unequally distributed in the United States; (2) that, even if all qualitative differences between elementary and secondary schools were eliminated, inequalities in educational attainment would persist; and (3) that in the last analysis neither educational opportunity nor educational attainment is at the heart of social and economic success in adult life, but rather such factors as luck and "subtle, unmeasured differences in personality and on-the-job competence."

In the autumn, Jencks' study of inequality fanned the fires of the debate

Jencks and his associates argued vigorously that their findings should not be taken as an attempt to discredit the schools. There are compelling moral and social reasons, they insisted, for spending more money than ever on schools and for trying to desegregate them as promptly as possible. What seemed clear to them, however, was that better schools would not eliminate differences in educational achievement and that better schools would neither eliminate nor even substantially reduce social and economic inequalities in the larger society. The only way to attack those problems, the authors concluded, would be "to establish political control over the economic institutions that shape our society." This, they admitted, "is what other countries usually call socialism."

The Jencks study, flying as it did in the face of liberal faiths that dated from the time of Horace Mann, set off a vituperative and far-reaching controversy. Some commentators thought it high time that Americans abandoned their cherished myths about education and equality and dealt instead with hard realities in their discussions of social policy. Others contended that the very same studies Jencks had cited, when properly interpreted, indicated a far more direct and profound relationship between education and adult success than Jencks himself allowed, and warned that the interpretations presented in *Inequality* flowed more from the political convictions of the author than from an objective analysis of the data.

In the end, much would doubtless depend on how Americans joined an important but limited body of social science findings that could be interpreted in very different ways, to their larger beliefs about the role of education in reconciling the often-conflicting demands of liberty, equality, and fraternity. Americans in 1972 were far and away the most schooled people in history. And what would probably prove decisive for social policy was their own collective sense of how well or how poorly their own schooling had contributed to the richness and the satisfaction they themselves were finding in the lives they led.

Christopher Jencks

Related Articles

For further information on education in 1972, see Section Two, The Prescott Experiment and Always Testing; and Section Three, Education.

It appeared that several of the arts—popular music, painting, theater, and the movies—were marking time, waiting for something new and vital to explode

Anyone required to write an annual report on the arts for any publication whatsoever would do well to protect himself from the loud laughter of his friends and former admirers with a prefatory note. "Everything herein," it would state, "is subject to the general understanding that no movement in the arts takes place within the span of a calendar year."

There appears to be some doubt among the heathen, and even among true believers, that the calendar—or even the states of the union, for that matter—were invented by the Almighty. Similarly, one may doubt that any decisive trend—in literature, painting, music, the movies, or whatever—is ordered from on high to take place within a given year. At least, we can be sure of one thing: It cannot be seen to be happening *at the time*, though much later we can look back and see that certain works of art or certain performances sparked an explosion that would dispose of a tradition, or start a new one. Such explosions, we can now confidently say, happened with the Armory Show in New York City in 1913, which caused many American artists to change their styles to reflect the modern European trends; with the first performance of Igor Stravinsky's *The Rite of Spring*, also in 1913; and with the arrival of the Beatles in the 1960s. The fact that the people interested in painting, in classical music, and in popular music were enormously excited by these events does not in itself prove that the events were historic. People interested in the arts are notoriously inclined to be enormously excited most of the time. And, conversely, a yawn of apathy from the experts also proves nothing about a new movement they reject. We should all be warned by a passage in an article on modern painting written in 1947 for a world-famous reference work. The subject was Abstract painting (originally known by the odd name of *Orphism*). And there we read that Orphism, or Abstract painting, in which the painters sought to paint without subject, expired for lack of interest. Well, it may have snoozed awhile, but it shook

Focus on The Arts

Alistair Cooke

itself awake and bestrode the art world like a Colossus through the 1950s and 1960s. In the '70s, it appears to have run its course, certainly its fashion, and we are now going through the usual historic experience of a strong reaction, a swing to the other extreme; so that young painters who 10 years ago would have been slapping a blob of color on a vast white rectangle in the hope of being mistaken for Adolph Gottlieb are now painfully painting crab grass and old barns in the hope of being bought at the going Fairfield Porter rates.

The good old urge to freak out the squares has been reborn

What we can say, with all due caution and a ceremonial crossing of the fingers, is that several of the arts–pop music, painting, theater, the movies–*appeared* to be marking time in the early 1970s, to be treading water until some pioneer decides to take the next big plunge. In the meantime, there were various alarums and excursions that heralded nothing very new or vital.

The unveiling of the John F. Kennedy Center for the Performing Arts in Washington, D.C., though celebrated with a special Mass composed for the occasion and attended by a trumpet flourish of celebrities, is not likely to compare with the unveiling of the Parthenon or the opening of Dublin's Abbey Theatre.

Jesus Christ Superstar was a highly touted theatrical attempt to give the most sacred myth a circus production. It was a logical development of the good old urge, reborn in the past two decades, to shock the bourgeoisie or freak out the squares–the continuation of a movement that started with Federico Fellini's *La Dolce Vita* in the movies and Kenneth Tynan's *Oh, Calcutta!* in the theater. There are people who angrily insist that the American theater was revolutionized by the Living Theater, in which the actors broke through the convention of the proscenium arch, mingled with the audience, and pretended to creativity by improvising any particular emotion that struck them as they encountered the paying customers in row D. As with all shocks, the charge had to be constantly increased to reproduce the original outrage; and we stepped up the dose so violently, from four-letter words and irreverent costumes to hard-core pornography and *Jesus Christ Superstar*, that the bourgeoisie were no longer shocked but numbed with boredom.

The star in *Superstar*

So what we have seen in the past year or two, in the Broadway theater especially, has been an increasingly frantic effort toward novel *effects* by way of staging. New ideas and new philosophies do not sprout every spring, and the avant-garde have consequently had to dress up as dazzlingly as possible some "shocking" ideas that are now fairly outworn. "Show biz," I think, is the key phrase to the last decade in the theater. We have, since Arthur Miller and Edward Albee, practically nothing new to say; so we have to go in for bizarre or sumptuous sets and gimmicks.

The movement, reaching for its apogee, achieved instead its nadir in a musical piece called *Via Galactica*, which had preliminary publicity worthy of the first Apollo space launch. It had no discoverable plot, but the elements it threw together were chic in the extreme: the earth a thousand years from now; everyone has turned blue. People control their emotions with spinning-saucer hats. The stage is awhirl with space ships, flashing galaxies, and humans no longer earthbound (to produce the effect, they bounced around on trampolines). The critics admitted they had never seen anything like it and begged the public to go–in spite of the dense plot, aimless dialogue, indifferent acting, and muddled music–just for the trick effects. Everyone agreed it was visually stunning–for about half an hour. After that, the audience was stunned into boredom. The show closed after seven performances, and Broadway producers and "angels" sat around more stunned than anybody at the thought of $925,000 gone down the drain. This disaster may have done some good in reviving Hamlet's embarrassingly old-fashioned prescription that "the play's the thing."

Motion pictures are exploiting the dark well of the unconscious

That is one lesson that the motion pictures, at any rate, have learned for keeps. In spite of their obvious advantage over the theater in exploiting fantasy and gadgetry, the movies–from Georges Méliès' *Trip to the Moon* in 1902 to *2001: A Space Odyssey* of considerably more recent vintage–have not forgotten for long that a close-up of recognizable human beings is more exciting to most audiences than a long shot of a planet. Lately, however, in our admittedly violent time, they have become absorbed in, or obsessed with, the brutal extremes of realism. And, in a surprisingly large number of films, the new freedom to represent intimate sexuality has combined with the itch for violence to produce the ultimate violation of personal intimacy; namely, rape. It started, innocently enough, a dozen years ago in a Sophia Loren film, *Two Women*. But the climactic–and at that time greatly daring–rape scene was no less, but no more, than a familiar assertion of the horror of war. In 1972, in *A Clockwork Orange*, sexual attack is used –in fact it is stylized–to symbolize the final humiliation of one human being by another, who performs the act as a kind of ritual purgation of anxiety.

What we are now seeing, in many movies made with much pretense to courage and "unflinching" realism, is the acting out in life of the aggressions that Freud said ought to be acted out on the psychoanalyst's couch so that life could be saved from such damaging disturbance. We do not need to be a Freudian or an anti-Freudian to grant that much of the material that contemporary movies exploit is an eruption from the dark well of the unconscious. To stir up a person's unconscious and allow it to explode is a very dangerous proceeding, unless there is somebody on hand who knows how to control it. We have accepted Freud's discovery of the id–the chaotic, instinctive, untamed part of the unconscious. We are now busy watching the ego wallow in it. But we are not prepared to allow any outside control of these eruptions through either the social conscience (the superego) or any social institution. (At least, we weren't prepared until late in 1972, when the greatly publicized "silent majority" found its voice, voted conservative, and was very soon echoed by the Supreme Court of the United States. But I anticipate.)

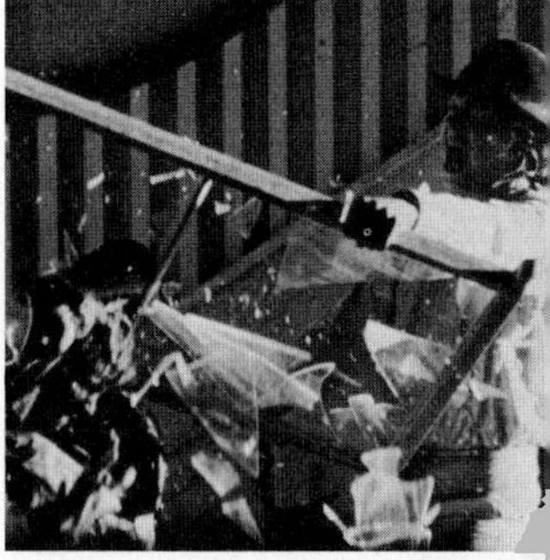

Violence in *Clockwork*

What is plain enough is that while many serious film makers are seriously concerned with violent sex as a contemporary symbol, many commercially minded men are preoccupied only with exploiting it. Probably the most commercially successful wedding of antisocial violence and social intimacy is *The Godfather*, which is drawing audiences around the world as vast as those that celebrated the comic violence of the James Bond films. *The Godfather*'s juicy formula is carefully calculated: it is to mix equal parts of *Bonnie and Clyde*'s red blood (in living color) with the broth of family feeling in *Cheaper by the Dozen* or *Life with Father*. A new, and ominous, response in the audiences is the actual cheering that sometimes breaks out in reaction to the vivid brutality of the film's murders.

We do not know whether imagined violence breeds the real thing

This brings up the general question, which is currently agitating presidential commissions and city fathers and is beginning to exercise state legislatures: What is the effect of these violent images on the audience? In other and simpler words, are these liberal and concentrated doses of sex and violence—in movies, on television, in night clubs—"bad for people"? Does imagined violence breed the real thing in life?

The trouble with finding the true answer to that difficult question is the dogmatism of the opposing groups that instantly leap to answer it. Whole teams of sociologists, psychiatrists, and psychologists are on hand to pooh-pooh the mere suggestion that life will imitate art so crudely.

On the other hand, church groups, women's clubs, and clerics and such are as instantly convinced, without demonstrable proof, that the prisons are choking—or ought to be—with people who have just learned a new criminal technique from a movie or a television program.

The simple and humbling truth is that we do not know the answer. And there seem to be very few people around who are willing to undertake a disinterested and exhaustive survey of the criminal population in an effort to *find* the answer. The liberal-minded psychologists generalize from their own premise as unscientifically as the embattled church groups.

Godfather and sons

But in any confused or alarmed society, the people in authority do not postpone action until the truth is made plain. And the reaction is now underway against the 1960's junket of permissiveness. In many states, too, new bills are being drafted to give communities the power to censor movies and other public exhibitions. Such a move, in the form of a proposition, was included on the California ballot in November, 1972. It went so far as to specify that a community could prohibit the public display, either on film or in the flesh, of those parts of the body once known as "privates." The proposition lost by 2 to 1. But within the month, the U.S. Supreme Court came to the rescue with a decision that could start a landslide of prohibitive legislation. While bringing no new light to bear on the murky question of what constitutes obscenity, the nation's highest court gave to the states the right to withdraw liquor licenses from clubs that tolerate acts of "gross sexuality" among entertainers, waitresses, or patrons. The majority, by 6 to 3, held that liquor licenses exist in the first place in order to regulate public conduct and that they are regularly withdrawn on the evidence of disorder.

This ruling aims an oblique blow at pornographic exhibitions usually considered gross, and it would seem safe to assume that other states will doubtless devise other glancing blows. And if the Supreme Court has correctly interpreted the election returns, these indirect attacks on obscenity will be upheld. There is a scramble on in the state legislatures to draw up obscenity statutes under various disguises. If we don't hear much about them as yet, the reason is one given by the attorney general of Oklahoma for seeming to be slow in responding to a general desire to restore the death penalty: "The trouble is to write a law the Supreme Court will like."

The problem is to write a law that the Supreme Court will like

Related Articles

For further information on the arts in 1972, see the following articles in Section Three:

Architecture
Awards and Prizes (Arts Awards)
Canadian Library Association
Canadian Literature
Dancing
Deaths of Notable Persons
Fashion
Fonda, Jane
Hackman, Gene
Interior Design
King, Carole
Library
Literature
Literature for Children
Motion Pictures
Museums
Music, Classical
Music, Popular
Nobel Prizes
Photography
Poetry
Pulitzer Prizes
Radio
Recordings
Television
Theater
Visual Arts

Focus on Sports

Jim Murray

In 1972, the question was: When did athletes become instruments of national policy, fair game for the street fanatics, the nationalists, and the haters?

(The scene is a hotel in New York City. An elevator lands in the cordoned-off lobby and out step a group of grim-faced young men with size 19 collars, shielding their faces with their sleeves and hats. They are ushered to a fleet of waiting limousines with guns bristling out of them like automotive porcupines and are whisked away in a wail of motorcycle escorts. An arrest of a narcotics ring? No. These are members of the New York Colts football team on their way to a secret rendezvous in the Super Bowl with the Dallas Dogies. Where the game will be played, and when, is a state secret. The reason: A group of insurrectionists calling themselves "The Aaron Burr Society" has threatened to kill the entire team from end to end, platoon by platoon, unless the U.S. government accedes to their demand that they be given Louisiana to set up their own country. The Super Bowl will be televised nationally from a location known only to a handful of men and only after all identifying geographical, institutional, or meteorological telltales have been masked or hidden.)

(ERIE, PA., Nov. 30, National Press Service–Mrs. Pearlie Ann Mason today sued the United States government for $800 million and moved to set aside the draft of her son Fred (Gallops) Mason into the national athletic pool. Mrs. Mason said the national player draft–which was put into effect to restore spectator sports to the national scene after they had all but disappeared following the bombing of the Moscow Olympics by Patagonian terrorists seeking redress for setbacks in their tribal war with the Hu-Hu's–was unconstitutional despite passage of the 34th Amendment to the Constitution enabling it. "The youth of America are defecting to Canada to escape this unjust claim on their young lives," Mrs. Mason declared. She added, "I didn't raise my son to be a split-end or any other hazardous occupation where he will be called upon to risk his life in the cross hairs of every fanatic in this hemisphere. The government has no right to force a young man into uniform–be it football, baseball, track, tennis, or crew." The White House countered that it was in the gross national interest to have athletic games continue: "Some of us have to make the sacrifice. Unfortunately, it has to be those who can run faster, jump higher, or swing harder than their peers.")

What happened in Munich and Romania had all the trappings of movie fantasies

Are the above just fanciful distortions? Orwellian logic? Hyperbolic overkill? Clockwork Orange? Okay. Consider the following absurdity that came clattering in over the news wire one morning in September, 1972:

(MUNICH, Sept. 5–An Arab terrorist team in athletic sweat suits and stocking caps vaulted into the Olympic Village here today, shot two members of the Israeli Olympic delegation, and held nine others hostage for more than 16 hours until their demands were met that the entire party be given safe conduct out of Germany via helicopter and jet. At Fürstenfeldbruck airfield, ambushed by German sharpshooters, the terrorists slaughtered the remainder of the Israeli athletes, and five of their own number were slain. Three were captured.)

Are *those* credible happenings? *Believable* episodes? No, surely they are right out of a Stanley Kubrick screen fantasy. A Sam Peckinpah cinematic outrage. The credits will come up in a moment and say "Alfred Hitchcock." Or, consider this melodrama:

(BUCHAREST, Oct. 10–The United States Davis Cup team–which rejected Romanian requests that it leave the two Jewish members of the team at home, as well as any Jewish officials, coaches, or fans–has arrived in this Romanian capital, where they are kept sequestered and virtual prisoners on the 17th floor of the Inter-Continental Hotel. They have their own elevator, which is usable only by coded card. The Romanian secret police have sealed off not only the floor the American tennis players are living on, but also the floor above and the one below. Armed patrols scour the corridors. Food, drink, and American motion pictures are brought in, and the athletes are forbidden to look out the windows or otherwise present an inviting silhouette. Under heavy guard, they are whisked to and from the cup matches in bulletproof limousines.)

Davis Cup stars at play in Bucharest

Is *that* just another Transylvanian horror story? Frankenstein Takes Up Tennis? Dracula Drinks from the Davis Cup? No, unfortunately, unlike the two flights of imagination about New York City and Erie, Pa., the Munich and Bucharest scenes are verities straight out of 1972, not 007 shoot-'em-ups. John Wayne doesn't solve these with the Seventh Cavalry or a green beret and a Bren gun.

In 1972, the question was: When did athletes become instruments of national policy, fair game for the street fanatics, the morbid nationalists, the haters? You shoot archdukes, not tennis players, right? You stone embassies or invade the Bureau of Indian Affairs Building, not the Israeli sports compound, right? You kidnap generals, not weightlifters, right? You attack a troop train, not a trainer.

Wrong. Athletes are the new "royal families" of our culture. They are the targets in this real-life Day of the Jackal. A national athlete lying dead sends a far greater chill down the spine of the average citizen than does a martyred prime minister.

How did it happen? Well, the finger points first, as it so often does in this century, at that most formidable demon in all history: Adolf Hitler. At the Nazi Olympic Games of 1936, a tyrant marshaled an entire nation to bray to the entire world the superiority of an evil ethic. The pageantry in Berlin was a showcase of political ideology. The Olympics had been cast as a forum for political and social propaganda. Unnoticed in all the furor over the Fuehrer's refusal to shake hands with the American black track star Jesse Owens was the fact that two Jewish sprinters were quietly dropped from the United States relay team.

The Olympics changed from just fun to a serious clash of ideologies

The athlete really became a surrogate for power in 1952 when Russia, suddenly dropping its long-standing scorn of this capitalistic decadence, entered a team–a formidable team–in the Helsinki Olympics. Immediately, the Games degenerated into mini-war. Journalists began to keep a grim medal-count. Chins dropped when the Russians would outgold us. We began to see it as a significant statistic of the Cold War: the high jump today, the world tomorrow. What would they take over next, Wall Street?

The Russians were taken lightly, at first. We figured they would outlift us with the freight-car wheels or win the dancing-sitting-down exhibition. But in 1960–in an event we *cared* about, the high jump–an extraordinary event took place. We sent to the Rome Olympics a bona fide 7-foot high-jumper–not him, his jump. He spent the two weeks before the Games started "psyching out" the Russians–that is, jumping 7 feet conspicuously in front of them. *They* were rumored to have leaped 7 feet, too, but we all knew about Communist propaganda, now, didn't we? They'd invented baseball, too, hadn't they? Well, *both* Russians outjumped our John Thomas, who, to this day, has never beat them for a gold.

An Arab terrorist bargains in Munich

Suddenly it became not just a bunch of guys running around in their underwear, but a deadly serious clash of ideologies. I mean, if the Battle of Waterloo was won on the playing fields of Eton, might not World War III be lost in the high jump? Shape up, fellows, was the American plea.

It was in this atmosphere of bogus national self-interest that the Games went to Mexico City in 1968 amid rumors of student unrest. Avery Brundage, president of the International Olympic Committee, gravely troubled, paid a visit to the president of Mexico. If revolution were to break out or student demonstrations to break up the Games, perhaps it would be better to transfer them to Los Angeles, which was waiting in the wings? The president of Mexico shook his head. The students will not demonstrate, he promised. So, consider a news story as incredible as this one that followed:

(MEXICO CITY, Oct. 2, 1968–An undisclosed number of women, children, and students were killed here tonight in a bloody shoot-out between police and some of the 6,000 demonstrators, mostly students, who were in the Plaza of the Three Cultures. The students, protesting the military occupation of the National Autonomous University campus, had gathered for a march on the National Polytechnic Institute and were cheering in the plaza when a helicopter suddenly appeared overhead and dropped a flare. As if at a signal, white-gloved, carbine-bearing policemen appeared on balconies surrounding the plaza and opened fire into the crowd of demonstrators. A one-hour gun battle ensued, with tanks supporting the police effort. Conflicting reports put the dead at from 28 to 200, with 300 to 500 wounded. The Mexican government later admitted to a death toll of 48, which eyewitnesses, mostly foreign journalists, said was low. Some 1,500 persons were jailed.)

It was a hard look that Sports was taking at itself in 1972

1984? No, that was 1968. Pre-Orwell. The Mexico Olympics, with the Avenida de los Insurgentes lined with impassive-faced troopers, opened 10 days later without incident, just as promised. But slaughter had come to the Olympics; it was not new in 1972.

And then, in the middle of the Olympics in Mexico, Tommie Smith and John Carlos of the U.S. team mounted the victory stand and raised black-gloved fists in mute protest at the treatment of blacks in America. Within minutes their gesture, as haphazard and schoolyardish as it was, had become a major historical incident, flashed to all corners of the world in bated-breath headlines.

That was it. Pandora's box was open, and the seeds of hate and vengeance loosed on the world. Men of good will who could only have applauded the courageous stand against injustice by Carlos and Smith could only deplore the picture it showed the world of the Olympics as a forum for political purposes, the athlete as a standardbearer for his people. Men of good will? Men who–with their international bickering and their power plays to ban sports teams because of the public policies of their governments–have themselves helped politicize the Games.

Olympic service for Israeli dead

And what now? Are the paths of athletic glory to lead but to the grave, too? Could even the shelving of the national anthems, the flag-waving, and the other trappings of patriotism return the Games to the noble ideals of Baron Pierre de Coubertin or even the ancient Greek ideal?

Must the Olympic Games perish or be played inside a ring of cannon or on a lone and secret, shark-surrounded isle? It was a hard look that Sports was taking at itself in 1972. And hard answers must be found, or Sports may find itself staring permanently down the barrel of a submachine gun held by a shadowy character in a stocking cap. His nationality is unimportant. He belongs to a universal brotherhood. His name is Fear.

Related Articles

For further information on sports in 1972, see SPORTS and the articles on individual sports in Section Three.

Section Two

Special Reports

Seven articles and the exclusive YEAR BOOK Trans-Vision® give special treatment to subjects of current importance and lasting interest.

A New Look At Early Man in North America

By Stuart Struever

Changing goals and methods of the "New Archaeology" are producing new ideas about the life of early man

On the surface, Theodore Koster's cornfield is so ordinary it would never draw a second glance. It is small, covering only about 3 acres, and it is tucked away in a remote corner of Illinois about 45 miles north of St. Louis. With the old frame farmhouse and outbuildings, it snuggles close to the limestone bluffs that run along the Illinois River.

Yet, for centuries, what is now the cornfield has covered an archaeological treasure. In four years of digging there, scientists and students working with me have unearthed one of the most important prehistoric sites yet discovered in North America. We have uncovered at least 15 prehistoric settlements, stacked in layers one over another. Koster's cornfield is producing the most complete picture yet developed of how early man lived in North America.

We have excavated 34 feet below the present surface and have found evidence that man lived at this site more than 8,000 years ago, long before the Egyptians built the first pyramids or the ancient Britons erected Stonehenge. The people who lived at the Koster site had facial and skeletal characteristics of the present-day American Indian. Their ancestors came across one of the series of recurring land bridges between Siberia and Alaska.

The artifacts we have found in the soil show that a series of villages

The pioneers who built this stone house in Illinois became the 16th culture to occupy the sheltered valley that is the Koster site.

Koster Site

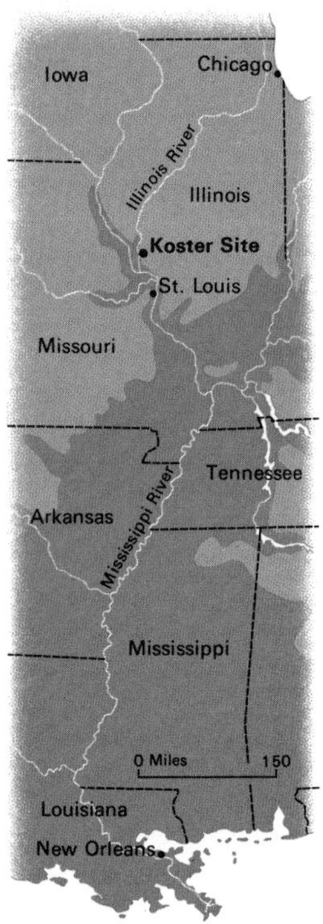

once stood at the site. Each one was abandoned and gradually covered with dirt and rocks that washed down from the bluffs. The mantle of soil preserved intact not only the remains of stone tools and hunting gear, but also bones, nuts, seeds, and other food remnants. As a result of this remarkable preservation and the techniques of the "New Archaeology," we have shattered many of the beliefs about early man that have been held for generations.

The location first came to our attention in the summer of 1968 when I was searching the area for evidence of early Indian settlements. Harlin Helton, a neighboring farmer and amateur collector, brought me some Indian arrowheads and broken bits of pottery. He said they came from the Koster cornfield. Although the finds were not particularly significant, I was interested because Koster's plow had unearthed many others in the same field. This suggested that there might be a prehistoric Indian settlement buried there. Moreover, Gregory Perino of the Gilcrease Institute in Tulsa had unearthed an Indian burial ground in another field close by. The area was a good site for a settlement. It is sheltered from the winds by high bluffs, and there is a spring nearby that supplies water throughout the year. We decided to do some exploratory digging the following summer.

At first, the Koster site appeared to be only 18 inches deep, because we could find no evidence of human occupation in the soil immediately below the uppermost level. However, we dug through this "sterile" soil and discovered an underlying layer that contained bits of bone and other refuse from human habitation. Further probing during the summer of 1969 revealed several alternating layers of human occupation and sterile levels. By mid-September, we had discovered six successive prehistoric communities or "horizons."

We have returned to the Koster site every summer since then, with crews of scientists, technicians, and student workers, and with earth-moving equipment. We have set up dormitory and research facilities in Kampsville, a small river town about 9 miles north of the Koster site. Old frame houses and stores in Kampsville have been turned into laboratories where scientists analyze and identify material uncovered at the site. We are now unpeeling, one by one, the layered ruins of at least 15 prehistoric Indian occupations. Horizon 13, which lies 29 feet below the present ground surface, has been radiocarbon dated at 5100 B.C., and we know that Horizon 14 is about the same age and Horizon 15 is much older.

In the past, historians and archaeologists took little interest in the lower Illinois River Valley. They explored the few monuments left by the prehistoric Mound Builders and did some exploratory digging, but, for the most part, they focused their interest on excavating ancient temples and graves in the Near East, Europe, and Central America. But important as it is, that work has focused little on prehistoric man's day-to-day behavior and processes of social change.

In an effort to discover how man adapted to his ever-changing envi-

The author:
Stuart Struever is a Northwestern University anthropology professor. He heads the program to uncover the remains of ancient civilizations in central Illinois.

An aerial view of the Koster site, *top,* shows its location near the Illinois River. North wall of the main trench, *left,* has dark-stained bands of soil that were formed by ruins of the site's many successive communities. Author Struever, *above,* examines the skeleton of an 18-month-old infant from soil dated at 5100 B.C.

ronment, four colleagues and I established the Foundation for Illinois Archaeology and its Illinois Archaeological Program in 1957. We planned to focus on the period of Indian prehistory from about 500 B.C. to A.D. 800, a period of dramatic changes in the record of early man in Illinois. We were interested not in just one time period and one small area, but in the development of archaeology itself, using Illinois as our laboratory. We particularly wanted to know how and when agriculture started and how this was related to the increased cultural complexity of Indian societies that emerged about 100 B.C. So far, we have located 510 prehistoric village and burial sites in an area of about 2,800 square miles centering on the lower Illinois River Valley.

Koster's cornfield has added new dimensions to our understanding of prehistoric life in the valley. We now believe, for example, that the first use of cultivated plants probably started there between 800 and 500 B.C. Our work is also beginning to change the picture of early man painted by archaeologists of the past. The Koster evidence has shown that early man was not primarily a hunter and eater of big game. He gathered plants, too, and in many cases depended more on plants than on animals for food.

Our work has also shown that life for early man was not necessarily nasty, brutish, and short. Instead, man adapted to many kinds of environments and used natural resources efficiently. The Illinois River Valley was, indeed, a land of plenty where people ate reliable subsistence foods that supported a stable culture for about 5,000 years.

We also know now that these prehistoric hunter-gatherers were not nomads. Long before they took up agriculture, they moved in patterned, seasonal cycles from one settlement to another, and some of them lived in permanent villages. There is evidence that the prehistoric people who lived at the site knew about agriculture for at least 2,000 years before they finally began cultivating plants to produce most of their food.

The remains found at the Koster site indicate that this region had a relatively stable environment from about 5000 to 2000 B.C. During this time, only hickory nuts among plant foods appear to have been important to the people. Small quantities of other plant foods, such as hazelnuts, pecans, walnuts, and seeds, have been found, indicating that the inhabitants ate these foods but did not rely on them. This contrasts with the later period, when they used hazelnuts, pecans, walnuts, and seeds extensively.

Studies have shown that a small population could live well by concentrating on a few abundant, nutritionally complete foods that were easy to collect, such as hickory nuts. As long as the population did not grow much, there was no reason for the people to change their diet. But when the population increased, the people who lived at the Koster site apparently began using other foods. This appears to differ with the

Koster Site

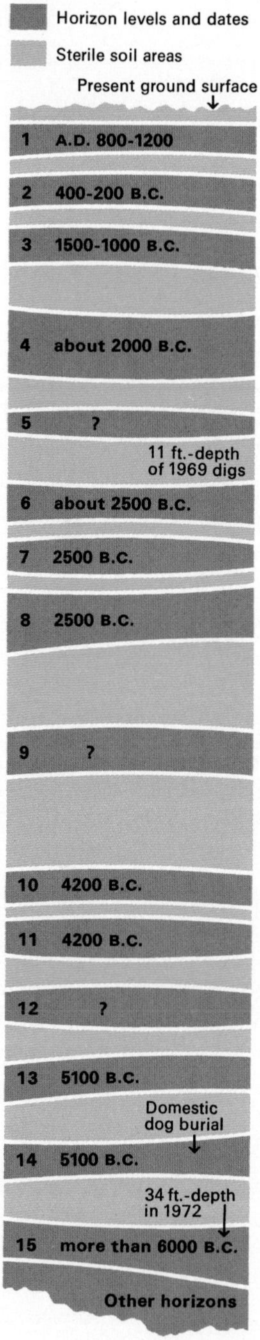

Horizon levels and dates
Sterile soil areas
Present ground surface
1 A.D. 800-1200
2 400-200 B.C.
3 1500-1000 B.C.
4 about 2000 B.C.
5 ?
11 ft.-depth of 1969 digs
6 about 2500 B.C.
7 2500 B.C.
8 2500 B.C.
9 ?
10 4200 B.C.
11 4200 B.C.
12 ?
13 5100 B.C.
Domestic dog burial
14 5100 B.C.
34 ft.-depth in 1972
15 more than 6000 B.C.
Other horizons

Each student-excavator is responsible for digging a certain area, and throws all soil onto screens where artifacts can be recovered.

view of the English economist Thomas R. Malthus, who said in 1798 that food supply could not keep up with population growth. Instead, it may be that increasing population caused man to increase productivity and eventually provided a motive for the change to agriculture. In any case, the later village sites we found at Koster are larger and show that man began to rely more on seeds and other foods. People began to raise corn in the lower Illinois valley about 100 B.C. Yet it was not until about A.D. 800 that they became fully dependent on agriculture.

We have also learned that the amount of leisure they had was not a major factor in determining the level of culture of these early men. Most archaeologists have assumed that once prehistoric men learned to domesticate plants and animals, they could then produce large food surpluses, thus freeing many people in the community to experiment with various activities thought to characterize higher civilizations, such as art, mathematics, and written language. We now have evidence that prehistoric hunter-gatherers actually had more leisure than modern industrial man, which raises questions about the role of leisure time in the development of civilization.

These radically new ideas about early man in North America are a direct result of the change in the goals and methods effected by the New Archaeology. This approach emphasizes that archaeological evidence taken from the ground can tell us more about prehistoric man than just identifying the tools he used and the food he ate. It can also help us to understand his social, political, and economic behavior. By studying culture, environment, and human biology as interdependent systems, we believe that archaeologists will eventually be able to explain changes that have occurred in these systems throughout the long prehistoric record.

In the past, archaeologists have tried to trace and describe events in the history of prehistoric groups. The new archaeologist tries to *explain* them. Instead of just listing historical events, he seeks the underlying causes that link them. In this sense, the New Archaeology is more scientific than the old. It seeks general laws of human behavior and culture change. The new archaeologist no longer chooses a site to dig just because, like Mount Everest, it is there. His choice of region, site, and methods of research are determined by the theories he wishes to test.

We may ask, for example, if there are universal prerequisites to warfare in human history. Must certain conditions exist before large-scale conflict begins, and what sets these forces in motion? We have found no evidence of warfare in the Illinois River Valley until about A.D. 800. Our problem is to discover why warfare started then and why men lived there peacefully before that time.

In addition, the new archaeologist does not regard any one artifact as typical of a culture. He recognizes that every culture is a system of interacting parts, and all remains have a relationship to the culture, even the garbage from prehistoric trash heaps. We know that archaeologists cannot continue to dig a few small holes into the remains of a prehisto-

Conveyor belt efficiently removes the soil from Horizon 11 (4200 B.C.), *above left,* as students carefully put artifacts into bushel baskets, *above.* Some of the soil is washed in the river, *left,* to separate bits of animal bone and plants. These pieces are then taken to a laboratory.

At the central data lab in nearby Kampsville, hundreds of artifacts are sorted, identified, and logged in every day of the digging season.

ric community and then accurately picture what life was like in that community. That is somewhat the same as a future archaeologist digging a hole into Wall Street and trying to reconstruct the way of life for all of New York City from what he finds. How could a few artifacts from Wall Street help us to understand athletic events in Yankee Stadium, or the life of people in Brooklyn's Bedford-Stuyvesant district, or in shipping areas along the Hudson River? The archaeologist must sample the complete range of human activities that make up an ancient society—houses, religious buildings, cemeteries, market areas, athletic fields, and all the rest.

This can be done only if every part of a site is excavated and more specialists are involved in the digging and analysis. At our Kampsville Research Center, a zoologist studies all animal remains to determine how each animal was killed and its age at the time it died. A botanist examines plant remains to determine climatic conditions and the time of year particular plants were used for food. An osteologist studies human skeletons to determine the age and sex of individuals and the diseases that might have killed them. A malacologist analyzes snails to determine what the prehistoric climates were like, and, of course, several archaeologists man specialized archaeology laboratories where they study the tools and other prehistoric artifacts that are recovered. This on-the-spot collaboration provides faster and more effective feedback among the specialists, providing each with new insights as he relates his own findings to the total problem. In addition to these research operations in the Kampsville laboratories, other specialists working in university laboratories collaborate with our program. These include a pollen analyst, a geologist, a geographer, and a botanical specialist.

Processing data has always been the most time-consuming aspect of archaeology. Too often, it takes years before a report can be published. The material recovered from an archaeological site must be carefully packed in boxes or bags for later study in a museum or university laboratory. Often, when archaeologists analyze data months after they have left the field, they discover they overlooked an important area during the excavation. For our work, we have set up a direct line link-

How Artifacts Are Processed

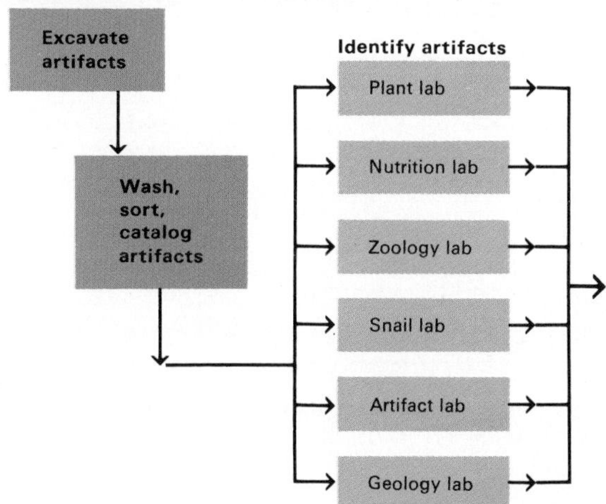

Manfred Jaehnig, who can be seen through the window, *top left,* heads the snail lab. He sorts the tiny fossil snails from the soil, *top right,* and identifies them in an effort to determine environmental conditions over the centuries. These and other data are then fed into a computer system, *above left and above.*

ing the laboratories in Kampsville to a computer at Northwestern University, and we can now process information almost as soon as it comes from the ground. We can get information feedback and correct observations immediately in order to plan the excavation work. Most important, the computer performs elaborate and time-consuming statistical analyses of our data.

We have also had to devise some new techniques to get all the information possible from the Koster site. One of these is a simple flotation technique we developed to recover tiny animal bones, seeds, and other small remains that are usually lost in the normal screening of soils that is done at any archaeological site. During the excavation, we encountered a pit that contained the charred ashes of some prehistoric fire. At the suggestion of a botanist, we gently poured the dirt and ashes into water in the hope that any hidden carbonized plant remains would float. To our surprise, a few charred seeds came to the surface. We now

Text continues on page 72.

From the top of the knoll behind the village that stood on the Koster site 4,500 years ago, the river valley spreads below. The season is fall, and a shallow ephemeral lake formed by the river is fast evaporating. The gray mud belt around the water gives evidence of the lake's contours earlier in the year. The perennial spring that flows past the village has created several acres of reeds and sedges as it spreads out over level ground. The women of the village are returning from a hickory nut-gathering expedition at day's end, carrying their booty in woven baskets. They are accompanied by a pet dog. Their houses are about 12 by 18 feet in floor space, with the floors nearly 18 inches below ground level. The walls are made of

woven twigs covered with mud plaster, and the roofs are thatched. When archaeologists began to excavate this village, which is found in Horizon 6 at the Koster site, they found several limestone roasting pits about 15 feet in diameter, which were used for roasting deer. There were also racks for smoking fish. The people had flint knives and other tools, as well as hunting weapons, and they made bone sewing tools, including needles, awls, and punches. Small beads made from imported hematite, or iron ore, and teardrop-shaped plummets that may have been weights for fishing nets were also found. About the village were many large *metates,* pieces of glacial stone with a distinctive groove in the center, that were used to grind nuts.

The people who lived at the Koster site about 4,500 years ago obtained their food in a wide variety of ways. Women gathered mussels from the riverbed, *above left,* and men hunted deer in the fall, *left.* The hunters used dogs to run the deer to exhaustion, and then killed the deer by using *atlatls* (spear throwers). The men also caught ducks by carefully stalking them after sunset and casting nets over them, *above.* The nets were equipped with special weights that made them easier to throw. The women gathered fish, *below,* by forming a line and stamping in the water to scare the fish into swimming into the shallow inlets where they could be scooped up in wicker sieves and tossed onto the shore. Other of the women then gathered them up and took them home in wicker baskets.

use this flotation technique routinely on samples of soil from all test levels. After using water to separate the plant remains, small bones, and shells from the soil, we use a chemical-flotation process to separate animal from plant fragments. During the 1971 field season, some 4,700 half-bushel soil samples went through the water-separation and chemical-flotation system. The animal and plant fragments recovered this way were sent to the botany and zoology laboratories in Kampsville.

Of course, most of the soil taken from the site is not put through this flotation process. Instead, it is dumped on a wire screen to sift artifacts out of the loose dirt. The pieces are then put into bags and sent to the field headquarters in Kampsville. After being washed and dried, they are sorted and weighed at the Central Data Processing Lab there.

The information from this sorting and counting process is fed into the computer, and the artifacts and debris are then sent to the various Kampsville laboratories or to university laboratories to be identified and cataloged. During the 1971 season alone, the zoology laboratory at Kampsville, under the direction of zoologist Frederick C. Hill of Northwestern University, identified more than 45,000 deer, fish, and animal bones as well as mussel shells taken from the Koster site.

The fossils, artifacts, food remains, and other bits of information we have found show that the people who lived at the time represented in each of the 15 horizons had some cultural differences from the others. An example of how much we have learned from just one layer of earth is the record of Horizon 6. These people occupied the site at about 2500 B.C.—the same time the great pyramids of Egypt were built. Obviously, a good-sized village stood there for a long time. The people enjoyed a comfortable, relatively secure life in a virtual land of milk and honey with tremendous food resources around them in the valley, and the

Baked-clay fireplace, *below,* was constructed in about 2500 B.C. by people of the same civilization as the man whose skeleton is being carefully uncovered, *below right.* Students are using bamboo picks.

taking was easy. They lived at the Koster site year-round, or perhaps left briefly during the summer. Their village covered at least 2 acres. They built their houses by setting branches or logs on end in wall trenches. Pieces of mud daub with fiber impressions indicate that they piled twigs and grass over the branches and mortared with mud, forming wattle and daub houses. Some primitive groups in Africa and Asia still live in such houses.

We found large grinding stones that weighed as much as 40 pounds that may have been used to process foods such as nuts. They are too heavy to have been carried far, which provides indirect evidence that this was a permanent settlement. We know that the people lived there during the fall, winter, and early spring because of the food remains. Deer teeth found in Horizon 6 indicate that some of the deer were from 4 to 6 months old when they were killed. Deer are born in May or June, so the site must have been occupied during the fall. The presence of large numbers of hickory nuts, which ripen in October, also supports this conclusion. The mature deer antlers and bones from fully mature migratory waterfowl that we found also indicate that people lived there during the winter and early spring.

We have found evidence of many types of activities in various parts of the village. Near a wall pit, we found a large grinding stone set into a hollow and held in place by chunks of limestone. Nearby was a small fire pit lined with limestone slabs and containing the charred remains of hickory nuts.

Another fire-pit area apparently was used to roast game for the entire village. We found a number of large pits that were lined with limestone and contained charcoal, charred animal bones, and scorched rocks. We also found clay-lined pits where people probably boiled fish. Individuals or groups butchered game, cracked mussels, tanned hides, chopped wood, and made tools at other places.

There were skilled workmen living there during this period, too. One can imagine a toolmaker squatting at the edge of the village chipping flakes from a piece of flint to shape a perfect spear point. Another may have been making an ax head or drilling a hole through a piece of metal to make some jewelry. Occasionally, we have found a flint core, surrounded by flakes chipped from it.

We collected many types of stone tools from Horizon 6, including large ground-stone axes that were used to chop wood. In addition to spear and arrow points, there were a variety of knives, scrapers, drills, and gouges that were used for butchering and processing hides and foods. We found teardrop-shaped plummets that probably served as weights in the casting nets used to catch waterfowl or fish. What we first believed were limestone pendants—chunks of limestone with holes bored through them—may actually have been fishnet weights.

Many of the tools we found in Horizon 6 were made of bone. The ornate, engraved bone pins may have been decorative hairpins, while the awls and needles were probably used in working hides.

Koster's student workers range from junior high school pupils to college graduates. Some living conditions are not ideal, but after the daily grind of digging in the hot sun, they have time for study and relaxation.

The people who lived at the time of Horizon 6 ate hickory nuts, fish, thin-shelled mussels, and deer most of the time. But their diet also included small quantities of other plant foods as well as ducks, Canada geese, wild turkeys, turtles, and small mammals. We also discovered corn pollen in Horizon 6. This indicates that early man cultivated maize in this region 2,000 or 3,000 years earlier than had been previously believed.

They must have used massive harvesting techniques to catch the fish. This is indicated by the density and range in size of fish bones we found in this layer. The zoology laboratory identified bones from 22,000 fish that were taken from an area 6 feet square and 3 inches deep. Some of them were from fish only 1 inch long. The fish may have been harvested by draining backwater lakes, by poisoning the water, or by stirring up the mud and thus bringing the fish to the surface for air.

These early people may also have been traders. We found a copper bead that must have come from copper deposits near Lake Superior, and an ornament made of galena, a lead ore, that probably came from western Illinois or southwestern Wisconsin.

Like the people before and after them, these Horizon 6 settlers found this sheltered valley an ideal place to live. It offered protection from winter winds, perennial spring water, and an abundant supply of plant and animal food. The rock outcrops of the bluffs provided flint for tools. There is no evidence that the settlers suffered from famine, violence, or war. At the last, they buried their dead in a tiny graveyard at the edge of the village, where we found 20 adult skeletons. From all this information about Horizon 6, we believe we can reconstruct the village site and learn how community life was organized 2,500 years before Christ. Each other horizon has its own distinctive characteristics, and each yields evidence of the cultures that occupied it.

The Foundation for Illinois Archaeology is a modest but real beginning of the type of institution that we must have to fully reconstruct prehistoric ways of life from the excavated record. In 1972, we had a team of 120 people at Koster. Eight professors headed the digging operations and the laboratories. There were 64 trained student assistants, 40 inexperienced students, and a support staff of 8 maintenance and kitchen personnel. In addition to working at the Koster site, the team excavated and analyzed material at three smaller sites nearby.

One of the keys to our program has been the success of our archaeological field school. This serves a broad educational function—a function that makes it more valuable than simply a trade school for training future archaeologists. Most teachers today are uncomfortably aware that many good students never become completely absorbed in any vocation. A great many graduates drift almost casually into roles that come easily, have little challenge, and offer little excitement. For some, at least, the field school marks the first step in another direction—a commitment to learning and a sense of the importance of the goals of research—that may continue to excite them throughout life.

The field school's emphasis on multidisciplinary training offers students a chance to learn from collaborating scientists the techniques of zoological, botanical, or geological analysis, as well as methods of excavation and data analysis. In this way, it provides clinical training for those who want to become archaeologists, botanists, geologists, or zoologists. It also provides the archaeological student with a perspective on the potentialities and limitations of these disciplines, and trains college, high school, and even junior high school students.

Their experience is total. They find themselves working harder than they ever believed possible. The field crews awaken at dawn to board trucks that take them to the site, where they dig all day under the blazing sun. The laboratory crews, too, work in conditions that are somewhat less than ideal. They tediously pick out fragments of bone with tweezers while the afternoon sun bathes the laboratory buildings in withering heat. The old drugstore now serves as a computer lab, and the town's hardware store has been converted into our artifact lab. Its shelf-lined walls are useful, even though the floors sag.

Most of the students are working for three college-level course credits from Northwestern University. They are light-years away from the usual campus distractions of football, fraternities, and dances. Even the formal academic atmosphere of classrooms, exams, and professors with posted office hours is missing.

There are no halls of ivy at Kampsville. Learning is an around-the-clock experience, acquired over a catfish sandwich at Millie's or a drink from the tin cup at the Koster well. Throughout a grueling day of digging in the sun, or picking out fragments of bone in a lab, there is intense preoccupation with archaeology.

The students learn how to wash, sort, catalog, repair, and otherwise prepare thousands of excavated items for analysis. They participate in all aspects of the processing system. More importantly, they learn why such a system is essential to the eventual success of the research project. Some students spend 50 or 60 hours a week in a laboratory analyzing excavated material. They soon learn how difficult it is to extract information from a mass of excavated remains.

Yet it is in this atmosphere of rural isolation, under difficult living conditions, that students and faculty can work together and share an expansion of knowledge most effectively. For many students, something important happens here—an intellectual awakening, the beginning of self-knowledge, and a crystallizing of ideas.

In sum, our research into human-cultural-environmental interrelationships at Koster has proved fruitful. Yet we have only scratched the surface. No one knows what we may find next year at the site or what equally revealing archaeological sites in the lower Illinois River Valley await our discovery. And, 5,000 years from now, perhaps some future archaeologist will find the remains of our work—our broken tools and garbage heaps—and reconstruct the life of the students and teachers of the field school at Kampsville.

Conservation Of Our Past Heritage

An archaeologist hastily excavates at the edge of a Florida highway before bulldozers churn the soil and destroy all traces of any ancient civilization.

Modern technology is rapidly destroying the record of more than 12,000 years of human occupation in North America. This unreplenishable resource of historical heritage is being scattered, plowed under, and cemented over for housing developments, shopping centers, roads, reservoirs, strip mines, recreation areas, and man-made lakes. Sites containing Indian mounds and ridges are leveled to make farmland more productive. Thousands of acres in America are being cleared annually for the first time, and ancient sites are often destroyed in the process. Less than 50 years of archaeological exploration probably remain before the majority of prehistoric sites are obliterated.

The problem is one of conservation, although that word usually only conjures up thoughts of land, animals, and vegetation, and not ancient communities. However, this conservation problem cannot be solved by replanting or replacing. When an archaeological site is destroyed, we have forever lost part of our precious historical heritage.

Most of the ancient sites lie in the most rapidly expanding metropolitan areas. This is particularly true of the great Mississippi and Illinois river valleys, where large human populations lived for thousands of years and developed the most complex prehistoric cultures. Many of these prehistoric sites face destruction when roads and bridges now in the planning stages are built to link the river valleys to St. Louis; Springfield, Ill.; and Davenport, Iowa.

Many important sites have also been ruined for scientific study by relic collectors and vandals. Removing artifacts or disturbing a site can wipe out the evidence archaeologists need to understand the culture of its prehistoric occupants.

The crisis in prehistoric-site preservation can be blamed partly on laws that are outmoded, limited in range, and inadequately enforced. There are, however, several federal laws in existence, including the National Historic Preservation Act of 1966, that provide funds to conduct archaeological surveys and to list the prehistoric sites in participating states. Arkansas and a few other states have also provided funds to find and preserve archaeological treasures before sites are destroyed. But just as in any other conservation effort, public concern determines the effectiveness of these programs.

In order to involve the public, the Society for American Archaeology has created the Committee on Public Archaeology, comprised of an archaeologist from each of the 50 states. The committee has listed six ways a concerned layman can aid in the preservation of sites and in alerting state and federal agencies, the public, and land developers regarding the urgency of preserving sites until they can be studied and their information can be recorded. These are:

- Write to the archaeology department of a large university in your state to find out how you can help, how you can learn more about archaeology, and what is being done in your state to preserve prehistoric sites. Most important, inform the department immediately if you know of a site facing destruction.
- Join your local or state archaeological society.
- Find out how the Historic Preservation Program, created as a result of the National Historic Preservation Act of 1966, is being implemented in your state. Write your lawmakers, if necessary, about pending legislation.
- Distribute copies of the booklet *Stewards of the Past* to landowners, contractors, and others in your area whose work includes alteration of the land. The booklet may be ordered from Carl Chapman, Department of Anthropology, University of Missouri, Columbia; James B. Griffin, Museum of Anthropology, University of Michigan, Ann Arbor; William B. Haag, Department of Geography and Anthropology, Louisiana State University, Baton Rouge; Charles R. McGimsey III, Arkansas Archaeological Survey, University of Arkansas, Fayetteville; or Stephen Williams, Peabody Museum, Harvard University, Cambridge, Mass.
- Refuse to buy or sell prehistoric artifacts.
- If you have a collection, be sure it is properly identified and recorded.

Your Day (Or Years) In Court

By Jack Star

The nation's court system is beginning to crack under the strain of too many cases and red tape, jeopardizing the right to a prompt and a fair trial

A bustling judge presided for seven months in 1972 in a special courtroom in Chicago's Civic Center that no witnesses or spectators ever entered. The jury room, piled high with lawsuit files, had no room for a jury. Yet the judge called four or five cases every 15 minutes, prodding attorneys to speed up their work in a frantic fight to break the logjam of pending cases in Cook County courts.

In the predawn blackness of Oct. 11, 1972, rebellious inmates of the District of Columbia jail seized the head of the D.C. Department of Corrections and nine other hostages. One of their major grievances was their long wait for trial or court hearings. They released the hostages after officials agreed to send them for immediate court hearings.

These cases are symptomatic of a growing illness that plagues our judicial system. In every part of the United States, it can take years for a court case to come to trial. The delays are so great that they threaten the very foundation of American justice. They whittle away at the citizen's belief that he can get justice through the courts.

The cases in Chicago and Washington, D.C., are extreme, but representative. Throughout the United States, it takes almost 22 months for a personal injury case to reach a jury—once the defense lawyer has filed

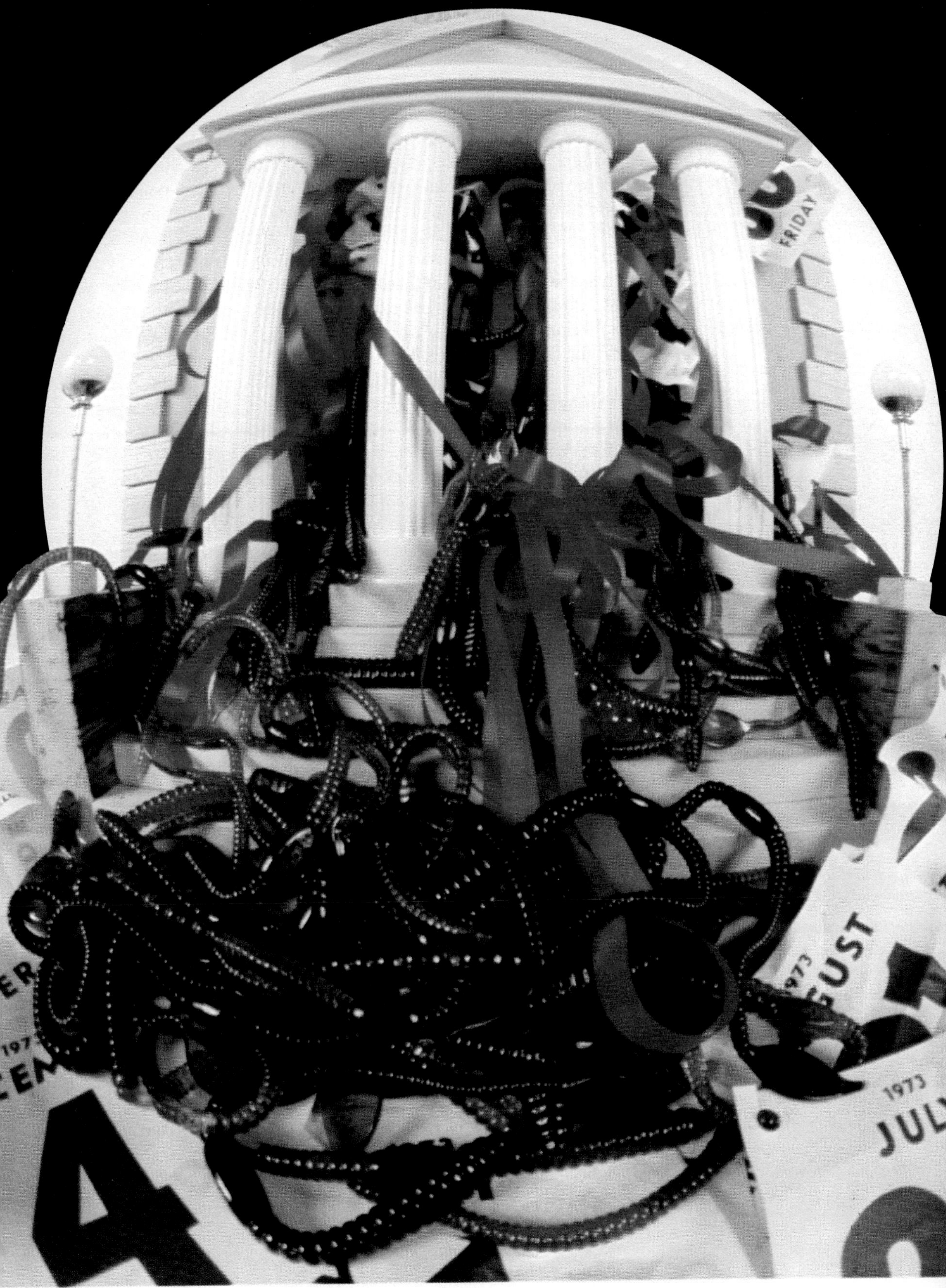
FRIDAY
1973
1973
1973

his answer to the suit, which can add another 5 or 6 months to the total wait. In Chicago and New York City, it takes over four years for a civil case to come to trial. And there are backlogs in many federal courts.

What brought the judicial system to this crisis? Experts point to a number of factors. The most obvious is our growing population; there are more people to get into disputes—and to resort to the civil courts in an effort to resolve them. In addition, crime has been increasing even faster than the population, so there are more criminal trials. Observers also cite what they call the "law explosion." Every year, Congress, the states, and municipalities pass thousands of new laws. Enforcing them adds still further to the courts' workload.

The delays in our courts have become so bad that many judges and lawyers wonder whether the court system can take much more strain without collapse. Chief Justice Warren E. Burger has asked, "Is a society that frequently takes 5 to 10 years to dispose of a single criminal case entitled to call itself an 'organized' system?" The court crisis, like most crises, has stimulated reform attempts. But not all authorities find all the reforms acceptable. The Chicago experiment was one of these.

"We decided that a reasonable time to prepare a case was a year," said youngish, optimistic Benjamin S. Mackoff, administrative director of the Circuit Court of Cook County, who has been trying to reform the creaky system. In many ways, the backlog of civil cases in Cook County is typical of those throughout the nation. Mackoff described the Chicago experiment:

"We programmed our computer to mail out a notice ordering the rival lawyers to come to a special courtroom when their case was a year old. We had five- and six-year-old cases awaiting trial where the summons hadn't even been served, or the defendant's lawyer hadn't replied to it. These old cases were clogging the system. We thought we could avoid this with our newest cases, the 14,000 filed in 1971."

A visitor to the special Civic Center courtroom might have despaired of Mackoff moving the average lawsuit into court in a year's time—but perhaps his computerized efforts could reduce the long delays. Judge Paul F. Elward, a plump, pleasant, and very brisk man, presided in the special courtroom. One by one, he called up the still dewy 1971 cases. With a long check list and a ball-point pen in his hand, he brought the opposing lawyers before him and quickly ticked off points: "Let's see, summons issued? Defendant served? Defendant appearance? Defendant answer? We've got all those. How about the interrogatories [the pretrial questions the opposing lawyers can ask each other's client]? We've got all those, huh? Is there a need for a medical exam?"

Many lawyers seem in no hurry to complete these tedious prerequisites for trial. "Lawyers are creatures of habit," one explained. "Once they get used to taking five years to handle a case, they like taking five years." Besides, 85 per cent of Cook County's 35,000 pending cases in-

The author:
Jack Star is a former newspaperman and was the Midwest editor of *Look*. He has written extensively on crime and problems of the courts. The American Bar Association has presented him with a Silver Gavel Award for his reporting on law.

The "law machine"—Congress, states, and municipalities—churns out new laws every year. Enforcing them adds to the courts' burden.

volve automobile accidents, another circumstance in which the county is typical. Between 50 and 90 per cent of the nation's civil lawsuits are auto negligence cases; they make a massive contribution to the jam-up in the courts. In 1970, for example, the United States had 16 million accidents that caused about 2 million injuries. Enormous numbers of lawsuits result, although only 3 per cent of them ever go all the way to a court verdict. So what's involved here is a form of arbitration, or pressure for a compromise. The threat of an adverse verdict is the goad for settling "out of court."

"Remember," said Judge Elward, "the average time from an accident to filing of the suit is 18 months. Add another 12 months until it comes before me and that's a 30-month delay to start with. Of 2,596 cases I have called, *no one* has walked in the door ready for trial. But, if this call does nothing else, it gets the legal machinery started. After four, five, six calls they're finally ready for trial."

Not all lawyers were happy with such pressure. One who failed to come up with some interrogatories as ordered two months earlier stood unbelieving while Elward fined him $100 for wasting the court's time.

Judge Elward's action in the Chicago experiment illustrated the frustrations of battling the huge logjam. He illustrated it better, perhaps, than he intended—when he gave up the fight. Many of the attorneys who felt Elward's pressure asked for a change of venue, an order shifting their case to another court, but Elward refused. One of them appealed to the Illinois Supreme Court, however, and got a ruling that such requests had to be granted. Elward concluded that his power had been emasculated by the ruling. He asked to be reassigned, and the experimental program was dropped.

As Mackoff explained it, Judge Elward's experiment was one jaw of a vise squeezing reluctant lawyers toward either trial or compromise. The other jaw consisted of a group of pretrial judges whose bench experience fits them to recognize possibilities for compromise. In his chambers, Judge Sigmund Stefanowicz, one of seven pretrial judges in the Cook County court system, tightened the vise in a conference with lawyers representing the parties involved in a relatively minor automobile collision. While I watch, the entire conference lasts five minutes:

Back in 1968, the plaintiff's car was rammed from behind, causing $713 damage. Normally, such cases are settled for the property damage plus three times "specials" (loss of wages, doctor bills, hospital bills)—$785 in this case. The plaintiff wanted $3,500. Threatened with a trial within a month at which an unpredictable jury might soak his client $5,000, the insurance company lawyer now offers to pay $3,035 (the traditional formula worked out to $3,068). The plaintiff's lawyer thinks this is a fair offer. "My client has been trying to settle with the insurance company since 1968," he says wistfully. "Fine, fine," says Judge Stefanowicz. "It's a good compromise." But an observer can't help wondering why it took so long.

A lawyer's view of delays, however, is different from the layman's. I watch silver-haired Philip H. Corboy, president of the Chicago Bar Association and a leading personal injury lawyer, win a whopping $752,500 for his client, a settlement that came toward the end of a long trial. The client, previously blinded in one eye, had lost his remaining eye when struck by a flying splinter from a defective tool six years earlier. "This case could not have been tried in less than two years," explains Corboy. "We were too busy with other cases."

An attorney may even find delays useful. "It takes time for a case to ripen," Corboy says. "Besides, we had no settlement offer at all until three weeks ago, just before the jury was picked, when they made an offer of $165,000." Attorney Corboy takes sharp exception to criticism that brands trial lawyers as dilatory. But there is no denying that lawyers can constitute a bottleneck, because trial work tends to gravitate to a relatively few specialists. "I'm overwhelmed," one complains. "I've got 800 cases pending and trials before five judges simultaneously."

But does this have to be? Judge Joseph J. Butler, who assigns the civil cases for trial in Chicago, recalls how one such problem was solved: "The lawyers for one insurance company, an outfit with five times as many cases here as any other company, were found to have 150 pending 1966 cases and 700 pending 1967 cases. They were willing to cooperate, so we sent them before the same judge, day after day, for three months— with the files kept right in the courtroom to save time. Within three months, they disposed of 600 cases. That judge, who was our number-one man, had gotten rid of only 89 cases in a previous three-month period under the old ways of doing things."

The jam-up is not limited, however, to civil courts, where cases involving individuals' private rights are heard, where plaintiffs seek recovery for damages done to them. It is no snap to get a hearing in criminal court, either, which deals with offenses considered harmful against society as a whole. The average delay between arrest and trial in New York and Philadelphia is over five months; in Ohio, it is over six months; in Chicago, six to nine months. It is easy to find men who have been in jail awaiting trial for as long as two years, unable to raise the $500 needed to post a $5,000 bond. Prosecutors may be dilatory, but sometimes the defense itself contributes to the delays. "What's the point of hurrying to trial if the state has a good case?" asks a defense lawyer. "My man is as well off in the county jail as in the state penitentiary. Besides, memory dims and prosecution witnesses disappear with the passage of time."

As a result, American jails house a huge population of unconvicted prisoners, such as those who rebelled in the District of Columbia jail. When the 1970 census was taken, 83,000—or 52 per cent—of the prisoners in the nation's county and city jails had not been convicted of any crime; they were awaiting trial.

As much in criminal cases as in civil proceedings, scheduling all the elements to be ready for trial at the same time seems an almost insuperable problem. Chicago Judge Kenneth E. Wendt, for example, tries

manfully but unsuccessfully to expedite the flow of cases. But he points out that his courtroom goes unused a good part of the time. "I have over 100 cases pending on my calendar," he says. "I set eight or nine a day, hoping that *one* of them will be ready for trial."

On one typical morning, Judge Wendt waited from 9:30 until 10:15 A.M. for the public defender, assigned to defend those who cannot afford a lawyer, to show up. When he finally arrived, breathless and embarrassed about causing the delay, he explained that he had been called to an important conference. Now, however, it is the assistant state's attorney's turn to be embarrassed. "Your honor," he says, "we were all set on this matter and now it seems the fingerprint expert is on furlough." The clerk calls a new case, and this time the prosecutor is enraged, not embarrassed. "I gave six subpoenas to the sheriff last week to be served on the witnesses," he says, "but for some reason, instead of being served they turned up this morning on my desk." Judge Wendt shakes his head sadly. He's heard all this before. "In the past seven days," he explains, "we've had only three real trials."

With all the proposed innovations, all the new approaches being tried to break the towering jam-up, all the endless red tape, the essential question still remains unanswered: What happens to justice? The picture presented on a steaming summer day in the aging Criminal Court Building on Chicago's grimy West Side makes a courtroom visitor suspect that the whole system of justice is foundering. This is an "easy" day in one of the building's two Felony Courts, where nearly half of all of Chicago's serious crimes get their hearing. On this morning, only 130 cases are waiting to be called.

All the action is at the bench, where a knot of policemen, public defenders, prosecutors, stenographers, and court deputies wait for prisoners to be brought in from the crowded lockup. "Quiet! Quiet in the court!" the clerk shouts hopelessly for the tenth time. Judge Robert J. Sulski, a conscientious man in a limp, black robe, hunches forward over the high bench at 11:37 A.M., straining to hear the commonplace drama unfolding beneath him. It's the first hearing of the day. The previous two hours were consumed by legal red tape.

A frail, 67-year-old woman tells how she had just cashed her welfare check and bought some food stamps in a currency exchange when a youth grabbed her around the neck and took her remaining $111. She told detectives she recognized the youth as a resident in her housing project. At the police station, she picked out his photograph in a "mug" book. The defense lawyer, a young man in a mod checked coat, cross-examines firmly. He is no Perry Mason, but he quickly makes the point that the old woman had contradicted herself—the police report shows she had first told the investigating officers that she could not recognize the man. Now Judge Sulski must decide whether to hold the youth over to the grand jury, which probably would indict him, after which the

A society on wheels, the United States has more auto accidents each year. The resulting lawsuits contribute to the jam-up in the courts.

Plea-bargaining, with opposing attorneys agreeing on charges and sentences,is helping to prop up the pillars of justice by relieving congestion in the courts. Some experts say it should be brought into the open as a formal part of court procedure.

case would go to trial. He decides not to. When there is only the word of the victim, the identification must be more positive. "No probable cause," the judge rules, discharging the accused robber.

A young black man, charged with burglary, listens to his lawyer ask that the case be dismissed because this is his sixth appearance in court and the prosecution still isn't ready. The prosecutor calls a detective to testify: "Your honor," the detective says, "we can't find the complainant." As is not uncommon in a big-city ghetto, the complainant's tenement has been torn down and he has left no forwarding address. "Discharged," says the judge. In a loud whisper, he tells me, "Thirty per cent of my cases are discharged for want of prosecution."

I begin to catch on to the overworked Judge Sulski's role. He is Peter, the little Dutch boy who stuck his finger into the leaking dike to save the nation from being flooded. It is the judge's job to sidetrack as many of the prospective felony cases as he can to spare the grand jury and the overwhelmed 17 Criminal Court trial judges. To a degree, he is succeeding. Every year, the Chicago police arrest more people, but there were one-third fewer indictments in 1971 and 1972 than in 1968.

The preliminary hearings such as Judge Sulski's help bring about this reduction by discharging some of the accused, by downgrading some charges to lesser offenses, and by accepting guilty pleas from 30 to

40 per cent of the defendants. Once past the preliminary hearing and after indictment, still more of the defendants "cop a plea," bringing the overall average to that of most American courts—90 per cent guilty pleas. Long surreptitiously practiced, this process—pleading guilty in return for a reduced charge and sentence—is formally called *plea-bargaining*. It is one of the desperation measures that keep the judicial system afloat, and it has the backing of Chief Justice Burger. He points out that at present only 10 per cent of all cases actually go to trial. But if less plea-bargaining reduced guilty pleas to 80 per cent, it would raise the trial figure to 20 per cent. The nation would have to double its judicial manpower and facilities—judges, court reporters, bailiffs, jurors, and courtrooms, Burger says.

Plea-bargaining is also defended by U.S. District Judge William J. Campbell, formerly chief judge for the Northern District of Illinois. Campbell, in fact, believes "plea-bargaining should be acknowledged, legitimatized, and encouraged....Judges should meet in chambers with the prosecutors and the defense attorney—if any meaningful plea-bargaining is to be accomplished. The defendant's agreement can come later in court and on the record. Agreements or understandings reached at such conferences should, of course, be made part of the record and not piously denied or cavalierly winked at when the agreed sentence is imposed."

Despite its obvious success and its many defenders, there is growing uneasiness about relying on plea-bargaining to keep the judicial system from collapse. Hans Mattick, criminologist at the University of Illinois at Chicago Circle, says the system leads to inappropriately severe charges. "The police overcharge, knowing they'll be plea-bargained down," he says. Norval Morris, director of the University of Chicago's Center for Studies in Criminal Justice, says, "We cannot tolerate a system where 90 per cent of the serious criminal cases are disposed of in the manner of a Moroccan market place."

At the opposite pole stands Assistant State's Attorney Charles C. Leary, who is in charge of the prosecution's side of plea-bargaining in Chicago's Felony Court, where penitentiary sentences are normally imposed. Says Leary, "If your case is worth 5 to 10 years upstairs [in a trial court], I can get you 3 to 7 down here. If we tried every case, we'd be in worse shape than the courts hearing personal injuries.

"It's my task to hold the line on indictments, to send only 'good' cases to the grand jury. Suppose a man uses a shotgun to hold up a tavern. In Illinois, armed robbery is punishable by a minimum of five years in prison. Suppose the man is arrested three days later and seven tavern patrons identify him. The defense lawyer is looking for probation—the holdup man is only 22 years old, it's his first felony, and he comes from a good family. Sorry! With seven victims identifying him, our case is strong and we'll go to court. If we had only a single witness, though, I'd think about a compromise. We don't like single 'fingers'."

In such an eventuality, with a relatively weak case, Leary might consider reducing the charge to simple robbery. This might mean offering the defendant three years' probation, with the first six months or the first year to be spent in the County Jail, in return for a plea of guilty. The judge can overrule Leary, but it occurs to an observer that the prosecutor, operating alone in the judge's shabby chambers while court is in session elsewhere, exercises tremendous authority. In effect, he is, all by himself, another judicial system—with inadequate safeguards.

Ironically, some safeguards in our judicial system contribute to the problem of court logjams. One such safeguard is the appeal, in which a case already decided by a court is transferred to a higher court for review. The process was established to further guarantee that an individual accused of a crime receives justice in the courts.

Toward Speedier Justice

By Warren E. Burger
Chief Justice of
The United States

American courts need help in their struggle to withstand an unprecedented explosion in the number of cases filed. Cases filed in federal district courts have increased by more than 50 per cent in 10 years. The workload of the United States Court of Appeals has increased almost 250 per cent, while the nine justices of the Supreme Court of the United States must review twice as many cases as they did 10 years ago and three times as many as 20 years ago.

Both state and federal courts risk falling so far behind that meaningful justice is often denied. Caseload growth must be curbed or performance capability greatly increased. Otherwise, the attraction to the best-qualified lawyers of becoming a judge could well diminish. The quality of justice could be jeopardized.

Courts can be protected from this potential deterioration by resolving some disputes that now go to the courts through other institutions, such as special administrative agencies, mediation, and arbitration.

In order to assure that Congress, in creating new rights to sue, weighs the added burden to the courts along with the benefits, it should be required that each new proposed law be accompanied by an impact statement. The statement would estimate the effects of such legislation on the courts. One way to accomplish this would be through a joint judiciary council—appointed equally by the President, Congress, and the judiciary—to prepare impact statements and generally advise Congress and the executive branch on the needs, problems, and jurisdiction of the courts. This could also be accomplished by the congressional committees on the judiciary.

Where the constitutionality of a state or federal statute or an Interstate Commerce Commission action is challenged, a cumbersome three-judge court now has the right of direct appeal to the Supreme Court without intermediate review by a court of appeals. These special courts should be eliminated, and appeals should go from the district judge to a court of appeals. Many other cases, which now go to the federal courts because the citizens involved are from different states, could also be handled more satisfactorily by state courts.

Attorneys are frequently allowed to delay commencement and completion of cases. Judges can speed dispositions by setting time limits for cases and firmly scheduling hearings and trials. Other organizational improvements that are helping to improve judicial efficiency are coming through the adoption of improved docketing procedures. They include the early assignment of every case to a specific judge, thereby focusing responsibility for case management. They include omnibus or single hearings, which dispose of all pretrial motions at one time, thus avoiding a se-

In early 1971, I interviewed Presiding Judge Joseph A. Power of the criminal division of the Cook County Circuit Court. Not much has improved, he says, when we talk again in mid-1972. There are 2,000 men in Cook County Jail, three-fourths of them unconvicted prisoners—awaiting indictment hearings or trials. The average caseload for each judge is about 120 cases. And on top of this already heavy load, the court must reconsider 40 to 50 cases a week—some as much as 20 years old—in which men serving prison terms are seeking reviews.

The prisoners usually claim that their lawyers were incompetent. Quite often, the lawyer is not around to defend himself—he is dead. "Even if there are no grounds for an appeal," says Judge Power, these cases "take hundreds of man-hours for assorted court personnel to han-

ries of delaying motions before trial. And they include pooling and central control of court reporters, and procedures to use jurors more efficiently. Efficiency is not a primary objective of the judicial system, but without reasonable efficiency and sound organization, courts cannot perform their function of dispensing justice.

Experienced court executives can help chief judges improve court operations, as some state courts have demonstrated. Such executives have long been used in a number of courts, but only in 1972 did the federal courts obtain a limited amount of such assistance. More of it is needed.

Geographic realignment of federal judicial circuits is needed, and a commission has been created to make recommendations to Congress on boundaries as well as on the structure and procedures of the federal courts of appeals.

More practical guidance, stemming from applied research and planning for the judiciary, is needed. There is considerable support for the creation of a National Institute of Justice, somewhat comparable to the National Institutes of Health. This could help to develop and coordinate a comprehensive research program. It could propose long-range judicial objectives and planning based on an overview of both state and federal needs. Increased research, development, and planning will help strengthen training and advisory programs of the Federal Judicial Center, created in 1968, and such newer organizations as the Institute for Court Management, created in 1970, and the National Center for State Courts, created in 1971.

Rehabilitation of people convicted of crimes is a vital phase of the total administration of justice, a phase that needs help. Many prisons have so deteriorated that they tend to perpetuate instead of correct criminal behavior. Expansion of probation staff and training services would save money over costly prison confinement, and it would help to rehabilitate those found guilty. Prisoners who show promise of rehabilitation should be separated from incorrigibles and permitted to learn their way out of prison by comprehensive educational and vocational programs. The 1972 proposal of President Richard M. Nixon to create a National Corrections Academy to train prison personnel was an important step to improve U.S. correctional systems.

Considerable progress has been made, particularly during the past three years, in trying new methods and initiating new legal and judicial institutions. But the need for improvement that lies ahead is enormous. Judges and court personnel increasingly recognize the need for modernizing the administration of justice. They will, however, need strong public support to achieve this modernization. If the pursuit of justice is, indeed, one of our noblest goals, we must give it more support.

Victimless crimes and acts that are not crimes add to the logjam in the courts. Some–such as divorces, child-custody cases, gambling, and drunkenness–could be taken out of the courts to be settled elsewhere.

dle, what with the transcripts and all. Maybe we should give everybody one appeal automatically and dispose of everything at once, while the case is still fresh. We have a right to a speedy trial. Why can't we get one on the appellate level?"

Statistics point up the problem. Delays in state and federal appeals courts average two years. In some cases, they even reach five years. Since 1961, appeals from state prisoners to federal courts have increased from 1,020 a year to 12,145. There is terrible pressure, even on the Supreme Court of the United States. It must now deal with 4,000 appeals a year, compared with 1,100 in 1950. And, if we create more trial courts (one way suggested to combat rising crime and the court logjam), appeals courts will be even more crowded.

Most of the proposals made to ease the court load—the single automatic appeal, for example—would require major changes in the judicial system. Robert W. Meserve, veteran Boston lawyer and president of the American Bar Association (ABA), sees changes in the U.S. Con-

stitution as a possibility. "We can avoid some civil delays by a constitutional amendment to cut down on jury trials," he says. "In England, there is no right to a civil jury trial except in slander and in libel." Several Canadian provinces have done away with civil juries, and Canada's court delays, on the whole, are not as long as those in the United States. It takes only about two years for a civil case to come to trial in Toronto and only one year in Vancouver, for example.

In criminal cases, Meserve and others advocate stopping the prosecution of so-called "victimless criminals"—gamblers, prostitutes, drug addicts, homosexuals, for example. Over 2 million arrests annually are for public drunkenness. These constitute more than twice the total of all seven serious crimes tabulated by the Federal Bureau of Investigation—murder, forcible rape, robbery, aggravated assault, burglary, theft over $50, and auto theft.

"I'm not a softie in this field," says Meserve, "but take drug addiction as a cause of crime. Many violent crimes are caused by people satisfying a drug habit. You can send a junkie to jail, but have you cured the problem? The system is dealing only with the symptoms."

Chief Justice Burger suggests that some matters might be better administered outside the courts. They include divorce and child-custody questions, the adoption of children, receiverships of insolvent debtors, and land title registration. Simpler, no-fault divorces are now a reality in about six states. And surely auto accidents, which take up 17 per cent of the time of state courts and 11 per cent in federal courts, and generate awesome piles of paperwork for the court system, can be more simply and better handled.

Curiously, Meserve is cool toward the idea of no-fault auto insurance—giving an accident victim compensation from his own insurance company, no matter who is at fault. This scheme, which theoretically could remove all of the less serious accidents from overburdened courts, is now in effect in about half a dozen states. Automobile policy rates are down 43 per cent in Massachusetts—which has no-fault insurance—but Meserve says the no-fault plan has done little to reduce the number of lawsuits. "Maybe not," one legal scholar replies, "but our present no-fault laws are not tough enough. What we need is a no-nonsense federal no-fault law."

Glenn R. Winters, executive director of the American Judicature Society (more than 47,000 lawyers, judges, and laymen promoting efficient justice), believes that lazy or inefficient judges and procrastinating lawyers can be identified by using computers to keep track of their cases. The computers would also spotlight situations in which "an inner circle of trial lawyers builds big reputations and ends up with more trial work than they can handle." But George F. Westerman, staff director of the ABA's section for judicial administration, is far less hopeful. "You can't just give computers to the courts," he says. "More radical reform is required. The alternative to civil jam-ups is to go to some sort of compulsory arbitration, but lawyers are not willing to give up their fees just to streamline the legal system. As for the criminal courts, they should be reserved for true crimes. We're arresting too many people."

In a landmark 1972 decision, the Supreme Court ruled that no person may be imprisoned for a misdemeanor—disturbing the peace or breaking a traffic law, for example—unless he has been represented by counsel or has waived that right. In its famous *Gideon v. Wainwright* decision of 1963, the court had ruled that any indigent accused of a felony has that right; the new ruling is far more sweeping. It may increase court congestion, unless large numbers of lawyers are found to defend persons accused of such minor crimes as spitting on the sidewalk, using obscene language, loitering, begging, and public drunkenness.

Under another new ruling, petty offenders too poor to pay a fine can no longer be sentenced to serve out the fine in jail. "The result here will be no penalty at all because most petty offenders are too poor to pay fines," says Frank Jones, executive director of the National Legal Aid and Defender Association. "If these men have lawyers, there are going to be fewer guilty pleas," he says. "We are going to start winning acquittals and appeals, and people are going to realize that the street drunk should be handled administratively."

In an effort to speed justice, the Supreme Court, in May, 1972, swept aside the requirement, dating back to 14th century English common law, that jury verdicts in state courts must be unanimous for criminal convictions. All states can now establish other norms. For some time, Oregon has permitted a conviction when the jury votes 10 to 2, and Louisiana, 9 to 3. But, even if legislatures take advantage of this opportunity, authorities doubt that they will remove a major cause of delay. Cases that go all the way to a jury, which then can't reach a unanimous verdict, cause relatively little problem. A more promising solution lies in cutting jury size, because jury selection is a tedious, time-consuming process. Some federal jurisdictions and several states allow 6-member juries in civil cases, some states use fewer than 12 jurors in minor criminal cases, and Florida, Louisiana, and Utah do so even in felony trials.

An important product of the judicial system's problems is the fading public confidence in the courts. This is not eased by such critics as New York City's Police Commissioner Patrick V. Murphy, who says that "the court system must accept the giant share of the blame for the criminal rise in crime." In 1970, when New York had 94,000 felony arrests, it held only 552 felony trials—mainly because of plea-bargaining. Fewer than a quarter of New York's reported felonies even end in an arrest. So Murphy scoffs at the notion that criminals are deterred by the certainty "that once caught they will be promptly prosecuted, convicted if found guilty, and jailed."

Former Supreme Court Justice Tom C. Clark maintains that the courts lag because there are more policemen, thus more criminal charges filed, while the system's capacity remains constant. "The charge that sentences are light is without foundation," Clark says. "A survey of sentencing in America shows it to be number one in severity of sentences imposed of any country in the Free World. Rather than our sentences being light, a prime reason for the crime wave is the increasing number of recidivists [crime repeaters], which indicates a total failure of our prison system."

A special judicial committee studying court delays in New York City at the start of 1972 found nearly 5,000 prisoners there awaiting trial or sentencing—an increase of 48 per cent in only half a year. It recommended 30 new criminal courts and 4 new grand juries to handle the jam-up. Other cities are following New York's example, adding more courts, more prosecutors, even more computers. But we still have a growing population, thus more problems and more disputes that cry for justice. Pessimistic observers of the rickety structure that is our judicial system say even these moves will be less than adequate. They suggest the most important reforms are those that can, in some way, sharply limit the numbers of us who must go to court.

Traditional Africa

In a Modern World

A *Year Book* Trans-Vision® and Special Report

Africa: A Proud Heritage

There are many misconceptions about Africa that have only recently been dispelled. The most pervasive of these is that Africa was a changeless and primitive continent before Europeans began exploring what was called the "Dark Continent" in the late 1700s. The white man has tended to regard the story of his involvement there as the "history" of Africa. Consequently, that "history" was concerned mostly with coastal colonial settlements. According to most early white observers, Africa's interior was in savage chaos, inhabitated by illiterate societies or "tribes." There could be no history, they concluded, where there was no civilization.

A new view of Africa developed after World War II when scholars began to look at Africa from within and to view foreign factors against the background of African peoples and their cultures. They discovered a rich history, much of which was unknown or only vaguely familiar to the rest of the world. The Trans-Vision® unit that follows is a very brief outline of that history. Africa is perhaps the most intriguing of the continents. Its history includes the earliest history of man, for it was there that the earliest known man lived. From its vast deserts, rain forests, and grasslands arose the earliest great civilizations of the past. In the words of leading African historian Basil Davidson, Africa is truly "black mother" to the world.

Africa: Old and New

African historian Philip Curtin explains in this Special Report how Africa has sought to preserve the most valuable aspects of its older, traditional way of life during several decades of change and "modernization" in the move toward its own future.

Africa: A Proud Heritage

Above, a giraffe grazes amid vegetation typical of African savannas. *Left,* oases in the Sahara.

The Land

The history of Africa is tied to its unique environment. It is the only continental land mass whose northern and southern extremes are nearly equidistant from the equator. As a result, it is the most tropical of the continents, with about 9 million of its 11.7 million square miles lying within the tropical zone. This tropical environment formed the cradle for mankind.

But Africa is not all lush tropical rain forests. Vast savannas, or grasslands, cover more than 40 per cent of the continent, and provide its characteristic vegetation. These grasslands vary from drier regions near deserts, which contain scattered trees, bushes, and short grass, to wetter areas near rain forests where the grass may grow from 6 to 8 feet high. Africa's grasslands provide for its abundance of wild game and are the setting for its pastoral societies. The major areas of Africa's grasslands lie between the Sahara and the equatorial rain forests, and between the Congo River Basin and South Africa.

Deserts cover another 40 per cent of the continent. Africa has three main desert regions–the Sahara, which stretches 3,000 miles from the Atlantic Ocean to the Red Sea; the Somali, from Kenya northeastward along the coast; and the Kalahari, which lies in Botswana and South West Africa (Namibia). But only a portion of this huge desert area is barren and desolate. Much of it consists of shrub and grass areas suitable for some limited grazing. The remainder of Africa consists of rain forests, 8 per cent of which are equatorial. The highlands of Ethiopia, the mountains of northwestern Africa, and the moist, temperate regions of southern Africa also have forests.

An arcuate, or curved, line drawn from the mouth of the Congo River around the southern and eastern margins of the Congo Basin to the Ethiopia-Sudan border in the northeast would divide Africa into highland and lowland zones. The highlands lie south and east of this imaginary line. They consist mainly of a complex of plateaus from 3,000 to 5,000 feet above sea level, with occasional higher areas and mountains. The lowland area, north and west of the line, consists of plains and basins ranging from 500 to 2,000 feet above sea level. A few higher mountains and plateaus lie in this area. Mount Cameroon, in Cameroon, for example, rises 13,354 feet.

The highlands of eastern Africa are rent by faults, or breaks in the earth's crust, a chain that runs nearly the length of the continent. This is the Great Rift Valley system. In Kenya and Uganda, the system splits into the Eastern Rift and the Western Rift. Between them lies Africa's greatest lake, Lake Victoria. Africa's highest peaks – Mount Kilimanjaro (19,340 feet) in Tanzania and Mount Kenya (17,058 feet) – are also in the rift zone.

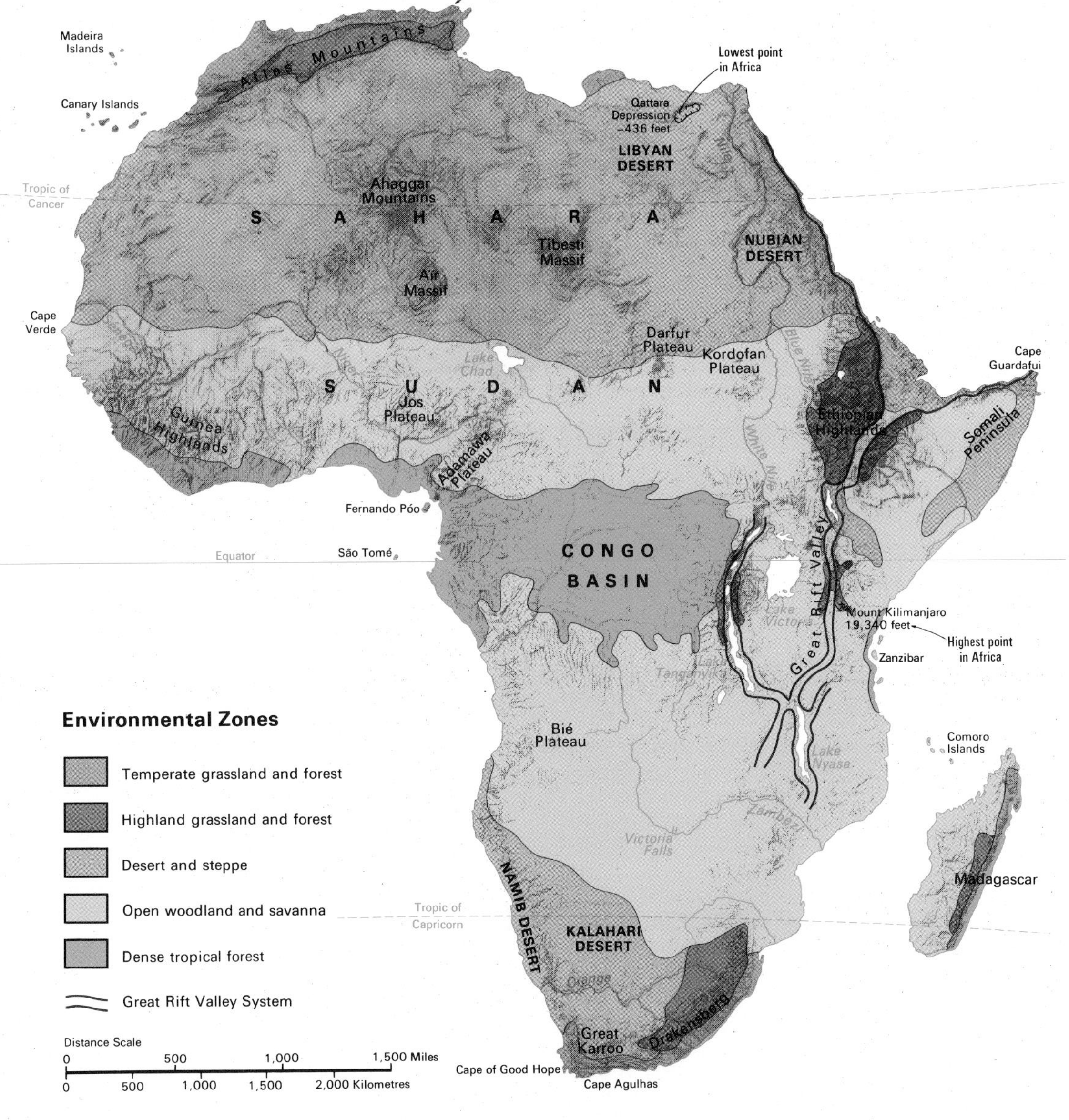

Man's Beginnings in Africa

Aided by recent advances and discoveries from a wide variety of disciplines, archaeologists have pushed the veil of history back 4 to 5 million years to discover that the birthplace of modern man's ancestors was in Africa.

The first fossil primate remains in Africa were discovered in South Africa. In 1924, Australian Raymond A. Dart blasted out a site on the high dry plateau of South Africa and found "the complete facial skeleton of an infant...which looked amazingly human. . . . The brain was so large and the face so human," Dart wrote, "that I was confident that here, indeed, was one of our early progenitors that had lived on the African continent; and, as it had chosen the southern part of Africa for its homeland, I called it *Australopithecus africanus* (the South African ape)."

Dart placed his discovery midway between the apes and the oldest identifiable human fossils and deduced that it had lived about 1 million years ago. *A. africanus* was about 4½ feet tall, weighed about 60 or 70 pounds, and had a brain capacity about one-third that of modern man. It walked upright and it was capable of simple tool making.

Dart's colleagues rejected his theory of man's origin. They believed man's birthplace was in Asia. But Dart had started a widespread controversy that would soon be resolved in his favor. In 1936, the famous South African zoologist Robert Broom discovered an adult man-ape in a cave near Johannesburg, South Africa. This was a primitive fossil creature with both human and subhuman characteristics who lived perhaps 3½ million years ago. This find seemed to confirm both Dart's discovery and his conclusion. Other scientists – including Louis S. B. Leakey and his wife, Mary, British anthropologists who in 1959 discovered a fossil skull on the oldest bed of Olduvai Gorge, near Lake Victoria, in Tanzania – confirmed Africa as the birthplace of man.

More recent discoveries have increased our knowledge of early man and his ancestors. Eastern Africa has been the richest area for these discoveries. From fossils of manlike creatures, their stone tools, and other objects found in successive layers of Olduvai Gorge and other sites, scientists conclude that the ancestor of both man and the ape came into being in Africa about 20 million years ago during the Miocene Epoch. Dart's *A. africanus* developed some 15 million years later. It was followed in a few more million years by *Homo habilis* (skillful man), discovered by the Leakeys in the Olduvai beds. *Homo habilis* had a slightly larger brain capacity, and there is evidence that suggests he was the first systematic toolmaker. *Homo habilis* was followed by the even larger-brained *Homo erectus* (erect man) and, about 150,000 to 200,000 years ago, by Neanderthal man in northern Africa and a closely connected race of Rhodesioids (*Homo sapiens rhodesiensis* or Rhodesian man) in southern Africa.

About 35,000 years ago, *Homo sapiens sapiens* (modern man) appeared. His emergence was due primarily to a process of natural selection, during which he had developed a large brain as a means of survival.

The early ages of man are still wrapped in scientific doubt. There are many pieces of the jigsaw puzzle that have yet to be fitted together. It is not until the Mesolithic, or Middle Stone Age, period that scientists feel sure of their ground. By about 14,000 B.C., modern man was well entrenched in

About A.D. 100: The Bantu Migration

The drying of the Sahara reduced communication between the north and the south to a bare minimum. Except for a few trade routes, such as those that crossed the Sahara to the Niger markets, the peoples who had once shared a comparatively homogeneous existence now found themselves divided by an expanse that would eventually cover 3 million square miles, extending some 3,200 miles from east to west, and from 800 to 1,400 miles from north to south.

Those Saharan dwellers who moved north quickly adapted to the cultures of Egypt and Syria, which were also influencing the entire Mediterranean world. Some were absorbed into the cultures of the African kingdoms of Kush and Aksum that grew as Egypt declined. Eventually, they all became, to a greater or lesser extent, heirs of the civilizations of Greece and Rome. The émigrés who moved south, however, were cut off from these stimulating contacts. In the harsh environment where they found themselves, survival became a primary consideration. Their mastery of this environment resulted in a movement of people that, because of the numbers and the distances involved, remains unique in world history.

At about the time of Christ, Bantu-speaking peoples began a progressive diffusion, moving south and southeast from what is now eastern Nigeria into the Congo River Basin of central Africa. These early Bantu-speakers had mastered agriculture, introduced into the Lower Nile area about 5,000 B.C., and, for some three centuries, had had knowledge of ironworking. The earliest known iron in the Bantu homeland of western Africa is associated with the Nok culture in northern Nigeria. The use of iron in the Nok culture dates to approximately 400 B.C., and the Bantu in all probability learned their ironmaking skills from the Nok people.

Knowledge of agriculture and ironworking helped the Bantu people to prosper and multiply as they began pushing through the rain forests and into the broad plateau south of the Congo Basin – an area much like their homeland. From there they spread rapidly and widely – eastward into the highlands, and southward where they encountered the Bushmen. But the Bushmen, as well as the Pygmies of the Congo Basin, were no match for the Bantu and they were forced to give way to the spreading Bantu groups. By about A.D. 500, Bantu communities had settled far to the south and east. By A.D. 1000, the powerful Bantu had peopled much of the lower half of Africa and were still migrating southward, into what is now South Africa.

About A.D. 1000: The Impact of Islam

In the 700s, Islam, the religion of the great Moslem Empire that spread quickly from Arabia to north Africa, began also to have an important influence on the east African coast and on all of north Africa, and eventually it extended southward to the area the Europeans called the land of Zanj. By the late 800s, Islam had spread into the eastern and western Sudan, as well as the Middle East and southern Spain.

In north Africa, Islam found itself beset with political division in the Fatimite caliphate and its influence began to diminish. Islam was still the principal outside influence in Africa, however, and provided the major link with Asia and Europe. Moslem merchants and traders crossed the desert into the western Sudan, and Islam was introduced into the west African kingdoms and into Kanem around Lake Chad. In west Africa, the kingdom of Ghana, in the grasslands of the western Sudan between the upper Senegal and Niger rivers, reached the height of its power around 1000. The great kingdom of Ghana covered the greater part of western Africa, and its trade extended as far as Spain and Portugal. For more than 300 years, until its decline in the 1000s, Ghana was known throughout the north African world as "the Land of Gold." By developing a valuable two-way traffic of gold and ivory from the south for the scarce commodity of salt from the north, Ghana's kings were able to support huge armies and to live in a splendor befitting "the Lords of the Gold."

The Moslem merchants spread Islamic teachings as they moved over the Saharan trade routes into west Africa, and Islam brought to Africa a new knowledge of the world to the north, new and important spiritual influences, and the skills of reading and writing. Whatever written history exists of the ancient kingdoms of Africa and the beginnings of modern-day Africa after 1000, were written in Arabic, the language of Islam. Moslem traders, however, did not reach the kingdoms south of the central forests. As a result, these areas developed without the aid of writing or the other skills Islam brought to the western kingdoms.

Thus, long before European colonization, Africa had prosperous kingdoms and had attained impressive civilizations. They flourished on agriculture; they mined and traded large amounts of gold; they had mastered metalworking, spinning, weaving, and dyeing. Some cities had attained international fame, and tales of their magnificence and splendor reached far across the civilized world. They were true centers of learning and religion, attracting scholars, theologians, merchants, and legal experts from distant lands.

Text continues on page 114

these 3,000 years, rivers and lakes increased in size and importance. As they did, settlements sprang up and agriculture flourished. During this phase, too, the Sahara was not a desert but an area of grasslands, lakes, and rivers. Because of these climatic changes, man learned to perfect the survival skills of hunting and gathering and fishing, and became more specialized and efficient in them.

It was during this period that man began to portray his life style and esthetic sense through rock paintings and engravings. The earliest rock paintings have been dated to 4300 B.C. and are attributed to early Bushmen of eastern and southern Africa. Stone Age man also used pottery and domesticated animals, raising huge herds of cattle and grazing them in the lush grasslands where he lived. He also began to bury his dead, an indication that he had religious beliefs.

About 2000 B.C., rainfall began to diminish in the Sahara region. Bit by bit, drought parched the once-verdant land, and its inhabitants were forced to seek sustenance elsewhere. Some migrated northward; others moved southward. The almost insuperable barrier that was formed between the two groups by the largest desert in the world was to have an enormous impact on African history.

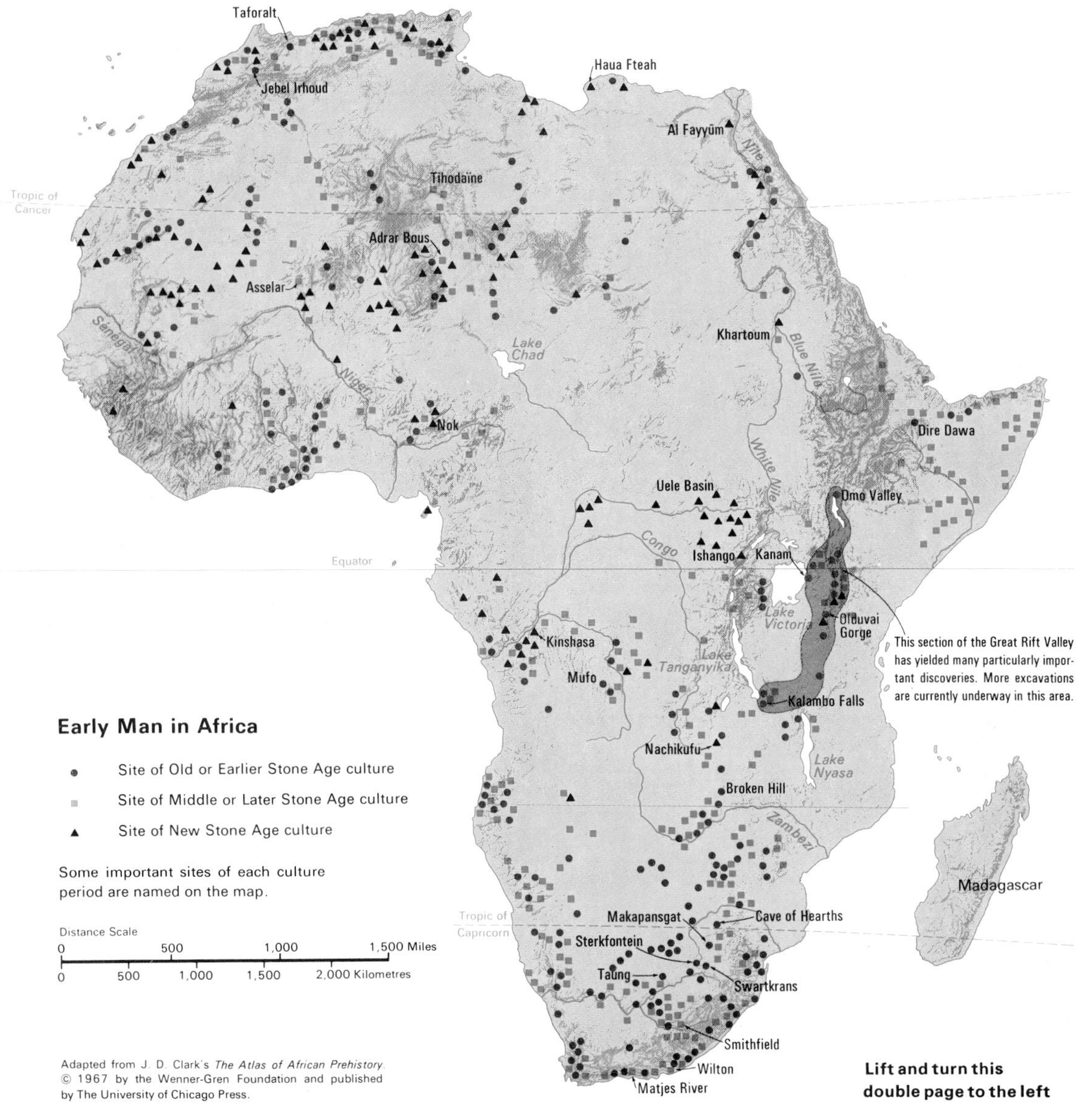

Adapted from J. D. Clark's *The Atlas of African Prehistory.* © 1967 by the Wenner-Gren Foundation and published by The University of Chicago Press.

Lift and turn this double page to the left

Africa. The man-apes had become almost extinct. Modern man had developed a family and community life and numbered about 2 million. He was able to make relatively sophisticated hand axes and other stone tools and weapons, knew how to gather and use plants for food, and had become a regular user of fire.

During the late period of the Stone Age, which lasted until about 3000 B.C., several different types of people lived in Africa. Most numerous were the Negroids in western Africa, ancestors of today's black Africans. Next in numbers were the ancestors of the smaller Bushmen and Pygmies from present-day Ethiopia southward along the highland backbone of eastern Africa and into southern Africa. Africans whose ancestors probably came from southwestern Asia lived in northern Africa, and those whose ancestors probably migrated from Europe settled along the Mediterranean Sea. By 2000 B.C., the Negroids had become the most widespread group on the continent, and they are the chief subjects of the rest of Africa's kaleidoscopic, multi-faceted history.

Toward the end of the New Stone Age, important changes in Africa's climate affected the development of the culture and skills of Stone Age African man. After about 8000 B.C., the Sahara became extremely dry, but this was followed by a more humid period, known as the Makalian wet phase, from about 5500 B.C. to 2500 B.C. During

Dancers and musicians cavort in Stone Age rock painting near Lake MacIlwaine in Rhodesia.

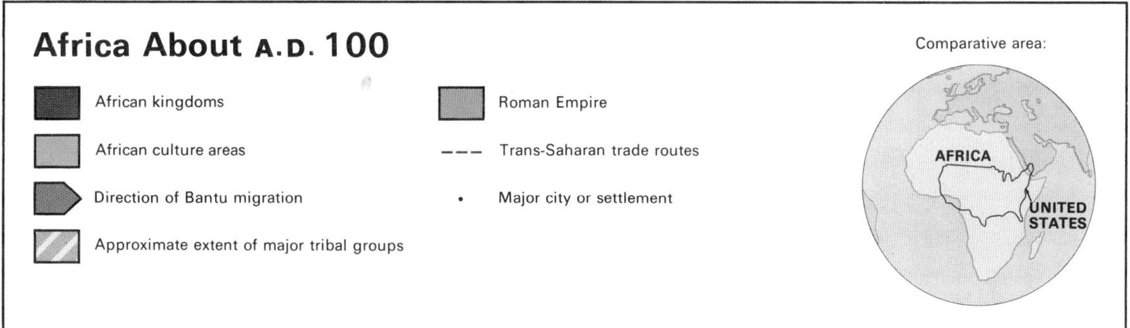
Africa About A.D. 100
African kingdoms
African culture areas
Direction of Bantu migration
Approximate extent of major tribal groups
Roman Empire
Trans-Saharan trade routes
Major city or settlement
Comparative area:
AFRICA
UNITED STATES

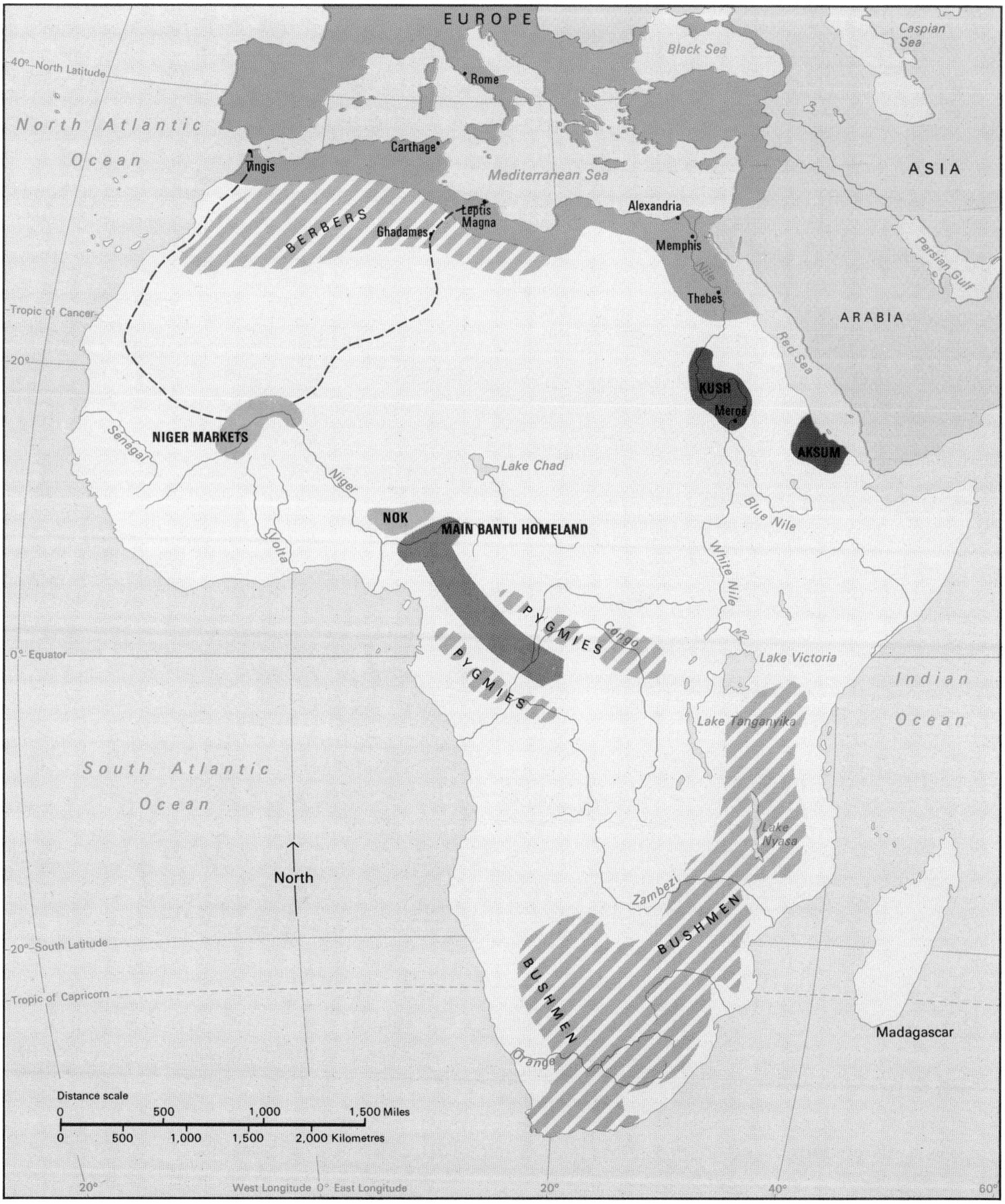

EUROPE
Black Sea
Caspian Sea
Rome
40° North Latitude
North Atlantic Ocean
Carthage
Tingis
Mediterranean Sea
ASIA
Alexandria
Leptis Magna
Ghadames
BERBERS
Memphis
Nile
Persian Gulf
Thebes
Tropic of Cancer
ARABIA
Red Sea
20°
KUSH
Meroë
AKSUM
NIGER MARKETS
Senegal
Lake Chad
Niger
Blue Nile
NOK
MAIN BANTU HOMELAND
Volta
White Nile
PYGMIES
Congo
0° Equator
PYGMIES
Lake Victoria
Indian Ocean
Lake Tanganyika
South Atlantic Ocean
Lake Nyasa
North
Zambezi
BUSHMEN
20° South Latitude
BUSHMEN
Tropic of Capricorn
Madagascar
Orange
Distance scale
0 500 1,000 1,500 Miles
0 500 1,000 1,500 2,000 Kilometres
20° West Longitude 0° East Longitude 20° 40° 60°

The Study of Africa's History

Although the serious study of African history began only about two decades ago, Africans have always been conscious of their past. The importance they attach to the role of their ancestors as the source of morality and custom enhanced this sense of history. As a result, they built up a knowledge of the past in the form of what is now commonly known as oral tradition.

The old men within various African communities were the custodians of these traditions. They were expected to recall significant individuals and events that had influenced the life of their people and to relay the information to their descendants. In those areas of Africa where Islam had been introduced, the past was not merely retained in oral form but also was recorded in Arabic texts.

These African historical sources were available to the European explorers, traders, and travelers who began to visit Africa during the 1700s. A number of them recorded some of the oral traditions as part of the accounts of their journeys, but no serious attention was paid to this aspect of their work at that time. European historians accepted only documentary evidence as a valid source of history. However, after the imposition of colonial rule on Africa toward the end of the 1800s, it became evident that a stable system of government required a good understanding of Africa and the structure and functions of African institutions. So colonial authorities asked anthropologists to undertake research in Africa. In fulfilling this task, these scholars could not neglect the oral traditions of the Africans and began to record them or to revive the traditions collected earlier. By the period between World War I and World War II, administrative need and academic curiosity had combined to kindle interest in the study of African societies.

European scholars were preoccupied with anthropological studies, and the product of their efforts was scarcely historical in character. Some, such as G. G. Seligman in *The Races of Africa* or M. Delafosse in *The Negroes of Africa*, attempted a general synthesis. The majority, however, concentrated on regional or local surveys of African cultures. At the same time, organizations such as the International African Institute in England, the Society of Africanists in France, and the Belgian Royal Colonial Institute were founded to encourage intensive research.

Meanwhile, black intellectuals in the United States began to take greater interest in their cultural roots as a reaction against the assumption that they belonged to a race without history. Afro-American scholars also launched the Association for the Study of Negro History, whose *Journal of Negro History*, edited by Carter G. Woodson, provided a forum for the publication of articles relating to African history. But these scholars were restricted by the axiom that only what is documentary is historical. They concentrated on the few written sources available.

After World War II, a new orientation in the study of African history emerged among Africans and then gradually gained acceptance among Western scholars. This orientation was part of the growth of nationalism in Africa; Africans educated in the metropolitan universities of Europe demanded that history teaching in Africa should emphasize the achievements of Africans, not the activities of Europeans. Instead of writing academic theses on colonial policies, some Africans chose themes–such as *Trade and Politics in the Niger Delta* (K. O. Dike) and *The Egba and Their Neighbours* (S. O. Biobaku)–that focused attention on African initiatives and the interaction of African societies. Rather than rely on written sources alone, they boldly consulted the oral traditions and thus opened up the possibility of integrating the traditional African approach to history with Western historiography. With this new approach, what had previously been recorded about Africa by travelers, explorers, missionaries, and colonial administrators gained new importance. Shorn of the racial prejudices embedded in them, the accounts provided essential material for cross-checking oral traditions and made it possible for scholars to attempt a credible chronology of African history.

It was soon discovered that other disciplines within the social and natural sciences could contribute toward extending the range of knowledge of the African past. Anthropologists helped in clarifying how African institutions might have evolved. Linguists were able to classify African languages and thereby throw considerable light on the pattern of diffusion of African peoples throughout the continent. Archaeologists unearthed a wealth of information relating to the early cultures of Africa. Even botanists made a contribution to the unrecorded pattern of relationships among African peoples by studying African food crops.

Today, there is a wealth of published information on the history of Africa from the earliest times to the present. Two books that reflect the new approach to African history and, at the same time, offer a good general synthesis are *A Short History of Africa* by R. O. Oliver and J. D. Fage (Penguin Books, 1962) and *Africa: History of a Continent* by Basil Davidson (Macmillan, 1966). These could be usefully supplemented with *Africa*

Lift and turn to the right to expose page 114

About 1500: The Great Kingdoms

About 1100, the African east-coast trading cities entered an era of prosperity through peaceful maritime trade. Arabs, established in the Barbary States and the Mameluke Empire, developed a series of ports in east Africa for the trading of ivory, slaves, and gold. In the mid-1440s, Portuguese ships began to navigate Africa's coastal waters. Portuguese explorers reached the mouth of the Congo River on Africa's west coast in the 1480s. In 1497 and 1498, Vasco da Gama led an expedition around the Cape of Good Hope to India. Within 10 years, the Portuguese had visited all of coastal Africa, had displaced the Arabs from the east coast, and controlled parts of the west coast.

In west central Africa, the great Bantu kingdoms of the Kongo and Luba and Lunda were reaching their peak. At Zimbabwe, in southeastern Rhodesia, for example, the Bantu built a complex so elaborate it was once thought to have been built by "outsiders," not Africans. By the 1500s, the Bantu had reached the southern farming region of present-day South Africa and occupied most of central and southern Africa.

In west Africa, the powerful and wealthy kingdom of Mali had long ruled the rich savanna lands between the Sahara and the forests. By the late 1400s, though, Songhai, located around the middle Niger River, had replaced Mali as the strongest kingdom. Until its defeat by Morocco in 1591, Songhai ruled an area that extended west to the Atlantic Ocean and as far east as Lake Chad. Songhai's city of Timbuktu became one of the medieval world's great centers of learning.

Other important west African kingdoms were the Hausa states, which lay between Bornu-Kanem and Songhai, the Benin and Oyo empires of the Yoruba and Edo peoples in what is now southwestern Nigeria, and the Ashanti empire in the Akan forestlands west of the Volta River.

About 1800: The Slave Trade

From 1500 to 1800, European ships opened new trade lines and new communication links. But, during that time, most of the European newcomers were traders. Wary of "fever," and in need of maximum protection, they avoided the interior and stayed close to the coast. To brave even this degree of risk required a large financial reward, and this existed in the form of gold and slaves.

The major impact of Europeans on Africa south of the Sahara was the introduction of the slave trade by the Portuguese. It provided workers for Portuguese and Spanish sugar plantations in the Caribbean. Eventually, the major destination for slaves was the new colonies in North America.

How many men, women, and children were sold as slaves is unknown. Perhaps as many as 3 to 5 million were sold in the New World. An estimated half-million were sent to the United States and Canada alone via the West Indies. But thousands died from brutal overcrowding and neglect on the long ocean voyage, and thousands more died en route from the African interior to the coastal slave ports. And, to this staggering toll must be added those killed in the wars waged among Africans to obtain the slaves. It was not until the 1880s that the slave trade ended. It had been the largest forced migration in history.

Africa in 1956: Eve of Independence

The "scramble" for colonies in Africa began about 1880. Parts of Africa were already under colonial influence, and the interior had been cautiously explored beginning in the 1770s. But competition for the riches of Africa did not begin until about 1880, when European governments began to stake out claims throughout the continent. These claims, generally unrelated to geographical, political, or social realities, often cut across tribal boundaries.

Although some African rulers gave in peacefully to European powers, many resisted. The Europeans treated the ensuing wars of resistance as "rebellions" and put them down swiftly with superior weapons. By 1900, European powers controlled most of Africa.

Colonial rule lasted for about 50 years. There were only four independent African countries–Ethiopia (free throughout its history except for a brief period during World War II), Liberia (1847), Egypt (1922), and the white-controlled Union of South Africa (1910).

The march to independence began in 1951, when Libya achieved independence. Perhaps the most significant date, however, was March 6, 1957, when Ghana achieved independence in the first transfer of power from colonial rule to black Africans. Thereafter, the independence movement accelerated, and, one by one, the former European colonies won their freedom.

Today, there are 43 independent African countries (see "Africa Today" map on facing page).

These new countries of Africa are possessors of a proud heritage. But they have many problems of economics, government, and unity ahead of them. The next period of African history will see this vast continent loom large in the affairs of the world.

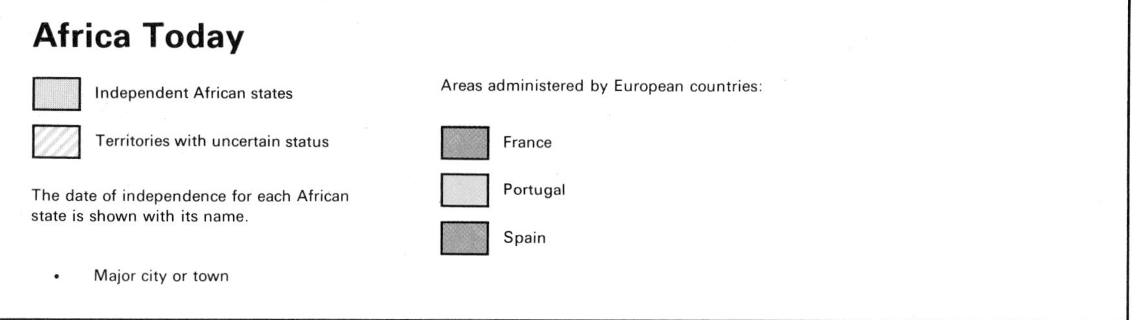

Africa Today

Independent African states

Territories with uncertain status

The date of independence for each African state is shown with its name.

• Major city or town

Areas administered by European countries:

France

Portugal

Spain

EUROPE
Black Sea
Caspian Sea
40° North Latitude
North Atlantic Ocean
Ceuta (Spain)
Melilla (Spain)
Tunis
Algiers
TUNISIA 1956
Mediterranean Sea
Madeira Islands (Portugal)
Rabat
Casablanca
MOROCCO 1956
Tripoli
Suez Canal
Alexandria
ASIA
Canary Islands (Spain)
ALGERIA 1962
LIBYA 1951
Cairo
EGYPT 1922
The Sinai Peninsula is part of Egypt. The area has been occupied by Israel since 1967.
Persian Gulf
SPANISH SAHARA
Nile
ARABIA
Tropic of Cancer
Lake Nasser
Red Sea
20°
MAURITANIA 1960
MALI 1960
NIGER 1960
Ethiopia has been independent for about 2,000 years.
Dakar
SENEGAL 1960
CHAD 1960
Khartoum
GAMBIA 1965
Niger
Lake Chad
SUDAN 1956
PORTUGUESE GUINEA
UPPER VOLTA 1960
AFARS AND ISSAS (France)
GUINEA 1958
ETHIOPIA
DAHOMEY 1960
NIGERIA 1960
GHANA 1957
Addis Ababa
SIERRA LEONE 1961
IVORY COAST 1960
Ibadan
LIBERIA 1847
Accra
Lagos
CENTRAL AFRICAN REPUBLIC 1960
SOMALIA 1960
CAMEROON 1960
TOGO-1960
EQUATORIAL GUINEA-1968
UGANDA 1962
KENYA 1963
Congo
0° Equator
São Tomé (Portugal)
GABON 1960
CONGO 1960
Lake Victoria
Indian Ocean
ZAIRE 1960
RWANDA 1962
Nairobi
BURUNDI 1962
Kinshasa
CABINDA (Angola)
Lake Tanganyika
TANZANIA 1964
Zanzibar
Dar es Salaam
South Atlantic Ocean
Luanda
Date of union between Tanganyika and Zanzibar.
MALAWI 1964
Comoro Islands (France)
ANGOLA (Portugal)
Lake Nyasa
ZAMBIA 1964
North
Zambezi
South West Africa is governed by South Africa. The United Nations declared an end to South Africa's mandate in 1966.
SOUTH WEST AFRICA (NAMIBIA)
RHODESIA
MOZAMBIQUE (Portugal)
Tananarive
20° South Latitude
BOTSWANA 1966
MALAGASY REPUBLIC 1960
WALVIS BAY (South Africa)
Tropic of Capricorn
Pretoria
Johannesburg
Rhodesia declared independence from Great Britain in 1965.
SWAZILAND 1968
Durban
LESOTHO 1966
SOUTH AFRICA 1910
Distance scale
0 500 1,000 1,500 Miles
0 500 1,000 1,500 2,000 Kilometres
Cape Town
20°
West Longitude 0° East Longitude
20°
40°
60°

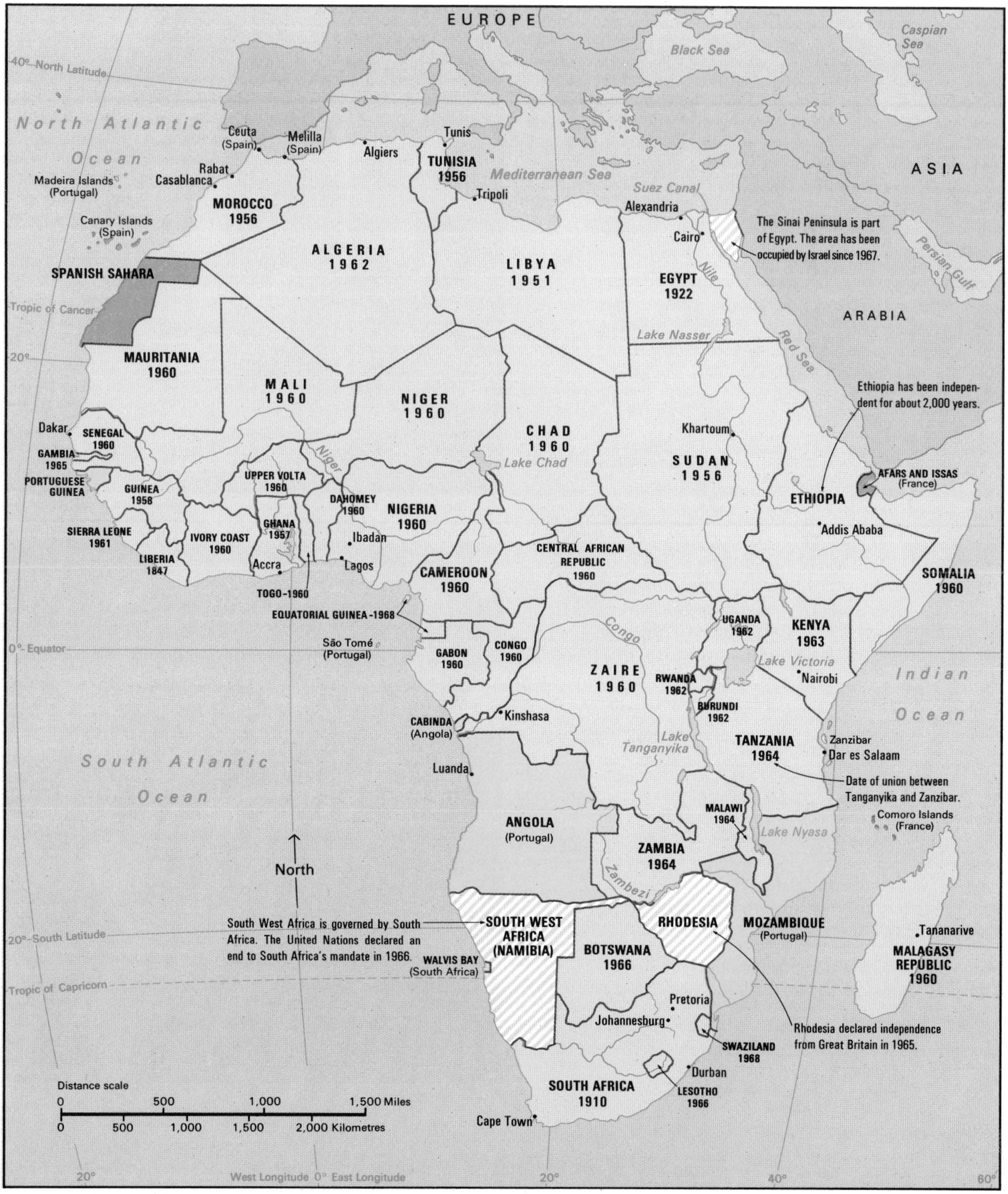

and Africans by Paul Bohannan and Philip Curtin (The Natural History Press, 1971), a good survey of African culture history. The collection of texts edited by Davidson, *The African Past: Chronicles from Antiquity to Modern Times* (Penguin Books, 1964), is an exciting reminder of the range of new documentary sources.

Many new regional histories also are available. For West Africa, the older one-volume survey by J. D. Fage has been rewritten and published under the title *A History of West Africa: An Introductory Survey* (Cambridge University Press, 1969). The first of a two-volume *History of West Africa*, edited by J. A. Ajayi and M. Crowder (Longmans, 1972), promises, when completed, to be a standard work of reference based on the new approach to African history. Jan Vansina's *Kingdoms of the Savannah* (University of Wisconsin Press, 1966) should be consulted for west-central Africa, especially for its use of oral tradition. The first volume of a projected multivolume work on the *History of South Africa*, edited by Monica Wilson and Leonard Thompson (Oxford, Clarendon Press, 1969), has started to replace Eric A. Walker's massive work, *A History of Southern Africa* (Longmans, 1957). An easy-to-read historical overview of the region is available in Leo Marquard's *The Story of South Africa* (Faber and Faber, 1955). For East Africa, there is a readable up-to-date collection of short essays in *Zamani, a Survey of East African History* by B. A. Ogot and J. A. Kieran (East African Publishing House, 1968). More detailed is the three-volume Oxford survey, *History of East Africa* (Clarendon Press, 1963-1965). For the reader interested in northeastern Africa, two books–*A Short History of the Sudan* by Mandour El Mahdi (Oxford University Press, 1965) and *A History of Ethiopia* by A. H. M. Jones and E. Monroe (Oxford University Press, 1955)–should stimulate the mind of the beginner.

Prepared by the staff of *The World Book Year Book.*

Consultants:
Kenneth O. Dike, professor of history, Harvard University.
Donald E. Vermeer, associate professor of geography and anthropology, Louisiana State University.

"The Study of Africa's History" written by Sylvanus J. S. Cookey, lecturer in history, University of California, Los Angeles.

Printed in U.S.A. by the Trans-Vision® Division, Milprint Incorporated.

Lone Moslem meditates in Moorish palace in Morocco; South African paints design on wall.

Ibeji sculpture is draped with a mantle of cowrie shells; newly dyed wool festoons a Marrakech market.

Dancing Swazi warriors prepare for manhood rite; Ghanaian in regal attire attends a holiday festival.

Africa: Old and New

By Philip D. Curtin

Africa's move toward modernization is not simply an exchange of new for old, but a blending of the two

On my first trip to Africa, in 1955, I was driving along a main road near Ibadan in western Nigeria when I came unexpectedly on a village where a "traditional festival" was clearly in progress. Dancers and musicians were decked out in their most colorful festive clothes. After watching for a time, I gathered enough courage to ask a young man in an especially splendid costume if I could take his picture to capture this glimpse of the African past.

When I had finished shooting, he performed a most untraditional African gesture, however, and handed me his calling card. On it was printed the information that he was the local Ford dealer and offered full garage facilities along with a line of new and used cars. The "traditional festival" was the installation of the first elected district council.

The old and the new blend in the art of modern Africa. Yoruba sculpture of a colonial officer in a Model-T type automobile shows how new elements are incorporated into traditional art forms.

This kind of change has been going on in Africa for several decades. It began even before the relatively recent struggles for independence of the 1950s and 1960s. The result has been a mixture of style and reality in which the older African culture can mask a modern reality, or a modern façade can hide the vital survival of many of the older, traditional ways of life.

Like everything else about this vast continent, Africa's change is too varied to be described easily, much less understood. A common tendency is to oversimplify the change with two brightly contrasting images—the "traditional" Africa of "tribesmen," "chiefs," "witch doctors," and wild jungle animals versus the "modern" Africa of concrete and stainless steel skyscrapers, traffic jams, oil refineries, and environmental pollution. We call this mythical process of change "modernization," and we tend to characterize it as a one-way street in which the "traditional" fades out gradually while the "modern" brightens and comes into clearer focus. In fact, both images are only half-truths; the change is far more complex than a simple substitution of the new for the old.

The image of traditional Africa suffers most from a lingering myth. The myth—that Africa is an uncivilized, barbarian, and static continent—served the purposes of Americans and Europeans. It helped to explain and justify the slave trade. Christian missionaries used it to show the depths of "pagan ignorance" in order to warrant generous public support for their work. Imperialists used it to show that their "trusteeship" over the "savages" was a necessary step toward a better world. Romantic writers liked to contrast the "savage" or "primitive" Africa with their familiar civilized world.

The influence of the myth was far-reaching. In motion pictures, such as the Tarzan series, the savage aspect lurked in the constant threat of wild animals; Africans were little more than cardboard figures in the background. This use of the African backdrop was certainly not intended to tell viewers anything about the real Africa, nor were the familiar cartoon figures of masked witch doctors or cannibals around the stewpot more than abstract figures of primitive life. It only served to reinforce the myth of savage Africa in the public mind. People easily recognized and were comfortable with the stereotype.

The image of modern Africa is equally mythical, but in another way. Most North Americans and Europeans tend to think of modernization as "becoming like us." But how much like us? What part of our own culture is essential to modernity, and what part is merely incidental? Neither Westerners nor Africans seem to really know. After their conquest by the West in the 1800s, Africans tried to discover what made the Europeans so powerful. The European response presented to ordinary Africans was simple—"Civilization equals Christianity." But the message carried by the early missionaries went beyond such things as dressing in the European style, singing Western-style hymns, and getting rid of extra wives. It took a long time for the Europeans to discover that Africans wanted not to imitate the West but to understand the key

The author:
Philip D. Curtin is a professor of history at the University of Wisconsin and a former president of the African Studies Association. His books include *The Image of Africa, The Atlantic Slave Trade,* and, with Paul Bohannan, *Africa & Africans.*

Door carving showing a European officer making his rounds on a bicycle is a good example of how Africa's history can be seen in its art. The attendant at left holds a fly whisk; the one at right holds a rifle.

to Western success and power. For Africans, Western conquest meant the beginning of a serious consideration of what they might borrow from the West without destroying their own values. This meant discovering what to reject, as well as what new initiatives needed to be invented from scratch.

By now, most Africans agree that they want modernization. Most also agree that modernization means developing a society capable of high levels of production and consumption in order to remove the material constraints standing in the way of what they feel is a better life. Africans have observed how economic modernization has occurred in Japan, Russia, western Europe, and the United States. But it is unlikely that many Africans would choose any of these examples as a model of the kind of society they want. Most Africans would prefer to preserve the most valuable aspects of their old way of life, even at some economic cost. But they do not always agree on which things are really essential. In Moslem areas, for example, religion would have a very high priority. Almost everywhere, Africans would be reluctant to see the disappearance of the extended family, which acts as a broad network of solidarity and mutual aid; anyone who starved in traditional Africa did so because his kinsmen were starving, too. The extended family has served as insurance, but insurance has its costs. The cost in traditional Africa was a continuing liability to help pay for other people's ill fortune. Modernization has tended to limit these liabilities and to limit the possible benefits for the unfortunate. It is difficult for Africans to decide how far this change should be allowed to go.

The language question is equally tough. The subtle advantages and disadvantages of a national language are unlikely to occur to people who speak English, the most widely written and spoken language in the world today; but anyone whose mother tongue has only a few million speakers needs a second language to communicate with the wider world. Scientific knowledge is communicated in only a few of the world's languages—English, French, German, and occasionally others. The world's best work in literature is translated into these languages. A book on a specialized subject, or one written for any but the broadest audience, generally must be published in one of these world languages if it is to pay for the cost of its production. This is as true in Greece or Scandinavia as it is in Burundi or Lesotho.

Nevertheless, Burundi and Lesotho are fortunate because they have a single national language. Some 800 languages are spoken in Africa south of the Sahara. Few African countries (and none of the larger ones) have a single home language spoken by even half their population. For a stable sense of common nationality, they must have a common language that every citizen understands. But *which* language?

The answer is not as clear as one might expect. The most efficient answer would be simply to adopt one of the world languages. Where no single African language is clearly dominant, a common language for internal as well as international communication simplifies language education and avoids possible friction between those who speak different local languages. But the cost is not negligible. The rich oral literature found throughout the continent and the historical traditions of the people are all bound up in a mother tongue, which also preserves modes of thought, proverbs, and sayings designed to guide conduct and transmit the values of society. To accept another language for education and general communication risks losing much of this cultural heritage. This is what occurred in most of Scotland and Ireland and somewhat less so in Wales and Brittany.

Many of the hundreds of African languages, each with only a few thousand speakers, are on their way to extinction within a century or so. This makes it all the more important that some of the major African languages be kept in use and modernized.

African states have gone in different directions. Ethiopia, the one country that kept its independence through the period of European conquest, used Amharic with an ancient alphabet of its own as a national language; yet the Ethiopians adopted English as the language of education beyond the elementary school level. The most common solu-

The traditions of an older Africa reappear today. A modern African girl's hair style, *below,* is the same as that on a Yoruba sculpture, *bottom,* which has been adorned with a modern airplane earring.

tion during the 1950s and 1960s was for each newly independent country to adopt the language of the former ruling colonial power because many people already knew it. Most of the new nations of western Africa adopted either French or English. In eastern Africa, however, Swahili was already a common second language for millions of people, though it was the mother tongue for only a few thousand on the coast and the offshore islands. Most of the languages of the region are in the Bantu language group. This means that Swahili, also a Bantu language, is comparatively easy to learn. Because of its strictly African character, it also has sentimental value. But the choice of Swahili imposes costs as well. In addition to a home language, most eastern Africans are forced to learn Swahili for internal communication and English for higher education and external communication. On the other hand, most Africans have always had to learn two or three languages other than their own.

Even ordinary farmers who lived in the same village all their lives had to communicate in market places where people gathered from a wider region. Those who traveled more widely, such as traders, had some knowledge of half a dozen or more languages through such languages of trade as Swahili, Hausa in northern Nigeria, or Malinke in Mali. These were common second languages over thousands of square miles. Moslem clerics, learned in Islamic law, had much the same problem as a modern African scientist. A cleric living in Bornu, now the northeast corner of Nigeria, would have spoken Kanuri at home, and all through that kingdom. He would have known Hausa as the dominant trade language of the region, and Arabic as the language of religion and almost all written communication. The progress of Western-style education along with the concentrations of population after the colonial period simply multiplied the number of specialists sharing this problem.

Western education also brought new problems. Compared to Asia or Latin America, African societies before the colonial period were not sharply

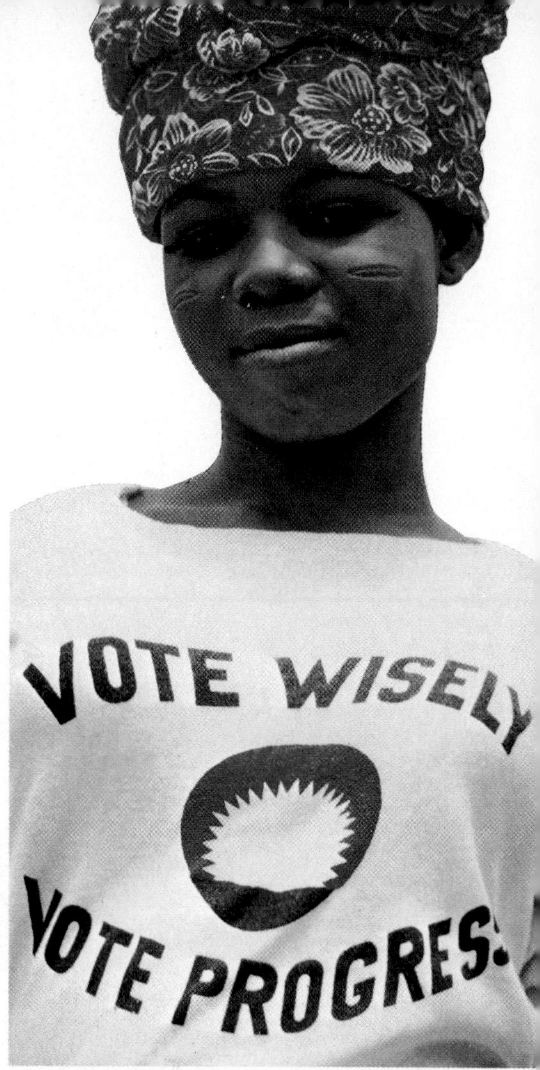

Africa's modern forms of political expression are symbolized by a campaigner, *above right,* and a speech by Malawi President Hastings Banda, *right,* contrast sharply with its warrior roots, *facing page.*

divided into unequal social classes. Aristocracies existed, but they often held political power or social prestige without demanding a vastly unequal share of the national wealth.

Then a new kind of aristocrat appeared during the colonial period. Africans with a good Western-style education were given preference in government jobs or with European firms. As decolonization came along after World War II, they moved into the positions vacated by departing European civil servants. These positions often carried more power and more income than the old aristocracy enjoyed.

As time passed, the first generation of university graduates was followed by a second with similar ambitions, but now the best jobs were already filled by men little older than themselves. The result was a rising friction between generations. So far, the friction has been muted by the fact that universities have accepted students and granted scholarships on the basis of ability, not merely money or position. But the men in power are tempted to ensure university places for their own children, which could lead to an inherited aristocracy of education.

It is also difficult to adjust education to national needs without limiting individual freedom to choose a career. A common European tradition, transmitted to Africa in the colonial period, placed a higher value on a university degree in the liberal arts than in engineering or techni-

The most dominant form of government in Africa is military dictatorship, typified by bemedaled President Jean Bokassa of the Central African Republic and Nigerian soldiers in training.

cal training—and higher prestige in this case meant higher salaries as well. Africans chose liberal education in history, literature, and the like, so that there were sometimes more people trained in these fields than suitable jobs available. Meanwhile, the African governments still have to depend on Europeans and Americans for much-needed technical skills. This is a waste of resources, and African governments have little to waste. Yet, they rightly hesitate to order people into occupations that people would not have chosen for themselves.

Cities pose a different range of problems for African modernization. Most of the old Africa was rural, even in northern Africa and parts of western Nigeria, which had an ancient urban tradition. Modernization has not only speeded the growth of cities, but has concentrated its influence in the urban areas. These are the centers of government, new industries, transportation and distribution, intellectual life, entertainment, radio and television, and consumer services catering to the wealthy and the foreigners. In the eyes of rural people, whose lives are not touched so directly by the changes of recent years, the cities *are* the modern world. Cities seem from a distance to offer the opportunity to enjoy at least some of the advantages of modern life. Wages are higher there (though so are prices). As a result, people have crowded into the cities in search of opportunity. But for

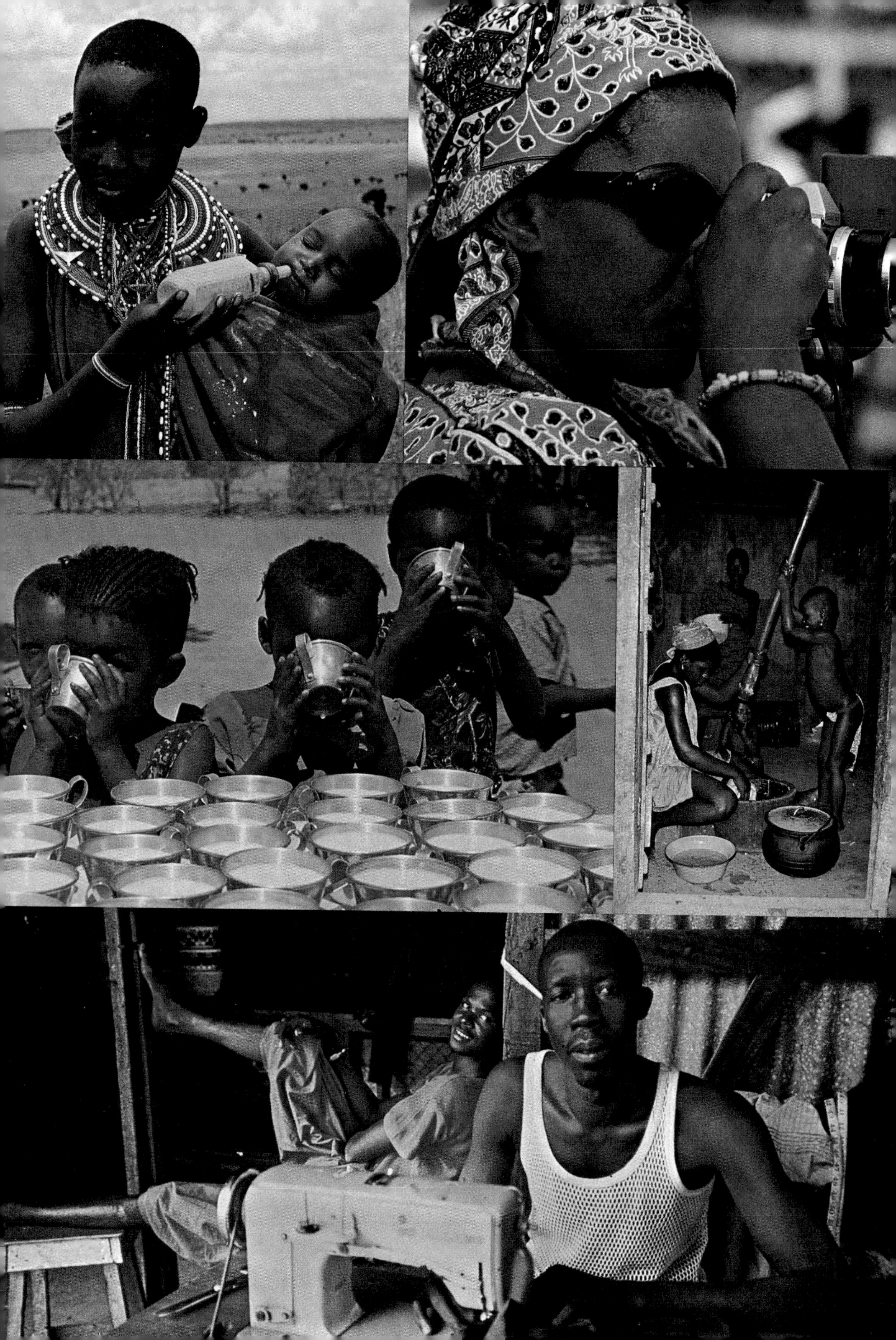

many, the opportunity does not exist because they lack both education and skills. As a result, unemployment rates in urban areas are often as high as 25 to 50 per cent of the work force.

Contrasting with the glitter of bright lights and the air-conditioned steel and concrete buildings are the shantytowns of the urban poor, whose poverty becomes all the more oppressive within sight of the luxury of the wealthy. The results of city growth are overcrowding, bad sanitation, petty crimes and crimes of violence, and disease—a rapid rise in urban disorder that is all too familiar in our own cities as a result of "modernization."

African governments have tried to deal with the problems associated with urban growth in several different ways. Urban crime has reached such critical proportions recently that some countries have responded with violent laws to suppress violence. Nigeria, for example, recently imposed the death penalty for armed robbery. The Central African Republic has instituted public physical punishment for thieves in its capital of Bangui. Other countries have tried to keep the unemployed in rural areas where they can be supported by their kinsmen. This has long been the policy in the Republic of South Africa, where the minority of overseas Europeans (whites living outside of Europe) who control the government deny the black majority the right to move about freely or to live in the cities; Africans may live in the cities only if they have a job. If they are no longer employed, they are threatened with expulsion to a rural area. In fact, Africans perform all unskilled labor in South Africa. This means that they are necessarily a majority of the urban population. Nevertheless, government policy claims that the cities are the special province of the overseas Europeans; Africans may live there only on sufferance and only in special ghettos called "locations." Such stringent control over population movement is possible only in a police state such as South Africa, and even there it can only add to social tension in the cities.

Urban Africans are employed at wage rates required by law to be much lower than those of overseas Europeans doing the same kind of work. Their life is so tightly controlled by police regulations that they feel the same kind of deprivation felt by the urban unemployed in the free countries of tropical Africa. Urban social problems of the slums are therefore just as serious there as they are farther north, in spite of full employment in the cities.

The heart of the problem is the concentration of the modern sector of the economy in the cities. Cabinet ministers, professors, lawyers, engineers, and specialists from overseas who live and work in the city make as much money as they would in Europe. Service and consumer industries gather to supply their needs at international standards of quality and price. But the lower level of economic development in Africa means, of course, that per-capita income for Africans is much lower than it is in Europe. High incomes exist alongside low incomes. The effect is one of exaggeration—as though one of the world's most devel-

Africans still do things in traditional ways, but school milk programs and modern devices such as plastic bottles, cameras, and sewing machines are common.

oped economies shared the same land with one of the least developed; not continents apart, but side by side. The contrast between city and country life, and even between life in the modern suburbs and in shantytowns is profound. From Dakar to Mombasa, from Khartoum to Cape Town, the comparison of luxurious skyscraper apartments with the sand-blown, unpaved streets of the slums is unavoidable. Even when the two are not actually side by side, the poor can hardly avoid seeing the symbolic towers of the rich.

This economic imbalance may not be unjust in one sense: The specialists in the modern sector may add more to national income than the value of their own salaries, but this is beside the point. If the whole region is to be modernized without intolerable social stress, some way has to be found to develop the countryside as a counterbalance to the attractions of the cities. Several African governments have begun to recognize the problem. Solutions vary from broad projects for decentralized development to plans to increase the attractiveness and facilities of smaller towns and cities, or simply to distribute more generally such essentials as health care and education. Whatever the success of the particular schemes now being tried, the inequity itself is a useful reminder that many present-day problems are indeed worldwide. Concentration of the poor in isolated sections of cities creates the same problems for Johannesburg, Kinshasa, Lagos, and Lubumbashi as it does for New York City and Detroit. The simple problem of persuading competent doctors to practice in rural areas is the same in northeastern Zambia

Most of Africa's growth and its most dramatic changes have occurred in such cities as Nairobi, Kenya, *below,* and Lagos, Nigeria, *facing page*. To rural Africans, cities represent modernization.

and northern Maine, eastern Senegal and West Virginia, southern Ethiopia and northern Wisconsin.

Modern problems also overrun "traditional" Africa in a type of conflict that is sometimes called "tribalism." The term "tribe" has no definite and fixed meaning, beyond the general sense of a people who are like one another or have a common interest. When "tribe" is used to describe Africans, however, it tends to call up the myth of savage Africa. We tend to assume that "primitive" people belong to a tribe just as "modern" people belong to a nation or a state. When the press writes of "tribal rivalries" among Ibo, Yoruba, and Hausa in Nigeria, the reader immediately leaps to a series of conclusions—mostly wrong—about past and present Nigeria. First, he will probably assume that Ibo and Yoruba "tribes" have been the centers of these people's primary allegiance for a very long time. He will also probably assume that these two "tribes" have been century-old rivals, and he will certainly assume that the "tribalism" represents an instance of the old Africa interfering with modern progress.

In fact, Ibo (more accurately Igbo) is a language term referring to a group of somewhat different but mutually intelligible dialects spoken east of the lower Niger River. Although Ibo was long known as a single language, a survey in the late 1840s of the people living in this region showed that no one thought of himself as an Ibo. Each identified his own group as a smaller entity, just as Canadians and Americans identify with their own countries rather than as common members of the

Even with modernization, flamboyant colors are still evident in Africa. *Clockwise in center on the following two pages:* Young men dress up for market; rituals take on a modern flair; bundles of clogs on sale in Mali market place; cheap and colorful pots replace traditional crafted ones. Modern appliqué, *left and right of center photos,* shows animals and creatures from Yoruba mythology.

Traditional Africa looks to education for change. Education is by far the most important vehicle for modernization in Africa. Still, less than 1 per cent of all Africans attend such institutions as the University of Ibadan, Nigeria, *above*. Only half of the African children go to grade schools, *facing page*.

English-speaking world. Yoruba also originally identified a similar group of related dialects. Neither Yoruba-speakers nor Ibo-speakers ever belonged to a single political unit until they were conquered by Great Britain and made part of the colony of Nigeria. They had never engaged in "tribal warfare" against each other. In fact, they had no common frontier, nor did either of them have a common frontier with the Hausa, the third major "tribe" of Nigeria. Their common culture and common language were increasingly recognized in the late 1800s. But the sense of being Yoruba, or Ibo, became a political force only during the colonial period, and even then its real importance hardly began before 1930.

What actually happened in Nigeria is typical of rising modern tensions in other parts of Africa. People rooted to the old life of village farmers, who produced nearly all they consumed, were concerned with kinship but paid little attention to ethnic differences. During the colonial period, some people moved to the towns and cities, plantations, and mines. There they entered an alien world, with all too few kinsfolk nearby for support. It was only natural to turn for mutual assistance to others with whom they had something in common, and common language and customs were an obvious tie. This is what built the Ibo sense of identity.

During the early colonial period, the Ibo were the first to take advantage of missionary education. Soon they had spread out all over Nigeria in government, trade, and education. As they encountered competition with other people, they began to help one another, but not as "Ibo" at first. In such towns as Onitsha and Enugu in or near Iboland, nearly everybody was Ibo, so that people sought out others from their home village or village group. Mutual assistance thus began with units much smaller than an all-Ibo identity. But, as the Ibo moved farther afield within Nigeria—to Lagos, which was dominantly Yoruba, or to the Hausa-speaking cities of the north—they began to help one another *as Ibo*. This is when the intense feeling of Iboness came into existence. When they moved still farther from home, the Ibo often banded together with others as Nigerians—in London, say, or in other parts of western Africa. But the field of action that counted most was Nigeria, and when it became independent in 1960, competition increased between people of different cultures simply because there was no longer an alien government to mediate.

When the Ibo tried to secede from Nigeria, in the late 1960s, and create an independent nation called Biafra, a civil war began that many observers mistakenly believed was the result of ancient "tribal" rivalries—hence a throwback to the traditional Africa. In fact, the attempted secession of Biafra grew out of thoroughly modern conditions of ethnic rivalry that stemmed from the colonial period. There was a generally traditional element behind the conflict, however—the pattern of Ibo norms and values that stressed initiative, adaptability, and hard work as desirable qualities in a mobile society. These qualities

Mobil

made for Ibo success in the urban setting, and they also helped to build resentment among others whose values stressed other kinds of behavior.

Elsewhere in Africa, so-called "tribal" conflict takes other forms with equally modern roots. For example, conflicts occurred in those parts of Africa where the colonial power cooperated closely with local aristocrats and helped to keep them in power. Some of the bloodiest civil wars in recent years have been revolts by the working class or peasants against a ruling class that could no longer depend on overseas support. This was the case in Zanzibar in 1964, when people who called themselves "Afro-Shirazi" revolted and massacred many of those they called "Arabs." These labels, however, were deceptive. "Arab" in Zanzibar usage meant a member of the aristocracy who traced his ancestry back to Arabia, as opposed to a recently arrived "Arabian." The "Arabs" were similar to the "Afro-Shirazi" in language, religion, customs, and appearance. The crucial difference was that the Arabs were formerly the masters of the clove plantations, while the common people were descended from their slaves.

Much the same misunderstanding surrounds "tribalism" in Burundi and Rwanda. There, the aristocrats, who have been driven out in recent years, were called Tutsi, or Watusi, and the peasantry were called Hutu, or Bahutu. Because the Tutsi were tall and could often (though not always) be recognized on sight as members of the aristocracy, the easy explanation was to call a peasants' revolt "tribal" warfare. In fact, the Hutu and the Tutsi in these two countries speak the same language, have the same religion, and generally share the same customs. The revolts were tragic for individual Tutsi, many of whom were personally blameless for past wrongs. They were the revolts of a peasantry that felt it had been oppressed by the aristocracy during the colonial period, not a swingback to the animosities of the more distant past.

Just as the urban problems in Africa represent special versions of the general urban problem throughout the world, the so-called "tribal" conflicts represent different kinds of conflict between different groups of people elsewhere. If to be modern is to be "like us," then the struggle for justice on the part of a former slave class on Zanzibar is not unlike some of the American experience in recent years.

Nevertheless, Africa will continue to move toward its own future. And Africa's future will most certainly not be a carbon copy of the West, nor yet a return to the African past, but a modification of that past in the light of ongoing experience.

There are problems to be solved, but the problems should not be allowed to obscure the immense African achievement of the past decade. The dominant opinion in Africa today ranges upward from a guarded optimism to the kind of attitude I encountered recently in Nigeria. On hearing my polite expression of approval, my Nigerian friend came back: "But you came too soon. Five years from now we could *really* show you something."

Congested traffic at a construction site in the Ivory Coast is typical of the difficulties Africa faces in trying to grow as the need to modernize outstrips the economy's ability to keep pace.

Always Testing

By Richard E. Snow

Giving and taking tests has become a way of life in the United States, from childhood to retirement

You slide behind the wheel and buckle the safety belt with nervous fingers. Perhaps you wipe moist palms on the seat before turning the ignition key. After a quick glance at the official sitting beside you, a clipboard on his lap, you start the car moving slowly across the pavement. You have come in quest of a driver's license. To get it, you must pass a test.

Tests have become increasingly important in the lives of virtually everyone in the modern world. Most of us are subjected to many tests throughout our school days, during military service, and when we apply for a job.

New test systems, with their punch-card answer sheets and electronic scoring, seem strange and complex. Their widespread use seems to set modern life apart from antiquity. But achievement examinations are actually nothing new. Indeed, they were a basic part of selection and promotion procedures for the civil service system in ancient China's earliest dynasties. In the Western world as early as 1845, Horace Mann, the pioneer American educator, was arguing that systematic written tests should replace oral university examinations.

Yet, today, tests are coming under increasing attack. Critics charge that some probe improperly into a person's private feelings and beliefs, that they are based on the responses of the majority and thus discriminate against minorities, or that they are based on a nonrepresentative sample. A psychologist has complained that one test, "in which blacks are compared with the white Minnesota sample, would lead us to be-

Tests given in classrooms play an important part in a person's life, but tests are also being used widely today in business and industry.

lieve that the majority of Negroes are manic-depressive schizophrenics." To consider these and other issues, we need to understand why we take tests and what they do.

Perhaps the most familiar test today is the one you take to get a driver's license. In it, both knowledge and performance are tested. The written test measures your knowledge of signs, rules of the road, and the like; and the road test, your performance in handling a car. The performance test cannot adequately measure knowledge, nor the written test, driving skill.

Neither test is a perfect measure. The performance test cannot include all possible driving situations, and the written test cannot include all possible questions. Nonetheless, the tests usually work fairly well, ensuring that all licensed drivers have at least minimum driving knowledge and skill.

The tests' primary purpose is to qualify drivers, but they can also serve diagnostic functions and help to evaluate driving instruction. The driver who misses only one or two questions can go back to the instruction book to fill gaps in his knowledge. If many applicants miss the same question, officials may revise the book to make that information clearer and easier to learn. All tests, not just driving tests, can serve these multiple purposes—qualification, evaluation, and diagnosis—but different individuals and institutions emphasize different purposes.

School tests in the United States today are used more for evaluating instruction and for diagnosing individual students' strengths and weaknesses than they are for selecting, promoting, and graduating students. Colleges and professional schools, however, do use tests as well as grades made earlier in school to select for admission those students most likely to do well. And many schools require final qualification tests before granting diplomas. Lawyers, physicians, engineers, and other professionals are qualified in a similar way so the public can rely on their knowledge and skills. School tests, like driving tests, assess knowledge and skills. They are more often concerned with conceptual and problem-solving skills, however, than the psychomotor skills of driving. Teachers construct achievement tests for use in their own classes. Standardized mental ability and achievement tests are also given on a school-, district-, or statewide basis, usually to evaluate the quality of instruction. Many guidance counselors use tests to identify students' vocational interests.

Industry uses tests mainly to choose among the applicants for a job, but also to evaluate job training. The military services and many government offices use tests for classification. They identify individuals' strengths, weaknesses, and preferences to help choose the most suitable areas of job specialization. In hospitals, mental health clinics, and counseling centers, psychological tests form an essential part of the diagnostic process. Test information helps the investigation and treatment of a variety of mental and physical illnesses. And tests provide a vital tool for research in the sciences of human behavior.

The author:
Richard E. Snow, an associate professor of education at Stanford University, is a visiting professor at the University of Leiden in the Netherlands for the 1972-1973 school year.

A person must pass a performance and a knowledge test to get a driver's license. In the performance test, *left*, he demonstrates his car-handling skill for the examiner. The knowledge test checks his understanding of road signs and other information. The shape of each road sign has a meaning for a driver. Do you know what the signs *below* indicate? Answers on Page 149.

Even newspapers, magazines, and television sometimes carry so-called "tests" that claim to measure your personality, your chances for marital happiness or business success, or something. These are usually demonstrations created for their entertainment value—and they can be entertaining. But if they are relied on as sources of valid information, they can also be misleading. They are not formal tests, evaluated according to accepted rules.

Basically, a test is a measuring instrument similar in some ways to a thermometer or a bathroom scale. The readings of an instrument that only looks like a thermometer may be interesting—or even entertaining. But if it is not a reliable thermometer, its readings can be misleading or even dangerous.

Each test, to measure an aspect of human behavior, must require people to do things showing that aspect. So any test is a sample of situations, like the collection of questions or the sequence of performance situations in the driver's license tests. Mental and performance tests are designed to distinguish those persons who know or can do a specific thing from those who do not know or cannot do it. They try to measure maximum performance—the best a person can do at the time. Others measure personality, attitudes, or interests by asking people what they typically do or how they typically feel in various situations. These are usually called "inventories," rather than tests, to emphasize that they rely on individuals to report about themselves instead of testing their knowledge or skill. The word "test," however, is often applied to both kinds of measure, whether it shows maximum or typical behavior.

Most widely used tests are "standardized." That is, they are (1) systematic procedures to observe human behavior and (2) describe it in terms of a numerical scale or category system with (3) fixed administration, apparatus, and scoring methods so that the same procedures can be reproduced exactly each time they are used.

Tests are designed this way so that we can rely on their accuracy, just

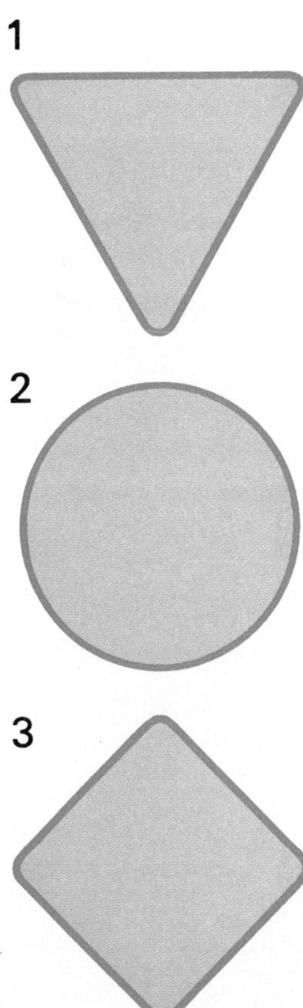

as we rely on thermometers or bathroom scales. We need also to be able to use them easily, evaluate them readily, and interpret them validly. Standardization helps provide these qualities. But we must not expect absolute precision, even from standardized tests, any more than we would expect it from a bathroom scale used, for example, to measure the weight of precious gems.

Scoring most tests is not really complicated. On a school achievement test, for example, the total of correct answers given by each person tested is a measure of his knowledge of the topics in the test. At the same time, the total of a group's incorrect answers for each question indicates its difficulty. In addition, the particular questions or groups of questions answered correctly indicate the aspects of a field in which each student is most knowledgeable.

Scoring tests often involves more than simply totaling the number of correct responses. But for inventory measures, there are no correct answers; the questions might deal with whether you "like to read books," "are a good mixer socially," or "are a person who can be relied upon." Here, the scoring system compares your answers to those of specified groups of people. An interest inventory, for example, is scored to show how similar your preferences are to those of lawyers, or salesmen, or foresters, or other groups. Reacting to such statements as "I enjoy beautiful gardens," or "Camping in the rough is great," or "It's fun to eat fruit right from the tree," you might see how similar your score is to the scores that might have been obtained by Adam and Eve. (Presumably, they would have agreed with such statements, at least in their early days.) In this same way, tests can be made to measure such traits as "responsibility" with a statement like "I can be counted on to get things done." Or they can be used to measure such personality traits as "sociability" or "introversion."

Traditionally, standardized educational and psychological tests have been classified into a few general categories. Besides "personality" or "interest inventories," they include "aptitude," "special abilities," and "achievement" tests.

Aptitude tests measure a person's potential or ability to acquire—with proper training—certain degrees of skill or knowledge. Such scholastic aptitude tests as the famous college board examination are often used to predict how well a student will do in advanced schooling. An achievement test, on the other hand, measures how much of some skill or knowledge he has already acquired. When no basic changes in teaching or training methods are expected, achievement—past performance in the same subject—may best predict future success. Hence the distinction between aptitude and achievement is not always important, since many achievement tests can also be used as measures of aptitude. Most school proficiency tests are, however, called achievement tests, whenever during an instructional program they are administered.

Aptitude measures that are not directly based on prior learning, however, may give better estimates of a learner's potential when new teaching methods, such as independent study, or discussion groups, or television or computers, are used. This kind of aptitude has been referred to as *fluid* ability, to distinguish it from *crystallized* ability shown by prior achievement. One way to view mental tests is according to how much they are influenced by prior learning. At one extreme are those that measure abstract intellectual abilities and learning skills that are not directly learned. In the middle are general aptitude and achievement measures. At the other extreme are subject-matter proficiency measures, such as arithmetic tests, that depend heavily upon prior learning in specific school subjects. Considering various tests in terms of their position in such a range keeps the concepts of aptitude and achievement from seeming so distinct. Instead, these concepts define a range of tests.

There are many tests of general mental ability. Some are called measures of "intelligence," others, of "general scholastic aptitude," but both would be better called simply "ability" tests. Some may be individually administered, often to diagnose forms of mental retardation or brain damage or to identify gifted children. They can be given only by trained psychologists.

Others are intended for groups and can be administered by experienced teachers or school officials. They are often used as screening devices, so the more expensive and more accurate individual tests need not be given to everyone. Schools sometimes

Blocks of varied shapes help in testing young children. This girl must match the pattern of the tester's set. Experts say a person's cultural background has little effect on such a test.

Below, find a figure in each group with a feature setting it apart. This question is fair for all cultural groups. Answer on Page 149.

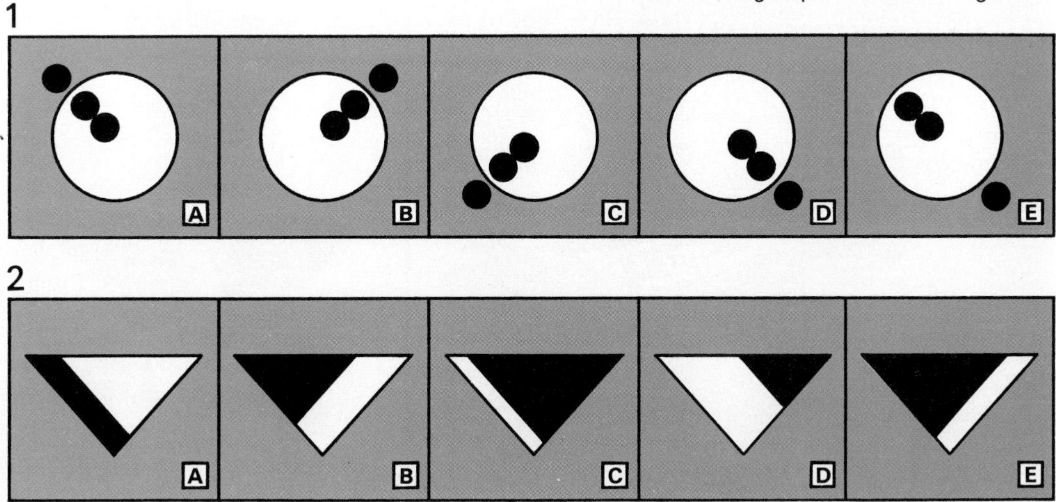

use them to group students with similar abilities or to predict later school success.

Many individual and group tests give several part scores. The Lorge-Thorndike Intelligence Test, for example, provides several subtests that combine to give verbal and nonverbal intelligence quotients, or IQ scores. The Wechsler Intelligence Scale for Children involves 11 subtests, scoring such items as comprehension, block design, picture arrangement, and recognition of similarities. Special ability tests may measure spatial, verbal, or numerical ability. The widely used Differential Aptitude Tests include examination of verbal, spelling, grammar, numerical, abstract reasoning, spatial, mechanical, and clerical abilities. Others focus on the abilities that are involved in artistic or musical talent, special psychomotor or perceptual abilities, or fluent, flexible, or creative thinking.

Scientific research on the nature of human abilities has produced a theory that interrelates specific ability tests in larger and larger clusters, with a few major abilities at the broadest, most general level. Another theory separates mental tests according to four kinds of content, five kinds of mental operation needed to succeed on tests, and six kinds of mental product called for by tests. Combining different elements from the three different groups suggests that there are at least 120 separate kinds of mental ability. Different people might well be strong in some and weak in others. You could be weak in, say, memory for symbolic systems (like remembering telephone numbers), yet you might do well in what some psychologists call divergent production of semantic units (for example, thinking of many different uses for a brick). Psychologists are continuing to work on such theories. They try to identify the best

Psychological tests may have no "right" answers. They may ask you to tell a story suggested to you by a picture, *below*. Or, they may ask what you see outlined in a symmetrical ink blot, *below right*. A dog's face? A flower? Your answers help an analyst to understand you better.

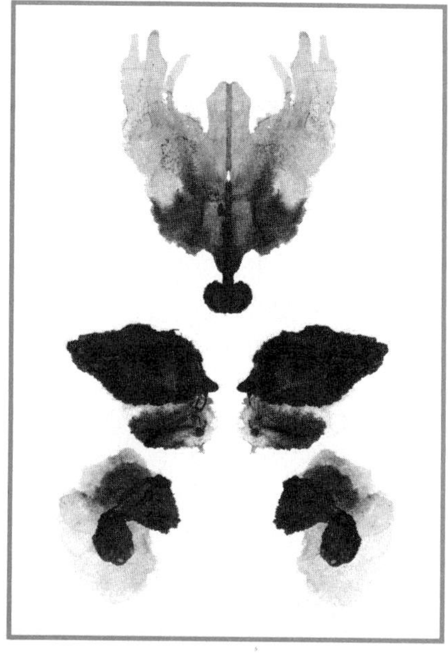

kinds of tests for different practical purposes, but they also use tests to study the nature of human abilities.

It seems likely that humans differ from one another in many kinds of special abilities. But we are often inclined to simplify our descriptions of others. Comments like "He is quite intelligent, but not very creative" are common. And for practical purposes, a simple, overall summary of a person's general ability is often needed. An IQ test provides such a summary by including several different kinds of questions in one test and arriving at a total score. Unfortunately, people often consider the IQ as the single mark of an individual's worth. The term *intelligence* is often interpreted as indicating innate capacity instead of learned skill. Some scientists have tried also to develop similar overall measures of what is often called *creativity*. People think of creativity, too, as a single, inborn trait.

But neither intelligence nor creativity is a single human trait. Both terms refer to complexes of abilities—overlapping complexes not well measured by simple tests. What goes to make up each is not completely clear, but most experts agree about some of the components. In intelligence, they include verbal comprehension, spatial ability, memory, and flexibility and adaptability in problem solving. Obviously, the process of creativity also uses these intellectual abilities, but some experts emphasize that fluency with words and ideas as well as flexibility and adaptability in thinking clearly seem included. Sudden insights may sometimes be involved in creativity, but hard mental work is more common; the would-be creator who just waits for inspiration will probably have a long wait. Probably no single collection of test situations can adequately sample all of the kinds of abilities that might be included in intelligence and creativity. And there is no test in existence today that can distinguish between hereditary and environmental sources of ability.

So we should recognize that an IQ score or any other summary test score may be useful only for some purposes. It may signify a characteristic that is important in some situations, but it hardly exhausts the list of those that might be important in others.

Personality and interest inventories usually aim at providing some kind of clinical or counseling diagnosis of emotional structure or interest patterns. They serve to identify—for students, parents, schools, and community services—special predispositions and preferences. Considering such factors helps to design instructional or counseling programs to fit individual needs.

Some inventories are used to diagnose emotional disturbances. Others serve strictly to help choose college or vocational training programs that fit an individual student's interests. Employers sometimes use personality inventories for selecting job applicants, but this is a practice that is now rare in education and government. After hearings were held by the Congress of the United States several years ago, the Peace Corps and the Civil Service Commission stopped the routine use of tests like

This test measures the ability to spot flaws in small objects quickly and accurately. Persons applying for jobs as assembly-line inspectors must take such tests. In the illustration on the right, can you spot within a few seconds the pieces that do not match the perfect specimens, which are at the far left of each line? Answers are given on Page 149.

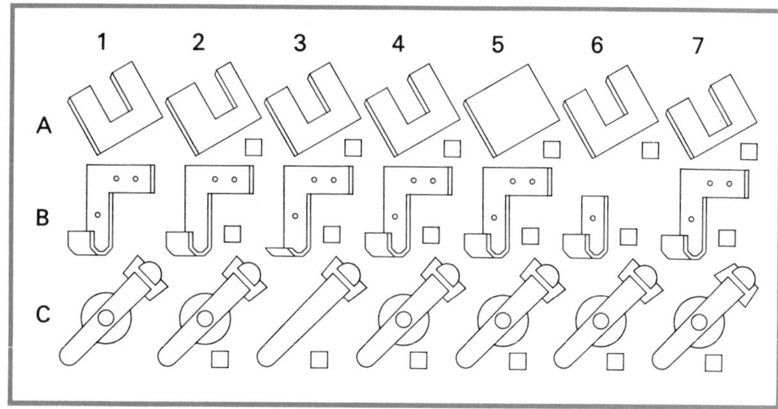

the Minnesota Multiphasic Personality Inventory. Critics said such tests probed areas that an employee or student has a right to keep to himself.

Personality measures have been used for many years and appear valid for some purposes, but experts are far less agreed about their meaning and value than they are about those of ability measures. There are many quite different measures of personality. Even inventories that claim to measure the same personal characteristic may yield scores with different meanings. Some say personality measurement is especially complicated because those tested can fake on inventories—report feelings and opinions different from those they actually have. A person is less likely to fake knowingly on interest inventories, where the test is for his own personal or vocational use. But even honest answers to personality questions may have underlying reasons that vary greatly from person to person. This makes interpretation difficult. Research is improving our understanding of human personality, but it will be some time before many questions about personality measurement can be answered clearly.

Tests today are not only used widely. Some are misunderstood widely. Some tests are misused and some testing practices, highly regarded in the past, have come under attack.

Written tests became popular in education in the 20th century because of their objectivity. Oral recitations and teacher ratings were unsystematic, potentially biased ways to measure achievement. Similarly, the traditional employment interview in government and industry was supplemented—and sometimes even supplanted—by standardized tests. The tests could be shown to be more reliable, more valid, and more efficient for most purposes. For both employment and educational uses, democratic principles argued for standardized tests; they were considered relatively free of class and racial biases. As John W. Gardner, former secretary of health, education, and welfare, put it, "The tests couldn't see whether the youngster was in rags or in tweeds, and they couldn't hear the accents of the slum."

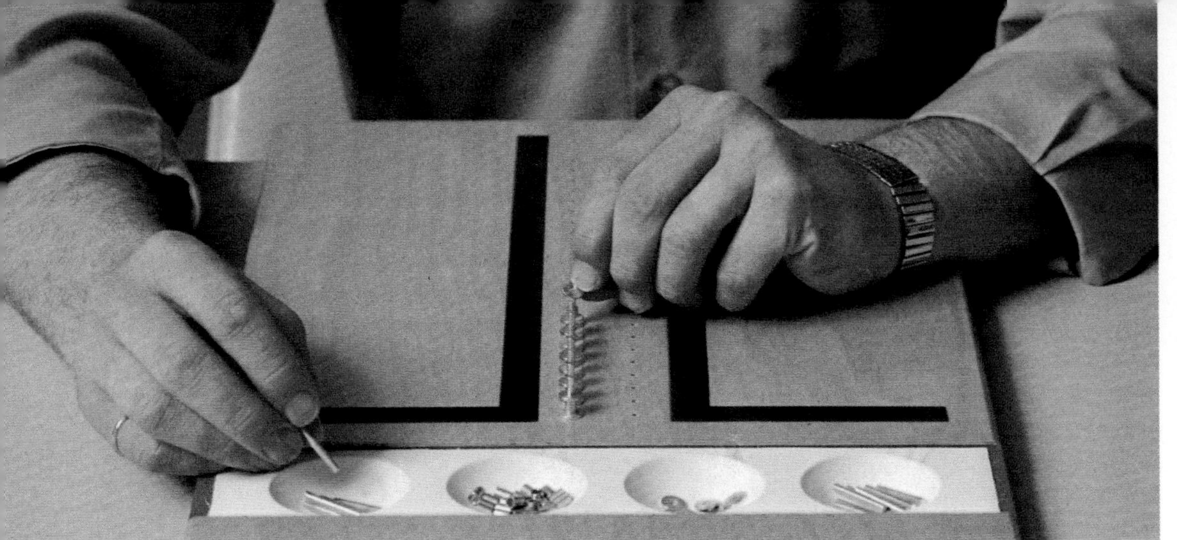

An applicant for a job in which manual dexterity is important may face the Purdue Pegboard, a manipulative test that makes him repeat certain operations as often as possible in 30 seconds.

It is ironic, then, that tests are now attacked as instruments of unfair discrimination against members of minority ethnic groups and the poor. On the average, such people tend to score lower on some mental tests than do members of the white middle class. To some, this means the tests are culturally biased. Civil rights groups have objected, usually on behalf of minority-group parents. School boards have debated, court cases have been filed, and legislation has been proposed to restrict or stop the use of tests for this reason. Even the Scholastic Aptitude Test, which is used almost universally by colleges today to choose students, is coming under attack on these grounds. Some colleges have considered dropping it.

True, some tests contain culturally biased items. Because of efforts over the years to make questions more difficult, obscure words, uncommon objects, and other irrelevant difficulties have found their way into some commonly used tests. Such items do tend to discriminate against those from impoverished or ethnically different backgrounds.

It is unlikely, for example, that a slum child is familiar with such words as "chalice" or "chortle," or has seen a crystal chandelier. Unless the test is meant to measure knowledge of such things, using them introduces unnecessary and potentially biasing difficulties. If a reasoning test's questions include such items, the slum child's score will probably be lower than if it used words and pictures common to his experience. This will give an unfair estimate of his reasoning ability. As published tests are revised, such items are gradually being recognized and eliminated. But continued vigilance and scientific work is needed to discover the subtle biases that can exist.

It is clearly illegal and immoral for employers to discriminate on the basis of race. But a test is not unfair simply because blacks, for example, tend to score lower than whites. The key issue is the selection test's relevance to job performance. If it is clear that the test accurately measures skills needed to perform a job successfully, and if these skills cannot be readily trained, then an employer can rightfully use the test to select as employees those most likely to succeed on the job. Even the rejection of a disproportionate number of one racial group does not, by itself, show improper bias. But the burden of proof is on the employer to show that the test really is relevant to the job and not just to, say, performance in the training program for the job. Verbal tests may sometimes predict only how fast a person will learn the job in a particular training program, not how well he will ultimately do it. Thus, the test may be irrelevant, but it is not unfair. It is the *use* of an irrelevant test that constitutes unfair discrimination.

In the classroom, it is feared that children from ghetto or poverty backgrounds are discriminated against by tests designed for white, middle-class society. They do poorly on the tests, are placed in slow-learning groups, and progressively fall further and further behind in educational development. But if the tests genuinely reflect the level of knowledge and skills needed in today's complex technical society, they are not unfair. If children from slum areas are really weaker in verbal, or reasoning, or other thinking abilities, and these abilities are needed in life, then such problems should be recognized, identified, and studied. Remedies need to be found. Educational procedures need to be designed to develop the required abilities.

Again, it is the wrong *use* of tests—to relegate some children to instruction from which they do not profit—that constitutes unfair discrimination. The remedy, then, is to devise educational techniques that suit children who, for whatever reason, are ill suited for traditional methods. We need education that truly adapts to important individual differences in learners. We need tests that can identify these differences. To eliminate tests because they show the effects of environmental handicaps would be comparable to killing the messengers that bring bad news.

Personal privacy is another issue on which tests are now being attacked. Some critics regard tests, particularly personality measures, as unethical invasions of privacy often involving coercion and deceit. A congressional committee was told of one widely used personality test that asked job applicants for their reactions to statements such as "I pray several times every week" and "I feel sure there is only one true religion." It had been used by the Department of Labor, the Department of State, and the Peace Corps.

Certainly any test used without the informed consent of the person tested is in some degree an invasion of privacy. And it is vitally important that our constitutional safeguards against potentially harmful invasions be maintained. But the issue often must be decided in terms of the use to which the test information is to be put.

Intrusive, personal questions may be deemed acceptable if the responses will directly help the person tested, perhaps in diagnosing emotional disorders or in personal counseling. Employers should have the right to ask questions critically related to job performance, if such a relationship can be proved. A test for astronaut applicants, for instance, could be valuable if it revealed tendencies toward claustrophobia. Perhaps the public has the right to ask intrusive questions about the personalities of those it entrusts with great power. Even high-level political officeholders may eventually find themselves subject to some kinds of tests.

Fully informing the person tested about the test's intent is not always possible. Test interpretation is complicated. It requires extended professional training. Too much information may only confuse the person being tested and interfere with the test's purposes. Some tests require at least temporary deception in order to tap particular aspects of personality. Inventories of interests or personality, for example, need to guard against some respondents' tendency to provide answers that seem most socially desirable or approved. The factor that particular questions are aiming at, then, may have to be concealed from the person who is being tested.

Just as with medical procedures we rarely understand, we must in some cases rely on the wisdom and ethics of the professional practitioner. We need safeguards against the misuse of tests by quacks, by self-interested or disreputable persons, even by well-meaning but untrained persons. But these restraints should allow full proper use of tests to benefit individuals and society. And they should foster continued scientific research into human behavior.

There are scientifically proven ways of determining a test's worth for any particular current purpose or proposed use. Fundamentally, these methods are the same as those that would be used in checking the accuracy of your thermometer or bathroom scale. A specialist compares the test with other measures of the same characteristic. He conducts trials to see if the test is reliable and functioning as theory predicts, and to see if the scores are useful for the purposes intended. The American Psychological Association and other groups have established standards for educational and psychological tests to specify procedures for constructing, publishing, and using tests. Anyone can publish a "test," just as anyone can publish a song, but reputable publishers adhere scrupulously to the standards.

Even so, tests are far from perfect. We all have found some test questions that seemed stupid, or ambiguous, or unfair, just as we can always see shortcomings in the many other familiar technologies of our present-day world. In the future, restrictions on testing are likely to grow as society increases its concern about discrimination in both education and industry. In education, tests will probably be used more and more to evaluate schools, less and less to evaluate individuals. In industry, there will be more research on tests that simulate working conditions. Such tests may be better, and the public may accept them better, because of their obvious relationship to the job.

Thus, tests and testing are widely questioned today. But the consensus seems to be that we are better off with them than without them—as long as we continue to pursue safeguards for the present and improvements for the future.

Test answers:
Page 141: From top to bottom, the sign shapes signify Yield, Railroad Crossing, and Warning.
Page 143: 1-E has the double dot and the single dot spaced apart; 2-A shows a white segment with three sides and a dark segment with four.
Page 146: A has parts 2, 5, and 7 flawed; B has parts 2, 3, and 6 flawed; in line C, parts 3 and 7 are flawed.

ELIZABETH C. STANTON
SUSAN B. ANTHONY
GLORIA STEINEM
BETTY FRIEDAN
LUCY STONE
AILEEN HERNANDEZ
5TH AVE
UNITED
FRANCES WILLARD
WILMA SCOTT HEIDE
CARRIE C. CATT
MARTHA GRIFFITHS
JULIA WARD HOWE
ALICE PAUL
BELLA ABZUG

The Second Feminist Revolt

By June Bundy Csida

A new women's revolution is well on its way toward completing work started by the earlier suffragettes

When congressional and presidential elections were held in November, 1872, the feminist leader Susan B. Anthony and 15 other defiant women went to the polls in Rochester, N.Y., and cast their votes along with the men. However, Anthony was soon arrested for daring to "knowingly, wrongfully, and unlawfully vote for a representative to the Congress of the United States." In 1872, it was literally a crime for women to vote.

The scene was entirely different in 1972. At the Democratic National Convention in July, black Congresswoman Shirley A. Chisholm (D., N.Y.) was nominated for President of the United States. Jean Westwood was named Democratic National Chairman, the first woman in history to hold this position. A month later, Anne Armstrong, cochairman of the Republican National Committee, became the first woman to deliver a keynote address at a major national political convention. And, an unprecedented number of women held delegate seats at both conventions.

One hundred years had passed since Anthony was arrested for voting. The early feminists' dream of suffrage for women had been a reality for the past 52 years. Yet, in 1972, a new wave of feminists were highly visible and highly active. Not content with merely the right to vote, women were seeking new pathways to power in both the Democratic and the Republican parties. An increasing number of women were demanding more employment opportunities in business and the professions and equal pay for equal work. An old revolution had caught fire again, and women started coming together as a political force in a manner not seen since the days of the suffragettes.

There have been two phases to the women's revolution in the United States. The first phase began in 1848; the second, in the mid-1960s. In July, 1848, feminists Elizabeth Cady Stanton and Lucretia Coffin Mott convened the historic Woman's Rights Convention at Seneca Falls, N.Y. These women, active abolitionists, were inspired to hold a woman's convention after they had been refused seats at a world antislavery convention in London—just because they were women. They decided then that women were just as much enslaved by white men as were blacks.

The Woman's Rights Convention issued a declaration stating: "...We hold these truths to be self-evident: that all men and women are created equal...." And, Stanton made the first public demand for woman suffrage. Many of the early feminists considered the vote insignificant compared to the need for other women's rights reforms. But Stanton and Anthony believed that the vote would give women the political power to reach all their other goals.

In the early 1800s, women had many duties but few rights. A married woman had no right to property, even if it was her own by inheritance. If she worked, her wages belonged to her husband. If she left home—even if she was forced to leave because of intolerable circumstances—she forfeited everything, including her children. A dying man could even give or will his children away from his widow.

Out of the antislavery movement during the mid-1800s came individuals dedicated to improving the lives of women. They tirelessly circulated petitions, sent feminists on lecture tours, and lobbied congressmen to change repressive laws. Their cause was very unpopular. Preachers likened them to prostitutes; angry mobs pelted them with everything from prayer books to rotten eggs because of their "unladylike" behavior.

However, like the women's liberationists of today, these early feminists were anything but a homogeneous group. Conservative and radical factions disagreed on basic issues, such as whether or not divorce laws should be liberalized. They fought over whether they should try to win suffrage through the passage of individual state laws or by one national law. There were even some feminists who worked ardently for most women's rights, but who did not believe women should be given the vote.

Differences among feminists became so great that in 1869 the movement split into two rival organizations: the radical National Woman Suffrage Association, headed by Anthony and Stanton; and the conservative American Woman Suffrage Association, headed by Antoinette Brown, a minister; Julia Ward Howe; and Lucy Stone. Each faction had its own newspaper—*The Revolution* for the radicals, the *Woman's Journal* for the conservatives.

Then, in 1872, the year Anthony dared to vote, the first woman dared to run for President. She was the flamboyant Victoria Claflin Woodhull, an ambitious, egocentric woman who believed in free love, spiritualism, and magnetic healing.

The author:
June Bundy Csida is editor of *NOW Acts,* the newsletter of the National Organization for Women, and is a former *Billboard* editor.

Woodhull spent her early years as a fortuneteller in the Midwest. In 1868, she and her sister, Tennessee Claflin, moved to New York City and won the favor of the wealthy financier Commodore Cornelius Vanderbilt, who set them up as stockbrokers. The sisters acted as the aging tycoon's mediums, giving him tips on the stock market from the "spirit world."

Understandably, the feminists were wary of Woodhull. But they were also weary of battling against seemingly hopeless odds. For almost a quarter of a century, Anthony, Stanton, and other staunch feminists had tried in vain to win a hearing from Congress. Therefore, they were impressed when Woodhull appeared before the House Judicial Committee on Jan. 11, 1871, and demanded enfranchisement of women under the provisions of the 14th and 15th amendments, which granted the vote to Negro men. So Anthony and Stanton briefly allied themselves with the charismatic Woodhull. The conservative feminists were outraged at this.

Woodhull soon alienated her suffragist supporters. She attempted to take over the National Woman Suffrage Association and behaved scandalously both on and off the speaker's platform. On election day, 1872, presidential candidate Woodhull of the newly formed Equal

Conditions for working women have improved greatly since the turn of the century. But about 75 per cent of clerical workers today are still women, and few are in management.

Rights Party was languishing in jail. She was charged with obscenity for printing—in her own newspaper, *Woodhull and Claflin's Weekly*—an exposé of the famous preacher Henry Ward Beecher's alleged affair with a married parishioner. To make matters worse, Beecher was a former president of the American Woman Suffrage Association. It was an unhappy chapter in the history of the movement. Also, by linking feminism with free love, Woodhull had severely damaged the cause of women's rights.

Although basic differences continued to exist, the two rival organizations united in 1890 to form the National American Woman Suffrage Association, with Stanton as its first president. By the turn of the century, the women's movement had made great strides. Women were receiving college educations and had achieved some marriage and divorce reforms. Nevertheless, when Stanton died in 1902 and Anthony in 1906, only four states—Colorado, Idaho, Utah, and Wyoming—had given women the right to vote.

The final push for woman suffrage was left to a new generation of feminists. Carrie Chapman Catt, a school administrator, and Anna Howard Shaw, a minister and a physician, took over the National American Woman Suffrage Association. These later feminists often linked themselves to other causes, such as union organization and social reform. Frances E. Willard had rallied the Woman's Christian Temperance Union to the suffragist cause in 1878, so many feminists were against the use of alcohol. Therefore, men interested in the liquor trade were vehemently opposed to granting women the vote.

Since women were being exploited as cheap labor, this phase of the feminist revolt was also opposed by businessmen for economic reasons. But social worker Jane Addams and Stanton's daughter, Harriot Blatch, enlisted the support of women workers in factories and sweatshops. Alice Paul, one of the most militant feminists, organized thousands of women to march on Washington, D.C., and sent demonstrators to picket the White House. Finally, under the politically shrewd leadership of Catt, who controlled the powerful National American Woman Suffrage Association and its 2 million members, the conservative and radical feminists achieved their common goal. On Aug. 26, 1920, the 19th Amendment was ratified, giving women the vote.

Most feminists assumed the battle was won with the right to vote. They were wrong. By the 1970s, women still had not fully realized the other suffragist goals: equal pay for equal work, equal employment opportunities, equal education, equal political representation, equal treatment under the law, and child-care centers for working women.

By 1970, women constituted 37 per cent of the total work force, but they were still paid less money than men. In 1970, the wage gap between men and women was actually wider than it was in 1955. According to the Women's Bureau of the U.S. Department of Labor, full-time women workers in 1970 earned, on the average, only $3 for every $5 earned by men. Women college graduates, on the average, earned less

The Women's Liberation Movement gained momentum as women began to realize the problems that they share. Consciousness-raising groups played a major role in this process.

than male high school drop-outs. Men earned almost twice as much as women when their educational backgrounds were equal.

This was largely because most women workers were in low-skilled, low-paying jobs. Few women were engaged in professional or career-type work. As of 1971, women made up more than 75 per cent of the clerical work force but held only 17.2 per cent of the higher-paying managerial positions. Among managers, only 19 per cent of the women earned more than $10,000, as compared to 60 per cent of the men. Even the so-called traditional occupations for women were dominated by men in the better-paying, authoritarian roles. In elementary and secondary schools, for example, about 70 per cent of all teachers were women, but 80 per cent of all school administrators were men.

In 1971, about 12.2 million mothers had jobs, and more than 2 million of these working mothers were heads of households. All working mothers had a total of 5.6 million children of preschool age. But licensed day-care service was available for only about 780,000 children.

The situation for women in government and politics was equally discouraging. In 1916, before the vote was extended to all women in the United States, Jeannette Rankin, a Republican from Montana, be-

Since Victoria Woodhull ran for President in 1872, few women have sought or won high elective office. Only two have tried to win the presidential nomination of a major party. But they began emerging as a political force in 1972 at the national, state, and local levels.

came the first woman elected to the House of Representatives. Between then and 1972, 80 women have served in Congress, including 11 in the Senate. However, many of them were intended to serve out the terms of their late husbands or some other deceased congressman. Two of them were never seated because Congress was in recess and did not return before their short terms expired. Rebecca Latimer Felton, the first woman member of the Senate, was appointed in 1922 to fill the unexpired term of a dead senator from Georgia. Her actual term in the Senate lasted one day.

During the half century after women won the right to vote, only three women were elected to serve full terms in the Senate: Hattie W. Caraway (D., Ark.), who served from 1931 to 1945; Maurine Brown Neuberger (D., Ore.), who served from 1960 to 1967; and Margaret Chase Smith (R., Me.), a former member of the House of Representatives, who served in the Senate from 1949 to 1973. And, only two women had served in the Cabinet: Frances Perkins, secretary of labor from 1933 to 1945; and Oveta Culp Hobby, secretary of health, education, and welfare from 1953 to 1955.

After Woodhull's disastrous presidential candidacy in 1872, another woman, Belva Ann Bennett Lockwood, ran for the presidency as the Equal Rights Party's candidate in 1884 and 1888. Not until 1964, however, did a woman declare herself a candidate for nomination by a major political party. In that year, Senator Smith won 27 delegate votes at the Republican National Convention.

Women fared even worse in local politics. As of 1972, Hartford, Conn.; Oklahoma City; Portland, Ore.; Sacramento, Calif.; and Seattle were among the few major U.S. cities that had ever elected a woman mayor. And, only three states—Alabama, Texas, and Wyoming—had elected women governors.

In 1961, President John F. Kennedy set up a Commission on the Status of Women, headed by Eleanor Roosevelt, the widow of President Franklin D. Roosevelt. The commission's report, issued in 1963, concluded that women were discriminated against in virtually every aspect of life. Essentially the same conclusions were drawn by the Report of the President's Task Force on Women's Rights and Responsibilities in 1970 and by a similar study released by the Department of Health, Education, and Welfare in 1972.

Meanwhile, in 1963, Betty Friedan's best-selling book, *The Feminine Mystique*, was published. This consciousness-raising manual for "trapped" suburban housewives, was awakening—or reawakening—latent feminists across the country, and so the rebirth of feminism began.

Betty Friedan observed that after World War II, American women again turned their attention to the home, even though they had the vote and the power to gain education and enter the professions. They began marrying at very early ages. The birth rate soared. Then, by 1960, many of these women had grown increasingly unhappy, developing mysterious ailments, visiting psychiatrists, tranquilizing them-

Women were mustered into the State Guard for the 1890 statehood celebration in Wyoming, which granted women suffrage in 1869. The Army and the Navy established the first women's corps in 1942, and the first women were promoted to the rank of general in 1970 and to admiral in 1972.

selves. Psychoanalysts and social scientists tried to explain this problem in the psychosexual terms of Sigmund Freud: Anatomy is destiny, and American women had not learned to adjust to their sexual role. But Friedan felt these theorists ignored the fact that women have minds.

"It is my thesis," she wrote, "that the core of the problem for women today is not sexual but a problem of identity—a stunting or evasion of growth that is perpetuated by the feminine mystique." She theorized that complex social forces, the advertising industry, and the media (notably women's magazines) had created and perpetuated the feminine mystique: A woman, no matter how gifted or intelligent, finds her greatest glory and fulfillment by giving up all interest in the affairs of the world and devoting her life solely to husband and children. Friedan pointed out that women were literally and figuratively trapped in this image of themselves as mindless, beautiful creatures, with no personal identity and no real role at all.

The Feminine Mystique is generally credited with doing as much to ignite the current women's liberation drive as *Uncle Tom's Cabin* did for the antislavery movement before the Civil War. Other books, such as Caroline Bird's *Born Female* (1968), Kate Millet's *Sexual Politics* (1969), and Germaine Greer's *The Female Eunuch* (1970), also acted as catalysts in the social chemistry of the feminist revival today.

The modern Women's Liberation Movement is as much a state of mind as a visible, organized drive to attain certain social and political goals. At the heart of the movement is the consciousness-raising group —women who meet to discuss their problems and air their grievances. No one knows how many of these small groups exist, or have existed, independently of a larger organization.

The oldest and largest of the new feminist activist groups is the National Organization for Women (NOW). Since it was founded in 1966 by Friedan and 27 other women, NOW has grown to include 400 chapters with 20,000 members. NOW's goal is "to take action to bring women into full participation in the mainstream of American Society, *now*, assuming all the privileges and responsibilities thereof in fully equal partnership with men." Friedan was president of NOW from 1966 to 1969, when she was succeeded by Aileen Hernandez, a former government official. Behavioral scientist Wilma Scott Heide became NOW's president in 1971.

Today, women's liberation groups vary in character from the relatively moderate to the ultraradical. Among the more conservative groups are NOW, Federally Employed Women (FEW), and the Women's Equity Action League (WEAL). At the other end of the liberation spectrum are a small number of militant fringe groups such as the Red Stockings, the Society for Cutting Up Men (SCUM), and Ti Grace Atkinson's The Feminists. There are also individual women who object to the label "women's liberation," but who, nevertheless, support the concepts and principles of the movement.

Women's liberation began as a largely white middle-class movement. But eventually, black and Chicano feminists started forming their own groups in an effort to focus on the special liberation problems of minority women. Some minority women believe they should concentrate on liberating the minority man before they tackle their own problems. Others point out, however, that minority men, on the average, are already doing better in the labor market than white women, let alone minority women. In 1970, the median full-time wage for minority men was $6,598 as compared to $5,490 for white women, and—lowest of all—$4,674 for minority women.

At first, the new feminist movement provided more rhetoric than results. However, by suing em-

Not all women support the feminist cause. In the past, some were against woman suffrage; today, some oppose the liberation movement.

ployers for discriminating against women in jobs and pay, staging sit-ins and demonstrations, and holding public rallies, the new feminists battled ever-more effectively for women's rights. In many ways, their actions paralleled those of their counterparts during the 1800s. They borrowed tactics from the early suffragists: staging protest marches, sponsoring lecture tours by feminist leaders, working for politicians who favored the feminist cause, and allying themselves with other minority causes. Like the earlier feminists, they also published their own newspapers and magazines. Among the outstanding feminist publications today are two newsletters, *The Spokeswoman* and *The Woman Activist*, and a new national magazine, *Ms. The Spokeswoman* is edited by Susan Davis in Chicago. *The Woman Activist*, edited by Flora Crater, is a monthly bulletin from Washington, D.C. Along with other feminist news, *The Woman Activist* provides complete reports on how every member of Congress voted on measures affecting women's rights.

In 1971, many of the new feminist factions finally began joining together. The National Women's Political Caucus (NWPC) was formed in July of that year, as a bipartisan coalition of Democratic and Republican women, pledged to involve more women in politics on a full-time basis. The NWPC provided a prime example of the power that women can wield when they set aside party barriers and work together. Its members include such diverse types as Betty Friedan, journalist Gloria Steinem, Congresswoman Bella Abzug (D., N.Y.), Congresswoman Chisholm, former Republican National Committeewoman Elly Peterson, actress Shirley MacLaine, and Congresswoman Martha Griffiths (D., Mich.).

The greatly increased number of female delegates to the 1972 Democratic and Republican national conventions demonstrated NWPC's political force. Largely as a result of NWPC pressure, almost 40 per cent of the Democratic delegates were women, as compared to 13 per cent in 1968; and almost 30 per cent of Republican delegates, compared to 17 per cent in 1968. Women speakers were prominent on the podium at both conventions, and both parties adopted strong women's rights planks, including provisions for child-care centers. In the 1972 elections, more women ran for public office than ever before—64 for the House, 6 for the Senate, and an unprecedented number for state, county, and city offices.

Although Senator Smith was defeated in her re-election bid and the voters elected an all-male Senate, five new congresswomen were added to the nine incumbent women in the House of Representatives. And never before were so many women elected at the state and local levels.

It was truly a breakthrough year in 1972 for the Women's Liberation Movement. Not only were women making revolutionary gains in politics, but they also were appearing in jobs that had previously been held exclusively by men. The first women were accepted for training as Federal Bureau of Investigation agents. The first woman undercover inspector was hired by the Internal Revenue Service, and more and more

The new feminists use many techniques, like marches and rallies, that they learned from the suffragists. They are trying to win such rights as equal pay for equal work, and day-care centers for children.

policewomen were assigned tasks traditionally reserved for men, including squad car duty.

In a drive to recruit more women in anticipation of "man" power demands of an all-volunteer Army and Navy, the military was not only in step, but ahead of Congress. In 1972, Alene B. Duerk, director of the Navy Nurse Corps, was named the first woman admiral. The Army named its first women generals, Anna May Hays and Elizabeth P. Hoisington, in 1970. Jeanne M. Holm became the first woman Air Force general in 1971.

In August, the Nixon Administration issued a fact sheet stating, "There are now more women in full-time, policy-making positions in the federal government than ever before in our nation's history." However, that gave women little more than 100 of an estimated 12,000 policy-making positions, those paying $28,000 or more a year.

Nevertheless, President Richard M. Nixon has made several appointments that were firsts for women, including that of Barbara H. Franklin as the President's chief recruiter of women. The Nixon Administration appointed the first women chairmen of the Federal Maritime Commission, of the National Endowment for the Arts, and of the U.S. Tariff Commission. The Administration also named the first woman examiner in chief of the U.S. Board of Patent Appeals and the first women members to the President's Council of Economic Advisers and the Atomic Energy Commission.

Ironically, in these and other areas of advancement, the feminist movement has benefited from what was intended as an antifeminist joke. When the 1964 Civil Rights Act was being debated in Congress, a Southern congressman, Howard W. Smith (D., Va.), introduced the word "sex" into Title VII of the act. He hoped this would discourage his fellow congressmen from voting for the bill, which was primarily intended to ban racial discrimination in employment. The 1964 Civil Rights Act was passed by Congress anyway, with Title VII forbidding employers to discriminate against employees on the basis of race, color, religion, national origin, or sex. This has given the new feminists legal leverage to push their demands.

In March, 1972, President Nixon signed another bill, giving the Equal Employment Opportunity Commission (EEOC) the authority to sue employers in federal court for not complying with the provisions of Title VII. Under continuous pressure from feminist groups, the EEOC has stepped up action on sex discrimination cases.

Beginning in 1972, the enforcement of Executive Orders banning sex discrimination in government employment and by employers holding federal contracts provided the women's movement with an even greater weapon. The 1969 Higher Education Act, Executive Order 11478, empowered the Department of Health, Education, and Welfare's Office for Civil Rights to review discriminatory practices at universities receiving federal grants. As a result, lawsuits were filed against more than 350 institutions. In 1972, this act was amended to include prohibitions against sex discrimination in university admission policies and to extend the provisions of the Equal Pay Act of 1963 to women in professorial, managerial, and administrative positions.

By demanding the enforcement of existing laws, the feminists have begun making significant gains for women. However, a major feminist goal is a constitutional guarantee of equal rights for women.

An equal rights amendment was first introduced in Congress, on behalf of Alice Paul and her militant National Women's Party, in 1923. It was repeatedly voted down until March, 1972, when Congress finally passed the Equal Rights Amendment by an overwhelming majority and sent it on to the states for ratification. Congresswoman Griffiths played an important role in getting Congress to act on the amendment. One of the most significant aspects of this feminist victory was that, for the first time, old-line women's organizations such as the League of Women Voters, the Young Women's Christian Association, the Junior League, and even the Girl Scouts, joined forces with the newer women's liberation groups to promote a common cause.

The proposed amendment very simply reads: "Equality of rights under the law shall not be denied or abridged by the United States or by any state on account of sex." This has been the object of controversy and heated debate since 1923. Foes of the amendment predicted passage would wipe out protective labor laws for women and put them on the firing line in Vietnam. Those in favor of the amendment contended that most of the protective labor laws merely restrict women's opportunities for overtime work or higher pay. They proposed that the genuinely beneficial women's labor laws should also be extended to men. With preparations underway for an all-volunteer Army, the question of women being drafted to bear arms has largely been laid aside. By the end of 1972, the amendment had been ratified by 22 states. It has until 1979 to win ratification by three-fourths (38) of the states.

The significant gains of the new feminists have not met with universal acclaim. As in the days of the suffragists, not all feminists are women and not all women are feminists. While the suffragists were fighting for the vote, antifeminist women were fighting against it. They claimed that politics was a rough and dirty business, certainly no place for respectable women. And, today, some of the most vocal opposition to the new feminist movement comes from women who view feminism not only as a threat to marriage but possibly as an indictment of their whole way of life. The most extreme example of this opposition is seen in such antifeminist groups as Happiness of Womanhood, Men Our Masters, and the Pussy Cat League.

Other women oppose feminism on the grounds that it is incompatible with God's or nature's "ordained role" for women. Still others believe the movement is harmful to children because it might encourage young mothers to work outside the home. Also, liberalization of laws governing abortion, or "the right of a woman to control her body," is one of the most controversial issues advocated by the Women's Liberation Movement. Much debate has centered around this subject, which arouses strong antagonism on ethical and religious grounds, and this antagonism often spills over into other areas in which the movement is fighting for women's rights. However, a record 64 per cent of those polled in June, 1972, by the Gallup Organization believed abortion should be a matter for decision between a woman and her physician.

In spite of the news coverage and publicity that the new feminists have received, many Americans are still either not familiar with women's liberation or are under the misconception that the entire movement advocates the extremist positions of its most radical members. But recent surveys indicate that attitudes toward women's liberation are rapidly changing. A 1972 Harris Poll showed that only 36 per cent of all women are opposed to women's rights organizations, as compared to 42 per cent in 1971. The poll also indicated that 42 per cent of all men favor feminist programs. Although the Women's Liberation Movement has made great tangible gains in government, politics, and new job opportunities for women, one of the most encouraging aspects of feminist progress in 1972 was this indication that an increasing number of men and women were sympathetic to the movement—not because they were particularly appalled by the plight of women, but because they recognized feminism merely as one wing, and an important wing, of the movement for human rights.

See also Section Four, Woman.

Ecumenism In the '70s

By Martin E. Marty

Religious conflicts and a lack of leadership have the unity movement on a rocky road

The movement for religious unity, hailed just a decade ago as the wave of the future, seemed to be faltering in 1972. Both the religious and the public press predicted the end of the ecumenical trend, while the National Council of Churches of Christ in the United States of America reported that many of its programs had to be curtailed because of a lack of funds. At the same time, metropolitan interchurch councils, including those in Chicago, Kansas City, New York, and St. Louis, were in serious difficulty

A Greek Orthodox service and a religious dance group represent two diverse approaches to the understanding that the ecumenical movement has sought to unify.

and lacked denominational support. In her August, 1972, opening address to the World Council of Churches, Princess Beatrix of the Netherlands put the problem this way: "In the past, you have committed yourselves to bridging gaps between churches. Now there are gaps to be bridged within churches." Yet this was not the whole story. If unity seemed impossible among the denominational and church leaders, there were signs, at least, of interfaith cooperation in many local communities, and the dream clearly remained in the hearts and minds of most local churchmen.

The movement, however, was lacking a strong figure to rally around. The death of Pope John XXIII in 1963 removed this century's most widely recognized symbol of the movement toward religious unity. While Protestant and Eastern Orthodox Christians had been developing a unity movement for a half century, it was Pope John's convoking of Vatican Council II (1962 to 1965) that awakened the larger world to the idea of ecumenism. The term, which originally referred to anything that affected the whole inhabited world, had, in modern times, come to be associated chiefly with the goal of bringing the Christian churches together.

As leader of the largest Christian body, the 550-million-member Roman Catholic Church, the pope had become progressively interested in reaching out to "separated brothers" in Protestantism and Or-

The Crusades, which set Christian against Moslem, also caused internal discord in the Christian religious community, a discord that today's ecumenical movement is seeking to overcome.

The author:
Martin E. Marty is associate dean of the University of Chicago School of Divinity, a noted author and historian of religion, and winner of a 1972 National Book Award.

thodoxy. In some respects, his spiritual embrace included "all men of good will," "the human family," people for whom he sought "the brotherly unity of all." After his death, Vatican Council II approved a statement that spoke positively of all the major religions of the world, taking special note of Judaism.

Since then, the spirit of unity has become ever-more-widely understood and celebrated, even to the point of being taken for granted. Christians now greet each other more openly than before across denominational lines and express fresh and positive interest in non-Christian religions. But conflicts between peoples of differing religious outlooks and cultures have continued as if there had never been attempts to see "the family of man" as a united whole.

The advance of the uniting spirit and the setbacks to the unitive movements both point to the larger expectations that most people bring to religion. The spiritual traditions of most groups speak of a quest for a truth that can, in the final sense, be described only as "one." Believers who share a single ultimate truth are eventually expected to come together and to display their unity to the world. In the Christian Scriptures, for example, Jesus is remembered as praying that His disciples "may be made perfect in one" (John 17:23). And an early Christian letter asserted that there was "one body and one Spirit. . . one Lord, one faith. . ." (Ephesians 4:4, 5). In Islam, God is One, "the be-

In order to succeed, the ecumenical movement must comprehend the gap between highly liturgical worship, such as a Roman Catholic Mass, *below left,* and more spontaneous forms, *below,* as at Youth Explo '72 in Dallas in June.

The Reformation, which split the Western Christian church, began around the time Martin Luther signaled his break with the Roman Catholic Church in 1520 by publicly burning the papal bull of excommunication.

lievers are brethren." And while Jews historically have seen themselves as the "chosen people," they have also believed that all men are somehow related to the one God.

Just as well known as the drive for oneness, however, has been the parallel record of almost limitless religious divisions. Not only have Roman Catholic and Protestant Christians been divided since at least 1517 and Western and Eastern Christians since 1054, but these Christians have also tended to segregate or persecute Jews for most of the 2,000 years since the Christians and Jews parted. In Europe and the Middle East, hostilities between Christians and Moslems have broken into war many times. All these religions pursued their own courses through the centuries, their adherents generally lacking curiosity about or positive regard for Buddhism, Hinduism, or other world religions.

Each major religion is also divided. After the death of Mohammed in A.D. 632, the Moslem community split into three groups and subsequently there were other schisms. Hinduism evolved into many cults and sects, and helped give birth to an elaborate caste system in India. Buddhism divided into Mahayana and Hinayana forms after the death of the founder, Siddhartha Gautama (Buddha), and there have been still more subdivisions. Protestantism in the United States alone has more than 200 distinct church bodies, while American Judaism has its Orthodox, Conservative, Reform, Liberal, and Reconstructionist wings.

These divisions among the religions grow out of a set of claims that compete with the visions of human unity. While truth may finally be one, it is argued, man's knowledge of it may be incomplete and distorted as long as he lives. He cannot unite spiritually with others until both find truth, and truth can be found only if others convert and join the true believers.

When Christians from Europe and North America went into other parts of the world in the 1800s, they tended to stress division. Some

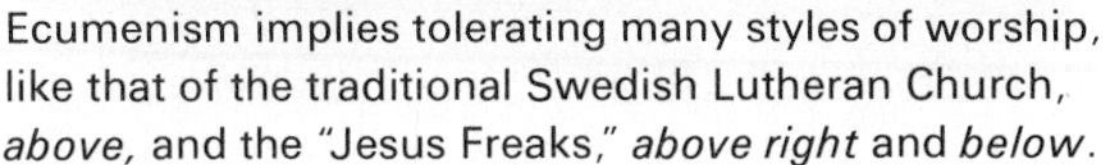

Ecumenism implies tolerating many styles of worship, like that of the traditional Swedish Lutheran Church, *above,* and the "Jesus Freaks," *above right* and *below.*

missionaries accompanied military conquerors or colonial businessmen. More often they were independent, guided by a sincere belief that they were called to take their faith elsewhere and convince people who practiced other religions of the truth of Christian belief. The missionary effort could not be undertaken without a spirit of competition, because the sending churches were themselves divided.

The inevitable result was a divided Christian Church everywhere in the world and an awareness of new tensions between Christians and the Africans, Asians, and, sometimes, North and South Americans who withstood attempts at conversion. But since fragmentation had gone about as far as it could tolerably go, the 20th century leaders devoted themselves more frequently to what British Anglican Archbishop William Temple called "the great new fact of our era," ecumenism. This "fact" took form in the formation of the World Council of Churches in 1948, Vatican Council II, various national and local councils of churches, and mergers or organic unions of several once-divided denominations.

Most people, of course, do not customarily think of the issue of church unity on a global scale. They tend, rather, to make up their minds about such issues on the basis of more intimate and more localized experiences. The young American today, possibly because of the ecumenical trend of our times, lives in a world of much greater religious tolerance than the one in which his parents matured. Only with difficulty can he think back to the biases that prevailed in the world his parents grew up in. Young people today frequently marry those of other faiths. Where their parents could do so only secretly or with disapproval, today's newlyweds may receive blessings of the priest, minister, or rabbi representing the faith of each marital partner.

Their parents may also be members of an organization promoting brotherhood—the National Conference of Christians and Jews or a similar agency. The young American who has been involved in social-

At the end of the Six-Day War in June, 1967, Israel once again controlled all of the city of Jerusalem, and Hasidic Jews prepared soldiers for worship at the hallowed Wailing Wall, *top*. The triumph was in sharp contrast to historical events such as the notorious expulsion of Jews from Spain, *above,* that took place in 1492.

action causes or joined in freedom marches or racial demonstrations has done so in company with people of other faiths. In school, they may have used a version of the Bible endorsed and annotated by Catholic, Jewish, and Protestant authorities.

Among highly literate and churchgoing families, living-room dialogues about differing religions may have been a common experience, and television has brought images of religious concord into homes. Students at a state university have the option of attending religion courses in the growing departments that have been set up for such purposes. Most attention there will probably be given to Asian and African religions, and the treatment will be sympathetic and positive. Wherever one looks, he finds that a premium seems to be placed today on understanding and unity.

Yet, at the same time, the young American today sees that the world has become increasingly divided. People may marry across denominational lines, but the lines themselves remain as firm as ever. There have been few successful new mergers of churches, and almost no new institutions exist to help people give permanent expression to interreligious brotherhood. Despite all the progress made across Christian and Jewish lines, many Jewish leaders feel that the dialogue produced little understanding. Witness, they say, the indifference many Christians showed the Jewish plight during the Six-Day War in Israel in 1967. And while television still projects hopes for unity, many of the pictures on its screen show people in all parts of the world killing each other, and often in the name of religious difference and definition.

What the young person experiences in his or her locality is a fairly accurate picture of what was accomplished in the public and official sphere during the 1960s. Pope Paul VI, successor to Pope John XXIII, presided over the completion of Vatican Council II. Before its end, the Catholic bishops made gestures of reconciliation to the Eastern Orthodox Church and showed themselves to be friendly to Protestants. They also approved statements surprisingly favorable to Judaism. The new pope made a number of reconciling trips: to Jerusalem in 1964, where he met Jordanian and Israeli leaders and embraced Eastern Orthodox leader Athenagoras I; to largely non-Christian India, also in 1964; to the United Nations in New York City in 1965; and finally, in 1969, to the headquarters of the World Council of Churches in Geneva, Switzerland. While these visits may have accomplished little in a formal way, they symbolized his continuing interest in the non-Catholic world.

These attempts to reconcile religious differences constantly faced hard realities. The world experienced another decade of wars, most of them accompanied by religious issues. In the Middle East, the Arab world with its Moslem faith carried on a *jihad* (holy war) with Israel. Israel responded by making

Both the World Council of Churches meeting in Uppsala, Sweden, *below,* and the Vatican Council II meeting in St. Peter's Church in Rome, *bottom,* struggled with the problems and possibilities of ecumenism for today.

claims that Jews had a religious mandate to occupy their land. While economic and other considerations were an obvious part of this conflict, both sides used religious appeals to justify their cause. In traditional Moslem law, if a land has ever been part of the *dar al-Islam* (the sphere of Islam), it dare never be separated from it.

Tension between Hindus and Moslems in India and Pakistan led to massacres and wars, and finally played a major role in the war that created the new nation, Bangladesh, late in 1971. More complicated was the story in Vietnam, where Roman Catholic emigrés from North Vietnam united with some Buddhist groups against the Communists—perceived as a religious foe. In Northern Ireland, Protestants battled Catholics, and though nonreligious factors were also present there, religion helped heat up the divisions and conflicts.

Most people do not associate these wars having religious overtones with religion itself and may not see how they are related to the problem of religious unity. But they serve as a parable of the much more quiet, yet still frustrated, picture of discussions within ecumenical organizations. Indeed, there have been more setbacks than gains in effecting church unity.

The World Council of Churches, which embodied many Protestant and Orthodox hopes for cooperation, came upon hard times in the late 1960s. Some people seemed uninterested in it because of its complex bureaucratic organization and its remoteness from the average congregation. The council itself was torn apart, becoming a forum for the international conflict between East and West, in which Russian Orthodoxy had a strong voice. Controversy between "developed" and "developing" nations broke into the open at a council-sponsored conference held at Geneva in 1966. Church delegates from the developing, or Third World, nations condemned many European and American practices, such as the Vietnam policy of the U.S. government, a condemnation that was widely publicized and rejected by many of the Euro-American churches.

What was true of the World Council of Churches was also the case with its U.S. branch, the National Council of the Churches of Christ in the United States of America. Its enemies criticized its generally liberal social-action policies, particularly those related to aiding integration in the South. Members of participating churches withheld funds, forcing the National Council to limit its activities and cut its staff. Meanwhile, pro-National Council churchmen seemed to be losing some of their enthusiasm for its cause.

While Vatican Council II inaugurated an era of new friendliness between Catholics and non-Catholic Christians, there has been almost no progress since then toward organic union of the separated Christian groups. Occasionally, small groups of officially sponsored theologians have announced new accords between Catholics and, say, Lutherans or Anglicans on various Christian teachings. But these announcements did not lead to new formal activities. Vatican Council II also turned

The variety in Catholic worship that grew from Vatican Council II ranges from a traditional service, *left,* to home Masses, *below*.

Attempting to meet 20th century needs, a drive-in Oklahoma prayer station welcomes all motorists.

loose forces that led to troubles within Catholicism. Many priests and nuns left their professions, church attendance declined, and Catholic theologians argued in public with their bishops over teachings about birth control and papal infallibility. The faithful lay people became confused, hostile, or indifferent. These internal problems forced Catholics to look inward and not toward their "separated brothers."

No better symbol of ecumenical troubles is available than the growth and decline of the Consultation on Church Union. This body was formed in response to a call by Presbyterian leader Eugene Carson Blake in 1962 to explore the formation of one united Protestant church. At first, it included just two churches (Protestant Episcopal and Presbyterian), but it grew during the 1960s to nine black and white denominations. Despite official church backing, however, most members of the constituent churches showed little enthusiasm and some condemned it. In August, 1972, the United Presbyterian Church in the United States of America, the original host, withdrew from the consultation. The beginning of the end of that venture was then prophesied.

Despite a stance aimed at embracing many points of view, Hinduism has split into many sects. Members of the Jains, a sect formed about 500 B.C., worship at the feet of a gigantic idol on Vindhyagiri Hill in India.

Instead of new mergers and stronger councils, polarization increased within denominations. Liberals fought conservatives at national gatherings of most of the denominations, with fundamentalists and conservatives joining forces against ecumenically minded social activists. Moderates barely prevailed in vote after vote on public policy during the 1971 assembly of the Presbyterian Church in the United States, and when the meeting closed, several conservative congregations and

Aspects of Hinduism have taken hold among youths in the United States. Here, members of the Hare Krishna sect celebrate in their Los Angeles church.

individuals split from the main body. The Lutheran Church–Missouri Synod, often described as America's most polarized church, was almost equally divided in every vote at the 1971 convention. The moderates of that body, however, successfully denied the synod's conservative president, Jacob A. O. Preus, his wish to have synodical statements of doctrine possess "binding force" on a virtual par with that of the Bible and historic Lutheran confessions or creeds.

In both 1970 and 1971, the Southern Baptist Convention, largest Protestant group, held tense and divided sessions. One of the main issues was the publication by a church board of a controversial commentary on the book of Genesis, which offended conservatives because it suggested that Moses was not the author and that the book was composed of several "parallel narratives." The 1969 meeting of the Nation-

Particularism of a black service, *top,* and a Jewish Defense League protest, *above,* are balanced by unity efforts such as an avant-garde San Francisco church, *above right,* with rabbi, priest, and minister.

al Council of Churches was disrupted by a radical group that called itself "Jonathan's Wake," which demanded a decentralization of the program and a redirection of endowments. Another radical group calling itself "Yellow Submarine" made similar demands and threatened to close down the United Presbyterian General Assembly in 1970.

Issues of war and peace, housing and race, and other social involvements tended to split religious organizations. The names of Martin Luther King, Daniel and Philip Berrigan, and Angela Davis evoked either passionate support or hostility on the part of various Christian and Jewish factions.

People of many faiths go to the religious revival meetings of evangelist and healer Oral Roberts.

Not all these difficulties of official, or institutional, ecumenism should be seen as a rejection of the desire for spiritual unity. Some observers detected in them positive attempts by religious people to fight back against paper unity, complex organizations, impersonal bureaucracies. What was called a "new localism" prevailed. People wanted to be part of intimate groups that they could affect or control. They seemed to be more interested in personal contacts, small groups, local congregations, and new kinds of cells, than they were in organizations that spoke or worked for them in Rome or Geneva or New York City. The "Underground Church," composed of small gatherings outside the parish structures, was a short-lived but widely publicized Catholic quest for such intimacy after Vatican Council II, and such a clustering of cells also found parallels in Protestant circles.

For all the frustrations, the overall record in Western Christianity in

relations between believers remains one of startling improvement. A vivid instance of the changed spirit comes from Latin America. As recently as 1946, a Catholic archbishop in Argentina had said that his was "a Catholic country. Those in this country who abandon Catholicism are traitors. And traitors are shot in the back." Yet in 1964, when Panamanian mobs attacked a Protestant church because they regarded it as an American intrusion, a Catholic bishop stood in the church door and shouted, "This is not American property. This is God's house." If they would burn it, he added, they would also have to burn their Catholic cathedral, because "both of them belong to the same Lord." The two incidents may not be completely representative, but they symbolize the change that has occurred in this era of ecumenism.

Almost every new movement during the past decade provided complications for conventional ecumenism. The new self-consciousness on the part of various ethnic and racial groups produced divisions, with the black and white background mattering most. Movements for black power and black self-determination were accompanied by calls for a black theology. Albert Cleage, the clergyman leader of Detroit's Shrine of the Black Madonna called for the "religiocification" of the black movement, and went so far as to argue that the people of the Old Testament and Jesus were literally black, and that the Christian story applied essentially to nonwhites.

While religious claims were not important in the Women's Liberation Movement, the efforts at "consciousness-raising" by this movement did include attempts to advocate a particular women's theology instead of what they saw to be the male-dominated Jewish and Christian heritages. Young people who separated into "Jesus People" movements often parted with their denominations. One interviewee responded to a question about conventional organizations: "We do not go to church; we are the church." Roman Catholic "neo-Pentecostalism," a movement that stressed prayers and speaking in tongues, attracted thousands. While this movement provided fresh experience for Catholics, the participants also remained aloof from many institutional interests of their host church, while they openly united with Pentecostalists from non-Catholic churches.

Ecumenism is largely a Christian concept and necessity, perhaps because Christianity has become the most visibly divided religious force in the world. But the equivalent of ecumenical concerns affected most of the world's other religions, too. And everywhere the attention paid to new needs for unity was contradicted by the satisfaction people found in sectarianism, particularism, nationalism, and isolationism.

In Japan, religious leaders urged that the nation must come to a kind of spiritual unity, and the Buddhist majority offered its services as a kind of integrator. But Buddhism itself is torn by sects and competes with Shinto, a former state religion once ruled by the emperor. More significantly, hundreds of new religions divided the Japanese, from Tenrikyo through the highly aggressive and fast-growing "value-creating society" called Soka Gakkai. China achieved a semblance of unity under the authority of Maoism, which scholars claimed was a quasi-religion. Maoism, however, was imposed with a force that took a toll of people's freedom to choose alternatives, and the antitraditional Maoist Cultural Revolution that erupted in 1966 led most non-Chinese to back away from using Maoism as a model for future spiritual unity.

There were scholarly attempts by Buddhists to unite their two main strands, Hinayana and Mahayana Buddhism. In 1950, the World Fellowship of Buddhists for World Buddhism was formed and it now has about 50 national organizations. There are also three other Buddhist ecumenical groups. But these have not altered age-old traditions of separation among most adherents.

Among major religious forces, none should be better equipped to stimulate visions of unity than Hinduism, which has a philosophy designed to embrace separate and differing points of view. But Hinduism's practice rarely catches up with this philosophy, and there has been little expression of new Hindu unity during the last decade. Meanwhile, the Hindus have been at war with the Moslems.

Islam suffers the reputation of being belligerent, but it is generally unitive in outlook, and a spirit of tolerance characterizes many groups in the Moslem world. Their unity has been cemented on practical bases in recent years by common opposition to Israel. But Islamic sects remain, and they have not been united. In any case, the religion has not effected any new ties to the non-Islamic world.

While it is hard to foresee a simple positive course for unity movements within and among the various religions, the dream itself has by no means died. On the practical and personal levels of society, a type of religious unity does take place. It may well be that tomorrow's ecumenism may have less of an organizational and more of a specific character, through which people will respond to immediate causes and occasions to give expression to unity.

Modern life leaves local and personal groups little choice but to link up. Even the anti-ecumenical forces among Protestants that opposed the World and National Council of Churches have banded together in a unity movement known as the National Association of Evangelicals. Although their motto has been "Cooperation Without Compromise," they have actually compromised away many old divisive practices. Conservative Protestants in the Campus Crusade, the Full Gospel Business Men's International, and the Billy Graham Crusades have cooperated extensively on an ecumenical basis. Instead of being present at the end of the age of ecumenism, we may be witnessing only the altering of its terms and bases.

Surprising new forms of conversation have also emerged during the decade. Most notable of these efforts have been the Marxist-Christian dialogues that some theologians have called "Secular Ecumenism." These events have brought together Protestant and Catholic Christians and various kinds of Marxists in Europe and North and South America. Neither partner to the talks has yielded much of anything, but they have increased understanding of what is at stake in the cessation of hostilities between Christians and Marxists.

Despite frustrations and setbacks, men will continue to seek some form or other of religious or spiritual unity. There have been many prophets of such world integration in the 20th century. Arnold J. Toynbee, the historian, projected a kind of synthesis of purified existing religions. Jesuit priest Pierre Teilhard de Chardin expected a kind of convergence between liberal Catholicism and scientific evolutionary world views.

All the while, of course, formal religion itself may decline. Human unity may come about without the aid of religion, and wars in the future may be fought without religious sanctions. Whatever happens, the trends of recent years suggest that for the foreseeable future, at least, people will have to learn to live dissatisfied with simple isolation but short of world integration. As the German novelist Thomas Mann said: "The world has many centers; that is, the human experience is available to many interpretations. We are in a situation where no one of these centers can assume it speaks the final word for all men in all times."

Religion in the 1970s sometimes produces conflict, as it does in Londonderry, Northern Ireland, *below,* and sometimes rapture as in the festival, Youth Explo '72, *above*.

The Prescott Experiment

By William Trombley

A fledgling college in the Arizona desert attempts to teach students the lessons of both man and nature

Calling the roll at Prescott College would be a waste of time. During a typical week, half of the student body may not attend any classes. Instead, they are likely to be off climbing mountains, shooting river rapids in kayaks, or hunting for archaeological finds on Indian reservations in Arizona. A number of American colleges and universities have begun to stress outdoor experience as a means of building self-reliance in young people, but none has carried the back-to-nature movement as far as Prescott has.

"It isn't very popular to say these days, but we are trying to build leadership here," says Ronald C. Nairn, former president and now chancellor of Prescott College. "We don't care if they become head of the Rotary Club or the Black Panthers as long as they are leaders.

"In the outdoor program, I believe we have a very simple vehicle by which students can do this. They come up against themselves. There's no cheating here. When you turn into Diamond Creek on the Colorado River, words like commitment take on real meaning. You know there are 14 tough rapids between you and Lake Mead and no way to avoid them. That's commitment."

Prescott's location is ideal for the outdoor program. The 620-acre campus of this newly accredited liberal arts college is situated in the

high desert country of northern Arizona. The school is 90 miles northwest of Phoenix and about 7 miles from Prescott, a town of 15,000 at the edge of Prescott National Forest. The Colorado River and Grand Canyon National Park are within a four-hour drive. Mountains and smaller rivers are much closer.

Although the outdoor experience is important at Prescott, the college also has strong academic programs. But, since shooting rapids and climbing mountains are more colorful activities than studying, Prescott has been plagued with the image of a "kayak college."

"Those of us who have strong academic programs going have heard about that until we're sick to death," says biologist Charles L. Douglas. "It's good press, and we've gotten quite a lot of donations because of it, but it has hurt us. We get some students who just want to rappel down cliffs all the time."

Most Prescott students alternate periods of academic study with periods of intense outdoor activity. But a few, such as Jeff Salz, a junior from West Orange, N.J., admit they have become very book disoriented. "I spend most of my time on the outdoor stuff," says Jeff. The experience of sophomore Nancy Whiteman of Denver is probably more typical. "I switch back and forth from the physical work to the academic work," she says. "It makes a good contrast."

There is a definite philosophy behind the outdoor program, which fits into Prescott's fundamental idea that education should be a continuing journey—not an end in itself. In 1968, Prescott began to stress outdoor activity. The college borrowed many of its ideas from Outward Bound, an international outdoor program that seeks to teach self-sufficiency to persons of all ages by exposing them to real dangers and real challenges in real situations.

Roy Smith, a 32-year-old Englishman who had worked for Outward Bound, came to Prescott and set up the school's Outdoor Action program. He and Nairn decided the program was needed because "we thought something vital was missing from education—adventure, initiative, responsibility. Those things were not fostered in the regular academic curriculum. In fact, they were ignored."

"Modern youngsters can verbalize so well they get out of most things by talking," Smith says, "but the outdoors is an extremely honest environment. You have to perform."

The students seem to agree. "The way to get an education is to face difficulties," says Jonena Hearst, a junior from Pocatello, Ida. And in that respect, the college itself has been receiving an education.

Today, well-established universities with large endowments are having difficulty making ends meet. Prescott's financial situation is far more precarious, because it is a new, experimental college with few alumni and no endowment. Also, Prescott's tuition and fees are relatively low for a private college. The $3,400 tuition, which includes room and board, provided only about 45 per cent of the income needed to handle the 370 students enrolled for the 1972-1973 school year. So,

The author:
William Trombley is an education writer for the *Los Angeles Times*, specializing in the area of higher education.

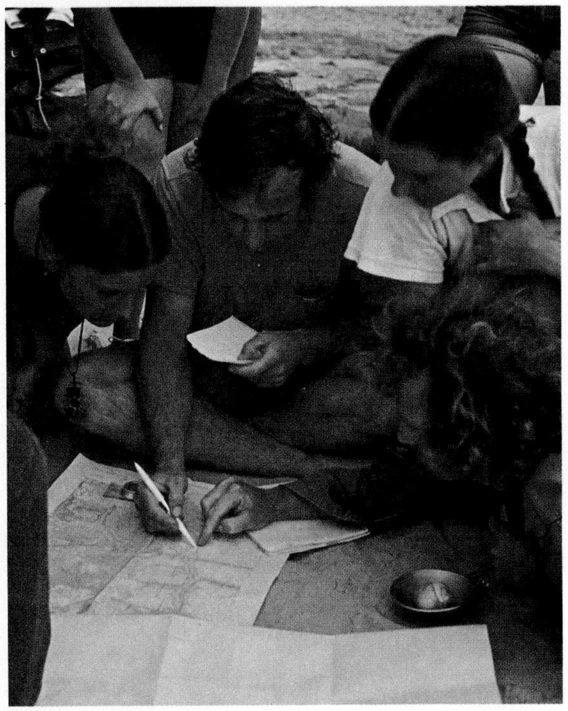

During freshman orientation, a group of Prescott students, *above,* plan the day's hike. Freshmen learn to survive in wilderness areas, cook their own food over open fires, *below,* and shoot rapids in rubber rafts, *below left*. Throughout their college days, Prescott students pursue demanding activities, such as rappelling down cliffs, *left*.

A fine arts student, *above,* can take a special studies course by working off-campus as an apprentice to a working artist. Facilities such as the college library, *right,* provide more traditional learning methods. The casual dress of students, *below,* illustrates the informal air on Prescott's campus.

not only has Prescott experimented with ways of educating students, it has also had to experiment with basic administrative structure and with methods of raising funds.

Prescott College first opened its doors to students in September, 1966, under Nairn's guidance. At that time, serious efforts were being made on some American campuses to break away from the academic specialization that had dominated colleges and universities for the past three decades.

Nairn, after earning a Ph.D. in political science at Yale and then teaching at several universities, had grown increasingly distressed at the narrowness of academic specialties. He hoped Prescott would be different, that it would concentrate on interdisciplinary education, the relating of one field of study to another. He began to develop a curriculum along those lines as soon as he arrived to take over the presidency in the summer of 1965.

Curriculum was the least of Prescott's problems at that time, however. The Congregational Church and local residents had been trying to start the college for several years. When Nairn arrived, Prescott owed $150,000 but had only $22,000 in the bank. And many townspeople were angry because the college had been promised to them for several years, but no progress had been made. Nairn decided the only way to relieve what he recalls as "intense pressure and tension in the community" was to build and open a college quickly—without the kind of planning that usually goes into a new educational venture.

He raised money, hired architects, engaged a skeleton crew of faculty members, and plunged in. Nine months later, Prescott was inviting prospective students and their families to visit the campus, even though nothing had been built on the desert site. "A lot of them asked, 'What kind of con game is this?' " Nairn recalls. "But I told them there would be buildings, and there were buildings."

Nairn wanted to offer a different type of educational experience at Prescott. But there was very little time to ponder innovational programs. So he took a radical approach.

"You don't do these things with a bunch of faculty meetings," he says. "One faculty meeting made it clear to me that if it was left to them we might have a curriculum in five years, if we were lucky. So I sat down myself and conceived the idea of these centers and told the faculty this is the way it's going to be."

Nairn organized the curriculum into four study areas or centers: the Center for Arts and Literature, the Center for Contemporary Civilization, the Center for Man and Environment, and the Center for Systems and Sciences. He hoped this approach would foster interdisciplinary studies, rather than traditional specialized education, in which a student concentrates on one subject, such as physics, and largely ignores other fields.

The following September, true to his word, Nairn opened the college. It was a cluster of small, terra-cotta buildings that clung to the

A student in a biology laboratory discusses bird specimens with his instructor. Students at Prescott receive personal attention, because the ratio of students to teachers is quite low.

tough desert landscape. Seventy-two students and 20 faculty members were on hand then. Five and a half years later, in March, 1972, Prescott—with an enrollment of more than 300 students—was accredited by the North Central Association of Colleges and Secondary Schools.

Since it opened, Prescott has been a constantly changing institution. In 1971, Nairn added the Center for the Person, emphasizing personal development rather than academic achievement. The Center for the Person flourished for a year, but now offers only a few courses. Also, the Center for Contemporary Civilization, which attempted to cover the problems and processes that are common to all nations, has lapsed into inactivity.

Much of Prescott's academic strength rests in the Center for Man and Environment. This center offers training in anthropology, biology, and geology, and a great many opportunities to combine outdoor activities with conventional methods of study.

The Center for Arts and Literature presents a standard humanities program that is weak in history but strong in literature. Pedro Aisa, professor of Spanish literature, takes his Cervantes students on horseback into the nearby mountains. There, drinking from goatskins and sleeping under the stars, the students acquire a sense of what Spain was like in Cervantes' time, during the late 1500s. Classes like Professor Aisa's are exceptional, however. Most of the courses in this center are quite traditional in their approach.

The Center for Systems and Sciences includes chemistry, physics, mathematics, and systems analysis. This center tries to encourage the study of whole systems rather than their component parts. This leads to an understanding of the systems and how they function. For example, chemistry students begin with the study of environmental chemistry, discussing the problems of a modern industrial society. Then they work their way backward to more theoretical material.

The student experience at Prescott is different from that at any other school. And this is clear right from the beginning. Freshmen are introduced to an unusual orientation program that takes them into the rugged country of Arizona, Colorado, and Utah. For three weeks they hike, climb, boat, and take survival training. At the end of orientation, each student must survive a "solo" period of three days alone in the wilderness. They take nothing with them but a few matches and a small amount of water.

The solo is quite a shock to Prescott freshmen, but most of them seem to relish the experience. "At night it was really nice, peaceful," says Kathy Keller, a senior from Boulder, Colo., who went through freshman orientation in September, 1968. "The first night I slept, but the rest of the nights I stayed up to look at the stars. For once, I was not tired. I was more peaceful."

When Kathy emerged from the wilderness she could not recall her own last name immediately. "I guess I was onto things more real than that," she says.

The strenuous life does not end with freshman orientation. Throughout their Prescott careers, students alternate periods of academic work with outdoor activity—backpacking, kayaking, climbing, sailing, scuba diving, rafting, and horseback riding.

The college also blends outdoor experience with more traditional academic work by emphasizing field studies in such subjects as anthropology, archaeology, biology, and geology. A hard day's drive away is Baja California, where the college maintains a marine biology field station. On one Baja field trip, students under the direction of biologist Jane B. Taylor discovered several new marine species in the Gulf of Mexico. Geologist Vernon Taylor leads groups of his students in journeys down the Colorado River in rubber rafts to study the geology and ecology of the Grand Canyon.

Marine biology students combine their outdoor skills with their regular studies as they search for specimens in the Gulf of California, *left.* Others get experience in archaeology excavating Indian ruins, *below.*

Prescott students have taken to the field to study everything from the local bird population to the economic impact of proposed new highways. "We try to place students on jobs that professionals in the field are doing," says Professor Douglas, chairman of the Center for Man and Environment. For example, students are currently engaged in what Douglas calls "salvage archaeology" on Black Mesa, located on an Indian reservation in northeastern Arizona, where coal is being strip mined. "It's not adequate archaeology," Douglas says, "but it's very good training for the students."

Other students are working with the Kaibab Paiute Indians to develop the economic potential of their reservation. "A lot of young people these days say they want to work with people," says Nairn. "Well, that's a fine feeling, but few do anything about it. We're going to say, 'OK, you say you're interested in human problems. Here are some. Go to work.' " So, Prescott students and Indians work side by side to excavate adobe and stone ruins near the tribal headquarters. They hope the excavation site will turn out to be a profitable tourist attraction, providing income for the Indians.

In order to facilitate these field experiences, Prescott's academic calendar is divided into two standard academic quarters and three one-month "blocks," when students concentrate on a single project. During

Geology students, *facing page,* travel down the Colorado River to the Grand Canyon to study the area's rock formations in their natural setting.

the 1972 winter block, for example, eight Prescott students climbed volcanoes in Mexico, while another group of six and an instructor set up camp on the Amazon River to study the tropical birds in that area. A qualified wilderness expert goes along on all of these expeditions.

Because the student-faculty ratio is low (8 or 9 students to 1 instructor) and Prescott has no graduate students, undergraduates spend a great deal of time with faculty members. They are also able to participate in research projects that would be confined to the graduate level in most universities.

Small classes, outdoor activity, and the opportunity to engage in advanced research are not the only attractions of Prescott College in the eyes of students. They also like its informality. Both males and females generally dress in work shirts and jeans. And most school officials take a casual attitude toward rules and regulations. Yet, Prescott students appear to have few serious behavior problems.

"This is one of the straightest schools in the country as far as people flipping out and tripping out and getting completely self-indulgent goes," says Jeff Salz, who has sampled life on several campuses. "Maybe it's the outdoor program. I know that has helped me."

Academically, Prescott is not as adventurous as some of the other experimental colleges that have sprung up in the United States in recent years. There are no grades at Prescott, but students must complete 42 courses successfully to graduate. They must take at least two courses in each major academic area— arts and literature, man and environment, systems and sciences.

Students are encouraged to develop their own academic programs in close consultation with faculty advisers. A typical program would include on-campus seminars, off-campus field projects, independent reading and study, and even courses at other institutions.

Prescott's drop-out rate is high, partly because some students develop academic interests that go beyond the expertise of the college's 40-member faculty. Others feel that the small college in the desert is too isolated. "There's a problem if people stay here for four years," says Peggy Weir, a junior from Washington, D.C. "This is kind of a micro-level. If you don't go to the cities for awhile and really get shocked, you just get a distorted view of things."

Although students like Prescott's interdisciplinary, problem-oriented approach, it is difficult to find professors to teach such courses. "They are all traditionally trained in their separate disciplines and they find it very hard to give them up," says Robert W. Harrill, a young chemist who directs the Center for Systems and Sciences.

The problem of academic specialization has plagued Prescott since its earliest days, according to Nairn. He believes education should be concerned with "the essences of human existence," not with the accumulation of detail in specialized fields of knowledge. However, he has not been able to supervise curriculum development closely. It has drifted toward the specialization he so dislikes. "I tried to develop inte-

A group of business executives meet in an outdoor session during a Schole seminar. In addition to providing executives with physical and mental stimulation, the seminars provide a unique source of income for Prescott College.

grated liberal arts education in the college and I failed," he says. "We have been caught up in specializing and it's going to be very, very difficult to break out of it."

Disappointed that, in his opinion, interdisciplinary liberal arts education had not flourished in the college, Nairn continued experimenting. In 1970, he started two affiliated units, the Prescott Institute, intended to offer academic credit for work experience as well as for traditional learning, and the Schole. Schole is a Greek word that refers to "a learned discussion in an intense and sustained search for truth." Nairn resigned as college president to direct the new Prescott affiliates. But the two new units caused such confusion and administrative problems that in 1972 Nairn decided to dissolve them and simply offer their programs through the college.

The Schole seminars offer discussions on such broad topics as "The Mind of Modern Asia" and "Violence, Revolution, and War." At first these seminars were intended primarily for business executives, but now Prescott students may attend, at no additional cost, to further their studies in the humanities.

Schole seminars are also a novel means of generating revenue for the college. Business executives are offered the two-week seminars, which include outdoor activities, at a cost of about $3,000. Nairn is confident that executive participation in these seminars will prove to be an important source of income for the college.

What was once the Prescott Institute is now another new part of Prescott College, called the First Year, for which Nairn has ambitious plans. He hopes to develop a program of experiential education for freshmen, in which they will be granted academic credit for their work experiences and field expeditions, as well as for their classroom and laboratory learning.

The First Year program is intended to help students find out what they want from education, or if college is for them at all. Through work programs and apprenticeships, some students may find that formal higher education, in any form, does not fill their particular needs. "We intend to put a lot of pressure on them during this time so they can find out what they really want to do," says psychologist Layne Longfellow, director of First Year.

In spite of its struggle to stay financially afloat, its problems with administrative structure, and difficulty in finding qualified faculty, Prescott has one asset that many other institutions might well envy—fierce loyalty among its students. This was evident at Prescott's 1972 commencement, an informal affair attended by the college's graduates, their families, and friends.

Instead of the usual graduation ritual, Prescott held an informal seminar about higher education and the nature of this small college. The discussion was led by Longfellow.

The dialogue began stiffly but quickly loosened up as Longfellow, who was dressed casually and held a cup of coffee in one hand, described other colleges and universities he had seen, either as a student or as a professor. They were schools, he noted, where little attention was paid to anything but a student's academic prowess. By contrast, he said, "Prescott College makes an attempt to educate man's soul and man's body, as well as man's mind."

Some of the parents at the seminar were worried. "The trouble is, we don't really know how to set up an innovative college," said one of them, who was a Los Angeles university professor. "I am concerned that we not destroy what is best in the old traditional approach if we don't have a replacement."

But graduate Marilyn Vache from Phoenix, who transferred to Prescott to complete her junior and senior years, said Prescott should forget about building up the academic side of the college. "That just takes money and people. The quality Prescott has is an opportunity to wake people up. They should concentrate on that."

Shelley Beall, who transferred from Prescott to Arizona State University to earn a teaching certificate in her senior year, praised her preparation at Prescott. "For me this was a place to grow up, a place to know people, to learn how to work with people," she said.

Another graduate added, "The reason I came to Prescott was that at this college you could do and not just prepare." Marilyn Vache summed up the student experience that Prescott—in spite of all its difficulties and shortcomings—has apparently succeeded in offering. "I came here from public schools with 12 years of atrophied muscle, both in my body and my brain," she said. "My two years at Prescott have been spent waking up those muscles."

Section Three

The Year On File, 1972

Contributors to THE WORLD BOOK YEAR BOOK report on the major developments of 1972 in their respective fields. The names of these contributors appear at the end of the articles they have written. A complete roster of contributors, giving their professional affiliations and listing the articles they have prepared, appears on pages 6 and 7.

Articles in this section are alphabetically arranged by subject matter. In most cases, titles refer directly to articles in THE WORLD BOOK ENCYCLOPEDIA. Numerous cross references (in bold type) are a part of this alphabetical listing. Their function is to guide the reader to a subject or to information that may be a part of some other article, or that may appear under an alternative title. *See* and *See also* cross references appear within and at the end of articles and similarly direct the reader to related information contained elsewhere in THE YEAR BOOK.

ACHEAMPONG, IGNATIUS KUTU (1931-), led an army coup that overthrew the civilian government of Ghana's Prime Minister Kofi A. Busia on Jan. 13, 1972. Busia was in England when the coup occurred. Colonel Acheampong then dissolved Parliament, banned all political parties, and set up a National Redemption Council, with himself as chairman, to rule the country.

Dissatisfaction with Busia's handling of Ghana's economic troubles, particularly a 44 per cent devaluation of the new cedi, led to the revolt. After seizing power, Acheampong revalued the new cedi, lowered food prices, and postponed payments on Ghana's $1-billion foreign debt.

Acheampong was born in Kumasi, Ghana. After graduating from high school, he taught school for several years and then attended an officer training school in England. Acheampong joined Ghana's army when he was 27 years old.

During his army career, he served with the United Nations forces in the Congo and later studied at the U.S. General Staff College at Fort Leavenworth, Kans. In 1966, he helped oust the late President Kwame Nkrumah.

At the time of the coup against Busia, Acheampong was commander of the first infantry brigade in Accra, the capital. Acheampong and his wife live on an army base in a suburb of Accra. They have seven children. Darlene R. Stille

ADVERTISING. Despite a substantial upturn in revenue, 1972 was a year of continuing turmoil for the advertising business. The year started on a gloomy economic note. Agency profits had hit a 10-year low in 1971 and, at the beginning of 1972, some large agencies were fighting for survival. The general economic squeeze, aggravated by federal price controls, caused many firms to tighten their advertising budgets. One of the largest agencies, Lennen & Newell, barely managed to avert complete collapse in February after the loss of several large accounts. The agency reorganized under the Federal Bankruptcy Act after such major losses as the $12-million Lorillard tobacco account and the $7-million Florida Citrus Commission promotion account.

Account shifts continued at high levels throughout the industry, but total billings turned strongly upward. By August, the authoritative Media Research Department of McCann-Erickson predicted that 1972 would be the beginning of a five-year boom. The agency estimated total advertising expenditures for all media would jump from 1971's $20.6 billion to $22.5 billion in 1972, and would surpass $25 billion by 1973.

The year's biggest gains were for television spots, up 13 per cent over 1971, followed by newspaper advertising, up 10 per cent. The estimated increase of 9.3 per cent for all ad expenditures for the year nearly doubled the 1966-to-1971 5 per cent growth.

Government Action. Offsetting the glowing economic signs were increasing federal pressures for major changes in advertising practices. The Federal Trade Commission (FTC) was the principal thorn in the side of the industry. Once known as the "Little Old Lady of Pennsylvania Avenue," the revived regulatory agency pressed its new program of requiring documentation of advertising claims to help buyers make "rational choices" and deter unsupportable claims.

The FTC asked for substantiation from manufacturers of toothpaste, cold remedies, cough remedies, laundry products, and tires. But, after studying the results, the FTC concluded that the program was an "extremely inefficient vehicle for furnishing product information to consumers." A staff report submitted to the Senate on May 1 indicated that about 30 per cent of the documentation was too technical for the average person to understand. And, the FTC said, there were "serious questions" about the adequacy of another 30 per cent.

In October, the agency announced its first action resulting from the year-old documentation program. It came in a proposed complaint accusing General Motors (GM) of falsely claiming that its Vega is "the best handling passenger car ever built in the United States" and in claiming that the Buick Opel has a chassis that never requires lubrication. The FTC said GM had "no reasonable basis to support those claims when they were made."

The FTC also continued to push "corrective" advertising with its second consent order; its first involved Profile bread in 1971. On May 4, Ocean Spray Cranberries and Ted Bates, its advertising agency, agreed to devote 25 per cent of 1973's advertising budget to correcting impressions left by previous ads that cranberry juice had more food energy than orange or tomato juice. Two sugar industry associations also agreed to run corrective ads.

Perhaps the biggest departure from past practices came in a formal complaint on April 26 against the four largest breakfast cereal manufacturers. The companies were accused of using advertising funds to "illegally monopolize" cereal sales. The four companies – Kellogg, General Mills, General Foods, and Quaker Oats – control 91 per cent of all cereal sales in the United States. It was the first government effort to prove that industry concentration derived from advertising power is illegal.

The Federal Communications Commission (FCC) also became increasingly embroiled in advertising matters. It received petitions, including one from the FTC, urging it to enforce its "fairness doctrine" by requiring stations to air "counter" ads to refute controversial claims made in product commercials. A White House agency, the Office of Telecommunications Policy, opposed the FTC bid.

In Congress, hearings were held in May on "Truth-in-Advertising" bills that would require ad-

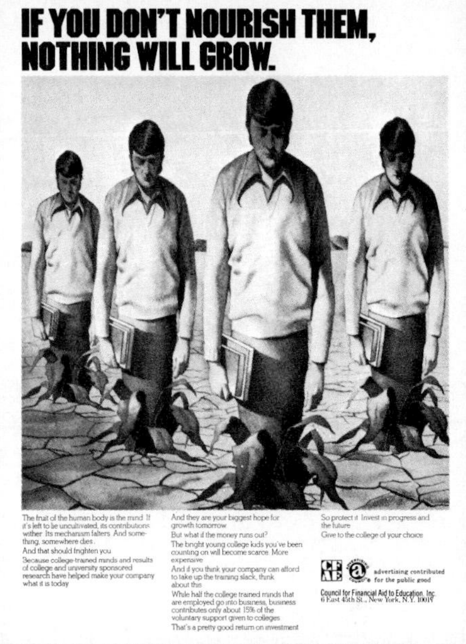

Ads for traffic safety and aid to higher education were among many that advertising agencies prepared voluntarily for The Advertising Council.

vertisers to supply documentation of claims to persons requesting it. However, the bills died without reaching the floor after encountering industry and Administration opposition, as well as skepticism from consumer advocates who felt that the rules might be easily circumvented.

One of the more prominent citizens groups, Action for Children's Television (ACT), scored a notable victory in July when the three main promoters of children's vitamin products on Saturday television programs agreed to its demands that the commercials be discontinued. In October, the FCC held hearings on ACT's earlier petition urging the FCC to set guidelines for children's programming. On October 18, the Television Code Review Board of the National Association of Broadcasters agreed to develop guidelines on children's advertising and require documentation on all commercials "to support the validity and truthfulness of claims."

Industry Responses. The year saw full implementation of the self-regulation program set up by the advertising industry in October, 1971, to adjudicate citizens' complaints about specific ads through the National Advertising Review Board (NARB). Complaints are first received and analyzed by the National Advertising Division (NAD) of the Council of Better Business Bureaus. Cases not settled to the satisfaction of the complainant or advertiser may be appealed to the NARB. Arthur E. Rowse

AFGHANISTAN. The drought that had crippled Afghanistan's economy and brought starvation to its people moved into its third year in 1972. Its effects were compounded by an unusually harsh winter in which many wheat farmers ate their seed wheat to survive. In January, the World Food Program approved a $2.2-million grant to provide 20,000 metric tons of wheat for an estimated 250,000 destitute Afghans. The United States also gave 100,000 tons. But the India-Pakistan War of 1971 had blocked shipments into landlocked Afghanistan; even after these were resumed, bureaucratic inefficiency and red tape further delayed distribution.

By mid-June, about half the Afghan livestock population had been slaughtered by its owners. It included some 15 million karakul sheep, the country's main source of foreign exchange. There is no official count of the number of Afghans who starved to death, but malnutrition was common.

Pakistan's President Zulfikar Ali Bhutto paid a state visit to Afghanistan. King Mohammed Zahir Shah told Bhutto during his visit that the only obstacle to improved relations was Pakistan's refusal to grant self-determination to the Pushtun tribes in northwest Pakistan. They live near the Afghan border and are ethnically related to the Afghans.

The India-financed Child Health Institute in Kabul began operations. William Spencer

See also Asia (Facts in Brief Table).

AFRICA

Racial conflicts, coups, and economic growing pains plagued Africa in 1972. Much of the continent was caught up in racial conflicts, from the bloody civil strife in Burundi and the Asian deportations in Uganda to the chronic black-against-white struggle in Rhodesia and South Africa. Most of the trouble arose from prejudice and racial stereotyping. But the question of which racial or tribal group was to rule the affected African nations – and therefore have the advantage in education, jobs, and wealth – was also a major factor.

Burundi Massacres. Burundi suffered one of the worst civil conflicts in recent African history. The government estimated that between 50,000 and 100,000 persons were killed in an antigovernment uprising and the retaliations that followed. The strife arose between two tribal groups that have long been enemies, the Hutu (Bahutu) and the Tutsi (Watusi). The tall and regal Tutsi have dominated the smaller Hutu for centuries – during colonial times and since modern Burundi won its independence from Belgium in 1962.

The bloody massacres in early 1972 followed the return of exiled King Mioame Ntare V, who had been deposed by President Michel Micombero in November, 1966. Micombero had promised the king amnesty, but Ntare was arrested on March 30, after he returned to Burundi.

Trouble broke out on April 29, when the official radio station announced that the king had been killed while trying to escape. At the same time, Micombero dismissed his Cabinet and sent military officers to govern Burundi's provinces. These events apparently triggered a Hutu revolt in which at least 5,000 Tutsi reportedly were killed. Then, the army set out to destroy all Hutu opposition.

What followed was described by outside observers as a massacre. The government claimed that most of the dead were Tutsi. However, unofficial sources believed that the Tutsi-controlled army systematically exterminated Hutu leaders. Troops reportedly executed thousands of Hutu men, women, and children – anyone who could read and write – thus ensuring that a similar uprising could not occur for many years. By mid-June, the Hutu opposition was completely crushed, leaving only the prospect of continued bitterness between the two tribes.

Asians Expelled. General Idi Amin Dada, Uganda's president, announced on August 5 that Asian residents who held British passports would be given three months to settle their affairs and leave Uganda. The sudden influx of Indian refugees caused political unrest in Great Britain – which accepted Ugandan Asians holding British citizenship – and threatened widespread consequences in other parts of Africa. See Great Britain.

The difficulty between Africans and Asians in Uganda goes back to colonial days, when the British brought in Indians to build a railroad. The Indians stayed on and became shopkeepers and accountants. They eventually settled throughout eastern Africa and became commercial promoters and financiers for Africa's developing economic system.

When Amin overthrew President Apollo Milton Obote in 1971, Indians controlled most of Uganda's industry and dominated its business and the professions. Obote favored gradual Africanization through education, quota systems in the civil service, and requirements that industries hire Africans. But the African population resented the Indians' high standard of living. So, Amin's announcement that they would have to leave Uganda was favorably viewed by most black Ugandans.

The United Nations (UN) attempted to debate Amin's policy, but most African nations claimed it was an internal Ugandan problem. This attitude created fears about the future of Asians living in Kenya, Tanzania, and Zambia. On August 21, Kenya warned aliens that they would have to leave the country unless they stopped "sabotaging" the economy, and a government official said he approved of Amin's policy. But both Tanzania and Zambia tried to reassure Asians living there. However, the Indians were cautious, knowing that such matters depend on personal attitudes more than official policies, and that governments and policies change suddenly in Africa. See Kenya; Tanzania; Uganda; United Nations; Zambia.

Changes of Government. In Ghana, the armed forces overthrew Prime Minister Kofi A. Busia on January 13, while he was receiving medical treatment in London. Colonel Ignatius Kutu Acheampong, leader of the revolt, established a National Redemption Council to rule the country. The council was composed of military, business, trade union, and religious representatives. See Acheampong, Ignatius K.; Ghana.

Following riots by students and workers, President Philibert Tsiranana turned over the government of the Malagasy Republic to General Gabriel Ramanantsoa on May 18. Citizens voted for a military regime on October 7, and Ramanantsoa assumed full power as chief of state. See Malagasy Republic.

Kwame Nkrumah, president of Ghana from 1960 to 1966, died of throat cancer in Romania on April 27. Although they often disagreed with him, African leaders praised him as "a great citizen of the world who raised the stature of the black man."

Anxiety etches deep lines on the faces of weary Asian refugees arriving in London after being expelled from Uganda by President Idi Amin Dada.

President Sékou Touré of Guinea, where Nkrumah had lived in exile, offered to return the body to Ghana if the 1966 revolution was repudiated and Nkrumah's followers returned to power. But Ghana's National Redemption Council refused to do this, and funeral services were held in Conakry, Guinea, on May 13 and 14. Negotiations on the matter continued, however, and Guinea returned the body to Ghana on July 7. The body then lay in state on July 8 in Accra, Ghana's capital, while thousands of Ghanaians came to pay their respects, and Nkrumah was buried at his birthplace, the village of Nkroful, on July 9.

Tanzam Railroad. One of the most important economic and political programs in Africa neared completion in 1972, as trains began operating on a section of the new Tanzania-Zambia railroad. Construction of the 1,116-mile railway, being built by China, was ahead of schedule in spite of the rugged terrain it must cross.

China, a growing influence in Africa, had granted $400 million in interest-free loans for the railroad and supplied the necessary skilled labor. The rail link could provide landlocked Zambia with military equipment imported from China. But its principal purpose is economic – the railroad will bring Zambia into closer contact with the countries of the East African Community.

Regional Cooperation was threatened several times by disagreements between members of regional organizations. Tension between Tanzania and Uganda threatened to break up the East African Community, particularly after Ugandan exiles living in Tanzania launched an attack on Uganda in September. However, the two nations settled their differences peacefully on October 5.

On April 19, Zaire withdrew from the Common Organization of Africa, Malagasy-Mauritius (OCAM). Zaire called the French-speaking OCAM a club of neocolonialist countries and said that continued membership would jeopardize Zaire's relations with other African nations. See ZAIRE.

The first formal alignment between French-speaking and English-speaking African nations occurred on May 1, when Nigeria and Togo agreed to form the Nigerian-Togolese Economic Community. See NIGERIA.

On April 3, a new regional group, the West African Economic Community, was established. It was composed of seven French-speaking nations: Dahomey, Ivory Coast, Mali, Mauritania, Niger, Senegal, and Upper Volta.

Pan-African Peacemaking. Several serious national and international disputes were settled with the aid of the Organization of African Unity (OAU) and neutral African leaders. Emperor Haile Selassie I of Ethiopia played a major role in working out the accords that ended the long-standing civil war in Sudan. The peace agreement between the Sudanese government and rebels in southern Sudan was signed in Addis Ababa, Ethiopia, on March 27. See SUDAN.

The end of the civil war also brought about better relations between Sudan and neighboring countries, notably Ethiopia and Somalia. The Sudan-Uganda border, which had been closed for 17 years because of the war, was reopened on May 11.

President Hamani Diori of Niger mediated a dispute between Chad and Libya. Chad charged that Libya was involved in a 1971 attempted coup against the government of Chad. The two nations re-established diplomatic relations on April 12.

On June 8, the leaders of Zaire and Congo (Brazzaville) achieved a reconciliation between two rival liberation groups working to free Angola from Portuguese rule – the Popular Movement for the Liberation of Angola and the Revolutionary Government of Angola in Exile. As a show of unity, the leaders of both guerrilla organizations addressed the annual OAU summit conference in Rabat, Morocco, on June 14. See ANGOLA.

The OAU aided in a border dispute between Gabon and Equatorial Guinea. It gained a general agreement for a peaceful settlement in talks in Kinshasa, Zaire, on September 18, and the OAU assigned a four-nation commission to work out the details.

Somali President Mohamed Siad Barre sponsored peace talks between Tanzania and Uganda in October, and Somali observers monitored Tanzanian and Ugandan troop withdrawals to at least 6 miles on either side of the border.

Liberation Movements. The OAU's liberation committee met at Kampala, Uganda, in May and decided to grant aid to all black guerrilla organizations active against the white minority government of Rhodesia. This included the Zimbabwe African National Union (ZANU), the Zimbabwe African People's Union (ZAPU), and the Front for the Liberation of Zimbabwe, formed in October, 1971. The two older organizations, ZANU and ZAPU, announced on March 23 that they were setting up a joint military command.

The Mozambique Liberation Front (Frelimo) escalated guerrilla activities against the Portuguese colonial government in 1972. Frelimo raiders stepped up hit-and-run tactics in the Tete district. On February 9, they blew up a truck, killing nine persons. In November, they were responsible for 20 explosions along a railroad line, threatening Rhodesia's link with the Indian Ocean.

A major Frelimo objective was to disrupt construction on the giant Cabora Bassa Dam on the Zambezi River, which will supply electric power to South Africa when it is completed in the 1980s. The rebels operated from guerrilla bases in Malawi, Tanzania, and Zambia, enabling them to escape across the border from pursuing Portuguese troops.

The new Frelimo activities directly threatened the interests of white-ruled Rhodesia and South Africa.

Facts in Brief on the African Countries

Country	Population	Government	Monetary Unit*	Foreign Trade (million U.S. $) Exports	Imports
Algeria	15,401,000	President Houari Boumediene	dinar (4.5 = $1)	1,009	1,257
Angola	5,720,000	Governor-General Fernando Augusto Santos de Castro	escudo (27.2 = $1)	431	423
Botswana	708,000	President Sir Seretse Khama	rand (1 = $1.27)	21	47
Burundi	3,850,000	President Michel Micombero; Prime Minister Albin Nyamoya	franc (82.5 = $1)	19	30
Cameroon	6,230,000	President Ahmadou Ahidjo	CFA franc (255.79 = $1)	206	249
Central African Republic	1,620,000	President Jean Bedel Bokassa	CFA franc (255.79 = $1)	31	34
Chad	4,000,000	President François Tombalbaye	CFA franc (255.79 = $1)	28	62
Congo	1,010,000	President Marien N'Gouabi; Vice-President Aloise Moudileno-Massengo	CFA franc (255.79 = $1)	31	57
Dahomey	2,910,000	President and Premier Mathieu Kerekou	CFA franc (255.79 = $1)	42	76
Egypt	35,892,000	President Anwar al-Sadat; Prime Minister Aziz Sidki	pound (1 = $2.30)	789	890
Equatorial Guinea	310,000	President Francisco Macias Nguema	peseta (63.65 = $1)	30	21
Ethiopia	26,580,000	Emperor Haile Selassie I; Prime Minister T. T. Aklilou Abte-Wold	dollar (2.3 = $1)	126	189
Gabon	521,000	President Albert Bernard Bongo	CFA franc (255.79 = $1)	121	80
Gambia	380,000	President Sir Dawda Kairaba Jawara	dalasi (1.92 = $1)	13	24
Ghana	9,900,000	National Redemption Council Chairman Ignatius Kutu Acheampong	new cedi (1.28 = $1)	433	411
Guinea	4,200,000	President Sékou Touré; Prime Minister Lansana Beavogui	sily (22.47 = $1)	55	70
Ivory Coast	4,610,000	President Felix Houphouet-Boigny	CFA franc (255.79 = $1)	456	399
Kenya	11,950,000	President Jomo Kenyatta	shilling (7.14 = $1)	219	515
Lesotho	1,170,000	King Motlotlehi Moshoeshoe II, Prime Minister Leabua Jonathan	rand (1 = $1.27)	4	31
Liberia	1,240,000	President William R. Tolbert	dollar (1 = $1)	222	157
Libya	2,161,000	Revolutionary Command Council President Muammar Muhammad al-Qadhaafi; Prime Minister Abd al-Salam Jallud	pound (1 = $3.04)	2,683	712
Malagasy	7,210,000	President Gabriel Ramanantsoa	franc (255.79 = $1)	147	213
Malawi	4,950,000	President Hastings Kamuzu Banda	kwacha (1 = $1.30)	72	109
Mali	5,345,000	President and Prime Minister Moussa Traoré	franc (511.5 = $1)	35	55
Mauritania	1,250,000	President Moktar Ould Daddah	CFA franc (255.79 = $1)	79	48
Morocco	16,690,000	King Hassan II; Prime Minister Mohamed Karim Lamrani	dirham (4.66 = $1)	499	698
Mozambique	7,767,000	Governor-General Eduardo de Arantes e Oliveira	escudo (27.2 = $1)	170	299
Niger	4,350,000	President Hamani Diori	CFA franc (255.79 = $1)	32	58
Nigeria	59,300,000	Federal Military Government Head Yakubu Gowon	pound (1 = $3.04)	1,640	1,506
Rhodesia	5,792,000	President Clifford Dupont; Prime Minister Ian D. Smith	dollar (1 = $1.40)	388	395
Rwanda	3,920,000	President Grégoire Kayibanda	franc (92.1 = $1)	22	33
Senegal	4,220,000	President Léopold Sédar Senghor; Prime Minister Abdou Diouf	CFA franc (255.79 = $1)	125	218
Sierra Leone	2,666,000	President Siaka P. Stevens; Prime Minister Sorie Ibrahim Koroma	leone (1 = $1.30)	100	113
Somalia	2,980,000	Supreme Revolutionary Council President Mohamed Siad Barre	shilling (6.93 = $1)	34	63
South Africa	21,596,000	President Jacobus Johannes Fouche; Prime Minister Balthazar Johannes Vorster	rand (1 = $1.27)	2,203	4,436
Sudan	17,051,000	President Jafir Muhammad Nimeri	pound (1 = $2.87)	329	332
Swaziland	458,000	King Sobhuza II; Prime Minister Makhosini Dlamini	rand (1 = $1.27)	67	57
Tanzania	14,328,000	President Julius K. Nyerere; Prime Minister Rashidi Kawawa	shilling (7.14 = $1)	251	338
Togo	2,216,000	President Etienne Eyadema	CFA franc (255.79 = $1)	49	70
Tunisia	5,646,000	President Habib Bourguiba; Prime Minister Hedi Nouira	dinar (1 = $2.07)	219	346
Uganda	10,626,000	President Idi Amin Dada	shilling (7.14 = $1)	235	191
Upper Volta	5,730,000	President Sangoulé Lamizana; Prime Minister Gerard Kango Ouedraogo	CFA franc (255.79 = $1)	16	50
Zaire	18,600,000	President Mobutu Sese Seko	zaire (1 = $2.00)	735	533
Zambia	4,700,000	President Kenneth David Kaunda; Vice-President Mainza Chona	kwacha (1 = $1.40)	679	626

*Exchange rates as of Nov. 1, 1972

And this raised the specter of future military intervention by one or both of these countries.

White-Ruled Africa. The possibility of dialogue between South Africa and black nations faded in 1972. Most black leaders abandoned the idea; Prime Minister Busia of Ghana, a proponent of dialogue, was ousted.

A special session of the United Nations (UN) Security Council met in Addis Ababa from January 28 to February 4. It was the first ever held in Africa. The council passed a resolution empowering UN Secretary-General Kurt Waldheim to begin negotiations with South Africa for the independence of Namibia (South West Africa). The South African government welcomed Waldheim when he visited Namibia in March, but showed no intention of relinquishing control of Namibia. The government adopted even more repressive policies during the year, particularly following student riots. See NAMIBIA; SOUTH AFRICA.

The Addis Ababa meeting of the Security Council also considered Great Britain's proposed settlement with the white government of Rhodesia, which unilaterally declared its independence from Great Britain in 1965. Britain vetoed a UN resolution condemning the proposed agreement, which would gradually give Rhodesian blacks the vote but would not provide for black-majority rule within this century–if ever.

In January, a British commission headed by Lord Pearce went to Rhodesia and sampled black and white opinion on the settlement. The blacks were overwhelmingly opposed, and staged demonstrations throughout Rhodesia to dramatize their dissatisfaction. The Pearce commission found that the settlement was not acceptable to all Rhodesians and recommended that it be abandoned. Great Britain followed the commission's recommendation, in spite of white Rhodesian protests.

Crime in Africa. The migration of Africans from rural to urban areas and the overcrowding and high unemployment that results have created a crime problem in parts of Africa. As a deterrent, some governments instituted harsh penalties. One of the most extreme examples occurred in the Central African Republic on July 31, when President Jean Bedel Bokassa ordered troops to beat 46 prisoners with wooden clubs. Four of the men were beaten to death, and the 42 battered survivors were put on public display the following day.

The Central African Republic had declared severe penalties for thieves earlier in July: loss of one ear for the first offense, both ears for the second, the right hand for the third, and death for the fourth. In October, Bokassa announced that tax evaders and unemployed persons not attending school would face prison terms of from 3 to 10 years. George Shepherd

See also Section Two, TRADITIONAL AFRICA IN A MODERN WORLD.

AGNEW, SPIRO THEODORE, was re-elected as Vice-President of the United States on Nov. 7, 1972. President Richard M. Nixon had announced on July 22 that Agnew would be his running mate, ending months of speculation. The Republican National Convention at Miami Beach, Fla., on August 23 cast 1,345 of its 1,348 votes for Agnew. Mr. Nixon's choice of Agnew was not popular with liberal Republicans but it pleased the party's conservatives.

The Vice-President traveled extensively in the United States during 1972 and made a 10-day journey to Japan, Thailand, and South Vietnam in May. He appeared at Republican fund-raising events, represented the President at ceremonial functions, and defended Mr. Nixon's policies. He also campaigned a great deal before the elections.

Agnew arrived in Tokyo on May 12 to act as U.S. representative in ceremonies marking the transfer of Okinawa and other islands in the Ryukyu chain from U.S. to Japanese rule. He then flew to Bangkok, where he discussed the Indochina situation with Thailand's leaders. He went on to Saigon for conferences with President Nguyen Van Thieu and U.S. officials.

The "Old" Agnew. Many of Agnew's speeches made early in the year were in the hard-hitting style of the "old" Agnew. He continued his attacks on the news media and on critics of the Administration. On April 21, Agnew accused Senator Edward M. Kennedy (D., Mass.) and three Democratic presidential hopefuls–Senators George S. McGovern of South Dakota, Edmund S. Muskie of Maine, and Hubert H. Humphrey of Minnesota–of staking their political careers on a hoped-for failure of President Nixon's Vietnam policies. Lawrence F. O'Brien, then Democratic national chairman, replied on April 26 that Agnew was practicing "a 1972 version of Republican McCarthyism."

Agnew hit at McGovern again in a speech at a Republican fund-raising dinner in New York City on June 30. He called him "one of the greatest frauds ever to be considered as a presidential candidate by a major American party" and "the darling of the advocates of American retreat and defeat."

The "New" Agnew. In his acceptance speech to the Republican Convention on August 23, and in a press conference the next day, a "new" Agnew took form. He said, "If I seem conciliatory, I am." He stated that he had not enjoyed the controversial role he played in the 1968 and 1970 campaigns, but carried it out because he wanted to be "an effective team player." It would not be necessary, he said, for him to act as "the cutting edge" of the Republican attack in 1972.

Agnew was generally regarded to have an inside track for the 1976 Republican presidential nomination. Political analysts suggested his new, less-abrasive style was intended to make him a more popular figure for the 1976 campaign. William McGaffin

AGRICULTURE made more news in 1972 than it had in several years. Secretary of Agriculture Earl L. Butz, fresh from a controversial Senate confirmation in December, 1971, vowed to put agriculture in the public eye. The farm vote was expected to be an election issue, and Butz became one of the most active of President Richard M. Nixon's surrogate speakers.

Agricultural trade, especially in wheat and corn, became the symbol of warming U.S.-Russia diplomacy. Some grain was also sent to China, and at year's end, India also seemed assured of receiving large amounts of U.S. farm products.

Food-price policy walked a tightrope as the Federal Price Commission threatened to control farm-level prices, and agricultural leadership grudgingly responded by holding many farm prices down. Retailers claimed that high farm prices caused high food prices. Farmers claimed that high profit margins in food stores were at fault. Farmers were also concerned about inflation. William J. Kuhfuss, president of the American Farm Bureau Federation, said in September, "Inflation is a serious threat to economic stability in our economy today–not only for farmers, but also for all citizens. . . ."

The farm press was full of disquieting stories. An outbreak of hog cholera gave Midwest farmers their biggest scare since the corn-blight problems of 1970. The corn and soybean harvests were more difficult and further behind schedule than they had been in decades. A mold that grew on corn made many hogs sick. A shortage of natural gas forced much grain-drying equipment to shut down. United States cattlemen objected to relaxed restrictions on beef imports, which brought increased competition. The relaxed restrictions were the result of concessions made earlier by the United States Department of Agriculture (USDA) to try to hold down fast-rising beef prices to U.S. consumers. Labor union battles within agriculture drew widespread attention; the lettuce boycotts were mentioned at both of the major national political conventions.

The Grain Deals with Russia were clouded by controversy. Some farmers claimed that grain dealers made excessive profits when prices for wheat rose sharply as Russia bought more and more. Assistant Secretary of Agriculture Clarence D. Palmby resigned after he and Secretary Butz negotiated the trades with Russia. When he went to work for a large grain company, critics voiced questions of impropriety. Secretary Butz contended in September that sales to Russia had increased the value of farmers' crops by nearly $1 billion.

Consumerism and Agriculture. Consumer-protection law changes and private class-action suits involving agriculture covered a wide range of issues. Agricultural colleges and the USDA were bombarded by consumer-interest groups concerned with a variety of problems. A devastating report, "Hard Tomatoes, Hard Times," released on May 31 by the Agribusiness Accountability Project added fuel to the fire. The report claimed that the land-grant colleges and the USDA had sold out to agribusiness and nonfarm interests, and were paying homage to efficiency while ignoring rural social problems and the family farmer. Representatives of the land-grant colleges countered such attacks by pointing out that the U.S. worker had a wider variety of more wholesome and better packaged food for a smaller part of his paycheck than any consumer ever had before. Top USDA economist Don A. Paarlberg said, "The chief gainer from increased agricultural efficiency is the consumer."

Controversy arose even within the agriculture establishment. For example, a group called the USDA's Young Executive Committee questioned many farm policies established by their own organization. Moreover, they said, "Failure to obtain public agreement on the basic goals for agriculture has resulted in the formulation of individual programs with conflicting objectives."

Farm Prices Grow. Prices–including both those paid by farmers and those received by them–were substantially above 1971 levels. The index of prices received by farmers in October was 129 (1967=100), more than 13 per cent higher than in October, 1971. The index of prices farmers paid was also 129 (1967=100), up 7 per cent from 1971.

Bob Brigham, *Life* © 1972 Time Inc.

Wheat from the United States arrives in the Russian port of Odessa as part of the biggest grain transaction ever between the two nations.

Meat animals posted the biggest rise in prices farmers received, up 24 per cent from October, 1971, to October, 1972. Prices received for beef cattle averaged $34.20 per hundredweight (cwt), and for hogs, $27.50 per cwt. Wheat and rice prices were both far above 1971 levels. Wheat's $1.89 per bushel on October 15 compared to $1.30 on the same date in 1971. Rice was $6.72 per cwt, compared to $5.37 in 1971. The rice price was only 26 cents per cwt below the all-time high established in 1948.

These higher prices helped the farmer increase his share of the consumer's food dollar from 38 cents in 1971 to 40 cents in 1972. Yet, despite the higher prices paid for farm products, American families continued to spend less on food. In 1972, the average American family spent only 15.5 per cent of its income for food, compared to 15.8 per cent in 1971, 16.6 per cent in 1970, and 20.0 per cent in 1960.

Crop Production reached a record high index of 114 (1967= 100), up 2 per cent from 1971 and 14 per cent from 1970. The increase was led by cotton, with an index of 186 compared to 141 in 1971, and by oil, up 27 points to an index of 136. Feed grains and food grains showed some decline from 1971, because cool and wet weather during the latter part of October and early November hampered harvesting efforts. Soybean production continued to expand, reaching another record of 1.351 billion bushels, up 181 million bushels from last year.

Cotton production jumped sharply to 13,955,100 bales, up about 33 per cent from the 10,473,000 bales in 1971. Rice production was up almost 1 per cent, peanut production up 9 per cent to a new record, and tobacco production up 1.5 per cent from 1971. Citrus fruit production was also up. Oranges gained 30 per cent, and lemons were up 32 per cent, but tangerines were down 8 per cent and grapefruit down 2 per cent.

The overall record output of crops was due, in large part, to record high yields. For 28 major field and fruit crops, the average yield was 5 per cent above 1971 and 15 per cent above 1967.

Livestock Production hit an all-time overall high. Beef production rose 2.7 per cent, but pork production fell 4.3 per cent. Broiler and turkey production, however, were at record high levels, both up 6 per cent from 1971. Milk production was also up from 1971.

On September 1, hogs and pigs on farms numbered 46.468 million head, down 1 per cent from Sept. 1, 1971, and down 8 per cent from Sept. 1, 1970, Surveys showed, however, that farmers expect to farrow 7 per cent more sows during early 1973.

The Farmer's Financial Status improved during 1972. Farm receipts were boosted, with higher prices for crops and livestock more than offsetting a $3-billion rise in farm-production expenses. Overall, net farm income rose almost $3 billion to a record high of nearly $19 billion.

Farmers' assets rose 7.7 per cent to $338.9 billion on Jan. 1, 1972. Debts rose 9 per cent to $66.6 billion, leaving the net worth of farmers at $272.3 billion. Over the past 10 years, farmers' assets have risen an average of 5.9 per cent per year, while net worth has averaged a 4.8 per cent increase and debts a 13.2 per cent increase annually. However, a consensus of studies showed that farmers now contribute only 15 per cent of the value of food by the time it gets to consumers. Marketing and processing account for 50 per cent of the total.

Farm Exports and Imports. United States farm exports set another record in the year ended on June 30, totaling more than $8.05 billion. The new record was 4 per cent above the previous high, which was established in 1971. The export market in fiscal 1972 took the output from 1 of every 5 acres of cropland harvested in the United States, and accounted for about 14 per cent of farmers' cash receipts. More than 50 per cent of the U.S. production of rice and soybeans was exported as was 40 per cent of the wheat, cattle hides, and tallow, and about 30 per cent of the tobacco and cotton.

Judging by statistics from the latter half of 1972, exports for the year ending on June 30, 1973, will skyrocket far beyond the new record, perhaps as high as $10 billion. Shipments to Russia will make up much of the increase. Russian purchases of United States farm products were forecast at $1.2 billion for the year, compared to only $150 million for the year ending on June 30, 1972.

The expansion in U.S. farm exports is a result of several important factors: a low world grain harvest in 1972, especially the Russian wheat crop; liberalization of trade policies with Russia and the People's Republic of China; and generally good U.S. supplies of grain, and the capacity to move these grains in large quantities.

Imports also continued rising. During the fiscal year ended on June 30, 1972, U.S. agricultural imports totaled more than $6.042 billion, up 4 per cent from 1971. Most of the increase came from cattle, meat, sugar, some fruits and vegetables, tobacco, and wine. Meat imports rose in value by 8 per cent to over $1 billion. Imports of fresh-chilled boneless beef, the largest item within the meat category, went up 14 per cent to $599 million.

Public Agricultural Policy revolved largely around who would control agriculture. Secretary Butz said in September, "The question of who will control farming in America is the key issue which agriculture must face in this decade." Bigness frightened many farmers. For example, it was reported that 0.4 per cent of the nation's cattle feedlots, or only 146 lots, had 25 per cent of the nation's beef in 1972 – and 190 of the lots produced more than 50 per cent of all beef. The same problem arose in crops. For example, more than 30 per cent of the nation's soybeans were produced on only 30,000 farms.

Antitrust law and agricultural policy came sharply into conflict in 1972. For example, cooperatives have always been given special privileges in agricultural policy and related legislation. Secretary Butz told a farm audience in September, "Farm cooperatives have a special spot in my heart." He issued a memorandum on October 27 that started with this preamble: "Farmers have learned that by working together they can achieve results far greater than by working individually."

Farmers pushed harder than ever for bargaining legislation in 1972. Agricultural policy has been previously designed to raise producer prices through price supports, marketing orders, and cooperative activities. Now, group bargaining was the issue. The possible conflict of agricultural policy with antitrust laws, which control the size and monopolistic practices of business enterprises, was brought even more into the open in 1972 when farm prices were generally exempt from the economic stabilization program imposed on other groups. However, the Nelson Family Farm Act introduced in Congress in 1970 would prohibit many contractual and other arrangements between powerful large producers and small farmers. Such arrangements were being fostered by traditional agricultural policy. In 1972, there were at least 14 lawsuits pending against the large, newly established regional dairy cooperatives. Plaintiffs represented a large group of government and private interests. A United States Department of Justice advisory opinion on the so-called Holly Farms case said that this large broiler contractor would probably jeopardize the exempt status of the National Broiler Marketing Association cooperative if it became a member.

The Farm-Labor Force continued to decline in number. The total number of farmworkers dropped from 4.446 million in 1971 to 4.390 million in 1972. This is contrasted with a farm-labor force of 7.057-million in 1960. The decline in farm laborers from 1971 occurred among farm-family workers, because the number of hired farmworkers increased slightly, from 1.165 million to 1.175 million. The number of hired workers has changed very little since 1969, but a continuing decline in family workers has reduced the total farm labor force by more than 4 per cent in that time.

Average wages for hired farmworkers remained far below industrial wages, but they increased from \$1.54 per hour in October, 1971, to \$1.65 per hour in October, 1972.

Farm-labor productivity has continued to advance. Data released in 1972 showed that only 6 man-hours of labor were required to produce 100 bushels of corn from 1966 to 1970, while more than 50 man-hours of labor were required during the years from 1945 to 1949.

Although the farm-labor force declined, the total U.S. farm population halted its long-term decline,

Agricultural Statistics, 1972

Output of Major U.S. Crops
(millions of bushels)

Crop	1962-66†	1971	1972*
Corn	3,862	5,540	5,400
Sorghums	595	895	896
Oats	912	876	731
Wheat	1,230	1,640	1,559
Soybeans	769	1,169	1,351
Rice (a)	742	843	851
Potatoes (b)	275	319	294
Cotton (c)	125	104	140
Tobacco (d)	2,126	1,707	1,733

†Average; *Preliminary
(a) 100,000 cwt.; (b) 1,000,000 cwt.;
(c) 100,000 bales; (d) 1,000,000 lbs.

U.S. Production of Animal Products
(millions of pounds)

	1957-59†	1971	1972*
Beef	13,704	21,904	22,500
Veal	1,240	546	450
Lamb and Mutton	711	554	530
Pork	10,957	14,795	13,885
Eggs (a)	5,475	5,978	5,938
Chicken	5,292	10,766	11,411
Turkey	1,382	2,262	2,400
Total Milk (b)	123.2	118.6	120.5

†Average; *Preliminary
(a) 1,000,000 dozens; (b) 100,000,000 lbs.

World Crop Production
(million units)

Crop	Units	1971	1972*	%U.S.
Barley	Metric tons	130.4	127.8	7.1
Corn	Metric tons	291.3	(NA)	48.3[1]
Oats	Metric tons	54.7	49.1	21.6
Wheat	Metric tons	323.2	300.5	14.1
Rice	Metric tons	294.2	(NA)	1.3[1]
Coffee	Bags[2]	71.4	72.9	0.3
Cotton	Bales	57.0	60.4	23.2
Soybeans	Metric tons	43.4	49.0	73.2

*Preliminary; (NA) not available.
[1]Based on 1972 data; [2]132.276 lbs.

at least temporarily. The 1972 farm population was estimated at 9.5 million, up from 9.425 million in 1971. The farm population held at 4.6 per cent of the total U.S. population.

The continuing build-up of people in cities and urban communities brought many new community development problems to agricultural leaders. The USDA and State Cooperative Extension Service devoted 34 per cent more time to rural-development activities in fiscal 1972 than in 1971.

World Agricultural Production leveled off somewhat in 1972 after a decade of continued expansion. Total world grain production had grown from 771-million metric tons in 1961 to a record 1.11 billion metric tons in 1971. In 1972, however, total grain output was estimated at 1.06 billion metric tons. Wheat production slipped sharply from 323.2 million metric tons in 1971 to 300.5 million metric tons in 1972, due in large part to an estimated 25 per cent drop in Russian production. Feed grain production was also down, primarily because less U.S. acreage was planted in these crops. Cotton and coffee showed increased production in 1972 and soybean production again jumped sharply, led by the record U.S. crops. Charles E. French and Larry L. Nelson

AIR FORCE, U.S. See National Defense.
AIR POLLUTION. See Environment.
ALABAMA. See State Government.
ALASKA. See State Government.

ALBANIA became more isolated from the rest of the Communist world in 1972, but continued to open up toward non-Communist Europe. Albania retained close economic links with its big ally, China, and China extended its heavy financing of Albania's economic development under a trade agreement signed in Peking on April 11. But a chill between the two countries followed China's improved relations with the United States. See China.

Albania vigorously opposed the policy of playing one set of "imperialists" against another. Albanian leaders seemed to fear that friendlier relations between China and the superpowers could weaken Albania's position.

Trade Relations. Commercial and cultural relations continued to develop with Yugoslavia's autonomous, largely Albanian, Kosovo province. In 1972, Yugoslavia became Albania's third most important trade partner, after China and Italy. Better relations developed with Italy, France, Switzerland, and the Scandinavian countries. Albania signed a long-term trade agreement with Austria in April.

On February 26, party leader Enver Hoxha launched a new government campaign officially described as a "cult of the masses." It was aimed at bringing the people closer to the government and reducing the power of the bureaucracy. Chris Cviic

See also Europe (Facts in Brief Table).

ALBERTA. See Canada.

ALGERIA marked the 10th anniversary of its independence from France in 1972 by taking an active role in regional affairs and going all-out for industrial development. President Houari Boumediene visited Morocco and reached two agreements with King Hassan II. They defined the Algerian-Moroccan border west of Tindouf, the scene of conflict in 1963, and they agreed on joint exploitation of the Gara-Djebilet iron mines. Boumediene visited Tunisia and met with President Habib Bourguiba for the first time. The two agreed to develop jointly the El-Borma natural gas field that straddles their common border. Algiers was host to a summit conference of the Libyan, Algerian, and Egyptian chiefs of state on July 17. The three agreed to press for removal of all naval power from the Mediterranean Sea.

The Boumediene regime marked its seventh anniversary on June 19 by beginning the land-reform program called for in the October, 1971, Agrarian Reform Charter. The first 100 hectares (about 247 acres) of donated land were distributed to landless peasants. Even more emphasis was placed on industrial development. Algerian planners set 1980 as the date by which the country should be an advanced industrial state.

Economic Indicators suggested that the date was not unrealistic. During Cuban Premier Fidel Castro's visit in May, the El Hadjar Steel Works at

Dense crowds of Algerians greeted Cuba's Fidel Castro and Algeria's Houari Boumediene as Castro was escorted to Algiers for a May visit.

Annaba went into operation. President Boumediene also dedicated the 360-mile gas pipeline from the Hassi Rmel fields to the Skikda liquefaction plant and a new oil pipeline to the nearby refinery. Algeria reported at the Arab Oil Congress in May that its natural gas reserves exceeded 100-million cubic feet, 10 per cent of the world's supply. Algeria concluded long-term sales agreements for its gas with West Germany, Belgium, and Spain, among others.

Algeria had earlier made a $1.5-billion contract with the El Paso Natural Gas Company, but at year's end, that agreement had not been approved by the U.S. Federal Power Commission.

Trade Agreements, mostly repayable in crude oil, were signed with Guinea, Senegal, Ghana, Cameroon, and Congo (Brazzaville). A two-year trade pact with Russia would increase reciprocal trade to $590 million by 1974. Russia also agreed to purchase the bulk of Algeria's unsold wine stocks, although Algeria would benefit from preferential tariffs from the European Community on its wine crop.

Algeria received loans from Romania, after the state visit in March of President Nicolae Ceausescu, and from Czechoslovakia, for industrial equipment. The United Nations Development Program in June granted Algeria $73 million for long-term industrial development. William Spencer

See also AFRICA (Facts in Brief Table).

AMERICAN LEGION. See VETERANS.

AMERICAN LIBRARY ASSOCIATION (ALA). Katherine Laich, lecturer and coordinator of programs at the school of library science, University of Southern California, became president of the ALA at the 92nd annual conference held in Chicago from June 25 to July 1, 1972. Jean E. Lowrie, director of the Department of Librarianship, Western Michigan University, Kalamazoo, took office as vice-president and president-elect. In August, library scientist Robert Wedgeworth from Rutgers, N.J., succeeded the retiring ALA executive director, David H. Clift.

The ALA Council set up an ad hoc joint committee of ALA's American Association of School Librarians and the National Council of Teachers of Mathematics to explore the impact of the expected change to the metric system in the United States. The ALA Council also established a Round Table on Government Documents, and a Federal Librarians' Round Table. In addition, the council approved the merging of the Adult Services Division and Reference Services Division and adoption of new standards for accreditation.

The ALA Intellectual Freedom Committee received a $14,000 J. Morris Jones-World Book Encyclopedia-ALA Goals Award for a prototype educational workshop in intellectual freedom. The ALA Committee on Accreditation was awarded $10,000 for a seminar to prepare evaluators of graduate programs of library education.

The ALA's Washington office, its Legislation Committee, and many ALA members, applauded the signing into law of the Education Amendments of 1972. The measure authorizes federal funding for library training and research.

As part of their efforts for recognition of the right to photocopy books under certain conditions, the ALA filed a brief of exceptions in the U.S. Court of Claims in connection with two cases in which photocopying is alleged to be a violation of copyright.

International Book Year (IBY). The ALA endorsed several IBY projects, including a bookmobile of the Americas, a black caucus to provide cultural exchange between American and African librarians, and an exchange program between Howard University, Washington, D.C., and Fisk University, Nashville, Tenn., and libraries in Botswana and Malawi. Also, the ALA Office for Intellectual Freedom, cooperating with the Association of American Publishers, reissued a revised and updated Freedom to Read Statement.

ALA Publications in 1972 included: *A Strategy for Public Library Change; A Multi-Media Approach to Children's Literature: A Selective List of Films, Film Strips, and Recordings Based on Children's Books; Print, Image and Sound: Essays on Media; Job Dimensions and Educational Needs in Librarianship; American Theatrical Arts;* and *Public Libraries in Cooperative Systems: Administrative Patterns for Service.* Curtis Swanson

AMERICAN PARTY candidates made a poor showing in the 1972 presidential election on November 7. Alabama Governor George C. Wallace decided not to bolt the Democratic Party and head a third-party ticket, as he had done in 1968. The American Party's presidential candidate, John G. Schmitz, and his running mate, Thomas J. Anderson, won only 1,080,541 popular votes, 1.4 per cent of the total vote. They carried no states, and received no electoral votes. See ELECTIONS.

Schmitz, a conservative Republican congressman from California, and Anderson, a farm-magazine publisher from Pigeon Forge, Tenn., are both members of the John Birch Society. They were chosen by the 1,500 delegates at the party's nominating convention in Louisville, Ky., on August 4 and 5. Wallace had told the convention by telephone on August 4 that he could not accept a draft to run again because of his physical condition.

Wallace spoke to the convention from his room in a Birmingham, Ala., rehabilitation clinic. He was undergoing treatment there for paralysis suffered in an assassination attempt at a Laurel, Md., political rally on May 15. See WALLACE, GEORGE C.

The American Party, formerly called the American Independent Party, had candidates on the ballots in 32 states and ran 9 candidates for the Senate and 49 for the House in 1972. However, none was successful. William McGaffin

ANDERSON, JACK (1922-), a syndicated newspaper columnist, embarrassed the Nixon Administration in 1972 with his revelations. In January, Anderson published secret papers showing that the United States had strongly opposed India in its war with Pakistan over Bangladesh, while at the same time issuing misleading public statements to the contrary. He received the Pulitzer Prize in national reporting for his disclosures.

In February, Anderson charged that the government had settled an antitrust suit against the International Telephone and Telegraph Corporation (ITT) in a way favorable to ITT. At about the same time, he said, ITT pledged to give part of the funds needed to hold the Republican National Convention in San Diego. The disclosures caused the corporation to shred papers in its files and prompted inconclusive U.S. Senate hearings. See REPUBLICAN PARTY.

Anderson also reported on August 1 that Senator Thomas F. Eagleton, then the Democratic candidate for Vice-President, had been arrested for drunken driving. He later retracted that charge and apologized for making it without documentation. See EAGLETON, THOMAS FRANCIS.

Jack Northman Anderson was born in Long Beach, Calif., but grew up in Cottonwood, Utah. He joined Drew Pearson's staff on the "Washington-Merry-Go-Round" column in 1947, and took over the column when Pearson died in 1969. Joseph P. Spohn

ANDREOTTI, GIULIO (1919-), was sworn in as prime minister of Italy on Feb. 18, 1972, succeeding Emilio Colombo. His Christian Democratic Cabinet resigned nine days later when it failed to get a vote of confidence, but he formed a three-party Cabinet on June 26 that won immediate approval.

Andreotti was born on Jan. 14, 1919, in Rome. Although he grew up in poverty, he earned a law degree from the University of Rome by the time he was 21 years of age.

While preparing an article for a student newspaper, Andreotti met and befriended Alcide De Gasperi. By 1945, when De Gasperi became prime minister, Andreotti was one of his closest aides. Andreotti became a deputy to Parliament in 1947. He served as undersecretary in the governments of De Gasperi and his successor from 1947 to 1953.

From 1954 to 1970 Andreotti held several important posts, including heading the ministries of interior, finance, treasury, defense, and industry and commerce. He has served as chairman of the Christian Democratic Party in the Chamber of Deputies since 1968.

Andreotti likes to write and is a Latin buff. He heads a center for research on the famous Roman orator and politician Cicero, who was from the rural area between Rome and Naples that Andreotti represented for 20 years. He is married and has four children. Michael Reed

ANGOLA. Under United Nations pressure to grant more self-government to its overseas provinces, Portugal elevated Angola and another province, Mozambique, to the status of states on June 23, 1972. Angolans will now elect a legislative assembly and an advisory council. The assembly meets twice a year to legislate on internal affairs, collect taxes, and prepare budgets. The governor-general, appointed by Portugal, now ranks as a minister of state and holds office for four years, with possible two-year extensions. Portugal continues to supervise government administration and the economy.

Portugal also adopted trade and financial measures designed to improve economic relations with Angola and Mozambique. Under the old colonial economic ties, Angola and Mozambique had developed large balance of payment deficits. To reduce the deficits, Angola was forced to cut its Portuguese imports.

Differences among the nationalist guerrillas weakened their efforts against Portugal. However, President Mobutu Sese Seko of Zaire and President Marien N'Gouabi of Congo (Brazzaville) mediated talks between the rival Popular Movement for the Liberation of Angola and the Revolutionary Government of Angola in Exile and announced an agreement on June 8. George Shepherd

See also AFRICA (Facts in Brief Table).

ANIMAL. See CONSERVATION; INTERNATIONAL LIVE STOCK EXPOSITION; ZOOLOGY; ZOOS AND AQUARIUMS.

ANTHROPOLOGY. Man's ability to create speech was an area of human evolution that was widely discussed by anthropologists in 1972. The question that the scientists considered was whether man's ability to speak is simply an extension of the animal ability to vocalize, or a uniquely human characteristic that required fundamental anatomical changes during man's evolution.

Anthropologist Philip Lieberman of the University of Connecticut, anatomist Edmund S. Crelin, Jr., of the Yale University School of Medicine, and electrical engineer Dennis Klatt of the Massachusetts Institute of Technology used detailed computer analyses of animal and human speech-producing organs to study the issue. They focused on the ability of adult men, newborn infants, chimpanzees, and Neanderthal men to produce the critical vowel sounds *a*, *i*, and *u*. They concluded that adult man's speech-making capabilities are significantly different from those of the other three.

The study suggests that the ability to speak is different from the making of animal sounds, and that anatomical as well as cultural evolution contributed to the development of this skill. For example, when the La Chapelle-aux-Saints Neanderthal man, whose skull was used in the study, lived in France about 40,000 years ago, he could communicate verbally only about one-tenth as rapidly and probably much less effectively than modern man can.

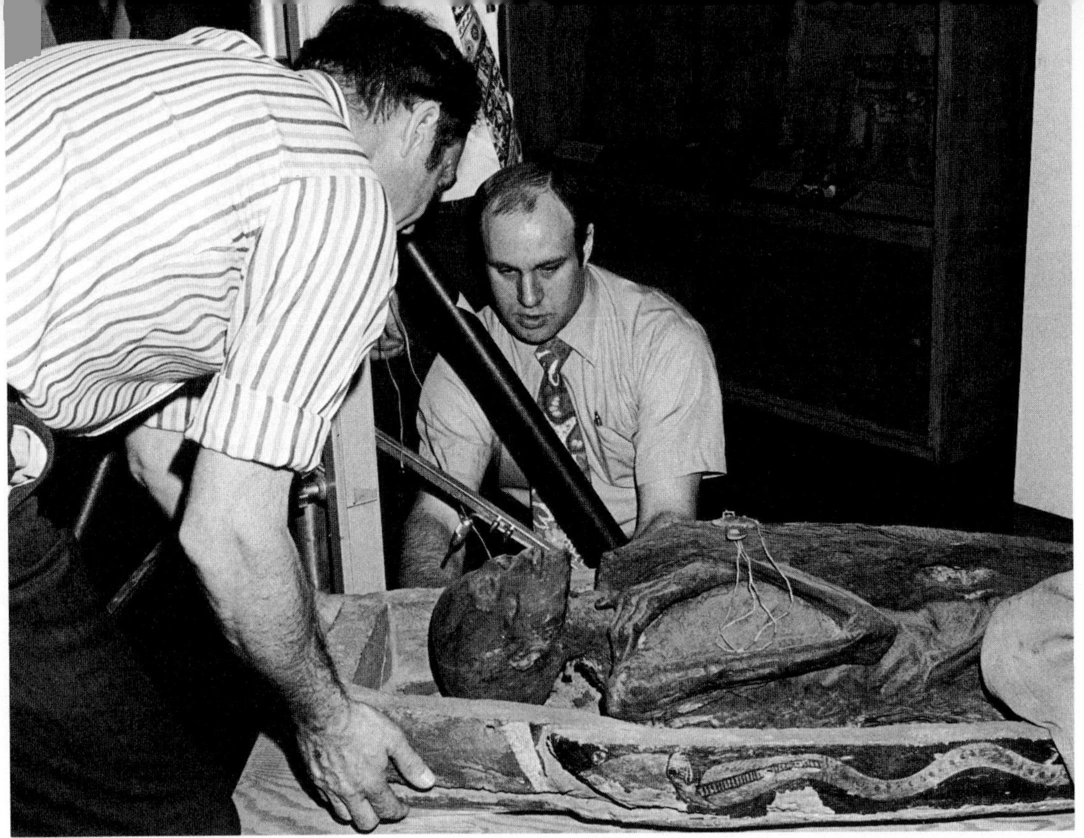

University of Michigan scientists X-ray the mummy of an ancient Egyptian in search for any signs of such diseases as arthritis and arteriosclerosis.

Anthropologist F. Jane Hill of Wayne State University studied the interaction of linguistic and biological evolution, emphasizing the important effects that language abilities, once acquired, had on human evolution. She noted that adults have more difficulty learning new languages than children do, and that when a new language is learned after 12 years of age, it is almost invariably learned with an accent. She concluded that at an early stage in human evolution, when population density was low, these factors would have created linguistic barriers between human groups and thereby would have contributed to intergroup competition. It has long been known that biological evolution proceeds more rapidly under conditions of competition. Moreover, the existence of linguistic barriers between groups would have acted as a selective pressure favoring those individuals who could speak best. This, in turn, would have resulted in an even more rapid development of speech.

Early Man in Africa. Louis S. B. Leakey, who pioneered the study of man's early ancestors in Africa, died on October 1. Leakey was responsible for the discovery of important evidence bearing on man's early evolution, and he stimulated investigations by many other anthropologists.

His son, Richard Leakey, reported in November the discovery of bone fragments on the east shore of Lake Rudolf in Kenya. These were from the skull of a man who lived about 2.6 million years ago. Richard Leakey had previously found stone tools in this same area, but not the associated skeletal material. The skull is much closer in shape to that of modern man than any other skulls of comparable age yet discovered. It is even closer to modern man than the 1.75-million-year-old *Homo habilis* skull found in 1963 by Louis Leakey in Olduvai Gorge, Tanzania. The reconstruction of the skull tends to support the argument that man's ancestors lived at the same time as the Australopithecines, but evolved independently.

Environment and Intelligence. In a recent contribution to the growing debate over a possible genetic basis for differences in intelligence between "races," especially blacks and whites, anthropologist Ashley Montagu summarized a substantial body of evidence demonstrating the impact of environmental factors on intellectual skills. Montagu showed that an inadequate diet can impair learning skills both for the prenatal and growing child. He also presented a number of studies showing that the improvement of a deprived sociocultural environment leads to improved intellectual skills. Fred Plog

ANTI-POVERTY PROGRAM. See POVERTY; SOCIAL SECURITY; SOCIAL WELFARE.

ARAB EMIRATES, UNION OF. See UNION OF ARAB EMIRATES.

ARAB REPUBLICS, FEDERATION OF. See EGYPT; LIBYA; SYRIA.

ARABIA. See SAUDI ARABIA.

ARCHAEOLOGY. A 1972 study of obsidian tools produced by the Olmec shed new light on trade relations in the ancient world. The Olmec civilization existed along the eastern coast of Mexico between 1100 and 400 B.C. Scholars have long debated the extent to which the Olmec art style, which was widespread in Central America, was accompanied by a similar distribution of economic and political institutions. In an attempt to resolve this problem, archaeologists Robert Cobean of Harvard University, and Michael Coe, Edward Perry, Karl Turekian, and Dinkar Dhakar of Yale University studied many obsidian tools found at the Olmec site of San Lorenzo Tenochtitlán in Veracruz state. They used X-ray emission spectroscopy in making their studies.

The archaeologists found that as Olmec culture developed, a trade network grew in which obsidian was brought to San Lorenzo from increasingly greater distances. Some obsidian samples came from sources in Guatemala and northern Mexico that are 500 miles from San Lorenzo.

Survey Archaeology. Archaeological field research has traditionally been associated with extensive excavation. Yet, over the last decade, much time and energy have been devoted to making site surveys, systematically mapping potential archaeological sites with only limited supplementary excavation. A variety of results published in 1972 illustrate the kinds of information that archaeologists have obtained with this technique.

Archaeologists excavating the ancient city of Sarepta in Lebanon in 1972 found a Phoenician temple in the upper left-hand corner of the site.

Pedro Armillas of the State University of New York at Stony Brook reported on his extensive study of the chinampas near the modern city of Xochimilco, Mexico. Chinampas, often mistakenly called floating gardens, are narrow rectangular islands of earth and decaying vegetation that were built by the Aztecs in marshy areas to make them suitable for agriculture. Armillas estimates that the chinampa system covered some 22,000 acres and provided food for about 100,000 persons when it was most extensive, about A.D. 1400, Armillas also believes the chinampas produced food for both the farmers living among these unique fields and for the inhabitants of urban centers, such as Tenochtitlan. The regular layout of the chinampas, as well as an equally regular pattern of causeways and canals connecting population centers in and near them, leads Armillas to conclude that the system is the product of a highly organized reclamation effort.

In another survey of early Mexican agriculture, Alfred Siemens of the University of British Columbia and Dennis Puleston of the University of Minnesota used aerial photographs and foot surveys in a portion of Campeche state to determine the type of agriculture the Maya used. Archaeologists have generally believed that the Mayan inhabitants of Central America relied on slash-and-burn agriculture for most of their subsistence resources. This simple agricultural technique, which involves the clearing of small plots in the forest that are abandoned after a few years use, is not, however, generally associated with other civilizations as large and complex as the Maya. The archaeologists traced canal systems and ridged fields that suggest the Maya, at least in this area, used a far more complex and intensive agricultural system than the simple slash-and-burn pattern.

Bushmen. John Yellen and Henry Harpending of Harvard University studied the relationship between the settlement pattern, social organization, and subsistence strategies of the modern !Kung Bushmen of South Africa and those of Late Paleolithic populations that inhabited the same area. They found that the !Kung are a highly mobile hunting-gathering population with shifting ties among family groups. The Late Paleolithic sites in the same area showed significant parallels between !Kung camping locations and those of the Late Paleolithic groups. Moreover, the archaeologist's analysis of artifacts from these sites showed great similarity over the entire territory. Sites quite distant from each other had stone tool remains that were of the same sort as those found at nearby sites. The scientists concluded that the tools and settlements were consistent with the organization of populations such as that of the !Kung. They also believe that societies similar to the !Kung have occupied this South African territory for a long time.

Fred Plog

ARCHITECTURE. The imaginative architectural design of the Olympic site for the 20th Olympiad's Summer Games in Munich, West Germany, won recognition in 1972. Unifying the site and providing the greatest visual excitement was a 370,000-square-foot, tentlike roof of transparent acrylic designed by 47-year-old Frei P. Otto. Actually a series of cable-hung ceilings, this vast, plastic covering–probably more an engineering tour de force than an architectural breakthrough–partly enclosed the 80,000-seat Olympic stadium and completely sheltered the other two major stadiums, the sports arena and the swimming area. The temporary roof appropriately expressed the temporal nature of the games.

The design integrated all of the structures into a sculptured landscape and made their post-Olympics use more practical. The 19-story high-rise and the two- and three-story concrete buildings that housed women athletes became student housing after the games. The high-rise, stepped concrete structures that housed male competitors are now condominium apartments. The sports stadiums were designed so they can be used for local events with little conversion work needed.

Prototype Airports. During 1972, the problem of moving passengers and handling baggage at airports became critical as the massive new jets made their presence felt. Just getting from automobile to airplane was of most concern. The long walk from parking areas, the congestion at the terminal ticket counters, and the equally long hike to the airplane often last longer than the flight itself. Two prototypes for a new generation of airports have been designed so that passengers can avoid all of this by driving directly to their departure gates.

The Kansas City International Airport was officially dedicated on October 21 and went into operation in early November. Architects Kivett & Myers have the spur of the main highway from Kansas City lead into the center of the complex. The spur then circles a 219-foot-high control tower, a power plant, and administration offices, and provides access to three secondary rings on the perimeter. Each ring, 1,000 feet in diameter, accommodates 900 cars and has entrances to 20 aircraft positions or gates. The total walking distance from automobile to airplane is only 75 feet.

The aircraft side of each ring is three stories high, the passenger side is two stories high. The lowest level handles airline operations, and the two upper levels are for passengers.

At the new Dallas-Fort Worth Regional Airport, by architects Hellmuth, Obata & Kassabaum, passengers also drive directly to departure gates. The facility is designed as a long transportation spine from which extend 14 horseshoe-shaped air termi-

Alley Theatre in Houston, designed by Ulrich Franzen, received one of the 1972 Honor Awards from the American Institute of Architects.

The Weyerhaeuser Headquarters, which blends in with the Tacoma, Wash., landscape, received an award from the American Institute of Architects.

nals. Each has parking for 1,200 cars and can handle 24 planes simultaneously. The airport is being constructed in stages and will not be completed until the year 2000. When finished, it will cover an area larger than Manhattan Island.

AIA Policy Statement. The annual convention of the American Institute of Architects (AIA) was held in May in Houston. Almost 2,000 convention delegates adopted a controversial policy statement on national goals. Described by AIA President Max O. Urbahn as "revolutionary," the report has these basic thrusts: The nation must end segregated living. Low- and moderate-income families must be subsidized at levels equivalent to tax-deduction subsidies now provided to higher-income homeowners. Land development must increasingly be brought under public control. And state governments should control local building, zoning, and health codes to better plan and regulate land use.

The last two recommendations received the most criticism from the delegates. Delegates generally conceded that the great amount of grass-roots-level persuasion by report chairman Archibald C. Rogers and his team was responsible for the ultimate convention support.

Pietro Belluschi, 72, received the AIA's 1972 Gold Medal. The Italian-born architect is best known for the buildings he designed in the Pacific Northwest. His museums, churches, private homes, and high-rises reflect his passion for simplicity. Architectural regionalism has been a constant theme of his.

An Unusual Exhibition ran from September 26 to October 22 in New York City's Metropolitan Museum of Art. Entitled "Synagogues from Damascus to Newport," it consisted of eight large architectural models. The earliest was the Dura-Europas Synagogue in Syria (A.D. 245), and the latest was Peter Harrison's Touro Synagogue in Newport, R.I. (1763). Minor miracles of construction, the scale models are the first of a group being created for the museum of Yeshiva University in New York City.

New Buildings continued to claw their way to the sky. Topped out during the year were Minoru Yamasaki's World Trade Center in New York City at 1,350 feet and Edward Durell Stone's Standard Oil of Indiana Building in Chicago at 1,136 feet. But Skidmore, Owings and Merrill's Sears Tower, also under construction in Chicago, will become the world's tallest in 1973 at 1,450 feet.

A new book provided the most controversy during the year. Architect Robert Venturi's pop art theories culminated in *Learning from Las Vegas* (M.I.T. Press), in which he derides his "arty" colleagues for being boring and sterile. Claiming that a billboard has more contemporary meaning than the Cathedral of Notre Dame in Amiens, France, he finds American urban sprawl vital and admirable. Rob Cuscaden

See also AWARDS AND PRIZES.

ARGENTINA. Former President Juan Domingo Perón returned to Argentina on Nov. 17, 1972, after 17 years in exile. A former army officer, Perón had ruled Argentina as dictator-president for nine turbulent years ending in 1955. His return, sanctioned by the military government of President Alejandro Agustín Lanusse, was tied to the first presidential election in 10 years, scheduled for March, 1973.

Lanusse, in announcing the presidential elections, had indicated he would not be a candidate and that power would be handed over to elected authorities on May 25, 1973, thus ending almost seven years of military rule. The Perónist movement, with its impressive labor strength, was regarded as the largest political force in Argentina. Because of this, the regime sought an understanding with Perón, then living in Madrid, that would smooth the way toward the election. The talks were inconclusive, however, and on July 7 Lanusse presented a final challenge to Perón by announcing that all presidential candidates must become permanent residents in Argentina by August 25 and remain in the country until the new government took office. Perón, a candidate of his Justicialist Party, rejected the ultimatum. One of Perón's first acts after his return was to meet in Buenos Aires with 70 representatives of the country's political parties. Their goal was a workable agreement between the Perónists, the anti-Perónists, and the military. Only thus could a successful election be held. In December, he rejected a nomination for the presidency and returned to Madrid.

A Wave of Assassinations–including political leader Mario Roberto Uzal, industrialist Oberdan Sallustro, and General Juan Carlos Sanchez–in the spring infuriated the government and shocked the country. The left wing terrorists, known as the People's Revolutionary Army, wanted to embarrass and discredit the regime. They especially disliked any possibility of an accord between the government and the Perón group concerning the elections; instead, they advocated the overthrow of the military as well as the "capitalist system" in Argentina.

Political turmoil reached a peak during the week of August 22, when demonstrations in several cities resulted in the arrest of hundreds of students and labor and political leaders. The outburst stemmed from the killing of 16 suspected guerrillas in a prison at the naval air base near Trelew, in the southern province of Chubut. Antigovernment leaders called the killings a deliberate "massacre." The army insisted the victims were subversives trying to escape.

The Economy. Earlier in the year, major disturbances erupted in various cities. They were symptomatic not only of political tensions, but also of resentment against economic conditions. The economy was in full recession in almost every sector except beef production. While the internal deficit rose, inflation soared; there were partial peso devaluations throughout the year, and foreign exchange reserves reached critically low levels. By the end of August, the national treasury's cash deficit exceeded the same period in 1971 by 107.2 per cent. The January-June gross domestic product was up 4.4 per cent over the same six-month period in 1971. The rise was largely due to a 9.1 per cent increase in industry, a 5.2 per cent increase in mining, and a 9.5 per cent rise in construction. Agriculture, however, was down 6.7 per cent.

The first six-month balance of payments was in the red by $242 million, as compared to $104 million in mid-1971. Gross monetary reserves at the end of August totaled only $115 million as compared to $499 million in August, 1971. The net figure, however, was a $542.6-million deficit.

Foreign Loans. Throughout the year, Argentina sought to spur the economy and ease its debt situation by encouraging an influx of foreign capital. By midyear, the International Monetary Fund had granted an aggregate $362.8 million, and various international and foreign institutions had loaned a total of $398.5 million for iron, power, and pulp and paper projects, a gas pipeline, railways, and purchases of machinery and equipment. In October, a group of 14 U.S. banks agreed to lend $145 million to bolster Argentine reserves. Mary Webster Soper

See also Latin America (Facts in Brief Table).

ARIZONA. See State Government.

ARKANSAS. See State Government.

ARMED FORCES OF THE WORLD. The United States and Russia on May 26, 1972, signed a strategic arms limitation treaty limiting antiballistic missile systems, and an interim five-year agreement freezing offensive nuclear weapons at their present levels. The treaty recognized parity between U.S. and Russian strategic forces. The Soviet Union had more megatonnage than the United States in its nuclear warheads and a 3 to 2 lead in the number of strategic missiles. However, the United States had more nuclear warheads, and U.S. warheads could be aimed more accurately. The United States had 5,900 deliverable warheads to 2,500 for Russia. The United States also had a 3 to 1 lead in strategic bombers and the advantage of three overseas Polaris missile submarine bases.

According to U.S. estimates made for the Strategic Arms Limitation Talks (SALT) agreement, Russia had 1,618 intercontinental ballistic missiles (ICBM's) in operation or under construction. The Russian Navy had 512 submarine-launched ballistic missiles on all of its missile submarines in operation.

The United States had 1,000 Minuteman ICBM's, 54 Titan II ICBM's, and 41 Polaris missile submarines with a total of 656 missiles. The United States also had 450 strategic bombers compared to 140 for Russia. So, total strategic nuclear weapons, including the bombers and the missile warheads,

President Nixon exchanges copies of the Strategic Arms Limitation Treaty with Communist Party Leader Leonid Brezhnev in Moscow on May 26.

meant the United States had a 2 to 1 lead over Russia.

New Strategic Weapons. Russia continued to cloak its new large ICBM's in mystery. These ICBM's were believed to be either improved SS-9s or an entirely new missile. Russian engineers were apparently working on a new multiple independent re-entry vehicle (MIRV) warhead for the SS-9, which will be operational in two or three years.

Russia may be building a new version of the Polaris-type missile submarine. The Soviet vessel contains 12 launchers for a larger, longer-range missile, the SSN-X-8, which has a range of 3,000 miles.

The U.S. *Trident* missile submarine was expected to be operational by mid-1978. It will carry 24 missiles having a range of more than 4,000 miles. Conversion of 31 of the 41 Polaris submarines to carry Poseidon missiles with MIRV warheads was to be completed by mid-1976. Work on 12 of the submarines was completed in 1972. Conversion of 550 of the 1,000 Minuteman ICBM's to MIRV warheads is scheduled for completion in mid-1975. More than 200 of the converted Minutemen were ready by mid-1972. Russia had more than 3,000 jet interceptors and more than 10,000 surface-to-air missiles (SAM's). The United States had about 500 jet interceptors and 500 SAM's.

The People's Republic of China may have intermediate- and medium-range ballistic missiles with ranges of from 1,500 to 2,500 miles. China is believed to have tested an ICBM with a 3-megaton warhead and a potential range of 6,000 miles.

China had one diesel-powered missile submarine, built during the early 1960s, but no submarine-launched missiles. It had 40 medium-range bombers and 150 light bombers, some of which could carry nuclear bombs. Its air defenses included more than 3,000 jet interceptors and several hundred SAM's.

In Sea Power, the United States continued to lead, although the Russian Navy was catching up. The U.S. Navy had 247 major surface warships–including 14 attack carriers, 2 antisubmarine carriers, 7 helicopter carriers, 9 cruisers, 56 missile destroyers, 94 other destroyers, and 65 escort ships –and 138 submarines.

The Russian Navy had 223 surface warships–including 2 helicopter carriers, 28 cruisers, 11 surface missile destroyers, 30 air-defense missile destroyers, 40 other destroyers, and 112 escort ships–and 345 submarines.

China had 4 destroyers, 4 escort ships, and 40 diesel-powered attack submarines, in addition to its diesel missile submarine. Great Britain had 84 surface warships, with 2 aircraft carriers, 3 helicopter carriers, 3 cruisers, 8 missile destroyers, 3 destroyers, and 65 escort ships. Britain also had 36 submarines, including 4 nuclear-powered missile submarines, 6 nuclear-powered attack submarines, and 26 diesel-powered attack submarines. France, the fourth naval power, had 54 surface ships and 20 submarines, including 1 nuclear-powered missile submarine. In tactical air forces, the United States led with more than 5,000 aircraft. Russia had 4,200; China, 800.

Land Forces. China had the largest army, with 2.6 million ground combat troops, and Russia had 2.2 million troops. The United States had 1 million, including Marine troops but excluding troops assigned to strategic units. China had 122 divisions; Russia, 160 divisions; and the United States, 13.

Russia had 31 divisions stationed in Warsaw Pact nations: 20 in East Germany, 2 in Poland, 4 in Hungary, and 5 in Czechoslovakia. Nearly a million Russian troops were stationed on the Chinese border. The East European Warsaw Pact nations had 59 divisions–10 Bulgarian, 12 Czechoslovak, 6 East German, 15 Polish, 9 Romanian, and 7 Hungarian.

North Atlantic Treaty Organization (NATO) defenses in Europe included 4⅓ U.S. divisions, 2 Belgian divisions, 4 Danish brigades, 12 West German divisions, 5 Greek divisions, 5 Italian divisions and 4 mountain brigades, 2 Netherlands divisions, 1 Norwegian infantry brigade, 2 Portuguese divisions, 17 Turkish divisions, 5 British brigades in Germany and 5 brigades in Great Britain. France has 5 divisions, but no troops committed to NATO. Lloyd H. Norman

ARMY, U.S. See NATIONAL DEFENSE.

ART. See ARCHITECTURE; DANCING; LITERATURE; MUSIC, CLASSICAL; POETRY; VISUAL ARTS.

Comparative Military Manpower

	United States	Russia	China
Army	849,824	2,250,000	2,600,000
Air Force	713,718	810,000†	185,000
Navy	792,297*	500,000	160,000
Total	2,355,839	3,560,000	2,945,000

*Includes 199,601 Marines as of Sept. 30, 1972.

†Includes a strategic rocket force of 375,000.

The Strategic Balance in 1972

	United States	Russia
ICBM's	1,054	1,618
Polaris-type missile submarines	41	26*
Polaris-type missiles	656	416
Other missile submarines	0	32
Other submarine missiles	0	96
Long-range bombers	450	140
Deliverable nuclear warheads	5,900†	2,500

*With 17 more under construction.

†Includes triple warheads on 250 Minuteman III ICBM's and 192 missiles with 10 warheads each on Poseidon submarines.

ASIA

A will-o'-the-wisp of peace hovered briefly over war-ravaged Indochina in 1972. It first appeared in October, when U.S. presidential adviser Henry A. Kissinger announced, after weeks of secret negotiations with the North Vietnamese, that "peace"–as he put it–"is at hand." And so it seemed. But by the end of December, the promise of an end to hostilities had crumbled like so many before it and with its disintegration had vanished, in a deadly rain of bombs, the hopes of a lasting peace that was ardently desired in almost every corner of the civilized world.

The tragic near-hit climaxed a year during which there were momentous shifts in the political patterns of Asia. Each shift, beginning in February with a reversal of United States foreign policy toward the People's Republic of China, was as unexpected as it was dramatic. None, however, was as portentous for the future of Asia as the emergence of China, India, and Japan as the three major power centers of the continent. This development foreshadowed in an

The war in Southeast Asia remained a grim reality in 1972. Here, South Vietnamese rumble toward An Loc to relieve a besieged garrison.

oblique way the talk of peace that was to come in October.

In the contest for power and independence, Japan emerged as the most decisive entity of the three, primarily because of its tremendous economic strength, its defensive security, and its ability to act as a broker, financially and otherwise, for many of the Asian countries. Its unique position, backed by its huge financial assets, thus allowed Japan to adopt a highly flexible approach to the problems of Asia. This reversal of its previous role as a follower of U.S.-set foreign policy took place in part because of hard decisions made by Russia and the United States. But it also reflected the basic strengths of Asia itself.

India's Emergence as a power followed a Russian decision to back India in its conflict with Pakistan in December, 1971. The decision involved the implementation of a Russian-Indian Defense Treaty that provided the Indians with armaments. It also entailed casting two key vetoes in the United Nations Security Council that effectively blocked a cessation of hostilities until India's victory was assured. The splitting of Pakistan into two states–and the subsequent creation of Bangladesh out of one of them–left India the dominant power in South Asia. See BANGLADESH; INDIA; PAKISTAN.

Continuing Russian naval exercises in the Indian Ocean seemed to many to presage a victory for Russian influence in the subcontinent. Yet, as the year unfolded, it clearly revealed basic weaknesses in Russia's global position that made the pursuance of such an objective unfeasible. See EUROPE; MIDDLE EAST.

Realizing this, President Richard M. Nixon and Kissinger implemented a series of decisions made in 1971. They wanted to end direct U.S. military involvement in Southeast Asia and thereby lessen the enormous strain that military costs placed on the U.S. economy. Thus, the President made his historic visit to China in February, 1972. See PRESIDENT OF THE UNITED STATES.

The talks between Mr. Nixon and Chinese leaders Mao Tse-tung and Chou En-lai were guardedly cordial. But their joint communiqué indicated several important steps had been taken in an effort to establish more normal relations between the two countries.

The communiqué, issued on February 27 in Shanghai, indicated that both sides made concessions. The chief stumbling block to China-U.S. relations has always been Taiwan, which is occupied by Chiang Kai-shek and his Nationalist Chinese government. This problem was removed from contention by the American acknowledgment that Taiwan is a part of mainland China. Further, the communiqué stated that the United States "will progressively reduce its forces and military installations on Taiwan as the tension in the area diminishes." See TAIWAN.

President Nixon had previously ordered the U.S. Seventh Fleet to cease patrolling the Formosa Strait. With Taiwan removed from the area of contention,

Prime ministers Mujibur Rahman of Bangladesh and Indira Gandhi of India shake hands at signing of 25-year friendship treaty in March.

both sides agreed to broaden understanding between their peoples. Both sides agreed, too, to keep open channels of communications, including the sending from time to time of a senior U.S. diplomatic representative to Peking. They also agreed to develop bilateral trade. Thus, in one week, the United States and China had reversed 22 years of hostile isolation from each other. It was a gigantic diplomatic coup that had vast repercussions, not only in Asia, but also throughout the world.

Key Issues Involved. For years, Japan had followed to a great extent the American lead in its relations with the Asian countries. This was especially true insofar as China was concerned. The success of President Nixon's visit to China, then, necessitated some fast political reshuffling on the part of the Japanese. In anticipation of this, Russia's Foreign Minister Andrei A. Gromyko was sent to Tokyo a month before the President went to Peking. The Russians and the Japanese negotiated minor agreements in such areas as fishing rights and cultural exchanges. But the key issue involving the return of Kunashiri, Etorofu, Shikotan, and Hobomai–four northern islands seized from Japan by Russia in 1945–remained unsettled. China, however, had already indicated that it supported such Japanese claims. This, plus the China-U.S. reconciliation, helped propel Japan into the Chinese orbit. Subsequently, after conferring with U.S. Assistant Secretary of State for East Asian and Pacific Affairs Marshall Green, who explained the China-U.S. accord, Japan's Prime Minister Eisaku Sato announced that "Taiwan [is] a part of the People's Republic of China."

Sato's resignation on June 17 brought to the Japanese prime ministership a tough businessman–Kakuei Tanaka (see Tanaka, Kakuei). In meetings with President Nixon in Honolulu on August 31 and September 1, Tanaka reaffirmed continuing close relations with the United States, but he also began to redefine Japan's own position concerning China. From September 25 to 29, Tanaka visited Peking for a series of meetings with Premier Chou En-lai. They proved to be fruitful ones. In a subsequent communiqué, Prime Minister Tanaka acknowledged "the sufferings and depredations" the Chinese people had been subjected to by the Japanese from 1937 to 1945 during the Sino-Japanese War. Japan, in a final gesture toward China, also altered its formal trade and treaty relationships with Taiwan to put them on a more informal basis. See Japan.

The Indian Image Improves. India, meanwhile, initiated special moves to consolidate its new position as the undisputed major power in South Asia and lessen its dependence on Russia. Prime Minister Indira Gandhi quickly recognized Bangladesh as an independent nation and began preparations to send back into the new nation the millions of refugees who had sought asylum in India during the India-Pakistan War. India's negotiations with the defeated Pakistan government proved more difficult. But the replacing of President Aga Mohammed Yahya Khan with Zulfikar Ali Bhutto–who was given virtually dictatorial powers–paved the way for a settlement. See Bhutto, Zulfikar Ali; Pakistan; Rahman, Mujibur.

The Indian minister of external affairs, S.S. Singh, denied accusations that the India-Russia treaty was a threat to any other country's interests, and he insisted that it did not preclude a normalization of relations between India and China. To bear this out, he called for a resumption of cultural and trade relations between the two nations.

Russian Role Perplexes. Meanwhile, the Soviet Union's overall response to these developments was somewhat obscure. Russia continued to vilify the Chinese, especially because of the Chinese-American rapprochement. At the same time, it tried to strengthen Russian relations with the Japanese. Yet it also continued to work out additional agreements with the United States, most notably on strategic arms limitations (see Armed Forces of the World). Perhaps these cooperative efforts to achieve a détente were due to unknown internal factors in Russia or even to fear of close Sino-American relations. At any rate, the new American policies in Asia were clearly put to the test by the bitter conflict in Vietnam.

The War. The year began with a resumption of American bombing in North Vietnam. The objectives of the raids were airfields and supply depots that might be used to support a new offensive against South Vietnam. The new offensive was not long in coming. With dramatic suddenness, the North Vietnamese mounted a full-scale invasion of South Vietnam on four fronts on March 30. Evidently the Communists had decided on a quick, massive drive to crush the South Vietnamese government before it could develop its forces into an independent entity capable of resisting the Hanoi government without U.S. aid. During the first few weeks, the Communists achieved solid gains, but gradually the South Vietnamese halted the drive.

Escalating the War. It was at this point that President Nixon decided on a strategy designed to halt the Communists and help bring an end to the war. On May 8, the President ordered a large-scale air and naval blockade of North Vietnam. Units of the U.S. Seventh Fleet quickly mined the waters off Haiphong and other North Vietnamese ports. Carrier-based American aircraft, as well as U.S. bombers based in Thailand, blasted roads and key bridges linking North Vietnam with China.

The Soviet Union decided against any attempt to run the blockade, rerouting ships that were headed toward North Vietnam. China, while warning against air incursions of its borders, made no real effort to halt the disruption of its links with the North.

"Think what a society they could have if they put all this effort into something constructive. . . ."

Facts in Brief on the Asian Countries

Country	Population	Government	Monetary Unit*	Foreign Trade (million U.S. $) Exports	Imports
Afghanistan	18,388,000	King Mohammed Zahir Shah; Prime Minister Mohammed Musa Shafiq	afghani (83 = $1)	86	117
Australia	13,320,000	Governor-General Sir Paul M.C. Hasluck; Prime Minister Edward Gough Whitlam	dollar (1 = $1.19)	5,230	5,266
Bahrain	235,000	Amir Isa bin Salman Al Khalifa; Prime Minister Khalifa bin Salman Al Khalifa	dinar (1 = $2.27)	180	109
Bangladesh	75,840,000	President Abu Sayeed Chowdury; Prime Minister Sheik Mujibur Rahman	taka (7.3 = $1)	no statistics available	
Bhutan	892,000	King Jigme Singhi Wangchuk	Indian rupee	no statistics available	
Burma	29,445,000	Union Revolutionary Council Chairman and Prime Minister Ne Win	kyat (5.4 = $1)	124	126
China	801,380,000	Communist Party Chairman Mao Tse-tung; Premier Chou En-lai	yuan (2.25 = $1)	2,100	2,100
Cyprus	652,000	President Archbishop Makarios III	pound (1 = $2.60)	116	263
India	592,694,000	President V. V. Giri; Prime Minister Indira Gandhi	rupee (7.28 = $1)	2,108	2,520
Indonesia	132,681,000	President Suharto	rupiah (415 = $1)	1,242	1,174
Iran	31,229,000	Shah Mohammed Reza Pahlavi; Prime Minister Amir Abbas Hoveyda	rial (75.75 = $1)	2,642	1,871
Iraq	10,376,000	President and Prime Minister Ahmad Hasan al-Bakr	dinar (1 = $3.04)	1,538	694
Israel	3,154,000	President Zalman Shazar; Prime Minister Golda Meir	pound (4.2 = $1)	919	1,764
Japan	106,994,000	Emperor Hirohito; Prime Minister Kakuei Tanaka	yen (304.6 = $1)	24,040	19,727
Jordan	2,600,000	King Hussein I; Prime Minister Ahmad al-Lawzi	dinar (1 = $2.80)	32	215
Khmer Republic (Cambodia)	7,310,000	President Lon Nol; Prime Minister Hang Thun Hak	riel (186.26 = $1)	15	78
Korea (North)	15,100,000	President Kim Il-song	won 1.11=$1)	175	150
Korea (South)	34,130,000	President Chung Hee Park; Prime Minister Kim Jong Pil	won (400 = $1)	1,068	2,394
Kuwait	921,000	Emir Sabah al-Salim al-Sabah; Prime Minister Jabir al-Ahmad al-Sabah	dinar (1 = $3.04)	2,407	678
Laos	3,180,000	King Savang Vatthana; Prime Minister Souvanna Phouma	kip (600 = $1)	7	114
Lebanon	3,213,000	President Suleiman Franjieh; Prime Minister Saeb Salaam	pound (3 = $1)	242	671
Malaysia	11,740,000	Paramount Ruler Abdul Halim Muazzam; Prime Minister Abdul Razak	dollar (2.86 = $1)	1,636	1,434
Maldives	114,000	President Ibrahim Nasir; Prime Minister Ahmed Zaki	rupee (6.4 = $1)	no statistics available	
Mongolia	1,412,000	People's Revolutionary Party First Secretary and Premier Yumjaagiyn Tsedenbal	tugrik (3.68 = $1)	83	115
Nepal	11,647,000	King Birendra Bir Bikram Shah Deva; Prime Minister Kirti Nidhi Bista	rupee (10.1 = $1)	30	46
New Zealand	2,936,000	Governor-General Sir Arthur E. Porritt; Prime Minister Norman E. Kirk	dollar (1 = $1.19)	1,359	1,346
Oman	720,000	Sultan Qabus bin Said; Prime Minister Asim ibn Muhammad Jamali	Saidi rial (1 = $2.67)	no statistics available	
Pakistan	64,604,000	President Zulfikar Ali Bhutto	rupee (11 = $1)	666	917
Philippines	42,678,000	President Ferdinand E. Marcos	peso (6.78 = $1)	1,104	1,315
Russia	250,867,000	Communist Party General Secretary Leonid I. Brezhnev; Premier Aleksei N. Kosygin; Supreme Soviet Presidium Chairman Nikolai V. Podgorny	ruble (1 = $1.21)	13,806	12,476
Saudi Arabia	8,384,000	King and Prime Minister Faisal	riyal (4.14 = $1)	2,361	693
Sikkim	205,000	Maharaja Palden Thondup Namgyal	Indian rupee	no statistics available	
Singapore	2,234,000	President Benjamin H. Sheares; Prime Minister Lee Kuan Yew	dollar (2.86 = $1)	1,755	2,828
Sri Lanka (Ceylon)	13,397,000	President William Gopallawa; Prime Minister Sirimavo Bandaranaike	rupee (6.4 = $1)	327	334
Syria	6,663,000	President Hafiz al-Asad; Prime Minister Mahmoud al-Ayubi	pound (4.3 = $1)	195	440
Taiwan	15,160,000	President Chiang Kai-shek; Vice-President C.K. Yen; Prime Minister Chiang Ching-kuo	new Taiwan dollar (40.1 = $1)	1,998	1,884
Thailand	39,249,000	King Phumiphon Aduldet; Prime Minister Thanom Kittikachorn	baht (21=$1)	833	1,281
United Arab Emirates	180,000	President Zayid bin Sultan al-Nuhayan; Prime Minister Maktum ibn Rashid al-Maktum al-Falasa	Bahrain dinar and Qatar ryal	no statistics available	
Vietnam (North)	22,643,000	President Ton Duc Thang; Premier Pham Van Dong	dong (2.71 = $1)	98	180
Vietnam (South)	19,799,000	President Nguyen Van Thieu; Vice-President Tran Van Huong; Prime Minister Tran Thien Khiem	piastre (410 = $1)	8	494
Yemen (Aden)	6,210,000	Republican Council Chairman Abdul Rahman Iryani; Prime Minister Muhsin al-Ayni	ryal (4.69 = $1)	13	143
Yemen (San'ā')	1,390,000	Presidential Council Chairman Salim Ali Rubayya; Prime Minister Ali Nasir Hassani	dinar (1 = $2.67)	105	158

*Exchange rates as of Nov. 1, 1972

The blockade of the North Vietnamese ports and the disruption of transportation links became increasingly effective. The Communist offensive slackened for want of supplies, and in the face of stiffening resistance by the South Vietnamese. The Hanoi government eventually agreed to resume peace talks with the United States. The offensive they had launched three months earlier had obviously not attained its objective. The American blockade was hurting their effort; they were not getting the support they had expected from Russia, its satellites, or China.

Peace Within Reach. On October 26, Kissinger announced an agreement had been drawn up calling for an Indochina cease-fire and a political settlement in Vietnam. Among its provisions, the agreement called for the withdrawal of U.S. forces within 60 days of a cease-fire; all captured military personnel and foreign civilians would be repatriated within the same period as that allocated for the troop withdrawal. The agreement also affirmed in general the right of self-determination to the South Vietnamese, who would decide their political future through free and democratic elections under international supervision. It was also implied that the United States would sign the agreement by October 31. It was not until November 2, however, two days after the deadline, that President Nixon declared the United States would sign the agreement only when all remainng differences were cleared up. He did not specify the unresolved issues.

Failure Again. President Nguyen Van Thieu, meanwhile, had denounced the proposed agreement, calling it "a sellout of South Vietnam." Thieu insisted that his minimum demand before approving a halt in the fighting was the total pullout of Hanoi's troops from his country.

On November 26, Kissinger and Le Duc Tho of North Vietnam resumed private discussions to work out a final Indochina peace agreement. These ended without agreement. On December 4, the talks resumed. But nine days later they again concluded without positive results. The principal stumbling block seemed to be South Vietnam's demand, rejected by Hanoi, that North Vietnam either withdraw all its troops from South Vietnam or at least acknowledge their presence in the country as illegal. On December 18, the Nixon Administration announced a resumption of full-scale bombing of North Vietnam and remining of North Vietnam's ports, and it warned that this policy "would be continued until such time as a settlement is arrived at." When the bombing was finally halted on December 31, about 1,400 strikes had been carried out by giant U.S. B-52s and other bombers. The halt coincided with an announcement by President Nixon that Kissinger would resume negotiations in Paris on Jan. 8, 1973. John N. Stalker

See also the various Asian country articles.

ASTRONAUTS. The Apollo moon-landing program drew to a close in 1972, clouded by incidents involving commercial exploitation of the space program. In September, the National Aeronautics and Space Administration (NASA) released a report that told how *Apollo 15* astronauts took 632 specially stamped and canceled envelopes to the moon – 400 of them unauthorized. Ninety-nine of these covers were sold to a German stamp dealer for an average of about $1,500 each, but NASA said that the three astronauts did not accept the $7,000 each that had been promised to them as part of the transaction.

As a result of the incident, *Apollo 15* astronauts David R. Scott and Alfred M. Worden were officially reprimanded, dropped from the astronaut corps, and given other jobs in NASA. The third crew member, James B. Irwin, was also reprimanded, but he had previously announced plans to resign and pursue a career in religious teaching.

It was also revealed that 50 out of 200 medals carried to the moon by the *Apollo 14* crew were turned over to the Franklin Mint, a Philadelphia firm. The firm melted 25 of these down, and struck several thousand small coins from the metal.

The Last Apollo Missions. Astronauts made the last two Apollo flights in 1972. In April, the *Apollo 16* crew of John W. Young, Thomas K. Mattingly II, and Charles M. Duke, Jr., brought back a record 210 pounds of rock and soil from the Descartes Highlands. *Apollo 17*, in December, was manned by astronauts Eugene A. Cernan, Ronald E. Evans, and scientist-astronaut Harrison H. Schmitt. See SPACE EXPLORATION.

The *Skylab* Crews. In January, NASA announced the flight crews for *Skylab*, the first U.S. earth-orbiting space station. There will be three *Skylab* missions over an eight-month period in 1973. Each will be manned by a three-man team. The crews consist of a commander, a science pilot (scientist-astronaut), and a pilot. Listed in that order, the astronauts for the first flight, a 28-day mission, are Charles Conrad, Jr.; Joseph P. Kerwin, M.D.; and Paul J. Weitz. The second flight crew is Alan L. Bean; physicist Owen K. Garriott; and Jack R. Lousma, and they will be in orbit 56 days. The third team, also due to spend 56 days in orbit, consists of Gerald P. Carr; solar physicist Edward G. Gibson; and William R. Pogue.

Personnel Changes. After exhaustive tests, physicians gave Donald K. Slayton a clean bill of health in April and restored him to the list of active astronauts. One of the original seven astronauts, Slayton was grounded because of a heart flutter in 1962. Resigning from the space corps in 1972 were Edgar D. Mitchell, lunar module pilot on *Apollo 14*, and Richard F. Gordon, Jr., *Apollo 12* command module pilot. Physicist Philip K. Chapman and geophysicist Anthony W. England also resigned, leaving 40 astronauts on active status. William J. Cromie

ASTRONOMY. A proposal to construct a Very Large Array (VLA) radio telescope system in the United States received top priority by the Astronomy Survey Committee of the National Academy of Sciences in 1972. In June, the committee published a list of the problems they consider the most important to research during the next 10 years. The committee, headed by astronomer Jesse Greenstein of the California Institute of Technology, brought out clearly the close relationship between astronomy, physics, and chemistry resulting from recent discoveries of cosmic explosions and molecules in space.

The VLA, for which the National Science Foundation has obtained $3 million to begin design work, will be composed of 27 individual radio-collecting dishes, electronically connected so they can function as a single large telescope. They are to be arranged in a Y-shape, with nine radio telescopes spaced out along each 13-mile-long branch. The antennas will be on railroad tracks so they can be moved to vary the distance between receivers. The VLA will make it possible to map cosmic radio wave sources with from 10 to 100 times finer detail than any previous work. It will be the radio telescope equivalent of the 200-inch Hale optical telescope at Palomar Observatory near San Diego, Calif.

The VLA will require 10 years to complete, but should be in partial operation by 1976. It will be built on a flat, dry lake bed in the Plains of San Agustin, 50 miles west of Socorro, N. Mex., a site chosen for its level ground, moderate altitude, and freedom from man-made radio interference.

Jupiter and Beyond. Spacecraft *Pioneer 10* was launched toward Jupiter on March 2. The 21-month trip is expected to take the craft to within 87,000 miles of Jupiter. It will pass behind the planet's natural satellite Io, allowing scientists to test for the presence of an atomosphere there. Cameras will scan the planet and record a close-up view of its Great Red Spot. Sensors will detect the magnetic field of Jupiter and of the space through which *Pioneer 10* travels. The spacecraft is scheduled to arrive in the vicinity of Jupiter in December, 1973.

After passing Jupiter, *Pioneer 10* will eventually leave the solar system and travel out into the Milky Way. On the very small chance that it may someday be found by other intelligent beings, the spacecraft carries a small plaque describing human beings and the location of the solar system in our galaxy.

Close-up of Mars. Another spacecraft, *Mariner 9*, transmitted television pictures from an orbit around Mars. A severe dust storm on Mars prevented the cameras from recording the terrain for several weeks. The dust finally cleared, revealing a cratered, geologically active landscape.

The Martian craters appear to have been formed by two different processes–meteorite impact and volcanic activity. Rims of the Martian craters are smoother than those on lunar craters, showing the effects of wind erosion in the atmosphere on Mars. Several gigantic canyons, many times larger than the Grand Canyon, were also found. They apparently resulted when surface layers collapsed after loss of support from below. In places, the formations resemble riverbeds, but Mars does not have appreciable amounts of water. Wind and dust erosion can sometimes cause features similar to those caused by water erosion.

Mariner 9 also took the first pictures of Mars's natural satellites, Deimos and Phobos. Both are small, irregularly shaped bodies, heavily cratered by meteorite impact. Phobos, the closest to Mars, is about 16 by 13 miles, and Deimos is about 7½ by 8½ miles.

Landing on Venus. A 2,600-pound *Venera 8* spacecraft, launched by Russia on March 27, landed on the planet Venus on July 22. It transmitted data about its surface for 50 minutes before the spacecraft disintegrated under the tremendous heat and pressure of the planet's atmosphere. The landing was the latest in a series of Russian attempts to gather data about Venus.

The findings of *Venera 8* contained the first data on several aspects of the planet's physical and chemical character. *Venera 8* found that the Venusian surface resembles the earth's granitic rocks, and that some sunlight penetrates the dense cloud cover to reach the planet's surface. *Venera 8* recorded a surface temperature of 470°C. (880°F.) and atmospheric pressure 90 times greater than on earth. (Earth's is about 14.7 pounds per square inch.) The Venusian atmosphere is 97 per cent carbon dioxide, and *Venera 8* detected tiny amounts of ammonia in it at elevations of from 20 to 30 miles. Russian scientists also said winds blow in the direction that the planet rotates. The wind speeds decline from 160 feet per second at an altitude of 28 miles to 6 feet per second at 6 to 7 miles.

Thunder on the Sun. Solar observers found sound waves traveling outward at high speeds from dark spots in the sun's upper atmosphere. Such sunspots are cooler regions in the sun's atmosphere where magnetic disturbances and solar flares occur. They appear dark against the hotter background of the visible disk.

The sound waves, called Stein waves after Allen Stein, the California Institute of Technology student who first noticed them, originate in the coolest, darkest part of the sunspot and move outward at speeds of from 18,000 to 25,000 miles per hour. They are noted after mysterious flashes occur in the sunspot, and they apparently carry energy out into the solar atmosphere. Some astronomers have compared them to thunder after a lightning flash.

A Solar Eclipse occurred on July 10 that was visible in parts of Canada. The moon's shadow traversed a narrow path starting in Alaska and moving across the Northwest Territories, Quebec, New

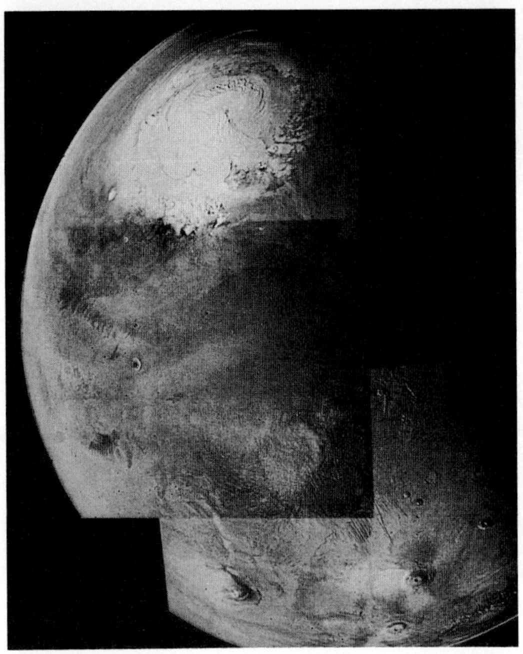

Northern hemisphere of Mars, from the polar cap to slightly south of the equator, shows in a mosaic of three photos taken by *Mariner 9* on August 7.

Brunswick, Prince Edward Island, and Nova Scotia. Rockets were launched from Fort Churchill, Canada, to observe the eclipsed sun over Hudson Bay, and large groups of observers gathered at Cap-Chat, Que., on the south bank of the St. Lawrence River to see the event. Weather conditions, however, were disappointing at eclipse time. Observers on the cruise ship *Olympia* were able to see the eclipse from a clear sky region in the Atlantic Ocean about 1,000 miles east of New York City. About 800 people had signed up for the cruise specifically to see the eclipse, and the *Olympia* was able to maneuver to an area where the sky was clear. The next eclipse of the sun will be on June 30, 1973, when the shadow will pass across the Sahara.

Cygnus X-3. Early in September, a faint radio star flared with a huge gain in its radio wave energy output. The burst of energy made the previously weak source about 200 times brighter and the sixth strongest source of cosmic radio waves in the sky for a few days. Observers have never seen a radio source change so markedly in such a short time. Canadian astronomers first spotted the change using a radio telescope at Algonquin Park in Ontario. Observatories throughout the world, and the X-ray satellite observatory *Uhuru*, joined in a massive program to document this unprecedented event.

Astronomers do not know what caused the outburst. However, the original star was known to be unusual, because it was a strong source of X rays. Its name means it is the third X-ray source in the constellation Cygnus. That region of the sky is heavily obscured by interstellar dust so that the object cannot be seen by optical telescopes. Two tentative explanations have been advanced for the flare-up. It could be matter collapsing rapidly into what is called a black hole. Or, it might be caused by a starquake, the celestial counterpart of an earthquake, in which a nearly dead star suddenly shrinks in size to readjust its internal structure.

New Neighborhood Galaxies. Four newly discovered, faint collections of stars were added to the small group of galaxies to which our Milky Way belongs. Astronomer Sidney van den Bergh of the David Dunlap Observatory in Toronto, Canada, located them on long-exposure, finely detailed photographs of the sky near the Andromeda constellation, a giant spiral star system similar to our own galaxy, the Milky Way. The Andromeda and the Milky Way are the dominating pair in a collection of about 20 galaxies that, together, form the Local Group.

The four new members of the Local Group are faint, dwarf systems – each about 2.5 million times brighter than the sun and containing only a few hundred thousand stars. They are thought to be companions of the Andromeda system. Laura P. Bautz

ATOMIC ENERGY. See ENERGY.

AUSTRALIA elected a new government on Dec. 2, 1972, after one of the most turbulent Parliaments in Australian history. The 27th Parliament had seen John Gorton fall almost overnight in March, 1971, from the prime ministership to the back-benches. His own party ousted him in favor of William McMahon, whose policies were frequently under fire from the opposition Labor Party.

Then, Edward Gough Whitlam and his Labor Party scored an unexpected victory in the elections, winning a comfortable majority of seats. For the first time in 23 years, the Country-Liberal Party coalition was out of office. Whitlam, the eighth Labor prime minister in Australia's history, took office on December 5. Lance Barnard became deputy prime minister. See WHITLAM, EDWARD GOUGH.

On his first day in office, Whitlam announced an end to the military draft, one of the main issues that had brought him to power. Three days later, he took steps to identify his government more closely with the working people. He abolished the custom of federal nominations for British knighthoods and other royal honors. He relinquished use of a Bentley – a British-made prestige car usually used by Australia's prime ministers – for a Ford Galaxie produced at a Ford plant in Australia. He also announced he would refuse an appointment to the Privy Council in London, a position to which he is entitled as prime minister. He was the first Australian to do so.

Edward Gough Whitlam, accompanied by his wife, casts his ballot in the December 2 election that led to his becoming Australia's prime minister.

Domestic Problems. Whitlam faced a sluggish economy and an unemployment picture that seesawed between highs and lows throughout the year. Spiraling wages and prices further complicated the problem.

The annual conference of the nation's six state premiers, which was presided over by Prime Minister McMahon, was held in Canberra on February 14. Chief among the topics discussed were measures to stimulate the economy and relieve unemployment. The measures included increased financial grants to the states, restoration to manufacturers of an investment allowance on new plants and equipment, increased unemployment grants in country areas, and a substantial increase in unemployment benefits.

Figures released in January by the ministry for labor and national service indicated that unemployment was the highest in 10 years. It had reached 2.16 per cent of the 5.6 million labor force. By March, it had fallen to 1.75, with only 97,877 registered as unemployed. But by July 17, it had risen to 3 per cent, or nearly 100,000, the highest June unemployment total in 11 years. By September, however, it had fallen to 1.58 per cent.

Labor Difficulties. The fluctuation was due in part to labor problems. A two-week strike by electric power workers in February put 200,000 Australians out of work and forced automobile plants in South Australia, New South Wales, and Queensland to shut down. At one point, factories were closing at the rate of about 100 a day. Other strikes were equally disruptive.

To avoid these disruptions, the Arbitration Commission, on May 5, authorized a pay increase of $2.38 a week for most of the Australian work force. The commission also raised the minimum wage for adult males by $5.60 to $60.73 a week. On June 14, about 83,000 federal government workers received a 7.5 per cent wage increase. This raised the federal base adult grade salary from $4,124 to $4,430 a year. And in midyear, Australia's 16,000 waterfront workers won a 35-hour workweek. They were the second industrial group to get this concession. Coal miners gained the 35-hour workweek in 1971.

Mineral Wealth. A promising discovery of uranium at Yeelarrie, in Western Australia, was announced on January 12. A few days later, an oil strike was reported at Fly Lake in the northeast corner of South Australia. New nickel deposits were found in the Agnew and Spargoville areas in Western Australia. In August, an estimated 1 billion tons in coal reserves were discovered in the Bowen area of Queensland. Initial explorations revealed about 210-million tons of good grade iron ore in the Pilbara region of Western Australia.

A record beef export year was predicted, with overseas sales reaching about $446 million. There were an estimated 20 million head of cattle in

Australia, and production was running at about 1-million tons a year. On the other hand, a survey showed the fewest sheep in nine years. Preliminary figures released in July showed there were only 163.9-million head; this was about 13.8 million fewer than in 1971.

Other Activities. On October 21, Governor General Sir Paul M. C. Hasluck activated a switch to open the Snowy Mountains Hydroelectric Scheme's main power station, Tamut Three. The ceremony came almost 23 years to the day after the project began. Australia's largest national development, it cost $943 million.

Australia's newest stretch of railroad was officially opened by Prime Minister McMahon in South Australia in October. A 47-mile stretch of standard-gauge track, the new line links the steel and shipbuilding center of Whyalla with Port Augusta and every capital city in mainland Australia.

At ceremonies held in Sydney on January 21, the government marked the official end of the United States rest and recreation program in Australia. In the previous four years, about 280,000 American troops serving in Vietnam spent leaves in Australia. Meanwhile, the last Australian combat troops returned to Sydney from South Vietnam on March 12. Only about 120 Australians engaged in noncombatant roles remained in Vietnam. Paul C. Tullier

See also ASIA (Facts in Brief Table).

AUSTRIA won a three-month head start on other European Free Trade Association (EFTA) countries when it signed a free trade agreement on July 22, 1972, with the European Community (Common Market). The interim tariff arrangements for industrial goods became effective in October. They cut industrial tariffs between Austria and Common Market countries. Generally, the agreement was to take effect in 1973.

Chancellor Bruno Kreisky went to Paris in February and in March to discuss terms with the French. He also went to Brussels in February for talks with Franco Maria Malfatti, president of the European Commission, the Common Market's governing body.

Kreisky emphasized that Austria's main difficulty concerned paper, special steels, and agricultural products. He also demanded duty-free arrangements in industrial trade with the newly enlarged Common Market. Kreisky told the Common Market countries that Austria's paper industry would die, throwing 20,000 Austrians out of work, if arrangements proposed by the market were implemented.

Tariffs on what Austria considered "sensitive" goods, including paper and steel, are to be dismantled slowly. Kreisky said the pact would support "an autonomous policy based on existing realities."

International Security. During a visit to West Germany on May 23 and 24, Kreisky discussed East-West relationships with Chancellor Willy Brandt. They also discussed plans for an international conference on European security.

Substantial changes in Austria's income tax system were announced on April 14. The new plan abolished children's allowances, but gave tax rebates for children and raised ceilings on tax-free earnings. The highest tax rate–applied to annual incomes over $40,000–was cut from 68 to 62 per cent.

Economic Activity expanded moderately, though the fast growth of 1970 and 1971 slowed somewhat. Higher import prices spurred inflation. Austrian unemployment remained low, at 2.7 per cent of the nation's labor force. The gross national product grew at a rate of 5.5 per cent.

Austria relies on tourist income to cover almost all its foreign trade deficit. In 1971, about 86 per cent was covered with the money spent by 67 million visitors. Work started on a United Nations (UN) complex in Vienna to house the International Atomic Energy Agency and the UN Industrial Development Organization.

On May 3, Peter Jankowitsch, a member of the foreign service since 1957, presented his credentials as Austria's new permanent representative to the United Nations. He presented them to his predecessor, Kurt Waldheim, who became UN secretary-general on Jan. 1, 1972. Kenneth Brown

See also EUROPE (Facts in Brief Table); WALDHEIM, KURT.

AUTOMOBILE. New car sales in the United States set an all-time record of 10,820,000 in 1972. The previous high was the 10,246,300 sales in 1971.

Both U.S. models and imports set sales records in the United States market, with 9,230,000 domestic cars and 1,580,000 imports sold.

On a percentage basis, the import manufacturers lost ground for the first time in several years. They got about 14.6 per cent of U.S. sales, a drop from their 15.3 per cent in 1971.

The Compact Cars provided much of the action in the sales race. The General Motors (GM) Vega, Ford's Pinto, and American Motors Corporation (AMC) Gremlin did battle with the imports–notably Volkswagen (VW), Toyota, and Datsun. Chrysler continued to import its Dodge Colt for sale in that segment of the market, but Plymouth Cricket sales faltered.

Registration figures gathered by R. L. Polk & Company, auto-industry statisticians, showed VW was still king of the import sales market, based on totals for January to October, 1972; they showed 364,772 VWs sold. Toyota was the runner-up with 213,651 sold during the nine months.

Henry Ford II, chairman of the board of Ford Motor Company, was one of the first to assess the Free World car and truck market for 1972. He predicted the final total would top 32 million units, 8 per cent above the 30 million of 1971.

Other auto-industry spokesmen agreed that new car sales in the United States would top 11 million in 1973, another new high. But they added an "if." The "if" centered on negotiations that will take place between the U.S. auto industry and the United Auto Workers (UAW), whose three-year contracts expire in September, 1973.

Quickie Strikes at U.S. auto plants, most of them GM plants, slowed 1972 production. The main issues in dispute were the speed of assembly lines and the number of workers needed to man them. Discussion spread among automobile executives, union leaders, and government officials about the often-repeated view that assembly-line work is monotonous and should be reformed. See MANUFACTURING.

Richard C. Gerstenberg, GM board chairman, defended working conditions for his firm's 400,000 hourly paid workers. He said the average GM worker is paid $5.09 an hour. Gerstenberg's figures showed the average GM hourly worker earns $12,466 a year before taxes. He said the actual payroll cost to GM is $15,400 when fringe benefits are included.

Union Gains. UAW President Leonard Woodcock said average industry-wide wages for 70,000 auto workers reached $5.05 per hour in 1972. "Henry Ford's once-historic $5 a day now has become the UAW's better-than-$5-an-hour average straight-time rate," Woodcock said.

The Wankel rotary engine, smaller and simpler than the traditional piston engine, made its U.S. debut in the Japanese-built Mazda auto.

Irving Bluestone, UAW vice-president and head of its GM department, distinguished between annual earnings and working conditions, citing a University of Michigan study of auto workers. He said it showed "even a good-paying job can be a boring, deadly, and dull routine drag." He indicated that 1973 negotiations would eye working conditions closely.

The 1973 Cars. Working under numerous federal guidelines, the auto industry continued its trend away from major annual styling changes. Money went into auto safety and antipollution devices.

Only one brand-new car – the compact Oldsmobile Omega – was introduced in the 1973 line-up of 277 models. There were 289 models in 1972.

Generally, Detroit automakers settled for face-lifting jobs on the 1973s – a bit of metal here or there and some extra paint. But they labored long and hard – and sometimes with short tempers – to meet federal requirements on such items as a 5-mile-an-hour bumper system, material flammability, and the reduction of oxides of nitrogen exhaust pollutants.

New Bumpers. The federal government required that 1973 cars be equipped with bumpers that can withstand a 5-mile-an-hour front impact or a 2½-mile-an-hour rear impact into a fixed barrier without damage to safety-related items on the car. These included the fuel tank and the exhaust, cooling, lighting, and door-latching systems.

Auto men said Washington's demands for stronger bumpers and for antipollution items sent costs up steadily. Henry Ford said the mandated programs would add $750 to the cost of a car between 1972 and 1976. Gerstenberg estimated the amount at $872.

Price Maneuvers. These changes provided the opening for the auto companies to ask the federal Price Commission for price hikes. After the new cars were introduced, government and the industry jockeyed on the prices. The auto-pricing picture was jumbled in the early weeks of the 1973 model run; the firms were torn by their desire to recover extra costs, yet remain competitive.

Chrysler, for example, raised its auto prices $20 in mid-October and $40 more in December to pay for the extra safety and antipollution devices. In December, the company also sought an additional $97 increase to cover costs of wages and materials, and $9 for additional government-ordered safety items. That request was under study at the year's end.

GM asked the commission for a 1.53 per cent increase – $54 per car – and got it after considerable study. Ford asked for $91.53, or 2.78 per cent, and got $62.55 a car, or 1.9 per cent, in early December. AMC raised its prices $37.59 and sought a second boost of $38.22 to recover the extra costs.

Customer Satisfaction was the target of a major AMC move in introducing its 1973 cars. AMC had drawn attention when its 1972 models included an unconditional guarantee on all parts except tires for 12 months or 12,000 miles with no cost to the buyer.

For its 1973s, AMC added two more items of customer appeal. One provided an allowance of up to $150 for food and lodging for a 1973 AMC car owner and its occupants if the car is kept overnight at an AMC dealer 150 miles or more from the motorist's home. And for an additional $149 within 90 days of purchasing his new car, the buyer could extend the coverage to 24 months or 24,000 miles.

Experimental Engines. Carmakers had boasted of pollution controls instead of power in 1972. Buyers complained they made winter starting more difficult and cut down acceleration. On 1973s, manufacturers tried some minor devices that, they said, improved the performance of those cars equipped with antipollution systems. But Detroit ran into objections from the Environmental Protection Agency.

Experiments with alternate forms of power plants went on. Chrysler, which spent millions of dollars in the mid-1950s trying to develop an inexpensive, workable gas-turbine engine, won a federal contract in November to develop a sixth generation of its engine. It was considered a possible replacement for the piston engine used in virtually all of today's cars.

The German-developed Wankel rotary engine drew particular attention in August when GM's Gerstenberg said that limited production of a Wankel-powered Vega was possible in two years. A Wankel-powered Japanese import, the Mazda, was already on sale. Charles C. Cain III

AUTOMOBILE RACING. Race cars ran faster than ever in 1972. And nowhere did they improve more than on the United States Auto Club (USAC) Championship Trail, particularly in its showcase race, the $1,011,846 Indianapolis 500 on May 27.

In 1971, Peter Revson of New York City, set an Indianapolis record by averaging 178.696 miles per hour (mph) for four laps (10 miles) of qualifying. In 1972, all 33 qualifiers, including Revson, broke the record. Bobby Unser of Albuquerque, N. Mex., was the fastest, averaging 195.940 mph in an Olsonite-Eagle with an Offenhauser engine, prepared by Dan Gurney's All-American Racers.

Unser, Revson, and Mark Donohue of Newton Square, Pa., were the three leading qualifiers, all at speeds faster than 191 mph. Donohue, driving a McLaren-Offenhauser entered by Roger Penske, won the race and the top prize of $218,768. Jerry Grant was dropped from 2nd place to 12th on a protest. In a hurried final pit stop, Grant refueled from the supply of a teammate.

One reason the cars were faster was the slightly higher and slightly larger rear airfoils, often called wings. The air pressure exerted on the wings kept the cars glued to the track, allowing them to hold the road at 175 mph going through the corners. In addition, cars were more streamlined, and the new treadless tires put more rubber in contact with the track.

Joe Leonard of San Jose, Calif., driving a new Parnelli-Offenhauser, won the 11-race USAC series, as he did in 1971. A. J. Foyt of Houston, a perennial winner in major USAC races, had better luck elsewhere. He won the USAC dirt-track series and the two richest races on the National Association for Stock Car Auto Racing (NASCAR) Grand National circuit for late-model stock cars.

NASCAR Season. For the 1972 season, NASCAR streamlined its program. It split off the shorter and less-lucrative races into two series and limited its Grand National series to 31 races, each from 250 to 500 miles long.

Foyt won the $196,175 Miller High Life 500 on March 5 at Ontario, Calif., and the $183,700 Daytona 500 at Daytona Beach, Fla., on February 20. He drove a 1971 Mercury prepared by Glen Wood. David Pearson of Spartanburg, S.C., drove a similar Mercury to major victories at Cambridge Junction, Mich. (twice); Darlington, S.C.; Talladega, Ala.; Dover, Del.; and Daytona Beach.

In all, Bobby Allison of Hueytown, Ala., won 10 races; Richard Petty of Randleman, N.C., 8; and Pearson, 6. Allison, driving a Chevrolet, won the most money, $271,395. All year long, he dueled with Petty, who drove a Dodge in most of his races. Finally, Allison won his fourth series point title. William H. G. France, who organized NASCAR in 1948, retired in January as its president. His son, William C. France, succeeded him.

George Follmer of Arcadia, Calif., won the two other major American series – the Canadian-American (Can-Am) Challenge Cup and the Trans-American (Trans-Am) – both conducted by Sports Car Club of America. His Trans-Am victory in a Javelin was anticipated. His Can-Am victory in a Porsche was surprising.

Can-Am Series. To start with, Team McLaren had won Can-Am honors the five previous years, and this time it planned to add Jackie Stewart of Scotland, the 1971 world champion, until he became ill. But even with a new and faster car, the McLaren team could not keep up with the Porsches of Follmer and Donohue, who, between them, won 7 of the 9 races at tracks in the United States and Canada. Follmer replaced Donohue, who was hurt July 3 and missed much of the season.

The 5-liter turbocharged, open-cockpit Porsches were similar to the closed-cockpit Porsches that won the world manufacturers championship in 1970 and 1971. Porsche abandoned the manufacturers series when the engine size was ordered reduced to 3 liters, and Ferrari won the 10 manufacturers races it entered. A French Matra-Simca won the 11th and most famous, the 24 Hours of Le Mans.

The World Driving Champion was Emerson Fittipaldi, a 25-year-old Brazilian named for the American poet Ralph Waldo Emerson. He drove a Lotus-Ford to victory in 5 of the 12 Grand Prix races for Formula One 3-liter roadsters. Frank Litsky

AVIATION. After two of the most difficult years in its history, the U.S. aviation industry's fortunes improved somewhat in 1972. Airline traffic increased, but problems of excess capacity, rising operating costs, and low fares held profits down. Security measures to deal with the growing threat of hijackers and extortionists became a growing source of economic and public pressure on the industry, as did social concern over airport noise and the environmental impact of airports.

Profits of Domestic Scheduled airlines improved slightly in 1972. The modest upturn resulted from the traffic growth that began in the last half of 1971, continued efforts to limit capacity additions (seat-mile increases) to 5 per cent, and a 2.7 per cent domestic fare increase granted by the Civil Aeronautics Board (CAB) in early September. Estimated 1972 net income for trunk lines approached $225 million. This was a dramatic increase over 1971's $78 million and 1970's loss of $52 million.

The improved earnings levels of carriers resulted in a 6.2 per cent rate of return on investment. This level was far short of the CAB's "fair and reasonable" level of 12 per cent.

A number of industry experts were concerned about how to get the $5.9 billion needed for new equipment by 1975. In December, Edward E. Carlson, president of United Air Lines, the nation's largest carrier, said that a threat of nationalization hung over the industry if it did not resolve its financing difficulties and cooperate in developing a national air-transportation plan that would help to meet the nation's increasing air-transportation needs.

Air Cargo Traffic registered its strongest gain in three years. For the first nine months of 1972, total scheduled cargo flown by 22 U.S. airlines increased 10 per cent over the same period in 1971. Some factors contributing to the increase:

- The new, wide-bodied aircraft could carry more cargo in belly compartments, with cargo capacity increased from 500 pounds to 3,000 pounds. Some airlines introduced new rate incentives in an effort to fill the increased capacity.
- The improved handling of small packages broadened the market for air cargo.
- The greater availability of temperature-controlled containers permitted longer hauls of perishables.

Airline Mergers, which in 1971 appeared likely to have a major influence on the industry, declined in importance during 1972. The American Airlines-Western Airlines merger was rejected by the CAB and by President Richard M. Nixon. The decision had the effect of placing a red light in front of "mergers of equals."

It appeared that the CAB would consider only extreme financial need as the grounds for merger approval. The Delta-Northeast merger, which went into effect on August 1, and the Allegheny-Mohawk merger, in May, were both in this category.

Airports. Public pressure to close jet airports at night increased throughout the nation. Protesters claimed that night jet flights were disturbing the sleep of those who lived near airports. Strong efforts to impose curfews were evident in Boston, Chicago, Los Angeles, Miami, Minneapolis, New York City, San Diego, and other U.S. cities. The trend, however, was even more pronounced abroad. More than 25 jetports in Europe–including terminals in Amsterdam, Frankfurt, London, and Paris–either banned or severely restricted night operations. Curfews were also imposed in Tokyo, Hong Kong, and Sydney.

Some aviation authorities predicted that the United States was heading for an airport crisis. They stressed that the nation had virtually stopped building airports, despite an anticipated tripling in airline passenger travel during the 1970s. Although nearly all of the 23 major U.S. cities and many of the medium and smaller cities have demonstrated a need for new or expanded airports, only one major airport, in Kansas City, was completed. Another, in Dallas-Fort Worth, was under construction.

Hijacking attempts of U.S. aircraft grew in number and became increasingly bizarre and violent during the year. Aviation and government officials searched for effective deterrents as pilots went on a worldwide protest strike in June and psychiatrists debated whether protective measures encouraged or discouraged hijackers.

The weaknessess in existing ground security systems were reflected by 31 hijacking attempts of U.S. planes in 1972, compared to 27 in both 1971 and 1970. However, successful skyjacking decreased to 10 from 12 in 1971, and 18 in 1970. Experts believed the reduced number of successful hijackings reflected experience gained in dealing with the problem by law enforcement agencies, the Federal Aviation Administration (FAA), airline pilots, and airline management.

Nevertheless, the continuing seriousness of the air piracy problem caused the Administration to take the furthest-reaching federal antihijacking measures to date. Citing a "new breed of hijackers . . . unequaled in their ruthlessness and their wanton disregard for human life," President Nixon issued an emergency order on December 5 requiring the nation's airlines to inspect all carry-on luggage and electronically search all passengers for weapons, by Jan. 5, 1973.

The Administration further directed that each of the nation's 531 commercial airports must station an armed officer from a local law-enforcement agency at boarding gates by February 5.

By the end of the year, the majority of the nation's airlines had petitioned the CAB for authority to raise all air fares by $1 ($2 for round-trip tickets) to meet the $103-million projected costs of implementing the plan in 1973–an estimated $56 million in

A one-day strike by airline pilots on June 19 shut down many of the world's airports. But most U.S. pilots obeyed a court order to stay on the job.

capital and labor for the airlines and $47 million for airport operators to provide 4,500 armed officers at boarding gates.

Late in the year, negotiations on antihijacking measures were being conducted between the United States and Cuba through the Swiss government. The discussions indicated promise of eliminating Havana as a sanctuary for hijackers of both planes and ships. See also MIDDLE EAST.

SST Service. On May 25, British Overseas Airways Corporation (BOAC) announced that it would begin 3½-hour service between New York City and London in the summer of 1975. The airline made the announcement after becoming the first carrier to purchase the British-French supersonic *Concorde.*

Meanwhile, U.S. airline officials indicated that they planned to look long and skeptically before buying the *Concorde.* Aviation authorities were dubious about the profit-making capability of the 104-seat, 1,350-mile-an-hour plane. At $60 million with spare parts, one *Concorde* would cost more than twice as much as a 350-seat, 600-mile-an-hour Boeing 747. Airline experts also indicated concern over whether the *Concorde* will be permitted to operate at U.S. airports because of the thunderous noise of its engines and the sonic booms it creates.

International Air Fares. In December, it appeared that bargain air fares would soon be in force for travel between North America and Europe. The International Air Transport Association announced on December 13 that airlines would be able to set their own rates on transatlantic routes beginning Feb. 1, 1973.

Air Safety. U.S. scheduled airlines, which account for nearly 45 per cent of all total revenue passenger miles flown by scheduled carriers throughout the world, continued to have a far better safety record than their foreign counterparts. The data below is from the Air Transport Association of America and the International Civil Aviation Organization:

Fatalities On Scheduled Flights

Year	U.S.	Foreign	Total
1968	305	607	912
1969	132	814	946
1970	2	777	779
1971	174	793	967

The air transport operations of foreign carriers experienced the highest number of deaths in their history during 1972. There were seven incidents in which the crash of a single plane caused more than 100 deaths including the first-, third-, and fourth-highest death tolls ever recorded for single-plane crashes. A total of 979 people were killed in these seven crashes, with 443 of the fatalities occurring on charter flights. The worst single plane disaster on record took place on October 13 when a Soviet Ilyushin jet airliner crashed near Moscow, killing all 176 persons on board.

A bomb set by extortionists who demanded $2 million wrecked an empty TWA jetliner at the Las Vegas, Nev., airport in March.

Within the United States, there were five fatal accidents involving scheduled carriers. A total of 163 passengers were killed. The number of fatalities per 100 million passenger miles was a relatively safe 0.11.

Air Fares. At year-end, lower-cost air transportation appeared likely in 1973 for both domestic and international travelers. In December, the International Air Transport Association announced that airlines would be able to set their own rates on transatlantic routes beginning Feb. 1, 1973. It was expected that as a result of this action, scheduled domestic carriers would be offering lower-cost round-trip fares through new travel group charters (TGC's) that would compete with charter flights. TGC's permit travel organizers to put together groups of 40 or more members of the general public willing to book and post 25 per cent of their fare 120 days in advance, with final payment 45 days in advance. The TGC approach was subject to court approval.

General Aircraft. Sales of private planes rose for the first time since 1969. During 1972, sales increased from $321 million to $500 million, with 9,200 units being delivered compared to 7,466 in 1971.

Commercial Aircraft manufacturers experienced a better year than they had anticipated after the rate in decline of industry sales that began in 1969 finally came to a halt. Sales increased only slightly to $2.56 billion for 210 units, compared to $2.59 billion for 228 units in 1971. Kenneth E. Schaefle

AWARDS AND PRIZES presented in 1972 included the following:

Arts Awards

American Institute of Architects. ***Gold Medal,*** Pietro Belluschi, consulting professor of architecture, University of Oregon, and designer of more than 1,000 ecclesiastical, residential, and commercial buildings. ***Fine Arts Medal,*** George Rickey, sculptor of long, stainless steel stilettos in many museum and university courtyards. ***Industrial Arts Medal,*** Charles Eames, noted designer of chairs, architect, and producer of documentary films. ***Research Medal,*** Christopher J. Alexander, professor of architecture, University of California, Berkeley.

Brandeis University. ***Creative Arts Medal Awards,*** Louis I. Kahn for architecture, Merce Cunningham for dance, Katherine Anne Porter for fiction, and Alfred Lunt and Lynn Fontanne for theater arts.

Capezio Dance Award. Reginald and Gladys Laubin and La Meri, three leaders in ethnic dance.

National Academy of Design. ***Benjamin Altman Prize, Figure Painting*** Gregorio Prestopino ($2,500); ***Landscape Painting,*** John Hultberg ($2,500).

National Academy of Recording Arts and Sciences. ***Grammy Awards: Record of the Year,*** "It's Too Late" by Carole King. ***Album of the Year, Pop,*** "Tapestry" by Carole King; ***Classical,*** "Horowitz Plays Rachmaninoff." ***Best Score for a Motion Picture,*** Isaac Hayes for *Shaft*. ***Best Song of the Year,*** "You've Got a Friend" by Carole King. ***Best Pop Vocal Performance, Group,*** The Carpenters for *The Carpenters; **Female,*** Carole King for "Tapestry"; ***Male,*** James Taylor for "You've Got a Friend." ***Best Comedy Recording,*** Lily Tomlin for "This Is a Recording." ***Best Rhythm and Blues Vocal Performance, Male,*** Lou Rawls for "A Natural Man"; ***Female,*** Aretha Franklin for "Bridge Over Troubled Water"; ***Song,*** "Ain't No Sunshine." ***Best Country Vocal Performance, Male,*** Jerry Reed for "When You're Hot, You're Hot"; ***Female,*** Sammi Smith for "Help Me Make It Through the Night." ***Song,*** "Help Me Make It Through the Night."

National Academy of Television Arts and Sciences. ***Emmy Awards: Best Actor and Actress in a Single Dramatic Performance,*** Keith Michell in "The Six Wives of Henry VIII," and Glenda Jackson for "Elizabeth R." ***Best Supporting Actor and Actress,*** Jack Warden in "Brian's Song" and Jenny Agutter for "The Snow Goose." ***Best Actor and Actress in a Dramatic Series,*** Peter Falk for "Columbo" and Glenda Jackson for "Elizabeth R." ***Best Actor and Actress in a Comedy Series,*** Carroll O'Connor and Jean Stapleton for "All in the Family." ***Best Supporting Actor and Actress in a Comedy Series,*** Edward Asner for "The Mary Tyler Moore Show"; Valerie Harper for "The Mary Tyler Moore Show" and Sally Struthers for "All in the Family." ***Best Director of a Single Program,*** John Rich for the Sammy's Visit episode of "All in the Family" with Sammy Davis, Jr. ***Best Program of the Year,*** "Brian's Song." ***Best Comedy Series,*** "All in the Family." ***Best Variety Series,*** "The Carol Burnett Show." ***Best Variety Series and Talk Show,*** "The Dick Cavett Show." ***Best New Series and Best Dramatic Series,*** "Elizabeth R."

National Association for American Composers and conductors. ***Henry Hadley Medal,*** Virgil Thomson, composer and critic, for distinguished services to American music.

National Institute of Arts and Letters and American Academy of Arts and Letters. ***Gold Medal for History,*** Henry Steele Commager, lecturer, Amherst College. ***Gold Medal for the Novel,*** Eudora Welty, author of *Losing Battles* (1970). ***Award of Merit Medal for Painting,*** Clyfford Still. ***Richard and Hinda Rosenthal***

Foundation Award for Painting, Barkley L. Hendricks. ***Rosenthal Foundation Award for the Novel,*** Thomas McGuane for *The Bushwhacked Piano*. ***Marjorie Peabody Waite Award,*** Vittorio Rieti, composer. ***E. M. Forster Award,*** Frank Tuohy, fiction writer. ***Loines Award for Poetry,*** William Jay Smith. ***Zabel Award*** (fiction), Donald Barthelme. ***Brunner Memorial Prize in Architecture,*** Richard Meier.

Journalism Awards

American Newspaper Guild. ***Heywood Broun Award,*** Aaron Latham, *The Washington Post*, for a series examining the failures of Junior Village, the capital's home for homeless children.

National Cartoonists Society. ***Reuben,*** Milton Caniff, Publishers Hall Syndicate and King Features, for "Steve Canyon."

George Foster Peabody Awards. ***Broadcast News,*** John Rich, NBC Radio and Television, for two decades of reporting on China and the Far East. ***Radio: Education,*** WHA, Madison, Wis., for "innovative classroom use of radio to help bring about an understanding of America's current problems." ***Public Service,*** NBC Radio, for "Second Sunday." ***Television: Education,*** WQED, Pittsburgh, for "The Turned On Crisis."

Sigma Delta Chi, Professional Journalistic Society. ***Newspaper Awards: General Reporting.*** James B. Steele and Donald L. Barlett, *The Philadelphia Inquirer*, for their investigation of low-income-housing programs. ***Editorial Writing,*** Joanna D. Wragg, *The Ledger*, Lakeland, Fla., for editorials urging reform of Lakeland Housing Authority. *Washington Correspondence*, Neil Sheehan and *The New York Times*, for "their coverage, enterprise, and rigorous effort in obtaining, evaluating, and publishing the 'Pentagon Papers.'" ***Foreign Correspondence,*** Peter Arnett and Bernard Gavzer, the Associated Press, for stories on the source of heroin for American soldiers in South Vietnam. ***News Photography,*** Dong Jun Kim, *Seoul* (Korea) *Shinmun*, for photo of guest leaping to his death during hotel fire. ***Editorial Cartooning,*** Hugh Haynie, *Louisville Courier-Journal*, for cartoon of ill-fed, ill-clothed black child saying, "Oh, yes, sir. They're very nice moon rocks, thank you sir." ***Public Service,*** *Boston Globe* and its "Spotlight Team," for investigation of municipal corruption in Somerville, Mass. ***Magazine Awards: Reporting,*** Arthur Hadley, free-lance writer, *Playboy* magazine, for "Goodbye to the Blind Slash Dead Kid's Hooch," an article on the winding down of the war in Vietnam. ***Public Service,*** *New Orleans Magazine*, for article by Rosemary James on the status of criminal justice in New Orleans Parish. ***Radio Awards: Reporting,*** John Rich, Tokyo-based correspondent for NBC, for stories on the visit of the U.S. table tennis team to China. ***Public Service,*** WBZ Radio, Boston, for examining Massachusetts' drug problems. ***Editorializing,*** WSOC-AM, Charlotte, N.C., for editorial on school busing. ***Television Awards: Reporting,*** Robert Schakne, CBS News, for coverage of uprising at Attica (N.Y.) State Prison. ***Public Service,*** CBS, for a seven-show series that discussed bureaucratic and executive control over the dissemination of information and that focused on the "Pentagon Papers." ***Editorializing,*** Robert Schulman, WHAS-TV, Louisville, for series on effects of strip mining in eastern Kentucky. ***Research in Journalism,*** John C. Merrill and Ralph L. Lowenstein, University of Missouri journalism professors, for their book, *Media, Messages, and Men*. ***Distinguished Teaching in Journalism,*** Alvin E. Austin, professor of journalism, University of North Dakota.

Literature Awards

Academy of American Poets. ***1972 Fellowship,*** James Wright, professor of English, Hunter College, New York City, for "distinguished poetic achievement." ***Lamont Poetry Selection Award,*** Peter Everwine, Fresno State College, Fresno, Calif., for *Collecting the Animals*.

American Library Association. ***Beta Phi Mu Award,*** Margaret E. Monroe, professor and former director of the University of Wisconsin Library School, for distinguished service to education for librarianship. ***Caldecott Medal,*** Nonny Hogrogian, author-illustrator of *One Fine Day*, for the most distinguished American picture book for children in 1971. ***Francis Joseph Campbell Citation,*** Frederick A. Thorpe and Keith Jennison, publishers, for library services for the blind. ***Melvil Dewey Medal,*** Jerold Orne, university librarian, University of North Carolina, for distinguished contributions to librarianship. ***Joseph W. Lippincott Award,*** Guy R. Lyle, director of libraries, Emory University, "for devotion to the improvement of libraries and librarianship. ***Newbery Medal,*** Robert C. O'Brien, for *Mrs. Frisby and the Rats of NIMH*, the most distinguished contribution to American literature for children in 1971.

National Book Committee. ***National Book Awards: Arts and Letters,*** Charles Rosen, pianist, for *The Classical Style: Haydn, Mozart, Beethoven*. ***Children's Literature,*** Donald Barthelme, for *The Slightly Irregular Fire Engine or the Hithering, Thithering Djinn*. ***Biography,*** Joseph P. Lash, for *Eleanor and Franklin: The Story of Their Relationship, Based on Eleanor Roosevelt's Private Papers*. ***Contemporary Affairs,*** Stewart Brand, for *The Last Whole Earth Catalog: An Access to Tools*. ***Fiction,*** Flannery O'Connor, who died in 1964, for her book *Flannery O'Connor: The Complete Stories*, published in 1971. ***History,*** Allan Nevins, who died in 1971, for his *Ordeal of the Union Series*, an eight-volume history of the Civil War. ***Philosophy and Religion,*** Martin E. Marty, for *Righteous Empire: The Protestant Experience in America*. ***Poetry,*** the late Frank O'Hara, for *The Collected Poems*, and Howard Moss, for *Selected Poems*. ***Science,*** George L. Small, for *The Blue Whale*. ***Translation,*** Austryn Wainhouse, for Jacques Monod's *Chance and Necessity: An Essay on the Natural Philosophy of Modern Biology*. ***National Medal for Literature,*** Lewis Mumford, "for the excellence of his total contribution to the world of letters."

Poetry Society of America. ***Alice Fay di Castagnola Award,*** Erica Jong and Myra Sklarew, for works in progress. ***John Masefield Award,*** Donald Junkins, professor of English, University of Massachusetts, for *A Remembrance: Chadbourne Hall, 1949, a Three-Cent Jefferson Stamp Brings a Letter from My Father*. ***Shelly Memorial Award,*** Galway Kinnell, for his published work.

Nobel Prizes. See Nobel Prizes.

Public Service Awards.

Freedoms Foundation. ***George Washington Award,*** General of the Army Omar N. Bradley, America's only living five-star general, for "his long, dedicated, and selfless service to his country."

National Association for the Advancement of Colored People. ***Spingarn Medal,*** Gordon Alexander Parks, "in recognition of his unique creativity, as exemplified by his outstanding achievements as a photographer, writer, film maker, and composer."

Planned Parenthood—World Population Center. ***Margaret Sanger Award,*** Alan F. Guttmacher, president, Planned Parenthood Federation of America, for courageous leadership in voluntary family planning.

Reinhold Niebuhr Prize, Willy Brandt, chancellor of West Germany, and Theodore M. Hesburgh, president of Notre Dame University.

Rockefeller Public Service Awards for "distinguished service to the government of the United States and the American people." ***Administration,*** Vernon D. Acree, commissioner of customs, Bureau of Customs, Department of the Treasury. ***Human Resource Development and Protection,*** Samuel C. Adams, Jr., assistant administrator, Bureau for Africa, Agency for International Development. ***Intergovernmental Operations,*** Barbara M. White, career minister for information, United States Information Agency. ***Professional Accomplishment and Leadership,*** Wallace P. Rowe, chief, Laboratory of Viral Diseases, National Institutes of Health; and Laurence N. Woodworth, chief of staff, Joint Committee on Internal Revenue Taxation, U.S. Congress.

United Nations Educational, Scientific, and Cultural Organization. ***Kalinga Prize,*** Pierre Anger, for the popularization of science.

Pulitzer Prizes. See PULITZER PRIZES.

Science and Technology Awards

American Chemical Society. ***Priestley Medal,*** Harold C. Urey, 1934 Nobel laureate in chemistry, and professor emeritus, University of California, San Diego, for "distinguished services to chemistry."

American Institute of Physics. ***Dannie Heineman Prize for Mathematical Physics,*** James D. Bjorken, Stanford Linear Accelerator Center, "for his contributions to particle theory."

American Physical Society. ***Bonner Prize in Nuclear Physics,*** John D. Anderson, Lawrence Radiation Laboratory, and Donald Robson, Florida State University, "for their contributions to the discovery and understanding of nuclear analog resonances." ***Buckley Solid State Physics Prize,*** James C. Phillips, Bell Telephone Laboratories, Murray Hill, N.J., "for his synthesis of theoretical and empirical knowledge of band structures and optical properties."

Atomic Energy Commission. ***Enrico Fermi Award,*** Manson Benedict, professor of nuclear engineering, Massachusetts Institute of Technology, in recognition of pioneering leadership in the development of the nation's first gaseous diffusion plant and contributions in the development of the nuclear reactor. ***Ernest O. Lawrence Memorial Awards,*** Charles C. Cremer, Los Alamos Scientific Laboratory, for "leadership in the development of novel small-weapon design concepts"; Sidney D. Drell, Stanford University, for "theoretical investigations of the range of validity of quantum electrodynamics"; Marvin Goldman, University of California, Davis, for "contributions to the understanding of the effects of bone-seeking radionuclides"; David A. Shirley, University of California, Berkeley, for contributions "to the chemical nature of matter employing interactions of the nucleus with its electronic environment"; and Paul F. Zweifel, Virginia Polytechnic Institute and State University, for "contributions to the theory of the slowing down and thermalization of neutrons."

Robert J. Collier Trophy, Colonel David R. Scott, Lieutenant Colonel James B. Irwin, and Major Alfred M. Worden, *Apollo 15* astronauts; and Robert R. Gilruth, director, Manned Spacecraft Center, Houston, for achievement in aeronautics.

Columbia University. ***Louisa Gross Horwitz Prize,*** Stephen W. Kuffler, professor, Harvard Medical School, for "outstanding experiments" that have provided information of fundamental importance concerning the nervous and visual systems.

Albert Einstein Award, Eugene P. Wigner, 1963 Nobel laureate in physics, professor of mathematical physics, Princeton University, for outstanding contributions to the physical sciences.

Franklin Institute. ***Franklin Medal,*** George B. Kistiakowsky, Harvard University, professor of chemistry, "for his pioneering research in the thermodynamics and kinetics of the reactions of organic molecules . . . and for his service to his country and to mankind as scientific adviser at high government levels."

Geological Society of America. ***Penrose Medal,*** Wilmot H. Bradley, retired, U.S. Geological Survey, for his studies of the paleoecology and sedimentation of the Green River Formation. ***Arthur L. Day Medal,*** Frank Press, professor and head, Department of Earth and Planetary Sciences, Massachusetts Institute of Technology, for his contributions to seismology.

Harmon International Aviation Trophies. Geraldine Cobb for "a series of humanitarian flights during 1971 over the Amazon River Basin; Lieutenant Colonel Thomas B. Estes and Lieutenant Colonel Dewain C. Vick, USAF, "for their long-distance, nonstop flight of 15,000 miles at three times the speed of sound"; Andre Turcat, France, and Brian Trubshaw, Great Britain, chief test pilots and directors of flight tests for the *Concorde* test programs.

Albert and Mary Lasker Foundation Awards. ***Albert Lasker Medical Research Awards*** for advances in cancer chemotherapy. Emil Frei III, physician in chief, Children's Cancer Research Foundation, Boston; Emil J. Freireich, Anderson Hospital and Tumor Institute, Houston; James F. Holland, chief of medicine, Roswell Park Memorial Institute, Buffalo; and Donald Pinkel, medical director, St. Jude Children's Research Hospital, Memphis, for their work on acute lymphatic leukemia; Paul Carbone and Vincent T. DeVita, Jr., National Cancer Institute; and Emil Frei III for work on Hodgkin's disease; Roy Hertz, professor of obstetrics and gynecology, New York Medical College, Valhalla, for work on choriocarcinoma; Min Chiu Li, director of medical research, Nassau Hospital, New York; Edmund Klein, chief, department of dermatology, Roswell Park Memorial Institute; and Eugene J. Van Scott, professor of dermatology, Skin and Cancer Hospital, Temple University, Philadelphia, for work on skin cancers; Joseph H. Burchenal, director of clinical investigation, Memorial Hospital, New York; Denis Burkitt, surgeon, Medical Research Council, London; V. Anomah Ngu, professor of surgery, Centre of Health Sciences, Cameroon; and John L. Ziegler, National Cancer Institute, for work on Burkitt's lymphoma; Isaac Djerassi, director of research hematology, Mercy Catholic Medical Center, Darby, Pa., for work on drug side effects; Emil J. Freireich for work on infection. ***Special Award,*** C. Gordon Zubrod, director, division of cancer treatment, National Cancer Institute, for leadership in creating "an effective national cancer chemotherapy program."

National Academy of Engineering. ***Founders Medal,*** Edwin H. Land, president and director of research, Polaroid Corporation, for his development of cameras, films, and processes for instant photography and for his invention of synthetic polarizers for light.

National Academy of Sciences (NAS). ***Alexander Agassiz Medal,*** Seiya Uyeda, professor of geophysics, University of Tokyo's Earthquake Research Institute, for his "outstanding contributions to the tectonic and thermal history of the earth." ***Henryk Arctowski Medal,*** Francis S. Johnson, director, Center for Advanced Studies, University of Texas, Dallas, for studies of solar activity. ***Cottrell Award,*** Arie J. Haagen-Smit, emeritus professor of bio-organic chemistry, California Institute of Technology, for his "highly innovative studies on the formation of smog and his untiring efforts to shape the air-pollution control policies of the nation." ***Arthur L. Day Prize and Lectureship,*** Hatten S. Yoder, Jr., director, Geophysical Laboratory, Carnegie Institution of

Washington, for developing an apparatus that enables scientists to investigate a wide range of phenomena within the earth's crust. ***NAS Award in Applied Mathematics and Numerical Analysis,*** Kurt O. Friedrichs, distinguished professor of mathematics, New York University's Courant Institute of Mathematical Sciences, for his contributions to many of the most difficult questions in applied mathematics. ***NAS Award in Microbiology,*** Charles Yanofsky, professor, Department of Biological Sciences, Stanford University, for his efforts in elucidating the basic biochemical mechanisms responsible for the genetic control of enzyme synthesis in bacteria. ***U.S. Steel Foundation Award in Molecular Biology,*** Howard M. Temin, professor of cancer research, University of Wisconsin's McArdle Laboratory for Cancer Research, for his work "leading to the discovery of reverse transcription," which may lead to a better understanding of how viruses produce cancer. ***Charles Doolittle Walcott Medal,*** Elso S. Barghoorn, professor of botany and curator of paleobotany, Harvard University, for providing a picture of life on earth more than 3.4 billion years ago. ***James Craig Watson Medal,*** André Deprit, NASA Goddard Space Flight Center, for his "adaptation of modern computing machinery to algebraic rather than arithmetical operations."

Vernon Stouffer Foundation. ***Stouffer Prize,*** Vincent P. Dole, Rockefeller University, New York City; John W. Gofman, University of California, Berkeley; Robert S. Gordon, Jr., National Institutes of Health, Bethesda, Md.; and John L. Oncley, University of Michigan, Ann Arbor, for their research in determining how fat and cholesterol are transported in the blood.

Theater and Motion Picture Awards

Academy of Motion Picture Arts and Sciences. ***"Oscar" Awards: Best Picture,*** *The French Connection*, 20th Century-Fox. ***Best Actor,*** Gene Hackman in *The French Connection*. ***Best Supporting Actor,*** Ben Johnson in *The Last Picture Show*. ***Best Actress,*** Jane Fonda in *Klute*. ***Best Supporting Actress,*** Cloris Leachman in *The Last Picture Show*. ***Best Director,*** William Friedkin for *The French Connection*. ***Best Foreign Language Film,*** *The Garden of the Finzi-Continis*, directed by Vittorio De Sica. ***Special Oscar,*** Charles Chaplin, for "the humor and humanity" he brought to dozens of films for more than 50 years.

Antoinette Perry (Tony) Awards: ***Best Dramatic Play,*** *Sticks and Bones*. ***Best Dramatic Actor,*** Cliff Gorman in *Lenny*. ***Best Dramatic Actress,*** Sada Thompson in *Twigs*. ***Best Director of a Dramatic Play,*** Mike Nichols for *Prisoner of Second Avenue*. ***Best Musical,*** *Two Gentlemen of Verona*. ***Best Actor in a Musical,*** Phil Silvers in *A Funny Thing Happened on the Way to the Forum*. ***Best Actress in a Musical,*** Alexis Smith in *Follies*. ***Best Director of a Musical,*** Hal Prince and Michael Bennett for *Follies*. ***Best Score,*** Stephen Sondheim for *Follies*.

New York Drama Critics' Circle Awards. ***Best Play of 1971-1972,*** *Sticks and Bones*, produced by Joseph Papp. ***Best American Play,*** *Sticks and Bones*, written by David Rabe. ***Best Foreign Play,*** *The Screens*, written by Jean Genêt. ***Best Musical,*** *Two Gentlemen of Verona*, produced by Joseph Papp.

New York Film Critics Awards: ***Best Actress,*** Jane Fonda in *Klute*. ***Best Actor,*** Gene Hackman in *The French Connection*. ***Best Film,*** *A Clockwork Orange,* Warner Brothers. ***Best Director,*** Stanley Kubrick for *A Clockwork Orange*. ***Best Screenwriting,*** Penelope Gilliatt for *Sunday Bloody Sunday*, and Larry McMurtry and Peter Bogdanovich for *The Last Picture Show*. Lillian Zahrt

See also Canadian Literature; Chemistry; Literature for Children.

BAHAMAS. See West Indies.

BAHRAIN continued to expand its ties abroad in 1972. This newly independent Arab sheikdom became the 126th member of the United Nations Educational, Scientific, and Cultural Organization and the 119th member of the World Bank. It also established diplomatic relations with France, Mongolia, Syria, and Japan.

Bahrain agreed to allow the United States Middle East Fleet to continue using its naval base facilities. Some other Arab states had complained that Bahrain was being used as a base for imperialism. Originally, the agreement was between the United States and Great Britain, then in control of Bahrain. The British later withdrew from the Persian Gulf.

In March, workers at Manama Airport and the Bahrain Aluminum Plant went on strike to protest the hiring of foreign workers. Demonstrations were put down by police, and a government decree prohibited strikes or public assemblies. In May, the government accepted workers' demands for limits on foreign workers and for improved fringe benefits.

In June, a 45-member Constituent Council was formed to write a constitution. The council will have 22 elected members and 23 that the sheik will appoint. A voter registration drive got underway in August in preparation for the December council elections. William Spencer

See also Middle East (Facts in Brief Table).

BALLET. See Dancing.

BALTIMORE. Rioting broke out on July 17, 1972, in the Maryland State Penitentiary in downtown Baltimore, when 75 inmates seized 4 hostages and set fires in the prison to protest living conditions. Three prison guards and one inmate were hospitalized for injuries suffered during the disturbance. The disorder ended after Maryland Governor Marvin Mandel and U.S. Representative Parren J. Mitchell (D., Md.) met with the rioters and promised there would be no reprisals against the prisoners. Prison guards then walked off their jobs briefly, contending that the governor's actions would lead to further trouble.

The first criminal conviction of a U.S. congressman in 15 years was handed down by a judge in Baltimore on February 23. Congressman John Dowdy (D., Tex.) was sentenced to 18 months imprisonment and fined $25,000. He was found guilty of receiving a $25,000 bribe to block a U.S. Department of Justice probe into a Maryland home-improvements firm.

A U.S. district court ruled on April 19 that a contract between a Baltimore A & P supermarket and the meat-cutters union violated the regulations of the federal Pay Board. It was the first suit brought by the Department of Justice to enforce the Pay Board's regulations. The disputed contract called for a 15 to 22 per cent pay increase. The Pay Board's ruling allowed only a 7 per cent increase.

Governor Mandel proposed to the state legislature on March 28 that a new multisports arena be built in the Baltimore area. The new facility would cost between $95 million and $194 million.

The Uniform Crime Reports released on August 29 showed that Baltimore's crime rate ranked seventh among the nation's major metropolitan areas. The area had a high rate of violent crimes, with 929.3 crimes per 100,000 persons.

A new method for early detection of lead poisoning was tested on more than 600 children between the ages of 1 and 5 in a Baltimore neighborhood during the summer. It can also uncover a form of anemia common to children in low-income areas.

In June, tropical storm Agnes caused extensive damage in Baltimore and killed three children, when the car in which they were riding was washed off a highway. Baltimore Mayor William Schaeffer asked the federal government to declare the city a disaster area. On June 23, the state of Maryland was declared eligible for disaster relief funds.

Median family income in Baltimore was $8,815 per year, one of the lowest figures reported for a major U.S. city. Despite this, employment in the city increased substantially, reaching 822,000 jobs by May. Average gross weekly earnings of production workers also increased by $10.51 between May, 1971, and May, 1972, to $162.41. J. M. Banovetz

BANGLADESH. When Sheik Mujibur Rahman returned to Dacca on Jan. 10, 1972, a million people shouted in joy, "Glory to the Father of the Nation." The newly created Bengal state was only a few weeks old, and Sheik Mujibur himself had just emerged from 9½ months in a West Pakistan prison. On that day, every miracle seemed possible.

The infant state needed miracles. The land – East Pakistan until Dec. 16, 1971 – lay ravaged by the West Pakistan troops and their hirelings. Some 9-million people who had fled to India were returning, often to homes that had been burned. Factories stood still; bridges were down; the port of Chittagong, through which food had to enter, lay wrecked.

International Aid. Within 52 hours of his arrival, Sheik Mujibur had given up the nation's presidency reserved for him, and taken over as prime minister. Almost as soon came recognition by foreign states, led by India and the Russian bloc. The United States, which sided with West Pakistan during the war, granted recognition in April. Foreign aid was prompt. Most was supplied by India, whose army withdrew in March, along with 91,000 captured West Pakistan troops. But, by November, U.S. assistance was running at $217 million, or roughly one-third of all aid.

The situation remained critical, however. Shortages persisted, and the prices of rice, kerosene, and

A tumultuous outpouring of humanity greeted Sheik Mujibur Rahman, center, holding picture, when he returned triumphantly to Dacca on January 10.

clothing doubled and trebled. Essential exports were hindered by disrupted transport, inefficiency, and smuggling of rice, fish, and jute into India. The nationalized industries ran below capacity.

Sheik Mujibur's ruling Awami (People's) League began to show signs of corruption and divided ideology, and purges did not seem to help. The powerful Student Union split into "Mujibists" and radical "Scientific Socialists." The problem of law and order became more acute as ex-guerrillas took over power in the provinces. A million Biharis, or non-Bengali Moslems, who fled to India in 1947 and later returned to become West Pakistan's tools, had a harrowing time in 1972; several thousand were killed. In October, the Home Ministry said that 41,000 persons had been arrested for collaboration with West Pakistan and "some" executed.

On November 4, the Constituent Assembly adopted a 153-article Constitution, to go into force on December 16, the first anniversary of the West Pakistan surrender. Elections were also set for March 7, 1973. In these, Mujibur could expect strong opposition. Though he was still popular, there were vigorous demands for his resignation after he returned from Europe in September. Radicals demanded more socialism, industry remained stagnant, and lawlessness continued. Mark Gayn

See also ASIA (Facts in Brief Table); RAHMAN, MUJIBUR.

BANKS AND BANKING. In a historic break with tradition, the Bank of England abolished its bank rate in October, 1972. For 270 years, the bank rate served as the peg for monetary and fiscal policy in Great Britain. It was replaced with a new "fluctuating last resort rate." The first official "minimum lending rate" was set at 7.25 per cent–up from the 6 per cent bank rate that had obtained since June 22. The change was part of a package of reforms directed at stimulating banking competition in Great Britain by breaking the tradition of tying interest rates to the bank rate. Banks were ordered to end interest rate-fixing agreements. Bank reserve requirements were substituted for direct controls on lending.

In another historic action, Great Britain allowed the pound sterling to float, effective June 23, from its central rate of $2.61 plus or minus 2.5 per cent. The central rate was established in the Smithsonian Agreement of December, 1971. Rapid monetary growth and inflation in Britain precipitated the sterling crisis. The rate subsequently fell to less than the August, 1971, dollar-devaluation level of $2.40.

Other major currency rates were maintained against the dollar by having foreign central banks buy or sell dollars. The effect was an average devaluation of about 9 per cent from the dollar parity rates that existed before its convertibility to gold was suspended. The devaluation of the dollar, along with reduced inflation in the United States, generated increased foreign demand for U.S. investments and goods. The dollar was no longer an overvalued currency relative to its parity, as it had been during the preceding decade.

Competition Among Banks and financial intermediaries remained intense in 1972. An increasing number of institutions provided 24-hour-a-day automatic banking service. Several banks in various U.S. cities introduced fully computerized payment schemes. Clerks feed sales information into computer terminals at the point of sale that are activated by magnetic credit cards. The data are transferred electronically to a bank computer, which credits the merchant's account instantaneously and processes the buyer's account for regular monthly billing. A group of California banks offered statewide computerized payments. They also planned to allow electronic transfers of payroll dollars to accounts of employees. The banks hoped to eliminate 15 million written checks each month. An electronic transfer costs about 5 cents compared with the 16 cents required to process a regular check.

Net bank credit topped $500 billion in 1972 for the first time. Compared with a decade earlier, commercial banks increased loans and investments in state and local government securities but decreased U.S. government securities. Time deposits passed demand deposits as the major source of funds.

Savings Institutions. Savings banks and savings and loan associations showed somewhat less growth in savings during the 10 years ending in mid-1972 than did commercial banks, but they grew substantially and remained the major source of housing credit. Savings institutions had a banner year in 1972. Savings flowed in at record rates–and flowed out to help finance record home building. Credit demands were met without much change in mortgage rates. To allow savings institutions to keep pace with commercial banks, regulatory authorities approved the limited use of savings accounts to make payments to third parties. Massachusetts became the first state to permit savings banks to issue credit cards as well as limited checking against savings deposits. The Federal Home Loan Bank Board dropped prohibitions against satellite offices and electronic tellers at federally chartered savings and loan associations.

Interest Rates, which had moderated in 1970 and 1971 from the century-high levels of the late 1960s, were somewhat higher in 1972. Rate increases were moderated by large Federal Reserve (Fed) security purchases and purchases by foreign governments that had acquired billions of dollars during the 1971 crisis. Official holders accumulated about $30-billion of U.S. securities in the 18 months ending in mid-1972, an increase of 150 per cent. European central bankers were critical of low interest rate policies in the United States; but Fed Chairman Arthur Burns retorted that European rates were simply too high.

In 1971 and the first half of 1972, the Fed bought securities at about an $8-billion annual rate, nearly twice the rate of 1969-1970. Bank reserves – which the Fed adopted as a new guide for day-to-day open-market operations – increased greatly, and so did the amount of bank credit and the money supply.

Canada Lowers Rates. The quickening pace of business-loan demands in Canada led chartered banks to increase the rates paid for deposits above the 6 per cent prime lending rate, which they were afraid to raise for political reasons. Banks were permitted to uniformly lower deposit rates. The higher rates had attracted unwanted U.S. dollars and kept the Canadian dollar and the price of Canadian goods high relative to the U.S. market.

The Inflation Threat. There was growing concern in financial markets that the inflation rate in the United States, which had been cut from 6 to 3 per cent since 1969, would accelerate again and bring about both tighter money and increased taxes. President Richard M. Nixon pledged that taxes would not go up unless Congress introduced inflationary spending. The President sought unprecedented authority to contain federal spending within a $250-billion maximum by curtailing certain items through executive decision. Congress denied him the authority in its final action before adjourning in October for the election campaign.

The Fed inaugurated a major restructuring of bank check collection and reserve requirement regulations in November. Member bank requirements were based solely on the size of the bank, with lower requirement ratios for smaller banks. The Fed took this step despite the recommendation of the Hunt Commission on Financial Structure and Regulation in 1971 that requirements be uniform for all banks. Higher requirements on large banks have the same effect as a tax, and operate to prevent savings in costs due to the scale of operations being passed on to the customers.

The changes reduced average requirements from about 8.5 to 7.5 per cent for member banks and freed about $4.5 billion in reserves for member banks to lend. Part was absorbed by Fed sales of securities to banks, and part by speeding up debiting accounts of banks on which checks are being collected.

New Supercrat. George P. Shultz replaced John B. Connally as secretary of the treasury in June, 1972 (see SHULTZ, GEORGE P.). After the election, Shultz was named to head a Cabinet Committee on Economic Policy in the reorganized Nixon Administration. Connally had played a key role in formulating President Nixon's New Economic Policy in August, 1971, and had tried to link general relation of trade barriers against U.S. goods with international monetary reform. Shultz received a warm reception at the International Monetary Fund (IMF) meetings in October when he proposed a new international payments system.

Shultz proposed that the dollar be treated the same as other currencies and not as the standard against which parities for other currencies are set. This was the arrangement from the end of World War II until Aug. 15, 1971. Shultz also proposed that gold and the IMF's issue of Special Drawing Rights Certificates, or paper gold, be the international standard. The proposal would retain the wider bands in exchange rates around parities that were adopted temporarily in the Smithsonian Agreement. The new bands allowed a deviation of plus or minus 2.25 per cent around the central rate, in comparison with a range of only 1 per cent previously. For the United States, there had been much less flexibility, because it was obligated to buy or sell gold at $35 an ounce. On May 8, the United States formally raised the gold price to $38 an ounce, but continued to ban sales of its remaining $10.5 billion of gold.

The most hopeful aspect of the U.S. reform proposal was in linking adjustments in exchange rate parities to chronic balance of payments disequilibrium. Nations with continuing surpluses would either have to appreciate their currency values relative to the international standard or face sanctions restricting trade. Overall, the proposal called for more flexibility in foreign exchange rates as a routine rather than a last resort measure. William G. Dewald

See also Section One, FOCUS ON THE ECONOMY.

BARBADOS. See WEST INDIES.

BARRETT, DAVID (1930-), a liberal former social worker, was elected premier of British Columbia in a dramatic upset on Aug. 30, 1972. The election ended the 20-year rule of the conservative Social Credit Party and Premier William A. C. Bennett, about 30 years Barrett's senior. Barrett's New Democratic Party (NDP) won 38 of the Legislative Assembly's 55 seats. He described the NDP as "in the [President Franklin D.] Roosevelt tradition." The NDP had previously held only 12 seats in the Assembly. See CANADA.

Barrett was born in Vancouver, B.C., and attended high school there. He graduated from Seattle University in 1953, and received a master's degree in social work from St. Louis University in 1956. From 1955 to 1957, he served as a St. Louis Juvenile Court probation officer. In 1957, he joined the staff of the Haney Correctional Institution in British Columbia. Later he became supervisor of counseling services for the province's John Howard Society, which seeks to improve prisons.

Barrett entered politics after losing his job as a corrections officer. He was fired by the provincial corrections department because of his political activism and because he criticized the department. In his first political campaign, he was elected to British Columbia's legislature in September, 1960.

Barrett and his wife have two sons and a daughter. They live in Port Coquitlam, B.C. Ed Nelson

BASEBALL. The Oakland A's combined 19 mustaches, 1 mule, 1 overpowering owner, and green and gold uniforms that would have done justice to a softball team to produce a victory in the 1972 World Series. They defeated the favored Cincinnati Reds in a tense seven-game series. The Reds beat the world champion Pittsburgh Pirates in five games in the National League play-offs, scoring the winning run in the decisive game on a wild pitch. The A's defeated the Detroit Tigers in five games to win the American League pennant.

The A's won the first two games of the World Series, lost the third, and won the fourth. Then the Reds won the fifth and sixth games. In the decisive seventh game, played October 22 in Cincinnati, the A's won 3-2. Then A's owner Charles O. Finley and manager Dick Williams stood on the dugout roof kissing their wives.

The World Series was unusual in many ways. Six of the seven games were decided by one run, a record. The combined batting performances (.207 for Oakland, .208 for Cincinnati) were the poorest ever. Some blamed the starting times of the first night games in World Series history. Those two games began at 5:15 P.M., Oakland time, so that they might be televised in prime evening time in the East, and the batters had difficulty seeing the ball in the twilight.

The A's hero was Fury Gene Tenace, a second-string catcher most of the season, who became a starter in the stretch drive. He hit only five home runs during the regular season. In the series, he hit four, equaling a record shared by Babe Ruth and Lou Gehrig, among others. He became the first man to hit home runs the first two times he went to bat, and those homers won the first game, 3-2. Tenace batted in 9 of the A's 16 runs, and his .913 slugging average set a series record. Among his rewards as the series' outstanding player was a new car. He welcomed it, saying, "The one I have isn't even paid for yet."

Tenace's season salary was $18,000, low by baseball standards. Finley gave $5,000 raises during the series to Tenace, Joe Rudi, and Mike Hegan, but Commissioner Bowie Kuhn ruled they were really bonuses and therefore illegal.

Finley, a self-made insurance millionaire from Chicago, was too flamboyant for many other club owners. In preparation for a Mustache Night promotion, he offered $300 to any player who grew a mustache (19 of the 25 did). He gave the team a mule as a mascot and named it Charlie O. after himself. He became his own general manager and called Dick Williams, his 10th manager in 12 years, "the first manager I've had." He raised Williams' salary three times during the year to $80,000.

Vida Blue. Finley got nowhere with one player, Vida Blue. In 1971, his first full season, the left-

Final Standings in Major League Baseball

American League	W.	L.	Pct.	GB.
Eastern Division				
Detroit	86	70	.551	
Boston	85	70	.548	½
Baltimore	80	74	.519	5
New York	79	76	.510	6½
Cleveland	72	84	.462	14
Milwaukee	65	91	.417	21
Western Division				
Oakland	93	62	.600	
Chicago	87	67	.565	5½
Minnesota	77	77	.500	15½
Kansas City	76	78	.494	16½
California	75	80	.484	18
Texas	54	100	.351	38½

Leading Batters

Batting Average—Rod Carew, Minnesota	.318
Home Runs—Dick Allen, Chicago	37
Runs Batted In—Dick Allen, Chicago	113
Hits—Joe Rudi, Oakland	181

Leading Pitchers

Games Won—Gaylord Perry, Cleve.; Wilbur Wood, Chicago	24
Win Average—Jim Hunter, Oakland (21-7)	.750
Earned-Run Average—Luis Tiant, Boston	1.91
Strikeouts—Nolan Ryan, California	329

Awards

Most Valuable Player—Dick Allen, Chicago
Cy Young—Gaylord Perry, Cleveland
Rookie of the Year—Carlton Fisk, Boston
Manager of the Year—Chuck Tanner, Chicago

National League	W.	L.	Pct.	GB.
Eastern Division				
Pittsburgh	96	59	.619	
Chicago	85	70	.548	11
New York	83	73	.532	13½
St. Louis	75	81	.481	21½
Montreal	70	86	.449	26½
Philadelphia	59	97	.378	37½
Western Division				
Cincinnati	95	59	.617	
Houston	84	69	.549	10½
Los Angeles	85	70	.548	10½
Atlanta	70	84	.455	25
San Francisco	69	86	.445	26½
San Diego	58	95	.379	36½

Leading Batters

Batting Average—Billy Williams, Chicago	.333
Home Runs—Johnny Bench, Cincinnati	40
Runs Batted In—Johnny Bench, Cincinnati	125
Hits—Pete Rose, Cincinnati	198

Leading Pitchers

Games Won—Steve Carlton, Philadelphia	27
Win Average—Gary Nolan, Cincinnati (15-5)	.750
Earned-Run Average—Steve Carlton, Philadelphia	1.98
Strikeouts—Steve Carlton, Philadelphia	310

Awards

Most Valuable Player—Johnny Bench, Cincinnati
Cy Young—Steve Carlton, Philadelphia
Rookie of the Year—Jon Matlack, New York
Manager of the Year—Sparky Anderson, Cincinnati

hander won 24 games and lost 8 and was voted the American League's Most Valuable Player and outstanding pitcher. His salary was $14,500. For 1972, he asked for $115,000. Finley offered $50,000. Blue came down. Finley stood pat. In April, wearing an open-necked sports shirt, blue slacks, and blue sneakers, the 22-year-old Blue announced his retirement from baseball to become vice-president of a company that manufactured bathroom fixtures. His salary as vice-president was $50,000 a year. On May 2, he left the company and signed with the A's for $50,000 plus $13,000 in assorted bonuses.

On May 28, he made his first start. On June 18, he gained his first victory, making his won-lost record 1-3 (on that date in 1971, it was 14-2). He finished the year at 6-10, angry at Finley and the world. "Everybody wanted a piece of the cake last year," said Blue, "but this year there's no cake."

The Play-Offs. Three of the four division races were unexciting. The A's won the American League West by 5½ games; the Reds, managed by Sparky Anderson, won the National League West by 10½; and the Pirates took the National League East by 11. But in the fourth race – the American League East – only a half-game separated the Tigers, Boston Red Sox, Baltimore Orioles, and New York Yankees on Labor Day. With only five days to go, the Orioles were eliminated, the victims of weak hitting and a lack of leadership. With four days to go, the Yankees were eliminated. With three days to go, the Red Sox led the Tigers by a half-game and went to Detroit to play the Tigers in the last three games. The Tigers won the first two and ended up taking the title by a half-game.

Fury Gene Tenace, who hit only five home runs in the regular season, hit a record-tying four in the World Series to lead Oakland to victory.

In normal years, half-games could not settle pennant races. But in 1972, things were hardly normal. Major league players, seeking improved pension and medical benefits, went on strike during the exhibition season. By the time the strike was settled, on April 13, 86 regular-season games had been missed. They were not made up, so different teams played different numbers of games. As it turned out, the Tigers played (and won) one more game than did the Red Sox.

The Flood Case. Baseball had mixed success in another off-the-field battle. The Supreme Court of the United States, ruling on Curt Flood's suit that challenged the reserve system, upheld baseball's exemption from antitrust laws and thus declared the reserve clause legal. The clause ties a player to one club indefinitely. However, the majority opinion called the antitrust exemption an "aberration" and an "anomaly," and it urged Congress to act. *Business Week* magazine called the decision "applesauce . . . baseball is a business in every sense of the word. It is part of the entertainment industry."

All-Stars. The Associated Press All-Star team consisted of pitchers Steve Carlton of Philadelphia and Gaylord Perry of Cleveland, Cincinnati catcher Johnny Bench, first baseman Dick Allen of the Chicago White Sox, Cincinnati second baseman Joe Morgan, shortstop Don Kessinger of the Chicago Cubs, third baseman Ron Santo of the Cubs, and outfielders Billy Williams of the Cubs, Roberto Clemente of Pittsburgh, and Cesar Cedeno of Houston. All were National Leaguers except Perry and Allen, who were traded from the National League to the American before the season began.

Bench led the major leagues in home runs (40) and runs batted in (125). Allen, playing for his fourth team in four years, led the American League in home runs (37) and runs batted in (113), and was third in batting (.308). In the National League, Williams was first in batting (.333), second in runs batted in (122), and third in home runs (37) and hits (191).

Carlton, pitching for a last-place club, posted a 27-10 record. The 6-foot 5-inch left-hander led the major leagues in complete games (30) and the National League in starts (41), innings pitched (346), strikeouts (310), and earned-run average (1.98).

Wilbur Wood of the White Sox and Perry led the American League with 24 victories each. Milt Pappas and Burt Hooton of the Cubs and Bill Stoneman of Montreal pitched no-hit, no-run games. In Pappas' performance, against San Diego, he was one strike away from a perfect game when he walked a pinch hitter on a 3-2 pitch.

Baseball's first player strike in April closed the lid early on spring training and delayed the regular season opening about 10 days.

Clemente became the 11th player in history and the third active player to reach 3,000 career hits. Henry Aaron of Atlanta and Willie Mays of the New York Mets are the others. The 38-year-old Aaron hit 34 home runs and ended the year with a career total of 673–41 short of Babe Ruth's hallowed record of 714. San Francisco traded 41-year-old Mays to the Mets, and Mays said it was "like coming back to paradise." He had been with the Giants in New York before they moved to San Francisco.

Leo Durocher was forced out as manager of the Cubs in July and a month later replaced Harry Walker at Houston. Ted Williams retired as manager of the Texas Rangers, the weakest team in the majors. Managers Preston Gomez of San Diego, Frank Lucchesi of the Phils, Bill Rigney of the Twins, and Luman Harris of Atlanta were fired during the year. After the season ended, California dropped Del Rice. Yogi Berra became manager of the Mets when Gil Hodges died during spring training, and Jackie Robinson, Hodges' Brooklyn Dodger teammate and the first black player in the major leagues, died in October. See DEATHS (Close-Up).

Hall of Fame. Berra, Sandy Koufax, and Early Wynn were voted into the National Baseball Hall of Fame. In addition, a veterans committee named Vernon (Lefty) Gomez, Ross Youngs, and Will Harridge, and a Negro Leagues committee named Josh Gibson and Buck Leonard. Frank Litsky

BASKETBALL. The attempted merger of the two major professional leagues and its resultant bonanza in player salaries overshadowed actual competition during and after the 1971-1972 season. The National Basketball Association (NBA) and the American Basketball Association (ABA) wanted to merge, but the players opposed merger, and Congress imposed such stiff terms that the two leagues were stymied.

Los Angeles produced two champion teams–the Lakers in the NBA and the University of California, Los Angeles (UCLA), among the collegians. En route to the NBA title, the Lakers won 33 consecutive games (the previous record was 20). UCLA, with 30 victories, was the only undefeated team among the 210 ranked as major by the National Collegiate Athletic Association (NCAA).

Merger Problems. The 17-team NBA and the 11-team (since reduced to 10) ABA agreed in 1971 to merge and thus end a bidding war for players. But Congress held up the merger at the behest of the NBA Players' Association.

In 1972, a Senate subcommittee headed by Sam J. Ervin (D., N.C.) held merger hearings. The subcommittee wrote a bill that would allow a merger, but included severe restrictions. There would be no option or reserve clause. A new player would be limited to a one-year contract plus a one-year option. The home team, which had always kept all the gate receipts, would have to share them on at least a 70-30 basis. ABA teams, which had agreed to pay an indemnity to join the NBA, would pay less money or no money if their business was bad. If there was no merger, the terms would not apply. The terms, especially the loss of the option clause, were too harsh for the rival leagues. However, the bill never reached the Senate floor.

Meanwhile, the war for talent went on. So did the lawsuits that tried to keep players from jumping leagues. The ultimate legal move was a $300-million antitrust suit filed on March 22 in which the ABA charged the NBA with conspiring to "monopolize and eliminate competition" in professional basketball.

The older league spirited away three ABA stars–Julius Erving and Charlie Scott of Virginia, and Jim McDaniels of Carolina–and a fourth, Rick Barry of the New York Nets, was ordered to honor a contract he had signed in 1969 with the Golden State Warriors of the NBA. All signed long-term contracts. Erving signed with Atlanta for $250,000 a year, Scott with Phoenix for $340,000, McDaniels with Seattle for $250,000, and Barry with Golden State (based in Oakland, Calif.) for $218,000. It meant a fine standard of living for such youths as Erving, 22, and Scott and McDaniels, both 23.

The Erving Case. Erving was unhappy at Virginia, where he felt that $125,000 a year for four years was not enough. "I was naïve when I turned pro," he said. Erving left college in 1970 to play in

Final Standings in Major League Basketball

National Basketball Association

Eastern Conference			
Atlantic Division	**W.**	**L.**	**Pct.**
Boston	56	26	.683
New York	48	34	.585
Philadelphia	30	52	.366
Buffalo	22	60	.268
Central Division			
Baltimore	38	44	.463
Atlanta	36	46	.439
Cincinnati	30	52	.366
Cleveland	23	59	.280
Western Conference			
Midwest Division			
Milwaukee	63	19	.768
Chicago	57	25	.695
Phoenix	49	33	.598
Detroit	26	56	.317
Pacific Division			
Los Angeles	69	13	.841
Golden State	51	31	.622
Seattle	47	35	.573
Houston	34	48	.415
Portland	18	64	.220

Leading Scorers	G.	FG.	FT.	Pts.	Avg.
Kareem Abdul-Jabbar, Milw.	81	1,159	504	2,822	34.8
Nate Archibald, Cincinnati	76	734	677	2,145	28.2
John Havlicek, Boston	82	897	458	2,252	27.5
Spencer Haywood, Seattle	73	717	480	1,914	26.2
Gail Goodrich, Los Angeles	82	826	475	2,127	25.9

American Basketball Association

Eastern Division	W.	L.	Pct.
Kentucky	68	16	.810
Virginia	45	39	.536
New York	44	40	.524
Floridians	36	48	.429
Carolina	35	49	.417
Pittsburgh	25	59	.298
Western Division			
Utah	60	24	.714
Indiana	47	37	.560
Dallas	42	42	.500
Denver	34	50	.405
Memphis	26	58	.310

Leading Scorers	G.	FG.	FT.	Pts.	Avg.
Charlie Scott, Virginia	73	956	525	2,524	34.5
Rick Berry, New York	80	829	641	2,518	31.4
Dan Issel, Kentucky	83	969	591	2,538	30.5
John Brisker, Pittsburgh	49	520	248	1,417	28.9
Ralph Simpson, Denver	84	917	457	2,300	27.3

College Champions

Conference	School
Atlantic Coast	North Carolina
Big Eight	Kansas State
Big Ten	Minnesota
Ivy League	Pennsylvania
Missouri Valley	Louisville-Memphis State (tie)
Ohio Valley	Eastern Kentucky-Morehead State-Western Kentucky (tie)
Pacific-8	UCLA
Southeastern	Kentucky-Tennessee (tie)
Southwest	Texas-Southern Methodist (tie)
Western Athletic	Brigham Young

Wilt Chamberlain, left, was named the most valuable player as the Los Angeles Lakers beat the New York Knicks for the NBA championship.

the ABA. On April 10, Milwaukee chose him on the first round of the NBA draft. Atlanta said it had signed him the night before as a free agent. Erving played two exhibition games for Atlanta.

NBA club owners voted that Erving belonged to Milwaukee, and Commissioner Walter Kennedy fined Atlanta $25,000 for each of the exhibition games in which Erving played. Atlanta and Erving thereupon sued the NBA for $2 million on antitrust charges, and Milwaukee sued Atlanta for $3 million. A federal court told Erving he could only play with Virginia until an arbitrator settled the case, and Erving returned reluctantly.

The Bidding War helped those who remained with their teams to get more money, too. Kareem Abdul-Jabbar of Milwaukee, the NBA's scoring champion and Most Valuable Player, signed for an estimated $500,000 a year; Wilt Chamberlain of Los Angeles for $350,000; Walt Frazier of the New York Knickerbockers for $340,000; Jerry West of Los Angeles for $300,000; and Elvin Hayes, traded from Houston to Baltimore, for $230,000.

Chamberlain and West helped the Lakers stay unbeaten for more than two months (Nov. 5, 1971, to Jan. 9, 1972). Los Angeles, Milwaukee, Boston, and Baltimore won the NBA division titles. Los Angeles, coached by Bill Sharman, beat the Knicks in five games in the play-off finals. Chamberlain was voted Most Valuable Player in the play-offs.

The Indiana Pacers won the ABA play-off finals from the New York Nets in six games. Kentucky and Utah were the division champions, and 7-foot 2-inch Artis Gilmore of Kentucky was voted both Player of the Year and Rookie of the Year.

College Scene. The Associated Press ranked UCLA first in the nation, North Carolina second, Pennsylvania third, Louisville fourth, Long Beach State fifth, South Carolina sixth, Marquette seventh, Southwestern Louisiana eighth, Brigham Young ninth, and Florida State tenth. United Press International agreed, except to reverse the ranking for Long Beach State and South Carolina.

UCLA won the national championship, beating Florida State, 81-76, in the final of the NCAA tournament. It was UCLA's sixth consecutive national title and the eighth in nine years, all under coach John Wooden.

In every poll, Wooden was voted Coach of the Year and 6-foot 11-inch Bill Walton, UCLA's sophomore center, Player of the Year. Walton, a defensive star, had tendonitis in both knees and had to heat them before games and ice them afterward. Dwight Lamar of Southwestern Louisiana was the leading scorer among major colleges, averaging 36.3 points per game. He was chosen for most all-America teams along with Walton and Henry Bibby of UCLA, Jim Chones of Marquette, and Ed Ratleff of Long Beach State. Frank Litsky

BELGIUM. An 11-month-old coalition government collapsed on Nov. 22, 1972, because of the problems dividing the Flemish- and French-speaking populations. It had been formed on January 14, ending a government crisis that had lasted since the Nov. 7, 1971, elections. Gaston Eyskens, who headed the previous coalition, formed the new Cabinet after 10 weeks of intensive consultations and was sworn in January 21 for a fourth term as prime minister. That crisis and the one later in the year arose over cultural autonomy for two linguistic groups, Dutch-speaking Flemings and French-speaking Walloons, and efforts to move toward regionalism and eventually federalism.

The new government soon was in trouble with farmers and with women. On January 25, angry farmers led a young bull into the Parliament lobby to call attention to their demand for higher farm prices. In Parliament, women deputies walked out briefly because there was no woman minister in the 19-member government.

Budget Deficit. A deficit 1972 budget was announced in February to get the economy moving faster. But with both prices and unemployment rising, the economy continued to lag. Belgians expected the 1973 enlargement of the European Community (Common Market) to increase exports of the Belgium-Luxembourg Economic Union. The competitive position of many exports was strengthened when a temporary exports tax was abolished early in 1972. It amounted to 0.8 per cent of global annual exports. Export totals were disappointing, and tax receipts fell after a value-added tax was introduced.

In talks in London on May 2, Eyskens and Foreign Minister Pierre Harmel successfully pressed their claim that Brussels should continue as "capital" of the European Community. France wanted the headquarters moved to Paris. On July 10, Russian Foreign Minister Andrei Gromyko visited Brussels to discuss the proposed conference on European security. On December 27, Belgium became the first North Atlantic Treaty Organization member to grant full diplomatic recognition to East Germany.

Fishing Agreement. Belgium and Iceland reached an agreement in September that allowed Belgian fishing trawlers to work at certain times in waters within 50 miles of Iceland. Effective September 1, Iceland unilaterally extended its territorial fishing limit. Belgian trawlers defied the new limit.

Netting of wild birds was banned in Belgium beginning August 1 following protests from organizations in Great Britain, the Netherlands, Switzerland, and West Germany. An estimated 20 million songbirds had been lured into nets each year, and Minister of Agriculture Leo Tindemans said Belgium had been ignoring conventions for the protection of birds that it had signed. Kenneth Brown

See also EUROPE (Facts in Brief Table).

BHUTTO, ZULFIKAR ALI (1928-), was sworn in as president of Pakistan on Dec. 20, 1971. He replaced Agha Mohammed Yahya Khan, who was forced to resign after Pakistan's defeat in its war with India. Within weeks, Bhutto took several bold steps to strengthen his power. See PAKISTAN.

Bhutto was born into an aristocratic family on Jan. 5, 1928, in Larkana, Pakistan. He received a bachelor's degree with honors in political science from the University of California, Berkeley, in 1950, and a master's degree with honors in law from the University of Oxford, England, in 1952. In 1953, he returned to Pakistan, where he practiced law and taught constitutional law.

Bhutto served as a delegate to the United Nations General Assembly in 1957. President Ayub Khan named him minister for commerce in 1958. By 1963, after holding several important government posts, Bhutto had become foreign minister. Later, through his Pakistan People's Party, Bhutto led a popular movement against the president. He was arrested in 1968, and spent three months in jail.

In 1970, Bhutto's party won most of the West Pakistan seats in a new National Assembly. Thus, he established himself as the elected political leader of West Pakistan. When war with India began in 1971, Bhutto's growing power and great popularity forced President Yahya Khan to appoint him deputy prime minister and foreign minister. Michael Reed

BIOCHEMISTRY. Two important developments in 1972 highlighted research in biochemistry. In England, scientists clarified the nature of vitamin D and its activity in the body. In the United States, a research team succeeded in making a model of a cell structure that is so small it has never been seen clearly.

Vitamin D is associated with rickets, a disease characterized by faulty bone formation because of abnormalities in calcium and phosphorus absorption. Scientists have long known that exposure to sunlight helps children with rickets. Physicians believed that they had learned why when scientists discovered that a compound formed by ultraviolet irradiation of a substance called ergosterol cured rickets. However, ergosterol is found in plants and not in human beings. So they began to search for another form of vitamin D. They found a derivative of cholesterol that has a four-ringed structure in which one of the rings contains a system of double bonds. This form of vitamin D, too, was effective against rickets.

In 1969, scientists found that another cholesterol derivative discovered in the human body was even more active in combating rickets. The body produces this substance from the original derivative.

However, new work reported in 1971 indicates that the picture is even more complicated. Experimenters D. E. M. Lawson, D. R. Fraser, E. Kodicek, R. H. Morris, and Dudley H. Williams of the University of Cambridge in England discovered that the second derivative is converted in the liver into a third compound. In addition, this compound is carried by the blood to the kidneys, where it is transformed into a fourth, more active, form called 1,25-dihydroxycholecalciferol. This substance then acts on the intestines and bones, which are involved in calcium metabolism.

The new research has also revealed several previously unknown details about the metabolism, distribution, and use of vitamin D and its derivatives. This new information makes it apparent that the vitamin actually functions more as a hormone than as a vitamin.

Ribosome Model. In all living cells, the synthesis of proteins, such as enzymes and protein hormones, occurs in tiny structures called ribosomes. In September, 1971, biologists Yoshiaki Nonomura, Günter Blobel, and David D. Sabatini of Rockefeller University in New York City proposed a model for the three-dimensional shape of a ribosome. Their work may generate new laboratory activity throughout the world as other scientists attempt to check the validity of the model and relate ribosome form to its function.

In nucleus-containing cells from mammals, including human beings, most of the ribosomes are in the cytoplasm, or extranuclear material. They are usually attached to the many folds of a structure called the endoplasmic reticulum, although many are found within other structures including the cell nucleus. Frequently, they are strung together in bead-like fashion to form what are called polyribosomes or polysomes.

When protein is being synthesized, a ribosome receives a molecule called messenger RNA, which was constructed in the cell nucleus according to the directions of a gene. The messenger RNA is absorbed by the ribosome and dictates the order in which amino acids, the building blocks of proteins, are joined. Thus, genes indirectly dictate the structure of a living organism's proteins.

Although scientists understand these biochemical events, they do not know how the structure and composition of ribosomes relate to their function. Ribosomes from all types of cells appear to be essentially similar in structure. They consist of two subunits of unequal size. But they are so small that scientists cannot see them in detail, even through the most powerful microscopes. How, then, could their physical structure be determined?

The Rockefeller University biologists used an electron microscope to make an extensive study of the structure of rat liver ribosomes and their subunits. They treated the polysomes from rat liver with the antibiotic puromycin, which causes polysomes to break down into their individual ribosomal units. Then, after using a technique called negative contrast staining, they examined the units under the electron microscope. In the staining process, the released ribosomes are mixed with the substance uranyl acetate and dried. Because uranyl acetate is neither adsorbed nor bound by the ribosome, and is not penetrated by electrons, it surrounds the ribosome and outlines its structure. The ribosome can then be viewed through the microscope, which uses electrons in forming the images that it produces.

Even under these conditions, the tiny ribosomes were not clearly defined. But, by carefully examining many ribosomes in this way, the scientists were able to construct a three-dimensional Plasticine ribosome model that could account for the differences noted among the ribosomes they studied and in the same ribosome when viewed at several different 60° angles.

The smaller subunit of the rat liver ribosome appears to be an elongated, slightly bent, and roughly spherical body with an indentation across its width that divides it into two regions of unequal size. The larger subunit is roughly a partly flattened sphere. The smaller subunit sits on the flattened surface of the larger subunit and close to the edge. The scientists suggested that the messenger RNA is attached to the ribosome during protein synthesis either through the indentation in the smaller subunit or through a small channel that runs between the two subunits.

Earl A. Evans, Jr.

BIOLOGY. Research efforts involving muscles were among the major developments in biology in 1972. One group of scientists developed a new experimental system that should allow more detailed and accurate studies of nerve-muscle junctions. Other investigators reported experiments showing what makes muscles contract and that the major substances involved also probably cause movement in many other kinds of cells and tissues.

Muscle-Nerve Relationships. Any normal, intact skeletal muscle in humans and other mammals contracts when it receives a stimulus from the appropriate nerve. A chemical substance called acetylcholine probably helps to transmit the stimulus to the muscle cell at the junction of the nerve and muscle cells. The muscle cell is highly sensitive to acetylcholine at the point where the two cells meet. If the nerve is cut, this high sensitivity disappears and the entire muscle membrane becomes somewhat sensitive to acetylcholine. If the muscle cell is reconnected to the nerve, a high-sensitivity area occurs again, and the general sensitivity is lost.

In June, 1971, biologists Alan J. Harris, Steve Heinemann, David Schubert, and Helgi Terakis of The Salk Institute for Biological Studies in La Jolla, Calif., reported on a study of the effect of contact between a nerve cell and a muscle cell. Most impressive was the experimental technique that these scientists developed. Although the cells were grown and studied outside any living organism, they behaved normally, making them ideal for study.

Harris and his colleagues grew rat muscle and nerve cells in the laboratory and then put them together. Using minute microelectrodes inserted into the muscle cells, the investigators recorded changes in muscle-cell membrane electrical potential as acetylcholine was applied to various sites. They found that the membrane of muscle cells in which the nerve was cut were uniformly slightly sensitive to acetylcholine. But when a nerve cell made contact with a muscle cell, high sensitivity to acetylcholine developed at the site of contact.

Muscle Contraction. Scientists believe that three species of interacting molecules play a part in muscle contraction. They are adenosine triphosphate (ATP) – which is continuously formed as the body metabolizes sugar, fat, and protein – and two so-called contractile proteins, actin and myosin. Evidence for the sequence of events that takes place in muscle contraction was uncovered in experiments reported by biophysicists Richard W. Lymn and Edwin W. Taylor of the University of Chicago in 1971.

In the muscle cell, actin and myosin filaments fold into one another like the fingers of two hands, and ATP is attached to the actin molecules. When a nerve signals a muscle to contract, calcium ions

The baby mice, left, developed from embryos that were frozen, then thawed and transferred to the uterus of a foster mother, right.

stored in the muscle cell apparently are released. The calcium triggers projections from the myosin molecules to attach and detach from the adjoining actin filaments in such a way that transient chemical bridges are formed between them. In the process, the actin filament is pulled into the myosin filament, shortening the muscle. In this state, however, myosin molecules convert ATP into adenosine diphosphate and energy. The energy is used to restore calcium to the muscle cells, and the muscle returns to its original, relaxed state.

Other studies found either actin, myosin, or both, or substances similar to them in cells, tissues, and organelles (specialized parts of cells) that move. Biologist Nadyd Gawadi, of the University of Cambridge, found actin in certain filaments that move chromosomes in dividing locus testis cells. Biologists O. Behnke of the University of Copenhagen and A. Forer and J. Emmersen of the University of Odense in Denmark, found actin or an actinlike protein in the same structures in crane fly spermatids and in crane fly spermatid tails.

Robert S. Adelstein, Thomas D. Pollard, and Walter M. Kuehl, researchers at the National Institutes of Health in Bethesda, Md., isolated actinlike and myosinlike proteins from thrombosthenin. Thrombosthenin is a group of contractile proteins found in human blood platelets. Earl A. Evans, Jr.

BLINDNESS. See HANDICAPPED.

BOATS AND BOATING. Pleasure boating continued its uninterrupted prosperity in 1972. More people spent more money on boats, boating equipment, and their upkeep than ever before.

Industry sources estimated that 46 million people participated in recreational boating during the year, using 9.2 million boats. About 5.4 million of these were outboard motorboats. These boats used 7.4 million motors, 585,000 of them purchased in 1972. Boatmen spent an estimated $3.9 billion for new and used boats, motors, equipment, fuel, insurance, maintenance costs, and club memberships.

Offshore Competition. Bobby Rautbord of Miami Beach, Fla., won the world offshore championship in a series of 22 races in 13 nations. Four of these were held in the United States. Rautbord won five races, and Carlo Bonomi of Italy, the European champion, won four.

Rautbord and Bonomi drove 36-foot Cigarette hulls manufactured by Don Aronow of Miami. Bob Magoon of Miami Beach and Sanford (Sandy) Satullo of Fairview, Ohio, who dominated the U.S. offshore championship series, also used Cigarette hulls. Magoon, an eye surgeon, retained the title. Satullo won his first four races.

Unlimited Hydroplanes, the world's fastest and noisiest racing boats, are 2-ton monsters powered by airplane engines that generate up to 4,000 horsepower and sometimes reach 200 miles per hour (mph) on straightaways. *Atlas Van Lines*, owned by Lee Schoenith of Detroit and driven by Bill Muncey, won 6 of the 7 championship races in 1972.

In qualifying for the Gold Cup race in Detroit in June, Muncey broke the world record by averaging 120.948 mph for the three qualifying laps. Muncey also won the race. The American Power Boat Association rejected the record on a technicality, but it was academic. Six weeks later, in qualifying for the Seattle Seafair Trophy race, Bill Sterrett, Jr., driving *Pride of Pay 'N Pak*, averaged 125.581 mph. Again, Muncey won.

In Yachting, the world's most prestigious yacht race, a 635-mile run from Newport, R.I., to Bermuda, attracted 178 yachts worth $15 million. They were worth somewhat less at the finish because so many of them had been battered by 50-knot, gale-force winds and tides that reached 14 feet.

Windward Passage, a 73-foot ketch, led most of the way until five sails were blown out. The overall winner was *Noryema*, a new 48-foot fiberglass sloop owned by Ron Amey of England and sailed by Ted Hicks. The trip took nearly four days.

Immediately after the race, 48 yachts sailed the 2,700 miles from Bermuda to Spain. *Noryema* won Class C honors. The overall winner, in a little over 16 days, was *Carina*, a 48-foot sloop owned by Richard B. Nye of New York City. Frank Litsky

Alain Colas of France, in a 67-foot trimaran, *Pen Duick IV*, won the 2,810-mile race from Plymouth, England, to the New England coast.

BOLIVIA seemed more stable, politically and economically, in 1972 than at any other time in recent years. Under President Hugo Banzer Suarez, the government was fully supported by both the Bolivian Socialist Falange and the rival Nationalist Revolutionary Movement and, most important, by the armed forces. The all-important tin prices were up, as was agricultural production. Gas exports and foreign loans flowed in at a satisfactory rate.

There were some exceptions. Despite a national illiteracy rate of about 65 per cent, the country's universities, which had been shut down during Banzer's successful coup in August, 1971, remained closed. A subsequent law had ended the schools' autonomous status and placed them directly under the presidency to remove them from politics. Banzer, however, reportedly delayed their reopening to prevent the students from organizing against him.

In March, the government launched a drive against left wing extremists. Among other moves, it ordered 119 employees of the Russian Embassy to leave the country after accusing them of espionage and dealing with subversive elements. In mid-March, the government also announced a "war to the death" against extremists, including members of the guerrilla-type National Liberation Army. A state of siege was proclaimed in November.

The Economy. The government, despite these diversions, maintained its stability and continued its efforts to achieve a 6 to 8 per cent growth rate. The Central Bank's gold and foreign exchange assets at midyear stood at $53.4 million, up from $39 million a year earlier. The U.S. Agency for International Development authorized three loans totaling $30-million for public works, private industrial development, and rural communities, while the Inter-American Development Bank lent $46.3 million for housing, a highway, an airport, industrial growth, and telecommunications.

The nation's most important highway was opened in mid-September, extending 125 miles from Cochabamba to Villarroel port on the Ichilo River–which eventually connects with the Amazon River. It goes through previously inaccessible wet areas of tropical Bolivia. The United States provided the $51 million required to build the road, which is expected to speed the industrial and commercial development of some 80,000 square miles–almost one-fifth of the country. It will be the first such connection between western Bolivia and the rich but isolated department of Beni, which borders Brazil.

On April 29, Bolivia began exporting natural gas to Argentina through its $56,250,000, 330-mile, 24-inch Santa Cruz-Yacuiba pipeline. This development made Bolivia South America's first gas-exporting country. Mary Webster Soper

See also LATIN AMERICA (Facts in Brief Table).

BOOKS. See CANADIAN LITERATURE; LITERATURE; LITERATURE FOR CHILDREN; POETRY.

BOSTON public schools were plagued with charges of segregation throughout 1972. In January, the U.S. Department of Health, Education, and Welfare (HEW) gave the Boston school committee until February 9 to draw up a school desegregation plan. The committee failed to act, so HEW cut off $10 million in annual federal aid to Boston's schools in June. In addition, the National Association for the Advancement of Colored People filed suit in March to obtain desegregation orders that would involve suburban as well as city schools.

Meanwhile, the Boston school system sued the Massachusetts state department of education for state aid being withheld because Boston failed to comply with Massachusetts' racial imbalance act. On September 6, the state of Massachusetts released $6.6 million in federal funds to the Boston public school system.

Communications. On January 21, the Federal Communications Commission (FCC) transferred the operating license for television station WHDH-TV from the Herald Traveler Corporation to Boston Broadcasters, Incorporated. The FCC claimed that the Herald Traveler Corporation owned too many communications media in the Boston area. Profits from the television station had enabled the corporation to cover the operating losses of its newspaper, the *Boston Herald Traveler.*

After 125 years of publication, the *Herald Traveler* printed its final edition on June 18. The paper was sold to the Hearst Corporation, publishers of the rival *Boston Record American,* on May 17 for $8.6 million. The closing of the *Herald Traveler* left the city with only two daily newspapers. There had been nine in 1940.

Boston Motorists reaped unexpected benefits from Massachusetts' no-fault auto insurance law in 1972. Rates had been reduced by 15 per cent for 1971 and an additional 27.6 per cent for 1972. Then, on June 5, the state Supreme Court ruled that the rates should have been cut an additional 27.6 per cent for 1971 as well, and ordered that amount deducted from 1972 premiums.

Governor Francis W. Sargent halted construction of new expressways around Boston until the area's total transportation needs can be determined. He urged that more emphasis be placed on mass-transit programs.

On January 6, longshoremen in Boston and other Eastern ports ended a 58-day strike with a tentative settlement calling for a 15 per cent increase the first year. However, the Pay Board trimmed the first-year raises to range from 9.8 per cent to 12.1 per cent.

The cost of living in the Boston area rose 3.7 per cent between April, 1971, and April, 1972. Average gross weekly earnings for production workers went up 8.7 per cent between May, 1971, and May, 1972. However, unemployment increased by 2,100 persons during the same period. J. M. Banovetz

BOTANY. A technique for developing hybrid plants was announced in June, 1972, by Peter S. Carlson, Harold H. Smith, and Rosemarie D. Dearing of Brookhaven National Laboratory in Upton, N.Y. The technique may someday be used to produce plants that have both potatoes and tomatoes on the same stalk, and other unusual varieties.

The scientists, in this case, fused two different species of tobacco that naturally form hybrids. They did not choose two species that have never been hybridized because they wanted to be able to compare their produced hybrid with the naturally occurring one. Protoplasts, cells with the cell wall removed, were isolated from leaf cells, grown separately, and then stimulated to fuse. The hybridized cells were then selected from the mixed population of parent and fused cells by using a growth medium that would support only the hybrids. They were induced to regenerate into new plants that proved to be identical to naturally occurring hybrids.

Plant Defense. Potato tubers contain certain proteins that inhibit the digestive enzymes of insects that feed on the plant leaves, according to Terry R. Green and Clarence A. Ryan of Washington State University. They reported in February that they had discovered this inhibitor substance in the tuber leaves in highly variable concentrations. By inflicting controlled damage to the leaves, they were able to manipulate the concentration of this inhibitor. When a leaf was damaged, the enzyme inhibitor accumulated rapidly in both damaged and undamaged leaves of the plant. Because digestibility of food is an important consideration in the selection of food by leaf-eating insects, the researchers conclude that the enzyme inhibitor is probably a type of defense mechanism.

Moving Chloroplasts. The filamentous algae, *Mougeotia*, are composed of single plate-shaped chloroplasts. These orient themselves to light in one of two ways depending on the light conditions. In blue light or white light of high intensity, the edges of the chloroplasts face the light. In red or white light of low intensity, the flat sides face the light. In 1972, botanists Gottfried Wagner, Anneliese Laux, and Wolfgang Haupt of the University of Nuremberg, West Germany, discovered that protein fibrils in the cells caused this movement. They used cytochalasin, an inhibitor of protein fibrils, to test this theory. Algae cells were irradiated with light so that all chloroplasts oriented themselves in profile. Cytochalasin was then added to the water in which the algae lived, and 15 minutes later the algae were put in red light and the number of chloroplasts that turned their flat side to the light was recorded. There was almost no change in orientation when the concentration of cytochalasin was high. This indicates that the protein fibrils must cause the chloroplast movement in *Mougeotia* cells. Barbara N. Benson

BOTSWANA. See AFRICA.

BOWLING. Don Johnson of Akron, Ohio, and Nelson Burton, Jr., of St. Louis – for many years leaders on the professional bowling tour – were big winners in 1972. Surprisingly, so were Mike Durbin of Chagrin Falls, Ohio; Bill Beach of Sharon, Pa.; Anthony (Teata) Semiz of River Edge, N.J.; and Paul Colwell of Tucson, Ariz. – all part-timers on the tour.

The Professional Bowlers Association (PBA) conducted 35 tournaments with a gross value of over $2-million. In all, 13 were held in the winter and 22 in the summer and fall.

Johnson, the bowler of the year in 1971, started 1972 by winning the $100,000 U.S. Open (the successor to the All-Star Tournament) in January in New York City. For three hours before the finals, he kept his fingers in a raw potato to heal blisters. In November, he won the $85,000 Brunswick World Open in Chicago, and he led in annual earnings with $56,648. Burton, who won the Miller Tournament in Milwaukee, among others, was second with $55,930.

Durbin, who had left the tour to become a resident professional in his hometown, returned in the $125,000 Tournament of Champions in late March in Akron. On the first day, he averaged 250 for 16 games, a world record, and he won the tournament and its top prize of $25,000, bowling's highest. Then, at home, on the last night of a league season, he rolled 248, 300, and 300. He set a world-record average of 238-31 for the season's 102 league games.

When Beach won the American Bowling Congress (ABC) Masters tournament in April in Long Beach, Calif., he was happy he had closed his barbershop to bowl in the tournaments. "My wife and I felt it was worth the gamble," he said. In the ABC classic division for professionals, Semiz triumphed in singles (754 for three games) and all-events (1,994 for nine games). When he is not on the tour, Semiz works as a pipe coverer in a New York skyscraper. Colwell, an Air Force sergeant, saved up enough leave time to enter seven PBA tournaments. He won two and took prize money in three others, earning $16,100.

It was a frustrating year for Ray Orf, a 30-year-old professional. Bowling with his 7-year-old son in a mixed league on February 6 in his native St. Louis, Orf started with a spare and then rolled 35 consecutive strikes. His games of 290, 300, and 300 gave him a three-game total of 890, an all-time competitive record. But ABC refused to recognize the score, saying that the lanes accidentally had received too much dressing. Orf then sought redress in court.

Women's Competition. Lorrie Koch of Carpentersville, Ill., an office clerk, became the first amateur to win the U.S. Open, then turned pro. Millie Martorella of Rochester, N.Y., took the Women's International Bowling Congress (WIBC) all-events title. Dottie Fothergill of North Attleboro, Mass., won the WIBC Queens tournament and lost the women's professional championship by three pins to Patty Costello of New Carrollton, Md. Frank Litsky

BOXING. Heavyweight champion Joe Frazier of Philadelphia and Muhammad Ali of Cherry Hill, N.J., his predecessor and major antagonist, were boxing's dominant figures in 1972, Ali for fighting almost everyone and Frazier for fighting almost no one.

In 1971, Frazier outpointed Ali in a $20-million production in New York's Madison Square Garden. That fight paid each fighter $2.5 million, by far the largest purses in history. Negotiations continued through 1972 for a rematch, with each man demanding $3.5 million.

Frazier's Foes. Frazier defended his title twice against unranked foes distinguished more for their courage than for their ability to fight. On January 15 in New Orleans, on the eve of the Super Bowl football game, Frazier beat Terry Daniels of Dallas in four rounds. He knocked the former Southern Methodist University football player down four times. One observer called the fight "routine slaughter." On May 25 in Omaha, the ringside physician stopped Frazier's fight with Ron Stander of Council Bluffs, Iowa, after the fourth round.

Ali chastised Frazier for fighting such obscure opponents. "I kept the game alive this year," said Ali, and he had a point. From April 1 to November 21, he fought in Tokyo, Vancouver, Las Vegas, Dublin, New York City, and Lake Tahoe. In succession, he outpointed Mac Foster of Fresno, Calif., in 15 rounds and George Chuvalo of Toronto in 12; stopped Jerry Quarry of Bellflower, Calif., in 7; Alvin (Blue) Lewis of Detroit in 11; Floyd Patterson of New Paltz, N.Y., in 7; Bob Foster of Albuquerque, N. Mex., in 8. Not incidentally, Ali took home purses of $250,000, $200,000, $500,000, $250,000, $200,000, and $250,000.

Other Champions. At year's end, Bob Foster of Albuquerque, N. Mex., and Frazier were the only world champions from the United States. Foster knocked out Vicente Rondon of Venezuela; Mike Quarry of Arcadia, Calif.; and Chris Finnegan of England in light-heavyweight title bouts during the year. He has defended the title 11 times.

Carlos Monzon of Argentina, the world middleweight champion, knocked out three challengers—Denny Moyer of Portland, Ore., in 5 rounds; Jean-Claude Bouttier of France in 12; and Tom Bogs of Denmark in 5. Monzon, 30, has not lost in eight years.

Four from Panama won world titles. They were Alfonso Frazer (junior-welterweight), Roberto Durañ (lightweight), Ernesto Marcel (featherweight), and Enrique Pinder (bantamweight).

The World Boxing Association and the World Boxing Council, two governing bodies in steady conflict, recognized different champions in 5 of the 11 weight divisions. There was slight movement to merge the two organizations.

Frank Litsky

World Champion Boxers

Division	Champion	Country	Year Won
Heavyweight	Joe Frazier	U.S.A.	1968
Light-heavyweight	Bob Foster	U.S.A.	1968
Middleweight	Carlos Monzon	Argentina	1970
Junior-middleweight	Koichi Wajima	Japan	1971
Welterweight	Jose Napoles	Mexico	1971
Junior-welterweight	Bruno Arcari	Italy	1970
(disputed)	Alfonso Frazer	Panama	1972
Lightweight	Roberto Duran	Panama	1972
(disputed)	Rodolfo Gonzalez	U.S.A.	1972
Junior-lightweight	Ricardo Arredondo	Mexico	1971
(disputed)	Ben Villaflor	Philippines	1972
Featherweight	Ernesto Marcel	Panama	1972
(disputed)	Jose Legra	Spain	1972
Bantamweight	Enrique Pinder	Panama	1972
Flyweight	Masao Oba	Japan	1970
(disputed)	Venice Borkorsor	Thailand	1972

BOY SCOUTS. See Youth Organizations.

BOYS' CLUBS. See Youth Organizations.

BRAZIL. Festivities marking the 150th anniversary of Brazilian independence from Portugal were held in São Paulo on Sept. 7, 1972. The high point of the ceremonies, presided over by President Emílio Garrastazú Médici and Prime Minister Marcello Caetano of Portugal, was the return of the remains of Emperor Pedro I from Portugal to the Independence Monument in São Paulo. The emperor had rejected Portugese rule and declared Brazil a nation in 1822.

The independence celebrations included the biggest military parade in Brazilian history. They were the direct outgrowth of a concerted effort by the nation's military leaders to emphasize the strides that Brazil had made since they took control in 1964. Under their leadership, the country was well established on a course of sustained and powerful economic expansion. Massive investments have been made in industry, mining, petroleum, electricity, transportation, and agriculture, while trade continues to climb and inflation has been controlled. The gross national product grew in 1972 to an estimated $45-billion, about $1 billion higher than in 1971. The inflation rate was around 15 per cent, and the foreign debt approached $7 billion. Gross foreign reserves climbed to an estimated record $3 billion, up from $1.7 billion at the start of the year. Exports were expected to reach $4 billion, of which some $1 billion was in manufactured goods. In the first six months, exports climbed almost 33 per cent, imports 21.8 per cent, agricultural production 11 per cent, and industrial output 13.5 per cent, and the balance of payments surplus was a hefty $801 million, compared with $550 million for all of 1971.

But the country's "economic miracle" had its price: More than 8 per cent of employable Brazilians over the age of 15 were out of work early in the year, while wages, for the most part, were pitifully low. Industrial mechanization meant that less manpower was needed in the higher-paying sectors. There were other drawbacks inherent in the military's control. Civil liberties and the right to dissent had all but vanished. Because of the ruling generals' decisions, Brazil postponed state elections scheduled for 1974, and the regime maintained not only its curbs on the basic freedoms, but also its special powers to purge politicians and hold suspected subversives indefinitely without trial. Censorship was tightened.

Economic Moves. To spur the economy, Brazil created Latin America's largest private bank by approving the merger of two institutions into a giant partnership called the Brazilian Bank Union with resources of $1.6 billion. The republic also sent trade missions to Africa, Europe, and the People's Republic of China. Over 1,000 businessmen from other countries attended the "Brasil Export '72" trade fair in São Paulo in September.

Agricultural Gains. Brazil challenged Cuba's sugar-export position in 1972 with shipments expected to total $450 million, up from $150 million in 1971. Big new sugar customers were Russia and China. The republic launched a three-year campaign to plant 600 million coffee trees. Throughout the year, Brazil maneuvered with other major coffee producers to obtain higher prices for the bean.

On August 5, the regime introduced agrarian reform by authorizing the expropriation of land for redistribution in Pernambuco, Paraíba, and Ceará states. All three are located in the poverty-stricken northeast area where nearly 30 per cent of the rural population is either unemployed or underemployed.

Major Engineering Project. The first major stretch of a new road, an 800-mile link of the Trans-Amazon Highway, was officially opened on September 30. The project is on schedule, and the entire 3,400-mile stretch from Recife on the Atlantic Ocean to the Peruvian and Bolivian borders was expected to be finished in 1973.

A massive engineering program, it would thrust into areas laden with minerals, petroleum, timber, and other untapped resources. Included among the latter was an estimated 11 billion tons of iron ore found near Marabá, Pará. It is perhaps the world's biggest deposit. The highway, when completed, will be part of a giant 9,000-mile network of roads that will crisscross the Amazon Basin and link the republic with its 10 neighbors. Mary Webster Soper

See also Latin America (Facts in Brief Table).

BRIDGE. See Building and Construction.

BRIDGE, CONTRACT. Italy's celebrated Blue Team, which had won 12 previous world championships, emerged from a two-year retirement to win the Fourth World Bridge Team Olympiad at Miami Beach in June. Italy defeated the defending world champion Aces who are based in Dallas, Texas, by 65 points.

By winning the Harold A. Vanderbilt knockout team championship, March 27, at the American Contract Bridge League (A.C.B.L.) spring national tournament in Cincinnati, the Precision Team staked a claim as one of the foremost teams in U.S. bridge history. The victory gave the Precision Team three national team titles – two Spingold Cups and a Vanderbilt Trophy – in four attempts. Precision Team members were Steve Altman, Gene Neiger, Alan Sontag, Joel Stuart, and Peter Weichsel, all of New York City, and Tom Smith of Greenwich, Conn. The Precision Team's bid for a third consecutive Spingold Cup title failed at the A.C.B.L. summer tournament at Denver in August. The cup went to a team composed of B. Jay Becker, his son Michael Becker, Jeff Rubens, and Andy Bernstein, all of New York City. Never before had a father and son played on a Spingold winner. Theodore M. O'Leary

BRITISH COLUMBIA. See Canada.

BRITISH COMMONWEALTH OF NATIONS. See Great Britain and articles on various countries of the Commonwealth.

BUILDING AND CONSTRUCTION expenditures reached an estimated new high of $122 billion in 1972, 12 per cent over the 1971 figure of $107 billion. The U.S. Bureau of the Census attributed some of the increase to inflation, but more of it to the high rate of residential construction. Over 2.3 million conventional housing units and some 600,000 mobile homes were built in 1972. As a result of the Nixon Administration's Phase 2 price curb beginning in November, 1971, cost inflation in the construction industry declined during the year.

At the end of September, the skilled labor and the materials components of *Engineering News-Record* magazine's Building Cost Index had gained only 8.3 per cent and 4.9 per cent, respectively, since September, 1971. This compared with gains of 11.9 per cent and 20.9 per cent in the comparable 1970-1971 period. Machinery costs, as measured by the Bureau of Labor Statistics Price Index, showed only a 3.4 per cent rise in the year that ended in August, compared with a gain of 6.1 per cent over the previous year. Only lumber costs were out of line, and this was caused by a limited supply and the pressure of increased homebuilding. In October, the Cost of Living Council asked the Department of Justice and the Federal Trade Commission (FTC) to determine whether the lumber industry's pricing policies were in violation of controls.

Despite a rise in interest rates in the early fall, the

A 2,500-ton, 370,000-square-foot plastic roof covered the sports arena, swimming pool, and most of the huge Olympic stadium in Munich.

cost of borrowing remained well below the prohibitive levels of two years ago. As a result of this, contractors could pass on to owners and agencies the effects of the moderation in price increases and lower borrowing costs. The effects were particularly noticeable in highway construction. Reflecting tighter bids, the highway bid price of the Federal Highway Administration (FHWA) index rose only 0.2 per cent during the year ending with the second quarter of 1972, 10 per cent more than the same period in 1971.

Building Codes and Specifications. In August, the nation's three major model building code organizations–based in Birmingham, Ala; Chicago; and Whittier, Calif.–formed a coordinating body for joint action. The new organization, the Council of American Building Officials (CABO), will sponsor model performance standards, develop model mechanical and plumbing codes, and provide research reports on nationally distributed building products, systems, and industrialized buildings.

Outstanding Buildings. A long-delayed plan to extend the west front of the U.S. Capitol was unanimously approved in March by a seven-member commission after an engineering study reassured the commission that the Capitol walls are in no danger of collapse. The $60-million extension will add about 285 offices and conference rooms.

The 656-foot-high Maine-Montparnasse office tower, nearing completion in Paris, will be the tallest building in Europe and the only one encasing an operating subway. The $140-million, 58-story building will be part of a five-acre, $300-million office and retail store complex.

Bridges. A new Mississippi River bridge opened in July after many construction problems posed by floodwaters and shifting river channels. The $50-million, 3.2-mile bridge carries Interstate 40 across the river between Memphis, Tenn., and Crittenden County, Arkansas. The 3,660-foot spans include twin 900-foot tied-arch trusses, designed to provide alternate routes in case the river shifts its course.

The longest concrete-arch bridge in North America was completed in August. The structure spans a deep gorge northeast of Yakima, Wash., to carry Interstate 82 across Selah Creek. The twin concrete arches, 549.5 feet long, carry two 12-foot-wide lanes 330 feet above the bottom of the gorge, a precaution against the torrents that fill the gorge after snowmelt.

A prestressed concrete box-girder bridge neared completion in Japan. Its record 754.5-foot, free-standing main span will carry two lanes of traffic across the mouth of Urate Bay in Kōchi on the island of Shikoku. It is 72 feet longer than West Germany's Bendorf Bridge and slightly longer than the projected 750-foot Three Sisters Bridge over the Potomac.

An FHWA report issued in January, described one-sixth of all the highway bridges in the United States as "critically deficient." However, none of the 89,900 structures in this category is considered completely unsafe. For a start, FHWA recommended replacing 50 of the most dubious bridges. The program was ordered after West Virginia's Silver Bridge over the Ohio River collapsed in December, 1969, with tragic loss of life.

Dams. The U.S. Corps of Engineers began construction of New Melones Dam, an irrigation, power and flood-control project on the Stanislaus River near Sonora, Calif. The 1,560-foot-long rock-fill dam project will replace Melones Dam, a 46-year-old concrete arch that will be inundated by the new dam's reservoir. New Melones, 625 feet above the stream bed, will be nearly three times as high as the old structure and the second highest rock-fill dam in the United States. Only the 770-foot Oroville Dam on the Feather River, also in northern California, is higher.

In February, the Bureau of Reclamation awarded a contract to start construction on its 10-year, $1.2-billion Central Arizona project. The giant project, a series of dams first proposed more than 20 years ago, has been the center of a controversy involving questions of ecology, water diversion, and power needs. It will distribute 1.2 million acre-feet of water annually through 377 miles of open canals, tunnels, and pipes reaching almost to the Mexican border.

In August, President Richard M. Nixon authorized the U.S. Corps of Engineers to inspect all of the nation's more than 28,000 dams to ensure their safety. The inspection program will involve hiring 200 additional engineers, and will cost an estimated $150-million. Follow-up inspection every three years, required by the new law, will cost $7 million a year.

Tunnels. At the end of the year, contractors were completing a $47.5-million sunken-tube tunnel under the mouth of the Mobile River at Mobile, Ala. The 3,000-foot-long tunnel will carry four lanes of Interstate 10 traffic 600 feet under the shipping channel through the seven largest sunken-tube sections ever used in the United States. Located 500 feet south of the existing Bankhead Tunnel, the new project will ease the heavy traffic that has plagued motorists for more than a decade.

A unique tunneling project in New York City combined the sunken-tube method with conventional blasting techniques. The city's $69.5-million 63rd Street Tunnel, which will eventually carry both Long Island Railroad trains and New York City subway trains between the boroughs of Queens and Manhattan, was holed through on October 10. The 3,140-foot tunnel consists of four 375-foot steel tubes, two end-to-end in the west channel and two in the east channel of the East River.

Mary E. Jessup

Only Moslems may enter the holy city of Mecca, so building of hotel there is monitored by non-Moslem technicians 8 miles away using closed-circuit TV.

BULGARIA remained Russia's model ally in 1972, but showed new flexibility in both foreign and domestic policies. In January, Todor Zhivkov, Communist Party first secretary and chairman of the State Council, announced measures designed to raise Bulgarian living standards. They included better welfare payments and an average 6 per cent annual increase in incomes. Planned reform of the secondary school system and the system of advanced professional education was announced in February. The party leadership continued to maintain a very tight grip on the cultural situation, however. One of the most vocal proponents of the hard line in culture was the secretary of the writers' union, Georgi Dzhagarov. Private medical practice was abolished effective on October 1.

International Relations. The most striking development in Bulgaria's foreign policy was the steady improvement in relations with Yugoslavia. In August, senior Bulgarian Communist Party officials visited Skopje, capital of the long-disputed Macedonian region of Yugoslavia. The Bulgarian press, though, remained discreetly silent about their nation's traditional, and sometimes vigorous, claims on Macedonia.

Bulgaria and Romania agreed on September 27 to build jointly a huge hydroelectric complex on the Danube River. Work on this project, which will help irrigate nearly 250,000 acres of land and provide 3.8-billion kilowatt-hours of electricity per year, is to start in 1975.

On May 3, a Turkish DC-9 airliner was hijacked by Turkish urban guerrillas and landed in Bulgaria. The hijackers were granted political asylum, but the plane and passengers were returned to Turkey. Bulgaria and Turkey remained wary of each other, however. Turkey suspected Bulgarian agents of backing antigovernment guerrilla activity in Turkey. In October, four more young Turkish guerrillas seized a Turkish Boeing 707 with 69 persons aboard. They held the plane at the Sofia airport. Unable to negotiate successfully with Bulgarian or Turkish officials, they surrendered and were held for trial.

Trade Grows. A Bulgarian tourist official was expelled from Great Britain in February on suspicion of espionage. In retaliation, a commercial counselor at the British Embassy in Sofia was expelled from Bulgaria. Nevertheless, Anglo-Bulgarian trade continued to develop during the year. On March 23, Britain agreed to deliver $1 million worth of British hogs and technical services to Bulgaria. In September, a British firm granted Bulgarians a seven-year license to produce huge straddle-lift container-handling vehicles in Bulgaria. Bulgaria's close and growing economic integration with Russia also continued. Economic ties with Chile received a boost in June when Bulgaria granted the Latin American nation $23 million in credit. Chris Cviic

See also EUROPE (Facts in Brief Table).

BURMA. After 10 years of military dictatorship under General Ne Win, Burma returned to civilian government in 1972. On April 20, Ne Win resigned as army chief of staff to become prime minister (see NE WIN). All but one of the senior members of the ruling Union Revolutionary Council gave up their military ranks. The moves paved the way for the drafting of a new Constitution, which was announced on April 22. The Constitution established a Socialist Republic of Burma. It provides for a one-party system, with an elected, unicameral People's Congress of 600 members.

Government Measures. The government's actions reflected a sharp expansion of the Burmese Socialist Programme Party. They also indicated a concern for the problem of ethnic minorities by creating three new states for the Mons, the Chins, and the Arakanese. But little autonomy was given to these states.

There was still insurgency among the Shan states, with the Karens and the Kachins conducting sporadic raids against government forces. But the rebels lost their titular head, former Prime Minister U Nu, who resigned from the National United Liberation Front. After that, U Nu was reduced to writing letters favoring revolution to the editors of foreign newspapers.

Ne Win's government continued its drive toward socialism by nationalizing some 69 mills and factories in the Rangoon area during the year. In order to limit opposition to such programs, even more severe restrictions were placed on the press. To remove judicial restraints, lawyers were prohibited from serving as judges, and people's judges were appointed. This created a kind of rough lay justice for the country.

The Economy stagnated as production of rice dropped, and Burma could not meet its export commitments, thus limiting its ability to meet foreign-exchange requirements. Japan and West Germany extended considerable credits in an effort to stimulate development. Japan provided financing for extensive offshore oil test drilling operations and also set up new air routes to provide service between Rangoon and Tokyo.

Japan continued to be the leading exporter to Burma, followed closely by West Germany, which extended about 45 million marks (about $14.2 million) in credits for industrial expansion during the year. Russia tried to enter the Burmese market by sponsoring a large-scale trade fair, but the results were limited. The possibility of a rapprochement with China was enhanced by Ne Win's visit to Peking in September. John N. Stalker

See also ASIA (Facts in Brief Table).

BURUNDI. See AFRICA.

BUS. See TRANSPORTATION.

BUSINESS. See ECONOMY, THE; LABOR; MANUFACTURING; Section One, FOCUS ON THE ECONOMY.

CABINET, U.S. After his re-election on Nov. 7, 1972, President Richard M. Nixon asked all Cabinet and White House staff members to submit their resignations. Five incumbent Cabinet members retained their old posts for the second Nixon Administration and one was given a new position. Earlier in the year, there were also several Cabinet changes.

Kleindienst Controversy. On February 15, Attorney General John N. Mitchell announced he was resigning to manage President Nixon's re-election campaign. Mr. Nixon named Deputy Attorney General Richard G. Kleindienst as Mitchell's successor. However, he was linked to the International Telephone and Telegraph Corporation (ITT) case. ITT had contributed between $200,000 and $400,000 to the Republican Party, allegedly in return for favorable treatment by the Department of Justice in antitrust suits. See REPUBLICAN PARTY.

Kleindienst's confirmation was postponed while the Senate investigated his involvement in the ITT affair. He was confirmed on June 8. See KLEINDIENST, RICHARD G.

Other Changes. Secretary of Commerce Maurice H. Stans resigned on January 27 to become President Nixon's chief campaign fund-raiser. Stans was replaced by Peter G. Peterson, formerly on the White House staff. See PETERSON, PETER G.

Secretary of the Treasury John B. Connally resigned on May 16. George P. Shultz, director of the Office of Management and Budget, took over the treasury post on June 12 (see SHULTZ, GEORGE P.). Caspar W. Weinberger became the new director of management and budget.

Second-Term Cabinet. The President began composing his second-term Cabinet on November 28, when he nominated Secretary of Health, Education, and Welfare (HEW) Elliot L. Richardson as secretary of defense and Weinberger as the new HEW secretary. Roy L. Ash was named the new director of the Office of Management and Budget.

On November 29, Peter J. Brennan, president of the New York Building and Construction Trades Council was nominated to replace James D. Hodgson as secretary of labor. On December 6, textile manufacturer Frederick B. Dent was named to replace Peterson as secretary of commerce. Undersecretary of Commerce James T. Lynn was nominated for secretary of housing and urban development on December 5, replacing George W. Romney, and oil executive Claude S. Brinegar was chosen for secretary of transportation on December 7, replacing John A. Volpe.

Cabinet members who kept their posts were: Secretary of State William P. Rogers, Secretary of the Interior Rogers C. B. Morton, Secretary of the Treasury Shultz, Secretary of Agriculture Earl L. Butz, and Attorney General Kleindienst. Darlene R. Stille

CALIFORNIA. See LOS ANGELES-LONG BEACH; SAN FRANCISCO; STATE GOVERNMENT.

CAMBODIA. Marshal Lon Nol, who had abolished the monarchy and proclaimed Cambodia the Republic of Khmer in 1970, swore himself in as the republic's first elected president on July 3, 1972. The elections, which were held on June 4, followed Lon Nol's take-over of the government on March 22. At that time, he abruptly dismissed the constituent assembly and canceled the Constitution it was preparing. He proclaimed himself president and announced the formation of a new 17-man Cabinet. His action followed a political crisis brought on by student-led demonstrations against the proposed appointment of Sisowath Sirik Matak, a close adviser to Lon Nol, as prime minister.

During Lon Nol's inaugural address in Phnom Penh, gunfire could be heard in the distance. The fighting, only 18 miles from the capital, symbolized the territorial chaos that prevailed in Cambodia. The government controlled at most one-half of the country.

Communist forces had shown repeatedly during the year that they could occupy territory at will. The major reason was what many considered widespread corruption within the Cambodian Army, and not the fierceness of Communist attacks. A substantial number of the troops frequently went unpaid and consequently they either mutinied or deserted. "Phantom" soldiering, a common practice of claiming more soldiers than existed in order to make profiteering easier, also weakened an already inadequate army.

Following a major defeat by the North Vietnamese at Tchenla II in the spring, the Cambodian troops seemed content to let the invaders deploy their units in the eastern and southern provinces while themselves avoiding any real contact with the enemy. Instead, some attempt was made to recapture Angkor Wat—the site of ancient ruins and a great historic symbol in northwestern Cambodia. But Angkor Wat was of no significant military value. Even this modest effort met with no real success. Although the government managed to hold Phnom Penh, it was largely because the Communists made no real effort to take it.

Election and Rice. On September 3, Cambodia held its first National Assembly election in six years. Most voters, however, were apathetic because only 10 of the 126 seats were contested. In most districts, the only candidates were those belonging to Lon Nol's Social Republican Party. The elections coincided with a serious rice shortage, which added to the political and military chaos. Most observers attributed the shortage to a lack of government planning and the closing by Communist forces of key roads linking the rice-growing areas to Phnom Penh.

A settlement of the war would eliminate the Vietnamese from Cambodia. But the nation would still face dissension from within. John N. Stalker

See also ASIA (Facts in Brief Table).

CANADA

The strong majority government in Canada since 1968 came to an end on Oct. 30, 1972, when Prime Minister Pierre Elliott Trudeau's Liberal Party suffered a crushing setback at the polls. The Liberals lost 38 seats in the House of Commons, emerging with only two more members than Progressive Conservatives, led by Robert L. Stanfield. The Liberals were left holding only 109 seats, far short of a 133-seat majority. So Canada re-entered a period of minority government comparable to its experience under John G. Diefenbaker and his successor, Lester B. Pearson, whose death late in 1972 cast a momentary pall over all the parties (see DEATHS OF NOTABLE PERSONS). For the Conservatives, the result was a solid electoral victory, a gain of 35 seats since 1968.

Trudeau lost heavily in English-speaking Ontario and the west, but this result did not mean that Canadians had rejected his policy of promoting national unity by extending French-language rights. A more accurate explanation probably was that Canadian

Prime Minister Pierre E. Trudeau and his wife leave press conference after he said he would lead minority government in the new Parliament.

voters expressed their dissatisfaction with the Trudeau Government's failure to correct the highest annual rate of unemployment since 1961 and the renewed climb in the cost of living. As a shaken Trudeau and his ministers prepared to meet a new House of Commons, where support was essential for their continuance in office, it was apparent the economy had top priority in Canada.

The Campaign was unexciting. Governor-General Roland Michener, on Trudeau's advice, dissolved Parliament September 1. Trudeau then called the election for October 30 and began his restrained drive for the voters' support.

The prime minister played down his personal appeal, which had so aroused voters four years earlier. His sober, almost philosophical campaign emphasized his faith in Canadian dualism as the only enduring basis for Canadian unity. Under Stanfield, the 58-year-old Halifax lawyer who had led the party since 1967, the Conservatives hammered away at the government's failure to curb unemployment or to control the rising cost of living. See STANFIELD, ROBERT L.

The New Democratic Party attacked big business. Party leader David Lewis said an unjust system of grants, deferrals, and tax deductions let large corporations evade their share of taxation. He called for thorough tax reform to eliminate "corporate welfare bums." The fourth party, the Social Credit movement, recommended a national guaranteed wage and higher welfare benefits.

Conservative leader Robert L. Stanfield and his supporters dealt a sharp electoral setback to Canada's ruling Liberal Party.

The Liberal strength of 109 seats was concentrated heavily in Quebec, where the party won 56. Ontario rebuked the Trudeau Government by cutting the party from 64 seats to 36. But results in the western provinces provided the Liberals' greatest shock. Western voters reported feeling Trudeau's Government was oriented toward the nation's East. "When Trudeau talks Canadian unity, he's thinking one thing while we're thinking another," one had complained. The Liberals' Western contingent fell from 25 members to 7. Not a single Liberal was elected to any of Alberta's 19 seats.

The Conservatives, in electing 107 members of the House of Commons, won 35 per cent of the popular vote – up 4 per cent from 1968. They retained a majority of seats, 22, from the Atlantic provinces and won 14 more in Ontario for a total of 40 from the largest province. In the west, they picked up 44 seats, including 8 in British Columbia, a province from which they had been excluded in 1968. Their greatest failure was in Quebec, where their new provincial leader, Claude Wagner, a former Liberal, was able only to elect himself and one other candidate. The separatist Parti Québécois did not participate in the election.

With 31 members elected, the New Democratic Party gained 9 seats. It won 17 per cent of the popular vote. It gained in Ontario and British Columbia, but again was shut out from seats in the Maritime Provinces and Quebec. The Social Credit movement captured 24 per cent of the popular vote in Quebec, but only 7 per cent in the country at large. All 15 of its winning members were elected from Quebec.

The campaign brought 74 per cent of the eligible voters – about 9 million persons – to the polls. Those between the ages of 18 and 21 voted for the first time in a federal election.

Trudeau Stays On. A chastened Prime Minister Trudeau refused Stanfield's call to resign. In mid-November, he announced that Parliament would meet on Jan. 4, 1973.

Under the parliamentary system, a Government holds office depending not on popular support, but on the will of the people's representatives seated in Parliament. A Government stands or falls on the response Parliament gives to its legislative proposals. With the two major parties at virtually equal strength in the Commons, it was apparent that the 31 New Democratic Party members held the balance of power. This fact would undoubtedly bring about a heavier emphasis on economic and social measures in the Trudeau Government's 1973 policies.

Cabinet Shuffle. After the election, Trudeau, preparing for "the massive job ahead of us," announced a major Cabinet shakeup. On November 27, he shifted the portfolios of 10 ministers and brought 8 new men into the Cabinet. Eleven ministers retained their posts, including External Affairs Minister Mitchell Sharp. The new ministers included Jeanne Sauvé, minister of science and technology; Warren Allmand, solicitor general; Hugh Faulkner, secretary of state; Stanley Haidasz, minister of state; Marc Lalonde, minister of health and welfare; Daniel J. MacDonald, minister of veterans affairs; André Ouellet, postmaster general; and Eugene Whelan, minister of agriculture.

The year 1972 had begun with a wide reshuffling of the Trudeau Cabinet. On January 28, 10 of its 29 members were transferred to new positions. Edgar Benson, architect of the controversial 1971 tax reform, left the finance portfolio and moved to national defense. The tax reform bill had been amended 150 times before final passage in the last days of 1971. Later, on September 1, Benson resigned from the Cabinet and was appointed president of the Canadian Transport Commission. John Turner, minister of justice, took over the key finance portfolio. At the dissolution of Parliament on September 1, two members of the Cabinet, Arthur Laing and Joseph Julien Jean-Pierre Côté, were named to the Senate, together with John James Greene, the former minister of energy, mines, and resources, who had retired from the government in January following a stroke.

Parliament Slowed. The fourth and final session of the 28th Parliament opened February 17 with the Government listing 29 items of proposed legislation. Fewer than 10 had been passed when the session was dissolved. Measures still pending when the session ended included one for a new screening agency to regulate foreign take-overs of Canadian companies. Others were an election expenses act, a new economic competition policy, legislation to ensure privacy in the electronic age, and an amendment to the labor code making technological changes negotiable issues. Legislation for the Family Income Security Plan – to which the Government gave high priority – was held up through a technicality on July 7. Action on it was deferred, probably temporarily, by the Government.

Parliament had to deal with two dockers' strikes during the summer – one at St. Lawrence River ports and one on the Pacific coast. The strike of 3,200 longshoremen at three Quebec ports lasted eight weeks, resisting federal mediation attempts. Legislation passed on July 7 outlawed strikes and lockouts by unions or management for three years at the ports of Montreal, Quebec, and Three Rivers. At the end of the summer, Parliament was called back into session for two days to pass the West Coast Ports Operations Act to reopen six British Columbia ports. The measure ended a strike that had threatened Canada's grain exports.

Provincial Relations with the federal government were quiet during the year. The provincial premiers held their 13th annual conference in Halifax on August 3 and 4. The premiers of the five eastern provinces (with Quebec participating for the first time) discussed the sharing of revenues from offshore oil and gas royalties. They rejected Ottawa's claim to jurisdiction over the offshore resources and its proposal to divide revenues on an equal basis among the 10 provinces. The eastern provinces indicated that they did not favor asking the Supreme Court of Canada to clarify jurisdiction. They preferred to settle the matter in negotiations with Ottawa.

United States Relations. On April 13, U.S. President Richard M. Nixon visited Canada, returning Trudeau's Washington visit of December, 1971. Accompanied by Mrs. Nixon and Secretary of State William P. Rogers, he spent three days in the Canadian capital. President Nixon struck a realistic note when he addressed Parliament. He admitted there were "real problems" between the two countries, but added that they could be solved by patient negotiations. The Nixon-Trudeau talks were expected to lead to a resumption of the trade discussions between the two governments.

On the last day of the President's visit, the two leaders signed the Great Lakes Water Quality Agreement to bring about an "early and substantial improvement" in the condition of such lakes as Erie and Ontario. It was estimated that Canada would have to spend at least $250 million in upgrading municipal sewage facilities, while the United States might be committed to spending $2 billion. Water-quality standards were laid down, and the two nations agreed that the International Joint Commission would undertake research, supervisory, and monitoring functions.

Foreign Investments. On May 2, the Trudeau Government unveiled its long-awaited policy statement on control of direct foreign investment in Canada. The statement proposed a board to review the purchase of Canadian companies by foreign concerns. Under the review process, it would approve only investments of significant benefit to Canada. The Commons Standing Committee on Finance, Trade, and Economic Affairs brought a modified version to Parliament, but it failed to gain approval and the statement was shelved until a new session.

The Trans-Alaska Pipeline System (TAPS) was another controversial subject in 1972. Canada opposed the pipeline because of its threat to the environment of the north and the danger it presented of oil pollution along Canada's Pacific coast as tankers moved south to Cherry Point, Wash. An oil spill on June 4 at Cherry Point emphasized the hazards of shipping oil down the rugged British Columbia coast and into the narrow waters of Puget Sound. Canada continued to press an alternative pipeline route for Alaskan oil through the Mackenzie Valley east of Alaska. But the U.S. rejected a Mackenzie Valley route in early May when it approved the TAPS project.

The Ministry of Canada
In order of precedence

Pierre Elliott Trudeau, prime minister
Paul Joseph James Martin, leader of the government in the senate
Mitchell Sharp, secretary of state for external affairs
Allan Joseph MacEachen, president of the queen's privy council
Charles Mills Drury, president of the treasury board
Jean Marchand, minister of transport
John Napier Turner, minister of finance
Jean Chrétien, minister of Indian affairs and northern development
Donald Stovel Macdonald, minister of energy, mines, and resources
John Carr Munro, minister of labor
Gérard Pelletier, minister of communications
Jack Davis, minister of the environment and fisheries
Jean-Eudes Dubé, minister of public works
Stanley Ronald Basford, minister of state for urban affairs
Donald Campbell Jamieson, minister of regional economic expansion
Robert Knight Andras, minister of manpower and immigration
James Armstrong Richardson, minister of national defense
Otto Emil Lang, minister of justice and attorney general of Canada
Herb Gray, minister of consumer and corporate affairs
Robert Stanbury, minister of national revenue
Jean-Pierre Goyer, minister of supply and services
Alastair William Gillespie, minister of industry, trade, and commerce
Stanley Haidasz, minister of state
Eugene Whelan, minister of agriculture
Warren Allmand, solicitor general of Canada
Hugh Faulkner, secretary of state of Canada
André Ouellet, postmaster general
Daniel J. MacDonald, minister of veterans affairs
Marc Lalonde, minister of national health and welfare
Jeanne Sauvé, minister of state for science and technology

Premiers of Canadian Provinces

Province	Premier
Alberta	Peter Lougheed
British Columbia	David Barrett
Manitoba	Edward R. Schreyer
New Brunswick	Richard B. Hatfield
Newfoundland	Frank Moores
Nova Scotia	Gerald A. Regan
Ontario	William G. Davis
Prince Edward Island	Alexander B. Campbell
Quebec	J. Robert Bourassa
Saskatchewan	Allan Blakeney

Commissioners of Territories

Northwest Territories	Stuart M. Hodgson
Yukon Territory	James Smith

Overseas Affairs. China attracted the greatest attention among Canadians in 1972. In August, External Affairs Minister Mitchell Sharp led 600 Canadian officials, businessmen, and athletes to Peking for a Canadian trade fair. The fair was the first of its kind since Canada established diplomatic relations with China in 1970. It won about $25-million worth of business for Canada, including the sale of 5,600 tons of Canadian nickel. These sales and others were expected to produce a total of $250-million in Canadian exports to China. That total would put Canada in third place among China's trading partners, behind Japan and Hong Kong.

At a three-hour meeting during the fair, Premier Chou En-lai told Sharp that China found it profitable to import wheat in order to free some of its rice for export at favorable international prices. He hinted that Canada can count on China to continue buying much Canadian wheat as long as the price is competitive. Chou also expressed appreciation for Canada's help in gaining recognition of China in the Western world and for supporting China in its 1971 bid for United Nations membership.

A modest home in Gravenhurst, Ontario, was the goal of a pilgrimage by every Chinese delegation to Canada. It was the birthplace of Dr. Norman Bethune, the Canadian surgeon who lost his life in 1939 while serving with the Chinese Communist armies in their struggle against Japan.

Deficit Budget. John Turner, named to the finance portfolio on January 28, presented his first budget on May 8. It provided large tax cuts for the manufacturing and processing industries and gave financial support to the old, the sick, and the disabled, but offered little in tax relief for the average citizen. Turner said his main concern was to create jobs through "incentives for Canadian industry." Expenditures for fiscal 1972-73 were set at about $16.1 billion and anticipated revenues at $15.7-billion, leaving a deficit of about $450 million.

Financial help for the aged came in a measure to lift the $80 freeze on monthly old-age pensions. In the future, they would be increased each April 1 to offset any increase in the consumer price index. The income supplement for needy pensioners was also raised and coupled to changes in living costs. Starting in January, 1973, the top rate of corporate income tax for Canadian manufacturing firms would be cut.

The Economy. Although the Canadian economy was troubled by high unemployment in 1972, almost every other indicator improved. The gross national product grew by about 10 per cent to $102 billion; about 6 per cent represented real output. Exports were high, aided by the economic improvement in the United States, which usually creates a demand for Canadian products. Automobile production was impressive, profiting from the free-trade provisions of the Auto Agreement of 1965. Canadian forest

Premier-elect David Barrett talked to newsmen at a celebration after his party swept to a victory in August election in British Columbia.

products, oil, newsprint, iron ore, and aluminum were also in demand in different markets. Grain shipments for the crop year ended July 31, 1972, set a new record at 791 million bushels. These included large wheat sales to Russia and China. For the first nine months of the year, exports totaled $14.1 billion, a gain of 8.4 per cent from the same period a year earlier, while imports came to $13.5 billion, a gain of 19.8 per cent. Canada's deficit on nonmerchandise transactions, however, was expected to turn this surplus into an overall deficit of perhaps $1 billion for 1972. The Canadian dollar steadily appreciated in 1972, as short-term capital, responding to higher interest rates, flowed into Canada.

Unemployment continued to be the major economic problem in 1972. A principal reason was the explosion of the labor force, which grew faster than in any other nation in the Western world. Although 300,000 more jobs were created in the year ended June 30, unemployment rose steadily over the summer, when it would normally have declined. In September, it stood at 7.1 per cent of the labor force on a seasonally adjusted basis. This was the highest rate in 11 years and one that recalled the severe 1961 slump.

Inflation was another distressing problem. Canada had held the line satisfactorily for several years, but prices shot up in 1972. The consumer price index, based on 1961 prices, gained 5.3 per cent in the year ending in October. It reached 142.0; in October, 1971, it had been 134.9. Higher food prices were a major reason.

The Provinces

Alberta, with almost 90 per cent of Canada's proved oil reserves, unveiled a new tax on the assessed value of reserves in April. The tax was expected to yield over $50 million to the provincial government in 1973 and would avoid the necessity of renegotiating long-term leases for oil royalties.

British Columbia provided the year's biggest surprise in provincial politics on August 30 when the New Democratic Party (NDP) defeated the Social Credit government of William A. C. Bennett. Bennett had been in office for more than 20 years. During its long life, the Bennett government had alienated a number of influential groups, such as physicians, teachers, and organized labor.

The new premier was David Barrett, 41, a former social worker (see BARRETT, DAVID). Elected leader of the NDP in 1970, he successfully broadened its appeal among British Columbia voters. Although Bennett was elected in his own district, 11 of his 15 Cabinet ministers were defeated. The new government was sworn in on September 15, and met the legislature in a special session a month later. Barrett announced that he intended to turn the British Columbia Telephone Company, controlled by U.S. interests, into a government corporation.

Manitoba. Support for nonpublic schools reappeared as the province's most controversial political issue. Premier Edward R. Schreyer's effort to provide more state aid to private and parochial schools was turned down in the legislature even though he had said at one time that he would resign if not supported. Sidney Green, minister of natural resources, resigned on March 2 in opposition to Schreyer's policy, but he later rejoined the Cabinet. The House also opposed Schreyer's proposal to refer the subject to a special legislative committee. The issue has plagued Manitoba for almost a century, but was shelved once more.

New Brunswick faced serious economic difficulties in 1972. The federal Government announced that it was banning commercial salmon fishing after May 1 in an effort to restore declining supplies. Much of the decline was blamed on heavy fishing by Denmark in the Davis Strait. This affected 900 fishermen in New Brunswick who would be paid compensation. In January, it was discovered that New Brunswick's richest man, K. C. Irving, had left the province to settle in the Bahamas, presumably for tax reasons.

Conservative Premier Richard Hatfield fired an energetic but troublesome colleague, J. C. Van Horne, his minister of tourism, on August 16. The premier said Van Horne, who had challenged him for the party's leadership in 1969, had knowingly overspent his department's budget.

Newfoundland. Premier Joseph R. Smallwood resigned on Jan. 18, 1972, after the Liberal Party's disputed election defeat. He had been premier for almost 23 years. The confused and disputed election results ultimately gave 20 seats to Smallwood's Liberals and 21 to the Conservatives under a new leader, Frank Moores, 39 (see MOORES, FRANK). Moores was sworn in as premier three hours after Smallwood resigned, and formed a 15-member Cabinet. The Liberals soon replaced Smallwood as party leader with his 31-year-old minister of health, Edward Roberts. In an election on March 24, the new government won a resounding vote of confidence and 33 of the legislature's 42 seats. But it faced a formidable task in dealing with severe unemployment and the failure of important local industries on the island.

Nova Scotia. Peter Nicholson, holding both the finance and education portfolios in Premier Gerald A. Regan's Liberal government, presented his second budget on March 29. Departmental estimates were cut to hold expenditures to $549 million. Revenues of $545 million were budgeted.

The government took over the privately owned Nova Scotia Light and Power Company, which supplies half of the province's electric power, in January. The company's 1,000 employees were to be absorbed into the Nova Scotia Power Commission. A second attempt in three years to give dental technicians, commonly called denturists, the right to sell false teeth directly to the public was defeated in the legislature on April 24.

Ontario, Canada's largest province, radically reorganized its government on January 5. Three "super-ministers" were appointed to coordinate policies among groups of related departments in the areas of social development, resources, and justice. A fourth appointment, with executive functions in finance and intergovernmental affairs, was made at the same time. Premier William G. Davis picked ranking members of his Progressive Conservative Cabinet for the four posts. Changes followed shortly. On August 31, provincial treasurer Darcy McKeough resigned from the ministry of finance and intergovernmental affairs because of his personal involvement in an application for approval of a planned Chatham subdivision. He had processed it routinely in 1969 while serving as minister of municipal affairs. On September 8, Allan Lawrence, the provincial secretary for justice, resigned to run for a House of Commons seat, and won.

The budget was presented on March 28. Revenues for fiscal 1972-73 were estimated at $4.45 billion and expenditures at $5.05 billion, leaving a lower deficit than in 1971.

Prince Edward Island had Canada's lowest average personal income in 1972. A federal report

Justin Trudeau, young son of Canada's prime minister, enjoys a brief moment of play with his mother as they wait for Trudeau at an airport.

showed that it was $2,188. The nationwide average was $3,045.

The province's extreme dependence on the federal government showed in the budget presented on March 16. It predicted revenues of $109 million. About 55 per cent would be federal grants and fund transfers.

Quebec. A strike of 200,000 public service employees in April, 1972, provided a turbulent test for Prime Minister J. Robert Bourassa's Liberal government. It had recently granted civil servants the right to strike. A common front of teachers and public service unions led to the closing of hospitals and the withdrawal of many government services for 11 days before the National Assembly stepped in to send government employees back to work on April 21. Three radical leaders were jailed for disobeying court injunctions during the strike–and an even wider wave of labor disturbances was touched off. Faced with internal revolt against their extreme policies, the three eventually agreed to forego their martyrdom and appeal their sentences. They were released on bail on May 23. Negotiations for a new contract for public employees dragged on through the summer with the government threatening to impose a contract if agreement was not reached. One group, composed largely of nonmedical hospital workers, reached an agreement on October 16. Employees of Quebec's state-operated liquor stores settled on October 17. Teachers, however, held out until the December 15 deadline. Using a new law, part of the April legislative action, the government then decreed a new, five-year contract for the teachers.

The settlement provided for smaller student-teacher ratios and larger salaries–a total of about $50 million more than had last been offered the teachers. By the end of the five-year period, teacher salaries are to cost Quebec about $750 million per year, and an estimated 3,500 additional teachers will be needed.

Saskatchewan. Premier Allan Blakeney's New Democratic Party government met its first full-scale session of the legislature from February 24 to May 5. In a major government reorganization, departments of consumer affairs, environment, and culture and youth were set up and an ombudsman was appointed. The most far-reaching measure was a plan to create a government land bank to which farmers could sell their land and from which other farmers could rent or buy land. The measure was intended to save small family farms in the wheat-growing province.

Facts in Brief: Population: 22,516,000. Government: Governor General Roland Michener; Prime Minister Pierre Elliott Trudeau. Monetary Unit: Canadian dollar. Foreign Trade: exports, $18,271,-000,000; imports, $16,813,000,000. David M. L. Farr

See also CANADIAN LIBRARY ASSOCIATION (CLA); CANADIAN LITERATURE; MICHENER, ROLAND; TRUDEAU, PIERRE ELLIOTT.

CANADIAN LIBRARY ASSOCIATION (CLA) held its 27th annual conference in Regina, Saskatchewan, from June 10 to 16, 1972. More than 1,000 persons attended. The central conference theme was Canadian books. The most significant session of the conference was devoted to the final report of the CLA structural committee. The only substantial change the committee recommended was to include the chairman of the Canadian Library Trustees Association on the CLA board of directors. This was unanimously accepted, with agreement that a separate Trustees Division was desirable. A committee was named to draft a constitution.

The Canadian Association of Public Libraries became a division of CLA in June, 1972, incorporating the Canadian Association of Children's Librarians, Adult Services, the Young People's Section, and the Administrators of Large Public Libraries Committee. CLA received a grant of $20,000 from the secretary of state of Canada to provide financial assistance to local, regional, and national library activities in observance of International Book Year. Bernard McNamee was appointed CLA executive director in May, 1972.

Medals and Awards. The Book of the Year for Children Medal was awarded to Ann Blades for *Mary of Mile 18.* The Amelia Frances Howard-Gibbon Medal for illustrators was awarded to Shizuye Takashima for *A Child in Prison Camp.* The Merit Award of the Canadian School Library Association, established in 1972 to recognize outstanding contributions to the development of school library service in Canada, was presented to Mrs. M. Alison Vaness, supervisor of libraries, Calgary school board. The Merit Award of the Canadian Library Trustees Association went to Fred J. McNamara, East York Public Library board. The fourth Howard V. Phalin-World Book Graduate Scholarship in Library Science was awarded by a CLA standing committee to Mrs. Katherine H. Packer, assistant professor of library science at the University of Toronto. The scholarship was sponsored by World Book-Childcraft of Canada, Limited.

Films and Publications. Two outstanding library films were released: *At Long Last,* which depicts the National Library of Canada in action, and *Chut,* which portrays the services of the National Library of Quebec. *Research Collections in Canadian Libraries–I, Universities* was published in English and French by the National Library of Canada. It is divided into regional sections, the first on the Prairie Provinces and the second, the Atlantic Provinces. This work analyzes and evaluates university collections.

Library Education. The University of Toronto School of Library Science became the new Faculty of Library Science under its own dean. The first director of the school, Miss Winifred G. Barnstead, received an honorary doctor's degree when the new building was opened in June. Elizabeth Homer Morton

CANADIAN LITERATURE concentrated on politics and government more than usual in 1972. This reflected the nation's concern with these subjects, inspired partly by an impending federal election and changes brought about by the provincial elections of 1971 and 1972.

How Canadians Govern Themselves by Joseph Schull, *Canada's Parliament* by George Bain, *The Canadian Constitution* by W. J. Lawson, and *How Parliament Works* by E. Russell Hopkins are new or reprinted government publications released in 1972. They provide the essential information about the government for all types of readers.

The Election Process in Canada by Terance H. Qualter explains federal and provincial government and principles of the electoral process. *Political Party Financing in Canada* by K. Z. Paltiel answers questions regarding fund-raising and related subjects. *Federal-Provincial Diplomacy; the Making of Recent Policy in Canada*, edited by Richard Simeon, examines the growing power of the provinces and the federal government's position in regard to it. *Apex of Power; the Prime Minister and Political Leadership in Canada*, edited by Thomas A. Kockin, is a collection of material on the growing power of the office of prime minister. *The Trudeau Question* by William A. Wilson dispassionately notes Prime Minister Pierre Elliott Trudeau's successes and failures.

Fiction. *Lives of Girls and Women* by Alice Munro is a series of penetrating fictional biographies. *Pandora*, a first novel by Sylvia Fraser, describes alienation between a young child and her parents. The book's most vivid scenes are those of childhood and wartime Ontario. Good anthologies and collections of tales or short stories include *The Fruit Man, the Meat Man and the Manager* by Hugh Hood, *Saturday Night at the Bagel Factory and other Montreal Stories* by Don Bell, *When He Was Free and Young and He Used to Wear Silks* by Austin Clark, and *Fourteen Stories High; Best Canadian Stories of 1971*, edited by David Helwig and Tom Marshall.

Poetry. *Volvox; Poetry from the Unofficial Languages of Canada*, edited by J. Michael Yates, is translated from Persian, Turkish, Romanian, Hungarian, and German. It is as good an anthology as any ever published in Canada. Some of the poets included are Rachel Korn, Nicholas Catanoy, George Faludy, and Robert Zend. Other worthy collections include *Between Tears and Laughter* by Alden Nowlan, *Selected Poems* by Al Purdy, *The Years; Poems* by Raymond Souster, *Sunrise North* by Elizabeth Brewster, *The Armies of the Moon* by Gwendolyn MacEwan, *The Collected Poems of Irving Layton*, *Collected Poetry* by Louis Dudek, and *Touch: Selected Poems, 1960-1970* by George Bowering.

Biography. In *Letters to Limbo*, Sir Robert Laird Borden, prime minister of Canada from 1911 to 1920, reveals a relatively unknown inner side to his character. *Beaverbrook* by A. J. P. Taylor shows this Canadian businessman-turned-British-lord as an attractive, complex character. *Wilfrid Laurier, the Great Conciliator* by Barbara Robertson provides an anecdotal history of the first French-Canadian prime minister of Canada. *Laura Secord, the Legend and the Lady* by Ruth McKenzie, *Cape Breton Harbour* by Edna Staebler, *Raisins and Almonds* by Fredelle Bruser, *Pictures out of My Life* by Pitseolak, and *A Child in Prison Camp* by Shizuye Takashima are episodes in the lives of women.

History. *Canada's Five Centuries* by William Kaye Lamb has been described as the finest volume in the field of Canadian history, one "calculated to open up new realms of wonder and imagination for young readers." The narrative text is profusely illustrated with maps, rare photographs, paintings, and illustrations collected by Lamb when he was dominion archivist.

Governor-General's Literary Awards for books published in 1971 went to Pierre Berton for *The Last Spike* (English nonfiction), John Glassco for *Selected Poems* (English poetry), Mordecai Richler for *St. Urbain's Horseman* (English fiction), Gerald Fortin for *La Fin D'un Régne* (French nonfiction), Paul-Marie Lapointe for *Le Rél Absolu* (French poetry), and Gérard Bessette for *Le Cycle* (French fiction).

Stephen Leacock Memorial Award for humor went to Max Braithwaite for *The Night We Stole the Mountie's Car.*

Elizabeth Homer Morton

CELEBRATIONS and anniversaries observed in 1972 included the following:

Arbor Day Centennial. Although it is celebrated on different dates in different parts of the United States and Canada, the first Arbor Day was on April 10. In 1872, Nebraska newspaper publisher J. Sterling Morton had that date set aside as Nebraska's Arbor Day, the first Arbor Day anywhere. After Morton died, the Nebraska legislature changed the date of Arbor Day to his birthday, April 22. In 1972, Mrs. Richard M. Nixon celebrated Arbor Day by planting a fern-leaf beech tree on the White House grounds near the West Wing.

Brazil Independence Sesquicentennial. On Jan. 9, 1822, after the Portuguese government ordered Regent Dom Pedro home from Brazil, he declared Brazil independent, and became Emperor Pedro I. After his death, he was buried in Portugal. To celebrate the 150th anniversary of independence, Brazil asked Portugal to return Pedro's remains. They arrived by ship in April and were exhibited in every major Brazilian city, then buried on September 7 beside Pedro's first wife, Empress Leopoldina, at the Iparanga Monument on the outskirts of São Paulo. Almost everyone in Brazil participated in the celebration. In Brasília, the capital, a 3,000-square-foot Brazilian flag flew atop a 300-foot pole. Schools and offices closed. Church bells tolled and factories blew whistles. In addition, the government minted commemorative gold coins, and more than a million free souvenir newspapers dated Sept. 7, 1822, told how Prince Pedro had "just declared Brazil independent."

Dodge City Centennial. More than 200 persons gathered at Dodge City's famed Boot Hill on Aug. 21, 1972, for yet another burial. This one was different, though–there was no corpse. Instead, a 2,700-pound vault filled with memorabilia from 1972 was buried. This was a highlight of Dodge City's six-day celebration of its 100th birthday. The theme of the centennial was "Cow Town to Now Town." The activities were a far cry from the brawls and shootings of the days when Wyatt Earp, Bat Masterson, and Doc Holliday tried to keep the peace with blazing six-guns. There were contests, pageants, picnics, parades, rope tricks, an air show, and a revival meeting. Many women wore bonnets and long gingham dresses, and the men had string ties and beards.

National Parks Centennial. See CONSERVATION (Close-Up).

Norway Unified 1,100 Years. About A.D. 872, Harold Fairhair won the battle of Hafsfjord and became undisputed monarch of the territories that now

The remains of Dom Pedro I, the emperor who declared Brazil independent, were returned by Portugal during Brazil's sesquicentennial.

comprise Norway. Harold's most important achievement was having his authority recognized in most parts of the country. This was the first and probably most significant of a series of events that ultimately unified Norway militarily, territorially, and politically. In 1972, there were celebrations of the 11th centenary throughout Norway. Some of the more important events included an exhibition of Norwegian art from the Viking Age and the Middle Ages, from foreign collections, at Oslo's Historical Museum from March 23 to June 15; a recitation to music of an especially commissioned work on the theme "Harold Fairhair and the Unification of the Realm" at the opening of the 1972 Bergen International Festival on May 24; and televised jubilee festivities attended by King Olav V and other dignitaries at Hafsfjord, about 100 miles south of Bergen, and the nearby cities of Stavanger and Haugesund on June 17 and 18. In addition, commemorative medals were struck and sold in Norwegian banks.

Ralph Vaughan Williams Centennial. Great Britain celebrated the 100th birthday of composer Ralph Vaughan Williams by issuing a stamp bearing his portrait. A Vaughan Williams Centenary Festival was presented throughout the year in Dorking, Surrey, where the composer lived for 20 years. There was also a Ralph Vaughan Williams Exhibition at the British Museum in London from September 29 to January 7, and the London Philharmonic Orchestra played Centenary Concerts at the Royal Festival Hall on October 12 and at Westminster Abbey on November 9.

Spanish Riding School of Vienna 400th Anniversary. The first documented mention of the Spanish Riding School was in 1572. In addition to teaching the classical art of riding, it also educated the children of nobility, future diplomats, and generals. So prized were the skills taught there, that several riding masters were raised to the nobility and entered the diplomatic service. Today, the school preserves the classical riding principles, and promotes the breeding of Lipizzans, the magnificent breed of horses used at the school. The school celebrated its anniversary with a graphic art exhibition called "Horse and Rider" and several riding performances.

Pennsylvania Supreme Court's 250th Anniversary. When Charles II gave Pennsylvania to William Penn in 1681, there was no provision for a local final court of authority. All appeals had to be made to the king or Parliament, 3,000 miles away in England. Finally, in 1722, Great Britain established a Pennsylvania Supreme Court. To celebrate that event, the current Supreme Court of Pennsylvania, oldest in the United States, sat in its former home, Independence Hall, on May 22, 1972. Members of the Philadelphia Bar Association, dressed and acting as William Penn and his strong supporter David Lloyd, addressed the court in argument against the historic lack of a local supreme court. Michael Reed

CENSUS, U.S. The U.S. Bureau of the Census reported in July, 1972, that more than half of the families in the United States now have annual incomes of $10,000 or more. The report showed that median family income in 1971 rose to $10,290. For the first time in U.S. history, the median figure was above $10,000. This means that half of the families earned more than $10,290, and half earned less.

The median income in 1971 was 4.2 per cent higher than the 1970 median of $9,870. However, since consumer prices also rose in 1971, median family income was about the same as in 1970 in terms of what the dollar could buy. The 1971 median income when the head of the family worked full time all year was $12,440.

The report also showed that in 1971 there were 10.4 million families with annual incomes between $15,000 and $24,999 and 2.8 million with incomes of $25,000 and over. About 19 per cent of the 53.3-million U.S. families had less than $5,000 a year.

Minority Income. The median family income for blacks in 1971 was $6,440, about 60 per cent that of white families. It had been $6,280 in 1971. However, other census reports showed that black Americans continued to make substantial social and economic advances. A small segment of black families made significant gains in achieving income parity with whites. These were young black working couples living in the North and West. Among these families, the wives actually earned about 30 per cent more than their white counterparts and made a larger contribution to the family income.

Median income for families of Spanish origin rose to $7,550 in 1971. The 1970 median level for these families was $7,330. About 9.2 million persons were identified as being of Spanish origin in the 1970 census. About 2.4 million persons of Spanish origin, one-fourth of the population group, were living below the poverty level in 1971. The 1971 poverty level for a nonfarm family of four was $4,137.

The Population Growth Rate in the United States fell below 1 per cent in 1971 for the second time since 1940. The rate also fell below 1 per cent in 1968. The net increase in U.S. population in 1971 was 0.98 per cent, compared to 1.09 per cent in 1970.

The decline in the growth rate was due to a continued decline in the birth rate. In 1970, there were 18.2 births for every 1,000 Americans, but this rate dropped in 1971 to 17.2 births for every 1,000 Americans, the lowest ever recorded.

On December 31, the total U.S. population including the armed forces overseas was estimated at 210.2 million, an increase of 1.6 million since January 1. The estimated population gain in 1972 resulted from 3.2 million births, 2 million deaths, and a net immigration of almost 400,000. Henry Smith

CENTRAL AFRICAN REPUBLIC. See AFRICA.

CENTRAL AMERICA. See LATIN AMERICA.

CEYLON. See SRI LANKA.

CHAD. French involvement in the seven-year-old civil war in this former French colony appeared to be nearing an end in 1972. Early in January, French President Georges Pompidou visited Chad, which is now a member of the French Community. During a state dinner given in his honor by President François Tombalbaye, Pompidou reiterated his promises to respect agreements under which French military aid had been supplied to the Chad government since 1960. At that time, an armed rebellion by nomadic rebels had erupted in the northern and eastern parts of the country. In a later address to the Chad National Assembly, Pompidou also promised that France would continue to help Chad develop its road, rail, and air transport as well as its natural resources.

On May 18, the government announced that French troops would begin leaving the country on June 1. The statement gave official recognition to the fact that the war – and French involvement – had ended. Only an estimated 400 to 600 rebels were believed still at large, and they were so isolated from outside support that the Chad forces could handle the situation themselves.

By October, half of the 2,500-man French contingent had returned to France; and on September 1, General René Cortadellas, commander in chief of the French-Chadian forces, turned over his command to a Chadian, Colonel Félix Challoum. The remaining troops had either been reclassified as military advisers and integrated into Chad's army or assigned to permanent French bases, established in 1960 at Fort-Lamy and at Mongo. All of the French helicopters and fighters would be based at Mongo, in the south central region.

Meanwhile, a large number of Chadians were arrested on undisclosed charges in July and August. Included among them were politicians, businessmen, and such high-ranking officials as former Prime Minister Ahmed Koulamallah. According to a government statement, the arrests followed the discovery on June 5 of a group of rebels hiding in a village near Fort-Lamy. As a result of the arrests, a vigilante committee was formed at Fort-Lamy.

Foreign Relations. Under President Tombalbaye, Chad continued to pursue a pro-Arab policy. On April 12, the country resumed diplomatic relations with Libya. The two countries had severed relations in August, 1971. In November, Tombalbaye announced that Chad had formally broken relations with Israel. Simultaneously, he announced diplomatic recognition of the People's Republic of China.

President Tombalbaye dedicated and officially opened the University of Fort-Lamy on June 6 in elaborate ceremonies attended by high dignitaries from several African countries. The new university, a part of the president's "cultural revolution," offers courses in arts and economics. Paul C. Tullier

See also AFRICA (Facts in Brief Table).

CHEMICAL INDUSTRY. A surge in corporate profits, beginning in late 1971 and continuing throughout the year, served to bolster the working capital of U.S. chemical companies in 1972. However, because of higher costs of raw materials, fuel, power, and labor, profits were still lower than in the mid-1960s. At the same time, the Price Commission insisted on a price increase ceiling of 8 per cent and refused to allow 1966-1967 as a base period for calculating profit margins, as the industry requested.

Organic chemical production boomed in 1972, with benzene and ethylene showing sizable gains. Plastics were also strong with gains of up to 33 per cent. Synthetic resin output increased an average of 24 per cent, which induced a sharply higher output of numerous intermediate chemicals and monomers. Much of the increase in plastic resins was caused by the 75 per cent increase in sales of plastic pipe. Synthetic fibers made a good showing because of the rebound in carpet markets and home furnishings and steady growth in automotive and apparel markets. Industrial gases had a spotty year. Oxygen production was down about 3 per cent, perhaps because of low steel production. Acetylene production was off about 19 per cent. However, nitrogen sales continued to grow at the rate of 9 per cent. Also up were hydrogen at 6 per cent and carbon dioxide at 14 per cent. Fertilizer sales were much better than expected. Volume was up only about 3 per cent, according to the Fertilizer Institute. However, exports increased 16 per cent over 1971's shipments. Ammonia, which was in oversupply at the start of the year, finished strong.

Energy Crisis. Probably the most important development to surface in 1972 was the impending scarcity of energy. The chemical-process industries account for more than 50 per cent of industrial gas use. Plants that produce ammonia, methanol, and carbon black are especially vulnerable because natural gas is used both as a fuel and as a principal feedstock. Lack of gas was cited as a factor in Shell Chemical's decision to close its two Pacific Coast ammonia plants in 1972. Some short-range solutions to the problem involve using liquid feedstocks such as naphtha for conversion into substitute natural gas. A long-term solution, the gasification of coal, might also result in valuable chemical intermediate byproducts.

Environmental Issues. Skyrocketing costs of pollution control showed up in the latest survey by the Manufacturing Chemists Association, which reported that its 137 member companies will spend a total of $1.34 billion for control equipment from 1972 to 1975. The high cost of pollution control held down profits in the chemical-process industries.

The Food and Drug Administration (FDA) began to regulate cosmetic manufacturing and labeling in accordance with a voluntary, six-month trial-regulation plan proposed by the industry. The agency banned the use of diethylstilbestrol (DES) in animal feeds, hexachlorophene in soaps and deodorants, and lead in paints. Household paints containing more than 0.5 per cent cannot be sold after Dec. 31, 1972.

Phosphates in detergents were banned in Chicago; Dade County, Florida; and Buffalo, N.Y. Food additives that were under investigation for possible hazard to humans included saccharin and sodium nitrite.

To meet new pollution-control regulations, ink producers developed inks that polymerize under ultraviolet light, thus eliminating release of solvents into the atmosphere.

Scientists at Argonne National Laboratories near Chicago determined that nature out-pollutes man when it comes to carbon monoxide emission. Natural sources account for more than 3.5 billion tons of carbon monoxide per year–90 per cent of the world's total.

Pesticides exhibited a pattern of slackening growth reflecting the impact of environmental pressure on the industry. To date, three companies–Lebanon, Commercial Solvents, and Nease–have left the industry. Canceled or in danger of cancellation by the Environmental Protection Agency Pesticides Regulation Division were many uses for DDT, Mirex, aldrin, dieldrin, lindane, polychlorinated biphenyls, TDE, chlordane, endrin, heptachlor, strobane-T, and toxaphene.

Tougher legislation for pesticides in general slowly evolved in Congress as a proposed revision of the 1947 Federal Insecticide, Fungicide, and Rodenticide Act. At year's end, the House had cleared a bill but the Senate version was still in committee.

Research and Development spending, about $1.89 billion, was 3 per cent higher than in 1971. The National Science Foundation funded a new program, "Research Applied to National Needs" (RANN) with $54.1 million dollars. RANN is designed to create new chemical-process industry segments to make the United States more competitive with foreign technologies. Enzyme technology was the first application of interest to the chemical industry.

Foreign Trade. The chemical trade balance, while still in the black at $1.98 billion, was poor when compared to 1971's $2.22 billion.

The Department of the Treasury tightened enforcement of the Anti-Dumping Act of 1921. The act is designed to prevent selling foreign goods at or below cost to develop a U.S. market. Early in the year, the department had 35 anti-dumping cases pending, including railroad parts and vehicles from Canada, stainless sheet steel from Japan, sulfur from Mexico, wool and polyester-wool from Japan, and perchloroethylene from France, Spain, and Italy. The treasury ruled that Mexican sulfur has, in fact, been dumped in the United States. Damages will be assessed if the U.S. Tariff Commission determines that U.S. producers were hurt. Edward Abrams

CHEMISTRY. National Aeronautics and Space Administration (NASA) scientists announced in July, 1972, that the earth's main supply of oxygen probably comes from the dissociation of water vapor, not photosynthesis. In dissociation, the water vapor breaks down into its component parts, and oxygen is set free into the atmosphere. This process occurs in the upper atmosphere, and is caused by solar ultraviolet radiation. The NASA scientists discovered this during studies of films taken by an ultraviolet camera-spectrograph that was left on the moon by the *Apollo 16* astronauts. The dissociation of water is also believed to be responsible for the earth's geocorona, a massive cloud of atomic hydrogen that envelops the earth.

New Isotope. A team of scientists at Brookhaven National Laboratory on Long Island, New York, announced in April that they had produced phosphorus-35, the seventh known radioactive isotope of phosphorus. The scientists, David R. Goosman and David E. Alburger, disclosed that the isotope resulted when a sample of oxygen-18 was bombarded with fluorine-19 ions. As each oxygen nucleus absorbed a fluorine nucleus, it emitted two protons to become phosphorus-35. The new isotope has a half-life of only 48 seconds and decays to sulfur-35 by emission of beta rays.

Synthesis of L-Isomers. A Monsanto research team, headed by William S. Knowles, developed a method for direct chemical synthesis of pure L-amino acids, including L-phenylalanine, which is used in low-calorie sweeteners. They used a soluble complex of rhodium with substituted phosphine ligands as a catalyst. They also synthesized L-dopa, a derivative of L-phenylalanine. L-dopa is often used to treat Parkinson's disease.

Tumor Inhibitor. Chemist Morris Kupchan and his associates at the University of Virginia succeeded in isolating maytansine from plant materials. This is a chemical that is effective in inhibiting the growth of tumors. According to Kupchan, maytansine is the most promising of the more than 100 naturally occurring anticancer drugs that have been discovered so far. At the same time, it has a low toxicity. Mice infected with lymphocytic leukemia were able to tolerate a 50- to 100-fold increase in dosage. The common range of currently used anticancer drugs permits only a two- to three-fold increase.

Maytansine occurs in *Maytenus ovatus*, a shrub that grows widely in Ethiopia and Kenya. The drug was extracted with alcohol from dried leaves, fruits, roots, or stem material. A study of the structure of maytansine disclosed that it is a new type of ansa macrolide, a group of compounds that are usually isolated from microorganisms. The antibiotics rifamycins and streptovaricins belong to this class.

According to Kupchan, tumor inhibition occurs when a maytansine selectively destroys enzymes involved in the cell division reactions. This stops the rapid multiplication of cancer cells. Those who worked with Kupchan were W. A. Court, C. J. Gilmore, R. C. Haltiwanger, A. Karem, Y. Komoda, R. M. Smith, G. J. Thomas, and R. F. Bryan.

Antiviral Agent Synthesized. Virazole, a chemical active against viruses, was synthesized by John T. Witkowski of International Chemical and Nuclear Corporation's Nucleic Acid Research Institute in Irvine, Calif. It was found to be effective against Asian flu and the common cold in cell culture experiments, and treatment with Virazole in animal studies significantly increased the survival rates of mice infected with viral pneumonia and influenza.

Viruses cause a vast array of deadly diseases and ailments, from polio, smallpox, and rabies to mumps, cold sores, and the common cold. Viruses also may cause some forms of arthritis, cancer, heart disease, diabetes, and mental disorders. But no comprehensive drug has yet been developed for the treatment of viral diseases.

In order to multiply, a virus invades a cell and issues chemical instructions for synthesizing viral DNA or RNA and vital protein to the host cell. These then combine to form more virus. Virazole inhibits the rate of DNA synthesis, and thus interferes with the virus's ability to reproduce. Alfred W. von Smolinski

See also Awards and Prizes; Biochemistry; Nobel Prizes.

CHESS. Bobby Fischer became the first American to hold the official world chess championship on Sept. 1, 1972. He won the title when the defending world champion, Boris Spassky of Russia, resigned in the 21st game of their championship series in Reykjavík, Iceland. Fischer's victory ended the Russian world chess supremacy that had lasted 35 years.

In their title match, Fischer won seven games, each worth one point. Spassky won three, including a forfeit when Fischer failed to show up for the second game. Eleven games ended in a draw. Each draw was worth half a point to each player. Fischer's final score was 12½ points, Spassky's, 8½. The final 3 games of the scheduled 24 did not have to be played.

Fischer displayed several outbursts of temperament before and during the match. He refused to appear in Iceland until the prize money was increased, and the match was delayed two days. He did not appear for the opening ceremonies, but later apologized in a letter to Spassky.

Fischer won a total of $154,677.50 for his victory. He received $78,125 from the Icelandic Chess Federation and an additional $76,552.50 put up by James D. Slater, a British financier and chess enthusiast, as a further inducement when Fischer refused to appear. Spassky received $98,812.50, of which $45,937.50 came from Slater.

Money was only one of the controversies that

Bobby Fischer, right, won the world chess title from Boris Spassky in Iceland on Sept. 1, 1972. But when they met in 1970, shown, Spassky won.

marked the match. The championship site was a matter of dispute, as were the television film rights and camera placement. Fischer's forfeit came when he failed to appear for the second game in protest against filming of the match.

Spassky was restrained and impassive, but his second, Efim Geller, issued a statement on August 22 claiming that Fischer's American followers might be using "electronic devices and chemical substances" to impair Spassky's play. Most observers refused to take these charges seriously.

Praising Fischer's fighting spirit and "excellent technique," Spassky said after the match that he hoped to play Fischer again and did not think him "a power that cannot be conquered."

The Fischer-Spassky match attracted more attention than any chess games in history and boomed interest in chess in the United States. Demand for chess sets and instruction books outran supply.

Walter Browne of Australia won the 73rd U.S. Open Championship in Atlantic City in August, with 10½ points out of a possible 12. He also won the National Open in Sparks, Nev., in March. The 21st National Annual Chess Championship in New York City, in April and May, ended in a tie for first among Lubomir Kavalek of Washington, D.C.; Robert Byrne of Ossining, N.Y.; and Sammy Reshevsky of Spring Valley, N.Y. Russia won the Chess Olympics in Skopje, Yugoslavia, in October. Theodore M. O'Leary

CHICAGO. Mayor Richard J. Daley suffered several political setbacks in 1972. First, his preferred candidates for governor and state's attorney were defeated in the Democratic primary election in March. Then, he and 58 other members of the Illinois delegation to the Democratic National Convention were unseated in July. And finally, the Democratic incumbent state's attorney, Edward V. Hanrahan, lost to a Republican in the November election.

Hanrahan was under a conspiracy indictment stemming from a 1969 police raid in which two Black Panther Party leaders were slain. He first had Daley's backing to run again for the state's attorney post, but lost it because of the indictment. Nevertheless, Hanrahan stayed in the race and defeated his Democratic primary opponent. Daley then supported Hanrahan against Republican Bernard Carey. Although cleared of the indictment on October 25, Hanrahan lost the election, in part because of a heavy black vote for his opponent.

Police Problems. A federal investigation resulted in the indictment and conviction of several policemen for extorting payoffs from Chicago tavern owners. In November, Police Superintendent James B. Conlisk, Jr., set up a special 50-man unit to uncover police department corruption.

In May, a black group led by Congressman Ralph H. Metcalfe (D., Ill.) charged Chicago police with harassment and brutality in the black community and called for Conlisk's resignation. Conlisk then held public meetings in various parts of the city in a relatively unsuccessful attempt to improve police-community relations.

Protesting their working conditions, Chicago policemen demanded a bill of rights and a wage contract. In October, they staged a speed-up in traffic-ticket writing. Conlisk conditionally agreed to their demands on November 15.

Former Alderman Fred Hubbard was arrested in Los Angeles in September and returned to Chicago to stand trial for embezzlement. The government charged that, while director of the Chicago Plan, Hubbard took $100,715.99 in federal funds. The plan was designed to place more blacks in the construction industry. A new Chicago Plan pledging jobs for 9,820 minority workers by 1976, was announced by the U.S. Department of Labor on October 18.

Budget and Economy. Mayor Daley proposed a record $993-million city budget for 1973. It called for expanded services, but a 7.5 per cent cut in property tax levies.

Employment was up slightly. Production workers' income rose 8.7 per cent between May, 1971, and May, 1972, while the cost of living went up only 2.6 per cent. Uniform Crime Reports released on August 29 showed that Chicago's crime rate was slightly below the national average. J. M. Banovetz

CHILD WELFARE. The battle for legislation to provide day-care programs for children continued through 1972. There has been demand for high-quality developmental programs open to all children, probably on a sliding-fee basis. Congress rejected President Richard M. Nixon's 1972 proposals as little more than custodial programs for children that would enable welfare mothers to work. In August, House and Senate conferees agreed to include $542-million for child care, open to public-assistance recipients only, in the total Labor-Health, Education, and Welfare (HEW) appropriations bill for 1973. But the President was expected to veto the appropriation bill because it was $1.7 billion over the Administration's budget request.

The Ford Foundation, noting that 5 million mothers with children under 5 years old would be working by 1975, made substantial grants to three demonstration programs for preschool children. The need was also emphasized by a survey of 700 day-care centers serving 25,000 children in 77 communities. The surveyors reported "a terrifying collection of incidents of child abuse and neglect."

Community Mental Health Centers (CMHC). A preliminary report by Ralph Nader's task force on mental health charged in April that CMHC, which include mental health services for children, had failed to supplant state mental health hospitals with local prevention and care. It suggested that, because of domination by psychiatrists, the medical model of operation used was inappropriate for treating persons upset by lack of jobs, housing, and other social and life-support needs. The report came as Congress was considering renewed appropriations for the centers. In the same month, the National Institute of Mental Health announced that $10 million had been allocated to staff children's services in CMHC and to develop innovative, preventive programs to aid disturbed children in their home environments.

Foster Care. The second national conference of foster parents, held in Denver from May 5 to 7, brought together 1,195 foster parents and interested persons from 45 states. Some 200 foster-parent associations formed at local and state levels in the past few years were represented. The Children's Bureau of HEW had estimated in April that there were 300,000 children in foster homes.

Adoption. Efforts to increase the adoption of hard-to-place children continued. Huge numbers of handicapped, older, and minority-group children are unplaced. By 1972, public funds to help families willing to adopt such children were available in 14 states.

The Children's Bureau issued a report describing 20 adoption recruitment programs for black children. On August 30, parents and children from interracial adoptive families discussed their way of life on NBC television's "Today Show."

New Professional Child-Care Workers. A new profession is being created for those without prior college training who are interested in working with young children. Practitioners will be called Child Development Associates. Supported by an $802,000 grant from the Office of Child Development, 10 pilot programs got underway in the fall of 1972. They aim at training 100,000 associates over the next five years. Programs will lead to a credential after from six months to two years. Associates will be qualified to work in a professional capacity in day-care centers, Head Start programs, nursery schools, and other preschool programs.

Raising IQs. In 1972, psychologist Rick Heber of the University of Wisconsin at Madison published results of research providing renewed evidence that early cultural enrichment experiences can significantly raise the IQs of some children. Heber worked with poor children whose mothers had IQs below 70. One group received extensive care, stimulation, and affectionate handling by a trained staff from birth, with increasing emphasis on intellectual stimulation as the children developed. A similar group received no staff attention, developing under the sole care of their mothers and families. Those in the enriched environment scored an average of 33 IQ points over the control group, and exceeded the average among majority-group children. Frances A. Mullen

CHILDREN'S BOOKS. See LITERATURE FOR CHILDREN.

CHILE. President Salvador Allende Gossens, the first elected Marxist in Latin American history, fought for his political life in 1972. At the risk of provoking a civil war or a military coup, he plunged ahead with a drastic Socialist revolution, even though he had no clear mandate. However, he insisted on accomplishing his aim through the democratic process.

Rural violence, widespread unrest, and mounting anger spread among even Allende's own constituents. There were strikes, frequent street demonstrations and clashes, and major Cabinet changes, including the resignation of all 15 members on October 31. Numerous acts of sabotage were reported, and states of emergency were declared frequently. On August 21, housewives in Santiago staged a pot-banging demonstration in protest against food shortages. On the same day, most of Chile's 150,000 shopkeepers closed in a one-day protest against Allende's Socialist policies as well as to protest living costs which had soared 99.8 per cent between January and September as compared with a 22.1 per cent rise in all of 1971. Monetary reserves hit rock bottom, bankruptcy loomed, and production lagged. Chile also encountered growing difficulty in selling copper, which accounts for from 70 to 80 per cent of its foreign exchange earnings. The economy limped along through deficit financing and with aid from Communist nations.

Supporters of Marxist President Salvador Allende Gossens march in Santiago, Chile, on September 4 to celebrate second anniversary of his election.

Allende Blamed "Fascists" for his difficulties at home, and accused the United States of waging international economic warfare against Chile because of its seizure of properties owned by U.S. firms without compensation. Most of his troubles, however, came from his Socialist efforts, which united all major opposition parties in a Federation of Democracy that was committed to present a single slate of candidates in the March, 1973, congressional elections.

On October 10, a truckers' strike caused severe shortages of basic foods and gasoline. Sympathy strikes sprang up among small businessmen, shopkeepers, farmers, professional people, taxi and bus drivers, gas workers, and students. The government reacted by putting 20 of the country's 25 provinces, including Santiago, the capital, under modified martial law. Simultaneously, it seized radio and television stations and forced food shops and pharmacies to open. The strike finally ended in November.

On April 7, President Allende vetoed a constitutional amendment that would have curbed his powers to take over industries. In October, the government took control of two Dow Chemical subsidiaries; the Senate, in July, approved the expropriation of the Chilean Telephone Company, 70 per cent of which was owned by International Telephone & Telegraph Corporation. Mary Webster Soper

See also LATIN AMERICA (Facts in Brief Table).

CHINA, NATIONALIST. See TAIWAN.

Japanese Prime Minister Kakuei Tanaka bows and raises his cup to drink a toast with Chinese Premier Chou En-lai in Peking in September.

CHINA, PEOPLE'S REPUBLIC OF. The official newspaper, *People's Daily*, told the Chinese people on the first day of 1972 that "the situation is excellent." At least in part, the claim was justified. Visitors to China noted a more relaxed mood, and there were more goods on store shelves, denoting economic progress. For the first time since 1966, women wore brighter clothes, the stage presented a few new plays, and new books of fiction appeared in the stores. But China still faced a number of problems, and probably none harsher than that left by the "September Crisis" of 1971 in which Communist Party Chairman Mao Tse-tung's political heir, Lin Piao, lost his power and probably his life.

The Economy offered the brightest side of national life. In 1970 and 1971, its rate of growth ran at about 10 per cent. In 1972 it probably did almost as well, but there was also a growing emphasis on quality and sophistication. Many practices denounced during the Cultural Revolution as "counterrevolutionary" were restored. Workers were once again offered material incentives, and managers were restored to good grace and authority. During the late 1960s, the worker was enjoined to be "Red" rather than "expert." Now, he was pressed to improve his technical skills.

Natural calamities, especially drought, brought grain production down from its record 1970 heights. Premier Chou En-lai himself estimated the decline at about 10 million tons from the 246 million tons of grain and potatoes gathered in 1971. The deficit was made up in part by huge foreign purchases, including 3.75 million tons of wheat from Canada and 500,000 tons of wheat and 300,000 tons of corn from the United States, but the party did appeal to each Chinese in December to save a mouthful of grain each day, to help build up the reserves.

Commune officials, who often tended to be heavy-handed in the past, were warned to heed the suggestions and complaints of villagers. They were also told that once the peasants had delivered their grain quotas to the state, they should be allowed to grow and sell what they wished on their tiny private plots, which total roughly 5 per cent of China's cultivated land. Peasants were also permitted to engage in sideline occupations, such as basket making, for profit. Official reins remained tight, but, by and large, the peasants could expect their voices to be heard and their income to be increased.

China still insisted on balancing its imports with exports, and on paying cash. But now credits were available, especially in Japan. And if they wished, the Peking leaders could change to the buy-now-pay-later program that most countries use in international trade. Apart from the grain, China's most notable purchase of the year was a September order for 10 Boeing 707s at a cost of $150 million. These planes were in addition to 20 British Tridents ($173 million) and three faster-than-sound Anglo-French *Concorde* jetliners ($170 million) ordered earlier in the year. The purchases reflected Peking's determination to build an international airways system for China. Chinese official traders began to crisscross the world in search of good buys, including entire industrial plants. But China's foreign trade was still below 4 per cent of its gross national product of from $120-billion to $125 billion.

Dealing with the World. It was in foreign relations that Peking scored its greatest triumphs. The year's highlight was President Richard M. Nixon's visit to China, February 21 to 28, which Mr. Nixon himself described as "the week that changed the world." Cool in the beginning, the welcome became more cordial after Mao met the visitor in the Chairman's study for an hour's "serious and frank" conversation. Few specific agreements were reached, but this renewal of the dialogue broken in 1949 was of momentous importance for both countries.

A communiqué issued in Shanghai on February 27 said the United States had agreed to "progressively withdraw its forces and military installations on Taiwan as the tension in the area diminishes," with total withdrawal as the "ultimate objective." Both countries agreed on "contacts and exchanges" in science, technology, culture, journalism, and sports. They also agreed to "stay in contact through various channels . . . and continue to exchange views on issues of common interest." In pursuit of this agreement, the President's adviser, Henry A. Kissinger, flew to Peking in late June, for his fourth visit in less than a year.

The President's concluding comment on the communiqué was an expression of gratitude for the "gracious hospitality" shown him by the Chinese government. Encompassed in that remark was his gratitude not only for the food and the comfortable quarters made available to the American visitors, but also for the security and communications arrangements, and for the extraordinary efforts the Chinese made to facilitate the transmission of television coverage of many of Mr. Nixon's activities in China.

After President Nixon made the major breach in the wall of China's isolation, others followed. Great Britain formally agreed in March to establish full diplomatic relations with China, after the British had acknowledged that Taiwan was a "province" of China. In late September, Japan's new prime minister, Kakuei Tanaka, went to Peking to ask for forgiveness for Japan's years of aggression in China, to arrange for opening diplomatic relations, and to lay the groundwork for future trade. Japan was quickly followed by West Germany. By the year's end, more than 20 nations had extended recognition to Peking.

An hour-long meeting with Communist Party Chairman Mao Tse-tung highlighted President Nixon's unprecedented trip to China early in 1972.

CHINA, PEOPLE'S REPUBLIC OF

China's growing contacts with the capitalist world created problems. The young radicals of the Cultural Revolution had to be reassured that their leaders were not betraying the faith in dealing with President Nixon. Even more difficult were Peking's relations with its Asian allies. North Vietnam, which depended on China for guns and food in fighting the U.S. forces, reacted sharply to Peking's new cordiality toward Americans. It reacted even more bitterly when President Nixon ordered North Vietnamese ports mined and towns bombed, and China (like Russia) did nothing to challenge the U.S. action.

Feud with Moscow. Observers agreed that the leaders in Peking must have taken a fresh look at the Asian scene and at China's interests in late 1969 or early 1970. They apparently decided that the United States was no longer the prime threat, but that Russia was. Out of this grew the decision to seek closer relations with the United States. A by-product was the agreement among the leaders that an easing of relations with the Americans was more important to China than Hanoi's victory on the battlefield, especially since the U.S. forces were leaving Vietnam in any case. Thus, Peking continued its dialogue with the United States even as U.S. planes and ships were devastating North Vietnam. Some experts argued that it was this "betrayal" by Peking (and by Moscow) that led leaders in Hanoi to seek an end to the war in late 1972.

Traffic-control tower in Shanghai controls mainly bicycles. The city has few cars, and most people use bikes, buses, or pedicabs.

At the United Nations, where Peking took its seat in October, 1971, its delegates pursued a cautious course. Their prime effort seemed to be to win the leadership of the Third World, and they consistently sided with the African and Arab blocs. In August, China used its first veto in the Security Council to bar the admission of Bangladesh to the United Nations.

But the harshest words at the United Nations were invariably reserved for Russia, which the Chinese denounced as a "superpower" seeking to establish its "neocolonialist" sway over weaker states. Peking constantly referred to the million Russian troops allegedly posted along the Chinese border. In October, foreign reporters were given a tour of Peking's subway system, revealed to be a well-equipped air-raid shelter, 26 feet underground and capable of accommodating 4 million of the capital's 7 million inhabitants. Similar shelters were said to exist in all other major cities. Visitors were led to believe this was China's response to the Russian threat on the northern border.

"September Crisis." The political scene in 1972 seemed to be dominated by the so-called Lin Piao Affair, which in September, 1971, removed from power the man Mao himself had picked in April, 1969, as his successor. Both Mao and Premier Chou told visitors that Lin Piao and his wife, Yeh Chun, had plotted to assassinate Mao, and that when the plot failed, they died in an airplane crash in Mongolia on Sept. 12, 1971, as they tried to escape. Other military leaders who vanished at about the same time included Chief of General Staff Huang Yung-sheng, Air Force Commander Wu Fa-hsien, and Navy Commissar Li Tso-peng. Premier Chou told a group of visitors that the three had seized an aircraft for an escape, but were eventually brought back to Peking by the suspicious pilot. There, as they opened fire on approaching police, the pilot shot and killed the rebellious trio. An estimated 50 senior military officers were purged as a result of the alleged assassination plot.

Once the Lin Piao group was eliminated, Peking launched a campaign of public reindoctrination that lasted throughout 1972. It denounced Lin Piao as a "swindler." Some of the speeches, as well as party documents that made their way abroad, suggested the dispute between Lin Piao and the other leaders dated back to a secret conference in August, 1970, and covered a wide range of subjects, from foreign relations to national priorities. In the yearlong series of debates that followed, the Lin Piao group found itself opposed by a powerful coalition that won Mao's support.

The key figure in the coalition was Premier Chou. But allied with him were the party "radicals," who included Madame Mao (Chiang Ching) and some Communist Party leaders in Shanghai, as well as some of the regional army commanders. A union of leaders with varying interests, the coalition was cemented by the conviction that Lin Piao was not fit to succeed Mao and that he had to be forced out.

Who After Mao? Lin Piao's ouster revived the problems of succession. China was ruled in 1972 by a group of Old Revolutionaries – Mao himself was 79; Chou En-lai, 74; military leader Yeh Chien-ying, 76; and Vice-Premier Li Hsien-nien, 68. But with the exception of the Shanghai leaders, who had no national power base, there were apparently no younger men waiting on the sidelines. The crucial question of who after Mao? – and, even more, who after Chou En-lai? – could not be easily answered.

Chou gave no hint of the identity of those who might compose a future collective leadership when he spoke to a group of American newspapermen in October. He also gave no hint as to when present vacancies in the government might be filled. He argued that China had an abundance of middle-aged and younger potential leaders.

"The world hears only of Chairman Mao, Premier Chou, and a few other old leaders at the top and those who committed mistakes," he said, "but those who can do the leading work really are quite numerous." Mark Gayn

See also ASIA (Facts in Brief Table).

CHRONOLOGY. See Pages 8 through 14.

CHURCHES. See EASTERN ORTHODOX CHURCHES; JEWS; PROTESTANT; RELIGION; ROMAN CATHOLIC.

CITY. Long-needed relief for the nation's cities, chronically faced with budget crises, finally arrived in December, 1972, when the U.S. Department of the Treasury began mailing out the first checks under the federal government's new revenue-sharing program. President Richard M. Nixon formally signed the new program into law on October 20. It is retroactive to Jan. 1, 1972. Cities, counties, and townships were scheduled to receive a total of $20.1-billion between December, 1972, and Dec. 31, 1976. The new law appropriated a total of $30.2 billion for use by the nation's state and local governments. The funds are to be disbursed as follows:

Year	States (in billions)	Local governments (in billions)	Total (in billions)
1972	$1.8	$3.5	$5.3
1973	2.0	4.0	6.0
1974	2.0	4.1	6.1
1975	2.1	4.2	6.3
1976	2.2	4.3	6.5

The Distribution Formulas for revenue-sharing funds are based on population, per capita income of residents, and tax effort – the relationship between the taxes levied by a governmental unit and the aggregate income of that unit's residents. First, the total sum being paid in any given time period is divided among the 50 states on the basis of a state distribution formula. Then, two-thirds of the allocation for each state is reallocated to that state's local governments. All counties, townships, cities, villages, towns, and boroughs qualify for revenue sharing. Special units of local government, such as school districts, will not share directly in the program.

City governments may use the funds for what the law defines as high-priority expenditures. These include law enforcement, fire protection, building-code enforcement, environmental protection, mass transportation, streets and roads, health, recreation, libraries, social services, financial administration, and capital expenditures. The use of revenue-sharing funds by local governments for education or for "matching" funds to secure other federal aid is specifically prohibited. However, state governments may use their revenue-sharing funds to provide increased aid to public schools.

Although the initial legislation expires in five years, revenue sharing is expected to become a permanent system of aid to city governments. The President chose to sign the bill, which ushered in a historic new era in American federalism, in Philadelphia's Independence Hall. The program's final passage came after years of effort by the nation's mayors to find a formula that would use the federal government's superior taxing powers to produce revenue for local services – without being subject to the restrictions and regulations that traditionally accompany fed-

Workers lunch at an outdoor cafe in City Hall Plaza, which has become a revitalizing focal point in downtown Boston's commercial life.

eral aid programs. The new program is expected to provide relief for floundering municipal budgets and revitalize the nation's cities.

Lower Urban Density. The U.S. Bureau of the Census published its summary of general social and economic characteristics in October. According to this profile, as of 1970, about 67 per cent of the nation's population lived in urban areas, with the urban population occupying about 1.53 per cent of the total land area in the United States. But the nation's urban population increased by 19 per cent from 1960 to 1970, while the urban land area increased by 35 per cent. As a result, the population density of urban areas declined from 3,100 persons per square mile in 1960 to 2,750 persons in 1970. The rapid exodus from central cities to roomier suburbs caused the decline.

At the same time that people were moving to suburban residential areas, businesses were moving to outlying commercial and industrial areas. New York's Regional Plan Association estimated that half the jobs in the New York metropolitan area were outside the city in 1972, and that 90 per cent of all new jobs will also be outside the city.

In the Baltimore area, 63 per cent of all employed suburbanites worked in the suburbs, and 23 per cent of the city's work force commuted to suburban jobs. As of 1972, there were 37 office parks, or complexes, in Atlanta's suburbs, and more than half of all commercial business in the Chicago metropolitan area was transacted in the suburbs.

The American Institute of Architects (AIA) on January 24 called for more public control over urban growth and suggested the establishment of a national growth policy. Under the AIA plan, the federal government would purchase and set aside 1 million acres of land for planned communities that could accommodate from 500 to 3,000 families each. The plan also called for converting the government's Highway Trust Fund into a general fund for community development.

City Campuses. The Carnegie Commission on Higher Education released a report on December 5 recommending that colleges and universities in big cities deepen their involvement in urban problems. The commission report also requested that these institutions make their programs more accessible to city residents.

The report urged urban campuses to adopt an open-admission policy, taking students who might not qualify for admission otherwise. It also urged them to establish "satellite campuses" in suburban areas, which have a shortage of such facilities. The commission suggested that colleges and universities involve themselves in programs to help solve city problems and establish metropolitan higher-education councils to coordinate urban-development projects with industry, government, and community groups.

Health Problems. Two studies released in 1972 suggested possible links between urban air pollution and health problems. New York University biochemists Robert Shapiro and Barbara Braverman told the American Chemical Society on August 28 that sulfur dioxide, a major component of air pollution, can disrupt normal genetic mechanisms. The researchers said there is a possibility of long-range genetic damage to people living in urban areas.

Another study, reported on October 2 to an American Medical Association conference on the effects of pollution, noted a "considerable correlation between urban living and lung-cancer deaths not attributable solely to smoking rates."

The Senate Public Works Committee, in its report on the 1972 Federal Aid Highway Act, noted that "at least 67 cities must curtail motor traffic as part of their overall strategy" to meet federal air-pollution standards. The standards were set in the 1970 Clean Air Act and must be met by 1975.

One obvious solution to the air-pollution problem caused by exhaust emissions is public mass transit. Yet the plight of public-transit systems continued to worsen despite increased federal aid. In New York City, transit labor alone cost 8 per cent more than the revenue produced by fares. The Chicago Transit Authority expected a $50-million operating deficit in 1972 and warned in December that it would be

After plea by Chicago Mayor Richard J. Daley, U.S. Conference of Mayors voted in June to support President Nixon and pray for the war's end.

virtually bankrupt by Feb. 15, 1973. Throughout the United States, urban transit system costs have increased 50 per cent since 1960, while revenue has gone up only 20 per cent.

Urban Violence. There were large, and often violent, antiwar demonstrations on college campuses in major cities in May. They followed President Nixon's announced decision to bomb North Vietnam and mine its harbors. More than 1,800 persons were arrested in disturbances throughout the nation. Large demonstrations occurred in Albuquerque, N. Mex.; Berkeley and San Jose, Calif.; Boulder, Colo.; Chicago; Madison, Wis.; and Minneapolis.

Crime in the cities continued to increase, but the rate of increase declined for the third straight year. In its Uniform Crime Reports, released on August 29, the Federal Bureau of Investigation reported a 7 per cent rise in serious crimes in 1971, down from the 11 per cent increase in 1970. And, in the first quarter of 1972, the crime rate was only 1 per cent higher than in the same period of 1971. The number of crimes committed in 28 of the nation's 50 largest cities increased, but it decreased in the other 22.

Crime rates increased most sharply (11 per cent) in the suburbs. The lowest rate of increase (2 per cent) occurred in cities with a population of more than 250,000 persons. See CRIME.

A new menace–marauding teen-age gangs–arose on the streets of some of the nation's largest cities. In the past, such gangs have been a problem periodically in slum and ghetto neighborhoods. But the current gangs promised to be more deadly. They have replaced their old weapons–such as switch-blade knives, tire chains, and zip guns–with pistols, shotguns, grenades, and submachine guns.

Gang warfare was blamed for 40 deaths in Philadelphia in 1971 and for 15 killings in New York City during the first three months of 1972. In some cases, gang membership and drug use were closely related. In others, particularly in black neighborhoods, some vigilante-style gangs attempted to stop the flow of narcotic drugs.

Indian Ghettos. After 20 years of encouraging Indians to move into cities, the federal government renounced its Indian relocation policy on January 12. Officials announced that the $40-million annual training and job-assistance programs would concentrate on Indian reservations. There, the programs would be tied closely to development plans controlled by Indians. The Bureau of Indian Affairs, in announcing the policy shift, noted that efforts to relocate Indians in urban areas had created large Indian ghettos in Chicago, Cleveland, Denver, Los Angeles, and San Francisco. See INDIAN, AMERICAN.

On March 14, voters in Dade County, Florida, which includes Miami, rejected a proposal to change their metropolitan county's governing structure from a county commission-manager system to a commission and an elected chief executive. J. M. Banovetz

CIVIL RIGHTS. The school bus–boycotted, buried, and overturned by irate parents–was a tangible symbol of civil rights controversy in 1972. Busing to achieve racial integration in schools was a major concern for the executive, legislative, and judicial branches of the federal government, and became a volatile issue in several state presidential primaries.

President Richard M. Nixon, long opposed to busing, proposed a moratorium on all new court-ordered busing until July, 1973, and strict limits on how the courts could deal with school desegregation in the future. As an alternative to busing, he recommended that $2.5 billion in federal funds already appropriated be used to upgrade the most impoverished schools to equalize educational opportunities.

Roy Wilkins, director of the National Association for the Advancement of Colored People (NAACP) strongly criticized President Nixon's antibusing stand in a speech on May 25, and stated that proposed antibusing legislation was an attempt to "turn back the clock on civil rights."

Nevertheless, Congress passed a bill on June 8 that would delay court desegregation orders, requiring the transfer of pupils from one school to another, until all judicial appeals had been exhausted, or until Jan. 1, 1974. See CONGRESS.

The U.S. Commission on Civil Rights issued a report on May 2, claiming Mexican-American students are oppressed by the public schools in five states. The report stated that a Chicano student in Arizona, California, Colorado, New Mexico, and Texas is denied "the use of his language, a pride in his heritage, and the support of his community." Among the commission's recommendations was bilingual classes in English and Spanish.

Black Civil Rights activists were engrossed in politics in 1972. At the Democratic and Republican National conventions, there were more black delegates than ever before. Congresswoman Shirley A. Chisholm (D., N.Y.) became the first black woman to seek the presidential nomination of a major party. A black lawyer, Patricia Roberts Harris, chaired the powerful Democratic credentials committee.

The first National Black Political Convention, with some 8,000 participants of all political persuasions, was held in Gary, Ind., in March. After heated debate, the convention adopted a Black Agenda, which called for a guaranteed annual income of $6,500, reparations to blacks from white society, and more children's day-care centers. Reflecting a tendency toward a politics based solely on race, the agenda also called for a Black Political Assembly that would endorse candidates, conduct voter-registration drives, and deal with "the white-power political institutions."

The economic side of black civil rights was featured in September at Chicago's Black Expo, a minority trade and cultural exposition sponsored by Operation PUSH (People United to Save Humanity), which was founded by Jesse Jackson in 1971.

The Congressional Black Caucus heard testimony in March denouncing racism and discrimination at the executive level in radio and television broadcasting. The witnesses called for more black programming, a voice in policy-making decisions, and eventually a share by blacks in the ownership of stations.

The Women's Liberation Movement made important political gains in 1972. More women than ever were delegates to the Democratic and Republican National conventions. At the Democratic convention, not only was a woman nominated for President, but Frances (Sissy) Farenthold of Texas received a substantial number of delegate votes for the vice-presidential nomination.

Another major success was congressional passage on March 22 of the Equal Rights Amendment, which would prohibit discrimination on the basis of sex. The amendment was then sent to be ratified by the states. As of December, 22 of the necessary 38 states had ratified the amendment. See U.S. CONSTITUTION.

In a petition presented to the Federal Communications Commission in May, the National Organization for Women (NOW) protested that television is

Poet Imamu Amiri Baraka (LeRoi Jones) chairs a session of the first National Black Political Convention held in Gary, Indiana, in March.

saturated with programs that demean women. NOW charged that one major network provided "not one program of any intellectual, educational, or informative content . . . during the hours reserved for women viewers."

Equal Job Opportunities. Representatives of NOW and the NAACP accused the Nixon Administration of backing down on its commitment to provide equal employment opportunities for women and minorities. On September 25, NOW and the NAACP publicized a memorandum from Secretary of Labor James D. Hodgson to his department heads, stating that Administration policies "do not provide for quotas or proportional representation" based on population ratios.

Under a Department of Labor order that went into effect in April, most federal contractors and subcontractors were required to set goals and timetables for hiring women and minorities at all work levels. In his memorandum, Hodgson claimed the order's guidelines were meant only to aid companies in planning corrective action, not to set quotas or determine if companies were discriminating.

Some critics also charged that the Administration was abandoning established programs, such as the Philadelphia Plan, for opening jobs in the construction industry to blacks. The Administration denied the charges.

The Courts and Rights. The Supreme Court modified several established civil rights decisions in 1972. The court ruled that a jury in a state court need not be unanimous to convict a suspect of a crime. It also ruled that a witness can be forced to testify in a government inquiry without being granted total immunity from prosecution. In another ruling, the court held that journalists have no constitutional right to withhold confidential information from grand juries. However, the Supreme Court took a long-awaited step when it ruled that the death penalty was "cruel and unusual punishment," and therefore not permissible under the United States Constitution.

Two of the year's most publicized trials had civil rights implications. The Harrisburg, Pa., trial of Philip Berrigan, a Roman Catholic priest, and six other peace activists charged with plotting to raid draft boards, bomb Washington, D.C., heating tunnels, and kidnap presidential adviser Henry A. Kissinger ended in a mistrial on April 5.

On June 4, Angela Y. Davis, an outspoken young Communist, was acquitted by a California jury of charges of murder, kidnaping, and conspiracy.

Senator Sam J. Ervin, Jr., (D., N.C.), head of the Senate Judiciary Subcommittee on Constitutional Rights, filed a brief with the Supreme Court in February detailing Army spying on civilians. Ervin's friend-of-the-court brief told how congressmen, governors, and other elected officials had been under Army surveillance from 1967 to 1970.

In August, the subcommittee issued a 97-page report saying that the Army spying was "far more extensive than we had imagined." For example, a file was kept on a Massachusetts woman simply because she wrote letters to government officials and newspapers protesting the futility of a Civil Defense program in the face of the world arms race. The subcommittee report concluded that the Army spy program was a waste of time and money and infringed on the rights of civilians.

In Other Countries. A new United Nations panel, created in 1971 to examine complaints from individuals about violations of human rights, had received 27,000 letters by September, 1972. Although the proceedings of the five-member panel were kept secret, the investigators reportedly found serious violations of human rights in Greece, Iran, and Portugal.

In Uganda, President Idi Amin Dada ordered about 55,000 British Asians out of the country. In South Africa, white students protesting against discriminatory policies in education were punched, kicked, and tear-gassed by riot policemen.

Russian Jews wishing to emigrate to Israel were harassed by the Russian government. Some were required to pay exorbitant reimbursements for their education.

Louis W. Koenig

See also COURTS AND LAWS; EDUCATION; and Section Two, SECOND REVOLT OF THE FEMINISTS.

CLEVELAND. An election crisis occurred in Cleveland during the May 2 Ohio primary, when polling places in 127 Cuyahoga County precincts failed to open their doors to voters at the scheduled hour. The Cuyahoga County election board had failed to distribute voting machines and ballots on time. As a result, the federal courts ordered all polling places in the county to remain open until 11:59 P.M. Despite the time extension, 16 polling places never opened.

City Employees. Confronted with a continuing financial crisis, Mayor Ralph J. Perk issued an executive order, effective in February, directing city employees to take a 10 per cent across-the-board cut in hours worked and pay received. This allowed the mayor to balance the city's $89.3-million budget without dismissing 1,400 city workers. The city had been forced to lay off 2,500 men since 1970 because of the lack of funds. Later, hope appeared for Cleveland's financial crisis when the new federal revenue-sharing program became law.

Cleveland's firemen began a work slowdown on June 9. They were protesting the federal Pay Board's rejection of their promised $773 annual pay increase, because their workweek was reduced from 56 to 48 hours at the same time. Together, the two changes were equivalent to a 7 per cent pay increase, and this was a violation of the 5.5 per cent guideline established by the Pay Board. During the slowdown, the firemen answered fire calls but did not clean up debris after fires or maintain the firehouses. The city's police, meanwhile, kept their 40-hour work-week and were allowed to keep their $773 annual pay increase.

Cleveland sanitation workers protested their working conditions with a one-week strike that ended on October 3. During the strike, 1,500 tons of garbage accumulated each day.

A special "savings" account was set up for federal postal workers in Cleveland so that they could pay the 1 per cent municipal income tax levy. Because the local levy could not be withheld from federal paychecks, officials estimated that some 10,000 federal workers owed the city about $1.5 million. Under the savings account scheme, employees pay municipal tax deductions into the "savings" account, and the city withdraws the funds.

The owners of the American League baseball clubs approved unanimously, on March 22, the sale of the Cleveland Indians franchise to businessmen who promised to keep the club in Cleveland.

Employment rose slightly in the city in 1972, and the average weekly earnings of production workers increased 8.6 per cent between May, 1971, and May, 1972. According to the U.S. Bureau of the Census, median family income in Cleveland was $9,107 in 1971. J. M. Banovetz

CLOTHING. See FASHION.

COAL. See MINES AND MINING.

COIN COLLECTING. In August, coin collectors began to watch for double-die pennies erroneously struck and issued by the Philadelphia mint. The 1972 date on the face of the coins had a second impression above the primary impression. On the obverse side, the motto "In God We Trust" was also doubled and widely separated. First reports had the double-die pennies selling at $4,000 for a roll of 50 uncirculated specimens. Some uncirculated specimens were bringing about $50 apiece. An estimated 100,000 double-die pennies were produced.

The National Aeronautics and Space Administration (NASA) revealed in October that a 1793 American cent had been hidden on the *Gemini 7* spacecraft when it made its 14-day earth orbit in 1965. Howard Manners, then a NASA flight surgeon, slipped the coin into a flight bag at the request of William Ulrich, then a Minneapolis coin dealer. Ulrich sold the coin in August, 1972, for $5,000 in cash and a $10,000 lot to William F. Steinberg, a Fort Lauderdale, Fla., coin dealer. NASA said that astronauts Frank Borman and James Lovell, Jr., did not profit from the transaction.

Interest diminished in the 40 per cent silver Eisenhower dollars, so the U.S. mint extended the deadline for ordering proof specimens of the dollars from June 30 to July 15. The 1972 coins went on sale May 1. By mid-June, 1.5 million requests had been received, whereas more than 4.2 million of the 1971 dollars were sold. Mary Brooks, director of the U.S. mint, announced in August that the Eisenhower dollar would join the customary cent, nickel, dime, quarter, and half dollar as part of U.S. proof sets beginning in 1973. The addition will increase the price of proof sets from $5 to $7.

Collectors began bidding on November 1 for more than 2 million of the 90 per cent silver dollars struck at Carson City, Nev., between 1878 and 1891. The General Services Administration, charged with auctioning the coins, invited a committee of numismatic experts to view a number of the uncirculated coins. The experts reported that the coins were in excellent condition. The numismatic value of these and 91,000 other silver dollars to be disposed of has been estimated at from $75 million to $120 million.

Work started in 1972 on converting the old San Francisco mint into a museum and sales office for coin collectors. This 98-year-old structure was one of the few buildings to survive the 1906 earthquake and fire. Some 3 million collectors do business with the Numismatic Sales Division of the U.S. Treasury.

At the American Numismatic Association convention in August, World Wide Coin Investors of Atlanta paid $50,000 for an 1894 proof dime struck at the San Francisco mint. Only 24 of these coins were struck, and only 5 are known to exist. The sellers were coin dealers Abner Kreisberg and Jerry Cohen of Beverly Hills, Calif. Theodore M. O'Leary

COLOMBIA. The Liberal and Conservative parties that make up the ruling National Front as a coalition retained political control in Colombia in 1972. In the national elections, held on April 16 to fill about 8,800 posts in 906 provisional councils and 22 municipal assemblies, the Liberal Party won 40 per cent of the vote and the Conservatives 28 per cent. The National Alliance Front, a bipartisan party composed of defectors from the two main parties, took 24 per cent. The remaining 8 per cent was captured by candidates of about a dozen other parties and factions. It was the first election since 1957 to be held outside the National Front agreement that shares power and alternates the presidency between the two main parties.

There was considerable unrest in academic circles during the year. On February 21, thousands of teachers in technical and intermediate schools went on strike because of a dispute over wages. They were joined on March 6 by the National Association of Secondary Schools, increasing the number of striking teachers to 40,000 in about 6,000 schools. An additional 70,000 primary-school teachers joined the strikers on March 20. By the end of March, about 4 million students were affected by the walkout.

At the same time, students at the National University in Bogotá and other universities began boycotting classes, demanding a revision of university statutes or more effective participation in university government. Between April 11 and April 17, thousands of students and teachers took to the streets, demonstrating, setting fire to vehicles, and clashing with police and troops. The violence did not subside until April 17, when the government agreed to raise the teachers' salaries and repeal the Teaching Statute, a controversial decree that rigidly regulated teachers' salaries and promotions.

The Economy. Business was sluggish, suffering from tight credit and a shortage of working capital and investments, while inflation increased. Monetary reserves kept rising, however, reflecting improved export earnings from coffee and manufactured goods. At the end of August, gross holdings totaled $295.9 million, up from $265.3 million at the start of the year and $213.2 million as of Aug. 31, 1971. Inflation climbed 11.3 per cent in the year ended May 31. This hurt the nation's labor force of almost 5.8 million persons, of whom 97.9 per cent earned under 5,000 pesos and of whom, more eloquently, 44.7 per cent earned less than 500 pesos. International institutions and private banks granted Colombia $245 million in loans in July for tourism, investment programs, urban improvements, and education, and to promote exports, agriculture, and livestock. Mary Webster Soper

See also Latin America (Facts in Brief Table).

COLORADO. See State Government.

COMMON MARKET. See Europe.

COMMUNICATIONS. Satellites have made a growing mark since 1965 in international telecommunications. In 1972, they made their first impact on the domestic scene. The world's first geostationary satellite for domestic communications–Telesat Canada–was launched on Nov. 9, 1972.

Named *Anik* (Eskimo for "brother") and scheduled to begin commercial operations in early 1973, the satellite is stationed 22,400 miles above the equator. Telesat, a corporation specially formed to provide domestic satellite communications service in Canada, will operate 35 ground stations throughout the country to provide telephone, telegraph, television, data, and other forms of communications. Canada's satellite will allow communication service to the remote Far North areas, which until now have not been able to fully benefit from advancing communications techniques.

The United States was still undecided at year's end as to the course it will follow in providing domestic satellite communications service. The Federal Communications Commission received proposals initially from eight applicants and, in a close 4-to-3 vote, adopted a "domsat" (domestic satellite) policy in June, 1972. But appeals and alternate suggestions from those who wish to provide the service delayed any final action. It was anticipated that domestic satellite service would not get underway in the United States for at least two years.

Russia was also moving forward with domestic satellite service. In 1972, Russia launched three more *Molniya* satellites, which operate in a random, rather than synchronous, orbit. Since 1965, Russia has launched 23 communications satellites.

Internationally, satellites were the principal area of communications services growth in 1972. By year's end, the 83-member International Telecommunications Satellite Consortium (Intelsat) had four *Intelsat 4* satellites in operation–two over the Atlantic, and one each over the Pacific and Indian oceans, linking 80 antennas at 64 earth stations in 49 countries.

Two events brought home the advances achieved in international telecommunications:

- President Richard M. Nixon's historic visit to mainland China in February was closely followed by television. China cooperated with U.S. interests to set up earth stations in Peking and Shanghai, establishing a television link between China and the rest of the world for the first time, just a few months after telephone and telegraph service was restored.
- The Olympic Games in Munich, West Germany, used a record 1,005 half-channel hours of satellite time in August and September for international telecasts. The new record was more than double the television usage of satellites for any event since commercial satellite service went into effect on June 28, 1965.

A flat chip of oxidized silicone is the image sensor of a new, solid state, low-voltage video camera built by Bell Laboratories engineers.

Cable Links. Along with the growth of satellite facilities, plans were moving ahead to provide on-the-ground links between countries. Approval was given in July for construction of a sixth transatlantic cable, between the United States and France, and construction went ahead on another cable under the Atlantic Ocean between Canada and Great Britain. The first cable linking Europe and South America was completed in October, and another step in the comprehensive plan for cable facilities to serve the Pacific area was taken in October when a follow-up proposal was made to build a facility between Hawaii and Okinawa, via Guam.

Telephone Service. At year's end, the number of telephones in service throughout the world was estimated at more than 300 million. Of this total, about 128 million are in the United States. Bell System companies accounted for some 105 million and the nation's 1,800 independent telephone companies had some 23 million in service.

The task of making overseas calls was simplified for telephone users in several countries in 1972 by the expansion of international direct-distance dialing. Great Britain and some western European countries enlarged their direct-dialing facilities. In the United States, telephone users in 16 exchanges in New York City were able to dial 20 countries. Thomas M. Malia

CONGO (BRAZZAVILLE). See AFRICA.

CONGO (KINSHASA). See ZAIRE.

CONGRESS OF THE UNITED STATES. Powerful Democrats in control of both houses in the second session of the 92nd Congress clashed repeatedly in 1972 with President Richard M. Nixon as he tried to persuade Congress to go along with his Administration's policies. The Senate's effort to regain some control over the warmaking power of the government and to end the war in Vietnam failed because of support in the House of Representatives for the Administration's program.

As the November, 1972, elections approached, the President asked Congress for authority to limit spending in fiscal 1973 to $250 billion, regardless of the appropriations passed by Congress. The Senate refused. The President promptly announced that he would not release funds in excess of $250 billion in fiscal 1973. He labeled the 92nd Congress "spendthrift" and vetoed several large appropriation bills that he said would "breach the budget."

With the issue clearly drawn, Congress on October 4 overrode the President's veto of a bill granting a 20 per cent increase in railroad retirement benefits. On October 18, Congress passed a $24.6-billion appropriation to fight water pollution—again over the President's veto. Then, on October 27, the President vetoed nine measures that he felt would breach the budget, including a $30-billion appropriation for the departments of Labor and Health, Education, and Welfare. On the same day, he also vetoed authorizations for public works, flood control, mining and minerals research, airport development, improved burial and cemetery benefits for veterans, higher pay for U.S. marshals, expanded health care for veterans, and vocational rehabilitation. In all, the President vetoed 26 bills. Of the 318 measures the President proposed to the second session, Congress passed 141, or less than 44 per cent.

The Second Session of the 92nd Congress convened on Jan. 18, 1972. In the Senate, there were 54 Democrats, 44 Republicans, 1 Conservative, and 1 Independent. The House of Representatives had 254 Democrats, 178 Republicans, and 3 vacant seats.

Mike J. Mansfield (D., Mont.) continued to serve as majority leader in the Senate; Robert C. Byrd (D.,W.Va.), as Democratic whip. Minority leader in the Senate was Hugh D. Scott, Jr. (R., Pa.), and Robert P. Griffin (R., Mich.) was again minority whip.

In the House, Carl B. Albert (D., Okla.) retained his post as speaker, and Hale Boggs (D., La.) served as majority leader. Gerald R. Ford (R., Mich.) was minority leader, and Leslie C. Arends (R., Ill.) was minority whip. However, Boggs and Congressman Nick Begich (D., Alaska) were missing and presumed dead after a plane in which they were flying disappeared over Alaska on October 16. The 92nd Congress recessed for the Democratic and the Republican conventions. It adjourned October 18.

Two of Ralph Nader's "raiders" organize material for their study and evaluation of Congress and the performance of individual congressmen.

Members of the United States Senate

The Senate of the first session of the 93rd Congress consists of 56 Democrats, 42 Republicans, 1 Independent, and 1 Conservative, compared with 54 Democrats, 44 Republicans, 1 Independent, and 1 Conservative for the second session of the 92nd Congress. Senators shown starting their term in 1973 were elected for the first time in the Nov. 7, 1972, elections. Those shown ending their current terms in 1979 were re-elected to the Senate in the same balloting. The second date in each listing shows when the term of a previously elected senator expires. For organization purposes, the one Independent will line up with Democrats, the one Conservative with Republicans.

State	Term
Alabama	
John J. Sparkman, D.	1946–1979
James B. Allen, D.	1969–1975
Alaska	
Theodore F. Stevens, R.	1968–1979
Mike Gravel, D.	1969–1975
Arizona	
Paul J. Fannin, R.	1965–1977
Barry Goldwater, R.	1969–1975
Arkansas	
John L. McClellan, D.	1943–1979
J. William Fulbright, D.	1945–1975
California	
Alan Cranston, D.	1969–1975
John V. Tunney, D.	1971–1977
Colorado	
Peter H. Dominick, R.	1963–1975
Floyd K. Haskell, D.	1973–1979
Connecticut	
Abraham A. Ribicoff, D.	1963–1975
Lowell P. Weicker, Jr., R.	1971–1977
Delaware	
William V. Roth, Jr., R.	1971–1977
Joseph R. Biden, Jr., D.	1973–1979
Florida	
Edward J. Gurney, R.	1969–1975
Lawton Chiles, D.	1971–1977
Georgia	
Herman E. Talmadge, D.	1957–1975
Sam A. Nunn, Jr., D.	1973–1979
Hawaii	
Hiram L. Fong, R.	1959–1977
Daniel Ken Inouye, D.	1963–1975
Idaho	
Frank Church, D.	1957–1975
James A. McClure, R.	1973–1979
Illinois	
Charles H. Percy, R.	1967–1979
Adlai E. Stevenson III, D.	1970–1975
Indiana	
Vance Hartke, D.	1959–1977
Birch Bayh, D.	1963–1975
Iowa	
Harold E. Hughes, D.	1969–1975
Richard Clark, D.	1973–1979
Kansas	
James B. Pearson, R.	1962–1979
Robert J. Dole, R.	1969–1975
Kentucky	
Marlow W. Cook, R.	1968–1975
Walter Huddleston, D.	1973–1979
Louisiana	
Russell B. Long, D.	1948–1975
J. Bennett Johnston, Jr., D.	1973–1979
Maine	
Edmund S. Muskie, D.	1959–1977
William D. Hathaway, D.	1973–1979
Maryland	
Charles McC. Mathias, Jr., R.	1969–1975
J. Glenn Beall, Jr., R.	1971–1977
Massachusetts	
Edward M. Kennedy, D.	1962–1977
Edward W. Brooke, R.	1967–1979
Michigan	
Philip A. Hart, D.	1959–1977
Robert P. Griffin, R.	1966–1979
Minnesota	
Walter F. Mondale, D.	1964–1979
Hubert H. Humphrey, D.	1971–1977
Mississippi	
James O. Eastland, D.	1943–1979
John Cornelius Stennis, D.	1947–1977
Missouri	
Stuart Symington, D.	1953–1977
Thomas Francis Eagleton, D.	1968–1975
Montana	
Mike J. Mansfield, D.	1953–1977
Lee Metcalf, D.	1961–1979
Nebraska	
Roman Lee Hruska, R.	1954–1977
Carl T. Curtis, R.	1955–1979
Nevada	
Alan Bible, D.	1954–1975
Howard W. Cannon, D.	1959–1977
New Hampshire	
Norris Cotton, R.	1954–1975
Thomas J. McIntyre, D.	1962–1979
New Jersey	
Clifford P. Case, R.	1955–1979
Harrison A. Williams, Jr., D.	1959–1977
New Mexico	
Joseph M. Montoya, D.	1964–1977
Pete V. Domenici, R.	1973–1979
New York	
Jacob K. Javits, R.	1957–1975
James L. Buckley, Cons.	1971–1977
North Carolina	
Sam J. Ervin, Jr., D.	1954–1975
Jesse A. Helms, R.	1973–1979
North Dakota	
Milton R. Young R.	1945–1975
Quentin N. Burdick, D.	1960–1977
Ohio	
William B. Saxbe, R.	1969–1975
Robert Taft, Jr., R.	1971–1977
Oklahoma	
Henry L. Bellmon, R.	1969–1975
Dewey F. Bartlett, R.	1973–1979
Oregon	
Mark O. Hatfield, R.	1967–1979
Robert W. Packwood, R.	1969–1975
Pennsylvania	
Hugh D. Scott, Jr., R.	1959–1977
Richard S. Schweiker, R.	1969–1975
Rhode Island	
John O. Pastore, D.	1950–1977
Claiborne Pell, D.	1961–1979
South Carolina	
Strom Thurmond, R.	1956–1979
Ernest F. Hollings, D.	1966–1975
South Dakota	
George S. McGovern, D.	1963–1975
James G. Abourezk, D.	1973–1979
Tennessee	
Howard H. Baker, Jr., R.	1967–1979
William E. Brock III, R.	1971–1977
Texas	
John G. Tower, R.	1961–1979
Lloyd M. Bentsen, Jr., D.	1971–1977
Utah	
Wallace F. Bennett, R.	1951–1975
Frank E. Moss, D.	1959–1977
Vermont	
George D. Aiken, R.	1941–1975
Robert T. Stafford, R.	1971–1977
Virginia	
Harry F. Byrd, Jr., Ind.	1965–1977
William L. Scott, R.	1973–1979
Washington	
Warren G. Magnuson, D.	1944–1975
Henry M. Jackson, D.	1953–1977
West Virginia	
Jennings Randolph, D.	1958–1979
Robert C. Byrd, D.	1959–1977
Wisconsin	
William Proxmire, D.	1957–1977
Gaylord A. Nelson, D.	1963–1975
Wyoming	
Gale W. McGee, D.	1959–1977
Clifford P. Hansen, R.	1967–1979

Members of the United States House

The House of Representatives of the first session of the 93rd Congress consists of 240 Democrats and 192 Republicans (not including representatives from the District of Columbia, Puerto Rico, Guam, and the Virgin Islands), with 3 seats vacant, compared with 254 Democrats and 178 Republicans, with 3 seats vacant, for the second session of the 92nd Congress. This table shows congressional districts, legislator, and party affiliation. Asterisk (*) denotes those who served in the 92nd Congress; dagger (†) denotes "at large."

Alabama

1. Jack Edwards, R.*
2. William L. Dickinson, R.*
3. William Nichols, D.*
4. Tom Bevill, D.*
5. Robert E. Jones, D.*
6. John H. Buchanan, Jr., R.*
7. Walter Flowers, D.*

Alaska

† Vacant

Arizona

1. John J. Rhodes, R.*
2. Morris K. Udall, D.*
3. Sam Steiger, R.*
4. John B. Conlan, R.

Arkansas

1. Bill Alexander, D.*
2. Wilbur D. Mills, D.*
3. J. P. Hammerschmidt, R.*
4. Ray Thornton, D.

California

1. Don H. Clausen, R.*
2. Harold T. Johnson, D.*
3. John E. Moss, D.*
4. Robert L. Leggett, D.*
5. Phillip Burton, D.*
6. William S. Mailliard, R.*
7. Ronald V. Dellums, D.*
8. Fortney H. Stark, D.
9. Don Edwards, D.*
10. Charles S. Gubser, R.*
11. Leo J. Ryan, D.
12. Burt L. Talcott, R.*
13. Charles M. Teague, R.*
14. Jerome R. Waldie, D.*
15. John J. McFall, D.*
16. B. F. Sisk, D.*
17. Paul N. McCloskey, Jr., R.*
18. Robert B. Mathias, R.*
19. Chet Holifield, D.*
20. Carlos J. Moorhead, R.
21. Augustus F. Hawkins, D.*
22. James C. Corman, D.*
23. Del M. Clawson, R.*
24. John H. Rousselot, R.*
25. Charles E. Wiggins, R.*
26. Thomas M. Rees, D.*
27. Barry M. Goldwater, Jr., R.*
28. Alphonzo Bell, R.*
29. George E. Danielson, D.*
30. Edward R. Roybal, D.*
31. Charles H. Wilson, D.*
32. Craig Hosmer, R.*
33. Jerry L. Pettis, R.*
34. Richard T. Hanna, D.*
35. Glenn M. Anderson, D.*
36. William Ketchum, R.
37. Yvonne B. Burke, D.
38. George E. Brown, Jr., D.
39. Andrew J. Hinshaw, R.
40. Bob Wilson, R.*
41. Lionel Van Deerlin, D.*
42. Clair W. Burgener, R.
43. Victor V. Veysey, R.*

Colorado

1. Patricia Schroeder, D.
2. Donald G. Brotzman, R.*
3. Frank E. Evans, D.*
4. James P. Johnson, R.
5. William L. Armstrong, R.

Connecticut

1. William R. Cotter, D.*
2. Robert H. Steele, R.*
3. Robert N. Giaimo, D.*
4. Stewart B. McKinney, R.*
5. Ronald A. Sarasin, R.
6. Ella T. Grasso, D.*

Delaware

† Pierre S. du Pont IV, R.*

Florida

1. Robert L. F. Sikes, D.*
2. Don Fuqua, D.*
3. Charles E. Bennett, D.*
4. William V. Chappell, Jr., D.*
5. Bill Gunter, D.
6. C. W. Young, R.*
7. Sam M. Gibbons, D.*
8. James A. Haley, D.*
9. Louis Frey, Jr., R.*
10. L. A. Bafalis, R.
11. Paul G. Rogers, D.*
12. J. Herbert Burke, R.*
13. William Lehman, D.
14. Claude D. Pepper, D.*
15. Dante B. Fascell, D.°

Georgia

1. Ronald Ginn, D.
2. Dawson Mathis, D.*
3. Jack T. Brinkley, D.*
4. Ben B. Blackburn, R.*
5. Andrew Young, D.
6. John J. Flynt, Jr., D.*
7. John W. Davis, D.*
8. Williamson S. Stuckey, Jr., D.*
9. Phillip M. Landrum, D.*
10. Robert G. Stephens, Jr., D.*

Hawaii

1. Spark M. Matsunaga, D.*
2. Patsy T. Mink, D.*

Idaho

1. Steven D. Symms, R.
2. Orval Hansen, R.*

Illinois

1. Ralph H. Metcalfe, D.*
2. Morgan F. Murphy, D.*
3. Robert P. Hanrahan, R.
4. Edward J. Derwinski, R.*
5. John C. Kluczynski, D.*
6. Harold R. Collier, R.*
7. Vacant
8. Dan Rostenkowski, D.*
9. Sidney R. Yates, D.*
10. Samuel H. Young, R.
11. Frank Annunzio, D.*
12. Philip M. Crane, R.*
13. Robert McClory, R.*
14. John N. Erlenborn, R.*
15. Leslie C. Arends, R.*
16. John B. Anderson, R.*
17. George M. O'Brien, R.
18. Robert H. Michel, R.*
19. Thomas F. Railsback, R.*
20. Paul Findley, R.*
21. Edward R. Madigan, R.
22. George E. Shipley, D.*
23. Charles Melvin Price, D.*
24. Kenneth J. Gray, D.*

Indiana

1. Ray J. Madden, D.*
2. Earl F. Landgrebe, R.*
3. John Brademas, D.*
4. J. Edward Roush, D.*
5. Elwood H. Hillis, R.*
6. William G. Bray, R.*
7. John T. Myers, R.*
8. Roger H. Zion, R.*
9. Lee H. Hamilton, D.*
10. David W. Dennis, R.*
11. William H. Hudnut III, R.

Iowa

1. Edward Mezvinsky, D.
2. John C. Culver, D.*
3. H. R. Gross, R.*
4. Neal Smith, D.*
5. William J. Scherle, R.*
6. Wiley Mayne, R.*

Kansas

1. Keith G. Sebelius, R.*
2. William R. Roy, D.*
3. Larry Winn, Jr., R.*
4. Garner E. Shriver, R.*
5. Joe Skubitz, R.*

Kentucky

1. Frank A. Stubblefield, D.*
2. William H. Natcher, D.*
3. Romano L. Mazzoli, D.*
4. Marion Gene Snyder, R.*
5. Tim Lee Carter, R.*
6. John B. Breckinridge, D.
7. Carl D. Perkins, D.*

Louisiana

1. F. Edward Hébert, D.*
2. Vacant
3. David C. Treen, R.
4. Joe D. Waggoner, Jr., D.*
5. Otto E. Passman, D.*
6. John R. Rarick, D.*
7. John B. Breaux, D.*
8. Gillis W. Long, D.

Maine

1. Peter N. Kyros, D.*
2. William S. Cohen, R.

Maryland

1. William O. Mills, R.*
2. Clarence D. Long, D.*
3. Paul S. Sarbanes, D.*
4. Marjorie S. Holt, R.
5. Lawrence J. Hogan, R.*
6. Goodloe E. Byron, D.*
7. Parren J. Mitchell, D.*
8. Gilbert Gude, R.*

Massachusetts

1. Silvio O. Conte, R.*
2. Edward P. Boland, D.*
3. Harold D. Donohue, D.*
4. Robert F. Drinan, D.*
5. Paul W. Cronin, R.
6. Michael J. Harrington, D.*
7. Torbert H. MacDonald, D.*
8. Thomas P. O'Neill, Jr., D.*
9. John J. Moakley, D.
10. Margaret M. Heckler, R.*
11. James A. Burke, D.*
12. Gerry E. Studds, D.

Michigan

1. John Conyers, Jr., D.*
2. Marvin L. Esch, R.*
3. Garry Brown, R.*
4. Edward Hutchinson, R.*
5. Gerald R. Ford, R.*
6. Charles E. Chamberlain, R.*
7. Donald W. Riegle, Jr., R.*
8. James Harvey, R.*
9. Guy Vander Jagt, R.*
10. Elford A. Cederberg, R.*
11. Philip E. Ruppe, R.*
12. James G. O'Hara, D.*
13. Charles C. Diggs, Jr., D.*
14. Lucien N. Nedzi, D.*
15. William D. Ford, D.*
16. John D. Dingell, D.*
17. Martha W. Griffiths, D.*
18. Robert J. Huber, R.
19. William S. Broomfield, R.*

Minnesota

1. Albert H. Quie, R.*
2. Ancher Nelsen, R.*
3. Bill Frenzel, R.*
4. Joseph E. Karth, D.*
5. Donald M. Fraser, D.*
6. John M. Zwach, R.*
7. Bob Bergland, D.*
8. John A. Blatnik, D.*

Mississippi

1. Jamie L. Whitten, D.*
2. David R. Bowen, D.
3. G. V. Montgomery, D.*
4. Thad Cochran, R.
5. Trent Lott, R.

Missouri

1. William L. Clay, D.*
2. James W. Symington, D.*
3. Leonor K. Sullivan, D.*
4. William J. Randall, D.*
5. Richard Bolling, D.*
6. Jerry Litton, D.
7. Gene Taylor, R.
8. Richard H. Ichord, D.*
9. William L. Hungate, D.*
10. Bill D. Burlison, D.*

Montana

1. Richard G. Shoup, R.*
2. John Melcher, D.*

Nebraska

1. Charles Thone, R.*
2. John Y. McCollister, R.*
3. David T. Martin, R.*

Nevada

† David Towell, R.

New Hampshire

1. Louis C. Wyman, R.*
2. James C. Cleveland, R.*

New Jersey

1. John E. Hunt, R.*
2. Charles W. Sandman, Jr., R.*
3. James J. Howard, D.*
4. Frank Thompson, Jr., D.*
5. Peter H. B. Frelinghuysen, R.*
6. Edwin B. Forsythe, R.*
7. William B. Widnall, R.*
8. Robert A. Roe, D.*
9. Henry Helstoski, D.*
10. Peter W. Rodino, Jr., D.*
11. Joseph G. Minish, D.*
12. Matthew J. Rinaldo, R.
13. Joseph J. Maraziti, R.
14. Dominick V. Daniels, D.*
15. Edward J. Patten, D.*

New Mexico

1. Manuel Lujan, Jr., R.*
2. Harold L. Runnels, D.*

New York

1. Otis G. Pike, D.*
2. James R. Grover, Jr., R.*
3. Angelo D. Roncallo, R.
4. Norman F. Lent, R.*
5. John W. Wydler, R.*
6. Lester L. Wolff, D.*
7. Joseph P. Addabbo, D.*
8. Benjamin S. Rosenthal, D.*
9. James J. Delaney, D.*
10. Mario Biaggi, D.*
11. Frank J. Brasco, D.*
12. Shirley Chisholm, D.*
13. Bertram L. Podell, D.*
14. John J. Rooney, D.*
15. Hugh L. Carey, D.*
16. Elizabeth Holtzman, D.
17. John M. Murphy, D.*
18. Edward I. Koch, D.*
19. Charles B. Rangel, D.*
20. Bella S. Abzug, D.*
21. Herman Badillo, D.*
22. Jonathan B. Bingham, D.*
23. Peter A. Peyser, R.*
24. Ogden R. Reid, D.*
25. Hamilton Fish, Jr., R.*
26. Benjamin A. Gilman, R.
27. Howard W. Robison, R.*
28. Samuel S. Stratton, D.*
29. Carleton J. King, R.*
30. Robert C. McEwen, R.*
31. Donald Mitchell, R.
32. James M. Hanley, D.*
33. William F. Walsh, R.
34. Frank Horton, R.*
35. Barber B. Conable, Jr., R.*
36. Henry P. Smith III, R.*
37. Thaddeus J. Dulski, D.*
38. Jack F. Kemp, R.*
39. James F. Hastings, R.*

North Carolina

1. Walter B. Jones, D.*
2. L. H. Fountain, D.*
3. David N. Henderson, D.*
4. Ike F. Andrews, D.
5. Wilmer D. Mizell, R.*
6. L. Richardson Preyer, D.*
7. Charles G. Rose III, D.
8. Earl B. Ruth, R.*
9. James G. Martin, R.
10. James T. Broyhill, R.*
11. Roy A. Taylor, D.*

North Dakota

† Mark Andrews, R.*

Ohio

1. William J. Keating, R.*
2. Donald D. Clancy, R.*
3. Charles W. Whalen, Jr., R.*
4. Tennyson Guyer, R.
5. Delbert L. Latta, R.*
6. William H. Harsha, R.*
7. Clarence J. Brown, R.*
8. Walter E. Powell, R.*
9. Thomas L. Ashley, D.*
10. Clarence E. Miller, R.*
11. J. William Stanton, R.*
12. Samuel L. Devine, R.*
13. Charles A. Mosher, R.*
14. John F. Seiberling, D.*
15. Chalmers P. Wylie, R.*
16. Ralph S. Regula, R.
17. John M. Ashbrook, R.*
18. Wayne L. Hays, D.*
19. Charles J. Carney, D.*
20. James V. Stanton, D.*
21. Louis Stokes, D.*
22. Charles A. Vanik, D.*
23. William E. Minshall, R.*

Oklahoma

1. James R. Jones, D.
2. Clem R. McSpadden, D.
3. Carl B. Albert, D.*
4. Tom Steed, D.*
5. John Jarman, D.*
6. John N. Happy Camp, R.*

Oregon

1. Wendell Wyatt, R.*
2. Al Ullman, D.*
3. Edith Green, D.*
4. John Dellenback, R.*

Pennsylvania

1. William A. Barrett, D.*
2. Robert N. C. Nix, D.*
3. William J. Green, D.*
4. Joshua Eilberg, D.*
5. John H. Ware III, R.*
6. Gus Yatron, D.*
7. Lawrence G. Williams, R.*
8. Edward G. Biester, Jr., R.*
9. E. G. Shuster, R.
10. Joseph M. McDade, R.*
11. Daniel J. Flood, D.*
12. John P. Saylor, R.*
13. Lawrence Coughlin, R.*
14. William S. Moorhead, D.*
15. Fred B. Rooney, D.*
16. Edwin D. Eshleman, R.*
17. Herman T. Schneebeli, R.*
18. H. John Heinz III, R.*
19. George A. Goodling, R.*
20. Joseph M. Gaydos, D.*
21. John H. Dent, D.*
22. Thomas E. Morgan, D.*
23. Albert W. Johnson, R.*
24. Joseph P. Vigorito, D.*
25. Frank M. Clark, D.*

Rhode Island

1. Fernand J. St. Germain, D.*
2. Robert O. Tiernan, D.*

South Carolina

1. Mendel J. Davis, D.*
2. Floyd D. Spence, R.*
3. W. J. Bryan Dorn, D.*
4. James R. Mann, D.*
5. Thomas S. Gettys, D.*
6. Edward L. Young, R.

South Dakota

1. Frank E. Denholm, D.*
2. James Abdnor, R.

Tennessee

1. James H. Quillen, R.*
2. John J. Duncan, R.*
3. LaMar Baker, R.*
4. Joe L. Evins, D.*
5. Richard H. Fulton, D.*
6. Robin L. Beard, Jr., R.
7. Ed Jones, D.*
8. Dan H. Kuykendall, R.*

Texas

1. Wright Patman, D.*
2. Charles Wilson, D.
3. James M. Collins, R.*
4. Ray Roberts, D.*
5. Alan Steelman, R.
6. Olin E. Teague, D.*
7. Bill Archer, R.*
8. Bob Eckhardt, D.*
9. Jack Brooks, D.*
10. J. J. Pickle, D.*
11. W. R. Poage, D.*
12. James C. Wright, Jr., D.*
13. Robert D. Price, R.*
14. John Young, D.*
15. Eligio de la Garza, D.*
16. Richard C. White, D.*
17. Omar Burleson, D.*
18. Barbara C. Jordan, D.
19. George H. Mahon, D.*
20. Henry B. Gonzalez, D.*
21. O. C. Fisher, D.*
22. Robert R. Casey, D.*
23. Abraham Kazen, Jr., D.*
24. Dale Milford, D.

Utah

1. K. Gunn McKay, D.*
2. D. Wayne Owens, D.

Vermont

† Richard W. Mallary, R.*

Virginia

1. Thomas N. Downing, D.*
2. G. William Whitehurst, R.*
3. David E. Satterfield III, D.*
4. Robert W. Daniel, Jr., R.
5. W. C. Daniel, D.*
6. M. Caldwell Butler, R.
7. J. Kenneth Robinson, R.*
8. Stanford E. Parris, R.
9. William C. Wampler, R.*
10. Joel T. Broyhill, R.*

Washington

1. Joel Pritchard, R.
2. Lloyd Meeds, D.*
3. Julia Butler Hansen, D.*
4. Mike McCormack, D.*
5. Thomas S. Foley, D.*
6. Floyd V. Hicks, D.*
7. Brock Adams, D.*

West Virginia

1. Robert H. Mollohan, D.*
2. Harley O. Staggers, D.*
3. John M. Slack, D.*
4. Ken Hechler, D.*

Wisconsin

1. Les Aspin, D.*
2. Robert W. Kastenmeier, D.*
3. Vernon W. Thomson, R.*
4. Clement J. Zablocki, D.*
5. Henry S. Reuss, D.*
6. William A. Steiger, R.*
7. David R. Obey, D.*
8. Harold V. Froehlich, R.
9. Glenn R. Davis, R.*

Wyoming

† Teno Roncalio, D.*

Nonvoting Representatives

District of Columbia

Walter E. Fauntroy, D.*

Guam

Antonio Won Pat, D.

Puerto Rico

Jaime Benitez, D.

Virgin Islands

Ron de Lugo, D.

The Federal Election Campaign Act of 1971 was the first bill passed in the second session. The bill, passed by the Senate on Dec. 17, 1971, passed the House on Jan. 19, 1972, and was signed by President Nixon on February 7.

The new law replaced the Corrupt Practices Act of 1925. It limited the amount of money any candidate for federal office could spend on his campaign. Contributions and expenditures of more than $100 had to be made public after the law went into effect on April 7.

On January 20, President Nixon delivered his State of the Union message to Congress. He asked for increased spending for defense and a new method of financing for U.S. schools, and again asked Congress to act on welfare reforms. He called on Congress to establish a revenue-sharing plan, to reorganize the federal administration, and to improve health care and the environment.

Budget and Appropriations. President Nixon's budget for fiscal 1973 was submitted to Congress on January 24. According to the President, the $246.3-billion budget he proposed was aimed at "a new prosperity for all Americans without the stimulus of war and without the drain of inflation." The President offered no new tax proposals. Estimated receipts for fiscal 1973 were $220.8 billion, but the budget deficit was estimated at $25.5 billion.

Senate Armed Services Committee hears testimony from Defense Secretary Melvin R. Laird, right, during hearings on status of the Vietnam War.

Because of the deficit, the President asked Congress on January 25 to raise the national debt ceiling temporarily to $480 billion. On March 15, Congress raised the ceiling to $450 billion through June 30. On June 30, it extended the temporary ceiling to October 31. On October 28, the President signed a law raising the debt ceiling again, to $465 billion.

Mounting defense costs made it impossible to balance the budget without major tax increases, and made it increasingly difficult to keep the federal deficit within bounds. On September 13, Congress approved a $20.9-billion authorization bill for weapons. It was $2.3 billion less than the President had requested. On September 14, Congress appropriated $74.3 billion for defense, the largest defense appropriation passed since World War II. It was, nevertheless, $5.2 billion less than the President had requested.

Treaties and Agreements. Several treaties on arms control were submitted to the 92nd Congress. On February 15, the Senate voted 83 to 0 to ratify a treaty barring the deployment of nuclear arms on the ocean floor beyond the 12-mile territorial limit.

On August 3, the Senate voted 88 to 2 to ratify the Strategic Arms Limitation Treaty (SALT) between the United States and Russia, which limits antiballistic defensive missile systems. Congress passed a resolution on September 25, approving the so-called interim agreement between the United States and Russia, which set a five-year freeze on most offensive nuclear weapons. See NATIONAL DEFENSE.

During the second session of the 92nd Congress, the Senate attempted without success to limit the President's warmaking powers and authority to conduct the war in Indochina, and tried to reassert its influence in the area of foreign policy. Congress passed a bill on August 14 making it mandatory for the secretary of state to submit the texts of all international agreements to both houses of Congress within 60 days. The President signed the bill on August 22. However, a bill limiting to 30 days the President's use of the armed forces without congressional approval did not pass, nor did measures calling for the withdrawal of all U.S. forces from Indochina by a "date certain."

Revenue Sharing and Social Welfare. Revenue sharing, a program specifically urged by the President, was approved by Congress on October 13. The law made $30.2 billion in federal funds available to state and local governments over a five-year period. The President signed the law in Philadelphia on October 20. See STATE GOVERNMENT.

Two important changes were made in the social security program in 1972. On June 30, the House completed congressional action on an $8-billion measure raising social security benefits by 20 per cent. The new law also provided automatic cost of living raises. The increased benefits went into effect on September 1. Higher payroll taxes were approved to provide funds for the increases. See SOCIAL SECURITY.

A $6.1-billion social security-welfare bill was passed by Congress on October 17. It provided for 144 changes in health and welfare benefits, most of which will become effective in 1974. Raises were provided for widows receiving benefits, for all male social security recipients, for many retired low-income workers, for the disabled, and for persons who continue to earn income after they retire. Tax rates and the taxable wage base for social security taxes were raised as of Jan. 1, 1973, to help cover increased costs.

On September 5, Congress extended Office of Economic Opportunity programs for three years, but did not approve the creation of an Independent Legal Services Corporation, which the President had opposed. The President's proposed welfare reforms were not passed by the 92nd Congress.

On June 8, Congress passed a $19.5-billion measure providing funds for schools and for students at every educational level in the United States. The President signed it on June 23. The bill included major innovations in federal programs for higher education and established a National Institute of Education. The new law also provided for a delay of 18 months in carrying out lower court orders requiring the use of buses to desegregate public schools. Permanent legislation forbidding the use of buses to achieve racial balance was passed by the House at the urging of the President, but was defeated by liberal forces in the Senate. Congress also authorized $1 billion for furthering school desegregation in fiscal 1973.

Antipollution Legislation. In addition to passing the $24.6-billion bill for sewage treatment, on October 12, Congress raised a measure giving the Environmental Protection Agency (EPA) the power to regulate the use and sale of pesticides. The measure also provided compensation for manufacturers whose products are banned by the EPA. The President signed it on October 21.

On October 28, the President signed a bill passed by Congress on October 18 authorizing the EPA to establish limits on noise from interstate buses, trains, and other noisemakers, such as jackhammers, compressors, automobiles, and motorcycles. The measure also called for a nine-month study of the possible regulation of airplane and airport noise. Also on October 28, the President signed a bill banning the dumping of hazardous materials into the ocean. See ENVIRONMENT.

Consumer Protection. On October 11, a House-Senate conference committee agreed on a Product Safety Bill. It was signed by President Nixon on October 27. The bill created an independent commission to establish and enforce safety standards for thousands of consumer products. The commission can establish mandatory standards to protect consumers against "unreasonable" dangers in products for homes, schools, recreation, and other uses. The commission can forbid the sale of products that cannot be made "reasonably safe."

Congress also passed a measure empowering the secretary of transportation to require that automobile bumpers provide "maximum feasible protection" against damage to the vehicle. The measure was signed by President Nixon on October 20.

Other Measures passed in the second session:

- The director of the Special Action Office for Drug Abuse Protection was empowered to act as steward of federal funds for 13 agencies involved in the war on narcotics, with a $1-billion budget for the next three years to fight drug abuse.
- The Equal Employment Opportunity Commission received the authority to take cases to court and, therefore, file its own suits in job-discrimination cases based on race, sex, or national origin.
- The Senate completed congressional action on March 22 on a constitutional amendment prohibit-

the small society

ing discrimination based on sex by any law or action of federal, state, or local government. See U.S. CONSTITUTION.

- The dollar was devalued by raising the price of gold from $35 an ounce to $38 an ounce.
- An appropriation of $3.5 billion was provided to increase veterans' benefits, mostly for education.

Congressional Hearings. While it was looking into the credentials of General Creighton W. Abrams for the post of Army chief of staff, the Senate Armed Services Committee investigated the conduct of Major General John D. Lavelle. He allegedly ordered unauthorized bombing raids on North Vietnam in November, 1971, and was subsequently demoted to the rank of lieutenant general and retired. The committee found no proof that Abrams knew of the raids. His nomination was approved by the committee on October 6 and it was then confirmed by the Senate on October 12.

During hearings on the nomination of Richard G. Kleindienst to the post of attorney general, the Senate Judiciary Committee investigated charges that special favors had been granted to International Telephone and Telegraph by the Department of Justice. On April 27, after six weeks of hearings, the committee approved the nomination, 11 to 4. It was approved by the Senate on June 8, by a vote of 64 to 19. See KLEINDIENST, RICHARD G. Carol L. Thompson

CONNECTICUT. See STATE GOVERNMENT.

CONSERVATION. The United Nations (UN) Conference on the Human Environment, held in Stockholm, Sweden, from June 5 to 16, 1972, reflected growing international concern with world environmental problems. Maurice Strong, secretary-general of the conference, summed up the views of most of the 114 nations represented: "We need to achieve an international and communal sense of urgency which we can translate into dynamic global action."

The conference adopted a Declaration of Principles to serve as a guide for the fight against pollution. It also unanimously approved creation of a permanent UN organization to work on world environmental problems, and plans for a $100-million environmental action fund. The participating nations recommended a ban on all nuclear testing, and an "Earth Watch" system–a global network of monitoring stations–to provide advance warning of emerging threats to the environment. They also urged the storage of genetic samples in national seed banks to preserve the world's most endangered species of wildlife. See ENVIRONMENT (Close-Up).

On September 21, Russia and the United States signed an agreement calling for joint environmental studies and exchange of conservation information. The pact was based on an understanding reached in May during President Richard M. Nixon's visit to Russia. Russell Train, chairman of the U.S. Council on Environmental Quality, termed the accord "the most comprehensive agreement on the environment ever entered into by two countries."

Conservation Organizations in the United States stepped up their challenges to federal actions they believed endangered the environment. However, the observance of Earth Week from April 17 to 24 was, to quote Secretary of the Interior Rogers C. B. Morton, "underwhelming." To make things worse, the Supreme Court of the United States dealt a sharp setback to conservationists on April 19 by upholding an appeals court decision that the Sierra Club did not have standing to sue in court. The organization had tried to block construction of a $35-million resort on U.S. Forest Service land in the Mineral King area near Sequoia National Park in California. However, the club won a second round in the legal battle in August when a federal judge upheld its contention that the Forest Service had not filed an environmental impact statement on the resort project.

Conservation's Election Scorecard. The League of Conservation Voters, participating actively in election-year politics, claimed a major victory in September when U.S. Representative Wayne Aspinall (D., Colo.), chairman of the House Interior and Insular Affairs Committee, was defeated in the Colorado Democratic primary. The league had listed Aspinall as its principal target, claiming he had used his powerful post to give preference to developmental interests over conservation.

In the November 7 general election, 43 of 57 congressional and gubernatorial candidates backed by the league won. However, two candidates that the league had vigorously supported lost. They were Governor Russell W. Peterson, Delaware, who had pushed through that state's model shoreline-protection law, and John D. Rockefeller IV, a strip-mining foe, who ran for governor of West Virginia.

Voters signaled broad public support for environmental measures, supporting proposals for protecting their natural surroundings. New York voters approved, by 2 to 1, a $1.15-billion bond issue to finance facilities that will provide cleaner air and water. In Florida, voters authorized spending $240-million to buy land for outdoor recreation. Massachusetts and North Carolina voters passed measures recognizing environmental protection as a state duty. South Dakotans banned the hunting of mourning doves. Washington voters approved regulation of shoreline use and development.

Parks and Outdoor Recreation. The National Park System marked the centennial on March 1, 1972, of the establishment of Yellowstone, the first national park (see Close-Up). The Department of the Interior's Advisory Board on National Parks claimed in April that more than 200 million annual visits to the parks had created a crisis. In September, the Conservation Foundation reported that overcrowding and pressures on roads and campsites were threatening to impair the atmosphere in some parks. The

100 Years Without "Progress"

Old Faithful Inn and tourists in 1922

In such a place as this, man can fortify himself morally and spiritually. He can free himself from the so-called progress that is framed in concrete roads, bathed in polluted water and air, dressed in wash-and-wears, and heralded in a deafening cacophony of sounds.

The place is Yellowstone National Park, more than 2 million acres of superlative scenery in Wyoming, Montana, and Idaho that was set aside a century ago as the first national park in the world. The success of the idea can be measured by the fact that more than 1,200 national parks and reserves have since been established in over 100 nations. The U.S. National Park System now operates 278 park areas, 35 of them national parks. Canada has 24 national parks and 19 national historic parks.

Despite reports of traffic jams and crime in some of the more crowded national parks, by far the greatest part of all national parks is still essentially undisturbed by civilization and awaits anyone who will forsake the crowded lodges and campsites. By walking a few miles, you can camp beside your own private lake, sharing it only with the creatures that find refuge in the park and drink from the clear, pure water.

The loudest sound will be the rumble of thunder, a warning to move your sleeping bag from beside the dying fire into your snug, dry tent. It is so still in the morning that you can hear a trout breaking water to capture a struggling insect.

On Jan. 5, 1972, President Richard M. Nixon designated 1972 National Parks Centennial Year. But, even before that–on July 10, 1970–he had endorsed a centennial celebration by signing Public Law 91-332, which created a National Parks Centennial Commission and empowered it to execute "a suitable plan for commemoration of the 100th anniversary of the beginning of the worldwide national park movement. . . ."

The centennial celebration began on March 1, the same date on which President Ulysses S. Grant signed into law the act that created Yellowstone National Park. It centered around the official theme: Parks, Man, and His Environment. In Washington, D.C., Secretary of the Interior Rogers C. B. Morton and Postmaster General Elmer T. Klassen marked the first day by officially issuing the first of eight centennial commemorative stamps. The 8-cent stamp pictures Old Faithful, the famous Yellowstone geyser. This ceremony was followed by the National Parks Centennial Banquet in Washington, at which Morton was the principal speaker.

The most important event in the celebration was the second World Conference on National Parks. More than 500 persons representing almost 100 nations attended the meetings, which began at Yellowstone on September 18 and continued at nearby Grand Teton National Park from September 20 to 27. At these meetings, park officials discussed current problems and plans for the future. Some of the specific areas covered were tropical, polar, marine, and mountain park management, wildlife and resource management, visitor services, staff training, and interpretation of the environment.

Other centennial events included a symposium on the future of national parks, held from April 13 to 15 at Yosemite National Park in California; an exhibition of 19th century paintings featuring national parks, held at the Smithsonian Institution in Washington, D.C., from June 23 to August 27; and a display of paintings by Thomas Moran, who first painted the wonders of Yellowstone, shown at Colorado State University, Fort Collins, from July 1 to September 30.

Hundreds of other events were held throughout the National Park System. They ranged from a series of summer seminars at Rocky Mountain National Park, Colorado, to an open house and goat roast at Navajo National Monument, Arizona.

A centennial medallion was offered for sale in silver and bronze. The medallion shows Old Faithful on one side and two other Yellowstone scenes and the earth on the other. The medallions can be purchased at national parks or by mail from the National Park Service. Sale proceeds are used to help defray the costs of centennial celebration activities. Michael Reed

An effort to save the Philippines' remaining 50 monkey-eating eagles gets the support of Charles A. Lindbergh, second from right, "Lone Eagle" of 1927 flight.

report recommended: (1) a moratorium on road-building, parking lots, and other automobile-oriented improvements in the parks; (2) a study aimed at developing alternative methods of intrapark transportation so that private vehicles could be banned; (3) a "Buy Back America" program to purchase land for new parks at the edge of American cities with a $2-billion annual fund raised by taxes from land sales and a 5 per cent excise tax on recreational vehicles and outdoor equipment; (4) a reorganization of the National Park Service, including its merger with the Bureau of Outdoor Recreation and the Bureau of Sports Fisheries and Wildlife; and (5) the shift of commercial facilities outside the parks.

President Nixon signed legislation on October 28 authorizing establishment of the 26,172-acre Gateway National Recreation Area at the entrance to New York Harbor and the 34,000-acre Golden Gate National Recreation Area in and around San Francisco Bay. Legislation approved on March 1 designated a 132-mile stretch in northwestern Arkansas as the Buffalo National River. The river will be protected as a free-flowing stream and the scenic value of adjoining land preserved. The nation's first National Lakeshore, Indiana Dunes on the shores of Lake Michigan, was established on September 8.

In an omnibus bill signed on October 28, the President approved legislation establishing the Cumberland Island National Seashore in Georgia, the Glen Canyon National Recreation Area in Arizona and Utah, the Fossil Butte National Monument in Wyoming, and the Thaddeus Kosciusko National Historical Site in Pennsylvania. The bill also designated a segment of the Saint Croix River in Minnesota and Wisconsin as part of the National Wild and Scenic Rivers System.

Wildlife. On October 27, President Nixon approved a 15-year moratorium on taking or importing whales, sea otters, dolphins, and other ocean mammals. Conservationists supported the legislation, but objected to the provision exempting porpoises "killed incidental to the commercial fishing of tuna" (see Fishing Industry). On October 19, President Nixon signed legislation giving the secretary of the interior power to enforce bans on shooting eagles, wolves, or other wildlife from aircraft. An executive order issued by the President on February 8 barred the use of poisons on all public lands, except in emergencies.

The Department of the Interior on March 30 put eight species of wild "big cats"–cheetahs, leopards, tigers, snow leopards, jaguars, ocelots, margays, and tiger cats–on the list of endangered foreign wildlife. Neither these animals nor their furs can be imported into the United States. However, the Fund for Animals charged in September that the department had undermined its own order by permitting big-game hunters to bring home their kills. Andrew L. Newman

CONSTITUTION, U.S. See U.S. Constitution.

CONSUMER AFFAIRS. Interest in consumer affairs continued high in 1972. The number and intensity of consumer problems proliferated, largely because increasing technical sophistication made products more difficult to evaluate and repair and because selling methods often tested ethical and legal limits. Food prices, advertising claims, product safety, insurance, and credit practices received the most attention.

Consumer advocates began to focus on more basic issues, such as the effect of monopolistic practices on retail prices and the availability of competing products. Although business and government officials tried to cope with consumer concerns, their efforts did not seem to have any noticeable effect in reducing controversy and confusion in the minds of the buying public.

Administration v. Inflation. By far the most widely discussed consumer issue was inflation. Election-year politics spurred public debate over whether President Richard M. Nixon's economic controls were strong enough to stem the rising cost of living. Administration spokesmen insisted that the controls were working well. They chose to compare earlier annual increases of 6 per cent in the Consumer Price Index (CPI) to the 3.4 per cent rate achieved in the first full year of controls ending in November, 1972. Critics, pointing to the Administration's original target of only 2.5 per cent increase in prices, declared that the program was still weak.

Food prices were the fastest-rising component of the CPI. By July, beef and pork prices had reached all-time highs – 12 and 20 per cent respectively, over year-earlier levels. Prices of many fruits and vegetables also rose faster than the average of all prices, reflecting the fact that most raw agricultural commodities were exempt from controls.

Caught between its concern for consumer prices and its election-year desire to capture the "farm" vote, the Nixon Administration responded by lifting regulations limiting imported meat products and launching some publicity campaigns designed to get private citizens to resist price increases more actively. In August, the President's consumer adviser, Virginia Knauer, distributed a series of television spots urging Americans to "shop harder" by comparing price and quality more carefully before buying. The Price Commission urged radio and television listeners to "be a price fighter" by reporting apparent violations of economic controls to the government. Later, the Price Commission was forced to grant substantial price increases for bread products, largely because of increased costs of wheat attributed to the huge sale of American grain to Russia. Toward the end of the year, food prices eased off somewhat, reducing pressure on the Administration to take further anti-inflationary steps. See ECONOMY, THE.

Congressional Legislation. Although the 92nd Congress passed several important consumer measures, its output fell far short of expectations. The most far-reaching law enacted in 1972 was the Consumer Product Safety Act, signed by President Nixon on October 28. The new statute sets up a federal agency headed by five commissioners appointed by the President. It aims to bring the safety of virtually all consumer products not already subject to government supervision under federal control. The law also empowers the government to ban products it deems unsafe. A feature of the law allows private citizens to go to court to force the agency to act in the public interest if it is found negligent in this respect. It also forbids commissioners and staff officials to have any commercial interests that conflict with their official duties.

The Federal Water Pollution Control Act Extension, passed over President Nixon's veto, sets a target date of 1985 for the complete cleanup of the nation's waterways. The President said he agreed with the bill's aims but objected to the projected costs, estimated at $24.6 billion. A few weeks after reluctantly signing the bill, he announced that he would withhold about half of the authorized funds for the next two fiscal years. See ENVIRONMENT.

The biggest legislative disappointment for consumer advocates was the defeat of bills to set up a new Consumer Protection Agency and to establish a nationwide system of no-fault automobile insurance.

Regulatory Agencies. The two most prominent consumer protection agencies, the Federal Trade Commission (FTC) and the Food and Drug Administration (FDA), ran into serious obstacles that appeared to curtail their effectiveness on behalf of consumers. Federal Judge Aubrey E. Robinson, Jr., ruled on April 4 that the FTC lacked the authority to issue rules defining unfair and deceptive trade practices. The agency had set up a series of rules, in such areas as the labeling of light-bulb life and clothing-care instructions, rather than prosecute each case separately.

The FTC came under increasing attack by business – and officials from other branches of government – for requiring "corrective" advertising and demanding documentation of advertising claims.

On April 26, the FTC aroused new opposition by filing antitrust charges against the four largest breakfast-cereal makers. The companies were accused of gaining a virtual monopoly through extensive advertising and then of concentrating their positions further by dominating the advertising media. The firms were also accused of deceptively promoting the nutritional value of their products.

As the year ended, the future of FTC action as a vigorous protector of consumers became clouded further by reports that key personnel would be replaced by others more friendly to business.

The FDA also ran into determined opposition from the courts and in political circles. At the same time, consumer advocates became more critical of the agency's efforts to police the food and drug industries. Several court decisions served to delay the agency's continuing efforts to remove ineffective and hazardous medical drugs from sale.

State Activities increased considerably. The *Report on the Office of the Attorney General*, a publication of the National Association of Attorneys General, declared that "consumer protection has generated more interest among attorneys general in recent years than any other single area of activity." Some 36 states had laws against "deceptive acts or practices" similar to the national FTC law. Antitrust action also increased, with many states bringing their first cases in this field to court. Among their targets were companies producing oil, snack food, farm machinery, and dairy products. Some 43 states joined in the $100-million settlement of antibiotic-drug price-fixing charges brought by the federal government.

State legislatures continued to build a network of consumer laws. One survey of large states showed that most of the new laws paralleled congressional activity. The most popular areas were food labeling and credit practices. Next most popular were bills to establish and strengthen consumer affairs offices. Others dealt with warranties, sales practices, automotive problems, and flammable fabrics. About 20 per cent of the bills involved attempts to require more information in advertising, labeling and contracts. Some states even took the lead. California, for example, set up laws going far beyond federal regulations governing flammability of clothing and furniture. Several municipalities and counties passed regulations limiting the level of phosphates in detergents.

Citizens and Business Action. A growing number of business firms responded to consumer complaints by setting up "consumer hot lines" and by designating high-level officials to improve product quality and customer relations. Prominent among them were automobile manufacturers. Most publicized was Ford's campaign for "No Unhappy Owners." Trade associations were also busy in this respect. Leading these developments was the Council of Better Business Bureaus (CBBB). During the year, the organization launched a massive radio campaign, with more than 1,000 participating stations, to present consumer tips to the public. CBBB also formed a National Advisory Committee on Consumer Arbitration to help guide the expansion of arbitration panels around the country.

Consumer Groups. The number of voluntary citizen membership groups continued to hover around 70. Most of the activity occurred at the community and neighborhood levels, and government officials opened many new offices of consumer affairs. Every state except Montana and Tennessee had at least one such agency, a gain of three during the year. The number of county consumer offices went from 18 to 37, city offices from 17 to 27. Arthur E. Rowse

See also ADVERTISING.

COSTA RICA. See LATIN AMERICA.

COURTS AND LAWS. Capital punishment as historically imposed in various states was declared unconstitutional by the Supreme Court of the United States on June 29, 1972. In *Furman v. Georgia*, the court ruled 5 to 4 that "the imposition and carrying out of the death penalty in these cases constitutes cruel and unusual punishment in violation of the 8th and 14th amendments."

The nine justices issued separate opinions on the matter, leaving some confusion over the implications of the ruling. But it was clear that the court was not ready to prohibit all capital punishment under all circumstances. Two justices based their opinions on the "arbitrary" and "freakish" way in which the penalty had sometimes been imposed. State courts accepted the high court ruling with great reluctance. By the end of the year, fewer than half of the 631 prisoners on death row had had their sentences formally voided.

Many states initiated efforts to restore the death penalty after the ruling. Most of them concentrated on eliminating "arbitrariness" by making death mandatory for certain crimes. On November 7, California voters approved an initiative attempting to reinstate capital punishment. In December, the Florida Legislature approved a new death penalty law designed to meet Supreme Court objections. But those who opposed the death penalty were confident

Don Wright, *The Miami News*

that all attempts to revive capital punishment would be voided by the high court.

Grand Juries. The Supreme Court refused to restrict the power of grand juries in forcing a witness to testify. On June 29, in *Branzburg v. Hayes*, the court ruled 5 to 4 that the First Amendment does not privilege newsmen to withhold confidential information from a grand jury. Many reporters vowed they would rather serve jail terms than comply with the ruling. By the end of the year, four reporters had served brief terms as a result of the court's decision.

Also on June 29, the court decided 5 to 4 in *Gravel v. United States* that the Constitution's congressional speech or debate clause does not grant immunity from grand jury subpoenas to a senator or a senator's aide who may commit illegal, nonlegislative acts. The *Gravel* case arose from the controversial Pentagon Papers case.

On May 22, the court ruled 5 to 2 on two different cases that the government need not offer a witness complete immunity from criminal prosecution in return for his grand jury testimony. The witness can still be prosecuted if the indictment is based only on evidence other than his grand jury testimony. The court also held that it was not unconstitutional to force a grand jury witness to testify under threat of imprisonment.

Government Surveillance. On June 19, in *United States v. U.S. District Court*, the court ruled 8 to 0 (with Justice William H. Rehnquist not participating) that the government's electronic surveillance of U.S. citizens suspected of subversion was unconstitutional, unless approval had been obtained from a federal judge. So the government was required to produce the results of all such wiretaps upon request. Rather than comply, the justice department dropped charges against several defendants.

On June 26, by a 5 to 4 vote in *Laird v. Tatum*, the court rejected claims that First Amendment rights were infringed upon by the Army's program of gathering information on civilians and possible civil disturbances.

Criminal Law. Several high court rulings limited criminal suspects' rights. On June 12, by a 6 to 3 vote, the court expanded a policeman's right to stop and frisk a person suspected of carrying a weapon, even though the search was prompted by an unnamed informant.

On June 7, in *Kirby v. Illinois*, the court held 5 to 4 that a suspect was not necessarily entitled to have an attorney present at a police line-up held before he was indicted or charged with a criminal offense. On May 22, in *Johnson v. Louisiana*, the court decided 5 to 4 that state laws allowing convictions of criminal defendants by a less-than-unanimous jury were constitutional.

However, in *Argersinger v. Hamlin* on June 12, the court unanimously extended the right to free counsel to indigents charged with misdemeanors carrying a jail term as penalty. Local authorities must either provide counsel or stop imposing sentences on persons convicted of misdemeanors.

Death-row inmate in Texas State Penitentiary holds newspaper headlining U.S. Supreme Court ruling that death penalty is unconstitutional.

In Other Important Cases, the court held:

- On May 15, 7 to 0, that Amish parents need not send their children to public school beyond the eighth grade.
- On June 12, 6 to 3, that a Moose lodge, being a private club, could be issued a state liquor license, even though it refused to serve a Negro invited as a guest.
- On June 19, 6 to 3, that professional baseball's exemption from antitrust laws should be removed by Congress–if it is removed at all–and not by the courts.
- On October 10, 8 to 1, that an Ohio plan giving direct tuition grants to parents of children who were attending private and parochial schools was unconstitutional.

Court Turmoil. On January 7, Lewis F. Powell, Jr., of Richmond, Va., a former American Bar Association (ABA) president, and Rehnquist, of Phoenix, Ariz., an assistant U.S. attorney general, were sworn in as the 99th and 100th U.S. justices. They were President Richard M. Nixon's third and fourth appointments to the Supreme Court, and observers believed they helped turn the court toward more conservative rulings in several constitutional and criminal cases.

During the year, Powell was criticized for a letter he had written while still a private attorney, urging business to fight against public challenges from consumer advocates. Powell was also forced to disqualify himself from 15 cases in 1972 because of conflicting stock ownership.

Serious conflict-of-interest questions were raised about Rehnquist, who cast the deciding vote in 5-to-4 rulings on the congressional immunity and Army spying cases. While an assistant attorney general, Rehnquist had been chief government spokesman in defending the Army surveillance practices.

In August, the ABA adopted a new judicial ethics code specifying: "A judge formerly employed by a governmental agency should disqualify himself in a proceeding if his impartiality might reasonably be questioned because of such association." In October, Rehnquist issued a defense of his participation, saying that Supreme Court justices had "a duty to sit" in close cases. He added that the government's briefs in both of the cases in question were prepared by sections of the justice department other than the one he had headed.

In December, a panel appointed by Chief Justice Warren E. Burger recommended that a National Court of Appeals be set up to decide what cases should be heard by the Supreme Court. Remaining cases would be heard by the new court.

Two new Supreme Court justices, William H. Rehnquist, left, and Lewis F. Powell, Jr., right, were sworn into office on January 7.

Criminal Acquittals. On April 5, a Harrisburg, Pa., jury failed to reach a verdict on kidnap-conspiracy and related charges against Philip F. Berrigan, a Roman Catholic priest, and six others. The government then dropped the cases. But Berrigan and a codefendant were found guilty of smuggling letters out of prison and both were sentenced to serve a year in prison.

On June 4, an all-white jury in San Jose, Calif., acquitted black militant Angela Y. Davis of murder, kidnap, and conspiracy charges stemming from a 1970 shoot-out at the Marin County courthouse.

On October 25, a Chicago judge acquitted Cook County State's Attorney Edward V. Hanrahan and 13 codefendants of conspiring to obstruct justice, following a December, 1969, police raid on an apartment in which two Black Panthers were killed.

On November 21, the U.S. appeals court in Chicago reversed the convictions of five defendants in the so-called Chicago 7 conspiracy trial, stemming from violence at the 1968 Democratic National Convention. A jury had found five guilty of crossing state lines to incite riot and had acquitted two others. The appeals court ruling was sharply critical of the way presiding Judge Julius J. Hoffman conducted the trial. In addition to citing technical errors, the three-judge appeals panel criticized Hoffman for his "deprecatory and often antagonistic attitude toward the defense."

David C. Beckwith

CRIME. The number of serious crimes reported to police in the United States was only 1 per cent higher during the first nine months of 1972 than for the same period in 1971. Attorney General Richard G. Kleindienst said this was the smallest percentage increase recorded since 1960. According to the Federal Bureau of Investigation (FBI) statistics issued on August 29, crime increased by 7 per cent in 1971, the lowest yearly rise in the crime rate since 1965.

But the decline was in crimes against property. The statistics showed a growing number of violent crimes. There were 17,630 murders committed in 1971, or 11 per cent more than the 15,860 committed in 1970. Forcible rape was up 11 per cent and aggravated assault, 10 per cent.

The FBI's figures showed that the average American's chances of being the victim of a serious crime had nearly tripled since 1960. In 1960, there were 1,126 serious crimes per 100,000 persons – 159 violent crimes, and 967 crimes against property. By 1971, the rate had grown to 2,907 crimes per 100,000 persons – 393 violent crimes and 2,514 crimes against property. The crime rate increased 2 per cent in large cities and 11 per cent in the suburbs.

Drug Arrests in 1971 increased 11 per cent over 1970 and 469 per cent over 1966. Of about 400,000 persons arrested on narcotics charges in 1971, 313,000 were under the age of 25.

To combat the growing drug problem, President

Richard M. Nixon created a new Department of Justice agency, the Office of Drug Abuse Law Enforcement, on January 18. He named Myles J. Ambrose, former commissioner of customs, director of the effort to rid the nation of drug pushers. On March 25, Ambrose named 33 U.S. cities where special teams of federal, state, and local police would work to curtail the distribution of heroin.

Campaign Issues. In the 1972 presidential race, Democratic candidate George S. McGovern contended that President Nixon had failed in his promise to restore law and order in the cities. The Republicans replied that the nation had made progress in its war against crime and cited the early 1972 FBI figures as proof.

The presidential campaign was marred by the attempted assassination of Governor George C. Wallace of Alabama. He was shot on May 15 while campaigning at a shopping center in Laurel, Md. The gunshot wounds left Wallace paralyzed from the waist down. See WALLACE, GEORGE C.

Arthur H. Bremer, a 21-year-old from Milwaukee, was arrested at the scene and later convicted of shooting Wallace and three other persons attending the rally. On August 4, he was sentenced to 63 years in prison, but the penalty was reduced to 53 years by an appeals court.

Airline Hijackings continued to be a formidable problem throughout the world. From 1968 through 1971, there were 175 hijackings. The 31st hijacking of a U.S. plane in 1972 occurred on November 10. Three men, all with criminal records, boarded a Southern Airways DC-9 in Birmingham, Ala., and during a tense 28 hours forced the crew to make nine landings in eight cities in three countries. The hijackers finally surrendered, along with about $2 million in ransom money, to Cuban authorities in Havana.

Gangland Murders. On April 7, Joseph Gallo, an underworld chieftain, was shot to death in a New York City restaurant, touching off a series of gangland killings. Gallo was reportedly responsible for the shooting of Joseph Colombo in 1971. A few weeks after Gallo's death, a Colombo gang member turned himself in to the FBI and confessed the details of the revenge slaying. A rash of murders followed, ending with the July 16 killing of Thomas Eboli, a leader in the Mafia family of the late Vito Genovese. Eboli was the 10th victim found since April. Reportedly, the gang warfare consolidated the power of the highest-ranking Mafioso, Carlo Gambino.

Eugene Gold, district attorney of Brooklyn, launched an attack on organized crime in the New York City area. Early in 1972, Gold hid an electronic listening device and tapped the telephones in a junkyard trailer that was used as a Mafia meeting place. Police also photographed persons entering and leaving the trailer. On the basis of evidence gathered during the six-month surveillance, 677 persons were subpoenaed in October to appear before a grand jury.

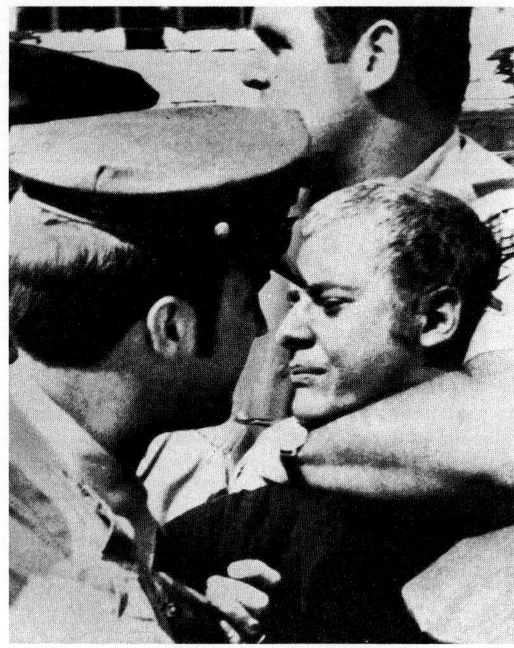

Police surround and subdue Arthur Bremer in a Laurel, Md., shopping center after he shot Alabama Governor George C. Wallace on May 15.

Other major crimes committed in 1972 included the following:

- On January 7, police found eight time bombs in banks in Chicago, New York City, and San Francisco. They were allegedly placed by a 33-year-old Army deserter.
- Three persons were killed on April 2 during a shoot-out between rival narcotics gang members at a night club in Atlantic City, N.J.
- Eight Americans were slain at a golf club on St. Croix, Virgin Islands, on September 6, during a robbery that netted less than $1,000. Five suspects were later arrested.
- In October, 10 men were arrested in Chicago and charged with a series of nine murders, including the killing of four persons in suburban Barrington Hills. Police said several of the suspects were Vietnam veterans who belonged to a secret organization called De Mau Mau.
- In November, five members of a wandering family were linked to at least seven rapes and murders in Colorado, Oregon, Texas, and Utah. While these investigations were underway, three of the family members were indicted by a Denver grand jury for a 1971 murder.
- Warfare blamed on two youth gangs fighting for control of drug traffic in Gary, Ind., claimed at least 23 lives in 1972, and a federal task force was sent in to deal with the violence.

Art Petacque

CUBA. Daily life remained somewhat shabby in 1972. Although more food and clothing were available and the prices of basic necessities remained low, the cost of such goods as sunglasses, cosmetics, electric appliances, and radios was very high. These items were available in the shops, but only a small percentage of Cubans could afford them.

The economically crucial sugar harvest, which brings in up to 80 per cent of Cuba's exchange earnings, totaled only about 4.1 million tons. This was considerably less than the 5.9 million harvested in 1971 and the 8.5 million in 1970. Production was hampered by management problems and a severe drought. Nevertheless, higher prices abroad helped Cuba to earn $560 million from its sugar exports.

Electric power shortages remained a source of continuing inconvenience. The situation was particularly serious in the country's western electric grid that covers four of Cuba's six provinces, including metropolitan Havana. Blackouts occurred there almost daily.

International Relations. Between May 3 and July 6, Premier Fidel Castro made a 10-nation tour of Africa and Eastern Europe, visiting Guinea, Sierra Leone, Algeria, Bulgaria, Romania, Hungary, Poland, East Germany, Czechoslovakia, and Russia. His official state visit to Russia, the first since 1964, emphasized the steady improvement in relations between the two countries. Castro returned to Cuba with assurances that Russia would continue to supply heavy economic and military aid. On July 11, the assurances were confirmed when Cuba was elected a full member of the Council for Mutual Economic Assistance, the trade and economic alliance established by Russia and its East European allies.

Russian aid to Cuba continued to flow at the rate of about $2 million per day. It was estimated that about one-third was in military assistance. Havana's debt to Moscow was believed to have reached well over $4 billion over the past decade.

During the year, Cuba and Peru formally re-established diplomatic ties. Relations were also established with Somalia and Zambia. There were indications, too, that Cuba's relations with the United States might be improving and that a dialogue between the two countries might be re-established. In April, U.S. Secretary of State William P. Rogers hinted that the United States might ease its coolness toward Cuba if the Castro regime ended its interventionism, support of revolutions, and "close and active military ties with the Soviet Union." On July 10, a U.S. delegation attended an oceanographic conference in Havana, the first time the U.S. had been represented at an international meeting in Cuba in nearly 12 years. Mary Webster Soper

See also LATIN AMERICA (Facts in Brief Table).

Cuban Premier Fidel Castro made an unprecedented two-month, 10-country tour of Africa and Europe in 1972. Here, he shakily mounts a camel in Algeria.

CYPRUS. Archbishop Makarios III retained his post as president in 1972 despite strong pressures for his departure. General George Grivas, 74, former underground leader, failed to force Makarios to make way for a man more committed to *enosis* (union with Greece). The three bishops of the Greek Orthodox Church of Cyprus were equally unsuccessful. Three times they called upon Makarios to resign the presidency, because, they said, he could not be both political and spiritual head of his people. He rejected their demands.

The Greek government had more success. On March 10, Makarios met a Greek request to place the "considerable quantity" of Czech arms he had imported under control of the United Nations (UN) peacekeeping force.

Spyros Kyprianou, foreign minister since independence in 1960 and a prime target of Greek hostility, resigned on May 5. Cabinet changes on June 16 brought in seven new ministers.

Intercommunal tension remained "deeply worrying," according to UN Secretary-General Kurt Waldheim. Talks between the Greek and Turkish Cypriots began on July 3 to try again to find an acceptable solution to the future administration and constitution of Cyprus. The UN Security Council agreed that the peacekeeping force should remain until Dec. 15, 1972. George Scott

See also MIDDLE EAST (Facts in Brief Table).

CZECHOSLOVAKIA. Political repression continued in 1972, but Czechoslovakia's economic position improved. The government announced the arrest of alleged "antistate elements" on January 11, and some foreign journalists were expelled from the country. Trials were held in July and August in Prague and Brno for 46 persons charged with subversion in connection with 1968 reform policies. All were identified as supporters of former Communist Party First Secretary Alexander Dubček. Thirty-eight defendants were convicted and received jail sentences of up to six years.

The Trials caused sharp criticism among Western Communists and other left wing groups. The French Communist Party's Politburo condemned them as a breach of solemn promise by the Czechoslovak party leader, Gustav Husak, that no political trials would be held.

A journalists' union revealed in April that 1,222, or 40 per cent, of the union's 1968 membership had been purged from the profession. Government pressure also continued against artists, actors, and other liberal intellectuals. The famous Prague theater, Behind the Gate, was closed in June, and a number of actors and directors lost their jobs. But the regime continued to claim that only those who had broken the law would be prosecuted. The Roman Catholic Church came under strong pressure, with expulsions from theological colleges, regulations forbidding priests to practice after age 60, and the harassment of younger priests. The authorities also prevented the church from replacing bishops who had died.

Economic Progress was more encouraging. Industrial production rose by an average of 7 per cent. Prices remained relatively stable, and incomes continued to rise. Imports of consumer goods ensured a constantly improving supply on the domestic market. Production costs remained high, however, as did the rate of industrial absenteeism and labor turnover. The investment bank of the Russian-led economic union, Council for Mutual Economic Assistance (COMECON), granted the Czechs a $2.05-billion loan on June 25 to modernize and expand truck production. Czechoslovakia's economic cooperation with other COMECON countries, especially Russia, Poland, and East Germany, increased significantly during the year.

Trade with most of the West slumped, although not that with West Germany, Czechoslovakia's most important Western trading partner. Despite several rounds of talks, however, the two failed to re-establish normal relations. The major stumbling block seemed to be Czechoslovak insistence that the 1938 Munich Agreement be recognized as invalid from its beginning. It had forced Czechs to give up territory to Nazi Germany. In September, the biggest-ever Warsaw Pact maneuvers were held on Czechoslovak soil. Chris Cviic

See also EUROPE (Facts in Brief Table).

DAHOMEY. The army seized power on Oct. 26, 1972, and Mathieu Kerekou, a 39-year-old paratrooper, became president and premier. Reports indicated that many government and political leaders had been arrested. The coup was the second attempted in 1972. A previous attempt, on February 23, by army mutineers failed. Lieutenant General Maurice Kouandeté, deputy secretary-general of defense, and 11 others implicated in the plot were arrested. Kouandeté was sentenced to death on May 16, and the others received prison sentences.

Justin Ahomadegbe was overthrown in the October coup. He had succeeded Hubert Maga as president on May 7 in accordance with a charter adopted in 1970. The charter provided that members of the three-man Presidential Council rotate as head of state for two-year terms. Ahomadegbe had announced that the Cabinet, the Consultative Assembly, and the Supreme Court would continue to function until elections could be held.

Dahomey was one of seven French-speaking African nations that signed a treaty in Bamako, Mali, on June 3, setting up the West African Economic Community. The other members are Ivory Coast, Upper Volta, Mali, Mauritania, Niger, and Senegal. The organization planned to promote regional trade among its members. Paul C. Tullier

See also AFRICA (Facts in Brief Table).

DAIRYING. See AGRICULTURE.

DALLAS was the scene of Explo '72, probably the biggest fundamentalist revival meeting in the history of religion in the United States. An estimated 75,000 young people converged on Dallas on June 12 for the six-day evangelical conference to attend training seminars, prayer meetings, and a music festival. The Campus Crusade for Christ sponsored Explo '72 at a cost of $2.7 million. Evangelist Billy Graham was named honorary chairman of the event.

New Airport. Construction was underway on the Dallas-Fort Worth Regional Airport. Operations were scheduled to begin in mid-1973, when four terminal buildings were to be completed. An additional nine terminals will be built later, without interruption of airport service. The facility will not be finished until about the year 2000.

When completed, the new airport will be larger than Manhattan Island and capable of handling more daily passenger flights than the present combined capacities of Kennedy, La Guardia, and Newark airports. Despite its projected size, passengers using the facility will not have long walks. An automated transit system will carry about 9,000 persons per hour between terminals and parking lots, limiting the average walk to about 75 feet.

The system uses enclosed, rubber-tired cars, which travel along a concrete-walled guideway. Each car holds up to 40 passengers. A trip between the parking lot and terminals will take about eight minutes.

School Busing. In August, the U.S. Fifth District Court of Appeals overturned a federal district court order directing the Dallas public school system to implement a racial integration plan using school busing. The U.S. Department of Justice had intervened in the case in April, asking the court to follow President Richard M. Nixon's guidelines on busing. The guidelines were contained in a measure signed into law on June 28, instituting an 18-month delay on court-ordered busing for the purpose of integration. See Congress of the United States.

Dallas was named 1 of 33 U.S. cities in which special federal, state, and local law enforcement teams would conduct intensive drives to stop the spread of heroin and other narcotics. However, according to the Uniform Crime Reports released on August 29, the city's crime rate was a relatively low 3,808.9 crimes per 100,000 persons.

Nonagricultural employment in Dallas increased by 23,000 persons between May, 1971, and May, 1972. The cost of living in the city rose 3.3 per cent from February, 1971, to February, 1972, but the average gross weekly earnings of production workers went up only 2.9 per cent to $130.33 per week between May, 1971, and May, 1972. Nevertheless, the city's cost of living remained slightly below the national average, while median family income was a relatively high $10,019. J. M. Banovetz

DAM. See Building and Construction.

DANCING reached rare heights during the New York City Ballet's Stravinsky Festival held from June 18 to 25, 1972. Out of 31 ballets presented in 7 performances at the New York State Theater in Lincoln Center, 21 were premières. Their scores ranged in time from Stravinsky's *Sonata* (1902) to *Requiem Canticles* (1966).

Speculation that George Balanchine, director of the company and long-time friend of Igor Stravinsky, had lost his golden touch was shattered on the first evening of the festival, when his *Violin Concerto* and *Symphony in Three Movements* were first seen. Both were proclaimed masterpieces. His other new ballets were *Danses Concertantes,* an excerpt from *Le Baiser de la Fée* and from the 1902 *Sonata*, *Scherzo à la Russe, Duo Concertant, Choral Variations on Bach's "Vom Himmel Hoch,"* and *Pulcinella*, co-directed with Jerome Robbins. By number and quality, Balanchine dominated the festival. Robbins contributed four new works, including the delightful *Circus Polka* for 48 children, with himself as ringmaster.

After summer engagements in the United States, City Ballet presented a few of the new Stravinsky ballets in Munich, West Germany, in August, during the Olympic Games cultural program and then performed in Russia and Poland from September 21 to October 21. Many festival works went into regular repertory during the winter season.

Robbins' major work for the company was *Watermill*, which premièred on February 3. With Japanese music and Oriental-style decor, iconography, and meditative atmosphere, some thought it a profound statement about the natural world and man's place in it; others called it fancy hocus-pocus. In any case, it provoked talk, as did a revival of Michel Fokine's *Les Sylphides*, called *Chopiniana* by City Ballet, on January 20. The traditional woodland setting and filmy white costumes were abandoned in favor of a bare stage and practice clothes in an effort to reconstruct the romantic masterpiece in modern, neoclassical terms.

American Ballet Theater (ABT). Just before the ABT opened in New York City on January 4, its leading dancer, Erik Bruhn, announced his retirement. The 43-year-old Dane was considered the world's greatest *danseur noble*. The season was distinguished, however, by two new Eliot Feld ballets, *A Soldier's Tale* and *Eccentrique*, both to music by Stravinsky. Paolo Bortoluzzi, an Italian dancer from Maurice Béjart's Belgian troupe, joined the company in time for its New York summer season from July 4 to August 13. Fokine's *Le Spectre de la Rose* was revived for this floridly romantic dancer. In addition to performing at the Kennedy Center in Washington, D.C., in the spring and fall, ABT visited several cities for engagements of at least one week, reversing its former schedule of cross-country, one-night stands. The organization began construction of a new school in New York in June, and an apprentice company, Ballet Repertory Company, was formed on July 1.

The City Center Joffrey Ballet's year was highlighted by revivals of Feld's *Meadowlark*, Leonide Massine's *Le Beau Danube*, Robbins' *Interplay*, and Alvin Ailey's *Feast of Ashes*. Two new ballets were also shown in Chicago in February before the company danced in New York from February 23 to April 2. Following June engagements on the West Coast, in the Midwest, and at the Wolf Trap Farm's summer festival in Washington, D.C., the company was back in New York City from October 4 to November 12. Joffrey II, an affiliate for young dancers, gave lecture demonstrations at schools and danced in New York's Central Park in September.

Dancers from Abroad. Britain's Royal Ballet danced at the Metropolitan Opera House from April 24 to June 1. Most of the new ballets, including the full-length *Anastasia*, were by Kenneth MacMillan, the new artistic director, and were poorly received. Some thought that splendid performances compensated for the lack of choreographic creativity. Others wondered if MacMillan had enough stature to lead such an important institution.

Visiting Canada in June were several members of the Bolshoi Ballet of Moscow. Maya Plisetskaya led the troupe, although her new *Anna Karenina*, which premièred in Moscow on June 11, was not performed on the tour.

Martha Swope, *Time* © Time Inc.

Dancers of the New York City Ballet perform *Requiem Canticles*, the late Igor Stravinsky's last big work, for the Stravinsky Festival in June.

Appearing in the United States for the first time in four years was the Netherlands Dance Theater at the Brooklyn Academy, March 28 to April 9. The company, trained in ballet and modern technique, is considered the most avant-garde in Europe. American critics, however, did not find their modern ballets avant-garde by American standards, even though their first offering, Glen Tetley's *Mutations*, was danced in the nude.

Maurice Béjart's Ballet of the 20th Century, another modernistic ballet group from Europe, created a sensation with Béjart's *Nijinsky–Clown of God* when it was first presented in Paris in the winter. The production was brought to Madison Square Garden's Felt Forum in October.

A Marathon of Modern Dance–with 20 companies in all–was held at the American National Theater and Academy (ANTA) on Broadway from October 2 to November 11. Although modern-dance concerts usually feature one choreographer, in part because there are few repertory companies, at least two troupes shared each ANTA bill. From the West Coast came the groups of Bella Lewitzky, Donald McKayle, and Gloria Newman. Young choreographers representing the newest trends in modern dance, such as Twyla Tharp, Cliff Keuter, Elizabeth Keen, and Viola Farber, were also seen. The Martha Graham company, much anticipated because it had not danced at all for more than a year, canceled because of managerial disagreements, but the group led by José Limón, another giant in modern dance, performed. Limón, 64, died soon after, on December 2.

A developer of "chance" choreography, in which the segments of a dance or dances may be altered according to a prearranged plan and danced in continuous sequence, Merce Cunningham programmed several Events on his company's tours and two-week February season at the Brooklyn Academy of Music. The Events were successful experiments and seriously challenged the traditional concept that each work of art is an organic whole that loses meaning and structure when disassembled. Of Cunningham's entirely new dances, *Landrover* was especially beautiful and dynamic.

With support from private foundations and the National Endowment for the Arts, many modern dance groups toured the country's colleges, some settling into brief residencies. The Alvin Ailey company, however, announced in August that it was becoming a permanent member of the City Center. Changing its name to the Alvin Ailey City Center Dance Theater, it performed there for three weeks in November, when it revived *Kinetic Molpai*, a work by Ted Shawn. A founder of modern dance and director of the Jacob's Pillow summer dance festivals in Massachusetts, Shawn died on January 9 at the age of 80.

Nancy Goldner

DEATHS OF NOTABLE PERSONS in 1972 included those listed below. An asterisk (*) indicates the person is the subject of a biography in THE WORLD BOOK ENCYCLOPEDIA. Those listed were Americans unless otherwise indicated.

***Alinsky, Saul D.** (1909-June 12), a sharp-tongued, radical social organizer who helped the poor and powerless. He organized Chicago's Back-of-the-Yards Neighborhood Council.

Athenagoras I (1886-July 6), Ecumenical Patriarch and leader of the Eastern Orthodox Churches. He had worked for its reunion with the Roman Catholic Church.

Austin, Gene (1900-Jan. 24), popular crooner and composer of the 1920s. His theme song, "My Blue Heaven," sold more than 12 million records.

Babin, Victor (1908-March 1), dual pianist with his wife, Vitya Vronsky. Since 1961, he had been director of the Cleveland Institute of Music.

Balenciaga, Cristóbal (1895-March 23), one of the most influential designers of women's clothing.

Barlow, Howard (1892-Jan. 31), conductor of the Firestone Orchestra in the popular radio and television "Voice of Firestone" series from 1943 to 1961.

Bates, Theodore L. (1901-May 30), founder of Ted Bates & Company, worldwide advertising agency that pioneered in the hard-sell use of television after World War II.

Battle, John S., Sr. (1890-April 9), governor of Virginia from 1950 to 1954. He served on the U.S. Civil Rights Commission from 1957 to 1959.

Begich, Nick (1932-Oct. 16?), Democratic congressman from Alaska since 1971. He and Rep. Hale Boggs (D., La.) were reported missing when an airplane they were on disappeared in Alaska on October 16.

Welsh Guardsmen carry coffin of the Duke of Windsor, formerly King Edward VIII, during funeral services at Windsor Castle in June.

Bell, George M. (1911-July 19), leading newspaper publisher in Canada and an internationally known horseman. He held an interest in seven papers.

Berryman, John (1914-Jan. 7), prize-winning poet. He won a Pulitzer Prize in 1965 for his book *Seventy-Seven Dream Songs* and the National Book Award in 1969 for *His Toy, His Dream, His Rest.*

Blocker, Dan (1928-May 14), who played the role of Hoss Cartwright on the "Bonanza" television series.

Boggs, Hale (1914-Oct. 16?), a Democratic congressman from Louisiana since 1941 and majority leader since 1971. He and Rep. Nick Begich (D., Alaska) were passengers on an airplane that disappeared on a flight from Anchorage to Juneau, Alaska, on October 16.

Bolton, Oliver P. (1917-Dec. 14), former Ohio Republican congressman and a member of the only mother-and-son team to serve in the House of Representatives at the same time. He was elected in 1952, 1954, and 1962.

Boyd, Louise A. (1887-Sept. 14), the first woman explorer ever to fly over the North Pole.

Boyd, William (1898-Sept. 12), who rose to stardom in movies and television as Hopalong Cassidy.

Brown, Fredric (1906-March 11), mystery and science-fiction author. His first mystery, *The Fabulous Clipjoint*, won the Edgar Allan Poe award of the Mystery Writers of America in 1947.

Bush, Prescott S. (1895-Oct. 8), Republican senator from Connecticut from 1952 to 1963 and a partner in the firm of Brown Brothers Harriman & Company.

***Byrnes, James F.** (1879-April 9), called "assistant President" by President Franklin D. Roosevelt when he was director of the Office of War Mobilization during World War II. Byrnes also served as secretary of state; associate justice of the Supreme Court of the United States; U.S. representative and senator; and governor of South Carolina.

Carroll, Leo G. (1892-Oct. 16), versatile British-born actor whose roles included Cosmo Topper in television's "Topper" series and Mr. Waverley on the "Man from U.N.C.L.E." series.

Carter, Hodding (1907-April 4), outspoken Mississippi newspaper editor and publisher. He won a Pulitzer Prize in 1946 for editorials against racial prejudice.

Casadesus, Robert M. (1899-Sept. 19), French pianist and composer. He had given more than 3,000 concerts throughout the world.

***Chevalier, Maurice** (1888-Jan. 1), perhaps the most popular entertainer from France in the 1900s. An actor, singer, and dancer, he was a jaunty and debonair performer who always wore a straw hat.

***Chichester, Sir Francis** (1901-Aug. 26), who sailed around the world alone in the ketch *Gipsy Moth IV* at the age of 65.

Clemente, Roberto (1934-Dec. 31), Pittsburgh Pirates baseball star. He died in the crash of a plane carrying relief supplies to Nicaragua.

Clyde, George D. (1898-April 2), former two-term governor of Utah.

Collins, George W. (1925-Dec. 8), Democratic congressman from Illinois. He died in the crash of an airplane approaching Chicago.

***Colum, Padraic** (1881-Jan. 11), Irish lyric poet, playwright, essayist, and author of children's books. He moved to the United States in 1914 and became a citizen.

Correll, Charles J. (1890-Sept. 26), who played Andy on the "Amos 'n' Andy" radio show from 1928 to 1960. The show was once the most popular on radio.

Dalton, John M. (1900-July 7), former governor of Missouri.

***Day-Lewis, Cecil** (1904-May 22), poet laureate of England. He also wrote more than 20 mystery stories and thrillers under the name of Nicholas Blake.

The Man Who Made Decisions

Harry S. Truman (1884-1972)

Adapted from the editorial page of the Chicago *Sun-Times* of Dec. 27, 1972.

Harry S. Truman was a common man elevated in uncommon times to the leadership of the American people. He liked the presidency, and wasn't frightened by it. He worked hard at it, and while he may at times have seemed less a man of destiny than a creation of politics, history is certain to judge him well.

During Mr. Truman's often stormy seven years and nine months in the White House, his decisions helped mold the world as it is today and helped erect the structure around which much of the world of tomorrow will be shaped.

Mr. Truman was to a large degree an American cliché: farm boy, family man, small town merchant, county politician of fierce and abiding loyalties; a hard-working, honest man who was a veteran, and a Mason, and a churchgoer; a scrappy Missourian who liked music, poker, and pie à la mode. Yet, his era uprooted clichés.

Franklin Delano Roosevelt died in the late afternoon of April 12, 1945. At 7:09 P.M., the ordinary Mr. Truman accepted the charismatic leader's burdens as the nation's 33d President.

During the next four months and two days, he announced the surrenders of Germany and Japan, and inbetween disclosed the awesome episode that had brought Japan to defeat: The atomic bomb had been invented and used; the atomic age had begun.

Mr. Truman had a heightened sense of history that alerted him to the immense human need that existed in the wake of World War II. He was many times to be accused of pooh-poohing the Communist threat at home, but he was never in doubt that the Communists were a danger.

Under the Truman Doctrine, military and economic aid were given to Greece and Turkey, enabling them to ward off the grip of Communism. The North Atlantic Treaty Organization transformed U.S. theories of peacetime troop deployment. The Marshall Plan was a massive infusion of dollars that helped lift Europe from the postwar doldrums and prepared the way for economic revival.

Mr. Truman's capacity to confront crises was tested to perhaps the greatest degree in 1950. He was at home in Missouri when the Communist troops invaded South Korea. He left for Washington, and later said:

"Flying over the flatlands of the Middle West and over the Appalachians that summer afternoon, I had a lot of time to think. I turned the problems over in my mind in many ways, but my thoughts kept coming back to Munich. . . . Here was another probing action, another testing action. If we let the Republic of Korea go under, some other country would be next, and then another. And all the time, the courage, the confidence of the Free World would be ebbing away, just as it did in the 1930s."

That decision, he said, was the most difficult he had to make during his tenure in office, but he was convinced he was right and he believed his action may have forestalled a third world war.

Mr. Truman's decisions, for all their impact, were not always unanimously accepted as correct. He fired General Douglas MacArthur from command in Korea. He battled striking railway workers and miners and seized the steel mills in an attempt to bar a strike in them. Legislators riddled his Fair Deal program, and he termed the 80th Congress the "worst."

He was beset by other problems. His tenure covered the rise of McCarthyism, the trial of Alger Hiss, the spying of the Rosenbergs.

The "five percenter" scandals erupted, and mink coat and deep-freeze became dirty Washington words. Mr. Truman was accused of surrounding himself with cronies who were not worthy of the friendship of a President. But Mr. Truman was a salty man who refused to be disloyal to those who had known him when.

These were traits of the common man, and in 1948, when it seemed Mr. Truman was, at best, a candidate for nonentity, the nation's other common men sent him back to the White House in a rousing, surprise victory.

In his last days, Mr. Truman's tenaciousness impressed his doctors, one of whom said his fight against death "was a reflection of his attitude toward life." He was human and tough and fallible, and he will be sorely missed.

Athenagoras I was the Ecumenical Patriarch of Orthodox Christians and a force for Christian unity.

Actor Dan Blocker was a national favorite as Hoss, strong-man son in the "Bonanza" television series.

James F. Byrnes played an active role in every part of political life for nearly half a century.

Delderfield, Ronald Frederick (1912-June 24), best-selling British novelist who had been a newspaperman and playwright. His novels chronicled British life.

De Wilde, Brandon (1941-July 6), motion-picture actor who won fame as the child star in the 1953 western, *Shane.*

***Dies, Martin** (1900-Nov. 14), Democratic congressman from Texas from 1931 to 1945 and from 1953 to 1959. He was first chairman of the controversial House Special Committee to Investigate Un-American Activities.

Dykstra, John (1898-March 2), president of the Ford Motor Company from 1961 to 1963.

***Edward VIII,** Duke of Windsor (1894-May 28), who abdicated the British throne in 1936 to marry an American commoner, Mrs. Wallis Warfield Simpson.

Ellender, Allen J. (1890-July 27), president pro tem of the U.S. Senate and Democratic senator from Louisiana. He had served in the Senate since 1937 and was chairman of the Appropriations Committee.

Ellington, Buford (1907-April 3), Democratic governor of Tennessee from 1959 to 1963 and from 1967 to 1971.

Feis, Herbert (1893-March 2), State Department adviser from 1932 to 1947 and member of its policy-planning staff in the early 1950s. His book, *Between War and Peace: The Potsdam Conference* (1960), won the Pulitzer Prize for history in 1961.

Fleischer, Nat (1886-June 25), founder of *The Ring* magazine, which issued monthly ratings of boxers in all divisions.

Forand, Aime J. (1895-Jan. 18), retired Rhode Island Democratic congressman who served 11 terms.

Frederik IX (1899-Jan. 14), king of Denmark. He was famed as an informal monarch who answered the telephone himself and knew how to handle a vacuum cleaner.

***Friml, Rudolf** (1879-Nov. 12), composer of *Rose Marie, The Firefly, The Vagabond King,* and some 30 other operettas. Poet Ogden Nash once wrote about the Czechoslovakia-born composer: "I trust that your conclusion and mine are similar: 'Twould be a happier world if it were Frimler."

***Ganz, Rudolph** (1877-Aug. 2), Swiss-American symphony conductor, composer, and pianist. He made his debut at the age of 22, and was president of Chicago Musical College from 1933 to 1954.

Gentele, Goeran H. A. (1917-July 18), newly appointed Swedish-born director of the Metropolitan Opera in New York City. Gentele and two daughters were killed in an automobile accident in Sardinia.

Gilbreth, Lillian M. (1878-Jan. 2), pioneer engineer of time-and-motion study. She was the real-life mother featured in the book and movie *Cheaper by the Dozen,* which described her family of six sons and six daughters.

Giobbe, H. E. Cardinal Paolo (1880-Aug. 14), a leader in the Vatican diplomatic corps for 33 years. An Italian, he was the oldest member of the Sacred College of Cardinals.

***Golschmann, Vladimir** (1893-March 1), music director of the Denver Symphony Orchestra. Born in Paris of Russian parents, he was conductor of the St. Louis Symphony Orchestra from 1931 to 1957.

Goodman, Paul (1911-Aug. 2), iconoclastic writer, social critic, and reformer. His books include *Growing Up Absurd* (1960) and *Compulsory Mis-Education* (1964).

Gove, Philip B. (1902-Nov. 15), editor of the controversial *Webster's Third New International Dictionary* (1961). He championed the cause of more freedom in spoken and written English, and edited the dictionary from the standpoint that "correctness rests upon usage."

Graham, Frank Porter (1886-Feb. 16), former president of the University of North Carolina, later a U.S. Senator, and a United Nations mediator.

Grant, William T. (1876-Aug. 6), founder of the W. T. Grant Company department-store chain. He retired as its chairman in 1966.

Griebling, Otto (1896-April 19), "Otto the clown" with the Ringling Brothers and Barnum & Bailey circus for about 50 years, a native of Germany.

***Grofé, Ferde** (1892-April 13), composer of American orchestral suites, including *Grand Canyon Suite* (1931).

Grossinger, Jennie (1892-Nov. 20), Austrian-born hotelier who transformed a family hotel in New York's Catskills into the world-famous resort "Grossinger's."

Gulbenkian, Nubar S. (1896-Jan. 10), flamboyant Turkish financier and one of the world's richest men. His fortune was based on Middle Eastern oil interests.

Handley, Harold W. (1909-Aug. 30), Republican governor of Indiana from 1957 to 1961.

Hartnett, Charles Leo (Gabby) (1900-Dec. 20), a member of baseball's Hall of Fame. His 20 years in major-league baseball included 19 as catcher with the Chicago Cubs.

***Hayden, Carl T.** (1877-Jan. 25), Democratic U.S. senator from Arizona. He served 42 years in the Senate, longer than any other man, after 14 years in the U.S. House of Representatives.

Jackie: Ever An Agitator For Equality

Jackie Robinson

As the first black man to play major-league baseball, Jackie Robinson assured himself of immortality. Sociologically speaking, he was perhaps the most significant athlete in United States history.

In 10 years (1947 to 1956) with the Brooklyn Dodgers, most of them as a second baseman, he batted .311, and his baserunning excited a nation. He helped the Dodgers win six National League pennants and the 1955 World Series before he retired. In 1962, the first year he was eligible, he was voted into the Baseball Hall of Fame.

Yet for all his success, Jackie Robinson was forever aggressive and restless. He and his Dodger teammates were the subjects of Roger Kahn's 1972 best seller, *The Boys of Summer*. The title came from Dylan Thomas' line, "I see the boys of summer in their ruin," and Jackie's life had its ruin.

At 53, he had heart trouble, high blood pressure, and diabetes. He was blind in one eye and going blind in the other. His son, Jackie, Jr., who had overcome drug addiction, was killed in a 1971 automobile accident.

Through it all, Jackie Robinson insisted, "I've got nothing to complain about." But until he died on Oct. 24, 1972, he was complaining – not of his lot, but of the plight of black people.

To the end, Robinson fought for his people and equality. He was honored before the second game of the 1972 World Series in Cincinnati. It was just 10 days before his death and Jackie, now feeble, had to be helped onto the field by his old teammate, Peewee Reese. He thanked baseball for all it had done for him, then added: "I won't be satisfied until I look over at the coach's box at third base and see a black manager there."

He was involved in banking, insurance, and construction, all black-financed. He was an integrationist when black radicalism was more fashionable. As reporter Heywood Hale Broun said, "He lived a life richer in honor than in happiness."

"Jackie Robinson established the black man's right to play second base," wrote columnist Red Smith. "He fought for the black man's right to a place in the white community, and he never lost sight of that goal."

Red Barber, the former Dodger broadcaster, agreed and wrote, "All his life, Jackie Robinson said what was in his heart and what was on his mind; he was so immediately honest he was often severely abrasive." After a dressing-room discussion, Don Newcombe, Robinson's teammate and also black, once said, "Robinson, not only are you wrong, you're loud wrong."

Robinson was born Jan. 31, 1919, in Cairo, Ga., the son of a sharecropper and the grandson of a slave. He grew up in Pasadena, Calif., and excelled in four sports at the University of California, Los Angeles (UCLA). He was the first UCLA athlete to win four letters in a single year. Robinson later earned an Army wartime commission, and then joined the Negro National League as a shortstop.

Until then, there had been no black players in modern major-league baseball or basketball and few in football. In 1946, Branch Rickey, the visionary general manager of the Dodgers, signed Robinson to play for the Dodger minor-league team at Montreal.

In 1947, Robinson was promoted to the Dodgers. He endured resentment from teammates, from opponents, and from spectators. The St. Louis Cardinals threatened to strike if Robinson played against them. He played – and they did not strike.

Those early years, he said, "produced understanding among whites, and it gave black people the idea that if I could do it, they could do it, too, that blackness wasn't subservient to anything. . . . But I remain a black in a white world. Many people resented my impatience and honesty, but I never cared about acceptance as much as I cared about respect."

Jackie Robinson died only weeks before publication of his autobiography, *I Never Had It Made*. The publisher, G. P. Putnam's Sons, said of him:

"His driving spirit transformed him and transformed those who watched and played with him. His youth was our youth and we cheered ourselves in him. He was a man, and no barrier of color or prejudice could diminish his manhood and the great joy he brought to those who became part of his triumphs."

Frank Litsky

Maurice Chevalier, a jaunty yet elegant French boulevardier, was a great international favorite.

Mahalia Jackson was considered one of the world's foremost gospel singers. She died on January 27.

Howard Johnson built a business featuring "28 flavors of ice cream" into a tourist service empire.

Heatter, Gabriel (1890-March 30), former radio news commentator. He was famous for his optimistic expression, "Ah, there's good news tonight."

Hill, William S. (1886-Aug. 28), served nine terms as a Republican congressman from Colorado.

Hodges, Gil (1924-April 2), manager of the New York Mets baseball team. He starred as the Brooklyn Dodgers first baseman from 1947 to 1961.

***Hoover, J. Edgar** (1895-May 3), until his death he was the only director the Federal Bureau of Investigation had. He was appointed to head the bureau when it was created in 1924. See Close-Up.

Hopkins, Miriam (1902-Oct. 9), stage and screen star, mostly during the 1930s. Her stage appearances included *Jezebel* and *The Skin of Our Teeth.*

Irvin, Rea (1881-May 28), cartoonist and creator of the first cover of *The New Yorker* magazine. His best-known creation was the curious Edwardian figure Eustace Tilley. Irvin was the magazine's first art director.

Jackson, Mahalia (1911-Jan. 27), gospel singer who inspired audiences around the world. She was held in affection as much because of her personal openness and unassuming manner as because of her powerful voice.

Johnson, Howard (1897-June 20), restaurateur who built an empire on providing service to tourists. He expanded his business from a small drugstore to a nationwide chain of roadside restaurants and motels.

Kawabata, Yasunari (1899-April 16), only Japanese winner of the Nobel Prize for literature (1968). He was described as a passive individual and a lyric sensualist.

Kellner, Ida (1889-Sept. 20), violinist and the first woman to play in a major U.S. symphony orchestra. She had been assistant concertmaster of the Detroit Symphony Orchestra.

***Kendall, Edward C.** (1886-May 4), biochemist who shared the 1950 Nobel Prize in physiology and medicine with two others for the discovery of cortisone, then called compound E in 1936, and for research in adrenal hormones.

Klein, Abraham M. (1909-Aug. 21), Canadian poet, novelist, and attorney. He was awarded the Canadian Governor-General's Medal for Poetry for his book *The Rocking Chair* (1948).

***Knight, Frank H.** (1885-April 15), who taught economics at the University of Chicago from 1928 to 1958. He was called the founder of the Chicago School in economics.

Lawrence, William H. (1916-March 2), for 20 years a White House reporter and war correspondent for *The New York Times* before joining the American Broadcasting Company as a television political commentator in 1961.

***Leakey, Louis S. B.** (1903-Oct. 1), anthropologist and paleontologist who made important discoveries, especially in Olduvai Gorge, Tanzania, concerning man's origins. Born in Kenya, he was the son of English missionaries.

Le Compte, Karl M. (1887-Sept. 30), who served as a Republican member of Congress from Iowa from 1939 until his retirement in 1959.

Levant, Oscar (1906-Aug. 14), pianist, actor, Academy Award-winning composer, and humorist. A famed insomniac, he aimed barbed wit at his own hypochondria. He wrote *A Smattering of Ignorance* (1940), *Memoirs of an Amnesiac* (1965), and *The Unimportance of Being Oscar* (1968).

***Limón, José** (1908-Dec. 2), Mexican-born dancer and choreographer who came to the United States at the age of 7. He was credited with helping to improve the stature of men in dance, which he sought to make a "virile preoccupation."

Little, Tom (1898-June 20), editorial cartoonist for the *Nashville Tennessean.* He joined the paper's staff in 1916 and began cartooning in 1936. Little won a Pulitzer Prize in 1957.

Lloyd, Woodrow S. (1913-April 8), premier of Saskatchewan, Canada, from 1961 to 1964. Later, he served with the United Nations Development Program in Korea.

Long, Edward V. (1908-Nov. 6), Democratic senator from Missouri from 1960 to 1969. He lost in the 1968 primary to Thomas F. Eagleton.

Lovre, Harold A. (1904-Jan. 17), who served as a Republican congressman from South Dakota from 1949 until he was defeated by George McGovern in 1956.

Lübke, Heinrich (1894-April 6), president of the Federal Republic of (West) Germany from 1959 to 1969 in Chancellor Konrad Adenauer's administration.

Mahendra, BirBikram Sha Deva (1920-Jan. 31), king of Nepal, a social reformer, and a poet.

Marek, Kurt W. (1915-April 12), German writer on films and art history and, under the pseudonym C. W. Ceram, on archaeology. His work included *Gods, Graves and Scholars* (1951).

***Mayer, Maria Goeppert** (1906-Feb. 20), Polish-born, first woman physicist to win the Nobel Prize since Marie Curie in 1903. She shared the 1963 prize for her discoveries on the structure of atomic nuclei.

Yasunari Kawabata was a Japanese novelist and the winner of the 1968 Nobel Prize for Literature.

© National Geographic Society

Anthropologist Louis S. B. Leakey discovered the remains of the oldest known manlike creature.

Poet Marianne Moore often formed her own patterns in preference to conventional rhyme and meter.

McCormack, Buren H. (1909-March 28), executive vice-president, director, and chairman of Dow Jones & Company, owners of *The Wall Street Journal*.

McElroy, Neil H. (1904-Nov. 30), who was president of Procter & Gamble when President Dwight D. Eisenhower appointed him secretary of defense in 1957.

***Moore, Marianne** (1887-Feb. 5), a prizewinning, self-disparaging poet who described herself as an "observer." Among many awards, she won the Bollingen Prize in Poetry, the National Book Award for Poetry, and the Pulitzer Prize, all in 1952.

***Nkrumah, Kwame** (1909-April 27), former president of Ghana and the first man to lead a former African colony to independence after World War II. He was president from 1960 until he was deposed in 1966.

Norell, Norman (1900-Oct. 25), dean of American fashion designers, frequently called the "American Balenciaga."

Ntare V (1947?-April 29), deposed king of Burundi. Overthrown by Michel Micombero in 1966, he returned from exile in March, 1972, and was held under house arrest in Gitega, Burundi.

Nunn, Henry L. (1878-Sept. 15), cofounder of the Nunn-Bush Shoe Company and employee-relations innovator.

Ohrbach, Nathan M. (1885-Nov. 19), Vienna-born merchandiser whose eight Ohrbach stores set the pace for the giant discount-store movement. He was brought to the United States at the age of 2.

Parsons, Louella (1881-Dec. 9), first of the Hollywood gossip columnists. She began her career as a $5-per-week society editor.

Patchen, Kenneth (1911-Jan. 8), author, avant-garde poet, and artist. His verse was called cryptic, often angry, and pacifistic.

***Pearson, Lester B.** (1897-Dec. 27), prime minister of Canada from 1963 to 1968, winner of the 1957 Nobel Peace Prize, and president of the United Nations General Assembly in 1953. He was a man with a ready wit, and the public became familiar with his nickname "Mike" and his jaunty bow ties. From 1961 to 1964, he was a member of THE WORLD BOOK YEAR BOOK Board of Editors.

Philbin, Philip J. (1898-June 14), for 14 terms a Democratic congressman from Massachusetts.

***Pound, Ezra Loomis** (1885-Nov. 1), expatriate American poet who was one of the major forces in 20th-century literature. His *Cantos*, begun about 1915, have been termed by some critics the most important long poem in modern literature. He spent more than a decade in a mental hospital after treason charges were filed against him by the United States because of his radio broadcasts in behalf of Italian Fascists in World War II.

***Powell, Adam Clayton, Jr.** (1908-April 14), political and religious leader of New York City's Harlem area. He was elected to Congress in 1944. In 1967, Congress excluded him from his seat on the charge he had misused public funds. He was re-elected in 1968, and the Supreme Court of the United States ruled in 1969 that his exclusion had been unconstitutional.

Rabin, Michael (1936-Jan. 19), violin virtuoso who first appeared as a soloist at Carnegie Hall at the age of 13.

Rado, Sandor (1890-May 14), born in Hungary, founder of the first school of psychoanalysis at an American university, the graduate school of psychoanalysis at the Columbia University College of Physicians and Surgeons.

Ramspeck, Robert (1890-Sept. 10), a Democratic congressman from Georgia from 1929 to 1945.

Rank, J. Arthur (1888-March 29), founder of the Rank Organization, which financed many of the best-known British films.

***Robinson, Jackie** (1919-Oct. 24), who made history in 1947 by becoming the first Negro player in modern major-league baseball. An all-around athlete in college, his baseball career in the majors was with the Brooklyn Dodgers. He was elected to baseball's Hall of Fame in 1962. See Close-Up.

***Romains, Jules** (Farigoule, Louis) (1885-Aug. 14), French poet, novelist, and satirical dramatist.

Rutherford, Margaret T. (1892-May 22), comedienne on stage, in films, and on television for more than 40 years. She was made a Dame of the British Empire in 1967.

Ryan, William F. (1922-Sept. 18), founder of the Democratic Reform movement in New York City and a liberal congressman from Manhattan for 12 years.

Saarinen, Aline B. (1914-July 13), art critic and television commentator. The widow of architect Eero Saarinen, she broke into television on the NBC "Today" show and in 1971 was named chief of the Paris bureau of NBC News.

Sanders, George (1906-April 25), veteran motion-picture villain whose portrayals blended cynical charm with cruelty. Born in Russia of British parents, he appeared in more than 90 movies in a film career that started in 1936.

Segni, Antonio (1891-Dec. 1), former president of Italy, who also served twice as prime minister.

J. Edgar Hoover: An American Legend

J. Edgar Hoover

In 1913, 18-year-old John Edgar Hoover decided that he did not want to be a Presbyterian minister and enrolled in night school to study law. During the day, he worked as a $30-a-month messenger in the Library of Congress. He earned a law degree in 1916 and joined the Department of Justice in 1917. Two years later, during the era of the "Red Raids," he was made head of a new intelligence unit to study "subversives" and assemble a card file on 450,000 suspected "radicals." In 1924, at the age of 29, Hoover was named to run the most inefficient agency in the Department of Justice, the Federal Bureau of Investigation (FBI).

Under J. Edgar Hoover, the modern tradition of law enforcement was born. Hoover cleaned up and modernized the FBI, turning it into one of the most efficient crime-fighting agencies in the world. He introduced the centralized fingerprint file, which now contains more than 200 million prints. He established a national crime laboratory, the first application of scientific methods to police work, and he set new standards for recruiting agents. For 48 years, Hoover and the FBI were indistinguishable. He served under 8 presidents and 16 attorneys general; through the Prohibition Era and the Great Depression; through the gang wars of the 1920s; through the espionage of World War II; through the civil rights marches, the campus unrest, and the anti-Vietnam War protests of the 1960s.

The man became an institution. His power in and out of the bureau was awesome. He ran a one-man show. It was not until 1971, when House Majority Leader Hale Boggs (D., La.) called him a "feudal baron," that a word of criticism of the venerable director appeared in the Congressional Record.

His power rested not only on fear of reprisal but also on the careful cultivation of a public image. Junior G-Man clubs for boys; a best-selling ghost-written book on the Communist menace, *Masters of Deceit* (1958); movies; comic strips; radio serials; and a television show starring Efrem Zimbalist, Jr., whom Hoover personally selected – all these showed his profound understanding of how to promote a legend. The FBI: gangbusters in peace, spy catchers in war, ever-vigilant, straight-shooting protectors of the people.

But in the late 1960s, critics of Hoover began to contend that the FBI was no longer solely a fact-finding and law-enforcement agency. They charged that it had become a political force in America. Hoover's ultraconservative philosophy, they maintained, committed the bureau to time-consuming "surveillance" of blacks and leftist groups, while organized crime went unchecked and civil rights laws largely unenforced.

A bachelor, Hoover lived alone in Washington, D.C., after the death of his mother in 1938. His favorite pastime was attending the races with his close friend, associate FBI director Clyde Tolson. He also had lunch and dinner with Tolson six days a week for nearly four decades. He ate the same lunch – fruit salad and coffee – every day at Harvey's restaurant until it was razed, and then he ate at the Mayflower Hotel. He always had a Jack Daniels highball before dinner.

On May 3, 1972, at the age of 77, the most enduring and powerful public official in American life died of hypertensive cardiovascular disease. His flag-draped coffin was carried through the rain the following day to the Rotunda of the Capitol, where it rested on Abraham Lincoln's catafalque. He was the first civil servant and the 22nd person in American history to be so honored. Inside the great Rotunda, supreme court justices, senators, and representatives gathered in tribute. Twenty-five thousand mourners filed past his coffin. Treasury Secretary John B. Connally bore a wreath of carnations and cornflowers from President Richard M. Nixon. Chief Justice Warren E. Burger spoke: "John Edgar Hoover, who was known to his intimates as Edgar, and to two generations of Americans as J. Edgar Hoover, was a man who epitomized the American dream of patriotism, dedication to duty, and successful attainment. The country has lost one of the great public servants in all its history. He has justly been, and will be, an American legend." Allan Davidson

Lester B. Pearson, winner of a Nobel Peace Prize, was Canada's prime minister from 1963 to 1968.

Belgian statesman Paul-Henri Spaak was a spokesman for international understanding.

Walter Winchell was a famous newspaper gossip columnist and a radio personality.

***Shapley, Harlow** (1885-Oct. 20), astronomer who directed the Harvard Observatory from 1921 to 1952. He demonstrated that the Milky Way was much larger than had been thought.

***Shawn, Ted** (1891-Jan. 9), dancer and dancing master sometimes called the father of modern dance. He studied ballet as therapy for paralyzed legs, later married his partner Ruth St. Denis.

***Sikorsky, Igor I.** (1889-Oct. 26), aviation pioneer who developed the world's first practical helicopter, which made its first flight in 1939. Born in Russia, he came to the United States in 1919.

Smith, Betty (1896-Jan. 17), novelist who wrote the best seller *A Tree Grows in Brooklyn* (1943).

Smith, Joseph Fielding (1876-July 2), president of the Church of Jesus Christ of Latter-day Saints and spiritual leader of the world's 3 million Mormons. Hyrum Smith, his grandfather, was a brother of Joseph Smith, founder of the church.

Smith, Ralph T. (1915-Aug. 13), appointed in 1969 to finish the unexpired term of the late Illinois Republican Senator Everett M. Dirksen.

Smith, Wendell (1914-Nov. 26), television and newspaper sports reporter and author who played a major role in the signing of Jackie Robinson as the first black baseball player in the major leagues in 1947.

Snow, Edgar P. (1905-Feb. 15), journalist who became an international expert on China after interviewing its revolutionary leaders in 1936. He wrote *Red Star over China* (1937), *The Other Side of the River* (1962), and *The Long Revolution* (1972).

***Spaak, Paul-Henri** (1899-July 31), Belgian statesman and a chief architect of European unification and Western solidarity since World War II. He helped to write the United Nations Charter and was first president of its General Assembly. In 1938, at the age of 39, Spaak became Belgium's youngest prime minister. Later, he took part in forming or serving virtually every international organization in Western Europe. He was a member of THE WORLD BOOK YEAR BOOK Board of Editors from 1964 to 1970.

Stark, Lloyd C. (1886-Sept. 17), governor of Missouri from 1937 to 1941. He helped to break up the Tom Pendergast political machine in Kansas City, Mo., and sought the Democratic nomination to the United States Senate, but was beaten by the incumbent, Harry S. Truman.

Summerfield, Arthur E. (1899-April 26), postmaster general of the United States from 1953 to 1961 under President Dwight D. Eisenhower's Administrations and chairman of the Republican National Committee. He also managed the Eisenhower campaigns.

Tamiroff, Akim (1899-Sept. 17), Russian-born actor who played hundreds of movie roles in a 35-year career.

***Theiler, Max** (1899-Aug. 11), South African research physician and bacteriologist, developer of a vaccine against yellow fever. He won the 1951 Nobel Prize in physiology and medicine.

Tisserant, Eugene Cardinal (1884-Feb. 21), French dean of the Roman Catholic Sacred College of Cardinals. He supervised the elections of Pope John XXIII and Pope Paul VI.

Traubel, Helen (1903-July 28), famed Wagnerian soprano of the Metropolitan Opera in New York City.

***Truman, Harry S.** (1884-Dec. 26), 33rd President of the United States, from 1945 to 1953. See Close-Up.

***Van Doren, Mark** (1894-Dec. 10), poet, novelist, playwright, critic, and retired Columbia University English professor. He won the 1940 Pulitzer Prize for poetry.

***Von Békésy, Georg** (1899-June 13), physicist whose research into the mechanism of hearing won the Nobel Prize for physiology and medicine in 1961.

***Webster, Margaret** (1905-Nov. 13), British actress and director born in New York City.

***Weeks, Sinclair** (1893-Feb. 7), secretary of commerce from 1953 to 1958 under President Dwight D. Eisenhower.

Wellington, Duke of, Gerald Wellesley (1885-Jan. 4), former British diplomat, noted art connoisseur, and great-grandson of the man who defeated Napoleon in the Battle of Waterloo.

Wheat, Zack (1888-March 11), Brooklyn Dodgers slugger from 1909 to 1926. He was elected to the Baseball Hall of Fame in 1959.

Willis, Edwin E. (1904-Oct. 24), Democratic congressman from Louisiana for 20 years until 1969. In 1966, as chairman of the House Committee on Un-American Activities, he began an investigation of the Ku Klux Klan.

***Wilson, Edmund** (1895-June 12), prolific writer on literature, history, anthropology, and economics. He was one of the leading literary and social critics of his time.

***Winchell, Walter** (1897-Feb. 20), fast-talking newspaper columnist and radio newsman. He was considered the creator of the modern gossip news column. His career began in 1920. He retired in 1969. Ed Nelson

DELAWARE. See STATE GOVERNMENT.

DEMOCRATIC PARTY. Democratic hopes of regaining the White House, which they lost in 1968, were crushed by the landslide victory of President Richard M. Nixon over George S. McGovern on Nov. 7, 1972. The 50-year-old South Dakota senator suffered the worst defeat ever experienced by a Democrat. He did not even carry his own state. He won only Massachusetts and the District of Columbia and received 37.5 per cent of the popular vote. President Nixon took 49 states and 60.7 per cent.

However, the Democratic Party demonstrated that it was still strong by retaining control of Congress. The 93rd Congress had 56 Democrats, 42 Republicans, 1 Independent, and 1 Conservative in the Senate; and 240 Democrats, 192 Republicans, and 3 vacancies in the House of Representatives. The party also made a net gain of 1 state in the 18 races for governor. This increased the total of Democratic governorships from 30 to 31. See ELECTIONS.

Race for Nomination. Before the primary elections began in early 1972, nine Democrats other than McGovern were also running for their party's presidential nomination: Senators Edmund S. Muskie of Maine, Hubert H. Humphrey of Minnesota, Henry M. Jackson of Washington, and Vance Hartke of Indiana, and former Senator Eugene J. McCarthy of Minnesota, Congresswoman Shirley A. Chisholm of New York, Governor George C. Wallace of Alabama, Mayor John V. Lindsay of New York City, and Mayor Sam Yorty of Los Angeles.

Senator Thomas F. Eagleton stood by, head bowed, as Senator George S. McGovern told newsmen that Eagleton was stepping down as his running mate.

Muskie was considered the strongest candidate, but his campaign began to lose momentum during the first primaries. On April 27, after making a poor showing in Wisconsin, Muskie announced his withdrawal from the primary races.

Meanwhile, McGovern began making some surprising gains. He had developed a reputation as a party reformer because he helped to reshape the Democratic convention rules after the 1968 convention to admit more youths, women, and blacks as delegates. He broadened his appeal early in 1972 by calling for populist reforms, by advocating that the welfare system be reformed to give each person $1,000 a year, and by taking a generally left-of-center line on such issues as abortion, amnesty, marijuana, and defense spending.

As a result, many alienated and minority groups embraced him as an exponent of the so-called New Politics and a man who would shake up the old boss-ridden political system. Before the national convention began, he had won 10 state primaries and captured almost all the delegate votes he needed.

McGovern's success was matched by that of Wallace, who won the Michigan and Florida primaries by campaigning against the busing of schoolchildren to achieve racial balance. However, Wallace's presidential hopes were shattered when he was shot and paralyzed while addressing a political rally in Laurel, Md., on May 15. See WALLACE, GEORGE C.

When the Democratic National Convention convened in Miami Beach, Fla., on July 10, the McGovern forces were clearly in control, even though a stop-McGovern movement had set him back temporarily. The Democratic credentials committee had taken away 151 of the 271 delegates he had won in California on June 6. His opponents argued that he violated the party's far-reaching reform rules when he took all of the California delegates instead of sharing them with the other candidates according to their percentage of the votes. However, the convention returned the 151 California delegates to him, and he easily won a first-ballot nomination on July 12. This was the last break McGovern had in what turned out to be an ill-starred campaign.

The McGovern Issue. The convention itself made enemies for him. Instead of the usual collection of party regulars, big-city bosses, and labor chieftains, many of the delegates were youths, women, and blacks, attending their first convention.

Chicago Mayor Richard J. Daley, a kingmaker of past conventions, was not allowed to attend this one. The credentials committee ruled that his elected Illinois delegation was in violation of the party's reforms. George Meany, AFL-CIO president who had soured early on McGovern, was present at the convention only to work against him. McGovern further offended the party regulars when he named Utah national committeewoman Jean Westwood as chairman of the Democratic National Committee, replacing Lawrence F. O'Brien. Although Daley later agreed to work for McGovern's election, Meany refused to endorse him, and organized labor was divided on the McGovern issue. McGovern never succeeded in uniting his party.

The worst setback to McGovern's campaign was the disclosure that his 42-year-old vice-presidential running mate, Senator Thomas F. Eagleton of Missouri, had undergone psychiatric treatment. He was hospitalized three times between 1960 and 1966 for nervous exhaustion and fatigue. On two occasions, Eagleton had received electric shock therapy. Eagleton revealed his past medical record in Custer, S. Dak., on July 25. See EAGLETON, THOMAS F.

McGovern's immediate reaction to Eagleton's surprising announcement was a pledge of "1,000 per cent" support. A few days later, McGovern decided to drop Eagleton on the grounds that the controversy interfered with the real issues of the campaign. However, by first supporting and then dropping Eagleton, McGovern's credibility was called into question.

His leadership image was damaged further when he failed to persuade a half dozen prominent Democrats, including Senator Edward M. Kennedy, to replace Eagleton as vice-presidential candidate. He finally settled on Sargent Shriver, Kennedy's brother-in-law. Shriver was confirmed as the vice-presidential candidate at a special meeting of the Democrat National Committee in Washington, D.C., on August 8. See SHRIVER, SARGENT.

In the campaign that followed, McGovern attempted to make an issue out of alleged Republican corruption. He pointed out that the Republicans had changed the site of their convention to Miami Beach, Fla., after the originally planned San Diego site became controversial. The International Telephone and Telegraph Corporation had given between $200,000 and $400,000 to the San Diego convention, allegedly in return for favorable treatment by the Department of Justice on an antitrust suit.

Then, five men were caught breaking into the Democratic National Headquarters at the Watergate office-apartment complex in Washington, D.C., on June 17. They were apparently attempting to install electronic eavesdropping equipment. Seven men were ultimately indicted in connection with the case. Two of them, G. Gordon Liddy and E. Howard Hunt, were Republicans who had worked at the White House. Another, James W. McCord, was the security agent for both the Committee to Re-Elect the President and the Republican National Committee. However, these issues did not seem to arouse the public. See REPUBLICAN PARTY.

At the same time, McGovern was busy redefining his positions on such explosive issues as amnesty, abortion, marijuana, tax reform, and defense cuts. He wanted to present a more moderate position on

Presidential candidate George S. McGovern, right, presents his new running mate, Sargent Shriver, who replaced Thomas F. Eagleton on August 8.

Alabama Governor George Wallace, paralyzed by a would-be assassin, addresses the Democratic National Convention in Miami from a wheel chair.

these issues than he had during the primaries, and thus erase his image as a radical. Instead, he raised questions about his credibility and decisiveness.

Among the many disappointments for McGovern in the election returns was the fact that he did so poorly with the 25 million young persons who were eligible to vote for the first time in 1972. Many did not vote, and a majority of those who did apparently voted for President Nixon.

The Democrats managed to retain a majority in Congress because of heavy ticket-splitting among the electorate. Many Democratic voters cast their ballots for a Republican President, but remained loyal to their party's congressional candidates. Also, President Nixon, not wishing to alienate these Democratic voters, campaigned very little on behalf of Republican congressional candidates.

Money Woes and In-Fighting. The Democrats entered the 1972 campaign with a $9.3-million debt left over from 1968. On July 8 and 9, the party sponsored a 19-hour telethon, which grossed about $3.7-million. McGovern conducted a direct-mail campaign to solicit small donations from private citizens.

After the election, the Democrats renewed the internal fighting that began at the convention. Conservative Democrats rallied to win back control of the party from McGovern's supporters. At a national committee meeting on December 9, they forced Jean Westwood to resign. William McGaffin

DENMARK saved its bacon, and Europe's, by voting decisively on Oct. 2, 1972, to join the European Community (Common Market). About 63.5 per cent of the Danes voted for entry in the referendum. A week earlier, when neighboring Norway voted "no," Danish Prime Minister Jens Otto Krag had warned that a similar rejection by Denmark would cause considerable devaluation of the krone and cuts in public spending. Denmark sells about $675 million worth of agricultural produce a year, including bacon, to Common Market countries. Loss of these outlets would have ruined the farmers.

A French newspaper reported on April 5 that a Russian diplomat had offered to finance the campaign by a group of Danes opposed to joining the Common Market. The Danes soon confirmed that the offer had been made, but they said that they had rejected it categorically.

In a government-sponsored campaign before the vote, Krag had let it be known that the Cabinet favored entry despite Norway's opposing view. The day after the referendum, Krag resigned "for personal reasons." A trade union leader, Anker Henrik Jorgensen, succeeded him. See JORGENSEN, ANKER HENRIK.

Balance of Payments. Common Market membership is expected to reduce Denmark's chronic and serious balance of payments deficit. Soon after

After being proclaimed Danish queen, Margrethe II and Prince Henrik wave to crowds while their son Frederik peeps through balcony opening.

taking office in 1971, the Krag government imposed a temporary surcharge on most imports. The surcharge fell from 10 per cent in the first half of 1972 to 7 per cent for the last six months. It will stay at 4 per cent until April, 1973, when it expires. This action was expected to cut the deficit of $1.048 billion by about one-third.

Old-age and disability pensions were increased in the fall of 1972, and income tax adjustments boosted revenue. Further social benefits, including sickness payments, were planned for 1973. During 1971, consumer prices rose by 6 per cent. But legislation preventing firms from passing on wage increases succeeded in holding the 1972 increase below this figure.

First Queen. King Frederik IX, who had reigned since 1947, died on January 14 at the age of 72, and Denmark got its first crowned woman sovereign, Frederik's daughter Margrethe, 31. She is known, however, as Margrethe II. See MARGRETHE II.

The Danish foreign ministry said on October 2 that it was formally protesting the action of Russian marines who had boarded a Danish fishing boat in the Baltic Sea September 27. Denmark said the Russians removed a Russian defector at gunpoint.

On June 1, the Danish Folketing (parliament) voted 121 to 0 to approve legislation that calls for fines for airlines whose planes fly over Denmark at supersonic speeds. Kenneth Brown

See also EUROPE (Facts in Brief Table).

DENTISTRY. Scientists pursued several promising leads in 1972 in trying to find ways to reduce the high rate of tooth decay and periodontal (gum) disease. They focused increasing emphasis on the harmful role of dental plaque in the development of these disorders. Plaque, a sticky, transparent film composed of bacterial colonies, constantly forms on teeth. A number of antibacterial agents have proved highly effective in controlling plaque in animal experiments conducted at the National Institute of Dental Research in Bethesda, Md. However, these drugs have not been sufficiently tested for human use.

The American Dental Association (ADA) has recommended that an overall prevention program should include oral cleaning with toothbrush and dental floss once a day, using a fluoride dentifrice, and restricting the intake of sweets. Drinking fluoridated water can also be beneficial, they said. They stressed that the program should be implemented under the professional direction of a dentist and requires complete cooperation of the patient.

The ADA continued to press to have dental care, primarily for children, included in any national health program that may finally be adopted by Congress. An ADA-sponsored bill that would initiate pilot programs for childrens' dental care was passed by the U.S. Senate but stalled in the House of Representatives.

Dental Disaster Squads. State disaster teams composed of dentists may be the way to identify mass disaster victims quickly and accurately, the head of the nation's first dental disaster squad has suggested. Lester L. Luntz of Hartford, Conn., pointed out in March that dental identification of mutilated or burned accident victims has become a universally accepted method when all other means of identification fail. But frequently, identification is delayed because of the lack of dentists experienced in the proper techniques and perhaps because equipment to conduct the special examinations is not readily available. A highly trained team of experts in every state would be the answer, Luntz said. Connecticut dentists pioneered this idea and proved its effectiveness by quickly identifying all 29 fatalities in a 1971 plane crash in New Haven.

Dental Hearing Aid. Earl W. Collard of the school of dentistry at the University of California at Los Angeles told the International Association for Dental Research, meeting in Las Vegas, Nev., March 24, that he has developed a miniature wireless intra-oral transducer that can be clamped onto a tooth. The device converts radio signals into vibrations that are transmitted through the teeth to the hearing center of the brain, where they are received as sounds. He suggested that such a device could serve as an effective and completely concealed hearing aid. Lou Joseph

DETROIT. A U.S. district court judge ordered the most sweeping school desegregation plan in the nation's history in Detroit on June 14, 1972, The order, affecting public schools in Detroit and 53 suburbs, stated that full desegregation of the Detroit public schools could come only by including suburban students in an integration scheme.

Suburban Desegregation. Judge Stephen J. Roth ordered a panel of nine education experts to draw up a specific integration plan to take effect in the fall of 1973. The court set these guidelines:

- Within each cluster of schools and districts, the racial makeup of each school and class should reflect the racial balance of the cluster.
- Each school faculty should be at least 10 per cent black, preferably with a biracial administration.
- Busing of children should be kept to the minimum consistent with complete desegregation.

However, on December 8, a U.S. court of appeals, while agreeing the schools were segregated, refused to approve the plan because not all of the 53 districts were included in the hearings. The case was sent back to the lower court.

Because of revenue shortages in 1972, the Detroit school board tried to reduce the school year from the 180 days required by state law to 117 days. A federal judge blocked the move. Estimated school revenues were only $170 million. The board said $295 million would be needed for the full academic year.

A Housing Scandal erupted when a congressional investigation disclosed that speculators were buying structurally unsound houses and reselling them–with the help of Federal Housing Administration loans–to low-income purchasers. Many buyers eventually lost the property because they could not meet mortgage payments and make needed repairs. Because of defaults on mortgages, the federal government owns about 7,000 Detroit homes, many of them abandoned. The number could rise as high as 23,000, blighting entire neighborhoods.

County Sues Ford. In July, Wayne County brought the most far-reaching environmental protection suit ever filed in Michigan. It charged that the Ford Motor Company violated at least 143 county air-pollution control regulations. The company replied that it had spent $25 million in pollution controls in the area since 1963.

Henry Ford II announced plans for a 32-acre development project on the downtown Detroit riverfront. It would include offices, apartments, a 70-story hotel, enclosed shopping malls, and a pond.

Employment in Detroit rose slightly, from 1,473,900 persons in May, 1971, to 1,478,800 in May, 1972. Detroit's average gross weekly earnings of production workers rose substantially during the same period, from $195.84 to $226.37 J. M. Banovetz

DICTIONARY. See Section Five, DICTIONARY SUPPLEMENT.

DIMITRIOS I (1914-) was elected Patriarch of the 250-million-member Eastern Orthodox Christian Church in July, 1972. He succeeded the late Athenagoras I.

Dimitrios Papadopoulos was born in Istanbul, Turkey. He attended a Greek school in Therapia, Turkey, and his theological education began when he was 17 at Halki, an island monastery and seminary near Istanbul that has produced many of Eastern Orthodoxy's leading prelates and theologians. He speaks French, Greek, and Turkish.

He became a deacon in 1937 and worked in an Istanbul parish before going to Greece on a two-year preaching assignment. He returned to Turkey in 1939 and was ordained a priest in 1942, serving in the Greek parish of Ferikoy, an Istanbul suburb. In 1964, he was consecrated a bishop, and on Feb. 15, 1972, he was appointed metropolitan archbishop of Imroz and Bozcaada, islands in the Aegean Sea.

Dimitrios I is regarded as a mildly liberal theologian in a church that is noted for its conservatism. He has shunned church politics in favor of pastoral duties, but he is expected to seek Christian unity as faithfully as his predecessor. Observers believe his attention to pastoral duties rather than worldly pursuits turned the election in his favor. He is unmarried; only celibates are eligible for the rank of bishop in the Eastern Orthodox Church. Foster Stockwell

DIPLOMATIC CORPS. See U.S. GOVERNMENT.

DISASTERS. A series of earthquakes devastated Managua, the capital of Nicaragua, on Dec. 23, 1972. The entire downtown area was leveled. Officials estimated that more than 10,000 persons were killed by the quakes or the fires that followed, and that additional thousands were injured.

The worst flooding in U.S. history struck the Eastern United States in June. Hurricane Agnes, which turned into tropical storm Agnes, brought heavy rains that caused the flooding. Parts of Florida, Maryland, Ohio, Pennsylvania, New York, Virginia, and West Virginia were declared disaster areas. According to the Office of Emergency Preparedness, Agnes killed 8 persons in Florida, 20 in Maryland, 48 in Pennsylvania, 31 in New York, 13 in Virginia, and 2 in the District of Columbia. The storm left 27,000 persons homeless.

Other major disasters in 1972 included the following:

Aircraft Crashes

Jan. 6—Near Bacalar, Mexico. A Mexican DC-6 airliner crashed in the Yucatán jungle, killing all 23 persons aboard.

Jan. 7—Ibiza Island, Spain. A Caravelle jet owned by Iberia Air Lines crashed into a mountain while attempting to land on the Mediterranean island. All 6 crew members and 98 passengers were killed.

Jan. 18—Victoria, Tex. Nine persons were killed when a private Lear jet struck a utility pole, crashed, and burned.

Jan. 21—Northern Colombia. Thirty-five persons were killed when a DC-3 crashed and burned in the Andes Mountains.

Jan. 21—Bogotá, Colombia. A Urraca Airlines turboprop crashed while taking off during a rainstorm. All 20 persons aboard were killed.

Jan. 26—Northwestern Czechoslovakia. Twenty-seven of the 28 persons aboard a Yugoslav Airlines DC-9 were killed when the jetliner exploded. Sabotage by Croatian Nationalists was suspected.

March 3—Albany, N.Y. A Mohawk Airlines turboprop crashed into a house while attempting to land. Two crewmen, 14 passengers, and 1 occupant of the house were killed; 36 persons were injured.

March 14—Near Dubai, Union of Arab Emirates. A Danish chartered plane returning to Denmark from Ceylon crashed while attempting to land, and all 112 persons aboard were killed.

March 19—Near Aden, South Yemen. Twenty-two persons were killed when a Yugoslav jet chartered by Egyptian Airways struck a mountain and exploded.

April 16—Amaseno, Italy. All 18 persons aboard were killed when an Italian ATI Airline propjet crashed in a mountainous area 50 miles south of Rome.

April 18—Addis Ababa, Ethiopia. Thirty-six persons were killed and 24 injured when an East African Airways VC-10 struck a farmhouse during take-off.

May 6—Palermo, Italy. An Alitalia DC-8 hit a mountain while trying to land. All 115 passengers and crew members aboard were killed.

May 18—Kharkov, Russia. A Soviet airliner crashed in the Ukraine, killing all 108 persons aboard.

May 21—Lobito, Angola. Twenty persons were killed and three injured when an Angola Airlines turboprop overshot the runway while trying to land and crashed.

May 29—Near New Orleans, La. Eleven persons were killed when a helicopter carrying workers to an offshore oil rig crashed in a swamp 60 miles southwest of New Orleans.

A housing development near Bull Run, Va., is inundated by floodwaters caused by tropical storm Agnes, which struck the East Coast in June.

June 14—Near New Delhi, India. The crash of a Japan Air Lines DC-8 killed 85 of the 89 persons aboard and 2 persons on the ground.

June 15—Near Pleiku, South Vietnam. A bomb exploded on a Cathay Pacific Airlines jet en route from Bangkok to Hong Kong. The plane crashed, and all 81 persons aboard were killed.

June 18—London. In the worst air disaster in British history, 118 persons died when a British European Airways jet crashed taking off from Heathrow Airport.

June 29—Lake Winnebago, Wis. Two small commercial planes collided in flight and fell into the lake, killing all 13 persons on board.

July 11—Northern Norway. A Royal Norwegian Air Force plane hit a mountain, killing the 18 persons aboard. Poor visibility was blamed for the crash.

July 29—Villavicencio, Colombia. A midair collision between two Avianca Airlines planes killed 37 persons.

Aug. 14—Near East Berlin, Germany. A chartered East German airliner exploded and crashed in a suburban area, killing 156 persons.

Aug. 27—Southeastern Venezuela. Twenty-four persons died when their plane crashed in dense jungle.

Sept. 13—Near Katmandu, Nepal. The crash of a Royal Nepalese DC-3 killed 31 persons.

Sept. 24—Sacramento, Calif. A privately owned, rebuilt jet fighter crashed into a crowded ice cream parlor near the end of the runway while attempting to take off. Twenty-two persons, 12 of them children, were killed.

Oct. 2—Sochi, Russia. An Ilyushin-18 crashed and exploded, killing all 100 persons aboard.

Oct. 13—Near Moscow. A Russian jetliner crashed while attempting to land. All 176 persons aboard were killed in the worst disaster in aviation history.

Oct. 13—Chile. A plane crashed in the Andes Mountains, killing 29 of the 45 aboard.

Nov. 5—Near Sofia, Bulgaria. Thirty-four persons were killed when a Bulgarian airplane hit a mountain.

Nov. 28—Moscow. A Japanese DC-8 crashed on take-off, killing 62 persons.

Dec. 3—Santa Cruz De Tenerife, Canary Islands. A chartered Spanish airliner crashed after take-off, killing all 155 persons aboard.

Dec. 8—Chicago. A jet crashed while attempting to land and tore through houses near Midway Airport. Forty-three persons on the plane and two residents of a house were killed.

Dec. 8—Pakistan. A Pakistani airliner crashed in the foothills of the Himalaya, killing all 33 persons aboard.

Dec. 29—Florida. A Lockheed L-1011 crashed in the Everglades near Miami, killing 100 persons.

Bus and Truck Crashes

Jan. 21—Near Bogotá, Colombia. Twenty persons were killed when a bus and truck collided.

Feb. 5—Mahasu, India. Nineteen persons died when a bus plunged into a Himalayan gorge 300 miles north of New Delhi.

Feb. 18—Near Cairo, Egypt. A bus carrying students plunged off a bridge into a canal, killing 77 persons.

March 4—Near Mināb, Iran. Thirty-two persons drowned when a bus fording the Kae River near the Persian Gulf was swept away by strong currents.

March 30—Kuala Lumpur, Malaysia. Ten persons, including 7 children, were killed and 27 others injured when a freight train struck a school bus.

May 13—Bean Station, Tenn. A double-deck Greyhound bus struck a tractor-trailer truck, killing 14 persons and injuring 15 others.

May 15—Minia, Egypt. At least 50 persons drowned when a bus carrying Christian pilgrims ran off the road and plunged into the Nile River.

June 11—Near Alexandria, La. Twelve persons were killed when a pickup truck carrying 14 passengers was struck from the rear by a tractor-trailer truck.

July 3—Amritsar, India. A head-on collision between a bus and a truck killed 27 persons and injured 37 others.

July 10—Ayacucho, Peru. A truck carrying passengers plunged into a ravine, killing at least 15 persons.

Aug. 28—Northern Iran. Two buses collided, killing 39 persons and injuring 40 others.

Aug. 27—Northern Ecuador. A bus rolled into a 150-foot-deep ravine, killing 19 persons.

Sept. 21—Pernik, Bulgaria. Eleven members of a Czechoslovak parachute team died when a train struck their bus at a grade crossing.

Nov. 6—Seoul, South Korea. A bus skidded into a stream, killing 20 persons and injuring 70 others.

Dec. 26—Near Fort Sumner, N.Mex. A cattle truck struck a bus, killing 19 persons.

Earthquakes

April 10—Southern Iran. An estimated 5,000 persons were killed and about 60 villages were devastated by a major earthquake and 1,000 aftershocks.

Dec. 23—Managua, Nicaragua. A series of earthquakes killed at least 10,000 persons.

Explosions and Fires

Jan. 16—Tyrone, Pa. An explosion and fire in a hotel killed 13 persons.

Feb. 24—São Paulo, Brazil. Sixteen persons were killed when fire raged through a 29-story department store and office building.

March 6—Barcelona, Spain. An explosion destroyed a 10-story apartment building, killing at least 12 persons.

March 11—Minsk, Russia. About 100 persons were killed by a fire and explosion at a factory.

March 30—Rio de Janeiro, Brazil. A series of explosions in an oil refinery killed 21 workers and injured 48.

May 13—Osaka, Japan. Fire destroyed three floors of a seven-story department store and killed 23 persons.

May 13—Osaka, Japan. One hundred and sixteen persons were killed when a blaze swept through a penthouse night club. It was the worst fire in Japan since World War II. Nineteen of the victims died when they jumped from the seventh-floor roof.

June 28—Bombay, India. An explosion aboard a Greek-owned oil tanker docked for repairs killed 22 persons and injured 30 others.

July 2—Near Seoul, South Korea. A fire in a farmhouse killed 13 children and injured 7 others. The blaze broke out when a child poured gasoline into a kerosene lamp.

July 5—Sherborne, England. Fire swept through a mental hospital ward, killing 30 patients.

Sept. 23—Rhodes, Greece. An electrical short circuit started a fire that killed 31 persons in a restaurant.

Oct. 1—Off the coast of South Vietnam. An explosion in a gun turret aboard the U.S. cruiser *Newport News* killed 20 sailors.

Oct. 29—Barcelona, Spain. An explosion in an apartment building killed 12 persons.

Nov. 30—Rome. An explosion in an illegal fireworks factory killed 15 persons.

Dec. 2—Seoul, South Korea. Thirty-nine persons were killed when fire swept through a theater.

Dec. 14—Weirton, W. Va. Nineteen men were killed and 10 injured by explosions in a coke plant.

Floods

Feb. 26—Man, W. Va. A mountainside dam burst, releasing a reservoir of mine waste and water. The flash flood of sludge that resulted along Buffalo Creek killed 118

Rescuers search for victims in the wreckage of a train that derailed on a mountain curve near Saltillo, Mex., killing 208 persons.

Debris litters the area along Buffalo Creek near Man, W. Va., where a dam burst in February, causing a flash flood that killed 118 persons.

persons, leveled 14 mining camps, and left about 5,000 persons homeless.

March 11-12—Palpa, Peru. At least 12 persons drowned in flooding caused by torrential rain.

June 10—Rapid City, S. Dak. Ten inches of rainfall in two days sent Rapid Creek over its banks and collapsed a dam. The floods that swept through the city killed 237 and caused an estimated $120 million in property damage. Eight other persons were missing.

June 18—Hong Kong. After three days of rain, flooding, and landslides, 87 persons were known dead and more than 100 were feared buried under the mud slides.

June 18—Southern Japan. Heavy rains caused flooding and landslides that killed 10 persons.

July 2-5—Southern Japan. At least 105 persons were killed and 90 injured during flooding and landslides caused by heavy rains.

July 31—Philippines. More than two weeks of incessant rain caused widespread flooding and landslides on the island of Luzon, killing 427 persons and leaving about 2 million homeless.

Aug. 1—Eastern India. Flooding killed at least 100 persons in the states of Assam, Bihar, and West Bengal.

Aug. 9—Nepal. Monsoon rains, floods, and landslides over a two-week period killed 105 persons.

Aug. 18-19—Seoul, South Korea. Floods and landslides caused by the worst rains in the nation's history killed 296 persons in the city and outlying areas.

Mine Disasters

May 2—Kellogg, Ida. A fire in the Sunshine Silver Mine killed 91 miners who were trapped 3,700 feet below the surface.

June 6—Wankie, Rhodesia. A violent explosion in Rhodesia's largest coal mine collapsed tunnels and released deadly methane gas, killing 427 miners.

July 22—Blacksville, W. Va. A fire in Consolidation Coal Company's Blacksville No. 1 mine trapped nine miners. An explosion two days later forced rescuers to halt operations, and the mine was sealed off.

Shipwrecks

Jan. 3—Persian Gulf. Forty persons drowned when a launch carrying falcons and hunting equipment for the ruling sheik of Qatar sank during a storm near the island of Qais.

Jan. 9—Off British Columbian Coast. An African freighter sank in heavy seas about 120 miles west of Vancouver Island and its 42 crewmen were lost.

Feb. 2—Gulf of Mexico. The *V.A. Fogg*, a tanker carrying volatile benzine residue, exploded and sank near Galveston, Tex. All 39 persons aboard were killed.

March 5—Gulf of Mexico. The *San Nicolas*, a Liberian freighter bound for New Orleans, broke up and sank, killing 28 crew members.

May 11—Off Argentina. A collision between a Liberian oil tanker and a British freighter killed at least 84 persons, and 10 others were missing.

Aug. 26—Near Saint-Nazaire, France. A docked Greek oil tanker, *Princess Irene*, exploded and sank after being struck by lightning. At least 18 persons were missing and presumed dead, and 26 others were injured.

Aug. 30—Mirzāpur, India. About 80 persons drowned when a riverboat capsized on the Ganges River.

Sept. 13—Northern Malaysia. At least 30 persons were killed when a ferry capsized while crossing the Krani River.

Nov. 15—Near Piraeus Harbor, Greece. A Greek tanker collided with a Greek Navy vessel, killing 45 persons.

Tornadoes, Typhoons, and Storms

Jan. 8—Philippines. At least 67 persons were killed by Typhoon Kit.

Jan. 26—Bogotá, Colombia. Torrential rains triggered a landslide that killed an estimated 70 persons.

March 18-19—Japan. Blizzards and severe storms throughout Japan caused the deaths of at least 118 persons.

April 1—Bangladesh. A tornado twisted through Mymensingh District, 60 miles north of Dacca, killing 200 persons and injuring 360 others.

Sept. 16—Honshu Island, Japan. A typhoon struck Japan's Pacific coast, killing at least 13 persons.

Oct. 22—Kashmir. More than 50 persons were missing and presumed dead when snow and high winds buried them in a mountain pass.

Train Wrecks

Jan. 16—Near Lárisa, Greece. A collision between a freight train and a passenger express killed 16 persons and injured 60 others.

March 31—Near Potgietersrus, South Africa. A passenger train derailed on a bridge and several coaches fell into a riverbed below, killing 38 persons and injuring 174 others.

May 17—São Paulo, Brazil. Twelve persons were killed and 50 injured when a passenger train hit a stalled truck at a grade crossing.

June 4—Jessore, Bangladesh. A speeding passenger train struck the rear of a train stopped in a station, and at least 27 persons were killed and 87 injured.

June 16—Soissons, France. Part of the roof of a mile-long railroad tunnel collapsed; and two passenger trains, traveling in opposite directions, hit the debris, derailed, and collided, killing 107 persons and injuring 90 others.

Aug. 6—Liaquatpur, Pakistan. A passenger train struck the rear of a freight train stopped at a station. Sixty-five persons were killed and more than 100 injured.

Sept. 29—Near Malmesbury South Africa. Forty-eight persons were killed when a train derailed.

Oct. 5—Saltillo, Mex. A speeding train derailed on a mountain curve, killing 208 persons. The train's crewmen were charged with drinking.

Oct. 30—Chicago, Ill. An express commuter train rammed into the rear of a local backing up at a station. Forty-five persons were killed.

Oct. 31—Eskisehir, Turkey. Twenty persons were killed when two trains collided.

Nov. 6—Western Japan. Fire broke out on an express train, killing at least 40 persons.

Other Disasters

March 5—Kigoma, Tanzania. Twelve persons drowned and 25 others were missing after a motorboat capsized.

April 10—Nepal. Fifteen South Korean mountain climbers were killed by an avalanche in the Himalaya.

April 11—Canary Islands. The Spanish government announced that a freakish wind gust killed 12 Spanish paratroopers during a training drop.

July 10—Chandka Forest, India. Elephants, apparently crazed by heat and drought, rampaged through five villages, killing at least 24 persons.

July 12—Betten, Switzerland. Thirteen persons were killed and two injured when an aerial cable car slid backwards into a concrete cable station.

Sept. 16—Naga, Philippines. At least 76 persons were killed when a wooden bridge that was crowded with Roman Catholics who were celebrating a religious festival collapsed.

Nov. 7—Brunswick, Ga. Cars and trucks plunged into the Brunswick River when a freighter crashed into a bridge. Ten persons were killed.

Dec. 20—Rio De Janeiro. A supermarket roof collapsed, killing 15 shoppers. Darlene R. Stille

DOMINICAN REPUBLIC. See LATIN AMERICA.

DRUGS. Addictive drugs remained a major worldwide concern in 1972. On March 21, President Richard M. Nixon signed into law a bill establishing by statutory authority a Special Action Office for Drug Abuse Prevention, which the President had set up by executive order in June, 1971. The law authorized spending $1 billion over the next four years to prevent drug abuse. Another $75 million was earmarked for scientific research over three years.

Administration officials, originally hopeful that Turkey's agreement in 1971 to stop growing the opium poppy would reduce drug importations, were not as optimistic in 1972. With 57 countries growing poppies and producing heroin, narcotics officials termed the whole effort at stopping poppy cultivation "nonsense." In 1971, the United States seized 1,541 pounds of heroin, compared with 488 pounds in 1970. However, U.S. Narcotics Bureau agents estimate that the half-million addicts in the United States use from 6 to 10 tons of heroin a year.

Methadone. Controversy continued over transferring addicts from heroin to the theoretically safer drug methadone. According to a study at Rockefeller University in New York City, reported in April, from two-thirds to three-fourths of the 14,000 addicts who relied on methadone maintenance returned to society as productive members. On the other hand, a spokesman for the New York Medical Examiner's

Drug Routes into the United States

 Principal growing area

Drug route

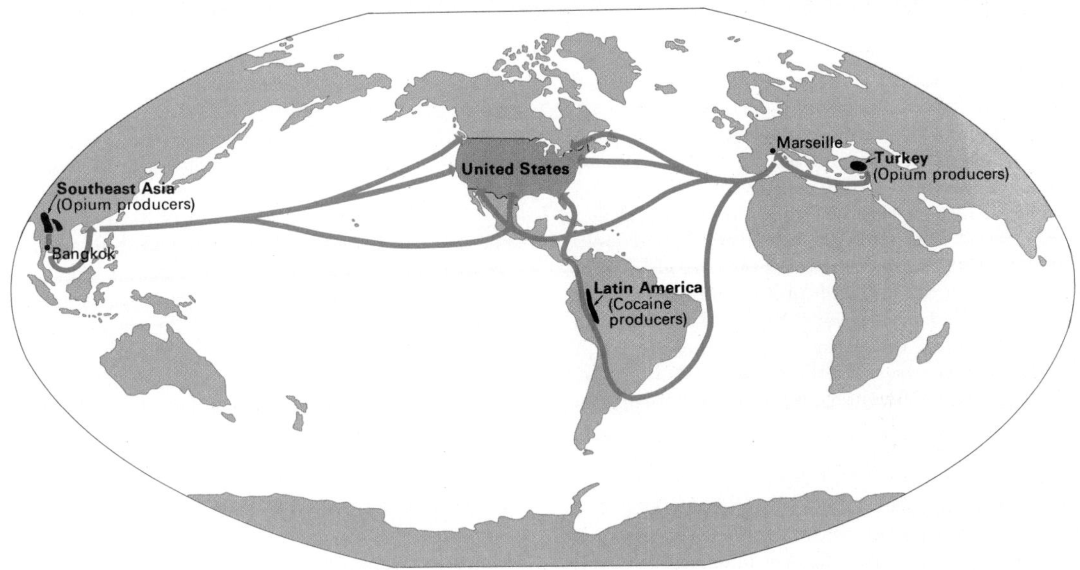

Office called methadone the second biggest cause of death among narcotics users.

In an effort to resolve some of the uncertainties involved in the use of methadone, the government announced new guidelines for maintenance programs on April 3. The more than 450 programs in the nation will be reviewed, and the drug, a prescription drug, will be reclassified to take it out of the hands of private practitioners and pharmacies.

Drug Investigations. In 1970, the Food and Drug Administration (FDA) banned the use of the artificial sweetener cyclamate because tests show it causes cancer in mice. In 1972, the sweetener saccharin and a number of other drugs were under investigation. The FDA completed an effectiveness study of nearly 3,000 prescription drugs in February. As a result of this study, the domestic production quota of amphetamines was reduced to about 17 or 18 per cent of the 1971 quota. These drugs have been widely used as diet pills to reduce appetite. During the fiscal year, the FDA recalled nearly 2,000 potentially dangerous drugs and drug-containing products from the market.

A World Health Organization (WHO) expert blamed confusion in drug labeling for the thalidomide tragedy that deformed thousands of European babies during the 1960s. Alexandre Manulla said that it took several months after the disastrous effects of thalidomide were recognized to get it recalled. It took so long because thalidomide was sold under many different trade names rather than a recognized standard name. Switzerland, he cited as an example, has some 40,000 pharmaceutical products today that may be known by 80 or more trade names. WHO is trying to simplify the situation by designating a single international name for each drug. The United States, Great Britain, and France are among several nations already using such an international designation.

Safety Packaging was delayed by a shortage of child-proof containers. In October, FDA officials said that the nation's 55,000 retail pharmacists would have until Jan. 22, 1973, to comply with new regulations for packaging aspirin, dangerous drugs, and certain liniments. The original deadlines had been August 14 for aspirin, September 21 for methyl salicylate or wintergreen oil, and October 24 for 4,300 types of such controlled drugs as amphetamines, barbiturates, and narcotics. FDA officials said a field survey that is underway indicated that the packaging-supply backlog may be even more extensive than agency officials estimated, and that the deadline might have to be extended for manufacturers of bottled aspirin, the leading cause of child poisonings. An FDA pharmacist said the shortage of containers had probably been aggravated by pharmacists deciding to put all prescriptions in child-proof containers. Mary E. Jessup

DUERK, ALENE BERTHA (1920-), director of the U.S. Navy Nurse Corps, became the first woman admiral in United States history. She was sworn in as a rear admiral on June 1, 1972.

Born in Defiance, Ohio, Rear Admiral Duerk graduated from the Toledo Hospital School of Nursing in 1941. A year later, she enlisted in the Navy and served as staff nurse at the Portsmouth (Va.) Naval Hospital. After she was commissioned an ensign in 1943, she served on the hospital ship U.S.S. *Benevolence* in the Pacific. The highest award she received for her World War II service was the Naval Reserve Medal. Released from service in 1946, she was called back to active duty during the Korean War. In 1948, she received a B.S. in Ward Management and Teaching from Western Reserve University in Cleveland. She became a captain in July, 1967.

Rear Admiral Duerk administers nursing services for 39 hospitals and several dispensaries from the headquarters of the Navy chief of the Bureau of Medicine and Surgery in Washington, D.C. As director of the 2,550 female and 250 male nurses, she is in charge of training, education, and the assignment of nurses to duty stations.

Since Rear Admiral Duerk became director in May, 1970, she has traveled in the Far East and throughout the United States. Her favorite pastimes are gardening and cooking German and Chinese foods. Lillian Zahrt

EAGLETON, THOMAS FRANCIS (1929-), a U.S. senator from Missouri, was briefly the 1972 Democratic vice-presidential candidate. He was the first vice-presidential candidate in history forced to withdraw apparently against his own wishes.

On July 25, 11 days after his nomination as the running mate of Senator George S. McGovern (D., S. Dak.), Eagleton told a news conference that he had been hospitalized in 1960, 1964, and 1966 for nervous exhaustion and had received electric shock therapy. He said his health was now excellent.

McGovern admitted that he was unaware of Eagleton's medical history, but promised Eagleton "1,000 per cent" support. Then, columnist Jack Anderson charged on July 27 that Eagleton had a record of drunken-driving arrests. Eagleton angrily denied this. Nevertheless, some McGovern staff members and several newspapers called on Eagleton to withdraw, and he did so on July 31. On August 1, Anderson acknowledged that the unverified drunken-driving charge was false and publicly apologized.

Eagleton was born on Sept. 4, 1929, in St. Louis, Mo. He received a law degree from Harvard in 1953 and was elected St. Louis circuit attorney in 1956, Missouri attorney general in 1960, lieutenant governor in 1964, and U.S. senator in 1968. He married in 1956 and has two children. Darlene R. Stille

See also DEMOCRATIC PARTY.

EARTHQUAKES. See DISASTERS; GEOLOGY.

EASTERN ORTHODOX CHURCHES. Athenagoras I, Patriarch of Constantinople and the first among all the heads of Eastern Orthodox Churches, died on July 6, 1972, in Istanbul, Turkey, at the age of 86. He had been elected to the post in 1949, after serving for 15 years as the Greek Orthodox Archbishop of North and South America. The late patriarch helped to achieve a major breakthrough in ecumenical relations when he met Pope Paul VI of the Roman Catholic Church in Jerusalem in 1964 and in Rome and Istanbul in 1967.

Athenagoras I did not succeed, however, in improving the status of the Ecumenical Patriarchate in Turkey. He was unable to prevent the closing in 1971 by the Turkish government of the theological school on the island of Halki near Istanbul, and the massive exodus of Greeks from Istanbul. After his death, the Turkish government openly opposed the election as his successor of any of the leading members of the Holy Synod of the Ecumenical Patriarchate, virtually forcing the Synod to elect as patriarch the hitherto unknown Dimitrios, 58-year-old Metropolitan of Imroz and Bozcanda, Turkish islands in the Aegean Sea. See DIMITRIOS I.

In the United States, the biennial Clergy and Laity Congress of the Greek Archdiocese of North and South America, adjourned its meeting in Houston in July when the death of Patriarch Athenagoras I was announced. The congress was discussing the new situation created in the Greek parishes in America by massive immigration to the United States from Greece. This has created tensions between the more Americanized Greeks and the newcomers.

Changes in Leadership. In May, the Diocese of Pittsburgh and West Virginia of the Orthodox Church in America elected a new bishop. He is Theodosius (Lazor), a native of Canonsburg, Pa., who was formerly Bishop of Sitka and Alaska.

Metropolitan Vladimir (Nagosky), Primate of the Orthodox Church in Japan, resigned his office in March and returned to the United States after 10 years of leading the 150,000-member Japanese Orthodox Church. He was given the title of Archbishop of Berkeley (Calif.) and auxiliary to the Archbishop of San Francisco and the Western States.

On August 10, Metropolitan Andrey (Velichko), the fomer head of the Bulgarian parishes in America, died at the age of 85 in Sophia, Bulgaria.

The Second International Conference of Orthodox Theologians was held at St. Vladimir's Orthodox Theological Seminary in New York City in September. Theologians from Greece, Poland, Romania, Russia, Turkey, the United States, and Yugoslavia took part.

In Russia, Metropolitan Nikodim, the chief spokesman for the Russian Orthodox Church abroad, resigned as head of the Patriarchate's Department of External Affairs and was replaced by Archbishop Juvenaly. Alexander Schmemann

ECONOMY, THE. Operating under mandatory wage and price controls for the first full "peacetime" year in history, the U.S. economy turned in a creditable, though not sterling, performance in 1972.

However, there was no general agreement as to whether the controls had contributed significantly to the year's gains. The gross national product (GNP), which is the most broadly based of the economy's performance measures, rose by almost 10 per cent over 1971 to $1.155 trillion. Of the total increase, only about 3.5 per cent was the result of inflationary forces. The balance represented a net gain in the production of goods and services. On the other hand, the unemployment rate was stubbornly high at year's end, about 5.3 per cent of the civilian labor force. It was slightly more than 6 per cent at the end of 1971.

Some analysts took the position that the relatively low rate of production capacity in use and late 1971's high rate of unemployment–along with normal increase in productivity associated with the early months of a recovery–would have combined to hold down prices while permitting substantially expanded output without government intervention. Other analysts argued that if there had not been a system of controls, the preceding two years of inflationary expectations would have led to higher wage demands and a much greater willingness on the part of business to raise prices.

Whatever the merits of these opposing arguments may be, the hard fact remains that the rate of inflation in the United States was well below that in most other industrialized countries for the first time in several years. Both business and consumers entered 1973 with a much better record behind them than had existed since 1967, and they were apparently looking forward with optimism to continuing progress on all fronts in 1973.

A Brightening Outlook. Almost all segments of the economy shared in the general prosperity, but with wide variations. For example, while wages rose overall about 6 per cent, construction workers and West Coast longshoremen reaped gains of 14 to 15 per cent. Personal income rose to $950 billion, a level that apparently encouraged consumers to spend more freely. Savings dropped to 6.4 per cent compared with 1971's abnormally high level of 8.2 per cent. Per capita disposable income rose to $3,755, about 4.5 per cent above its 1971 level. More important, however, was the growth of this income in real purchasing power. At 2.5 per cent, it represented greater growth than in any of the preceding four years. The increase, of course, could be explained by the rise of only 2 per cent in consumer prices. In 1970 and 1971, prices rose more than 5 per cent.

Farmers found their income up nearly 20 per cent over 1971. Net income per farm rose from $6,050 to $6,750, a jump of more than 11 per cent. At the same time, farm prices increased more rapidly than did the prices of goods purchased by farmers, so that the so-called comparity ratio rose to more than 80 per cent by the end of the year. Pretax corporate profits rose to a new high of $91 billion, and after-tax profits hit $52 billion. This led to some complaints that wage and price controls had effectively restrained wage income but not profits.

This argument, however, ignored the fact that corporate profits (before taxes) have been a steadily declining percentage of the GNP. In 1966, they made up 11.5 per cent of the GNP; in 1972, it was about 9 per cent. Nevertheless, investors were clearly satisfied with the recovery as the stock market rose to record highs in November and December. One week after the election, the Dow Jones average of 30 industrial stocks closed over the 1,000 mark for the first time. In the weeks immediately following, it moved to even higher ground. See Stocks and Bonds.

The Labor Force. Unemployment dropped, and more than 82.4 million Americans were employed at year's end–nearly 2.3 million more than 1971. Yet, the benefits arising from these developments were not shared equally among all elements of the labor force. Unemployment among nonwhite workers was almost 10 per cent and nearly 18 per cent among teen-agers. On the other hand, only 2.6 per cent of experienced married workers were out of work, barely more than could be expected from the normal turnover associated with people changing jobs.

With the rate of unemployment hovering at a troublesome 5.3 to 6 per cent, computerized job services tried to find Americans work.

Picketing consumers in Erie, Pa., protest rising food prices at a local supermarket. Even with controls, the price of food rose in 1972.

This relatively spotty record highlighted one of the continuing problems of the American economy. With a 4 per cent unemployment rate commonly associated with the concept of "full employment," more than 1 million new jobs would have been required in 1972 to achieve that goal. As long as unemployment is concentrated among less-experienced workers, any such increase in the number of jobs available will inevitably create a heavy upward pressure on wages and thus renew fears of inflation.

Most observers conceded that further efforts to bring unemployment down among nonwhites and teen-agers were badly needed, but no one seemed quite sure how that might best be accomplished.

The task of creating enough jobs to provide work for all who seek it is complicated by a steadily rising proportion of women seeking jobs. Even the rapidly growing economy of 1972 was unable to fully meet the problem, and it is most unlikely that rates of growth in the total economy in excess of 6 per cent can be maintained for any prolonged period of time.

Of the more than 82 million jobholders in 1972, 19 million were employed in manufacturing and 32 million in service, finance, and trade. For the first time in more than a decade, agricultural employment, at 3.4 million, held steady instead of declining. The rise in government employees was halted, with 13 million Americans working for federal, state, or local governmental agencies.

Debt and Credit. The great bulk of Americans seemed to have almost unlimited confidence in the future. They pushed retail sales up by 10 per cent and took on an increasing burden of consumer debt, which neared $155 billion by year's end. This was about $20 billion higher than at the end of 1971. Nearly 70 per cent of the credit was in the form of installment purchases, which unquestionably helped to fuel the purchases of durable goods. Output of durable goods jumped 10 per cent during the year. About 47 per cent of installment credit and 40 per cent of noninstallment credit was held by banks.

Strong Housing Demands also indicated the generally prosperous conditions. More than 2.4 million new dwelling units were built in 1972. The number of new starts was expected to fall slightly in 1973, but analysts confidently estimated that it would not drop below 2 million.

Mobile homes are not included in these totals and increasing numbers of Americans choose to house themselves in them. It seems apparent then, that the total number of housing units going up is more than sufficient to catch up on the accumulated backlogs and meet the rates of new family formation. Whether these units are of the right types, and in the right locations, to meet the most pressing immediate requirements is another matter. Strong resistance developed during the year to the construction of low-income housing in many parts of the country, espe-

Selected Key Economic Indicators

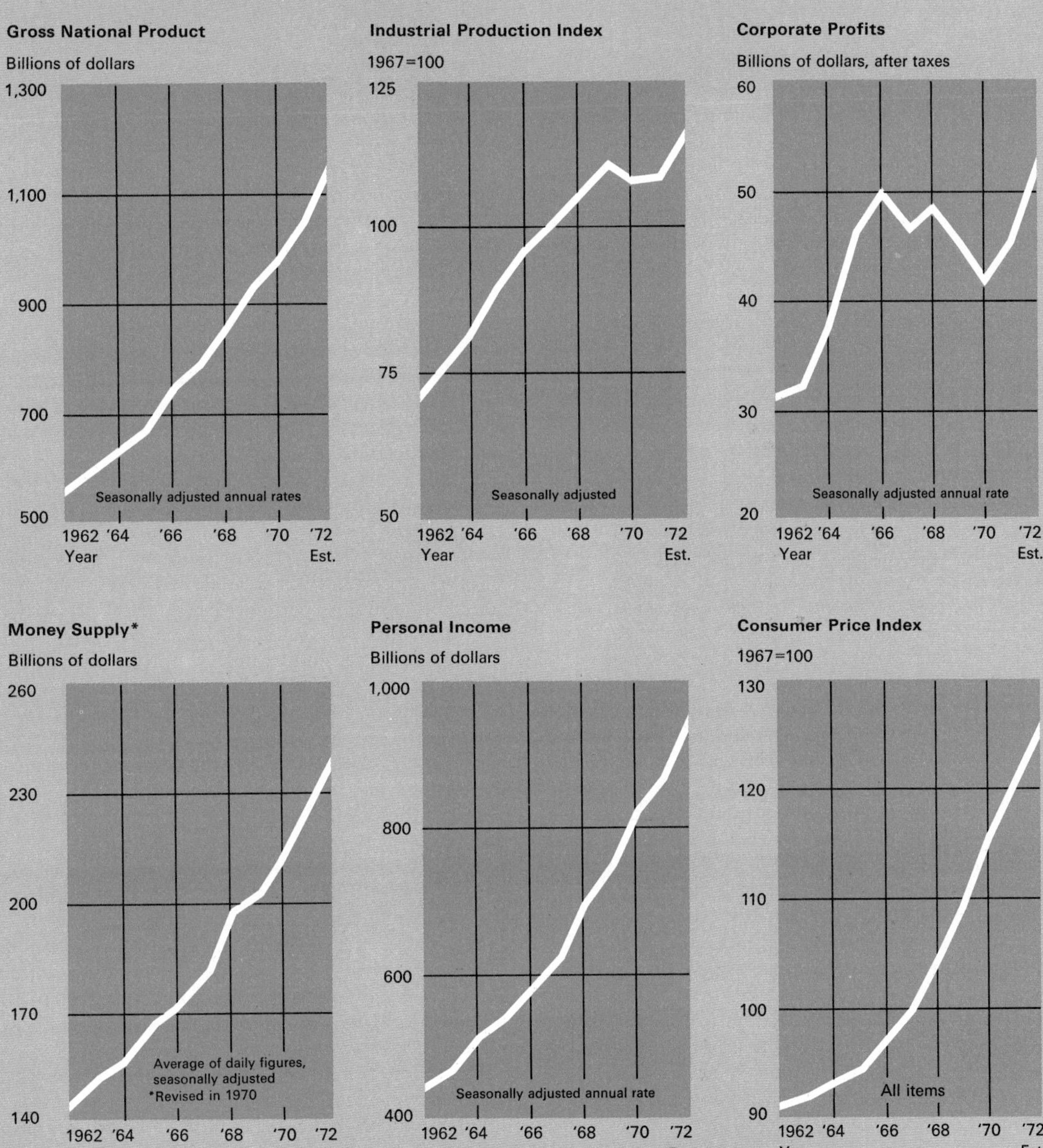

The most comprehensive measure of the nation's total output of goods and services is the *Gross National Product* (GNP). The GNP represents the dollar value in current prices of all goods and services plus the estimated value of certain imputed outputs, such as the rental value of owner-occupied dwellings. *Industrial Production Index* is a monthly measure of the physical output of manufacturing, mining, and utility industries. *Corporate Profits* are quarterly profit samplings from major industries. *Money Supply* measures the total amount of money in the economy in coin, currency, and demand deposits. *Personal Income* is current income received by persons (including nonprofit institutions and private trust funds) before personal taxes. *Consumer Price Index* (CPI) is a monthly measure of changes in the prices of goods and services consumed by urban families and individuals. CPI includes about 300 goods and services. All 1972 figures are *Year Book* estimates.

cially in the affluent suburbs. So it can be argued that progress in eliminating slum housing was certainly less apparent than the gross numbers of new units would seem to indicate.

Industrial Production rose by almost 10 per cent. The Federal Reserve (Fed) index stood at 116.7 in October (1967=100) as compared with 106.8 in October, 1971. Durable goods and mining, both with increases of more than 10 per cent, led the sectors. Business continued to expand rapidly and replace machinery and equipment. Spending for these items reached a record $89.6 billion. Gross private domestic investment totaled $180 billion, of which $54 billion went for housing and the balance for a variety of commercial and industrial purposes.

The Money Supply was the instrument for all of this activity, of course. According to economic theory, given the proper confidence among consumers and an appropriate set of incentives, all that is needed to keep the economic machine operating smoothly is the appropriate supply of money. Of course, just what is an appropriate supply of money, how to determine proper incentives, and how to guess the existing state of consumer confidence ahead of time, are problems that have never been practically solved. Monetary authorities look to such things as interest rates and price levels to make an estimate of how much money should be made available to keep the economy balanced.

In 1972, the money supply rose by 6 per cent to $242 billion. Interest rates declined slightly during the year – although they moved up near the end – and the economy moved forward in a relatively steady fashion. Those who feared inflationary pressures suggested that the money supply expand less rapidly, and those who were worried about the level of unemployment called for more rapid growth. However, the Fed did a reasonably successful job of keeping the economy on an even keel.

The International Picture was not as satisfactory. The U.S. dollar's direct ties to gold had been severed and new currency relations were established in 1971 in an effort to correct a serious imbalance of payments running against the United States. But these measures were not fully successful in restoring international currency stability.

The effective devaluation of the U.S. dollar in 1971 – ranging from a high of 12 per cent relative to the German mark and the Swiss franc down to 2.7 per cent against the French franc – apparently did little to correct the U.S. position in 1972. For the second year in a row, merchandise imports exceeded exports by almost $5.5 billion. The total balance of international payments saw the United States running about $8 billion in the red, but a decline in inflationary pressures in the United States offered some hope for the future.

For the first time in several years, inflationary pressure in the United States was distinctly less than that of other industrialized countries. This fact unquestionably helped to keep U.S. goods more competitive in foreign markets. Should this trend continue, prospects for bringing U.S. payments into balance would improve distinctly.

Government Finance. Federal sharing of revenues with state and local governments began in 1972, with a program calling for a $30-billion return over a period of five years from the federal treasury. The move had a double objective: to reduce the property tax burden, which in many areas had climbed to levels that threatened to spark serious taxpayer revolt, and to provide some much-needed funds for the solution of urgent problems in the nation's metropolitan areas. Strangely, at the same time that federal funds were being returned to state and local governments, the federal budget was running a deficit of about $25 billion, while state and local governments were showing a surplus in the neighborhood of $10 billion.

By any conventional standards, the federal deficit looked extraordinarily large. Yet it actually showed a slight surplus on what economists term the "full employment" basis. This is an estimate of what total receipts and expenditures would have been had the economy actually been operating at full capacity, measured at a level of 4 per cent unemployment. According to this concept, it is appropriate for the government to run deficits and thus stimulate economic activity during periods of less than full employment. Certainly most economists support the concept. But many insist that the measure is too imprecise and subject to too many uncertainties to provide the precise tool needed to manage the economy.

President Richard M. Nixon apparently shared some of this concern when he took executive measures in October to prevent the spending of funds appropriated by Congress in an effort to keep total budget expenditures for the fiscal year ending June 30, 1973, within a $250-billion limit. A substantial increase in social security benefits in September made this task even more difficult.

Overseas Economic Developments received more than normal attention in 1972. Many major events occurred that could well shape the future relationships among the major nations. Drawing the most attention was the announcement in July of a 3-year, $1-billion wheat sale by the United States to Russia.

For many years, the productivity of Russian agriculture has been a major headache for Kremlin leaders and, when 1972 proved to be a disastrous year, acute food shortages appeared in the offing for Soviet consumers. The agreement apparently developed as a result of Russian needs and the willingness of the United States to extend normal Commodity Credit Corporation terms of sale to the Soviet Union.

Price Commission Chairman C. Jackson Grayson and Irma Angevine of Consumer Federation of America visit store to check for price increases.

The program offered a much-needed outlet for U.S. grain, which had faced a declining market in Western European countries as a result of the agricultural support system adopted by the European Community (Common Market). Unhappily, there were charges immediately after the agreement that the U.S. Department of Agriculture had failed to make known its full impact rapidly enough, enabling grain exporters to purchase wheat at lower prices than would otherwise have existed and thus to make large profits. At least one major grain exporter revealed, however, that it actually had lost money on the Russian sale.

Of equal interest for future U.S.-Russian relationships, was the October announcement that the United States had agreed to purchase large quantities of Siberian natural gas for shipment to the United States over the next decade. The basic elements in this arrangement apparently were the tremendous projected shortage of natural gas in the United States and the Russian need for advanced American technology.

The arrangement sparked a great deal of controversy. Some quarters criticized it as creating a dangerous dependence upon Russia for basic energy requirements, and others as being essentially a bilateral barter arrangement such as many of the trade agreements between Russia and its Eastern European satellites. However, defenders of the agreement pointed out that the mutual advantages to the two countries promise to provide a base for further reducing political tensions. And, from the United States point of view, increasing dependence on foreign, and probably interruptable, sources of energy was inevitable over the next decade.

It was hoped that natural gas would provide a clean source of energy for an increasingly ecologically conscious society and that this would lead to more conventional arrangements between independent American businesses and Russia. Whether related to the natural gas deal or not, this prospect seemed brighter when Russia agreed in November to permit the manufacture of American soft drinks there.

The Common Market. Equally significant for long-run relationships among industrialized nations was the decision of Great Britain, Ireland and Denmark to join the Common Market as of Jan. 1, 1973. Norway, the fourth applicant for admission, surprisingly voted against seeking admission in a national referendum in September. Observers attributed the vote more to Norwegian nationalism than to the economic consequences. Immediately after the decision, the Norwegian government began to negotiate special relationships that would permit Norwegian goods into the Common Market on a basis comparable to those for full market members. See DENMARK; NORWAY.

Similar agreements were being worked out with the European Free Trade Association (EFTA), of which Great Britain had been the principal member. It appeared likely that all of Western Europe would be in what could easily become the world's second largest economic unit within a few years.

Some analysts believe that this economic integration will ultimately lead to political union, but whether this occurs or not, the advantages of a widespread and prosperous market free of barriers to trade, labor, and capital will inevitably result in higher standards of living. Principal losers in the enlarged economic community will probably be American farmers. Already faced with declining markets in Europe as a result of agricultural protectionism, U.S. farmers will unquestionably find it more difficult to sell in Great Britain. A major importer of U.S. agricultural goods, the British must now mold their own agricultural policies to those of the Common Market. It may well have been, in fact, the importance of the British market for Danish agricultural products, especially bacon and dairy foods, that influenced the Danish vote to join the market.

In the long run, however, the expansion of the Common Market will probably be of major benefit to the United States. Ever since its creation in 1958, U.S. trade with the area has grown steadily. Despite the tariff barriers facing American producers and not their competitors within the market, the balance of trade has continued to be favorable to the United States. See EUROPE.

In the Western Hemisphere, attention centered on Marxist-oriented Chile. Mounting economic difficulties there led to massive strikes by middle-class shopkeepers and nearly complete disruption of the economy. See CHILE.

In the Eastern Hemisphere, oil producing and exporting countries in the Persian Gulf area have been steadily increasing their demands for ownership of the vast holdings of foreign oil producers. Agreements were signed in 1972 that would ultimately transfer 51 per cent ownership to the governments involved. Over the long run, the agreements are bound to mean drastically higher prices for energy consumers in both Western Europe and the United States, and the threat remains that nationalization might completely end the oil companies' control.

Rich v. Poor Nations. In an international context, most of the less-developed nations continue to press for more industrialization, recognizing that only through this process can they close the wide gap between the rich and the poor. Not unreasonably, they believe that only the affluent can sacrifice the production of goods and services now to improve the quality of the environment. They either do not accept alarming predictions that society will be destroyed if we do not drastically reduce present rates of growth in production and population, or they cannot endorse them in the face of popular pressures at home, where the wide gap between rich and poor nations is unacceptable. Without denying the importance of the environmental problems that our industrial society creates, it must be admitted that there is a major difference between slowing or halting growth in a country such as the United States and in one where failure to grow will lead to starvation.

International Trade. Despite monetary uncertainties, the volume of transactions between countries continued to rise. Exports and imports ran about 17 per cent higher than in 1972. The industrialized countries' share in this growing trade again rose, and constituted 71 per cent of the total. This reflected the problem less-developed countries faced in getting the necessary resources to build up their industrial base. The major foreign trading nations were, as usual, the United States, West Germany, Japan, France, Canada, and Great Britain.

The imbalance between the developed and the less-developed countries is illustrated by the fact that the total of exports from all the African countries could not equal the exports of a relatively small nation such as the Netherlands. Industrialized countries tend to trade most heavily among themselves. As a result, the leading purchasers of United States goods were Canada, Japan, West Germany, Great Britain, and France, in that order, and the leading suppliers were Canada, Japan, West Germany, Great Britain, and Italy. Warren W. Shearer

See also LABOR; MANUFACTURING; MONEY. Section One, FOCUS ON THE ECONOMY.

ECUADOR. A three-man junta led by Army Brigadier General Guillermo Rodriguez Lara seized the government on Feb. 15, 1972. Deposed President José María Velasco Ibarra, who was charged with "exploiting the people," was flown to Panama. It was the fourth time he had been ousted since 1933. The junta immediately proclaimed a "revolutionary and nationalist" government and placed the country in a state of siege. It closed schools, put public transport under the armed forces, and imposed a night curfew and censorship. It also suspended the general elections scheduled for June 4 and restored the Constitution of 1945, which was drafted by leftists.

Ecuador's economic future brightened considerably on August 15, when the first petroleum from the new Texaco-Gulf oil fields was exported. It transformed the republic overnight from an agricultural nation into one of Latin America's biggest oil producers. The crude oil traveled from the heart of the Amazon jungles over the lofty Andes Mountains to a new Pacific coast terminal at Balao, near Esmeraldas port, via a 313-mile, $150-million Texaco-Gulf pipeline opened on June 26. The line can handle 250,000 barrels a day (bpd), and eventually will carry 400,000.

A second pipeline is to be built by Cayman del Ecuador to the Pacific port of Manta, and a score or more of oil firms were spending $80 million in 1972 exploring and developing new sources of the low-sulfur crude oil that is highly prized in pollution-conscious markets. By 1973, aggregate production is expected to reach 250,000 bpd, and plans are to increase this to 325,000 bpd by 1974 or 1975 and to 400,000 by 1977 or 1978.

Fishing Dispute Eases. The 14-year-old "tuna war" off Ecuador's Pacific coast subsided into an uneasy "cease-fire" during the year primarily because there was little left to fight about. Most of the tuna mysteriously left the 200-mile sea area that the republic claimed as sovereign waters. The U.S. tuna boat fleet had refused to recognize the territorial claim. The fish had migrated to new feeding grounds in the central Pacific and farther north off the coast of Central America and Mexico, pursued by dozens of U.S. clippers. As a result, very few U.S. fishing vessels were seized by Ecuador in 1972 and fined for not having Ecuadorean fishing licenses.

The nation struggled with trade imbalances and chronic budgetary deficits. It increased its gross monetary reserves to $83.7 million on August 18 from a low of $21 million in March, mainly as a result of a $40-million loan received May 1 from the Manufacturers Hanover Trust of New York City. Stepped-up investments by U.S. oil firms also helped. Various U.S. and international organizations loaned $40.7 million for agricultural, electric power, water supply and/or sewage, industrial, and textile projects. Mary Webster Soper

See also LATIN AMERICA (Facts in Brief Table).

EDUCATION struggled with rising costs and slackening growth in enrollments in 1972. Its mood was one of uncertainty and retrenchment. Taxpayer resistance to spending increased. In the colleges, where actual enrollments were still rising, the effects of overexpansion had become serious. It led to unfilled space for an estimated 500,000 students and to continuing budget deficits.

The busing issue dominated much of the public school debate. Opponents of busing insisted that they were largely concerned with what they saw as threatened damage to their children's education. But civil rights spokesmen insisted that this stance was actually window dressing for segregationist efforts to halt, or even reverse, school desegregation.

After years of unrest, the mood on college campuses had become so calm and generally nonpolitical that some observers called it apathetic. Others suggested that, instead, the newly won 18-year-old voting rights may have diverted more student energy into traditional political activity, particularly in a presidential election year.

Experiment Fails. Early in the year, the federal Office of Economic Opportunity (OEO) announced that a much-heralded educational experiment had failed. In the $5.6-million experimental program, called performance contracting, private firms set out to teach reading and mathematics to 13,000 children from low-income families. Company fees were to be governed by program success. The OEO said on January 31 that a study compared children who had taken part in the program with a control group of 10,000 similar students who had not. It said no significant differences were found.

Five of the six firms involved in the experiment disputed the government findings. Final payments were still being negotiated at the end of the year.

The Busing Issue. In a March 16 television address, President Richard M. Nixon called for a moratorium on any new, court-ordered busing programs until Congress and the courts clarified circumstances under which it might be necessary. The President personally opposed school busing for racial balance. Civil rights spokesmen charged that his proposal would turn the clock back and encourage a return to segregation.

School segregation was particularly difficult to end in metropolitan areas where minorities were clustered in the central city and whites in the suburbs. On January 10, a federal judge ordered a merger of the Richmond, Va., school system with those of two suburban counties to overcome that problem. The move would have involved the busing of thousands of children. But the two counties appealed his decision. On June 6, Chief Judge Clement F. Haynsworth was joined by four other appeals court judges in overturning the Richmond order.

Meanwhile, in Detroit, another federal judge declared that "relief of segregation in the public schools

Some education specialists said student tastes were shifting from traditional academics to more practical courses such as auto mechanics.

. . . cannot be accomplished within the corporate geographical limits of the city." He directed the state board of education to establish a metropolitan-area desegregation plan. On June 14, he ordered a massive busing program under which about 310,000 of Detroit's 780,000 students would ride buses across city lines.

The judge in Detroit had barred the U.S. Department of Justice from joining in the case before him, but it joined with the state board in appealing his decision. On August 24, appeals court judges stayed his order indefinitely.

Members of Congress were also concerned with the growing dispute. They passed an important bill providing federal aid to higher education in June, but not until an antibusing amendment had been added. The House later passed a much tougher antibusing bill that essentially followed President Nixon's proposals. But three attempts failed to shut off debate in the Senate, and the bill died. Another similar effort by the Nixon Administration was expected.

The vice-chairman of the U.S. Civil Rights Commission testified on April 11 that annual school busing costs had risen to about $1.7 billion. But about 95 per cent of the increase was due to population growth, 3 per cent to school centralization, and only 1 per cent to safety, desegregation, and other purposes. Desegregation was estimated to be a factor in only 3 per cent of all school busing.

Unequal Financing. One of the major issues of school financing became the question of how to narrow, if not close, the gap between wealthy and poor school districts. The issue is complicated by the fact that the tax rate in the poorer communities often is actually higher than in neighboring wealthier ones, while the expenditure per pupil remains much lower. Across the nation, the average annual expenditure per pupil had doubled during the previous decade. It reached $929 in 1972.

In its final report in March, the President's Commission on School Finance did not suggest a massive commitment of federal funds for schools, as many educators had hoped it would. But it did recommend that states take over a major part of the public school financing instead of merely supplementing local expenditures – the current practice in nearly every state. This could be achieved, the commission suggested, if the federal government provided the states with from $4.6 billion to $7.8 billion over the next five years as an incentive for taking over the financial responsibility in the nation's 17,500 school districts. Education organizations still hoped the federal government would accept responsibility for about one-third of the schools' costs. In addition to the support level, debate began over its form – whether federal funds would be for special programs or would represent a general sharing of revenue.

High school students watch intently as stream water is tested for pollution. New courses increase their focus on contemporary problems.

Although no action was taken during the year to implement such major funding revisions, pressure built up as courts supported greater equalization of school spending. The California Supreme Court held in 1971 that existing funding in two districts was discriminatory because it made the quality of a child's education a function of his parents' wealth. The districts concerned were Baldwin Park, with an annual expenditure of $577 per pupil, and nearby Beverly Hills. With relatively less effort by wealthier individual taxpayers, Beverly Hills could afford $1,232 per pupil. Similar cases were filed in Texas and New Jersey. The Supreme Court of the United States was expected to rule on one or several such tests, resolving the legal issue. As one result, school financing systems in perhaps 49 of the 50 states could be declared unconstitutional. In the view of many observers, the issue involved not only the financing but in addition, ultimately, the very control of public education.

In November, the Lawyers' Committee for Civil Rights Under Law held a special conference, coaching attorneys on how to sue local school boards under Title I of the Elementary and Secondary Education Act of 1965. Title I helps to finance compensatory education for children – many of them from poor neighborhoods – whose education appears inadequate. It assumes that local boards provide equal support for individual schools. But it is not always equal, the committee said. Instead, many districts use the aid for other purposes – to bring school financing closer to equality.

College Finances. The budget crisis in higher education continued unabated. Observers estimated that more than 30 institutions, most of them small, independent colleges, will have been forced to close by the end of 1972. The Carnegie Commission on Higher Education urged the nation's colleges and universities to increase productivity and trim budgets.

It called for a moratorium on virtually all new Ph.D. programs as one way to save money and deal with the excess of persons with advanced degrees.

Although it was unlikely to bring immediate relief, some hope continued for more federal aid to higher education. The landmark 1972 higher-education bill, if fully funded, would provide substantial help for both institutions and needy students.

The bill authorizes spending more than $16 billion within five years. Most of the new money would go to colleges and universities according to the number of federally aided students and the total amount of federal scholarship money on each campus. Thus, it rewards colleges that admit needy students, linking federal aid to social service.

Once the new law is fully operative – the timetable depends on when actual appropriations are voted – it will also activate a new form of "entitlement grants." They would help every student from a family below a certain income level toward a higher education.

Cost of Public School Education

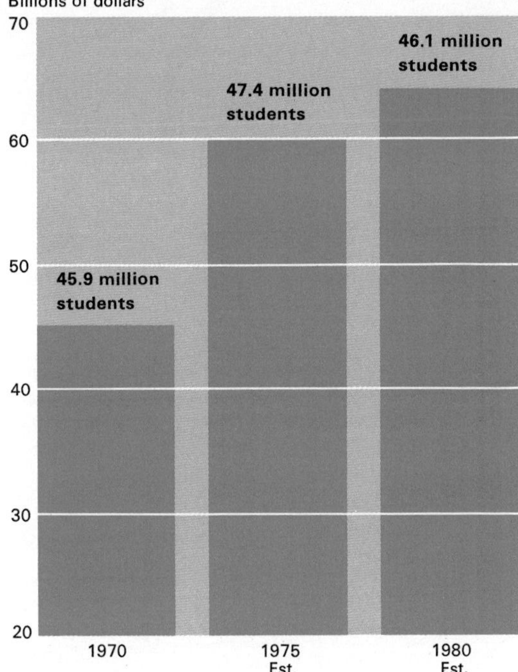

Source: The President's Commission on School Finance

The guaranteed annual scholarship support would be $1,400 minus what a student's family can "reasonably" be expected to provide. The entitlement would gradually be eliminated as the annual family income reached about $13,000.

Teachers and Enrollment. Teachers at all levels totaled 2.9 million in the fall of 1972, including 664,000 college faculty members. The National Education Association (NEA) reported a record 111,000 teachers were unemployed. No state had reported a substantial shortage of teachers since 1969. The most serious oversupplies were in social studies, English, elementary-school teachers, foreign languages, health and physical education, home economics, business education, and art. The nation's largest school districts had an average of nine applicants for each teaching position.

The average teacher's salary for the 1971-1972 school year was $9,690, about 5 per cent above the average for the previous year. Average salaries ranged from Mississippi's $6,518 to Alaska's $14,124. Michigan, California, and New York had averages above $11,000. New York City's United Federation of Teachers negotiated a new contract that will bring annual salaries to slightly more than $20,000 for teachers with 7½ years of service.

The total enrollment in public and private institutions rose for the 28th consecutive year, reaching 60.4 million. But the increase was the smallest one during that entire period of steady growth. Even more significant, total elementary enrollment declined for the third consecutive year.

The 1973 high school graduating class is expected to total 3.1 million. It will be the largest class in the history of American public education and about 100,000 more than in 1972. An estimated 958,000 bachelor's degrees will be conferred during the academic year, 55,000 more than in 1972. There were expected to be 256,000 new master's degrees and 38,000 doctorates.

Education Costs. Tuition at the nation's colleges and universities continued to rise, but the rate of increase in the 1972-1973 academic year seemed to be slowing for the first time in a decade. It was estimated at somewhere between 2.5 per cent and 4.9 per cent, compared with 8 per cent in 1971-1972.

Faculty Unions. The trend toward an organized teaching profession continued. In New York, the United Federation of Teachers, an affiliate of the AFL-CIO, merged with the New York State Teachers Association, a unit of the NEA that in the past had strongly opposed the concept of labor organization for the teaching profession. The new organization, the United Teachers of New York, is the largest such unit in the country. It was seen by some observers as an indication of a trend to a national merger of the former rival groups. Fred M. Hechinger

See also Section One, Focus on Education.

EGYPT. President Anwar al-Sadat suddenly ordered all Russian military advisers out of Egypt on July 18, 1972. He announced that Russian military installations, some of which had been off-limits even to senior Egyptian officers, would become the property of the state. Sadat said the unexpected move was necessary because Russia refused to supply advanced weapons and aircraft that Egypt wanted.

Russia complied promptly and discreetly with the order. About 15,000 advisers and dependents were airlifted home within two weeks. About 500 Soviet technicians who were working on industrial aid projects were allowed to stay in Egypt. Late in the year, efforts at reconciliation began. See Middle East.

Ousting the Russians won Sadat a burst of popularity at a time when his regime was under attack for failing to solve economic problems and for its "no war, no peace" policy with Israel. Some Egyptians appeared to feel the relaxation of tensions between Russia and the United States indicated Russia was losing its enthusiasm for the Arab cause.

On January 16, Sadat named Aziz Sidki, former minister of industry and petroleum, prime minister to head a new austerity Cabinet created to prepare for war with Israel. See Sidki, Aziz.

The Cabinet's appointment did little to appease Egypt's militant anti-Israeli students. They went on strike in January, demanding formation of a student militia. A banner at Cairo University campus, under

"Nothing personal—but could I ask you to leave?"

student control, proclaimed, "We want a confrontation–not a confrontation Cabinet."

Arab Federation. Egypt fared better in its relations with other Arab states. The Federation of Arab Republics (Egypt, Libya, Syria) moved toward union. Meeting on June 23, the three heads of state set up a federal supreme court and a joint trade union council. Egypt and Libya agreed on August 2 to total unification by Sept. 1, 1973. On September 18, the two agreed on Cairo as capital of the proposed union.

Other Developments. On August 13, a parliamentary committee approved a new law making the Arab Socialist Union Egypt's only political party and, for the first time, making it a criminal offense to join or try to establish new parties. Sadat also restored citizenship and voting rights to 12,000 Egyptians, most of them Communists and members of the outlawed Moslem Brotherhood, who had been disenfranchised since 1962. In October, the practice of arbitrary confiscation of property without compensation was abolished.

Sidki's austerity program let Egypt pay $340 million on its foreign debts of $1.86 billion on August 19. Two major oil finds and discovery of 784 million tons of phosphate in the Western Desert offered hope that the plan to double national income by 1982 could succeed. William Spencer

See also MIDDLE EAST (Facts in Brief Table).

ELECTIONS. The American people voted overwhelmingly on Nov. 7, 1972, to give Richard M. Nixon a second term as President. Mr. Nixon's reelection by a landslide victory of historic proportions kept a Republican in the White House but left the Democratic Party in control of Congress. President Nixon defeated his Democratic opponent, Senator George S. McGovern of South Dakota, by carrying 49 of the 50 states. McGovern won only in Massachusetts and the District of Columbia.

The Nixon Landslide. President Nixon's share of the popular vote was 60.7 per cent. McGovern received 37.5 per cent, 1.4 per cent went to American Party candidate John G. Schmitz, and 0.1 per cent to People's Party candidate Benjamin Spock. Mr. Nixon received 47,168,963 votes; McGovern, 29,169,615; Schmitz, 1,080,541; and Spock, 78,801. The Electoral College, which met on December 18, cast 520 votes for President Nixon and 17 for McGovern. One vote was cast for John Hospers of the Libertarian Party.

Mr. Nixon accomplished his landslide by breaking up the old coalition of black, Jewish, and Roman Catholic voters that had been a Democratic mainstay since the days of President Franklin D. Roosevelt. He also picked up a large part of the blue-collar and youth vote. Yet despite the President's impressive victory margin of 17,999,348 votes, his landslide had its shortcomings.

The Democratic majority in the House and the Senate, which had ruled throughout President Nixon's first four years, remained in power. It was the first time in any U.S. election that a party winning the presidency with a sweep such as Mr. Nixon's failed to take both houses of Congress.

The Republicans had hoped to pick up the five seats they needed to take control of the Senate in the 93rd Congress. Instead, they lost two. In the new Senate that convened on Jan. 3, 1973, the Democrats outnumbered the Republicans 56 to 42, with 1 Independent lining up with the Democrats and 1 Conservative with the Republicans. In the House of Representatives, the Republicans gained only 14 of the 39 new seats they needed to gain control. The new House had 240 Democrats to 192 Republicans, with 3 vacancies because of deaths.

Limited Victory. The Nixon landslide, as Republican National Chairman Robert J. Dole observed, was "a personal triumph for Mr. Nixon but not a party triumph." Although Mr. Nixon was the first Republican ever to carry Hawaii, the first to win Arkansas in 100 years, and the first since Reconstruction to sweep the once-solid Democratic South with runaway margins, his political coattails had very limited pulling power.

This was largely due to ticket splitting on an unprecedented scale and partly to the type of campaign he conducted. To avoid offending Democratic voters, whose support he sought for re-election, he confined his campaigning for other Republican candidates to only a few key races.

Many Democrats who voted for President Nixon did so because they disliked or feared McGovern. At the same time, these voters split their ticket and voted for Democratic candidates for the House and Senate.

Only 55 per cent of those eligible to vote went to the polls. This was the lowest voter turnout percentage in 24 years.

Mr. Nixon's task of winning re-election was also eased by Alabama Governor George C. Wallace's absence from the contest. Wallace had been a strong contender in the Democratic primary campaign. He won five primaries, finished second in six others, and received a total of 3,755,424 primary votes before he was shot and partly paralyzed in an assassination attempt at a political rally in Laurel, Md., on May 15. Wallace bowed out of the race after losing the Democratic nomination and declined to run for President on the American Party ticket, as he had done in 1968. Consequently, Mr. Nixon picked up many votes that would otherwise have gone to Wallace.

Primary Contests. In the early months of 1972, the crowded field of Democrats contending for their party's presidential nomination included, not only Wallace and McGovern, but also Senators Edmund

Happy crowd members wave the symbol for "four more years" at President Richard M. Nixon after his landslide re-election victory in November.

Democrat Daniel Walker, *above*, won fame by hiking through Illinois and defeated Richard Ogilvie, *top right*, the incumbent Republican governor. *Below left*, 74-year-old Margaret Chase Smith, the only woman in the U.S. Senate, lost to 48-year-old William D. Hathaway, a Democratic congressman, *below center*. John D. Rockefeller IV, *below right*, a promising young Democrat, lost the West Virginia governor's race.

S. Muskie of Maine, Hubert H. Humphrey of Minnesota, Henry M. Jackson of Washington, Mayor John V. Lindsay of New York City, and Congresswoman Shirley A. Chisholm of New York.

McGovern was considered a minor candidate. When the primaries opened, he rated only 5 per cent in the public opinion polls. However, McGovern gathered strong support through his populist appeal and his image as a left-of-center apostle of the so-called New Politics. He also had an excellent organization of tireless young workers. He wound up winning 10 of the 23 presidential primaries, and on June 30 was fewer than a dozen votes short of the 1,509 delegate votes he needed to win the nomination at the Democratic National Convention.

The Presidential Campaign. McGovern won the Democratic nomination, but many Democrats were dissatisfied with him as the candidate. George Meany, AFL-CIO president, refused to endorse him, and organized labor was sharply divided over whether to support McGovern.

Also, McGovern had alienated many of the regular Democrats by excluding them from the national convention. A major setback came with the disclosure by Senator Thomas F. Eagleton (D., Mo.), the vice-presidential candidate, that he had undergone psychiatric treatment. McGovern subsequently replaced Eagleton with Sargent Shriver. See DEMOCRATIC PARTY; EAGLETON, THOMAS F.; MCGOVERN, GEORGE S.; SHRIVER, SARGENT.

In the campaign that followed, McGovern modified his position on many issues, but he failed to win the unified backing of his party. He covered 26 states, making repeated visits to the large industrial states of the North and East and to California and Texas. But instead of making President Nixon the issue, as he had hoped to do, McGovern himself became the issue.

Mr. Nixon maintained an unusually low profile during most of the campaign. He let Vice-President Spiro T. Agnew and other Republican notables do the speaking for him. He did not oblige McGovern by coming out slugging with partisan rhetoric, and refused to debate him. Instead, the President campaigned on the progress he had made toward peace and prosperity. Mr. Nixon's campaign strategy and the divisions in the Democratic Party over McGovern resulted in the President's landslide re-election. See REPUBLICAN PARTY

The Congressional Elections were another story. The Democrats managed to hold both the House and the Senate, which the Republicans thought they had a good chance of winning. Eight new Democrats and only five new Republicans were elected to the Senate for the 93rd Congress. Four of the Democrats upset Republican incumbents. Democrat Floyd K. Haskell beat Gordon L. Allott of Colorado. Joseph R. Biden, Jr., defeated Republican Senator J. Caleb Boggs of Delaware. Biden did not reach the minimum age of 30 until after his election; Boggs was 63. Democrat Richard Clark upset Republican Senator Jack R. Miller of Iowa. Former Democratic Representative William D. Hathaway, 48, defeated Senator Margaret Chase Smith, 74, of Maine, the only woman in the Senate.

The other four new Democratic senators were James G. Abourezk of South Dakota; Sam A. Nunn, Jr., of Georgia; J. Bennett Johnston, Jr., of Louisiana; and Walter Huddleston, who defeated Louie B. Nunn for the seat of retiring Republican Senator John Sherman Cooper of Kentucky. In the five senate races won by Republican newcomers, only one Democratic incumbent lost his seat. Senator William B. Spong, Jr., of Virginia was upset by Republican Congressman William L. Scott.

In North Carolina, Democratic Congressman Nick Galifianakis lost to Republican Jesse A. Helms for the seat of retiring Democratic Senator B. Everett Jordan. In Idaho, William E. Davis lost to Republican Congressman James A. McClure in a contest for the seat of retiring Republican Senator Len B. Jordan. In Oklahoma, Republican Dewey F. Bartlett defeated Congressman Ed Edmondson for the seat of retiring Democratic Senator Fred R. Harris. In New Mexico, Republican Pete V. Domenici won over Democrat Jack Daniels in a bid to succeed retiring Democratic Senator Clinton P. Anderson.

As a result of the election, the Senate will again be more liberal than the House and a continuing problem for the Nixon Administration, even though all five of the new Republicans elected to the Senate are conservatives. Five of the eight new Democrats in the Senate are more liberal than the Republicans they replaced. Two conservatives succeeded conservatives, and one moderate took the seat of a moderate. Four of the conservative Republican senators who lost their seats were strong Nixon supporters.

The Solid South. The Republicans picked up 13 congressional seats formerly held by Democrats. Seven of these were in the once-solid Democratic South. In Mississippi, Republicans Thad Cochran and Trent Lott broke into what had been an all-Democratic congressional delegation. David C. Treen became the first Louisiana Republican elected to the House since Reconstruction.

In South Carolina, Republican Edward L. Young beat Democrat John W. Jenrette, Jr. In Tennessee, Republican Robin L. Beard, Jr., defeated Democratic incumbent William R. Anderson. Republican Robert W. Daniel, Jr., won the seat of retiring Democratic Congressman Watkins M. Abbitt of Virginia. And one of three new Florida congressional seats produced by reapportionment was won by Republican L. A. Bafalis.

Three blacks were among the Democrats elected to the House, raising the total number of blacks in the 93rd Congress – including 1 in the Senate – to 16. The three newcomers were State Senator Barbara C. Jordan of Texas, the first black woman elected to Congress from the South; Yvonne Brathwaite Burke of California; and Andrew Young of Georgia, a former aide to the late Martin Luther King, Jr.

In Gubernatorial Races, the Democrats registered a net gain of 1 seat, bringing the total of state governorships under their control to 31. They won 11 of the 18 governors' seats contested in 1972. One of their outstanding victories was in Illinois, where Daniel Walker upset incumbent Republican Richard B. Ogilvie.

Of the seven races the Democrats lost, the one that drew the most national attention was in West Virginia. Secretary of State John D. Rockefeller IV, the one Rockefeller millionaire who is a Democrat and a populist, lost to West Virginia's Republican Governor Arch A. Moore, Jr.

Even though the Republicans won only seven gubernatorial races, they managed to score some surprises. In Indiana, Republican Otis T. Bowen defeated his favored Democratic opponent, former Governor Matthew E. Welsh.

In North Carolina, James E. Holshouser defeated Democrat Hargrove Bowles, Jr., to become the state's first Republican governor since 1901. In Missouri, Christopher Bond at age 33 became the nation's youngest governor-elect after his victory over Democrat Edward L. Dowd. William McGaffin

See also AMERICAN PARTY; STATE GOVERNMENT; Section One, FOCUS ON THE NATION.

ELECTRIC POWER. See ENERGY.

ELECTRONICS. The growing importance of technology in new industrial applications continued to be a major trend in 1972. Postal automation, the textile industry, airlines, and rapid-transit systems were particularly affected.

An experimental, automated post office in Cincinnati, Ohio, has computer-controlled machines that automatically cull, cancel, sort, and batch mail. In the textile industry, computers are now being used to design, as well as produce, fabrics. Airlines are also expanding their use of computers in air-traffic control and freight movement.

San Francisco's Bay Area Rapid Transit System (BART), which began operation in 1972, is controlled by a Westinghouse Prodac 250 computer. The computer not only controls the trains' speed, but also keeps a constant check on track traffic, train identification, and switching functions.

Solid State. Advances in solid state technology have served mainly to refine existing techniques. This progress makes semiconductor devices faster, more efficient, and, in many cases, cheaper. For example, reduced power consumption and higher operating speeds are claimed for one such new technique called "silicon on sapphire," pioneered by Inselek, Inc. In this technique, the substrate, or base, layer of an integrated circuit uses a layer of sapphire in addition to the usual silicon. Computer memory devices are among the typical applications. Refinements in metal-oxide semiconductor technology are also permitting integrated circuits to be made more complex in their functions, with no increase in size.

Medical Electronics. The rapid growth of medical electronics spawned an even greater need in 1972 for engineers trained in this specialty. In what was perhaps the year's most important development, engineers at the Medtronic Company created a spinal stimulator. The device sends radio frequency waves to the brain and thereby eliminates back pain by blocking spinal pain pulses.

Digital readouts, which display data in direct, numerical form, are replacing needle-type meters in more and more applications. These clear, unambiguous displays greatly reduce the chance of human error in reading instruments, and they can be more easily used with digital computer and control equipment. Instruments with wider ranges of functions are also now available, partly because of the adoption of large-scale integration techniques, which permit the fabrication of more complex circuits.

Consumer Electronics. The ability to integrate more functions on a single integrated circuit (IC) chip has also influenced consumer electronics, most notably in the calculator field. Single IC's combining all basic calculator functions have brought electronic calculator prices down to as low as $60, and have made possible more complex calculators, almost as small as a cigarette pack, for $100 or less. Similar developments have made possible IC watches that have no hands, gears, or motors, and are read in direct digital form like the calculators.

The emphasis in television continued on simplified color tuning and on modular chassis construction for easier, less-expensive repairs. Both the Sony U-Matic and Avco Cartrivision video cassette recording systems went on the market in 1972. Avco and its licensees concentrated on the home market, while the Sony system was aimed toward audio-visual applications. Ampex abandoned its Instavideo system, and RCA announced a new system to be marketed in 1973. Both Sony and Advent unveiled color television projection systems, while RCA and Bell Labs showed all-solid-state television camera prototypes. Magnavox marketed a system that allowed games to be played with moving spots of light on the television screen.

In audio, Columbia's SQ and RCA's Quadradisc four-channel record systems made their debut, operating on separate and incompatible principles. Meanwhile, Electro-Voice adapted its system for greater compatibility with SQ, and the Japanese industry adopted both SQ and the Sansui "Regular Matrix" system as standards.

Ivan Berger

EL SALVADOR. See LATIN AMERICA.

EMPLOYMENT. See ECONOMY, THE; EDUCATION; LABOR; SOCIAL SECURITY; SOCIAL WELFARE.

Inexpensive, battery-operated, pocket electronic calculators using highly sophisticated circuitry were one of the hottest consumer items in 1972.

ENERGY. The term "energy crisis" took on added meaning in 1972 as industry, commerce, and the home builder and owner felt its effects. The cost of raw fuel and electricity increased, and some suppliers even refused to deliver added quantities. Raw fuel, in a form acceptable to meet environmental requirements, was in tight supply. Natural gas headed the list of most-wanted fuels, prompting suppliers to seek ways of shipping gas over great distances.

In late October, a joint venture between the United States and Russia to ship natural gas to the United States was announced. Early plans called for using liquefied natural gas (LNG). The liquefaction process will take place on the eastern Siberian border, and tankers will then carry the liquid product to the United States.

With both supply and prices of fuels fluctuating, the electric power industry was hard put to plan its fuel needs and capacity commitments. Among the many contributing factors were rising inflation, strict air-pollution standards, continued growth and demand for energy in all forms, declining domestic oil and gas exploration, and new environmental and safety restrictions in coal and uranium mining.

A study by National Economic Research Associates, released on August 15, concluded that the basic forces operating in the energy economy will continue to push fuel prices higher. However, these pressures should be significantly eliminated in the next decade, the study said, by new technologies that should make coal, oil, and uranium more acceptable forms of raw energy.

National Power Survey. Plants fired by fossil fuels such as coal continued to be the workhorse of the electric power industry. Despite temporary setbacks and some decline in ordering during the 1960s, nuclear units have become an economic choice for many utilities, and the long-term outlook was bright. Optimism was evident in the 1970 National Power Survey of the Federal Power Commission published in June, 1972. The survey covered generation, transmission, distribution, and load-forecasting. According to the survey, announced nuclear plant orders from January, 1966, to June 1, 1970, totaled about 73,000 megawatts (mw), surpassing the most optimistic estimates of the electric power industry.

The survey attributed recent declines to the traditional cyclic buying pattern followed by utilities in purchasing generating equipment, and the increased cost of nuclear plants. The additional cost was caused by a number of factors, including an overloading of the industry's fabricating capability, increased labor costs, and a realization that the cost of construction had been seriously underestimated.

New Power Concepts receiving serious consideration included magnetohydrodynamics, fuel cells, thermionics, thermoelectrics, and electrogasdynamics. Controlled fusion offered the possibility of direct conversion of nuclear energy to electricity, but it is unlikely to occur in this century. The industry showed renewed interest in solar energy, considering such methods as the sunlight-algae-methane-steam cycle and sunlight-thermal-energy-steam cycle. Fuel cells and magnetohydrodynamics seem to offer the most attractive possibilities by the year 2000 to compete in power production.

An experimental fuel cell on the roof of a one-family house in Brooklyn converts natural gas into electricity without combustion.

Nuclear Power. As of Oct. 1, 1972, operable nuclear capacity in the United States was about 16,000 megawatts electrical. Of 152 total units, 31 had operating licenses; 33 had licenses pending; 16 had construction permits; 37 had permits pending; and 35 units have been announced.

The most recent Atomic Energy Commission (AEC) prediction of installed nuclear capacity in 1980 ranges from 130,000 megawatts electrical (mwe) to 170,000 mwe. The plants now scheduled for operation by 1980 have a total capacity of121,000 mwe. All 152 plants announced as of October 1 have a total capacity of about 132,000 mwe, but some of them are not scheduled for operation until 1981 or 1982. To reach the AEC forecast of 150,000 mwe of installed capacity by 1980, all plants now scheduled for operation by then must be completed and operating successfully, and about 29,000 mwe of new, presently unannounced, capacity must also be in operation. Realistically, the most recent forecasts of installed nuclear capacity in 1980 will not be met; 100,000 mwe appears to be a more likely figure.

Growth Rate. With the U.S. economy snapping back to its traditional growth pattern, kilowatt-hour (kwh) sales in the 50 states in 1972 nearly doubled 1971's. Even though 34,451 mw of net generation additions were made by year's end, the reserve margin during the peak period slipped to about 19 per cent, commonly considered too thin for reliable operations. The slippage stemmed largely from delays in permits. Such delays, if extended through 1973, could lead to the "power crisis" predicted by some spokesmen for the summer of 1974.

To meet the needs of a growing population, utilities in the 50 states must build and put into commercial operation 1,022,700 mw of new generatingcapability between 1972 and 1990. And these generation additions will require matching transmission and distribution expansion. The cost of this future growth is expected to be staggering. Investments of nearly $18-billion in 1972 were expected to climb steadily to a total of $494 billion by 1990. And these projections are in 1972 dollars. If inflation continued at an average of 3.25 per cent a year, the total new capital would soar to $696.4 billion.

The Electric Utility Industry had another modest year measured in terms of revenue, profit, and output. Figures for the year ended Dec. 31, 1972, were:

	1971	1972	% gain
		(in millions)	
Total capacity (kw)	389	425	9.25
Total production (kwh)	1,721,000	1,850,000	7.50
Utilities output (kwh)	1,618,000	1,750,000	8.30
Utilities revenue*	$21,000	$24,100	14.80

*For investor-owned companies

Electric energy sales by U.S. utilities responded vigorously to the economic recovery of early 1972, gaining about 9 per cent above 1971. All classes of consumers contributed to this sharp increase. The largest numerical contribution came from the industrial sector, which boosted its consumption by 9.1 per cent. This vigorous industrial activity was reflected in commercial kwh sales, which were up 7.9 per cent over 1971.

Residential Sales benefited from higher rates of household formations, from 680,000 new housing units heated with electricity, and from the growing use of self-defrosting refrigerators, which use far more electricity.

Housing starts began to turn upward in 1972, and the trend was expected to continue. Completion of new housing usually converts promptly into new residential customers. Projections indicate an average gain of nearly 1.4 million such customers per year through 1980, followed by a gradual slowing to end slightly under 1.2 million by 1990.

The Gas Turbine market grew in 1972, despite predictions that sales would taper off by 1972 and average from 2,500 to 3,500 mw a year until about 1980. About 4,000 mw of gas-turbine generating sets were sold in the first half of 1972 alone.

New Coal Deposits

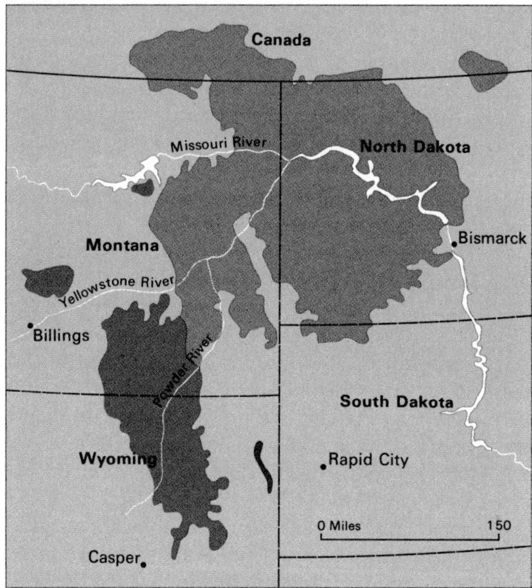

At least one manufacturer predicted orders would continue at the rate of from 6,000 to 7,000 mw a year through 1974. A slight dip in sales may follow this period, assuming a significant number of large nuclear units go into operation. Then, after utilities have had sufficient time to reassess their generation mix and future requirements, orders were expected to increase and probably exceed levels attained during the early 1970s.

Industrial Generation. Industrial steam-turbine generator orders placed between June 1, 1971, and May 31, 1972, dropped severely. The story was the same in the first half of 1972. This sudden change of pace was caused by a lag in the response to U.S. economic growth, existing or anticipated fuel supply problems, the high cost of money, and government pressure to reduce industrial pollution. Despite the depressed market, most industrial turbine-generator manufacturers were optimistic that sales would increase dramatically in 1973. An increase in in-house power generators was expected to be a factor.

Environmental Quality. Investor-owned electric utilities spent more than $2 billion in 1972 to enhance environmental quality in the United States. This figure compared with $1.5 billion spent in 1971 on various aspects of environmental quality. The totals include capital investment, operating expenses, and research and development.

Capital investment for air and water quality facilities, underground electric lines, and aesthetic and recreational purposes was estimated at $1.5 billion in 1972, compared with $1.1 billion in 1971. The 1972 capital investment for environmental purposes is more than twice the $736 million spent in 1970.

The 1972 electric utility company environmental investment represents 11.5 per cent of the total construction expenditures – about $13.2 billion – for new investor-owned electric plant and equipment. This represented an increase of 2.2 per cent over 1971's expenditures.

Capital Spending. The year marked a turning point for major capital spending by utilities. This was in contrast to the previous five years when top executives of electric power companies squirmed under pressures from environmentalists, government agencies, stockholders, and moneylenders while electric utility construction business boomed. Spending on new generating capacity had declined steadily from 1959 through 1964. However, from 1966 through 1971, it jumped at an average rate of almost 30 per cent annually. One indicator pointed to an easing of this $12.1-billion-a-year segment of the construction industry. The University of Maryland's interindustry forecasting model, which makes long-term forecasts of the overall economy and of 185 different industries, predicted the growth of utility construction, adjusted for inflation, will rise at a rate of less than 4 per cent a year through 1975. James J. O'Connor

ENGINEERING. Unemployment, the continued aerospace industry slump, and government cutbacks in research and development continued to be the major concerns of the engineering profession in 1972. A skills-conversion study released in June by the National Society of Professional Engineers (NSPE) showed 92,000 unemployed engineers. However, the study concluded that 7,000 could be employed in professional-level jobs by the end of 1973 and 47,000 more could be working by the end of 1975. The study was conducted under a $750,000 contract with the U.S. Department of Labor and with the aid of six other professional engineering groups.

Engineering Enrollments. Despite employment potential in such areas as transportation, pollution control, power resources, and urban and environmental development, disenchantment with engineering as a career increased. This was reflected in a dramatic decline in engineering enrollments for the 1971-1972 academic year, according to a study released in April by the Engineering Manpower Commission (EMC) of the Engineers Joint Council. The survey, covering 282 U.S. engineering schools offering bachelor's or higher degrees in the various engineering fields, showed 26,000 fewer engineering students than in 1971.

Another EMC report, in February, showed that engineering degrees conferred during the academic year ending in June, 1971, also was leveling off. There were only 43,167 bachelor's degrees conferred – 200 more than in 1970. Only at the master's level was there an appreciable increase. Electrical and mechanical engineering continued to be the leading fields at all degree levels, followed by chemical and industrial engineering. The EMC survey listed 536 women, 462 U.S. blacks, and 5,268 foreign nationals among the total number of engineering graduates.

Engineer Demand. Companies recruiting on college campuses cut hiring of June, 1972, graduates in half, according to an annual tally of recruiting companies made by Frank S. Endicott, director of placement at Northwestern University. For engineers with a bachelor's degree, hiring was only 5 per cent above June, 1971, levels, and it was actually down 3 per cent for graduates with master's degrees. The picture was especially depressing against the background of 1971, when companies recruiting on college campuses cut their hiring in half. According to the College Placement Council in Bethlehem, Pa., each recruiting company was making only one-third as many job offers as it did in 1967.

Despite the scramble for jobs, beginning salaries continued to rise in 1972. The monthly pay offered to male engineering graduates averaged $884; to women graduates, $880. The 1971 NSPE survey showed the median salary for the 33 per cent of NSPE members that responded to the survey was $18,210, up 11 per cent from 1969. Mary E. Jessup

ENVIRONMENT. Despite general agreement that the attack on environmental problems must be stepped up, there were sharp battles in 1972 over the nature and scope of programs to deal with them. In the United States, the battles were between conservationists and advocates of development and between President Richard M. Nixon and the Congress.

On the international scene, 1,200 delegates from 114 nations met in the first world Conference on the Human Environment in Stockholm, Sweden, in June. They approved a declaration of principles that hopefully will serve as a guide for an international campaign against pollution. See Close-Up.

President Nixon stressed in his February 12 message presenting the Administration's environmental protection program to the Congress that the pursuit of environmental quality will require both courage and patience. "Problems that have been building for many years will not yield to facile solutions," he said.

Water Pollution. A yearlong battle between Congress and the President over water-pollution legislation seemingly climaxed on October 18, when Congress overrode the President's veto of the clean waters bill. Then, in an unusual move on November 22, the President ordered $6 billion cut from the program for 1973 and 1974. Whether he could legally enforce such an order was still in question at the end of the year.

In his veto of the measure, which aims at eliminating pollution discharges by 1985, Mr. Nixon charged that the bill was "budget-wrecking." It authorizes spending $24.6 billion over the next nine years to build municipal sewage-treatment plants, and increases the federal share of the cost from 55 to 75 per cent. The bill also requires industrial plants to meet limits based on the "best practicable technology" by July, 1977, and on the "best available technology" by 1983. It also establishes a new method of controlling pollution. Previously, states were responsible for setting water-quality standards on a stream-by-stream basis. These standards were aimed not at banning all discharges, but at limiting effluents to a level that would not degrade the water. Under the new legislation, industrial firms must get permission from the states to make any discharges into streams.

Legislation approved on October 28 empowered the federal government for the first time to control the dumping of municipal wastes at sea. Under the Marine Protection Research and Sanctuaries Act, the dumping of some hazardous substances is banned and other dumping is controlled through a new permit system. The bill is aimed at the increasing practice of coastal cities and industries to evade stream-pollution controls by dumping their sewage sludge in the ocean. At an international conference on November 13 in London, 79 nations signed a global agreement banning the ocean dumping of oil, mercury, and cadmium compounds and establishing a permit system to limit the dumping of other wastes.

Air Pollution. Court battles and conflicts between the states and the Environmental Protection Agency (EPA) highlighted efforts to meet the 1975 deadline for stringent ceilings on major air pollutants. Fewer than a third of the 55 states and other jurisdictions had received total approval of their plans.

A major issue was whether areas where the air is now cleaner than required by law could permit air quality to fall to the level allowed by federal standards. Environmentalists argued in the U.S. Court of Appeals in October that the Clean Air Act prohibits any significant deterioration in air purity.

In June, the EPA ordered the Ford Motor Company to make a complete rerun of the 50,000-mile emission tests required to check conformance of new automobile engines to 1973 clean-air standards. The reruns were ordered after the company admitted its employees had done unauthorized maintenance work on test engines during the first tests. Ford reran the tests, and most of the engines were then approved.

Land Protection. Legislation to protect coastal wetlands and estuaries was approved on October 28. Under the new Coastal Zone Management Act of 1972, states will receive federal funds to develop land-use plans for coastal areas. Such areas have increasingly been subjected to exploitation for recreational and industrial development.

Congress failed to approve major overall land-use legislation that would have provided $170 million to help the states develop controls for long-range use of privately held land. The legislation passed the Senate on September 19, but the House did not consider the bill. However, supporters believe the groundwork has been laid for enactment of the measure in 1973. Legislation to control coal strip mining also died in the closing days of Congress, but environmentalists predicted that tough strip-mining controls would be enacted in the next session.

The California Supreme Court reaffirmed on November 7 a September 28 ruling that state and local governments must complete environmental impact reports before approving private construction projects that may significantly affect the environment. Conservationists hailed the decision, but private developers called it a threat to the housing industry.

The Department of the Interior on September 13 set aside nearly 79 million acres (about 123,000 square miles) of land in Alaska for possible additions to national park, forest, and wildlife refuge systems. The total area involved, almost half the size of Texas, would double the land assigned to such facilities.

Noise Control. Under the Noise Control Act of 1972, signed by the President on October 28, the EPA is empowered to set limits on noise from trucks, buses, and railroad trains. Federal standards can also be set to control the noise from newly manufactured products ranging from jackhammers to snowmobiles. The

Pollution Control Costs—1970-1979

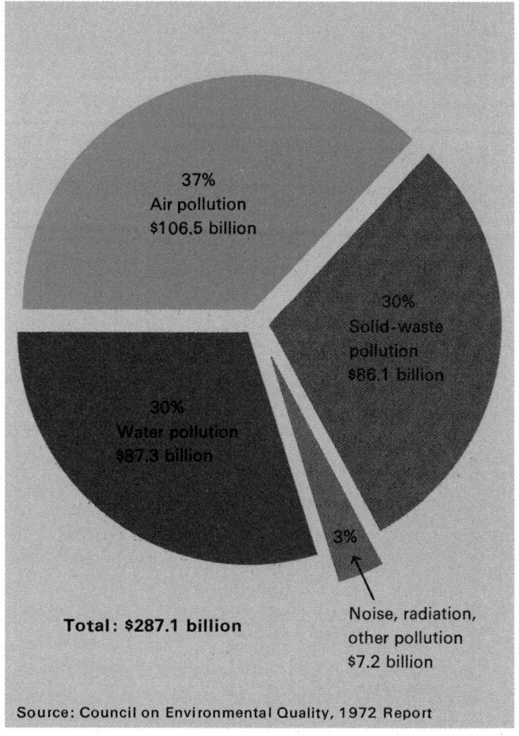

One Earth Faces Up To Danger

"Only One Earth" was the theme of the United Nations (UN) Conference on the Human Environment in Stockholm, Sweden, in June, 1972. The phrase was appropriate, not only because it captured the flavor of the new environmental concern, but also because it made no promises of earth-shattering accomplishments.

After the conference, expressions of dissatisfaction were common. Some critics said it had not dealt exhaustively with issues that many considered vital–such issues as population pressures, the generation and consumption of energy, or what some called the ultimate polluter: war. Others, however, felt the meeting had accomplished just about everything it had set out to do, because most of the recommendations on the agenda had been approved, although in watered-down form in some cases.

Paradoxically, the conference began long before it opened on June 5, and its influence continued after it closed June 16. It was the result of a Swedish proposal to the UN in December, 1968, and it followed planning meetings held throughout the world. That it achieved as much as it finally did was widely credited to one man, Canadian industrialist Maurice F. Strong.

At age 33, Strong was president of Power Corporation of Canada, Ltd., one of the country's largest holding companies. At 40, he had charge of Canada's $400-million foreign-aid program. On Jan. 1, 1971, at 42, he officially became undersecretary-general of the UN and secretary-general of the environment meeting. From then until it opened, he traveled the globe laying the groundwork and reassuring less-developed nations that world environmental safeguards need not throttle their efforts at industrial growth and progress. In the 18 months before the conference, he never spent more than eight consecutive days at his new home in Switzerland.

During conference preparations, it became clear that the division between rich and poor countries was far more serious than that between East and West. Many poorer nations, straining for industrial prosperity, were convinced environmental concerns were a luxury they could ill afford. Among other things, they feared that the developed countries' moves to defend the environment might restrict international trade and, hence, their own development.

As the meeting began, there seemed abundant reason to restrain any optimism. Arriving delegates were greeted by a huge windmill built by a group of Swedes to symbolize their opposition to atomic power. Cynics said that, instead, the windmill illustrated the quixotic nature of any world attack on pollution.

But the conference accomplished much. It struck a mortal blow to parochialism about the environment. The approximately 1,200 official delegates –from 114 countries and representing about 90 per cent of the world's 3.8 billion people–recognized environmental protection as a serious, worldwide problem. And they implicitly recognized that a nation is responsible for the effects of its own environmental problems on other countries.

Russia and several of its East European allies boycotted the conference, protesting East Germany's exclusion. Members of the UN or any of its agencies were welcomed, but East Germany did not qualify on either count. Delegates expected that Russia would join the world effort in due course.

By the time the conference closed, it had agreed on the need for "earthwatch," a worldwide monitoring system to keep track of air and water pollution. After long and earnest discussions, a declaration of 26 principles was adopted and a 27th was referred to the General Assembly. Planners had proposed 23, but most were modified and several added.

The documents turned out to be neither pious platitudes nor denials of responsibility. All were sent to the General Assembly for ratification, with compliance purely voluntary. But the consensus was so wide that they were already considered to have both moral and practical force.

As the meeting closed, one delegate's comment seemed to sum up its effect: "I used to think environment was a rich man's fad. Stockholm has taught me better."

Ed Nelson

"...the Human Environment"

Youthful environmentalists erected a tent city outside Stockholm and put on "eco-skits" during the UN Conference on the Human Environment.

legislation was weakened just before passage when the Senate eliminated a ban on supersonic passenger aircraft landings in the United States.

Pesticides. The Federal Environmental Pesticide Control Act of 1972, signed by the President on October 21, provides the first major reform in pesticide laws in 25 years. The new legislation prohibits the use of any pesticide in any way that is inconsistent with the information on its label. It also extends federal regulation to cover all pesticides, including those distributed or used only within a single state.

Environmentalists are expected to try to get Congress to rescind a provision in the act that compensates a manufacturer if his product is belatedly found unsafe and removed from the market. Because of this provision, the Sierra Club called the bill "far more protective of the pesticide industry than it is of the environment."

A ban on using the pesticide DDT on crops, effective on December 31, was announced by the EPA on June 14. The move permits DDT to be used only for disease control. Spokesmen for farmworkers contended that substitute pesticides could endanger workers who harvest crops.

Energy Environment Crisis. With energy demands continuing to grow, the nation was faced with increasingly hard choices between developing new sources of power and the environmental hazards they often create. An American Petroleum Institute spokesman said at the institute's annual meeting on November 13 that environmentalists would have to compromise on energy-development issues, because the "energy picnic is over." C. Howard Hurdesty, vice-president of Continental Oil Company, said: "We want low-cost, low-sulfur fuel oil, but we don't want terminals on our shores. We want more coal, but don't want surface mining. We demand adequate supplies of electricity, but resist siting of nuclear plants. . . . Our environmental concerns are more deeply rooted than our energy concerns. So far, we are not willing to accept the fact that some trade-offs, some compromises will be necessary to keep these inconsistencies from destroying our way of life."

On May 11, Secretary of the Interior Rogers C. B. Morton announced he would grant right-of-way permits for the proposed trans-Alaska pipeline. The pipeline would transport oil from Prudhoe Bay on the Arctic Ocean to Valdez, an ice-free port on the southern coast of Alaska. Environmental groups, which successfully stalled the pipeline's construction for more than two years, charged Morton's decision was "arbitrary and capricious."

In August, a federal judge dissolved the injunction that had blocked construction work on the pipeline. The environmentalists promptly appealed the ruling to the Circuit Court of Appeals. Andrew L. Newman

See also CONSERVATION.

EQUATORIAL GUINEA. See AFRICA.

ESPIONAGE. Some "small fry" spies were caught by counterintelligence nets in 1972. In London, Sublieutenant David James Bingham of the Royal Navy was sentenced to 21 years in prison on March 13 after he admitted selling secrets to Russia. Bingham, 31, entered the navy at 16 and had made top grades in electronics and in officers' school.

Bingham's wife, Maureen, said, "I nagged him into becoming a spy." She said she prodded him to sell naval secrets to the Russians to get money to pay household debts and to finance her bingo playing. They owed more than $5,000 at one time. She said she went to the Russian Embassy in 1970 with a note offering antisubmarine intelligence. Bingham said he turned information over to an assistant Russian naval attaché at the London Embassy. Bingham photographed British sonar used to detect submarines, the fleet operations tactical manual, and details of the nuclear depth charge.

U.S. Air Force Master Sergeant Walter T. Perkins, 37, of Tyndall Air Force Base in Florida was sentenced to three years in prison on August 11 for stealing secret papers for the Russians. The senior noncommissioned officer in the intelligence section of the air defense weapons center, Perkins was arrested at the Panama City, Fla., airport with five secret documents in his attaché case. The Air Force charged he was trying to deliver documents on radar detection and U.S. missile systems to Russian agents.

Great Britain protested to Russia on August 26 about a Russian spy ring that allegedly operated in Hong Kong and recruited agents throughout the Far East. The spy plan reportedly was found in the trousers of Alexander Trusov, a Russian posing as a marine repair superintendent. According to the report, Trusov recruited a Hong Kong businessman to get information in return for contracts with Russian importing agencies. Two other Russian agents involved another Hong Kong businessman. The Russians were expelled and the businessmen arrested.

Other Cases. Cairo, Egypt, newspapers printed rumors in mid-February that a spy ring had operated against Egypt's government and other Arab regimes. The network allegedly involved the U.S. Central Intelligence Agency, an unidentified American woman diplomat who was arrested late in 1971, an Egyptian of Greek origin, and several intellectuals opposed to President Anwar al-Sadat. The ring was allegedly attempting to gather data on Russian aircraft and missiles for the United States and Israel.

In New York City, a Russian employee of the United Nations, Valery I. Markelov, 32, was arrested by the Federal Bureau of Investigation on February 15 for allegedly trying to obtain secrets of the Navy's latest jet fighter, the F-14 "Tomcat" made by Grumman Aerospace Corporation at Bethpage, Long Island. Markelov was held on $500,000 bail but, on May 19, was permitted by a federal district court to go to Russia while his case is pending. Lloyd H. Norman

ETHIOPIA took an increasingly active part in African and international affairs in 1972. Emperor Haile Selassie I continued to be one of the most influential African statesmen.

The United Nations Security Council opened its first session on African soil in Addis Ababa on January 28. At the opening session, Selassie warned the Security Council that repression in southern Africa was leading to increased violence. He said the danger of spreading conflict was imminent and warned of far-reaching consequences for the world. The emperor compared the Rhodesian rebellion and the spread of South African military power to the Italian aggression against his country during the 1930s, and he urged the Security Council to forestall that danger by "timely action." Most of the session was devoted to discussion of a request, submitted by the Organization of African Unity (OAU), that the council take over the administration of Namibia. See South Africa.

Ethiopia Played a Key Role in the settlement of the civil war in southern Sudan (see Sudan). The reconciliation agreement was signed in Addis Ababa in February. The settlement was facilitated by the emperor's first formal visit to Sudan, from Dec. 31, 1971, to Jan. 3, 1972. The visit improved relations between the two countries, which have frequently been in conflict over boundaries. More than 1,000 miles of their joint boundary is not precisely located.

Ethiopia had been accused of supporting southern rebels in Sudan's civil war. A heavy flow of Sudanese refugees into Ethiopia further aggravated relations between the two nations.

Sudan had been charged with supporting the Eritrean Liberation Front (ELF), a rebel band operating in Ethiopia's only coastal province. In 1972, Sudan agreed to close down any offices that the ELF "might have set up" there. Agreement on the basic terms for settlements with rebel groups in both areas was the most important outcome of Haile Selassie's visit.

On January 17, the emperor visited western Africa – Sierra Leone and Nigeria. He signed an agreement for cultural exchange with both countries. At the ninth anniversary meeting of the OAU on May 24, Selassie rejected the notion of a peaceful settlement in Rhodesia. He urged increased international and African intervention (see Rhodesia). Despite Ethiopia's past reputation for moderation and pro-Western orientation, the international activity added to the country's growth as a radical leader among African states.

Russian economic aid was extended during the year to include the construction and equipment of a plant-disease laboratory near Ambo. Russia will supply all the technicians for the next five years. France said it would hold its strategic base at Djibouti. The city is also the terminal of Ethiopia's only railroad link to the sea. George W. Shepherd

See also Africa (Facts in Brief Table).

EUROPE

The European Community (Common Market) expanded to 9 nations on Jan. 1, 1973, and not 10, as had been planned. In a national referendum that was held on Sept. 24, 1972, Norway voted to stay out, to the dismay of the six members and three other prospective member nations. Fears that the Danish vote on October 2 would give a similar result proved unfounded, however.

Norway's "No." After an emotional campaign, 1,079,282 of Norway's voters said "no" to Norwegian membership and 923,521, "yes." Most of the "noes" came from rural areas and the young. Of the eligible voters, 75 per cent cast ballots. The rejection of such a major program backed by Prime Minister Trygve M. Bratteli toppled his government. Bratteli put off resignation of his minority Labor Government until October 7 in order to present the 1973 budget.

The result of the vote spread gloom in Europe. Sicco Mansholt, new president of the European Commission, called it "a step back from Europe. It is a warning for us," he said. "We have not yet created a social and democratic Europe." Norway announced on September 29 that it would seek the best possible free-trade treaty with the Common Market. See NORWAY.

Denmark's "Yes." Observers feared that Denmark would follow Norway's lead in its referendum on October 2. But much more was at stake for the Danes. Without Common Market outlets for their dairy products, valued at $650 million a year, Danish farmers would be in difficulty. Prime Minister Jens Otto Krag threatened heavy devaluation of the krone if the Danes said "no." But the vote was solidly in favor of joining: 1,955,932 (63.5 per cent) for entry to 1,124,106 (36.5 per cent) against. After expressing "pleasure and gratification," Krag resigned for what he called "personal reasons" on October 3.

The Norwegian and Danish votes suggested further international complexities would develop. The Scandinavian countries had built up an interdependent trade bloc, but the Common Market would now include only Denmark. See DENMARK.

Ireland's "Yes." Britain decided, despite protests by the Labour opposition, not to hold a referendum on entry. On May 10, about 70 per cent of the Irish Republic electors voted, 1,041,890 to 211,891, for joining.

The four applicant countries, Great Britain, Ireland, Denmark, and Norway, had signed the acces-

Norwegians opposed to the Common Market staged a torchlight parade in Oslo in September. Norway's "no" caused dismay in Western Europe.

stem Nei!

sion treaty in Brussels on January 22. But ratification by each was still necessary. The treaty-signing ceremony was delayed for 45 minutes when a German woman threw ink at British Prime Minister Edward Heath as he entered Egmont Palace.

On January 21, in Strasbourg, France, when Heath received the $90,000 prize awarded by the German Freiherr von Stein Foundation for his contribution to European unity, he said that the world "will stop and listen" to the new Europe. "Europe will be strong in the councils of the world," he added, "for, as great powers polarize, who can ignore the voice that speaks for 250 million people?"

Market Summit Meeting. Member nations made plans in February for a summit conference in Paris in October. It was to tackle relations with nonmember countries, strengthening of the community's institutions, political cooperation, and economic and monetary union in the enlarged community. Several times during the summer, the meeting was in doubt. President Georges Pompidou of France wanted a proposed European monetary and economic union at the top of the agenda.

Another problem was the deteriorating political situation in West Germany, where the defection of individual ministers had deprived the government of a reliable majority. Chancellor Willy Brandt told French Foreign Minister Maurice Schumann in Bonn on August 23 that he wanted the Common Market summit to resolve the European issues before he confronted a German general election. In November, Brandt won a resounding victory, generally seen as expressing approval of his efforts to get along with East Germany. See GERMANY, WEST.

At the Paris summit in October, political leaders of the nine Common Market members committed their nations to creating a European regional fund of an unspecified size by the end of 1973. They also agreed to "coordinate their regional policies" at once. At the same time, they agreed that "a high priority should be given to the aim of correcting, in the community, the structural and regional imbalances which might affect the realization of economic and monetary union."

The leaders also agreed to set up a European monetary fund by April, 1973, and called on central bank governors for proposals on pooling resources. Finance ministers were ordered to produce plans within a month to combat inflation.

Agreement to become a "European Union" by 1980 was reached after the Netherlands was placated. Before it agreed, it had demanded commitments to give the European Parliament more power.

Monetary Union. Earlier in the year, financial ministers of the then-six Common Market members had worked on plans to narrow margins of fluctuation

Parisians study Socialist Party poster asking Frenchmen not to vote in April national referendum on enlargement of the European Community.

Facts in Brief on the European Countries

Country	Population	Government	Monetary Unit*	Foreign Trade (million U.S. $) Exports	Imports
Albania	2,380,000	Communist Party First Secretary Enver Hoxha; Premier Mehmet Shehu; People's Assembly Presidium Chairman Haxhi Lleshi	lek (4.62 = $1)	60	98
Austria	7,500 000	President Franz Jonas; Chancellor Bruno Kreisky	schilling (22.9 = $1)	3,172	4,195
Belgium	9,822,000	King Baudouin I; Prime Minister Gaston Eyskens	franc (43.8 = $1)	12,392 (includes Luxembourg)	12,853
Bulgaria	8,670,000	Communist Party First Secretary and State Council Chairman Todor Zhivkov; Premier Stanko Todorov	lev (1.85 = $1)	2,182	2,119
Czechoslovakia	14,685,000	Communist Party First Secretary Gustav Husak; President Ludvik Svoboda; Premier Lubomir Strougal	koruna (15 = $1)	4,180	4,010
Denmark	5,025,000	Queen Margrethe II; Prime Minister Anker Jorgensen	krone (6.95 = $1)	3,685	4,614
Finland	4,752,000	President Urho Kekkonen; Prime Minister Kalevi Sorsa	markka (4.1 = $1)	2,357	2,795
France	52,003,000	President Georges Pompidou; Prime Minister Pierre Messmer	franc (5 = $1)	20,594	21,323
Germany (East)	17,407,000	Communist Party First Secretary Erich Honecker; State Council Chairman Walter Ulbricht; Prime Minister Willi Stoph	mark (3.15 = $1)	5,076	4,960
Germany (West)	63,454,000	President Gustav Heinemann; Chancellor Willy Brandt	Deutsche mark (3.175 = $1)	38,941	34,255
Great Britain	56,551,000	Queen Elizabeth II; Prime Minister Edward Heath	pound (1 = $2.34)	22,340	24,000
Greece	9,100,000	Regent and Prime Minister George Papadopoulos	drachma (30 = $1)	662	2,096
Hungary	10,424,000	Communist Party First Secretary Janos Kadar; President Pal Losonczi; Premier Jenö Fock	forint (27.63 = $1)	2,500	2,989
Iceland	220,000	President Kristjan Eldjarn; Prime Minister Olafur Johannesson	króna (88 = $1)	150	210
Ireland	3,057,000	President Eamon de Valera; Prime Minister John Lynch	pound (1 = $2.34)	1,316	1,834
Italy	54,970,000	President Giovanni Leone; Prime Minister Giulio Andreotti	lira (580.75 = $1)	15,102	15,960
Liechtenstein	21,000	Prince Francis Joseph II	Swiss franc	no statistics available	
Luxembourg	346,000	Grand Duke Jean; President and Prime Minister Pierre Werner	franc (43.8 = $1)	12,392 (includes Belgium)	12,853
Malta	319,000	Governor General Sir Anthony Mamo; Prime Minister Dom Mintoff	pound (1 = $2.67)	45	157
Monaco	25,000	Prince Rainier III	French franc	no statistics available	
Netherlands	13,493,000	Queen Juliana; Prime Minister Barend W. Biesheuvel	guilder (3.2 = $1)	13,971	15,510
Norway	3,973,000	King Olav V; Prime Minister Lars Korvald	krone (6.6 = $1)	2,558	4,084
Poland	33,701,000	Communist Party First Secretary Edward Gierek; State Council Chairman Henryk Jablonski; Premier Piotr Jaroszewicz	zloty (38 = $1)	3,872	4,038
Portugal	9,990,000	President Américo Deus Rodrigues Thomaz; Prime Minister Marcello Caetano	escudo (27.2 = $1)	1,033	1,772
Romania	20,929,000	Communist Party General Secretary and State Council President Nicolae Ceausescu; Prime Minister Ion Gheorghe Maurer	leu (16 = $1)	1,851	1,960
Russia	250,867,000	Communist Party General Secretary Leonid I. Brezhnev; Premier Aleksei N. Kosygin; Supreme Soviet Presidium Chairman Nikolai V. Podgorny	ruble (1 = $1.21)	13,806	12,476
Spain	34,299,000	Chief of State (El Caudillo) and Prime Minister Francisco Franco; Vice President Luis Carrero Blanco	peseta (63.65 = $1)	2,939	4,942
Sweden	8,241,000	King Gustaf VI Adolf; Prime Minister Olof Palme	krona (4.7 = $1)	7,464	7,082
Switzerland	6,490,000	President Roger Bonvin	franc (3.77 = $1)	5,740	7,219
Turkey	37,941,000	President Cevdet Sunay; Prime Minister Ferit Melen	lira (14 = $1)	677	1,171
Yugoslavia	21,225,000	President Josip Broz Tito; Prime Minister Djemal Bijedic	dinar (17 = $1)	1,778	3,316

*Exchange rates as of Nov. 1, 1972

A woman protestor throws ink on Prime Minister Edward Heath as he arrives at a Brussels palace to sign Britain's entry into the European Community.

between their currencies. At a Brussels meeting of the European Commission on March 15, the figure of 2.25 per cent on either side of parity was suggested. Britain's decision on June 24 to float the pound beyond these limits was seen on the continent as a setback to hopes for a unified monetary policy. Pompidou pressed Britain to bring the pound back to a fixed alignment with other European currencies.

New Common Market proposals for higher farm prices averaged 8 per cent for 1972 crops. They led to protests by Italy and France. Common Market ministers of agriculture were split, and the issue was unresolved. On September 25, the foreign ministers earmarked $250 million over five years to help in backward farming areas. The money will be used mainly to give new jobs to farmers leaving the land. Most of a draft budget of $5 billion for 1973 will be used to finance the market's agricultural policy.

EFTA Agreement. After four months of talks, treaties were signed in Brussels on July 22 merging the Common Market with the European Free Trade Association (EFTA). The treaties established a free-trade area covering about 90 per cent of the trade between the enlarged market and the EFTA countries. The treaties were effective on Jan. 1, 1973. The six EFTA countries–Sweden, Switzerland, Austria, Portugal, Finland, and Iceland–gained tariff concessions.

Sicco Mansholt of the Netherlands, who forged the Common Market's agricultural policy, became president of the European Commission when Franco Maria Malfatti of Italy resigned on March 22. In his first address to the European Parliament in Strasbourg on April 19, Mansholt called for a guaranteed minimum income within the Common Market and removal of obstructions to travel.

East-West Security. European security seemed strengthened by growing agreement between East and West Germany. On November 6, negotiating teams for the two agreed on a treaty to set up formal relations. But formal ratification was still necessary.

Preparations for an East-West security conference began in June after President Richard M. Nixon and Russian Communist Party leader Leonid I. Brezhnev pledged in Moscow in May to prevent nuclear war. The United States told the North Atlantic Treaty Organization (NATO) that negotiations for reductions in troop strengths in central Europe should proceed "on parallel tracks" with the conference.

A 34-nation meeting in Helsinki from November 22 to 27 agreed on procedure for a conference on security and cooperation in June, 1973. Each nation will take part on an equal and independent basis. Decisions will be reached on a consensus basis, defined as the absence of any objections.

The NATO powers on November 16 invited the four Warsaw Pact powers to open exploratory talks on mutual and balanced force reductions in Central

Europe on Jan. 31, 1973. In Bonn on November 23, U.S. Senator Edward M. Kennedy (D., Mass.) addressed the North Atlantic Assembly. He called for a strengthening of the alliance and condemned a "sense of complacency" that he said existed.

In February, NATO Secretary-General Joseph Luns called for the continuance of the 300,000 U.S. troops in Europe. NATO forces in northern and central Europe number 580,000, compared with 960,000 for the Warsaw Pact. Luns said the security system based on cooperation between North America and Europe had brought "an unprecedented period of peace."

NATO held its biggest land, sea, and air exercise in history in and off northern Norway in September. Code-named Strong Express, the exercise involved 350 ships, including 3 aircraft carriers, 65,000 men from 12 countries, and 700 aircraft. The high point was a series of amphibious landings on the Norwegian coast. Sensitive to Norwegian memories of World War II, only a few German troops landed.

The Malta Crisis. Britain failed to reach a settlement with Malta for the continued use of military and naval bases on the island. Prime Minister Dom Mintoff ordered the British to leave by January 15, and thousands of service families were airlifted out. On January 14, British Defense Secretary Lord Carrington flew to Rome for talks with Luns, and NATO added to Britain's offer of $23.25 million. Tough bargaining ensued, Mintoff held out for $45 million, but admitted that Malta faced severe hardship without rental of the island bases. A final combined NATO offer of $35 million was accepted in March. But in December, Mintoff noted the pound, allowed to float, was somewhat devalued. He said the rent should go up. See Malta.

Environment Conference. Europe's growing concern over pollution reached a high point in June when the first world Conference on Human Environment was opened in Stockholm, Sweden, by United Nations Secretary-General Kurt Waldheim. He asked that funds the world spends on arms be diverted to "the problems of mankind." In references to China and France, he criticized nuclear testing above and below ground. See Environment (Close-Up).

Environmental concerns were also dealt with outside the conference. On February 15, in Oslo, 12 European countries bordering the North Sea and North Atlantic called for prevention of marine pollution by dumping from ships and planes.

The Fishing War. Iceland extended the limits outside which other countries' fishermen could take fish from 12 to 50 nautical miles, effective September 1. This disturbed European countries with fishing industries, and Britain announced that it would refer the matter to the International Court of Justice at The Hague. Iceland rejected a request by the Common Market to reconsider the new limit in return for a 50 per cent cut in tariffs on fish products. Talks were held through the summer to try to reach a compromise, but Great Britain said it would not accept "any extension of the present limit, not even of 25 or 20 miles." The International Court ruled on August 17 that, pending a final judgment, Iceland must not interfere with trawlers fishing outside the old 12-mile limit. Iceland refused to accept the ruling. British trawlers were harried in September, and some trawls were cut. Icelandic protection vessels photographed those fishing within the limits and warned that offenders would be arrested if they entered Icelandic ports. Iceland later made a special arrangement with Belgium allowing Belgian trawlers to take limited catches within the 50-mile limit. See Belgium.

Germ Warfare Banned. Great Britain, Russia, and the United States–at the Geneva disarmament conference–negotiated a convention outlawing biological weapons. Documents were signed on April 10 in London, Moscow, and Washington by 70 other nations.

Assassination at Games. Arab guerrillas calling themselves Black September shocked the world in September when they disrupted the Olympic Games in Munich to kill two Israeli Olympic team members and kidnap nine others. The nine held as hostages by the guerrillas were also shot later (see Olympic Games). Kenneth Brown

See also various European country articles.

EXPLOSION. See Disasters.

FAIRS AND EXPOSITIONS. There was something for everyone at the more than 10,000 local, regional, national, and international fairs and expositions held throughout the world in 1972. They offered a bewildering variety of merchandise ranging from needlework to steel. People interested in establishing an export program or expanding an existing one had almost 1,000 worldwide trade fairs at their disposal to help sales-promotion efforts. Among them were several so-called solo exhibitions scheduled by the U.S. Department of Commerce for United States firms only. One, held in São Paulo, Brazil, by the Illinois Department of Business and Economic Development, resulted in sales of nearly $7 million.

The Canton Trade Fair, produced by the People's Republic of China, invited United States concerns to take part for the first time. About 15, most of them small trading companies, sent representatives to the month-long exhibition, which opened April 16. At the Canton Fair, foreign traders buy about $1-billion worth of Chinese products each year. The fair attracts traders from about 100 countries, and this spring it included more than 2,000 Japanese representatives from 1,400 companies. Some 20,000 foreigners attended it, entering by train from Hong Kong, filling Canton's hotels, and taxing to the limit the city's capacity to supply taxis and interpreters.

Seattle Trade Fair. The 22nd annual Eunimart, an international trade fair featuring consumer products, was held from August 11 to 20 in Seattle. It was the first time that Russia exhibited in a U.S.-based trade fair. The Soviet Union needed 15,000 square feet of space to exhibit electronics, diamonds, furs, hunting equipment, vodka, and caviar. While at Eunimart, the Russian delegation signed a $40-million contract with International Harvester. Thirteen foreign countries participated in the fair. There were 1,800 exhibitors who attracted 4,000 buyers, and a record 118,000 paid admissions.

Transpo '72, the U.S. Department of Transportation's (DOT) exposition, was held at Washington's Dulles International Airport from May 27 to June 4. The exposition fell far short of its predicted attendance. Billed as the biggest event of its kind in history, the $11-million exposition drew only 438,603 visitors who paid a total of $959,000. About 1.5 million visitors had been predicted by DOT Secretary John Volpe. Exhibitors paid $1.63 million for space rental.

The 24th annual postwar Frankfurt (West Germany) Book Fair was held from September 28 to October 3. A total of 3,581 publishers from more than 50 nations displayed 214,000 books at the fair, 80,000 of them new.

In spite of a shortened 1972 season, Montreal's "Man and His World" attracted good crowds for the fifth year. By far the most popular pavilion was that of the People's Republic of China, which drew 437,353 visitors. The only sponsored cultural exhibit in North America, China's pavilion featured a blend of classical culture and contemporary craftsmanship.

U.S. Expo in Doubt. With the calendar moving inexorably toward July 4, 1976, the American Revolution Bicentennial Commission (ARBC) in May rejected a proposal from Philadelphia, the last candidate, to hold a World's Fair in 1976. The proposed fair would have been a focal point of the nation's 200th birthday celebration. On September 8, the ARBC adopted reforms in an effort to satisfy congressional critics who were holding up appropriations. The commission, increased to 50 members, voted to meet six times a year instead of four, and also created nine advisory panels comprising national leaders in the arts, advertising and public relations, and transportation and communications, as well as representatives of youth, ethnic, and other key groups. At the same time, ARBC endorsed New York City's Showboat as a centennial project. The Showboat, a children's theater, will play from piers and bulkhead sites throughout the city's five boroughs and serve as a national model for other cities throughout the United States.

Bicentennial projects suggested by the general public to the commission increased from 15 in 1970 to more than 1,500 in 1972. Work began in June on the site for America's first world exposition on the environment. The exposition is scheduled to open in May, 1974, in Spokane, Wash. Lynn Beaumont

FARM MACHINERY. See MANUFACTURING.

FASHION relaxed a bit in 1972, worrying less about hemlines and waistlines, shifting into the casual mood of sportswear for both daytime and evening styles. According to designers, the busy modern woman wanted to look at ease, uncontrived, and certainly never obvious after years of self-conscious modes of dress and accessories. An important aspect of being fashionable in 1972 was not to look as if one had spent either too much time or money on clothes.

The sweater was a pivotal point of this effortless effect. It was the year's most important fashion ingredient, cropping up as a beach cover-up, the basis of city costumes, the bodice of haute-couture satin evening gowns. After sweaters, a woman could choose between long or short dresses, skirts or pants, belted waists or no waists, bare halters or covered-up caftans. Such designers as Yves Saint Laurent showed most of their daytime styles at midknee level, but they included several midcalf and ankle-length skirts.

Great Variety. Female delegates at the Democratic National Convention in Miami illustrated the variety of attire available to the American woman. They turned up in everything–floor-length dresses; tailored, short separates; faded blue jeans. Critics blamed designers for failing to provide fashion direction. Actually, the wide range of choices represented the cost-conscious consumer's triumph over the couturier as sovereign.

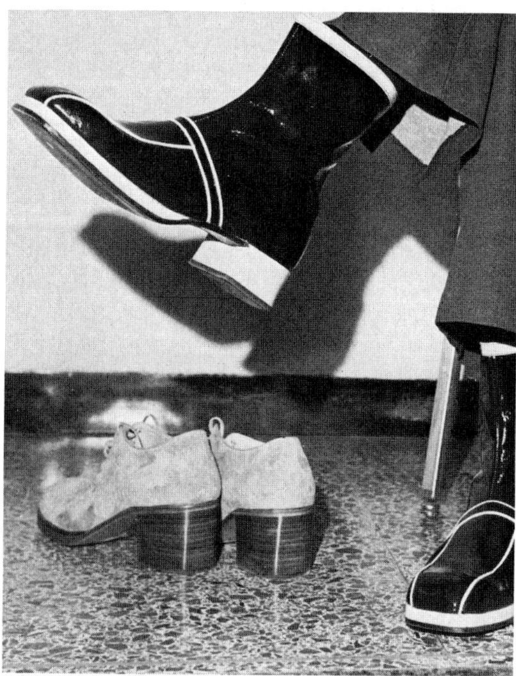

Fashion went to men's feet in 1972 as shoes with wild colors, thick platforms, and 3-inch heels became popular with young and old alike.

The most successful designer of 1972 was Halston. His clothes, whisked up by such fashion leaders as Liza Minnelli and Jacqueline Kennedy Onassis, were elegant versions of established American classics – shirtwaist dresses, cashmere pullovers and cardigans, wrapped jackets and pants. So big was the influence of the unstudied, sportive American shapes on what women around the world wore in 1972, that experts claimed New York City, rather than Paris, was the fashion capital of the world. Yet, while Paris couture declined, some of the year's most innovative clothes came from that city's kicky young ready-to-wear boutiques, such as Kenzo Takada's JAP.

Loosening Up. The ease-is-of-the-essence fashion philosophy affected the way a garment met the body. After a decade of drawing clothes closer to the figure, designers began to let go. Snug-bodiced fashions were rivaled by a revival of the chemise, the blouson, caftans, smocks, tents, toppers, battle jackets, and baggier sweaters. Elasticized and drawstring waistlines, shirred yokes, deeper armholes, and dolman, raglan, and kimono sleeves helped ease silhouettes. Trousers, still vital in a fashionable woman's wardrobe, spoke the new trend in three languages: Italian – wide-flowing, skirtlike, and called palazzos; French – pleated and cuffed, with highrise waistbands; American – straight, sharply tailored, often based on the cut of trusty old jeans.

Ease also meant no hard edges, no sharp contrasts, no chopped-up colors. Textures softened into cashmere, shetland, angora, lambswool, mohair, brushed-wool plaids, cuddly, lamblike acrylic piles, fluffy, long-haired furs. Hushed hues and pastels served as further softening agents. Mauve, peach, apple-green, pink, yellow, and baby-blue tended to be used in all-of-a-tone costumes, such as a pink-checked shirt with a pink-striped sweater over a pink plaid skirt. Natural and neutral shades of white, wheat, camel, and gray melted into one another in luxurious fabrics or connected sporty separates of citified nonchalance.

Accessories underlined the monotone scheme. Among the favorites were tortoise, ivory, amber, pewter, silver, braided-leather cubes, buttons strung together, whale and tiger teeth. But pearls were the most popular embellishment for ears, necklines, and wrists. Brimmed cloche hats replaced knitted caps, little flat envelopes tried to oust the ever-present shoulder bags. Clogs, wedgies, cork-soled platforms, and chunky, high heels continued to alarm podiatrists. There was a tendency toward shorter hair styles for both men and women.

Men's Fashions were dominated by the gentlemanly ideal, as the wild prints and fancy sartorial treatments of recent years gave way to traditionally masculine materials and shapes. Bold plaids livened up sport jackets; rich, modulated tones in houndstooth checks, Donegal tweeds, and Prince-of-Wales plaids were used for business suits. Summer-weights

Chopped-off, patched, bleached, or never washed, blue jeans were customized by millions or bought in a host of new colors and fabrics.

revived such favorites as crinkly seersucker, khaki, and all-white Mark Twain-type "ice cream suits."

Other he-man conceits making comebacks – beefy sweaters with more texture in shetland, mohair, Norwegian-type knit; and hefty woolens cut into stalwart stormcoats, battle jackets, peacoats, and lumberjack shirts. The buttoned-down shirt returned in 1972 with a more generously proportioned collar. Ties turned to smaller, timeless motifs: stirrups, anchors, paisleys. The two-button, waist-and-shoulder-expressed construction reigned for jackets, but there was a drift back to pleated pants and boxy, raglan-sleeved coats with just-below-the-knee hems. Footwear became more flamboyant. Men wore higher heels and white loafers on city streets.

Fashion Awards. The Coty American Fashion Critics' Awards on October 19, accorded Hall of Fame stature to Bonnie Cashin for pioneering the current move away from escapism to easy clothes for active, constructive living. Halston, for his elegant approach to such fashion classics as the twin-sweater set, received a Return Award. The 1972 "Winnie" went to newcomer John Anthony for his realistic tailored silhouettes. A special award was given to Mountain Artisans, a crafts group in Appalachia, W.Va., directed by Dorothy Weatherford. They were recognized for reviving and reinterpreting the traditional American crafts of patchwork and quilting in dresses and skirts. Kathryn Zahony Livingston

FINLAND struggled with a continuing political crisis through much of 1972. The nation voted in January to elect a new government – the 55th in Finland's 55 years of independence – to replace that of Ahti Karjalainen, which resigned in October, 1971. Nine parties vied for the 200 seats in Parliament. However, the election produced little change, and the political parties remained divided on basic issues. Non-Socialist parties retained a majority of 16 seats.

The five center-left parties failed to form a coalition government, and, on February 21, President Urho Kekkonen asked Rafael Paasio, leader of the Social Democrats, to form a minority government.

Government Resigns. Paasio's government lasted only until July 19. It decided then that, as a minority government, it could not take the responsibility of signing a free-trade agreement with the European Community (Common Market). After a four-week deadlock, a compromise on August 29 brought a majority coalition of the Social Democrat, Liberal, Center, and Swedish People's parties to power. Social Democrat Kalevi Sorsa, 42, a former foreign minister, was sworn in as prime minister on September 4.

The Common Market. Finland anxiously watched the outcome of referendums held in neighboring Denmark and Norway on joining the Common Market. Since World War II, Finland has feared isolation on the north and west that would make it more dependent on Russia. Despite objections by its own Communist-dominated People's Democratic League, Finland, a member of the European Free Trade Association (EFTA), concluded negotiations with the Common Market for tariff concessions.

Swedish ties to the market and Great Britain's membership in it added to the pressure on Finland, because they were the biggest customers for Finnish exports. At the end of the year, however, Finland had not decided whether to accept the agreement the market offered. It was similar to the one accepted by several other nonmember countries.

Active Neutral. Helsinki was the site for preparatory talks in November for a 1973 European Security Conference. But Kekkonen's work to build a more active Finnish role as a neutral country worried Russia. Russia vetoed the Finnish candidate for United Nations secretary-general, Max Jakobson. And Finland's Communist-dominated political party, the People's Democratic League, opposed Common Market ties. It held that they would hurt Finnish workers by opening Finland's borders to lower-cost goods from market countries.

Finland and East Germany signed a preliminary agreement on September 6 in Berlin establishing diplomatic relations. Foreign Minister Karjalainen said that Finland would recognize both German states on November 19. Kenneth Brown

See also EUROPE (Facts in Brief Table).

FIRE. See DISASTERS.

FISHING. See HUNTING AND FISHING.

FISHING INDUSTRY. The International Whaling Commission meeting in London on June 30, 1972, agreed to reductions in the 1973 quotas for catches of sperm, finback, and sei whales. The reductions range from 38 per cent for fin whales to 8 per cent for sperm whales, both in the North Pacific Ocean. The commission rejected, however, a U.S. suggestion that a 10-year moratorium on whale hunting be declared.

Fears that the Atlantic salmon is doomed to extinction led to efforts to reduce catches of the "king of fish." Denmark, which has been taking large catches in the salmon's main feeding area in the Davis Strait off western Greenland, agreed in February under U.S. pressure to gradually reduce its catches. In June, the International Commission for Northwest Atlantic Fisheries adopted salmon quotas that will reduce catches from 800 tons in 1972 to zero in 1976. However, Canada, in whose streams 50 per cent of the salmon spawn, contended these measures will work too slowly. In June, Canada banned all commercial salmon fishing in its Atlantic waters.

Spurred by reports that more than 200,000 porpoises are killed yearly when they are trapped in tuna fishing nets, the National Marine Fisheries Service launched a $250,000 research program in June to help protect the porpoises. Preliminary tests of net modifications to permit the trapped porpoises to escape lowered mortality 75 per cent. However, conservationists charged the tuna industry was responding sluggishly to federal efforts.

An infestation of unusually poisonous plankton hit the New England coast in early September. The microorganism, called the red tide because it colors the water rust-red, poisoned clams and mussels. Massachusetts declared a public health emergency on September 15 and banned the sale of shellfish. Clam digging was halted along the New England coast for several weeks. Clam diggers and seafood restaurants in New England suffered economic losses estimated in the millions, and President Richard M. Nixon on September 28 declared Massachusetts and Maine to be disaster areas.

Hurricane Agnes dumped unprecedented amounts of warm fresh water into the prime Chesapeake Bay and Virginia fishing waters and caused damage to the fishing industry that may total more than $33-million over the next four years.

United States commercial fishermen caught 5 billion pounds of fish and shellfish in 1971 that were valued at $643 million, the highest catch in history. The lobster catch, however, declined seriously in 1972, causing a hike in prices. Prices rose as high as $12 a pound early in 1972, and the National Marine Fisheries Services called on the Atlantic States to join a long-range program to avoid depletion of the supply. Andrew L. Newman

FLOOD. See DISASTERS.

FLORIDA. See STATE GOVERNMENT.

FONDA, JANE (1937-), actress and ardent activist, took time out from her career as a motion-picture star and went to North Vietnam in July, 1972, to observe, firsthand, the effects of U.S. bombing. While there, she made daily broadcasts to American servicemen over Radio Hanoi. Although several U.S. congressmen accused her of treason and of undermining the morale of American servicemen, she continued to speak out against the war.

Earlier in the year, Ms. Fonda, who has also backed the causes of Indians, blacks, and migrant workers, received both the Academy of Motion Picture Arts and Sciences Award and the New York Film Critics' Award for best actress for her portrayal of a tough, intelligent call girl in *Klute*. It was perhaps her best performance to date in a series of films that began with *Tall Story* (1960), and includes starring roles in *A Walk on the Wild Side* (1962), *Period of Adjustment* (1962), *La Ronde* (1964), *Barbarella* (1968), and *They Shoot Horses, Don't They?* (1970).

Since October, 1970, she has been lecturing throughout the United States and donating the proceeds to the Vietnam Veterans Against the War. She also has led a 15-member troupe in presenting a "Free the Army" show near U.S. military bases.

Ms. Fonda was born in New York City on Dec. 21, 1937, to actor Henry Fonda and Frances Seymour Brokaw. In 1965, she married French film director Roger Vadim; they have a daughter. Lillian Zahrt

Gallon plastic bottles of grape concentrate sell quickly in shops that cater to the rapidly growing number of home winemakers.

FOOD. In efforts to protect the consumer, United States government agencies moved quickly and forcefully into the food field in 1972. Especially notable were Food and Drug Administration (FDA) attempts to implement truth in labeling, to encourage further vitamin and mineral fortification of basic foods, to ensure the purity of products by close surveillance of production and distribution, and to keep down the prices of goods that are in constant demand. On March 29, the FDA released its listing of how much impurity is allowed in food. See Close-Up.

Proposals on labeling advanced in 1969 by the White House Conference on Food, Nutrition, and Health were enthusiastically implemented wherever possible, and they produced a veritable information explosion. Guidelines were proposed to manufacturers and packagers for nutritional labeling of their products. The government was trying to establish a voluntary but uniform labeling system that would reveal percentages of nutritional content. Producers were also asked to state facts concerning perishability on labels and to suggest proper storage conditions. The FDA made substantial headway, despite strong industry resistance to doing too much too fast.

Consumption of several nutrients has gradually declined in the United States. Vitamin B_1 (thiamin) and C (ascorbic acid) and iron and phosphorus intake has fallen, probably because of a decline in the consumption of such prime sources as pork and citrus fruits. To halt these general declines, the FDA encouraged the addition of more iron and protein to bread; more vitamins B_1, B_2, and B_6 to cereals and infant formulas; and more vitamin C to beverages and dessert powders.

The Public Health Service warned that pork processed in the United States should be frozen and then cooked thoroughly at a high temperature to kill the parasites that cause trichinosis in hogs and human beings. When mussels and clams were infected by a "red tide" of poisonous algae in the North Atlantic Ocean, much of the public stopped eating seafood.

Food Prices. Price controls appeared to halt or slow inflation on almost everything but food. The Federal Trade Commission charged the four largest producers of breakfast cereals with monopolizing the industry and maintaining artificially high prices. The Administration tried to halt the rise in meat prices by providing incentives to foreign countries to compete on the U.S. market and by instituting a system designed to pass on the reductions in wholesale prices as quickly as possible to consumers. The Cost of Living Council also moved rapidly to hold down coffee prices by working out international agreements to increase supplies. Meanwhile, the Price Commission permitted only a few food processors to increase prices, and it urged the food industry to hold its requests for increases to a minimum.

What's Fit To Eat?

The American palate has had several shocks in the past few years, but none so severe as the revelation in 1972 that it has regularly been subjected to rodent hairs and fly eggs. Impurities in foods were generally assumed to be caused by accident, oversight, or carelessness in violation of existing laws, until the U.S. Food and Drug Administration (FDA) released its list of so-called filth allowances in March.

Recently, U.S. citizens have had good reason to question the quality of the foods they eat. In 1969, foods and drinks containing cyclamates, a sugar substitute Americans had been consuming for years, were suddenly whisked off supermarket shelves when scientists found that cyclamates cause cancer in rats. A host of other chemical additives came under suspicion. On the average, each person in the United States consumes 5 pounds of additives a year.

In addition to chemicals deliberately placed in foods, there was the problem of harmful chemical contaminants from the atmosphere finding their way up the food chain. High concentrations of mercury were present in swordfish and tuna. Americans had also come to accept the fact that some foods contain natural elements that could prove harmful. For example, egg yolks contain large amounts of cholesterol, which builds up inside arteries and can lead to heart disease.

FDA scientist tests lettuce

In 1971, a fatality caused by botulism toxin in canned soup raised questions about how effectively food-processing companies are inspected. There also had been occasional reports about rodent hairs being found in frozen TV dinners.

Then, in 1972, the FDA released its master list of filth allowances for food. The public was shocked to learn that peanut butter meets federal standards if it contains no more than 50 insect fragments or 2 rodent hairs for approximately every 3 ounces. Tomato juice is fit to drink if there are no more than 10 fruit fly eggs per 100 grams (about 4 ounces). One in every 10 coffee beans may be infested with insects, and insect fragments are fairly common in ground spices.

The agency's list had been a closely guarded secret since the first contaminant limit was set in 1911. Under growing pressure from consumer groups and the news media, the FDA finally released the information. Officials quickly pointed out that these were maximum contaminant levels, not guidelines for the food industry. The information had previously been kept secret because FDA officials feared that the food industry, if aware of the limits, might relax sanitation standards rather than seek perfection.

However, a report released by the U.S. General Accounting Office (GAO) in April stated that sanitary conditions in food-processing plants were deteriorating. The GAO's investigators found that unsanitary conditions existed in 40 per cent of the 97 plants they inspected. The FDA admitted this was representative of the industry as a whole. Inspectors found filth in raw materials, and food-processing equipment and work areas were dirty and poorly maintained.

They also found that the FDA's list of 32,000 food manufacturers was outdated and incomplete. After checking a sampling of firms on the FDA list, they reported that 22 per cent of them were no longer in business. Meanwhile, new food plants may have been established, but never added to the list and, therefore, never inspected. Also, the FDA has only 210 inspectors to check all of the food-processing plants in the nation.

The U.S. Department of Agriculture recognizes that "food poisoning ranks second only to the common cold as the most frequent cause of illness" in the United States. Yet, a private study group found salmonella organisms–bacteria that cause food poisoning–in more than half of the government-inspected poultry they examined.

The FDA claims it is technically impossible to market foods that are completely pure. According to officials, the allowable amounts of contaminants present no health hazards, and actual contaminant levels in processed foods are far lower than the maximum allowances on the government list. Nevertheless, many people were disturbed about consuming even one rodent hair with their peanut butter.

Darlene R. Stille

Foreign Food. While the United States fought to regulate the production and distribution of food more equitably, the developing nations of the world were striving for enough production to meet demand. The United Nations Food and Agriculture Organization reported that food production in the developing countries declined. The agricultural exports of these countries were down 3 per cent.

Nonetheless, foreign foods continued to invade the U.S. market at an ever more rapid rate. Imports of vanilla beans and mustard, sesame, poppy, and caraway seeds increased sharply. Rosemary, laurel, and oregano imports also rose. Much of the attraction for exotic herbs may be attributed to the growing interest in gourmet foods and ethnic cooking. President Richard M. Nixon's much-publicized state dinner in the People's Republic of China triggered new interest in Chinese cuisine. Groceries and restaurants in the Chinatowns of America began importing food products from the People's Republic of China.

The supermarkets of Europe continued to lead the continent to the freezer. Even in Hong Kong – the home of good, fresh food in the East – the customer in the supermarket was inclined to purchase and eat an ice cream cone while shopping. Such small, relatively rich countries as Denmark, Switzerland, and Belgium, were intrigued by the convenience of frozen dishes and entire meals. But their markets have gone a step further – customers may rent apartments, or cars, as well as buy food there.

Food Trends. The frozen food industry increased sales in the United States by adopting new packaging techniques. Multipacks – with dinners large enough to satisfy mother and father and with smaller portions for the youngsters – were designed for families. On the assumption that people do not like to eat directly from a metal foil container, packagers put dinners in attractive serving trays designed to look like white dinner plates. Ecko Company also made a container that was orange on the outside and white within to look like a casserole and to be used for such foods as lasagna. More elaborate oven-ready dinners, such as stuffed cabbage or stuffed pork chops, also made their appearance in grocery freezers. Reuben sandwiches and similar creations were also frozen and ready for the oven.

Beef, lamb, and poultry consumption increased, pork and fish held their own, and veal declined in the United States. The average American ate 114.8 pounds of beef (113.8 in 1971), 3.4 pounds of lamb (3.1), 42.9 pounds of chicken (42.3), and 8.9 pounds of turkey (8.5). The average per capita consumption of eggs declined by 4, to 318. Milk, butter, and cream consumption declined, but cheese increased from 11.5 to a record 13.2 pounds per person. Per capita consumption of fresh fruits declined by about 2 pounds and fresh vegetables by about 3 pounds. Frozen and canned fruits and vegetables did not gain correspondingly. Their increases were limited to fractions of pounds. Potato consumption increased 2 pounds per person to 120.9 pounds. Beer was still the most popular drink, but the consumption of wine advanced sharply.

Time magazine ran a cover story on U.S. wines. The story told of the improvement in domestic wines, and supported the contention with some favorable comparisons between U.S. and European wines by a panel of winetasters.

Natural, or organic, foods became more popular than ever. The number of health food stores, which handle these products, increased from 1,200 in 1968 to 3,000 in 1972.

New Products were not as important as variations of established products. Prepared buttered waffles, eggs, and bacon were introduced that could be heated in the toaster to make breakfasts easy. Add-your-own-meat dinners became popular as consumers sought to trim their budgets by buying meat more carefully and making it stretch further. Soy protein continued to dominate in the development of substitute and synthetic foods. Textured proteins were produced that resemble and taste like French-fried clams, sliced and diced meat, sausage, and tidbits of meat for dips, omelets, and casseroles. More like the real thing than the real thing itself were the vegetable protein garnishes made as substitutes for bell peppers and mushrooms. Alma Lach

INSTANT LOANS

Friendly Finance Corp.

MAULDIN

Miami's bruising Larry Csonka turned this plunge into a 49-yard Super Bowl run. Csonka carried the ball 15 times, gained 112 yards.

FOOTBALL. The Miami Dolphins, created as an expansion team in 1966, made National Football League (NFL) history in 1972. The Dolphins became only the third NFL team ever to finish a regular season undefeated and untied, the first to gain that distinction in 30 years, and the first to do it in a 14-game season. Then they beat the Cleveland Browns, 24 to 14, and the Pittsburgh Steelers, 21 to 17, to win the American Football Conference (AFC) championship and qualify for the Super Bowl.

Miami kept its record perfect by beating the Washington Redskins, National Football Conference (NFC) champions, 14 to 7, in the Super Bowl game in Los Angeles on Jan. 14, 1973. Miami's defense throttled Washington's offense. The Redskins' touchdown came with about three minutes left to play. Defensive back Mike Bass ran 49 yards with a fumble after a Miami field goal attempt had been blocked.

The Dolphins bore the perfectionist imprint of Don Shula, their 42-year-old coach and general manager. They set an NFL season record of 2,960 yards rushing, breaking a mark established by the 1936 Detroit Lions in the single-wing era. They became the first NFL team to have two 1,000-yard runners in one season. Larry Csonka ran for 1,117 yards and Eugene

(Mercury) Morris for 1,000. Things went so well for them that tight end Marv Fleming once caught a touchdown pass and found a $10 bill in the end zone. Before the season started, the Baltimore Colts put Earl Morrall, their 38-year-old second-string quarterback, on waivers. The Dolphins claimed him for $100, and when Bob Griese suffered a broken right leg and dislocated right ankle in the season's fifth game, Morrall became the regular.

The Redskins, like the Dolphins, had a strong-willed coach plus a quarterback pressed into service when the starter was injured. The coach was George Allen, so single-minded that against the New York Giants, leading by a touchdown and with only seconds remaining in the game, he called time out to try to score another touchdown. (He succeeded.) His major cogs included Bill Kilmer, who replaced the injured Sonny Jurgensen at quarterback, and Larry Brown, a superb runner. They led the Redskins to their first division title in 27 years, and the defense stopped the Green Bay Packers and Dallas Cowboys without a touchdown in the NFC play-offs.

The Cowboys, who had won the Super Bowl in January, 1972, were good but erratic, and their best quarterback, Roger Staubach, missed almost the entire season with a shoulder separation. Still, they did well in a season in which such veteran teams as the Minnesota Vikings, Kansas City Chiefs, Baltimore, Detroit, and the New York Jets did not, mostly because of aging and injured defenses.

The surprise teams were the Steelers, with a 6-8 won-lost record in 1971 and 11-3 in 1972, and the Packers, who went from 4-8-2 to 10-4. The Steelers won the first division title in their 39-year history, mainly because of a rugged defense and a rookie fullback named Franco Harris, one of 10 children of a black American soldier and his Italian war bride. The Packers overcame an indifferent passing game with the bruising running of John Brockington and MacArthur Lane and an inspired defense.

A Runner's Year. Csonka, Morris, Brown, Harris, and Brockington were 5 of the 10 men who gained 1,000 or more yards rushing. This was in sharp contrast to the five previous seasons, which had produced only 14 of the 1,000-yard performances. The upsurge in running resulted from an almost innocuous rule change that was designed to help passing by diminishing the effectiveness of zone defenses.

To offset a drop in touchdown passes and scoring, the club owners had moved the inbounds markers, also known as hash marks, 3½ yards closer to the center of the field. All plays began at or between these markers, so the change gave the offense more room on the playing field in which to maneuver. As intended, it helped the passing game. It also did wonders for running.

"Give the hash marks a lot of credit," said Csonka, "but don't short-change anyone who hits a thousand. You still take a beating."

1972 College Conference Champions

Conference	School
Atlantic Coast	North Carolina
Big Eight	Oklahoma
Big Sky	Montana State
Big Ten	Ohio State-Michigan (tie)
Ivy League	Dartmouth
Ohio Valley	Tennessee Tech
Mid-America	Kent State
Missouri Valley	Louisville-West Texas-Drake (tie)
Pacific Eight	Southern California
Southeastern	Alabama
Southern	East Carolina
Southwest	Texas
Western Athletic	Arizona State
Yankee	Massachusetts

The Bowl Games

Bowl	Winner	Loser
Bluebonnet	Tennessee, 24	Louisiana State, 17
Cotton	Texas, 17	Alabama, 13
Gater	Auburn, 24	Colorado, 3
Liberty	Georgia Tech, 31	Iowa State, 30
Orange	Nebraska, 40	Notre Dame, 6
Rose	Southern California, 42	Ohio State, 17
Sugar	Oklahoma, 14	Penn State, 0
Sun	North Carolina State, 32	Texas Tech, 28

All-America Team (as picked by UPI)

Offense

Ends—Johnny Rodgers, Nebraska; Charles Young, Southern California.
Tackles—Jerry Sisemore, Texas; Pete Adams, Southern California.
Guards—John Hannah, Alabama; Ron Rusnak, North Carolina.
Center—Tom Brahaney, Oklahoma.
Quarterback—Bert Jones, Louisiana State.
Running Backs—Greg Pruitt, Oklahoma; Otis Armstrong, Purdue; Woody Green, Arizona State.

Defense

Ends—Willie Harper, Nebraska; Bruce Bannon, Penn State.
Tackles—Greg Marx, Notre Dame; Dave Butz, Purdue.
Middle Guard—Rich Glover, Nebraska.
Linebackers—Randy Gradishar, Ohio State; Jamie Rotella, Tennessee.
Defensive Backs—Brad Van Pelt, Michigan State; Cullen Bryant, Colorado; Randy Logan, Michigan; Conrad Graham, Tennessee.

Other Changes. The Colts took all kinds of beatings, on the field and off. Before the season, in a deal unparalleled in sports annals, owner Carroll Rosenbloom traded franchises with the Los Angeles Rams (the players stayed where they were). The new owner of the Colts, Robert J. Irsay, hired Joe Thomas as general manager. Thomas, who had survived open-heart surgery a year before, watched impatiently as the Colts lost four of their first five games.

Then he decreed a youth movement, saying, "If we're going to lose, we might as well lose with young players and let them grow and mature together." He told coach Don McCafferty to bench 39-year-old Johnny Unitas, perhaps the best quarterback in NFL history, in favor of 25-year-old Marty Domres. When McCafferty resisted, Thomas fired him and promoted John Sandusky to head coach. Unitas was benched, the Colts finished with a 5-9 record, and Unitas vowed never to play again for the Colts.

"Thomas told me, 'I don't want you to take this as

a slap in the face,' " said Unitas. "But what the hell else is it but a slap in the face. I'm no clock runner-outer."

The season began with four new head coaches–Lou Saban at Buffalo, Abe Gibron at Chicago, John Ralston of Stanford at Denver, and Bill Peterson of Rice at Houston. McCafferty at Baltimore and John Mazur at New England were ousted during the season, and Bob Hollway at St. Louis and Ed Khayat at Philadelphia after the season.

There was turnover of another sort at San Diego, where the Chargers set an NFL record of 21 off-season trades. One acquisition was Duane Thomas, the talented but unpredictable Dallas running back known for unannounced departures. He left the team in training camp, rejoined it in midseason, missed a practice, and was deactivated. "Obviously," said coach Harland Svare, "he's got some problems that won't permit him to play now."

Canadian Football. The Canadian Football League (CFL) enjoyed its first wide exposure on U.S. television, though the weekly telecasts ended after eight of the scheduled 20 weeks because of a lack of national advertisers. But the CFL did not appear sure where it wanted to go. It has applications from a dozen U.S. cities, but it feared U.S. domination. It also feared that the NFL would award franchises to Montreal and Toronto, two of its key cities. And it feared formation of a proposed league encompassing U.S. and Canadian cities.

Standings in National Football Conference

Eastern Division	W.	L.	T.	Pc.
Washington	11	3	0	.786
Dallas	10	4	0	.714
N.Y. Giants	8	6	0	.571
St. Louis	4	9	1	.321
Philadelphia	2	11	1	.179
Central Division	**W.**	**L.**	**T.**	**Pc.**
Green Bay	10	4	0	.714
Detroit	8	5	1	.607
Minnesota	7	7	0	.500
Chicago	4	9	1	.321
Western Division	**W.**	**L.**	**T.**	**Pc.**
San Francisco	8	5	1	.607
Atlanta	7	7	0	.500
Los Angeles	6	7	1	.464
New Orleans	2	11	1	.179

National Conference Individual Statistics

Scoring	TDs.	E.P.	F.G.	Pts.
Marcol, Green Bay	0	29	33	128
Ray, Los Angeles	0	31	24	103
Fritsch, Dallas	0	36	21	99
Mann, Detroit	0	38	20	98
Gogolak, N.Y. Giants	0	34	21	97
Cox, Minnesota	0	34	21	97

Passing	Att.	Comp.	Pct.	Yds.	TDs.
Snead, N.Y. Giants	325	196	60.3	2,307	17
Tarkenton, Minn.	371	215	58.0	2,651	18
Berry, Atlanta	277	154	55.6	2,158	13
Kilmer, Wash.	225	120	53.3	1,648	19

Receiving	No. Caught	Total Yds.	Avg. Gain	TDs.
Jackson, Phila.	62	1,048	16.9	4
Tucker, N.Y. Giants	55	764	13.9	4
Malone, Atl.	50	585	11.7	2
C. Taylor, Wash.	49	673	13.7	7

Rushing	Atts.	Yds.	Avg. Gain	TDs.
Brown, Wash.	285	1,216	4.3	8
Ron Johnson, N.Y.	298	1,182	4.0	9
Hill, Dall.	245	1,036	4.2	6
Brockington, G.B.	274	1,027	3.7	8

Punting	No.	Yds.	Avg.	Longest
Chapple, L.A.	53	2,344	44.2	70
Eischeid, Minn.	62	2,651	42.8	61
James, Atl.	61	2,609	42.8	59
Blanchard, N.Y.	47	2,006	42.7	58

Punt Returns	No.	Yds.	Avg.	TDs.
Ellis, G.B.	14	215	15.4	1
Bertelsen, L A.	16	232	14.5	0
McGill, S.F.	22	219	10.0	0
Barney, Det.	15	109	7.2	0

Standings in American Football Conference

Eastern Division	W.	L.	T.	Pc.
Miami	14	0	0	1.000
N.Y. Jets	7	7	0	.500
Baltimore	5	9	0	.357
Buffalo	4	9	1	.321
New England	3	11	0	.214
Central Division	**W.**	**L.**	**T.**	**Pc.**
Pittsburgh	11	3	0	.786
Cleveland	10	4	0	.718
Cincinnati	8	6	0	.571
Houston	1	13	0	.071
Western Division	**W.**	**L.**	**T.**	**Pc.**
Oakland	10	3	1	.750
Kansas City	8	6	0	.571
Denver	5	9	0	.357
San Diego	4	9	1	.321

American Conference Individual Statistics

Scoring	TDs.	E.P.	F.G.	Pts.
Howfield, N.Y. Jets	0	40	27	121
Gerela, Pitt.	0	35	28	119
Yepremian, Miami	0	43	24	115
Muhlmann, Cin.	0	30	27	111

Passing	Att.	Comp.	Pct.	Yds.	TDs.
Morrall, Miami	150	83	55.3	1,360	11
Lamonica, Oak.	281	149	53.0	1,998	18
Johnson, Den.	238	132	55.5	1,783	14
Unitas, Balt.	157	88	56.1	1,111	4

Receiving	No. Caught	Total Yds.	Avg. Gain	TDs.
Biletnikoff, Oak.	58	802	13.8	7
Taylor, K.C.	57	821	14.4	6
Myers, Cin.	57	792	13.9	3
Hill, Buff.	52	754	14.5	5

Rushing	Atts.	Yds.	Avg. Gain	TDs.
Simpson, Buff.	292	1,251	4.3	6
Csonka, Mia.	213	1,117	5.2	6
Hubbard, Oak.	219	1,100	5.0	4
Harris, Pitt.	188	1,055	5.6	10
Garrett, S.D.	272	1,031	3.8	6
Morris, Mia.	191	1,000	5.2	12

Punting	No.	Yds.	Avg.	Longest
Wilson, K.C.	66	2,960	44.8	69
Walden, Pitt.	65	2,846	43.8	72
Cockroft, Cleve.	81	3,498	43.2	65
Lee, Balt.	57	2,410	42.3	60

Punt Returns	No.	Yds.	Avg.	TDs.
Farasopoulos, N.Y. Jets	17	179	10.5	1
Casanova, Cin.	30	289	9.6	1
Leigh, Mia.	22	210	9.5	0
Dunlap, S.D.	19	179	9.4	0
Parrish, Cin.	15	141	9.4	1

In the CFL championship game for the Grey Cup, played on December 3 in Hamilton, Ont., the Hamilton Tiger-Cats defeated the Saskatchewan Roughriders, 13 to 10, when Ian Sunter came off the bench to kick a 34-yard field goal on the final play of the game.

Attendance. NFL attendance increased for the 20th time in 21 years, and college attendance rose for the 19th consecutive year. The NFL attracted 10,612,864 spectators to its 182 regular-season games, an average of 58,312. The preseason games, once played before near-empty stands, averaged a record 52,951. College attendance reached 30,828,802; this was a 1.23 per cent increase over the figure for the preceding year.

The College Champion was the University of Southern California (USC). Of the 121 football teams in the National Collegiate Athletic Association (NCAA) university division, only Southern California was undefeated and untied. In the Trojans' 11 regular-season victories, their smallest margin was 9 points. Southern California, coached by John McKay, unveiled an exciting sophomore running back in Anthony Davis. In a 45 to 23 triumph over Notre Dame on national television on the final Saturday of the regular season, Davis ran for six touchdowns. Two of them came on kickoff returns of 97 and 96 yards.

In McKay's 13 years at Southern California, his teams had won 100 games and lost only 33. Seven of his teams won Pacific Eight conference titles, six went to the Rose Bowl, three had undefeated and untied seasons, and three won national championships.

On December 2, the day of the Southern California-Notre Dame game, Auburn upset Alabama, 17 to 16, spoiling Alabama's undefeated and untied season. The previous Saturday, Michigan suffered its first defeat, 14 to 11, to Ohio State. Nebraska, the national champion in 1970 and 1971, lost its season opener, 20 to 17, to the University of California, Los Angeles (UCLA). The UCLA hero on that occasion was its new quarterback, Mark Harmon, son of Tom Harmon, the former great Michigan halfback.

In United Press International's final ratings, made after the regular season, the 35 coaches on the selection board unanimously named USC as national champion. Oklahoma (10-1) was ranked second, Ohio State (9-1) third, Alabama (10-1) fourth, Texas (9-1) fifth, Michigan (10-1) sixth, Auburn (9-1) seventh, Penn State (10-1) eighth, Nebraska (8-2-1) ninth, and Louisiana State (9-1-1) tenth.

Southern California upheld its top ranking by beating Ohio State, 42 to 17, in the Rose Bowl on Jan. 1, 1973, in Pasadena, Calif. On the same day, Nebraska defeated Notre Dame, 40 to 6, in the Orange Bowl in Miami, and Texas upset Alabama, 17 to 13, in the Cotton Bowl in Dallas. On New Year's Eve, Oklahoma beat Penn State, 14 to 0, in the Sugar Bowl in New Orleans.

Leading Players. Nebraska, coached by Bob Devaney, produced two outstanding players in Johnny Rodgers, a 5-foot 9-inch, 170-pound wingback, and Rich Glover, a middle guard. Rodgers was voted the Heisman Trophy as the nation's leading player, Glover the Outland Trophy as the best interior lineman. Devaney, a head coach for 16 years, retired after the Orange Bowl game.

Rodgers finished his college career with 5,586 total yards (running, pass receiving, and kick returning), an NCAA record. He averaged 13.8 yards a play, another record, and he scored a touchdown every nine times he handled the ball. Rodgers had been convicted of holding up a gas station in 1970. "I would've hated to think that I didn't win the Heisman Trophy because of what had happened to me," he said.

Howard Stevens, who played two years at Randolph-Macon College and his last two at the University of Louisville, became the first collegian to rush for more than 5,000 yards (he totaled 5,297) in his career. He also set a career scoring record of 418 points. Prophetically, the 5-foot 5-inch, 165-pound Stevens wore number 1 on his uniform. The most exciting running performance of the season was by USC's Davis against Notre Dame. The best aerial performance was by Tony Adams of Utah State, who set an NCAA one-game record of 567 yards passing in a 44 to 16 victory over Utah. Frank Litsky

FOREST AND FOREST PRODUCTS. A proposal by the Council on Environmental Quality to curb clear-cutting in federal forests was blocked in January by protests from the timber industry. Conservationists sought a ban on the practice of cutting all trees on selected tracts. They charged it defaced forest areas and caused erosion and stream siltation. The lumber industry contended further limitations on clear-cutting would force a price-supply crunch in the midst of a record building boom.

On June 24, however, the U.S. Forest Service adopted a plan to restrict clear-cutting on its timberlands. The action came in response to guidelines set forth on March 30 by the Senate Subcommittee on Public Lands.

Wage and price controls were reimposed on 62,000 lumber companies on July 17. The Cost of Living Council said these exempt lumber firms had increased prices much more rapidly than those under control. Triggered by the continued rise in housing construction, lumber prices increased 14 per cent in the year ended in June. The Administration also announced in July that timber cutting on federal lands would be increased in 1972 to yield about 300 million more board feet of softwood lumber. Lumber production in 1972 was estimated at about 38 billion board feet. Andrew L. Newman

FORMOSA. See Taiwan.

FOUR-H CLUBS. See Youth Organizations.

FRANCE. Prime Minister Jacques Chaban-Delmas and his Cabinet surprised France and its neighbors by resigning on July 5, 1972, after three years in office. Pierre Messmer, a tough, orthodox Gaullist who had been minister for overseas territories immediately formed a new government. See MESSMER, PIERRE.

A key factor in Chaban-Delmas' resignation was the preparation by the Gaullist party, the Democratic Union for the Republic, for a general election in March, 1973. There had been growing dissension within the party over a tax scandal, control of radio and television, and the lukewarm response to a referendum on enlarging the European Community (Common Market). Chaban-Delmas was regarded by many as an election liability. On June 27, the French Communist and Socialist parties agreed on a program for a popular front government–the first such pact since 1936. The two parties said they would fight the election under this joint manifesto.

The Tax Scandal involved charges that Chaban-Delmas had not paid income tax. He went on both French television channels on February 15 to answer his critics. The satirical weekly *Le Canard Enchaine* had published his tax returns. They showed that, quite legally, he had paid no income tax for the years 1966 to 1970. The opposition parties exploited the situation. Gaullists denounced the Communists, who led the attack on the prime minister, as "permanent enemies of the Fifth Republic." Chaban-Delmas described the attacks on him as "attempts to bring about my resignation and undo my policy of reform." He explained his tax payments at length. In France, tax evasion is known as a "national pastime"; measures were taken on July 3 to curb it, however, by enforcing laws on the publication of income tax assessments.

A secondary factor in the resignation was controversy over the government-controlled radio and television system, ORTF, which always has been the prime minister's responsibility. Two parliamentary committees reported corruption and mismanagement in the organization, and the chairman and director-general of ORTF resigned immediately. In its own inquiry, ORTF's board found no evidence of corruption, but noted certain "administrative and professional errors."

The Common Market. President Georges Pompidou called a referendum on Great Britain's entry into the Common Market on April 23. He emphasized that the electorate would be deciding the wider issue of Europe's future organization, and said he needed the people's confidence to "safeguard France's independence effectively." In spite of a three-week campaign, the public reacted with apathy. About 45 per cent of the registered voters stayed away or cast blank ballots. Of those who voted, 68.11 per cent said "yes" to enlarging the Common Market and 31.89 said "no." Pompidou said the enlargement had been ratified, but many authorities were disappointed that the proportion of nonvoters was the highest since universal suffrage was introduced in France in 1848.

Pompidou played a leading role in plans for extending the Common Market. But he preferred a looser confederation than some members favored. In Luxembourg on May 4, he developed his *Europe des Patries* theme–which seeks to preserve national identities within a wider Europe. He called for a "similar harmonization of foreign policy that will one day be common toward all outsiders, whoever they may be." This was indispensable, he said, for a united Europe. On May 15, the rediscovery by Britain and France of their old closeness was the theme of Pompidou's banquet speech during the state visit to France by Queen Elizabeth II. Pompidou caused consternation among Common Market leaders by saying on June 2 that he would not take the responsibility of inviting nine other heads of government to Paris in the fall to discuss the enlarged market if the result were to be "merely vague declarations of intent." Later in the month, his position was clarified: Preparatory foreign ministers' meetings should hold out some prospect of monetary and economic union, or, he felt, a summit meeting would be useless. On September 15, Pompidou gave the go-ahead for the summit. In his letter to the nine

President and Madame Georges Pompidou, in center, were honored at dinner in British Embassy in Paris during visit of Queen Elizabeth II and Prince Philip.

Loomis Dean, *Time* © 1972 Time Inc.

Astonished visitors to France's famous Élysée Palace found that op art was dominating parts of President Pompidou's official residence.

heads of state, he said the conference, starting October 19 in Paris, would "define a certain number of new routes for concerted action among our 10 countries." The meeting agreed on a goal of European union by 1980. See EUROPE.

Labor and the Economy. Strikes occurred in a variety of industries during the year. A journalists' strike in February stopped the publication of all Paris newspapers, and a 48-hour stoppage in April silenced radio and television. More serious was a two-week strike of Breton dairy farmers, depriving millions of milk. The strike ended with new price agreements.

After prices rose 0.8 per cent in a month, the government announced measures on August 30 designed to keep the annual rate of increase below 4.5 per cent. Price control on home products was promised with a plea to the Common Market to allow increased food imports. On September 6, Messmer outlined a social program giving increased benefits for the old and underprivileged.

Australia and New Zealand were among countries that protested a series of French nuclear tests on the atoll of Mururoa from June 19 to August 2. France answered its critics by stating that no other country had imposed such strict restraints on itself for its experiments. Kenneth Brown

See also EUROPE (Facts in Brief Table).

GABON. See AFRICA.

GAMBIA celebrated its seventh year of independence on Feb. 18, 1972. A week earlier, President Dawda Kairaba Jawara, leader of the People's Progressive Party (PPP), had dissolved Parliament in preparation for a general election, the first held since Gambia became a republic in 1970.

On March 29, general elections were held for the House of Representatives. The ruling PPP won 28 of the 32 seats at stake, while the opposition United Party took 3. The remaining seat was won by an independent member of the PPP. In an unexpected move, President Jawara immediately reconstituted his Cabinet by adding one and appointing two new ministers. One of them, Sir Alieu Sulayman Jack, had previously served as speaker of the House.

Gambia's relations with neighboring Senegal posed both external and internal problems. Senegal complained of smuggling, a practice made easy by the fact that the border is largely unmanned and unmannable. Although a ministerial meeting between the two governments improved relations somewhat, the tensions remained. In the fall, Vice-President Sheriff M. Dibbu resigned because his brother was involved in a smuggling incident. He was caught in Senegal with a quantity of transistor radios. Construction began on new port facilities at Bathurst. They included a 400-foot extension to the quay and access roads. Paul C. Tullier

See also AFRICA (Facts in Brief Table).

GAMES, MODELS, AND TOYS. Continued concern about ecology was reflected in the number of toys relating to the environment that were marketed in 1972. One of these, the Johnny Horizon Environmental Test Kit, enabled youngsters to make simple tests for air and water pollution. A kit called Nature's Window could be used by children to grow small gardens and watch each step in the growing process. With Weather Forecaster, they could employ principles used by the National Weather Service. Other toys oriented to the ecology included Smoky the Bear sets, miniature greenhouses, and an ecology stamp book.

A skeptical view of the ecological trend in toys was taken by Mortimer R. Feinberg, professor of psychology at City University of New York. "I don't think the kids really give a damn about the ecology," he said, "but the parents do, and so the manufacturers are playing into the parents' value structure."

The Afro-American History Mystery was one of four new "soul" games designed primarily for blacks. An increasing number of schools were using the games as teaching tools for black and white pupils.

New Regulations. Toymakers faced new regulations introduced by consumer interests and government agencies. In California, a state law went into effect on July 1 prohibiting the manufacture and sale of toys related to violence, such as bombs, grenades, and torture instruments. It was the first such law in the United States. In June, the U.S. Food and Drug Administration (FDA) announced the recall of more than 200,000 toys banned as hazardous to children. The FDA also planned to issue strict mandatory standards for bicycles sold in the United States. There has been a sharp increase in bicycle-associated deaths. Consumer advocate Ralph Nader and Mrs. Juliette Smith of Washington, D.C., mother of a young son, were among those joining in a federal court suit filed on September 4 asking that manufacturers be forced to reimburse purchasers of toys and other products declared hazardous by the U.S. government.

Model Making. Bucky Servaitis of Kettering, Ohio, lost his grand national championship to Brian L. Webster of Manchester, Tenn., at the 41st National Model Airplane Championships at the Glenview (Ill.) Naval Air Station in July. But Servaitis retained his open national championship. Webster retained his senior national championship, while the junior national championship went to Kenneth A. Bauer of Orange, Calif. The Dixie Whiz Kids retained their team championship, and the Chicago Aeronuts took the club team championship. William Werwage of Parma, Ohio, and the U.S. stunt team won in the Control Line world championships at Helsinki, Finland, in July. Merrick Andrews of Bogota, N.J., was the individual winner at the indoor world meet in England. Theodore M. O'Leary

GARDENING. New data revealed in 1972 may bring a reassessment of the dangers of DDT. Use of the pesticide has been heavily restricted because scientists said it could not be decomposed by bacterial action, and because it accumulates in plants and animals.

However, Edward R. Laws, Jr., at Johns Hopkins Hospital, reported statistical evidence that indicates persons exposed to high levels of DDT for from 10 to 20 years have less chance of getting cancer than those with normal exposure. In addition, scientists at Cornell University reported that they have observed complete breakdown of DDT by microorganisms that normally occur in the soil.

All-America Plants of 1972 included the "Carved Ivory" zinnia, "Gold Galore" semidwarf marigold, "Circus" and "Summer Carnival" salmon and white petunias, and a hollyhock that flowers the first year from seed. All-America gladioli were "Cameo" (rosy-edged, yellow-throated), and "Miss America" (ruffled pink). Among the roses, "Gypsy" (orange-red), "Electron" (bright pink), and "Medallion" (yellow), all hybrid teas, also won awards. Other introductions included "Sunkiss" portulaca (five colors), "Ballerina" California poppy, "Ruffled Pink" verbena, "Hot Pants" salvia, and "Elfin Orchid" impatiens.

Awards. In Swarthmore, Pa., the Arthur Hoyt Scott Foundation's celebrated medal was awarded to May Theilgaard Watts, naturalist emerita of Morton Arboretum near Chicago. The American Horticultural Society awarded its Liberty Hyde Bailey Medal to Henry T. Skinner, director of the National Arboretum, Washington, D.C. The Distinguished Achievement Medal of Pennsylvania's Horticultural Society went to Edgar T. Wherry, botanist-ecologist-conservationist of the University of Pennsylvania.

Boston's Massachusetts Horticultural Society presented the following awards: the Thomas Roland Medal to Robert E. Young of the University of Massachusetts for breeding improved vegetables: the Jackson Dawson Medal to William E. Snyder of Rutgers University, New Brunswick, N.J., for advancing plant propagation; and the Large Gold Medal to Walter Beinecke, Jr., for conserving and restoring the open spaces and historic sites of Nantucket Island, a popular resort island that lies off the coast of Cape Cod, Mass.

Research. August de Hertogh of Michigan State University discovered that by holding tulips in frozen storage after they root and timing their removal, they can be made to flower in any month. The United States Department of Agriculture found a new lure for Japanese beetles, phenethyl propionate + eugenol, that is twice as effective as the next best lure and, in addition, lures the beetles five times as long. Edwin F. Steffek

GEOLOGY. Nearly 370 million years ago, a primitive land vertebrate clumsily slithered across a small sand bar in what is now the state of Victoria in Australia, perhaps in search of food or the sanctuary of a nearby pond or stream. In so doing, it played a highly significant role in the parade of life on earth. The footprints left in the sand became fossilized and were discovered early in 1972 by James Warren and Norman A. Wakefield, geologists at Monash University in Clayton, Australia.

The footprints are the earliest yet found in the fossil record. They were made by one of the early amphibians, intermediaries between fish and reptiles, a group today represented mostly by frogs, salamanders, and newts. Chained to the water because they had to lay their eggs there, amphibians were the first to attempt life on the land, but they were only partly successful. The early ones were fish-like in general appearance and closely resembled a group known as the lobe-finned fishes, or crossopterygians.

Until the discovery of these Australian footprints, the earliest record of land vertebrates came from skeletal remains in Greenland in rocks of late Devonian age, about 350 million years ago. The Australian footprints were found on a slab of fine-grained, purplish sandstone of the Genoa River Formation in eastern Victoria, in the southeast corner of Australia. The Genoa River Formation grades laterally into marine strata that have been assigned to the Frasnian Epoch of the late Devonian Period on the basis of the fossils of marine invertebrates found in the rocks. The Genoa River Formation rocks are at least 20 million years older than the Greenland formations.

The only other reported occurrences of late Devonian amphibians are dubious marks on the surface of rocks in Pennsylvania, and a fossil skull from the late Devonian rocks of Sacumenac Bay in Canada. The skull is intermediate in nature between lobe-finned fishes and amphibians.

The Australian footprints consist of three trackways, all occurring on the same layer of rock. The first set consists of 10 impressions of the left limbs and 9 impressions of the right. The hindlimb had five toes while the forelimb apparently had only three. However, it could be that the animal walked in such a manner that all of its toes did not make an impression in the sand.

In the middle of another trackway, the impression of the undulating body or tail mark is clearly visible. From the size of the footprints, the width of the forelimb, and the distance from the forelimb to the hindlimb, the animal was probably just under 2 feet long. The undulating body mark and these dimensions indicate that the animal was *Ichthyostega*, a primitive amphibian, the bones of which have been found in the terrestrial, late Devonian rocks of Greenland.

Oldest Rocks. In late 1971, a team of researchers from the University of Oxford in England and the Geological Survey of Greenland headed by L. P. Black of Oxford found the oldest rocks on earth. The rocks, dated at 3.98 billion years old, were found southeast of Godthab, Greenland. Previous to this, certain South African rocks from 3.4 to 3.5 billion years old were thought to be the oldest.

The new discovery came from southern Greenland and not in other parts of the country because most of Greenland was affected by volcanic action in the middle of the Precambrian Era, more than 2-billion years ago. This obscured older rock. The southern portion of Greenland apparently was not affected by this volcanic action.

Dinosaurs. Scientists have long thought that all dinosaurs were cold-blooded reptiles. However, geologist Robert T. Bakker of Harvard University published convincing observations in July that some dinosaurs were warm-blooded animals.

Anatomically, the locomotor apparatus of the large dinosaurs such as the *Triceratops*, the duck-billed dinosaurs, and the *Stegosaurus* is similar to that of such modern large mammals as the elephant and the rhinoceros. Their legs stood vertical beneath the body, and scientists conclude that they could move about as fast as elephants. This being the case, the energy metabolism necessary for large dinosaurs to move at high speeds must have been similar to that of a large mammal.

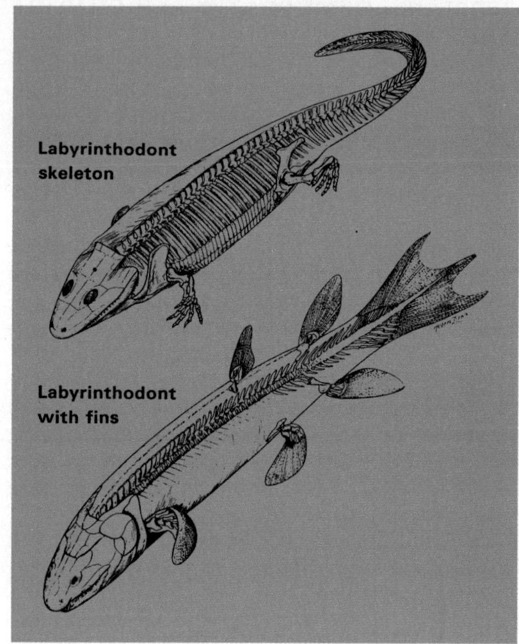

The oldest known fossilized footprints of a primitive amphibian, such as the one shown, were discovered in Australia in 1972.

A warm-blooded animal must eat more to fuel its high rate of metabolism. Studies of modern animal communities indicate the ratio of predators to prey is low among warm-blooded animals. Among cold-blooded animals, a given number of prey can sustain proportionately more predators. Studies of large dinosaur fossils also suggest a low predator-to-prey ratio, which compares favorably with warm-blooded animal communities.

Large warm-blooded animals that live in warm climates are nearly hairless. The elephant, rhinoceros, and hippopotamus are examples. Dinosaurs, as fossil dinosaur skin shows, were also hairless. In other words, dinosaurs more closely resembled large mammals than huge lizards, even though they were reptiles and not mammals. They probably became extinct because of a drop in temperature at the end of the Cretaceous Period 65 million years ago. Those animals that could withstand a prolonged drop in temperature survived. These included such small, hairy, warm-blooded animals as primitive mammals and lizards that could decrease their metabolism and body functions to survive. However, large, hairless animals, such as the dinosaurs, could not survive the prolonged temperature drop. If the African steppes of today underwent a prolonged drop in temperature, the large, hairless, warm-blooded elephants would not be able to survive. Thomas X. Grasso

GEORGIA. See State Government.

GERMANY, DEMOCRATIC REPUBLIC OF (EAST), struggled for world recognition in 1972. On January 10, State Council Chairman Walter Ulbricht called for recognition from all countries that had demanded the four-power Berlin settlement, which became effective in June. Guarantees of European security were unthinkable, he said, without a "sovereign East Germany." He said the entry of both German states into the United Nations (UN) and its agencies was "a task for this year." An East German observer delegation was invited to the World Health Organization assembly in May because East Germany displayed "sufficient attributes of statehood." But, on May 19, the assembly rejected a proposal for East Germany's admission, 70 votes to 28 with 25 abstentions. Russia strongly supported admission, but West Germany opposed it. The decision barred East German participation in the June UN Conference on Human Environment in Stockholm, Sweden, which was open only to members of the United Nations or UN agencies.

A German Treaty. The two Germanys concluded a general traffic treaty on April 16 and exchanged ratifications on October 17. The agreement, the first treaty ever signed by the two states, relaxed border traffic restrictions for both goods and passengers. But, by mid-December, reports spread that East Germany was pressuring citizens not to issue the invitations required for West Germans to visit the East. A more basic treaty to create "normal" relations between East and West Germany was signed in East Berlin on December 21.

German Reunions. For the first time since 1966, East Germany granted passes allowing West Berliners to visit East Germany at Easter and Whitsunday, the seventh Sunday after Easter. Conditions at the crossing were more relaxed than at any time since Germany was divided. Neither vehicles nor passengers were searched. Over Easter, 449,597 West Berliners crossed over for up to three days and 629,000 more crossed on Whitsunday. Highly emotional reunions between people who had not met for six years were commonplace. East Germany received $2.15 million in visa fees.

Nationalization. The government speeded up its take-over of semiprivate and private businesses during the year. Gerhard Gruneberg, a member of the Socialist Unity Party's Politburo, said 94 per cent of the owners of semiprivate firms and 73 per cent of the owners of private industrial and building firms had agreed to sell their businesses to the state.

A law allowing women abortion on demand during the first three months of pregnancy was approved on March 9. By August, recorded abortions had increased fivefold. Kenneth Brown

See also EUROPE (Facts in Brief Table).

Thousands of Germans enjoyed happy reunions at Easter when East Germany relaxed border rules. About 450,000 West Germans visited East Germany.

GERMANY, FEDERAL REPUBLIC OF (WEST). The most serious political and constitutional crisis since World War II arose in April, 1972, following the discovery that neither the government nor the opposition had a reliable majority in the legislature. For a time, the future of friendship treaties with Russia and Poland, concluded in 1970 but awaiting ratification, was in doubt. But a premature general election on November 19 gave Chancellor Willy Brandt's government a resounding triumph.

The first setback for Brandt came on February 9 when the *Bundesrat* (Upper House) defeated by one vote an advisory approval of the friendship treaties. On March 1, Brandt's majority in the *Bundestag* (Lower House) dwindled to four. His 1969 majority of 12 had shrunk as a series of supporters defected to the opposition over his renewal of friendly relations with the East.

State Elections in Baden-Württemberg on April 22 were considered a plebiscite on the treaties. The Christian Democratic Union (CDU) won 65 local seats to 45 for the Social Democratic Party (SDP) and 10 for the Free Democratic Party (FDP). Encouraged, the CDU set out to topple the federal government. Brandt's SDP-FDP coalition faced its biggest threat since taking office in 1969. Trade unionists, angry at the threat to Brandt, threatened strikes. Short work stoppages occurred in steelworks in Duisburg, Herford, and Emden, widely scattered industrial centers. The CDU no-confidence motion failed by two votes on April 27 and legislators gave Brandt a standing ovation. He was cheered by 50,000 people in West Berlin when he defended his foreign policy, but in Bonn, right wing demonstrators marched in protest against the treaties.

Treaties Debated. Debate on bills to ratify the East-West treaties began on May 10. Brandt told the Bundestag that the treaties would "complement proven friendship with the West by reconciliation with the East."

The first formal treaty between the two Germanys was ratified in October. It eased travel restrictions for citizens of one Germany who wanted to visit the other. The friendship treaties with Russia and Poland were ratified on May 17, but with only 248 affirmative votes in the Bundestag. They represented just half of its 496 members.

Christian Democratic leader Rainer Barzel had been unable to rally conservative support for the treaties. He directed his deputies to abstain from voting to maintain party unity. More than 200 did.

Minister of Finance Karl Schiller clashed with Cabinet colleagues over tax proposals. He wanted to cut public spending, but other ministers disagreed. On July 6, Brandt "reluctantly" accepted Schiller's resignation. Schiller also resigned from the SDP on September 24.

The Bundestag rejected Brandt's request for a vote of confidence on September 22, necessitating the November election. Brandt and his Cabinet stayed away from that session, ensuring defeat.

The election returned the SDP-FDP coalition to the government with 54.3 per cent of the popular vote. Brandt's SDP, for the first time, won more votes than the conservatives, 45.9 per cent to 44.8 per cent. The Bundestag re-elected Brandt chancellor on December 14, 269 votes to 223. On December 13, it had elected its first woman speaker, Annemarie Regner, who is the former secretary of the SDP's founder.

East-West Relations. A general traffic treaty negotiated between the two Germanys on April 26 gave more than a million West Germans the opportunity to cross into East Germany (see GERMANY, EAST). The first direct flight from West to East by a West German civil airliner took place on September 3. West Germany and Poland agreed on September 14 to re-establish full diplomatic links. A basic good-neighbor treaty between East and West Germany was signed on December 21.

West Germany hosted the Olympic Games in Munich, but they were marred by the deaths of 11 Israeli Olympic team members in an Arab terrorist raid on September 5. Brandt intervened personally in an attempt to save the lives of nine held hostage, but they were killed in an airport gun battle. See OLYMPIC GAMES. Kenneth Brown

See also EUROPE (Facts in Brief Table).

GHANA. A military junta seized power in a bloodless coup d'état on Jan. 13, 1972. An 11-member National Redemption Council headed by Colonel Ignatius Kutu Acheampong dissolved Parliament and ousted Prime Minister Kofi A. Busia. At the time of the coup, Busia was in London for a medical checkup. See ACHEAMPONG, IGNATIUS KUTU.

The junta's actions were prompted by widespread dissatisfaction with the Busia government's political and economic policies. In particular, they deplored the corruption and arbitrary dismissals in government, as well as Busia's policy of expelling foreign businessmen.

The new regime quickly canceled a 44 per cent devaluation of the Ghanaian cedi, repudiated a debt of $94 million left over from the days of former President Kwame Nkrumah, and declared a 10-year moratorium on repaying several hundred million dollars in other foreign debts. It also lowered the prices of such staples as sugar, flour, and soap as it moved against traders who were hoarding them.

The body of former President Nkrumah, whose regime had been ousted in a military-police takeover in 1966, was returned for burial in Ghana on July 7. Nkrumah, who had been living in exile in neighboring Guinea, died in April. Paul C. Tullier

See also AFRICA (Facts in Brief Table).

GIRL SCOUTS. See YOUTH ORGANIZATIONS.

GIRLS' CLUBS. See YOUTH ORGANIZATIONS.

GOLF. In 11 years as a professional golfer, Jack Nicklaus won almost every tournament and honor worth winning. But in 1972, the 32-year-old Nicklaus had his finest year. His goal was the never-achieved professional grand slam – a sweep of the United States Open, British Open, Professional Golfers' Association (PGA), and Masters championships. He did not achieve it, but he made a strong run. He won the Masters and the U.S. Open. He lost the British Open to Lee Trevino by only one stroke. Then, fresh from a finger operation, he tied for 13th in the PGA championship.

By March, Nicklaus had surpassed Arnold Palmer as the sport's all-time money-winner, and by August, he had surpassed his own 1971 record of $244,490 in tournament earnings. He finished the year with more than $290,000. Nicklaus also led the PGA circuit in tournament victories and tournament points, and the PGA named him Golfer of the Year.

Nicklaus won seven tournaments and finished second four times. He earned purses totaling $233,000 in those seven victories alone – in the Bing Crosby in January, Doral-Eastern in March, Masters in April, U.S. Open in June, Westchester Classic and U.S. match play in August, and Walt Disney in December.

As columnist Red Smith wrote in *The New York Times:* "When he is on his game, he is the best golfer in the world. This has been true for a long time, but until this year there were many who resented the truth and rejected it. Until this year, he was an upstart and an interloper, the crasher who had dared to expose Arnold Palmer as merely human. . . . Even those who hated his guts were saddened when he missed by a stroke in the British Open."

Jane Blalock filed a $5-million federal court suit against the LPGA to continue playing during 1972 after they suspended her for "unethical practices."

Try for Grand Slam. The grand-slam tournaments began with the Masters in April at Augusta, Ga. Nicklaus led every round, finishing the 72 holes with a score of 286 for a three-stroke victory over Tom Weiskopf, Bruce Crampton, and Bobby Mitchell. At the finish, the crowd gave him a standing ovation.

Next came the U.S. Open in June over the Pebble Beach (Calif.) links, a picturesque, windswept course that juts into the Pacific Ocean. Nicklaus, with a 290, beat Crampton by three strokes. It was Nicklaus' 13th major victory (4 Masters, 3 U.S. Opens, 2 British Opens, 2 PGA's, and 2 U.S. Amateurs), tying the record held by his idol, Bobby Jones.

In the British Open, held in July at Muirfield, Scotland, Nicklaus played well but not quite his best. "I made some swings I'm not familiar with," he said. With two holes to go, he was tied with Trevino. Then Trevino chipped into the cup on the 17th hole and finished with a 278 to Nicklaus' 279.

Finger Infection. Back home in Columbus, Ohio, on July 24, Nicklaus had a manicure. Within hours, his right index finger became infected, and the next day he underwent surgery and had to withdraw from the PGA team championship, which he and Palmer had won the two previous years.

A physician warned Nicklaus that reinfection was possible if, instead of resting, he hit hundreds of golf balls in practice. Despite that, he went to the PGA championship in August at Birmingham, Mich., and played at less than his best. Gary Player of South Africa, with a 281, beat Tommy Aaron and Jim Jamieson by two strokes. Nicklaus finished with 287.

"I actually haven't played a lot this summer," he said. "I made my schedule at the beginning of the year. I felt that the four major championships were being played on four courses I liked, so I keyed things on them. I didn't win all four, but if you're looking for a reason for my winning otherwise, maybe it's that. A lot of guys concentrate hard, but I try not to play so much that I lose concentration."

Another Winner. Trevino, the 1971 Golfer of the Year, remained happy, uninhibited, and successful, winning more than $200,000. In addition to the British Open, the 31-year-old El Paso, Tex., golfer won the Danny Thomas-Memphis Classic, and the Greater Hartford and Greater St. Louis opens. In October, without a word to anyone, he walked off the course in the middle of the third round of the Texas Open, complaining of slow play.

"An hour after I'd left," he said, "I'd have given $5,000 not to have done it and to be able to go back and play it out. I should be fined or suspended."

During 1972, the Ladies Professional Golf Asso-

Jack Nicklaus, winner of almost every tournament he entered during 1972, winces after making shot on the 4th green during the Doral-Eastern in Miami in March.

ciation (LPGA) staged 29 tournaments worth $968,400, up 50 per cent from the 1971 gross. Kathy Whitworth, the LPGA president from Richardson, Tex., and Jane Blalock of Portsmouth, N.H., won five tournaments each. They became the first players in LPGA history to earn $50,000 in one year. Kathy Ahern of Denton, Tex., won the LPGA championship tournament by six strokes and finished second to Susie Maxwell Berning of South Lake Tahoe, Calif., in the women's U.S. Open.

The 26-year-old Miss Blalock, voted Rookie of the Year in 1969 and Most Improved Player in 1970 and 1971, had problems as well as success. The LPGA suspended her for a year for "actions inconsistent with the code of ethics." Supposedly, she had moved the ball out of a spike mark during a tournament, and though the LPGA would not use the word "cheating," there were hints of other rules violations. Miss Blalock denied any wrongdoing and filed a $5-million antitrust suit against the LPGA. A federal court allowed her to continue playing, though her earnings were placed in escrow.

The outstanding amateur golfer was 20-year-old Ben Crenshaw of Austin, Tex. He won the Eastern Amateur and the Porter Cup, tied for first in the National Collegiate championship, took amateur honors in the Masters, and tied for second in the U.S. Amateur tournament, which was won by Marvin (Vinnie) Giles III. Frank Litsky

GOULD, SHANE ELIZABETH (1956–), strengthened her ranking as the world's best female swimmer by winning three gold medals in the 1972 Olympic Games in Munich, West Germany. The 15-year-old Australian won the 200-meter and 400-meter free-style races and the 200-meter individual medley, setting a new world record in each race. She was upset in the 100-meter free-style by Sandra Neilson of the United States, but won a bronze medal for finishing third. See OLYMPIC GAMES (table).

A broad-shouldered blonde, Miss Gould is 5 feet 7½ inches tall and weighs about 126 pounds. She began her assault on world swimming records earlier in 1972. Beginning in April, she set new world marks in all five of the free-style distances, 100, 200, 400, 800, and 1,500 meters. She is the first swimmer in 30 years to hold all of the women's free-style records.

Miss Gould was born in Sydney, one of four daughters of an airline executive. As a child, she lived for six years with her family in the Fiji Islands, where she soon learned to climb coconut palms. Her coaches believe this helped to develop her unusually strong shoulders and chest.

When the family returned to Australia in 1966, Miss Gould began training for competitive swimming. In preparation for the Olympics, she trained four hours a day, two hours before and two hours after her high school classes. Joseph P. Spohn

GOVERNORS, U.S. See STATE GOVERNMENT.

GRAY, L(OUIS) PATRICK III (1916–), was named acting director of the Federal Bureau of Investigation (FBI) on May 3, 1972. Gray succeeded J. Edgar Hoover, who died on May 2 at the age of 77. See DEATHS OF NOTABLE PERSONS (Close-Up).

Gray is a long-time friend of President Richard M. Nixon and worked for him in his 1960 and 1968 election campaigns. In 1969, he became executive assistant to Health, Education, and Welfare Secretary Robert H. Finch. In January, 1970, Gray returned to private law practice in New London, Conn., but he moved back to Washington later in the year as assistant attorney general.

Known for his dedication to detail and hard work and his intense patriotism, Gray's initial moves as interim director were quick and decisive. Within a week after his appointment by President Nixon, he announced that the FBI would recruit women as special agents. He also announced plans to hire more minority group agents, to liberalize dress and grooming requirements, and to expose more of the bureau's operations to public scrutiny.

Gray was born in St. Louis, Mo., and grew up in Houston, Tex. He attended Rice University before being admitted to the U.S. Naval Academy in 1936. He received a B.A. degree from the academy in 1940 and a law degree from George Washington University Law School in 1949. He retired in 1960 as a captain after 20 years of service. Allan Davidson

GREAT BRITAIN

Prime Minister Edward Heath announced a 90-day freeze on wages, prices, rents, and stock dividends on Nov. 6, 1972. Heath had always argued against such methods of economic management, but when talks between Government, employers, and unions about a voluntary incomes policy collapsed, he had little choice. He was faced with rampant inflation–wage rates were rising at 17 per cent a year, prices were up 8 per cent and still climbing, and unemployment was intolerably high at 3.4 per cent. A sense of crisis mounted. The pound fell as low as $2.32 from $2.60, where it stood before it was floated in June.

The Labour Party and unions opposed the freeze, but public-opinion polls showed the country generally favored it. The Government rushed the necessary new legislation through Parliament, which provided heavy fines for violators.

Earlier in the year, Chancellor of the Exchequer Anthony Barber tried to double economic growth to 5 per cent a year. On March 21, he announced big tax cuts totaling about $3.14 billion. They were chiefly in personal income and purchase taxes. He also introduced a package of measures to give British industry the strongest investment incentives in the world. Heath's Government–by restoring investment grants, by pouring aid into depressed regions and creating an Industrial Development Executive, and by appointing a special minister for industrial development–repudiated the self-help philosophy with which it had won power.

Bitter Industrial Conflict also marked the year. The depleted condition of many union treasuries after the strife of 1970 and 1971 had been expected to dampen labor militancy in 1972. But in the first nine months, 22.2 million working days were lost through strikes, compared with 13.5 million in all of 1971, which had been the worst year since the 1926 general strike. Union militants could argue that strikes paid off. Striking workers–such as coal miners, dockworkers, railwaymen, and electrical and automobile workers–won average raises of 29 per cent over two years, 5 per cent above the industrial average and far above the Government's unofficial 8 per cent guideline.

The year began with a strike in the nationalized coal mines, the first official nationwide strike in the industry since 1926. The coal strike lasted from January 9 to February 28, and it brought regular brownouts to most of Britain. A court of inquiry recom-

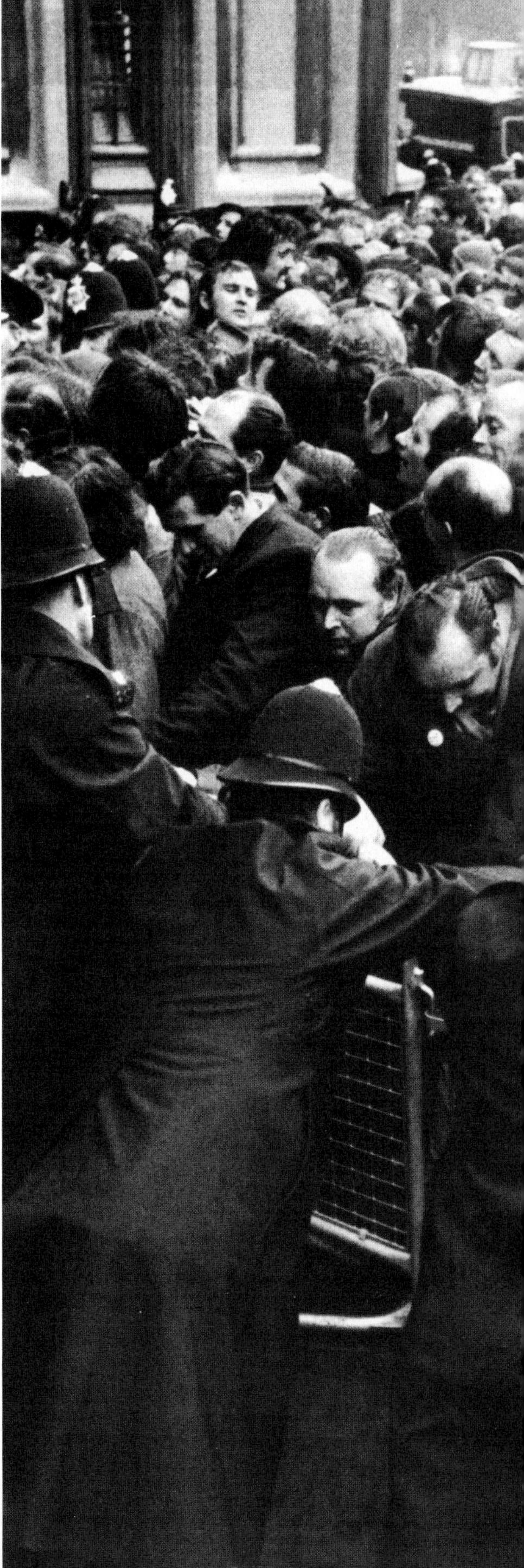

Thousands of striking miners marched on the Houses of Parliament in February. They were demonstrating against Prime Minister Heath.

mended pay raises, but the union rejected them—and won still more concessions. The final raise averaged about 25 per cent.

The 1971 Industrial Relations Act took full effect on February 28. Efforts to use its machinery to cool disputes and chasten militants led to bitter confrontations between the Government and organized labor and dramatic union clashes with the law.

Railroad workers resorted to a slowdown on April 17 after the National Industrial Relations Court (NIRC), set up under the new labor law, ordered cooling-off periods—the first in British history. In an NIRC-ordered vote, workers backed their leaders. The railroads offered acceptable terms.

Court Ignored. Britain's biggest union, the Transport and General Workers' Union (TGWU), tried to ignore the NIRC and paid heavily for it. The trouble started when Liverpool dockworkers refused to let trucks bring large cargo containers onto the docks. The move was part of their campaign to save their jobs, which are threatened by the use of freight containers. They ignored TGWU advice to obey NIRC orders and stop the action—and the TGWU was fined about $13,000 in March. It failed to pay, and a second fine, 10 times as large, was imposed in April. The union paid up.

The TGWU was again at the wrong end of an NIRC decision on May 12. Its members were still refusing to handle the container trucks at Liverpool, and the trucking companies asked for another ruling. The union pleaded that, having told the dockworkers to stop, it could not be held responsible for their misbehavior. In a historic judgment, the court gave the union 21 days to discipline its members or face new contempt charges. The union tried to comply, though it had no direct power over the stewards.

At the Chobham Farm container depot in east London, dockworkers refused to let container trucks enter, and the drivers—also TGWU members—won an NIRC order to end the picketing. The dockworkers balked and, at the end of July, five were jailed. Tension rose, but four days later, the court found a legal reason to release the men without losing face. On August 17, Britain's 42,000 dockworkers voted to end another containerization strike, one that had lasted more than three weeks. They won better job guarantees for workers who lost their jobs because of the use of cargo containers.

Throughout the year, the Trades Union Congress (TUC) opposed the new labor law and demanded its repeal. The Government insisted the act had come to stay, but did not resort to court action again to cool industrial disputes. In June, the Government and the TUC had their first face-to-face talks in 16 months. On July 18, they were joined by employers' representatives for the first three-way talks on inflation. The three parties met frequently and discovered common ground, but they found no voluntary anti-inflation formula. Heath then proclaimed the freeze.

Two days later, Britain's second biggest union, the engineering workers, was fined over $10,000 for contempt of court. It had failed to explain to the NIRC the exclusion of a union member from a branch meeting. One man's grievance escalated into a major collision between union and court, with a second fine for contempt provoking retaliatory strikes.

Joining Europe. Against this background of domestic unrest, Heath's Conservative Government drove the European Communities Bill, adapting British law to European Community regulations, through Parliament. The measure won final approval on July 13. That cleared the last obstacle to Britain's entry into the European Community (Common Market); Heath had achieved a chief objective.

He did it in the face of formidable opposition. Opinion polls showed that most people were against Britain joining Europe. The campaign for a popular referendum to advise on entry gathered unexpected strength, but Heath insisted that Parliament must decide the issue. There, as the bill went through its various stages, the Government teetered near defeat. The final House of Commons vote on July 13 supported membership, 301 to 284. Nearly 100 attempts to amend the bill had been beaten, but by margins as low as 4 and 6 votes.

In October, Heath attended the nine-nation summit meeting of the enlarged Common Market. He talked tough and won agreement for a regional policy that would help Britain's hardest-hit industrial areas.

Altar candles illuminate a Church of England meeting during a British power cut. A long, bitter miners' strike caused power shortage.

Internal Struggles over the Common Market issue beset both major parties. The Government rode out a sustained rebellion in the House of Commons by a small faction within its own party. The split in the Labour Party opposition came to a head on April 10 with the resignation of deputy party leader Roy Jenkins, former chancellor of the exchequer. He was a leader of Labour's pro-market minority. The Labour Party's shadow cabinet had decided to back a rebel Conservative's amendment to hold a referendum before entering Europe. Several other party leaders followed him out in protest.

On October 4, at its annual conference, the Labour Party came close to declaring outright opposition to Common Market membership. It called on the next Labour government to renegotiate the Brussels treaties and to let the British people vote on the issue.

Labour's morale took an even bigger blow than the Government's in the by-election at Rochdale on October 26. Cyril Smith, a local businessman and former Labour mayor of the town, became a Liberal Party candidate for Parliament. He turned a Labour majority of 5,171 into one of 5,093 for himself. Then, south of London on December 7, a young Liberal turned a Conservative majority of 12,696 into a Liberal one of 7,410 in the biggest by-election upset since 1934. With eight seats in Parliament, the Liberal Party scented another revival of its fortunes.

Cabinet Changes. On July 18, Home Secretary Reginald Maudling resigned. Testimony given during bankruptcy proceedings involving international architect John Poulson revealed that Maudling, while his party was out of power, accepted the chairmanship of one of Poulson's companies in return for payment to a charity supported by his wife. He later resigned. Maudling said he had done nothing deserving criticism. But a Metropolitan Police investigation into Poulson's affairs had been set up. As home secretary, Maudling was the ultimate authority over that police force, and felt he could not continue in office during the investigation. Robert Carr took over the home office but continued also as leader of the House of Commons until Heath announced a major Government reshuffle on November 5.

A high-flying, self-made, 41-year-old millionaire, Peter Walker, moved over to head the vast trade and industry department after outstanding success as secretary for the environment. He replaced former business chief John Davies, who was picked to carry out detailed Common Market negotiations in Brussels following British membership. Geoffrey Rippon, who had negotiated the terms for British entry, took charge of the environment department. James Prior, former agriculture minister, relieved Carr as leader of the House.

Uganda Crisis. In early August, President Idi Amin Dada of Uganda created a new problem for

Rhodesian Bishop Abel Muzorewa tells London demonstrators that proposed Rhodesian-British settlement terms are unacceptable to blacks.

Britain. He declared that all Asian residents with British passports were to be expelled from Uganda, because they sabotaged the economy. He said they must be out of the country within three months, and that they were Britain's responsibility. Britain, while acknowledging its legal and moral obligations toward the Asians, tried unsuccessfully to persuade Amin to extend the deadline.

General concern over the housing shortage and unemployment in Britain fed fears about the immigrants' effect on the nation. Nevertheless, a Uganda Resettlement Board was created, and in mid-September the airlift to Britain began. Old military bases became reception camps. Many refugees were given food, warm clothing, money for necessities, and help in finding homes and jobs.

Rhodesian Settlement Dies. A complex deal to formalize Rhodesia's independence from Britain collapsed in 1972. It had been accepted by the Rhodesian government and, providing it received Rhodesian people's approval, by Britain. A special commission went to Rhodesia in January to get Rhodesians' views. Despite officials' efforts to confine them, the commissioners went far afield during their two-month investigation. Their report, published on May 23, said white Rhodesians supported the settlement by more than 14 to 1, but blacks opposed it by more than 36 to 1. It said that blacks perceived Rhodesia's government as committed to white supremacy, that their mistrust of it outweighed all other considerations.

Rhodesian Prime Minister Ian D. Smith called the report naïve, inept, and irresponsible. He said no further negotiations would be held.

Britain's Sir Alexander F. Douglas-Home said that the country would observe United Nations-ordered trade sanctions, although few other nations did so. United States laws had been passed to buy Rhodesian chrome. Over right wing protests, Parliament agreed on November 9 to keep the sanctions in effect for another year. See Rhodesia.

Arab Terrorism came to England in the form of letter-bombs late in the year. One of them, mailed from the Netherlands, killed an agricultural counsellor at the Israeli Embassy in London on September 23. In November, Jewish companies and individuals received letter-bombs sent from India and one man was injured. A special bomb squad was set up.

Edward, Duke of Windsor, who provoked a constitutional crisis in 1936, died in Paris on May 28. He came to the throne as King Edward VIII, on Jan. 20, 1936, but abdicated on December 11 to marry an American divorcée, Mrs. Wallis Warfield Simpson. Another member of the royal family, Prince William of Gloucester, was killed on August 28 in a plane crash. He was 30, unmarried, and ninth in line to the throne. George Scott

See also Europe (Facts in Brief Table).

GREECE. Six U.S. destroyers dropped anchor off the port of Piraeus on Sept. 2, 1972, the first step in making the Athens area the U.S. Navy's largest Mediterranean home port. Some 300 dependent Navy families landed in Athens three days later. Destroyer Squadron 12 arrived under a controversial agreement that allows a U.S. carrier task force with 6,700 men and 3,100 of their dependents to be based in the Athens area.

Some Greeks were offended by the special privileges–including conditional judicial immunity, tax exemptions, and duty-free imports–given the U.S. servicemen and their families. Greek courts were to waive priority of jurisdiction at the request of American authorities unless a case had "special significance." In March, the United States sold two squadrons of Phantom F-4 fighter-bombers to Greece.

Power Spreads. Prime Minister George Papadopoulos, who is also foreign minister and defense minister, took over as regent on March 21. He dismissed George Zoitakis, regent since 1967, for "unjustified interference" in the government's work. Zoitakis had refused to sign a decree increasing the police force. The firing was seen as a step toward abolition of the monarchy. In July, a mass-circulation, progovernment newspaper said in a front-page editorial that the government did not want King Constantine to return. It suggested Papadopoulos be made president for life. A Constitution promulgated in 1968, after the king fled to Rome, said he would return after the next elections, but elections have not been scheduled.

Improved contacts between the ruling junta and the West seemed to be developing. On January 29, Jean-Noel de Lipkowsky, French secretary of state for foreign affairs, arrived for an official four-day visit. He received a warm reception. The British defense secretary arrived on September 6 for two days of talks. Papadopoulos repeated his intention to implement the 1968 Constitution.

Torture Charged. Two private international agencies reported on October 17 that Greece continued to torture political prisoners. The International Commission of Jurists and Amnesty International rejected testimony given to the Congress of the United States by Henry J. Tasca, U.S. ambassador to Greece. Tasca reportedly testified that the Red Cross found no evidence of systematic torture when it last visited prisoners in Greece. The agencies countered that the Red Cross did not publish reports on such visits, but they said they knew it had transmitted to the Greek government "accounts . . . of torture of political prisoners." Kenneth Brown

See also EUROPE (Facts in Brief Table).

GUATEMALA. See LATIN AMERICA.

GUINEA. See AFRICA.

Prime Minister George Papadopoulos, left, celebrating Greek Easter, dances with soldiers in Athens. Papadopoulos was named regent on March 21, 1972.

GUYANA. The long-standing border dispute with Venezuela continued to disturb relations between the two countries in 1972. In January, about 3,000 Venezuelan "pioneers" were reported settling in the Amazon jungle along the Guyana-Venezuela border. Their presence was expected to discourage foreigners, including Guyanese, from exploiting the mineral-rich area. Guyana was accused by Venezuela of sending troops into the area to create unrest among Venezuelan Indians. Both countries, however, continued to try to solve their problems.

In February, Guyana was extended permanent "observer" status by the Organization of American States. Venezuela, which had previously blocked the move, abstained from doing so. In May, Venezuela also ended its policy of excluding Guyana from Caribbean affairs. It agreed that Guyana should be among the 15 nations that attended a weeklong conference on Caribbean maritime problems, which was held in the waters off Santo Domingo.

Guyana continued to establish ties with the Communist countries. In March, a seven-member permanent trade mission from the People's Republic of China established headquarters in Georgetown. The mission will promote trade relations and economic cooperation between the two countries. The Guyanese government planned to establish a similar mission in Peking. Paul C. Tullier

See also LATIN AMERICA (Facts in Brief Table).

HACKMAN, GENE (1931-) won the 1972 Academy of Motion Picture Arts and Sciences Award and the New York Film Critics' Award for best actor for his portrayal of a tough narcotics cop in *The French Connection.* It was the third time he had been nominated for an Oscar. The others were as best supporting actor in *Bonnie and Clyde* (1967) and *I Never Sang for My Father* (1970).

A former Marine whose boyhood hero was Errol Flynn, Hackman briefly studied acting in California in the mid-1950s. After a series of odd jobs in New York City, he joined the Premise, an off-Broadway theater. His work there led to a series of Broadway plays including *Who'll Save the Plowboy?, A Rainy Day in Newark,* and *Children from Their Games,* culminating in 1964 with a leading role opposite actress Sandy Dennis in *Any Wednesday.*

His Broadway reputation established, he made his film debut in *Lilith* (1964) and appeared in such television shows as the "U.S. Steel Hour," "The F.B.I.," "Naked City," and "CBS Playhouse." Good and bad movie parts followed fast, including *The Split* (1968); *Riot!, Marooned, Downhill Racer,* and *Gypsy Moths* (1969); *Doctors' Wives* (1971); and *Prime Cut* (1972).

Hackman was born in San Bernardino, Calif., on Jan. 30, 1931. He and his wife have a son and two daughters. He enjoys motorcycling, skiing, and flying. Lillian Zahrt

HAITI. The atmosphere of intimidation that existed under the late President François Duvalier seemed to be lifting in 1972 under his son, President Jean-Claude Duvalier. The Ton Ton Macoutes, the private security police of the former president, had virtually disappeared, and terrorism against political dissidents had stopped. The newspapers, too, were being allowed to publish some criticism of the government.

Optimism was further encouraged when the president commuted the death sentences of the men who had been implicated in a plot against his father in 1970. The father had been adamantly opposed to such concessions. Even more indicative was the solution of an interfamily power struggle involving the president, his mother, and his elder sister, Marie-Denise Dominique. It was resolved when the president dismissed Max Dominique, his sister's husband, as ambassador to France. The pair did not return to Haiti and Mrs. Dominique was replaced as secretary to the president by Aguste Dijon, a former classmate of the president.

The Economic Health of the nation appeared to be improving. Two loan agreements totaling $1.8-million were signed in January with the Inter-American Development Bank (IADB) of the Alliance for Progress. The loans were to be used to finance a two-part, $5.1-million farm and industrial growth program. Throughout the year, too, representatives of the International Monetary Fund, the World Bank, and the IADB visited the country to investigate the possibilities for further loans, grants, and investments. Some investments had already been made, and two new tourist hotels were being planned in Port-au-Prince. The results of this activity were reflected in the gross national product, which reached about $375 million in 1971 and was expected to increase by from 6 to 8 per cent in 1972.

Haiti continued its efforts to improve relations with other countries, a direct reversal of previous policies. On March 10, President Anastasio Somoza Debayle of Nicaragua met with President Duvalier in Port-au-Prince. Later, the two governments issued a joint communiqué agreeing to exchange military information and commercial missions and to assist each other in technical matters. Haiti resumed diplomatic relations with the Dominican Republic, its neighbor on the island of Hispaniola. Haiti also resumed diplomatic relations with Costa Rica, and delegations of Haitians were sent to Honduras and other countries to encourage commerce.

A seven-man U.S. military mission visited Port-au-Prince from July 26 to August 4 to discuss a Haitian request for from $5 million to $10 million in U.S. arms. The mission reported its findings to a congressional subcommittee for its consideration, but because of a lengthy debate, no decision had been reached by year's end. Paul C. Tullier

See also LATIN AMERICA (Facts in Brief Table).

HANDICAPPED. In the fiscal year that ended on June 30, 1972, some 326,000 persons were rehabilitated, or returned to productive activity, in the United States. This was a 12 per cent increase over the previous fiscal year and the highest annual total ever achieved.

Texas led the states with 21,907 persons rehabilitated, a 41 per cent gain over the previous year. Following in order were Pennsylvania (20,252), Illinois (14,315), North Carolina (13,696), Florida (13,253), and California (12,990).

Rehabilitation Engineering Centers. A major effort to use new engineering concepts to benefit the disabled was announced in March, 1972, by Secretary Elliot L. Richardson of the Department of Health, Education, and Welfare. A national system of rehabilitation engineering centers will be created under the program. At the centers, engineers will work with physicians in treating patients with the most modern rehabilitation technology. Richardson called the program "a coalition for positive action at the patient level," and added, "It is an alliance of medical expertise and space age technology whose goal is to restore a wider world to the handicapped and disabled."

The first two centers will be at the Ranchos Los Amigos Hospital in Los Angeles, which is affiliated with the University of Southern California, and at Moss Rehabilitation Hospital in Philadelphia, affiliated with Temple and Drexel universities. Each will receive $350,000 in federal funds the first year. Two or three additional rehabilitation centers will probably be established.

A new computerized system prints 20 to 30 pages of braille per minute. This is more than 150 times faster than other methods.

New Advisory Committee. The organization of a new National Advisory Committee on Services for the Blind and Visually Handicapped was completed in 1972. The committee will advise on policies and procedures dealing with vocational rehabilitation, social services, aging, prevention of blindness, the multi-handicapped blind, and the Randolph-Sheppard vending-stand program, under which blind persons operate vending stands on government property. The organizations represented on the committee are American Association of Workers for the Blind, American Council of the Blind, National Federation of the Blind, Association for the Education of the Visually Handicapped, and National Council of State Agencies for the Blind.

New Devices. A wheel chair with an "ear" for voice commands may prove to be a new way of getting around for paralyzed persons. The experimental vehicle was designed by Paul H. Newell, Jr., head of biomedical engineering of Texas A&M University at College Station. It was designed for quadriplegics unable to use any other kind of motorized wheel chair.

In the voice-operated wheel chair, the patient wears a throat microphone. A barely audible hum with a particular pitch guides the chair forward. A rise in pitch steers it right. A lower note sends it left. Prototypes of the new chair are now being tested.

Other new wheel-chair controls under study and in use include a chin-operated control unit, and a puff-and-blow control unit that is operated like a harmonica. The patient blows into the proper hole to activate the desired direction signal.

The President's Committee on Employment of the Handicapped observed its 25th anniversary in 1972. Through committee programs, experts in environmental design, business, labor, medicine, and education have labored to see that their fields are sensitive to the needs of the disabled. At a silver anniversary meeting held on May 4 and 5, 1972, in Washington, D.C., there was a presentation representing the latest in 25 years of advances in rehabilitation aids.

New Park Guide. A new *National Park Guide for the Handicapped* was published in 1972. It is designed to help the blind, the deaf, those confined to wheel chairs, and other handicapped persons to enjoy the National Park System. For example, for wheel-chair visitors the booklet devotes particular attention to door widths, rest-room facilities, ramps, handrails, guardrails, terrain surface distance, and inclines. The guide is sold for 40 cents by the Superintendent of Documents, U.S. Government Printing Office, Washington, D.C. 20402. Joseph P. Anderson

HARNESS RACING. See Horse Racing.

HAWAII. See State Government.

HEALTH AND DISEASE. The National Academy of Sciences charged in September, 1972, that thousands of Americans die needlessly each year because of inadequate emergency medical care. Accidental injuries impose "a staggering demand" on the nation's health services, the academy said, and it termed such injuries the leading killer of Americans from 1 through 38 years old. The academy further charged that "thousands of lives are lost through lack of systematic application of established principles of emergency care."

It proposed establishing an emergency telephone reporting system, improving the quality of ambulance service, and creating a nationwide corps of properly trained emergency medical technicians. The primary need, the report said, is for greater federal responsibility in outlining the key medical services needed in all emergencies.

Venereal Disease remained a major health problem in virtually all parts of the United States, though there was reason for cautious optimism that a new era in venereal disease control may be on the horizon. J. Donald Miller, director of state and community services at the federal Center for Disease Control in Atlanta, Ga., reported that the federal government was putting an additional $16 million into the venereal disease control effort. He said that the statistics show that gonorrhea incidence has risen 15 per cent during 1972, and the number of primary and secondary syphilis cases is the highest in 22 years.

A decade ago, a task force appointed by the surgeon general of the U.S. Public Health Service believed syphilis might be eliminated as a public health hazard by 1972 or 1973. Instead, 100,000 new cases of infectious syphilis were reported in this country during the period from July, 1970, to July, 1971. More than 2.5 million new gonorrhea cases occurred during the same period. Miller said that on a graph, the curve is that of a classic epidemic completely out of control.

"Hope for stamping out the epidemic lies in an increasing public concern over the problem," he said. Early detection, successful use of new antibiotics, and education on the use of high-quality prophylactics as disease preventatives are all measures that, hopefully, will ultimately stem the rising tide of the disease.

Drugs. A World Health Organization advisory group reported that opium, morphine, and codeine are "no longer indispensable in the practice of medicine." The 13-member panel said synthetic compounds are as effective as opiates in relieving pain, and in some respects superior to them.

The group added that there is substantial evidence that some synthetic drugs are as effective against a cough as codeine, and to some extent have been used in place of codeine. They said that synthetic drugs are equivalent or superior to the opiates in dealing with diarrhea.

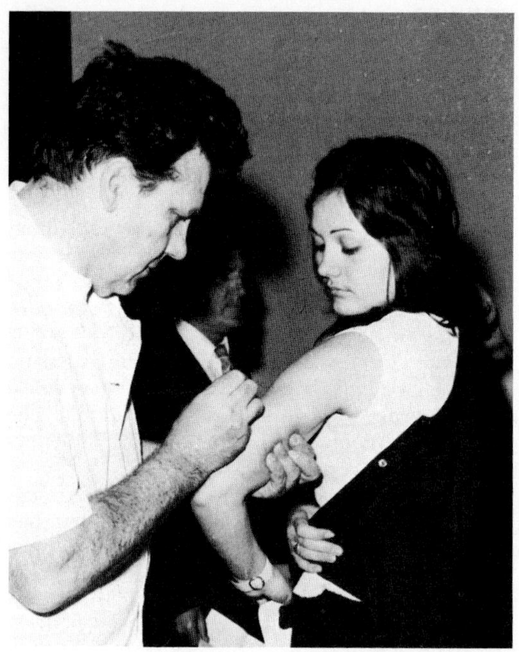

More than 25 per cent of the 20 million Yugoslavs were vaccinated against smallpox in 1972 after a disease outbreak claimed the lives of 22 persons.

Cancer deaths among blacks in the United States have shown an "alarming increase" in recent years compared to deaths in the U.S. white population, according to a research team at the Howard University College of Medicine. Using data from the vital statistics of the U.S. Department of Commerce for the period from 1949 to 1967, the investigators found that cancer mortality rates for nonwhites (91 per cent of whom are black) rose from 138 to 182 for each 100,000 persons, an increase of 32 per cent. Cancer deaths among whites rose from 149 to 154 during the same period, an increase of 3 per cent.

According to Jack E. White, professor of surgery and director of the Cancer Research Center at Howard University College of Medicine, "In 1949, the cancer mortality rate for nonwhites was 8 per cent lower than for whites, while in 1967 it was 18 per cent higher–an astounding change for a short period of only 18 years."

White and his colleagues believe that environmental influences are the chief factor in the alarming rise of cancer mortality in blacks over the 18-year period. Such factors as food preparation and dietary habits (greater consumption of fried foods, for example), use of tobacco and alcohol, occupational hazards (greater exposure to cancer-causing agents), and urbanization may be involved. Richard P. Davies

HIGHWAY. See BUILDING AND CONSTRUCTION; TRANSPORTATION.

HOBBIES. A blood-red Duesenberg automobile, custom-built in 1933 for actress Greta Garbo, brought a record price of $90,000 at an auction of classic cars in Auburn, Ind., on Sept. 3, 1972. Kruse Auctioneers, who conducted the sale, said it was the highest price ever paid for an automobile. The successful bidder, Charles R. Wood of Lake George, N.Y., said his acquisition of the car "was an old dream come true." The car had changed hands several times since Miss Garbo owned it. About 150 classic cars were sold at the auction for more than $1 million.

In another auction sale involving a classic car once owned by a motion-picture star, James R. Nethercutt of Sylmar, Calif., paid $22,000 in Hollywood on March 6 for a gray, maroon-trimmed Avions Voisin Victoria owned by the late Rudolph Valentino. The actor had the automobile built in 1923 for his honeymoon with Natasha Rambova.

Ten letters from the late author Ernest Hemingway brought $5,975 from various buyers when they were sold on March 9 in New York City by the Charles Hamilton Galleries, Inc. The letters were written from Cuba between 1949 and 1953 to the late Charles Poore, a book critic. A letter in which Hemingway discussed his novel *For Whom the Bell Tolls* brought $1,900, the highest price paid for any of the letters. A gallery spokesman described the letters as written in "off-the-cuff, man-to-man style."

Nostalgia exhibit held in Chicago in July drew thousands of interested hobbyists, particularly collectors of old comic books and movie posters.

At another auction conducted by the Hamilton Galleries on July 1, an unidentified New York City physician paid $1,250 for a letter that Lee Harvey Oswald, assassin of President John F. Kennedy, wrote to his mother from Russia in 1962, and $500 for a letter written in 1931 to Adolf Hitler by Eva Braun, who became his mistress. It was believed to be the first Eva Braun letter to be auctioned in the United States. At the same auction, a three-page letter written by the British scientist Charles Darwin in 1848 brought $725, and an autograph by the recluse American industrialist Howard Hughes went for $80.

Two flintlock breech-loading repeating pistols brought a record price of $145,000 when sold at an auction in London on July 18 to an anonymous buyer. The pistols were mounted in silver in the early 1900s by Michele Lorenzoni of Florence, Italy. Formerly in the imperial Russian collection in the Hermitage in Leningrad, the pistols were part of a firearms collection assembled by the late William Renwick of Tucson, Ariz.

Memorabilia associated with the late Walt Disney and the characters he created brought $15,000 at an auction in Los Angeles, May 14. Among the many items, a Mickey Mouse and Pluto snow shovel, made in 1935, went for $125. Theodore M. O'Leary

See also COIN COLLECTING; GAMES, MODELS, AND TOYS; STAMP COLLECTING.

HOCKEY. The National Hockey League (NHL), which had monopolized the professional sport since 1917, received two serious challenges in 1972. One came from the World Hockey Association (WHA), a 12-team league that was formed in November, 1971, and played its first game 11 months later. The WHA spirited away more than 60 NHL players and became a second major league. The other challenge came from an unexpected source–Russia. In an eight-game series against the Russian Olympic champions, an NHL All-Star team representing Canada barely won, 4 games to 3, with 1 game tied.

The WHA began play in the 1972-1973 season with eight teams (New York, New England, Philadelphia, Cleveland, Chicago, Minnesota, Houston, and Los Angeles) in the United States and four (Quebec, Ottawa, Winnipeg, and Alberta) in Canada. It introduced a 10-minute, sudden-death overtime period to reduce the number of tie games, and it amended the playing rules to help the offense. The WHA also hit the NHL where it hurt most, attempting to sign the best NHL players and contending that the reserve clause in the NHL player contract was invalid. On November 8, a U.S. judge in Philadelphia agreed that the reserve clause cannot be used to prevent NHL players from jumping to the WHA.

NHL Jumpers. The new league signed such NHL stars as Bobby Hull, Derek Sanderson, Gerry

Former Chicago Black Hawks ace Bobby Hull and his wife display the $1-million check he received for signing with the World Hockey Association.

Cheevers, Bernie Parent, and Johnny McKenzie. The Winnipeg Jets of the WHA gave Hull a total of $2.75 million and a 10-year contract as player-coach, with $1 million in cash immediately. The Chicago Black Hawks of the NHL went to court to keep the high-scoring Hull, and Hull was enjoined from playing or coaching in the WHA until the November 8 ruling freed him. The Philadelphia Blazers of the WHA also spent money freely. They signed Sanderson, the Boston Bruins' center, for $2.65 million over five years. They signed Parent, the Toronto goalie, for $700,000 over five years. They signed McKenzie, the tenacious Boston forward, as player-coach for $300,000 over three years.

President Clarence Campbell of the NHL seemed unconcerned, saying in Parent's case, "I'll be impressed when he gets the dough." But NHL club owners found themselves caught in a bidding war, and they paid dearly. For example, the New York Rangers of the NHL gave new contracts of $200,000 a year to Brad Park, Rod Gilbert, and Vic Hadfield, and $150,000 to Walt Tkaczuk. Three years before, they paid salaries of $12,000 to Park and $14,000 to Tkaczuk. A lawyer close to the scene said that almost every NHL player would at least double his salary in 1972.

Canada-Russia. Thirty-five of those highly paid stars formed Team Canada to oppose the Russians in four games in Canada and four in Moscow in Sep-

Standings in National Hockey League

East Division	W.	L.	T.	Pts.
Boston	54	13	11	119
New York	48	17	13	109
Montreal	46	16	16	108
Toronto	33	31	14	80
Detroit	33	35	10	76
Buffalo	16	43	19	51
Vancouver	20	50	8	48

West Division	W.	L.	T.	Pts.
Chicago	46	17	15	107
Minnesota	37	29	12	86
St. Louis	28	39	11	67
Pittsburgh	26	38	14	66
Philadelphia	26	38	14	66
California	21	39	18	60
Los Angeles	20	49	9	49

Scoring Leaders	Games	Goals	Assists	Points
Phil Esposito, Boston	76	66	67	133
Bobby Orr, Boston	76	37	80	117
Jean Ratelle, New York	63	46	63	109
Vic Hadfield, New York	78	50	56	106
Rod Gilbert, New York	73	43	54	97
Frank Mahovlich, Montreal	76	43	53	96
Bobby Hull, Chicago	78	50	43	93
Yvan Cournoyer, Montreal	73	47	36	83
John Bucyk, Boston	78	32	51	83
Bobby Clarke, Philadelphia	78	35	46	81
Jacques Lamaire, Montreal	77	32	49	81
Fred Stanfield, Boston	78	23	56	79
Marcel Dionne, Detroit	78	28	49	77
Pit Martin, Chicago	78	24	51	75
Richard Martin, Buffalo	73	44	30	74

Leading Goalies	Games	Goals against	Avg.
Tony Esposito, Chicago	48	82	1.76
Gary Smith, Chicago	28	62	2.41
Gerry Desjardins, Chicago	6	21	3.50
Chicago Totals	78	166	2.12
Lorne Worsley, Minnesota	34	68	2.12
Cesare Maniago, Minnesota	43	112	2.64
Gilles Gilbert, Minnesota	4	11	3.02
Minnesota Totals	78	191	2.44
Gilles Villemure, New York	37	74	2.08
Ed Giacomin, New York	44	115	2.70
New York Totals	78	192	2.46

Awards

Calder Trophy (best rookie)
Ken Dryden, Montreal.

Hart Trophy (most valuable player)
Bobby Orr, Boston.

Lady Byng Trophy (sportsmanship)
Jean Ratelle, New York.

Norris Trophy (best defenseman)
Bobby Orr, Boston.

Ross Trophy (leading scorer)
Phil Esposito, Boston.

Smythe Trophy (most valuable in Stanley Cup play)
Bobby Orr, Boston.

Vezina Trophy (leading goalie)
Tony Esposito and Gary Smith, Chicago.

tember. Although the WHA jumpers were barred and Bobby Orr, the NHL's best player, was recovering from surgery and unavailable, the Canadians were sure they would win all eight games. They laughed at the Russians' inexpensive skates and helmets. But when they played, all laughing stopped.

In the first game, in Toronto, Team Canada took a 2-0 lead in the first 6½ minutes, but the Russians won, 7-3, on conditioning, speed, and better passing. As Johnny Peirson, a former NHL player, said, "It's nice to be in on history, but I didn't think it would be Dunkirk."

After four games in Canada, the Russians led, 2 games to 1, with 1 tie. The Russians then won the first game in Moscow, giving them a 3-1 series lead. Team Canada won the last three games, however, each on a goal by Paul Henderson of Toronto.

Bruins' Success. In the NHL's 1971-1972 season, the Bruins won the East Division title, the Black Hawks won the West, and the Bruins defeated the Rangers in the Stanley Cup play-off finals. Orr won three trophies – Most Valuable Player in the regular season, most valuable in the play-offs, and outstanding defenseman. He was second in scoring to teammate Phil Esposito, who led for the third time in four years. Orr had knee surgery in June and was used sparingly as the new season began. Frank Litsky

HOME FURNISHINGS. See INTERIOR DESIGN.

HONDURAS. See LATIN AMERICA.

Major U.S. Horse Races of 1972

Race	Winner	Value to Winner
Arlington-Wash. Futurity	Shecky Greene	$103,020
Beldame Handicap	Susan's Girl	67,680
Belmont Futurity	Secretariat	82,320
Belmont Stakes	Riva Ridge	93,540
Champagne Stakes	Stop the Music	87,900
Coaching Club American Oaks	Summer Guest	66,360
Florida Derby	Upper Case	107,760
Garden State Stakes	Secretariat	179,199
Hollywood Derby	Riva Ridge	59,900
Hollywood Gold Cup	Quack	100,000
Jockey Club Gold Cup	Autobiography	68,220
Kentucky Derby	Riva Ridge	140,300
Man o' War Stakes	Typecast	70,380
Preakness Stakes	Bee Bee Bee	135,300
Santa Anita Handicap	Triple Bend	105,000
Washington, D.C. Int'l.	Droll Role	100,000
Woodward Stakes	Key to the Mint	69,300

Major U.S. Harness Races of 1972

Race	Winner	Value to Winner
Cane Futurity Pace	Hilarious Way	$53,596
Hambletonian	Super Bowl	59,545
Kentucky Futurity	Super Bowl	30,915
Little Brown Jug	Strike Out	52,982
Messenger Pace	Silent Majority	77,366
Roosevelt International	Speedy Crown	62,500
Yonkers Futurity	Super Bowl	46,548

HORSE RACING. Clear-cut champions emerged only from the 2-year-old crop of horses in 1972. La Prevoyante, a Canadian-bred filly, and the colt Secretariat outclassed their competition consistently and impressively.

La Prevoyante was undefeated, racing both in Canada and in the United States; Secretariat, which came from the same Meadow Stable as Kentucky Derby winner Riva Ridge, lost just twice. This included a disqualification in the Champagne Stakes as the result of bumping Stop the Music, which was declared the winner.

Riva Ridge Was Foiled in its quest for the Triple Crown when longshot Bee Bee Bee won the Preakness in May. Bee Bee Bee ran in front all the way on a sloppy track. Riva Ridge was fourth in the Preakness, after taking the Kentucky Derby by three and a quarter lengths over No Le Hace and Hold Your Peace. He rebounded in the Belmont Stakes in June, winning by a length and a half over Ruritania.

Riva Ridge's chances of becoming Horse of the Year were diminished, however, by its performance in later races. Canonero II, the 1971 Kentucky Derby winner, defeated Riva Ridge before an injury forced Canonero's permanent retirement to stud. Archrival 3-year-old Key to the Mint pressed Riva Ridge for honors by beating him in the Woodward Stakes, and also won the Travers and Brooklyn Handicap.

Among the more distinguished handicap division performances were those of two West Coast horses, the 4-year-old filly Convenience and 6-year-old mare Typecast. They alternated in finishing ahead of each other in California stakes so frequently that a match race was arranged at Hollywood Park on June 17, with a winner-take-all purse of $250,000. Typecast was favored, but lost to Convenience by a head. Typecast subsequently beat males in the Hollywood Park Invitational Turf Handicap and in the Man o' War Stakes. Summer Guest, Susan's Girl, and Numbered Account stood out among the 3 year olds.

Racing's reputation suffered from the discovery of several "ringers" – runners competing under the identity of inferior horses to accomplish betting coups – and derogatory testimony before a House Select Committee investigating corruption in sports. Policing agents within racing uncovered evidence and instituted legal prosecution in the ringer cases. No action resulted from the congressional hearings, held in May and June.

Harness Racing. Super Bowl won the Hambletonian, Kentucky Futurity, and Yonkers Futurity – Triple Crown of Trotting. The top older trotter was Speedy Crown, winner of four consecutive races at Roosevelt Raceway. In pacing, Strike Out won the Little Brown Jug. Albatross went over the $1-million earnings level and paced the fastest mile ever in a race – 1 minute 54 3/5 seconds at Sportsman's Park in Chicago. Jane Goldstein

HOSPITAL. The Department of Health, Education, and Welfare issued interim regulations effective Nov. 4, 1972, that hospitals receiving federal funds under the Hill-Burton Act provide charity care equal to 3 per cent of their operating costs, minus Medicare and Medicaid, or 10 per cent of the Hill-Burton assistance the hospital receives. The proposal caused great concern among hospital directors. Officials of the American Hospital Association said hospitals would have to raise rates to private patients in order to comply. Final regulations were to be determined in March, 1973.

Hospitals struggled to live within the 6 per cent rate increase guidelines established by the U.S. Price Control Commission. As of late summer, more than 574 institutions were still waiting for the government to review their requests that they be allowed to exceed that limit.

The American Hospital Association registered 7,097 hospitals with 1.56 million beds during 1971. The hospitals employed 2.9 million people and had expenditures totaling $28.8 billion, which was an increase of $3.3 billion.

Passavant and Wesley Memorial hospitals in Chicago combined to become a 1,000-bed institution. A total of 140 such mergers were reported between 1962 and 1970. Madison B. Brown

HOTEL. See TRAVEL.

HOUSING. A potential crisis loomed in the U.S. housing industry in 1972 as the federal government became the unwilling owner of more and more inner-city homes. Mortgage foreclosures involving housing programs for poor families rose from 3,686 in 1970 to 5,995 in the first half of 1972. Meanwhile, the number of such mortgage defaults rose from 12,641 at the end of 1970 to 34,972 by June 30, 1972.

The foreclosures were on mortgages granted to poor families under the Housing Act of 1968, which set ambitious housing goals for the nation and caused the Department of Housing and Urban Development (HUD) to lower its standards for insuring home mortgages in inner cities. Because of skyrocketing housing costs, officials estimated that some 25 million households are eligible for some sort of housing subsidy.

An FHA Scandal rocked the housing industry and HUD's Federal Housing Administration (FHA) in 1972. Federal indictments were handed down in several cities, including Detroit, Los Angeles, Newark, New York, Philadelphia, and St. Louis. The indictments charged real estate firms, lending institutions, and FHA officials with falsifying records and reports on homes sold to poor families at inflated prices. An official estimated that the government could lose $200 million in the New York area alone because of the fraudulent practices.

The real losers, however, were the impoverished

Lee Balterman, *Life* © 1972 Time Inc.

An 18-year-old St. Louis public-housing building, the victim of crime, overcrowding, and official neglect, is dynamited to make way for a park.

inner-city residents who were enticed into purchasing overpriced houses. Real estate dealers, loan officers, and government officials conspired to falsify the prospective buyer's credit and earnings reports. They also submitted inflated assessments on the houses to secure FHA-insured mortgages. But many buyers later found that their mortgage payments were too high and that their new homes badly needed repair. As a result, they defaulted on payments, the mortgages were foreclosed, they were evicted, and the government was left holding worthless mortgages on abandoned buildings.

HUD Action. In response, HUD Secretary George W. Romney ordered administrative reforms and set higher standards for approving insured-mortgage applications. The new standards threatened to reduce the number of these mortgages by nearly 50 per cent.

A movement began growing in Congress to drastically alter the housing programs, to which the government has committed about $100 billion. In September, the House Rules Committee killed a $10.6-billion housing bill that would have extended the housing subsidy programs for two years. In October, Romney called for an end to all federally subsidized housing programs or, at least, for allowing the states to administer the programs.

HUD and the Veterans Administration (VA) released a yearlong study of closing costs on housing transactions. The study concluded that self-serving and wasteful practices in the real estate and lending industries were unnecessarily costing home buyers and sellers millions of dollars annually. HUD and the VA instituted procedures designed to hold down closing costs in transactions involving FHA-insured mortgages.

Housing Starts continued at record levels throughout 1972. A record seasonally adjusted annual rate of 2.68 million starts was reached in February. Housing starts then fell off somewhat, but the rate at which new homes were being built was still higher than in 1971. A total of 2 million new housing units were started in 1971. The sharpest gain in 1972 was in single-family homes, most of them in suburban areas. The rate of starts for buildings with five or more family units also increased.

The construction of suburban apartment complexes intended primarily for young single persons gained momentum in 1972. The rising average marriage age and expanding suburban job opportunities contributed to the popularity of this type of housing.

Condominiums accounted for 16 per cent of the nation's housing starts in 1971. In 1972, that figure rose to about 27 per cent. There was a demand for condominiums in every type of housing area, from the inner city to resort and retirement centers. Condominiums were particularly popular as a second home, accounting for 40 per cent of all new developments started in this field in 1972. J. M. Banovetz

HOUSTON

HOUSTON. Rapid growth in the Houston area continued throughout 1972, as a steady influx of large corporations generated new jobs and demands for more homes and offices. Among the corporate offices planning to move to Houston were Signal Oil and Gas Company of Los Angeles; Raymond International, a New York City construction firm; APCO Oil Company from Oklahoma City; and a division of Jones and Laughlin Steel Company from Tulsa, Okla. The business activity has created more than 4,000 high-salaried jobs.

Continuing Growth. Work started on the development of a new, 74-acre Houston Center. When completed, the center will cover 33 blocks of the downtown area. The development, which includes office buildings, hotels, stores, and apartments, will all be built on a platform 50 feet above ground level. Parking garages and transportation facilities will be under the platform, separating pedestrians from vehicles. The project has been under construction since January.

Family income and buying power reflected the area's growth rate. Department store sales increased by 11.3 per cent between August, 1971, and August, 1972, and construction activity was up 6.5 per cent between March, 1971, and March, 1972. Nonagricultural employment rose 4.4 per cent between May, 1971, and May, 1972, and the earnings of factory workers rose 6.6 per cent, to $8,888, during the same period. The U.S. Bureau of the Census reported that the median income for a family living in Houston was $9,876 in 1971, slightly less than the national average.

Despite the growth, Houston's downtown district was threatened by the outlying areas, which enjoyed the greatest share of the business increase. The last two large theaters in the downtown area were scheduled to close, and a major store, Lord and Taylor, announced that it was opening new facilities in an outlying shopping center.

The federal government's new revenue-sharing program promised to help pay for expanding municipal services to accommodate the city's growth. Houston Mayor Louie Welch predicted that the added funds would be used for such improvements as new streets, utility lines, and public transportation and also would enable Houston to avoid a tax increase.

The Crime Rate in Houston declined by 2 per cent in 1971 but still remained substantially above the national average. According to the Uniform Crime Reports released in August, the city's crime rate was 3,519 crimes per 100,000 persons, compared to the national average of 2,907. To help cut the rate still further, Houston was named by the U.S. Department of Justice's Office of Drug Abuse Law Enforcement in March as one of the cities in which special teams of federal, state, and local law-enforcement officers would work to stop the distribution of heroin and other narcotic drugs. J. M. Banovetz

HUNGARY continued its economic reform in 1972 against the background of rumored political and economic differences with Russia. On February 11, Communist Party leader Janos Kadar paid an unscheduled visit to Moscow. Premier Jeno Fock later admitted he had been unable to obtain a firm commitment of a supply until 1985 of Russian raw materials for expanding Hungarian industry.

Russian and Czechoslovak newspapers continued to draw attention to "petit-bourgeois phenomena" in Hungary. In May, Fock said there were no political differences of opinion between the two countries – a statement that the Russian press echoed. The Hungarian press noted repeatedly that there was no special Hungarian "road to Socialism." This and Kadar's pointed references in October to Hungary's loyalty to the principle of central planning suggested attempts to ease Russian misgivings about Hungarian economic policies. Hungary's growing trade links with the West particularly concerned Russian leaders. United States Secretary of State William P. Rogers paid a cordial visit to Hungary in July.

On October 13, Hungary and the United States reached a preliminary agreement on old debts. Hungary agreed to pay $20 million toward claims for property owned by U.S. nationals that was damaged during World War II or nationalized by Hungary since then. In return, the United States said it would back Hungary's request for most-favored-nation status on Hungarian exports to the United States. The agreement must be approved by each nation's government.

Growing Western Ties. In May, the first joint U.S.-Hungarian firm, with equal ownership in each country, was formed in Amsterdam, the Netherlands. It was to promote a Hungarian biochemical invention. New, relatively liberal regulations covering the formation of joint companies with up to 49 per cent foreign participation were published in October. For the first time, they allowed for joint production as well as sales companies.

Hungary continued to play an active role in the Warsaw Pact. In February, it signed a new friendship and mutual assistance treaty with Romania. The domestic political scene remained tranquil, except for a student demonstration on March 15 in Budapest. It marked the anniversary of Hungary's popular 1848 revolution. It had been beaten down by Russian soldiers in 1849.

The government managed to keep inflation in check and to increase exports 20 per cent, while imports went up only 5 per cent. But the growth of labor productivity was still hampered, despite stringent measures against delays and inefficiency, by unfinished investments that tied up scarce capital. In November, the party sought to check a widening gap between income groups. It decided to raise the lowest incomes by 8 per cent and the highest by 4 to 5 per cent.

Chris Cviic

See also EUROPE (Facts in Brief Table).

HUNTING AND FISHING. Hunters and fishermen in the United States spent more than $208 million for licenses, tags, permits, and stamps in 1972, an increase of $16 million over 1971. Fishing-license holders increased by 1,316,814 to a record 25,751,494. Fishermen spent $99,922,221 for licenses, $9 million more than in 1971. Hunting-license holders rose to 15,977,588, an increase of 607,107. And, hunters spent a record $108,597,570 for licenses and permits, an increase of nearly $7 million.

However, license-tag sales are only an indication of the growth of the two sports. Many states do not require fishing licenses for those over retirement age and those below certain ages. Some who hunt and fish in more than one state may be counted more than once. A safe estimate would probably be that the United States had about 50 million fishermen and about 20 million hunters in 1972.

License revenues help states finance fish and wildlife conservation and management activities, and federal funds are allocated according to the number of licenses sold in each state. For the fiscal year ended June 30, 1972, the federal government apportioned $47,890,000.

DDT Ban. One of the most important developments in the outdoor field was the ban on the use of DDT for all but limited public-health use. William D. Ruckelshaus, administrator of the Environmental Protection Agency (EPA), announced the ban in June. It was effective Dec. 31, 1972. The action followed petitions by conservation groups asking that commercial shipments of DDT across state lines be stopped. The groups are seriously concerned for the health of man as well as fish and wildlife, because scientific evidence indicates that DDT accumulates in the cells of man and in a variety of plants and animals.

Salt-Water Fishing. The Outdoor Writers Association of America, meeting at Mazatlán, Mexico, in June, expressed concern over the numbers of big-game fish species being taken from ocean waters by Japanese commercial fishing vessels. Japanese commercial fishing had doubled and redoubled in the 1960s, particularly in the eastern Pacific Ocean, according to John S. Gottschalk, associate director for recreational resources of the National Marine Fisheries Service. Legislation preventing such commercial fishing in U.S. waters seems imminent.

International agreements signed by Canada, Great Britain, Norway, the United States, and other countries curtailed commercial netting of Atlantic salmon and increased salmon sport fishing. The change was most noted in Canadian waters, where nets were removed from river mouths. Commercial netting of Atlantic salmon near the polar icecap, most of which is done by the Danes, will be reduced. Denmark agreed on December 20 to phase out high-seas salmon fishing by 1976.

Jack Samson

See also FISHING INDUSTRY.

Russia's Irena Rodnina and Alexei Oulanov won a gold medal at the Olympic Games for their stunning performance in the figure skating for pairs.

ICE SKATING. European men and women won most of the major ice skating honors in 1972. The most successful Americans were three young women from Illinois – Northbrook's Dianne Holum, 20, and Anne Henning, 16, in speed skating and 18-year-old Janet Lynn of Rockford in figure skating.

Miss Holum won the 1,500-meter gold medal and Miss Henning the 500-meter gold medal in the Winter Olympics, held in February in Sapporo, Japan. Then, with Miss Henning back in high school, Miss Holum placed second in the world sprint championships in Eskilstuna, Sweden, and third in the world championships in Heerenveen, the Netherlands. She also won the 500-meter title in Heerenveen.

Sweep for Schenk. The most impressive speed skater of all was Ard Schenk, a tall, handsome, 27-year-old Dutch physiotherapist who won 3 of the 4 Olympic titles at Sapporo. In capturing his third consecutive world championship, he became the first man in 60 years to sweep the four races – 500 meters, 1,500 meters, 5,000 meters, and 10,000 meters. The Dutch were so grateful that they named a tulip after him. In August, Schenk and 13 other Europeans signed professional contracts for a series of European competitions in 1973.

The Netherlands provided both world and European champions – Schenk among the men and Attje Keulen-Deelstra, 34, among the women. The world sprint champions were Leo Linkovesi, 24, of Finland, and Monika Pflug, 17, of West Germany. Miss Pflug, an Olympic champion, was injured in an accident in June, but was winning again in November.

In Figure Skating, the three major competitions were the Olympic Games and the world and European championships. The same skaters won all three – Ondrej Nepela of Czechoslovakia in men's singles, Beatrix Schuba of Austria in women's singles, and Irena Rodnina and Alexei Oulanov of Russia in pairs.

None wanted to continue. Nepela, a 21-year-old law student, hoped to retire, saying simply, "I'm getting tired." Miss Schuba, 20, turned professional, and Miss Rodnina and Oulanov were involved in romances with other Russian skaters.

In the Olympics, the U.S. championships at Long Beach, Calif., in January, and the world championships at Calgary, Canada, in March, the radiant Miss Lynn drew the biggest cheers. Her dazzling, acrobatic exhibitions of free skating helped her gain her fourth straight U.S. title.

Ken Shelley and Jo Jo Starbuck of Downey, Calif., won their third consecutive U.S. pairs title and placed third in the world championships and fourth in the Olympics. Shelley won the U.S. singles title and was fourth in the Olympics. Frank Litsky

See also OLYMPIC GAMES.

IDAHO. See STATE GOVERNMENT.

ILLINOIS. See CHICAGO; STATE GOVERNMENT.

IMMIGRATION AND EMIGRATION. Congress in 1972 attempted to impose penalties on U.S. employers who knowingly hire illegal aliens. The bill passed the House on September 12. However, it expired in the Senate Judiciary Committee, where it was held without action until the end of the 92nd Congress. Under the bill's provisions, the U.S. attorney general would serve warning on an employer that he had violated the law, after the first offense. After the second violation, the employer would be fined $500 for each alien that he knowingly hired.

United States officials estimated there were about 1.5 million illegal aliens in the country. Many were Mexicans employed at substandard wages on large farms and ranches. Under the present law, an alien is deported once he is apprehended, but no action is taken against his employer.

To keep their citizenship alive, children living abroad and born to a U.S. citizen and an alien parent must spend a certain amount of time in the United States when they are between the ages of 14 and 28. This period was reduced from five years to two years by an amendment to the Immigration and Naturalization Act passed by Congress on October 14.

In fiscal 1972, 384,685 immigrants were admitted to the United States, compared with 370,478 in 1971. During the same period, 116,215 aliens became citizens; 116,266 were deported. William McGaffin

INCOME TAX. See TAXATION.

INDIA. New Year's Day of 1972 found India still aglow with the joy of a victory won a fortnight earlier. There was plenty to celebrate. The "14-Day War" of December, 1971, left Pakistan defeated and cut to half its former size. India held more than 90,000 Pakistani prisoners. And – although all this had been achieved at a cost of 2,473 men killed, 6,653 wounded, and 2,238 missing, with a cost to the treasury of about $500 million – the victory united the nation as never before. In the words of a New Delhi editor, "Every Indian felt himself 10 feet tall."

It was also a time of triumph for Prime Minister Indira Gandhi. Her Congress Party had swept the national polls in March, 1971, under her slogan of "Down with Poverty!" In March, 1972, the party exploited the war victory for a similar sweep in the state (provincial) elections. It won 1,926 provincial assembly seats, followed by the pro-Moscow Communists, who took 112 seats, and the rightist Jan Sangh, with 104. The victory at the local polls was all the more important because Mrs. Gandhi had now driven most of her own party's old and conservative bosses out. More powerful than her father, Jawaharlal Nehru, had been, the prime minister was now free to carry out her radical program of renovating India and its society.

Economic Reversals. It soon became apparent, however, that fortune had turned hostile. Monsoon rains came late, and the drought was severe. Suddenly, a country that only a few months earlier had expected to have surplus grain realized it did not have enough. The stockpile of 9 million tons left over from 1971 shrank rapidly. Some 930,000 tons of it was shipped to Bangladesh. By November, the leaders in New Delhi were warning that grain would have to be imported. The problem was made more acute by the United States, which leaned toward Pakistan in 1971, and now had all but cut off aid to India. The feared shortages soon began to drive the prices up, and there were riots.

The grain shortage was matched by the continued stagnation in industry, whose growth rate was put at less than 3 per cent. Not the least of the problems was the crushing cost – estimated at about $640 million a year – of servicing India's foreign debts, and the reluctance of the "have" nations to give or even lend generously. With the family-planning program lagging, the population of about 560 million kept growing by about 14 million a year.

Perhaps the most dangerous political problem was tied to the failure to keep the promise of "Down with Poverty!" Its essential part was the pledge to set low ceilings on landholdings, and to give the land thus obtained to the perhaps 100 million landless peasants. Mrs. Gandhi's difficulty was that while she had changed the top crust of the Congress Party, its lower echelons were still controlled by landlords and well-

Prime Minister Indira Gandhi attends ceremony at the Red Fort in New Delhi in August to mark the 25th anniversary of India's independence.

to-do peasants fiercely opposed to any major changes in land ownership. There were other considerations as well. In November, troops were rushed to the state of Andra Pradesh to quell riots provoked by job discrimination in favor of people from the former princely state of Hyderabad.

Turn to the Left. Abroad, as at home, India leaned to the left. Its relations with the United States drifted from bad to worse, with Washington, D.C., showing no great inclination to improve them. By contrast, the ties with Moscow grew stronger. The very close bonds with Bangladesh were marred only by growing Bengali resentments against India's dominant influence.

Simla Accord. The deadly feud with Pakistan was seemingly ended in July when Prime Minister Gandhi met President Zulfikar Ali Bhutto at the mountain resort of Simla, near New Delhi. There, Mrs. Gandhi agreed to withdraw Indian troops from nearly all occupied areas. Although the two leaders agreed to avoid war over Kashmir, there were repeated clashes on the border. But it was not until December 7 that the two countries resolved a deadlock that had developed over designating a cease-fire line. They agreed to regard the new line as a tentative boundary pending a final settlement as to who has sovereignty over Kashmir. Mark Gayn

See also ASIA (Facts in Brief Table).

INDIAN, AMERICAN. About 500 protesting American Indians, calling themselves the Trail of Broken Treaties caravan, seized control of the Bureau of Indian Affairs (BIA) Building in Washington, D.C., on Nov. 2, 1972. A week of protest had been scheduled by the militant American Indian Movement, and its leaders demanded that the federal government provide food and lodging for them in the capital. They vowed to hold the BIA building until adequate facilities were provided.

The Indians presented government officials with a list of 20 demands, including the enforcement of existing treaties, reforms in ownership and control of natural resources on Indian lands, and replacement of the BIA with an Indian-operated agency. Negotiators talked for several days, but made no progress. The demonstrators charged that the government was interested only in evicting them. A district court ordered the Indians to leave, but an appellate court delayed the order to avoid a police confrontation.

On November 7, the White House stepped into the dispute. Aides of President Richard M. Nixon promised that the protesters would not be prosecuted for taking over the building, and agreed to set up a panel to study Indian grievances.

The Indians left the following day but took along Indian artifacts and paintings and thousands of government documents. They said the papers con-

A group of militant American Indians guard the entrance to the Bureau of Indian Affairs Building, which they seized and occupied in November.

tained evidence against former Western senators and congressmen who had exploited the Indians. Damage to the BIA Building was estimated at more than $500,000. Some tribal leaders criticized the militants for their actions and the government for not conferring with elected Indian leaders.

In December, there was an extensive shakeup in the BIA and related Department of Interior agencies. Louis R. Bruce, commissioner of Indian affairs, and his deputy, John O. Crow, were two of the officials removed from their posts.

Indian Gains. On November 11, a U.S. district court ordered the Department of the Interior to revise its regulations affecting water diversion from the Truckee River, which feeds Pyramid Lake in Nevada. The court ruled that enough water must flow into the lake to keep it at its present level.

Pyramid Lake lies on a Paiute reservation, and is the main economic support of these Indians. The diversion of water from the Truckee River to irrigate land near Reno has caused the lake water level to drop about a foot a year, endangering fish in the lake. The water level has dropped 70 feet since 1908.

The BIA on July 17 offered to place all of its operations affecting the Navajos under the tribe's own control. The action was viewed as a major step in keeping with President Nixon's pledge to increase Indian control of their own affairs. The Navajos, the nation's largest tribe, with 134,000 members, accepted the offer. However, Secretary of the Interior Rogers C. B. Morton, said that turning over control to the Navajos would require detailed planning.

Other Developments. On January 12, Commissioner Bruce announced that the government was ending its policy of encouraging Indians to relocate in large cities. The relocation program had created Indian ghettos in the cities. Bruce said that BIA programs were being revised to stress coordinated planning for reservation development, job training for Indians on their reservations, protection of Indian resources, construction of improved roads on reservations, and increased tribal control over Indian education.

Morton issued new regulations on June 23, extending preference to Indian BIA employees in promotion, training, and reassignment. On August 14, four non-Indian BIA employees filed a suit charging that the preference policy was unconstitutional and violated the Civil Rights Act of 1964.

In July, the government began distributing the $962.5 million allocated to Indians, Eskimos, and Aleuts as part of the Alaska native land claims settlement. In late August, officials of the Federal Trade Commission and the BIA began hearings at the Navajo reservation in Arizona to probe the practices of nearly 150 white traders. Indians charged that they were flagrantly cheated by whites trading on the reservations. Andrew L. Newman

INDIANA. See State Government.

INDONESIA. Although most Asian countries accepted China as a major force in Asia, General Suharto followed a far more cautious policy in 1972. Indonesia was the only Asian nation not seeking trade with China. In part, his wariness was caused by Indonesia's large Chinese minority of nearly 3 million, only half of whom were Indonesian citizens. A substantial number of them were suspected of being used by Peking.

Mindful of the disruptive role the now-banned Communist Party had played under the Sukarno regime, General Suharto sought a role independent from the world's power blocs. To this end, his government sharply protested an attempt by Russia in March to secure the use of facilities at the Singapore naval base adjacent to Sumatra. Indonesia also objected to a proposal made by Russia, Japan, Great Britain, and the United States to internationalize the Strait of Malacca. In addition, Indonesia refused any attempts to normalize relations with Peking until China returned Indonesian Communist refugees being sheltered in Peking. To counter what was regarded as a resurgence of Communist influence, Suharto encouraged international cooperation in Indochina through the Association of Southeast Asian Nations.

Foreign Aid. In February, Suharto visited Australia. He worked out important agreements involving Australian economic aid, including investments and technical assistance, as well as military support. This resulted in Australia supplying Indonesia with military aircraft and training facilities in Australia for members of the Indonesian Air Force. Suharto also conferred with President Ferdinand E. Marcos of the Philippines on Southeast Asia security matters.

Suharto continued to diversify his dependence on foreign aid. The United States, which furnished about $203 million in aid, was the largest supporter, but it was closely followed by Japan. The Japanese agreed to provide about $200 million in credits for oil development.

The Economy. Internally, Indonesia continued its tough economic policies to curb inflation, stimulate food production, reduce unemployment, and diversify production. Food production was up, exceeding 12.5 million tons of rice for the year, and Sumatran tobacco crops were back on the world market on a large scale. The economic picture was good, and the increase in savings enabled the government to cut interest rates.

The Suharto government kept a tight rein on political activities within the country. In August, 2,225 criminals were released, and the sentences of 8,222 other prisoners, including political offenders, were reduced to mark the 27th anniversary of Indonesian independence. But, a student protest against a government exhibition in Djakarta that same month was abruptly quashed. John N. Stalker

See also Asia (Facts in Brief Table).

INSURANCE. Legislatures of 39 states debated no-fault automobile liability insurance in 1972, but only 4–Connecticut, Maryland, Michigan, and New Jersey–enacted laws. Illinois' law, which was to become effective on Jan. 1, 1972, never went into operation. A circuit court judge held it unconstitutional on Dec. 29, 1971, and the state supreme court upheld that ruling on March 24. The four new states join Massachusetts and Florida as the only states that limit a victim's rights to bring suit under the traditional tort (or fault) liability system. The Michigan law is to become effective on Oct. 1, 1973. The others became effective on Jan. 1, 1973.

The major intent of these laws is to enable auto-accident victims to be reimbursed promptly by their own insurers for their net economic loss, including medical bills and salary, without regard to who was at fault in the accident. Who is subject to the law, what may be collected by a victim, and at what point the victim may sue for damages beyond that already received from his or her own insurer, are defined in varying ways in each of the state laws. Delaware, Minnesota, Oregon, and South Dakota have statutes providing no-fault benefits, but these laws do not restrict the victim's right to sue for damages.

Congressional Efforts. Attempts by Senators Philip A. Hart (D., Mich.) and Warren G. Magnuson (D., Wash.) to win enactment of a federal minimum standards no-fault law collapsed on August 8, when the Senate voted, 49-46, to send the bill to the Judiciary Committee, where it died. The broad Hart-Magnuson measure would have effectively eliminated all automobile tort liability suits. The Administration preferred enactment of no-fault laws by the states. Nevertheless, Administration spokesmen warned on several occasions that a federal system might be sought if the states failed to act promptly on the matter.

Bumper Standards. Major automobile insurers announced at midyear that they would grant discounts ranging from 5 to 20 per cent on collision insurance policies for 1973 model automobiles equipped with energy-absorbing bumpers. The bumpers must be capable of withstanding 5- to 10-mile-per hour crash impacts without damage to the vehicle. Several manufacturers had bumpers based on federal standards on their 1973 models.

Workmen's Compensation. The National Commission on State Workmen's Compensation Laws, authorized by the Occupational Safety and Health Act of 1970, reported its findings on July 31. "The present performance of the program is unsatisfactory . . . and extensive reforms are essential," the commission said. The commission found that many state benefits are "inadequate" and "inequitable."

The commission set July 1, 1975, as the target date for voluntary state compliance with recommended benefit liberalizations, and a permanent federal commission to aid the states in the task. Emanuel Levy

INTERIOR DESIGN and home-furnishings selections combined a note of fashion, color, and comfort in 1972. The highlight of the year was a return to the mood of the 1920s, with overstuffed chairs and cushy sofas. Most offerings were small in scale and covered in bright prints and patterns.

Manufacturers made available a choice of styles–from Early American through Mediterranean, transitional, contemporary, and far-out modern. But it was Mediterranean that was the top seller in every category except overstuffed. Mediterranean designs were smaller in scale and less decorative in trim and carvings than in recent years.

Contemporary furnishings were made of steel, wood, leather, glass, fabric, metals, cane, cork, and all types of plastics. The glossiness and brightness of the 1960s was gone from contemporary styles, and more natural materials were used with the man-made plastics, steel, and glass.

The Southern Furniture Market, held from October 20 to 27, in High Point, N.C., presented curved seating without sharp corners. New designs emphasized space, size, and furniture arrangements. One seating group consisted of eight pieces of polyurethane, all in cubical shapes and in sizes that could be used interchangeably for seats, backs, and arms. Natural finishes and a trend toward more informal living was evident in all styles.

Colorful Fabrics. Soft pastels and blends of subdued patterns and stripes predominated in upholstery fabrics. Texture continued to be important throughout the year, and lush velvet was the most popular. Manufacturers emphasized the durability of coverings and used synthetics such as olefins, acrylics, polyesters, and nylon. Mixtures of cotton and rayon fibers were featured on the higher-priced selections. Stripes predominated in fabric designs, and there was a trend toward jacquard stripes. Their colors were also bright, with such combinations as purple and gray and emerald green and white.

Oriental design influences dominated accessories, lamps, and lighting. Clocks, mirrors, consoles, and art objects were hand-carved and hand-painted ceramics or combinations of natural materials. Contemporary accessories made use of plastic, chrome, and glass, such as shining Parson's tables, chrome étagères, and glass cocktail and bunching tables.

Floor Coverings. Soft-surface floor coverings–carpeting and area rugs–had the look of luxury and promised hard, long wear. There were many plush textures, along with shags and low-level piles. Dyeing and printing techniques developed by manufacturers made exciting floral prints and patterns possible. Some lines were available in as many as 18 colors. Manufacturers considered nylon fiber to be the fastest-growing one in carpeting because it wears well, cleans easily, and is moderately priced.

Hard-surface floorings–linoleum, asphalt tile, and vinyl–also were colorful and had visual appeal.

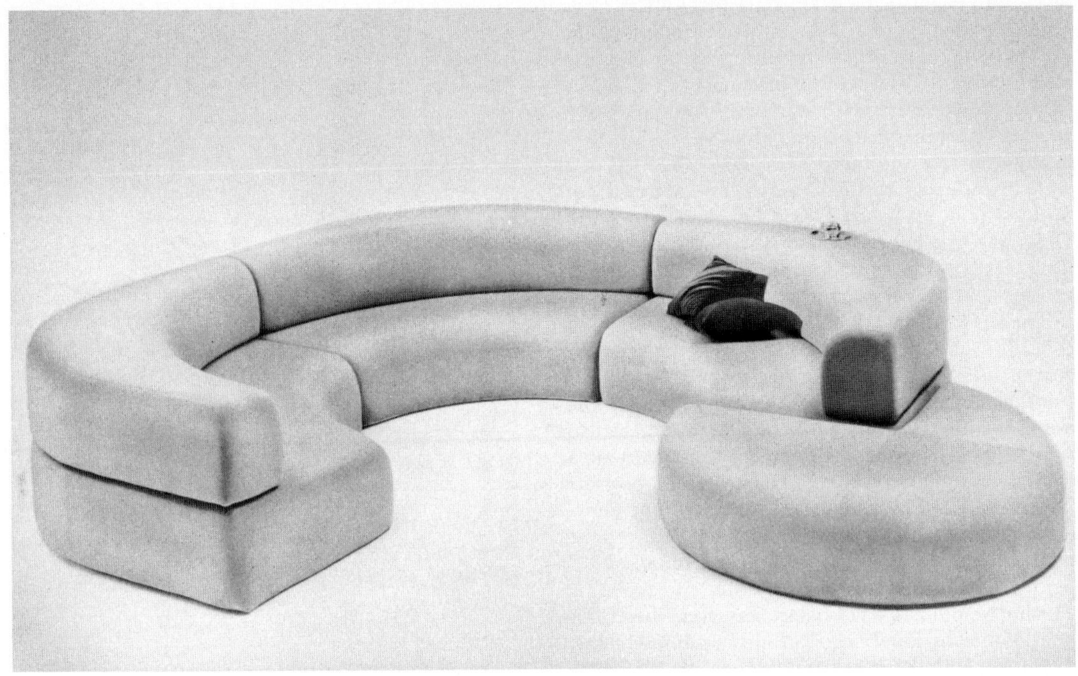

Polyurethane seating units without sharp corners were designed for Stendig by Ennio Chiggio so buyers may arrange them in any way desired.

There were floral patterns, geometrics, and mosaic and brick designs. Many featured easy-care and no-wax surfaces.

A report released in September by Wheat First Securities of Richmond, Va., ranked 1972 as the biggest in the furniture industry's history, based on the individual earnings of manufacturers.

Industry Awards. The Furniture Council of the Society of the Plastics Industry presented Poly Awards to manufacturers for innovative use of polymers in home furnishings. Awards were announced during the Winter International Home Furnishings Market in January at the American Furniture Mart in Chicago. The top award went to Burris Industries of High Point, N.C., for the "Olympia" upholstered chair utilizing molded polyurethane foam. Raymond A. Helmers, editor and publisher of *Furniture Design & Manufacturing* magazine was named Polymer Man of the Year.

The Home Furnishings Industry Institute in Chicago presented its first award for services to consumers to Jane Roggers on May 11, 1972. She was cited for the educational consumer-service program she executed as advertising director of the Dayton Company in Minneapolis, Minn.

Fabric designer Vera Neumann, known professionally as Vera, received the National Home Fashions League Trailblazer Award at the group's convention on May 20 in New York City. Helen C. Schubert

INTERNATIONAL LIVE STOCK EXPOSITION. A tiny, 12-year-old girl, blonde Kris Lindskog of Prophetstown, Ill., showed Bold Move, the crossbred Simmental-Hereford steer that won the grand championship 1972 International Live Stock Exposition held from November 23 to 28 in Chicago.

She later watched her 1,305-pound champion sell for $7.35 a pound at auction. The reserve grand champion, or runner-up, was a Hereford steer entered by Mike Gottschalk of Darien, Wis. Bold Move was also judged champion in the junior show.

The grand champion barrow (hog), named KOK, weighed 220 pounds and sold for $35 a pound. The purebred Chester White was owned and shown by William Baumgartner & Sons of Windsor, Ill. Reserve champion barrow, a crossbred Chester White-Duroc, was shown by Dave Huinker of Ames, Iowa. A crossbred Hampshire-Chester White, entered by Roger Maahs of Lincoln, Nebr., was champion barrow in the junior show.

Grand champion wether lamb was a 125-pound Hampshire belonging to Warren Finder, an 18-year-old from Stoughton, Wis. The lamb also was named champion in the junior competition.

A feeder cattle event in which five head of western calves are shown as a group was added to the 1972 show. The winners of the new event were Limousin-Shorthorn crossbreeds raised on the Hollers Ranch, near Cody, Nebr. Morris E. Rogers

INTERNATIONAL TRADE AND FINANCE. Economic relations among nations – trade, tourism, and exchanges of currency – showed a great underlying resiliency in 1972. This was reassuring after 1971's turmoil and crises, the worst in nearly a quarter of a century. Currency-exchange values were uncertain during the year and there were grave warnings of a wave of trade restrictions. Nevertheless, international business went on as usual, world trade continued to grow, and the stage was set for important negotiations in 1973 aimed at better international "rules of conduct" in both the monetary and trade fields.

The key to international transactions remained in the ability of traders and private citizens to exchange currencies. As 1971 ended, the Group of 10 – the 10 leading industrial nations – gathered in the Gothic administration building of the Smithsonian Institution in Washington, D.C. Under the threat of a drying up of international business and possible recessions, they agreed to a new set of currency-exchange rates. The new rates effectively reduced the international value of the U.S. dollar by about 12 per cent and raised the value of other currencies by varying amounts. Never before had there been this kind of international negotiation of exchange rates.

The World's Bankers and financiers were inherently skeptical, however, and they showed their doubts about the new pattern of exchange rates at various times in 1972. The resulting massive flows of funds in and out of the various currencies yielded a few more "crises" in 1972. The exchange rate of a particularly important currency, the British pound, was toppled within six months of the Smithsonian agreement as the markets decided it had been pegged too high. In late June, the British government set the pound free to "float" in daily trading in the currency-exchange markets. It floated mainly downward, providing an effective devaluation of the pound. International traders soon learned to cope with the situation and, at year's end, business was proceeding as usual.

Japan continued to show a huge surplus in trade and overall international payments, despite the agreement at the Smithsonian that the yen would be revalued upward against the dollar by 16.9 per cent. There was a huge flow of funds into Japan in 1972 in expectation of a further upward revaluation. As the year ended, it was widely anticipated that the yen's value would be altered upward again, creating a potentially thorny international problem for Japan.

In short, the world was growing more accustomed to uncertainty about currency-exchange rates than had been the case until the late 1960s. American tourists in Europe found that hotels (but not major banks) insisted on discounts when they exchanged U.S. dollars or dollar traveler's checks. Smart Americans soon learned to bring traveler's checks in German marks or Swiss francs, purchased before they left home. Japanese shipbuilding companies with long-term contracts took a big loss in profits from the upward change in the value of the yen.

United States Secretary of Commerce Peter G. Peterson, with glasses, strolls with Russian trade officials during U.S.-Soviet trade talks in August.

Switzerland imposed a "negative interest rate" – a penalty of 2 per cent every three months – on foreign accounts to keep unwanted dollars and other foreign currencies out. This further complicated international dealings for investors.

World Trade was hardly interrupted by these exchange complications. Trade between nations, measured by the value of exports, grew to an annual rate of $368 billion by mid-1972, up 18 per cent from mid-1971. Part of the increase merely reflected higher prices, however. Exports and imports continued to rise for the United States and other nations, although the currency-value changes altered trade in some ways. For example, fewer Japanese cars were sold in the United States. Equally important, perhaps, was the fact that neither the European Community (Common Market) nor any single major trading nation introduced important trade restrictions. Japan actually lowered its tariffs slightly and removed a few other import restrictions.

As trade, tourism, and international investment continued to flow, the year was marked by three major developments:

- Great Britain, Ireland, and Denmark qualified for membership in the Common Market 14 years after its birth – but only after lengthy and difficult negotiations. Norway also qualified, but that nation's voters rejected membership in a referendum in September. Sweden, Austria, Switzerland, and Finland – none of which wanted full membership – negotiated their own trade agreements with the market. The result was that after Jan. 1, 1973, nearly all of Western Europe will be gradually changing to a vast tariff-free trading area. Many restrictions still remained, however, on farm products moving between market members and nonmembers.

▪ The annual meeting of the International Monetary Fund (IMF) in Washington, D.C., in late September, formally set in motion machinery for negotiating a new world monetary system. The aim was to establish a more modern set of international rules on changes in currency-exchange rates and other measures for correcting the international balance of payments. This would remove the most serious flaw in the old system, which allowed chronic national deficits or surpluses. The old system resulted in repeated currency "crises" that caused difficulties for both traders and governments.

▪ A major change in trade relations was initiated between the United States and Russia. A formal trade agreement was signed, covering such matters as settlement of old World War II lend-lease debts and extension of new credits to Russia. Because of a very poor grain harvest, the Russians bought nearly one-fourth of the U.S. wheat crop, and other grains. Major deals were being negotiated covering such items as U.S. computers, Russian natural gas, and even U.S. machinery to produce table flatware. Trade possibilities with China began to open up as well, as President Richard M. Nixon abolished most of the restrictions on both U.S. exports and imports.

The Less-Developed Countries won nine seats on the Committee of 20 – 20 nations that will negotiate the reform of the monetary system. The best news of the year for the poor countries was the resumption of expansion and prosperity in the industrial countries, after stagnation and even recession in 1970 and 1971. This led to a predictable expansion of the exports of the less-developed countries.

The United States, despite the devaluation of the dollar at the end of 1971, showed an enormous trade deficit in 1972 of nearly $6 billion. However, the monthly figures began to pick up slightly as the year proceeded. There had never been any expectation that devaluation – raising the price of imports and reducing export prices – would work quickly to restore the U.S. trade surplus. Observers expected further improvement in 1973, particularly because the United States had the lowest inflation rate among the industrial countries in 1972. The inflation rate throughout Europe was double that of the U.S. third-quarter increase of 3.6 per cent in the consumer price index. Edwin L. Dale, Jr.

See also ECONOMY, THE; Section One, FOCUS ON THE ECONOMY.

IOWA. See STATE GOVERNMENT.

IRAN. A new Middle Eastern refugee problem arose in 1972 when about 60,000 Iranians were suddenly deported from Iraq after living there for years. Many reported their homes and possessions were seized before they were put across the border into Iran. In part, the move was a reaction to Iran's occupation of three islands – Abu Musa, Greater Tunb, and Lesser Tunb – at the head of the Persian Gulf in November, 1971. Iraq claimed, however, that the deportees had entered the country illegally and were competing with Iraqi citizens for jobs while paying no taxes.

Whatever the political reasons, Iranian social services were heavily strained, and extreme hardship was imposed on the refugees. Shah Mohammed Reza Pahlavi pledged funds to build permanent housing in new towns for the refugees.

Periodic border clashes took place during 1972, but Iran's major reaction followed the signing of an Iraqi friendship treaty with Russia in April (see IRAQ). Iranian armored forces crossed the border in strength and attacked Iraqi Army units, causing some casualties. The attack was a reminder of Iran's military superiority and a warning to Iraq not to encourage too much Russian activity in the Persian Gulf area.

President Richard M. Nixon paid a state visit to Iran on May 30 and 31. He assured Shah Pahlavi of continued U.S. support, as Iran placed orders for Phantom jets, SAM missiles, and modern weapons for its 150,000-man army. The shah sought to upgrade it to the strongest fighting force in the Middle East.

Internal Unrest resulted in part from the shah's dictatorial rule and in part from unfulfilled aspirations of the country's growing professional and managerial class and its unemployed intellectuals. In February, a military court in Teheran sentenced 6 alleged Communist guerrillas to death and gave 13 others long prison terms for subversion. Bombs exploded at the tomb of Reza Shah, the ruler's father, an hour before a scheduled wreath-laying ceremony during the Nixon visit. An American military adviser was seriously injured, and an Iranian bystander was killed.

State visits were exchanged with Saudi Arabia and Jordan, while the shah cultivated new links with Egypt. In April, the semiofficial Egyptian newspaper *Al-Ahram* published a 10-page supplement on Iran's development program, and an Iranian delegation attended the first session of the Libyan Arab Socialist Union.

A record-setting budget of $7.3 billion was approved by the Majlis (National Assembly) in March. The World Bank approved loans of $50 million to cover the Iran Industrial Bank's loans to Iranian industry during 1972 and 1973 and $32 million for planned improvements to Iran's Persian Gulf ports. The planned improvements include four deepwater berths for supertankers. William Spencer

See also MIDDLE EAST (Facts in Brief Table).

IRAQ parted company with the majority of oil-producing states on June 1, 1972, as it nationalized all assets of the Iraq Petroleum Company (IPC), a Western group and the principal oil company operating in the country. Iraqi oil shipments to Mediterranean refineries were halted at the same time. The action climaxed a dispute dating back to 1961 when the government of General Abdul Karim Kāsim, Iraq's premier, arbitrarily revoked some of IPC's exploitation rights and seized the North Rumaila oil fields. IPC then limited oil production, so that Iraq's average increase over a 10-year period – 68 per cent – was far below that of other oil-producing states.

A 17 per cent drop in production from 1971 totals during the first quarter of 1972 prompted a government ultimatum to IPC demanding back royalties, expanded production, and a part in management. When the ultimatum expired, IPC was shut down.

With oil providing 58 per cent of Iraq's revenues, the seizure represented a calculated risk that Iraq could manage its own oil operations. During the transition period, the Organization of Arab Petroleum Exporting Countries loaned Iraq $129 million, and Libya loaned $21.6 million (see MIDDLE EAST). As a hopeful sign, the Mosul and Basrah petroleum companies, IPC subsidiaries, continued to operate. The French member of the IPC consortium, Compagnie Francaise des Petroles, was allowed to buy 23.75 per cent of the Kirkuk oil fields' production over a 10-year period.

Russian Treaty. Russia made some political hay out of Iraq's differences with the West as represented by IPC. In April, Iraq and Russia signed a 15-year friendship treaty. Each was bound not to join any alliance directed against the other. Russian Premier Aleksei N. Kosygin visited Iraq to sign the treaty and to open a North Rumaila oil field that had been developed with Russian technical aid. He offered 100 scholarships for technical training in Russia.

As a by-product of Soviet-Iraqi friendship, the Iraq Communist Party was permitted to resume publication of its weekly newspaper. The Cabinet organized in May by President Ahmad Hasan al-Bakr included two Communist ministers. The naming of an American diplomat to open an "American interests section" in the Belgian Embassy in Baghdad suggested relations with the United States might be thawing.

The Economy continued to develop and diversify, despite uncertainty over the nation's oil industry. The new Misraq sulfur mine near Mosul began producing 250,000 tons annually. Barter agreements, repayable in Iraqi crude oil, were reached with Afghanistan, Bulgaria, Poland, and other countries. Iraq contributed $17 million to the Arab Fund for Economic and Social Development William Spencer

See also MIDDLE EAST (Facts in Brief Table).

Iraq seized control of the internationally owned Iraq Petroleum Company, valued at from $500 million to $800 million, on June 1.

IRELAND. Prime Minister Jack Lynch signed the treaty of accession to the European Community (Common Market) on Jan. 22, 1972, in Brussels. In a May 10 referendum, voters overwhelmingly approved market membership, 1,041,880 to 211,888.

The government had estimated that, as a member of the Common Market, Ireland would find its economy growing an average of 5 per cent a year from 1970 to 1978. Employment in industry and services would increase, while jobs in agriculture would continue to diminish. But in 1972, in the face of relentless inflation, and with Europe's highest unemployment rate – nearly 10 per cent – Finance Minister George Colley produced a cautious budget in April. It was not expected to lift growth above the 3 per cent rate.

"Bloody Sunday" in Londonderry, Northern Ireland – the January 30 killing of 13 Roman Catholic demonstrators by British soldiers – caused Ireland to recall its ambassador from London. On February 2, a crowd of 20,000 burned the British Embassy in Dublin. Ireland's government called on Great Britain to pull all troops out of Catholic districts in Northern Ireland and end the internment of suspected terrorists without trial. But when the British Government announced on March 24 that it would assume direct rule over Northern Ireland and hold periodic plebiscites on its reunification with Ireland, Lynch promptly expressed his approval. He called the move a "step forward in seeking a lasting solution" and ordered Ireland's ambassador back to London. Only extremists on each side objected.

The government intensified its crackdown on the illegal Irish Republican Army (IRA). On May 26, Lynch announced the establishment of a special criminal court where three judges would sit without a jury. This followed several cases in which the ordinary courts had acquitted IRA members. In its first four weeks, the special court sent more than 20 men to prison for up to six years, many on charges directly related to IRA membership. Bomb explosions on December 1 in Dublin killed two persons and injured over 100 but helped the government win passage of tough anti-IRA legislation.

Special Referendum. Lynch realized that Article 44 of the 1937 Constitution, recognizing the "special position" of the Roman Catholic Church – as well as laws against birth control and divorce – could stand in the way of Irish reunification. On May 4, he set up an all-party committee to review the constitutional position, and, on October 26, with church acquiescence, he agreed to a referendum on Article 44. On December 7, the voters decided – by a margin of about 5 to 1 – to delete Article 44 from the Constitution. In the same balloting, they decided to lower the voting age to 18. George Scott

See also EUROPE (Facts in Brief Table); NORTHERN IRELAND.

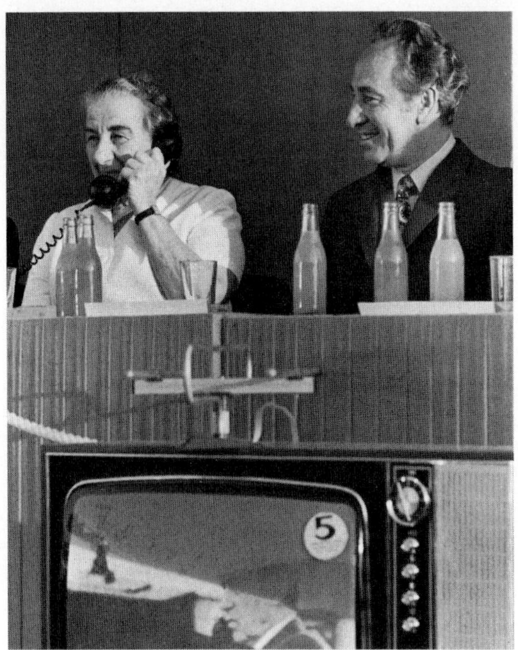

Prime Minister Golda Meir inaugurates Israel's first satellite ground station with a telephone conversation with President Nixon in July.

ISRAEL succeeded in shutting off Arab guerrilla attacks and sabotage in 1972. At the same time, it relaxed its rule and tried to allow residents of the Gaza Strip and Arab zones conquered in the 1967 Six-Day War to run themselves with as little interference as possible.

Israel tried to improve conditions in those areas that breed terrorism. It hoped to give many of the Gaza Strip's 270,000 refugees full status as tax-paying citizens, but encountered some Arab opposition. The special entry permits that had been required for all Arabs in the Gaza Strip were abolished, and work started on 1,200 new housing units there. Israel also allowed Arabs from occupied territories to visit Israel on vacation or for family reunions, and about 100,000 did so during the summer.

In May, Israel held an election in the occupied West Bank region of Jordan. Despite pressure exerted by Palestinian guerrilla organizations to boycott the elections, about 84 per cent of the eligible voters went to the polls and unseated many of the traditional Arab local leaders.

In March, King Hussein I of Jordan proposed setting up a new federated state composed of two equal regions, his Hashemite Kingdom of Jordan and the Israeli-occupied West Bank. His proposal was quickly rejected by Israel and received no support from other Arab nations. See JORDAN.

Arab terrorists struck two tragic blows during the year. Three gunmen sprayed the Lod airport near Tel Aviv with gunfire on May 30, killing 26 and injuring 76 persons. On September 5, 11 Israeli Olympic team members died in an Arab guerrilla assault in Munich, West Germany. See MIDDLE EAST; OLYMPIC GAMES.

New Settlements. Israel moved steadily ahead setting up settlements in land taken from the Arabs during the 1967 war. Typical of this effort was the construction work started at the Gulf of Aqaba, at the southern tip of the Sinai Peninsula. Israel was building 100 houses and workshops there.

"Israel will leave no vacuum in these areas," said Israel Galili, an influential member of Prime Minister Golda Meir's Cabinet. "No area is out of bounds to Jewish settlement."

Since the 1967 war, he added, the government has started 44 new communities for Israeli settlers. Fifteen are on the Golan Heights, captured from Syria; 15 are on the West Bank of the Jordan River; and 14 are in Sinai and the Gaza Strip.

Problems in Africa. Israel came to the parting of the ways with Uganda, a long-time friend in Africa, on March 30. Uganda's President Idi Amin Dada broke diplomatic relations with Israel, and expelled the 70-man Israeli military mission that had been training the Ugandan Army. In November, Chad also severed relations with Israel. Joseph P. Spohn

See also MIDDLE EAST (Facts in Brief Table).

ITALY struggled with political uncertainty and labor unrest in 1972. Emilio Colombo's four-party coalition government fell on January 15 after 17 months in office when Republicans deserted the coalition and Socialists threatened to follow them if a referendum on the 1970 divorce legalization was not quashed. Giulio Andreotti, Christian Democrat leader, took office as prime minister on February 18, but his one-party minority government was defeated on a vote of confidence on February 26 and resigned. President Giovanni Leone then disbanded Parliament and ordered elections on May 7 and 8.

The Communists called for a "united Left." Violence at rallies in Turin, Brescia, San Remo, and Salerno was blamed on neo-Fascists. On April 7, Foreign Minister Aldo Moro warned that a swing to neo-Fascism could lead to civil war. On April 28, nine days before the election, Andreotti wooed voters by approving pensions by pay increases. The election confirmed the Christian Democrats' supremacy, with slight gains for the Republicans and the extreme Right. His party then authorized Andreotti to form a center government without the Socialists.

The New Government, a three-party coalition of Christian Democrats, Social Democrats, and Liberals, was sworn in on June 26. It was Italy's 34th since World War II and the most conservative in a decade. Communists and Socialists pledged to bring it down as soon as possible.

The new government's first task was to revive the economy after the blackest year since World War II in 1971. The government decided in October to adopt the value-added tax on Jan. 1, 1973.

Labor Unrest. The gravest threat to the economy was a series of strikes that began with an almost total stoppage in Rome in February. It involved newsmen, printers, railroad and airline workers, and farm workers. Strikes continued through the year. Doctors struck in June for hospital reforms. Construction workers walked out in September. Postal service became so chaotic in November that Italians were warned not to mail holiday greetings.

Other Events. Michelangelo's *Pietà*, a white marble statue of the Virgin Mary and her dead Son, was mutilated by a man with a hammer in St. Peter's Basilica in May. On September 14, the Roman Forum and Colosseum were closed to visitors because of the danger of falling masonry. A severe cloudburst after years of insufficient maintenance had weakened the 1,900-year-old tourist sites. They were later reopened.

Venice continued sinking into its lagoon. The United Nations Educational, Scientific, and Cultural Organization raised $400 million to save the city, but Parliament could not agree on how to spend it. In Pisa, a commission decided to use a harness to prevent the Leaning Tower from falling. Kenneth Brown

See also EUROPE (Facts in Brief Table).

IVORY COAST. See AFRICA.

JAPAN. Relations with the People's Republic of China, the United States, and Russia underwent significant changes in 1972. Japan also changed governments. Prime Minister Eisaku Sato resigned on July 5, ending a record 7 years and 8 months in office. The Diet immediately named Kakuei Tanaka to succeed him. See TANAKA, KAKUEI.

Prime Minister Tanaka conferred with Chinese Premier Chou En-lai in Peking between September 25 and 30. On September 27, he also met with Chinese Communist Party Chairman Mao Tse-tung. In an official communiqué issued after the meetings, Japan acknowledged past war damages inflicted on the Chinese people and established diplomatic relations as of September 29. It also recognized the mainland government as "the sole legal government of China" and said it "understands and accepts" that Taiwan is China's territory. China, in turn, renounced any demands for war indemnities from Japan. The two governments agreed to settle all disputes by peaceful means and asserted that the normalization of their relations was "not directed against third countries." They also agreed to conclude a treaty of peace and friendship as well as a number of trade, navigation, aviation, and fisheries treaties.

As a result of the Chou-Tanaka agreement, relations between Japan and the Nationalist government on Taiwan were severed, but there was no indication that they would end their economic relations.

The most important development in relations with the United States was the restoration of Okinawa to full Japanese control on May 15. Final arrangements for the return were worked out at a meeting between Sato and President Richard M. Nixon at San Clemente, Calif., on January 6 and 7.

Agreement with U.S. On August 31 and September 1, Prime Minister Tanaka met with President Nixon in Hawaii. The two leaders reaffirmed the U.S.-Japan treaty of mutual cooperation and security, discussed the President's past visit and the prime minister's forthcoming visit to China, and agreed to "move toward a better equilibrium in their balance of payments and trade positions." It was simultaneously announced that the two governments had reached a series of economic agreements under which Japan would purchase more than $1 billion in agricultural products, aircraft, and uranium enrichment. They also announced they would form a working group to study the feasibility of jointly building in the United States a gaseous diffusion plant that would produce enriched uranium for peaceful uses. It would cost an estimated $1 billion.

Russian Foreign Minister Andrei A. Gromyko visited Tokyo in January. Japan and Russia agreed that they would discuss a formal peace treaty during the year and that their prime ministers would exchange visits. They also agreed that they would negotiate a scientific and technological treaty and explore further expansion of trade relations. Another visitor

Kakuei Tanaka, center, joins in the cheering after being elected leader of Japan's Liberal Democratic Party at its convention in Tokyo.

during the year was Prime Minister Edward Heath, the first British prime minister to visit Japan while in office. His four-day September visit was devoted primarily to discussions of economic matters.

National Election. Prime Minister Tanaka, seeking a mandate on his policies, dissolved Parliament on November 13 and called new elections. In the vote, held on December 10, he and his Liberal-Democratic Party won a solid victory.

In 1971, Japan's public and private economic assistance to developing countries topped $2 billion for the first time, just under 1 per cent of the gross national product. Official development assistance amounted to slightly over a quarter of the total.

Economically, Japan's rate of growth was only 5.7 per cent. However, the per capita annual income rose to $1,840, placing Japan about 13th in the world. The yen was revalued late in 1971 to a rate of about 300 to 1 U.S. dollar.

The Winter Olympics were held in Sapporo in February (see Olympic Games). In March, the government announced the discovery of mural paintings estimated to be about 1,300 years old in a tomb near Nara. John M. Maki

See also Asia (Facts in Brief Table).

JEWS. The division into Conservative, Orthodox, and Reform Jews persisted in 1972, although Conservative and Reform rabbis continued friendly relations. The Reform Jews prepared for the celebration in 1973 of the 100th anniversary of the Union of American Hebrew Congregations. About 700 congregations with 1 million adherents are presently affiliated with this body. The United Synagogue (Conservative) has 826 congregations with a claimed membership of over 1.25 million. The Union of Orthodox Jewish Congregations claims about 900 congregations with 1 million adherents.

In the United States, the increased role of women in Jewish religious life was evident. A women's organization, *Ezrath Nashim*, was established in the spring. The first woman rabbi, Sally J. Preisand, was ordained in June at the Hebrew Union College in New York City, and 14 women were elected as presidents of Reform Temples.

In the cultural sphere, *The Day-Jewish Journal* ceased publication, leaving the *Forward* as the only daily Yiddish newspaper in the United States. The number of Jewish all-day schools increased. Nevertheless, Jews continued to be divided on the issue of tax support for parochial schools. Gerson D. Cohen became chancellor of the Jewish Theological Seminary in New York, and Maurice Samuel, a leading Jewish literary figure, died on May 4.

A rabbi collects chips of stone from holes made in Jerusalem's sacred Wailing Wall during building construction. The drilling caused angry protests.

United States Jews focused deep concern on the plight of Russian Jews. On April 30, a "Solidarity Day with Soviet Jewry" was observed in over 100 U.S. cities. More than 100,000 persons marched in New York City.

In Other Countries. The Jewish community in Argentina was hit hard by the compulsory closing of Jewish credit unions. About 3,400 of the 15,000 Jews who left Chile when Salvador Allende Gossens assumed the presidency in 1970 have since returned to their homes.

The Jewish communities of Western Europe grew stronger organizationally and economically. In France, recent Jewish arrivals from North Africa integrated progressively into French life. In Italy, two new editions of the notorious anti-Semitic pamphlet *The Protocols of the Elders of Zion* were published, and Jews as well as Christians became concerned about the increased anti-Semitic propaganda of the Italian neo-Fascists.

Jews in Russia continued to apply for emigration. By the end of July, 18,000 Jews had left Russia, and almost 100,000 applications for exit permits were still pending. Then, on August 14, the Russian government imposed a heavy tax, up to $36,000, on exit permits. Despite arrests and involuntary military conscription, Jewish activists continued to protest the treatment of Jews by staging hunger strikes and sending petitions to Russian leaders and to the United Nations. *Ulpanim* (institutes for the intensive study of Hebrew) proliferated. A new rabbi was appointed to the Moscow synagogue.

The tiny Jewish communities in Poland, Czechoslovakia, and Bulgaria showed signs of disintegrating. In Romania, where Jewish religious activities are state-supported, the major event in the life of the Jewish community was a visit of Israel's Prime Minister Golda Meir in May.

In Arab Countries. There was a certain easing of tensions in Iraq, but Jews were brutally treated in Syria. Persecutions of Jews also continued in Egypt, and the chief rabbi there secretly fled. The ancient synagogue in Oran, Algeria, was confiscated and made into a mosque. In Tunisia, Moslem religious fanaticism resulted in attacks on Jews. The Jewish community in Morocco, hitherto well-treated, became concerned about its future because of recurrent attempts on the life of King Hassan II. On September 5, the world was shocked by the murder of 11 Israeli athletes and coaches at the Olympic Games in Munich. See OLYMPIC GAMES.

World Population. The estimated world Jewish population rose to about 14,236,000 at the end of 1971. About 7,169,000 lived in North, Central, and South America; 4,000,000 in Europe; 2,738,000 in Asia; 181,000 in Africa; and 77,000 in Australia and New Zealand. For the first time, the number of U.S. Jews passed the 6-million mark. Over 2,600,000 live in Russia, and 2,632,000 in Israel. Moses A. Shulvass

JOHNSON, LYNDON BAINES (1908-), 36th President of the United States, slipped further into retirement in 1972. He consulted with Senator George S. McGovern of South Dakota, the Democratic presidential candidate, about a vice-presidential candidate on August 3. On August 16, he endorsed the Democratic ticket, and met with McGovern and vice-presidential candidate Sargent Shriver at the LBJ Ranch on August 22. However, Mr. Johnson did not actively campaign because of his poor health.

He was admitted to the University of Virginia Hospital on April 7 after suffering a heart attack while visiting his daughter, Mrs. Charles Robb in Charlottesville, Va. He was released on April 11 and returned to Texas. He was also hospitalized for his heart condition on April 17, and again in June and July. In October, he attended the Lady Bird Johnson Awards ceremony in Stonewall, Tex., and helped present highway beautification awards.

In September, Mr. Johnson sold the family's television station in Austin, Tex., for $9 million. On December 6, the Department of the Interior announced that Mr. Johnson was donating 200 acres of his ranch to the National Park Foundation. At the Johnson Library in Austin on December 12, the former President mediated a dispute between black civil rights leaders at ceremonies opening his civil rights papers to the public. Carol L. Thompson

Attempted coup and assassination still lay ahead in 1972, but in March, Jordan's beleaguered King Hussein I was kissed by a citizen in Amman.

JORDAN. King Hussein I shocked the Arab world on March 15, 1972, when he proposed the federation of Jordan and the area now occupied by Israel into a new unitary state. It would be called the United Arab Kingdom.

He proposed that each region be autonomous within the kingdom, and each elect an equal number of representatives to a National Assembly. Amman would become the federal capital of the kingdom and Jerusalem, the regional capital of the west bank.

In the king's view, the new state would replace his own Hashemite Kingdom of Jordan and would restore the occupied west bank to the Arabs. Yet he felt it would not infringe on Israel's sovereignty.

Israel rejected the plan, and the reactions in other Arab capitals were generally hostile. They viewed it as a sellout of Arab interests, although one not quite as bad as a separate Jordanian peace treaty with Israel would have been. Egypt broke trade relations with Jordan, and Syria again closed its border, hampering Jordanian trade. Kuwait and Libya refused to resume the $65-million subsidy they had agreed to give to Jordan after the Six-Day War in 1967. The payments had been suspended after the Jordanian Army crushed the Palestinian guerrillas in 1970 and 1971.

Domestic Tranquillity. Despite the unfavorable reaction in other countries, most of Hussein's people stood by him loyally. This fact, plus the absence of Palestinian guerrillas, enabled the government to maintain order. The new Cabinet of Prime Minister Ahmad al-Lawzi, successor to the murdered Wasfi el-Tal, completed its first year without incident. The Jordanian National Union, the country's sole legal political organization, was renamed the Arab National Union, and elections were held for 240 of its members; the remaining 120 members were chosen by the king.

To mark his 20th anniversary on the throne, Hussein issued an amnesty for political prisoners and exiles. The observance was saddened by the death on July 8 of Hussein's father, former King Talal, in a psychiatric clinic in Istanbul, Turkey. A plot to overthrow Hussein, and apparently to kill him, was foiled in November. In December, Hussein divorced his British wife and married a Jordanian.

Aided by transfusions of foreign money, the economy survived the loss of Kuwaiti-Libyan support surprisingly well. The gross national product increased by 5.7 per cent, even with an 8.49 per cent devaluation of the dinar. The United States loaned $60 million, and Great Britain gave $6.48 million for a telecommunications network, while India guaranteed purchase of 360,000 tons of Jordanian phosphates for $3.6 million. Expansion of phosphate production was coupled with the discovery of copper deposits in southern Jordan. William Spencer

See also MIDDLE EAST (Facts in Brief Table).

JORGENSEN, ANKER HENRIK (1922-), the chairman of the General Workers Union and a member of parliament, was sworn in as prime minister of Denmark on Oct. 5, 1972. He succeeded Jens Otto Krag, who resigned for personal reasons. See DENMARK; EUROPE.

Jorgensen was born on July 13, 1922, in Copenhagen, where his father drove a horse-drawn streetcar. Orphaned when he was very young, Jorgensen was reared by an aunt and attended a school for orphans. His first job was as an errand boy. Later, he worked as a laborer, first in a shipyard and then a warehouse.

In 1950, Jorgensen's co-workers at the warehouse elected him deputy chairman of their branch of the General Workers Union, the largest union in Denmark. He was made general manager of the union in 1962 and chairman in 1968. His political career, meanwhile, began in 1961 when he was elected to Copenhagen's city council. He relinquished that post following his election to parliament on the Social Democratic Party ticket in 1964.

The new prime minister is short and stocky. A man of simple tastes, Jorgensen lives with his wife Ingrid and their 11-year old son Lars in a modest, four-room apartment in Copenhagen. The Jorgensens have three other children. Paul C. Tullier

KANSAS. See STATE GOVERNMENT.

KENTUCKY. See STATE GOVERNMENT.

KENYA. Outward prosperity and calm in urban areas masked a deep political unrest in 1972. The underlying turmoil surfaced in student disorders and in the postponement of elections within the Kenya African National Union, the ruling political party headed by President Jomo Kenyatta.

The party elections, scheduled for March 1, were postponed on the grounds that the All-African Trade Fair, held in Nairobi in March, would conflict with them. Then, in May, the minister of home affairs told Parliament that the elections were again postponed because not enough people had registered to vote. A small minority, he said, could not be allowed to determine public policies. Some observers believed the real reason was fear that violence might accompany any national election because of seething tribal and student unrest.

Students and Conspirators. Student unrest broke out in a riot on July 17 at the University of Nairobi. From July to October, 56 students were jailed during protests against government interference with academic freedom and the government's tribal favoritism.

A former Kenya Air Force pilot was sentenced to 10 years in prison on July 27 for conspiring with army officers and government officials to overthrow Kenyatta's government. The plot had been discovered in early 1971. Two days later, Kenyatta warned that sterner measures would be used against those who conspire to disrupt the country's peace and prosperity.

Economic Prosperity increased in certain sectors, such as tourism, banking, and the airline industry. East African Airways was promised management assistance from the U.S. Eastern Airlines. On January 6, the International Development Association granted Kenya a $22-million loan for roadbuilding.

However, Kenya braced for the economic impact of Uganda's take-over of Asian businesses. The chaos that resulted in the Ugandan economy was expected to be felt in Kenya, because many Asian businesses in eastern Africa are linked together. Also, Kenya is the primary supplier for Uganda's trade and industry. See UGANDA.

Kenya's trade with Western nations created balance-of-trade problems. In 1971 and 1972, Kenya's imports increased 60 per cent, and its balance-of-payments deficit with nations outside the East African Economic Community doubled. The increasing trade deficit was due largely to an average price increase of 10 per cent on imports from Western nations in 1971. Kenya's export trade suffered from the drop in world coffee and tea prices in 1971. The low prices continued in 1972, preventing a recovery in export trade. George Shepherd

See also AFRICA (Facts in Brief Table).

KHMER. See CAMBODIA.

KING, CAROLE (1942-), popular music composer, singer, and pianist, was the big winner of the National Academy of Recording Arts and Sciences Grammy Awards in 1972. She won 4 of the 10 top awards presented on March 14.

She was honored as the composer of "You've Got a Friend," which was named Song of the Year, while her recording of "It's Too Late" was judged Single Record of the Year. Both songs were in her album, "Tapestry," which was named Album of the Year. Her singing in that album was recognized as the Best Female Pop Vocal Performance.

Carole King was born Feb. 9, 1942, in Brooklyn, N.Y., the only child of a New York City fireman. She graduated from Brooklyn College in 1964, with a Bachelor of Arts degree in elementary education. She began writing songs when she was about 17 years old, and joined the song-writing staff of a popular music publishing firm in 1959. In 1961, she first came to wide popular attention with a record of "It Might as Well Rain Until September." She wrote the song, sang it, and provided the piano accompaniment for the record.

In 1970, Miss King married Charles Larkey, one of the musicians with whom she had formed a trio called City in 1968. Her third daughter was born Dec. 31, 1971. "I never wanted to become an artist," Miss King said, "but after a while it became the most efficient way to get songs to people." Ed Nelson

KIRK, NORMAN ERIC (1923-   ), led the New Zealand Labour Party to victory in national elections held on Nov. 25, 1972. He became the fourth Labour Party prime minister in New Zealand's history. He is on record as favoring the recognition of the People's Republic of China and also has indicated that he wishes to take New Zealand out of the Southeast Asia Treaty Organization. See New Zealand.

The new prime minister was born on Jan. 6, 1923, the son of a cabinetmaker. Kirk left school at the age of 12 and worked at a number of jobs to help augment the family's small income. He worked at various times as a scrub cutter, a railway cleaner, and a stationary engine operator. For a while, he worked as an engineer on a ferry in Auckland harbor.

His first public office was as mayor of Kaiapoi, a small town on South Island, when he was 30 years old. Thereafter, his rise in politics was rapid. He entered Parliament as a Labour member in 1957 and was elected titular president of the Labour Party in 1964. The following year, he successfully challenged the Labour Party leader, Arnold H. Nordmeyer, and became leader of the party.

Prime Minister Kirk, a handsome man known as "Big Norm," is over 6 feet tall and weighs more than 200 pounds. In 1941, he married Ruth Miller. Mrs. Kirk traveled with him throughout the campaign and is one of his most ardent fans. They have five children. Paul C. Tullier

KISSINGER, HENRY ALFRED (1923-   ), special assistant to the President for national security affairs, confirmed his position in 1972 as the "most indispensable man on Nixon's staff." The former Harvard University professor was President Richard M. Nixon's "secret agent" in a series of more than 20 Paris meetings with North Vietnamese diplomat Le Duc Tho and Xuan Thuy, Hanoi's chief delegate to the Paris peace talks. He also negotiated with heads of other governments, including Russia's Communist Party leader Leonid I. Brezhnev. One of the few men who has access to the President night and day, Kissinger often spends as much as four hours a day with him in briefings.

A leading authority on national defense policy and foreign affairs, Kissinger wrote the influential *Nuclear Weapons and Foreign Policy* (1957). He served as a consultant to former Presidents Dwight D. Eisenhower, John F. Kennedy, and Lyndon B. Johnson while teaching international relations at Harvard University, and joined the Nixon Administration in 1969. A hard-working intellectual, Kissinger has also gained a reputation as a Washington "swinger."

Kissinger was born in Germany. His family came to the United States in 1938 to escape Nazi persecution of the Jews, and he became a U.S. citizen in 1943. He married Ann Fleischer in 1949; they were divorced in 1964. Allan Davidson

KIWANIS INTERNATIONAL. See Service Clubs.

KLEINDIENST, RICHARD GORDON (1923-   ), became attorney general of the United States in 1972 after the longest confirmation hearings in history. The Senate Judiciary Committee approved his nomination to succeed John N. Mitchell in February. But Kleindienst asked that the hearings be reopened after his name was linked with charges that International Telephone and Telegraph Corporation (ITT) had pledged money to the Republican National Convention in return for settlement of three antitrust suits. His nomination was finally approved on June 8.

Kleindienst was born in Winslow, Ariz., where his father served as postmaster. After Air Force service in World War II, Kleindienst received a bachelor's degree (magna cum laude) in 1947 from Harvard College and a law degree in 1950 from Harvard Law School. He then returned to Arizona, where he practiced law.

In 1953 and 1954, he served in the Arizona legislature. Later, he led the Republican state committee. During the 1968 campaign, he directed field operations for the Nixon for President Committee and was general counsel of the Republican National Committee. He was appointed deputy attorney general after the 1968 election. Kleindienst is considered bright and politically skillful, very quick to make decisions and articulate them. He has been described as a tough law-and-order conservative. He and his wife have two sons and two daughters. Ed Nelson

KOREA, NORTH. Breaking its relative isolation, North Korea opened its doors to a limited number of Western journalists in 1972. It did so primarily to underscore its accomplishments. Although impressive, these were overshadowed by the militancy of the tight garrison state.

Kim Il-song – the prime minister and Communist Party leader whose 60th birthday on April 15 was marked by seven days of unstinting praise of his achievements – told visitors it is important "that we educate our people in the spirit of hating the enemy." The United States and Japan were identified in public displays as the main enemies.

North and South Korea announced on July 4 that they had established a coordinating committee to work for peaceful unification. It was the first official dialogue between the two governments since their creation as separate states in 1948.

The committee announced on November 4 that an agreement had been reached to establish political, economic, social, and cultural contacts, and avoid military confrontations. Further meetings were planned monthly at executive level.

The government announced in October that the draft of a new constitution had been completed as a preparatory step toward reunification of the divided peninsula. No specifics of the proposed revisions were given. Henry S. Bradsher

See also Asia (Facts in Brief Table).

KOREA, SOUTH. Unsettling political developments beset the nation in 1972. On October 17, President Chung Hee Park proclaimed martial law, suspended part of the Constitution, and dissolved the National Assembly. All political activities were suspended, press censorship was imposed, and all universities and colleges were closed. Park said these measures were designed to reform the political structure "so that South Korea could cope with the rapidly changing international situation and successfully carry on the current dialogue with North Korea for the peaceful unification of the country."

In addition, Park introduced constitutional changes that vastly increased the powers of the president and reduced the authority of the National Assembly. The president will now be elected by nonpolitical village delegates instead of directly. These and other changes won the voters' approval in a closely supervised referendum held November 21.

Park Stronger. The changes appeared tailored to benefit Park. He had been accumulating personal power ever since he became president after a military coup in 1961. Park, serving his third four-year term as president, would have been unable to succeed himself under the old Constitution. Under the new one, he could stay in office for life.

On December 23, Park was officially re-elected president by the National Conference for Unification, and he promised to seek peaceful reunification of Korea as soon as possible. North and South Korean Red Cross delegations had been meeting since 1971 to end 27 years of bitter hostility between the two countries and, in so doing, reunite an estimated 10-million families. Government leaders of the two Koreas had participated in the 1972 discussions.

Park was also concerned over efforts by the United States and Japan to improve their relations with the People's Republic of China. He warned that the international situation was such that "third, or smaller, countries might be sacrificed for the relaxation of tensions between the big powers." Despite his forebodings, the United States continued to maintain up to 43,000 U.S. troops in South Korea.

Economic Problems brought further government controls in 1972, including moves to reduce inflation, cut interest rates, and stabilize the international exchange rate of the won. South Korea had enjoyed a boom in recent years, with the average per capita annual income rising from $95 in 1959 to $223 in 1970. This progress, however, had created problems. As industrialization grew, agriculture lagged so much that it failed to satisfy the nation's needs. Consequently, food and raw materials constituted up to 80 per cent of imports. Imports more than doubled exports, increasing the foreign debt. Henry S. Bradsher

See also Asia (Facts in Brief Table).

North Koreans flip color cards in a stadium in Pyongyang to form a pictorial backdrop honoring the visiting president of Somalia.

KORVALD, LARS (1916-), became prime minister of Norway on Oct. 17, 1972. He was sworn in by King Olav V as head of a three-party majority coalition government. Korvald, chairman of the Christian People's Party (CPP), succeeded Trygve M. Bratteli, who resigned after the Norwegian people voted on September 25 not to join the European Community (Common Market). One of Korvald's major tasks will be to negotiate a free-trade agreement with the market countries for Norway. See EUROPE; NORWAY.

Korvald is the son of a Norwegian farmer. After attending local elementary schools, he studied at the State College of Agriculture and graduated in 1943. Korvald then became a teacher, and in 1952 he became rector of the Tomb Agricultural School. At about the same time, he became interested in politics and joined the CPP. In 1961, he was elected a member of the Norwegian Parliament. He became parliamentary leader of the CPP in 1965 and chairman of the party in 1967, a position he held at the time of his election to the prime ministership.

The new prime minister is a bachelor. He takes a marked Christian view of politics and is associated with the Biblically orthodox wing of the Evangelical Lutheran Church, the state church of Norway. Korvald is a tall, square-jawed man with iron-gray hair. He enjoys reading, preferring history and biographies. He also loves classical music. Paul C. Tullier

KUWAIT maintained its traditional policy of vigorous moral support for the Arab cause against Israel in 1972. It also continued its financial aid to less-fortunate Arab countries, making gifts and loans through the Kuwait Fund for Arab Economic Development (KFAED).

The KFAED loans were made to Morocco for construction of a sugar plant, to Bahrain for a water-distillation plant, and to Jordan and Sudan.

Emir Sabah al-Salim al-Sabah offered to commit all of Kuwait's income and assets to the battle against Israel once all Arab states were ready to act. A contingent of Kuwaiti volunteers went to Libya in July for military training. But the government remained prudent; eight members of the Popular Front for the Liberation of Palestine were deported after attempting to kill the Jordanian ambassador.

Kuwait's participation in the ownership agreement signed in October with Western oil companies promised greater prosperity than ever (see MIDDLE EAST). Kuwait held its oil production at about the 1971 level of 1 billion barrels. The record budget of $1.5 billion was entirely covered by oil revenues. The National Assembly approved a gift of $27.6 million to the Syrian armed forces and $1.2 million to Lebanon for the reconstruction of Lebanese villages destroyed in Israeli raids. It also legislated universal free medical care. William Spencer

See also MIDDLE EAST (Facts in Brief Table).

LABOR. Conditions brightened for American labor in 1972, the first year under President Richard M. Nixon's wage and price controls, with both the rates of inflation and unemployment showing improvement. The September Consumer Price Index (CPI) of the Bureau of Labor Statistics (BLS) was 3.3 per cent above the September, 1971, CPI, compared with price rises of 4.3 per cent in 1971, and 5.9 per cent in 1970. The unemployment rate stood at 5.5 per cent in September, about the same as the previous three months, but below the high of about 6 per cent between late 1970 and mid-1972.

The total number of employed persons increased considerably, however, to 82.2 million in September, a rise of more than 2.4 million over September, 1971. And workers' purchasing power increased significantly. Weekly real spendable earnings increased 4.5 per cent to $123.14 from September, 1971, to September, 1972. This index, which showed virtually no growth from 1966 to 1970, increased 2.8 per cent in 1971. It measures the spendable average weekly earnings for a nonsupervisory worker with three dependents in the private nonfarm economy, after deduction for social security and federal income taxes, and adjustment for changes in the CPI.

The table below reflects some of the major employment improvements, based on BLS preliminary estimates:

	1971	1972*
	(in thousands)	
Total labor force	**86,929**	**88,799**
Armed forces	2,816	2,455
Civilian employment	79,120	81,405
Unemployment	4,993	939
Unemployment rate	5.9%	5.7%
Change in real average weekly earnings (Private nonfarm sector)	2.8%	4.5%†
Increase in output per man-hour (Private nonfarm sector)	3.6%	5.3%†

*January–September average, seasonally adjusted except for armed forces data.
†Compared to the third quarter of 1971.

Collective Bargaining. Preliminary BLS figures for the first nine months of 1972 showed a continuation of the moderating trend of wage-rate increases that began in 1971. Settlements in major collective bargaining cases (1,000 or more workers) provided a mean increase of 6.6 per cent a year over the life of the contract, compared with an average of 8.1 per cent for 1971, and 8.9 per cent for 1970. First-year wage-rate adjustments declined even more sharply, averaging 7.2 per cent, as opposed to 11.6 per cent in 1971. The 1972 figures revealed particularly steep declines in construction-industry wage hikes. These settlements averaged 6.6 per cent over the life of the contracts, and 7.1 per cent in the first year, compared to corresponding increases of 10.8 per cent and 12.6 per cent in 1971.

Collective bargaining was relatively light in 1972. Only about 2.8 million workers were covered by major agreements either expiring or providing

The International Association of Machinists was one of the few unions that officially supported Senator George S. McGovern for President.

wage-reopening provisions during the year. This compared with 4.75 million in 1971, and nearly 4.7-million expected to bargain in 1973. In addition, the year's bargaining did not include such major industries as rubber, electrical equipment, automobile manufacturing, or trucking.

Factors tending to lower wage increases resulting from 1972 bargaining (when compared to recent years) included the Pay Board's 5.5 per cent guideline, continued moderation in the rate of inflation, and extensive use of cost-of-living escalator clauses. In 1972, 4.3 million workers were covered by these clauses, a substantial increase over the 2.8 million covered as recently as 1970. The latter two factors helped limit rank-and-file requests for substantial wage increases to "catch up" with inflation, so prevalent in the bargaining scene in recent years. The stabilization controls also influenced bargaining by shortening the duration of contracts, or by providing for more annual wage reopenings, enhancing the chances of more immediate bargaining, should controls be lifted. This trend was especially apparent in the construction industry.

Dock Settlements were reached early in the year for East and West Coast longshoremen. On Jan. 6, longshoremen at six Atlantic ports agreed to a tentative three-year pact that set the pattern for 45,000 members of the International Longshoremen's Association at Atlantic and Gulf Coast ports. The longshoremen had been working under a Taft-Hartley injunction that expired on February 14. The pact provided wage boosts of 70 cents an hour, retroactive to Nov. 14, 1971, with 40-cent hikes in October of 1972 and 1973. Management also agreed to 47-cent and 30.5-cent increases over the term in pension and welfare-fund contributions, respectively.

On May 8, the Pay Board pared the 70-cent first-year raise to 55 cents, while approving the settlement's second-year boost, and its benefit improvements in the first two years. As is its custom, the panel did not rule on the third-year provisions.

A West Coast settlement in February ended the longest dock walkout – 123 days – in the nation's history. An 80-day cooling-off period under the Taft-Hartley Act, effective October 6, halted the original walkout that began on July 1, 1971. The strike had resumed on January 17, despite Administration threats to intervene with legislative action. The 18-month agreement, ratified on February 19, covered 13,000 members of the independent International Longshoremen's and Warehousemen's Union (ILWU). It provided a 72-cent increase retroactive to Dec. 25, 1971, and 40 cents on July 1, 1972. A sticking point was resolved when management agreed to pay the ILWU a $1-a-long-ton royalty for all containers loaded or unloaded by non-ILWU workers (mostly members of the Teamsters Union) within 50 miles of each port.

On March 16, the Pay Board pared the West Coast settlement from what it valued as a 20.9 per cent first-year wage and benefit package to one worth 14.9 per cent. While still substantially above the board's standard, the approved package was justified under the "catch-up" exception rule. The panel also cited the increased productivity over the prior decade resulting from the industry's mechanization and modernization program. The reduction, by an 8 to 5 vote, with organized labor united in opposition, helped precipitate a labor walkout.

On April 15, the ILWU sued the Pay Board, asking a reversal of the panel's ruling that the slashed portion of the settlement could not be placed in escrow. According to the board, such an action would violate the stabilization program's purpose. On May 15, the ILWU and the Pacific Maritime Association accepted the settlement, which pared the first-year increase by 32 cents an hour, to 40 cents for longshoremen and 47.5 cents for clerks.

The Pay Board. Three labor members walked off the tripartite, 15-member Pay Board on March 22, precipitating an immediate test of its survival, and an ultimate test of its effectiveness. Leading the walkout was AFL–CIO President George Meany, accompanied by Steelworkers' President I. W. Abel and Floyd Smith of the Machinists. The next day, Leonard Woodcock, the president of the United Auto Workers, also left the board, leaving Teamsters' President Frank E. Fitzsimmons as the sole labor representative on the panel. The walkouts followed a special meeting of the AFL-CIO Executive Council called in response to the board's reduction of the West Coast longshore settlement. The council said the stabilization program was biased. It claimed that the panel was not truly tripartite, because the "so-called public members are neither neutral nor independent," resulting in a board dominated by a "coalition of business and public members."

President Nixon announced that the Pay Board would continue to function "as a single public unit, with those labor leaders who wisely wish to remain on it balanced by a reduced number of business leaders." He stated that he could not "permit any leader representing a special interest, no matter how powerful, to torpedo and sink the program. . . ." As a result, the panel continued to function with seven members. The five public members remained, and four business members resigned, leaving one business representative to balance Fitzsimmons.

Pay Board Rulings. On January 5, the Pay Board voted to reject five late 1971 settlements for 100,000 Auto Workers and Machinists. The contracts had provided a 51-cent first-year wage increase, including 34 cents that workers would have received under the prior three-year pacts if the escalator clauses had not contained 16-cent maximum cost-of-living hikes. The pacts also provided 3 per cent second- and third-year increases. On January 13, the board said it would approve the contracts if they were renegotiated to include only the 34-cent escalator "catch up" in the first year, deferring the remaining 17 cents as an addition to the 3 per cent due the second year. Both unions then sued to reverse the reductions.

On July 31, Federal District Judge George Hart agreed with the union's contention that the 34 cents should not be considered part of the new settlements, since that sum would have been paid under the prior agreements if there had been no cost-of-living adjustment. He remanded the contracts back to the board, asking that it consider the first-year increase to be 17 cents in determining whether it met Phase 2 guidelines. The panel appealed Judge Hart's ruling.

Among its other decisions, the Pay Board, in August, voted to retain "at this time" its 5.5 per cent-a-year ceiling on pay increases. In February, the panel had voted to allow an additional 0.7 per cent a year of the wage base in specified fringe benefits. It also allowed up to 1.5 per cent a year in situations where supplementary benefits had not been improved or added for three years.

On February 14, the Cost of Living Council, which supervises the stabilization program, exempted from wage controls all workers earning $1.90 an hour or less. The action set off a storm of criticism. It affected about 9 million workers, and was an attempt to comply with the Economic Stabi-

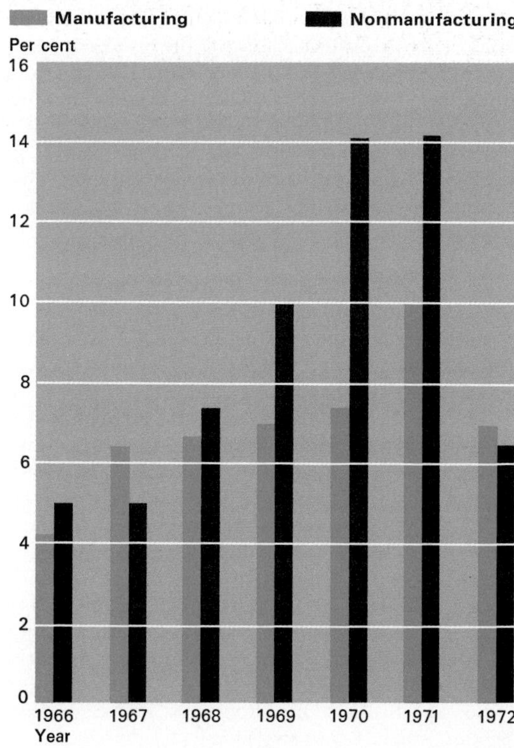

lization Act of 1970, as amended, to exempt the working poor from the controls program. Labor claimed that the cutoff should have been based on the 1970 BLS lower budget for an urban family of four–about $3.35 an hour. In response to suits filed by several unions, District of Columbia Judge William B. Jones ruled on July 14 that the council had exceeded its authority in setting the $1.90 cutoff. On July 26, the council raised the cutoff to $2.75 an hour.

Trouble for UMW. The United Mine Workers Union (UMW) and its president, W. A. (Tony) Boyle, were the subjects of controversial headlines throughout the year. On March 31, the 67-year-old labor chief was convicted of conspiracy and of making illegal political contributions from union funds. The verdict, reached by a federal district court jury in Washington, D.C., found Boyle guilty on all 13 counts of a federal indictment alleging violations of the Corrupt Practices Act, the Landrum-Griffin Act, and the Taft-Hartley Act. On June 27, Boyle was sentenced to five years in prison and fined $130,000.

On May 1, a Washington, D.C., federal district judge had ordered Boyle's 1969 election victory over Joseph A. (Jock) Yablonsky set aside. In his ruling, Judge William B. Bryant upheld Department of Labor charges that the election was marred by massive union election-law violations. On June 16, Judge Bryant ordered a new election in December.

On December 16, the Department of Labor, which had closely supervised the election and tabulated the ballots, announced that Arnold R. Miller, 49, defeated Boyle, receiving 55 per cent of the vote. Miller, presidential candidate of the insurgent Miners for Democracy, is a former West Virginia coal miner who headed the Black Lung Association after retiring from the mines as a victim of the disease.

Farmworkers, led by Cesar Chavez, stayed in the news. At a meeting of the AFL-CIO Executive Council in February, George Meany announced that the federation would issue a national charter to the 30,000-member United Farm Workers Organizing Committee. The Farm Workers, on February 29, then announced a breakthrough agreement with Coca-Cola's Food Division, capping a six-month organizing campaign in Florida. The contract was the first for migrant workers in Florida.

The union, which had successfully concluded a grape boycott in 1970, announced the start of another nationwide boycott in May affecting iceberg lettuce grown in California's Salinas and Imperial valleys. Chavez explained that the boycott was necessary because the growers would not recognize the union's right to bargain for the lettuce workers. When the boycott was announced, the union had reached agreements with four lettuce growers for 2,000 workers, and was trying to organize an additional 60,000 to 80,000 workers. Leon Bornstein

See also Section One, FOCUS ON THE ECONOMY; Section Three, ECONOMY, THE.

LAOS. The war in Vietnam continued to have bitter side effects on Laos in 1972. The primary cause was the supply trails running from North Vietnam through Laos and into South Vietnam. In 1971, a South Vietnamese incursion had partly wrecked these supply routes. But as soon as the dry season came in 1972, North Vietnamese Communist regulars went into action to reopen the supply routes. Two offensives were mounted, one to the north and the other to the south.

The northern offensive was aimed at the Jarres Plain, particularly at Long Cheng, about 80 miles north of Vientiane. As an indication of the importance of the drive, the Communists for the first time used heavy 130-millimeter guns, MIG aircraft, and heavy anti-aircraft fire to disrupt U.S. air support. Facing some 45,000 Communist troops was a force of Meo tribal guerrillas led by General Vang Pao and Lao forces recruited from Thailand together with Thai irregulars. These were largely supported by U.S. air power and financial backing.

The ensuing three-month battle saw Long Cheng change hands several times, and although the Laotians were able to hold on, the base became almost useless. The Communists cut the all-important junction of routes 7 and 13, thus breaking the link between the northern capital of Luang Prabang and the southern capital, Vientiane. In the south, Communist troops took the Bolovens Plateau and occupied a village on the Mekong route to South Vietnam. Their major aim was to intimidate Prime Minister Souvanna Phouma into asking the United States to stop bombing the Ho Chi Minh Trail in southern Laos. It was doubtful, however, that any such move would have succeeded even if Phouma had complied.

The toll in lives and the disruption of the economy caused more than a few problems for the Royal Laotian government. Vang Pao's Meo forces were composed of too many unpaid teen-age boys. Several small-scale mutinies indicated their general resentment against using Laotian forces to prop up the government in Vientiane. In fact, the government was probably in control of no more than 20 per cent of the country by the end of the year.

Economic Problems went from bad to worse during the year. Because the government subsisted mostly on American aid, it could do little to make any basic economic reforms on its own. War weariness was also reflected in actions by both the government and the army, in which constant consideration was being given to some sort of agreement with the Communists. Fears of a Communist take-over coupled with covert Thai incursions probably accounted for the exchanges that took place between Souvanna Phouma and Pathet Lao leader Souphanouvong during 1972. By the end of the year, their efforts to arrange a cease-fire were fruitless. John N. Stalker

See also ASIA (Facts in Brief Table).

LATIN AMERICA

The Latin American region presented a mixed picture of political, economic, and social paradoxes in 1972. Political turmoil stalked Argentina, Chile, El Salvador, and Guatemala. In Ecuador, President José María Velasco Ibarra was overthrown in a military coup d'état. In other Latin American countries, however, a certain political stability was maintained, notably in Uruguay, where a new head of state was inaugurated despite fierce terrorist activities.

Economic conditions in the various Latin American countries also created contradictions in the overall picture of progress. Although recession loomed in Argentina and Chile, Brazil maintained its strong economy, and Mexico, recovering from a recessionary period, was poised for greater growth. Both Bolivia and Ecuador anticipated huge financial gains from the opening of gas and petroleum pipelines.

Diplomats convene in the stately Hall of the Americas in Washington, D.C., for a meeting of the Organization of American States.

LATIN AMERICA

A much-anticipated second General Assembly of the Organization of American States (OAS) was held from April 11 to 21 in Washington, D.C. It called for strict observance of the principle of self-determination, and condemned military, political, and economic intervention. It also postponed indefinitely the readmission of Cuba to the OAS. Little of concrete value was accomplished, however, and most delegates merely restated their nation's long-time grievances against the United States. Ecuador accused the Congress of the United States of pursuing an "undeniably interventionist policy" because it suspended U.S. aid to Ecuador following seizure of U.S. fishing boats in Ecuador's coastal waters. Chile accused the United States of trying to block loans by international lending agencies.

U.S. Policy Unchanged. Despite these and other pressures, the United States continued to maintain its policy of realism and moderation toward Latin America, recognizing that the day of unchallenged U.S. political and economic dominance in Latin America has passed. Through its policies, too, it recognized that the area was rapidly changing, with a diversity of national approaches to political and economic matters. On some points, however, Washington held firm, notably in its announcement that it would follow a tougher attitude toward foreign nations that expropriate private U.S. holdings without "prompt, adequate, and effective compensation." Behind this attitude was the threat of eventual economic retaliation. Washington also decided–and did not hesitate to make it clear despite adverse Latin American reactions–that the time was not right to press Congress for long-promised tariff preferences for underdeveloped areas. A further indication of this firm stand centered around Washington's preoccupation with the flood of narcotics and other dangerous drugs entering the United States via Latin America. Under subtle but persistent U.S. pressure, Mexico and other republics cooperated with U.S. narcotics agents. In Bolivia, 15 cocaine-processing plants were discovered in September and millions of dollars worth of refined narcotics were seized. In Argentina in that same month, police smashed a smuggling ring that had shipped about 1,900 pounds of heroin into the United States. Paraguay agreed to the extradition of a leading narcotics trafficker who had been sought by U.S. authorities since late 1970.

The Inter-American Development Bank (IDB) closed its 13th annual meeting in Quito, Ecuador, on May 12 with an important communiqué. It adopted far-reaching measures aimed at eliminating some of the bitterness many republics had expressed toward the industrialized nations. Among some of the principal decisions were: (1) The IDB, capitalized at $6-billion, will ease the terms of its "soft loans" to poorer,

Facts in Brief on the Latin American Countries

Country	Population	Government	Monetary Unit*	Foreign Trade (million U.S. $) Exports	Imports
Argentina	25,414,000	President Alejandro Agustín Lanusse	peso (5=$1)	1,740	1,888
Bahamas	180,000	Governor Sir John Paul; Prime Minister Lynden O. Pindling	dollar (1=$1.03)	265	508
Barbados	265,000	Governor General Sir Arleigh Winston-Scott; Prime Minister Errol W. Barrow	East Caribbean dollar (1.84=$1)	39	118
Bolivia	5,326,000	President Hugo Banzer Suarez	peso (20=$1)	226	165
Brazil	101,556,000	President Emílio Garrastazú Médici	new cruzeiro (6.06=$1)	2,900	3,707
British Honduras	140,000	Governor Richard Posnett; Premier George Price	dollar (1.66=$1)	10	27
Chile	10,501,000	President Salvador Allende Gossens	escudo (20=$1)	1,247	931
Colombia	23,210,000	President Misael Pastrana Borrero	peso (21.9=$1)	732	844
Costa Rica	1,889,000	President José Figueres Ferrer	colón (6.62=$1)	232	350
Cuba	8,900,000	President Osvaldo Dorticos Torrado; Premier Fidel Castro	peso (1=$1.08)	1,043	1,300
Dominican Rep.	4,809,000	President Joaquín Balaguer	peso (1=$1)	243	358
Ecuador	6,736,000	President Guillermo Rodríguez Lara	sucre (25=$1)	238	303
El Salvador	3,952,000	President Arturo Armando Molina Barraza	colón (2.5=$1)	228	250
Guatemala	5,570,000	President Carlos Arana Osorio	quetzal (1=$1)	288	297
Guyana	836,000	President Arthur Robert Chung; Prime Minister L. F. S. Burnham	dollar (2=$1)	135	133
Haiti	5,165,000	President Jean-Claude Duvalier	gourde (5=$1)	46	57
Honduras	2,854,000	President Oswaldo Lopez Arellano	lempira (2=$1)	188	194
Jamaica	2,140,000	Governor General Sir Clifford C. Campbell; Prime Minister Michael Norman Manley	dollar (1=$1.30)	345	538
Mexico	56,179,000	President Luis Echeverría Alvárez	peso (12.49=$1)	1,501	2,451
Nicaragua	2,212,000	Three-member National Governing Council	córdoba (7.03=$1)	183	210
Panama	1,614,000	Chief Executive Omar Torrijos Herrera	balboa (1=$1)	121	391
Paraguay	2,630,000	President Alfredo Stroessner	guaraní (126=$1)	65	83
Peru	14,889,000	President Juan Velasco Alvarado; Prime Minister Ernesto Montagne Sánchez	sol (38.7=$1)	892	743
Puerto Rico	2,712,033	Governor Rafael Hernández Colón	dollar (U.S.)	1,680	2,681
Trinidad and Tobago	1,140,000	Governor General Sir Solomon Hochoy; Prime Minister Eric Eustace Williams	dollar (1.84=$1)	518	652
Uruguay	2,991,000	President Juan María Bordaberry Arocena	peso (680=$1)	206	222
Venezuela	11,595,000	President Rafael Caldera	bolívar (4.4=$1)	3,122	2,074

*Exchange rates as of November 1, 1972

less-developed member countries; (2) greater emphasis will be placed on loans involving two or more nations to spur the economic integration of the region; (3) the area's wealthier countries will buy up future IDB bond issues (Mexico agreed to purchase $25 million in new bonds); and (4) Canada was admitted as the 24th IDB member.

The five-member Central American Common Market (CACM) – consisting of Costa Rica, El Salvador, Guatemala, Honduras, and Nicaragua – deteriorated still further in 1972. Its troubles started in 1970, when Honduras cut off free trade with the CACM following the El Salvador-Honduras war. Costa Rica then became the outlet for goods originally destined for Honduras, and its debts had piled up. Subsequently, the other CACM members refused to extend loans to settle the obligations. Costa Rica retaliated by refusing to grant preferential exchange rates to CACM goods. This, in turn, prompted El Salvador, Guatemala, and Nicaragua to close their doors to Costa Rican products.

In October, an optimistic arrangement was signed to normalize Costa Rican trade relations with the other CACM countries. A complex system of exchange rates was worked out in an effort to make Costa Rican industry more competitive with that of other Central American nations.

Group Sets Precedent. In 1972, for the first time since the Andean Common Market was formed, its members – Bolivia, Chile, Colombia, Ecuador, and Peru – put into effect a 10 per cent across-the-board customs duty cut that was expected to spur intragroup trade. At the same time, a 20 per cent increase was applied on many types of goods imported from outside the market area.

On August 21, the Andean group took its first step toward sharing factories of basic industries among its members. The group agreed on what factories engaged in basic metalworking (except the sensitive automotive industry) would be shared by which republics. Involved in the move were 73 industrial divisions, ranging from tools and machinery to light airplanes, compressors, scissors, and toys. Each nation has been given from five to six years to demonstrate that its assigned production is going satisfactorily. Observers predict that the value of the Andean group's production will reach about $1.1 billion within a decade.

Central America

Costa Rica found it difficult to make ends meet during the year. The trouble stemmed primarily from the phenomenal rise in public expenditures. Although substantial tax increases approved by Congress in February were expected to add about 7 per cent to the normal growth of 1972 revenues, expenditures may have risen about 20 per cent. Offsetting this, however, a spurt in coffee prices boosted export earnings, and about $39 million in loans from various international institutions gave added impetus to agricultural livestock projects and power and telecommunication development.

El Salvador. About 100 soldiers and civilians were killed and 200 others wounded on March 25 in an unsuccessful uprising to overthrow the regime of President Fidel Sánchez Hernández. The revolt was led by Colonel Benjamin Mejia and by Jose Napoleon Duarte, a Leftist candidate defeated in the February 20 presidential election. A state of siege was declared and martial law was imposed.

On July 1, Colonel Arturo Armando Molina Barraza of the ruling National Conciliation Party became president. At his inaugural, which followed shortly after the state of siege was lifted, Molina Barraza promised to make public health, housing, unemployment, and agrarian problems his main concerns.

El Salvador was granted $21 million in loans during the year by various international institutions for roads, telecommunications, and drinking water systems. On August 14, President Molina said the government would immediately begin building the Rio Lempa hydroelectric dam project, delayed almost 20 years because two powerful El Salvador families had refused to allow their land to be flooded.

Guatemala. The gross national product expanded an estimated 5 per cent, and business was healthy. Coffee, sugar, and cotton all commanded high world market prices, while production for all three crops was good. The republic had its most valuable cotton crop in history, an estimated 353,000 bales valued at $51.2 million. It received $21.4 million from international agencies for rural health, agricultural, and industrial projects. In May, Guatemala paid $18-million for a controlling interest in the local electric power subsidiary of Boise Cascade Corporation, following the expiration of the firm's 50-year concession. Instead of insisting on payment in long-term bonds, a practice common elsewhere, the Guatemalan government deposited the sum in U.S. dollars in the Boise Cascade Corporation's bank account in New York City.

Olivero Castaneda Paiz, first vice-president of Congress and a leader in the fight against the Left wing guerrillas, was assassinated on June 25 in Guatemala City. His death was at first blamed on the Leftists, but it became apparent that internecine fighting had broken out on the Right when four of Castaneda's followers were gunned down in mid-July. At stake, apparently, was the presidency of Guatemala in 1974. Squabbling had already begun among conservatives over the choice of a successor to President Carlos Arana Osorio.

Honduras, struggling with its limited natural and human resources, remained one of Latin America's poorest countries. A grant of $16.3 million from the International Monetary Fund early in the year helped to support the economy. About $20.4 million in additional funds from various international groups helped pay for power facilities, a hospital, a medical school project in Tegucigalpa, and a number of governmental purchases.

On December 4, the army overthrew President Ramón E. Cruz and installed General Oswaldo Lopez Arellano for the five remaining years of the presidential term. Lopez, who also overthrew the government in 1963 and served as chief of state until Cruz was elected in 1971, will govern with decrees and laws issued through a Council of Ministers.

Nicaragua. President Anastasio Somoza Debayle turned over power to a three-man triumvirate on May 2 as his five-year term ended. The move was made in accordance with a pact signed earlier in the year between Somoza's ruling Liberal Party and the opposition Conservative Party. Under its provisions, Somoza was to step down when his term expired, and a three-man government will rule until a new constituent assembly could be formed following elections scheduled for September, 1974. However, Somoza continued as Nicaragua's strongman, in command of the armed forces as well as leader of the Liberal Party.

An economic boom appeared to be in Nicaragua's future, fueled mostly by higher cotton income and a record crop of 455,000 bales. A Special Development Fund was created in April to promote development in agriculture, livestock, fishing, industry, and agro-industry. It was to be managed by the Central Bank. The International Monetary Fund granted an $11.8-million stand-by loan, and the World Bank advanced $24 million for power projects.

Caribbean Islands

Dominican Republic. On June 21, President Joaquín Balaguer inaugurated a major $180-million ferro-nickel refining plant at Bonao in the center of the country. Eventually, the Canadian-built plant expects to produce about 60 million pounds of nickel a year, or 6 per cent of the present world output, bringing much-needed foreign exchange into the republic. Meantime, the New York and Honduras Rosario Mining Company received permission to dig a $20-million open-pit gold and silver mine. Production is expected to begin in 1974 at a 6,000-ton-a-day cyanide mill that will break down the ores.

The Tavera Dam was completed on April 3. Its capacity of 170 million cubic meters will enable more than 90,000 acres of land in the Yaque del Norte Valley to be irrigated. The first 40,000-kilowatt hydroelectric generator was scheduled to go into operation in October. Meanwhile, the nation received about $15.58 million in loans from various international agencies for electric power, sugar mills, transportation, and various industrial, mining, and farming projects. Mary Webster Soper

See also Latin American country articles.

LAW. See Civil Rights; Courts and Laws; Crime.

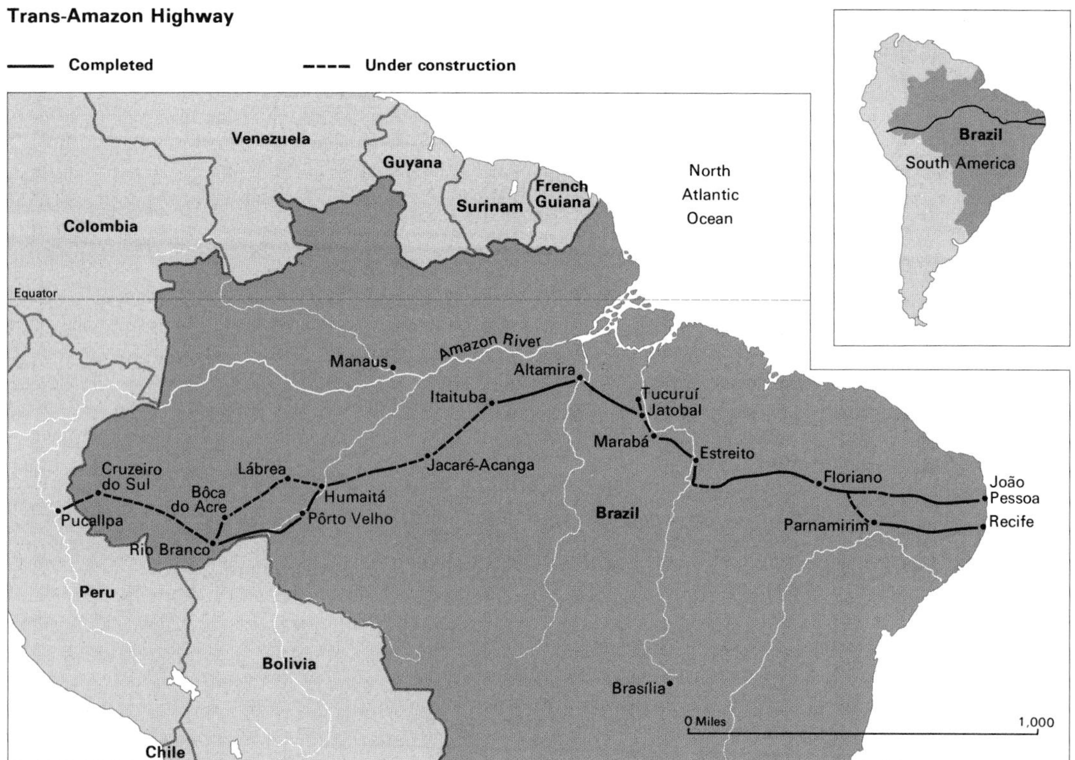

LEBANON. The focus of conflict between Israel and the Palestinian guerrillas shifted to southern Lebanon early in 1972. Guerrilla raids into Israel from Lebanese bases provoked counterattacks that caused extensive property damage as well as casualties. About 140 Lebanese villagers were reported killed or wounded during a four-day Israeli sweep from March 25 to 28. The Lebanese border village of Natiya was destroyed by Israel's air force.

Guerrilla Agreement. Despite the raids, Prime Minister Saeb Salaam declared on June 24 that Lebanon would not curb the guerrillas. "Let Israel hear this," he declared in a broadcast statement. "There will not be a clash between Lebanon and the Palestinians in any way." On June 27, however, Lebanon and the Palestine Liberation Organization (PLO) agreed to freeze guerrilla operations from Lebanese bases and make the Palestinians themselves responsible for internal discipline in the guerrilla camps. The Lebanese Army then moved back into areas previously controlled by the PLO.

Unsettling Presence. But the mere presence of Palestinians bent on revenge was an unsettling factor. Unable to strike directly at Israel, the commando organizations feuded among themselves. In July, a letter-bomb campaign injured several prominent Palestinian exile leaders and killed a leader of the Popular Front for the Liberation of Palestine. It was similar to the one launched against Israeli diplomats, officials, and Jews around the world.

Reports in late September said restrictions on Palestinian travel in Lebanon had quietly been relaxed. Prime Minister Salaam announced on September 25 that the Palestinians had agreed to avoid bringing "any harm to Lebanon" in its relations with Israel. Coupled with the record of Israeli reprisal raids, the statement seemed an effort to neutralize Lebanon.

Parliamentary Elections were held in three stages in April. Leftists made significant gains, though conservatives still dominated the parliament. On May 27, a new Cabinet took office under Prime Minister Salaam. In accordance with traditional ethnic balance, it included Moslems, Christians, and members of other sects.

The balanced Lebanese economy – dependent on tourism, banking, and transit trade – was relatively unaffected by the Palestinian-Israeli clashes. In July, Lebanon and Syria reached agreement on sharing water from the Orontes River.

Kuwait loaned Lebanon $14.4 million for industrial development. The United Nations granted $1.2 million toward the development of agriculture in southern Lebanon and for the government's "Green Plan." The plan calls for extensive reforestation and provides funds for farmers to purchase tractors. Lebanon re-established diplomatic relations with West Germany on March 30. William Spencer

See also MIDDLE EAST (Facts in Brief Table).

LEE, HAROLD BINGHAM (1899-), became the 11th president of the Mormon Church (Church of Jesus Christ of Latter-day Saints) in July, 1972. He succeeded Joseph Fielding Smith, who died on July 2. Lee had previously been president of the church's Council of the Twelve Apostles.

Lee was born on a farm in Clifton, Ida. He attended Idaho State Normal and the University of Utah, and became a grade-school teacher and principal in Salt Lake City, Utah. In 1933 he was elected to the Salt Lake City Commission. Also in that Great Depression year, he developed a plan to have unemployed church members harvest crops from Utah fields. The food was then distributed on the basis of family size.

In 1936, Lee assumed full-time church duties directing the Mormon welfare program. He has been active in directing the worldwide mission program, which currently assists 96,500 Mormons each year. Lee was named to the Council of Twelve Apostles on April 6, 1941. He also serves on the board of the Union Pacific Railroad and the Equitable Life Assurance Society as a representative of the church's stock interests.

In the last three years, much of his working time has been devoted to the Church Correlation Program, which tries to integrate the wide variety of Mormons' home studies, women's and youth organizations, publications, and sports activities. He is married and has two children. Foster Stockwell

LESOTHO. Developments of possibly major significance were afoot in Lesotho in 1972. At home, Prime Minister Leabua Jonathan made a concerted effort toward reconciliation with both King Motlotlehi Moshoeshoe II and the leader of the opposition Congress Party, Ntsu Mokhehle. Under the authoritarian rule of Jonathan, who seized control in 1970, Lesotho was a one-party state and neither the king nor Mokhehle had any voice in decisions.

In January, Jonathan ordered the release of 50 political prisoners who had been held for two years. Most of them were either members of the opposition or supporters of the king. At the same time, Jonathan agreed to exchange diplomatic representatives with South Africa at the consul-general level. In doing so, Lesotho became the first of the three former High Commission Territories (the others are Swaziland and Botswana) and the second black African country to send an official representative to South Africa. Mokhehle had long insisted that Lesotho's survival depended largely on South Africa's good will.

Lesotho continued to depend on British aid, which provided about half of the annual budget. Its efforts to encourage industrialization, despite all attempts to encourage foreign investors, remained negligible. Industry accounted for only about 1 per cent of the gross national product. Paul C. Tullier

See also AFRICA (Facts in Brief Table).

LIBERIA. See AFRICA.

LIBRARY. President Richard M. Nixon proclaimed 1972 International Book Year in the United States. It was part of an international observance in which more than 100 countries took part (see LITERATURE [Close-Up]). In his proclamation, the President recognized the importance of books and libraries in our society. "Books and libraries are among mankind's greatest sources of enlightenment," he said. "They contain the cultural inheritance of our forefathers and the core of our educational system."

New Libraries. The Martin Luther King Memorial Library was opened in Washington, D.C. It was designed by the renowned architect Mies van der Rohe. The dedication of the new $8.5-million William Pearson Scott Library at York University in Toronto was highlighted by a symposium on "The University – the Library." Distinguished men of letters Archibald MacLeish, Richard Blackwell, and Samuel Rothstein were the featured participants. About 250,000 education documents from the Johnson Administration were opened to the public at the Lyndon Baines Johnson Library in Austin, Tex., on January 25. When the library was dedicated in May, 1971, Mr. Johnson had said that the papers from his Administration would be unedited. "It will all be there with the bark off," he said. However, about five per cent of the education papers are still withheld for reasons of privacy.

In a special sale in August, the Chicago Public Library sold 18,000 books for 25 cents each, adding $4,500 to its general operating fund.

Library Grants. The National Historical Publications Commission granted $35,135 to the Cornell University libraries. The grant is to enable them to begin locating, photocopying, and listing all known manuscripts of the French soldier and statesman Marquis de Lafayette. The National Endowment for the Humanities, which administers federal funds, offered New York City's public library a grant of $750,000. The grant specifies payment of $1 for every $2 the library raises, up to $1.5 million, by June 30, 1973. The first contribution to the drive was $225,000 from the Vincent Astor Foundation.

Minority-Group Programs aimed at recruiting American Indians, blacks, Chicanos, and Puerto Ricans into the library profession were begun by various library schools and governmental agencies. Arizona State University, for example, will offer a three- or four-year course to 20 American Indian students. The students will be trained as school library media specialists to help alleviate the pressing needs for school staffs on the reservations. The Library Science Department at East Tennessee State University in Johnson City, Tenn., will recruit 20 Appalachian college drop-outs and train them to work with disadvantaged students in rural areas.

The meeting of the International Federation of Library Associations was held in Budapest, Hungary, from August 28 to September 2. Robert J. Shaw

See also AMERICAN LIBRARY ASSOCIATION.

LIBYA. President Muammar Muhammad al-Qadhaafi charted a bewildering course for his country in 1972. He made state visits to several African and Arab nations and issued forceful declarations of support for a variety of "liberation movements." But his most positive act was an agreement for total merger with Egypt, announced on August 2. The merger was scheduled for completion by September, 1973. The two countries agreed on Cairo as capital of the union. Unification of the two countries, already linked in the Federation of Arab Republics (with Syria), would combine Egypt's manpower and technical skills with Libya's wealth to form one of Africa's largest and most powerful states.

Qadhaafi's comments on world issues ranged from the plight of Moslems in the Philippines to criticism of Morocco's King Hassan II as a "tool of imperialism-Zionism." But they were not accompanied by positive support, except in the case of the Palestinian guerrillas. Libya did, however, terminate its military alliance with Great Britain in January. On February 6, the treaty by which the United States had leased Wheelus Air Force Base was formally abrogated. The United States had evacuated the base, on the outskirts of Tripoli, in 1970.

Cabinet Shuffled. Qadhaafi's obsession with foreign affairs and disagreements with his colleagues over the direction of the revolution led to a reorganization of the Cabinet on July 16. Minister of Industry Major Abd al-Salam Jallud replaced Qadhaafi as prime minister; with the exception of Jallud and one other officer, the entire Cabinet was composed of civilians. But the Revolutionary Command Council (RCC) of officers headed by President Qadhaafi remained the sole governing body.

On March 28, the RCC convened the first Libyan Arab Socialist Union. It was modeled on Egypt's Arab Socialist Union as the country's sole political organization. Qadhaafi defined the aims of the union as "social justice" and "the end of poverty, hunger, and ignorance." Later decrees banned strikes by workers and students and the formation of political parties outside the union.

Press censorship was abolished, but strict press regulations were issued. They followed a March trial of journalists charged with public corruption.

Diplomatic relations with Chad were restored as Libya halted support of the antigovernment Chad Liberation Front. Libya supported Malta during its dispute with Britain over naval base rental increases. Libya struck another blow at Britain with the nationalization of British Petroleum facilities and withdrawal of $552 million in Libyan deposits from British banks. On May 3, the government won an 8.49 per cent price increase, worth $170 million per year, from the oil companies. William Spencer

See also AFRICA (Facts in Brief Table).

LIONS CLUBS. See SERVICE CLUBS.

Alexander Solzhenitsyn, who won the 1970 Nobel Prize for literature, left seclusion to attend funeral of Russian poet Alexander Tvardovsky.

LITERATURE. Every sector of book publishing was thriving as 1972 drew to a close. Bookstore counters were loaded with attractive merchandise. Best sellers in fiction and nonfiction signaled new currents of contemporary interest. Lavish gift books were as handsome and expensive as ever. Fiction and nonfiction commanded higher and higher prices, with no indication of substantial buyer resistance. The vast flow of printed materials and a proliferation of new titles and fresh areas of interest were positive evidence of the robust health of the book trade.

Although booksellers use the best-seller list to promote sales, sophisticated readers know that such a gauge of public taste is in no way a measure of merit. Yet, there are times when the best-seller list has some significance, especially in the field of fiction, and this was true in 1972. The top fiction title on most national indicators in December was a simple but appealing little tale from the 1970 publishing season, Richard Bach's *Jonathan Livingston Seagull*. Of the top 10 titles, the one that remained on the best-seller list the longest was the 1971 book *The Winds of War* by Herman Wouk. The absence of a book with any genuine claim to literary significance on the 1972 lists could be interpreted as an indication that a kind of literary vacuum existed in the country. Indeed, it was an opportune time for a major novel to move into view. But none had come–unless, of course, the critics had missed out.

Fiction. Choosing the "best" novel was a task most reviewers were inclined to skip in 1972. There was a wide range of fairly good, good, and very good fiction works–some from first novelists, some from veterans–in both the novel and the short-story fields. But no really big one seemed to come along.

There was abundant talent on display–for example, in Philip Roth's *The Breast*. But it was difficult for many critics to view as a serious work of fiction his playful story of a professor who turned into a female breast. Two other veteran novelists preoccupied with literary hijinks served up novels that appeared to be elaborate puzzles rather than art. Vladimir Nabokov's *Transparent Things* was merely a brief *tour de force* that seemed to parody materials from his earlier novels. John Barth's densely constructed *Chimera* was a dazzling, often mystifying, creation in which he reworked the ancient myths of Scheherazade, Perseus, and Bellerophon.

Perhaps the best offering by an established American novelist was Eudora Welty's *The Optimist's Daughter*, a brief and beautifully written story of a dying Southern judge and the interpersonal conflicts that his situation arouses among his wife, daughter, and former wife.

Other veterans published solid but hardly spectacularly successful novels. Frederick Buechner's *Open Heart* is a truly funny effort with an underlying religious motif; Sumner Locke Elliott's *The Man*

Book Year Goal: Pass The Word(s)

The importance of the written word and the need to "pass it on" received international attention in 1972. The United Nations Educational, Scientific, and Cultural Organization (UNESCO) proclaimed 1972 International Book Year (IBY), and adopted the slogan of "Books for All."

René Maheu, director-general of UNESCO, urged all nations to join wholeheartedly in the special IBY observance. "The book is the most dependable and most convenient instrument of communications ever devised by man," he said. "With the book, the human mind for the first time was able to conquer time and then space . . . and we must not fail to recognize the role and place of the book in the service of the new spirit of community that the mass media have made possible."

UNESCO officials point out that industrialized countries have as much reason to promote books as do the developing nations. Surveys show that up to half the people in several European countries are nonreaders. Reading is far from a fixed habit in areas where other media such as radio and television are readily available.

IBY symbol

But IBY was not proclaimed because of fear that books are in danger of disappearing. Never before have so many books been available. The main problem is to pass them around, so that those who need them most–the people who live in the developing countries–can read and learn.

Book production has reached new heights in recent years. The introduction of paperbacks and other production and distribution advances have made it possible to market an ever-increasing number of relatively inexpensive books of good quality. Publishers produced more than one new book a minute–546,000 titles–in 1970. That was twice the total published in 1950.

Impressive as those figures are, they tell only part of the story. Publishing today is centered in the developed countries, and the people who live in the developing areas receive few books. The scarcity grows more acute for these people as their educational opportunities increase.

Four out of every five books are published in the United States, Europe, Russia, and Japan. Asia, which has 28 per cent of the world's population, published only 7.3 per cent of the books in 1970. Africa, with 9.6 per cent of the people, published 1.7 per cent, and Latin America, with 6.1 per cent of the people, published only 3.8 per cent of the books.

"There exists in the world today a tremendous need for reading," Maheu declared. "So great is this need that for large portions of the world's population one can speak of a veritable 'book famine.' The developing countries at present . . . must rely on book imports from abroad to help meet at least part of their needs. In the long run, their full requirements can only be met by setting up their own national publishing industries."

Maheu called upon governments and agencies administering aid programs to provide the technical and financial assistance that the developing countries need to promote their own publishing industry.

Expanding their own publishing capability to produce the kinds of books they need is especially important to developing countries. The subject matter of their new publications does not always meet development needs. For example, only about 10 per cent of the books published in Asia deal with scientific and technical subjects.

More than 100 nations have adopted IBY programs. The United States has outlined a library "twinning" program through which U.S. libraries could pair off with libraries in developing countries to exchange personnel and such material as books and indexes. Great Britain expanded its aid to developing countries for book publishing. Thailand began distributing free textbooks to students in rural areas. Malaysia and Rwanda started building national libraries, and Brazil opened community libraries. Egypt, Ethiopia, Dahomey, Indonesia, Kenya, and Nepal formed book-development councils. And, to encourage reading in France, the government presented six literary classics to each couple who got married during the year. If these plans succeed, the world may finally have "Books for All."

Joseph P. Spohn

Who Got Away is about a man who drops out to live his life backward; and Isaac Bachevis Singer's *Enemies, a Love Story* is a tale of Jewish refugees in New York City during the 1940s. Among the other noteworthy titles from experienced hands were *The Confessions of a Child of the Century*, Thomas Rogers' comic account of a young man's adventures in Harvard Square, Korea, Red China, and the Central Intelligence Agency; *Standard Dreaming*, by Hortense Calisher, an unusual and entertaining novel of New York City's Chinatown; *End Zone*, Don DeLillo's hilarious story of a football player who sees in the game some astonishing parallels to nuclear warfare; and *The Sunlight Dialogues*, John Gardner's huge philosophical view of changing life in a small New York town.

One of the year's most impressive first novels was Theodore Weesner's *The Car Thief*, about a Michigan delinquent who wants to get caught. Three other first novels with valid claims to attention were Steven Millhauser's *Edwin Mullhouse*, the fictional biography of a child artist by his best friend; David Rhodes's *The Last Fair Deal Going Down*, a zany Midwestern tale; and Alan Friedman's bawdy and brilliant *Hermaphrodeity*, the "autobiography" of a poet-archaeologist-businessman who is half man, half woman.

Importations. The biggest splash from abroad was made by the Russian novelist Alexander I. Solzhenitsyn's *August 1914*, a powerful tale of prerevolutionary Russia that easily made the best-seller list. So did the late R. F. Delderfield's *To Serve Them All My Days*, an accomplished novel of England between the wars as told by the headmaster of a public school.

Julio Cortazar, the Argentine author of *Hopscotch*, scored another American success with *62: A Model Kit*, a wildly imaginative tale of psychological misfits in an imaginary city of amusing horrors. From Japan came the late Yukio Mishima's *Spring Snow*, a novel of the Westernizing of Japan in the early 1900s. The Japanese novelist Yasunari Kawabata, 1968 Nobel laureate, published *The Master of Go*, in which the ancient game of Go symbolizes the conflict of tradition and change in Japanese life.

The 1969 Nobel Prize-winning novelist Samuel Beckett came up with a brief, typically puzzling tale in *The Lost Ones*. It told of a group of 200 "bodies" who were contained in a flattened cylinder and wondered how to get out.

Short-Story lovers enjoyed a particularly good year. Two of the more important younger writers were represented by fine collections. Joyce Carol Oates's *Marriages and Infidelities* ably displayed her remarkable talent for exploring the depths and heights of love and violence. John Updike's *Museums and Women and Other Stories* is a superbly crafted series of glimpses into suburban life and times.

Eudora Welty, seated, was presented the Gold Medal for Fiction at the awards dinner of the National Institute of Arts and Letters in January.

Other noteworthy collections included Penelope Gilliatt's *Nobody's Business*, Donald Barthelme's *Sadness*. Sol Yurick's *Someone Just Like You*, Richard Brautigan's *Revenge of the Lawn*, and Toni Cade Bambara's *Gorilla, My Love*.

Prize Stories 1972: The O. Henry Awards, edited by William Abrahams, contained a first-rate collection of short stories, including contributions by Barthelme, Oates, and 16 other writers. Doris Lessing's *The Temptation of Jack Orkney and Other Stories*, and Colombian Gabriel Garcia Marquez' *Leaf Storm and Other Stories* were among the best short-story collections from abroad.

Biography, Autobiography, and Memoirs. Any assessment of the literary year must include the fifth and last volume of Leon Edel's scholarly but enormously readable life of the novelist and critic Henry James. *Henry James: The Master, 1901-1916* is the climax of Edel's unremitting two decades of labor, a triumph in itself and a fitting conclusion to his life of the brilliant writer.

Two other novelists, George Orwell and Virginia Woolf, were the subjects of absorbing new studies. *The Unknown Orwell*, by Peter Stansky and William Abrahams, was the initial volume of a life of the English writer Eric Blair, who became known as George Orwell and, after many years of struggle, reached fame with *Animal Farm* and *1984*. The authors' psychological study of Orwell takes him through the first three decades of life–from Eton to the "down-and-out" days in Paris and London during the 1930s.

In *Virginia Woolf*, Quentin Bell, her nephew, provided the most illuminating biography yet published of the life and time of the Bloomsbury novelist. Still another English writer's life was surveyed in depth in *Midnight Oil*. This is the second volume in novelist and critic V. S. Pritchett's autobiography, which began with *A Cab at the Door*.

Among the important historical biographies, James Thomas Flexner's *George Washington: Anguish and Farewell (1793-1799)*, the fourth and final volume on the life of the Revolutionary War commander, covered Washington's second term as President and his retirement to Mount Vernon. Vincent Cronin's *Napoleon Bonaparte* was praised for its fresh insights into the life of the French general, and similar plaudits were bestowed on Cecil Woodham-Smith for her absorbing biography *Queen Victoria*.

More recent figures who were treated in praiseworthy biographical studies were Eleanor Roosevelt, the subject of Joseph P. Lash's *Eleanor: The Years Alone*, an account of her life after Franklin Roosevelt's death and a sequel to *Eleanor and Franklin*; the magazine publisher Henry Luce, the subject of W. A. Swanberg's exhaustive *Luce and His Empire*; and the first woman member of Parliament, whose story is told in Christopher Sykes' entertaining *Nancy: The Life of Lady Astor*.

Sir Rudolf Bing's *5,000 Nights at the Opera*, the witty, sometimes stinging memoir of the Metropolitan Opera's former general manager, found a wide and generally amused audience. So did another book about a show-business figure, Howard Teichmann's frank and funny biography *George S. Kaufman: An Intimate Portrait*.

There was human as well as scientific interest in three outstanding biographical works of the year–Margaret Mead's *Blackberry Winter*, an autobiographical account of the anthropologist's life until World War II; Banesh Hoffmann's *Albert Einstein: Creator and Rebel*, a penetrating study of the man and his scientific life; and Max Schur's *Freud: Living and Dying*, an excellent study of the father of modern psychoanalysis by the physician who attended him during the last decade of his life.

History, Politics, and Public Affairs. Several important series books in the historical field commanded attention during the year. The late Allan Nevins' final two volumes of the eight-volume Civil War history *Ordeal of the Union* appeared, with the subtitles *The War for the Union: The Organized War, 1863-1864* and *The Organized War to Victory, 1864-1865*. They completed what is certainly the most exhaustive and authoritative account of the Civil War in modern times.

Walter Johnson and Carol Evans, as editors, published *The Papers of Adlai E. Stevenson: Beginnings of Education, 1900-1941*, the first of a planned eight volumes that will include the late Illinois politician's letters and papers. George F. Kennan's *Memoirs 1950-1963*, the second volume of his account of his diplomatic career, covered his experience during the Korean War and his ambassadorships to Russia and Yugoslavia.

Several books in the field of historical Americana offered unusual glimpses into the past. Pierre Berton's *The Impossible Railway* is a fascinating account of the adventure of building the Canadian Pacific across the unmapped North a century ago. *The Children of Pride*, a mammoth collection of letters written by members of a large Georgia family during the period from 1854 to 1868 is brilliantly edited by Robert Manson Myers. It provided an intensely interesting picture of life in the Old South. Others are a facsimile reproduction of Benjamin Butterworth's profusely illustrated work, *The Growth of Industrial Art*, a 1902 government publication that illustrated the achievements of American enterprises to that time; and a selection of 88 photographs from Edward C. Curtis' 1907-1908 portfolio, *Portraits from North American Indian Life*.

The Vietnam War continued to occupy the attention of many writers. Among the year's better books in this field was David Halberstam's *The Best and the Brightest*, a searching examination of the steps through which America's President leaders, including John F. Kennedy and Lyndon B. Johnson and their associates, became trapped in the most unpop-

The greatest publishing hoax in years ended with jail sentences for Clifford and Edith Irving for his fake autobiography of Howard Hughes.

ular war since the Mexican War. Frances FitzGerald's *Fire in the Lake* was a penetrating study of the cultural and political history of the Vietnamese. It seemed to clarify as no one had done before the nature of the Vietnamese resistance to both the French and the Americans. Related books on the war in Vietnam were Neil Sheehan's *The Arnheiter Affair* and Seymour Hersh's *Cover-Up*, a disconcerting summary of the closely guarded report of the My Lai investigation by the Army.

There were few books on World War II in 1972, but the one that clearly was filled with the most interesting material was William C. Langer's *The Mind of Adolf Hitler: The Secret Wartime Report*. It is a psychoanalytical study done for the Office of Strategic Services in 1943 and never before published.

Letters, Essays, and Criticism. *Bernard Shaw: Collected Letters, 1898-1910* is the second volume of a planned series of four edited by Daniel H. Laurence. It established beyond doubt that George Bernard Shaw was a superb letter-writer.

Several other provocative personalities were represented in essay collections published during the year. Norman Mailer published two–*Existential Errands*, a collection of 28 letters, speeches, and articles from the preceding five years, and *St. George and the Godfather*, a paperback on the political conventions.

Two writers well known for their public clashes published collections of essays, each brilliant in its own way. William F. Buckley, Jr., the conservative editor and columnist, published *Inveighing We Will Go*, and Gore Vidal, *Homage to Daniel Shays: Collected Essays, 1952-1972*.

The late Edmund Wilson's *A Window on Russia* was filled with brilliant insights into Russian literature; and the late Paul Goodman brilliantly defended the richness of individual speech in his book *Speaking and Language*.

The suicide of the brilliant young poet Sylvia Plath inspired English author and critic A. Alvarez' *The Savage God*, a moving study of her tragic case as well as a record of Alvarez' own attempt at suicide.

In *The Coming of Age*, Simone de Beauvoir offers a penetrating, encyclopedic, and passionate discussion on the theme of aging. Edgar Allan Poe and the late Ezra Pound were the subjects of two fine critical appraisals–Daniel Hoffman's *Poe Poe Poe Poe Poe Poe Poe* and Hugh Kenner's *The Pound Era*.

The Literary Hoax of the Year ended disastrously for writer Clifford Irving, his wife Edith, and researcher Richard Suskind. The three admitted trying to defraud McGraw-Hill, Incorporated, of $750,000 with a fake autobiography of Howard R. Hughes. Mrs. Irving was jailed for two months. Suskind was sentenced to 6 months in prison and Irving to two and one-half years. Van Allen Bradley

LITERATURE, CANADIAN. See CANADIAN LIBRARY ASSOCIATION; CANADIAN LITERATURE.

LITERATURE FOR CHILDREN. The number of paperback editions of books formerly available only in hardback continued to increase in 1972. This included many of the Newbery and Caldecott Medal winners. If there was any discernible trend in subject matter, it was a focusing of interest on the American Indian. Greater interest in bicycling for all ages was reflected in the publication of more books dealing with all aspects of bicycles and bicycle riding.

Here are some of the outstanding books published in 1972:

Picture Books

The Castle of a Thousand Cats, by Harold Longman, illustrated by Don Madden (Addison-Wesley). Wonderfully humorous illustrations and an ingenious story line make this a delightful book. The reader may find himself chuckling aloud as he turns the pages. Any cat lover will find it irresistible. Ages 5 to 9.

Crash! Bang! Boom! by Peter Spier (Doubleday). A delightful picture book of noises by a very talented illustrator, this should prove as much fun for the read-alouder as for the child listener. Hundreds of noise-making activities are shown, from the "slup-slup" of a tongue licking ice cream to the "banga-banga-banga-bang!" of a riveting machine. Up to age 8.

Artist Leonard Baskin's startling drawing of "the cadaver-haunted vulture" illustrates the letter V in *Hosie's Alphabet.* Publisher: Viking.

How the Devil Gets His Due, adapted and illustrated by Harold Berson (Crown), is taken from an old French folk tale. The book has not only the appeal of a young peasant boy ingeniously outwitting the devil, but also the charm of humorous, action-filled pictures that set the tale in motion. Ages 5 to 9.

Mouse Tales, an I Can Read Book, by Arnold Lobel (Harper & Row). These seven tales have just the sort of absurd happenings, told with straight-faced humor and imagination, that a beginning reader should love.

D'Aulaires' Trolls, by Ingri and Edgar Parin d'Aulaire (Doubleday). This husband-and-wife team, experienced writers of children's stories, tell about all sorts of trolls, gnomes, and other mysterious creatures, and some of the fascinating traditions and stories that are told about these awesome beings. The pictures have an appropriate monumental and elemental quality, as well as humor and animation. Ages 6 to 10.

Milton the Early Riser, by Robert Kraus, illustrated by José and Ariane Aruego (Windmill/Dutton). The full-page color paintings in this book show the wide-awake panda Milton as he tries to get all sorts of extremely colorful and unusual animals to wake up and play with him. Up to age 8.

When Clay Sings, by Byrd Baylor, illustrated by Tom Bahti (Scribners). Perhaps more interesting to the adult than the child, this book is illustrated with designs derived from the prehistoric Indian pottery of the American Southwest. It would, however, give even the child some appreciation of the ancient Indians as real people. Any reader who enjoys good design will delight in the original, fanciful, and fascinating shapes that swim, leap, and dance across the book's imaginatively designed pages.

The Hare and the Tortoise and the Tortoise and the Hare; La Liebre y La Tortuga y La Tortuga y La Liebre, by William Pène Du Bois and Lee Po (Doubleday). Told in parallel columns of Spanish and English, this book has two stories – the traditional Aesop fable in which the tortoise is the victor, and an Oriental tale in which the hare outsmarts the tortoise. The full-color illustrations are filled with humorous and imaginative details. Up to age 12.

Anansi the Spider, by Gerald McDermott (Holt, Rinehart and Winston). This is a retelling of an African folk tale about five Ashanti brothers, each of whom possesses a special ability that proves invaluable in the rescue of their father. It is illustrated with highly stylized and original pictures. Up to age 8.

The Nuns Go to Africa, by Jonathan Routh (Bobbs-Merrill). This author-illustrator began painting three years ago. He chose nuns as his subjects because he didn't have to draw arms and legs for them. This African vacation sees them doing such unlikely things as getting caught in an elephant traffic jam, sliding

Miss Jaster consults with Wimple the Chief Constable after the mysterious disappearance of her zinnias in *Miss Jaster's Garden.* A Golden Book.

down a gorilla's roller coaster, and riding zebras, all narrated in a perfectly matter-of-fact manner which adds to the humor. Ages 5 to 9.

Over in the Meadow, illustrated by Ezra Jack Keats (Four Winds Press). Beautiful, full-color illustrations by a Caldecott Medal winner make this version of the old counting rhyme very appealing. Up to age 8.

We Are Having a Baby, by Viki Holland (Scribners). Excellent photographs show 4-year-old Dana's reactions to the arrival of her new brother – happy and interested at first, then not so sure. The sensitive approach and realism of the family portrayed should make this a good book to help a child anticipate a coming birth in the family. Up to age 8.

A Christmas Fantasy, by Carolyn Haywood, illustrated by Glenys and Victor Ambrus (Morrow), is a story of Santa Claus's life as a boy and how he got started in "the present business." The full-color illustrations have a Victorian charm and detail that seem appropriate. Ages 3 to 8.

Simon Boom Gives a Wedding, by Yuri Suhl, illustrated by Margot Zemach (Four Winds). Inspired by a Jewish folk tale, this is the story of a man who always wanted to buy the very best, and the strange and humorous results this sometimes produced. The full-color illustrations add greatly to the flavor and appeal of the book. Ages 5 to 9.

The Girl Who Loved the Wind, by Jane Yolen, illustrated by Ed Young (Crowell). Lovely paintings reminiscent of Persian miniatures, but modern in technique and feeling, make this story of the meeting of the wind and the overprotected daughter of an Eastern merchant a memorable one. Ages 5 to 9.

People, Places, and Things

Oh, Lizzie! The Life of Elizabeth Cady Stanton, by Doris Faber (Lothrop, Lee & Shepard), is a lively biography of a lively lady. It tells about the enthusiasms and difficulties of one of the intellectual leaders of the Woman's Rights Movement, who was also one of its most energetic and effective campaigners. Ages 10 and up.

From Lew Alcindor to Kareem Abdul Jabbar, by James Haskins (Lothrop, Lee & Shepard), follows the well-known basketball star from his earliest memories ("I was the large, economy-size child") through his high school and college years to his present professional status. It tells of some of the difficulties he encountered being 7 feet 2 inches tall and black. Ages 10 and up.

Flying Today and Tomorrow, by John Gabriel Navarra (Doubleday), has large photographs of many types of planes and simple explanations of some of the special characteristics of each. It should be a delight to the child who is fascinated by any type of flying machine. Up to age 10.

Science, Animals, and Skills

The Natural History of the Tail, by Lisbeth Zappler, illustrated by Jean Zallinger (Doubleday), is a fasci-

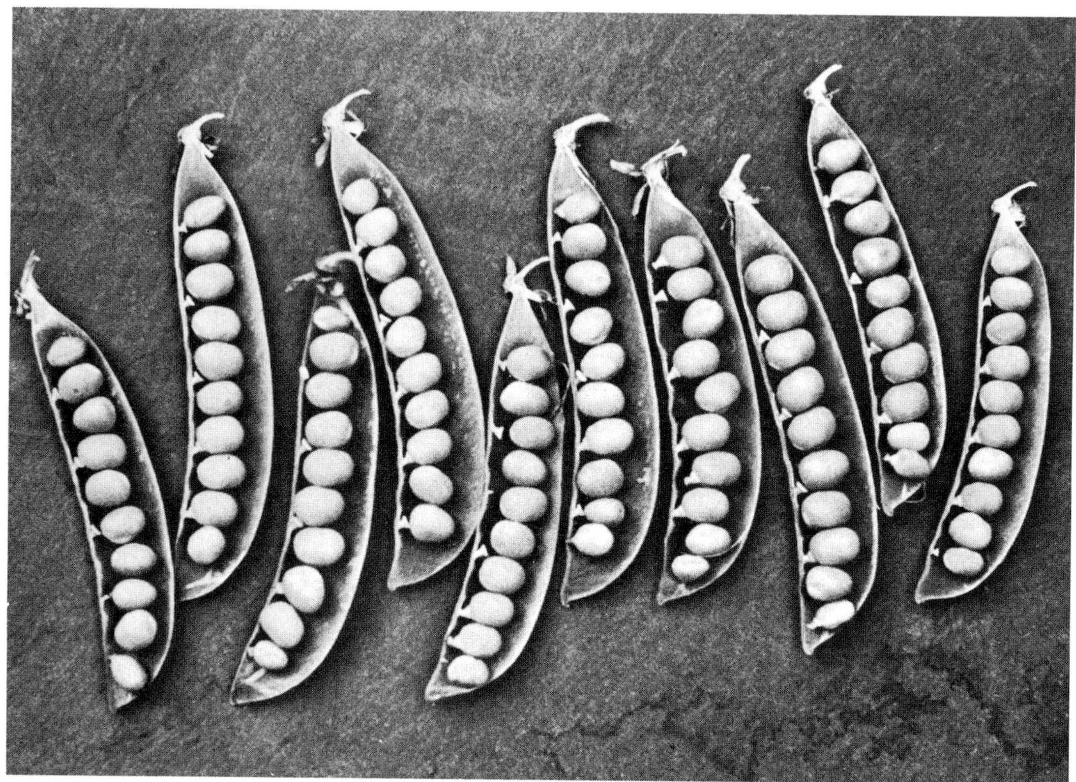

Ten pods each containing 10 peas are used to illustrate the number 100 in *Count and See* by Tana Hoban. Publisher: the Macmillan Company.

nating study of the tail. The book follows the early appearances of that appendage on primitive animals and birds up to present-day creatures. It discusses in readable and interesting fashion the uses various animals and birds make of their tails. Up to age 12.

Problem Pets, story and pictures by Lilo Hess (Scribners). Filled with excellent and appealing photographs, this book tells how to take care of the pets that people don't intend to acquire but sometimes do – baby birds, fawns, raccoons, foxes, skunks, and so on. It provides concise information on the care of wild animals in captivity. Ages 8 and up.

Those Other People the Porpoises, by Elgin Ciampi (Grosset & Dunlap). Many photographs of, and much unusual information about, individual porpoises in captivity, their life history and social behavior in the sea, their intelligence, and some possibilities of their future association with man, make this an interesting book. Ages 10 and up.

The Giant Panda, by Lynne Martin (Young Scott Books), tells about the discovery of the giant panda, discusses its habits and relatives, and gives full accounts of the pandas that have lived in the various zoos of the world. The photographs are very appealing. Ages 8 to 13.

Dandelion, Pokeweed, and Goosefoot; How the Early Settlers Used Plants for Food, Medicine and in the Home, by Elizabeth Shaeffer, illustrated by Grambs Miller (Young Scott Books). The title does not indicate the full range of this informative book, which explains the "international code" of Latin plant names. In an easy, conversational, and interesting manner, it gives various bits of information about 60 plants, concluding with sections on making tea and salads, and dyeing cloth. This book would be as fascinating to an adult as to a reader of the suggested 8 to 13 years of age.

Ed Emberley's Drawing Book: Make a World, by Ed Emberley (Little, Brown). Using a vocabulary of some 17 very simple shapes and letters, the author-illustrator shows how to draw hundreds of things, step by step. A fascinating book for anyone who likes to draw. Up to age 13.

The Bread Dough Craft Book, by Elyse Sommer, illustrated by Giulio Maestro (Lothrop, Lee & Shepard). Flowers, toys, jewelry, small pieces of sculpture, and a host of other items will quickly emerge from the hands of the enthusiastic reader as he follows the recipes and the easy directions for use of the modeling substance discussed in this book. Detailed information and helpful illustrations make this a book the craft enthusiast from 8 to 88 will enjoy.

Bikes, a How-to-do-it Guide to Selection, Care, Repair, Maintenance, Decoration, Safety, and Fun on Your Bicycle, by Stephen C. Henkel (Chatham Press). This book should have appeal for everyone interested in bicycles and bicycling, from elementary school students to adults. It has an interesting picture history of the bicycle, detailed information on the anatomy of the bicycle, how to care for and repair bikes, as well as chapters for both beginners and experts on how to ride a bike.

Action! Camera! Super 8 Cassette Film Making for Beginners, by Rick Carrier and David Carroll (Scribners), clearly and interestingly introduces the prospective film maker to his camera and to film terminology and techniques. It aims to teach the cameraman to edit his film in the camera, and it has three step-by-step film-making projects to help him learn professional techniques quickly. Up to age 12.

Fiction for the Middle Grades

The Little Broomstick, by Mary Stewart, illustrated by Shirley Hughes (Morrow). Plain Mary Smith finds herself in exciting and sometimes frightening circumstances when she decides to help her black cat Tib rescue his brother from a school for witches and helps him narrowly escape from being used by the witches as a subject in a bizarre transformation experiment.

The Mystery Next Door, by Audrey and William Roos, illustrated by Ingrid Fetz (Scribners). A breezy little mystery that not only has the rescue of an elderly lady held prisoner by her unscrupulous nephew, but also has the added interests of a 12-year-old heroine who is too fat and a 22-year-old hero who is skinny and unathletic. It all ends with everything taken care of–in rather pat fashion, perhaps, but nevertheless interestingly.

The Seven Wishes of Joanna Peabody, by Genevieve Gray, illustrated by Elton Fax (Lothrop, Lee & Shepard). Told by Joanna herself, this is the story of the seven wishes a little black girl makes when Aunt Thelma, the Special Spirit assigned to look after her, appears on television to tell her she has won the Seven Wishes Sweepstakes. The story mixes reality and magic in a very effective way, in large part because of the reality of the author herself. Humorous and delightful.

O the Red Rose Tree, by Patricia Beatty, illustrated by Liz Dauber (Morrow). Told in a sprightly and enthusiastic manner by a 13-year-old narrator, this story takes place in 1893 in the state of Washington. The heroine has adventures involving an Italian opera singer, a flood in Portland, and glimpses of Portland high society. The unusual energy and verve of the main characters make for entertaining reading for middle graders.

Dorrie and the Goblin, by Patricia Coombs (Lothrop, Lee & Shepard). Dorrie thought the little red-eyed goblin would be fun to have around, but soon found baby-sitting for a goblin–even a little one–was more adventuresome than she realized. Delightful illustrations by the author make Dorrie the Little Witch extremely appealing.

Teen-Age Fiction

The Pegleg Mystery, by Hal Evarts (Scribners). Full of action, suspense, and excitement, this story follows two high school seniors (one of whom is an Indian named Kelly) around California and Mexico on their motorcycle. Along the way, they run into an exciting mystery and across the path of a motorcycle gang looking for thrills.

The Henchmans at Home, by Hester Burton, illustrated by Victor G. Ambrus (Thomas Crowell). Each of these six stories highlights a happening in the lives of William, Ellen, and Rob Henchman over a period of nine years in the late 1800s. Excellent characterization and interesting use of incident make the reader feel he knows the family well–and cares about them.

Awards in 1972 included:

American Library Association Children's Services Division Awards: The *Newbery Medal* for "the most distinguished contribution to American literature for children" was awarded to Robert C. O'Brien for *Mrs. Frisby and the Rats of NIMH* (Atheneum). The *Caldecott Medal*, which is given to "the most distinguished American picture book for children," was presented to Nonny Hogrogian for *One Fine Day* (Macmillan). The *Mildred L. Batchelder Award* for "a book considered to be the most outstanding of those books originally published in a foreign country and subsequently translated and published in the United States" was received by Hans Peter Richter for *Freidrich* (Holt), translated from the German by Edite Kroll.

British Book Awards: The *Carnegie Medal* for "the most outstanding book of the year" went to *Josh* by Ivan Southall (Macmillan).

Book World's Children's Spring Book Festival Awards: The award in the Picture Book Division was won by *Little John* by Theodor Storm, retold by Doris Orgel, pictures by Anita Lobel (Farrar, Straus, and Giroux); in the ages 8 to 12 Division by *Cockleburr Quarters* by Charlotte Baker, illustrated by Robert Owens (Prentice-Hall); in the ages 12 to 16 Division by *Freaky Friday* by Mary Rodgers (Harper & Row).

National Book Committee Award: The National Book Award for children's books was presented to Donald Barthelme, author and illustrator of *The Slightly Irregular Fire Engine or The Hithering Thithering Djinn* (Farrar, Straus, and Giroux).

The Hans Christian Andersen Award, an international award, was given to Scott O'Dell for the total body of his work. Lynn de Grummond Delaune

LIVESTOCK. See AGRICULTURE; INTERNATIONAL LIVE STOCK EXPOSITION.

LOS ANGELES-LONG BEACH. The era of uncontrolled land development around Los Angeles drew to a close in 1972 as conservationist pressures began to show results. In September, the Los Angeles County board of supervisors ordered a building freeze on 1.8 million acres, one-third of the land suitable for development in the area. The board ruled that building permits will be granted for no more than one unit per acre. The board was acting under a 1970 state law requiring counties and cities to preserve open lands.

School enrollment in Los Angeles dropped for the third straight year in 1972. The 1972 enrollment of 622,000 students represented a 2.5 per cent decline from 1971's 637,000. Officials attributed the decline to a lower birth rate and families moving out of the area because of aerospace industry layoffs, or the 1971 earthquake scare.

High Crime Rate. Uniform Crime Reports released on August 29 showed the Los Angeles-Long Beach area had the third highest crime rate in the nation. The area's rate of 5,443.5 crimes per 100,000 persons was almost double the national average of 2,907. The violent crime rate, 794.8 per 100,000 persons, was also more than double the national average. Crime continued to increase at a 5 per cent rate in Los Angeles and a 9 per cent rate in Long Beach. Los Angeles led the nation in the number of bomb threats in 1971 with more than 700 bomb investigations.

The Los Angeles City Council approved an $11.2-million swap of city-owned land for federal government property. The city traded 4.1 acres valued at $3.2 million for 19.2 federally owned acres valued at $8 million. The federal government will use its newly acquired land for parking facilities to serve nearby federal buildings. Los Angeles will use its new property for park and recreational facilities.

Median Family Income in the area was reported by the U.S. Bureau of the Census to be among the highest in the nation. Los Angeles ranked sixth in the nation with a median family income of $10,503, while Long Beach ranked ninth with $10,282.

Employment in the Los Angeles-Long Beach area rose by about 42,500 jobs between May, 1971, and May, 1972, but unemployment was still rated as substantial by the U.S. Department of Labor. The income of the average factory worker, however, rose 9.4 per cent during the same period.

A two and a half month strike against station KTTV by the National Association of Broadcast Employees and Technicians was settled on November 3. Management kept the station operating during the strike. In November, a Los Angeles reporter was jailed for refusing a court order to disclose a news source. See NEWSPAPERS. J. M. Banovetz

LOUISIANA. See NEW ORLEANS; STATE GOVERNMENT.

LUMBER. See FOREST AND FOREST PRODUCTS.

LUXEMBOURG. Without a dissenting vote, the Luxembourg Chamber of Deputies reduced the minimum voting age from 21 to 18 on Jan. 13, 1972. At the same time, it reduced the minimum age qualification for holding office from 25 to 21.

President Georges Pompidou of France visited Luxembourg on May 3 and 4 and reported that he and Pierre Werner, Luxembourg's president and prime minister, considered an economic and monetary union to be of central importance for the European Community (Common Market). He reassured Werner that the "big brothers" of the enlarged community–France, Great Britain, and West Germany –would not dominate the smaller states.

After three years of talks, a 21-nation working party meeting in Luxembourg agreed in June on a draft convention that would better organize Europe's patent system. If ratified at a 1973 conference, the agreement will establish a central office to grant patents that would be valid throughout Europe.

Luxembourg's standard of living remained among the highest in Europe. The Grand Duke Jean and the Grand Duchess made their first state visit to Great Britain on June 13, and Queen Elizabeth II referred to Luxembourg's economic well-being. She said, "Today your modern steel industry and the high level of employment are a tribute to the talents of your political and industrial leaders." Kenneth Brown

See also EUROPE (Facts in Brief Table).

MAGAZINES. The biggest news event of 1972 was the decision by Time Inc. to discontinue publication of *Life* magazine with the December 29 issue because of continuing financial losses. Hedley Donovan, editor in chief of Time Inc., and Andrew Heiskell, chairman of the board, made the announcement on December 8. They said that *Life*'s appeal as an advertising medium had encountered severe competition from television since the late 1950s.

The weekly picture magazine, launched on Nov. 23, 1936, had pioneered news photojournalism in the United States (see PHOTOGRAPHY).

Consumer magazines reached a record high of $1.3 billion in advertising revenue in 1972, but publishers faced a major threat from sharply rising postal rates. The Board of Governors of the U.S. Postal Service ordered into effect on July 6 increases in second-class postage averaging 127 per cent. The increases are to be phased in over a five-year period. The Magazine Publishers Association, Incorporated, reacted strongly. Publishers did not dispute the need for reasonable increases to improve service. They held, however, that increases of from 20 to 30 per cent a year were "inordinately" high, pointing out that increases have averaged from 6 to 7 per cent a year over the past 15 years.

"The impact of the postage increases on the flow of ideas and opinion is likely to be catastrophic," wrote Tom Wicker, columnist of *The New York Times*, "for

January, 1972, heralded the birth of the new feminist magazine *Ms.*, but December sounded the death knell of *Life* magazine at the age of 36.

it is precisely upon the smaller, usually less-profitable publications that it will impose the heaviest burden." Andrew Heiskell of Time Inc. said, "Increases of such magnitude are sufficient to wipe out all profits and more. . . . To pass them on to the reader, along with other rising costs, will be to create a magazine industry for the affluent, only."

New Magazines. Despite concern over future prospects, more than 70 new magazines appeared during the year. The feminist magazine *Ms* was introduced in January. Gloria Steinem is president and Patricia Carbine, formerly of *McCall's*, is vice-president and secretary. The January 29 issue of *Saturday Review* marked its split into four monthly magazines, published in weekly rotation and covering arts, education, science, and society. Norman Cousins, former editor of *Saturday Review*, premièred a new biweekly, *World*, in July. In October, Time Inc. launched *Money*, its first new publication since *Sports Illustrated* appeared in 1954. *Money* is a monthly on personal and family finance. In September, publisher Hugh Hefner introduced *Oui* "for the man of the world." He intended the monthly to compete with London-produced *Penthouse*, which unabashedly imitates *Playboy* and doubled its circulation to more than 2 million during the year.

In November, CBS Publications, formerly the Magazine Division of Holt, Rinehart and Winston, which publishes *Field & Stream* and special-interest publications, brought out its first issue of *Epicure*, a new quarterly about food, wine, and travel.

Publishers Weekly and *Popular Science* observed their 100th anniversaries in 1972. *Reader's Digest* and *Better Homes & Gardens* celebrated their 50th anniversaries, and came out in successive months with the largest single revenue-producing issues in magazine history. *Better Homes*'s November issue reached $7.3 million in advertising revenue, slightly more than the *Digest*. *Fortune* and *Progressive Farmer* joined the trend toward smaller page size, effecting savings in paper and mailing costs.

Newsweek's chairman of the board Osborne Elliott resumed the post of editor on June 29, and Robert Stein returned to the editor's job at *McCall's*. On the 50th anniversary of *Foreign Affairs*, 79-year-old Hamilton Fish Armstrong retired as editor. Anthony Mazzola, former editor in chief of *Town & Country*, was named editor of *Harper's Bazaar*. *The New York Times*, through its subsidiary, *Golf Digest*, acquired *Tennis*. *The Times-Mirror*, through its Popular Science Publishing Company (which publishes *Popular Science* and *Outdoor Life*) acquired *Golf* and *Ski* from Universal Publishing & Distribution Company, which in turn acquired *On the Sound* from Seascape Publications. John H. Johnson, publisher and editor of *Ebony* and *Jet* magazines was named Publisher of the Year.

John K. Montmeat

MAINE. See STATE GOVERNMENT.

MALAGASY REPUBLIC. President Philibert Tsiranana relinquished his powers to General Gabriel Ramanantsoa, the army chief of staff, on May 18, 1972. The president, who had ruled the country since independence in 1960, acted after antigovernment riots and strikes by a coalition of students and workers.

The trouble stemmed from the arrest on May 12 of 400 student leaders who demanded changes in the country's educational system. They were especially dissatisfied with the French-oriented curriculum at the University of Madagascar in Tananarive and demanded a new one be substituted. Thirty-four of the rioting students were killed and 400 were injured by security police who tried to restore order. The students were joined on May 15 by workers who had reacted to a state of emergency proclaimed by the president by calling a general strike.

As the demonstrations persisted and grew more violent, President Tsiranana dissolved his government and placed all executive and emergency legislative powers in General Ramanantsoa's hands.

The Choice of Ramanantsoa was a popular one. He was considered an ardent nationalist who would reduce the level of French influence in the country. Most Malagasy deeply resented the fact that Tsiranana had permitted French private interests to retain some 70 per cent of investments other than real estate in the country and control of almost 67 per cent of Malagasy's foreign trade–the fastest-growing sector of the gross national product. There were about 50,000 French nationals on the island, and French still controlled the nation's commerce and the large sugar and coffee plantations. They also held key civil service positions and were able to manipulate both domestic and international government policy.

One of General Ramanantsoa's first moves was to form a new Cabinet of 10 ministers representing all parts of the island. Four members were military officers and six were civilians. He also promised to eliminate corruption and profiteering in government and to give the highest priority to social welfare in the most neglected areas of the country. All-out efforts were also promised to eliminate low wages, control rising prices, and increase the short supply of food.

Despite these assurances, unrest persisted, especially among President Tsiranana's few supporters. On August 29, Ramanantsoa proclaimed martial law. In a referendum held on October 7, the voters endorsed military rule for a five-year period. They also approved the president's departure from office and the closing of both legislative houses. On October 12, General Ramanantsoa assumed full control of the country. Paul C. Tullier

See also AFRICA (Facts in Brief Table).

General Gabriel Ramanantsoa, guarded by members of the armed forces, toured Tananarive in a jeep after he seized power in Malagasy in May.

MALAYSIA. The Strait of Malacca involved Malaysia in an international dispute in 1972. Malaysia and neighboring Indonesia each consider the strait as its property, claiming a 20-mile limit rather than the traditional 3-mile limit for its territorial waters. On March 7, the two countries, which share the waterway under a bilateral treaty signed in mid-1971, rejected a claim by the United States, Russia, Great Britain, and Japan that the strait constituted international waters. The four powers wanted to place the waterway under international administration. This would enable them to dredge the channel so it could be used by larger vessels. The Malaysian government insisted that control of the strait remain with it and Indonesia to ensure that their coastal waters and shores are not polluted.

On August 7, Malaysian Deputy Prime Minister Tun Ismail announced a cooperative agreement had been signed with Indonesia under which both nations would patrol the strait to curb subversive and smuggling activities. Patrol duties would be carried out under the command of a bilateral group known as the Western Regional Border Committee.

Ismail also announced the formation of an Eastern Regional Border Committee through which Malaysia and Indonesia hoped to control subversive operations along the borders separating Sarawak, a Malaysian province, from West Kalimantan in Indonesia. The insurgent forces that had plagued

Malaysia through most of the 1960s had reportedly trained and armed a cadre of 1,200 Chinese-dominated Communists in Thailand. Early in the year, this force had begun infiltrating the northwest coast of Borneo.

Foreign Affairs. On February 21, Queen Elizabeth II of Great Britain paid a state visit to Malaysia. While in Kuala Lumpur, the capital, the queen conferred with Prime Minister Abdul Razak and King Abdul Halim Muazzam. In June, former U.S. Secretary of the Treasury John B. Connally visited Malaysia as President Richard M. Nixon's special envoy on international trade and money matters.

Australian Prime Minister William McMahon visited Malaysia in June for talks with Prime Minister Razak. In a joint communiqué issued at the conclusion of the visit, the two nations agreed to continue their support of a five-power regional defense arrangement including Australia, Malaysia, Indonesia, New Zealand, and Singapore.

Malaysia, Indonesia, and Laos walked out of a nonaligned nations' meeting which was held in Georgetown, Guyana, from August 8 to 12. The three nations protested the decision to seat delegations representing the Viet Cong in Vietnam and the Cambodian government in exile. Paul C. Tullier

See also Asia (Facts in Brief Table).

MALI. See Africa.

MALTA. Prime Minister Dom Mintoff made brinkmanship pay off in 1972. He signed an agreement in London on March 26 sharply increasing the rent Malta receives for use of the island's military facilities by Great Britain and the North Atlantic Treaty Organization (NATO). Mintoff had threatened to expel British forces unless Malta received more rent.

At first, Britain refused to increase its share of the annual rental, and began to airlift servicemen and families back home. Other NATO countries, especially Italy, feared Russia would take over the base.

Talks held in Rome in January and February broke down four times before Mintoff went to London on March 4 for negotiations that led to the new, seven-year agreement. The annual rental paid by Britain and NATO was raised to about $35 million. In December, Mintoff asked a further increase, claiming the pound had lost some value.

Mintoff visited China in April and came home with a long-term, interest-free loan worth 100 million yuan (about $44.4 million). Most of it would take the form of development projects.

Mintoff's declared aim for Malta is economic self-sufficiency. But the abolition of special tax incentives to industrialists deterred any major new investment. Unemployment continued to rise. George Scott

See also Europe (Facts in Brief Table).

MANITOBA. See Canada.

Maltese citizens demonstrated in support of Prime Minister Dom Mintoff, who told Great Britain to pay higher rent or vacate its Malta military bases.

MANUFACTURING. The long downturn in industrial production that began in late 1969 and continued through 1971 came to a dramatic halt in October, 1972. The Federal Reserve Board industrial production index for October stood at 116.7 (1967=100), 9.3 per cent above October, 1971.

Commenting on the upswing, *The New York Times* indicated that an "increase of such magnitude is seen approaching boom proportions." Manufacturing production was also up 9.3 per cent, largely due to a 10.5 per cent rise in durable goods.

Output gains were widespread. Auto assemblies, at the annual rate of 9.1 million units, rose 7 per cent. Output of business equipment was 12 per cent above the 1971 low, although it was still 4 per cent below the 1969 peak.

New Orders and manufacturers' inventories for September confirmed the continuing recovery. Department of Commerce figures showed that new orders totaled $65.5 billion, up from $64.4 billion in August. New orders for durable goods reached $36.79 billion, up from $35.73 billion in August.

Total inventories were $105.29 billion at the end of September; shipments were $63.6 billion. The important ratio of inventories to shipments was relatively low – 1.66 compared with 1.82 a year earlier. With new September orders exceeding shipments, the backlog of orders rose to $82.2 billion, compared to $74.4 billion the year before.

The sharp advances in output put more of industry's unused plant capacity back to work. By the end of the third quarter, factories were operating at about 83 per cent of capacity, significantly higher than 1971's 75.5 per cent level.

Capital Spending and Productivity. The gains in capital spending that began during the third quarter of 1971 reached record levels in 1972. Investment for new plants and equipment spurted 10 per cent to an estimated $89.1 billion.

Manufacturing productivity increased at an annual rate of 3.3 per cent in the third quarter of 1972. This increase, in a traditionally slow quarter, was down from the high rate of 6.6 per cent of the second quarter, but well above the 2.1 per cent of 1971. Equally encouraging was the decline in unit labor costs in nonfarm industries, a key measure of inflationary pressures. Unit costs dropped by 0.8 per cent in the second and third quarters.

Labor. Despite the resurgence of the economy, unemployment hung stubbornly at 5.5 per cent in October. This was the level reached in June, 1972, after a decline from the year-end 1971 level of 6 per cent. Manufacturing added 126,000 workers in October, seasonally adjusted, following a gain of 87,000 in September. Manufacturing employment was at 19.1 million, the highest level in two years.

Idleness caused by strikes during the first nine months of 1972 plunged to 1.5 man-hours per thousand, from 2.5 a year earlier. This was the lowest level since 1966. The Labor Department attributed the decline to wage controls and to 1972's lighter bargaining schedule. In manufacturing, first-year wage increases in major labor agreements averaged 6.9 per cent, down from 10.9 per cent in the first nine months of 1971. See LABOR.

The Lordstown Syndrome, a term for rebellion by younger workers against the monotony of the automated assembly line, was a new phenomenon in 1972. It had been anticipated that automation would relieve the backbreaking drudgery of the assembly line and improve manufacturing efficiency. Although this has proved to be true, it has also accentuated the monotony of the assembly line and, in the view of union critics, "dehumanized work."

The issue burst into national focus at the General Motors (GM) plant in Lordstown, Ohio, a new, fully automated facility that turns out the compact Vega. By the end of the year, the Lordstown Syndrome had spread to GM plants in Norwood, Ohio; St. Louis; Janesville, Wis.; Arlington, Tex.; and Van Nuys, Calif. Workers, mainly the younger ones, rebelled against what they considered a production speed-up. Production disputes and management charges of worker sabotage underscored the growing problem of general worker discontent on assembly lines.

Technology. An electron-beam welding machine, first used in the nuclear and aerospace industries, moved onto the Ford and GM production lines in 1972. The electron beam heats rapidly, deeply, and precisely. It can weld a ⅛-inch-thick piece of steel at speeds of several hundred inches a minute, and the joint is thin and strong and needs little or no cleanup. Because heating is minimal, very little weakening or distortion of the metal parts takes place. The electron-beam welders handle from several hundred parts an hour to as many as 3,600 – one each second.

C. I. Hayes, Incorporated, a leading manufacturer of electrical heating equipment, introduced a revolutionary carburizing furnace. The head of a leading manufacturer's metallurgical force called it "the biggest advance in heat treating in 30 years."

Carburizing is a common heat-treating process used to harden the surface of a steel part without making it brittle. It requires a furnace heated to about 1750°F. by a delicately balanced atmosphere of air and either natural gas or propane. The metal's surface absorbs carbon from the gas, creating an outer shell of hardened steel.

Hayes has added a vacuum that draws off impurities from the surface of the metal. When coupled with vastly improved refractory and heating materials, carburizing temperatures reach 1900°F. and higher. The process time is cut in half. The furnace also uses plain natural gas as a carbon source, thus eliminating the intricate handling needed to control the atmosphere in an air-gas carburizer.

A subsidiary of Ingersoll-Rand developed a fluid jet cutter that cuts through nonmetallic materials

GM's automated assembly plant in Lordstown, Ohio, is the world's fastest, but line workers struck in March because of the pressure and monotony.

cleanly and quickly with a thin, powerful stream of specially treated water. The jet can cut through such diverse materials as paper, foam-backed carpeting, fiberglass insulation, and asbestos sheet and ceramic insulators at speeds of up to 2,000 feet per minute. The fluid jet can curve and twist in any direction. In addition, a cut can be started at any point, without a preliminary hole, and stopped at any point.

Machine Tools. Orders in September rose to the highest levels for any month since mid-1969. This indicated that the cautious recovery underway since the second quarter of 1971 was finally building up steam.

At the International Machine Tool Show in September in Chicago, industry saw the new computer numerical control (CNC) systems built around minicomputers. Development of the CNC systems, each of which has its own built-in minicomputer to run a machine tool, was held back because of relatively high costs. But with the price of minicomputers falling rapidly, the systems have now become more practical.

With CNC, the minicomputer uses the program stored in its memory to drive the machine tool. This control is faster than paper tape and eliminates tape-handling problems. Some observers claimed it might boost tool productivity by as much as 90 per cent. Moreover, its adherents say, changes in parts programs can be made at the machine rather than having to go back to a central computer (as in a direct numerical control system).

Electrical Manufacturing. The National Electrical Manufacturers Association estimated total 1972 shipments at a record $52.2 billion, a 9.9 per cent increase over 1971's $47.5 billion.

Consumer electrical products and industrial electronics and communications equipment each posted gains of about 10 per cent–from $10.5 billion to $11.6 billion and from $15.4 billion to $16.9 billion, respectively. In other major categories, lighting equipment registered a 16 per cent gain to $4.1 billion, industrial equipment posted a 5 per cent gain to $7.5 billion, building equipment was up 17 per cent to $2.1 billion, and power equipment was up 8 per cent to $5.8 billion.

Westinghouse Electric reported the development of a superconducting alternating-current generator that could provide a new standard of power generation. Spokesmen claimed the new system would be much more reliable, much smaller, and cheaper.

In a superconducting system almost all resistance to an electric current is lost. It occurs in several metals and in certain alloys when they are cooled to lower than −430° F. The superconducting generator gains its advantages from 2 miles of niobium-titanium alloy wire wound into the electromagnet. This wire carries about five times the electricity of conventional generator windings and produces a magnetic field three to four times greater than conventional generators. The new alloy replaces the iron used in conventional generators, and is anywhere from a third to a tenth the size and weight. Liquid helium, the coldest liquid known, is used to keep the unit at its super-low temperatures.

The Westinghouse superconducting prototype is only 5 feet long and 3.5 feet in diameter, but it can generate 5,000 kilowatts of electric power, enough to serve a town of 8,000 people.

Rubber. The Rubber Manufacturers Association estimated that 1972 rubber consumption would be 2.9 million long tons, a 7 per cent rise from 1971, and that synthetic rubber would account for 78 per cent of the total.

Record shipment of rubber tires–193 million, a gain of 4 per cent over 1971–was also indicated. Of this total, 51 million were to go to vehicle manufacturers and 142 million for replacement and export. Truck and bus tire shipments were expected to reach a record 32.8 million units compared to 29-million units in 1971.

Textile Sales were expected to exceed the 1971 level by 7 per cent. The American Textile Manufacturers Institute reported domestic mill volume at $24.5 billion, up from $22.9 billion in 1971. The institute indicated that shortage of textile labor was a problem, although employment increased to 996,000 from 962,000 in 1971. George J. Berkwitt

MARGRETHE II (1940-) was proclaimed queen of Denmark on Jan. 15, 1972, the day after her father King Frederik IX died of pneumonia and heart disease. Eldest of three daughters, she is the first woman sovereign in Danish history. Margrethe I ruled in the late 1300s and early 1400s, but was not crowned queen. It was not until 1953 that the country's Constitution was amended to include women in the line of succession. Although Margrethe's power is symbolic and limited to signing laws passed by the *Folketing* (parliament), she will have great influence over the Danes.

Margrethe is unusually well qualified for her role as queen. She studied French at the Sorbonne, constitutional law at the University of Copenhagen, sociology at the London School of Economics, and archaeology at Cambridge University. She has traveled around the world on archaeological expeditions and often did her own television programs on the scientific trips. She also helped do rescue work on The Temples of Abu Simbel in Egypt, which were threatened by the building of the Aswan Dam. She speaks five languages, and enjoys reading, classical music, ju-jitsu, skiing, tennis, and swimming.

In 1967, Margrethe married a French diplomat, Count Henri de Laborde de Monpezat, who is now known as Prince Henrik. They have two sons, Frederik and Joachim. Lillian Zahrt

MARINE CORPS, U.S. See NATIONAL DEFENSE.

MARSHALL, JOHN ROSS (1912-), was sworn in as prime minister of New Zealand on Feb. 7, 1972. He succeeded Keith J. Holyoake, who announced his retirement after 12 years in office at a National Party meeting on February 2. In elections held November 26, however, the Labour Party was swept into office and its leader, Norman E. Kirk replaced Marshall (see KIRK, NORMAN ERIC). Marshall had been in Parliament since 1946 and deputy prime minister since 1947. See also NEW ZEALAND.

Marshall was born in Wellington on March 5, 1912, the son of a civil servant. He was educated at a primary school in Whangarei and at Otage Boys' High School in Dunedin, and graduated from Victoria University in Wellington in 1934. He took a degree in law and one in political science.

Although a pacifist as a student, he enlisted in the army as a private in 1940, was commissioned, and eventually commanded an infantry company as a major in World War II. He ran for Parliament immediately after he was demobilized from the army.

His quietness, tenacity, and disdain for drama have made him a skilled diplomat as well as an able politician. He has frequently served as New Zealand's negotiator with other nations. Foster Stockwell

MARYLAND. See BALTIMORE; STATE GOVT.

MASSACHUSETTS. See BOSTON; STATE GOVERNMENT.

MAURITANIA. See AFRICA.

McGOVERN, GEORGE STANLEY (1922-), United States Senator from South Dakota, won the Democratic presidential nomination in July, but lost the election on Nov. 7, 1972. McGovern lost to President Richard M. Nixon in one of the greatest landslides in U.S. history. He won only in Massachusetts and the District of Columbia, with 17 Electoral College votes. McGovern had criticized the Vietnam War and heavy military spending. See ELECTIONS.

McGovern was born in Avon, a small farm town in southeastern South Dakota, the son of a Methodist minister. He grew up in Mitchell, S. Dak., and attended Dakota Wesleyan University there until 1942, when he became an Army Air Force cadet. As a World War II bomber pilot, he completed 35 combat missions over Europe and won the Distinguished Flying Cross. McGovern later earned master's and doctor's degrees from Northwestern University and taught history at Dakota Wesleyan. In 1953, he became executive secretary of his state's ineffective Democratic Party. It held no major state office and only two legislative seats. In 1956, he was elected the state's first Democratic congressman in 22 years. He lost his first bid for a U.S. Senate seat in 1960, but ran again and won in 1962 and 1968.

After his party's 1968 convention, McGovern helped set rules for wider participation. Ed Nelson

MEDICAID. See SOCIAL WELFARE.

MEDICARE. See SOCIAL WELFARE.

MEDICINE. Researchers at the Boston University School of Medicine in 1972 hailed a new surgical technique for removing cancerous and benign growths from human vocal cords. The technique involves the use of an apparatus they developed – a carbon dioxide (CO_2) laser. It is microscopically precise, allows nearly complete control of bleeding, permits virtually no postoperative draining, and stimulates more rapid healing than can be achieved by other methods.

M. Stuart Strong and Geza J. Jako, professors of otolaryngology at the school, believe that the CO_2 laser will be particularly useful in cases that require delicate surgery and in which preserving the vocal cords is especially important. They reported that the laser has been used in more than 30 cases to remove polyps, nodules, and small malignant tumors. The beam can be focused very precisely and the depth to which it goes can be controlled. "The ease with which the depth of tissue destruction could be controlled is striking," said Jako.

The CO_2 laser unit operates with an infrared wave length that is absorbed almost completely by most tissues. This allows sharp cutting with a focused beam. By adjusting power levels, researchers control the depth to which it cuts. They report a minimum of heat transfer and damage to adjacent tissues. The laser beam can be focused on a spot less than 1 millimeter in diameter, and its burning and vaporizing action will cut most tissues cleanly. Other investigators have shown that the beam can cut through bone and can control bleeding from stomach ulcers.

Transplants. A team of San Francisco surgeons reported wide success in transplanting leg veins. They performed the transplants on patients whose veins were not suitable for arterial reconstruction. The veins were removed from other patients who had undergone surgery for varicose veins, a fairly common operation. The veins were washed in an antibiotic solution and stored under frozen, sterile conditions at $-50°C$. for as long as three months before being used. Vein by-pass surgery is performed on patients with diseases of the heart, diabetic disorders, or inadequate arterial flow.

Drug Problems. Some addicts reportedly were encountering serious vascular difficulties. Because they were running out of usable veins for injecting the drugs, many were resorting to intra-arterial injections. Typical drugs used for intra-arterial injections are barbiturates, heroin, amphetamines, and codeine. Thomas M. Maxwell, a clinical instructor of surgery at the University of California, San Francisco, said therapeutic drugs that dilate the arteries or thin the blood are sometimes successful. But tissue damage from amphetamines and narcotics is often beyond repair, and amputation is necessary.

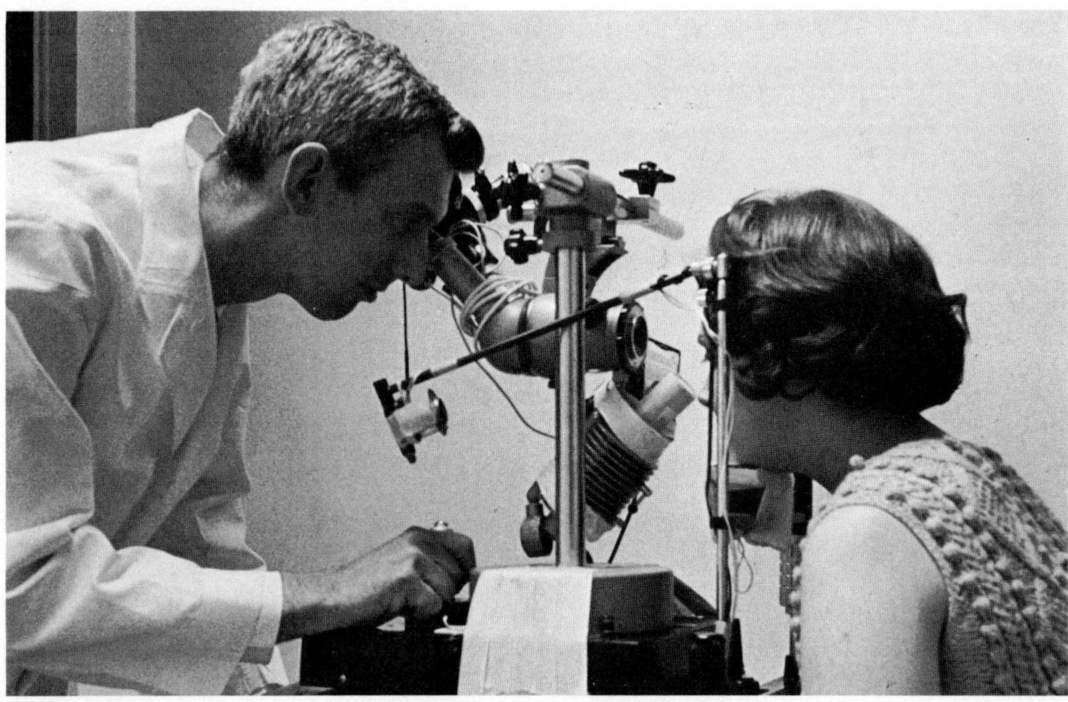

Neurologists using a new technique can now detect early signs of stroke by examining the eye's blood vessels, which resemble those in the brain.

The Sickle Killer

Sickle cell anemia, an incurable disease that evolved as a gene mutation centuries ago, finally began to receive serious attention in 1972. Two promising methods of treating the disease were being tested at several medical centers, and new legislation authorized spending $115 million by 1975 to bring the disease under control in the United States. In addition, a team of scientists in Boston announced in July that they were able to detect sickle cell anemia in fetuses that are aborted for medical reasons. Once they develop an intrauterine test that can detect the disease, genetic counselors can tell couples if their child will have sickle cell anemia.

Sickle cell anemia occurs almost exclusively among blacks. The mutant gene arose during human evolution in Africa as a protection against the malaria parasite, which invades human red blood cells. One in 10 black Americans inherits the sickle cell trait, while 1 in 500 suffers from the disease.

Sickle cell anemia is transmitted in two ways. If only one parent passes the sickle cell gene on, only part of the child's hemoglobin, a protein in the red blood cell, is defective. Such a child seldom has severe symptoms. If both parents pass it on, however, almost all the hemoglobin is defective, and the chances are 1 in 4 their baby will get the disease.

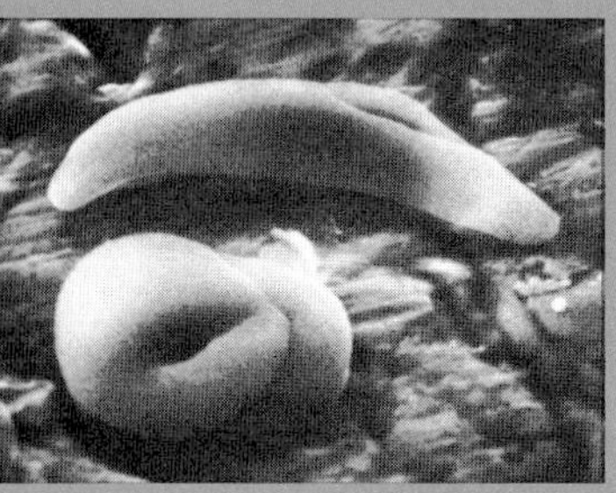

Sickle-shaped cell, top; normal cell, bottom.

In a child with the disease, the red blood cells retain their normal doughnut shape until physical or emotional stress suddenly reduces the oxygen in the blood below a certain level. A trip to the mountains, a fit of anger, or strenuous play can bring on an attack. When this happens, the blood cells take on an elongated sickle shape and clump together, blocking the flow of blood through the arteries and producing excruciating pain. Eventually, an attack will be fatal. Half of those with the disease die before they are 20.

Robert M. Nalbandian, a pathologist at Blodgett Memorial Hospital in Grand Rapids, Mich., has developed one of the most promising treatments. He injects a patient with very large amounts of urea, which reverses the sickling crises. Urea, a natural body chemical produced by the liver, ruptures the chemical bonds that hold proteins in place. Nalbandian believes this prevents the hemoglobin molecules from sticking together. Once the treatment is stopped, however, the cells sickle again.

At Rockefeller University in New York City, cell biologist Anthony Cerami and chemist James M. Manning are experimenting with potassium cyanate, a chemical generally found in solutions of urea. Their initial tests indicate that it inhibits sickling much more effectively than urea. In addition, its effects are permanent and only small amounts are necessary. Their experiments with dogs, mice, monkeys, and rats show that cyanate causes no ill effects, so they have begun clinical trials with human patients. Preliminary findings indicate cyanate increases the lifetime of the red blood cells and is well tolerated by man.

As more research funds become available, these and other treatments will be intensely examined. Clinical advances are useless, however, unless patients who could benefit can be identified and seek help voluntarily. Therefore, the U.S. Department of Health, Education, and Welfare has awarded $2 million to be shared by 19 clinics to provide screening facilities and education programs for from 10,000 to 20,000 persons a year. Another $6.5 million is being spent for 34 pure- and applied-research projects.

Such large-scale efforts are not without their critics. As with attempts to introduce birth control in some black communities, counseling has been called black genocide. However, there is no more reason for believing this than there is for labeling the prevention of births by whites with hereditary diseases such as Tay-Sachs disease or hemophilia as white genocide.

Doris L. Wethers, a black professor of pediatrics at Columbia University College of Physicians and Surgeons and a cofounder of the Foundation for Research and Education in Sickle Cell Disease, is cautious about making recommendations to patients: "I would certainly present them with the facts about their physical condition and let them know what alternatives there were. . . . The patients should have the final decision about what they do with their lives." Lillian Zahrt

Collaborative Research, Incorporated, of Waltham, Mass., has developed a method of detecting lysergic acid diethylamide (LSD). The system, developed for the Bureau of Narcotics and Dangerous Drugs, can detect microscopically small amounts of LSD in a sample of blood or urine.

The firm said commercial reagents would be available for clinical and hospital use by April, 1973. This is the first test that can detect the microgram quantities of LSD in a "street dose" of the drug, Theresa Harwood, director of the bureau's Biological Research Branch, explained. The assay also will aid in making the urinalysis of subjects in methadone maintenance programs.

Blood Measurement. Ultrasonic techniques for measuring blood flow may soon replace older methods in diagnosing certain heart and blood disorders. One apparatus, developed by a team of researchers at the University of Washington School of Medicine in Seattle, has three basic parts: a pulsed ultrasonic blood-velocity detector, a position-sensing arm and transducer, and an oscilloscope on which arterial cross sections can be viewed.

The device transmits a sound beam through body tissues. When the sound wave strikes a stationary object, one of two transducer crystals receiving the sound indicates no change in the reflected-sound frequency. If the sound wave strikes moving cells, the reflected frequency is altered. In this way, researchers can detect suspected or unsuspected vascular obstructions.

The views given by this ultrasonic device are valuable because atheromatous deposits (fatty, plaquelike substances that form inside arteries and precipitate disease and blockage) frequently occur on the inside arterial walls and are difficult to detect with X-ray techniques. The unit has provided information in examinations of patients with carotid artery lesions, aorta-coronary by-pass grafts, and a number of other arterial blockage disorders.

Cancer Viruses. Hope continued for a vaccine against some forms of human cancer. Research centered on C- and B-type viruses that have been linked to leukemia, sarcoma, and breast cancer. Such viruses – or viruslike particles – have been found in human tumor tissues or secretions, and they are structurally similar to agents known to cause cancer in some animals.

The day of the routine application of a vaccine for cancer prevention in man, however, could be decades away, according to Maurice R. Hilleman of the Division of Virus and Cell Biology Research at the Merck Institute for Therapeutic Research at West Point, Pa. "It's certainly not going to go like measles, mumps, or rubella," he said. "Yet it's worth the effort. Cancer kills 20 per cent of the population, and we have no assurance that it will continue to kill only 20 per cent." Richard P. Davies

See also HEALTH AND DISEASE.

MEMORIALS dedicated or announced in 1972 include the following:

Calvin Coolidge Memorial. A one-story memorial center honoring Calvin Coolidge, the 30th President of the United States, was dedicated on July 4. It is located at Plymouth Notch, a village in central Vermont where Coolidge was born on July 4, 1872. Coolidge's father owned a small store in the town and a nearby farm. John Coolidge, the only living son of the former President, spoke at the dedication.

Charles de Gaulle Memorial. French President Georges Pompidou, on June 18, led an estimated 30,000 people in dedicating a 150-foot-tall Cross of Lorraine memorial to General Charles de Gaulle, former president of France and leader of French resistance against Germany during World War II. The 1,500-ton, rose-granite cross towers 135 feet above a hilltop overlooking the town of Colombey-Les-Deux-Églises, where De Gaulle lived and is buried. The dedication date marked the 32nd anniversary of De Gaulle's historic broadcast to France from London calling on Frenchmen everywhere to rally to his Free French cause and continue the fight against Germany after France signed the 1940 armistice.

Frederick Douglass Memorial. "Cedar Hill" in Washington, D.C., the home of Frederick Douglass, was dedicated as a national shrine and opened to the public on February 14. Born a slave in 1817, Douglass became a noted author, speaker, and fighter for Negro rights. He helped recruit blacks for the Union Army during the Civil War, and later served as recorder of deeds in the District of Columbia and as U.S. minister to Haiti. His papers were placed in the Library of Congress in 1971.

Herbert Hoover Memorial. Julie Nixon Eisenhower participated in the formal opening of the Herbert Hoover National Historic Site at West Branch, Iowa. The site was dedicated on August 10, the anniversary of the former President's birth. It covers 148 acres in the small Iowa town where the nation's 31st President was born in 1874, and has the Herbert Hoover Presidential Library, and several restored buildings from his boyhood, including the cottage where he was born, a Quaker meeting house, and a blacksmith shop. The graves of the President and Mrs. Hoover are on a hill overlooking the site.

Joan of Arc Memorial. After 50 years of debate, the City Council in Rouen, France, on January 12, authorized the construction of a memorial to Saint Joan of Arc, who was burned as a heretic in Rouen in 1431. After Joan was canonized in 1920 and declared the patron saint of France, the city fathers decided to build a monument in the Place du Vieux-Marché, the old market square where she was executed. The first stone was laid in 1931 and blessed in 1956, but controversy has surrounded the design of the structure ever since. The now-approved monument will be a many-sail-shaped, wood-and-plastic structure by architect Louis Arretche. Foster Stockwell

MENTAL HEALTH. Several new drugs in 1972 beefed up the arsenal of psychiatric weaponry in the fight for mental health. Researchers told the Fifth World Congress of Psychiatry, held in February, 1972, in Mexico City, that significant progress has been made in the treatment of obsession, anxiety, depression, and mania by drugs.

One of those described was chlorimipramine, a widely used antidepressant. It effectively curbed obsessive symptoms in a group of patients tested at the Graylingwell Hospital in Chichester, England. After treatment with the drug, one patient–who reported a compelling need to check the gas, water, and electrical outlets in her house several times a day–improved almost immediately. According to Norman Capstick, the chief investigator at the hospital, most patients still have obsessions after taking chlorimipramine, but their obsessions do not bother them.

In another British study, James Raphael Kerry of Northern General Hospital in Sheffield, England, gave a favorable nod to medazepam, a drug used for the symptomatic relief of anxiety, over other tranquilizers. Patients who took this drug experienced fewer side effects, such as drowsiness and irregular muscular action. The drug relieves such anxiety symptoms as fear, depression, and loss of appetite.

A New Antidepressant, CIBA 34'276-Ba, was hailed by European and South American investigators as "clearly surpassing . . . all other psychoactive compounds . . ." previously used in the treatment of depression. Werner Gruter, professor of psychiatry at Marburg University in West Germany, said early results were so encouraging that he considers the compound to be the best drug for treatment of patients hospitalized or at home.

A study completed in April, 1972, affirmed the therapeutic value of lithium, a white metal, in the treatment of manic-depressive psychosis. J. Frank James, a member of a Duke University study team, reported that patients on lithium became worse when they changed to other drugs, and patients who had been taking other drugs improved when they were given lithium. Symptomatic improvements particularly evident in patients with such symptoms of mania as retardation, conceptual disorganization, excitement, grandiosity, and confused perception.

Drug Abuse Center. The first national center for training in drug abuse treatment, rehabilitation, and prevention opened in June, 1972, in Washington, D.C. Called the National Drug Abuse Training Center, it offers short- and long-term training programs for businessmen, educators, and laymen in the treatment of drug abuse and addiction. Athletes from the National Football League, the National and American Basketball associations, and the National Hockey League were among the first participants in the training sessions. The center is administered by the National Institute of Mental Health and the U.S. Office of Education. Richard P. Davies

MESSMER, PIERRE A. (1916-), a faithful follower of Charles de Gaulle, became prime minister of France on July 5, 1972. He is known as a political conservative and a tough administrator. As armed forces minister during the 1960s, he was charged with reviving a French Army demoralized by its defeats in Europe, Indochina, and Algeria.

When France fell to Germany in 1940 at the outset of World War II, Messmer was a young lieutenant in a colonial infantry regiment. He hijacked a freighter and forced it to take him to Gibraltar so he could join De Gaulle's Free French forces. He fought in North Africa and then was parachuted into Indochina, then occupied by Japan, to prepare for the return of French colonial rule there. However, he was captured by the Viet Minh, the Communist-led guerrilla army that opposed both Japanese and French control, and was held prisoner for about a year. During the 1950s, he held high colonial administrative posts in Indochina and Africa.

Messmer became minister for the armed forces in 1960, after French settlers rebelled against De Gaulle's policy of self-determination for Algeria. During his tenure, France slowly developed its own nuclear defense capability.

Messmer was born in Vincennes, a suburb of Paris. He studied in Paris to prepare for a career in the colonial service, and he also earned a law degree at the University of Paris. Joseph P. Spohn

MEXICO. A serious crisis within the ruling Institutional Revolutionary Party (PRI) ended Feb. 21, 1972, with the resignation of Manuel Sanchez Vite as party president. Sanchez Vite, who was considered a member of the party's conservative wing, had reportedly failed to carry out the "democratizing" policies promised by Mexico's President Luis Echeverría Alvárez. Sanchez' successor as head of the PRI, Jesus Reyes, was a member of the liberal faction.

Efforts were continued to eliminate corruption in government, which Secretary Horacio Flores de la Pena of the ministry of national patrimony called a "great national problem." Flores promised a campaign to eradicate it, and in February he invited citizens to file specific complaints against offending government officials and employees. The opposition National Action Party, however, criticized the moves, insisting that a full-scale, government-sponsored investigation should be launched rather than one dependent on voluntary moves by Mexico's citizens.

The Economy began recovering slowly from the recession experienced since mid-1970, and Mexico was poised once again for rapid and steady growth. Spurring the improvement was an estimated 30 per cent hike in public expenditures to $3.02 billion, as well as a relaxation of anti-inflation policies. Early rains gave promise of good crops, foreign trade improved, tourist receipts rose about 11.5 per cent, and

Mexican President Luis Echeverría Alvárez, left, is greeted by UN Secretary-General Kurt Waldheim during a June visit to United Nations.

most industries showed substantial increases in output and sales.

The Gross Domestic Product in the first six months registered a 6.4 per cent increase, versus a gain of just 3.2 per cent in the same 1971 period. Sales of household durables were up 17.7 per cent, new cars 10 per cent, and steel demand 10.1 per cent (with ingot output up 11 per cent). Although mining was off 14.7 per cent, there were substantial advances in petroleum and derivatives (13 per cent), petrochemicals (5.9 per cent), and manufactures (8.8 per cent).

On the other hand, many industries held back on new capital-spending programs. They were uncertain about government plans for the country, especially the need for economic and political reforms. Other factors included rising operating costs, labor and raw materials costs, and prospects of more government intervention in the private business sphere.

Mexico joined the growing list of Latin American nations claiming control of waters extending 200 miles offshore. The nation, which long has controlled the petroleum industry, also became owner of 51 per cent of the stock of the Mexican Telephone Company. It also acquired Azufrera Panamericana, of which the United States Pan American Sulphur Company owned 34 per cent. The company controls about 75 per cent of Mexico's sulfur production and 50 per cent of its known reserves. Mexico also took over financially troubled private banks so that, in September, the administration could announce it controlled 50 per cent of all banking resources.

Foreign Affairs. In the first six months, exports increased 22.2 per cent over the same 1971 span, with shipments of manufactures climbing 29.4 per cent and imports up 11.5 per cent. To boost trade, banking agreements were reached with Poland, Romania, and Yugoslavia, while high-level trade missions visited China, Japan, Honduras, and Nicaragua. Meantime, the United States opened a $450,000 trade center in Mexico City on February 14.

President Echeverría visited President Richard M. Nixon in mid-June. They discussed such problems as the salinity of the Colorado River, migratory agricultural workers, illicit drug traffic, trade curbs, and boundary disputes.

Mexico's Employment Problems grew worse during the year. About 3.5 million were unemployed, and another 5 million were at best marginally employed part of the year. With a runaway population expansion of 3.5 per cent a year, the government announced a major family-planning program.

In September, the government announced plans for the socioeconomic development of the Papaloapan Basin area of the Isthmus of Tehuantepec. Its projects include an $80-million dam to provide irrigation for 1,750,000 acres of land. Mary Webster Soper

See also LATIN AMERICA (Facts in Brief Table).

MICHENER, ROLAND (1900-) presided at the official opening of the fourth session of Canada's 28th Parliament on Feb. 17, 1972. As the queen's representative in Canada, Governor General Michener read the speech from the throne announcing the Trudeau government's legislative program.

The governor general began his official tours in March, visiting Whitehorse in the Yukon Territory, where he presented a new ceremonial mace to the territory's council and opened the 1972 Arctic Winter Games. In mid-May, Michener was in the Maritime Provinces, and he and Mrs. Michener received honorary degrees from universities in Fredericton and Halifax. Later in the month, Michener toured isolated fishing villages and logging centers along the rugged British Columbia coast.

A variety of ceremonial occasions occupied the governor general and his wife during the remainder of 1972. At the end of November, they visited Guelph, Ontario, for ceremonies marking the 100th birthday of Canadian poet John McCrae, who wrote "In Flanders Fields." At Government House in Ottawa, the Micheners entertained 28 ambassadors and high commissioners who arrived to take up diplomatic posts in Canada. President and Mrs. Richard M. Nixon stayed at the governor general's official residence from April 13 to 15 during their visit to Canada. D. M. L. Farr

MICHIGAN. See DETROIT; STATE GOVERNMENT.

MIDDLE EAST

The Arabs and Israel made little progress, if any, toward peace in 1972. Gunnar Jarring reactivated his United Nations (UN) mission in January. But numerous separate talks with Israeli, Jordanian, and Egyptian leaders in Cyprus and elsewhere failed to develop the favorable attitudes necessary for serious negotiations among the protagonists.

The military stalemate along Israel's borders continued, and the high cost of occupying Arab territories – estimated at $3.4 million a day – was a heavy burden on the Israeli economy. Yet, Israel was unprepared to relinquish Arab lands held since 1967 without firm guarantees of sovereignty.

Coexistence Unpopular. An Israeli poll chose Uri Avneri as the nation's most unpopular public figure. He was the principal advocate in the Knesset (parliament) of Arab-Israeli coexistence in Palestine. The former Labor Party secretary-general, Aryeh Eliav, got a similar reaction when his book *The Land of Splendor* advocated an independent Palestine Arab state composed of the West Bank and the Gaza Strip. It would incorporate all of Israel's Arabs. In March, King Hussein I of Jordan made a similar proposal. He advocated a United Arab Kingdom, the West Bank federated with Jordan. Israel would withdraw and the two sides would sign a peace treaty. Both sides were cool to the proposal.

Israel's refusal to enter any negotiation that might involve concessions to the Arabs stemmed in part from its absolute military superiority over the Arabs. Expelling Russian military advisers from Egypt in July pleased nationalist-minded Egyptians, but curtailed the effectiveness of the one Arab military force capable of a serious challenge to the Israelis (see EGYPT). The Arab nations did not attempt to renew the armed struggle with Israel. The border clashes that took place developed as Israel retaliated for attacks or for Palestinian guerrilla raids into its territory from Lebanese bases.

Spread of Terror. The only leverage the Arabs could exert on Israel was applied by the Palestine guerrillas. But guerrilla efforts were too disunited to generate a coordinated program of action. A series of "unity conferences" called by the Palestine Liberation Organization (PLO) produced little agreement; PLO chairman Yasir Arafat said in an interview on August 27, "Arab contradictions greatly affect our revolution." Arafat found himself increasingly thought of as a comparative moderate. A brief uprising against him broke out in a Lebanese camp on October 14.

Libya offered training as well as financial support to the guerrillas, and all the Arab states vocally backed the Palestinian cause. But no Arab leader would make the kind of commitment that might lead to a Palestinian government-in-exile and its international recognition as the standardbearer of a legitimate liberation movement.

Global Terrorism. Without a coordinated effort, some guerrilla organizations turned to global terrorism to dramatize their cause. They went beyond the Arab world and established links with extremist organizations elsewhere. On May 30, three Japanese members of Sekigunha (Red Army Group) shot into a crowd at the passenger terminal of Tel Aviv's Lod International Airport. At least 28 were killed, including a Canadian woman, 14 Puerto Rican tourists, and 2 of the gunmen. The Popular Front for the Liberation of Palestine claimed responsibility.

An even greater tragedy struck Israel on September 5. Terrorists from the Black September guerrilla organization attacked the quarters of the Israeli Olympic team in Munich, West Germany. Two Israelis were killed resisting the attack and nine others were taken hostage. All the hostages, five captors, and a West German policeman died hours later in a shoot-out at a deserted military airstrip where the guerrillas had arranged to take their prisoners. Three guerrillas were captured.

The non-Arab world quickly and universally condemned the Munich massacre but heroes' burials were given the five terrorists in Libya. The guerrillas showed no remorse. They said Munich should be equated with the Deir Yassin massacre of Arab villagers by Israeli forces in 1948. Israeli forces carried out retaliation raids and air attacks in Lebanon and Syria that brought a censure resolution before the UN Security Council. The resolution referred only to the cessation of military operations in the Middle East, however. It was vetoed on September 10 by the United States – using its second veto in UN history – on the ground that terrorist acts should be condemned equally with military action.

A Letter-Bomb campaign followed the Munich massacre. The first victim, an Israeli diplomat in London, was killed on September 19. The letter-bombs, no larger than a tea bag and rigged to explode when opened, were very difficult for security forces to stop. They turned up in cities throughout the world.

The nations of the world also seemed unable to act effectively against Arab (or any other) air piracy, despite a UN convention against hijacking. On Octo-

Israeli tanks and armored vehicles moved into Lebanon in a dawn raid on September 16 to retaliate for the murder of Israel's Olympic Games athletes.

ber 29, Black September guerrillas hijacked a Lufthansa airliner to Zagreb, Yugoslavia, and bargained successfully for the release of the three captured Munich terrorists against the lives of the passengers and crew.

Other Significant Developments offered a more promising future for the Middle East and hope for reduced tensions through economic progress. The expulsion of the Russian military advisers from Egypt left the Egyptian Army uncomfortably short of spare parts and new weapons withheld by Russia. Nevertheless, it struck a blow for Egyptian pride. Derogatory comments about Islam by visiting Soviet officials and the arrogance of Russian officers toward their Egyptian counterparts had reminded the Egyptians all too clearly of the British protectorate. The presence of technicians underscored the Russian economic commitment to Egypt, but it was clear that President Anwar al-Sadat's interest in a strategic marriage of mutual interests made no provision for the ideological dependence that Russia sought.

Inter-Arab Cooperation also appeared to be growing. The Federation of Arab Republics, which includes Egypt, Libya, and Syria, formalized a Presidential Council of the three heads of state on March 12. The council approved the establishment of a Federal Supreme Constitutional Court and several other unified coordinating agencies.

In late March, Libya took a hesitant step toward representative government by creating the Libyan Arab Socialist Union, modeled on the Egyptian Arab Socialist Union and Syria's National Progressive Front (see LIBYA). All three national organizations represent small steps away from traditional Arab leadership.

King Hassan II, however, had little success in welding Morocco's diverse political interests into an effective coalition. Only good luck and coolness under fire saved him from death or disaster in a second coup attempt in August. It was linked to his minister of defense, General Mohammed Oufkir. Subsequently, Oufkir committed suicide. See MOROCCO.

Another area of inter-Arab friction was removed with the acceptance of a cease-fire and agreement to unite Yemen (San'ā') and Yemen (Aden), properly called the People's Democratic Republic of Yemen. A unitary state of Yemen would remove one of the principal causes of peninsular friction. Socialist-oriented Yemen (Aden) had consistently backed rebels in Oman's Dhofar province against the Omani sultan and loudly advocated uprisings in the Union of Arab Emirates. The union added a seventh member, Ras al-Khaimah, in February.

Oil Formula. A significant restructuring of relationships between the Arab oil-producing states and

Facts in Brief on the Middle East Countries

Country	Population	Government	Monetary Unit*	Foreign Trade (million U.S. $) Exports	Imports
Bahrain	235,000	Amir Isa bin Salman Al Khalifa; Prime Minister Khalifa bin Salman Al Khalifa	dinar (1=$2.27)	180	109
Cyprus	652,000	President Archbishop Makarios III	pound (1=$2.60)	116	263
Egypt, Arab Republic of	35,892,000	President Anwar al-Sadat; Prime Minister Aziz Sidki	pound (1=$2.30)	789	890
Iran	31,229,000	Shah Mohammed Reza Pahlavi; Prime Minister Amir Abbas Hoveyda	rial (75.75=$1)	2,642	1,871
Iraq	10,376,000	President and Prime Minister Ahmad Hasan al-Bakr	dinar (1=$3.04)	1,538	694
Israel	3,154,000	President Zalman Shazar; Prime Minister Golda Meir	pound (4.2=$1)	919	1,764
Jordan	2,600,000	King Hussein I; Prime Minister Ahmad al-Lawzi	dinar (1=$2.80)	32	215
Kuwait	921,000	Emir Sabah al-Salim al-Sabah; Prime Minister Jabir al-Ahmad al-Sabah	dinar (1=$3.04)	2,407	678
Lebanon	3,213,000	President Suleiman Franjieh; Prime Minister Saeb Salaam	pound (3=$1)	242	671
Oman	720,000	Sultan Qabus bin Said; Prime Minister Asim ibn Muhammad Jamali	Saidi rial (1=$2.67)	no statistics available	
Qatar	92,000	Amir and Prime Minister Khalifa bin Hamad Al-Thani	ryal (4.41=$1)	185	35
Saudi Arabia	8,384,000	King and Prime Minister Faisal	riyal (4.14=$1)	2,361	693
Sudan	17,051,000	President Jafir Muhammad Nimeri	pound (1=$2.87)	329	332
Syria	6,663,000	President Hafiz al-Asad; Prime Minister Mahmoud al-Ayubi	pound (4.3=$1)	195	440
Turkey	37,941,000	President Cevdet Sunay; Prime Minister Ferit Melen	lira (14=$1)	677	1,171
United Arab Emirates	180,000	President Zayid bin Sultan al-Nuhayan; Prime Minister Maktum ibn Rashid al-Maktum al-Falasa	Bahrain dinar & Qatar ryal	no statistics available	
Yemen (Aden)	1,390,000	Presidential Council Chairman Salim Ali Rubayya; Prime Minister Ali Nasir Hassani	dinar (1=$2.67)	105	158
Yemen (San'ā')	6,210,000	Republican Council Chairman Abdul Rahman Iryani; Prime Minister Muhsin al-Ayni	ryal (4.69=$1)	13	143

*Exchange rate as of Nov. 1, 1972

Bloodstained baggage area at Tel Aviv airport testifies to the horror of an attack by guerrilla gunmen that killed 28 persons.

Western oil companies augured well for the future of both sides. Five Persian Gulf states in the Organization of Arab Petroleum Exporting Countries – Saudi Arabia, Kuwait, Bahrain, Qatar, and Abu Dhabi – banded together to bargain with the companies over participation in all phases of the oil industry. The new approach was considered an alternative to nationalization, which often meant reduced revenues. The participation formula provided for an immediate 25 per cent share for each signatory state in oil-company management. The share would rise to a controlling interest, 51 per cent, in 1983 and remain at that level until all current concessions expire early in the 21st century. The formula clearly foreshadowed a new era in company-state relations. Even the two major exceptions, Iraq and Libya, were generally disposed to accept the formula. In each case, only one oil company (BP in Libya and Iraq Petroleum in Iraq) was affected.

Civil War Ends. On March 6, the civil war between predominantly Christian Africans in southern Sudan and the Moslem Arab north finally ended. It had gone on for eight years and devastated the south. Hundreds of thousands of refugees fled to neighboring countries. In the peace settlements, the southerners agreed to forego independence in return for proportional representation and local autonomy within Sudan. See SUDAN. William Spencer

MINERALOGY. See GEOLOGY.

MINES AND MINING. Lindsay Johnson, consultant to the U.S. secretary of the interior, warned the annual meeting of the American Mining Congress in San Francisco in September, 1972, that the United States has demonstrated alarming dependency on the mineral resources of other nations since 1950. Although domestic demand for metals tripled between 1950 and 1971, Johnson explained, there was increasing dependence on foreign sources for many minerals and fuels. In that 20-year period, U.S. mineral production fell $8.6 billion short of domestic demand. By 2000, a deficit of $64 billion was forecast. According to the Department of the Interior, only coal, copper, phosphate, and sulfur were currently in adequate supply, although projections here, too, were not encouraging.

The Coal Industry. Despite recent comeback efforts by the coal industry, officials of the United Mine Workers of America said the industry is no longer producing at full capacity. Stiff new restrictions on air pollution cut the demand for high-sulfur coal and forced some mines to close. Nevertheless, production for the year was about 8 per cent over the 1971 output of 600 million tons.

Despite the lobbying efforts of environmentalists, legislation to regulate the nation's strip mines died in the last days of the 92nd Congress. The bill called for regulating surface mining of all minerals. In 1972, strip mining passed underground mining as the primary method of recovering coal.

Mine Safety. In August, the General Accounting Office (GAO) accused the U.S. Bureau of Mines of failing to assess and collect fines against mine operators for safety violations. The GAO reported that the bureau initially assessed $12.5 million in safety penalties against mine owners under the Federal Coal Mine Health and Safety Act of 1969. However, only $1.4 million had been collected.

The Bureau of Mines was criticized after a coal-mine refuse bank broke on February 26 near Man, W. Va., and 5 million cubic feet of water flooded the Buffalo Creek Valley, killing 118 persons. The Department of the Interior claimed on May 11 that it had warned five years earlier that the waste pile and 29 others in the state were unsafe.

New Supplies. The biggest new mine in South America was taking shape high in the Andes Mountains in southern Peru. The $418-million Cuajone copper complex, scheduled for completion in 1976, has a reserve of almost 500 million tons of ore.

Thiess Peabody Mitsu, Ltd., a British, American, and Japanese combine, announced that exploration has shown coal reserves of over a billion tons in central Queensland, Australia. Mines there are expected to export up to 9 million tons of coal a year. New Zealand was also having a mineral boom. By year's end, the country had signed contracts for the export of 20 million tons of irons and concentrate to Japan. See LABOR. Mary E. Jessup

MINNEAPOLIS-ST. PAUL, the Twin Cities of Minnesota, won the All-American City award for 1972. The annual award is sponsored by the National Municipal League.

St. Paul updated its municipal structure in 1972. It adopted city charter reforms calling for a strong-mayor form of government and giving the mayor a greater responsibility for directing the city's administrative agencies. A professional city administrator will assist the mayor. Voters approved the change on April 25, and it took effect on June 6.

School Disorders. Minnesota Governor Wendell R. Anderson called out the National Guard on May 11 to curb violence that erupted during demonstrations at the Minneapolis campus of the University of Minnesota. During the disturbances, 25 students and 3 policemen were injured, and 30 students were arrested. The students were protesting the mining of harbors and renewed U.S. bombing in North Vietnam.

A minor disturbance erupted at a Minneapolis high school on September 26, when black students demanded more black faculty members and educational programs. Rumors of more trouble prompted officials to temporarily cancel classes.

A committee of the Minneapolis Transit Commission on September 12 approved a report recommending construction of an automated transit system that will run 40-passenger vehicles on a 29.7-mile-long right of way. The commission chose an automated system after studies indicated that buses would be more expensive in the long run. The new system was expected to cost between $600 million and $1.21-billion.

Cost of Living. The average rent in the suburbs was the second highest in the nation. Suburban rents had increased by 80 per cent since 1962. The average selling price of a new single-family house in the seven-county metropolitan area was $38,500 in 1971. Only 11 new houses sold for less than $20,000 in 1971. At these prices, 85 per cent of the families living in the area could not afford to buy the average new house.

Despite the rapid increases in rents, the general cost of living in the metropolitan area rose only 3.2 per cent between April, 1971, and April, 1972. This was slightly below the national average. Nonagricultural employment increased by 3,200 jobs from May, 1971, to May, 1972. The average gross weekly earnings of production workers went up substantially, from $157.21 to $170.07, during the same period.

St. Paul had the nation's fifth highest median family income in 1972, $10,544. Median income for Minneapolis families, however, was a comparatively low $9,960.
J. M. Banovetz

MINNESOTA. See MINNEAPOLIS-ST. PAUL; STATE GOVERNMENT.

MISSISSIPPI. See STATE GOVERNMENT.

MISSOURI. See ST. LOUIS; STATE GOVERNMENT.

MONEY. The U.S. money supply increased relatively rapidly in 1972. Money, defined as currency and demand deposits, increased at a 7.6 per cent annual rate through October. Business cycle analysts, who emphasized rising monetary growth rates as an indicator of future national spending, interpreted this to mean economic expansion and perhaps renewed inflation. For comparison, money grew at an average annual rate of 5.9 per cent from 1966 through 1971, a period of considerable inflation. From 1952 through 1965, when there was very little inflation, the annual increase was 2.3 per cent.

The U.S. money supply averaged $242.4 billion in October, up $14.7 billion from a year earlier. Currency outside banks totaled $55.9 billion, and demand deposits were $186.5 billion.

Despite recent prophecies of its declining importance in the U.S. economy, currency continued to hold a strong position. Public holdings of notes and coin issued by the U.S. Department of the Treasury or by Federal Reserve Banks amounted to 23 per cent of the money supply in mid-1972. In 1929, currency accounted for only 17 per cent of the money supply. Coin – the most ancient of monies – actually staged a dramatic comeback in the last decade. Small change amounted to 11 per cent of currency in circulation in mid-1972, up from 8 per cent a decade earlier and from less than 5 per cent in the early post-World War

Real U.S. dollars were sold at a discount when Chicago's United of America Bank celebrated its 10th anniversary by holding a money sale.

II years. In Canada, coin comprised 12.3 per cent of currency outside banks in June.

Some banks experimented in 1972 with new electronic payments and credit hookups to help reduce the astronomical flow of checks. Demand deposits turned over at an annual rate of 85 times in 1972. This means that about $16 trillion in checks were being written and processed through the banking system. See BANKS AND BANKING.

Cash v. Credit. The use of credit cards reduced the number of money transactions to some extent. More than 275 million credit cards were outstanding in 1972. For merchants who do not issue their own cards, credit-card sales represent a source of ready cash from the institutions that issue the cards and handle the billing. However, credit and the transaction costs of credit-card sales are expensive enough to be reflected in prices, and discounts for cash purchases inevitably have begun to appear in recent years. One California-based company issued a "cash card" in New York City in 1972. For a small annual fee, the holder is entitled to cash discounts as high as 40 per cent from associated merchants. Businessmen were willing to take less on cash sales to avoid the trouble and expense of credit-card sales.

The table below shows kinds of U.S. currency in circulation on June 30, 1972. The large increase in dollar coins reflects the new Eisenhower dollars the Treasury Department began circulating at the end of 1971. The 482-million silver dollars (not issued since 1964) that remained in the hands of the public in 1972 were really not money in circulation at all. Rather, they were either locked up in coin collections or melted down for their metallic value, which has been greater than their monetary value since 1967. Government statisticians have recently recognized this fact and have deducted the amount of silver coins from currency in circulation figures.

U.S. Currency in Circulation And Demand Deposits, June, 1972

Currency in Circulation	Amount	Annual Per cent change
Federal reserve notes	$54,600,000,000	+6.4
Treasury currency		
Dollar coins	600,000,000	+31.3
Fractional coin	6,400,000,000	+6.6
U.S. notes	300,000,000	−.3
Monies in process of retirement	300,000,000	−1.4
Total currency in circulation	$62,200,000,000	+6.5
Less currency held by banks	8,900,000,000	+12.6
Currency held by public	$53,300,000,000	+5.6
Demand deposits held by public	177,000,000,000	+7.6
Money stock	$230,300,000,000	+7.1

Source: Federal Reserve Bulletin

The Federal Reserve System began issuing notes bearing the names of Romana Acosta Banuelos, the 34th treasurer of the United States, and George P. Shultz, who was named secretary of the treasury in May, 1972. William G. Dewald

MONTANA. See STATE GOVERNMENT.

MOORES, FRANK DUFF (1933-), became premier of Newfoundland in 1972, the first Progressive Conservative leader since the island became a Canadian province in 1949. He was sworn in on January 18, succeeding Liberal Joseph R. Smallwood. Moores also became minister of fisheries.

Moores's party won a disputed plurality in the Legislative Assembly in elections held on Oct. 28, 1971. Moores promptly dissolved the legislature when its session began on March 1, and called for new elections on March 24. In that election, Moores was unopposed and his party won 33 of the 42 seats.

Moores was born on Feb. 18, 1933, in Carbonear, a town of some 4,500 population on the island of Newfoundland about 30 miles from St. John's, the provincial capital. He attended the United Church Academy at Carbonear and St. Andrew's College in Aurora, Ontario. For 15 years after his graduation, Moores was active in the fishing industry in Harbour Grace, near Carbonear. He held office in several industry organizations.

Moores was elected to the Canadian House of Commons on June 25, 1968, in his first political campaign. He resigned all his business interests on entering politics. In 1969, he was elected national president of the Progressive Conservative Party of Canada.

Moores was married to Dorothy Pain of Toronto in 1952. They have seven children. Ed Nelson

MOROCCO. King Hassan II survived another assassination attempt on Aug. 16, 1972. Moroccan Air Force jet fighters strafed his plane as he returned from a visit to France. The king's damaged plane landed at Rabat Civil Airport, and the mutineers then strafed the airport and the royal palace. Eight died and 47 were injured, including 4 Cabinet ministers waiting to welcome the king. It was the second attempt on Hassan's life in 13 months.

Further support for the attempted coup did not develop, and Hassan quickly regained control. Kenitra Air Base, headquarters of the mutineers, was placed under armed guard. Two rebels sought asylum in Gibraltar, but the Gibraltar government returned them. General Mohammed Oufkir, minister of defense, who had helped to suppress the attempted military coup in July, 1971, was believed to be the mastermind behind this one. He reportedly committed suicide.

Ironically, the attack came at a time when Hassan seemed to have defused popular discontent. His opposition was in disarray. A four-month student strike ended on April 20 with the government agreeing to a 15 per cent increase in scholarships, the release of all detained students, and student participation in university housing management.

King's Leniency. Hassan also showed leniency toward those charged with the earlier attempt on his life. On February 29, all but 73 of more than 1,000

defendants were acquitted by a military court. Of the 73 convicted, 72 received prison terms and 1 a death sentence, which Hassan later commuted.

Hassan said on August 21 that he was puzzled about the motive for the air force attack. The next day, two newspapers published statements by the main opposition political party, Istiqlal, calling for more democracy and attributing unrest to the "path taken by the authorities." The papers were seized as they came off the presses.

The Political Opposition did its cause no good by refusing to engage in meaningful dialogue with Hassan on a more representative government. As a result, the king unilaterally proposed a new Constitution, Morocco's third in nine years, which was approved by 98.75 per cent of the voters in a March 1 referendum. There was no campaign against the new Constitution. It provides for a legislature, two-thirds of whose members are elected by the people. But Hassan could still dissolve the body and rule alone in an emergency.

The third Cabinet to hold office during the year was sworn in November 19. It was formed without the cooperation of the major political parties and was led by Hassan's brother-in-law, Ahmed Osman.

Morocco and the European Community came to agreement on working conditions for Moroccan nationals in Europe. William Spencer

See also AFRICA (Facts in Brief Table).

MOTION PICTURES. The great movie event of 1972 was *The Godfather*, the top-grossing film of the year and possibly of all time. In a nation apparently worried about violence in motion pictures, on television, and in its streets, the popularity of *The Godfather* made ironic commentary on American attitudes and values. The year began with angry outcries against the blood and gore of *A Clockwork Orange* and *Straw Dogs*, released in December, 1971; and the publication in March of the Surgeon-General's Report on Televised Violence further upset the public. Nevertheless, Americans paid well over $125 million to witness a three-hour testimony to the glories of gangsterdom.

Concerned chiefly with power struggles among rival gangland "families," which are, implicitly, units of the "Mafia" or "Cosa Nostra," *The Godfather* has two central themes: first, in the words of Balzac, that "Behind every great fortune there is a crime," and second, that beneath the bravado and butchery, gangsters are warm and loving human beings, good friends, good husbands, good fathers, and good sons.

The public did not complain about the brutality of the film; significantly, the cruelty is not sex-linked as in *Clockwork Orange* and *Straw Dogs*. Nor did the community of critics, who are often hostile to big, expensive movies (*The Godfather* cost $6 million to produce). They praised the film highly, and gave kudos to all concerned–director Francis Ford Coppola; scenarists Coppola and Mario Puzo, who wrote the best-selling novel on which the film is based; and stars Marlon Brando and Al Pacino.

The Godfather was not 1972's only blockbuster. *Cabaret*, an adaptation of the acclaimed Broadway musical of 1971, showed a domestic gross of more than $20 million. Liza Minnelli, daughter of film director Vincente Minnelli and the late Judy Garland, and evidently heir to her mother's charismatic gifts as a performer, stars in the film. The film was based on Christopher Isherwood's *Goodbye to Berlin* (1939) and a stage and screen version of the novella (both entitled *I Am a Camera*).

Cabaret was considered by many to represent a new direction in film musicals. Although stunningly visualized by director Bob Fosse, it is not so much *Cabaret*'s technique that distinguishes it as its content. Taking a woman of doubtful reputation for its heroine, exploring a bisexual love triangle, and setting this private decadence against the public decadence of Berlin during the 1930s, *Cabaret* deals with themes that are surprisingly mature for a musical. Despite the tradition of seriousness and social conscience (for example, *West Side Story* and *South Pacific*), American musicals have nearly always been conceived as "family entertainment."

Here was a musical with an R rating, the same rating given to *The Godfather*. This signified, accord-

In *The Godfather*, Marlon Brando plays a Mafia chieftain who survives a gangland gunning to enjoy his old age in a sunny suburban garden.

ing to the Motion Picture Association of America, that the film was not "acceptable to all audiences, without consideration of age," and that anyone "under 17 requires an accompanying parent or adult guardian."

The year, then, contributed dramatically to the demise of "family entertainment," with perhaps the loudest knell of all being rung by the release of the motion picture industry's first X-rated cartoon, *Fritz the Cat*. Based once again on a proven property – an unusual one, the popular underground comic strip created by Robert Crumb – the film is a pornographically explicit treatment of the social and, above all, sexual mores of young people during the 1960s. Vehemently antiyouth, it was received with delight by many critics and it did well at the box office.

The Black Films. A trend that began in 1971 and gathered greater force in 1972 was the production of films starring, and sometimes written and directed by, black artists, and addressed primarily to black audiences. Controversy raged about these films, most of which fell into the tried-and-true pattern of Hollywood "B" pictures. More than 20 were released during the year. They included romantic westerns such as *Buck and the Preacher*, starring Sidney Poitier and Harry Belafonte and directed by Belafonte; and *The Legend of Nigger Charley*, starring former football player Fred Williamson, in which black superheroes merely stepped into the boots of the white gunfighters of yesteryear. There were crime melodramas such as Gordon Parks' *Shaft's Big Score*, a sequel to the 1971 hit *Shaft*, in which Richard Roundtree plays a black detective in the tradition of Sam Spade. Another film, *Superfly*, ignited the box office; in less than three months, the film grossed $11 million. It also aroused the wrath of black and white critics alike because of its sympathetic treatment of a cocaine pusher. There were even horror films – *Blacula*, for example, in which an African prince is turned into a vampire by the famous Transylvanian himself. *Blacula*, however, was only a prelude; 1973 would see *Blackenstein* and *The Werewolf from Watts*, among others.

Since nearly all of these films dramatize encounters between good and victorious blacks and evil and defeated whites, racism excited anxiety. In addition, their titillating violence and sex, together with their lack of redeeming aesthetic quality, led critics to see them as exploitation films. Criticized by such diverse black groups as the National Association for the Advancement of Colored People (NAACP) and the Black Panthers, these films also had their defenders. They argued rather persuasively that black films have no greater responsibility to be moral or artful than white films, and that these movies at least provide black superheroes with whom black youths can identify.

However, the black movie scene was not all sex and violence. Twentieth Century-Fox released *Sounder*, a tender story of black sharecroppers from which Cicely Tyson emerged as an actress of considerable gifts and reputation. Paramount was responsible for a romanticized biography of blues singer Billie Holiday, starring Diana Ross, *Lady Sings the Blues*. And Cinerama released two rather serious, if ultimately unsatisfactory, dramas on the problems of black women: *Georgia, Georgia* and *Black Girl*. None of these films promised to distinguish itself at the box office as did those in the blood-and-guts tradition.

Liza Minnelli and Joel Gray sing about money in a scene from the film *Cabaret*, one of the most innovative movie musicals in years.

So successful indeed were these "blaxploitation" films that they, together with *The Godfather* and *Cabaret* and with such high-powered holdovers from 1971 as *The French Connection*, *The Last Picture Show*, and *Fiddler on the Roof*, made 1972 a somewhat economically encouraging year for the movie industry. Movie attendance increased by from 15 to 18 per cent over the 1971 figure of 820 million admissions. The year's total gross revenue was expected to surpass 1971's $1.35 billion by 20 per cent.

New Trends in Films. Not all of the excitement in Hollywood (by now, merely a metaphor, since fewer and fewer films were being made there) was commercial. There was growing interest in experimental and highly innovative films. Major companies, such as Columbia and Universal, distributed such commercially unlikely but aesthetically stimulating films as *Slaughterhouse Five*, *The King of Marvin Gardens*, *Images*, and *Play It As It Lays*. While their degree of artistic

© AMPAS

After receiving a long overdue Academy Award in April, Charlie Chaplin met Jackie Coogan, who starred with him in *The Kid* in 1921.

successfulness varies, all abandoned conventional narrative structures and conveyed plot and character by elliptical methods.

Also indicated was the almost startling pervasiveness of the *auteur* theory, a view of film that sees the director as the supreme artist behind any film and ultimately as its star. The names of François Truffaut, Federico Fellini, Eric Rohmer, Luis Buñuel, Alfred Hitchcock, and John Huston drew serious film audiences and excited critical interest in *Two English Girls*, *Fellini's Roma*, *Chloe in the Afternoon*, *The Discreet Charm of the Bourgeoisie*, *Frenzy*, and *Fat City*. Nearly all received ecstatic reviews; the works of Rohmer and Buñuel were especially applauded for their intelligence and artfulness. All of these films, with the exception of *Fat City*, are European imports. And when *The Emigrants*, directed by gifted Swede Jan Troell, is added to the list of impressive works from abroad, it is clear that the awards for the Best Foreign Film in 1972 had many worthy contenders.

But more importantly, the quality of and response to these films testified to the ever-increasing concern with aesthetic value. And this view of a film as art was solidifying itself in academia. The number of colleges and universities teaching film grew to 427, up from the 1970 total of 168. Joy Gould Boyum

See also AWARDS AND PRIZES; FONDA, JANE; HACKMAN, GENE.

MOZAMBIQUE. See ANGOLA.

MUSEUMS. Financial problems intensified in 1972 for many museums in the United States. The Detroit Historical Museum received enough income from the city to remain open only three days a week. To reduce an operating deficit, the Wadsworth Atheneum in Hartford, Conn., closed during August. At least nine museums reported thefts from their collections, which implied that they lacked funds to provide adequate security. Although Congress increased appropriations to the agencies making grants to museums, the museums urged more federal help. Congressional committee hearings considered, but did not act on, a Museum Services bill that would provide up to $40 million annually over a three-year period to help meet critical needs.

New Additions. In Boston, the Museum of Science and the Museum of Fine Arts completed large additions. In Seattle, the Museum of History and Industry added an auditorium, while the Pacific Science Center reconstructed a Northwest Coast Indian ceremonial house. Both the Indianapolis Museum of Art and the University of New Mexico's Maxwell Museum of Anthropology occupied $1-million extensions.

Besides completing a new educational wing, the University Museum in Philadelphia created a gallery for those who are blind or have impaired sight. Visitors can touch artifacts that are characteristic of many cultures. Attendants, labels in Braille and large type, and portable talking labels help handicapped visitors understand the objects.

A new museum at the base of the Statue of Liberty in New York City opened September 26. Called the American Museum of Immigration, it contains exhibits of possessions and life styles of immigrants to the United States. In October, the new Kimbell Art Museum, devoted to works of old masters, opened in Fort Worth, Tex. The collection includes works by Bellini, Goya, Rubens, Hals, and Matisse.

Extended Services. The Philadelphia Museum of Art involved students with local artists to beautify urban neighborhoods and to express themselves. Among the projects they completed is a three-story outdoor mural and a pavement painting covering more than 30,000 square feet. To encourage learning among students who had fallen behind in basic school subjects, the Guggenheim Museum collaborated with New York City schools to conduct after-school and Saturday workshops. The children studied an art of their own choice under professional artists.

Museologist Training. The number of courses on the theory and practice of museums increased. The Cleveland Museum of Art and Case Western Reserve University developed a two-year graduate program in art museum studies. The University of Michigan tailored a training plan to the needs of medium-sized art museums. The American Association of Museums began determining standards for courses in museology and organized brief intensive courses for museum workers. Ralph H. Lewis

MUSIC, CLASSICAL. Tragedy and violence saddened the music world in 1972. Two bombs, exploding within minutes of each other on January 26, heavily damaged the New York headquarters of Columbia Artists Management, Inc., and the nearby offices of impresario Sol Hurok. The second bomb killed Iris Kones, a receptionist, and injured Hurok and 13 other persons in Hurok's office. Anonymous telephone calls to the Associated Press and National Broadcasting Company after the blasts denounced Russian treatment of Jews and proclaimed the motto of the militant Jewish Defense League, "Never again!" Columbia and Hurok had, over the years, pioneered in importing Russian talent.

A sense of tragedy also emanated from nearly every stop of the Israel Philharmonic Orchestra during its 1972 tour of the United States. Security guards abounded. The programs for their concert at the John F. Kennedy Center for the Performing Arts in Washington, D.C., included a notation: "If you notice anything unusual . . . in the behavior of a member of the audience, please raise your hand high as a signal to a security officer."

The death of Goeran Gentele on July 18 stunned the music world. Less than a month after becoming general manager of the Metropolitan Opera, the former Swedish opera director was killed in an automobile accident while vacationing in Sardinia. The Met's directors chose Schuyler G. Chapin, the man Gentele had named his assistant, as interim successor.

Gentele's legacy was a much-discussed new production of Georges Bizet's *Carmen*, which opened the Met's 88th season on September 19. Mezzo-soprano Marilyn Horn was its star protagonist. The hullabaloo over the performance was so great that Deutsche Grammophon announced it would record the production in the United States. This would be the first full-scale opera recording in the United States since 1965. Because of high musician salaries in America, such recordings are normally made overseas.

Sir Rudolf Bing, Gentele's predecessor, kept himself in the public eye with his memoirs, which were published in late October. In his book, *5,000 Nights at the Opera*, he recounts his squabble with soprano Maria Callas and calls her 1956 debut in Bellini's *Norma* "the most exciting of all such in my time at the Metropolitan." He also discloses several feuds and pridefully points to 80 new productions during his 22-year reign. Waspish he could be, and distant, but Bing's artists honored him on April 22 with a rousing, old-fashioned, three-and-a-half-hour gala.

Fund-Raising. The National Endowment for the Arts awarded more than $5 million to 93 orchestras. The money was needed. Orchestras were pushing toward longer seasons, higher pay, and, therefore, bigger budgets and more frenetic fund-raising. The Cleveland Orchestra, for example, tied in with Lamar Hunt's World Championship Tennis for a tennis week in August as a benefit for the orchestra. The Cleveland Orchestra and Boston Symphony held local radio marathons. Comedian Jack Benny appeared as conductor and raised more than $50,000 for the Toronto Symphony.

Pianist Michael Ponti's debut recital in March in New York City marked his first visit to the United States after an absence of 17 years.

Artistically, orchestras thrived in the United States. The national press as usual gave fullest attention to developments in New York City: the unorthodox programming of conductor Pierre Boulez versus his New York Philharmonic audience, and Michael Tillson Thomas taking over the young people's concerts from Leonard Bernstein. But progress was more discernible elsewhere.

World premières across the country included: Walter Piston's *Flute Concerto* in Boston; Hans Werner Henze's *Heliogabalus Imperator* and an unnamed work by Jacob Druckman in Chicago; Duke Ellington's *Memories of Jacksonville* in Jacksonville, Fla; Dominick Argento's *A Ring of Time*, commissioned to honor the Minneapolis Symphony Orchestra in its 70th year, in Minneapolis; Charles Boone's *First Landscape* in honor of the San Francisco Orchestra's 60th anniversary in San Francisco; Grant Beglarian's *Diversions for Cello, Viola, and Orchestra* in Seattle, Wash.; and John La Montaine's *Wilderness Journey* in Washington, D.C.

The Philadelphia Orchestra introduced Dimitri Shostakovich's lumbering *Symphony No. 15* to America. Concert versions of operas seemed to increase in popularity, ranging from Richard Wagner's *Die Walküre* in Baltimore to the United States première of Arnold Schönberg's *Moses and Aaron* in concert form by the Chicago Symphony. The Los Angeles Philharmonic provided baroque, Beethoven, and Stravinsky marathons, a "Women in Music" concert, and performances for the Chicano community and the inmates of a California prison.

Despite increasingly unusual programs, the orchestras still gave primary allegiance to the standards. Beethoven and Mozart remained by far the most-often-performed composers, according to a survey by Broadcast Music, Incorporated. They were followed by Tchaikovsky, Brahms, Haydn, Wagner, Bach, and Dvořák. Stravinsky was 9th in the rankings, Aaron Copland 14th.

Operatic Activity. In Seattle, Thomas Pasatieri's opera *Black Widow* received its world première in March. The music is strongly melodic; the story is grim. A barren widow, obsessed with the idea of having a child, persuades her lover to marry a girl who will bear the child. When the baby is born, the widow moves in to control the household.

More than 60 years after it was written, ragtime composer Scott Joplin's opera *Treemonisha* was unearthed during an Afro-American Music Workshop at Morehouse College in Atlanta, Ga. A genuine grand opera, it has Verdi and French overtones, little ragtime, but a strong flow of Joplin's own racial heritage transformed into music. The Atlanta audience stood and cheered the opera's première on January 28.

Meanwhile, Opera /South, a black company based in Jackson, Miss., continued to grow. A November double bill featured two black composers: Ulysses Kay's *Juggler of Our Lady* and William Grant Still's *Highway 1, U.S.A.*

Virgil Thomson's *Lord Byron* was introduced at New York's Juilliard American Opera Center on April 20. *Chocorua* by Robert Selig, about an Indian chief in New Hampshire, debuted at the Berkshire Music Center in Massachusetts. On April 15, John Eaton's *Heracles* took second billing to its theater, the new, beautifully equipped Musical Arts Center on the Indiana University campus in Bloomington.

The first U.S. performances of the year included Frederick Delius' *A Village Romeo and Juliet* by the Opera Society of Washington and Hector Berlioz' mammoth, grandiose *Les Troyens* by Sarah Caldwell's Opera Company of Boston. The 300-year-old *La Calisto* of Francesco Cavalli, never before done in the United States, was showcased at the opening of the Patricia Corbett Pavilion at the University of Cincinnati's conservatory of music.

San Francisco's touring ensemble, Western Opera Theater, presented a Dollar Opera season – seven

Jubilant plantation dances and Afro-American music are part of Scott Joplin's newly discovered opera *Treemonisha.* It premièred in Atlanta.

performances with all seats unreserved at a dollar each. The Houston Grand Opera had a spring festival in a park. Performances were free and attracted approximately 50,000. In such efforts to reach a new public, Houston included a most untraditional *Postcard from Morocco* by Dominick Argento, and San Francisco highlighted Benjamin Britten's *Turn of the Screw*.

The move was away from the safe. In this spirit, Chicago's Lyric Opera revived Giuseppe Verdi's virtually unknown *I due Foscari*, and San Francisco, for its 50th anniversary season, presented Giacomo Meyerbeer's *L'Africaine*. In Dallas, Henry Purcell's *Dido and Aeneas* was provocatively paired with Ruggiero Leoncavallo's *I Pagliacci*. The New York City Opera produced Gaetano Donizetti's *Maria Stuarda*, for soprano Beverly Sills. The star supreme of the year, she was heard virtually everywhere and praised profusely wherever she appeared.

Departures from the usual repertoire were also evident in other lands. Florence's Maggio Musicale reintroduced Gioacchino Rossini's *William Tell*. Berlin audiences were pleased with *The Village Prima Donnas* by a Beethoven contemporary, Valentino Fioravanti. Drottningholm in Sweden spiced its summer fare with Cavalli's *Scipio Africanus* and Joseph Haydn's *Mondo della Luna*.

England's Glyndebourne Festival had *Il ritorno d'Ulisse in patria* by Claudio Monteverdi. And at Bayreuth, they finally performed Richard Wagner's first opera, *Das Liebesverbot* (The Fairies), 136 years after it was written, though in the nearby city auditorium and not at the Festspielhaus. At the Festspielhaus itself, an East Berlin director, Gotz Friedrich, dusted traditions severely in turning Wagner's *Tannhäuser* into a socialist parable. A male chorus was dressed in black uniforms resembling Hitler's storm troopers. At the opera's end, with Tannhäuser dying amid cries of "Hallelujah," klieg lights suddenly enveloped a stage filled with glaring workmen, their clenched fists raised in the air.

There were important opera premières overseas: Peter Maxwell Davies' *Taverner* at London's Royal Opera House, Wolfgang Fortner's *Elisabeth Tudor* at the Berlin Festival, Siegfried Matthus' *Another Spoonful of Poison, Darling?* at the Komische Opera in East Berlin, and Aarre Merikanto's *Juha* in Helsinki.

People. The musical world marked the retirement of Antonio Ghiringhelli after 27 years as general manager of La Scala. Conductor Otto Klemperer at 87 said he was ready to leave the concert platform, but that he still wanted to make recordings. Leopold Stokowski celebrated his 90th birthday several times to please his public. Soprano Roberta Peters was so enthusiastically received in *La Traviata* at the Bolshoi Theater in Moscow that officials gave her a medal usually reserved only for top artists who have served that institution for 25 years. Peter P. Jacobi

See also AWARDS AND PRIZES; RECORDINGS.

MUSIC, POPULAR. A national emergence of "soul music" and other kinds of music performed by black artists dominated the popular music world to an unprecedented degree in 1972. At one point, the five top-selling single records in the United States and 11 of the top 20 albums were by black artists.

Leading the way were composer-performer Isaac Hayes, whose main theme from the film *Shaft* won an Academy of Motion Picture Arts and Sciences Award (Oscar) and became a million-selling record; Aretha Franklin, who recorded an album of gospel music in a church; Sammy Davis, Jr., who landed on top of the charts for the first time with "Candy Man"; Bill Withers, a young singer-songwriter who, though already in his 30s, enjoyed wide acceptance with younger record buyers; the youthful Jackson 5; Marvin Gaye; Al Green; and Roberta Flack. Miss Flack's success with "The First Time Ever I Saw Your Face" symbolized the competition offered hard rock by a softer, gentler sound.

Among the white artists who also helped to create this trend were Gordon Lightfoot, Mac Davis, Carly Simon, and Kris Kristofferson. Nilsson's "Without You" and Neil Young's "Heart of Gold" both hit the top of the album charts, as did "A Horse with No Name" by a predominantly soft-rock group called America. Contributors to the "easy listening" sound also included B. J. Thomas with "Rock 'n' Roll Lullaby"; Three Dog Night with "An Old Fashioned Love Song"; Sonny and Cher singing "All I Ever Need Is You"; "Cherish" sung by David Cassidy; and "Hurting Each Other" by the Carpenters.

The Rock Groups used fireworks and other startling effects for a return to theatricality in their in-person performances. Along with glamorous imagery and glittering costumes came a bizarre quality characterized by some observers as "rock 'n' rouge" and "freak rock," sometimes with bisexual overtones. In keeping with this movement were David Bowie – the so-called Oscar Wilde of Rock – and a group that called itself Alice Cooper, although the leader was actually a man. From Britain came the garish T. Rex, and, in their first appearance in the United States since 1969, the Rolling Stones made an eight-week, 30-city tour. The Stones' U.S. concerts were often sold out within minutes after the tickets went on sale. "Exile on Main Street," both as a single and as the title number of an album, provided the Stones with sales far over the million mark.

Musical Comebacks. While some artists indulged themselves in freakish outfits and wild actions, a few took the opposite direction. Bobby Darin made a comeback by discarding his jeans and beads and working in a formal tuxedo, appealing to a somewhat older age group. Several record companies stimulated the pop music business by putting together touring shows that comprised artists who recorded for their label. One major company rented Madison Square Garden to showcase several of its middle-of-the-road artists.

The frenetic gyrations of Mick Jagger, *above,* turned on rock fans across the country during the tour of the Rolling Stones in July. Folk singer Don McLean, *left,* scored a hit with *American Pie,* his 8½-minute single recording.

Nostalgia was everywhere: on the stage, where both new musical shows and such revivals as *No, No, Nanette* evoked memories of earlier decades; on records, with stereo re-creations of monaural swing-era hits selling millions of albums; and in the resurgence of such early rock 'n' roll stars as Chuck Berry, who enjoyed his first big record hit in many years with "Dingaling."

One of the biggest concert attractions of the year was Neil Diamond, who was presented for a 10-day run in New York City by the Shubert Theatre Corporation. As a result of this and other similar ventures, the doors were opened for rock performers to play extended engagements in Broadway theaters previously reserved for "legitimate" productions.

The instrumental/vocal rock bands showed an inclination toward Latin and Afro-Cuban rhythms as many groups made extensive use of exotic percussion instruments. Malo, Santana, El Chicano, Sod, and War reflected this trend.

American Pie. Don McLean, a young singer and composer, was a best seller throughout 1972 with his version of a cryptic song called *American Pie.* Like McLean, many of the year's most important new stars were singers performing their own songs. Notable among them were John Prine, Steve Goodman, and Gilbert O'Sullivan.

Some artists, apparently overwhelmed by the magnitude of their success in previous years, sat out much of 1972 while records maintained their popularity. Among those who became relatively inactive were Carole King, who won four Grammy Awards in March, and James Taylor, who won one Grammy. Smokey Robinson, who leaped to fame during the 1960s as leader of The Miracles, announced that he had retired.

The Jazz Scene. Jazz rebounded sharply in 1972. The annual Newport Jazz Festival, after being closed down by a riot in 1971, transferred to New York City and expanded from four to nine days. It attracted capacity crowds to Carnegie and Philharmonic halls and to two midnight jam sessions at Radio City Music Hall in July. The Monterey Jazz Festival also attracted record crowds in September.

Jazz groups toured Japan and Europe with notable success. The big band of Thad Jones and Mel Lewis played in Russia. Duke Ellington, at 73, continued his feverish pace. On October 7, he was honored at Yale University, where 35 outstanding black musicians were awarded the Ellington Fellowship Medal.

Grammy Awards for best jazz performances in 1971 were presented to Ellington for "The New Orleans Suite" and to pianist Bill Evans for "The Bill Evans Album."

The National Endowment for the Arts stepped up its program by announcing grants totaling $250,000 to musicians, composers, and colleges for jazz-related projects.

Leonard Feather

NAMIBIA. For the first time, the white minority government of South Africa in 1972 showed some recognition of a United Nations (UN) role in Namibia (South-West Africa). UN Secretary-General Kurt Waldheim made a three-day visit to Namibia in March, and black African nationalists appealed to him for UN intervention to abolish South African rule in Namibia and establish an independent government. South Africa has refused to relinquish control of Namibia since the UN voted in 1966 to revoke its old League of Nations mandate.

After discussions with South African government officials, Waldheim announced an agreement had been reached on the aim of independence and self-determination for the people of Namibia. Some observers believe that South Africa is aiming for the partition of Namibia into separate black homelands, or Bantustans. These could later become independent or join with neighboring black nations, leaving the richest part of Namibia under white control. However, the African nationalists want a united and independent Namibia.

On September 5, Waldheim appointed Alfred M. Escher, a Swiss diplomat, as a special UN representative to aid the Namibians in gaining independence. Although Escher will not be allowed to set up an office in Namibia, South Africa agreed he and his representatives could visit it. George Shepherd

See also AFRICA (Facts in Brief Table).

NATIONAL DEFENSE. The United States slimmed its military forces to 2,355,839 as of Sept. 30, 1972, the lowest level in 22 years. However, the defense budget of $78.3 billion almost equaled the World War II peak of $79.8 billion, when the United States had more than 12 million men under arms. Pay increases and inflation contributed to the swelling defense costs. The burden of the Vietnam War eased, but the Department of Defense (DOD) was concerned about the decline of the United States as a world power, the soaring costs of manpower and sophisticated new weapons, and the uncertainties about a future threat from Russia and China.

As the United States phased out its involvement in the Vietnam War, troop strength in Vietnam was cut by more than half a million men. The last of the 112 ground-combat battalions departed on Sept. 1, 1972. On December 28, there were 24,100 U.S. troops in South Vietnam.

Declining Power. Admiral Thomas H. Moorer, chairman of the U.S. Joint Chiefs of Staff, said in his annual report in February that "the relative military power of the United States in the world has clearly peaked and is now declining.

"We will no longer have that substantial strategic superiority which in the past provided us with such a generous margin of overall military power that we could, with confidence, protect our own interests and those of our allies worldwide," Moorer said. "Henceforth, we will have to plot our course with much greater precision and calculate our risks much more closely."

Despite the dramatic shift in the military balance of power in Russia's favor during the last five years, Moorer said the United States still had better missile guidance and multiple independent re-entry vehicle (MIRV) warheads, and more strategic bombers. He said that Russia is ahead of the United States in ground-combat forces and is catching up in tactical air power, but is still somewhat behind U.S. naval power. However, the mere appearance of Russian superiority, Moorer warned, could have a debilitating effect on U.S. foreign policy and on the confidence of U.S. allies in U.S. strategic power.

President Richard M. Nixon's national security policy is based on the concept that the United States must maintain realistic deterrence against either nuclear or conventional wars. Therefore, the DOD insisted on improvements in the quality of strategic weapons and on technological superiority, even after the United States and Russia agreed on May 26, 1972, as a result of the Strategic Arms Limitation Talks (SALT), to slow the nuclear arms race.

The SALT Agreement. The two superpowers signed a treaty to limit each side to two antiballistic missile (ABM) defense sites, with no more than 100 missiles at each site. At the same time, they entered an interim five-year agreement to freeze their supply of strategic land-based intercontinental ballistic missiles (ICBM's) and submarine-launched ballistic missiles (SLBM's) to those currently in operation and under construction. Under terms of the SALT agreement, U.S. officials calculated that Russia could have 1,618 ICBM's, and 62 submarines carrying up to 950 SLBM missiles. The United States could have only 1,054 ICBM's and 44 missile submarines, carrying a total of 710 SLBM's.

The SALT agreement tried to establish approximate nuclear parity between Russia and the United States to slow the nuclear arms race. According to U.S. defense officials, if not halted by SALT, the Russians could have had more than 2,500 ICBM's and about 80 missile submarines by 1977.

The SALT agreements did not cover heavy bombers, nor such improvements as the MIRV warheads for existing ICBM's. The United States had 450 bombers against 140 for Russia. The United States also had 250 Minuteman III ICBM's with triple MIRV's, and 12 Polaris submarines equipped with Poseidon missiles carrying 10 or more MIRV's.

The U.S. advantage in bombers and MIRV warheads, plus three overseas bases for Polaris submarines, was considered enough to balance Russia's large numerical lead in ICBM's. So, U.S. defense officials were willing to accept this apparently lopsided formula for nuclear balance in exchange for Russia's agreement to freeze strategic missile deployment and limit ABM defenses to 200 missiles.

Construction continues on the Grand Forks, N.Dak., Safeguard antiballistic missile site, which is one of two allowed under the SALT agreement.

Better Weapons. As insurance against failure of the SALT agreement, Secretary of Defense Melvin R. Laird repeatedly urged Congress to speed development of the Trident missile submarine, which will cost nearly $1 billion, in fiscal 1973. The Trident would carry 24 missiles having a range of 4,000 miles, as compared with 16 missiles with a range of 2,750 miles on the Polaris-Poseidon submarines. The Trident program would cost about $13.5 billion for 10 submarines, including a naval base for their maintenance. Laird also asked Congress to keep the B-1 supersonic bomber program on schedule so that it could be deployed in the late 1970s.

To enhance the U.S. nuclear posture and bargaining position for future SALT talks, Laird also proposed that the U.S.:

- Develop a prototype for the "site defense" program, which would use ABM's to protect ICBM's.
- Develop a submarine cruise-launched missile that could evade Russian radar.
- Accelerate the shifting of B-52's to inland bases.
- Develop warheads that will be more accurate against enemy underground missile sites.
- Improve the intelligence satellites used to monitor Russian missile developments.

Laird recommended that, in addition to the Safeguard ABM site at Grand Forks, N. Dak., a second ABM defense site should be constructed around Washington, D.C. He halted construction of other ABM sites in the nation, under the terms of the SALT agreement.

Congress, however, delayed making a decision on the Washington, D.C., ABM site for another year. Senator John C. Stennis (D., Miss.), chairman of the Senate Armed Services Committee, said Congress did not approve the $235 million needed to start construction on the site because there was no accurate estimate of how much it would cost to complete the system. Congress did agree to provide $561 million in fiscal 1973 to complete the Grand Forks site.

Defense Costs. Strategic-weapons improvements and funds for the mining of harbors and for intensified bombing in North Vietnam added $2.2 billion on June 30 to the defense department's original $83.4-billion budget authorization request for fiscal 1973. Therefore, the total requested authority to commit funds for defense was $85.6 billion, compared with $77.1 billion for fiscal 1972. Actual spending for national defense in fiscal 1973, however, was estimated at $78.3 billion. This would have provided for a total military force by June 30, 1973, of 2,358,000 men. However, Congress passed a bill on September 15 ordering a 16,000-man cut in the total military strength to 2,342,000 by June 30, 1973.

The Navy was scheduled to receive the largest portion of the fiscal 1973 budget, $25.2 billion; the Air Force, $23.5 billion; and the Army, $22.1 billion.

The Navy requested $977 million for the Trident missile-submarine program and $299 million to start on the fourth nuclear-powered aircraft carrier. The Navy had production and cost inflation problems with its F-14 Tomcat jet fighter, its LHA landing helicopter amphibious assault ships, and its DD-963 destroyers. The Navy planned to purchase 313 F-14's at a cost of about $16 million each.

The Air Force was authorized $127 million to buy three Boeing 747 airborne command posts for the White House. These planes would be used to relay the President's orders in case of a nuclear war.

The Air Force planned to begin flight testing its new B-1 supersonic bomber by April, 1974. The 241 B-1's on order will cost an estimated $45.5 million each. The F-15 Eagle jet fighter was flight-tested in June. The 749 F-15 Eagles, including 20 research planes, will cost about $10.4 million each.

The Army, still struggling with mounting weapons costs, canceled its Cheyenne attack helicopter program on August 9. More than $400 million had been spent since 1966 to develop the Cheyenne. The Army wants to develop a smaller, less costly attack helicopter, and asked $33 million for this purpose.

The Marine Corps was granted $115 million for 24 British-made Harrier vertical take-off planes. The Marines had previously ordered 90 of these planes and plan to form three vertical take-off squadrons – one for each air wing.

End of U.S. infantry combat role in Vietnam War was marked when last combat battalion furled its colors during Da Nang ceremony on August 12.

Command Changes. Kenneth Rush, former U.S. ambassador to West Germany, succeeded David Packard on February 3, as deputy secretary of defense. John W. Warner, undersecretary of the Navy, became secretary of the Navy on May 4, 1972, replacing John H. Chafee. Lieutenant General Robert E. Cushman, Jr., became commandant of the Marine Corps on Jan. 1, 1972. On June 1, Alene B. Duerk was sworn in as the Navy's first woman admiral. See Duerk, Alene B.

On September 7, the Army ordered 25 generals into early retirement to open more positions for younger men. At the same time, President Nixon nominated Major General Alexander M. Haig, Jr., for Army vice-chief of staff. The 47-year-old Haig was promoted over 240 more senior officers.

General Creighton W. Abrams was nominated for Army chief of staff on June 20, to replace the retiring General William C. Westmoreland. He was confirmed on October 12 after a Senate committee cleared him of charges that he knew about unauthorized bombing of North Vietnam, ordered by General John D. Lavelle in late 1971 and early 1972.

Lloyd H. Norman

NATIONALIST CHINA. See Taiwan.
NAVY, U.S. See National Defense.
NEBRASKA. See State Government.

NEPAL. King Mahendra Bir Bikram Sha Deva died on Jan. 31, 1972, ending a 17-year reign during which he tried to modernize the isolated nation. He was succeeded by Crown Prince Birendra.

For several months, there was considerable confusion as to whether the 26-year-old king would be able to continue the somewhat autocratic rule of his father. Of particular concern was whether or not King Birendra could cope with a movement spearheaded by liberals and students to allow political parties in the Panchayat to open legislative sessions to the press and public. The ultimate test of the king's abilities came in August when parliamentary quarrels erupted over a no-confidence vote directed against the king's chief administrative officer, Prime Minister Kirti Nidhi Bista. The controversy raged for several weeks until the king issued a bluntly worded pronouncement that party factionalism was out and that the king was the final authority in the land. This prompted more opposition in the Panchayat and student demonstrations in the streets of Katmandu. The king moved swiftly to stifle this opposition. On August 17, he suspended 12 members of the Panchayat. About 200 antigovernment demonstrators, mostly students, were arrested. When the student unrest continued, he closed the universities. As the year ended, there was little doubt that King Birendra was firmly in control. John N. Stalker

See also ASIA (Facts in Brief Table).

NETHERLANDS. Discontent and frustration led to a political crisis in 1972. The center-right coalition government resigned on July 20, and a minority coalition took over until the people could vote in the general election on November 29. But election results were inconclusive; left- and right-wing parties were almost equally balanced in the lower house of the States-General, the Netherlands' legislature.

The government's troubles began in February when Prime Minister Barend W. Biesheuvel announced plans to free the three remaining Nazi war criminals serving life sentences. They were responsible for deporting 80,000 Dutch Jews who died in World War II concentration camps. Relatives of the victims and Jewish youths demonstrated in Amsterdam. The lower house voted against freeing the three. On March 5, the government decided to keep the war criminals in jail.

The political crisis arose on July 17 when two ministers representing the Democratic Socialist '70 Party resigned because the government planned to cut spending and raise university fees from $88 to $325 a term. With only minority support, the government resigned three days later. The four center-right parties, led by Biesheuvel, formed a caretaker government with the task of passing a budget to make up a deficit of about $927 million.

Inflation Problem. Queen Juliana referred to her country's political instability and persistent inflation when she opened a new session of the legislature on September 19. Her speech called for tying wage increases closely to the cost of living and setting prices to keep profit margins relatively constant. The Netherlands, with one of Europe's worst inflation problems, had seen wages rise annually by 10 to 12 per cent for the previous three years. Prices and taxes kept pace. The outgoing government limited wage and price increases for 1973 and levied several tax increases, including a form of sales tax and taxes on capital gains, corporations, and incomes.

Labor Unrest. Strikes in the shipbuilding and heavy metals industries lasted from February 4 to 20, when the 30,000 strikers accepted an arbitration award. Fearing a flood of laborers from Commonwealth nations, the Netherlands asked the European Community to restrict their entry when Great Britain joins in 1973. Holland had absorbed 300,000 Indo-Dutch who left Indonesia after independence, and had 150,000 foreign workers in its labor force. On August 11, Dutch and Turkish residents of Rotterdam clashed over housing difficulties.

Norbert Schmelzer and Andrei Gromyko, the Dutch and Russian foreign ministers, signed an agreement in The Hague on July 6. It calls for economic, industrial, and technical cooperation between the two countries. Kenneth Brown

See also EUROPE (Facts in Brief Table).

NEVADA. See STATE GOVERNMENT.

NE WIN (1911-) became Burma's first civilian chief of state in 10 years when he led his Cabinet out of the Burmese Army on April 20, 1972. He and most of the Cabinet's army members left the armed forces. Ne Win was no longer a general or Burma's defense minister, but he was still chairman of the ruling Revolutionary Council, prime minister, and head of the Burma Socialist Program, the country's only political party. The move prepared for the establishment of the Socialist Republic of Burma.

Ne Win was born Shu Maung (apple of one's eye) in Paungde, Burma. He studied for a medical career, but became active in a movement for Burmese independence from Great Britain in the 1930s. In 1941, he and others of a group called Thirty Companions were smuggled to Japan for military training. He took the name Ne Win (brilliant sun) then. When he decided the Japanese were not serious about Burmese independence, he turned against them.

In 1958, he headed a caretaker government to put down the threat of civil war. He cleaned up corruption and ruled until elections were held in 1960. When a new crisis arose, he led a coup on March 1, 1962, and set up a military dictatorship. Ed Nelson

NEW BRUNSWICK. See CANADA.

NEW GUINEA. See PACIFIC ISLANDS.

NEW HAMPSHIRE. See STATE GOVERNMENT.

NEW JERSEY. See NEWARK; STATE GOVERNMENT.

NEW MEXICO. See STATE GOVERNMENT.

NEWARK residents were treated in 1972 to the unique experience of a mayor busily trying to publish news of municipal corruption and wrongdoing in a city hall newspaper. Using Model Cities funds, Mayor Kenneth A. Gibson's office began publishing its own bimonthly newspaper in August to inform Newark's citizens about municipal programs aimed at correcting the city's problems. It provided detailed information on what services were available and how residents could make use of them. A staff member was also assigned to report on graft in the city, and spokesmen said the newspaper would print any evidence of wrongdoing uncovered in city hall. The first issue of the newspaper was mailed to 40,000 residents selected at random from the telephone book.

The strife-torn *Newark Evening News* went out of business on August 31. The newspaper, which was shut down by a strike on May 26, 1971, had resumed publication on April 10, 1972.

A *Newark Evening News* reporter, Peter J. Bridge, was jailed for 21 days beginning October 4 because he refused to answer grand jury questions about corruption in government. Bridge lost governmental immunity from prosecution by identifying the source of his information–a Newark Housing Authority official who said she had been offered a bribe. Bridge was jailed when he refused to answer other questions about the case.

Newark's Black Population reaped reapportionment benefits on April 12 when a three-judge federal court ordered a new congressional district plan into effect. The new plan created a predominantly black congressional district in and around Newark. It also gave one more congressional seat to New Jersey's growing suburban population. The federal court acted after the state legislature had failed to meet a court-imposed deadline for the approval of a reapportionment plan.

The city council on June 13 awarded itself the first pay raise in six years, upping salaries of its members from $10,000 to $15,000 a year. Mayor Gibson vetoed the increase, but the council overrode his veto.

A Major Financial Crisis plagued city hall. Special taxing powers granted by the state legislature to the city were due to expire at the end of 1972. The special taxing powers had generated $31 million in city revenues, and Mayor Gibson predicted bankruptcy for the city in 1973 unless some additional forms of revenue became available. Federal revenue-sharing funds, estimated at $8.4 million, fell far short of the city's needs.

Employment in Newark fell slightly, from 784,500 employed in May, 1971, to 778,900 in May, 1972. Average gross weekly earnings of production workers on manufacturing payrolls in Newark rose from $149.57 to $160.37, during the same period.

Former Mayor Hugh J. Addonizio was taken into custody on March 6 to begin serving a 10-year prison term for extortion. J. M. Banovetz

NEW ORLEANS learned in September, 1972, that it would not receive any federal funds for programs or projects that might increase the pollution discharged by facilities in the city. The action was taken by the federal Environmental Protection Agency (EPA). The EPA blamed New Orleans for the continuing flow of raw and inadequately treated sewage into the Mississippi River. However, the city took an innovative step to reduce the air pollution caused by automotive exhaust; it began to construct bicycle racks in commercial areas.

Crime Statistics. The Uniform Crime Reports released by the Federal Bureau of Investigation on August 29 showed New Orleans' crime index to be 4,439.3 crimes per 100,000 persons, compared with a national average of 2,907 crimes per 100,000 persons. There were 696 violent crimes per 100,000 persons.

Black militant H. Rap Brown, convicted of a federal gun-law violation in New York City in 1968, was resentenced to five years in prison by a New Orleans judge on June 2. Brown's defense attorney, William M. Kunstler, argued that the court proceedings were "arrogantly illegal." He claimed that Brown had been transferred from New York City to New Orleans for sentencing in violation of a court order. That same day, a three-judge federal appeals court rejected Kunstler's argument. Brown was immediately taken from New Orleans before another appeals judge could rule on a defense motion to prevent Brown's transfer back to New York City, where he was under indictment for a tavern holdup.

Garrison Election Bid. District Attorney Jim C. Garrison tried, but failed, to win the Democratic nomination for associate justice of the Louisiana Supreme Court. During his campaign, Garrison claimed that the 1971 federal indictments against him for bribery were "attempts at vengeance for his public statements that certain federal agencies were involved in a plot to assassinate former President John F. Kennedy."

Construction continued on the domed stadium, the Superdome, which is scheduled for completion in 1974. Although the facility was designed for football, baseball, hockey, concerts, and rallies, only the New Orleans Saints football team was committed to use the new stadium. The 80,000-seat Superdome will be able to accommodate more than 100,000 persons on special occasions and will have six large, closed-circuit television screens for instant replays of sports events.

The U.S. Bureau of the Census reported that the median family income for New Orleans was $7,445 per year. This was the lowest figure reported for a major U.S. city. Nonagricultural employment increased by 9,600 jobs to 382,300 between May, 1971, and May, 1972. Average weekly earnings of production workers also increased by $6.75 per week, reaching $151.07, during the same period. J. M. Banovetz

NEW YORK. See New York City; State Government.

NEW YORK CITY witnessed a bloody eruption of gangland fighting in 1972 that claimed the lives of at least 15 victims. The murders were allegedly the result of a gang war between followers of Joseph Colombo and Joseph (Crazy Joe) Gallo. Colombo had been shot and permanently incapacitated on June 26, 1971. Gallo, suspected of helping plot the attack on Colombo, was shot to death on April 7.

Drug Abuse. A federal report released on August 16 labeled New York City as the main distribution point for heroin smuggled into the United States from Europe. New York dealers reportedly pay $1-million for about 220 pounds of pure heroin and sell it for $22 million.

The state of New York and the Veterans Administration established a $2-million special program for treating an additional 1,100 New York City heroin addicts in 1972 and 1973. However, some 20,000 addicts in New York City were awaiting treatment.

Official Corruption. The Knapp Commission completed its two-year investigation of New York police corruption and reported on August 6 that police department corruption was widespread. It recommended the creation of a police anticorruption unit and the appointment of a special deputy attorney general to prosecute police and other officials. Governor Nelson A. Rockefeller accepted the recommendations and appointed a special prosecutor.

New York City transit officials in March marked the breakthrough of the East 63rd Street rail tunnel into the system under the East River.

In May, the state legislature created a commission to examine New York City's charter. The commission has until June, 1973, to present a new or revised charter, which must be approved by the city's voters.

A federal grand jury issued indictments on March 28 against 40 persons and 10 corporations, including Dun & Bradstreet Inc. They were charged with conspiring to falsify records in order to sell houses to low-income families at inflated prices – with Federal Housing Administration loans. See HOUSING.

The U.S. Department of Justice sued New York City and New Jersey on July 18 for failing to halt pollution of the New York Harbor. Allegedly, the city and state governments had not enforced existing codes requiring manufacturing firms to clean their wastes before flushing them into the city sanitation systems. The federal Environmental Protection Agency also sued New York City and New Jersey to force the cleanup of nearly 2 billion gallons of waste poured into the harbor each day.

Federal government statistics indicated that the cost of living was rising faster in New York City than in any of the nation's major cities. Living costs rose 55 per cent since 1955 and 30.3 per cent since 1967. Increases in the cost of food, up 27.4 per cent since 1967, also topped all other major cities. Average gross weekly earnings of production workers rose 6.1 per cent between May, 1971, and May, 1972, but employment fell by 80,000 jobs. J. M. Banovetz

NEW ZEALAND. The prime ministership changed hands three times in 1972. On February 2, Sir Keith J. Holyoake announced his retirement at a National Party caucus in Auckland. The resignation of the 68-year-old Holyoake, who had served for 12 years, paved the way for his successor, Deputy Prime Minister John R. Marshall. He was sworn in on February 7 (see MARSHALL, JOHN R.). But in the federal elections held on November 25, he was swept out by an unexpected victory of the Labour Party. Norman E. Kirk, head of the Labour Party since 1965, was named prime minister (see KIRK, NORMAN E.). It was the biggest election upset since the Labour Party won the elections in 1935.

Economic Problems. Prime Minister Kirk, like his predecessors, was concerned with giving greater representation to urban constituencies. In the past, farmers have been largely overrepresented in the government. Like his predecessors, too, he faced some compelling problems. First, there was a real problem with what could be termed wage inflation. The national unions in New Zealand had pressured the government and management into a series of wage hikes that set off a round of price increases that, in turn, could be disastrous to New Zealand's hopes for changing foreign trade patterns.

During Marshall's brief term, negotiations had been completed for a transition from the protected British Commonwealth market into the more competitive European Community (Common Market) on highly favorable terms for the country. But the price-wage inflation within the country would make the transition more difficult. The Kirk Government would need to check this inflation if plans for the new economic role of New Zealand were to be realized.

Seeking New Markets. The search for new markets continued mainly in the Pacific. New Zealand approached Australia and other Pacific countries seeking trade agreements. Of all the Pacific nations, Japan had the greatest potential. New Zealand exported more than $150 million in goods to Japan during the year, and this was expected to increase in the years to come. Metals were perhaps most important, now that steel and aluminum were being produced in quantity by new refineries. Timber exports assumed importance as reforested areas began to provide a regular supply.

New Zealand's food industry also comprised an important part of its export trade. Fish and frozen vegetables began to vie with the more commonplace wool and mutton products. But dairying, a highly efficient industry developed in response to British needs, had a more difficult time in finding new markets in the Pacific. Major efforts were made to change Asian diets to expand the market for these products, especially in Japan. John N. Stalker

See also ASIA (Facts in Brief Table).

NEWFOUNDLAND. See CANADA.

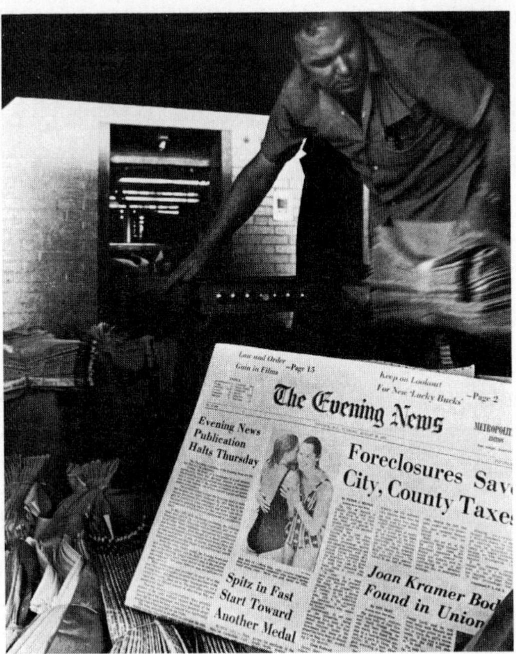

When *The Evening News* folded in August, Newark, N.J., became the largest city in the United States with only one daily newspaper.

NEWSPAPERS. Grave doubts arose in 1972 about the privilege of the press. The Supreme Court of the United States ruled on June 29 that newsmen do not have the constitutional right to refuse to testify before grand juries about information given to them in confidence. Offshoots of the decision came quickly. In October, reporter Peter Bridge was jailed for 21 days because he refused to answer a grand jury's questions concerning an article he wrote for *The Newark Evening News* concerning a housing scandal. In November, reporter William T. Farr was jailed because he refused to disclose sources of a 1970 article he wrote for the *Los Angeles Herald-Examiner* concerning the Charles Manson murder case. Newsmen in several other cities were subpoenaed in similar cases during the year.

The Supreme Court's Ruling reversed a lower federal court decision that Earl Caldwell, reporter for *The New York Times* in San Francisco, did not have to testify before a federal grand jury about conversations with national leaders of the Black Panther Party. It rejected Caldwell's contention that forcing him to give testimony would "suppress vital First Amendment freedoms . . . by driving a wedge of distrust and silence between the news media and the militants."

The Supreme Court decision also affirmed a ruling of a Kentucky Court of Appeals. The Kentucky court upheld the subpoenaing of Paul M. Branzburg, a reporter on *The Louisville Courier-Journal* when he was called to testify about violations of the drug laws he had observed while doing a series of stories. Branzburg, now with *The Detroit Free Press*, had argued that his testimony, if given, would "destroy the relationship of trust which he enjoys . . . thereby hampering the media's ability to cover news and activities of those involved in the drug culture."

Major Papers Fold. The suspension of publication by *The Boston Herald-Traveler* on June 18, *The Newark Evening News* on August 31, and the *Washington Daily News* on July 12 reduced daily newspaper circulation in the country. The *News* sold its name and other assets to the *Washington Evening Star*.

On January 1, there were 1,749 dailies and 61,743,141 readers of morning, evening, Sunday, and all-day newspapers in the United States. In contrast to the dailies, weekly newspapers posted a marked increase in circulation.

Meanwhile, publishers bid for congressional help in their battle against increased postal rates. Lawmakers, however, were unsympathetic to the publishers' cause. The resulting postal rate hikes caused circulation losses among from 500 to 600 small city papers that stopped mail deliveries to rural readers, although many subscribers were serviced direct by motor route contractors. Gerald B. Healey

NICARAGUA. See LATIN AMERICA.

NIGER. See AFRICA.

NIGERIA continued its remarkable recovery in 1972 from the financial and social disruptions caused by the civil war. The economy was booming with oil revenue and the inflow of foreign capital. In March, the World Bank loaned Nigeria $27 million to develop roads and repair eight bridges that were damaged during the war. However, a steep rise in unemployment and an estimated 6.5 per cent rise in the cost of living in 1971 and 1972 marred the favorable growth pattern.

On March 1, the government issued the controversial Nigerian Enterprises Promotion Decree. The decree forbids aliens to practice 33 specific trades, such as construction work, or engage in 22 types of business activity, such as advertising, after March 31, 1974.

Political calm lasted throughout the year. However, there were rumors of discontent among local government officials in the western part of Nigeria. The army kept 250,000 troops in the east, scene of the civil war, compared to the 11,000 stationed there before the war.

Nigeria worked to bring about a Green Revolution through scientific farming. Staff members began moving onto the $19-million campus of Nigeria's new International Institute for Tropical Agriculture at Ibadan. Forty scientists from 17 different countries will do research there on grains, such as corn and rice, and on protein-rich vegetables.

On August 24, the military government brought four state universities under federal control. This was designed to bring uniform standards to Nigeria's higher education programs.

Currency Change. A massive program was conducted in 1972 to educate Nigerians about the new monetary system that replaced pounds and shillings with decimal units called kobos and nairas on Jan. 1, 1973. The government used audio-visual aids to spread information about the new money in the nine languages and dozens of dialects spoken in Nigeria.

In another change, Nigerians switched in April from driving on the left side of the road to driving on the right. The change was made because all neighboring nations with which Nigeria has direct highway links drive on the right side.

Foreign Relations. The first step toward creating regional unity in western Africa was taken when Nigerian Major General Yakubu Gowon, head of the federal government, visited Togo in late April. On May 1, Gowon and Togo's President Etienne Eyadema announced the formation of the Nigerian-Togolese Economic Community. This was the first economic organization composed of a former British colony and a French-speaking African nation.

During his visit to Togo, Gowon also reconciled with President Felix Houphouet-Boigny, of Ivory Coast, who had supported secessionist Biafra during the Nigerian civil war. George Shepherd

See also Africa (Facts in Brief Table).

NIXON, RICHARD MILHOUS, enjoyed a year of remarkable personal triumph in 1972. Once an unpopular political figure, he won the 1972 election by a landslide – 60.7 per cent of the popular vote – signifying a broad mandate for his second term as chief executive. Although he had been an uncompromising foe of Communism, he initiated an era of reconciliation with China and Russia in 1972. And his personal emissary, Henry A. Kissinger, worked tirelessly, though unsuccessfully, throughout the year to end the United States longest and most unpopular war.

Mr. Nixon's re-election was a special victory, because it came just 10 years after his crushing defeat in the California governor's race, which supposedly marked the end of his political career. In 1972, Richard M. Nixon, the hard-fighting campaigner, was replaced by a retiring, aloof President Nixon. He campaigned mainly from the White House and only rarely made personal appearances. See Elections; Republican Party.

However, the President's every action was part of his larger campaign plan. Although, to many, he lacked personal magnetism, he was a hard-working, competent manager, and during his first term, he clearly worked to emphasize this competence.

To prepare for "a generation of peace," he traveled across the world seeking reconciliation in Peking and Moscow. Yet he insisted on "peace with honor" in Vietnam, and he received the support of most Americans when he announced in May he had ordered the bombing and mining of North Vietnam's harbors.

It was evident that Mr. Nixon still thought of himself as a loner. Soon after the election, he retired to Camp David, his Catoctin Mountain retreat in Maryland, to plan his second-term strategy. "On top of a mountain," he said, "it is easier for me to get on top of the job."

Personal Diplomacy. By his own count, Mr. Nixon, the most traveled President in U.S. history, had visited some 60 nations in his lifetime before making his historic visit to China in February. The President flew to Peking with Mrs. Nixon, an 87-member press corps, and color-television crews. Millions of Americans watched as he arrived in Peking, ending 22 years of hostility between the People's Republic of China and the United States.

During his weeklong stay in China, Mr. Nixon talked with Chairman Mao Tse-tung and held private conferences with Premier Chou En-lai. The Chinese entertained him with banquets, the ballet, table tennis matches, and gymnastics and a trip to the Great Wall.

Mr. Nixon visited Russia in May, during the tense aftermath of stepped-up U.S. bombing of North Vietnam and the mining of its harbors. Nevertheless, the carefully planned trip was successful. While in Moscow, Mr. Nixon signed several important treaties, including the strategic arms limitation agreements. He made a dramatic return to the capital by

Hubert le Campion, *Life* © 1972 Time Inc.

On her visit to Liberia in January, *above*, Mrs. Nixon dons a lappa suit and a head tie, the traditional costume, while ceremonial dancers look on. Julie Nixon Eisenhower, *above right,* tours Big Cypress Swamp in Florida, which President Nixon proposed acquiring as a fresh-water reserve. Tricia Nixon Cox, *right,* leads a door-to-door campaign in Columbus, Ohio, to aid her father's re-election effort.

addressing a specially convened joint evening session of Congress on June 1. See NATIONAL DEFENSE.

Vietnam Negotiations. In late October, Kissinger and the North Vietnamese announced they were nearing agreement to end the Vietnam War. Kissinger's statement on October 26 that "peace is at hand" gave an extra boost to Mr. Nixon's re-election effort.

However, the talks reached a deadlock, and on December 16, Kissinger announced that the negotiations had been broken off. On December 18, the United States resumed full-scale bombing of North Vietnam. On December 30, Mr. Nixon halted the bombing and announced that the peace talks would resume early in January. See ASIA.

The First Lady emerged as a public figure in her own right in 1972. In January, Patricia Ryan Nixon traveled to Ghana, Liberia, and Ivory Coast as a representative of the President. On January 3, she attended the inauguration of Liberian President William R. Tolbert.

Mrs. Nixon also accompanied the President to China and Russia. In both Peking and Moscow, she was an impressive good-will ambassador.

In September, Mrs. Nixon took to the campaign trail on behalf of the President. She made a 5,400-mile tour of several states, "taking the White House to the people." Carol L. Thompson

See also Section One, FOCUS ON THE NATION; FOCUS ON THE WORLD.

Fischetti, © 1972 *Chicago Daily News*

"We want to report a missing dream."

NOBEL PRIZES for literature, economics, and science were presented at ceremonies in Stockholm, Sweden, on Dec. 10, 1972. They were awarded by the Norwegian Storting (legislative) Nobel Committee, Oslo. No peace prize was awarded in 1972.

Literature Prize was awarded to Heinrich Theodor Böll, 54, for his contribution to "a renewal of German literature" in the postwar era. Böll was born in Cologne, Germany, where his father was a sculptor and carpenter. He served as a German infantryman in World War II and was wounded three times. His first two novels, both bitterly antiwar, were *The Train Was on Time* (1949) and *Adam, Where Art Thou?* (1951). Later novels, such as *Tomorrow and Yesterday* (1954), dealt with the aftermath of the war, the problems of men obsessed with death, and West Germany's postwar economic revival. He also wrote *Billiards at Half Past Nine* (1959), dealing with three German generations, and *The Clown* (1963), an expression of sorrow at the Germany he saw emerging from the war. His latest novel, *Group Portrait with Lady* (1971), centers mainly on the effects of war on his heroine, Leni, and the loss of her Russian lover-prisoner.

Economic Science Prize was shared by John R. Hicks, 68, of Oxford University in England, and Kenneth J. Arrow, 51, of Harvard University. Their theories have helped to assess business risk and government economic and welfare policies. The equilibrium theory for which they were specifically cited maintains that active forces cancel each other and produce a state of balance in the economy.

Chemistry Prize was shared by three chemists, Christian B. Anfinsen, 56, of the National Institutes of Health at Bethesda, Md., and Stanford Moore, 59, and William H. Stein, 61, of Rockefeller University in New York City. They received the award for unraveling the structure of the enzyme named ribonuclease. In 1959, Moore and Stein determined the full sequence of amino acids in ribonuclease. They found that it contains 124 amino acids and determined the location of the 1,876 atoms contained in these amino acids. Anfinsen is credited with the basic discovery of how ribonuclease is formed.

Physics Prize was shared by John Bardeen, 64, of the University of Illinois; Leon Cooper, 42, of Brown University; and John Robert Schrieffer, 41, of the University of Pennsylvania. They received the award for their 15-year-old theory of superconductivity, which measures the disappearance of electrical resistance in metals at lowering temperatures. The theory is usually called the BCS theory after the final initials of its three developers. This is Bardeen's second Nobel Prize. He shared the physics prize in 1956 for the development of the transistor. He is the first person to win a Nobel Prize twice in the same field.

Physiology and Medicine Prize was shared by Gerald M. Edelman, 43, a molecular biologist at

Rockefeller University, and Rodney R. Porter, 55, professor of biochemistry at Oxford University. The award was for their separate research on the chemical structure of antibodies, the blood proteins that play an important part in the body's defense against infection. They began their studies in 1959, but each approached the problem in a different way. Porter, a chemist, thought the antibody molecule was a single chain of amino acids, and he used an enzyme to break the links on the molecule's chain. Edelman, a physician who had developed a keen interest in physical chemistry at medical school, chose to break the antibody molecule by using chemicals such as urea and sulfur compounds that are considered standard materials for a protein chemist. Each method broke the large antibody molecule into smaller fragments, but the pieces resulting from one method differed from those produced by the other because the methods were not the same. Eventually the two men found that, instead of having a single chain structure, the antibody was more complex. It consists of heavy and light chains, according to molecular weight. By 1969, they had deciphered the structure of the entire antibody molecule. Foster Stockwell

NORTH ATLANTIC TREATY ORGANIZATION (NATO). See EUROPE.

NORTH CAROLINA. See STATE GOVERNMENT.

NORTH DAKOTA. See STATE GOVERNMENT.

NORTHERN IRELAND. Great Britain took over direct rule on March 30, 1972, ending 51 years of local government in Ulster. But the violence continued, and the death toll since the trouble began in 1969 mounted to more than 675 (see Close-Up). British Prime Minister Edward Heath's action followed three months of mounting violence, triggered by "Bloody Sunday," with the outlawed Irish Republican Army (IRA) exploding bombs indiscriminately in public places.

"Bloody Sunday" occurred on January 30 in the Bogside, a Roman Catholic area of Londonderry. British paratroopers shot and killed 13 persons and wounded 16 when a civil rights procession marching in defiance of a government ban, turned into a riot. Witnesses denounced the action as a massacre. Britain defended it as justifiable defense. Terrorism increased and spread to Great Britain on February 22 when a bomb exploded outside the officers' mess of a paratroop brigade at Aldershot. Five women kitchen workers, a Roman Catholic chaplain, and a gardener were killed; 19 others were injured.

Recognizing that "new and more radical measures" must be taken, Heath called Brian Faulkner, Northern Ireland's Unionist Party prime minister, to London for talks on March 22 and 23. Heath insisted that responsibility for law and order should be transferred to London. Faulkner refused to agree,

Londonderry's "Bloody Sunday" set off new violence in Northern Ireland. Thirteen were killed when British troops fired on Catholic marchers.

Legacy of Hate in the Emerald Isle

The two Irelands

The violence between Roman Catholics and Protestants in Northern Ireland that has taken more than 680 lives since August, 1969, is rooted in developments that span more than four centuries. From the very beginning, politics and religion have been mingled together in a volatile combination.

The Irish people have been predominantly Catholic since the 400s, when St. Patrick, an English missionary, brought Christianity to Ireland. Trouble began in 1541, when Henry VIII of England declared himself king of Ireland. Not only was Henry an Englishman, he was also a Protestant, and he tried to convert the Catholic Irish. And so, the politics of conquest were welded to a religious cause.

Henry's successors, determined to keep Ireland under English control, encouraged Englishmen to settle there. English kings and queens seized lands from the Irish and gave them to the English. This systematic take-over by English settlers, known as the Plantation of Ireland, caused the first armed revolts in the late 1500s.

Then, a Catholic, James II, became king of England in 1685. He abolished many of the anti-Catholic laws, but was deposed in 1688 by the Protestant majority. He fled to Ireland and organized an army to fight for the throne. The Protestant English chose William III of Orange as their king. William marched on Ireland and defeated James at the Battle of the Boyne, near Dublin, in 1690. After that, the ruling Protestant minority in Ireland took all political rights away from the Catholics and seized almost all of their land.

To this day, neither Protestants nor Catholics in Ireland have forgotten the Battle of the Boyne. Ancient religious hatreds have been kept alive to further aggravate the social and political differences.

Ireland was made a part of Great Britain in 1800. However, Irish patriots agitated for home rule during the 1800s and early 1900s. Violence erupted along sectarian lines, with Catholics for home rule and Protestants against it. In 1920 and 1921, Ireland was divided into two self-governing parts of Great Britain – Northern Ireland (Ulster) and the Irish Free State in the south. (In 1949, the Irish Free State broke *all* ties with Britain and declared itself the Republic of Ireland.) A Catholic majority lived in the south. A Protestant majority, fiercely loyal to Britain, lived in the north.

But many Catholic Irishmen were unhappy with the division and wanted all of Ireland to be united and free of England. So they formed the Irish Republican Army (IRA) during the 1920s. Once again, politics took on the armor of a holy cause.

Protestants in Ulster knew that if Ireland was reunited, the Catholics would be in the majority. For centuries, these Protestants of English descent had controlled the government and the economy. Many Protestants belonged to the Orange Order, a secret society formed in 1795. Through membership in the Orange Order, Protestants were assured better jobs and housing than Catholics. Also, Orangemen antagonized the Catholics by parading on Orange Day, every July 12, to celebrate William of Orange's victory. Naturally, the Protestants feared that they would lose control and become an oppressed and hated minority in a united, independent, and predominantly Catholic Ireland.

This was the situation when the Catholic civil rights movement began to gather force in 1968 and 1969. Although these Catholics were protesting discrimination in employment and housing, the Protestants saw it as part of the movement to reunite Ireland. Right wing Protestant ministers, such as Ian Paisley, preached against Catholicism with renewed vigor, and Catholics were attacked by Protestant mobs when they staged civil rights marches in 1968 and 1969. The violence has continued ever since, with British troops and IRA terrorists added to the fray.

The future of Northern Ireland looks bleak. Religious intolerance is ingrained in children from the earliest age. Catholics and Protestants are almost completely segregated, living in separate areas and attending separate schools. Old martyrs and causes are celebrated in song and legend. Political and social reforms may bring an end to the fighting. But no cure is in sight for the hatred and bigotry that infects both sides.

Darlene R. Stille

and he and his Cabinet resigned. Stormont, Ulster's parliament, was dissolved and London took over.

The new, ultraloyalist Protestant Vanguard Movement called a two-day general strike on March 27 and 28, nearly paralyzing the province. The Social Democratic and Labour Party, chief political voice of the minority Catholic community, and church leaders throughout Ireland welcomed the British initiative and called for an end to IRA violence.

Heath appointed William Whitelaw as secretary of state for Northern Ireland. In his first few weeks, Whitelaw acted quickly, imaginatively, and bravely. He began to release persons imprisoned without trial. He lifted the ban on processions, announced big aid programs, and promised to listen to all sides.

Bombs Again. The militant provisional wing of the IRA announced a cease-fire on June 26 but, on July 21, Belfast had its "Bloody Friday." Terrorist bombs killed 11 and wounded 120. The reinforced British occupied Catholic "no-go" areas and uncovered large stores of IRA arms and explosives.

Sectarian bitterness flared again. Protestant gunmen came into the open, wearing hoods and paramilitary uniforms much like those of the IRA. On October 15 and 16, they fought gun battles with British troops. Britain's peacemakers, now 17,000 strong, were threatened with attack from the two sides they had come to keep apart. George Scott

See also EUROPE (Facts in Brief Table); IRELAND.

NORWAY. The people of Norway turned their backs on the European Community (Common Market) in a decisive referendum on Sept. 25, 1972. The final vote showed 53.5 per cent (1,118,281 votes) against entry and 46.5 per cent (971,687 votes) for, with three-fourths of those eligible casting ballots. Support for Common Market entry was reasonably strong in most cities and towns. But among rural and younger voters, opposition was much stronger.

Prime Minister Trygve M. Bratteli had announced on August 23 that, although the referendum was only advisory, his minority Labor Government would resign if the answer were "no." The largest opposition party, the Conservatives, also favored entry and said they would not form a government if Bratteli's fell. Bratteli delayed his resignation until October 7 to present his 1973 budget. He was succeeded by Lars Korvald, 56, leader of the Christian People's Party.

Market Agreement. Korvald's first task was to seek a trade agreement with the Common Market to soften the blow that staying out of the market would cause to Norway's exports. Denmark's vote a week later to enter the Common Market was welcomed in Oslo as providing a stepping stone between Scandinavia and Europe. Renegotiation of Norwegian trade agreements with Great Britain and Denmark became necessary. Pending some special arrangement with the market, Norway faced high tariff payments. Danish Prime Minister Jens Otto Krag proposed consultations to achieve "some form of Nordic cooperation."

Proposals for Common Market membership had long stumbled over the apparent threat to Norwegian fishing grounds, which are critically important to the nation's economy. Under basic Common Market principles, the grounds would be open to fishing fleets from all market countries. But, negotiators for the market and for Norway agreed on January 14 to special arrangements to protect the fishing grounds until 1982 or longer. The vote showed the negotiations had been in vain, however.

Blow to NATO. The referendum was considered a setback for the North Atlantic Treaty Organization (NATO). The organization had considered using the Common Market as a framework to strengthen European defenses. But Norwegian participation was considered important to any discussion of northern security. Such participation became unlikely through the Common Market.

Prices Frozen. With prices up 7.9 per cent since August, 1972, and wages rising, the government froze prices on September 15, at their September 7 level. The budget, presented on October 6, increased social insurance spending by 20 per cent. Progressive taxation, to take more of wage and salary increases, was also announced. Kenneth Brown

See also EUROPE (Facts in Brief Table).

NOVA SCOTIA. See CANADA.

OCEAN. The U.S. deep-sea drilling project concentrated its 1972 coring operations in the Red Sea, Bay of Bengal, and Arabian Sea. This marked the first time any deep drilling had taken place in the Indian Ocean. The sediment taken from the Red Sea was described as remarkably similar to that from the Mediterranean Sea. The scientists discovered that the Ninety East Ridge, a north-south ridge in the east-central Indian Ocean that is now more than a mile beneath the surface, was above sea level millions of years ago. The sediments of this ridge contain beds of coal, lignite, and shallow-water oyster fossils.

The next phase of the deep-sea drilling project will be an expedition around the Antarctic, and the drilling ship *Glomar Challenger* was dry-docked in Durban, South Africa, in August to prepare it for rough seas and encounters with ice in the Antarctic regions.

IDOE Study. Scientists from 17 U.S. and foreign institutions completed a base-line study of hydrocarbons and heavy metals in marine organisms, sediments, and sea-surface films in the Atlantic Ocean, Caribbean Sea, Gulf of Mexico, and Pacific Ocean. The study was part of the Environmental Quality Program of the International Decade of Ocean Exploration (IDOE). The study disclosed that the pollutants PCB and DDT are now found in most marine animals and that abnormal concentrations of petroleum hydrocarbons are now found in ocean plants and animal communities. Scientists reviewing these findings at a workshop in Brookhaven, N.Y., in May, warned that this amount of ocean pollution constitutes a problem of global concern. They recommended research to determine inputs, dispersal paths, and present levels of these pollutants in coastal and open-ocean areas.

A study was made of ocean circulation during previous climatic periods under the Environmental Forecasting Program of IDOE. This revealed that the eastern course of the Gulf Stream was significantly farther south 17,000 years ago than it now is, far from the British Isles both in winter and summer.

The first cruise of IDOE's Geochemical Ocean Section Program began in July, 1972. Plans for the nine-month cruise call for the research vessel *Knorr* to follow a course that will take it from the Arctic Circle to the fringes of Antarctica, following a deep current that originates in the Norwegian Sea. Scientists will gather data on how the ocean mixes so they can determine how waste products that are added to the sea disperse.

On July 5, 1972, marine scientists from England, Mauritania, Portugal, Spain, and the United States began a 10-week expedition to explore the Mid-Atlantic Ridge in search of valuable mineral deposits and possible clues to the origin of oceanic crust and earthquakes. A part of an undersea mountain range, the Mid-Atlantic Ridge is the largest geographic feature on the earth.

International Conferences. The United Nations (UN) Seabed Committee completed its 1972 sessions in Geneva in August by compiling a list of subjects and issues that will be discussed during the 1973 UN Law of the Sea Conference. With an eye to this forthcoming conference, the National Academy of Sciences, on June 30, forwarded to the secretary of state a proposed position the United States should take on freedom of science in the oceans. It deals with the conduct of research in international waters and within areas of exclusive and limited national jurisdiction.

The International Whaling Commission met in London in June, and rejected a proposal by the United States for a 10-year moratorium on commercial whaling. The U.S. proposal was supported by Great Britain, Argentina, and Mexico. Japan, Russia, Norway, Panama, South Africa, and Iceland voted against it. Australia, Canada, Denmark, and France abstained. The UN Conference on the Human Environment, held in Stockholm earlier in June, had overwhelmingly approved the U.S. proposal.

The seabed arms treaty signed by the United States and 85 other nations became effective on May 18. It forbids placing nuclear weapons on the ocean floor beyond the 12-mile limit. Arthur G. Alexiou

OHIO. See CLEVELAND; STATE GOVERNMENT.

OKLAHOMA. See STATE GOVERNMENT.

OLD AGE. The Congress of the United States raised social security benefits 20 per cent in 1972 (see SOCIAL SECURITY). It also raised the limit on earnings by those receiving social security benefits from $1,680 to $2,100 per year before a reduction of benefits is required. In addition, Congress increased social security benefits by 1 per cent for each year that a person delays retirement from age 65 to 72.

The social security reform bill included a new program that established minimum payment for older Americans – $130 a month for single persons and $195 for elderly couples – and the law automatically changes the amount of the social security benefit payment if the purchasing power of the dollar changes. Thus, social security payments are protected against erosion of their value due to future reduction of the purchasing power of the dollar. Finally, some 740,000 railroad retirees and their dependents received increases in their monthly pensions of about 20 per cent.

Other Legislation. The actions followed the 1971 White House Conference on Aging, which also led to the passage of a Research on Aging Act and comprehensive Older Americans Services amendments. However, these were vetoed by President Richard M. Nixon in November.

The Research on Aging Act would have established a National Institute on Aging to conduct and support biomedical, social, and behavioral research related to the aging process. The amendments to the Older Americans Services Act would have created a 15-member Federal Council on Aging to advise the President on matters related to special needs of older Americans. Congress and President Nixon were expected to clash in 1973 over how much money to spend for services for the elderly.

World Conference. Gerontologists held their Ninth Triennial Congress of Gerontology in Kiev, Russia, in July. They focused most of their attention on biomedical research on aging, an area in which Russian scientists have made outstanding contributions. Controversy surrounded the research reports in this area, one group of researchers claiming that they had made progress in arresting the aging process, and another group doubting this.

Alex Comfort, director of research on aging at University College in London, said that the human life span can be lengthened by 10 or 15 years beyond 75 by applying biomedical research. He was supported by Bernard Strehler, a biochemist at the University of Southern California, who announced his conviction that "the weight of evidence indicates that the understanding of biological aging is imminent, and that a measure of control that will produce at least a 20- to 30-year extension of the healthy middle years of life is almost a certainty by the year 2001." Biologists point out, however, that millions of dollars must be spent for further research to achieve this result. Robert J. Havighurst

OLYMPIC GAMES. Every four years, the Olympic Games bring together the athletes of the world to meet in sports combat and human relationships. In the 1972 Summer Games held in August and September in Munich, West Germany, the combat was often magnificent and truly Olympian, and the human relationships among athletes were often rewarding.

Yet, these games fell short of Olympic ideals because of intrusions by political terrorists and Olympic officials. Judging was often far from objective as officials, especially from Eastern Europe, favored athletes from their own or allied nations. Wayne Wells, a wrestling gold medalist from Norman, Okla., explained it by saying, "It's the way they've been brought up. What's cheating to us is not cheating to them."

Much criticism centered on the actions of the International Olympic Committee (IOC) and its 84-year-old outgoing president, Avery Brundage of Chicago. The IOC faced a series of crises during the games. It answered them by:

- Barring the team from Rhodesia because black African nations threatened a boycott if it competed.
- Continuing the games after Arab terrorists invaded the Olympic grounds, and 17 persons, including 11 Israeli athletes and coaches, were killed.
- Banning two American runners from the Olympics for life for their indifference on the victory stand.
- Banning an asthmatic American swimming gold medalist and ordering his medal returned because he took a stimulant that he needed to help him breathe.

The Winter Olympics, held in February in Sapporo, Japan, had bad moments before they began. Brundage had threatened to disqualify about 40 skiers for professionalism. The nations with the leading skiers said that if that happened, their teams would not compete. Four days before the games, Brundage disqualified one skier – Karl Schranz of Austria – and the games went on.

The competition in Sapporo was excellent. At Munich, too, performances were stirring, and they captivated a worldwide television audience of hundreds of millions. The American Broadcasting Company (ABC) televised 61½ hours of the Olympics.

The Heroes. Television brought the heroes and heroines to life. It also revealed their flaws and the flaws of others that marred performances. For example:

Mark Spitz, a 22-year-old Indiana University graduate from Carmichael, Calif., broke seven world records while winning seven gold medals in swimming, the best performance in Olympic history. No previous Olympic competitor had won more than five gold medals in a single games. But Spitz seemed curt and uninterested at news conferences, and he refused to pose with his seven medals for photographs (he sold the rights to a German magazine). See Spitz, Mark.

Olga Korbut, a tiny, childlike, 17-year-old Russian gymnast, gave stunning performances that earned three gold medals. But in her specialty, the uneven parallel bars, the 4-foot 11-inch, 84-pound girl was relegated to second place because of the obviously biased judging by an East German in favor of the East German girl who won.

John Akii-Bua of Uganda, one of 43 children (his father had 8 wives), won the 400-meter hurdles in the world-record time of 47.8 seconds. When he started a victory lap, Olympic officials waved him off the track. Akii-Bua ignored them and floated around the track, leaping over real and imaginary hurdles and blowing kisses to the delighted crowd.

As Frank Shorter of Ranchos de Taos, N. Mex., entered the stadium track for the last lap and victory in the marathon, there was booing amid the cheering. Shorter did not know that the booing was for an intruder in track clothes who had just run into the stadium and was being put off the track.

Valery Borzov of Russia won the 100- and 200-meter dashes, beating an American in each. Larry Black of Miami, runner-up in the 200, ungraciously called Borzov a show-off and said he would not have won the 100 if Eddie Hart of Pittsburg, Calif., and Rey Robinson of Lakeland, Fla., had run. Hart and Robinson missed their quarterfinal heats because of a misunderstanding over the time schedule. Borzov shrugged his shoulders and said he "gave about 90 per cent of what I had to give."

American joy at winning the Olympic basketball title was premature. Officials gave Russia three chances to score the title game's winning goal.

Borzov was one of three gold medalists who gave the Soviet Union an unusual triple – the world's fastest athlete (Borzov), the world's best all-round athlete (Nikolai Avilov, who set a world record in winning the decathlon), and the world's strongest man (Vassili Alexeev, the superheavyweight champion in weight lifting).

Track and Field, the showcase sport of the 21 at Munich, produced much of the excitement and many of the sour moments. None was more sour than the aftermath of the 400-meter run, in which Vince Matthews of Brooklyn finished first and Wayne Collett of Los Angeles second. Matthews and Collett chatted and slouched on the victory platform while the national anthem was being played. Their conduct was too casual for the IOC, which banned them from the Olympics for life without a hearing.

Dave Wottle of Canton, Ohio, won the 800-meter final by inches. Later, he stood solemnly on the victory stand, his hand over his heart during the national anthem, forgetting that he was still wearing his distinctive golf cap. Rod Milburn of Opelousas, La., won the high hurdles but found little Olympic spirit at Munich and dismissed the games as "just another track meet." Randy Williams of Fresno, Calif., hurt a leg while warming up. So he put everything into his first leap (27 feet ½ inch) and made it good enough to win the long jump.

For some Americans, nothing went right. Bob Seagren of Los Angeles, the world recordholder and

The 1972 Summer and Winter Olympic Games featured many outstanding competitors from many nations. American teen-ager Ann Henning, *above*, foreground, set an Olympic record in winning the 500-meter race in Sapporo, Japan. Russian weight lifter Vassili Alexeev, *right*, became the world's strongest man by lifting 1,411 pounds. Other heroes, *opposite page, clockwise from upper left*, included Dan Gable, who won the lightweight free-style wrestling title; Mark Spitz, who set world records in winning each of his seven swimming titles; Cuba's Teofilo Stevenson, who beat the American favorite Duane Bobick to win the heavyweight boxing title; Olga Korbut, the petite Russian gymnast who won balance beam competition; and John Akii-Bua of Uganda, who set a world record in winning a gold medal in the 400-meter hurdles.

911

Official Results of the 1972 Olympic Games

(*) Indicates new Olympic record; (†) new world record; (††) ties world record

Winners of the Winter Olympics in Sapporo, Japan, in February

Event	Winner	Country	Mark
Men's Skiing			
Downhill	Bernhard Russi	Switzerland	1:51.43
Giant slalom	Gustavo Thoeni	Italy	3:09.62
Special slalom	Francisco Fernandez Ochoa	Spain	1:49.27
15-kilometer cross-country	Sven-ake Lundback	Sweden	45:28.24
30-kilometer cross-country	Vyacheslav Vedenine	Russia	1:36:31.15
50-kilometer cross-country	Paal Tyldum	Norway	2:43:14.75
40-kilometer relay	Voronkov, Skobov, Simaschov, Vedenine	Russia	2:04:47.94
Nordic combined	Ulrich Wehling	E. Germany	413.340 pts.
70-meter jump	Yukio Kasaya	Japan	244.2 pts.
90-meter jump	Wojeciech Fortuna	Poland	219.9 pts.
Women's Skiing			
Downhill	Marie Therese Nadig	Switzerland	1:36.68
Giant slalom	Marie Therese Nadig	Switzerland	1:29.09
Special slalom	Barbara Cochran	U.S.A.	1:31.24
5-kilometer cross-country	Galina Koulacova	Russia	17:00.50
10-kilometer cross-country	Galina Koulacova	Russia	34:17.82
15-kilometer cross-country relay	Moukhatcheva, Olunina, Koulacova	Russia	48:46.15
Men's Speed Skating			
500 meters	Erhard Keller	W. Germany	39.4s*
1,500 meters	Ard Schenk	Netherlands	2:02.96*
5,000 meters	Ard Schenk	Netherlands	7:23.61
10,000 meters	Ard Schenk	Netherlands	15:01.35*

Event	Winner	Country	Mark
Women's Speed Skating			
500 meters	Anne Henning	U.S.A.	43.3s*
1,000 meters	Monika Pflug	W. Germany	1:31.40*
1,500 meters	Dianne Holum	U.S.A.	2:20.85*
3,000 meters	Stein Baas-Kaiser	Netherlands	4:52.14*
Figure Skating			
Men's singles	Ondrej Nepala	Czecho-slovakia	9.0 ordinals (2,739.1 pts.)
Women's singles	Trixi Schuba	Austria	9.0 ordinals (2,751.5 pts.)
Pairs	Irena Rodnina and Alexei Oulanov	Russia	12.0 ordinals (420.4 pts.)
Biathlon			
Singles	Magnar Solberg	Norway	1:15:55.50
Relay	Tikhonov, Safine, Biakov, Mamatov	Russia	1:51:44.92
Bobsledding			
Two-man	Wolfgang Zimmerer, Peter Utzschneider	W. Germany	4:57.07
Four-man	Jean Wicki, Edy Hubacher, Hans Leutenegger, Werner Camichel	Switzerland	4:43.07
Ice Hockey		Russia	W4, L0, T1
Men's Luge			
Singles	Wolfgang Scheidel	E. Germany	3:27.58
Doubles	Paul Hildgartner, Walter Plaikner	Italy	1:28.35
	Horst Hornlein, Reinhard Bredow	E. Germany	1:28.35
Women's Luge			
Singles	Anna Marie Muller	E. Germany	2:59.18

Winners of the Summer Olympics in Munich, West Germany, in August and September

Event	Winner	Country	Mark
Track and Field			
Men			
100 meters	Valeri Borzov	Russia	10.14
200 meters	Valeri Borzov	Russia	20.0
400 meters	Vince Matthews	U.S.A.	44.66
800 meters	Dave Wottle	U.S.A.	1:45.9
1,500 meters	Pekka Vasala	Finland	3:36.3
5,000 meters	Lasse Viren	Finland	13:26.4*
10,000 meters	Lasse Viren	Finland	27:38.4†
3,000-meter steeplechase	Kip Keino	Kenya	8:23.6*
Marathon	Frank Shorter	U.S.A.	2h12:19.8
110-meter hurdles	Rod Milburn	U.S.A.	13.2††
400-meter hurdles	John Akii-Bua	Uganda	47.8†
20-kilometer walk	Peter Frenkel	E. Germany	1h26:42.4
50-kilometer walk	Bern Kannenberg	W. Germany	3h56:11.6
400-meter relay	Larry Black, Robert Taylor, Gerry Tinker, Eddie Hart	U.S.A.	38.2††
1,600-meter relay	Charles Asati, Hezahiah Nyamau, Robert Ouko, Julius Sang	Kenya	2:59.8
Decathlon	Nikolai Avilov	Russia	8,454 pts.†
High jump	Yuri Tarmak	Russia	7 ft. 3¾ in.
Pole vault	Wolfgang Nordwig	E. Germany	18 ft. ½ in.*
Long jump	Randy Williams	U.S.A.	27 ft. ½ in.
Triple jump	Victor Saneev	Russia	56 ft. 11 in.
Shot-put	Wladyslaw Komar	Poland	69 ft. 6 in.
Discus throw	Ludvik Danek	Czecho-slovakia	211 ft. 3 in.
Hammer throw	Anatoli Bondarchuk	Russia	247 ft. 8 in.*
Javelin throw	Klaus Wolfermann	W. Germany	296 ft. 10 in.*
Women			
100 meters	Renate Stecher	E. Germany	11.07
200 meters	Renate Stecher	E. Germany	22.4††
400 meters	Monika Zehrt	E. Germany	51.08

Event	Winner	Country	Mark
800 meters	Hildegard Falck	W. Germany	1:58.6*
100-meter hurdles	Annelie Ehrhardt	E. Germany	12.59*
1,500 meters	Ludmila Bragina	E. Germany	4:01.4†
400-meter relay	Christiane Krause, Ingrid Mickler, Annegret Richter, Heidemarie Rosendahl	W. Germany	42.8††
1,600-meter relay	Dagmar Kaesling, Rita Kuehne, Helga Seidler, Monika Zehrt	E. Germany	3:23.0†
Pentathlon	Mary Peters	Great Britain	4,801 pts.†
High jump	Ulrike Meyfarth	W. Germany	6 ft. 3½ in.*
Long jump	Heidemarie Rosendahl	W. Germany	22 ft. 3 in.
Shot-put	Nadezh Chizhova	Russia	69 ft.†
Discus throw	Faina Melnik	Russia	218 ft. 7 in.*
Javelin throw	Ruth Fuchs	E. Germany	209 ft. 7 in.*
Other Sports			
Archery			
Men	John Williams	U.S.A.	2,528 pts.*
Women	Doreen Wilber	U.S.A.	2,424 pts.
Boxing			
Light-flyweight	Gyoergy Gedo	Hungary	
Flyweight	Gheorghi Kostadinov	Bulgaria	
Bantamweight	Orlando Martinez	Cuba	
Featherweight	Boris Kousnetsov	Russia	
Lightweight	Jan Szczepanski	Poland	
Light-welterweight	Ray Seales	U.S.A.	
Welterweight	Emilio Correa	Cuba	
Light-middleweight	Dieter Kottysch	W. Germany	
Middleweight	Viatchesiav Lemechev	Russia	
Light-heavyweight	Mate Parlov	Yugoslavia	
Heavyweight	Teofilo Stevenson	Cuba	

Event	Winner	Country	Mark
Canoeing, Men			
Kayak singles	Aleksandr Shaparenko	Russia	3:48.06
Kayak pairs	Gorbachev, Kratassyuk	Russia	3:31.23
Kayak fours	Filatov, Morozov, Stezenko, Didenko	Russia	3:14.02
Kayak singles slalom	Siegbert Horn	E. Germany	4:28.56
Canadian singles	Ivan Patzaichin	Romania	4:08.94
Canadian pairs	Chessyunas, Lobanov	Russia	3:52.60
Canadian singles slalom	Reinhard Eiben	E. Germany	5:15.84
Canadian doubles slalom	Hofmann, Amend	E. Germany	5:10.68
Canoeing, Women			
Kayak singles	Yulia Ryabchinskaya	Russia	2:03.17
Kayak pairs	Pinayeva, Kuryshko	Russia	1:53.50
Kayak singles slalom	Angelika Bahmann	E. Germany	364.50 pts.
Cycling			
1,000-meter individual time trial	Niels Fredborg	Denmark	1:06.44
4,000 meters individual pursuit	Knut Knudsen	Norway	4:45.74
4,000 meters team pursuit	Colombo, Haritz, Hempel, Schumacher	W. Germany	4:22
Sprint	Daniel Morelon	France	
Tandem	Semenets, Tselovalnikov	Russia	
100-kilometer team time trial	Chouhov, Dardy, Komnatov, Likhachev	Russia	2:11:17.8
Equestrian			
Three-day event, individual	Richard Meade	Great Britain	57.73 pts.
Three-day event, team	Gordon-Watson, Parker, Meade, Phillips	Great Britain	95.53 pts.
Dressage, individual	Liselotte Linsenhoff	W. Germany	229 pts.
Dressage, team	Petushkova, Kizimov, Kalita	Russia	5,095.0 pts.
Jumping, individual	Graziano Mancinelli	Italy	8 penalty pts.
Jumping, team	Ligges, Wiltfang, Steenken, Winkler	W. Germany	32 pts.
Fencing, Men			
Individual foil	Witold Woyda	Poland	
Team foil		Poland	
Individual épée	Csaba Fenyvesi	Hungary	
Team épée		Hungary	
Individual saber	Viktor Sidiak	Russia	
Team saber		Italy	
Fencing, Women			
Individual foil	Antonella Ragno Lonzi	Italy	
Team foil		Russia	
Gymnastics, Men			
All-around	Sawao Kato	Japan	114.650 pts.
Team all-around	Kato, Kenmatsu, Kasamatsu, Nakayama	Japan	571.25 pts.
Horizontal bar	Mitsuo Tsukahara	Japan	19,725 pts.
Parallel bars	Sawao Kato	Japan	19,475 pts.
Rings	Akinori Nakayama	Japan	19,350 pts.
Side horse	Viktor Klimenko	Russia	19,125 pts.
Long horse	Klaus Koeste	E. Germany	18,850 pts.
Floor exercises	Nikolai Andrienov	Russia	19,175 pts.
Gymnastics, Women			
All-around	Ludmila Turischeva	Russia	77.025 pts.
Team all-around	Turischeva, Korbut, Lazakovitch, Burda, Saadi, Koshel	Russia	380.50 pts.
Balance beam	Olga Korbut	Russia	19,400 pts.

Event	Winner	Country	Mark
Long horse	Karin Janz	E. Germany	19,525 pts.
Uneven parallel bars	Karin Janz	E. Germany	19,675 pts.
Floor exercises	Olga Korbut	Russia	19,575 pts.
Judo			
Lightweight	Takao Kawaguchi	Japan	
Welterweight	Toyokazu Nomura	Japan	
Middleweight	Shinobu Sekine	Japan	
Light-heavyweight	Shota Chochoshvi	Russia	
Heavyweight	Willem Ruska	Netherlands	
Open class	Willem Ruska	Netherlands	
Modern Pentathlon			
Individual	Andras Balczo	Hungary	5,412 pts.
Team	Anishenko, Lednev, Shmelev	Russia	15,968 pts.
Rowing			
Single sculls	Yuri Malishev	Russia	7:10.12
Double sculls	Korshikov, Timoshinin	Russia	7:01.77
Pairs without coxswain	Brietzke, Mager	E. Germany	6:53.16
Fours without coxswain	Loreberger, Ruekle, Grahn, Schubert	E. Germany	6:24.27
Pairs with coxswain	Gunkel, Lucke, Neubert	E. Germany	7:17.25
Fours with coxswain	Berger, Faerber, Suer, Bierl, Benter	W. Germany	6:31.85
Eights with coxswain	Hurt, Veldman, Joyce, Hunter, Wilson, Earl, Coker, Robertson, Dickie	New Zealand	6:08.94
Shooting			
Moving target	Lakov Zhelezniak	Russia	569 pts.†
Trapshooting	Angelo Scalzone	Italy	199 pts.†
Free pistol	Ragnar Skanaker	Sweden	567 pts.*
Rapid-fire pistol	Jozef Zapedzki	Poland	595 pts.*
Free rifle	Lones Wigger	U.S.A.	1,115 pts.
Small-bore rifle (prone)	Ho Jun Li	North Korea	599 pts.†
Small-bore rifle (three positions)	John Writer	U.S.A.	1,166 pts.†
Skeet (clay pigeon)	Konrad Wirnhier	W. Germany	195 pts.
Swimming and Diving, Men			
Free style			
100 meters	Mark Spitz	U.S.A.	51.22†
200 meters	Mark Spitz	U.S.A.	1:52.78†
400 meters	Brad Cooper	Australia	4:00.27*
(Rick DeMont, U.S.A. [4:00.26] won, but was disqualified)			
1,500 meters	Mike Burton	U.S.A.	15:52.58†
Breast stroke			
100 meters	Nobutaka Taguchi	Japan	1:04.94†
200 meters	John Hencken	U.S.A.	2:21.55†
Butterfly			
100 meters	Mark Spitz	U.S.A.	54.27†
200 meters	Mark Spitz	U.S.A.	2:00.7†
Back stroke			
100 meters	Roland Matthes	E. Germany	56.58*
200 meters	Roland Matthes	E. Germany	2:02.82††
Individual medley			
200 meters	Gunnar Larsson	Sweden	2:07.17†
400 meters	Gunnar Larsson	Sweden	4:31.98*
400-meter free-style relay	Dave Edgar, Jerry Heidenreich, John Murphy, Mark Spitz	U.S.A.	3:26.42†
800-meter free-style relay	John Kinsella, Fred Tyler, Steve Genter, Mark Spitz	U.S.A.	7:35.78†
400-meter medley relay	Mike Stamm, Tom Bruce, Mark Spitz, Jerry Heidenreich	U.S.A.	3:48.16†
Springboard diving	Vladimir Vasin	Russia	594.09 pts.
Platform diving	Klaus Dibiasi	Italy	504.12 pts.
Swimming and Diving, Women			
Free style			
100 meters	Sandra Neilson	U.S.A.	58.59*
200 meters	Shane Gould	Australia	2:03.56†

continued next page

OLYMPIC GAMES

Event	Winner	Country	Mark
400 meters	Shane Gould	Australia	4:19.04†
800 meters	Keena Rothhammer	U.S.A.	8:53.68†
Breast stroke			
100 meters	Cathy Carr	U.S.A.	1:13.58†
200 meters	Beverly Whitfield	Australia	2:41.71*
Butterfly			
100 meters	Mayumi Aoki	Japan	1:03.34†
200 meters	Karen Moe	U.S.A.	2:15.57†
Back stroke			
100 meters	Melissa Belote	U.S.A.	1:05.78*
200 meters	Melissa Belote	U.S.A.	2:19.19†
Individual medley			
200 meters	Shane Gould	Australia	2:23.07†
400 meters	Gail Neall	Australia	5:02.97†
400-meter free-style relay	Sandra Neilson, Jennifer Kemp, Jane Barkman, Shirley Babashoff	U.S.A.	3:55.19†
400-meter medley relay	Melissa Belote, Cathy Carr, Deena Deardurff, Sandra Neilson	U.S.A.	4:20.75†
Springboard diving	Micki King	U.S.A.	450.03 pts.
Platform diving	Ulrike Knape	Sweden	390.00 pts.
Weight Lifting			
Flyweight	Zygmunt Smalcerz	Poland	744 lbs.
Bantamweight	Imre Foeldi	Hungary	832.23 lbs.†
Featherweight	Norair Nourikian	Bulgaria	887.35 lbs.††
Lightweight	Mukharbi Kirzhinov	Russia	1,104.11 lbs.†
Middleweight	Yordan Bikov	Bulgaria	1,069 lbs.†
Light-heavyweight	Leif Jenssen	Norway	1,118 lbs.*
Middle-heavyweight	Andon Nikolov	Bulgaria	1,157 lbs.*
Heavyweight	Yan Talts	Russia	1,278 lbs.
Super heavyweight	Vassili Alexeev	Russia	1,411 lbs.*
Wrestling (Free Style)			
Paperweight (105.6 lbs.)	Roman Dmitriev	Russia	
Flyweight (114.4)	Kiyomi Kato	Japan	
Bantamweight (125.4)	Hideaki Yanagida	Japan	

Event	Winner	Country
Featherweight (136.4)	Zagalav Abdulbekov	Russia
Lightweight (149.6)	Dan Gable	U.S.A.
Welterweight (163)	Wayne Wells	U.S.A.
Middleweight (180.4)	Levan Tediashvili	Russia
Light-heavyweight (198)	Ben Peterson	U.S.A.
Heavyweight (220)	Ivan Yarygin	Russia
Super heavyweight (over 220)	Alexandr Medved	Russia
Wrestling (Greco-Roman)		
Paperweight	Georghe Berceanu	Romania
Flyweight	Petar Kirov	Bulgaria
Bantamweight	Rustem Kazakov	Russia
Featherweight	Gheorghi Markov	Bulgaria
Lightweight	Shamil Khisamutdinov	Russia
Welterweight	Vitezslav Macha	Czecho-slovakia
Middleweight	Csaba Hegedus	Hungary
Light-heavyweight	Valeri Rezantsev	Russia
Heavyweight	Nicolae Martinescu	Romania
Super heavyweight	Anatoly Roshin	Russia
Yachting		
Dragon	John Bruce Cueno	Australia
Star	Anderson, Forbes	Australia
Flying Dutchman	Davis, Pattison	Great Britain
Finn	Serge Maury	France
Tempest	Drydrya, Mankin	Russia
Soling	Harry Melges	U.S.A.
Team Sports		
Basketball		Russia
Field Hockey		W. Germany
Team handball		Yugoslavia
Soccer		Poland
Men's volleyball		Japan
Women's volleyball		Russia
Water polo		Russia

1968 Olympic champion, finished second in the pole vault. He was forced to use a strange pole because his usual one had been banned as too new. George Woods of Warden, Ill., second in the shot-put in 1968, finished second again. He was beaten by a half inch on a questionable measurement. Jim Ryun of Lawrence, Kans., second in the 1,500-meter run in the 1968 games, was the victim of a spill and questionable strategy, and didn't even survive the heats.

The De Mont Case. At first, things went right for Rick De Mont, a 16-year-old high school senior from San Rafael, Calif. He won the 400-meter free-style swim by a hundredth of a second, and he was favored in the 1,500, in which he held the world record. But 15 minutes before the 1,500 final, he was disqualified from that race, and later his victory in the 400 was thrown out because he had failed a drug test.

The test showed samples of ephedrine, a stimulant not allowed in the Olympics. De Mont said he had taken the drug for years because of asthma, and he had informed the United States Olympic Committee (USOC) in writing weeks before. It turned out that the USOC had failed to discuss the subject with IOC physicians, and so De Mont became the first Olympic champion since Jim Thorpe in 1912 to be ordered to return a gold medal.

The Basketball Title. The young U.S. basketball team, playing the disciplined but unimaginative style of its 68-year-old coach, Hank Iba, seemingly had won the gold medal. With the U.S. ahead 50-49 and only three seconds left in the championship game, Russia took the ball under its basket. A long inbounds pass was deflected at midcourt and the game was apparently over, but a referee ruled that one second remained. The Russians tried again, the inbounds pass was short, the horn sounded, and the game again was apparently over. This time, an international basketball official ordered the clock reset to three seconds, the Russians tried again, and scored. The defeat was the first in Olympic history for a U.S. basketball team.

Why was the clock reset? The international official, a Briton, said the Brazilian referee had ordered it. The Brazilian said the other referee, a Bulgarian, had ordered it. The scorekeeper, a West German, said the Briton had ordered it.

Russian Successes. The United States, with 33 gold medals and 94 medals in all, was second in both categories to Russia (50 and 99). Soviet athletes also dominated the Winter Olympics (8 gold and 16 total), where the United States collected 3 gold medals and 8 overall. The United States was strongest at Munich in men's and women's swimming, men's track and field, free-style wrestling, rifle shooting, and archery. At Sapporo, it did well in women's speed skating.

The Russians were elated with their best overall performance since they joined the Olympic movement in 1952. Their newspapers spoke of "our victorious finish" as a victory for socialism and chided the United States as poor losers in basketball and unmannerly in other sports. According to *Komsomolskaya Pravda*, the successes of Soviet and other Iron Curtain athletes "show to the entire world the triumph of the personality liberated by socialism." The paper also admitted the importance of massive state-subsidized sports programs in the Communist nations.

The Israeli Tragedy stunned the Olympic Village on September 5. Eight Arab commandos broke into the Israeli team's dormitory about 5:30 A.M., killed two Israelis as they entered, and captured nine. Six other Israelis managed to escape. The Arabs threatened to kill the hostages unless 200 Arab commandos imprisoned in Israel were released.

About 16 hours later, the Arabs and their prisoners were taken to an airfield, supposedly to board a plane. But German police attempted to ambush the Arabs. Five of the Arabs and their nine prisoners were killed. The games were suspended for 24 hours, and 80,000 persons attended a memorial service in Olympic Stadium on September 6.

IOC Under Fire. Brundage and the IOC were assailed after the slayings. Brundage announced at the memorial service that the games would continue. In that speech, wrote Paul Zimmerman in *The New York Post*, Brundage was "a man selling campaign stickers at a funeral."

Of the IOC's decision to continue the competition, columnist Red Smith wrote, "Walled off in their dream world, appallingly unaware of the realities of life and death, the aging playground directors who conduct this quadrennial muscle dance ruled that a little blood must not be allowed to interrupt play."

Late in the year, the U.S. Olympic Committee came under fire for its direction of the U.S. Olympic program. The National Collegiate Athletic Association and two of its allies–U.S. Track and Field Federation, and U.S. Wrestling Federation–withdrew support from the committee and asked Congress to investigate its policies and practices. The Olympics suffered another blow in November when Colorado voters rejected a $5-million bond issue to finance the 1976 Winter Games. Frank Litsky

See also Section One, FOCUS ON SPORTS.

OMAN. See MIDDLE EAST.

ONTARIO. See CANADA.

OPERA. See MUSIC, CLASSICAL.

OREGON. See STATE GOVERNMENT.

PACIFIC ISLANDS, an area consisting mostly of tiny land dots in a vast ocean, continued to experience political change in 1972. To a large extent, this resulted from shifts in the international posture of the two major world powers that have dominated the area since 1945.

The most subtle, yet most pervasive, development was the emergence of Japan as a major economic and political influence in the Pacific Ocean area. This was due in part to the withdrawal of American influence and a simultaneous expansionist drive by Japanese capital. Perhaps the best example of Japanese resurgence was the reversion of Okinawa and other Ryukyu Islands to Japan on May 15 according to an agreement reached by the United States and Japan in 1971.

Economic expansion, however, was far more significant than territorial reversion. The ever-expanding Japanese tourist trade began to flood some island areas, notably Saipan and Hawaii. This was accompanied by large-scale investments in facilities to take care of the influx. Japanese business interests poured money into hotels and recreational facilities to handle the tourist trade. Investments in Hawaii alone amounted to over $150 million by the end of the year. Japanese long-range investment programs were also reflected in the number of major credits granted to oil and copper interests in Indonesia and in Bougainville.

Political Problems. Despite this expansion, political tidal waves continued to surprise observers of the island communities. Micronesia, a trust mandate of the United Nations (UN) under United States control, held lengthy talks with the Americans about its future status. During these talks, which took place in Honolulu from September 28 to October 8, the Micronesians sought more internal autonomy with eventual complete independence. The United States held out for more gradual autonomy and wanted to retain control of foreign affairs and defense. The talks ended with no real agreement.

Papua-New Guinea, administered by Australia under a UN mandate, held general elections in March for the 100-member House of Assembly. The results of the vote in the area, which includes New Britain and Bougainville, showed a decided gain for the advocates of immediate self-government. Yet no single party or group attained a majority.

A number of islands in the central Pacific were incensed in 1972 over the renewal of French atmospheric nuclear and atomic bomb testing off the Society Islands. Tests conducted off Mururoa Atoll in mid-June evoked a worldwide storm of protest, particularly by New Zealand and Australia. A suspicion that France planned to build an underground test site at Eiao in the Marquesa Islands prompted even greater protests, including some from Latin American nations. John N. Stalker

PAINTING. See VISUAL ARTS.

PAKISTAN will remember 1972 as the cruelest year in its 25-year history as an independent nation. Only a few months earlier, it had been the world's fifth largest nation, with 130 million people and a voice in international affairs. But all that had changed in two weeks in December, 1971. Half the nation, the east wing, had broken away to become Bangladesh. What remained was the west wing, with 55 million people. A quarter of the army was in Indian prisoner of war camps. The economy was badly disrupted, the government disorganized, and morale low.

On Dec. 16, 1971, defeated and in the depths of crisis, General Agha Mohammed Yahya Khan, president and "strongman," surrendered all power to Zulfikar Ali Bhutto, the 43-year-old maverick of national politics. One of the country's largest landowners, Bhutto was also its leading radical and had formed the opposition Pakistan People's Party (PPP), with a program of "Islamic Socialism." See BHUTTO, ZULFIKAR ALI.

Desperate Hours. Bhutto's initial moves had matched the needs of the desperate moment. He put Yahya Khan under house arrest, named a civilian Cabinet, initiated educational reforms, put basic industries under state control, and placed tight reins on the restless army. He also acted early to introduce the Socialist reforms he had promised during his years in the opposition. Crucial among them was a land-reform program under which large holdings were to be sharply cut in an effort to provide acreage for the landless.

On Jan. 2, 1972, the Bhutto government took control – but not the ownership – of 10 basic industries. The blow was aimed at the so-called "22 Families," said to own 80 per cent of the banking and 66 per cent of the industrial assets. Because of a fear of economic chaos, however, Bhutto quickly dropped sterner measures against the business community.

The crisis remained severe, however. West Pakistan had lost its biggest market in the east wing, as well as its most profitable money-earner, jute. Its treasury was empty, and in May, foreign lenders agreed to extend debt relief. On May 11, the rupee had to be devalued from 4.7 to the U.S. $1 to 11 to $1.

Seeking Friends. In February, Bhutto visited China, by now Pakistan's staunchest ally. Peking converted four loans into grants and eased the repayment of others. It continued to provide arms. Aid also came from the United States, which had leaned toward Pakistan during the war with India.

Relations with the lost half of the nation, now the republic of Bangladesh, remained icy. Bhutto himself ranged from insistence in December, 1971, that Bangladesh remain a part of Pakistan to the declaration in October, 1972, that the Pakistani would have to reconcile themselves to the loss. But, on Bhutto's plea, China vetoed Bangladesh's admission to the United Nations until the 90,000 Pakistani troops held in India were released. Bhutto also took his country out of the British Commonwealth because many of its members had recognized Bangladesh.

Domestic Unrest. Bhutto's thorniest problems, however, were still domestic ones. With millions unemployed, there was violence in the streets. In June, riots swept the Sind Province after a bill making Sindhi the only official language was pushed through the Assembly. In a compromise, Bhutto gave those who speak only Urdu 12 years to learn Sindhi. There were other clashes, between landlords and tenants.

Not the least of the problems lay in Baluchistan, whose leaders have long dreamed of an independent Pakhtoon State. When Bhutto named a new governor, the province exploded in violence.

On April 21, Bhutto lifted the martial law imposed nearly three years earlier, and became president under an interim Constitution. On October 20, a new draft of a permanent Constitution was approved following a four-day conference in Rāwalpindi. Ten leaders from all the parties in the National Assembly attended the meeting. The parliament, which would be known as the National Assembly, would consist of two chambers. The lower house would have 200 members, with 10 seats reserved for women; the upper house would have 60 members. The document also called for a prime minister as well as a president. Both would be responsible to the legislature. Mark Gayn

See also ASIA (Facts in Brief Table); BANGLADESH; Section Four, BANGLADESH; PAKISTAN.

PANAMA held its first election in four years on Aug. 6, 1972, when an unprecedented 88 per cent of the voters went to the polls to elect the 505-member Assembly of Community Representatives. Then, on September 13, the Assembly legalized the already wide *de facto* powers of General Omar Torrijos Herrera, permitting him to rule supreme for the next six years. Torrijos, who seized power in 1968, also remained head of the 10,000-man National Guard.

On September 11, the Assembly charged that the Panama Canal Zone is being "occupied arbitrarily" and it voted to reject the $1.93 million the United States pays annually to use it, thus reaffirming the nation's sovereignty over the zone. The Assembly also approved a new Constitution providing for indirect election of the president and taking no formal account of the U.S.-controlled Canal Zone – as its predecessor did. Meantime, negotiations with the United States for a new treaty to replace the 1903 pact made little progress.

Despite rising living costs and a number of unpopular taxes on gasoline, tobacco, and alcohol, the economy surged ahead, spurred by bigger outlays on public housing, communications, and utilities. On June 1, the government temporarily occupied Panama Power & Light, a Boise Cascade Corporation subsidiary, and later reached an agreement to acquire the concern. Mary Webster Soper

See also LATIN AMERICA (Facts in Brief Table).

PARAGUAY. A running dispute between the government of President Alfredo Stroessner and church authorities continued in 1972. On May 20, the Paraguayan Episcopal Conference charged that the government was carrying out a systematic harassment of the Roman Catholic Church. It specifically accused the Stroessner regime of expelling from Paraguay eight Catholic priests who had been wrongly accused of "subversive activities."

All of the priests had been involved in organizing the Christian Agrarian Leagues, an organization of cooperative work-study groups of Paraguayan peasants. The conference maintained the leagues had been organized by the priests to "dissipate the Paraguayan peasants' characteristic passivity and silent fatalism." It also charged that President Stroessner had countenanced the formation of pro-government vigilantes to harass the peasants who belonged to the groups. The government, in rejecting the complaint, insisted that the leagues were encouraging the peasants to rise up against the government.

Dispute Over Drugs. On September 2, Paraguay extradited to the United States a French-born Argentine, Auguste Joseph Ricord, believed to head a worldwide heroin organization with a huge market in the United States. Ricord's extradition came after 18 months of pleas and threats by Washington, during which time Paraguay became known as the "heroin crossroads of South America."

Stroessner, according to some critics, dragged his feet over the extradition request because his retention of power depended to a large degree on the lucrative smuggling "concessions" granted to his generals and top civilian aides in the Paraguayan government to keep them "happy." The accusations were based mostly on a secret study made by the U.S. Central Intelligence Agency. Washington reacted to Stroessner's seeming reluctance to act by cutting off Paraguay's sugar quota and passing a congressional resolution to end economic aid to nations failing to cooperate in solving the drug problem.

The Economy. Domestically, the country did fairly well in 1972. The gross national product was officially expected to climb 5 or 6 per cent, continuing the gains of the previous few years. Living costs rose 3 per cent in the first quarter – a modest uptrend compared with mounting inflation elsewhere in South America – but there were signs that the situation was under control. On April 15, President Stroessner conferred with Japanese Prime Minister Eisaku Sato in Tokyo. Later, Stroessner announced an agreement under which Japan would lend Paraguay $13 million for industrial development.

External trade did well in 1972, boosted by a recovery in cotton exports and continued high meat prices. And, thanks chiefly to the good trade performance, monetary holdings climbed to $26.64 million in August. Mary Webster Soper

See also Latin America (Facts in Brief Table).

PARENTS AND TEACHERS, NATIONAL CONGRESS OF (PTA), observed its 75th anniversary in 1972. The first PTA meeting was held Feb. 17, 1897, in Washington, D.C. The organization had an enrollment of 2,000 members then; its 1972 membership was over 9 million. An 8-cent postage stamp was issued to commemorate the anniversary. It pictures a blackboard on which is chalked "P.T.A. Parent Teacher Association 1897-1972."

The following officers were elected at the 1972 National PTA Convention, held from May 21 to 24 in New York City: Mrs. W. Hamilton Crockford, III, Richmond, Va., secretary; Mr. Cecil L. Poppe, Albuquerque, N. Mex., treasurer.

After 75 years of "noninvolvement in the control of basic policies," delegates to the 1972 convention amended PTA bylaws to provide that "the organization shall work with the schools to provide quality education . . . and . . . participate in the decision-making process establishing school policy, recognizing that the legal authority to make final decisions has been delegated by the people to boards of education." In keeping with the new policy, convention delegates passed a resolution favoring busing for school integration and issued a call for a "search for solutions that would by rational means reduce racial isolation through transportation." Joseph P. Anderson

PENNSYLVANIA. See Philadelphia; State Government.

PERSONALITIES OF 1972. For the fourth consecutive year, President Richard M. Nixon headed the list of men most admired by Americans, according to the Gallup poll. The other 9 in the top 10, in order, were: evangelist Billy Graham, the late President Harry S. Truman, presidential adviser Henry A. Kissinger, Senator Edward M. Kennedy (D., Mass.), Alabama Governor George C. Wallace, Vice-President Spiro T. Agnew, Pope Paul VI, Senator George S. McGovern (D., S. Dak.), and West German Chancellor Willy Brandt.

Dropped from the 1971 list were former President Lyndon B. Johnson, Senator Hubert H. Humphrey (D., Minn.), Ralph Nader, and Bob Hope.

The most admired woman was the President's wife. Mrs. Nixon was followed by Israeli Prime Minister Golda Meir, 1971's most-admired woman. The others were, in order: Indian Prime Minister Indira Gandhi, Mrs. Dwight D. (Mamie) Eisenhower, Mrs. Aristotle (Jacqueline Kennedy) Onassis, U.S. Representative Shirley Chisholm (D., N.Y.), Queen Elizabeth II, Senator Margaret Chase Smith (D., Me.), Mrs. Joseph (Rose) Kennedy, and Mrs. Martin Luther (Coretta) King.

Dropped from the 1971 most-admired list were Mrs. Lyndon (Lady Bird) Johnson and Mrs. John (Martha) Mitchell.

President Nixon and Kissinger also were selected as "Men of the Year" by *Time* magazine.

Lynne Cox, 15, of Los Alamitos, Calif., swam the English Channel in July, going from Dover to the French coast in 9 hours 57 minutes.

Bailey, Bill, of Fair Oaks, Calif., announced in April that his cheerful, upbeat *The Good News Paper*, distributed in all 50 states and 10 foreign countries, was going out of business. Characteristically, the last edition failed to report the news of the paper's demise–that would be bad news. Among the typical items printed in his only-good-news paper was this: "In the United States last year, 196,459,483 citizens did not commit a criminal offense. . . ."

Benítez, Manuel, a Spanish peasant who became the highest-paid athlete in the world, announced his retirement from the bull ring in February. After 12 years as a bullfighter, Benítez–known around the world as El Córdobés–estimated his income at $3 million a year. A 35-year-old bachelor, Benítez explained he was retiring "because I used to be an illiterate and I have suddenly discovered that there are many things in this world I would like to know about."

Berra, Yogi, New York Mets manager, added another Berraism to sports annals in 1972. The old malapro was handed a $25 honorarium check made out to "Bearer" after appearing on sportscaster Jack Buck's talk show in St. Louis. "How," he complained to Buck, "could you spell my name like that?"

Brown, Russell V., researcher at the University of Missouri, spent the year grappling with the question: If you lead a pig to liquor, will it drink? The answer, he discovered, is an unqualified yes–just about anything put in front of it. Pigs and humans, it seems, are among the few species that will drink alcohol voluntarily. Brown's research into the effects of alcohol on pigs led him to some drearily familiar findings. The pigs get drunk, stumble, burp, experience hangovers and withdrawal symptoms, and suffer liver damage.

Chaplin, Charles, returned to the United States in April after an absence of 20 years. The 82-year-old master of the silent screen and his wife Oona came for a 10-day visit to accept some belated honors and awards for his creation of what many consider the greatest comic character of our time. Chaplin left the United States in 1952 amid a storm of controversy over his private life and his espousal of leftist causes.

De Angelis, Anthony (Tino), the "salad oil king," disagreed with a fellow penmate, James R. Hoffa, when he was paroled from the Lewisburg, Pa., prison in June. De Angelis was sentenced to a 20-year term in 1965 for a $150-million soybean oil swindle. Hoffa had earlier described the prison as a pit of dehumanization. "Compared to other prisons," De Angelis said, "that place is a country club." He had personal reasons for being generous, though. When he entered Lewisburg, at the age of 50, he weighed 250 pounds and his heart was so weak he could not get life insurance. After a rigorous program of jogging, handball, and working in the kitchen, his weight dropped to 170, and–to the amazement of his doctors–his heart grew stronger. "I went in thinking I was never going to make it out alive," De Angelis recalled. "Well, I'm out now and I can say I had a very nice experience. In fact, it saved my life."

Draper, John Thomas, 30, was arrested in San Jose, Calif., in May by the Federal Bureau of Investigation and charged with being "Captain Crunch," titular head of an illegal network of "phone phreaks" whose major passion in life was to outwit the Bell Telephone System. The "phreak" network used unauthorized multifrequency signal equipment and other devices to gain access to Ma Bell's "tandems," or long-distance telephone circuits. Captain Crunch got his name from a toy whistle once found in "Cap'n Crunch" cereal. Phone phreaks discovered that the whistle had a perfect 2,600-cycle tone that opened the Bell tandems for free calls. Bell began to crack down on the phone-tripping culture after a lengthy and revealing article appeared in *Esquire* magazine in late 1971. In the article, Captain Crunch, who drives around the country in a Volkswagen bus that has a computer and a switchboard in the back, bragged: "It's possible for three phone phreaks to saturate the phone system of the nation. Busy it out. All of it. I know how to do this. But I'm not gonna tell."

Einstein, Albert, was revealed in 1972 as not only one of the world's great scientists, but also something of a poet. Among 452 pages of his notes auctioned in New York was a baffling quatrain:

"I shan't be absent, little cookie,
Though I'm not a sugar cookie,
What life has brought you up to now,
May sweeten the farewell somehow."

Fischer, Bobby, newly crowned world chess champion, is looking for a wife. He told *Life* magazine that he planned to start dating girls. But, the magazine said, "In love as in chess, Fischer is fussy about playing conditions. He likes tall girls with excellent figures, intelligent but not aggressive. . . ." Earlier in the year, singer Joe Glazer qualified Bobby as an American folk hero with "The Ballad of Bobby Fischer"*:

"He was born in nineteen forty-three
And right away I knew he'd made history
'Cause he opened his mouth on the day he was born
And instead of crying he said,
'Move that pawn.' "

*Copyright 1972 by Joe Glazer, used by permission.

Goodbrad, John D., told *The Wall Street Journal* in February that he is amazed that so many people are buying his product. "Our sales have been doubling every 60 to 90 days for the past two and one-half years," Goodbrad said with some puzzlement. Goodbrad's product is a grain, nut, and seed mixture called

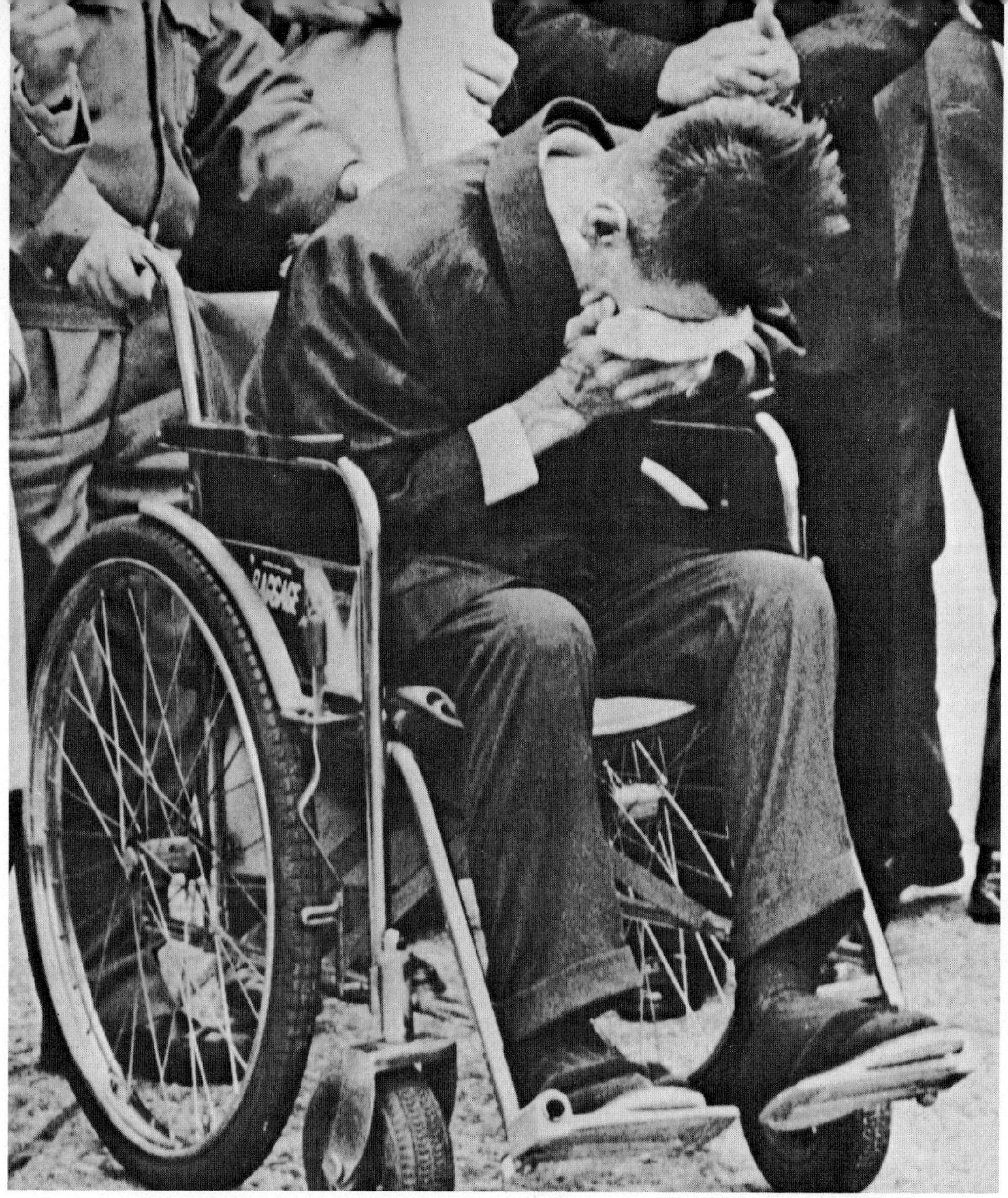

Japanese soldier Shoichi Yokoi, 57, is overcome by emotion on arriving in Tokyo after hiding in the jungle on Guam since World War II.

Crunchy Granola, described by the *Journal* as "something a horse might be fond of." Goodbrad's family business, Sovex, Inc., is now turning out 12,000 pounds of granola a day. Only a few years ago, the only granola crunchers were health-food faddists. Today, supermarkets sell it like it was cereal. It has even inspired a rock testimonial, "The Crunchy Granola Suite," by Neil Diamond.

Hall, Bob, 19, a student sky diver, leaped from an airplane in November. When both his parachute and reserve chute failed to open, he dropped 3,300 feet at 60 to 80 miles per hour and landed face down on an airport runway. "I screamed. I knew I was dead and that my life was ended right then. There was nothing I could do. It was all over." A few seconds later, he rose to a crouch. He suffered only a smashed nose and broken teeth. Having lived to tell about it, Hall suggested that his life did flash before his eyes. "My mind started doing weird things," he said. "All my life flashed before my eyes, it really did. I saw my mother's face, all the homes I've lived in, the military academy I attended, the faces of friends, everything."

Hiss, Alger, sent to prison for 44 months for perjury after a 1948 congressional investigation of Communist espionage, returned to the headlines in 1972. Denied an $80-a-month federal pension under a special bill named for him, Hiss, now 67, sued in a federal court in 1970. "The monetary aspect is not very large," the former state department official said, but the principle was important to him. In March, the court ruled that the provision, known as the Hiss Act, had been applied retroactively and was thus unconstitutional. The court ordered the government to pay Hiss his monthly pension, as well as back payments of $3,660 plus interest. Hiss told a *Life* reporter that he still clings to the hope that a public commission will re-examine his case on the basis of new evidence that he claims to have and will exonerate him. "The court's decision on my pension is one small step," he said.

Hunebelle, Danielle, wrote a book that purports to be an account of a love affair with presidential assistant Henry A. Kissinger. The book, *Dear Henry*, suggests, among other things, that Kissinger is something less than a paragon of neatness. "It has been my lot," she wrote, "to visit barracks and to enter dormitories without warning. I have also experienced the disorder of young children. But this naked room, in which two straight-backed divans had accumulated pell-mell not only clothes, shoes, and ties, but also a whole year's worth of underwear, appeared so repulsive that it was hard to imagine the second personality of the kingdom living there." Still, author Hunebelle assured a *Life* magazine reporter that she had no intention of saying anything that would be "embarrassing or bothersome for [Kissinger] in his present position."

Hunt, H. L., 83, one of the world's richest men, revealed his secret for staying healthy and active–creeping. Hunt, who still works from 7 A.M. to 10:30 P.M. six days a week, keeps in shape with "the greatest exercise ever. You get down on all fours and walk on your hands and knees and look at the little finger of each hand as you walk the hand forward. That turns your head from side to side. It's natural exercise, like when you were an ape." Hunt recommends 10 minutes of creeping every day.

Leopold Stokowski receives an antique silver box from the American Symphony Orchestra on his 90th birthday. Stokowski founded the orchestra at age 80.

Johnson, Richard J., "Mr. Average Voter," after months of agonizing, finally voted along with most of the rest of America for President Richard M. Nixon. Johnson, who lives in Rolling Meadows, Ill., a suburb of Chicago, was selected by national public television programs on the basis of his income and neighborhood to represent the views of middle-income voters. It was the first time in many years, he said, that he voted for a Republican presidential candidate.

Le Clair, Robert, 24, brunet, 36-30-32, won the first all-male beauty pageant in Boston. Le Clair, crowned "Adonis '72," is charming, personable, a gourmet cook, and an aspiring concert pianist.

Matthau, Walter, appeared in the nude (except for a hat and a flesh-colored G string) while playing the piano in the motion picture *Pete 'n' Tillie*. Explained Matthau: "The real secret of the scene is the middle-aged flab. I don't have any, but I'm such a good actor that I can look flabby."

Merrick, Thomas, California financier, wants to buy Italy's crumbling Colosseum for $1 million. But unlike the London Bridge, now in Arizona, or the Queen Mary, now in Long Beach, Calif., Merrick does not want to move the finest surviving example of ancient Roman architecture. He just wants to repair it and charge admission. Merrick sent an Italian agent, Fausta Vitalli, to Rome in October. "He's willing to bargain," Vitalli told Italy's superintendent of antiquities. "It's not love of archaeology that drives Merrick to try to buy the Colosseum, although he likes art. He sees a big deal in it."

Moorehouse, Geoffrey, 40, a former London newspaperman, set off in October to cross the vast Sahara alone on a camel. Moorehouse's trip, which will take a year, covers 3,600 miles. Admitting the prospect "petrifies" him, Moorehouse said: "I believe the most corrosive element attacking the greatness and goodness of the human spirit is fear, and its most insidious form, the fear of being afraid. In a sense the Sahara represents the ultimate of all my fears. If I can conquer the spiritual as well as the physical hazards embodied in the desert, then I believe I shall have something of value to tell mankind."

Noteboom, W. D., a biochemist at the University of Missouri at Columbia, discovered that the chemical value of the human body, like everything else, has gone up. His calculations show that the value of the body's chemicals is now $3.50–up considerably from the old figure of 98 cents.

Price, William, a Navaho Indian and Marine Corps master sergeant, retired in May after 30 years of service. Price gained some renown during World War II for developing a baffling code based on the Navaho language. Price recalled: "The Japanese had units of English-speaking men that not only listened to our radio and telephone conversations, but could even get into the conversation by imitating Brooklyn or Deep-South accents." The Navaho code created by Price and 200 other Navaho Marines at San Diego was, to Price's knowledge, never cracked.

Reel, James, of Rice University's Space Science Department, sent this invitation to friends in February. "You are cordially invited to attend a special seminar conducted by Mr. James Reel. Topic: Angular trajectory of multisolid mass elements as they relate to separate single mass in motion. Special note: Dr. LaGoose of the Canadian interior will be available after the oral presentation to aid in the evaluation of theoretical v. applied techniques of equipment calibration during experimentation." A footnote: "Translation: Let's go goose hunting Tuesday morning."

Sharin, Jack, of New York City, was somewhat perplexed during a taxicab ride from Chicago's O'Hare

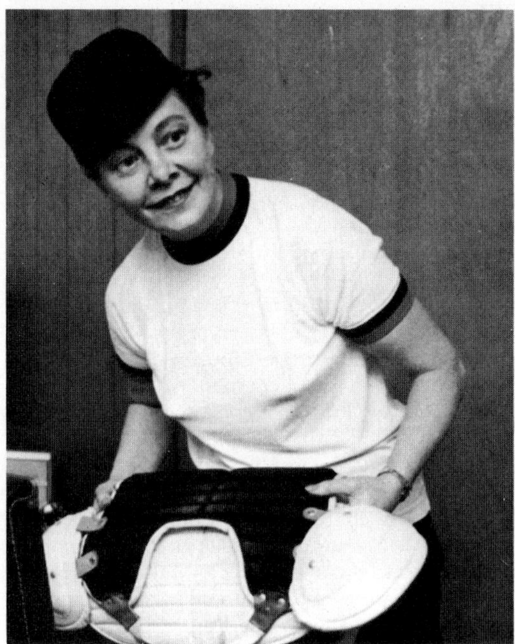

Organized baseball's first woman umpire, Bernice Gera, 40, quit after her first game in the New York-Pennsylvania League in June.

Airport when he noticed that nobody was driving the cab. The driver had fallen from the moving vehicle as it rounded a turn in the busy airport complex. Sharin squeezed through the tiny glass partition and grabbed the steering wheel. But when he tried to turn off the ignition to stop the car, he got stuck. While two fellow passengers acted as rear-view mirrors, Sharin managed to steer the cab onto an embankment, and it stopped. A few minutes later, a police car drove up with an apologetic cabdriver, who drove the New Yorkers to their destination.

Solzhenitsyn, Alexander I., Nobel Prize winner and author of the best-selling novel *August 1914*, announced in December that he was "financially desperate." His books are banned in Russia and his royalties are piling up in Switzerland, but he cannot get them. As word of the Russian author's plight spread, American authors Robert Penn Warren and Bernard Malamud announced that they wanted their Russian royalties paid to Solzhenitsyn. Hollywood writer Albert Maltz, who claimed Russia owed him $34,000 in back royalties for his book *The Cross and the Arrow*, told Russian officials to pay the money to Solzhenitsyn.

Spassky, Boris, breaking a month-long silence after his defeat by Bobby Fischer for the world chess championship, said, in *64*, the Soviet chess magazine, that he "was unable to explain some of his blunders." Of Fischer, Spassky said, "He has excellent technique, a great capacity to work, and a subtle awareness of the mood and physical state of the rival." But, the former Russian champion said, he does not consider Fischer "a power that cannot be conquered."

Tim, Tiny, was personally responsible for "drastically undermining" Consolidated Edison's "save-a-watt" electricity conservation program, according to Consolidated Edison board chairman Charles Luce. Luce told a Sierra Club conference in January that Tiny Tim's marriage to Miss Vicki on nationwide television in December, 1969, used up 200,000 watts.

Woodbery, D. H., 79, was the nation's worst-paid chief executive officer, according to *Forbes* magazine. Woodbery is president of the Havatampa Cigar Corporation of Tampa, Fla., which, according to *Forbes*, earned $3.8 million in 1971 on sales of $393.4 million. "For running it and serving as treasurer as well," the magazine reported, "Woodbery was paid $15,000–a good deal less than many a truckdriver." Woodbery, who could give himself a raise at any time, seemed unperturbed. "Actually," he said, "I haven't given too much attention to my finances. When I started the company, I borrowed a dollar from my brother. Poor fellow died a couple years back with my still owing him the dollar."

Yokoi, Shoichi, 57, a Japanese Army corporal, hid in the jungle on Guam for 28 years after World War II, fearing execution if he gave himself up. He was found in January, living on a diet of wild nuts, mangoes, papaya, shrimps, snails, frogs, and rats. Doctors at Guam Memorial Hospital pronounced him in normal health although slightly anemic from lack of salt. Yokoi was the third soldier found on Guam; the other two were discovered 17 years ago. "I'd like to be reunited with my family [in Nagoya] and then go up on a mountain and meditate for a long time," he told newsmen. A Tokyo department store's exhibition of Yokoi's hand-tailored, bark-and-root clothes drew a staggering 350,000 visitors. In November, Yokoi married a 44-year-old war widow. "We can communicate to each other by eyes, though we don't talk to each other much," Yokoi said. The couple planned to honeymoon on the romantic island of Guam. Allan Davidson

Johnny Rodgers, Nebraska's great running back, happily accepts the Heisman Trophy as college football's most outstanding player in 1972.

PERU. The Revolutionary Government of the Armed Forces marked its fourth year in office in 1972. Although it remained committed to social and agrarian reform, it continued its strong-arm rule.

One of the regime's major reforms involved a sweeping change in the educational system. On March 24, a law was enacted calling for bilingual education in Spanish and Indian dialects, equal opportunities for women, mandatory national service before graduation, and an active role for students in university administration. One immediate result of the last provision was demonstrations in the southern city of Puno on June 27 and July 3 by students protesting an unpopular university law. In the two melees, which included an attack on police headquarters, 4 persons were killed and at least 17 injured. Order was restored only after the government declared a state of siege and imposed a curfew.

During the year, the government sharply restricted television and radio programming and advertising that it did not consider "socially useful." Newspapers also came under fire when a statute was enacted prohibiting newsmen from publishing anything that could be construed as derogatory to the regime or the nation. On July 13, Pedro Beltran Ballen, head of *La Prensa*, Lima's only major independent newspaper, was given a suspended six-month term and fined for a story that the regime considered harmful to its relations with Chile.

Big Petroleum Finds contrasted with a disastrous anchovy shortage for a mixed economic picture during the year. Oil discoveries in the Amazon jungle meant that a 400- to 550-mile pipeline that can carry 250,000 barrels per day from the interior to the coast will now be built at a cost of from $200 million to $270 million. It is expected that more than $700-million will be spent on exploration and pipelines by various companies over the next five years. Meanwhile, the government declared that the matter of the expropriated International Petroleum Company properties was closed–thus squashing rumors of a possible deal to secure foreign mining finance.

Anchovy Shortage. Peru halted all fish meal exports indefinitely on October 1 because of an anchovy shortage. The shortage was caused by "El Nino," the warm Equatorial Current that pushes far south along the republic's normally cold-water coast every five or six years at Christmastime. When this occurs, marine species that cannot tolerate temperature changes move elsewhere. In the past, El Nino has disappeared in April and fishing habits return to normal. But in 1972, the Equatorial Current was still warm and strong in mid-August, and the anchovies did not return. The country had to dip into its stocks to fulfill contracts. The republic has been providing about 70 per cent of the world's supply of the protein-rich meal, which accounts for more than one-third of Peru's export earnings. Mary Webster Soper

See also LATIN AMERICA (Facts in Brief Table).

PET. Increasing affluence, the trend toward suburban living, and a growing desire of people for protection and companionship helped to produce a boom in the U.S. pet business in 1972. *The New York Times* estimated that the animal, fish, and reptile pet population in the United States had risen to 700-million, more than three times the human population. The Family Economics Bureau estimated that the pet population had increased three times faster than the human population over the period of the last decade.

The Pet Food Institute estimated that 3 out of 4 American homes own at least one pet, with fish comprising the largest single group. Americans spent $1.5 billion on dog and cat food in 1972.

Dog Shows. For the second consecutive year, a liver-and-white springer spaniel, Ch. Chinoe's Adamant James, owned by Milton E. Prickett of Lexington, Ky., took best-in-show honors at the Westminster Kennel Club show in New York City in February. The show drew 3,093 entries. Champion Janne-Chen's Maya Dancer, a Maltese owned by Mamie Gregory of Fort Lauderdale, Fla., was chosen best-in-show at the International Kennel Club show in Chicago in April.

Breed Standings. American Kennel Club registration figures showed that poodles were the most popular breed of dog in the United States for the 12th consecutive year. They were followed in order by German shepherds, beagles, dachshunds, miniature schnauzers, Saint Bernards, Irish setters, and Labrador retrievers. Collies were 9th, and Pekingese and Chihuahuas dropped to 10th and 11th.

Mimi, a miniature poodle owned by the Nicholas Emerito family of Danbury, Conn., won the Ken-L Ration gold medal as Dog Hero of the year. Mimi had always refused to walk up and down steep stairways. But when fire broke out in the Emerito house, the dog raced up and down the fiery stairs four times, barking to awaken the eight members of the family, all of whom managed to escape from the burning house.

Cats. In its 1972 All-America awards, *Cats* magazine named Joelwyn Columbyan, a silver tabby ash male owned by C. Raymond and Joan E. Sneed of Yorba Linda, Calif., *Cat of the Year*. Second best *Cat of the Year* was Lai-Nee La Prima Donna Giulia, a seal point Siamese female owned by Carl and Elaine Michelis of Austin, Tex. Third best *Cat of the Year* was Kitwillows' Red Rose, a red Persian female owned by John Stevens of Richmond, Canada. *Longhair Male of the Year* was Shawnee Tammey, a cream Persian male owned by Isabel Roberts of Clyde, N.Y. *Kitten of the Year* was Sandia's Dulcinea of Ebon Gaunt, a copper-eyed white Persian female owned by Bob and Alice Walters of Whitehall, Pa. *Alter of the Year* was Francine Little Princess, Jr., a blue-eyed white Persian spay, owned by Rose Marie McGarvey of Philadelphia. Theodore M. O'Leary

PETERSON, PETER GEORGE (1926-), was named secretary of commerce on Jan. 27, 1972, replacing Maurice H. Stans, who resigned to head fund-raising activities for President Richard M. Nixon's re-election campaign. In December, President Nixon said he would replace Peterson with Frederick B. Dent, a South Carolina manufacturer.

Peterson, a businessman, joined the Administration in 1971 as special assistant to the President for international economic affairs and executive director of the Council on International Economic Policy.

Peterson's rise in business was meteoric. After receiving an M.B.A. degree with honors from the University of Chicago Graduate School of Business in 1951, he became executive vice-president of a Chicago marketing firm. At 27, he became vice-president of a major advertising agency. At 32, he was invited to be a director of Bell and Howell Company by the company's president, Charles H. Percy. After Percy retired to enter politics, Peterson, at 41, became chairman of the board and chief executive officer.

Peterson was born in Kearney, Nebr. His father, originally named Petropoulos, was a Greek immigrant who owned a small restaurant. Peterson attended Nebraska State Teachers College and transferred to Northwestern, where he graduated in 1947.

Allan Davidson

PETROLEUM AND GAS. President Richard M. Nixon was forced to increase oil imports sharply in September, 1972, despite a decade of government efforts to limit them in order to protect and encourage the domestic industry. Lagging production of petroluem products simply has not kept pace with demand. The President's action means that imports of petroleum products will be permitted to rise from about 1.7 million barrels to about 2.3 million barrels a day east of the Rocky Mountains. In addition, the decision might nearly double the daily rate of imports of No. 2 fuel oil, which is widely used for heating houses in the Northeast.

Oil accounted for more than 40 per cent of all the nation's energy in 1972; natural gas was second at about 33 per cent. The Department of the Interior forecast that imports must rise far higher in the next decade and supply at least half of all the oil used in the United States. This would mean a fourfold increase in imports. Even the Alaska oil pipeline, which could add as much as 2 million barrels a day to the nation's supply, would not be able to satisfy a projected demand of 26 million barrels a day by 1985. In 1972, the nation used 16 million barrels a day.

Natural gas was also in dwindling supply. Wells were estimated to have only about a 15-year reserve. Government geologists predicted that gas made from coal must ultimately replace natural supplies.

Russian Gas for Western Europe

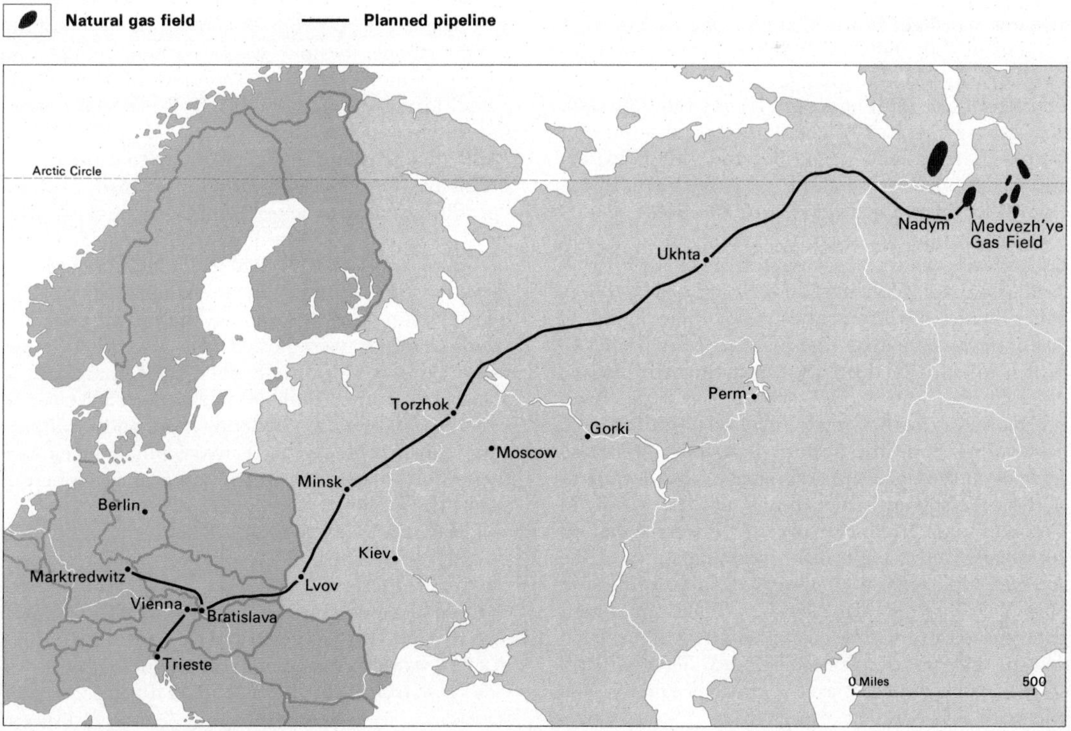

The Alaska Pipeline. The controversial Alaska pipeline moved a step nearer reality in 1972. In May, Secretary of the Interior Rogers C. B. Morton approved permits for the trans-Alaska pipeline to cross public lands. The federal government was still trying to get a court to lift its two-year-old temporary injunction against the $3-billion project. Indications were, however, that construction of the 786-mile pipeline from Alaska's Arctic North Slope to the ice-free port of Valdez in southern Alaska will be held up for at least a year. The project was still buried in suits brought by environmental groups and Alaskan fishing industries. In addition, several prominent legislators claim that an alternative Canadian route through the Mackenzie Valley to the Midwest would be superior from both an economic and environmental point of view. However, the Alaska Pipeline Service Company, the petroleum company combine proposing to build the project, hoped to begin construction early in 1973.

Other Sources. In the meantime, new sources of supply were being sought. In August, Shell and Exxon (formerly Esso) discovered a major new oil field 100 miles northeast of the Shetland Islands in the North Sea. The field, the most northerly oil find yet made in the North Sea, is thought to hold about 1 billion barrels of recoverable oil. Ultimate reserves in the North Sea oil fields are estimated at 12 billion barrels and over 50 trillion cubic feet of natural gas.

Foreign Sources. President Nixon's state visit to Russia in May resulted in an agreement, reached in London in July, that will provide some solution to oil and gas shortages in the United States. Under the agreement made between Russia's State Committee for Science and Technology and the Occidental Petroleum Corporation – a giant conglomerate with headquarters in Los Angeles – the corporation will supply patents and scientific and technological knowledge to Russia for the next five years in exchange for oil and gas valued at $3 billion.

A series of unencouraging conferences were held during the year with representatives of the oil-rich Arab countries. The situation was confused by differences among the Arab states. After the congress of Arab states was held in Algeria in late May, James E. Akins, director of the U.S. Department of State's office of fuels and energy, reported that the Arab producers were unwilling to increase output to keep pace with U.S. needs. Western plans for oil were also rejected at the summer conference of the Organization of Petroleum Exporting Countries held in Vienna in late June. However, 23 international oil companies and 5 major oil-producing states of the Arabian Gulf area finally reached an agreement in New York City in early October. Their agreement gave the oil-producing countries an active role in foreign oil operations on their land. They will receive 25 per cent of crude oil operations, and by 1982 will have a 51 per cent interest. Mary E. Jessup

PHILADELPHIA. In June, 1972, President Richard M. Nixon and the U.S. Bicentennial Commission rejected plans to hold the United States 200th birthday party in Philadelphia. Preliminary plans had been made for a 1976 Philadelphia World's Fair, to be held in connection with the bicentennial celebration. Instead, the occasion will be commemorated in local celebrations throughout the country.

Administrative Problems. In February, the Pennsylvania State Crime Commission issued a report charging that corruption existed throughout Philadelphia's police department and promising that a full-scale investigation would be made. Mayor Frank L. Rizzo, a former police commissioner, criticized the report as "an ill-advised publicity grab" made by the commission chairman and by Pennsylvania Governor Milton J. Shapp.

The city's police department was also troubled by charges of racial discrimination. In May, a U.S. District Court judge ordered the department to hire 1 black recruit for every 2 white recruits added between May 26 and July 1. However, the district court order was overturned by a U.S. Court of Appeals on September 14.

To recoup its $200-million investment in airport improvements, Philadelphia attempted to levy a $2 tax on each person using the new airport facilities. But the tax on arriving airline passengers was ruled unconstitutional and had to be discontinued in August. The city also lost $2 million on its new Veterans Stadium sports complex during the first year of operation.

A teachers' strike kept 285,000 students out of the public schools for four weeks in September. The Charles Klein Library of Temple University's law school lost most of its 150,000-volume book collection in a fire on July 25.

Crime and Vandalism continued to cause severe problems. The police department formed a special "graffiti squad" to arrest subway scribblers, who cause an estimated $4 million in damages each year.

A gang war between rival Philadelphia narcotics rings led to a shooting in an Atlantic City, N.J., nightclub on April 3. A reputed heroin pusher and 3 young women were killed and 11 others were wounded in the gunfire. Earlier, the Department of Justice had named Philadelphia as one of 33 cities in which special teams of federal, state, and local narcotics law enforcement teams would concentrate their efforts to crack the pipeline that spreads heroin across the nation.

The cost of living went up 2.8 per cent in Philadelphia between April, 1971, and April, 1972. Unemployment increased; in May, 1971, there were 881,700 persons employed, but only 878,600 had jobs in May, 1972. Average weekly earnings of production workers in manufacturing industries, however, rose from $150.42 to $158.80 during the same period. J. M. Banovetz

PHILIPPINES. President Ferdinand E. Marcos declared martial law on Sept. 23, 1972. It was the first time the measure had been imposed since the Philippines obtained its independence from the United States in 1946. More than 150 journalists and political opposition leaders were arrested. Marcos said the move was prompted by the threat of Communist subversion. He promised social reforms that would eliminate the ills on which Communism could thrive.

Marcos, the nation's first two-term president, had faced mounting unrest since 1970. His opponents had accused him of using the Communist threat to justify authoritarian measures. Bombings, five reported attempts on Marcos' life, and anti-U.S. demonstrations in Manila had added to the tension. An unsuccessful attempt on September 22 to kill Juan Ponce Enrile, secretary of national defense, was the official reason for invoking martial law. Nor did its invocation prevent an assassin from trying to kill the president's wife, Imelda, on December 7.

One of the gravest dangers facing the government, according to Marcos, was the New People's Army, a Maoist force of about 2,000 guerrillas and an estimated 100,000 followers. This force, led by Victor Corpus, a 28-year-old graduate of the Philippines Military Academy, included members of prominent families who deplored government corruption and gross social inequalities. Regional military units were increased, and the government launched a crackdown on private armies maintained by politicians and landlords. Marcos promised to remove "the corrupt, the inefficient, the ignorant, as well as those who are not essential" from a bloated civil service.

Reform Measures. In an effort to control soaring inflation, Marcos lowered prices for basic commodities. A land-reform decree issued on October 21 called for breaking up large estates, mainly in central and northern Luzon. Under the decree, about 715,000 tenants would take over an estimated 3.75 million acres of farmland on a 15-year purchase arrangement backed by a government-sponsored system of rural cooperatives. Large landholders were told they could retain 17.5 acres – but only if they farmed the land themselves. Guerrillas had been strongest in areas where landlords were the most powerful.

Prior to the declaration of martial law, a constitutional convention met on July 7. It had been trying to draft a new Constitution that would replace a 1935 charter adopted when the Philippines was a commonwealth of the United States. A major issue was whether to change from a presidential system, under which Marcos could not succeed himself for a third term, to a parliamentary form so he could remain in power as prime minister. The convention approved the change and rejected a proposal to bar presidents from future office. Henry A. Bradsher

See also ASIA (Facts in Brief Table).

Filipino students, dismissed from class, clamber aboard a bus. All the Philippines' schools were closed in September when martial law was declared.

PHOTOGRAPHY. A record 250,800 people from 116 countries visited photography's big international showcase, the biennial Photokina in Cologne, West Germany, from Sept. 23 to Oct. 11, 1972. After viewing the startling innovations displayed there, one was certain there would be two major changes in photographic equipment available by mid-1973.

The popular, interchangeable-lens, 35mm SLR will feature automatic exposure based on electronic shutters with infinitely variable timing, typically from 4 seconds to 1/2,000 of a second. Electronic flash units will offer automatic exposure control, using new alternate-capacitor circuitry. This method provides faster cycling – less time for the units to ready themselves for the next shot – and longer battery life.

The New Kodaks. Kodak unveiled a new family of cameras, films, and projectors at the Chicago Photo Trade Show on March 19. It included pocket Instamatic cameras only 1 inch thick that use drop-in cartridges of film in a new small 110 size. The higher priced of the five new models have automatic electronic shutters. However, a more significant technological advance was in the new films – Verichrome Pan for black and white, Ektachrome X and Kodachrome X for slides, and Kodacolor II for color prints – all with greatly improved grain and sharpness. While the pocket Instamatics were meant primarily for taking snapshots, some experts pre-

Pocket-size cameras made news in 1972. This is Kodak's Instamatic 20, one of five 1-inch-thick, cartridge-loading models it introduced.

dicted that the new 110 size–about the same as 16mm–would eventually replace 35mm, just as 35mm had earlier replaced 2¼x2¼.

Polaroid was less successful in getting its new cameras on the market. In April, Polaroid demonstrated its radical new SX-70 folding pocket camera for quick-repeat, instant-color prints that develop automatically outside the camera in full view of an observer. Because of production problems, however, the SX-70 was still not available for purchase at year's end.

International Agreements. On the international scene, the trend from competition to cooperation took new forms. Leitz of Wetzlar, West Germany, and Minolta of Osaka, Japan, agreed to share know-how and patents. Asahi Optical of Tokyo and Zeiss of West Germany set up a joint venture in lenses for eyeglasses in Tokyo, a possible prelude to camera-lens production there. Copal of Japan was licensed to produce 200,000 shutters in three years for 35mm cameras produced by Leica of West Germany. In Englewood, Colo., representatives of nine major Japanese photographic manufacturers met with officials of National Camera, America's only major camera-repair school, to work out methods for making service and technical information available to all camera technicians in the United States.

Magazine Photography. When *Life* magazine ceased publication on December 29, some observers said the era of the black-and-white photo essay in print was over (see MAGAZINES). What had in fact happened, however, was that the photo essayist had moved on to other media–even as reader interest was moving–while *Life* (and *Look*, which had died a year earlier) stuck stubbornly to their old patterns. With its more graphic, more immediate photo reporting in such vital areas as war and politics, television had captured the picture-magazines' audience. Many photographers schooled in the *Life* style had moved to news or documentary filming. Others were experimenting with books and portfolios. Some were working with still presentations for television, slide shows, and multimedia shows in preparation for the long-predicted emergence of video cassette systems. Confident that photojournalism remains viable, *U.S. Camera Annual*, one year older than *Life*, changed its format in 1972 to feature photo essays rather than individual photographs.

Still Photography. Whatever might be happening to the photo essay, still photography was growing, with 1 in 5 Americans using cameras to make some 5 billion pictures a year. Young people, especially, were "turned on" to photography, and more than 700 universities and other schools were offering photography courses. Galleries exhibiting and selling photographs were proliferating, and the National Endowment for the Arts granted fellowships of up to $5,000 to 60 photographers. Rus Arnold

PHYSICS. The most interesting developments in physics in 1972 involved the study of nuclear fusion, the process by which two nuclei merge with a consequent release of energy. Laser-produced fusion, which may someday permit controlled fusion on a large scale, was a new concept under study. A deepening mystery surrounded experimental efforts to verify theories of the fusion reaction that takes place in the interior of the sun.

Laser-Produced Fusion. Nuclear fusion has been studied on a small scale in physics laboratories since 1932. Only after the development of the hydrogen bomb, however, did scientists begin searching for a more controlled way of releasing and using the energy of nuclear fusion. This work has involved the study of plasmas. Plasmas are high-density gases of charged particles that are compressed and heated to millions of degrees, thereby causing fusion reactions to take place. Researchers have learned much about the physics of plasmas, and they have developed elaborate techniques to compress, heat, and contain them. Nevertheless, a fusion reactor has not yet been made to yield enough energy to be self-sustaining.

In 1972, important theoretical results were announced in connection with a new concept in fusion technique that previously had been classified secret by the U.S. Atomic Energy Commission. This involves bombarding a frozen pellet of suitable material with high-intensity light beams from a laser. In recent years, lasers have been developed that can deliver an enormous amount of energy within a billionth of a second. Physicists in various national laboratories, universities, and industries calculate that a suitable laser should be able to compress a portion of the pellet to thousands of times its original density, producing fusion on a practical scale. Both the government and industry will probably sharply increase funds for the investigation of this concept.

Delegates from Russia's Academy of Sciences visited the hydrogen bubble chamber at the Argonne National Lab near Chicago in October.

Physicists in Russia are believed to be conducting laser-fusion experiments now. In any event, it will likely be several years before this or any other fusion technique results in a reactor whose energy output exceeds the input necessary to sustain it. At that point, new energy transfer and storage techniques may be necessary before an operational fusion reactor would be an economic and practical reality. Nevertheless, such developments would be of incalculable value to mankind, offering a virtually inexhaustible source of power, free of serious operating hazards and environmental pollution.

Solar Neutrinos. Man cannot directly observe the nuclear-fusion reactions that take place in the sun's interior. Important information, however, can be obtained by observing neutrinos, the tiny particles that are emitted by nuclei produced in fusion. Neutrinos travel at the speed of light and can easily penetrate the matter of the sun and planets.

Raymond Davis, Jr., head of a research group at the Brookhaven National Laboratory in Upton, N.Y., designed an experiment in 1968 to detect solar neutrinos. He used a small electronic counter to measure infinitesimal amounts of radioactive argon produced when neutrinos interact with chlorine. The argon was produced in a tank containing 100,000 gallons of chlorine-rich, dry-cleaning solvent. In order to shield the apparatus from cosmic rays, which can also produce radioactive argon, all the equipment was placed nearly a mile underground in the Homestake Gold Mine in South Dakota.

The 1968 results indicated that the neutrino flux (rate of energy flow) was far less than that predicted by standard theories of stellar processes. In June, 1972, at a conference on neutrino astrophysics near Budapest, Hungary, Davis reported that after four more years of operation and several improvements in the apparatus, it now appears that the solar neutrino flux is less than one-tenth the predicted value.

There have been many speculations on the source of this discrepancy. If the experimental results are correct, perhaps the reactions do not proceed far enough to create the nuclei that emit neutrinos at a rate and energy suitable for detection. Perhaps the temperature of the sun's interior has a cyclic behavior and is presently at its minimum level. Maybe the neutrinos themselves decay on their way to the earth. This puzzle is certain to stimulate intense study in the future.

Thomas O. White

PITTSBURGH. Mayor Peter Flaherty and other area officials in January, 1972, asked the courts to halt construction work on new transportation facilities in the Pittsburgh-Allegheny County area. They were attempting to stop the Port Authority of Allegheny County from spending more funds on construction until it has received permits from all the governmental agencies with jurisdiction over its activities.

The suit would halt construction on transit projects financed by a $60-million grant from the U.S. Department of Transportation. The port authority was using the grant to develop a conventional bus system and Skybus, a personal rapid transit system consisting of rubber-tired vehicles that run on a concrete guideway.

United States Steel signed an agreement on September 25 with the federal Environmental Protection Agency (EPA) to begin work on a massive antipollution program at the U.S. Steel coke works in the Pittsburgh area. The EPA said the agreement concluded the nation's largest environment suit in terms of how much compliance would cost the company. U.S. Steel was given until 1977 to complete the work and meet air-quality standards.

A federal grand jury in Pittsburgh indicted two United Mine Workers (UMW) officials on October 17 on charges of conspiracy, obstructing justice, and obstructing federal investigation of the 1970 slaying of UMW leader Joseph A. Yablonski. The conspiracy indictment charged that the officials were involved in the conspiracy to murder Yablonski. A month before his death, Yablonski had been defeated in a heated campaign for the presidency of the UMW.

According to Uniform Crime Reports released on August 29, crime was at a relatively low level in the Pittsburgh area. Pittsburgh had 2,082.6 crimes per 100,000 persons, considerably below the national average of 2,907. The Federal Bureau of Investigation reported that crime in the city had dropped by 7 per cent since 1970. However, Pittsburgh was one of the cities to which the U.S. Department of Justice said it would send special teams of federal, state, and local law-enforcement officers to stop the spread of heroin and other narcotic drugs.

Economic Indicators in the city suggested that the local economy was improving even though the area's unemployment remained fairly high. Department-store sales increased 6.8 per cent between January, 1971, and January, 1972. Construction activity was up 14.9 per cent between March, 1971, and March, 1972. The city's cost of living rose only 3.1 per cent between April, 1971, and April, 1972. The average gross weekly earnings of production workers increased by 11.6 per cent, to $180.74 a week, between May, 1971, and May, 1972. The U.S. Department of Labor reported that the minimum income required for a family of four in the city was a low $7,078 a year.

J. M. Banovetz

PLASTICS. See CHEMICAL INDUSTRY.

POETRY. Dead in 1972 were two great masters of the art of poetry – Ezra Pound and Marianne Moore. Their deaths marked the end of a period of modern American poetry that was as rich, brilliant, and varied as any since Shakespeare, Christopher Marlowe, and Ben Jonson walked the streets of London. Yet, superb and good poetry continued to be written and published throughout the year; and all signs indicate that there are more good poets – older as well as the multitude of gifted, energetic younger poets – working today than at perhaps any other period.

In addition, the cornucopia of useful translations was full during the year, bringing such great and able poets as Pablo Neruda, Robert Desnos, Andrey Voznesensky, Gunner Ekelöf, and Tomas Transtomer to the American reading public. Finally, there were the countless readings by poets in art museums, bookstores, universities and high schools, and poets' homes, and in such underground locations as The Body Politic in Chicago and the Panjandrum Press in San Francisco's Mission District.

James Wright's excellent *Collected Poems* earned the Pulitzer Prize for 1972. Grandeur and wretchedness exist cheek-by-jowl in Wright's lyrics, which come from the most primary emotions – a world in which the soul is rooted in gentleness, rage, lust, cold loneliness, and love. The National Book Award was shared by the late Frank O'Hara's *Collected Poems*, which was beautifully edited by Donald M. Allen, and Howard Moss' *Selected Poems*. Due to his wit and insouciance, O'Hara could make verse out of the most mundane and seemingly "unpoetic" material.

Among the Younger Poets, the outstanding volume was probably *Nights of Naomi* by Bill Knott (1940-1966) – a poetry abrasive, ebullient in its humor, and stunning in its effect. Good books were also published by such young poets as George Amabalie, James Applewhite, Victor Bockris, Charles Boer, Joseph Bruchac, Michael Brownstein, Tom Clark, Kenward Elmslie, Dean Faulwell, Richard Friedman, Darrell Grey, Paul Hoover, James Koller, Jim Leonard, Morton Marcus, Jack Marshall, James McMichael, A. Poulin, Bob Rosenthal, Aram Saroyan, Charles Simic, Terry Stokes, James Tate, Diane Wakowski, and Andrew Wylie. Tom Veitch's splendid *Songs of a Cowboy Alchemist* won the annual Big Table Series of Younger Poets Prize. The Big Table Books were canceled by their publisher (Follett), however. Such fine little magazines as *Chicago*, *Gum*, *Milk Quarterly*, *Oink*, and *The World*, all edited by young poets, were gaining in reputation.

Among the Older Poets, John Ashbery's *Three Poems* was the most controversial volume – mysterious, opaque, at times prophetic. The most graceful was Lawrence Ferlinghetti's *Back Roads to Far Places;* the most muscular and pious, Allen Ginsberg's *The Fall of America*. Other poets who had volumes published in 1972 included A. R. Ammons, W. H. Auden, the late John Berryman, Gwendolyn Brooks, Charles

Russian poet Yevgeny Yevtushenko clowns with singers at New York City's Felt Forum in Madison Square Garden on his third visit to the United States.

Bukowski, Lucille Clifton, Richard Eberhart, Daryl Hine, Denise Levertov, Archibald Macleish, James Merrill, the late Sylvia Plath, James Schuyler, Anne Sexton, Louis Simpson, and John Hall Wheelwright.

John Frederick Nims's from *Sappho to Valery* was the outstanding book of translations. Exceptional anthologies included *Shaking the Pumpkin: Traditional Poetry of the North American Indian*, edited by Jerome Rothenberg; *The New Oxford Book of English Verse: 1250-1950*, edited by Dame Helen Gardner; *French Poetry Today*, edited by Simon Watson Taylor and Edward Lucie-Smith; *Neruda and Vallejo*, edited by Robert Bly; *200 Poems from the Greek Anthology*, edited by Robin Skelton; and *An Anthology of 20th Century Brazilian Poetry*, edited by Elizabeth Bishop and Emanuel Brasil.

Finally, the original manuscript of T. S. Eliot's *The Waste Land*, containing Pound's masterful editing, was published under the able editorship of the poet's widow, Valerie Eliot. Two reviews that merit attention were the spring issue of *The Seventies*, containing several important essays on poetics by Robert Bly; and the new *The American Poetry Review*, edited by Steven Berg in Philadelphia, which looks as if it might make an important contribution to poetry.

On October 10, Sir John Betjeman was named poet laureate of Great Britain. The 66-year-old author is one of Britain's most popular contemporary poets.

Paul Carroll

POLAND pursued a cautious reform policy at home and an increasingly bold foreign policy, developing new links with the non-Communist world in 1972. Industrial output increased 11 per cent over 1971; both exports and imports went up 20 per cent. But waste and inefficiency, especially in the industrial use of raw materials, continued to hamper efforts to increase productivity.

Strict price controls, combined with modestly rising monetary incomes, raised the urban wage earners' morale. On November 1, the price freeze introduced in 1971 and due to end on Jan. 1, 1973, was extended indefinitely.

Major Reforms included a local government program designed to give more power to the regions. Another would give the trade unions a greater voice in running the plants where their members work.

On both, however, the government showed signs of having second thoughts. Presumably, Russia and Poland's own conservative forces objected. The conservatives, however, lost some of their influence in parliamentary elections on March 19, when only 170 of the 460 deputies were re-elected. On April 7, General Mieczyslaw Moczar, a leading conservative, lost the presidency of Poland's powerful veterans' organization. But the presence of many conservatives in Communist Party posts continued to act as a brake on reform. Józef Cyrankiewicz was replaced as chairman of the state council by Henryk Jablonski.

Church Property Rights. In February, the Roman Catholic Church was granted full rights to church property in territories that had been held by Germany until the end of World War II in 1945. The Vatican created four new dioceses in those territories in June, thus giving its own recognition to Poland's Oder-Neisse frontier with Germany. In May, West Germany ratified the 1970 treaty in which West Germany officially recognized that frontier. This was followed by Poland's own ratification on May 26. Full diplomatic relations with West Germany were established on September 14.

President Richard M. Nixon paid a brief visit to Poland, on May 31 and June 1. During the visit, a consular agreement was signed by the two nations.

Aged Debts. On October 7, Poland agreed in principle to redeem–in part–the $41 million in bonds held by 10,000 Polish-Americans since the 1920s. The redemption would be a prelude to a further expansion of U.S.-Polish trade and industrial cooperation. A month later, the two signed agreements that could triple their trade.

In October, Communist Party leader Edward Gierek visited Paris and signed a 10-year agreement on economic cooperation. France promised to provide Poland with $300 million in credits for Polish purchases of French equipment. Chris Cviic

See also EUROPE (Facts in Brief Table).

POLLUTION. See ENVIRONMENT.

U.S. Fertility Rate

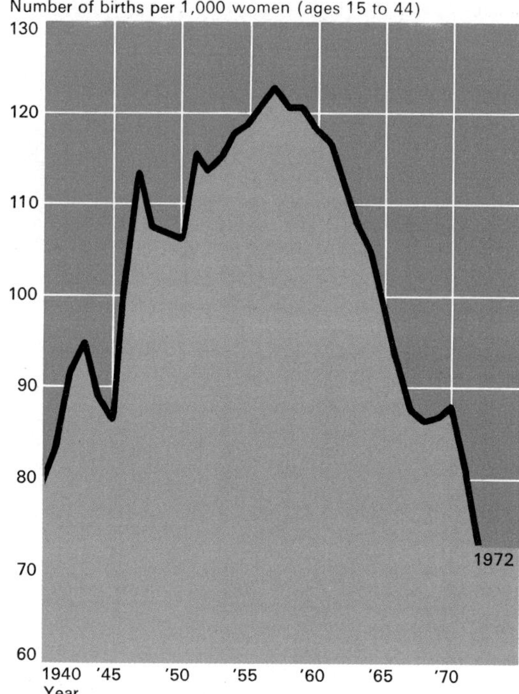

POPULATION, WORLD. United Nations (UN) estimates placed world population on Dec. 31, 1972, at about 3.8 billion, a gain of about 76 million during the year. With a total of 129 million births and 53-million deaths throughout the world in 1972, the birth rate was 34 births per 1,000 persons, and the death rate, 14. There were about 108 million births in the underdeveloped nations but only 20 million in the advanced, industrialized nations.

Chinese Population. Nearly a fifth of the human race joined the UN in late 1971 when China became a member. Chinese authorities placed China's 1972 population at between 750 million and 820 million. They estimated the annual rate of increase at about 2 per cent–a gain of between 15 million and 17 million a year.

Early in 1972, two family-planning survey teams sponsored by the Population Council and the International Planned Parenthood Federation visited China. Family planning has an urgent priority there, they reported, and China has perhaps the most comprehensive program of any nation. All forms of birth control are freely available to the Chinese public, ranging from contraceptive devices to abortion.

The U.S. government spent about $315 million on birth control in 1972. The planned parenthood organizations spent about $80 million; the UN, about $42 million. Worldwide spending on family-planning programs totaled about $500 million.

U.S. Population Control. The Commission on Population Growth and the American Future made its final report on March 27. It came out strongly for a stable population and recommended an expanded birth-control program, including making contraceptive devices, voluntary sterilization, and abortion more available. President Richard M. Nixon took issue with the commission's stand on abortion and on making contraceptives available to minors.

The U.S. birth rate declined by about 33 per cent between 1957 and 1972. Yet between 1960 and 1972, the number of women in the high-fertility age bracket (20 to 29 years) increased by nearly 5 million. This indicated a strong trend toward a stabilized population.

For the first time, the total fertility rate in the United States dropped below the "zero population growth" level of 2.1 children per woman of child-bearing age. The total fertility rate for the first nine months of 1972 was 2.08, compared to 2.39 for the same period in 1971. If this low fertility rate could be maintained for at least a generation, the U.S. population would stop growing around the year 2000.

Legal abortion expanded rapidly in the United States in 1972. Unofficial statistics from the 15 states in which abortion is performed most extensively indicated that at least 400,000 pregnancies were terminated in this manner. Robert C. Cook

See also CENSUS, U.S.

PORTUGAL changed the status of its overseas territories Angola and Mozambique from provinces to states on May 1, 1972. The only areas previously given this status were Goa, Damão, and Diu, which India annexed in 1961. The law was described as giving them greater autonomy "without affecting the unity of the nation." Under it, the states may set up legislative assemblies and advisory councils, plan their own budgets, and levy taxes. Lisbon retained the right to make treaties on their behalf.

Portuguese Walk Out. In Geneva, Switzerland, Portuguese delegates walked out of the annual conference of the International Labor Organization on June 27 after the group passed a resolution condemning Portuguese repression in Africa. Guerrillas, who have waged war in Angola, Mozambique, and Portuguese Guinea for 10 years, were offered amnesty on July 5. On July 10, the government announced that 1,500 guerrillas had been freed.

New censorship regulations went into effect on June 1. They give a commission the right to censor material before it is published during a state of emergency. A state of emergency has existed in Portugal since November, 1971.

Americo Deus Rodrigues Thomaz was re-elected to a third seven-year term as president on July 25 by a special electoral college. The action was seen as a hard-liners' victory. Thomaz was sworn into office August 9, and the next day, minor Cabinet changes were announced. Two liberal technocrats were replaced as secretaries of state for commerce and for national industry.

Some six hours before Thomaz was sworn in, bombs damaged power lines and towers in various parts of the country. About 30 per cent of Lisbon's power was affected. However, the inaugural ceremony went off on schedule.

Portugal signed an agreement on July 22 with other European Free Trade nations reducing tariffs. It was to reduce the impact when the European Community enlarged. Portugal was anxious about its tomato concentrate exports to Britain.

Industrial Expansion. Huge roadbuilding, port expansion, railroad expansion, and airport projects were planned. The greatest expansion will turn the fishing port of Sines into Portugal's biggest oil-reception and -processing center. The Setúbal area, south of Lisbon, will be the site of the new airport.

The cost of living rose 11 per cent in a year, worrying Prime Minister Marcello Caetano. Tourism receipts, increasing 16 per cent in a single year, added to disposable income and inflationary pressure. The government took stern steps against inflation in June. It gave the commerce minister authority to fix prices for a wide range of goods and services. He may also require businesses to submit price lists for other products for his approval. A new law also raised taxes on high incomes and profits. Kenneth Brown

See also EUROPE (Facts in Brief Table).

POSTAL SERVICE, U.S. Postmaster General Elmer T. Klassen announced on Aug. 28, 1972, that a planned postal-rate increase of 1 cent an ounce for first-class mail would not be needed. The increase, scheduled for 1973, would have provided an additional $450 million in revenue. A staff reduction of 37,750 workers made a rate increase unnecessary.

The staff reduction, which began on April 1, was accomplished by not replacing postal workers who quit or retired. Klassen hoped to get through 1973 without a postage increase. However, the Postal Service faces labor negotiations in 1973 with the four major postal unions. This could force higher rates if wages went up substantially.

Many Problems remained to be overcome by the quasi-public corporation, which completed its first year of operation on June 30. Some congressmen, dissatisfied with Postal Service performance, talked about giving it until mid-1973 to begin functioning properly.

Klassen, former president of the American Can Company, took over as postmaster general on January 1. He attempted to make the service run like a large corporation, but conceded that mail service deteriorated after he imposed the freeze on new hiring. "You cannot take an organization that has been living in a political environment and turn it around overnight," he said. The Postal Service, he added, was "passing through a period of necessary – if sometimes uncomfortable – adjustment." He said the service was still overstaffed and was also suffering from poor working conditions.

The old Post Office Department had a $2.2-billion deficit in its last year, fiscal 1971. The new Postal Service was given a congressional subsidy of $1.4 billion in fiscal 1972, but still suffered a net loss of $161.4 million.

Another worry for Postal Service officials was increasing competition from private mail-delivery systems. Some public utilities began hand-delivering monthly bills to save postage. Faced with huge rate increases, second- and third-class mailers were also trying to find new methods of delivery.

Parcel post also ran into trouble. The United Parcel Service handled as many packages as the Postal Service. "Before," said Klassen, "we handled twice as many as they did."

Some Improvements. Klassen reported that the Postal Service delivered 95 per cent of all local mail on a next-day basis. He planned to spend $6 billion during the next five years to improve machinery and facilities. A new system was introduced to speed up handling of special-delivery mail, which is now put in a plastic "speedy bag" to keep it from getting lost in the mainstream of the regular mail.

The Postal Service handled 87.2 billion pieces of mail in fiscal 1972 compared with 87 billion in fiscal 1971. It employed 706,000 persons and operated about 32,000 post offices. William McGaffin

POTTER, PHILIP ALFORD (1921-   ), was elected general secretary of the World Council of Churches on Aug. 16, 1972. He succeeded Eugene Carson Blake, who retired after serving six years.

Potter was born on the British West Indies island of Dominica on Aug. 19, 1921, the son of a Roman Catholic father and a Protestant mother. He was baptized a Protestant and given the name of a Catholic bishop. These circumstances, he later said, started his lifetime "passion for Christian unity, which has also become blended with a passion for the unity of mankind."

Extensive work in Christian youth movements, including four years with the World Council of Churches' youth division, and four years as a Methodist pastor in Haiti, have highlighted Potter's career as a churchman. Theologians Karl Barth, Reinhold and H. Richard Niebuhr, and Paul Tillich have profoundly influenced Potter's thinking. "My theology is Biblical, not systematic or dogmatic. I have faith in Christ who was born son of man while being Son of God, which makes that faith historical. I have a sense of belonging to all men beyond race and class."

Potter met his wife, the former Doreen Cousins, while he was studying to become a Methodist pastor at Canewood Theological College in Kingston, Jamaica. Mrs. Potter is the daughter of a Jamaican Methodist pastor. They now live in Geneva, Switzerland.

Foster Stockwell

POVERTY in underdeveloped countries continued to increase in 1972, despite production and income gains. A report presented by the International Bank for Reconstruction and Development (World Bank) at its annual joint meeting with the International Monetary Fund in Washington, D.C., in September, stated that despite billions of dollars in foreign aid and impressive economic growth, "the world's burden of poverty is increasing . . . ." The report listed rapidly growing population, extremely high unemployment, illiteracy, and inadequate health care as poverty-causing factors.

The wide variety of projects supported by the 117-nation World Bank, a specialized agency of the United Nations, reflected a shift in emphasis to the "poorest countries in the world" and the "poorest people" in those countries. In addition, there was increasing interest in helping member countries find ways to eliminate poverty.

In the United States, a leading citizens' group investigating malnutrition found that half the nation's poor were still going hungry, even though large gains have been made since its first study, "Hunger, U.S.A.," in April, 1968. An analysis completed in October, 1972, for the Citizens' Board of Inquiry into Hunger and Malnutrition showed that there are still major gaps in most federal programs. The report showed that 11.8 million persons were participating in the program, and 3 million others received food parcels instead of food stamps. That leaves some 11 million of the nation's 26 million poor people who are not being reached by federal programs. Furthermore, only about 8.4 million of about 10 million needy children were being served. Children in 18,000 schools without kitchen equipment could not participate. The citizens' board recommended that the poor receive cash assistance in place of food and stamps and that the federal government provide free lunches for all children, not merely for needy children.

Specifically, the report found that between 2.3 and 4.8 million children eligible to receive free school breakfasts do not participate in the free-breakfast programs and that only 49 per cent of the approximately 26 million who are eligible to receive food stamps are getting them. The report concluded that federal food programs "have failed to bring about an end to hunger and malnutrition in the United States and should be abandoned in favor of cash assistance to the poor."

Meanwhile, the "workfare" program that Congress approved in 1971 went into effect on July 1. This program requires about 1.5 million welfare recipients to register for work or for job training. In the first year of the program, the Department of Labor hoped to provide jobs or training for 200,000 persons receiving help under the aid to families with dependent children program.

Reducing America's Poor: A Faltering Crusade

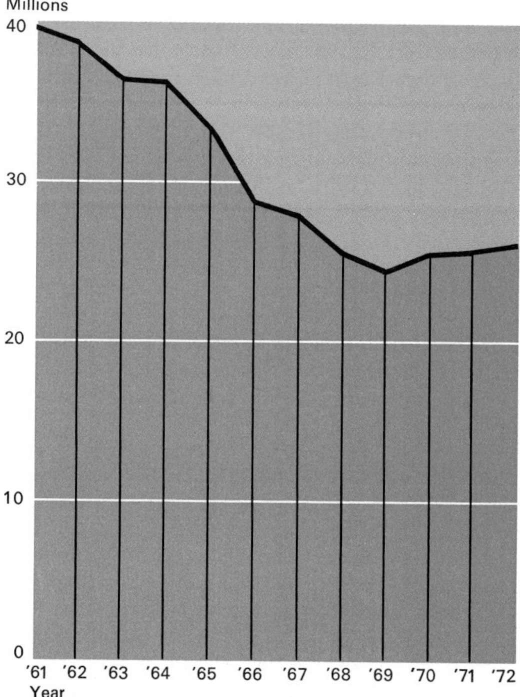

Source: U.S. Census Bureau

Action, created in 1971 to consolidate government voluntary-action programs, observed its first anniversary in July. During its first year, the Peace Corps, now an agency of Action, faced a severe financial crisis, and there was concern about the impact that the economy measures would have on programs and relations with host countries. By the end of the fiscal year, however, congressional support for 1973 was assured, and the planned "New Directions" for the Peace Corps became a reality.

The New Directions were evident. Host country citizens on Peace Corps staffs went up from 163 in 1971 to 315 in 1972. Multinational volunteer programs were developed that included more than 400 volunteers in 26 countries. More minority-group volunteers and staff members were added; one-third of the country directors now are members of minority groups. The Peace Corps now provides training in 56 languages and dialects – the most in history – and has programs that call upon more than 200 skills.

Cooperation among the agencies that make up Action – Peace Corps, Volunteers in Service to America (VISTA), Foster Grandparents, Retired Senior Volunteer Program (RSVP), Service Corps of Retired Executives (SCORE), and Active Corps of Executives (ACE) – benefited all Action programs. Applicants with skills not needed in one program have been referred to others.

University Year for Action (UYA) was created by Action in July as a new model of volunteer service. UYA students spend a full year working full time on poverty problems while their universities provide an academic program outside the classroom to support their volunteer work. They receive a full year of college credit. To be eligible, volunteers must be regularly enrolled graduate or undergraduate students at one of 30 participating universities.

The Office of Economic Opportunity (OEO) created a new Office of Economic Development, and made organizational changes to strengthen the agency's research and development efforts. Programs and staff previously under the Office of Program Development are now assigned to the new office, to the existing Office of Planning, Research, and Evaluation, and to the Office of Operations.

The Office of Health Affairs is being reorganized to place added emphasis on research and development and to enlarge the agency's capabilities. The new office will administer 40 economic development programs and plans to design a development loan-fund program to provide capital for high-risk ventures in rural and urban areas.

The reorganized office will devote most of its time to research, development, and evaluation programs. It will continue the transfer of proven operating programs to established federal agencies, such as the Department of Health, Education, and Welfare.

These changes were made to provide a sharper and more effective focus on President Richard M. Nixon's directive that the OEO serve as the federal government's research and development arm in dealing with the problems of poverty.

Partnership Project. The U.S. Junior Chambers of Commerce (Jaycees) and the OEO agreed to create an "action-oriented" partnership to help the nation's poor under a $275,000 OEO grant. During the year ending on June 30, 1973, 10 target cities will be selected to receive "major emphasis grants" and 80 or 90 others to receive smaller grants. Jaycee chapters in these areas will then receive grants with which they are to develop partnerships for the poor with local Community Action Agencies (CAA). Through such partnerships, the CAA's hope to make Jaycees services available to the poor.

Indian Scholarship Program. The OEO continued its strong commitment to help Indian communities obtain qualified professional leadership, attorneys, and administrators, and to help Indians prepare for policy-making administrative positions so they can control their own development programs. The latest step was a $325,000 grant from the OEO to the National Congress of American Indians. The grant, made in February, provides financial assistance to college graduates for graduate study.

Activities under the first year of the grant included active recruitment from tribes, other Indian organizations, and currently enrolled students; and coordination with colleges and universities to obtain maximum financial assistance for students.

Neighborhood Health Centers. A study completed in 1972 reported that about 75 per cent of all center users received preventive, not just crisis-oriented, health care and that users of the Neighborhood Health Centers generally were "highly satisfied" with the care they received.

The study judged 11 centers to be most successful. These centers tended to share certain common factors: Their communities were more involved in the center's activities; they put greater emphasis on sending health care teams into all parts of the service area to call on patients; they served relatively smaller numbers of people; and they spent relatively more money per patient. The more successful centers each served an average of 12,000 patients, while the other 10 centers each provided health care to an average of 23,000 persons.

Harvard Study. A controversial three-year study by a Harvard University research team headed by Christopher Jencks was published in October. It challenged a widely held belief of education reformers that there is a strong link between better schooling and future income for children of the poor. Rather, such efforts to provide better schooling for poor children have "surprisingly little effect" on their prospects for economic success as adults. Such intangibles as luck and personality, more than the development of cognitive skills, play a greater role, the report said.

Joseph P. Anderson

PRESIDENT OF THE UNITED STATES

President Richard Milhous Nixon proved himself to be a careful, far-sighted diplomat and a consummate politician in 1972. The major accomplishments of his fourth year in office were reconciliation with the People's Republic of China and a major arms agreement with Russia. But the biggest triumph by far was his landslide victory in the 1972 presidential election. Campaigning coolly from the White House on his record in foreign policy and his winding down of the Vietnam War, with muted appeals to middle-class Americans, President Nixon received support from Democrats as well as Republicans and won 60.7 per cent of the popular vote–without once referring to his opponent by name.

Campaign and Re-Election. The President was unanimously renominated by the Republican National Convention on August 22 in Miami Beach, Fla. His Democratic opponent was South Dakota Senator George S. McGovern.

President Richard M. Nixon, accompanied by Premier Chou En-lai, reviews Chinese troops after his arrival in Peking on February 21.

In the course of his campaign, the President strongly supported locally controlled schools and opposed the busing of schoolchildren to achieve racial balance. He spoke out against abortion, legalization of marijuana, welfare for those who refused to work, and amnesty for those who refused to fight in Vietnam.

But he maintained a very low profile throughout the campaign and rarely appeared on television. He made several paid political speeches on radio, but generally avoided the campaign trail. Mr. Nixon chose, instead, to stay at his desk in the White House, projecting an aloof and dignified image of a nonpartisan President who was above the demands of party politics. When the votes were counted on November 7, President Nixon had carried 49 states and received 47,168,963 votes. See ELECTIONS; REPUBLICAN PARTY; Section One, FOCUS ON THE NATION.

A Second Term. As he prepared for his second term in office, the President still faced a Democratic-controlled Congress, a growing federal budget deficit, continuing inflation and unemployment, and pressure to end all U.S. military involvement in Indochina. On November 9, the *Washington Star-News* printed an interview that the President had granted before the November 7 election. In the interview, Mr. Nixon promised that during his second term he would put an end to "the whole era of permissiveness" and stimulate "a new feeling of self-discipline" for Americans. "The average American," the President said, "is just like the child in the family" and should not be pampered too much. Mr. Nixon promised that there would be no tax increase and pledged to reduce the budget by trimming down the social programs instituted during the 1960s.

On November 8, the President announced that he planned a "significant" realignment of the executive branch. All members of the Cabinet, the White House staff, and other top-level members of the executive branch – totaling about 2,000 persons – were told to submit resignations, leaving the President free to streamline his staff. In late November, he began announcing changes.

Relations with Congress. The President clashed with the Democratic-controlled second session of the 92nd Congress in 1972, just as he had clashed with the first session. Of the 318 measures proposed by the President, the second session passed only 141. The Senate tried to challenge the President's conduct of the war, but was unsuccessful because of majority support for the President's policies in the House.

The mounting federal budget deficit triggered an open conflict between the President and the Senate. The President had asked Congress to allow him to limit federal spending in fiscal 1973 to $250 billion, regardless of appropriations already approved by Congress. The Senate refused to surrender this much financial control. The President then termed the Congress "spendthrift" and labeled its appropriations as "budget breaching." In the final days of the session, the President vetoed 9 bills. After Congress adjourned on October 18, he pocket-vetoed 11 more. One bill, a $24.6-billion appropriation to fight water pollution, was passed by Congress on October 18, over the President's veto.

The 92nd Congress did not act on the President's proposals for welfare reform and executive reorganization. However, it passed his revenue-sharing legislation. See City; State Government.

President Nixon repeatedly declared that he favored local control of schools and opposed the busing of schoolchildren to achieve racial balance. He made a nationally televised speech about busing on March 16, after Alabama's Governor George C. Wallace had won the Florida Democratic presidential primary by taking a strong stand against busing. President Nixon repeated his opposition to busing and asked the nation to press for congressional action forbidding court-ordered busing to achieve racial balance. On March 17, he asked Congress to declare a moratorium on busing – which it did – and requested legislation that would place permanent restraints on

President and Mrs. Nixon and Secretary of State William P. Rogers pause for the view—and for photographers—while touring the Great Wall of China.

the courts and the executive branch of the government to prevent further court-ordered busing. This Congress refused to pass. See CIVIL RIGHTS; CONGRESS OF THE UNITED STATES; EDUCATION.

Fiscal and Economic Problems. Mr. Nixon proposed a $246.3-billion budget with an estimated deficit of $25.5 billion for fiscal 1973. This was the second largest peacetime deficit in U.S. history, surpassed only by the estimated $38.8 billion for fiscal 1972.

Phase 2 of the President's economic stabilization plan, which began in November, 1971, continued through 1972, and the inflation rate slowed slightly. On January 27, the President announced that controls would remain in effect "until reasonable price stability can be maintained without controls." On March 22 and 23, four labor leaders resigned from the Pay Board to protest the board's decision on wage freezes. President Nixon subsequently reorganized the board into a seven-member public group. It had previously consisted of 15 members, representing business, labor, and the public. See ECONOMY, THE.

In April, President Nixon declared his support for government aid to the nation's private and parochial schools. But measures to set up tax credits for private-school tuitions did not pass in the Congress.

War in Indochina. President Nixon wound down the U.S. ground-combat phase of the war in Vietnam. When he took office in 1969, there were 500,000 Americans serving in Vietnam. Since then, the President had phased U.S. troops out of the war zones, and, on August 29, presidential press secretary Ronald L. Ziegler announced that by December 1, U.S. strength in Vietnam would be down to 27,000.

On June 28, the President announced that no new draftees would be sent to Vietnam unless they volunteered to serve there. He predicted that by July, 1973, an all-volunteer army would replace the present draft system, ending peacetime conscription.

As U.S. troops withdrew, the North Vietnamese opened a new offensive in March. The United States subsequently intensified the air war against North Vietnam. Air attacks on Hanoi and Haiphong harbor and other formerly off-limits targets began on April 16. On May 8, President Nixon announced that he had ordered the mining of North Vietnamese ports and the bombing of rail lines in North Vietnam to "keep the weapons of war out of the hands of the international outlaws" in Hanoi. On May 15, the Department of Defense revealed that the United States had also mined the rivers and waterways of North Vietnam. See ASIA; VIETNAM.

Negotiations for peace went forward despite these offensives and counteroffensives. On January 25, President Nixon told the American people that secret negotiations with North Vietnam had been underway for more than two years.

On October 26, the North Vietnamese announced that an agreement had been reached to end the hostilities. The tentative agreement was confirmed by Henry A. Kissinger, the President's adviser on national security affairs. Although the agreement was not signed on October 31 – as the North Vietnamese claimed had been promised – Kissinger reassured the American people that peace was at hand. Complex problems arose, however, bringing negotiations to a halt and it was not until late December that the President announced new talks would be resumed in Paris on Jan. 8, 1973.

To China and Russia. On February 17, President Nixon left Washington, D.C., for his historic visit to China, opening a new era of cooperation between Americans and Chinese. In Peking, the President talked briefly with Communist Party Chairman Mao Tse-tung and held about 12 hours of conferences with Premier Chou En-lai.

On February 27, the President and Premier Chou issued an 1,800-word communiqué promising a gradual increase in Sino-American contacts, but also acknowledging the real differences that divide the two giant powers. The President returned to Washington on February 28, after visiting Hangchow and Shanghai. See CHINA, PEOPLE'S REPUBLIC OF.

The President then concentrated on his May visit to Moscow, which was a masterpiece of diplomatic planning. More than a half-dozen treaties were signed while the President was in Moscow, all of them carefully prepared and ready for signature before his arrival. Not even the mining of North Vietnamese harbors, with the consequent threat to Russian shipping, interrupted the plans for the President's visit.

On May 23, the President and Chairman Nikolai V. Podgorny signed an agreement providing for joint cooperation in protecting the environment. On May 24, President Nixon and Premier Aleksei N. Kosygin signed an agreement providing for cooperation in outer space. On May 26, the President and Communist Party leader Leonid I. Brezhnev signed the Strategic Arms Limitation Talks agreements, banning or limiting nuclear arms (see ARMED FORCES OF THE WORLD). The other agreements signed provided for cooperation in health, scientific cooperation, and measures to prevent unintentional confrontations between military ships at sea. On May 26, the President and Russian leaders announced the establishment of a U.S.-Russian trade commission.

President Nixon visited Leningrad the next day, and on May 28, he addressed the Russian people on television.

The summit talks ended on May 29, and after a visit to Kiev, the President went on to Iran on May 30. President Nixon then stopped in Warsaw on May 31 to confer with Communist Party leader Edward Gierek and returned to Washington, D.C., on June 1.

The President went from the airport to a dramatic, specially convened joint evening session of Congress. He received a standing ovation as he described his tour and urged Congress to ratify the arms accords that he had signed in Moscow.

Presidium Chairman Nikolai V. Podgorny and a Russian honor guard greet President Nixon in Moscow as he begins his visit on May 22.

Other Foreign Policy Matters. The President conferred with Japanese Premier Eisaku Sato in January at the Western White House in San Clemente, Calif. He met with Turkish Prime Minister Nihat Erim on March 21 and with Jordan's King Hussein I on March 28 in Washington. He conferred with Prime Minister Pierre Elliott Trudeau on a state visit to Canada on April 14 and, on April 15, signed a joint agreement to counter pollution in the Great Lakes (see CANADA). The President sent former Secretary of the Treasury John B. Connally on a 15-nation tour in June, and he conferred with Mexican President Luis Echeverría Alvárez in Washington, D.C., on June 15 and 16.

He met Japan's new prime minister, Kakuei Tanaka, in Hawaii on August 31. He and Tanaka announced that Japan would buy $1.1 billion worth of U.S. goods over a two-year period to reduce the estimated $3.8-billion trade imbalance that existed between the two nations in 1972. Mr. Nixon addressed the annual meeting of the International Monetary Fund and World Bank in Washington on September 25, and declared that the United States would be "in the forefront of efforts to reform the international monetary system."

Appointments. On January 27, the President named Peter G. Peterson as secretary of commerce, replacing Maurice H. Stans (see PETERSON, PETER G.). Stans became chief fund-raiser for the Republican Party. On May 16, President Nixon named George P. Shultz as secretary of the treasury, succeeding John B. Connally, who returned to private life (see SHULTZ, GEORGE P.). His most controversial appointment was that of Richard G. Kleindienst to succeed John N. Mitchell as attorney general on February 15. Kleindienst finally won Senate approval on June 8 (see KLEINDIENST, RICHARD G.).

On May 3, the President appointed L. Patrick Gray III as acting director of the Federal Bureau of Investigation. Gray succeeded J. Edgar Hoover, who died on May 2 (see GRAY, L. PATRICK III). President Nixon named General Creighton W. Abrams as the new Army chief of staff on June 20. In late November and early December, Mr. Nixon announced the names of new Cabinet members he would submit to the Senate for confirmation when it reconvened in January, 1973: Elliot L. Richardson would become secretary of defense; Caspar W. Weinberger, secretary of health, education, and welfare; Peter J. Brennan, secretary of labor; Frederick B. Dent, secretary of commerce; Claude S. Brinegar, secretary of transportation; and James T. Lynn, secretary of housing and urban development. See CABINET, U.S.

Carol L. Thompson

PRINCE EDWARD ISLAND. See CANADA.

PRISON. See CRIME.

PRIZES. See AWARDS AND PRIZES; NOBEL PRIZES; PULITZER PRIZES.

PROTESTANT. Membership in the Protestant churches of the United States continued to decline slightly in 1972, while financial gifts grew. The increase in giving did not match the nation's 5 per cent inflation rise, however. The moderate decline in membership resulted in some clergy oversupply. Whereas many churches during the early 1960s had projected clerical shortages, they had not foreseen the decline in the birth rate and the dropping off in church attendance. Because of these factors and budgetary problems caused by inflation, fewer parishes could provide pulpits. Thus the Episcopal Church had an influx of 2,647 priests in 10 years, but it lost 588 congregations. The United Church of Christ had an oversupply of 500 for its 5,500 pulpits.

The situation varied somewhat from denomination to denomination, but there were reasons for seminaries to cut back on their enrollments so they did not add to the oversupply. Many argued that churches should encourage "tent-making" ministries patterned after that of St. Paul, who took "secular" employment to make his living.

Protestant evangelicals spent much of the year preparing for a major campaign, Key 73, which is designed to bring new converts into the churches. Protestants were divided over the campaign. More liberal churchmen did not like the assumptions of the conversion-minded and near-fundamentalist leadership, while moderates and moderate liberals generally linked up with the conservative majority. The presence of churchmen across this spectrum led some extreme fundamentalists to repudiate the common Christian effort.

Social Issues. There was not as much attention in 1972 to dramatic social ethical issues such as the Vietnam War and the racial struggles. However, the matter of amnesty for draft exiles in Canada, Sweden, and elsewhere drew the attention of church leaders and conventions. In general, the mainline denominational spokesmen and representatives were more ready than the polled majorities of other Americans to return these exiles en masse, perhaps without penalty or alternative service.

Church investments also concerned denominational leaders. Some churches had invested in corporations that do business with the racist regime in South Africa or are large-scale weapons manufacturers. Some churches began to move their investments to other firms, and some sent representatives – without much effect on policy – to annual meetings of stockholders.

Ecumenism Changing. The troubled World Council of Churches, the most extensive of modern ecumenical organizations, found new leadership during the year. Eugene Carson Blake, general secretary since 1967, retired. The Council in recent years was internally torn over the degree of commitments it could or should express toward underdeveloped countries and nonwhite forces. The selection of the new head symbolized the direction in which the organization would go. Philip Alford Potter, a black West Indian from the island of Dominica, was chosen. He was strongly in favor of church involvement in social issues (see POTTER, PHILIP ALFORD). The National Council of Churches, the U.S. parallel to the World Council, also chose a black leader. On December 7, W. Sterling Cary of New York City was elected president.

To advocates of a large-scale Protestant union, the most devastating news of the year came in May, when the United Presbyterian Church voted to withdraw from the Consultation on Church Union (COCU). Ironically, COCU had been initiated by Eugene Carson Blake at the time he headed this Presbyterian body. Much of the formal opposition to COCU came from theological conservatives who opposed what they believed to be liberalizing trends in both the doctrinal attitudes and social positions of the leaders of COCU.

Members in other denominations, notably the Episcopal and United Methodist churches, also indicated discontent. And the three black Methodist denominations in COCU expressed more interest in black identity than in a generalized form of Protestant unity. The ecumenical spirit was by no means dead, but the movement had come upon hard times.

In a most unusual move, the president of the 2.8-million-member Lutheran Church – Missouri Synod, J. A. O. Preus, accused the majority in the Concordia Seminary in St. Louis of deviating from the synod's historic position on Scriptural interpretation. Representing the conservative half of the deeply divided denomination, he charged that the seminary, under the leadership of John W. Tietjen, was liberal and employed destructive methods of interpreting Scripture. The issue was expected to play a prominent role when Preus comes up for re-election at the synod's convention in New Orleans in 1973.

The Jesus Movement. Protestantism's most publicized new form was the Jesus Movement, a name given to a wide range of responses to Christian concepts. The most-publicized version of the Jesus Movement's activities was Youth Explo '72, which attracted about 80,000 young people to Dallas' Cotton Bowl in June. To some, it seemed to be a superorganized rock festival with religious themes. To others, it was an expression of the spiritual yearnings and satisfactions of American youth. Evangelist Billy Graham graced numerous sessions. Bill Bright, leader of Campus Crusade for Christ International, was in charge, and he attracted a number of athletes and celebrities to the event. The adult community in Dallas reportedly found Youth Explo '72 a peaceful alternative to youthful protest movements.

One wing of the Jesus Movement, the Children of God, received disproportionate publicity because of its extremist character. This group asked members to "forsake all," including their families, "for the sake of the experience of God." It formed 60 communes that attracted 2,000 members. Some parents' groups began legal action against the Children of God, claiming that it had virtually seduced, hypnotized, and brainwashed their children. Some members of the sect came to it from the drug culture and were hardly representative of the movement as a whole.

The Media. Religious publishing continued to experience hard times. One or two evangelical organs prospered but most denominational and independent periodicals suffered. Despite the difficulties, there were some new enterprises. At the beginning of the year, *Worldview* was born under the auspices of the Council on Religion and International Affairs. *A.D., 1972*, a rather lavish periodical that serves both the Presbyterian Church in the United States of America and the United Church of Christ made an auspicious debut in the autumn.

A cinematic sensation of sorts was *Marjoe*, a film about the career of Marjoe Gortner, who for years had been a child-evangelist and then an effective adolescent fundamentalist preacher. Many evangelists complained that the film gave a distorted picture, because Marjoe had left the faith to seek a career in show business. In the film, he shows how he was exploited by his evangelist parents and how he and they took advantage of audiences for commercial purposes. The ethics of the film makers were also criticized, because revivalist audiences shown in the movie were not told of the change in Marjoe's way, or of the fact that he was putting on acts in filmed rallies.

World Protestantism. In Eastern Europe, Protestants continued to face difficulties, and, in Russia, where President Richard M. Nixon attended a Baptist worship service in Moscow in May, Baptists were suffering much the same as Russian Jews. Many Baptists have been jailed, and their denomination is divided over how to react toward the government. The division is over the matter of teaching Christianity to the young, one faction going along with the state's ban on religious education for the young, and the other resisting it.

In Scandinavia, the historic church-state ties were under review. For over 400 years, Lutheranism has been a state-supported church. However, there were moves toward disestablishment in Norway, Sweden, Denmark, and Finland, partly at the instigation of the churches themselves. Most people favored phasing out state support gradually over 10 or 20 years.

An ecumenical setback occurred in England when the Church of England rejected a plan for reunion with the Methodist churches that had been under discussion for more than 16 years. Only 65 per cent of the Church of England's General Synod approved the venture, whereas a 75 per cent majority was required. Chiefly at issue was the matter of the credentials of ministers and bishops. Martin E. Marty

See also Section Two, ECUMENISM IN THE '70s.

Studies by psychiatrist Ronald Fieve of Columbia University show that an inherited chromosome imbalance may sometimes cause manic depression.

PSYCHOLOGY. Extensive experiments were conducted in 1972 on the use of biofeedback to control involuntary functions of the mind and body. A research team at Harvard Medical School in Boston successfully used this learning technique to teach people how to regulate their own heartbeat and blood pressure. Psychologists David Shapiro and Gary Schwartz connected a cardiotachometer, an instrument that counts heartbeats, to a visual display board so that a light flashed every time the rate of the patient's heartbeat changed. They also used rewards. For example, in training a patient to decrease his heart rate, they gave him a reward whenever the light flashed indicating a slow rate. In this case, the reward was the knowledge that his heart rate was actually decreasing. However, the reward might be money or, in the case of training animals, food. Essential to the use of biofeedback techniques was the development of sensitive recording devices, electronic filters, special-purpose computers, and logic circuitry so that information regarding the biological function could be relayed quickly to the patient.

The list of physiological responses that individuals can learn to control at will is extensive. It includes the electric potential of the skin (a response used by "lie detectors"); speeding, slowing, or stabilizing the heart rate; increasing or decreasing blood pressure, brain-wave activity, or skin temperature; dilating and constricting blood vessels; muscle potentials; and salivation. Although the main focus of clinical interest has been on psychosomatic disorders, current studies are evaluating the usefulness of biofeedback in treating essential hypertension, cardiac irregularities, tension headaches, and circulatory disorders.

Aggression. Among most vertebrates, and particularly among mammals, males tend to be more aggressive than females. And the aggressive drive is activated in most mammals by the male hormones (androgens), while the female hormones (estrogens) either do not augment aggressiveness or may actively inhibit it. The golden hamster is different. The female of this species is larger and more aggressive than the male, except when directly stimulated by estrogens. Lenore Tiefer, a behavioral psychologist at Colorado State University, Fort Collins, says the female's larger body gives it a decisive advantage in fights with males, so males will not often start fights or fight back when attacked.

Two other investigators, A. P. Payne and Heidi Swanson at the University of Birmingham in England, have challenged this simple interpretation. According to their research, aggression in the male hamster can be increased if the testes are replaced by transplanted ovaries. They suggest that the hormone responsible for the increased aggression in hamsters is not estrogen, but progesterone. Robert W. Goy

PUBLISHING. See LITERATURE; MAGAZINES; NEWSPAPERS.

PUERTO RICO. The Popular Democratic Party (PDP) swept its candidate, 36-year-old Rafael Hernández Colón, to an upset victory in elections held on Nov. 7, 1972. Hernández Colón ousted Governor Luis A. Ferré of the New Progressive Party, and the Popular Democrats also won control of both houses of the legislature and 72 of the island's 78 municipalities. Jaime Benitez, the PDP's candidate for resident commissioner – a nonvoting seat in the U.S. House of Representatives – won over incumbent Jorge Luis Córdova Diaz. The elections were generally interpreted as reaffirmation of Puerto Rico's desire for commonwealth status rather than statehood or independence.

On September 14, President Richard M. Nixon nominated Puerto Rico's Secretary of Labor Julia Rivera de Vincenti as one of the 10 U.S. representatives at the 27th General Assembly of the United Nations (UN). She became the first Puerto Rican to serve on a General Assembly delegation.

The Rivera appointment came less than three weeks after the UN Committee on Colonialism had voted 12 to 0, with 10 abstentions, to study the political status of Puerto Rico in 1973. However, Governor Ferré rejected the UN decision as "undue interference in Puerto Rico's internal affairs." He said he would refuse to cooperate with any UN committee looking into the status of Puerto Rico. Paul C. Tullier

See also LATIN AMERICA (Facts in Brief Table).

PULITZER PRIZES in journalism, letters, and music were announced in New York City on May 1, 1972. The following awards were made:

Journalism

Public Service. A gold medal to *The New York Times* for publishing the controversial "Pentagon Papers," documents indicating how the United States became involved in the Vietnam War. The *Times* published them in June and July, 1971. The Supreme Court of the United States upheld the newspaper's right to publish them despite the attorney general's injunction efforts. It was the 38th Pulitzer Prize for the *Times*, which was cited for telling the people about how the government operates and for defending the people's right to know.

General Local Reporting. $1,000 to Richard I. Cooper, 25, and John W. Machacek, 32, of *The Rochester* (N.Y.) *Times-Union* for their coverage of the Attica prison riot on Sept. 13, 1971. They disclosed that the hostages had been killed by police bullets, not prisoners' knives. Cooper, a police reporter, received a B.A. degree in journalism from Michigan State University in 1969. Machacek covers city education for the newspaper and graduated from Marquette University in 1962.

Special Local Reporting. $1,000 to Ann DeSantis, Stephen A. Kurkjian, Timothy Leland, and Gerard M. O'Neill of *The Boston Globe* for investigative reporting that exposed widespread civic corruption in Somerville, Mass. DeSantis, 25, did graduate work at Harvard University before she became research assistant for the *Globe*'s Spotlight Team of investigative reporters. Kurkjian, 28, has a law degree from Suffolk University law school in Boston. Leland, 34, is assistant managing editor of *The Morning Globe* and founded the Spotlight Team in 1970. He graduated from Columbia University graduate school of journalism in 1961. O'Neill, 29, is a graduate of Boston University school of journalism.

National Reporting. $1,000 to Jack Anderson, the syndicated columnist, for disclosing policies of the Nixon Administration during the India-Pakistan War. He said that President Richard M. Nixon favored the Pakistani when the Indian Army was fighting for the independence of Bangladesh, a new nation in what had been East Pakistan. Anderson is a former Mormon missionary. He took over "The Washington Merry-Go-Round" column after Drew Pearson, its founder, died in 1969. See ANDERSON, JACK.

International Reporting. $1,000 to Peter R. Kann, 29, of *The Wall Street Journal* for his coverage of the India-Pakistan War, including forecasts, combat reporting, and a diary. He began covering the Vietnam War for the *Journal* in July, 1967, and in November, 1968, became its Asian correspondent, based in Hong Kong.

Editorial Writing. $1,000 to John Strohmeyer of *The Bethlehem* (Pa.) *Globe-Times* for an editorial campaign dealing with racial tensions in a situation of hostility encountered by Puerto Ricans and of police brutality. He attended the Columbia University journalism school, where he won a Pulitzer scholarship, and is a former Nieman fellow at Harvard University.

Editorial Cartooning. $1,000 to Jeffrey K. MacNelly, 24, of *The Richmond* (Va.) *News Leader* for a portfolio of cartoons during the year. Born in New York City, he attended the University of North Carolina and has been cartooning since college days.

Spot News Photography. $1,000 to Horst Faas and Michel Laurent of the Associated Press (AP) for "Death in Dacca," their series of photographs showing Bangladesh vengeance against the Pakistani. Faas, 39, also won a Pulitzer Prize in 1965. He joined the AP in Berlin in 1956, covered the Cold War in Germany, and the war in the Congo, and went to Vietnam in 1962. He is now assigned to Singapore. Laurent, 25, was in Czechoslovakia in 1968 when the Russians marched in, and got exclusive pictures in Dacca when Pakistani troops moved newsmen out.

Feature Photography. $1,000 to Dave Kennerly, 25, of United Press International (UPI) for photographs showing the loneliness and desolation of the Vietnam War. He asked for the Vietnam assignment after working as UPI White House photographer. He has seven years of professional experience.

Commentary. $1,000 to Mike Royko of *The Chicago Daily News* for a Monday-through-Friday column he has been writing since 1959. He was born in

A U.S. soldier moves through devastated countryside in one of the feature photographs of the Vietnam War that won David Kennerly a Pulitzer Prize.

Chicago on Sept. 19, 1932, and attended Wright Junior College in 1951 and 1952. After serving in the Air Force, he returned to Chicago to work as a reporter for the Lerner Neighborhood Newspapers and the Chicago City News Bureau before joining the *Daily News*. His 1971 book *Boss: Richard J. Daley of Chicago* received national attention.

Criticism. $1,000 to Frank L. Peters, Jr., 41, music critic of *The St. Louis Post-Dispatch* since 1967. He was born in Springfield, Mo., and was managing editor of the *Rome Daily American* in Italy before joining the *Post-Dispatch* in 1964.

Letters

Biography. $1,000 to Joseph P. Lash, 63, for *Eleanor and Franklin*, a study of the public and private relationship of President and Mrs. Franklin D. Roosevelt. The book also won a National Book Award and the Francis Parkman Prize of the Society of Historians. Born in New York City in 1909, Lash earned a master's degree from Columbia University in 1932. He was befriended by Mrs. Roosevelt during the 1930s, when he was active in Socialist politics.

Fiction. $1,000 to Wallace E. Stegner, 63, for *Angle of Repose*. Stegner has been professor of literature and creative writing and taught at the universities of Iowa, Utah, Wisconsin, Harvard, and Stanford. In 1972, he retired as director of the writing program at Stanford. He has written several novels set in the American West.

General Nonfiction. $1,000 to Barbara W. Tuchman, 60, for *Stilwell and the American Experience in China, 1911-1945*. It was a Book-of-the-Month Club selection. She graduated from Radcliffe College in 1933 and has written numerous books of history, including *The Guns of August*, which won a Pulitzer Prize for nonfiction in 1963. She has also written many magazine articles and book reviews.

History. $1,000 to Carl N. Degler, 51, for *Neither Black Nor White*, which deals with the question of slavery in Brazil and the United States. Degler was born in Orange, N.J., and earned a Ph.D. degree from Columbia University in 1952. He teaches at Stanford University. The author of *Affluence and Anxiety* (1968), he has been a member of the board of directors of the National Organization for Women since 1966.

Poetry. $1,000 to James Wright, 44, professor of English at Hunter College in New York City, for *Collected Poems*. He was born in Martins Ferry, Ohio, the son of a factory worker. In 1959, he received a Ph.D. degree from the University of Washington. His poems identify with the poor and the outcast.

Music. $1,000 to Jacob Druckman, 44, a member of the faculty of the Juilliard School of Music in New York City, for *Windows*, an orchestral piece. He is considered one of the leading American composers, and his music has been used by ballet companies, including the City Center Joffrey Ballet. Lillian Zahrt

QATAR. Sheik Ahmed bin Ali al-Thani, was deposed on Feb. 22, 1972, in a bloodless coup by his cousin and prime minister, Sheik Khalifa bin Hamad Al-Thani. Sheik Ahmed had held the throne since his father abdicated in 1960. Critics charged the sheik was not interested in Qatar's development. He was reported on a hunting trip in Iran at the time of the coup. His absence from Doha, the capital, during the 1971 independence celebrations also had caused criticism. He went into exile in Saudi Arabia.

Sheik Khalifa, the new ruler, moved swiftly to implement his pledge of national development. He raised the pay of civil servants and the army 20 per cent and boosted pensions 25 per cent. Price controls were imposed on basic consumer goods. The new national budget of 241 million ryals ($48 million) allocated 43 per cent for social services and 9 per cent for education. Qatar joined in the new ownership participation agreement with Western oil companies in October (see MIDDLE EAST).

In April, Khalifa established a National Advisory Council of 20 members as a first step toward representative government in Qatar. He also expanded the Cabinet. William Spencer

See also MIDDLE EAST (Facts in Brief Table).

QUEBEC. See CANADA.

RACING. See AUTOMOBILE RACING; BOATS AND BOATING; HORSE RACING; OLYMPIC GAMES; TRACK AND FIELD.

RADIO entered a new era of permissive programming in 1972. One of the most imitated and controversial new formats was the sex-oriented talk show in which female listeners discuss intimate details of their love lives by telephone with male "Talk Jockeys" (T.J.'s). The most popular "sex talk" jockey was Bill Ballance of KGBS in Los Angeles. His high-rated "Feminine Forum" was even piped into the Los Angeles Police Department. Critics condemned these new talk shows as "audio pornography." But by the end of the year, there were sensuous T.J.'s in Chicago, Cleveland, Dallas, and several other cities.

Middle of the road (MOR) programming, aimed at listeners from 25 to 49 years of age, continued to be the dominant music format. However, MOR no longer stood for vocalists such as Frank Sinatra, because all of the original rock-and-roll fans were over 30 in 1972. It meant early recordings by Elvis Presley, The Beatles, and other vintage rock stars.

Complaints and Controls. Radio was the target of as many complaints from citizen groups and government agencies as television throughout most of the year (see TELEVISION). However, the White House Office of Telecommunications Policy made a beginning on its 1971 promise to deregulate radio.

No relief was offered in the troublesome areas of license-renewal challenges, but, at year's end, the Federal Communications Commission (FCC) began releasing the results of its yearlong study on how to relax or eliminate much of its onerous red tape – logging, filing, and other technical rules for stations.

Black coalition groups, which took the lead in challenging station license renewals, took pride in the growth of black ownership of stations. The number of black-owned stations grew to 18 as compared to 5 in 1968. Three of them (WSOK in Savannah, Ga.; WLIB-FM in New York City; and WGRT in Chicago) were purchased in 1972. Plans for a black-owned National Black Network were announced in April by the Unity Broadcasting Network of New York.

The Mutual Broadcasting System (MBS) put two new network services into operation on May 1 – the Mutual Black Network and the Mutual Spanish Network. Each broadcast 100 five-minute news and sports shows weekly. C. Edward Little, Sr., succeeded Victor C. Diehm as MBS president on February 1.

Cox Broadcasting Corporation bought 50-year-old station KFI-AM in Los Angeles in July for $15-million, by far the largest price ever paid for a single radio facility. In May, the General Electric Company purchased WJIB-FM, Boston, from Kaiser Broadcasting for $3 million. It was the most ever paid for a single FM outlet.

Quadraphonic, four-channel sound gained acceptance. American Broadcasting Company affiliate WKRK in Baltimore, KAUM in Houston, and WRND in New Orleans were among the first to broadcast in four-channel sound. June Bundy Csida

RAHMAN, MUJIBUR (1921-), became the first president of Bangladesh in January, 1972, after a war of secession from Pakistan. See BANGLADESH in this section and in Section Four.

Mujibur, or "Mujib", was born in Tongipura, a city about 60 miles southwest of Dacca, one of six children of a middle-class Bengali farm family. He developed a strong antipathy to British rule as a youth, and was jailed for six days for agitating in favor of India's independence while he was still in grade school.

After earning a bachelor's degree at Islamic College in Calcutta, he entered law school at Dacca University. However, he was arrested for supporting a strike by the university's laborers, and later was expelled. This started a turbulent political career in which he spent 10½ of the next 23 years in jail.

Between jail terms, Mujib helped found the progressive Awami (People's) League of East Pakistan, and in 1954 he served briefly as the provincial minister in charge of industry and fighting corruption. When he demanded domestic autonomy for East Pakistan in 1966, he was arrested and taken to West Pakistan, only to be released in 1969. He was arrested again after an election in December, 1970, when he and the Awami League won a majority of seats in the Pakistan National Assembly. The election was voided, and war soon broke out. Foster Stockwell

RAILROAD. See TRANSPORTATION.

RECORDINGS. Quadraphonic, or four-channel, sound made extensive headway in 1972 in sales of records, tapes, and hardware (playing equipment). However, the existence of two systems discouraged many potential buyers. The rival systems are discrete quad sound, in which four separate channels of sound are transferred to an album, and the matrix method of recording, which has two channels on a disk that a decoder converts to four. This recalled problems that arose during the 1950s in the battle of 33⅓- and 45-rpm disk speeds. Perhaps manufacturers will eventually develop hardware capable of dealing with both methods of reproducing sound.

While Columbia Records and others aligned themselves with the matrix system, Radio Corporation of America Records (RCA) and a dozen others used the discrete method. Many listeners believed that the discrete method was superior. The matrix system, however, was able to reveal hidden tones in older, two-channel stereo recordings.

Sales Increase. Figures compiled during the year revealed that 4,277 albums had been released in 1971, a 6.5 per cent increase over the 1970 total. A higher proportion of double-pocket (two-LP) albums were sold. Single records totaled 5,372. Sales of prerecorded music for 1971 reached $1.74 billion, compared with $1.66 billion in 1970. Of these sales, $1.25 billion came from record sales and $493 million from tapes. Eight-track cartridge sales totaled $385-million and cassettes $96 million. Television performers such as the Partridge Family, the Brady Bunch, and Sonny and Cher were major attractions on records because of their television exposure.

Comedy on records, dominated for several years by Bill Cosby, took on a new direction as a team known as Cheech and Chong became popular. Their Mexican- and Chinese-American sketches and frequent references to drugs made a powerful appeal to the youth counterculture, and sales of their album "Big Bambu" reached well over $1 million.

Black singer Charlie Pride remained pre-eminent on the country music scene. It was an unprecedentedly strong year for soul music by black artists. James Brown, Jerry Butler, Michael Jackson, King Floyd, and numerous vocal groups ranked high on the best-seller lists. See MUSIC, POPULAR.

In Classical and Semiclassical music, there was a continually increasing audience for albums featuring Moog synthesizers. Among these were three by Walter Carlos, one of which comprised music from Stanley Kubrick's motion picture *A Clockwork Orange*. Leonard Bernstein's *Mass* headed the list among more orthodox classical works, along with an album of highlights from the Metropolitan Opera Gala honoring Sir Rudolf Bing; a selection of Chopin works by Van Cliburn; and Gustav Holst's *The Planets* by the Los Angeles Philharmonic. Leonard Feather

Singer and songwriter Carole King, one of the leaders of the soft-rock movement, won four Grammy Awards in March, 1972.

RED CROSS resources were strained to the limit in 1972, principally by unprecedented floods in the East that followed Hurricane Agnes, and a flash flood at Rapid City, S. Dak. The agency conducted disaster-relief operations in 13 states during the year, and by September 8, its commitments to aid disaster victims totaled $22.6 million. This was spent for food, shelter, medical aid, clothing, urgently needed household furniture, and home repairs. With both its disaster-relief budget and disaster-relief reserve exhausted, the Red Cross then raised over $15 million in a nationwide fund drive.

Red Cross chapters will recruit, train, and supervise up to 50,000 volunteers to work in Project Find, a federal food-distribution program designed to aid the elderly. The program was implemented in August.

Under the auspices of Red Cross Youth, 31 young people worked with Red Cross societies in other countries during the summer. Ten volunteers taught health and safety courses and helped to develop Red Cross programs in Malawi and Liberia, 6 trained health and safety instructors in Guatemala, and 10 went to West Germany, 3 to Sweden, and 2 to Finland.

The 47th National Convention of the American Red Cross was held May 1 to 3 in San Francisco. It discussed the role of the Red Cross in efforts to develop a national blood service, the need to expand volunteer manpower, and the development of new and innovative services. Joseph P. Anderson

RELIGION. About 3,000 Biblical scholars and theologians met in Los Angeles in September, 1972, to discuss religion and the humanizing of man. The International Congress of Learned Societies in the Field of Religion was described as the largest gathering ever held of higher academic students of religion. The scholars presented papers and deliberated on the status of the profession. Most of the participants were specialists in Biblical, theological, or historical studies. What most impressed observers was their variety and pluralism. All the major religions of the world are being studied by specialists in the United States, and most minor details of the life of each are subject to inquiry.

In recent years, analysts have begun to speak of "civil religion" as being an expression of the merging of religious and patriotic sentiment. Publication of *White House Sermons* early in 1972 provided an opportunity to learn what is said at the highest level of civil religious gatherings. The book brought together 24 Jewish, Protestant, and Roman Catholic sermons preached before President Richard M. Nixon in the East Room of the White House. Admirers of the custom were reassured by the nationalistic sentiment of the sermons; critics complained that what was missing was a Biblical emphasis that is prophetic and should be used to call under judgment the activities of political leaders.

Education Issues. The year's major church-state issues centered on education. Both presidential candidates came out for one form or another of "parochiaid" (state financial support for parochial schools) and it was an issue in many state legislatures, election campaigns, and court battles. Increasing taxation, inflated school costs, and the decline in the number of teaching nuns and clerics, all placed new burdens on Roman Catholic parents. Similar factors caused strain on the smaller number of non-Catholic parochial schools.

Rigid "separationists" believed that support for church schools, even for parents of children in the form of tax credits, blurred the historic line between church and state. Others considered this form of support legally legitimate, morally advisable, and practically valuable. They argued that survival of parochial schools would prevent new burdens on public education.

Another educational issue came to a head in a May 15 decision by the Supreme Court of the United States in *Wisconsin v. Yoder*. The Amish, a Mennonite sect that seeks to lead a separated life in rural America, has always resisted public education as well as social security and military service. The members of the sect prefer to teach their children in schools they control and see no point in having them attracted to "worldliness" by prolonged education in high schools. Wisconsin has a compulsory school-attendance law that the Amish rejected. The court ruled that the Wisconsin law violated religious freedom.

U.S. Church Membership Reported for Bodies with 150,000 or More Members*

African Methodist Episcopal Church	1,166,301
African Methodist Episcopal Zion Church	940,000
American Baptist Association	869,000
American Baptist Convention	1,562,636
American Lutheran Church	2,521,930
Armenian Church of North America, Diocese of the (including Diocese of California)	300,000
Assemblies of God	1,078,332
Baptist Missionary Association of America	193,439
Christian Church (Disciples of Christ)	1,386,374
Christian Churches and Churches of Christ	1,036,288
Christian Methodist Episcopal Church	466,718
Christian Reformed Church	286,094
Church of God (Anderson, Ind.)	152,787
Church of God (Cleveland, Tenn.)	287,099
Church of God in Christ	425,000
Church of Jesus Christ of Latter-day Saints	2,133,072
Church of the Brethren	181,183
Church of the Nazarene	394,197
Churches of Christ	2,400,000
Conservative Baptist Association of America	300,000
Episcopal Church	3,217,365
Exarchate of the Russian Orthodox Church in North and South America	152,973
Free Will Baptists	210,000
Greek Orthodox Archdiocese of North and South America	1,950,000
International Church of God in Christ (Evanston, Ill.)	501,000
Jehovah's Witnesses	416,789
Jewish Congregations	6,060,000
Lutheran Church in America	3,069,679
Lutheran Church Missouri Synod	2,788,110
National Baptist Convention of America	2,668,799
National Baptist Convention, U.S.A., Inc.	5,500,000
National Primitive Baptist Convention	1,645,000
Orthodox Church in America	1,000,000
Polish National Catholic Church of America	282,411
Presbyterian Church in the U.S.	949,857
Progressive National Baptist Convention, Inc.	521,692
Reformed Church in America	369,951
Regular Baptist Churches General Association of	204,357
Reorganized Church of Jesus Christ of Latter-day Saints	154,481
Roman Catholic Church	48,390,990
Salvation Army, The	335,684
Seventh-day Adventists	433,906
Southern Baptist Convention	11,824,676
Spiritualists, International General Assembly of	164,072
Unitarian Universalist Association	265,408
United Church of Christ	1,928,674
United Methodist Church	10,509,198
United Pentecostal Church, Inc.	250,000
United Presbyterian Church in the U.S.A.	3,013,808
Wisconsin Evangelical Lutheran Synod	383,263

*Majority of figures are for the years 1971 and 1972. Source: National Council of Churches, *Yearbook of American Churches for 1973.*

Evangelist Billy Graham, honorary chairman of Youth Explo '72, tries street preaching during the weeklong event held in Dallas in June.

Around the World. The year saw a new phenomenon in Buddhist ranks when it was announced that thousands of Buddhist monks have begun serving in the military in Cambodia. Many served as chaplains but some as soldiers. This runs counter to established Buddhist practice, but was justified as necessary for Cambodian survival in the face of anti-Buddhist Communists. President Lon Nol of Cambodia also expects the monks to exercise a kind of magical power on behalf of his forces.

The World Council of Churches helped to settle the Sudanese Civil War in March, with the assistance of Emperor Haile Selassie I of Ethiopia and the All-Africa Council of Churches. The settlement made Islam no longer the official state religion, though Arabic would still be the official language. The southern provinces, where many Christians live, will now have a regional assembly in the equatorial province.

Inter-religious warfare remained in the news throughout the year in Northern Ireland, where the opposing sides were ordinarily identified as Protestant and Roman Catholic. As the civil struggle there continually escalated and violence increased, many religious leaders on both sides spoke up in favor of nonviolence and settlement, but hostilities and terrorism persisted. Martin E. Marty

See also EASTERN ORTHODOX CHURCHES; JEWS; PROTESTANT; ROMAN CATHOLIC CHURCH; Section Two, ECUMENISM IN THE '70s.

REPUBLICAN PARTY. President Richard M. Nixon capped his political career with a landslide victory over Democrat George S. McGovern on Nov. 7, 1972, ensuring four more years of Republican rule in the White House. Mr. Nixon swept into a second term as President by carrying 49 states. He received 60.7 per cent of the popular vote and won an electoral-vote victory of 520 to 17. His landslide, however, was disappointing to the Republican Party, because it failed to gain control of Congress.

Mr. Nixon's victory represented a personal mandate rather than a mandate for the Republican Party. The Republicans tried to pick up the five seats they needed for a majority in the Senate, but instead, they suffered a net loss of two seats. The new Senate has 42 Republicans, 56 Democrats, 1 Independent, and 1 Conservative.

In the House, the Republicans gained only 14 of the 39 seats they needed to take control. The new House has 192 Republicans, 240 Democrats, and 3 vacancies.

In the races for governor, the Republicans ended up with a net loss of one state. This gave them control of only 19 state houses, while the Democrats hold 31.

No other presidential candidate has ever scored a victory of this magnitude without winning both houses of Congress for his party. President Nixon's failure to do so was largely the result of widespread ticket splitting. See ELECTIONS.

A New Majority. During the campaign, Mr. Nixon tried to avoid offending the Democrats, whose votes he sought for his "new American majority." In a speech televised from the White House minutes after his Democratic opponent had conceded on election night, the President asked Americans to "work together to achieve our common great goals" of peace and prosperity. He assured the nation that the United States was "moving swiftly," not only toward peace in Vietnam, but also toward the eve of "what could be the greatest generation of peace, true peace, for the whole world that man has ever known."

However, President Nixon could count on little political peace on Capitol Hill. He was expected to run into the same problems with a Democratic Congress that he had experienced in his first term. He would probably continue to prevail in foreign policy and defense matters, but he faced trouble in getting his domestic programs passed. However, he could count on support from a continuing coalition of Republicans and conservative Democrats in the House.

Convention and Campaign. The Republican convention met on August 21 in Miami Beach, Fla., instead of San Diego as originally planned. President Nixon had almost no opposition to his nomination. He had easily disposed of his primary campaign challengers. Liberal Congressman Paul N. McCloskey, Jr., of California had bid for the nomination, arguing that the President had not yet ended the war. Conservative Congressman John M. Ashbrook of Ohio had contended that Mr. Nixon had become too liberal.

In the balloting on August 22, President Nixon was nominated by a vote of 1,347 to 1. The one vote he did not get went to McCloskey.

There had been some discontent among liberal Republicans when Mr. Nixon announced before the convention that he wanted Vice-President Spiro T. Agnew to run with him again. But on August 23, the convention dutifully ratified Mr. Nixon's vice-presidential choice.

There was only one floor fight at the convention. The battle was over a delegate-reform proposal to increase representation at the 1976 convention for states with large populations. The battle was organized by liberals and moderates from populous states who wanted to prevent the small-state and Southern conservatives from assuring the 1976 presidential nomination of Agnew. Among the leaders of the fight was Senator Charles H. Percy of Illinois. He was considered a likely challenger in 1976 against Agnew. However, the large states lost the reform battle. Mr. Nixon remained aloof from the convention-floor battle and, for the first time in his political career, did not have to fight for his nomination.

During the campaign, the President exploited the gains he had made in foreign policy. He was greatly helped by the fact that Governor George C. Wallace of Alabama, partially paralyzed by an assassination attempt in May, did not run for President on a third-party ticket, as he had done in 1968 (see Wallace, George C.). Mr. Nixon picked up a large share of the blue-collar and Southern votes that would have gone to Wallace.

In addition, he won surprising support among the 25 million young persons eligible to vote for the first time in 1972. McGovern had been counting on solid support from them to help elect him.

Mr. Nixon received a political bonus 12 days before the election, when North Vietnam disclosed that a breakthrough had been achieved in the Vietnam peace negotiations. Presidential assistant Henry A. Kissinger confirmed the Hanoi disclosure on October 26 and said that "peace is at hand."

Contribution Controversy. While the Democrats struggled to pay off 1968 debts, the Republicans began the President's re-election effort with about $30-million in the party's treasury. The source of contributions to the Committee to Re-Elect the President became an issue for the Democrats. They charged that special-interest groups were making huge donations in return for favors from the Republican-controlled government.

On Feb. 7, 1972, the President signed the Federal Election Campaign Act of 1971, which required that, after April 7, all candidates disclose the sources of

In one of his rare 1972 campaign appearances, President Nixon reaches out to shake hands with admirers at the Providence, R.I., airport.

their campaign funds and how the funds were used. Democrats charged that former Secretary of Commerce Maurice H. Stans, the President's chief fund-raiser, urged large contributors to submit their donations before the April 7 disclosure deadline.

The campaign-fund controversy crystallized in February and March around the International Telephone and Telegraph Corporation's (ITT) contribution of between $200,000 and $400,000 through its Sheraton Hotel subsidiary to help finance the Republican convention in San Diego. Allegedly, the Department of Justice then settled an antitrust suit against ITT at terms favorable to ITT. As a result of the controversy over the ITT affair, the Republicans decided in May to move their convention to Miami Beach.

The Watergate Affair. Another scandal broke on June 17, when five men with electronic eavesdropping equipment were caught breaking into Democratic National Headquarters at the Watergate office-apartment complex in Washington, D.C. The break-in allegedly was led by Bernard L. Barker, a Miami real estate dealer and a former Central Intelligence Agency (CIA) operative. James W. McCord, a former CIA agent and security coordinator for the Committee to Re-Elect the President, was also apprehended at the scene.

In the investigation that followed, G. Gordon Liddy, a former presidential assistant on domestic affairs, and E. Howard Hunt, Jr., a former White House consultant, were also implicated in the political espionage activities. On September 15, all seven men were indicted by a federal grand jury.

Young Voters for the President greet President Nixon with a song as he arrives in Miami Beach for the Republican National Convention in August.

President Nixon and his chosen running mate, Vice-President Agnew, accept the nomination of the Republican National Convention in August.

Money found on the suspects at the time of the raid was traced by the Federal Bureau of Investigation to secret Republican campaign contributions made in Houston. The money had been sent from Houston to Mexico City, returned by a Mexican lawyer to Houston, flown to Republican headquarters in Washington, D.C., and then deposited in Barker's Miami bank account.

The Democrats filed a $1-million lawsuit against the five raiders. On September 11, they broadened the suit to include Stans, and they asked for $3.2 million in damages. The Republicans then filed a countersuit for $2.5 million, and Stans filed a separate suit on September 14, seeking a total of $5 million for being "falsely and maliciously" accused.

Meanwhile, John N. Mitchell, who had resigned as attorney general on February 15 to be President Nixon's campaign manager, announced on July 1 that he was leaving politics. His wife, Martha, had threatened to leave him unless he quit politics. Mitchell was replaced by Clark McGregor, a former adviser on congressional affairs. William McGaffin

See also DEMOCRATIC PARTY; Section One, FOCUS ON THE NATION.

RETAILING. After an October surge of 3.5 per cent and a dip of 0.2 per cent in November, retail sales closed strongly at the end of 1972. The massive latent buying power of the American public swamped the nation's retailers with the largest Christmas-buying binge in U.S. history, according to the National Retail Merchants Association. Their year-end investigation covered all types of retail outlets and was based on both government and private sources. Consumer spending in retail establishments was estimated at $47 billion in December, 1972, up nearly $5 billion over December, 1971. Consumer expenditures for the year were expected to be up about $35-billion over 1971's $409 billion.

Among the major reasons given for the huge upswing – a doubling in retail volume in less than a decade – has been the enormous gain in personal income, now approaching a trillion dollars a year. In addition, there was less pessimism on the part of consumers about the economy and inflation.

Sales were so impressive, in fact, that many manufacturers, particularly toymakers, reported shortages and sellouts. According to *The Wall Street Journal*, Determined Productions of San Francisco reported being "completely out" of its most popular toy, Woodstock, a stuffed bird. Mattel Inc., reported that late orders and unusually high demand caused pre-Christmas sellouts of parts of its Barbie Doll line.

Profits of major retail chains reflected the upsurge in sales. Sears Roebuck, J. C. Penney, and S. S. Kresge all reported their best Christmas business in history. Earlier in the year, Sears experienced a third-quarter gain of 14.4 per cent in earnings and a sales increase of 11.9 per cent, Penney reported an 18.5 per cent gain in net income, and Kresge 12.7 per cent on a 24.1 per cent increase in sales.

Not all was rosy for the retail industry, however. An annual private census of the industry by Audits & Surveys, Inc., a market research agency, reported in September, 1972, that 12,400 retailers closed their doors in 1971.

Catalog showrooms also appeared to be gaining popularity. Selling mostly hard goods and jewelry rather than apparel, these stores mostly display merchandise samples. Their catalogs serve as advertisements for showroom items. When a customer places an order, it is filled from an adjoining warehouse.

The showrooms were providing particularly strong competition for the so-called "discount stores," which, although growing in numbers, have reached near-saturation level in many markets. Faced with keen competition and the demands of a more affluent society, many discount operations tried to upgrade their interiors and expand their services and promotion. Joseph R. Rowen

RHODE ISLAND. See STATE GOVERNMENT.

With food prices up and competition keener, more and more stores changed to 24-hour-a-day service in 1972 in an effort to increase sales.

RHODESIA. The brief hope for a settlement of the independence issue between Rhodesia's white-minority government and Great Britain ended in disappointment in May, 1972. Rhodesia's black African majority overwhelmingly rejected a proposal offering British recognition if eventual black-majority rule were guaranteed. Under the complex terms of the proposal, the black Africans would have remained indefinitely under the control of a white regime.

The proposal had been worked out by British Foreign Secretary Sir Alec Douglas-Home and Rhodesian Prime Minister Ian D. Smith in November, 1971. However, the British wanted to be sure that both black and white Rhodesians approved the proposal. So, a 24-member commission headed by Lord Pearce, a former judge, went to Rhodesia in January to test public opinion on the matter.

The Pearce Commission found that while most whites accepted the proposed solution, the overwhelming majority of black Africans rejected it. They believed the pact did not accord blacks "dignity, justice, or fair opportunity." Blacks believed that the Smith government is committed to perpetuating white supremacy.

"The people of Rhodesia as a whole do not regard the proposals as acceptable as a basis for independence," the commission reported on May 23. The British government accepted the commission's recommendation to reject the settlement proposal. As a result, United Nations (UN) economic sanctions against Rhodesia remained in effect, and Britain was forced to seek a new basis for settlement. The Rhodesian government sharply rejected the Pearce commission conclusions, and Prime Minister Smith declared there would be no further negotiations.

Rioting and Arrests were reported in several Rhodesian cities in January after the Pearce commission arrived. An estimated 14 persons were killed by police, and more than 1,500 were arrested. The rioters, most of them blacks, opposed the independence proposal. On January 18, police arrested former Rhodesian Prime Minister Reginald S. Garfield Todd and his daughter Judith. Government officials said they were arrested because they were likely to incite further rioting. Both Todd, who served as prime minister from 1953 to 1958 under British colonial rule, and his daughter opposed the settlement. On February 24, they were released from prison and held under house arrest at their ranch.

The United States broke the UN sanctions against Rhodesia by importing chrome in 1972. In August, the Rhodesian team was barred from participating in the Summer Olympic Games at Munich, West Germany, because of the government's racial policies. George Shepherd

See also AFRICA (Facts in Brief Table).

ROADS AND HIGHWAYS. See TRANSPORTATION.

Black citizens let a fact-finding commission know their feelings about an accord between Great Britain and Rhodesia's white regime.

ROMAN CATHOLIC CHURCH. Tensions between the Vatican and progressive Dutch Catholics continued to mount in 1972. Pope Paul VI chose conservative Father Joannes Gijsen as bishop of Roermond, Holland, consecrating him at St. Peter's in Rome on February 13, over the opposition of the progressive Catholics. Although the pope had recommended that bishops resign at the age of 75, he himself did not resign on his 75th birthday, which was on September 26.

Effective on Jan. 1, 1973, Pope Paul suppressed the order of subdeacon, as well as the minor orders of porter, lector, exorcist, and acolyte, transferring these functions to laymen. The decree permits women who have been acting as lectors in reading the Scriptures to continue in that role.

Irish Religious Strife. The strife in Northern Ireland was intensified when British paratroopers fired on Catholic civil rights marchers on "Bloody Sunday," January 30, in Londonderry. Lord Widgery, British lord chief justice, exonerated the paratroopers after an investigation, but his report was severely criticized by William Cardinal Conway, primate of all Ireland. On October 4, British Prime Minister Edward Heath visited the pope and discussed the Catholic-Protestant conflict in Northern Ireland. See NORTHERN IRELAND.

On December 8, Ireland voted to abolish the "special position" of the Roman Catholic Church in the

When Pope Paul VI went to Venice in September, he became the first reigning pontiff in 172 years to visit that picturesque Italian island city.

country's Constitution. The provision on the church was opposed by 85 per cent of the voters, and the vote was seen as an important symbol of the desire for reconciliation with the Protestant majority in the neighboring province of Northern Ireland.

The trial of a priest, Philip Berrigan; a nun, Elizabeth McAlister; and five other defendants ended in a mistrial at Harrisburg, Pa., on April 5. The prosecution had charged that the defendants conspired to kidnap Henry Kissinger and blow up heating tunnels in federal buildings. However, they were convicted of smuggling contraband letters into and out of Lewisburg Federal Prison, where Berrigan had been jailed for destroying draft records. The conspiracy charges were dropped. Catholic antiwar activists saw the outcome of this highly publicized trial as a triumph for the peace movement. Berrigan was granted parole on November 29.

Ecumenical Developments. The Roman Catholic-World Council of Churches working group announced on June 5 that no decision had been reached as yet on Catholic membership in the world body. A new secretary of the joint Vatican-World Council of Churches commission for society, development, and peace (SODEPAX), was named on February 15. The appointment of Joseph Spae was generally considered a move to slow down the free-wheeling activism of SODEPAX.

The four Catholic dioceses of Missouri announced on July 21 that they will participate in Key 73, a yearlong 1973 evangelistic crusade in North America primarily supported by Protestant churches. A Vatican instruction, issued July 7, listed conditions permitting Protestants to receive Communion in Roman Catholic churches, and Jan Cardinal Willebrands, head of the Vatican Secretariat for Unity, on October 9 offered the first Roman Catholic Mass since the Reformation to be held at Lambeth Palace in London, England.

In Other Countries. On February 15, the bishops of Taiwan directed that Catholic churches in Taiwan might hold rites in which Catholics could honor their ancestors. The papal ban on participation in such rites had given rise to numerous persecutions of Catholics in China since 1742. In Spain, Vicente Cardinal Tarancon, chairman of the Spanish Bishops' Conference, announced on March 6 that the pope had openly encouraged "renewal efforts." This referred to a Spanish bishops' meeting that recommended severing many church-state ties and insisted on the church's right to speak on political questions. The conference recommendations had been attacked by the Vatican Congregation of the Clergy.

In the United States. In spite of President Richard M. Nixon's opposition to relaxed abortion laws, his Commission on Population Growth and the American Future supported such legislation, on March 15. The commission condemned present laws as interference with individual freedom. The President refused to endorse these recommendations, and the American bishops took sharp exception to the commission's report. Although both houses of the New York legislature had voted to repeal New York's legalized abortion law, Governor Nelson A. Rockefeller vetoed the bill on May 15. In a letter to Terence Cardinal Cooke, on May 8, President Nixon praised the cardinal for his opposition to relaxed abortion laws, saying he would "personally like to associate myself with the convictions you deeply feel and eloquently express."

Theodore Hesburgh, president of Notre Dame University and chairman of the U.S. Civil Rights Commission, said on March 1 that proposed antibusing amendments would undermine the 13th, 14th, and 15th amendments. He disagreed with President Nixon, and in November he resigned as chairman of the commission.

Because of the financial plight of parochial schools, Catholic leaders sought new legislation that would help these schools and at the same time meet the test of constitutionality. Catholic and non-Catholic nonpublic school leaders formed Citizen's Relief for Education by Income Tax (CREDIT) on March 28 to promote legislation for tax credits for parents of public-school children. President Nixon's panel on public education has supported such credits.

Appearing at a National Catholic Education Convention on April 6, Mr. Nixon asserted he would work for aid to nonpublic schools. The Supreme Court ruled 8 to 1, on October 10, that an Ohio law providing tuition reimbursement to parents of nonpublic-school children was unconstitutional. The decision, however, did not touch tax credits.

Faith and Doctrine. On March 29, Gabriel Cardinal Garrone, head of the Vatican Congregation for Catholic Education, attacked 34 European and North American theologians who had published a statement encouraging Catholics not to despair of the church in crisis nor to remain silent, but to act and seek solutions. The cardinal viewed the statement as encouragement to resist the decisions of the pope and bishops. A Pentecostal Conference at Notre Dame in June, was attended by some 11,000 Pentecostals. The 300 priests who concelebrated Mass on closing day, as well as the 600 nuns present, reflected the growing support for Pentecostalism in Catholic circles in America.

On September 14, the U.S. bishops sent to Rome their views on the question of allowing Catholics who have been divorced and remarried to receive sacraments. After two years of discussion, the Vatican ruled on October 12 that the Dutch bishops must discontinue the use of a new catechetical system in their dioceses because it perverts Catholic doctrines.

Ordination of Women. Archbishop Leo Byrne of St. Paul-Minneapolis said on April 13 that female sex is no bar to the priesthood, and that ordination of women should be given further study. A joint Roman Catholic and Presbyterian-Reformed group on April 28 recommended the ordination of women and "an equal participation in policy and decision making and voice in places of power." The National Assembly of Women Religious at their convention in Minneapolis in May voted in favor of the ordination of women, while the executive board of The National Coalition of Women Religious also urged the ordination of women, and "full independence" for women by 1976. The Committee on Women in Society and the Church, a U.S. bishops' committee, on September 26, described the proposed women's rights amendment to the U.S. Constitution as being too "doctrinaire."

Membership. According to *Vatican Annual* statistics released in March, the 1971 world membership of the Roman Catholic Church increased from 526-million to 533 million, but the total number of priests dropped from 351,000 to 347,000. According to the *Official Catholic Directory*, the 1972 Catholic population of the United States dropped to 48,390,990 from 1971's 48,557,389. There were 57,421 priests in the United States as against the 1971 total of 58,161. Converts decreased by 5,522 to 79,012. There were 146,914 sisters in 1972 and 3,105,417 students in Catholic elementary schools, 961,996 in Catholic high schools; and 22,963 seminarians. John B. Sheerin

See also RELIGION; Section Two, ECUMENISM IN THE '70s.

ROMANIA continued to expand its links with the non-Communist world and to improve its relations with the Russian-bloc countries in 1972. Meanwhile, the government experienced some abrupt administrative and personnel changes.

In March and April, President Nicolae Ceausescu visited eight African and Arab countries, including Egypt. He tried to mediate between Israel and the Arabs during a May visit to Bucharest by Israel's Prime Minister Golda Meir. United States Secretary of State William P. Rogers visited Bucharest in July.

Common Market Links? On September 20, Romania applied for membership in the International Monetary Fund and the World Bank. In October, President Ceausescu visited Belgium and Luxembourg and repeated Romania's request for a place in the European Community (Common Market) general-preference group. This group of about 100 developing nations is allowed to export goods to Common Market countries free of the usual tariffs that protect market production. Romania had first made the request on February 28, thus becoming the first Warsaw Pact country to give implicit recognition to the European Community.

Romania and Hungary ended their quarrel by signing a new treaty of friendship and mutual assistance in Bucharest in February. Romania signed a similar treaty with East Germany, its fiercest critic in Eastern Europe, in May.

New Power Project. On May 16, President Ceausescu and Yugoslav President Josip Broz Tito inaugurated the Iron Gates hydroelectric dam and navigation project on the Danube River – the biggest joint project by any two Communist states. The $450-million project generates a reported 11 billion to 12 billion kilowatt-hours of electricity annually.

The national Communist Party conference in July reaffirmed that there could be no "leading center" of international Communism. This was interpreted as a further statement of Romania's national autonomy. Nevertheless, the conference reaffirmed the party's leading role in all spheres of national life. Ceausescu was appointed head of the Supreme Council for Social and Economic Development, a new body charged with supervising efforts to complete five-year-plan targets on or ahead of schedule. In April, two regional party secretaries were fired for corruption and bribery. Corneliu Manescu, foreign minister for 11 years, was replaced in October by Gheorghe Macovescu, his deputy.

Monthly minimum wages were increased from 800 leu ($50) to 1,000 leu ($62.50) effective on September 1 and Ceausescu promised 1,100 leu ($68.75) by 1975. Old-age pensions and other welfare benefits were increased effective November 1. Chris Cviic

See also EUROPE (Facts in Brief Table).

ROTARY INTERNATIONAL. See SERVICE CLUBS.

ROWING. See SPORTS.

RUBBER. See MANUFACTURING.

RUSSIA took a major step toward a political and military accommodation with the United States in 1972. Meanwhile, it continued to ease relations with Western Europe while maintaining its grip on Eastern Europe. Elsewhere, Russia consolidated its influence in the Indian subcontinent and moved toward friendlier relations with Japan.

In domestic policy, the Soviet Union managed to weather a disastrous grain harvest without a political upheaval. Various forms of political dissent continued to flourish, however, despite strenuous efforts to stop them.

President Richard M. Nixon's visit from May 22 to 30 marked the beginning of a period of rapidly improving relations with the United States. The visit followed the President's trip to Peking. Its main achievement was the signing of accords covering a wide range of subjects. They included the limitation of antiballistic missiles and offensive weapons; cooperation in environmental protection, medical research, and public health; exchanges in science and technology; the exploration of outer space; and the prevention of accidents–and "incidents"–on the high seas. A declaration of 12 principles on the relations between the two powers was also adopted.

U.S. Grain Purchase. In July, Russia agreed to buy $750 million worth of American grain over a three-year period. The deal would help to make up for a bad harvest in Russia. A secret, three-day visit to Moscow by Henry A. Kissinger, President Nixon's top adviser, cleared the way for the October 18 signing of the three-year trade agreement. As a result of this pact, Soviet-U.S. trade is expected to exceed $15 billion per year by the end of the 1970s. On the same day, negotiators signed an agreement settling the Russian debt for goods supplied under the World War II lend-lease program. A shipping agreement, also signed in October, provided that one-third of the bilateral trade would be carried in American ships, one-third in Russian vessels, and one-third in ships of other nations. Of all grain deliveries, one-third is to be carried by American ships at rates 10 per cent higher than existing world rates. Forty ports in each country are to be opened to the ships of the other.

The Crop Failure. The disastrous grain harvest was the year's major economic problem. It was caused by extensive frost damage to the winter crops and prolonged drought in the summer. Heavy rains in both early and late autumn also handicapped harvest workers. Russia's total crop was an estimated 30 million tons short of an expected grain harvest of about 195 million tons.

To make up for those losses, the Russian government bought nearly $2 billion worth of grain from the United States, Australia, Canada, France, Romania, Sweden, and West Germany. On September

Flag-waving Muscovites and Communist Party chief Leonid I. Brezhnev, left, greeted President Tito of Yugoslavia when he visited Moscow in June.

President and Mrs. Richard M. Nixon attend a performance of *Swan Lake* at Moscow's Bolshoi Theater during their visit to Russia in May.

30, Premier Aleksei N. Kosygin, in a surprisingly frank speech to the State Planning Committee, called for stringent savings and reduction of waste in 1973 to make up for the lost crops.

Goals Reversed. Russia's current five-year plan, running through 1975, had set 1973 targets of 8.1 per cent growth in consumer-goods production and 7.8 per cent in heavy industry. It was the first five-year plan to give consumer goods a preferred place over industrial development. But the specific plan for 1973, presented to the Supreme Soviet in mid-December, reversed those priorities. It cut targeted consumer-goods growth to 4.5 per cent. The growth target for heavy industry was cut much less, to 6.3 per cent. The sharp reversal of emphasis apparently resulted from the crop failure.

Industrial output went up 6.9 per cent as planned, according to a government announcement, but labor productivity increased only 5.5 per cent during the year. Premier Kosygin disclosed in December that the nation's economy had grown less during 1972 than during any of the previous 10 years. Kosygin used national income figures, measures of the total value added to goods by labor through manufacturing. The measure is a key index in Russia but is not conveniently comparable to any national-growth measures used in the West.

Kosygin said that 1972 national income was 4 per cent higher than in 1971. A 6 per cent increase had been planned. It had not been as low as 4 per cent since 1963, another year in which the harvest had been unusually bad.

Personal income taxes were reduced as the Russians' minimum wage, in region after region during the year, was raised to the equivalent of about $85 per month. In what appeared to be a New Year's gesture to boost popular morale, the government announced on December 26 that no income tax would be levied on minimum salaries. The move seemed largely symbolic, since personal income taxes do not form a major part of government revenue in the Soviet Union.

Diplomatic Triumphs. In Europe, Russia's major diplomatic successes took place in West Germany. On May 14, the German parliament finally ratified nonaggression treaties signed with Poland and Russia in 1970. They confirmed the territorial status quo in Eastern Europe. The ratification followed a Russian diplomatic offensive that included the initialing of the first East-West German agreement on transport and communication questions. Russia also conducted a diplomatic drive aimed at helping Social Democrat Chancellor Willy Brandt win re-election in West Germany's national election on November 19. Moscow preferred Brandt as a negotiating partner at future European sessions.

On March 20, Communist Party leader Leonid I. Brezhnev hinted at the possibility of official Russian recognition of the European Community (Common Market). But he also hinted that the price would be recognition of the Russian-led COMECON trade bloc – the Council for Mutual Economic Cooperation – by Common Market countries. Inside COMECON, the long-term Russian policy of close, supranational integration continued to make slow proggress. At the COMECON meeting in Moscow in July, Premier Aleksei N. Kosygin criticized those who take a "narrow-minded, nationalistic view" of integration. But Cuba's entry as a full member and Yugoslavia's decision to collaborate more closely with the organization were Soviet successes. So was Iraq's decision to join as an observer member.

Balkan Relations. Moscow granted a $540-million credit to Yugoslavia in November, and this demonstrated growing Soviet interest in regaining influence in parts of the Balkans that had managed to break loose, such as Yugoslavia and Romania. Romania's President Nicolae Ceausescu showed himself less willing to incur Moscow's displeasure than he was in 1971, when he made his much-publicized trip to China.

Journeys by top Hungarian leaders to Moscow in February and March revealed the existence of Russo-Hungarian disagreements. The difficulty appeared to center on the prices and quantities of raw materials and fuels that Russia is to supply to Hungary by 1985. Russian attempts to improve relations with Turkey featured a weeklong official visit to Turkey by Presidium Chairman Nikolai V. Podgorny in April. But the effort came to nothing.

In the Middle East. Russia suffered a setback in Egypt on July 18 when President Anwar al-Sadat ordered the immediate withdrawal of Russian military advisers and experts serving with the Egyptian Army. The treaty of friendship signed with Iraq on April 9 compensated Moscow for the setback in Egypt. And, late in the year, Egypt began moves that were interpreted as a search for reconciliation. Egyptian Prime Minister Mahmoud Fawzi visited Moscow, and Soviet leaders were invited to Cairo.

In Asia, the Indian subcontinent brought Russia significant gains. Russia backed India in its war with Pakistan over the secession of Bangladesh, while China backed Pakistan. See BANGLADESH.

Russia recognized Bangladesh on January 24, becoming the first big power to do so. Leaders of all three countries – India, Pakistan, and Bangladesh – visited Russia in February and March in a series of steps that served to emphasize Russia's dominant role in the area.

On September 19, Russia concluded an economic agreement with India. It calls for close trade relations, Russian cooperation in India's economic ventures, and scientific and technological research. India apparently decided in favor of Russian economic aid when relations with the United States cooled during the Bangladesh crisis. United States aid was suspended during the fight with Pakistan. Russian industry began to take advantage of low Indian labor costs, supplying steel and cotton for processing in India.

Russia and China tried twice to resolve their longstanding border dispute. Meetings were held in March and again in October, but relations between the two powers showed little improvement. In September, about one-third of the Russian Army was said to be posted near the Chinese border.

Prospects for a Russian-Japanese peace treaty improved only slightly toward the end of the year. Japan's foreign minister, Masayoshi Ohira, visited Moscow. On his return home, he said Russia might be willing to turn back to Japan at least two of the four Kuril islands that were occupied by Soviet troops in the last days of World War II. Ohira implied such a step would be essential if a treaty were to be signed. In October, Japan and Russia agreed on a long-term plan under which Japan will help Russia exploit natural gas reserves in Siberia. In return, Japan will receive deliveries of gas and other natural resources. In late October, treaty negotiations were suspended for the rest of the year.

Internal Discord. The drive to crush political dissidents continued with the January trial of Vladimir Bukovsky, a writer accused of trying to "undermine" the Russian system. Bukovsky was sentenced to 12

"Oh, he's an intellectual with a doctoral degree—mark him at $37,500."

years in prison and banishment to a remote part of the Soviet Union – probably Siberia – for passing information to Western journalists about special psychiatric hospitals where dissidents reportedly are held. In January and June, two waves of arrests of Ukrainian nationalists were reported by Western correspondents. Prominent literary figures were among those arrested.

Russia's secret police, the KGB, received special powers on April 6 to deal with the dissidents. But the publication of the celebrated *Chronicle of Current Events* continued despite police searches. The *Chronicle* is an underground journal that carries stories reporting details on arrests, sentences, prison conditions, and other developments related to dissidents.

Nobel Drama. Novelist Alexander I. Solzhenitsyn, winner of the Nobel Prize for literature in 1970, criticized official persecution of writers in Russia. Solzhenitsyn was unable to deliver his acceptance speech personally in Stockholm because of his fear that the Soviet government might not let him return once he left Russia to go to Sweden.

He apparently accepted a plan to present the gold Nobel medallion to him at a private ceremony in a Moscow apartment in April. But the Russian Embassy in Sweden announced on April 4 that it had refused a visa for the Swedish Nobel official who was to make the presentation. In August, the Nobel Foundation published in its yearbook what it said would have been Solzhenitsyn's acceptance speech. The foundation refused to say how it had obtained the lecture. "Woe to that nation," Solzhenitsyn wrote, "whose literature is disturbed by the intervention of power. Because that is not just a violation of 'freedom of print,' it is the closing down of the heart of the nation, a slashing to pieces of its memory. . . ." Except for one novel, Solzhenitsyn's work is banned from publication in Russia.

Other dissenters refused to keep their silence. In August, a famous nuclear physicist, Professor Andrei D. Sakharov, wrote an open letter to Russian leaders asking them to abolish ideological indoctrination and introduce cultural freedom.

Jews wishing to emigrate to Israel continued to be harassed by the authorities, but emigration continued to increase steadily. Nearly 32,000 – more than the 1971 total – emigrated during 1972. On August 3, the government passed a decree imposing a so-called "brains tax" on those who wished to go to Israel. The tax was in addition to the $1,080 visa fee. It varied from $5,000 to $25,000 depending on the qualifications of the emigrant. But the Russian government withdrew slightly in October and waived the tax. As a result of pressure by the United States and others, 59 families against whom the "brains tax" would have been levied were allowed to leave without paying it. Chris Cviic

See also EUROPE (Facts in Brief Table).

RWANDA. See AFRICA.

SAFETY. Preliminary estimates indicated that 1972 recorded more traffic-accident deaths than any other year in the history of the United States. According to data collected by the National Safety Council, traffic accidents caused an estimated 56,700 deaths and a financial loss totaling about $16 billion.

Work continued toward safer highway conditions. An immediate and obvious change began in 1972 with the introduction of new highway and street traffic signs. New federal guidelines stipulated greater use of international traffic-control signs, hence greater use of pictures and symbols instead of word messages. Safety experts believe that symbols and pictures communicate faster and better with the driver.

Accidental Deaths and Death Rates

	1971		1972†	
	Number	Rate††	Number	Rate††
Motor Vehicle	54,700	26.5	57,600	27.7
Work	14,200	6.9	14,100	6.8
Home	27,500	13.3	27,000	13.0
Public	22,500	10.9	23,000	11.0
Total*	115,000	55.8	117,000	56.2

†For 12-month period up to Oct. 1, 1972.

††Deaths per 100,000 population.

*The total does not equal the sum of the four classes because *Motor Vehicle* includes some deaths also included in *Work* and *Home*.

Source: National Safety Council estimates

In a continuing effort to make the automobile safer, field tests began on passive restraints to hold the auto occupant in place during a crash. Passive restraints do not depend on an occupant's decision to operate the device. Air bags, triggered automatically to inflate by the impact of a crash, have been the leading form of passive restraints considered thus far. But the bags failed to inflate in demonstrations in Phoenix, Ariz., in April and in Detroit in May. Later demonstrations succeeded. They had been presented to show how the bags protected the occupants of crashing cars. A federal safety standard, frequently postponed, was scheduled to require such systems in all new cars starting Aug. 15, 1975.

A federal appeals court in Cincinnati ruled on December 5, however, that more refined testing standards were necessary before such devices could be required. The deadline was rescinded. The ruling, on petitions by four manufacturers, came in the first case in which the auto industry openly challenged a government safety standard in court.

Other Safety Problems. A children's sleepwear standard went into effect on July 29. It requires that garments that do not meet flammability standards must be so labeled. Such garments cannot be displayed on store shelves after July 29, 1973.

On November 1, the Food and Drug Administration (FDA) unexpectedly announced delays in the effective dates of safety packaging laws for aspirin, certain linaments, and dangerous drugs. Under a 1970 law, each could be sold only in childproof containers after a specific 1972 date. But the FDA decided that a shortage of containers made a later date – Jan. 22, 1973 – more practical.

Recreational Safety authorities reported that snowmobile fatalities climbed to 164 during the winter of 1971 and 1972. The projected death rate reached 1.3 per 10,000 snowmobiles.

Implementation of the Federal Boat Safety Act in 1972 required that life preservers approved by the U.S. Coast Guard be provided for all passengers on every water vessel, whether a paddle boat or luxury cruiser. The federal government authorized a survey of youth camps, which have long been without uniform safety codes, in an attempt to identify needed safety standards.

Work Safety. Most of the nation's industries completed their first full year under the Occupational Safety and Health Act in 1972. It covers nearly 60-million workers in more than 4 million places of employment.

During the 12 months ended on June 31, the Department of Labor inspected 29,505 business establishments employing nearly 6 million persons. About 25 per cent were in compliance with the law's safety and health standards, but 23,231 citations alleged 102,861 violations. Penalties proposed for the alleged violations totaled almost $2.3 million. Critics charged the department with unenthusiastic enforcement of the law. Howard Pyle

SAILING. See Boats and Boating.

ST. LOUIS. A federal experiment in renovating a large, low-income housing project began in St. Louis on March 16, 1972. An 11-story building in the Pruitt-Igoe housing project was destroyed by a controlled dynamite explosion to make way for a park.

The Pruitt-Igoe project, consisting of forty-three 11-story apartment buildings, was considered a model of low-income housing design when it was built at a cost of $36 million in 1955. But the densely populated units were plagued by crime, vandalism, and mismanagement. When renovation began, only 600 of its 2,800 units were occupied. Several of the buildings are to be demolished and others are to be converted into four- or five-story town houses.

The U.S. Department of Housing and Urban Development (HUD) budgeted $39 million for the rehabilitation effort. Even though an entirely new housing complex would cost an estimated $22 million, HUD refused to tear down the Pruitt-Igoe project. Housing officials were afraid that such a move would encourage other cities to request that their ghetto housing projects also be torn down.

St. Louis was the site of the People's Party presidential nominating convention in July. The delegates were originally split into two factions. One favored endorsing Democratic presidential candidate George S. McGovern rather than nominating a People's Party candidate, and the other was in favor of nominating Benjamin Spock, the noted pediatrician and antiwar leader. The convention finally settled on Spock as its nominee.

On July 12, 27 persons were injured when police battled demonstrating prisoners to end a sit-in in the city jail's chapel. Twenty-five prisoners stayed in the chapel for three days to protest conditions in the jail. After the incident, police were accused of using excessive violence in removing prisoners from the chapel.

St. Louis Hijacking. A hijacker commandeered an American Airlines plane at the city's airport on June 24 and demanded $500,000 in ransom. As the plane prepared to take off, a St. Louis businessman crashed his speeding car into the jet's landing gear, in an attempt to thwart the hijacking. This forced the hijacker and the plane crew to transfer to another plane. The hijacker, Martin McNally of Wyandotte, Mich., was captured after parachuting out of the plane over Indiana, and was convicted of air piracy in December.

Economic Indicators continued to paint a troubled picture for the city. Unemployment remained substantially high, and the number of persons employed in nonagricultural work dropped by 3,500 between May, 1971, and May, 1972. The average income of a factory worker increased 5.2 per cent during the same period. The U.S. Bureau of the Census reported in July that the median family income for the area was $8,182 in 1971. J. M. Banovetz

SALVATION ARMY in 1972 assessed its purpose, program, progress, and potential and identified several basic guiding principles for its members. The principles include: (1) maintain and confirm the high Salvation Army standards in regard to the dignity of men of all races, the sanctity of marriage, and the stand against the excesses that are prevalent in a permissive society; (2) maintain fundamental involvement in Christian evangelism; (3) continue to use local leaders wherever possible in programs, and make educational and practical service opportunities available to younger national officers; and (4) recognize the value of women officers and take steps to bring them into the top echelons of leadership.

In keeping with these principles, plans were formulated for two major projects for 1973. The first, named Key 73, has as its theme "Calling Our Continent to Christ." It will be the first interdenominational Salvation Army program of national scope, bringing together many kindred organizations for a spiritual outreach in North America. The second project, Family Focus 73, will encourage Salvation Army members to work at: (1) cultivating the art of family life; (2) enlarging the influence of the family within the community; (3) combating the breakup of family life and seeking to reunite broken families; (4) emphasizing Christian standards of chastity and fidelity; (5) encouraging family worship; and (6) introducing new families to God. Joseph P. Anderson

In August, the first tenants began moving into the 853-foot steel and concrete Transamerica pyramid, the tallest building in San Francisco.

SAN FRANCISCO. Passenger service began on Sept. 11, 1972, on the Bay Area Rapid Transit (BART) system, the first new U.S. public transportation system built in a major metropolitan area since 1908. The automated electric rail service opened on about 28 miles of track between Oakland and Fremont. BART, which cost an estimated $1.4-billion, is controlled by computers. Operators take over only if the automatic controls fail. See TRANSIT.

Transit Problems and Issues. The first accident occurred less than a month after BART opened. On October 2, a train crashed through a barricade when both the automatic and the manual backup brake controls failed to function. Five persons were injured.

On June 6, voters in the San Francisco Bay area rejected, by a 3-1 margin, a proposed $422-million bridge across the bay. Environmentalists opposed the bridge, contending that it would increase traffic congestion in the city and raise air-pollution levels. Without the bridge, they argued, more people would be encouraged to use mass transit.

The nation's first airline-hijacking deaths occurred at San Francisco International Airport on July 5. Two hijackers and one passenger were killed in a gun battle between the hijackers and Federal Bureau of Investigation (FBI) agents. The shooting began when FBI agents charged the plane in which the hijackers were holding a number of passengers and crewmen hostage.

Crime and Disorders. On May 12, 3,000 antiwar demonstrators clashed with San Francisco police in Union Square outside the St. Francis Hotel. Inside the hotel, California Governor Ronald Reagan and New York Governor Nelson A. Rockefeller were launching President Richard M. Nixon's re-election campaign in California. Two policemen and several protesters were injured in the skirmishing.

Mayor Joseph L. Alioto won acquittal in two separate court cases in 1972. On March 26, a county jury in Vancouver, Wash., cleared him of charges that he improperly split with the former state attorney general and his assistant $2.3 million in legal fees paid him by the state of Washington and 12 public utilities. On June 19, a federal judge in Tacoma, Wash., acquitted Alioto of bribery, conspiracy, and mail-fraud charges stemming from the same incident.

The Uniform Crime Reports released on August 29 showed San Francisco to have the second highest crime rate among major U.S. metropolitan areas. Miami ranked first. The bay area had 5,514.2 crimes committed per 100,000 persons in 1971, compared to the national average of 2,907 per 100,000.

San Francisco's median family income of $10,503 was considerably higher than the $9,626 reported for Oakland. Average gross weekly earnings of production workers increased $16.08 between May, 1971, and May, 1972. J. M. Banovetz

SASKATCHEWAN. See CANADA.

SAUDI ARABIA. Ahmad Zaki Yamani, minister of oil and minerals, played a key role in winning major concessions for Arabian oil producers in 1972. He was a leader in negotiations by which five members of the Organization of Arab Petroleum Exporting Countries (OAPEC) obtained a share in oil operations. The agreement gives Saudi Arabia, Kuwait, Bahrain, Qatar, and Abu Dhabi, 25 per cent shares in oil operations developed by Western companies. The shares are to increase to 51 per cent by 1982.

Saudi oil production continued to set new records. The 1971 production of 1.74 billion barrels had placed the country third among the world's oil producers, and output increased 26 per cent in the first half of 1972. The record budget of $3.15 billion reflected expanded allocations of 28 per cent for defense and $140 million in aid to other Arab countries. The Central Council of Ministers voted huge increases in spending for transportation, agriculture, education, and health programs.

Completion of the Al-Ahsa irrigation and drainage project in eastern Arabia brought 25,400 acres under cultivation for the region's 650,000 nomads. The government opened diplomatic relations with Sierra Leone and Oman and gave Uganda $276,000 for a mosque in Kampala. William Spencer

See also MIDDLE EAST (Facts in Brief Table).

SCHOOL. See CIVIL RIGHTS; EDUCATION; Section One, FOCUS ON EDUCATION.

SCIENCE AND RESEARCH. American scientists in 1972 saw an end to much of the instability that had troubled the research establishment for several years. President Richard M. Nixon's budget for fiscal 1973 granted the largest increases for research and development that had been allowed since the mid-1960s.

In keeping with a pledge Mr. Nixon made in his State of the Union message to Congress – to focus research on projects "where an extra effort is likely to produce a breakthrough, and where the breakthrough is most likely to make a difference in our lives" – most of the new funds went to applied, rather than basic, research endeavors. Various military projects, as well as research on new sources of energy, quieter jet planes, and protection from natural disasters, received new funding.

In medical research, much of the increase went for cancer studies following the President's commitment to a "Campaign to Cure Cancer." However, as the budget of the National Institutes of Health (NIH) was considered by Congress, several senators and congressmen backed additional funds for other research, particularly on heart and kidney conditions, so that the NIH budget soared to $2.724 billion – or $229 million more than the previous year and $125-million more than the President requested.

A report from the National Science Foundation (NSF) indicated that the job market for scientists had improved somewhat. This was caused in part by cutbacks in federal aid to graduate education, resulting in fewer graduates entering the job market.

Congress established the Office of Technology Assessment (OTA) in 1972. Patterned after the General Accounting Office (GAO), which issues reports to Congress on a variety of topics, the OTA will advise Congress on the technical aspects of bills it is considering. In the wake of controversies over the development of a supersonic transport and the space shuttle, several members of Congress felt the need for such a source of independent advice.

Urban Research Bill. Senator Edward M. Kennedy (D., Mass.), chairman of the Subcommittee on the National Science Foundation, emerged as a prominent congressional spokesman on scientific matters. With strong backing from the scientific community, he introduced a bill that would have given the NSF $1.8 billion for research into such urban problems as health care, waste disposal, and mass transit. In addition, the bill would have tied the country's total research expenditures to the size of the gross national product and mandated that funds for civilian research be at least as great as funds for military research.

The Senate passed the measure by a vote of 88 to 7, but it was allowed to die in committee in the House of Representatives following strong pressure against the bill from the Nixon Administration. Kennedy promised to reintroduce the bill in the next session of Congress.

Medical Experiments. A public outcry arose over the ethics of medical experiments on human beings after details of a 40-year study of the effects of syphilis were revealed in July. According to the story, a group of 400 black men in Alabama who had syphilis went untreated even after a cure was known. The study was conducted by the U.S. Public Health Service to determine through autopsies the effects of the disease. Half of the men were given treatment for syphilis and half were not – without their approval, since most were illiterate and did not understand the nature of the experiment.

Those in the untreated group were refused treatment even after penicillin became a widely available and effective therapy for syphilis. It was estimated that more than 100 men died of the disease because they were part of the untreated group in the study. Following reports of the study, Senator Kennedy attached a rider to the Defense Appropriations Bill prohibiting experiments on "uninformed and unvoluntary human beings."

Concern over the use of science was also generated by reports that the United States had tried to modify the weather as a weapon in the war in Vietnam. There was also concern over a GAO report that documented an alarming increase in the number of cases of public exposure to radiation, particularly from industrial sources.

Research in the United States

Expenditures = $28 billion, 1972 (Est.)

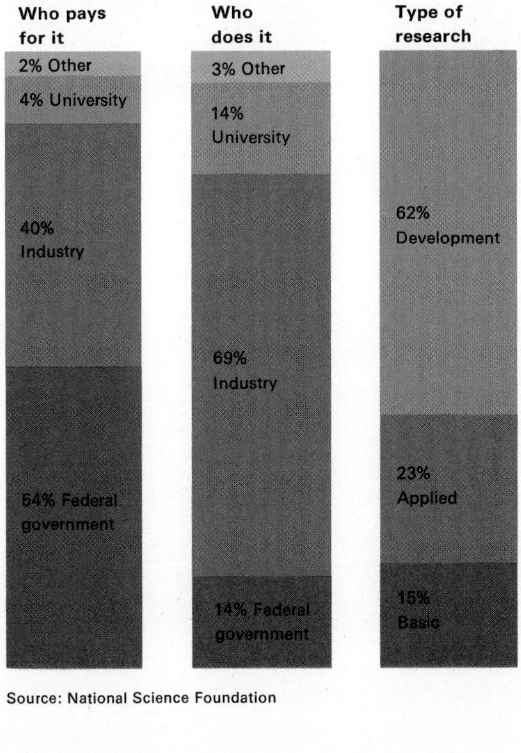

Who pays for it	Who does it	Type of research
2% Other	3% Other	62% Development
4% University	14% University	23% Applied
40% Industry	69% Industry	15% Basic
54% Federal government	14% Federal government	

Source: National Science Foundation

International Events. Following President Nixon's visit to China in February, a group of scientists from the Federation of American Scientists toured that country. Then, several months later, 10 prominent Chinese physicians came to the United States. In keeping with the spirit, Robert Q. Marston, director of the NIH, announced that the NIH would undertake an extensive investigation of acupuncture. Marston was removed from his post by Mr. Nixon in December as part of a general reorganization of the Administration.

In October, delegates to a 12-nation conference established an International Institute of Applied Systems Analysis, to seek solutions to problems created by the increasing industrialization of societies. The institute will study such problems as pollution, urban growth, and overpopulation.

Institute members include Bulgaria, Canada, Czechoslovakia, East Germany, France, Great Britain, Italy, Japan, Poland, Russia, the United States, and West Germany. Institute headquarters will be near Vienna, Austria. Russia will provide one-third of the annual operating costs of about $3.5 million, while the United States through the National Science Foundation will match that amount. The remaining third of the funds will come from the other nations. Robert J. Bazell

SCULPTURE. See VISUAL ARTS.

SENEGAL and Guinea ended a long-standing dispute with the aid of the Organization of African Unity on May 30, 1972. The two countries had been bitterly alienated since November, 1970, when Guinea accused Senegal of failing to act against dissidents in Senegal who were plotting to overthrow Guinean President Sékou Touré.

They signed a seven-point resolution agreeing to "respect the principle of nonintervention in the internal affairs of other states, ban all hostile propaganda, maintain regular and fraternal contacts between the two countries, and struggle against their common enemy – Portuguese colonialism."

An end to the difficulties with Guinea had been presaged in March when the presidents of Mali, Mauritania, and Senegal agreed to form a new Organization for the Development of the Sénégal River. Their objective was the economic development of the Sénégal River and its tributaries, which they all agreed were to be considered international waterways.

In April, Senegal's President Léopold Sédar Senghor was elected president of the Common Organization of Africa at its meeting in Lomé, Toga. Under his leadership, the member nations planned to create an exclusively French-speaking community that would stress social and economic ties. Paul C. Tullier

See also AFRICA (Facts in Brief Table).

Senegalese workmen in Dakar bag part of a massive peanut harvest destined for export. Senegal produces nearly 900,000 tons of peanuts every year.

SERVICE CLUBS presidents met in Oak Brook, Ill., on Aug. 25, 1972. Present were Lorin J. Badskey of Kiwanis International, George Friedrichs of Lions International, Roy P. Hickman of Rotary International, and Royce R. Pepin of Junior Chamber International, a world federation of 80 national Junior Chambers of Commerce. These leaders represented more than 2.5 million service club members. They agreed to encourage friendly communication and cooperation among all service organizations while each maintains its individual objectives.

Kiwanis International. The 57th annual convention, held from June 18 to 21 in Atlantic City, N.J., voted several changes in the club constitution. These included:

- An increase in the maximum per capita dues each club pays to its district from $7 to $8 per year, effective Oct. 1, 1972.
- A reduction of the minimum number of members required to charter a club from 25 to 20.

The delegates also elected Badskey, of North Webster, Ind., president and awarded the 1972 Kiwanis Decency Award to entertainer Art Linkletter for his leadership in the fight against drug abuse.

Kiwanis members in Canada and the United States celebrated the fifth annual Family Reunion Day on August 13. The observance reaffirms the importance of the family and its role as society's greatest stabilizing force and best hope for the future. Freedom of Enterprise Week was observed from August 27 to September 2 to dramatize the importance of the free enterprise system.

Lions International. Delegates to the 55th annual convention, held from June 28 to July 1 in Mexico City, approved the following changes in the club's constitution and bylaws:

- Membership shall be by invitation only.
- To seek any executive office in the club, a member must have served in the next lower executive office, except when filling a vacancy.
- Eligibility for the office of International Director was extended to club members in districts where attainment of the required number of clubs is improbable.
- Other forms of secret balloting than a printed ballot are permitted.

The international board of directors approved 10 comprehensive categories of service activities within which clubs can determine how best to serve their communities and mankind. The categories include sight conservation and work for the blind, hearing conservation and work for the deaf, and citizenship, educational, environmental, health, international, public, recreational, and social services.

George Friedrichs, of Annecy, France, was elected president of Lions International.

Rotary International observed Youth Activities Week from October 15 to 21. Interest and participation in youth service projects continued to grow. Interact–Rotary Club-sponsored groups of young people of high school age–served their schools and communities through creation of book banks and libraries, literacy campaigns and tutoring programs, work with handicapped and deprived children, and classes in languages, safety, and swimming. Other Rotary activities included forum discussions on topics of current interest, fund-raising for charities, rehabilitation of buildings in a home for the aged, and several welfare projects.

Rotary Clubs were urged to plan and conduct projects in the following areas for their 1972-1973 program year: career conferences to provide young people with vocational information and guidance from leaders in business, industry, and the professions; youth-exchange projects encouraging study in other countries; and surveys to determine the real needs and problems of young people in the community.

George Means retired as general secretary of Rotary International on Feb. 1, 1973. Harry A. Stewart, who had been serving as assistant general secretary, succeeded him.

The 63rd annual Rotary International Convention was held from June 11 to 15 in Houston. Roy Hickman, of Birmingham, Ala., was elected international president. Joseph P. Anderson

SHIPS AND SHIPPING. See TRANSPORTATION.

SHOOTING. See SPORTS.

SHRIVER, SARGENT (1915-), was the vice-presidential candidate of the Democratic Party in 1972. He was nominated at a special session of the Democratic National Committee in Washington, D.C., on August 8. Shriver replaced Senator Thomas F. Eagleton (D., Mo.), who was forced to withdraw from the ticket after disclosing he had received psychiatric treatment for mental depression and nervous exhaustion. See DEMOCRATIC PARTY; EAGLETON, THOMAS F.

Robert Sargent Shriver was born on Nov. 9, 1915, in Westminster, Md. He obtained a law degree from Yale in 1941, served as a U.S. naval officer during World War II, and then worked as a *Newsweek* magazine assistant editor in 1945 and 1946.

In 1948, Joseph P. Kennedy named him assistant manager of the Merchandise Mart in Chicago. From 1955 to 1960, he served as president of the Chicago Board of Education. Shriver married Kennedy's daughter Eunice in 1953. They have five children.

Shriver rose to national prominence in 1961, when President John F. Kennedy, his brother-in-law, named him the first director of the Peace Corps. He held that post until 1966. Under President Lyndon B. Johnson, he served as the first director of the Office of Economic Opportunity from 1964 to 1968. He was ambassador to France from 1968 to 1970. Since 1970, Shriver has had a private law practice in Washington, D.C. Darlene R. Stille

SHULTZ, GEORGE PRATT (1920-), was sworn in as the Nixon Administration's third secretary of the treasury on June 12, 1972. The former secretary of labor and director of the Office of Management and Budget (OMB), Shultz was named by President Richard M. Nixon to succeed John B. Connally.

An expert on labor economics and industrial relations and fiscal policy, Shultz was dean of the University of Chicago graduate school of business when President Nixon named him secretary of labor in January, 1969. He served in that post for 18 months until his OMB appointment.

Shultz was born in New York City and received a B.A. degree cum laude from the Princeton University School of Economics in 1942. He served as a Marine Corps officer in the Pacific during World War II and was discharged with the rank of major. He taught at the Massachusetts Institute of Technology (M.I.T.) from 1946 to 1957. He received a Ph.D. in industrial economics from M.I.T. in 1949.

He joined the Chicago faculty in 1957 as professor of industrial relations and was named dean of the business school in 1962. Shultz has written a number of articles, monographs, and books, among them *Strategies for the Displaced Worker* (1966), with Arnold R. Weber. Shultz married Helena M. O'Brien in 1946. They have three daughters and two sons and live in Arlington, Va. Allan Davidson

SIDKI, AZIZ (1920-), became prime minister of Egypt on Jan. 16, 1972, succeeding 71-year-old Mahmoud Fawzi. He immediately announced austerity measures to put Egypt on a war footing for its struggle with Israel.

Sidki was born into a middle-class family on July 1, 1920, in Cairo. He earned an engineering degree with honors at Cairo University in 1944, then went to the United States, where he earned a master's degree in city planning from the University of Oregon and a doctor's degree in economics from Harvard University. His doctoral thesis was on the prospects for industrialization in Egypt, then an almost totally agricultural nation.

Sidki returned to Egypt in 1951, a year before rebels ousted King Faruk I. In 1953, he became a planning adviser in the revolutionary regime. In 1956, President Gamal Abdel Nasser, who shared Sidki's dream of an industrialized Egypt, appointed him Egypt's first minister of industry. Other top ministry posts involving industrialization efforts followed, and hundreds of factories were built under Sidki's supervision.

On May 13, 1971, Sidki won the trust and gratitude of President Anwar al-Sadat when he denounced a powerful group within the government that had strongly challenged Sadat's power. Since that time, Sadat has assigned Sidki to a series of important posts. Michael Reed

SIERRA LEONE. The murder of a member of the ruling All People's Congress in Freetown on Aug. 28, 1972, resulted in the arrest of Salia Jusu-Sherriff, the leader of the opposition Sierra Leone People's Party. Jusu-Sherriff and six other members of the party were imprisoned pending trial.

Sierra Leone was active in international affairs during the year. Early in August, it protested the entry of Rhodesia in the 20th Olympic Games in Munich, West Germany. Along with Sudan, Tanzania, Ethiopia, Kenya, and others, it threatened to boycott the games (see OLYMPIC GAMES). In June, Sierra Leone was one of 40 African nations attending the 19th session of the Council of Ministers of the Organization of African Unity held in Rabat, Morocco (see AFRICA). Sierra Leone was visited by Cuban Premier Fidel Castro between May 3 and July 6. See CUBA.

The selection of Ishmael B. Taylor-Kamara as a vice-president of the General Committee of the United Nations (UN) was announced by UN Secretary-General Kurt Waldheim early in 1972. Taylor-Kamara was also the head of Sierra Leone's delegation to the UN.

A huge 969.8-carat diamond was discovered in the Kone area on February 14. The third largest ever found, it is valued at $11.7 million. Paul C. Tullier

See also AFRICA (Facts in Brief Table).

SKATING. See ICE SKATING; OLYMPIC GAMES.

SKIING. French and Austrian skiers swept most of the international honors in 1972. But in the year's showcase competition, the Winter Olympics, held in February in Sapporo, Japan, the skiers of both countries failed.

From December, 1971, to March, 1972, the world's best Alpine skiers competed in World Cup races in Europe, the United States, and Canada. After 21 races for men and a similar 21 for women (7 special slalom, 7 giant slalom, 7 downhill), Gustavo Thoeni of Italy and Annamarie Proell of Austria repeated as individual champions. France was first and Austria second in the Nations Cup standing, which combined men's and women's results.

The Winter Olympics saw Austria win only 4 and France only 2 of the 18 medals, and neither country won a gold. Switzerland dominated the Olympics with 6 medals, 3 of them gold.

The star of the Olympics was Marie-Therese Nadig, a 17-year-old, chubby, apple-cheeked Swiss skier. She won the women's giant slalom and the women's downhill, relegating the favored Miss Proell to second place. The victories were Miss Nadig's only important ones, but she was not surprised. "My worst fault," she said, "is egotism."

The other women's Olympic champion was Barbara Cochran of Richmond, Vt., who won the special slalom, the first gold medal for a U.S. skier in 20 years. Miss Cochran had a sister (Marilyn, 22)

Jan Bachlede of Poland speeds through a gate and takes first place in men's giant slalom at World University Winter Games in Lake Placid.

and brother (Bob, 20) on the Olympic team, and a sister (Lindy, 18) on the U.S. World Cup team.

In Olympic men's competition, Thoeni won the giant slalom and was second in the special slalom to Francisco Fernandez Ochoa of Spain. Bernhard Russi won the downhill, with three other Swiss skiers among the first six finishers. See OLYMPIC GAMES.

World Cup. Thoeni, a 21-year-old, part-time customs official, won the World Cup on the season's final day. He totaled 154 points to 142 for Henri Duvillard of France and 140 for Edmund Bruggemann of Switzerland. Mike Lafferty of Eugene, Ore., with 63 points, was ninth overall, and third in downhill. Miss Proell, 18, a farmer's daughter, scored 269 points to 187 for second-place Françoise Macchi of France. Miss Macchi, also 18, led until a pre-Olympic spill resulted in damaged knee ligaments and ended her skiing for the season.

Vladimir (Spider) Sabich of Kyburz, Calif., again dominated the American professional circuit, winning more than $50,000 of the $300,000 in purses. After the Olympics, Tyler Palmer of Kearsarge, N.H., America's best male slalom skier, turned professional.

Nordic Skiing. Galina Koulacova of Russia won three Olympic gold medals. Mike Elliott of Durango, Colo., and Martha Rockwell of Putney, Vt., gained three U.S. titles each, and Greg Swor of Duluth, Minn., won in U.S. jumping. Frank Litsky

SOCCER. Professional soccer in the United States and Canada finally showed progress in 1972. The North American Soccer League's eight teams played 14 games each, and the New York Cosmos won the championship, defeating the St. Louis Stars, 2-1, in the final in Hempstead, N.Y., on August 26. Attendance increased sharply in St. Louis, Dallas, and Toronto.

The Elizabeth (N.J.) Sports Club won the National Challenge Cup as U.S. champion for the second time in three years. Elizabeth defeated the San Pedro (Calif.) Yugoslavs, 1-0, on May 21 in Union, N.J., in the final of a 115-team competition.

Overseas, Ajax of Amsterdam won the Dutch National Cup, Dutch National League, European Cup, and the world club championship. Celtic of Glasgow won the Scottish League championship for the seventh consecutive year and the Scottish Association Cup and lost to Partick Thistle, 4-1, in the Scottish League Cup final. Derby County won the English League's powerful first division, and then bought David Nish, a gifted, 23-year-old fullback, from Leicester City for $551,250.

Poland won the Olympic championship, West Germany the European Nations Cup, the Glasgow Rangers the European Cup Winners Cup, Tottenham Hotspur of England the Union of European Football Associations Cup, and Leeds United the English Football Association Cup. Frank Litsky

SOCIAL SECURITY benefits were increased in two steps in 1972. President Richard M. Nixon signed a bill into law on July 1 that increased benefits 20 per cent across the board in September for 27.8 million Americans. The hike represents the largest dollar increase in the history of the social security program.

The new law also provides automatic benefit increases to match consumer price rises of 3 per cent or more per year, to protect recipients against inflation.

Tax Base Rises. The new law hiked the contribution and benefit base – the maximum amount of annual earnings that is counted for benefit and contribution purposes – from $9,000 a year in 1972 to $10,800 in 1973, and it will go to $12,000 in 1974. Thereafter, this amount will be adjusted automatically to keep pace with rising wages. This costs workers whose earnings are at or above the level of the maximum earnings base more, but it also increases their future social security benefits.

The Second Law, signed on October 30 by the President, had been debated in the Congress for two years. It was, in effect, a companion to the July legislation. Its provisions, most of which will not go into effect until July 1, 1973, will:

- Raise widows' and widowers' benefits from 82.5 per cent to 100 per cent, effective on Jan. 1, 1973.
- Increase monthly social security benefit payments from $84.50 to $170.00 for those who worked for 30 years or more in low-income jobs.

Increases in Social Security Benefits (1972)

Classifications Covered by New Law	If Average Annual Income Was: Under $924	$3,000	$5,400	$6,600	$7,800
	Monthly Benefits Would Be:				
Worker, age 65	$84.50	$174.80	$250.60	$288.40	$331.00
Wife, age 65	$42.30	$87.40	$125.30	$144.20	$165.50
Couple, both 65	$126.80	$262.20	$375.90	$432.60	$496.50
Wife, age 62	$31.80	$65.60	$94.00	$108.20	$124.20
Widow, age 60	$73.30	$125.10	$179.30	$206.30	$236.70
Widow, age 62	$84.50	$144.30	$206.80	$238.00	$273.10
Maximum for family	$126.80	$267.30	$467.90	$522.30	$579.30

Costs To Rise

Annual Income	Maximum* Tax on Each Worker, With Employers Paying a Matching Amount: 1972	1973	1974-77	1978-80	1981-85	By 2011
$3,000	$156	$176	$176	$182	$185	$219
$4,000	$208	$234	$234	$242	$246	$292
$5,000	$260	$293	$293	$303	$308	$365
$6,000	$312	$351	$351	$363	$369	$438
$7,500	$390	$439	$439	$454	$461	$548
$8,000	$416	$468	$468	$484	$492	$584
$9,000	$468	$527	$527	$545	$554	$657
$10,000	$468	$585	$585	$605	$615	$730
$11,000	$468	$632	$644	$666	$677	$803
$12,000 and over	$468	$632	$702	$726	$738	$876

*Tax figures shown here do not reflect automatic increases in the taxable wage base due to future inflation, which the law now requires.

Source: Social Security Administration

- Establish a 1 per cent bonus for each year a social security recipient works after age 65 before retiring. This provision becomes effective on Jan. 1, 1974.
- Improve benefits for men retiring at age 60 through 64.
- Permit social security retirees to earn up to $2,100 a year, instead of $1,680, without a reduction of benefits, effective on Jan. 1, 1973.
- Authorize issuing social security numbers to aliens entering the country if they are eligible for work, and to children upon entering first grade. This provision became effective on Jan. 1, 1973.

The social security bill will raise federal costs by more than $5 billion a year when fully effective after 1974. It is financed by payroll tax increases effective on Jan. 1, 1973. Under the new legislation, in 1973, the maximum social security tax paid by both employee and employer will rise to $631.80.

Senate Hearings. Senator Frank Church (D., Idaho), chairman of the Special Committee on Aging, announced that his committee will conduct hearings on "New Directions in Social Security." It will tackle such issues as how to make the payroll tax less onerous to workers; how to make retirement more secure for women; and how to deal fairly with the elderly in minority groups when so many do not live to age 65. It will also take up one of the biggest complaints of the elderly – that they are being forced to stop work at retirement age. Joseph P. Anderson

SOCIAL WELFARE. Congress rejected most of the reform measures presented in 1972. Most attention centered on "Workfare," a plan under which families headed by able-bodied parents whose children are all of school age would be ineligible for welfare. Instead, they would get federal jobs paying $1.20 an hour, or $48 a week. Critics of the plan called it "Slavefare."

The Administration of President Richard M. Nixon favored a bill passed by the House of Representatives in 1971 that would provide a guaranteed annual income of $2,400 for a family of four. It would also create 200,000 jobs and provide job training as it was needed. To encourage work, some payments would continue to be made as adults found employment, but the more recipients earned, the lower the payments would be.

This proposal was caught in a congressional crossfire between conservatives, who objected to the guaranteed annual income and urged that the work requirement be toughened, and liberals, who complained that requirements were too strict and the amount of guaranteed income too low. When it became apparent that supporters of the various plans, and modifications of them, would not reach accord, President Nixon announced that he would renew his efforts in the next Congress to "achieve a work-oriented program that will help all deserving people on a fair and equitable basis."

Changes Approved. There was agreement on a basic change in the welfare program as it affects the aged, blind, and disabled. A law passed in 1972 provides for federal take-over of the welfare systems for these people on Jan. 1, 1974. Under the old law, each state set its own qualifications and level of benefits.

The new federal benefits, payable to some 3 million persons, will be $130 per month for individuals and $195 for couples. Up to $20 a month in social security payments and $65 in earnings would be disregarded in determining whether beneficiaries have other income. The new law also provides that:

- States already paying above the new minimum for the aged, blind, and disabled (about one-half are) may maintain their present level of benefits, and the federal government will assume all of the states' costs.
- Those welfare clients covered who also receive some social security payments may keep at least $4 per month out of the new 20 per cent social security increase without a reduction of welfare benefits.
- Until the new federal program goes into effect in 1974, states are forbidden to deny Medicaid benefits to covered welfare clients because of any benefit raises from the 20 per cent social security increase.

Medicare and Medicaid. A new 1972 law made several major changes in Medicare and Medicaid. For example:

- About 1.7 million social security beneficiaries become eligible for Medicare payments, regardless of age, after they have been on disability insurance for 24 months. This provision is effective on July 1, 1973. This is the first extension of Medicare to any group of persons under 65 years old.
- Persons 65 or over, otherwise ineligible for Medicare hospital insurance, may enroll voluntarily and pay premiums ($33 per month) for coverage.
- Starting in 1974, raises in the Medicare "Part B Optional" medical insurance premium and in the Part B deductible are limited to from $50 to $60 per person per year.
- Under certain conditions, those eligible for Medicare can enroll in prepaid group health insurance programs, with the government paying the premiums.
- Coverage of chiropractic services is provided under Medicare.
- Medicare payments are provided for dialysis and kidney transplant for almost all Americans who need them. This coverage begins after the third month of treatment.
- Reimbursement up to $100 can be authorized for physical therapy services in a therapist's office.
- The requirement that a state must show it is trying to broaden the scope of its Medicaid services and liberalize eligibility requirements for medical assistance is eliminated.
- Doctor "peer review" groups will monitor physician practices under Medicare, Medicaid, and other federal medical programs to try to eliminate wasteful practices.

Joseph P. Anderson

SOUTH AFRICA, REPUBLIC OF. The white-minority government of Prime Minister Balthazar Johannes Vorster abandoned its relatively moderate policy toward the racial situation in South Africa in 1972 and took a sharp political turn to the right. Vorster's move to ease strict apartheid created unexpected problems. The liberal white United Party began making some political gains over Vorster's ruling Nationalist Party. Extreme right wing elements in the Nationalist Party plotted to overthrow Vorster, and black Africans began agitating for real control over their Bantustans, or tribal homelands. So, to regain tight political control, Vorster resumed tough, often brutal, methods of dealing with dissent.

Student Disorders erupted on both white and black university campuses in May and June. The students were protesting what they considered to be a violation of academic freedom by the apartheid system of education. Officials reacted by ordering mass expulsions and arrests.

The largest protests by white students occurred in Cape Town and Johannesburg. On June 2, police charged a group of white students demonstrating at a cathedral in Cape Town. Witnesses reported that police brutally clubbed and kicked the students. The police action was widely criticized, and huge rallies were held in Cape Town and Johannesburg on June 5 to protest police brutality. The police again moved against the crowds, using tear gas to disperse them.

The minister of police blamed militant left wing students and foreign agitators for the unrest. Nevertheless, the government was shaken by the unprecedented police clashes with young whites from wealthy, influential families.

Cabinet Changes. On August 1, five ministers resigned from the Cabinet. The most liberal of them was Theo Gerdener, minister of the interior. He was replaced by Connie P. Mulder, the right wing minister of information. Because the resigning ministers had been criticized for making statements opposing Vorster's hard-line policies, some observers viewed their resignations as an attempt to purge the Cabinet of liberal elements.

Church and State. Gonville ffrench-Beytagh, former Anglican dean of Johannesburg, won an appeal of his 1971 conviction under the Terrorism Act and was freed on April 14. He left for London the following day, fearing he might be arrested again or even assassinated.

In April, the black leaders of the Gazankulu and Transkei Bantustans criticized the government for overruling decisions made by tribal councils. They also demanded that more land area be added to their homelands.

George Shepherd

SOUTH AMERICA. See Latin America and articles on the various countries.

SOUTH CAROLINA. See State Government.

SOUTH DAKOTA. See State Government.

SOUTH WEST AFRICA. See Namibia.

SPACE EXPLORATION

Space exploration shifted in 1972 from pioneering ventures and high drama to providing benefits for the people on earth. The year saw the last two of the six manned Apollo lunar landings. From April 16 to 27, astronauts John W. Young, Thomas K. Mattingly, and Charles M. Duke, Jr., carried out the *Apollo 16* mission to the Descartes Highlands, southeast of the center of the moon's visible face. From December 7 to 19, astronauts Eugene A. Cernan, Ronald E. Evans, and Harrison H. Schmitt flew on *Apollo 17* to the Littrow Crater in the northeast part of the moon's face. Schmitt, a geologist, was the first scientist to make a U.S. space flight.

Each mission brought back lunar rocks and soil for laboratory analysis, and left nuclear-powered scientific stations to radio data to earth, hopefully for many years. Stations set up on the moon at three other locations since 1969 were still faithfully transmitting.

Just as did David R. Scott and James B. Irwin on the *Apollo 15* mission in 1971, the *Apollo 16* and *Apollo 17* astronauts used a battery-powered automobile to move about the lunar surface. Young and Duke drove their Lunar Rover 17 miles. Evans and Schmitt traveled 23 miles in their car in December.

As the Apollo program ended, scientists said the wealth of information it produced would keep them busy for from 5 to 10 years. They will try to piece together the sequence of events of the moon's 4.5-billion-year history and relate these events to the creation and early history of the sun, the earth, and the other planets.

Scientists and scholars gave varying assessments of the program's place in human history. Many agreed with historian Arthur Schlesinger, Jr., who declared: "The 20th century will be remembered, when all else about it is forgotten, as the century in which man first burst his terrestrial bonds and began the exploration of space." Anthropologist Margaret Mead and historian Arnold Toynbee saw the space experience as a turning point in history. But there were also dissenters. Sociologist Amitai Etzioni called Apollo a "moon doggle."

New Theories Proposed. But enough new data had been analyzed in 1972 for scientists throughout the world to find patterns, test new theories, and

Astronaut Charles M. Duke, Jr., collects moon samples at the *Apollo 16* landing site. Parked in background is the lunar roving vehicle.

revive and debate old controversies. There was some agreement on several major points, including:

- The now-quiet moon had an extremely violent early history that evidently lasted at least 1.5 billion years. The earth's early history was probably just about as violent.
- Like the earth, the moon has several layers. They formed because molten rock separated into various strata as the heaviest materials sank toward the moon's center and these materials then solidified at different times. The moon may also have a molten core of perhaps 300 miles in diameter.
- Most of the moon's craters were formed by the explosive impact of small asteroids and meteoroids hundreds of millions, or even billions, of years ago. The most cataclysmic impact, about 3.9 billion years ago, formed the Sea of Rains in the northwest sector of the hemisphere facing the earth. The impact splattered molten rock thousands of miles in all directions. At least two Apollo astronaut teams brought back samples of this now-cooled and solidified material.
- The events of the moon's first half-billion years remain a mystery. However, during the era between 3 billion and 4 billion years ago, intensive asteroid and meteoroid bombardments, vast flows of lava, and very rapid surface cooling between major impacts occurred.
- The next 2 billion years were relatively quiet. Then, about 900 million years ago, another gigantic object struck a bit northwest of the lunar center to form the spectacular crater Copernicus.

Many scientists believe that the earth was bombarded heavily at the same time as the moon. But, most of the evidence of the earth's early history has been obliterated by the development of mountains, the formation of ocean basins, weathering, and the washing of rivers, lakes, and seas.

Getting Down to Earth. Marking the shift from drama to more practical benefits from the space program, the United States launched the first Earth Resources Test Satellite (ERTS-1) on July 23 from a National Aeronautics and Space Administration (NASA) launch pad at Vandenberg Air Force Base, 100 miles northwest of Los Angeles.

The unmanned device went into an orbit that passed from 560 to 570 miles above the North and South poles. Designed to operate for a year, ERTS-1 carries a scanning camera that continuously photographs a 110-mile-wide strip of the earth's surface. It transmits its pictures in two visible light bands and two infrared bands. Stations at Greenbelt, Md.; Goldstone, Calif.; Fairbanks, Alaska.; and Prince Albert, Saskatchewan, receive all data from the satellite.

The satellite travels over every part of the earth every 18 days, except for small regions around the poles. Within the first few months of operation, it transmitted more than 20,000 images of this vast area. Some 300 teams of scientists in the United States and 34 other countries are studying the pictures to learn how satellite observations can be used to meet the needs of an exploding world population.

Analysis of the first pictures indicated the satellites may be useful for monitoring food crops, searching for mineral reserves, in aiding environmental protection efforts, checking wildlife and human habitation patterns, tracking glaciers and ice floes, and supporting search-and-rescue operations.

A more advanced series of earth-resource observation experiments was scheduled for the *Skylab* manned space station flights in 1973. Three three-man crews will visit the *Skylab*, a specially modified third-stage Saturn 5 rocket casing, on manned earth-orbital flights lasting from 28 to 56 days.

The Space Shuttle. Looking to the 1980s and beyond, NASA awarded a contract to the North American Rockwell Corporation in July to develop the main section, or orbiter, of the space-shuttle vehicle. The winged shuttle will take off vertically like a rocket, fly in earth orbit a week or more, and then land on a runway like an airplane. It will carry a crew of four and have space for about a dozen passengers or a heavy load of satellites and space equipment.

The space shuttle orbiter will be used repeatedly. Solid-propellant booster rockets will carry it to an altitude of 25 miles and then be dropped by parachute into the ocean. The boosters will be recovered, refueled, and reused. A large, external, liquid-fuel tank will accompany the orbiter to orbit, then return to destruction in a remote ocean area.

Because its most expensive parts are reusable, the space shuttle will save time and money. Developing the shuttle will cost an estimated $5.15 billion and take about six years.

International Space Rescue. President Richard M. Nixon and Russia's Premier Aleksei N. Kosygin agreed in Moscow in May to equip all future manned U.S. and Russian spacecraft with devices that will allow them to link in space. This will make it possible for U.S. astronauts and Russian cosmonauts to rescue one another should a space emergency arise.

In a series of meetings in Houston and Russia's "Star City," near Moscow, engineers, scientists, and astronauts of the two countries designed the docking mechanisms and scheduled the first flight test for July, 1975. Flight crews for the joint mission are to be selected in 1973. A leading candidate for the United States crew is Donald K. (Deke) Slayton, one of the original seven U.S. astronauts and chief of the astronaut corps. Slayton was grounded because of a heart murmur in 1962, but he made a complete recovery, and was restored to flight duty in March, 1972. He will be 49 years old in 1973.

The Planets. *Pioneer 10*, the first man-made object to fly beyond the orbit of Mars, was launched on

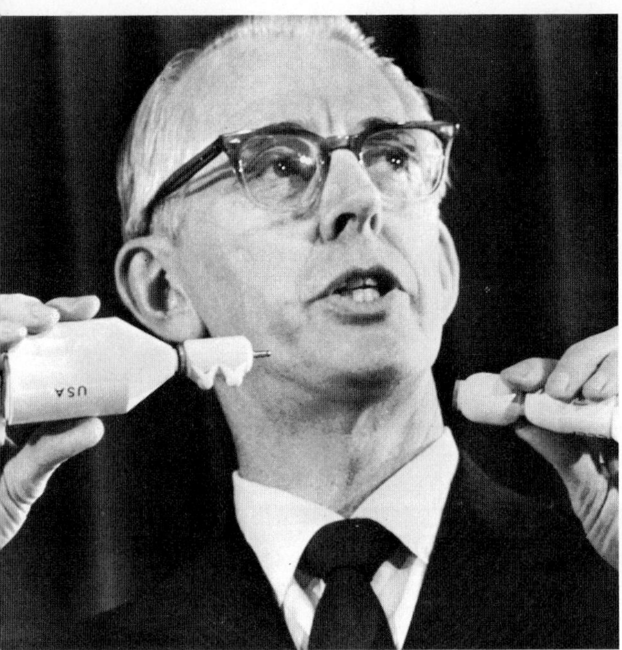

James Fletcher, NASA administrator, explains how United States and Russian spacecraft will link up in 1975 in a joint space enterprise.

March 2 on a 21-month journey past Jupiter. By the end of 1972, the 570-pound spacecraft had nearly completed its passage through the asteroids – the small, planetlike bodies between the orbits of Mars and Jupiter.

Preliminary reports from an experiment for which tiny gas-containing cells lined part of the outer surface of *Pioneer 10* indicated that no particles larger than 1/25 inch in diameter hit the craft. During the first half of its passage through the asteroids, the spacecraft evidently encountered more particles than expected in the range between 1/25 and 1/250 inch in diameter and fewer under 1/250 inch. In addition, early data from a telescope that viewed larger meteoroids and asteroids suggested that there might be more of them than scientists had expected.

After passing Jupiter in December, 1973, *Pioneer 10* will continue beyond the solar system and toward the constellations Taurus and Orion. Etched on a metal plate aboard *Pioneer 10* is a message that might be decipherable by intelligent beings should any come across it. The plate has pictures of a man and a woman and a set of symbols indicating the planet (earth) and the star (our sun) of the solar system from which it was launched.

Mariner 9 entered its orbit around Mars in November, 1971, but its instruments peered down at a storm that sent dust clouds 30 to 35 miles high, the most extensive storm observed on Mars since 1924. Mapping began after the dust settled in January, 1972. The craft took about 7,000 pictures, covering all of the Martian surface. Scientists and cartographers at the Center of Astrogeology in Flagstaff, Ariz., then pieced about 1,500 of the pictures together to produce the first detailed map of another planet. The map will be used to select landing sites for the two Viking spacecraft scheduled to land on Mars in 1976.

Further analysis of the *Mariner 9* pictures showed that dust storms cause the variations in Mars' appearance and that the planet may have had free-flowing water in the past. The pictures also showed that Mars is geologically active, with volcanic mountains and other formations larger than any on earth, including an equatorial crevass 2,500 miles long and three to four times as deep as the Grand Canyon.

When *Mariner 9* passed behind the sun in September, it was used in another experiment to test Albert Einstein's general theory of relativity. A powerful radio transmitter in Goldstone, Calif., sent a series of signals to the craft. The sun's gravity caused the path of the radio signals to curve, just as predicted by Einstein's theory. Scientists said remaining doubts about the Einstein theory were essentially eliminated by this and another experiment in which atomic clocks were flown around the earth earlier in the year.

Venera 8, a Russian spacecraft, left earth on March 27 and landed on Venus on July 22. The Russian news agency Tass said the craft found that Venusian surface rocks resemble the granite of earth and that some sunlight penetrates all the way through Venus' dense cloud cover. Russia also reported that the planet's atmosphere was 97 per cent carbon dioxide.

NASA launched the last of its Orbiting Astronomical Observatory satellites on August 21. The 2½-ton craft, named *Copernicus* for the Polish astronomer, carries a 32-inch reflecting telescope, the largest ever sent beyond the earth's atmosphere. It was put to work immediately to observe stellar dust clouds that Princeton University astronomer John E. Rogerson called "the ashes of stars that have died or the seeds of stars to be born."

Black Hole Confirmed. Meanwhile, astronomers said data from an X-ray satellite launched in 1970 proved almost certainly that the first of the long-suspected black holes has been discovered in the constellation Cygnus, the Swan. A black hole is a collapsed star with its mass packed so densely that gravity prevents the escape of visible light. Only X rays and other high-energy radiation can be emitted.

An instrument on Orbiting Solar Observatory 7, launched in 1971, detected the first direct evidence of thermonuclear reactions on the surface of the sun. Edward L. Chupp of the University of New Hampshire said the evidence came from gamma rays that were emitted during solar flares on August 4 and 7, 1972.

The first scientist on the moon, geologist Harrison H. Schmitt, stands beside a huge, split lunar boulder during the third *Apollo 17* moon walk.

People and Funds. NASA reprimanded the *Apollo 15* astronauts Scott, Irwin, and Alfred M. Worden on July 11 for lack of judgment in their "apparent intent . . . to gain personally" by carrying unauthorized personal items on the flight. All three left the astronaut corps following the reprimand. Among the things the astronauts had taken on the mission were stamps they planned to sell. See Astronauts.

Two space flight pioneers who had been among those principally responsible for the success of the Apollo moon landings moved to new assignments in 1972. Rocket expert Wernher von Braun, who headed the German project that led to the V-1 and V-2 rockets of World War II and then became an American citizen in 1955, left NASA in June to join the Fairchild Hiller Corporation. He had been in charge of long-range space planning since 1970. Robert R. Gilruth, director of the Manned Spacecraft Center in Houston, became the NASA director of key personnel. In the 1940s, Gilruth was one of the first American engineers to use rockets to launch advanced aircraft models through the sound barrier. He headed the Mercury and Gemini programs that preceded Apollo.

Congress appropriated $3.408 billion to NASA for fiscal 1972, compared with $3.298 billion in the previous year. It was the second successive increase for NASA, following five years in which its appropriation declined.

Jay Holmes

SPAIN. General Francisco Franco on July 18, 1972, named his old comrade-in-arms and vice-president, Admiral Luis Carrero Blanco, to succeed him when he dies. The action did not invalidate the 1969 steps marking Prince Juan Carlos as Spain's next king. But it appeared to provide for effective control to go to the dour, conservative Carrero. The 80-year-old Franco's action came as Spain went through a year of unrest in universities, in heavy industry, and in the Basque regions of the north.

Student Riots began on January 17 at the University of Madrid. The medical course there had taken six years plus a low-paid year of internship, but a new system extended the students' unpaid status through the seventh year. Medical students struck, refused to apologize, and were expelled. Universities throughout Spain closed. About 4,000 medical students were readmitted, but demonstrations nearly paralyzed the university. On July 30, the eve of widespread August vacations, Franco announced stern steps to restore discipline, but mass faculty resignations at Madrid's two universities followed in September.

Industrial Strife began in March with shipyard workers at El Ferrol, Franco's birthplace. Armed police arrived on March 14 and strikers, threatened with conscription into the navy, returned to work March 20. In Vigo, shipyard workers struck on May 24, and 16,500 workers from 23 plants struck on

September 17; 20 were arrested and 4,000 were fired from their jobs.

Basque Violence broke out in January, when Basques kidnaped the manager of a machine firm near Bilbao that had fired more than 100 strikers. The manager was freed when the company agreed to rehire the workers.

In February, a Basque demonstrator who had turned himself into a human torch and jumped from a balcony–but survived–was tried in Madrid. He reportedly was sentenced to four years in prison for illegal propaganda and to two and a half more years for causing harm to a policeman on whom he landed.

Economic Concerns centered on Spain's lack of international ties. It is ineligible for membership in the European Community because it does not have a democratic government. But at least half of its exports in 1973 will probably be subject to community tariffs. French President Georges Pompidou in September expressed support for Spanish membership "as soon as possible." Opposition has come from the Netherlands in the past, however.

Women's Rights inched ahead on July 5. The legislature dropped a civil code article prohibiting women under 25 from leaving home without parental approval except to marry or to enter "an institution approved of by the church." Kenneth Brown

See also EUROPE (Facts in Brief Table).

SPITZ, MARK ANDREW (1950-), won seven gold medals for swimming in the 1972 Olympic Games in Munich, West Germany. He is the first athlete to win more than five in one Olympiad. Spitz set a new world record in each of his races, winning the 100-meter and 200-meter free-style races, the 100-meter and 200-meter butterfly events, and swimming on the winning 400-meter and 800-meter free-style and the 400-meter medley relay teams. See OLYMPIC GAMES.

Spitz's great performance completely reversed his disappointing showing in the 1968 Olympics, when he failed to win a single individual race in Mexico City. His comeback began in 1971, when he shattered seven world records and became the first male swimmer to win four titles in one national Amateur Athletic Union meet. He won the 1972 Sullivan Award, given annually to the best American amateur athlete, for his 1971 performance.

Spitz was born in Modesto, Calif., and started swimming when he was 8 years old. He began taking private swimming instructions when he was 10. He swam in the Maccabiah Games in Israel when he was 15, and set his first world record (4:10.6 in the 400-meter free-style) when he was 16. Spitz entered Indiana University in 1969 and set more than 30 records as a member of the swimming team. He received his bachelor's degree in 1972. Joseph P. Spohn

General Francisco Franco takes part in the wedding of his favorite granddaughter to grandson of Alfonso XIII, Spain's last reigning king.

SPORTS administrators almost needed law degrees to keep up with their work in 1972. Dissident players and rival leagues sued the baseball, football, basketball, and hockey establishments, charging that their player contracts violated antitrust laws. Only baseball emerged unscathed.

In 1970, Curt Flood, a star outfielder who objected to being traded to another team against his wishes, sued baseball. In 1972, the Supreme Court of the United States ruled against Flood. It said that the reserve clause in his contract, which allowed his club to trade him without his consent, was legal, but only because the Supreme Court in 1922 had exempted baseball from antitrust laws. It said that no other sport enjoyed antitrust exemption, and it urged Congress to do something about baseball's exemption. After the season, the club owners offered to relax the reserve clause, but the players called the proposed changes insufficient. See BASEBALL.

The National Hockey League (NHL) reserve clause, similar to baseball's, was attacked in an antitrust suit by the new World Hockey Association (WHA). After more than 60 NHL players had jumped to the WHA, the NHL obtained court orders to stop some of them. A federal court ruled in November that the most famous of the jumpers, Bobby Hull, could play in the WHA pending final determination of the NHL suits. See HOCKEY.

A table tennis team from China plays a United Nations team in the Trusteeship Council Chamber during an April, 1972, tour of the United States.

The National Basketball Association (NBA) and the newer American Basketball Association (ABA) tried to convince Congress to allow them to merge. Meanwhile, the ABA pressed its $300-million antitrust suit against the NBA. See BASKETBALL.

There was no rival league to haunt professional football, but Joe Kapp, a former star quarterback, filed an antitrust suit against the National Football League. In 1970, Kapp had given up most of a $600,000, three-year contract rather than sign a standard player contract with the New England Patriots.

The United States Olympic Committee, criticized for faulty handling of athletes during the Olympic Games in Munich, West Germany, faced congressional investigation. Congress was also considering a bill to create a Federal Sports Commission that would regulate television policies, franchise movements, player drafts, and the various contracts in professional sports.

Among the Winners in 1972 sports competition were:

Curling. A freakish incident helped Canada retain the world championship in March at Garmisch-Partenkirchen, West Germany. When the U.S. champions from Grafton, N. Dak., seemed to have won the final, 10-9, the U.S. skip, Robert LaBonte, jumped with joy. Coming down, he accidentally moved one of his stones, which was then disqualified. Canada won the game and title, 10-9.

Fencing. Americans did poorly in the Olympics. The best, Paul Apostal of New York, was eliminated in the saber semifinals. In the U.S. championships, in July, at Waltham, Mass., Alex Orban of Yonkers, N.Y., won his fourth consecutive saber title.

Handball. Fred Lewis of Miami Beach, Fla., playing in his first national tournament, won the U.S. Handball Association four-wall championship after upsetting Paul Haber of Chicago, a five-time champion, in the semifinals. Steve Sandler of New York won the Amateur Athletic Union (A.A.U.) one-wall title for the seventh time.

Rowing. The Harvard freshman heavyweights won the Thames Challenge Cup and Kent (Conn.) School took the Princess Elizabeth Cup for schoolboys in the Henley Royal Regatta in England. The first U.S. national all-star eight defeated New Zealand twice in the West German championships, then finished second to the same New Zealand crew in the Olympics.

Shooting. Americans won 4 of the 9 Olympic medals in rifle shooting, including gold medals to Lones Wigger of Columbus, Ga., in the free rifle, and John Writer of Clarendon Hills, Ill., in the small-bore rifle, three position. In the U.S. small-bore, three-position championship, Wigger finished second to David Boyd of Quantico, Va.

Weight Lifting. Vassili Alexeev of Russia broke three of his four world records for superheavyweights by pressing 521¼ pounds, cleaning and jerking 523½ pounds, and totaling 1,421 pounds for three types of lifts in Russia's national championships. Ken Patera of Minneapolis, slowed by back and knee trouble, set a U.S. record in the U.S. championships by totaling 1,339¼ pounds.

Wrestling. The U.S. team surprisingly won six freestyle medals in the Olympics, including gold medals by Dan Gable of Waterloo, Iowa; Wayne Wells of Norman, Okla.; and Ben Peterson of Cumberland, Wis.

Peterson and 420-pound Chris Taylor, an Olympic bronze medalist, won National Collegiate Athletic Association (NCAA) titles and led Iowa State to the team championship.

Other Champions. *Archery*, world champions: men, John Williams, Cranesville, Pa.; women, Maureen Bechdolt, Loveland, Ohio. U.S. champions: men, Kevin Erlandson, Sacramento, Calif.; women, Ruth Rowe, Pittsburgh. *Badminton*, U.S. champions: men, Sture Johnsson, Sweden; women, Eva Twedberg, Sweden. *Biathlon*, U.S. champion: Pete Karns, Jackson, Wyo. *Billiards*, world pocket champion: Irving Crane, Rochester, N.Y. *Bobsledding*, European champions: four-man, Switzerland (Hanruedi Müller, driver); two-man, West Germany (Wolfgang Zimmerer, driver). *Canoeing*, U.S. champions: men's canoe (1,000 meters), Roland Muhlen, Newport Beach, Calif.; men's kayak (1,000 meters), Pete Weigand, Newport Beach, Calif.; women's kayak (500 meters), Mrs. Marcia Smoke, Niles, Ill. *Casting*, U.S. all-around champion, Steve Rajeff, San Francisco. *Court tennis*, world champion: Jim Bostwick, New York. *Cross-country*, A.A.U., Frank Shorter, Gainesville, Fla.; NCAA, Neil Cusack, East Tennessee State. *Cycling*, Tour de France winner: Eddy Merckx, Belgium. World champions: road, Marino Basso, Italy; sprint, R. van Lancker, Belgium. U.S. champions: road, John Howard, Springfield, Mo.; sprint, Gary Campbell, Paramount, Calif. *Field hockey*, U.S. champion: North Jersey. *Gymnastics*, U.S. Gymnastics Federation all-around champions: men, Yoshi Takei, Japan; women, Cathy Rigby, Los Alamitos, Calif., and Joan Moore, Philadelphia (tie). A.A.U. all-around champions: men, Makoto Sakamoto, Los Angeles; women, Linda Metheny, Tuscola, Ill. *Horseshoe pitching*, U.S. champion: Elmer Hohl, Wellesley, Ontario. *Karate*, world champion: L. T. Watanabe, Brazil. *Lacrosse*, U.S. champions: NCAA, Virginia; club, Carlings, Baltimore. *Luge* (tobogganing), U.S. champions: men, Terry O'Brien, Plattsburgh, N.Y.; women, Kathleen Homstad, Missoula, Mont. *Modern pentathlon*, U.S. champion: Charles Richards, Tacoma, Wash. *Motorcycling*, U.S. grand national champion: Mark Brelsford, San Bruno, Calif. *Parachuting*, world overall champions: men, Clayton Schoelpple, Hartwood, Va.; women, Barbara Karkoschka, East Germany. *Polo*, U.S. champions: open, Milwaukee; 20 goal, Red Doors Farm, Barrington, Ill. *Racquets*, world champion: William Surtees, Chicago. *Rodeo*, all-around champion: Phil Lyne, George West, Tex. *Roller skating*, world champions: men, Michael Obrecht, West Germany; women, Petra Hausler, West Germany. *Softball*, U.S. fast-pitch champions: men, Raybestos Cardinals, Stratford, Conn.; women, Raybestos Brakettes, Stratford, Conn. *Squash racquets*, U.S. champions: men, Victor Neiderhoffer, Berkeley, Calif.; women, Mrs. Nina Moyer, Pennington, N.J. *Squash tennis*, U.S. open champion: Dr. Pedro Baccallao, New York. *Surfing*, U.S. champions: men, Dale Dobson, San Diego, Calif.; women, Mary Setterholm, Corona Del Mar, Calif. *Table tennis*, U.S. champions: men, Dal Joon Lee, Parma, Ohio; women, Wendy Hicks, Santa Barbara, Calif. *Team handball*, U.S. champion: Adelphi University. *Volleyball*, U.S. Volleyball Association champions: men, Chart House, San Diego, Calif.; women, South Texas, Houston. A.A.U. champions: men, Sand and Sea, Santa Monica, Calif.; women, Region 13 Seniors, Los Angeles. *Water polo*, A.A.U. champion: Concord (Calif.) Dolphins. *Water skiing*, U.S. champions: men, Mike Suyderhoud, of Petaluma, Calif.; women, Mrs. Liz Allan Shetter, of Winter Park, Fla. Frank Litsky

See also articles on individual sports; OLYMPIC GAMES; Section One, FOCUS ON SPORTS.

SRI LANKA. Ceylon became the Socialist Republic of Sri Lanka on May 22, 1972. The first head of the new government was President William Gopallawa. Sirimavo Bandaranaike remained as prime minister. But the new name, which means "great and beautiful island," and the adoption of a new Constitution did little to solve the basic problems of civil unrest, unemployment, and worsening economic conditions.

The new Constitution, which was approved by the Constituent Assembly after 22 months of deliberation, provided for a one-house National Assembly, with members serving six-year terms. It also vested power almost solely in the Assembly, thus abandoning the more traditional separation of powers. The independence of the judiciary was sharply curtailed, and appeals to the Privy Council in London, the last link with Great Britain, were abolished. The Constitution deliberately excluded rights to private property, and called for the development of collective ownership of property, including land.

Domestic Problems. Yet constitutional change could not alter the facts of life in the country. About 14,000 to 16,000 members of the People's Liberation Front remained in detention camps, though some plans were made either to bring them to trial or to put them on parole. Organized crime, including ambushes and hold-ups, was rampant in the rural areas.

Fears that the ultra-leftist uprising of 1971 would be repeated kept the country on a military alert. Civil rights were sharply curtailed when the government in April adopted a bill that permitted the courts to use normally inadmissable evidence, such as confessions and hearsay, to try dissidents. The bill prompted the Communists to withdraw their support from the government. Yet the unrest continued, even spreading to the conservative Tamil districts in the north.

Economic Woes. The economy continued to slide downhill with a growth rate of less than 1 per cent as compared with a 2 per cent annual population increase. The economy was further hit by a depleted coconut crop and a sharp drop in world coconut oil prices. The rice crop was affected by a severe drought. The result was a trade deficit of about $6.25 million. To help solve the nation's foreign debt problem, the International Monetary Fund recommended a devaluation of the rupee, but Sri Lanka resisted this as a solution.

Meanwhile, the government continued its nationalization program, taking over several major tea plantations during the year. Legislation was also introduced in April limiting personal incomes to 2,000 rupees (about $310) per month.

From 12 per cent to 14 per cent of the work force was unemployed, and an even larger percentage was underemployed. In 1971, the government had promised to create 100,000 new jobs, but it had managed to establish only 8,000. John N. Stalker

See also ASIA (Facts in Brief Table).

STAMP COLLECTING. Publishers of two of the principal stamp catalogs, *Minkus World Wide* and *Scott Standard*, announced in June, 1972, that their 1973 editions would recognize the stamps of the People's Republic of China. European catalogs have always listed these stamps. But, until President Richard M. Nixon lifted trade barriers with mainland China on June 10, 1971, Chinese stamps had come under United States "trading with the enemy" restrictions. *Minkus* planned to list about 1,200 Chinese stamps issued since 1949, while *Scott* will include a comprehensive list of issues of the last 22 years.

The Moon Covers. In July, the National Aeronautics and Space Administration (NASA) acknowledged that *Apollo 15* astronauts David R. Scott, James B. Irwin, and Alfred M. Worden had augmented their officially approved cargo of 232 pieces of moon mail with an additional 400 envelopes. These were to be sold to collectors and the profits used to establish trust funds for the astronauts' children. Affixed to the envelopes were 10-cent stamps commemorating the *Apollo 11* mission, and other material of value to collectors.

An acquaintance of the astronauts received some of the envelopes and passed them to Herman E. Sieger, a German stamp dealer. The dealer sold them at an average of $1,500 each. NASA reprimanded the astronauts, but asserted that the astronauts refused the trust funds when they learned of the commercialization of the covers. On Sept. 15, NASA disclosed that 15 astronauts had been paid $37,500 for signing stamps and postcards.

Souvenir Cards. Growing interest in the collection of souvenir cards, issued to coincide with the issuance of stamps, was indicated when the first United Nations Postal Administration souvenir cards were issued. A total of 158,974 of them were sold on the day of issue. The U.S. Bureau of Engraving and Printing began issuing a limited number of these cards nearly 30 years ago. For the last six years, the Bureau and the U.S. Postal Service have been issuing the cards for distribution at stamp and coin shows. They have sold for $1 each, but with collectors now coveting them, the prices are going up. After a printing error on a 1971 card was discovered, its owner offered it for sale at $5,000.

The world's most valuable stamp, the famous British Guiana of 1856, has been listed in catalogs before, but never priced. In 1972, however, London stamp dealer Stanley Gibbons said the stamp would be priced at 120,000 pounds, roughly $288,000, in his 1973 *British Commonwealth* catalog. That is about $8,000 more than it brought at its last sale, in 1971 to Irving Weinberg of Philadelphia. A U.S. Postal Service survey in 1972 put the number of stamp collectors in the United States at 16 million, with men outnumbering women by 8 to 5. Theodore M. O'Leary

Mrs. Nancie R. Wall, librarian, arranges books on the shelves in the new stamp collectors library set up by the Philatelic Society at State College, Pa.

STANFIELD, ROBERT LORNE (1914-), leader of Canada's Progressive Conservative Party, fought Prime Minister Pierre E. Trudeau and the Liberal Party to a virtual stand-off in the national election in October, 1972. During the campaign, he traveled about 70,000 miles across Canada, making unemployment, inflation, and the "work ethic" the main issues. See CANADA; TRUDEAU, PIERRE ELLIOTT.

Stanfield was born on April 11, 1914, in Truro, Nova Scotia, a small industrial town where his family owned an underwear-manufacturing business. His father, Frank Stanfield, was once a provincial legislator and lieutenant governor, and this stirred an early interest in government in him. Stanfield attended public school in Truro, then studied political science and economics at Dalhousie University in Halifax. In 1939, he graduated cum laude from Harvard Law School. For eight years, while practicing law, he served as Nova Scotia's opposition leader in the provincial government. Subsequently, he served as premier of the province for 11 years.

The leader of the Progressive Conservative Party is tall, lean, and bald. His favorite pastime is gardening; he also enjoys attending the theater. Stanfield has been married twice. His first wife Joyce was killed in an automobile accident, leaving him with four young children. His second wife Mary is the daughter of a former justice of Nova Scotia. She and his children helped in his campaign. Paul C. Tullier

STATE GOVERNMENT. The November elections and such issues as school financing, revenue sharing, state lotteries, and the environment dominated state government concerns in 1972.

The Democratic Party scored election gains at the state level. There were 11 Democrats elected to governorships, increasing the Democrats' advantage by 1 to a 31 to 19 margin. Republicans took the governor's office from the Democrats in Missouri and North Carolina, while Democrats replaced Republicans in Delaware, Illinois, and Vermont.

The Democrats also increased their control of state legislatures, holding majorities in both houses in half the states. The Democrats retained majorities in the Senate and took control of the House in Montana, Nevada, Oregon, and Washington. They won control of both houses in Minnesota and control of the Senate and a tie in the House in South Dakota. Republicans took both houses in Connecticut from the Democrats, and gained full control in Illinois by winning the Senate and in Utah by winning the House. The outcome in the California Senate hinged on two special elections to be held in 1973. The California Assembly remained Democratic. In other changes, the Democrats won the Ohio House, and the Republicans won the Pennsylvania House and the Alaska Senate, which had been tied. See Elections.

Both women and blacks won more legislative seats. There are now 330 women and 225 blacks among the more than 7,500 legislators in the nation. These gains were not restricted to any one section of the country. Women scored heaviest in New Hampshire, winning 89 seats. Blacks are now represented in 23 state senates and 40 lower houses, with from 10 to 20 blacks elected in each of these states: Georgia, Illinois, Maryland, Michigan, Missouri, New York, Ohio, and Pennsylvania.

Money and Taxes. The adoption of federal revenue sharing in September was a major financial breakthrough for the states. Revenue sharing will provide $30.2 billion to state and local governments through 1976, with $5.3 billion being allotted in the first year. Both governors and state legislators made repeated appearances before congressional committees to promote this measure. The first payments were made in December, 1972, with one-third of the money going to the states and two-thirds to local communities. Equally important, in the opinion of many, was that revenue sharing may signal a change in the national mood, reversing the flow of power and resources to the federal government.

The imminence of revenue sharing, combined with a generally improved financial condition in most states, held state tax increases to a minimum in 1972. Only 4 of the 39 governors who gave State of the

Montana constitutional convention delegates in January wrote a model state charter only 12,000 words long. Montana voters approved it in June.

Selected Statistics on State Governments

State	Population*	Governor	Legislature***				State	Tax	Enrollment	
			Senate		House		tax rev.	rev. per	in schools	
			(D.)	(R.)	(D.)	(R.)	††††	capita	Elem.‡	High‡
Alabama	3,510	George C. Wallace (D.)	33	0‡‡‡	99	2†,‡‡‡‡‡	$818	$232.95	568	238
Alaska	325	William A. Egan (D.)	9	11	20	19†	102	314.10	62	23
Arizona	1,945	Jack Williams (R.)	12	18	22	38	595	306.12	331	133
Arkansas	1,978	Dale Bumpers (D.)	34	1	99	1	460	232.45	326	135
California	20,468	Ronald Reagan (R.)	19	19‡‡‡	50	29‡‡	6,740	329.31	3,186	1,887
Colorado	2,357	John A. Love (R.)	13	22	28	37	602	255.49	396	169
Connecticut	3,082	Thomas A. Meskill (R.)	13	23	58	93	989	320.75	484	183
Delaware	565	Sherman W. Tribbitt (D.)	10	11	20	21	257	454.39	95	40
Florida	7,259	Reubin Askew (D.)	25	14†	77	43	1,996	275.02	1,033	446
Georgia	4,720	Jimmy Carter (D.)	48	8	151	29	1,198	253.82	769	324
Hawaii	809	John A. Burns (D.)	17	8	35	16	389	480.67	130	53
Idaho	756	Cecil Andrus (D.)	12	23	19	51	200	264.64	125	60
Illinois	11,251	Daniel Walker (D.)	29	30	88	89	3,398	302.00	1,515	880
Indiana	5,291	Otis R. Bowen (R.)	21	29	27	73	1,187	224.39	867	364
Iowa	2,883	Robert Ray (R.)	22	27‡‡	44	56	759	263.41	454	199
Kansas	2,258	Robert Docking (D.)	13	27	45	80	528	233.75	346	157
Kentucky	3,299	Wendell H. Ford (D.)	25	11‡‡‡	72	27‡‡	861	260.97	509	211
Louisiana	3,720	Edwin W. Edwards (D.)	38	1	101	4	1,105	297.07	619	232
Maine	1,029	Kenneth M. Curtis (D.)	11	22	71	79‡‡	264	256.15	178	69
Maryland	4,056	Marvin Mandel (D.)	33	10	121	21	1,272	313.71	662	261
Massachusetts	5,787	Francis W. Sargent (R.)	33	7	186	52††	1,805	311.96	838	353
Michigan	9,082	William G. Milliken (R.)	19	19	60	50	3,033	333.92	1,503	710
Minnesota	3,896	Wendell R. Anderson (D.)	67**		134**		1,324	339.96	627	286
Mississippi	2,263	William L. Waller (D.)	50	2	119	2†	588	259.94	383	146
Missouri	4,753	Christopher S. Bond (R.)	21	13	97	66	1,047	220.33	725	298
Montana	719	Thomas L. Judge (D.)	27	23	54	46	183	254.27	111	68
Nebraska	1,525	J. James Exon (D.)	(Unicameral)**		49		319	209.50	231	102
Nevada	527	D. N. O'Callaghan (D.)	14	6	25	15	181	343.19	94	36
New Hampshire	771	Meldrim Thomson, Jr. (R.)	10	14	137	260‡‡‡‡	139	180.51	117	47
New Jersey	7,367	William T. Cahill (R.)	16	22‡‡‡	39	38†,‡‡‡	1,626	220.75	1,059	439
New Mexico	1,065	Bruce King (D.)	30	12	51	19	356	334.62	200	85
New York	18,366	Nelson A. Rockefeller (R.)	23	37	67	83	7,020	382.24	2,456	1,064
North Carolina	5,214	James E. Holshouser, Jr. (R.)	35	15	85	35	1,461	280.18	820	356
North Dakota	632	Arthur A. Link (D.)	9	41‡‡	22	79‡‡	158	249.69	98	47
Ohio	10,783	John J. Gilligan (D.)	16	17	58	41	2,189	203.04	1,698	741
Oklahoma	2,634	David Hall (D.)	37	10‡‡	75	26	645	245.05	433	193
Oregon	2,182	Tom McCall (R.)	18	12	33	27	508	232.77	322	156
Pennsylvania	11,926	Milton J. Shapp (D.)	25	24‡‡	96	105‡‡‡	3,863	323.91	1,622	749
Rhode Island	968	Philip Noel (D.)	37	13	73	27	301	310.85	136	54
South Carolina	2,665	John C. West (D.)	42	3‡‡	103	21	683	256.73	460	188
South Dakota	679	Richard S. Kneip (D.)	18	17	35	35	133	196.39	113	52
Tennessee	4,031	Winfield Dunn (R.)	19	13†	51	48	887	220.16	639	258
Texas	11,649	Dolph Briscoe (D.)	28	3	133	17	2,572	220.79	2,006	805
Utah	1,126	Calvin L. Rampton (D.)	13	16	31	44	308	273.46	213	93
Vermont	462	Thomas P. Salmon (D.)	8	22	60	89†	158	342.54	76	29
Virginia	4,764	Linwood Holton (R.)	33	7	71	25†††	1,189	249.53	765	309
Washington	3,443	Daniel J. Evans (R.)	30	19	57	41	1,175	341.15	557	248
West Virginia	1,781	Arch A. Moore, Jr. (R.)	24	10	57	43	529	297.24	284	120
Wisconsin	4,520	Patrick J. Lucey (D.)	15	18	62	37	1,628	360.19	675	325
Wyoming	345	Stanley K. Hathaway (R.)	13	17	17	44†	97	281.58	60	27

*Numbers in thousands, estimated as of July 1, 1972
**Nonpartisan
***As of Dec. 31, 1972

†Also one independent
††Also two independents
†††Also four independents
††††Amount in millions, for 1972

‡Numbers in thousands, for 1972
‡‡One vacancy
‡‡‡Two vacancies
‡‡‡‡Three vacancies
‡‡‡‡‡Four vacancies

West Virginia's Governor Arch A. Moore, Jr., presides as chairman at the opening of the National Governors' Conference on June 5, in Houston.

State messages requested increases in sales or income taxes, the two major tax sources for the states. As a result, state tax increases enacted in 1972 amounted to less than 2 per cent of 1971 tax collections, a decided contrast to the 1971 boost of 10 per cent.

For added revenue, 10 states raised motor fuel taxes 1 to 2 cents a gallon. They were Kentucky, Idaho, Maryland, Michigan, Missouri, Mississippi, New Jersey, New York, South Carolina, and Virginia. Six states boosted cigarette taxes, the greatest increases being 5 cents a pack in New Jersey and Oregon. Connecticut increased its sales tax from 6.5 to 7 per cent, making it the highest in the nation. California also raised its sales tax, from 5 to 6 per cent.

Personal income tax rates were raised by two states. New York imposed a surtax of 2.5 per cent on individual income tax liabilities and raised the top bracket from 14 per cent of taxable income over $23,000 to 15 per cent in excess of $25,000. Virginia raised the maximum tax rate from 5 per cent on taxable income over $5,000 to 5.75 per cent on amounts over $12,000. Corporate income tax rates were increased by California from 7.6 to 9 per cent, by Idaho from 6 to 6.5 per cent, by Nebraska from 20 to 25 per cent of the individual rates in 1973, by New Jersey from 4.25 to 5.5 per cent, and by Virginia from 5 to 6 per cent.

State tax collections yielded nearly $60 billion. This was a 17 per cent increase over fiscal 1971.

School Financing. A proliferation of school-financing cases in both state and federal courts followed the 1971 *Serrano v. Priest* and *Rodriguez v. San Antonio Independent School District* decisions in California and Texas. The decisions generally declared the financing methods for public schools to be discriminatory by making the quality of education dependent on wealth and property. The states, although undertaking various studies of alternative financing to the property tax, took little other action, preferring to await a ruling by the Supreme Court of the United States on an appeal in the *Rodriguez* case. Thirty states entered friend-of-the-court briefs in that case, asking the Supreme Court to summarily reverse the lower federal court's ruling that the Texas school financing system was unconstitutional.

The voters in four states opposed eliminating the property tax as a major source of funding for local schools. California and Colorado voters rejected property tax limitations, while those in Michigan and Oregon refused to ban use of local property taxes for financing school operations.

In another area of educational finance – the provision of aid to private and church-related schools – the states continued the trend of earlier years by passing new laws to compensate parents for non-public school tuition, despite adverse court decisions in this delicate area. Connecticut, Illinois, Missouri, New Hampshire, New York, and Ohio passed new measures. Some of the new laws were being challenged in court.

Lotteries and Gambling. In a search for new financing methods, several more states opened the way for state lotteries, which six states previously had shown to be profitable. Maryland and Michigan are starting lotteries, after voter approval in November. Iowa voters removed constitutional restrictions on lotteries. Washington voters authorized a lottery if approved by a 60 per cent legislative or voter majority. Montana voters endorsed legalized gambling at the option of the legislature. The Colorado electorate, however, defeated proposals for a privately operated, state-regulated lottery, and also for a state sweepstakes race.

The nation's first daily, state-operated lottery started in New Jersey. The daily lottery operates simultaneously with New Jersey's weekly lottery, which started several years ago and became the most successful weekly state lottery in the nation. Its weekly success wilted, however, as lottery competition from New York and Pennsylvania grew. New Jersey expects the daily lottery to produce about $25-million a year. The proceeds of New Jersey's daily and weekly lotteries, projected at $65-million a year, are to be spent for education and state institutions.

No-Fault Auto Insurance. With 49 state legislatures meeting in 1973, most will consider legislation for no-fault automobile insurance. The no-fault plan eliminates the need to prove who caused an accident. If a policyholder is injured, he can collect immediately from his own insurance company. Four states – Connecticut, Maryland, Michigan, and New Jersey – enacted such statutes in 1972. They join Massachusetts, Delaware, and Oregon, plus several other states that have enacted "limited" no-fault reforms. The issue is particularly important for the states because the U.S. Congress is expected to act on a federal no-fault law if the states show little interest. Massachusetts, the first state to adopt a no-fault insurance law, reported that its auto-accident cases had been cut about 50 per cent and that motorists had received $59 million in reduced premiums.

Environmental Action. Thirty-five of the 43 states holding legislative sessions in 1972 passed environmental-quality laws. Six strengthened strip-mining regulations, and several passed measures dealing with sewage-disposal processes and power-plant sitings.

New Jersey, one of the nation's most densely populated states and probably one of the noisiest as well, adopted the first comprehensive noise-pollution control law in January, 1972. It gave the state Department of Environmental Control the authority to draw up and enforce noise-pollution regulations.

Major environmental-control issues also won support in the November elections. California and Washington voters passed proposals to protect the coastline. Florida voters backed a $240-million bond issue for the acquisition of environmentally endangered lands. A $1.15-billion environmental bond issue was approved in New York.

Constitutions and Administration. Reorganization of the executive branch of state governments continued. Georgia consolidated about 300 agencies into 22 departments. Virginia set up six offices of secretary that took authority over all departments and agencies. Maine adopted legislation to implement reorganization in 10 to 13 departments. Arizona, Ohio, and Tennessee also proceeded with executive reorganization.

Voters' consent to constitutional amendments limiting the number of executive agencies was obtained in Idaho, Missouri, and South Dakota. The overall reorganization actions in Georgia, Maine, and Virginia brought to 14 the number of states that had carried out major reorganizations since 1965.

Iowa, Kansas, South Dakota, and Texas lengthened the term of governor from two to four years, leaving only four states that still have two-year terms. Constitutional amendments requiring the governor and lieutenant governor to be elected as a team were adopted in Kansas, Minnesota, and South Dakota, making a total of 17 states that now have team elections. Kansas and Minnesota also removed the lieutenant governor as the presiding officer of their senates.

Voters had mixed reactions toward other changes for legislatures. In Minnesota and Wyoming, the electorate voted to permit, but not to require, annual legislative sessions. Proposals for annual sessions lost in Alabama, Louisiana, and New Hampshire. Measures to increase legislative pay lost in Alabama, Arizona, Idaho, Nebraska, and Texas, and won in Utah.

In constitutional revision activity, Montana adopted a new Constitution and North Dakota rejected one. Proposals to hold constitutional conventions were defeated in Ohio and New York, but approved for Texas in 1974.

Rights and Regulations. As of December, 22 state legislatures had approved the 27th Amendment to the U.S. Constitution, the equal rights for women amendment. The measure seemed well on its way to ratification by the required 38 states. In addition, 16 more states lowered the voting age to 18, and two lowered it to 19.

Other Actions. Reapportionment of state legislatures was nearly completed. Fewer than 10 states still had to complete reapportionment in order to comply with the 1970 census.

The state supreme courts in South Dakota and Missouri found laws prohibiting abortions except when necessary to save a woman's life to be constitutional. In the November elections, liberalized abortion measures were rejected in Michigan and North Dakota. Washington, the other state to vote directly on abortion, passed a liberalized measure in 1970.

Robert H. Weber

STEEL INDUSTRY. American steelmakers produced about 67.5 million tons of steel during the first three quarters of 1972. This was a sharp decline from the 97.5-million-ton output for the same period in 1971. Spokesmen for the industry forecast a maximum production of about 95 million tons for the year, down markedly from the 1971 total output of 120.2-million tons. The outlook at year's end brightened when steelmakers announced anticipated shipments of 24 to 25 million tons, about 15 per cent above the first-quarter figure of 21.1 million tons.

The 1971 drop in steel production meant that Russia finally achieved its long-sought goal of becoming the world's largest steel producer. With an output estimated at 134.4 million tons, Russia moved ahead of the United States in production for the first time since 1895.

Steel Imports. The American Iron and Steel Institute (AISI) attributed part of the decline in U.S. output to record-breaking production by foreign steelmakers. Foreign shipments to the United States in 1971 were 18.32 million tons, more than the combined net tonnage produced by the third, fourth, and fifth largest U.S. steel producers. Imports were up nearly 5 million tons since 1970 and were almost 3 million tons above the 15.4-million-ton limit set for the year under the voluntary agreement with foreign producers pledged to limit their exports to the United States. This arrangement expired at the end of 1971 and was replaced in May, 1972, by a new three-year agreement with major European and Japanese producers.

The AISI gave additional reasons for the recent decline in U.S. production. The slowdown in the economy, drastic cutbacks in the aerospace and defense programs, and the continuing effects of the 30 per cent wage increase in the three-year contract awarded steelworkers on Aug. 1, 1971, all took their toll. In addition, air and water pollution-control programs pushed expenditures for environmental protection facilities to the $1.5-billion mark since 1951. Expenditures of an additional $4.5 billion were planned. About $500 million was budgeted for 1972.

Although automobiles continued to provide the major market for steel, the car-buying boom was not quite up to expectations. In addition, automobile manufacturers relied heavily on large quantities of imported sheet products.

World Outlook. At the sixth annual meeting of the International Iron and Steel Institute (IISI) in London in October, Charles H. Baker, secretary-general of the IISI, forecast that world steel production would reach 628 million tons in 1972 – a gain of 8 per cent over 1971. He also predicted a 6 per cent gain in 1973, which would bring world output from 660 to 670 million tons. Mary E. Jessup

U.S. Steel's new slitting and heat-treating line in Chicago winds cold-rolled flat steel onto coils at the rate of 250 feet per minute.

STEINEM, GLORIA (1934-), feminist, lecturer, and writer, in 1972 became the founding editor of a new magazine, *Ms.*, which is dedicated to the social and political concerns of women. The first issue appeared in January.

Gloria Steinem was born in Toledo, Ohio. Her mother was a newspaper reporter; her father, a summer-resort operator. When she was 11 years old, her parents divorced, and she lived with her mother in a Toledo slum.

To finance her education, her mother sold their home, and she graduated magna cum laude from Smith College in 1956, then received a fellowship for two years of study in India.

She began her writing career in 1960 with free-lance assignments for *Esquire* magazine, and became a frequent contributor to various women's magazines. She was also a scriptwriter for the television show "That Was the Week That Was" in 1964. In 1968, she began writing a political column for *New York* magazine.

That year, while attending a women's liberation meeting to gather information for her column, she became a convert to the feminist cause. She has become a leading lecturer and fund-raiser for the Women's Liberation Movement. She helped found the National Women's Political Caucus in 1971, and was active at the 1972 Democratic National Convention in Miami Beach, Fla. Darlene R. Stille

STOCKS AND BONDS. It took more than six years to do it, but it finally happened. The Dow Jones average of 30 industrial stocks finally broke through the "magic" 1,000 barrier, closing at 1,003.66, on Nov. 14, 1972. The blue-chip indicator's previous closing high was 995.15, reached Feb. 9, 1966. The year's high of 1,036.27 was reached on December 11.

For most of the year, however, the securities market reacted cautiously. Corporate profits surged to record levels during the year and encouraged some gains in stock prices. Yet, until November, these gains were more than offset by uncertainties over the negotiations to end the war, the presidential election, and the decisions of the Pay Board and the Price Commission. Added to this were inflation fears stemming from huge federal budget deficits and rapid monetary growth rates in 1972.

Security prices on the New York Stock Exchange (NYSE) advanced 14.58 per cent in 1972; prices on the American Stock Exchange (AMEX) rose 0.10 points. Standard and Poor's index of 500 stocks was up 15.3 per cent for the year.

Total New Issues of securities dropped during the first half of 1972 relative to the same period in 1971. The federal government, buoyed by unexpectedly large tax receipts from economic expansion and the new withholding rates, was able to reduce its offerings, although the estimated federal deficit in the fiscal year ending June 30 was an enormous $23 billion. This was the largest deficit since World War II.

1,000 Mark: Up and Over

Dow Jones industrial averages

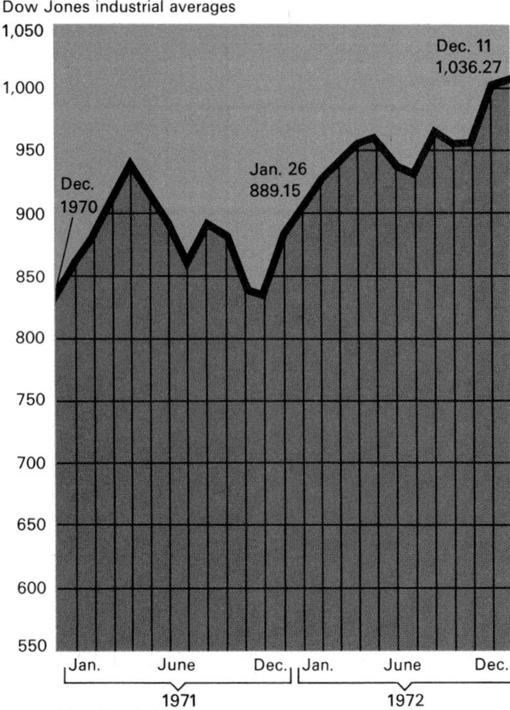

Monthly closings

Brokers, despite the quickening pulse of economic activity, had less than a banner year. Small investors, still smarting from losses in the 1969-1970 bear market, were increasing their savings and avoiding the risks of stock ownership. Stocks proved as vulnerable as bonds to inflation in the late 1960s and were actually more vulnerable than money in depository institutions. Stock yields were well below bond yields in 1972. Individuals unloaded mutual fund shares throughout the year, forcing open-end investment companies to maintain an unusually large cash position for redemptions. Individuals stopped selling more stocks than they were buying for the first time since the recovery from market lows in 1969, but this was insignificant in comparison with the roughly $50 billion in financial savings that were accumulated during the first half of the year.

Stock prices held up partly because of increased purchases on margin. This is often a sign that sophisticated investors expect market gains in the months ahead.

Institutional Investors kept pressure on brokers to reduce commission rates competitively on large transactions and to allow mutual funds, pension funds, insurance companies, and banks to make their own trades as members of stock exchanges. Institutions are presently barred from membership in the NYSE and AMEX, and must negotiate trades outside of major exchanges or pay commissions to brokers. The rapidly growing Philadelphia-Baltimore-Washington (PBW) Exchange is one of the few that allows institutional memberships. Commissions on transactions over $300,000 must be negotiated and, since 1971, these commissions have fallen from previously scheduled rates.

New Issue Guidelines. The Securities and Exchange Commission (SEC) asked the NYSE to draft guidelines in September for selling newly issued stocks. These stocks are generally unlisted on the major exchanges. The request triggered an industry squabble between the NYSE and the National Association of Securities Dealers (NASD). The 4,200-member NASD, which includes many brokers serving the over-the-counter market in unlisted securities, insisted that it be recognized as spokesman for, and supervisor of, the over-the-counter market, not the NYSE. Almost all of the 573 member firms of the NYSE are also members of the NASD.

The NASD moved closer to its planned nationwide stock-clearing system by hooking some regional exchanges into the network that clears unlisted stock among New York brokers. Stock clearing allows brokers to net out transactions so that delivery of only the excess securities sold is necessary. Lack of such a system contributed to the "back-office" crush in the late 1960s when the volume of over-the-counter sales was unusually high. William G. Dewald

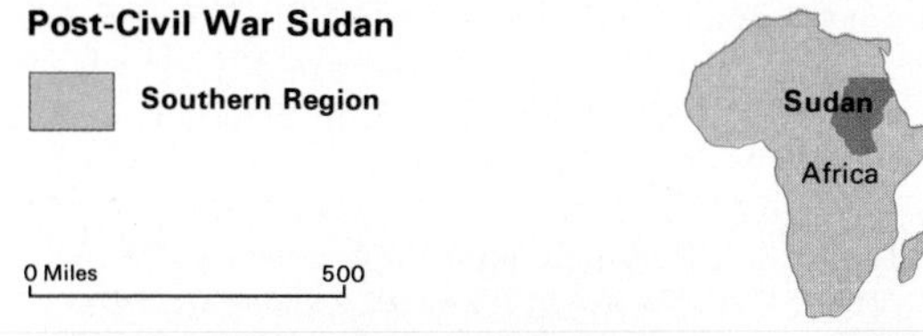

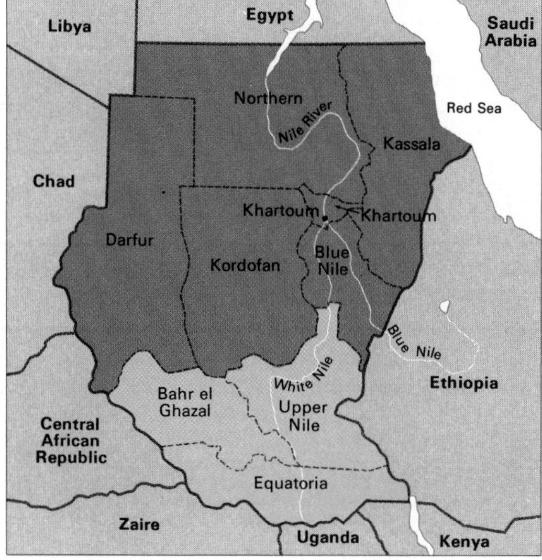

SUDAN. The Sudanese government and rebel forces in the south reached an agreement on March 6, 1972, ending the civil war that had raged since 1955. The Christian Africans in the south had wanted independence from the predominantly Moslem Sudanese government. The pact was negotiated in Addis Ababa, Ethiopia, under the sponsorship of Ethiopia's Emperor Haile Selassie I.

The Addis Ababa Agreement provided autonomy for the three southern provinces by uniting them into the region of South Sudan, governed by an elected assembly and an executive council. Executives would be appointed by Sudanese President Jafir Muhammad Nimeri upon the recommendation of the regional assembly. English was adopted as a working language along with the official Arabic language.

Southerners, including former rebel fighters, will be integrated into the Sudanese Army over a five-year period. At the end of that time, southerners should comprise at least half of the Sudanese armed forces in the south.

After ending the civil war, Sudan faced the gigantic job of restoring the south to normal. The United Nations (UN) High Commission for Refugees assumed responsibility for resettling some 200,000 Sudanese refugees in Ethiopia, Uganda, and Zaire. UN nations gave $10 million for refugee relief.

The first members were elected to Sudan's new parliament on October 10. The 207-member Sudanese People's Council was the first legislative body convened since Nimeri seized power in 1969.

Foreign Relations. Ending the civil war smoothed relations between Sudan and its neighbors. Sudan's border with Uganda was reopened, and the two states signed a mutual defense pact on June 28.

The Sudanese government made railroad-building agreements with Chad and the Central African Republic. Nimeri also announced in August that he intended to bring Sudan into the East African Community. On July 25, Sudan and the United States resumed diplomatic relations, which had been broken during the 1967 Arab-Israeli War. In April, Sudan and the Vatican agreed to establish full diplomatic ties.

The Economy continued to grow in spite of the drain on resources caused by war and reconstruction. In April, Sudan signed a trade agreement and an economic and technical cooperation pact with Romania. West Germany granted Sudan credits of $15-million to modernize railways and build a jute-processing plant. The World Bank in August approved loans of $1 million for a new textile plant and $11.25 million to reclaim 435,000 acres of saline land. William Spencer

See also AFRICA (Facts in Brief Table).

SUPREME COURT OF THE UNITED STATES. See COURTS AND LAWS.

SWAZILAND. See AFRICA.

SWEDEN. After 40 consecutive years of rule in Europe's most affluent nation, the Social Democrats struggled in 1972 to maintain their supremacy. It will be tested in a general election in September, 1973. With 118,000 workers (3.1 per cent) idle, unemployment was at its highest point since the 1930s. Inflation was virtually unchecked. Food prices rose about 7 per cent during the year and the cost of living about 8 per cent. Housewives staged a nationwide boycott in protest against rising food prices in February and March.

In May, the 17 Communist members, who hold the balance of power in Parliament, threatened to bring down the minority government over a proposal to raise the value-added tax (VAT) from 17.65 per cent to 20 per cent. The proposal was part of a "package deal" that included lowering taxes on average incomes (those from $6,000 to $14,000) and raising study allowances, child allowances, and pensions. Taxes on cigarettes, beer, liquor, and gasoline were to be raised. Prime Minister Olof Palme survived the test by compromising: The VAT increase was applied only to wines, spirits, and tobacco, but the payroll tax was raised from 2 to 4 per cent.

Tariff Agreement. With neighboring Denmark and Norway considering membership in the European Community (Common Market), Sweden obtained an agreement providing preferential rates for trade with Common Market members. The agreement saves Sweden $120 million in tariffs on imports from Common Market countries.

The treaty, signed July 22, was one of a series linking market countries with five nations of the European Free Trade Association. It gradually eliminates tariffs on most industrial goods in five annual steps beginning in 1973.

Powers of the Monarchy. King Gustaf VI Adolf would lose his remaining powers under a draft Constitution proposed on March 21. The monarchy would be retained, but the powers of Parliament would be strengthened. The new Constitution would abolish the king's Friday Council, which annually makes 30,000 decisions. Before it can take effect, the change will have to be passed by two legislatures with an election in-between.

A second committee reported in March on how to separate church and state. At present, a child of Swedish parents is automatically a member of the established Lutheran Church, to which 99 per cent of the population belong and pay taxes. The committee proposes to abolish the church's tax-levying and management roles by 1992.

Under a law passed on April 30 to take effect in 1973, every company with more than 100 employees must grant two places on its board of directors to trade union representatives. Kenneth Brown

See also EUROPE (Facts in Brief Table).

SWIMMING. Mark Spitz of the United States did even better in 1972 than he did in 1971, when he broke three world swimming records for men. He won seven gold medals in the Olympic Games in Munich in August, all in world-record time.

In the U.S. Olympic trials in August in Chicago, Spitz broke three world records a total of five times. Then came his string of Olympic gold medals and records – in the 100-meter free-style (51.22 seconds), 200-meter free-style (1 minute 52.78 seconds), 100-meter butterfly (54.27 seconds), 200-meter butterfly (2:00.70), and three relays.

Spitz, Gary Hall, and John Kinsella won two individual finals each in the National Collegiate Athletic Association (NCAA) championships in March in West Point, N.Y., leading Indiana University to its fifth straight title. Spitz also won three events, and Hall and Kinsella two each, in the Amateur Athletic Union (A.A.U.) national indoor championships in April in Dallas. Because it was an Olympic year, the A.A.U. held no outdoor championships in 1972.

Burton's Contribution. Spitz, at 22, and Mike Burton, at 25, were two of the oldest members of the U.S. Olympic team. Both came from Carmichael, Calif., and both were coached by Sherman Chavoor. Burton, in becoming the first man to retain the Olympic title in the 1,500-meter free-style, lowered the world record to 15 minutes 52.58 seconds.

Shane Gould set a world record in winning the Olympic 400-meter free-style race. The Australian teen-ager won three gold medals.

Shane Gould almost matched her stunning 1971 performance. She set women's world records in the 100-meter free-style (58.5 seconds), 200-meter free-style (2 minutes 3.56 seconds), 400-meter free-style (4:19.04), and 200-meter individual medley (2:23.07). She also won three Olympic finals, and was beaten in two others.

Record Breakers. World-record breakers among the men included Hall, Kurt Krumpholz, and John Hencken of the United States; Roland Matthes of East Germany, in both backstroke events; Nobutaka Taguchi of Japan; Brad Cooper of Australia; and Gunnar Larsson of Sweden. Record breakers among the women included Melissa Belote, Karen Moe, Keena Rothhammer, and Cathy Carr of the United States; Gail Neall of Australia; and Mayumi Aoki of Japan.

As usual, world records were broken often (16 of 16 among the men, 12 of 15 among the women). And as usual, the best swimmers were young. The average age of the U.S. Olympic team was 19½ for men and 17½ for women.

American swimmers again were supreme. Australians made the major challenges, and the East Germans, except for Matthes, were disappointing. The best divers included Klaus DiBiasi of Italy and Dick Rydze of the United States among the men and Micki King of the United States and Ulrike Knape of Sweden among the women. Frank Litsky

SWITZERLAND voted on Dec. 3, 1972, to join Europe's move toward economic integration. A free-trade treaty with the European Community (Common Market), submitted to the voters for approval by the government, won by 1,345,057 votes to 509,350. It was approved in all of the 25 cantons.

On September 24, Swiss voters rejected a constitutional amendment that would have stopped manufacturers from exporting Swiss arms. The amendment was narrowly defeated, 593,205 to 584,726. Swiss overseas arms sales were running at $33.5 million a year.

Defense Strategy. Swiss defense strategy, dating from 1966, included plans for new jet fighters. The government turned down the purchase of 60 American A7G Corsairs for $355 million and bought 24 refurbished Hunter jets from Great Britain for $25-million. Defense Minister Rudolf Gnägi said the move was necessary to trim government spending. But Air Force Commander Eugene Studer complained that the air force was becoming an "antique shop." The Hunters, plus 57 French Mirage-Milan fighters, will replace 210 Venoms, the main air force weapon for two decades. The Swiss National Council voted on October 2 to retain the cavalry, which the government had wanted to replace with armor. Twelve squadrons (2,000 horsemen) will be kept.

Monetary Measures. Steps were taken on July 4 and 5 to strengthen Switzerland's monetary defenses against both inflation and international speculators. They included an 8 per cent tax imposed on foreign deposits in Swiss banks after July 3 and a requirement that Swiss firms get national bank authorization to borrow money in other countries. The measures also required Swiss banks with more than $5.5-million in assets to deposit with the central bank 90 per cent of nonresidents' deposits since July 31, 1971.

A report by the Organization for Economic Cooperation and Development in February said little short-term change was likely in Switzerland's inflationary pressure. The outlook for exports and the balance of payments was called "uncertain." A severe labor shortage continued, attributable largely to restrictions imposed on immigrant labor in 1970.

Separatist Action. Jura separatists – the Front de Liberation Jurassien – bombed a Swiss Army munitions depot near Glovelier on July 16. Four days earlier, members of the movement occupied the Swiss Embassy in Paris for several hours. They seek a separate canton for the French-speaking Roman Catholic Jura region, now a part of the German-speaking Protestant canton of Bern.

Roger Bonvin, minister of transport, communications, and energy, was elected on December 6 to serve as president for 1973 under the Swiss system of rotating the office. He had previously held the office in 1962. Kenneth Brown

See also EUROPE (Facts in Brief Table).

SYRIA took an important step toward a more representative government on March 7, 1972. The formation of the Syrian Progressive National Front united four minority leftist parties from the governing coalition with the dominant Ba'ath Party. An 18-member Central Committee consisted of the president of the republic, 9 Ba'athists, and 2 members from each of the minority parties: the Arab Socialist Union, the Syrian Communist Party, the Socialist Unionists, and the Arab Socialist Party.

President Hafiz al-Asad enlarged his Cabinet on March 23 to 30 members – 15 Ba'athists and 15 non-Ba'athists. The latter included five independent ministers and four from the Arab Socialist Union. However, an amendment to the 1969 Provisional Constitution gave President Asad absolute power in case of a national emergency or when the main Syrian legislative bodies are not in session.

Provincial Councils were elected in March under a plan to decentralize administration, and there were some surprises. Only 8 Ba'athists were among the 98 elected to the Damascus City Council.

The Ba'ath Party celebrated its 25th anniversary in April. Asad reaffirmed Syrian support for the Palestinian movement against Israel. But there was little conflict, other than sporadic air clashes, until November 22, when an eight-hour series of air, artillery, and tank battles broke out between Syria and Israel on the Golan Heights.

Syria Nationalized all assets and facilities of the Iraq Petroleum Company (IPC) on June 19. The government formed the Syrian Company for Oil Transport to operate the IPC installations. The Organization of Arab Petroleum Exporting Countries loaned the country $16 million to compensate for lost oil revenues during the transition period.

President Asad visited Russia in July and signed an agreement setting up a joint commission to supervise Russian aid projects in Syria. He said Syria would not expel some 2,500 to 3,000 Russian advisers – as Egypt did – because their technical skills were needed and they did not represent a political threat.

In late December, Asad accepted the resignation of Prime Minister Abd al-Rahman Khalafawi and asked Vice-President Mahmoud al-Ayubi to form a government. On December 24, Asad announced formation of a 31-man Cabinet, in which Ba'athists would hold more than half the posts.

Favorable weather for agriculture aided the Syrian economy. The Homs fertilizer plant, a major industrial project in the 1971-to-1975 five-year plan, went into operation in May. It would produce 148,000 tons annually, enough to fill domestic needs. Phosphate production was expected to reach 300,000 tons in the first full year of operation. William Spencer

See also MIDDLE EAST (Facts in Brief Table).

TAIWAN. The shock waves that swept the country after its expulsion from the United Nations in 1971 continued in 1972. Most of the unease sprang from a decision by the United States and Japan to begin to normalize relations with the People's Republic of China. The U.S.-Peking accord, made during President Richard M. Nixon's February visit to China, in effect left any settlement of Taiwan's future status up to Taiwan and Peking. This was underscored by a U.S. pledge to withdraw its 8,000 troops still in Taiwan when tensions in Asia were reduced. An earlier agreement also called for an end to the use of the U.S. Seventh Fleet to patrol the Formosa Strait, which separates Taiwan from China. See CHINA, PEOPLE'S REPUBLIC OF; PRESIDENT OF THE UNITED STATES.

Similarly, a visit to Peking by Japanese Prime Minister Kakuei Tanaka put great strain on Taiwan's 20-year bilateral trade treaty with Japan. Japan has extensive investments on Taiwan, though many are hidden behind a façade of Taiwanese ownership. About 40 per cent – nearly $1 billion – of Taiwan's imports come from Japan annually. Japanese tourism is also a major industry, producing about 300,000 visitors each year. The news of mainland China's reconciliation with Japan and the United States thus caused a flight of investment money from Taiwan. Some observers estimated that more than $400 million left the island during the summer.

Carrying pictures showing Chiang Kai-shek some 20 years ago, Taiwanese schoolgirls march to celebrate his election to fifth term as president.

Japan, however, did not cancel its treaty with Taiwan, and commercial relations were expected to continue as before. Nor did the United States withdraw immediately. Given these two facts, Taiwan began to adjust to its new status. The government's reactions, mostly on the political front, were considered indications that the Nationalists on Taiwan were preparing for eventual reintegration with the mainland.

The major task facing the government during the year was a reform of the ruling Kuomintang (Nationalist Party) to give the Taiwanese greater representation in the party and the government. The party predictably elected the 85-year-old Chiang Kai-shek to his fifth six-year term as president on March 21. More important, Chiang's son Chiang Ching-kuo was elevated to the office of prime minister.

The 62-year-old prime minister, who is also director of the China Youth Corps, began by urging the young to be more critical and progressive. He aided the remodeling of the party's Central Committee by adding four key members of Taiwanese descent. And, as chairman of the Central Committee, he assumed the dominant role in the government.

In national and local legislative elections held on December 23, Kuomintang candidates won almost all of the contested seats. Most of the candidates, Kuomintang and opposition alike, were Taiwan-born, and many were young men. John N. Stalker

See also ASIA (Facts in Brief Table).

TANAKA, KAKUEI (1918-), was elected prime minister of Japan on July 5, 1972. He succeeded Eisaku Sato, who retired. He said he would continue close ties with the United States and improve relations with China and Russia. See CHINA, PEOPLE'S REPUBLIC OF; JAPAN.

Tanaka was born on May 4, 1918, in Nishiyama, a village in a poor farming region about 200 miles northwest of Tokyo. His father failed in both farming and business, and the family was poor. Tanaka left school in the sixth grade, and when he was 15, he went to Tokyo. He worked for room and board while attending a vocational school and English-language classes at night. At 18, he began work with a construction company. A few years later, he had his own company. Tanaka later became wealthy through real estate investments.

In 1947, at the age of 29, Tanaka was elected to parliament. He was named deputy minister of justice in 1949. He was named minister of postal services in 1957, finance minister in 1962, and secretary-general of the governing Liberal-Democratic Party in 1965. In this post, he organized successive election victories for his party. In December, 1971, Tanaka was given the post of minister of international trade and industry.

Tanaka is known for his vigor and flamboyance, unusual characteristics in his country. He is married and has a daughter. Michael Reed

TANZANIA. About 1,000 Ugandan refugees living in Tanzania launched an attack against Uganda on Sept. 17, 1972. The invaders managed to capture three small towns in southern Uganda before Ugandan army troops were able to stop them. The fighting was over by September 20.

Relations between Tanzania and Uganda had been strained since 1971, when the ousted President Apollo Milton Obote of Uganda took refuge in Tanzania. Many of Obote's supporters followed him there. After the border violations, President Idi Amin Dada, who had led the coup against Obote, accused Tanzanian President Julius K. Nyerere of plotting to invade Uganda. Nyerere, however, denied that any of his troops were involved in the September fighting.

After the aborted invasion, Uganda declared that Tanzanian troops were massing for an attack, and Tanzania accused Uganda of bombing a village near Lake Victoria. Finally, with Somali President Mohamed Siad Barre moderating the peace talks, the two countries announced on October 5 that they had reached a peaceful settlement of the dispute.

Other Disputes. The civil war in Burundi created a refugee problem in Tanzania. Reportedly, more than 25,000 Hutu (Bahutu) tribesmen sought refuge in Tanzania and other countries to escape tribal massacres in Burundi.

On July 21, Nyerere spoke out strongly against Amin's program of expelling Asians from Uganda. He said that Amin was practicing racism, "the same thing that Africans are deploring."

Vice-President Killed. Tanzanian First Vice-President Sheik Abeid A. Karume, ruler of the island of Zanzibar, was assassinated on April 7. Four gunmen shot Karume while he was visiting his Afro-Shirazi Party headquarters. Karume was replaced by Aboud Jumbe, formerly Zanzibar's minister of state.

One of Karume's political rivals, Abdul Rahman Babu, once head of Zanzibar's Umma Party, and about 300 party sympathizers were arrested on April 14 and questioned about the slaying. Fifty-two of them were released on July 14, but Babu was held in custody.

Babu was one of four prisoners who had been released by Nyerere on February 8 because of increasing criticism of the government's preventive detention powers. The four had been jailed for what the government considered security reasons.

Nyerere announced major Cabinet changes on February 17. Three ministers were dropped from the Cabinet, including Babu, who had been minister of economic affairs and development planning. Nyerere created the office of prime minister and appointed Rashidi Kawawa to the post. At the same time, he disbanded the ministry for rural administration. George Shepherd

See also AFRICA (Facts in Brief Table); UGANDA.

TAXATION. No new major tax reforms were proposed by the Nixon Administration or by Congress in 1972. Estimated receipts for the federal government were $220.8 billion for fiscal 1973, and estimates of the federal deficit were $25 billion to $26-billion, making the fiscal 1973 deficit the second largest in the nation's history. Despite President Richard M. Nixon's efforts to hold down federal spending and balance the budget, the cumulative federal deficit reached $87.3 billion during the first three years of his Administration.

On November 23, Deputy Secretary of the Treasury Charles E. Walker reported that, because the current economic boomlet was so "robust," the deficit for fiscal 1973 would probably be smaller than anticipated. He foresaw a deficit of $23 billion or less when the accelerating economy began generating more profits and, therefore, larger tax receipts.

Value-Added Tax was widely discussed as a way to equalize the financing of the nation's schools and to correct inequities between rich and poor school districts and rich and poor states. A form of national sales tax, the value-added tax is levied on the increase in value or price of a product at every stage in its manufacture and distribution. The cost of the tax is added to the final price and is eventually paid by the consumer. The tax is now widely used in Europe. In November, however, President Nixon reportedly rejected the tax, claiming it would raise too much revenue too fast.

Social Security Taxes rose in 1972 and will continue to rise in 1973. The taxable wage or salary base on which the tax is levied was increased from $9,000 in 1972 to $10,800 in 1973, and $12,000 in 1974. For 1973, the tax rate will rise from 5.2 per cent to 5.88 per cent each for worker and employer and, by the year 2011, to 7.3 per cent. The tax hikes will finance the automatic cost-of-living increases provided for by the new social security laws. From 1970 to 1972, social security benefits rose 51 per cent, requiring tax increases to cover these rising costs. See SOCIAL SECURITY.

Government Payrolls. The Tax Foundation, Inc., a private research organization, estimated an 88 per cent rise in federal, state, and local government payrolls during the 1960s. In addition to an increase in the total number of government employees, the average government worker's salary increased 64 per cent.

Internal Revenue Audit. On April 11, Internal Revenue Service (IRS) Commissioner Johnnie M. Walters announced a special auditing program to search for unallowable deductions, including inaccurate claims for deductions on medical expenses, casualty losses, and dividends. Walters estimated that the new program would bring $40 million a year in additional federal tax revenue.

In addition, the IRS planned to look into the work of commercial tax-preparation services. A preliminary 1972 check in the Southwest revealed that two-thirds of the returns prepared by such services were sloppy or fraudulent. Of 300 firms checked, 192 prepared returns that warranted rechecking. Forty-one persons were arrested and 44 were under indictment for fraud.

In 1973, the IRS planned to reissue the "short form" 1040-A after having dropped it for a few years. A new simplified instruction book was prepared by an IRS advisory committee. In 1971, Commissioner Walters was quoted as saying that even a fifth-grader could fill out the income tax form. But many fifth-graders who took up the challenge failed. The advisory committee included some fifth-grade teachers.

State and Local Taxes. In July, the Bureau of the Census reported that state government spending exceeded revenue from all sources for the first time in more than 10 years in fiscal 1971.

In fiscal 1972, state tax collections totaled $59.8-billion, 16.1 per cent more than 1971's $51.5 billion. Twelve states collected at least 20 per cent more in taxes than in 1971. The greatest percentage increases in state tax revenue were reported by, in order, Montana (34.6), Florida (25.8), Pennsylvania (24.9), Connecticut (24.3), and Ohio (23.5). Only four states reported increases of less than 5 per cent.

Nearly half of all state tax revenue was collected by only seven states. They were, in order, New York ($7.02 billion), California ($6.7 billion), Pennsylvania ($3.9 billion), Illinois ($3.4 billion), Michigan ($3.0 billion), Texas ($2.6 billion), and Ohio ($2.2-billion).

Per-capita state tax collections varied as usual. Nineteen states collected more than $300 per capita in fiscal 1972; 27 states collected between $220 and $300 per capita; 4 states collected less than $220.

Local tax collections totaled approximately $48.6-billion. This was approximately 18.7 per cent less than total state tax revenue.

General sales and gross receipts accounted for the bulk of fiscal 1972 tax collections. The 45 states that have a general sales tax experienced a 13.9 per cent increase over 1971. Selective taxes on motor fuels, tobacco, alcohol, and insurance were the second largest source of tax revenue, followed by individual income tax, which was up 28 per cent over 1971.

In the November elections, California, Colorado, Michigan, and Oregon defeated proposed constitutional amendments that would have eliminated or restricted use of the property tax for public school revenue. The Supreme Court of the United States was expected to rule in 1973 on the use of the property tax to finance public education. The court will decide whether the use of property taxes to finance education discriminates unconstitutionally against poorer communities. Carol L. Thompson

See also CITY; STATE GOVERNMENT.

TELEPHONE AND TELEGRAPH. See COMMUNICATIONS.

Redd Foxx, left, and Demond Wilson operate a Los Angeles junkyard in "Sanford and Son," one of the top 10 shows on television in 1972.

TELEVISION entered a new age of candor in 1972. Its bold programming of ethnic humor and heretofore taboo "adult" themes finally began to mirror the increasing permissiveness of society, although it was only a pale reflection of the anything-goes spirit of contemporary theater and motion pictures.

The trend was pioneered by "All in the Family," a situation-comedy series that spoofs bigotry and dares to be funny about such touchy topics as homosexuality, impotence, and menopause. "Family," 1972's top-rated show, was watched by more than 50 million people each week and won six Emmies.

The "Family" format was successfully adapted by three new comedies that were in the top 10. They were "Sanford and Son," starring Redd Foxx as a bigoted black junkman; "Maude," with Beatrice Arthur as a phony radical chic liberal; and "Bridget Loves Bernie," which involved a "mixed" marriage and Jewish-Catholic in-laws. One old favorite was scheduled to go off the air. The National Broadcasting Company (NBC) announced in November that "Bonanza" would go off the air in January, 1973.

Other Favorites. Movies, aired in prime network time seven nights a week, were bigger than ever in 1972. *Love Story*, with most of its sexy footage intact, chalked up a 42.3 Nielsen rating on October 1, making it the highest-rated movie of all time.

President Richard M. Nixon's historic trip to China in February was covered in remarkable depth. The networks also provided lengthy coverage of the Olympic Games in Sapporo, Japan, in February and in Munich, West Germany, in August and September; *Apollo 16*'s and *17*'s lunar landings in April and December; the Democratic and Republican conventions in Miami in July and August; and the November presidential elections.

Network and Independent Stations Sales were considerably better after two bleak years, but otherwise 1972 was even more ulcerous for broadcasters than 1971. One of the most serious threats was the increasing number of challenges to station license renewals. In May, the Federal Communications Commission (FCC) had a record backlog of petitions against more than 100 stations. Most of the complaints were filed by women's coalitions and minority groups, charging discrimination in employment and programming practices.

Commercial Controversies. In January, the Federal Trade Commission asked the FCC to apply its Fairness Doctrine to product commercials and require broadcasters to air counter-spots refuting claims of some commercials. Broadcasters fought the proposal, claiming it would cause a mass exodus of advertisers and bring financial ruin to the industry. Although no official FCC action had been taken by the end of the year, some stations had voluntarily telecast counter-ads.

© BBC

Glenda Jackson starred as the Queen of England in "Elizabeth R," an impressive new six-part dramatic series produced in Great Britain.

Broadcasters, still in shock from 1971's loss of cigarette advertising, were in danger of losing more than $300 million in advertising revenue from such nonprescription drugs as aspirin and vitamins. This was the result of continuing charges that these commercials might contribute to serious drug abuse.

The U.S. Department of Justice filed civil antitrust suits against the American Broadcasting Company (ABC), National Broadcasting Company (NBC), and Columbia Broadcasting System, Incorporated (CBS) on April 14. The suits seek to bar the networks from producing their own entertainment programs or financially assisting such programs by others.

President Nixon in September supported film craft union demands that the FCC force the networks to limit reruns to 25 per cent of prime evening time against a current estimate of 45 per cent. According to a study by *Broadcasting* magazine, the television networks actually telecast more repeats than first-run episodes on 27 prime-time series during the 1971-1972 season. Broadcasters claimed they had to repeat that many programs or go broke.

The Federal Election Campaign Act, putting a limit on campaign spending in the media, went into effect April 7. However, the barrage of political spots on television and radio was heavier than ever during the closing weeks of the presidential campaigns.

Television coverage of the 1972 Olympic Games in Sapporo, Japan, and Munich, West Germany, captivated viewers throughout the world.

TV Violence. In January, the office of the United States Surgeon General released its long-awaited study on the effect of television violence on children. The findings were both cautious and controversial. The consultants "tentatively" concluded "that there is a modest relationship between exposure to television violence and aggressive tendencies." Critics branded the government-funded study a "whitewash." Acting on a Senate Communications Subcommittee recommendation in March, the Department of Health, Education, and Welfare announced plans to fund the development of a "TV violence profile" grading system.

In August, John W. Macy, Jr., resigned as president of the Corporation for Public Broadcasting (CPB) two months after President Nixon unexpectedly vetoed a funding bill for CPB. His successor, Henry Loomis, said that he, like Mr. Nixon, believes in decentralization of the public broadcasting system. His plans called for minimizing news broadcasts of national affairs.

After years of debate, the FCC, in effect, lifted its long-time freeze on cable television (CATV). On March 31, CATV operators, formerly limited to areas covering about 9 per cent of the nation's television sets, were granted access to 60 per cent of the viewing audience. June Bundy Csida

See also AWARDS AND PRIZES (Arts Awards).

TENNESSEE. See STATE GOVERNMENT.

TENNIS. Back-room struggles for power overshadowed actual competition in 1972, and it was a shame. Ilie Nastase of Romania and Stan Smith and Billie Jean King of the United States had outstanding success, each earning more than $100,000 in tournaments.

Starting on January 1, the 33 male professionals under contract to World Championship Tennis (WCT) were banned from tournaments under the jurisdiction of the International Lawn Tennis Federation (ILTF). That kept the contract professionals (such stars as Rod Laver, Ken Rosewall, John Newcombe, and Arthur Ashe) out of the Wimbledon championships in England in July. Peace was restored, however, in time for them to play in the U.S. championships at Forest Hills, N.Y., in August and September.

Organization Problems. In an agreement reached in London in April, WCT promised not to renew player contracts when they expired. The last would run out in 1976, and then there would be no more contract pros. Starting in 1973, WCT would conduct 26 tournaments the first four months of the year, and the ILTF would run its tournaments for the last eight months. All players would be eligible to play in all tournaments under the same terms–prize money but no appearance money. That meant peace for men's professional tennis.

The women professionals started the year in un-

Billie Jean King holds aloft the Challenge Trophy she won in July by defeating defending Wimbledon women's champion Evonne Goolagong.

easy peace with the United States Lawn Tennis Association (USLTA) and ended it facing ostracism by both the ILTF and USLTA. Angry that men received much more prize money in the ILTF tournaments, they had formed their own circuit of 22 tournaments in 1971, under the sponsorship of Virginia Slims cigarettes and the sanctioning umbrella of the USLTA. In October, 22 women pros, including Mrs. King, Margaret Court, and Rosemary Casals, formed the Women's International Tennis Federation.

The Year's Stars. The 29-year-old Mrs. King dominated the women's circuit. She won her fourth Wimbledon championship, third U.S. Open, and first French Open. She also won the ILTF's Grand Prix series of 19 women's tournaments, and was ranked number one by the USLTA.

Nastase, 26, colorful and bad-tempered, won the men's Grand Prix and its $50,000 bonus. He defeated Ashe in five sets in the U.S. Open final in Forest Hills, and lost to Smith in five sets in a tingling, 160-minute Wimbledon final.

The 6-foot 4-inch Smith, 25, beat Nastase in five sets in the Davis Cup finals in October in Bucharest, Romania. Smith had a hand in all three victories as the U.S. defeated Romania, 3-2, and won the cup for the fifth consecutive year. Frank Litsky

See also Section One, Focus on Sports.

TEXAS. See Dallas; Houston; State Govt.

THAILAND. King Phumiphon Aduldet named Field Marshal Thanom Kittikachorn to the re-created prime ministership on Dec. 18, 1972. The marshal had seized power in 1971, abolished the Constitution, disbanded the Cabinet, and formed the National Executive Council (NEC), which ruled by decree. Kittikachorn was chairman of it.

The king's proclamation was countersigned by Major General Siri Siriyothin, who had been elected president of the National Assembly earlier the same day. The assembly, composed mostly of military officers, had been empowered to function as a Parliament under an interim Constitution promulgated on December 15. Its adoption and Kittikachorn's appointment ended the absolute rule of the NEC.

Government Crackdown. Prior to the government changes, the NEC had wielded total control. Earlier in the year, it had issued a series of sweeping decrees in a crackdown on crime and corruption. A massive attack on crime in Bangkok resulted in more than 10,000 arrests and the summary military executions of 20 notorious criminals. Night life was curbed, and a major effort was made to stop the traffic in narcotics. In July, a seizure of more than 4,000 pounds of opium, morphine, and heroin – valued at an estimated $213 million – was made in Chiang Rai. It was only one of a series of drives against the narcotics trade. Illegal gunrunning from Laos and Cambodia was also stopped.

Reform also meant greater restrictions on foreigners, including the imposing of a system of special work permits for aliens. New regulations governing foreign companies operating in the country required Thai participation – in some cases 51 per cent control – and the hiring of Thai nationals.

The Economy rallied slightly during the year due to two basic factors. The first stemmed from continued U.S. military activity. Although plans had been made to withdraw some 45,000 American support troops, they were canceled after a large-scale Communist offensive was launched in South Vietnam. The second factor involved the war between India and Pakistan that resulted in the creation of Bangladesh. Food shortages in the new nation enabled the Thais to clear out much of the huge rice surplus that had been carried over from 1971.

The NEC also began to take the threat of insurgency in both the northern and southern provinces seriously. Sir Robert Thompson, a top British expert on guerrilla warfare, helped to direct this campaign. The Thai Black Panther Division, withdrawn from South Vietnam and sent to Chiang Rai, fought major battles at Phu Hin and Long Kla during which about 600 rebels were killed. Seven districts of the province were evacuated to stop the insurgents from gaining local civilian support. Large forces were also sent to the south to knock out supply depots and rebel radio stations. John N. Stalker

See also Asia (Facts in Brief Table).

VALENTINE'S
LETTERWRITING SHOPPE

THEATER

Pippin brought a new dimension to the American musical in 1972. For years, there have been two main styles, slick or sloppy. This new musical, however, was innovative without being undisciplined. Through the metaphor of a magic show, *Pippin* tells of a quest by the son of the eighth century emperor Charlemagne. His school days over, young Pippin, played by John Rubinstein, seeks his role in the world, which is a stage show presided over by master of ceremonies Ben Vereen. He begins the proceedings by pulling a red scarf from the floorboards and transforming it into the emperor's court. As directed by Bob Fosse, Pippin's experiences are seen in terms of American show business. A military venture is a minstrel show, a love affair is a vaudeville adagio, and disembodied hands take a turn, performing a finger ballet.

The best of the conventional slick musicals was *Sugar*, which was based on the film *Some Like It Hot*. The highlight of the show was the clowning of Robert Morse as a musician who dons a female disguise and joins an all-girl band to escape pursuing gangsters. *Don't Bother Me, I Can't Cope,* a lively revue with songs by Micki Grant, depicted aspects of the black experience. *Grease* capitalized on the popularity of nostalgia by going back to the manners, morals, and music of the 1950s. Michael Cacoyannis directed a musical version of Aristophanes' satire on war, *Lysistrata*. It starred Melina Mercouri. *A Funny Thing Happened on the Way to the Forum*, a successful revival of the 1962 musical, featured Phil Silvers and Larry Blyden as the chief clowns this time.

New Works. Major American playwrights contributed new works to the 1972 theater scene. Tennessee Williams' *Small Craft Warnings* is a minor variation on the playwright's recurrent theme of vulnerability in a brutal world. In it, the rejects of society gather in a seedy bar and explain themselves in long monologues, seeking kindness from strangers.

Arthur Miller's *The Creation of the World and Other Business* is called a "catastrophic comedy," a comedy ending in disaster. Miller reveals timely as well as timeless implications in his account of Adam and Eve, the temptation and fall, the first birth, and the first murder. God and Lucifer debate vigorously while the action unfolds and Miller reflects on good and evil, man's capacity for choice. Directed by Gerald Freedman, it starred Zoe Caldwell as Eve and George Grizzard as Lucifer.

Younger playwrights also blended comedy and serious thought. Jason Miller's *That Championship Season* moved from off-Broadway to Broadway after drama critics chose it as the best play of the 1971-1972 season. Miller shows four middle-aged men meeting with their former basketball coach to celebrate in drink the 20th anniversary of their winning the state championship. But the former champs are losers in life, not winners, because they have been shaped by their coach's bigotry.

New English Plays successfully crossed the Atlantic. Rich in metaphor and parody, Tom Stoppard's *The Real Inspector Hound* spoofs inept drama critics and formula-written detective plays. Two critics watching a murder mystery literally get caught up in the action. In *Butley*, Simon Gray dissects an irascible intellectual who specializes in "spreading futility." Alan Bates gave a sympathetic interpretation of the cynical, wisecracking antihero.

From London's Royal Court, Washington, D.C.'s Arena Stage imported two impressive new plays. In *Moonchildren*, which moved to Broadway, Michael Weller thoughtfully depicts the obsessions and conflicts of a group of college students in 1965 and 1966. E. A. Whitehead's *The Foursome* centers on two young truckdrivers and the girls they meet on a weekend at the beach. They must play the game of courtship by rules that stress sexual attraction.

Good Revivals of major American plays marked three repertory seasons. The Repertory Theater of Lincoln Center contributed Arthur Miller's *The Crucible,* and scheduled Tennessee Williams' *A Streetcar Named Desire*, starring Rosemary Harris as Blanche DuBois, for April, 1973. The Circle in the Square, one of the oldest off-Broadway repertories, opened its first Broadway season on November 8 at its new Levine Theater. Its new production was Eugene O'Neill's *Mourning Becomes Electra* starring Colleen Dewhurst. O'Neill's *The Great God Brown* initiated the 1972-1973 season of the New Phoenix Repertory Company of New York City.

The New York Shakespeare Festival continued its free Shakespeare productions for outdoor city audiences under the guidance of Joseph Papp. *Hamlet* was marked by memorable performances from Stacy Keach in the title role and James Earl Jones as Claudius. A musical version of *Much Ado About Nothing* set in 19th century America moved to Broadway. The Festival's productions of *Sticks and Bones, That Championship Season,* and *Two Gentlemen of Verona* won Broadway's highest awards.

Comedies were plentiful, but few succeeded. Bob Randall's *6 Rms Riv Vu* was a lightweight situation farce. It featured the comic talents of Jerry Orbach as a husband who inspects a vacant apartment and is inadvertently locked in with a married woman. In *The Sunshine Boys,* Neil Simon depicts a retired vaudeville team of that name who get together for one last turn. Sam Levene and Jack Albertson starred under the direction of Alan Arkin.

Producer Joseph Papp's high-spirited rock version of *Two Gentlemen of Verona* became a critical and financial success on Broadway.

John Rubinstein stars as the son of the emperor Charlemagne in *Pippin,* a musical that opened on Broadway on October 23.

Repertory Theaters throughout the United States presented outstanding plays to ever-increasing audiences. Harold Pinter's *Old Times* drew crowds to the Goodman Theatre in Chicago. In New Jersey, Princeton's McCarter Theater premièred Sam Shepard's new play *The Tooth of Crime*. Shepard reflects the ills of society in the challenge and defeat of an aging pop singer by a younger one.

College and University Theaters displayed their best efforts at a spring drama festival at Washington's John F. Kennedy Center for the Performing Arts. They chose 10 productions from 30 winners in 12 regional contests. These included a 16th century Peking opera, *Black Dragon Residence*, offered by the University of Hawaii; Lillian Hellman's *The Little Foxes* by the North Carolina School of the Arts; and *365 Days*, a new play by H. Wesley Balk based on Ronald Glasser's book about his work with Vietnam evacuees in an Army hospital in Japan.

The National Endowment for the Arts allocated $2,983,500 to aid theaters in the 1972-1973 fiscal year. Recipients in the state of Washington included the Seattle Repertory Theater and Black Arts West, which trains drama groups. The Tyrone Guthrie Theatre in Minneapolis received its third four-year award from the Ford Foundation, a cash reserve grant of $618,828. Alice Griffin

See also Awards and Prizes (Arts Awards).

TOGO. See Africa.

TOLBERT, WILLIAM RICHARD, JR. (1913-), took office as president of Liberia on Jan. 3, 1972. He succeeded William V. S. Tubman, who died in July, 1971, after 27 years in office. Tolbert had been Liberia's vice-president since 1951.

Soon after he took office, Tolbert dismissed some Cabinet officers because of corruption and abolished the rice-importing monopoly that President Tubman had set up.

A wealthy rubber planter, Tolbert was born in Bensenville, Liberia, on May 13, 1913. He received his bachelor's degree summa cum laude in 1934 from Liberia College, now the University of Liberia. In 1935, he became a government clerk in the Liberian treasury, and was disbursing officer from 1936 to 1943. He was elected to the House of Representatives in 1943. Then, at 38, he was elected vice-president, the youngest man ever to hold that office.

Tolbert married Victoria A. David, daughter of an associate justice of the Supreme Court of Liberia, in 1936. They have eight children, including an adopted son who has no arms. Tolbert found him in a poor rural area. The boy has overcome his handicap enough to work as a clerk.

Tolbert is a Baptist, and was elected president of the Baptist World Alliance in 1965, the first black man to hold that position. Foster Stockwell

TORNADOES. See Disasters; Weather.

TOYS. See Games, Models, and Toys.

TRACK AND FIELD. Dave Wottle, Frank Shorter, Rod Milburn, Randy Williams, and Vince Matthews ranked among the world's outstanding track and field athletes in 1972. All were from the United States, all won Olympic gold medals in Munich, West Germany, and all overcame obstacles that might have stopped less-dedicated athletes.

Wottle, a slim, 21-year-old junior at Bowling Green State University in Ohio, was primarily a miler. On June 3, in the National Collegiate Athletic Association (NCAA) outdoor championships at Eugene, Ore., he won the 1,500-meter final (just short of a mile) in 3 minutes 39.7 seconds. On June 17, in the Amateur Athletic Union (A.A.U.) national outdoor championships in Seattle, he won the 800-meter final (almost half a mile) in 1 minute 47.3 seconds.

He insisted he was not trained to run the 800 meters. "I ran in the 800 just for some speed work for the 1,500," Wottle said sheepishly. "I don't know how to run an 800, anyway. I get confused."

On July 1, just before the 800-meter final in the Olympic trials in Eugene, Wottle still was saying, "I'm not a half-miler." Then he won the race in 1 minute 44.3 seconds, equaling the world record. The times of the next five men were 1:45.0, 1:45.1, 1:45.2, 1:45.3, and 1:45.4, making it the fastest mass finish ever at that distance. Said Ken Swenson, who ran third, "It was like going to a fire."

Wottle was lucky to be running. He was unable

to compete in 1971 because of stress fractures in both legs and bursitis in both knees. The bursitis struck again after the Olympic trials, but Wottle won the Olympic 800-meter final by a foot.

Shorter, Milburn, and Others. Shorter, a student at the University of Florida Law School, was the world's top-ranked marathon racer in 1971 and 1972. He formerly lived in Ranchos de Taos, N. Mex., where his father was a physician on an Indian reservation. He left there when rowdies harassed him as he ran on the country roads.

Milburn, a junior at Southern University in Baton Rouge, La., had not lost a high-hurdles final in two years until he finished third in the Olympic trials and barely made the team. He was angry at the world. "Everybody pressures me," he said. "I want to get away from people. They demand just too much. One reason I run is that it helps me forget other things."

Milburn did not enjoy training, and slacked off before the Olympic trials. But the day after he came in third, he was on the field with his coach at 9 A.M., trying to cure his problems. He succeeded, winning the 110-meter hurdles in the Olympics and equaling the world-record time of 13.2 seconds.

Williams, 19, who ended the year as the world's best long jumper, started it as only 23rd best in the United States. The University of Southern California freshman, one of only two teen-agers on the U.S. men's team, improved by almost 2 feet and won the Olympic title with a leap of 27 feet ½ inch.

Matthews was a 24-year-old Neighborhood Youth Corps worker in Brooklyn. In the Olympic trials, he beat Lee Evans, the world recordholder and 1968 Olympic champion, for the final berth in the 400-meter dash, and in Munich he was the surprise winner. He made it because he refused to quit when everything went against him. In 1968, he won a gold medal in the 1,600-meter relay. Then he retired until the winter of 1972, when he and other former stars formed the Brooklyn Over-the-Hill Athletic Association and bought uniforms with the club's initials of BOHAA. The A.A.U. rejected the name, saying it lacked dignity. Matthews then "discovered" that an Indian tribe named "Bohaa" once roamed Brooklyn, and this allowed the team to keep its uniforms.

All BOHAA lacked was a practice field and travel money. Matthews and his teammates climbed a 10-foot fence around a high school field every night to train. Coach Charlie Turner, a bus driver, took the $2,500 he had saved for a down payment on a home and gave it to his runners to get to the Olympic trials. Matthews' victory, he said, made it all worthwhile.

Pole Vault. Bob Seagren of Los Angeles and Kjell Isaksson of Sweden took turns raising the world record in the pole vault. Isaksson did 18 feet 1 inch and then 18 feet 2¼ inches. Both did 18 feet 4¼ inches

Polevaulter Bob Seagren of the Los Angeles Striders set a world record of 18 feet 5¾ inches in the Olympic trials at Eugene, Ore., on July 2.

TRACK AND FIELD

New World Track and Field Records Established in 1972

Event	Holder	Country	Where made	Date	Record
Men					
100 meters	Eddie Hart	U.S.A.	Eugene, Ore.	July 1	:09.9*
	Reynaud Robinson	U.S.A.	Eugene, Ore.	July 1	:09.9*
800 meters	Dave Wottle	U.S.A.	Eugene, Ore.	July 1	1:44.3*
3,000 meters	Emiel Puttemans	Belgium	Århus, Denmark	September 14	7:37.6
2 miles	Lasse Viren	Finland	Stockholm	August 14	8:14.0
3 miles	Emiel Puttemans	Belgium	Haysel, Belgium	September 20	12:47.8
5,000 meters	Emiel Puttemans	Belgium	Haysel, Belgium	September 20	13:13.0
10,000 meters	Lasse Viren	Finland	Munich	September 3	27:38.4
10 miles	Willy Polleunis	Belgium	Haysel, Belgium	September 20	46:04.2
20,000 meters	Gaston Roelants	Belgium	Haysel, Belgium	September 20	57:44.4
1 hour	Gaston Roelants	Belgium	Haysel, Belgium	September 20	12 mi.1,599 yd.
110-meter high hurdles	Rod Milburn	U.S.A.	Munich	September 7	:13.2*
400-meter hurdles	John Akii-Bua	Uganda	Munich	September 2	:47.8
3,000-meter steeplechase	Anders Gaerderud	Sweden	Helsinki	September 14	8:20.8
400-meter relay	Black, Taylor, Tinker, Hart	U.S.A.	Munich	September 10	:38.2*
800-meter relay	D'Ossola, Abeti, Benedetti, Mennea	Italy	Barletta, Italy	July 21	1:21.5
4-mile relay	Ross, Polhill, Taylor, Quax	New Zealand	Auckland, N.Z.	February 3	16:02.8
Pole vault	Bob Seagren	U.S.A.	Eugene, Ore.	July 2	18 ft. 5¾ in.
Triple jump	Viktor Saneyev	U.S.S.R.	Sukhumi, U.S.S.R.	October 19	57 ft. 2¾ in.
Discus throw	Ricky Bruch	Sweden	Malmö, Sweden	September 10	225 ft.
Javelin throw	Janis Lusis	U.S.S.R.	Stockholm	July 6	307 ft. 9 in.
Decathlon	Nikolai Avilov	U.S.S.R.	Munich	September 7-8	8,454 pts.
Women					
100 meters	Renate Stecher	E. Germany	Potsdam	June 3	:11.0*
	Eva Gleskova	Czechoslovakia	Budapest	July 1	:11.0*
200 meters	Renate Stecher	E. Germany	Munich	September 7	:22.4*
400 meters	Monika Zehrt	E. Germany	Paris	July 4	:51.0*
880 yards	Madeline M. Jackson	U.S.A.	Philadelphia	May 14	2:02.0*
1,500 meters	Ludmilla Bragina	U.S.S.R.	Munich	September 9	4:01.4
3,000 meters	Ludmilla Bragina	U.S.S.R.	Moscow	August 12	8:53.0
100-meter hurdles	Pam Kilborn	Australia	Warsaw	June 28	:12.5*
	Anneliese Erhardt	E. Germany	East Berlin	August 14	:12.5*
400-meter relay	Krause, Mickler, Richter, Rosendahl	W. Germany	Munich	September 10	:42.8*
1,600-meter relay	Kaesling, Kuehne, Seidler, Zehrt	E. Germany	Munich	September 10	3:23.0
High jump	Jordanka Blagoeva	Bulgaria	Zagreb, Yugo.	September 24	6 ft. 4¼ in.
Shot-put	Nadezhda Chizhova	U.S.S.R.	Munich	September 7	69 ft.
Discus throw	Argentina Menis	Romania	Bucharest	September 23	220 ft. 10½ in.
Pentathlon	Mary Peters	Britain	Munich	September 2-3	4,801 pts.

*Equals record

in one meet. Then Seagren did 18 feet 5¾ inches in the United States Olympic trials. Seagren was so intent on having the record that when he read that Isaksson would vault in El Paso, Tex., he spent $114 for a plane ticket, got into the meet, and regained the world record. Each of the two vaulters cleared 18 feet 4½ inches that day.

Jim Ryun, shy, sensitive, and plagued by uncertainty in recent years, ran more bad races than good. The 25-year-old world recordholder at 1 mile (3 minutes 51.1 seconds) ran miles in 3:52.8, 3:57.1, and 3:57.4. He also ran a mile in 4:14.2 and a 2-mile in 9:13.4, times that would not win high-level high school races. "He was a victim," said a friend, "of self-doubt that made each race a mentally exhausting, often lonely experience." Ryun's try for an Olympic medal ended when he bumped another runner and fell. In November, Ryun, Seagren, Evans, and Randy Matson were among many athletes who turned professional with the new International Track Association. The group planned to stage indoor and outdoor meets starting in March, 1973.

Chi Cheng, who held all four world sprint records for women, returned from California, where she had been living, to her native Taiwan for surgery to remove a withered hip muscle and move a tendon. "The pain," she said, "was terrible. Missing the Olympics was even worse."

Frank Litsky

See also Olympic Games.

TRANSIT. New federal assistance sparked progress in urban public transportation in 1972. The Urban Mass Transportation Assistance Program increased from $175 million in fiscal 1970 to $1 billion in fiscal 1973, ending June 30, 1973.

The year was also marked by a shift in public attitudes. Urban mass transportation no longer seemed to be looked upon as an unsuccessful venture for private business, but as an essential public service requiring public funds and assistance. Scores of local governments and many of the states were helping to support transit operations, recognizing that fares alone could not provide all the necessary support. A 1972 industry survey indicated that 64 transit systems had changed from private to public ownership in five years. In 1971, the latest year of the survey, only one system was abandoned. This compared with 26 abandonments of transit services in the four years preceding 1971, and a total of 268 abandonments since 1954.

There was also continued progress in research, development, and demonstration programs. These included such diverse transit plans as lanes exclusively for the use of buses, "dial-a-ride" curbside public transit service, "people movers," and air-cushion vehicles that ride on tracks.

Administration Proposal Defeated. Urban specialists and other supporters of increased federal aid for public transportation hailed a 1972 proposal by President Richard M. Nixon's Administration as a major breakthrough. Under the proposal, cities and states could use the money allocated to them from the urban systems portion of the fund for the capital costs of any form of ground transportation, including subways, rapid rail systems, and buses, as well as highways. The legislation failed to pass Congress, however, due to lack of a quorum in the House of Representatives.

On the minus side, the nation's transit systems continued to have rapidly mounting losses and declining numbers of passengers. According to the American Transit Association (ATA), the nation's transit systems had 8.3 billion riders and a deficit of $12 million as recently as 1965. In 1971, transit systems had only 6.8 billion riders, and deficits had soared to $411 million. The ATA's preliminary estimates for 1972 forecast a record low of fewer than 6.4-billion riders and deficits of more than $500 million.

The BART System. After 15 years of planning, construction, and delays, San Francisco's Bay Area Rapid Transit (BART) System began revenue passenger service on September 11. The $1.4-billion system began operating between Oakland and Fremont, the first, 28-mile segment of a projected 75-mile system.

In August, Carlos C. Villarreal, head of the Urban

San Francisco's $1.4-billion Bay Area Rapid Transit (BART) system began service on part of its 75 miles of track on September 11.

Mass Transportation Administration said "public response to the BART system will be a major factor in determining the future of transit in the urban environment." Unfortunately, within a few weeks after BART began revenue service, the line was plagued by system failures, accidents, and public criticism.

Nevertheless, transit experts referred to San Francisco as the "Renaissance city of urban transportation in America today" after inspecting the system. Transit advocates hoped BART would demonstrate that fast, clean, air-conditioned transit trains could lure an automobile-oriented society back to the use of public transportation. They also hoped it would demonstrate that, with labor-saving automation techniques, a major urban transit system could operate without a deficit.

At year's end, transit advocates anticipated that continued emphasis would be placed on developing balanced transportation in urban areas through increased spending on public transit facilities. They believed that such development would be spurred by the public concern over the energy crisis, noise and air pollution, and the impact of these on landscape, property, and people. This concern, they felt, gave support to the contention that improved public transit is the one form of urban mobility that can ease these problems. Kenneth E. Schaefle

See also AUTOMOBILE; AVIATION; SHIPS AND SHIPPING; TRANSPORTATION.

TRANSPORTATION. An improving domestic economy, expanding foreign trade, and the continuing impact of the federal government on transportation programs gave the transportation industry some modest relief in 1972 from the recent profit crunch.

However, 1972 was far from a turn-around year. Excess capacity, rapidly rising operating costs, unresponsive or lagging government regulation, and low profit margins continued to plague most segments of the industry. In addition, there was increased scrutiny and pressure on matters involving air and noise pollution, ecological and environmental balance, and employee and public safety.

The most financially troubled area continued to be urban transit. For the first time, losses of U.S. transit systems exceeded $500 million. It became increasingly obvious during the year that federal and state grants to upgrade equipment would not be enough to save some transit operations, and that additional federal or state funds would be needed for operating subsidies. See TRANSIT.

In December, the White House announced that John A. Volpe was leaving his position as secretary of transportation to become ambassador to Italy. Claude S. Brinegar, a senior vice-president with Union Oil Company in California, was nominated to become Volpe's successor.

The total U.S. transportation bill for 1972 was about $237 billion, a 7.2 per cent increase over 1971, according to preliminary estimates of the Transportation Association of America (TAA). The TAA's preliminary estimates of total U.S. mainland traffic volume were:

Freight (billions of intercity ton-miles)	**1971**	**1972**
Rail	744.0	781.2
Truck	422.0	443.1
Pipeline	444.0	461.7
Rivers and canals	205.0	215.2
Lakes	104.0	102.9
Air	3.5	3.8
Total	1,922.5	2,007.9
Passenger (billions of intercity passenger-miles)		
Auto	1,071.0	1,124.5
Private air	9.2	10.1
Public commercial air	110.6	121.6
Bus	25.5	25.7
Rail	10.0	10.5
Water	4.0	4.0
Total	1,230.3	1,296.4

The Airlines. United States domestic trunk airlines experienced a solid but unspectacular low-profit growth during 1972. Traffic increased about 10 per cent, compared with only 1.6 per cent in 1971 and no growth at all in 1970. However, it did not begin to approach the 15 to 19 per cent annual rate of growth of the mid-1960's.

The rate of return on investment for the airline industry, estimated at 6.2 per cent by the Air Transportation Association, fell far short of the 12 per cent that the Civil Aeronautics Board has stated to be fair and reasonable. See AVIATION.

The Railroad Industry experienced a moderate profit improvement. A 5 per cent increase in ton-miles resulted in an all-time high of 780 billion. Traffic growth and Interstate Commerce Commission (ICC) approval of rate increases helped revenues rise 6 per cent to $13.5 billion. Also beneficial were greater operating efficiencies, reduced employment, labor tranquillity, and savings on long-haul passenger service from Amtrak.

Nevertheless, most of the railroad industry's $800-million increase in earnings was consumed by rising operating costs, including two wage increases of 5 per cent each that became effective during the year. The industry's rate of return was 2.7 per cent, up slightly from 1971's 2.5 per cent, and 1970's 1.7 per cent. However, this level was still far below the 6 per cent return the ICC indicated the railroads would have to attain if they were to provide needed service improvements.

Deficit operations and the threat of bankruptcies still plagued a sizable segment of the industry.

The Surface Transportation Act, considered to be the type of legislation that could help the railroads redevelop their financial strength, was introduced in the Senate and supported by truckers and regulated water carriers as well as railroads. The proposed legislation provided for government loan guarantees

A $7-million research prototype of a 300-mile-per-hour air-cushion monorail vehicle was shown by the Department of Transportation in April.

administered by a federal agency, more timely procedures for abandoning unprofitable trackage, and prohibition of discriminatory rail property taxes. It earmarked 5 per cent of federal highway funds now allocated to states for grade-crossing protection.

Fireman Dispute Settled. The year will go down as a monumental one in the annals of railroad labor-management relations. One of the most significant agreements was the settlement in July of the 35-year-old fireman-manning dispute. The agreement permits long-term attrition in the number of firemen employed on diesel freights by the railroads. It brought to an end what was believed to be the longest labor-management dispute in American history. Albert Cheser, United Transportation Union president, hailed the agreement as a victory for "good-faith collective bargaining," and called on Congress and the Administration to scrap compulsory arbitration legislation. Industry observers believed the agreement signaled a new spirit of cooperation between railroad labor and management.

Railroad Merger. On August 10, the Illinois Central merged with the Gulf, Mobile and Ohio, the 40th rail merger since 1956. The new railroad, the Illinois Central Gulf Railroad, covers 9,400 miles and operates in 14 states from the Great Lakes to the Gulf of Mexico.

Amtrak's Record. After 18 months of operation, Amtrak's hopes of operating as a "for profit" corporation all but evaporated. In its first year of operation, Amtrak lost nearly $500,000 a day. Many sources close to Amtrak believed that it had little chance of survival without large and increasing federal subsidies or, as an alternative, a drastic cutback in the amount of service provided after July 1, 1973.

Amtrak recorded isolated successes, primarily in the Northeast corridor–the 430-mile span from Boston to Washington, D.C. However, on the whole, the public continued to spurn railroad passenger service in favor of automobiles, buses, and airplanes.

The Trucking Industry had a somewhat disappointing year. Although motor carriers benefited from a more buoyant economy, further expansion of territory, and continued efforts to reduce costs, rate increases did not keep pace with rising operating costs. In addition, productivity increases from larger trailers, more efficient terminals, and computer applications seemed to have run their course for the present.

Truckers earned $470 million, compared to $465-million in 1971 and a depressed $187 million in 1970. Net income was down to 2.7 per cent from 1971's 3.0 per cent. Both years were far short of the level the industry says is necessary to provide for improved financial strength in the future.

Interstate Highways. In December, it was reported that 80 per cent of the 42,500-mile interstate highway system was completed and open to traffic,

The luxury liner *Queen Elizabeth* was transformed into a gutted hulk in a fire on Jan. 8, 1972, while moored in Hong Kong harbor.

and that work was underway on another 18 per cent. More than 1,400 miles of the system were built during the year.

The interstate program had run into continuing delays in recent years because of criticism from environmental groups. At year's end, it faced an even more serious problem–lack of funds. Because Congress did not authorize appropriations in 1972, no money was allocated beyond mid-1973. At year's end, some states were already short of funds, and others were unable to make any firm plans for the future.

World Shipping. Confronted with declining orders for conventional vessels, shipbuilders placed increasing importance on developing such highly specialized craft as liquefied-gas carriers and floating platforms for the offshore oil industry. Both were areas of steadily mounting demand.

According to Lloyd's Register of Shipping, there were 1,969 merchant ships under construction on Sept. 30, 1972, a slight increase from the 1,939 on the same date in 1971. Shipbuilding orders, including those under construction, declined to 3,612 from 1971's 4,126.

Gross tonnage of vessels on the total world order book decreased to 78.9 million from September 1971's 84.1 million gross tons. The United States and France were the only leading shipbuilding countries to have increases over 1971. Kenneth E. Schaefle

TRAVEL. International tourism increased by 9 per cent in 1972, and accounted for about 198 million visits across international borders. Tourists spent over $24 billion in destination countries, fare payments, and private automobile outlay–by far the largest item in world trade.

The devaluation of the United States dollar made travel in the United States 8.6 per cent cheaper for visitors from abroad. The United States received 14.7 million foreign travelers, a 7 per cent gain over 1971. They spent an estimated $3.2 billion, which helped the United States retain its title as the world's number-one host country.

This record-breaking traffic, coupled with a 6 per cent increase in domestic travel and expenditures of more than $61 billion for transportation, lodging, food, and entrance fees, once again confirmed travel as the third largest United States industry. More than 85 million Americans made trips of seven days or longer, and more than 43 million went on camping vacations.

An estimated 25 million Americans traveled abroad and spent nearly $6 billion. This sent the travel deficit soaring to a new high of $2.8 billion. About 15.8 million Americans traveled to Canada, a gain of 5 per cent over 1971. Some 2.4 million traveled to Mexico, a gain of 11 per cent, and about 7 million went overseas, a gain of 11 per cent.

The United States hosted 10.3 million Canadian

visitors who remained for more than 48 hours. Another 1.3 million came from Mexico and 3.1 million from overseas.

President Richard M. Nixon's February visit to the People's Republic of China precipitated an extraordinary amount of interest in travel to that country. Aside from a small number of invited guests, however, no other Americans were admitted. Still, travel agents reported a marked increase in inquiries, and Americans continued to apply for visas through the ministry of information in Peking.

Travel Service Boost. After 10 years of operating with a slim budget of less than $4 million, Congress authorized the United States Travel Service $6.5 million to promote travel to the United States from abroad. More than $500,000 of this sum was disbursed on a matching-funds basis to state, city, and regional travel organizations for advertising and promotional campaigns.

The 1972 travel scene was brightened by the inauguration of low-cost, one-week European tour packages in effect from January 15 through April 30. They allowed Americans an eight-day vacation for as little as $270.

The Tourism Year of the Americas was proclaimed for 1972 to encourage all member countries to combine efforts to develop tourism and promote better understanding among the peoples of the Western Hemisphere and the rest of the world.

Low-Cost Charter Flights. The Civil Aeronautics Board (CAB) waived its requirement that low-cost charter travelers must belong to an affinity group, such as a club, union, or organization. On September 27, the CAB approved a new charter flight regulation. It permits a minimum of 40 unaffiliated people to travel together if they make reservations and a nonrefundable deposit of 25 per cent with a travel agent or airline three months in advance. In addition, they must fly both ways together and remain on the trip a minimum of 7 days in North America and 10 days elsewhere. Scheduled and nonscheduled airlines can offer these charter flights. The new regulations expire Dec. 31, 1975.

From the point of view of the traveling public, the most aggravating and confusing situation was the increasing variety of air fares. One airline listed nine different fares between New York City and Miami alone, and a British carrier introduced a daily "Skytrain" service between London and New York City for $79 during the winter months.

Illegal air charters continued to plague the industry, stranding hundreds of passengers abroad. But of even more concern was the evidence of widespread corruption in the air-travel industry. Major airlines, working with travel agents, offered illegal discount prices on unsold seats to fill their planes. The estimated 1972 revenue loss was more than $200 million.

In 1972, a total of 2.7 million American passports were issued. To ease congestion at passport service offices, U.S. citizens were allowed to apply for passports at some 800 post offices throughout the country.

A top tourist attraction, the Colosseum in Rome, was reopened to the public in October. It had been closed because of dangerous falling stones.

The Cruise Market continued to dominate the passenger steamship industry. Good prices, a wide selection of ships and itineraries, and the advent of new vessels, attracted 575,000 passengers who paid $300 million for their trips in 1972. A 91-day French Line world cruise, for example, carried 1,150 passengers to 27 ports around the world.

Amtrak, the nation's rail system, lost nearly $500,000 in 1972. But it resumed operating two deluxe international routes, one between Seattle and Vancouver, B.C., and one between New York City and Montreal. A survey conducted for Amtrak revealed that 64 per cent of the American people favored continuing intercity passenger train service. Some 16.5 million persons traveled by rail in 1972.

National Park Study. In September, a panel commissioned by the National Park Service recommended radical changes in the national park system. Among them were that the use of private automobiles be discouraged, that a moratorium be declared immediately on roadbuilding, and that resort accommodations, shopping centers, and homes on wheels be banned from national parks. With more than 200 million visitor-days being logged each year, the system's parks have been rapidly evolving into amusement centers rather than being preserved in their natural state.

Lynn Beaumont

TREPCZYNSKI, STANISLAW (1924-), deputy foreign minister of Poland and former head of the Polish Communist Party Secretariat, was elected president of the United Nations (UN) 27th General Assembly on Sept. 12, 1972. Only one other Communist country – Romania in 1967 – has provided a General Assembly president.

Prior to becoming a government minister, Trepczynski spent many years in the Polish labor movement, where he became recognized for his organizing skills. He is a fluent conversationalist in Russian, German, and French, and is an enthusiastic mountain climber.

Trepczynski is known as an imaginative, energetic, somewhat impatient activist who seeks quick solutions. "I try to find some common spirit with all those in the hall," he said. "Sometimes it is a joke or a gesture that will do it, but when I find that common spirit, I know it will go well." He admitted to a certain trepidation at being subjected to the long speeches the UN Assembly seems to favor.

Trepczynski was born in central Poland, where his father was a notary public and his mother a schoolteacher. He studied at the University of Łódź and received a master's degree in economics. His wife, Halina, is a pediatrician and the director of a children's hospital. They have two sons. Allan Davidson

TRINIDAD AND TOBAGO. See West Indies.

TRUCK AND TRUCKING. See Transportation.

TRUDEAU, PIERRE ELLIOTT. The Canadian prime minister suffered a personal setback in the Oct. 30, 1972, national elections when voters assigned his Liberal government a minority standing in the House of Commons. The Liberals were left with 109 seats, 24 short of a majority. But Trudeau brushed aside Conservative demands that he resign. See Canada.

In November, he made 18 Cabinet changes. "We intend to govern in a way that the Canadian people will see that we did understand their message in the election," he said. "We agreed to form a Cabinet where the best man will be in the right place at the right time." His appointments included the first woman to join a Trudeau Cabinet.

Trudeau's manifold duties as prime minister kept his work schedule filled during the year. On June 16, he inaugurated a $950-million hydroelectric project at Churchill Falls, Newfoundland. He played official host to U.S. President Richard M. Nixon during a two-day visit by the latter in April. At the end of their conference, the two leaders signed an agreement pledging joint efforts to combat pollution in the Great Lakes (see Environment). Trudeau was also one of the principal leaders in an international effort to help settle a number of Asians expelled from Uganda by President Idi Amin Dada in November (see Uganda). The prime minister tentatively accepted an invitation to visit China. David M. L. Farr

TRUMAN, HARRY S. (1884-1972), the 33rd President of the United States, died on Dec. 26, 1972. His final illness began on December 5, when he was hospitalized for pulmonary congestion. The former President then developed kidney failure, which led to his death. See Deaths of Notable Persons (Close-Up).

Mr. Truman's last year was spent quietly at his home in Independence, Mo. In spite of arthritis in his knees, he continued to take occasional strolls. On February 12, Secretary of the Interior Rogers C. B. Morton declared the property surrounding Mr. Truman's home a National Historic Landmark site.

Mr. Truman celebrated his 88th birthday on May 8 at home with his family and a few close friends, while 300 admirers honored him at a luncheon in Kansas City, Mo. The U.S. Senate passed a resolution lauding the former President on his birthday. On July 4, a large celebration in Independence was staged as a tribute to the former President.

The Trumans marked their 53rd wedding anniversary on June 28, and Mr. Truman suffered a fall that day at home. He was X-rayed at Research Hospital in Kansas City on June 30, but the doctors found no injuries. The former President was hospitalized on July 2. He underwent tests and treatment for an intestinal condition that had hospitalized him in 1971. For the first time, he cast an absentee ballot in the November 7 elections. Carol L. Thompson

TUNISIA. Improved health enabled President Habib Bourguiba to resume active leadership of the country in 1972. As a result, the long-debated question of presidential succession remained unsettled. The Political Bureau of the ruling Socialist Destour Party (PSD) proposed creation of an office of vice-president, to be elected for a five-year term concurrent with the president's. But disagreement among PSD factions and Bourguiba's fears about a breakdown in leadership after his final term ends in 1974 prevented the proposal's adoption.

Except for a short rest period in Switzerland, Bourguiba remained on the job. He exchanged state visits with Algerian President Houari Boumediene, and the two agreed to work for unity of the Maghreb – the area comprised of Tunisia, Algeria, and Morocco. They also agreed to try to make the Mediterranean "a sea of peace" with the removal of foreign naval power. Bourguiba made an official visit to France on June 28, his first since Tunisian independence in 1956, and signed four conventions governing Franco-Tunisian consular and legal relations.

Foreign Relations. Tunisia signed a treaty of friendship with Saudi Arabia and opened diplomatic relations with the Vatican, healing a breach that dated back to Tunisia's expropriation of Roman Catholic Church properties in 1964. Foreign Minister Mohammed Masmoudi traveled as much as Bourguiba in efforts to promote peace in the Middle

East. Masmoudi was awarded the International Statesman prize by the American Association for Third World Affairs for his work.

There was less student unrest than in previous years. However, the University of Tunis was closed from February to April, following demonstrations for the release of a jailed university lecturer. The demonstration was the first major objection directed against Bourguiba in his 15 years of leadership.

The Economy. Tunisia was troubled by inability to generate steady economic growth. Industry was too small to absorb the nation's expanding labor force, and the gross national product grew only 4 per cent instead of the projected 6 per cent. The country's heavy dependence on foreign investment produced a trade deficit.

Some solid economic gains were achieved, however. On July 7, the new Bir Litayem oil field near Sfax went into production. Its capacity of 400,000 tons would add 10 per cent to Tunisia's oil output. Tourism, the third biggest exchange earner after petroleum and phosphates, got a boost with new jet airports being opened at Tunis, Monastir, and Djerba Island. The huge Ghannouche chemical plant near Gabes, a key project in development of the drier area in the south, began producing phosphoric acid, most of it for export. William Spencer

See also AFRICA (Facts in Brief Table).

TURKEY struggled with a continuing government crisis in 1972. It was underscored by urban terrorism, martial law, and the inability of its leaders to reconcile their differences. Unable to institute reforms and control leftist militants, Prime Minister Nihat Erim resigned on April 17. He had "resigned" several times earlier, but this time he was replaced, and Defense Minister Ferit Melen became prime minister.

Erim was appointed in March, 1971, after an armed forces ultimatum to the government to reform or face a military take-over. He proposed 93 reform laws, but only 11 were passed. Erim finally asked for authority to legislate by decree, restricting individual and collective freedoms. He was refused, and resigned.

President Cevdet Sunay first asked Senator Ali Suat Hayri Ürgüplü to form a new Cabinet. Ürgüplü's choices were unacceptable to the armed forces, and Melen was given the post. Melen's Cabinet, approved on May 22, included eight Justice Party ministers and five from the main opposition, the Republican People's Party (RPP). Meanwhile, Ismet Inönü, the "Grand Old Man" of Turkish politics at 87, resigned as chairman of the RPP; he was succeeded by moderate socialist Bülent Ecevit, the party secretary-general. Ecevit defined the RPP as "democratic, not Marxist," and denounced extremism. The five RPP ministers quit the Cabinet on

More than 80,000 Turkish Army troops and police combed Istanbul on January 23 in a door-to-door search for wanted leftist terrorists.

November 4, accusing Melen of rightwing tendencies.

Violence and Terrorism continued despite mass arrests, military trials, and long prison sentences for crimes against the state. Martial law in 11 provinces was extended indefinitely on May 24.

Militants belonging to the outlawed Turkish People's Liberation Army (TPLA), an offshoot of the Dev Genc (Revolutionary Youth), carried out several spectacular exploits. On March 26, they kidnaped three North Atlantic Treaty Organization radar technicians – two Britons and a Canadian – and held them hostage for the release of three Dev Genc leaders sentenced to death. The hostages and 10 terrorists were killed in a shoot-out with police. TPLA members also hijacked a Turkish airliner to Bulgaria in May and attempted to kill the commander of Turkey's security forces. Government offices abroad were bombed. The breakdown in civil order and the recurrent government crises cast a dark shadow over the future of representative government in Turkey.

The World Bank loaned $18 million for land reclamation in the rich Adana Plain. Other loans were approved to provide city planning and a new water supply for Istanbul and a urea-ammonia plant expected to make Turkey self-sufficient in fertilizer by 1975. The United States offered $35 million to compensate Turkish farmers ordered to stop growing opium poppies. William Spencer

See also MIDDLE EAST (Facts in Brief Table).

UGANDA. President Idi Amin Dada, in an effort to achieve complete Africanization, ordered about 45,000 Asians out of Uganda in 1972. His original announcement on August 24 called for them to leave by November 8, but the date was later extended to November 22.

In the mass exodus that followed, more than 27,000 Asians were airlifted to Great Britain. Another 6,000 went to Canada, 6,000 to India, and 1,000 to the United States. The rest migrated to countries in Asia, Europe, and Latin America. By the end of November, only about 800 Asians remained in Uganda. They held valid citizenship papers and could not be forced to leave. However, the government ordered them to sell their holdings and move to rural areas. British "neocolonialists and imperialists," Amin announced, would be ousted next.

Domestic Turmoil. For generations, the Asians had dominated Uganda's commerce and industry. Without them, Uganda faced grave domestic problems. In Kampala, the capital, 80 per cent of the shops were closed. The city had the air of a deserted town; with the Asians gone, nearly one-third of the city's residential areas had been vacated. Schools that had almost 20,000 Asian children on their rolls before the exodus were now almost deserted. Many that had been staffed by Asian teachers were closed because no replacements were available. Even the social services were hard hit. Most of the hospitals and public health facilities had been staffed by Asian professionals; few native Ugandans were qualified to replace them.

There were other grave effects. Import-export concerns, most of which were operated by Asians, went out of business. With imports thus cut drastically, and the supplies of basic goods dwindling, prices doubled. Industry was at a standstill, and unemployment was widespread.

Despite these aftereffects, President Amin was considered a hero by the native Ugandans. Equally important, he had won the friendship of such countries as Libya and Saudi Arabia for expelling the Asians. His main problem, however, was how to sell the businesses and property left by the Asians to native Ugandans who had little money.

Border Hostilities erupted on September 17 between Uganda and Tanzania when a 1,000-man force of Ugandan exiles invaded Uganda from Tanzania. The invaders, known as the Uganda People's Militia, had spent several months secretly training in Tanzania, hoping to overthrow Amin's dictatorship. Amin charged that Tanzania had encouraged them. By October 1, the invasion had been repulsed and, on October 5, the foreign ministers of the two nations signed an agreement settling the dispute. Paul C. Tullier

See also AFRICA (Facts in Brief Table).

UNION OF SOVIET SOCIALIST REPUBLICS (U.S.S.R.) See RUSSIA.

UNITED ARAB EMIRATES (UAE) added a seventh member, Ra's al Khaymah, in February, 1972. The state was given six seats in the UAE Consultative Assembly. In return, Ra's al Khaymah withdrew its demands for equal representation and veto rights in the assembly with Abu Dhabi and Dubai, the largest and wealthiest members. The demands had kept Ra's al Khaymah from joining the union at its inception.

There was relatively little unrest within the UAE. The ruler of Sharjah, Sheik Khalid bin Mohammed al-Qasimi, was killed on January 24 during an attempted coup led by his cousin Sheik Saqr bin Sultarn. Sheik Saqr had been deposed by Sheik Khalid in 1965 and went into exile in Cairo, Egypt. The rebels were captured after a shoot-out at the royal palace, and President Zayid bin Sultan al Nuhayan said they would stand trial under union law. Sheik Khalid's younger brother, Sheik Saqr bin Muhammad al-Qasimi, was named ruler.

The UAE Consultative Assembly held its first session in February and began work on a permanent constitution. The Cabinet was enlarged with the addition of three new ministers from Ra's al Khaymah.

The largest UAE oil producer, Abu Dhabi, reached an ownership agreement with the Abu Dhabi Petroleum Company similar to those negotiated by other oil-rich Arab states. William Spencer

See also MIDDLE EAST (Facts in Brief Table).

UNITED ARAB REPUBLIC (U.A.R.). See EGYPT.

UNITED NATIONS (UN) entered its 28th year in 1972 with a new secretary-general at the helm. Kurt Waldheim, the Austrian diplomat who became the world forum's fourth chief on January 1, was determined to create new confidence in the organization through "preventive diplomacy."

Waldheim traveled to nearly 30 countries on five continents to personalize the diplomatic initiatives he took during his first year in office. But, despite his vigor and the broadening of the organization's political reality after the 1971 inclusion of the People's Republic of China, the UN found itself increasingly unable to deal with crucial conflicts in Vietnam, the Middle East, and Northern Ireland.

The Vietnam War caused difficulties with the United States for Waldheim. After President Richard M. Nixon announced on May 8 that he had ordered Haiphong and other North Vietnamese harbors mined, Waldheim warned the United States that it should exercise "utmost restraint." Then, on July 24, he made an unusual public statement criticizing stepped-up U.S. bombing of North Vietnam. He said that he had received evidence that U.S. planes had deliberately bombed dikes there. Waldheim was immediately rebuked by President Nixon and Secretary of State William P. Rogers, who characterized his remarks as "naïve."

When White House adviser Henry A. Kissinger predicted on October 26 that "peace is at hand," Waldheim offered the use of his "good offices" in the effort to achieve peace. The United States informed him that he would participate in final peace conferences. However, by mid-December, with all-out bombing of North Vietnam resumed after the secret Paris peace talks broke down, the secretary-general was again expressing "concern" at the negative developments.

Stanislaw Trepczynski, 48, deputy foreign minister of Poland who served as the 27th General Assembly president, opened and closed the session with castigatory remarks about Vietnam. He said the war "cannot be justified any longer on logical grounds by any stretch of the imagination." See TREPCZYNSKI, STANISLAW.

In the Middle East, the UN was also paralyzed in its efforts to find a solution to the impasse. Special UN mediator Gunnar Jarring traveled between New York City, Jerusalem, and various Arab capitals early in the year, but negotiations were officially described as "stuck," and he abandoned his efforts. Israel continued to reject as "spurious" all Security Council condemnations of "preëmptive strikes" against suspected Palestinian guerrilla campsites in southern Lebanon. See LEBANON.

The massacres of innocent travelers at Lod International Airport near Tel Aviv, Israel, on May 30,

Emperor Haile Selassie addressed the UN Security Council when it met in Ethiopia in January—its first session away from New York in 20 years.

and of 11 Israeli Olympic athletes in Germany on September 5, spurred Waldheim to tell the General Assembly that they could not remain a "mute spectator" to such acts. He asked the members to approve "measures to prevent terrorism and other forms of violence that endanger or take innocent human lives or jeopardize fundamental freedoms."

The Munich tragedy resulted in Israeli reprisal attacks on Lebanese villages. The United States, however, on September 10, cast its second veto in Council history to block a resolution asking for "restraint" by all parties. The United States said it vetoed the resolution because it did not include references to acts of terrorism. Despite vehement opposition from Arabs and Africans, the Assembly did inscribe the antiterrorism item after broadening it to include a search for the "underlying causes" of such violence. Secretary of State Rogers personally asked the Assembly to expedite action on an American proposal for a treaty requiring extradition and prosecution of international terrorists; but, after much discussion, the U.S. proposal was shelved in favor of a "study" of the matter until 1973. United States Ambassador George Bush said the action was "aimed at raising rather than lowering the level of violence in our troubled world." See MIDDLE EAST.

Meanwhile, the Assembly again passed a resolution demanding Israeli withdrawal from Arab territories as a prerequisite for negotiations. Only last-minute diplomatic maneuvering by the United States and its Western allies precluded an Israeli abandonment of even token UN involvement in future peace-settlement negotiations.

In Africa, concern with racial discrimination and colonialism in southern Africa was highlighted by a series of meetings. They began with an unprecedented session of the Security Council in Addis Ababa, Ethiopia, in late January. There, and at other committee meetings in New York, delegates agreed to increase economic and political pressures against Portugal and the Republic of South Africa. Decisions were also made to exert pressure on some Western countries, such as the United States and Great Britain that indirectly support Portugal and South Africa with trade and military aid.

Waldheim visited South Africa and Namibia – the former territory of South West Africa – in March. South Africa still controls Namibia despite UN revocation of its territorial mandate in 1966. Waldheim secured Prime Minister Balthazar J. Vorster's consent to the appointment of a UN special representative for Namibia who will prepare for self-rule there.

Great Britain vetoed a Security Council attempt in February to block its compromise with the white government of Rhodesia. Opponents of the compromise asked for a constitutional conference in which the African people would participate in forming the future government of their country. However, a British commission canvass showed that the black majority in Rhodesia rejected the agreement, and Britain abandoned it. The Council also passed two resolutions calling for tighter economic sanctions against the white-minority regime, and specifically criticizing the United States for importing chromium and nickel from Rhodesia. See RHODESIA.

Other Problems. The International Federation of Airline Pilots Associations threatened a worldwide strike on June 19 unless the UN took action to prevent increasing airplane hijackings and other threats to aviation. The Security Council met for 10 days on the issue, and on June 20 – one day after the strike was to take place – issued a unanimous consensus calling on all states to take measures to deter hijacking.

Meanwhile, burgeoning deaths, maimings, and property damage caused by terrorist acts in Northern Ireland brought a request from the Republic of Ireland for Waldheim to use his "good offices" to alleviate warfare there. Great Britain objected that the matter remained an "internal affair" not subject to UN jurisdiction. The objection was upheld. See NORTHERN IRELAND.

Relief operations for millions stranded in the aftermath of the 1971 India-Pakistan conflict were supervised by UN personnel. Requests for necessary supplies exceeded $600 million. The new nation of Bangladesh, born from the ruins of East Pakistan, applied for UN membership, but the resolution to admit the nation was vetoed on August 25 in the Security Council by China. Peking maintained that membership could be allowed only after a final settlement ensured the repatriation of 90,000 Pakistani prisoners of war still being held in India. See BANGLADESH; INDIA.

The UN Budget. Despite its defeat on the terroism issue, the United States clinched a major victory by persuading a majority of the Assembly to support its request for a cut in its regular dues from 31.52 per cent of the UN budget to 25 per cent beginning in 1974. Many delegates from developing countries saw the move as a sign of lessened American interest in the UN, but U.S. officials insisted that it was only fair that no member pay more than 25 per cent. The poorer countries immediately voted a decrease in their share from a .04 per cent to a .02 per cent minimum.

The likely membership of both East and West Germany in 1973 was expected to more than make up for the revenue difference caused by the U.S. cut. East Germany received permanent observer status in November, and sent Ambassador Horst Gunert as its first representative. Secretary-General Waldheim also planned to continue his belt-tightening programs, which resulted in a salary freeze and severe cuts in overtime for the Secretariat staff. The budget was increased from $213 million in 1972 to $224 million in 1973. The Assembly also exempted the People's Republic of China from paying a $27-million debt left by Taiwan (Nationalist China) when it was ousted in 1971. An attempt by China and Russia to discuss the removal of UN troops, most of them American, from South Korea was diverted by the United States. The United States contended that an inflammatory discussion would only disrupt reunification talks going on between North and South Korea.

Environmental Conference. A 12-day Conference on the Human Environment, held in June in Stockholm, Sweden, resulted in 114 countries agreeing to a Declaration on Environment. They also decided to establish a 110-country "earthwatch" in which global pollution problems would be recorded and monitored, and to create a special UN Environment Secretariat that the Assembly later decided should be located in Kenya, Nairobi. The conference took steps toward a convention against ocean dumping and the preservation of natural sites reflecting man's heritage. See ENVIRONMENT (Close-Up).

President Salvador Allende Gossens of Chile, in a special address to the Assembly, accused multinational corporations of "an underhand, indirect form of aggression" against developing countries. He specifically accused the International Telegraph and Telephone Company and the Kennecott Copper Corporation of such activities against his country.

The UN Development Program, with 10,000 international experts at work in 137 countries and territories in preinvestment projects, dropped Taiwan from its aid list at the insistence of the People's Republic of China. A marble plaque presented by Taiwan was left hanging in a UN corridor, but the nameplate identifying Taiwan as the donor was removed, also at China's request.

Santiago, Chile, was named as the site of a 1973 international conference on the law of the sea. Meanwhile, the World Court at The Hague received a new case filed by Great Britain against Iceland, which extended its fishing rights to a 50-mile circumference of the island in September. Britain insisted that Iceland could not unilaterally extend its fishing limits when most other countries honored a 12-mile limit.

Disarmament Talks. The UN Assembly approved plans for a worldwide disarmament conference, a proposal sponsored by Russia but opposed by the United States. China labeled the meeting an "empty talk club." However, China did not vote against the proposal, which most of the underdeveloped nations favored. The Assembly also decided that Aug. 5, 1973, the 10th anniversary of the partial test-ban treaty, would be the target date for a comprehensive test-ban treaty.

Despite United States opposition on the grounds that it would block freedom of information, Russia succeeded in getting Assembly approval in November for steps toward a convention governing the use of earth satellites for direct television broadcasting. Russia wanted approval to "jam" broadcasts of propaganda or material from other countries that it deems "erotic or immoral."

An effort led by France to secure safe-conduct cards for journalists traveling in war areas was blocked by delegates from the underdeveloped countries, who apparently feared espionage by agents of some of the more advanced countries. A UN university, the brainchild of former Secretary-General U Thant, was approved. Three new justices–Nagendra Singh of India, José Maria Ruda of Argentina, and Sir Humphrey Waldock of Great Britain–were elected to nine-year terms on the 15-man International Court of Justice. Judges Isaac Forster of Senegal and André Gros of France were re-elected.

Elections and Appointments. Australia, Austria, Indonesia, Kenya, and Peru were elected to two-year terms for 1973 and 1974 on the Security Council, replacing Italy, Belgium, Japan, Somalia, and Argentina. Waldheim appointed Helva Sipila, a Finnish attorney, as Assistant Secretary-General for Social and Humanitarian Affairs.

Former U.S. Congressman F. Bradford Morse (R., Mass.) was named undersecretary-general for political affairs and General Assembly, replacing the late Ralph Bunche, winner of the 1950 Nobel Peace Prize, as the UN's top U.S. official. In December, U.S. Ambassador to the UN George Bush announced that he would leave his post to become Republican National Chairman in early 1973. Former radio and television newsman and White House aide John Scali, 54, was named Bush's successor. Betty Flynn

U.S. CONSTITUTION. After 49 years of struggle by ardent feminists, Congress finally approved an amendment to the U.S. Constitution granting equal rights to women on March 22, 1972. The proposed amendment states that "Equality of rights under the law shall not be denied or abridged by the United States or any state on account of sex."

Opponents of the amendment, led by Senator Sam J. Ervin, Jr., (D., N.C.), predicted that ratification would create legal chaos in such areas as protective labor laws, sex-segregated educational programs in public schools, and criminal laws against sex offenses. However, the Senate passed it 84 to 5. The House had approved it in 1971, after Congresswoman Martha W. Griffiths (D., Mich.) by-passed the House Judiciary Committee and brought the amendment to the floor.

After the Senate vote, the amendment was sent to the states for ratification. Half an hour later, Hawaii became the first state to ratify it. By the end of 1972, 22 state legislatures had approved it. The amendment has until 1979 to win ratification by 38 states.

Opponents of school busing tried unsuccessfully to win congressional approval of an amendment that would prohibit forced busing to achieve racial integration in schools. The National Black Political Convention in March recommended an amendment giving blacks congressional representation based on population. Darlene R. Stille

U.S. GOVERNMENT. President Richard M. Nixon's landslide re-election on Nov. 7, 1972, promised to have far-reaching effects on the government. The President's victory enhanced his personal prestige and strengthened his authority. But the Democratic Party's victory in both houses of Congress foreshadowed sharp conflicts between Congress and the President in his second term. See DEMOCRATIC PARTY; ELECTIONS; REPUBLICAN PARTY.

Phase 2 of the President's economic stabilization program continued throughout 1972. However, economists disagreed on how effective it was in curbing inflation. See ECONOMY, THE.

The Executive Branch. The morning after his re-election, President Nixon asked for the resignations of some 2,000 high-level officials in the Cabinet, on the White House staff, and in the federal bureaucracy. This allowed the President to reorganize the executive branch and bring new talent into the Cabinet.

Although he made extensive changes, Mr. Nixon appointed only five new members to his Cabinet: Casper W. Weinberger as secretary of health, education, and welfare; Peter J. Brennan as secretary of labor; James T. Lynn as secretary of housing and urban development; Frederick B. Dent as secretary of commerce; and Claude S. Brinegar as secretary of transportation. Former Secretary of Health, Education, and Welfare Elliot L. Richardson was given a new post as secretary of defense. See CABINET.

On December 1, the Nixon Administration announced that George P. Shultz would stay on as secretary of the treasury and would also take on a new job as assistant to the President in charge of a new Council on Economic Policy. The primary members of the council will be the secretaries of agriculture, commerce, labor, state, transportation, and the treasury. The council will coordinate domestic and foreign economic policy. Observers viewed the creation of the new council as a move to by-pass Congress and, in effect, consolidate several Cabinet departments for efficiency – as the President had originally planned. Congress had earlier refused to approve Mr. Nixon's plan for reorganizing the executive branch and reducing the number of Cabinet posts from 11 to 8.

Other important executive appointments included the following:

- On November 28, Roy L. Ash, president of Litton Industries, was appointed director of the Office of Management and Budget.
- On November 30, Deputy Secretary of Defense Kenneth Rush was named deputy secretary of state.
- On December 13, the Administration announced the nomination of Joseph T. Snead, dean of Duke University law school, as deputy attorney general.
- On December 14, Mr. Nixon named Kenneth R.

Federal Spending and Revenue Receipts

Estimated U.S. Budget for Fiscal 1973*

	Billions of dollars
National defense	78.3
International affairs and finance†	3.8
Space research	3.2
Agriculture and rural development	6.9
Natural resources and environment	2.5
Commerce and transportation	11.6
Community development and housing	4.8
Education and manpower††	11.3
Health	18.1
Income security	69.7
Veterans benefits	11.7
General government	5.5
Interest	21.2
General revenue sharing	5.0
Allowances	1.3
Undistributed deductions	−8.6
Total	$246.3

*July 1, 1972, to June 30, 1973

†Includes foreign aid.

††Includes job training and safety programs.

‡Includes law enforcement.

U.S. Income and Outlays

Revenue receipts   Total outlays

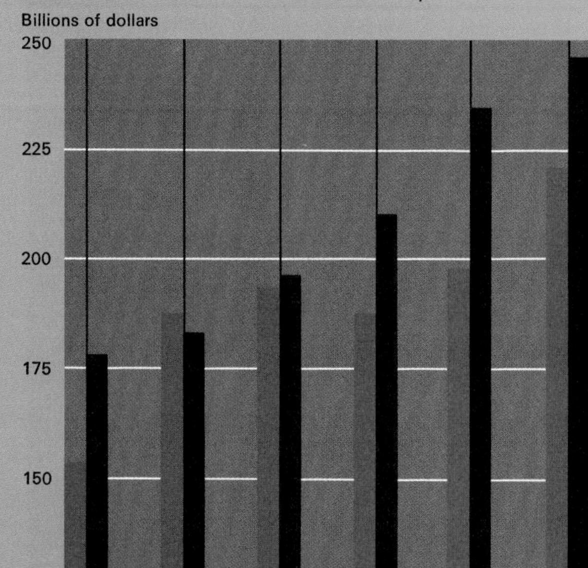

Source: U.S. Office of Management and Budget

Diplomatic Corps

Official ambassadors representing the United States of America in other countries and their counterparts to the United States, as of Dec. 31, 1972.

Country	From U.S.A.	To U.S.A.
Afghanistan	Robert G. Neumann	Abdullah Malikyar
Argentina	John Davis Lodge	Carlos Manuel Muniz
Australia	Walter L. Rice	Sir James Plimsoll
Austria	John P. Humes	Arno Halusa
Bangladesh	Hermann F. Eilts	Vacant
Barbados	Eileen R. Donovan	Valerie Theodore McComie
Belgium	Robert Strausz-Hupé	Walter Loridan
Bolivia	Ernest V. Siracusa	Edmundo Valencia-Ibañez
Botswana	Charles J. Nelson	Amos M. Dambe
Brazil	William M. Rountree	João Augusto de Araujo Castro
Bulgaria	Horace G. Torbert, Jr.	Christo Zdravchev
Burma	Edwin W. Martin	U Lwin
Burundi	Robert L. Yost	Nsanze Terence
Cameroon	C. Robert Moore	Francois-XavierTchoungui
Canada	Adolph W. Schmidt	Marcel Cadieux
Central African Republic	Vacant	Christophe Maidou
Chad	Edward W. Mulcahy	Lazare Massibe
Chile	Nathaniel Davis	Orlando Letelier
Colombia	Leonard J. Saccio	Douglas Botero-Boshell
Costa Rica	Viron P. Vaky	Rafael Alberto Zuniga
Cyprus	David H. Popper	Zenon Rossides
Czechoslovakia	Albert W. Sherer, Jr.	Dusan Spacil
Dahomey	Robert Anderson	Wilfred De Souza
Denmark	Vacant	Eyvind Bartels
Dominican Republic	Francis E. Meloy, Jr.	S. Salvador Ortiz
Ecuador	Findley Burns, Jr.	Alberto Quevedo-Toro
El Salvador	Henry E. Catto, Jr.	Julio A. Rivera
Ethiopia	E. Ross Adair	Kifle Wodajo
Fiji	Kenneth Franzheim II	S. K. Sikivou
Finland	Val Peterson	Leo Olavi Tuominen
France	John N. Irwin II*	Jacques Kosciusko-Morizet
Gabon	John A. McKesson III	Gaston-Robert Bouckat-Bou-Nziengui
Gambia	G. Edward Clark	Vacant
Germany, West	Martin J. Hillenbrand	Rolf Pauls
Ghana	Fred L. Hadsel	Harry Reginald Amonoo
Great Britain	Walter H. Annenberg	The Earl of Cromer
Greece	Henry J. Tasca	Basil George Vitsaxis
Guatemala	William G. Bowdler	Julio Asensio-Wunderlich
Guinea	Terence A. Todman	Sadan Moussa Touré
Guyana	Spencer M. King	Rahman B. Gajraj
Haiti	Clinton E. Knox	René Chalmers
Honduras	Hewson A. Ryan	Roberto Galvez Barnes
Hungary	Alfred Puhan	Karoly Szabo
Iceland	Frederick Irving	Gudmundur I. Gudmundsson
India	Daniel Patrick Moynihan*	Lakshmi Kant Jha
Indonesia	Francis J. Galbraith	Sjarif Thajeb
Iran	Richard Helms*	Amir-Aslan Afshar
Ireland	John D. J. Moore	William Warnock
Israel	Vacant	Yitzhak Rabin
Italy	John A. Volpe*	Egidio Ortona
Ivory Coast	John F. Root	Timothée N'Guetta Ahoua
Jamaica	Vincent de Roulet	Douglas Valmore Fletcher
Japan	Robert S. Ingersoll	Nobuhiko Ushiba
Jordan	L. Dean Brown	Zuhayr Mufti
Kenya	Robinson McIlvaine	Leonard Oliver Kibinge
Khmer Republic	Emory C. Swank	Sonn Voeunsai
Korea, South	Philip C. Habib	Dong Jo Kim
Kuwait	William A. Stoltzfus, Jr.	Salem S. Al-Sabah
Laos	G. McMurtrie Godley	Peng Norindr
Lebanon	William B. Buffum	Najati Kabbani
Lesotho	Charles J. Nelson	Mothusi T. Mashologu
Liberia	Melvin L. Manfull*	S. Edward Peal
Libya	Joseph Palmer II	Abdalla Suwesi
Luxembourg	Vacant	Jean Wagner
Madagascar	Joseph A. Mendenhall	Henri Raharijaona
Malawi	William C. Burdett	Gamaliel P. Bandawe
Malaysia	Jack W. Lydman	Vacant
Mali	Robert O. Blake	Seydou Traoré
Malta	John I. Getz	Joseph Attard-Kingswell
Mauritania	Richard W. Murphy	Moulaye El Hassen
Mauritius	William D. Brewer	Pierre Guy Girald Balancy
Mexico	Robert H. McBride	José Juan de Olloqui
Morocco	Stuart W. Rockwell	Badreddine Senoussi
Nepal	Carol C. Laise	Kul Shekhar Sharma
Netherlands	J. William Middendorf II	Baron Rijnhard B. Van Lynden
New Zealand	Kenneth Franzheim II	Lloyd White
Nicaragua	Turner B. Shelton	Guillermo Sevilla-Sacasa
Niger	Roswell D. McClelland	Abdoulaye Diallo
Nigeria	John E. Reinhardt	John M. Garba
Norway	Philip K. Crowe	Arne Gunneng
Pakistan	Vacant	Sultan Mohammad Khan
Panama	Vacant	Nicholas Gonzalez Revilla
Paraguay	George W. Landau	Vacant
Peru	Taylor G. Belcher	Fernando Berckemeyer
Philippines	Henry A. Byroade	Eduardo Z. Romualdez
Poland	Richard T. Davies*	Witold Trampczynski
Portugal	Ridgway B. Knight	João Hall Themido
Qatar	William A. Stoltzfus, Jr.	Abdullah Saleh Al-Mania
Romania	Leonard C. Meeker	Corneliu Bogdan
Russia	Jacob D. Beam	Anatoliy F. Dobrynin
Rwanda	Robert F. Corrigan	Fidèle Nkundabagenzi
Saudi Arabia	Nicholas G. Thacher	Ibrahim Al-Sowayel
Senegal	G. Edward Clark	Andre Coulbary
Sierra Leone	Clinton L. Olson	Philip Jonathan Gbagu Palmer
Singapore	Edwin M. Cronk	Ernest Steven Monteiro
Somalia	Matthew J. Looram, Jr.	Abdullahi Ahmed Addou
South Africa	John G. Hurd	Johan S. F. Botha
Spain	Horacio Rivero	Angel Sagaz
Sri Lanka	Christopher Van Hollen	Neville Kanakaratne
Swaziland	Charles J. Nelson	S. T. Msindazwe Sukati
Sweden	Vacant	Hubert de Besche
Switzerland	Shelby Davis	Felix Schnyder
Taiwan	Walter P. McConaughy	James C. H. Shen
Tanzania	W. Beverly Carter, Jr.	Paul L. Bomani
Thailand	Leonard Unger	Anand Panyarachun
Togo	Dwight Dickinson	Epiphane Ayi Mawussi
Trinidad and Tobago	Anthony D. Marshall	Sir Ellis Emmanuel Innocent Clarke
Tunisia	Talcott W. Seelye	Slaheddine El Goulli
Turkey	William J. Handley	Melih Esenbel
Uganda	Thomas Patrick Melady	Mustapha Ramathan
Upper Volta	Donald B. Easum	Telesphore Yaguibou
Uruguay	Charles W. Adair, Jr.	Hector Luisi
Venezuela	Robert McClintock	Andrés Aguilar
Vietnam, South	Ellsworth Bunker	Tran Kim Phuong
Yemen (San'ā')	William R. Crawford, Jr.	Vacant
Yugoslavia	Malcolm Toon	Toma Granfil
Zaire	Sheldon B. Vance	Lombo Lo Mangamanga
Zambia	Jean M. Wilkowski	Unia G. Mwila

*Ambassador designate

Sources: U.S. Dept. of State and Congressional Record

Cole, Jr., as executive director of the Domestic Council, replacing John D. Ehrlichman.

▪ On December 21, the White House said Atomic Energy Commission Chairman James R. Schlesinger would replace Richard M. Helms as director of the Central Intelligence Agency.

There was also a major shakeup in the Department of the Interior, following the take-over of the Bureau of Indian Affairs building by a group of militant Indians in November. See INDIAN, AMERICAN.

On May 3, L. Patrick Gray III was named acting director of the Federal Bureau of Investigation, replacing J. Edgar Hoover who died on May 2. See DEATHS (Close-Up); GRAY, L. PATRICK III.

The Legislative Branch. President Nixon's withdrawal of all but 24,100 U.S. troops muted congressional criticism of his Vietnam policy. However, Congress and the President clashed on the issue of fiscal control. Congress refused to allow the President to limit annual spending to $250 billion, regardless of appropriations, as Mr. Nixon had requested. Many congressmen believed this would weaken congressional control of U.S. government spending.

Nevertheless, the Environmental Protection Agency (EPA) announced on November 28 that Mr. Nixon had ordered the withholding of about half the funds that Congress authorized for sewage treatment facilities.

Major legislation passed by the second session of the 92nd Congress included: the Federal Election Campaign Act of 1971; a $30.2-billion revenue-sharing bill for distributing federal funds to state and local governments; a bill raising social security benefits 20 per cent; and a $19.5-billion aid to education bill with antibusing provisions. See CIVIL RIGHTS; CONGRESS; EDUCATION; SOCIAL SECURITY.

The Judicial Branch. On January 7, Lewis F. Powell, Jr., and William H. Rehnquist were sworn in as associate justices of the Supreme Court of the United States. They were Mr. Nixon's third and fourth appointees to the nation's highest court.

On June 29, the Supreme Court ruled that capital punishment – as it has been haphazardly administered by the states – constituted cruel and unusual punishment in violation of the Eighth Amendment to the U.S. Constitution. However, each justice wrote a separate opinion on the matter.

In other important decisions the court ruled: that Amish children do not have to attend school after the eighth grade; that it is unconstitutional for the government to conduct electronic surveillance on suspected domestic radicals without prior court approval; that journalists may not refuse to divulge their sources of confidential information to grand juries; and that the government need not grant a witness full immunity from prosecution in return for grand jury testimony. See COURTS AND LAWS. Carol L. Thompson

See also PRESIDENT OF THE UNITED STATES.

UPPER VOLTA. See AFRICA.

URUGUAY. Juan María Bordaberry Arocena became president on March 1, 1972. Inaugural ceremonies were held under tight security conditions because of an expected attack by left wing Tupamaro guerrillas. In his address, President Bordaberry vowed unyielding war against the terrorists.

Bordaberry found the country in grave economic condition, with foreign exchange funds nearly gone and welfare programs in a mess. Inflation was rampant and foreign investment was almost nonexistent. On March 10, Congress voted to lift most of the curbs imposed on civil liberties in June, 1969. On April 15, however, it approved a 30-day "state of internal war" – later extended – against the Tupamaro guerrillas, and the Uruguayan Army joined the police in their efforts to rout the leftists.

In May, goaded into a violent counterattack by a series of guerrilla-planned assassinations, the security forces launched a full-scale onslaught against them. By July, the number of people under arrest varied from the official figure of 1,600 up to 4,000. The security forces, meanwhile, destroyed numerous hideouts, large caches of arms and supplies, and underground medical clinics. They also uncovered guerrilla-run information and financial centers as well as a "people's jail" – an underground vault hidden with great cunning below the garage of a family town house in Montevideo where the Tupamaros were holding two politically prominent Uruguayans kidnaped 14 months earlier. On September 1, Raul Sendic, founder of the Tupamaro movement, was shot and captured by the police. But, while reverses affected the guerrillas, the leftists did succeed in dragging the security forces into politics for the first time since policemen staged a coup in 1933. The army as well as the leftists were equally disillusioned about politicians and their programs.

Business Remained Stagnant. Through June, beef exports were down to only 60,612 tons from 87,956 during the same period in 1971 and 105,823 tons in 1970. Cattle smuggling into Brazil was enormous, because prices were higher there. Living costs during the first nine months soared 56.5 per cent. To stimulate beef exports, a complete ban on the slaughter of cattle for domestic consumption was in effect between July 15 and November 15. A 20 per cent across-the-board wage increase was authorized on April 1, and another overall 20 per cent hike became effective at the end of September. Prices, however, also were raised for fuel, alcoholic beverages, cement, asphalt, and food and clothing. Devaluations of the peso occurred throughout the year, with a 50 per cent devaluation on March 2. With wage hikes constantly outdated by rampant inflation, labor unrest grew, resulting in many strikes. Mary Webster Soper

See also LATIN AMERICA (Facts in Brief Table).

UTAH. See STATE GOVERNMENT.

UTILITIES. See COMMUNICATIONS; ENERGY; PETROLEUM AND GAS.

VENEZUELA. An upcoming presidential election and a tense situation in the petroleum industry were major issues in 1972. The election, even though it was not scheduled until December, 1973, was by far the most disruptive issue. On May 23, Romulo Betancourt, who founded the Democratic Action Party in 1941, returned from Switzerland, presumably to announce he would be a candidate in the 1973 elections. He was followed on May 24 by former dictator Marcos Pérez Jiménez, now living in Spain, who made a brief visit to register his candidacy. Protests over the return of the two former presidents erupted across the nation between May 23 and June 2. One person was killed and dozens hurt as students rioted in Caracas, Maracaibo, Valencia, San Felix, and other cities. On July 20, Betancourt announced he would not be a candidate, presumably because of the protests. Congress began considering amendments that would prevent Jiménez from running.

Petroleum Problems. Up to September 13, petroleum output averaged 3,197,748 barrels per day (bpd), about 12 per cent below the same 1971 period. Among the causes were the mild winter in Europe and North America, which reduced demand; a decline in freight rates, which made it cheaper for the oil firms to transport supplies from the Middle East; and increases in local taxes and prices, which made the republic's oil increasingly expensive. This directly affected the economy, because petroleum revenues account for 20 per cent of the gross national product, almost 66 per cent of government income, and 90 per cent of all foreign-exchange earnings. In 1970, Venezuela was the world's leading oil exporter, but in 1972 it ranked third behind Saudi Arabia and Iran.

An uncertain atmosphere developed as the government tried to increase and stabilize its revenues to cover rising fiscal deficits, and the oil firms struggled with higher taxes and prices, tax penalties for quarterly variations in output, lower profits, and the knowledge that their concessions are due to expire starting in 1983. Perhaps more important, the regime's attitude did little to motivate oil concerns to spend money to develop badly needed new reserves.

No oil was found in southern Lake Maracaibo, reputedly rich in light crudes, and three firms temporarily stopped exploring there. This was disappointing, in view of a recent estimate that the nation's proven reserves, as of December, 1971, totaled 13.7-billion barrels, the lowest since 1960.

Gross monetary reserves increased to a record $1.5 billion on June 30, up 25.2 per cent over mid-1971 and attributed to higher oil receipts despite declining production. Business was good, commercial banks were strong, and inflation was no major problem. On the other hand, unemployment was serious. The oil industry provides only 28,000 jobs, while the population numbers 11 million. Mary Webster Soper

See also LATIN AMERICA (Facts in Brief Table).

VERMONT. See STATE GOVERNMENT.

VETERANS returning to civilian life in 1972 found increased job and training opportunities. However, about 25 per cent were not able to make a satisfactory adjustment. Studies made for the Veterans Administration (VA) and the U.S. Department of Labor revealed that many lacked adequate information on jobs and had little chance for effective counseling. Most important, the study showed the need for a comprehensive nationwide policy that can effectively deal with the many adjustment problems of veterans.

President Richard M. Nixon responded in May by extending his Jobs for Veterans Program for another year. He asked Secretary of Labor James D. Hodgson to continue as leader, and requested the Department of Defense, the VA, the Civil Service Commission, and the Department of Health, Education, and Welfare (HEW) to assist. In addition, the following special projects were inaugurated in 1972 to aid in the Jobs for Veterans Program:

- A hot-line telephone system to help veterans with such problems as bureaucratic red tape, unemployment, and drug abuse, and to give information on GI Bill benefits. Established in 13 cities across the country, this Veterans Referral Switchboard includes a well-publicized phone number that veterans can call when they need help.
- Overseas counseling by three-man teams from HEW, the VA, and the Labor Department. The teams operate at military bases in West Germany, Japan, South Korea, Okinawa, and South Vietnam – advising servicemen about to be discharged on jobs, training, educational opportunities, and other benefits to which they are entitled.
- A program for Spanish-speaking Vietnam veterans. Under the program, 12,000 men will be counseled, referred to skill and educational training centers, or placed in jobs. Bilingual Vietnam veterans were being recruited for staff positions to carry out this program.
- A construction-job clearing house to find jobs for veterans with construction skills. About 19,000 men skilled as carpenters, bricklayers, heavy-equipment operators, and in similar trades left military service in 1972. These men can be matched with jobs that are listed with the clearing house in Washington, D.C., which is operated jointly by the National Association of Home Builders and the Associated General Contractors of America.

Legislation. The Veterans' Compensation and Relief Act of 1972, which became law on July 1, provided an across-the-board increase of about 10 per cent in veterans' service-connected disability-compensation rates and dependency allowances, and an authorization for a clothing allowance of $150 per year for those who wear artificial appliances or braces or who are confined to wheel chairs. Effective July 1, 1973, it provides equal rates of compensation for those disabled in wartime and peacetime.

Other legislation provides those veterans totally and permanently disabled as a result of military service with increased government grants to purchase homes equipped with ramps for wheel chairs or other facilities to aid the handicapped.

Additional legislation provided lower premium rates for veterans insured under Federal Servicemen's Life Insurance. Effective July 1, 1972, the premium became $2.55 per month, a 45-cents-a-month reduction for $15,000 coverage.

Conventions. The American Legion held its 54th annual national convention in Chicago from August 18 to 24. Joe L. Matthews of Fort Worth, Tex., was elected national commander, and Gregory L. Hack, 16, of Lawrence, Kans., was elected president of the 1972 American Legion Boys Nation.

The Sons of the American Legion held its first national convention at the legion meeting, with 400 delegates, guests, and advisers from 24 states attending. Robert H. Faust was elected national commander.

The American Veterans Committee held its 29th convention from June 16 to 18 at Kerhonkson, N.Y. Raymond Bramucci of Hazlet, N.J., was re-elected national chairman.

Veterans of Foreign Wars held its 73rd annual national convention from August 18 to 25 in Minneapolis, Minn. Patrick E. Carr of Metairie, La., was elected commander in chief. Joseph P. Anderson

VIETNAM. President Nguyen Van Thieu tightened his grip on the government in 1972. Confronted by political and military problems of enormous magnitude, he dispensed with the U.S.-inspired democratic institutions and governed instead through the army and the exercise of direct personal power. Not since the assassination of Ngo Dinh Diem in 1963 had anyone become so independent of U.S. control or influence while at the same time remaining so dependent on American support. It was because of Thieu's firm control that his removal from the political scene had become a key demand of the North Vietnamese Communists negotiating a settlement of the war. See Asia; President of the United States.

The immediate catalysts behind Thieu's actions in 1972 were, first, an apparent thaw in U.S.-China relations epitomized by President Richard M. Nixon's visit to China in February; and, second, a massive military push launched by the North Vietnamese across the demilitarized zone on March 30. It was the biggest Communist offensive launched since 1968. As South Vietnam's troops pulled back in disarray under the fierce assault, Thieu acted to keep the civilian population from shifting loyalties.

On May 10, he imposed martial law, permitting the police to arrest and detain at will any suspected Communists or Communist sympathizers. On June 27, at Thieu's insistence, the Senate granted him the power to rule by decree in matters pertaining to national security and the economy. A previous decree had banned political demonstrations and strikes, restricted travel to foreign countries, and set a 10 P.M. to 5 A.M. curfew throughout South Vietnam.

Even more significant was Thieu's move to consolidate his power at the provincial level. On August 22, the government abolished democratic elections in the country's 10,775 hamlets. The decree superseded a 1966 law that provided for the election of hamlet and village officials. Under the new statute, the 44 province chiefs were to reorganize local government and appoint all hamlet officials.

Nor was freedom of the press exempt from Thieu's attentions. On August 5, he announced a decree restricting South Vietnam's newspapers. Newsmen as well as diplomats in Saigon considered the move an attempt to muzzle criticism of the Thieu regime. The decree required every daily newspaper to deposit about $47,000 with the government within 30 days. The money would be a guarantee to cover possible fines and violations of the already strict press rules.

Unemployment Rife. Economically, South Vietnam was in the throes of one of its worst recessions. The government attributed it to the drastic reduction of U.S. troops. During the peak period of U.S. involvement, in 1968, about 150,000 South Vietnamese had been employed by the Americans. These jobs had now virtually vanished. Hundreds of thousands

Russian Presidium Chairman Nikolai V. Podgorny embraces North Vietnam's Le Duan, right, head of the Workers' Party, during a Hanoi meeting.

Lazlo Toth, with beard, is captured after assaulting Michelangelo's *Pietà* with a hammer. He shattered the left arm and nose of the Virgin Mary's figure.

more had worked for small companies, now wiped out, whose services and products supplied U.S. demand. "Unemployment," according to the ministry of the economy, "was nothing short of catastrophic."

The estimated 500,000 refugees who depended on government aid to survive were a further drain on the economy. These refugees were costing the government about $100,000 a day to sustain. Much of this expense was closely connected with a growing shortage of such staples as rice. Although the country produced a record rice crop, it was unable to feed itself, and had to import between 100,000 and 200,000 tons.

North Vietnam was relatively uncommunicative about its internal political and economic situation. Le Duan, first secretary of the ruling Workers' (Communist) Party and Truong Chinh, chairman of the National Assembly, headed the government. General Vo Nguyen Giap directed the armed forces.

There was considerable diplomatic activity. Presidium Chairman Nikolai V. Podgorny of Russia flew to Hanoi on June 15 to discuss the resumption of peace talks in Paris. In a related move, Le Duc Tho, the North Vietnamese adviser to the talks, arrived in Peking on June 17 for talks with Chou En-lai. The peace talks resumed in July, but at year's end, no agreement had been reached. John N. Stalker

See also Asia (Facts in Brief Table).

VIETNAM WAR. See Asia.

VIRGINIA. See State Government.

VISUAL ARTS. A quiet expectancy and a darker nervousness was evident in the visual arts in 1972. Recent radical anti-art activity no longer seemed outrageous, and hopes for a radical new approach seemed more far-fetched than before. So the search for values in exhibitions often extended into the American past – both the recent past and its roots in the 19th century.

This search for a new innocence resulted in several extensive 19th century American exhibitions. The paintings of Eastman Johnson were seen at the Whitney Museum of American Art in New York City from March 28 to May 14. The Brooklyn Museum held shows featuring the water colors of both John Singer Sargent and Winslow Homer during the summer. One of the greatest of America's romantic landscapists, Albert Bierstadt, was honored by an exhibit organized by the Amon Carter Museum in Fort Worth, Tex., from January 11 to February 6. His paintings also appeared, along with 130 other works, from March 22 to May 28 in "The American West," the most important of these shows. Organized by the Los Angeles County Museum of Fine Art, it featured works by Frederic Remington, Charles M. Russell, George Catlin, and others documenting a world that even then was known to be dying.

The Brooklyn Museum mounted a large retrospective exhibition of Norman Rockwell, the man who may lay claim to the title of "America's favorite

Wrap-artist Christo hung his $700,000 orange curtain across Colorado's Rifle Gap on August 10. Hours later, high winds ripped it apart.

artist." Sixty years of work was seen from March 22 to May 14, and predictably enough, many of the paintings in the exhibition had appeared on covers of *The Saturday Evening Post*.

Major Exhibitions of 20th century American artists included the first full retrospective accorded James Rosenquist at the Whitney Museum in New York City. Sixty-six of the artist's often huge, mural-like, surreal-pop works were seen. Claes Oldenburg, one of the best known of the American pop artists, presented his large-scale sculptural enlargements of mundane life in "Object into Monument" at the Pasadena Art Museum from December 7 to February 6. Sam Francis was honored with a large retrospective of his glowing, nonrepresentational color images at the Albright-Knox Art Gallery in Buffalo, N. Y. Francis, who lived in Europe during the 1950s, is the least known of the abstract-expressionist wave that established the United States as the art power of the world at that time. Earlier in 1972, the Albright-Knox had displayed its own devotion to that style in an exhibition "Abstract-Expressionism: The First and Second Generations." Of the 56 paintings on display, the museum had purchased 46 between 1955 and 1960.

Such exhibitions, almost entirely culled from a museum's own resources, were not intended to be self-aggrandizing. On the contrary, they represented a response to the increasing financial pressures that have forced museums to abandon the traditional wide-borrowing pattern. Instead, they tried new organizational procedures for exhibitions, often with stunning results. For instance, the Solomon R. Guggenheim Museum in New York City presented a summer-long exhibition of the paintings of Vasily Kandinsky, one of the seminal figures of 20th century painting. All 133 works were from Guggenheim collections. The Museum of Modern Art (MOMA) in New York City displayed all of its Kurt Schwitters. The Art Institute of Chicago combined its holdings with those of city residents in "Small Bronzes from Chicago Collections" from July 22 to October 8.

Primitive Exhibits. Perhaps to counteract both the art world's present tiredness and the constant search for the new, works of art outside the European tradition got more attention than ever. Two exhibitions of American Indian art attracted more widespread attention than they would have a decade ago. "The Navaho Blanket" exhibition at the Los Angeles County Museum ran from June 27 to August 27. And the American Indian exhibition at the Minneapolis Institute of Arts reasserted the power of primitive vision that was essential in forming the new language of modern art when European artists looked to Africa and the South Seas about 1900. The Field Museum of Natural History in Chicago presented the first major Western display of the full range of Australian aborigine art.

In still another approach to the non-Western vision, the Metropolitan Museum offered a magnificent display from May 4 to June 4 of one of the greatest of Persian illuminated manuscripts: The 70 pages of the 16th century epic *Shah-nameh* was offered as "A King's Book of Kings." At the same time, the New York Cultural Center showed "Treasures of Persian Art," based on the Mahboubian Collection, the largest in the Western world.

Two of the outstanding exhibitions of European art presented French structural grace and Germanic literary allusion. The former exhibited the work of the well-known Georges Braque, whose large-scale cubist still lifes were seen at The Art Institute of Chicago from October 7 to December 3. The latter featured the little-known Ferdinand Hodler, a show organized by the Berkeley (Calif.) University Art Gallery.

Museum Activity in the United States was stimulated by the October opening of a major new building, the Kimbell Art Museum in Fort Worth, Tex., and by the announcement of several splendid gifts. W. Averell Harriman gave the National gallery of Art in Washington, D.C., 22 European masterworks of the late 19th and early 20th century. Five works by Paul Cézanne in the group brought the gallery's Cézanne holdings to 18, one of the world's great public displays of this important French artist.

In Los Angeles, the County Museum received a $10-million gift, the collection of Armand Hammer. The paintings will be seen in Dublin and London, and will circulate until the donor's death, when they will be permanently installed in Los Angeles. Also, Joseph H. Hirshhorn presented his museum in Washington, D.C., with 166 sculptures and 160 paintings; this was the first addition to the more than 6,000 works he gave in 1966.

The Two Greatest Acquisitions of the year were the Metropolitan Museum's portrait of a young boy by Goya, valued at $2.5 million, and a Greek ceramic *krater*, an open-mouthed mixing bowl from the 500s B.C., decorated in the "red-figure" style. The bowl, held by many to be one of the greatest examples of the art of the Greek potter and painter, cost $1.5 million.

The prices of important works of art continued to skyrocket. As the search for the finest examples of the art of an epoch become more intense, the works become more scarce and expensive. The works of previously neglected minor masters brought record prices. A Bellotto, a fine 18th century landscapist, sold for $771,000, while a 17th century Dutch still life by De Heem brought $104,000 and a landscape of the same period by Philips Koninch brought $200,000.

Several new highs were also recorded in auctions for 20th century works: A landscape by Oskar Kokoschka sold for $105,000, and the highest price ever paid for a work by a living artist – $260,000 – was paid for a carved wooden sculpture by Henry Moore.

In October, visitors to The Art Institute of Chicago enjoyed a major exhibition of cubist still lifes by Georges Braque, the 20th century French master.

The highest price paid for a work of art during the year – the third highest price ever recorded for a work of art – was the Norton Simon Foundation purchase for more than $3 million of a Zurbaran still life.

Desecration of the *Pietà*. Michelangelo's *Pietà*, one of the supreme masterpieces in the history of Western art, was severely damaged on May 21. A mentally deranged man attacked it in a chapel of St. Peter's Basilica in Rome. With 15 blows of a hammer, he shattered the left arm of the Virgin Mary and chipped parts of the nose, left eye, and veil. Restoration was successfully completed by the end of the year.

Sculpture Shows. The three most important shows highlighted the traditional idea of sculpture – the free-standing figure. The National Gallery presented the elongated and spiritual work of Wilhelm Lehmbruck, a German poet and sculptor who committed suicide in 1919 at the age of 38. Most of the works were lent by the three-year-old Lehmbruck Museum in Duisburg, his hometown. The other exhibitions, Jacques Lipchitz at the Metropolitan Museum of Art from June 6 to September 5, and MOMA's Matisse sculptures, February 24 to May 1, both celebrated the 20th century's abstract tradition. The Matisse exhibition marked the first time that all 69 of his known bronzes had been shown together. Joshua B. Kind

VITAL STATISTICS. See CENSUS, U.S.

WALDHEIM, KURT (1918-), an Austrian career diplomat, succeeded U Thant as secretary-general of the United Nations (UN) on Jan. 1, 1972. Waldheim was elected on the third ballot over Finnish Ambassador Max Jacobson, becoming the fourth secretary-general in UN history.

The tall, sharp-featured Waldheim is considered a model diplomat. He is a skillful negotiator and an exceptional linguist – necessary skills for performing what has been called "the most impossible job in the world." Although he is respected as a skilled diplomat, some fellow diplomats doubted that he could provide the strong leadership needed to restore the fading prestige of the United Nations.

Waldheim had been a member of his country's UN delegation since 1955. He was Austria's foreign minister from 1968 to 1970. In 1971, he was the conservative People's Party's unsuccessful candidate for the Austrian presidency, receiving 47.2 per cent of the vote.

Waldheim was born in St. Andrae-Wörden, a small town near Vienna. His father was a schoolteacher of Czechoslovak descent. At 19, he entered the Vienna Consular Academy to study to be a diplomat. Drafted into the German Army in 1939, he was released after suffering a leg wound on the Russian front. He earned a law degree from the University of Vienna in 1944.

Waldheim and his wife, the former Elisabeth Ritschel, have three children. Allan Davidson

WALLACE, GEORGE CORLEY (1919-), governor of Alabama and Democratic presidential contender, was shot at a Laurel, Md., shopping center on May 15, 1972. The attack left him paralyzed from the waist down. The assassination attempt occurred as Wallace was shaking hands with admirers after addressing a political rally. A man in the crowd fired a .38-caliber pistol at Wallace, wounding him in the stomach, left shoulder, and right arm and shoulder. One of the bullets lodged against his spinal cord, causing the paralysis. Three other persons also were wounded.

Arthur H. Bremer, 21, of Milwaukee, Wis., was captured at the scene and indicted for the crime. He pleaded not guilty by reason of insanity, but a jury convicted him on August 4. He was sentenced to 63 years in prison.

Wallace was at the height of his primary campaign when he was shot. The day after the shooting, he won the Maryland and Michigan primary elections, and ranked second in delegate strength behind Senator George S. McGovern (D., S. Dak.).

However, Wallace remained a candidate for the nomination and left the hospital to address the Democratic National Convention in Miami Beach, Fla., from a wheel chair on July 11. He received 385.7 delegate votes. Wallace said his physical condition forced him to refuse nomination as the American Party's presidential candidate. Darlene R. Stille

WARNER, JOHN W. (1927-), was sworn in as secretary of the Navy on May 4, 1972. He is the first secretary to have served in both the Navy and the Marine Corps.

Warner was born on Feb. 18, 1927, in Washington, D.C. He enlisted in the Navy at the age of 17, after attending Washington public schools. He completed a course in electronics at the Naval Research Laboratory in Washington, D.C., and was released from active duty in June, 1946, as an electronics technician, third class. He received a bachelor's degree from Washington and Lee University in 1949, majoring in general engineering, physics, and mathematics. Then, he entered the University of Virginia law school.

Warner's law training was interrupted for a second tour of military duty, this time as a Marine Corps communications officer in Korea. Released from active duty in 1952, Warner returned to law school and graduated in 1953. In 1956, he was appointed to the first of several posts he was to hold with the U.S. attorney's office in Washington, D.C. Warner worked for then Vice-President Richard M. Nixon in the 1960 campaign, then joined a private law firm. In 1969, President Nixon named him undersecretary of the Navy. In 1972, he also became Director of Ocean Affairs. Warner is married to the former Catherine Conover Mellon of Upperville, Va. They have three children. Michael Reed

WASHINGTON. See State Government.

WASHINGTON, D.C. Two major developments in 1972 promised to improve public transit in Washington, D.C. The new Metro rail system received $3 billion to develop and operate a 98-mile rail network. Metro was also guaranteed an additional $1.2-billion in construction bonds, to be repaid from future fare collections.

Secretary of Transportation John A. Volpe designated the Metropolitan Washington Council of Governments to coordinate public transit projects. The projects, costing more than $4.7 million, include:

- Improvements in bus operation and routing.
- Special off-hour scheduling and transit services for the elderly and handicapped.
- Shelters at 2,500 bus stops.
- Recommendations for government subsidies and other programs to prevent future service cutbacks.

Transpo 72, the world's first international transportation exposition, was held at Washington's Dulles International Airport from May 27 to June 4. All kinds of conveyances were on display, from computerized people movers to experimental air-cushioned vehicles.

A Teachers' Strike closed public schools in Washington from September 19 to October 3. Teachers demanded a 17 per cent pay hike and the restoration of 180 teaching positions that had been eliminated by budget cuts. A temporary restraining order was ignored until the teachers won a settlement.

The settlement provided for 182 new teaching positions, $350,000 more for classroom supplies, exemption from the requirement that teachers take additional courses to keep teaching certificates valid, and a promise that the requested pay increase would be sought. Legislation was then introduced in Congress for an immediate 7 per cent pay increase.

Protest Demonstrations. On February 17, a 3,300-car motorcade from Richmond, Va., drove to the capital in a demonstration against forced school busing. On March 25, 30,000 persons held a rally to protest President Richard M. Nixon's welfare and child-care policies. Hundreds of antiwar activists descended on Washington in April and May to protest the renewed bombing of North Vietnam and the mining of North Vietnamese harbors. A bomb exploded in the Pentagon on May 19, causing $75,000 damage, and in November a group of Indians took over the Bureau of Indian Affairs Building.

In August, Washington's police department opened a $90,000 command center for use during civil disorders. The center is designed to aid the police in directing their forces to potential trouble spots during demonstrations. Employment in the District of Columbia improved slightly between May, 1971, and May, 1972. Average gross weekly earnings of production workers went up almost $12 during that period. J. M. Banovetz

WEATHER. Colder than normal temperatures in the central United States and drought conditions in the Southwest ushered in 1972. Spring brought generous rain and below-normal temperatures to much of the North and East, with many record low temperatures recorded in June and July and variable but unseasonably cool conditions throughout the rest of the year. The Southwest drought was broken in June with the first rains since December for many locations, but drought conditions resumed in July.

On June 9, Rapid City, S.Dak., was struck by record-breaking floods that killed 237 persons and caused more than $100 million damage. Later that same month, Hurricane Agnes dumped rain from Florida northward into Maine and westward into Pennsylvania and New York. In its wake, it left nearly $2 billion in flood damage. See DISASTERS.

Weather Modification. Scientists at the Environmental Research Laboratories' Atmospheric Physics and Chemistry Laboratory in Boulder, Colo., were busy throughout 1972 trying to suppress lightning discharges over a 200-square-mile area in northeastern Colorado. They seeded thunderstorms with fine aluminized fibers that dissipated lightning by providing an alternate path for the electric currents caused by the storms. In one test, a storm's massive electric field was completely neutralized in 10 minutes by the seeding. The study was designed

The weather station at Grover, Colo., is the center for an experiment in cloud seeding to suppress hail. It is in an area of past record hailstorms.

to accurately measure the electric field strength from the ground for each lightning stroke within a 50-mile radius.

Atmospheric Visibility appears to be decreasing in the Eastern part of the United States. Data from Akron, Ohio; Lexington, Ky.; and Memphis, Tenn., showed that the frequency of restricted visibility periods has increased significantly over the last decade. This reverses the increased visibility trend reported from about 1930 to the mid-1960s, which was attributed to the conversion from coal to cleaner-burning gas and oil. The recent decrease in visibility is believed to be caused by a combination of increased pollution and natural causes.

Storm Warnings. The first of several automatic flash-flood warning systems was installed at Wheeling, W.Va., in May by the National Weather Service (NWS). The warning system consists of a high-water sensor placed at an upstream point on Wheeling Creek, and a downstream community alarm station from which warnings can be spread rapidly.

Portable electronic detectors, developed by scientists at the Environmental Research Laboratories, were tested at more than 15 sites in 10 tornado-prone states during the 1972 storm season. The monitoring equipment, which records distinctive electrical signals from tornadoes, was placed near weather radar stations to compare electrical activity with radar echoes. The research may help to establish the feasibility and reliability of using electrical observations as a tornado forecasting technique.

The NWS teletypewriter circuits in September began relaying abbreviated forecasts for 88 cities as an aid to travelers. The forecasts, which give a brief description of recent weather and predictions for the next 48 hours, were published by the city newspapers and broadcast by radio and television.

Weather Satellites. The National Aeronautics and Space Administration Earth Resources Technology Satellite (*ERTS-1*) was launched into a near-polar orbit on July 23. The orbit carries it around the earth 14 times a day, giving global coverage over an 18-day period. *ERTS-1* is an experimental spacecraft, intended to demonstrate the usefulness of repeated global sensing of conditions on and above the earth's surface. It will operate for about a year. National Oceanic and Atmospheric Administration (NOAA) scientists are using the *ERTS-1* data in studies of sea ice distribution, snow run-off potential, air and water pollutants, and severe storm detail.

On October 17, the fourth Improved Tiros Operational Satellite (*ITOS-D*) an environmental satellite, was launched for NOAA from Lompoc, Calif. Although similar in appearance to previous ITOS satellites, it has no cameras. It is the first in this operational series to rely entirely on scanning radiometers to obtain vertical temperature profile soundings of the atmosphere. William G. Collins

WEIGHT LIFTING. See SPORTS.

WEST INDIES. National elections held in two Caribbean countries in 1972 were marred by sporadic campaign violence and vandalism. In Jamaica, bombs were thrown, and Michael Manley, leader of the People's National Party (PNP), was fired at during a Kingston market rally on February 24. Because of outbursts of violence in the Bahamas, all bars, many businesses, and most schools were closed on election day.

The opposition PNP scored a major upset in the Jamaican elections on February 29. It captured 36 of the 53 seats at stake in the House of Representatives and ended the rule of the Jamaica Labor Party (JLP), which had been in power since 1962, when Jamaica gained independence. Manley, who had campaigned on the issues of corruption, unemployment, neglect of youth, and favoritism in government, was sworn in on March 2 as prime minister by Governor-General Clifford Campbell. Hugh Shearer, the outgoing prime minister, indicated he would withdraw as deputy leader of the defeated JLP.

In the Bahamas, Prime Minister Lynden O. Pindling crushed the opposition and took control of a large majority in Parliament. He campaigned on a promise of independence from Great Britain by July, 1973. Pindling's chief opposition, the Free National Movement, had also supported independence from Britain but maintained that the Bahamas would first have to become stronger economically.

Caribbean Conference. Barbados, Jamaica, and Trinidad and Tobago played leading roles in the 12th conference of heads of government of English-speaking Caribbean countries. The conference, held in Port-of-Spain, Trinidad, in October, adopted a number of major policies. Among them was one sponsored by the three nations and Guyana that favored establishing diplomatic and economic relations with Cuba. Prime Minister L. F. S. Burnham of Guyana read a statement by the four nations, all of whom belong to the Organization of American States (OAS), that noted the restrictions the OAS imposes on relations with Cuba. Burnham declared that each state had a sovereign right to enter into relations with any state and to seek meaningful cooperation with other states in the Caribbean.

Polio Outbreak. Despite political turmoil, the three Caribbean countries maintained their efforts to expand tourism in the area. Trinidad and Tobago, however, suffered a severe setback when an outbreak of poliomyelitis forced the government to close schools and cancel the annual February carnival.

Over a six-week period, 173 persons contracted polio and 10 died. The consequent halt in the flow of tourists cost the country an estimated $2 million. The government and the Pan American Health Organization launched an intensive vaccination program to bring the outbreak under control. Paul C.Tullier

See also LATIN AMERICA (Facts in Brief Table).

WEST VIRGINIA. See STATE GOVERNMENT.

WHITLAM, EDWARD GOUGH (1916-). In a major political upset, Edward Gough Whitlam and his Labor Party won the Australian elections held Dec. 2, 1972. In so doing, they defeated a conservative coalition of the Liberal and Country parties that had ruled Australia for 23 years. The new leader uses the name Edward only on formal occasions. Family and friends call him Gough. See AUSTRALIA.

The new prime minister was born on July 11, 1916, in the Melbourne suburb of Kew. His father was a lawyer who had once served as the Commonwealth Solicitor General, the second highest legal position in the government. Following in his father's footsteps, Whitlam attended the University of Sydney, where he earned degrees in the arts and law.

During World War II, Whitlam served in the Royal Australian Air Force. After his discharge, he entered law practice. He also became involved in Labor Party politics in Darlinghurst, a suburb of Sydney, and he entered the House of Representatives in 1952 as a Labor Party member. He was elected deputy leader of the opposition in 1960 and became its leader in February, 1967.

Whitlam married Margaret Dovey in 1942. They have three sons and a daughter. Paul C. Tullier

WILDLIFE. See CONSERVATION.

WISCONSIN. See STATE GOVERNMENT.

WRESTLING. See OLYMPIC GAMES; SPORTS.

WYOMING. See STATE GOVERNMENT.

YEMEN (ADEN). Border clashes and increasing domestic socialism during 1972 marked the fifth year of independence for the People's Democratic Republic of Yemen (PDRY), also called Yemen (Aden) and formerly called Southern Yemen. Fighting broke out several times in March with neighboring Yemen (San'ā'), and both countries complained to the Arab League. As a result of the incidents, the border was closed. This cut off the PDRY's main source of qat, which is a widely used narcotic leaf.

The Arab League arranged a cease-fire in October. Salim Rubai Ali Rubayya, chairman of the presidential council, met with Yemen's Republican Council chairman, Abdul Rahman Iryani, in Libya on November 25 to work out details for a merger of the two Yemens.

There also were border clashes with Oman, as Omani rebels used the PDRY for sanctuary. Several antigovernment groups seeking to overthrow the government formed an important element in this rivalry among Arab "brothers." As a result, the PDRY's ruling National Liberation Front (NLF) called a national congress that urged union with Yemen (San'ā') and the return of all PDRY exile leaders to cooperate with the government. In August, several anti-PDRY groups reportedly agreed to overthrow the "Marxist regime" in Aden, and a radio station called the Clandestine Voice of the Free South continued to attack the NLF from a clandestine transmitter hidden inside the country.

The NLF continued its "socialist transformation" of the country. In succession, it nationalized hotels, movie theaters, soft-drink manufacturing plants, office buildings, and all privately owned shops. A ministry of housing was created to oversee the transfer of property to "popular control committees." In addition, several associations, such as the Aden Women's Association and Girl Guides, were suppressed as being "tribal in character."

The country was plagued by a continuing financial crisis caused by meager resources and low agricultural yields. Most foreign travel was prohibited.

A few positive developments were reported, however. Foreign Minister Mohamed Salah Aulaqi's trip to Eastern Europe brought $20 million in loans from Hungary and Czechoslovakia. Russia gave 60 scholarships and $26.4 million to continue about 30 Soviet aid projects. China agreed to pay $2.4 million for 3,000 tons of Yemeni long-staple cotton. Libya granted a loan of $13.9 million, while Algeria provided technical equipment for the Aden Vocational Center plus $4 million for oil-exploration surveys by the joint Southern Yemen-Algerian Oil Production Company.

In November, the presidents of the two Yemen nations announced that they would unite within a year. William Spencer

See also MIDDLE EAST (Facts in Brief Table).

YEMEN (SAN'Ā') re-established formal diplomatic relations with the United States on July 1, 1972, after a five-year break. Yemen, which severed relations following the 1967 Arab-Israeli War, thus became the first Arab state to restore ties with the United States. The action came after U.S. Secretary of State William P. Rogers stopped in San'ā', the capital, in July, during his round-the-world tour. Rogers pledged that the United States would renew aid to Yemen, which had been suspended since 1968.

Intermittent border clashes clouded relations between Yemen and its neighbor, the People's Democratic Republic of Yemen (Aden). In September, Prime Minister Muhsin al-Ayni asked the Arab League to mediate their dispute. Ayni said that more than 100 Yemeni had been killed in the fighting and that the Yemen (San'ā') border town of Qataba had been bombed for 24 hours by planes controlled by the Aden government. In October, an Arab League mediation team obtained a cease-fire, and leaders of the two countries agreed to unite as a single nation within a year.

Yemen received support from various sources in efforts to rebuild its economy. Algeria gave $240,000 for a training school for technicians that would be located in San'ā'. Iraq and Libya contributed school buildings and equipment. Russia loaned Yemen $25-million. William Spencer

See also MIDDLE EAST (Facts in Brief Table).

YOUNG MEN'S CHRISTIAN ASSOCIATION (YMCA). The national council approved five-year operating goals in March, 1972. By 1978, the YMCA hopes to significantly influence those domestic and international conditions that affect the quality of human life.

To do this, the YMCA will work to (1) eliminate personal and institutional racism; (2) change conditions that foster alienation, delinquency, and crime; (3) strengthen physical and mental health; (4) strengthen family relationships and communications; and (5) work with people from other countries to build understanding and world peace.

The national council also discussed plans to obtain more members and form effective partnerships with other agencies, substantially increase financial resources, and use its physical and human resources more efficiently and effectively. The council also will work to improve the quality of juvenile justice in the United States. To achieve this, the YMCA will operate several programs and projects on national, regional, and local levels.

A new YMCA Water Safety and Lifesaving Program has been inaugurated to disseminate water-safety information to as many people as possible. The program is also designed to provide progressive training for Y leaders. Cooperation with the American Heart Association and other local service organizations should help ensure success. Joseph P. Anderson

YOUNG WOMEN'S CHRISTIAN ASSOCIATION (YWCA). On June 15, 1972, 107 voluntary and government organizations joined the YWCA of the United States in sponsoring the YWCA National Convocation on Racial Justice in New York City. The convocation was a step to achieve the YWCA's goal, voted at the organization's 25th national convention in 1970, "the elimination of racism wherever it exists and by any means necessary."

The convocation was attended by 3,000 national and community leaders from five continents who represented all racial backgrounds and many walks of life. They discussed ways to mobilize national organizations and arouse the national conscience to eliminate institutionalized racism.

Panel discussions focused on racism in American politics, economics, justice, foreign policy, housing, health care, education, and religion, and tried to evaluate the way agencies and groups can bring about change.

Since then, local YWCA's have sponsored "mini-convocations" on a regional and local level. These meetings have included regional and local representatives of many of the agencies and organizations that sponsored and took part in the national convocation with the YWCA. Much of what is being turned up has been brought to the attention of those who determine what issues are brought before the YWCA National Convention. Joseph P. Anderson

YOUTH ORGANIZATIONS continued the trend toward change in 1972. There were more changes in basic operating policies, greater flexibility in membership requirements, more decision making by members, and new and creative ways to attract today's more sophisticated youth.

Boy Scouts of America (BSA) highlights for 1972 include:

- Project SOAR (Save Our American Resources). Over 4 million Scouts, representatives of other organizations, and concerned citizens joined in this continuing drive against litter.
- Operation Reach. This effort to help solve the drug-abuse problem in America was begun in 1972 and will continue in 1973.
- Greater use of paraprofessional personnel in rural poverty and urban ghetto areas. This program, which enhances Scouting's outreach efforts, was expanded to reach American Indian boys. In addition, 20 paraprofessionals were employed to work in urban public-housing areas as youth coordinators.

The 62nd annual meeting of the Boy Scouts was held from May 17 to 19, in Los Angeles. Norton Clapp of Tacoma, Wash., was re-elected president.

Boys' Clubs of America (BCA) established a J. Edgar Hoover Freedom Award to perpetuate the late Federal Bureau of Investigation director's "memory and his inspiration to millions of American boys." Hoover served on the BCA board of directors for more than 30 years.

The 66th annual convention of the Boys' Clubs of America was held from June 4 to 8 in Washington, D.C. Delegates welcomed William R. Bricker of Milwaukee, Wis., as the new national director. Rodrigo Guerra, 16, of Pasadena, Calif., was named Boy of the Year.

Camp Fire Girls. The national council voted to open leadership ranks to men or women 18 years of age or older. However, Horizon Club leaders must be 20. In addition, a new leadership laboratory concept would allow high school students with leadership potential to train for placement as assistant leaders.

Four-H Clubs in 1972 offered two educational opportunities for young adults: the International Farm Youth Exchange (IFYE) and the Youth Development Project (YDP). Through IFYE, young adults from the United States can live and work with host families in other countries for from three to six months. Through YDP, young men and women with leadership experience can work with youth organizations similar to 4-H for a year in rural villages of developing countries. Participants have helped to establish libraries and regional camps.

The national 4-H Club conference was held from April 23 to 28 at the National 4-H Center in Washington, D.C.

Future Farmers of America (FFA). Six national officers, elected at the 1971 national FFA conven-

Scout modernization program includes new uniform with casual beret, at left. Scout in center wears uniform being replaced; at right is 1912 outfit.

tion, played a key role in FFA activities. They took a year's leave of absence from school to serve as student representatives of the FFA. Each traveled more than 100,000 miles to visit FFA chapters, attend state FFA conventions, and meet with government, business, and industry leaders.

National officers also played a key role in Operation Update programs, holding meetings in 27 locations across the United States. These programs were initiated to increase participation in FFA activities by informing FFA advisers and members of opportunities for awards in the FFA. FFA membership totaled more than 430,000 students.

The nation's top awards for farming and agribusiness, Star Farmer and Star Agribusinessman of America, were awarded at the FFA annual meeting in Kansas City, Mo. They went to David Galley, 20, a dairy farmer from Garrattsville, N.Y., and Edward Higley, 19, a logger from Brattleboro, Vt.

Girl Scouts of the United States of America increasingly dedicated its program to "inspiring each girl to develop her own values and sense of worth as an individual." Opportunities were provided for girls to share planned activities designed to help them learn to make decisions. For example, at the 1972 Girl Scout National Council convention, held in October, 1972, in Dallas, more than 360 Senior Girl Scouts participated in discussions to help set the future course of Girl Scouting.

Girl Scouts continued their "Action 70" program, a nationwide effort to combat prejudice. Girl Scouts were also involved in many drug-abuse prevention projects. For their efforts in this direction, Senior Girl Scouts of Troop No. 67, Oak Ridge, Tenn., received the Walter Donald Ross trophy given for outstanding community service by the World Association of Girl Guides and Girl Scouts. Other Girl Scout activities focused on conservation and environment problems. For example, through their nationwide Eco-Action program, Girl Scouts planned, created, and maintained environmental learning centers on property either owned or leased by their councils. There, they created mini-parks, playscapes, and nature trails. In a nationally sponsored "Career Preview," nearly 250 girls visited New York City in July to investigate such career possibilities as advertising, publishing, medicine, law, graphic arts, education, fashion, theater, broadcasting, ecology, and social work.

Girls Clubs of America (GCA) opened new clubs at the rate of about two a month during 1972. Many Girls Clubs with older members used mobile units and extension programs in storefronts and public-housing projects to reach school-age girls not being served by other youth agencies. By the end of 1972, membership had increased by 15,600, to 130,600. Two new regional offices were opened in Dallas and Philadelphia.

Girls, especially teen-agers, continued to take a greater part in program planning and their interest focused on environmental, behavioral, and social problems. More specifically, many of these Girls Club members took part in programs dealing with drug addicts, minority group members' problems, help for retarded and otherwise handicapped persons, and career and job counseling. Eco projects included clean-ups and glass, can, and paper collection for recycling.

Junior Achievement (JA) conducted a survey in 1972 that indicated that high school students who operated businesses of their own during a 30-week national training program understood several aspects of business far better than many adults. A survey published in 1972 showed that the adult estimate of profits is 28 cents on a dollar of sales. Teen-agers polled estimated it at 7 cents, closer to the actual 4 cents manufacturing profit that was left after taxes.

The 29th National Junior Achievers Conference was held in Bloomington, Ind., from August 13 to 18. Some 2,200 high school sophomores, juniors, and seniors selected from over 160,000 Achievers in all 50 states attended. There were also representatives from Canada, France, Puerto Rico, and Trinidad-Tobago. Christel Capdevielle, 17, of New Orleans, was named Miss Junior Achievement of 1972. James E. Tompert, 18, from Battle Creek, Mich., was elected President of the Year. Joseph P. Anderson

YUGOSLAVIA. A trend toward separatism in 2 of the nation's 6 republics posed serious problems for President Josip Broz Tito in 1972. The movement had been growing in Yugoslavia since 1970, when Tito decentralized economic and administrative power to give the individual republics control over everything but foreign affairs and military defense. Late in November, 1971, nearly 30,000 striking university students demonstrated in the Croatian capital of Zagreb, demanding autonomy for Croatia. The Croats, numbering about 4.3 million and comprising the nation's second largest ethnic group, believed they were being systematically exploited by the federal government on behalf of less-developed areas. They had insisted on greater political and economic independence.

Alarmed by the crisis, President Tito quickly abandoned his policy of tolerance toward the nationalistic trend and reasserted his authority as head of the Yugoslavian Communist Party. Under his orders, about 740 members of Croatia's Communist Party were ousted from their jobs or left the party. The purge was followed on January 22 by a three-day party conference in Belgrade, during which Tito announced a major party reorganization to forestall such crises as had erupted in Croatia. To tighten party discipline, the large cells of up to 1,000 members were replaced by smaller units. To ensure that each of the six republics and two territories would receive equal consideration in the distribution of federal income, the executive bureau of the party presidium was reduced from 15 to 8 members and each member was assigned a specific area.

A Second Source of concern was Serbia, which, with 8.5 million people, constitutes the largest republic in Yugoslavia. It, too, experienced a strong resurgence of nationalism in 1972. However, Tito did not permit a repetition of the Croatian crisis. In October, he accused the Serbian party leadership of following an independent line, ignoring central decisions, and defying his efforts to reinstate the Communist Party as the unchallenged leader in Yugoslavia. Under pressure, Serbian Communist Party Chairman Marko Nikezi resigned in October. And on November 2, Koca Popovic, the most prominent Serbian politician in the central government, resigned from the federal presidency.

Economic problems aggravated political tensions during the year. Inflation was rampant, there was a large balance of payments deficit, and enemployment was high. The government doubled its efforts to encourage foreign investment. In March, President Richard M. Nixon authorized the use of U.S. government funds to underwrite joint economic programs in Yugoslavia. In September, Yugoslavia and Iran signed agreements calling for greater cooperation in oil development, copper mining, and other ventures. Paul C. Tullier

See also EUROPE (Facts in Brief Table).

ZAIRE went to great lengths to change its image from Western-oriented to pure African in 1972. The process began in late 1971, when the name of the former Democratic Republic of the Congo was changed to the Republic of Zaire. President Mobutu Sese Seko then launched a general campaign to change the names of people, streets, rivers, and newspapers. Even the Easter Holiday was abolished. The changes often were confusing and sometimes met with resistance.

The Name Game. A new nationality law, published on January 3, required each Zairese child with a foreign father to adopt the Zairese name of the mother's family. On February 15, all citizens were ordered to take at least one authentic Zairese name. Civil servants, police, and army personnel were threatened with dismissal if they failed to comply. Mobutu dropped his first name, Joseph, and adopted the African name of Mobutu Sese Seko.

This campaign, intended to erase all traces of Zaire's colonial past and give the people pride in their African heritage, was extended to public places. For example, Mount Stanley became Mount Ngaliema. In Kinshasa, the capital, colonial monuments were removed. Roman Catholic priests were threatened with prison terms if they baptized babies with foreign-sounding names. Zaire also expelled thousands of African aliens.

Some resistance arose among Catholics, who were concerned about giving up their baptized names. An editorial in a Catholic weekly magazine questioned the wisdom of the so-called authenticity program. In response, Mobutu banned the Catholic weekly, expelled several missionaries, and temporarily closed seminaries.

A long-standing conflict erupted anew between Mobutu and the powerful archbishop of Kinshasa, Joseph A. Cardinal Malula. Mobutu accused the cardinal of subversion and of "putting banana skins on the path of the Zairese people." In January, Mobutu closed Cardinal Malula's official residence in Kinshasa. Pope Paul VI recalled the cardinal before the conflict became a major confrontation. But, on May 15, apparently after receiving a conciliatory letter from the cardinal, Mobutu authorized his return to Zaire.

Foreign Affairs. Mobutu sent troops and military aid to Burundi in May, during heavy tribal fighting there that followed an attempted coup. About 4,000 persons fled Burundi and sought refuge in Zaire.

On April 19, Zaire withdrew from the Common Organization of Africa, Malagasy, and Mauritius (OCAM). The government explained that membership in the French-speaking association might hamper efforts to broaden contacts with other African nations. Earlier, the official Zairese press had accused the OCAM of being a colonialist front and called for Zaire's withdrawal. George W. Shepherd

See also AFRICA (Facts in Brief Table).

ZAMBIA. President Kenneth David Kaunda outlawed the opposition United Progressive Party (UPP) on Feb. 4, 1972, and arrested 123 of its leaders, including his former friend, Simon Kapwepwe. Only a short time before, Kaunda had disciplined some of his own United National Independence Party (UNIP) members for physically assaulting Kapwepwe in retaliation for raids on UNIP offices. Kaunda claimed the arrests were necessary because of growing violence and subversive plotting on the part of the UPP and its leader, Kapwepwe.

On February 25, Kaunda announced that Zambia would become a single-party state, and outlined plans for the formation of the Second Republic. Kaunda claimed that the opposition parties were providing destructive, rather than constructive, criticism of the government. He appointed a 21-member national commission to draw up a new Constitution. Leaders of the largest opposition party, the African National Congress, declared Kaunda's plans were unconstitutional and refused to serve.

There was evidence, however, that Kaunda wanted the new Constitution to reflect the will of the people. Commission members toured the country during the year collecting recommendations from citizens.

Then, on December 13, Kaunda signed an amendment to the Constitution that made Zambia a one-party state. George W. Shepherd

See also AFRICA (Facts in Brief Table).

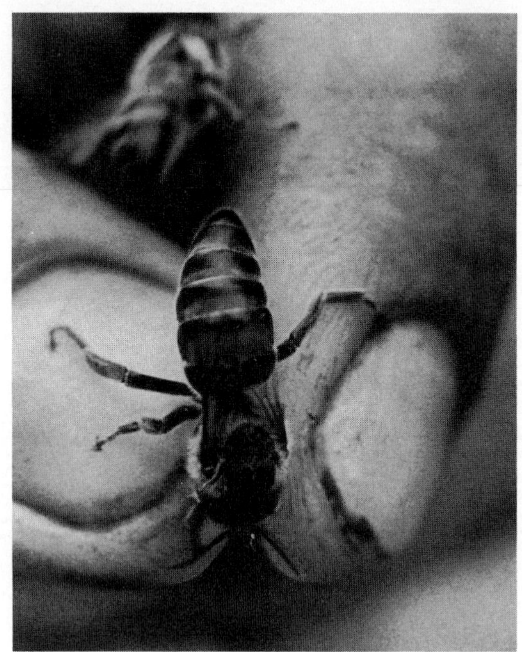

Brazilian honey bees, which originally bred from African and European strains, are spreading north and causing havoc because of their stinging ability.

ZOOLOGY. Australian zoologist D. R. Robertson of the University of Queensland discovered in 1972 that the tropical fish *Labroides dimidiatus* can change its sex under certain conditions. These fish are found on Australia's Great Barrier Reef. The females, it appears, cannot abide the absence of a dominant male. When the male dies or leaves a group of females, one of the females turns into a male to replace him. Within a matter of hours, the female's sex organs begin to change, and the fish takes on all the behavior patterns of a male. Robertson also found that occasionally two females can emerge as males in the same colony after the male has been removed. In such cases, the colony splits to form two new colonies.

Electrically Oriented Eels. Naturalists have proposed many theories of how eels make their magnificent migrations from ocean spawning grounds back to fresh water. In June, two scientists at the University of Maine in Orono demonstrated that American eels (*Anguilla rostrata*) probably migrate in response to electric fields in the water. Sentiel A. Rommel, Jr., and James D. McCleave induced a conditioned response, slowing the heart rate, by subjecting eels to weak electric fields. The motion of ocean currents across the earth's magnetic field generates weak electric fields. The Maine scientists implanted electrodes in the eels so they could take electrocardiograms regularly of the eels' heart action. They found that the eels were sensitive only to electric fields that were perpendicular to them, and not to parallel fields. The fields in ocean currents run across the current. Therefore, eels kept themselves oriented with the current by aligning their bodies to feel the transverse field. If eels can sense the polarity of an electric field, the scientists said, they can also tell upstream from downstream.

Bird's Eyes. Zoologists have never been certain of the purpose of a black pleated structure called the pecten found in the eyeballs of birds. Until recently, many believed that it had a nutritive function, because the pecten has an abundant blood supply. Horace B. Barlow of the University of California, Berkeley, suggested a new hypothesis in 1972 and produced some careful measurements to support his theory. He removed a pigeon's eyeball, kept it bathed in a saline solution, and then directed light into the eye from known angles and heights. He could see both primary and secondary shadows produced by the pecten through the lightly pigmented outer covering of the eye. He also precisely measured the angular position and amount of light falling on parts of the eyeball. The data support the hypothesis that the pecten acts as a baffle, shading some of the retina from light scattered from a bright image formed on the retina. For many positions of the sun, which is the brightest object in a bird's life, the pecten is particularly well situated to shade the eye from some of the light. Barbara N. Benson

ZOOS AND AQUARIUMS. Two giant pandas, Hsing-Hsing and Ling-Ling, a by-product of President Richard M. Nixon's visit to China, arrived in the United States in April, 1972. The young pandas are housed in the National Zoo in Washington, D.C., in air-conditioned quarters with connecting outdoor yards. They reportedly attracted a million extra visitors to the zoo. Another pair of pandas donated by China went to the Ueno Zoo in Tokyo.

The exact zoological classification of the giant panda is still a matter of debate, although extensive anatomical work indicates that it is a type of bear. Its natural diet consists largely of bamboo shoots, but animals in captivity also eat vegetables and meat. They do not live long. Both of the giant pandas familiar to the Western world, Chi-Chi in London and An-An in Moscow, died in 1972 at about age 15.

Other notable zoo and aquarium events of 1972 included the birth of a beluga whale at the New York Aquarium, and the birth of cheetahs at the Toledo (Ohio) and San Diego (Calif.) zoos. A mountain anoa (a type of buffalo) was born at the West Berlin (Germany) Zoo. A third generation of black lemurs was born at the St. Louis (Mo.) Zoo.

New Construction. The most ambitious zoo park was opened by the San Diego Zoological Society at San Pasqual, Calif., 40 miles north of San Diego. It covers 1,800 acres and is well stocked with African and Asian hoofed animals such as buffalo, antelope, elephants, and giraffes. The park also features a giant walk-through tropical birdhouse and large exhibits for gorillas and spider monkeys.

In May, the North Carolina legislature provided $2 million for planning and initial development of a state zoo on a 1,370-acre site on Purgatory Mountain. Commercially operated animal parks were also planned or under construction in several parts of the United States. One of the largest, Jungle Habitat, is a 1,000-acre drive-through park at West Milford, N.J.

Among the new exhibits in some of the older zoos was the World of Birds, which opened at Bronx Zoo in New York City in June. The multilevel building allows visitors to view the birds from several different heights without any glass or other barriers in the way. Five viewing points are at treetop level. The exhibits are naturalistic and have live, as well as artificial, plants and realistic fiberglass rock formations. Other new structures included a reptile house at Philadelphia; a tropical house at Assiniboine Zoo in Winnipeg, Canada; enclosures for large cats at Kansas City, Mo.; and a monkey and ape house in London.

Bird Embargo. In August, the U.S. Department of Agriculture stopped all shipments of exotic birds to the United States. The ban was ordered to protect domestic poultry from outbreaks of Newcastle disease.

George B. Rabb

Ling-Ling is one of the two pandas that were given to President Richard M. Nixon by the Chinese. It now resides in the National Zoo in Washington, D.C.

Section Four

World Book Supplement

In its function of keeping WORLD BOOK owners up to date, THE WORLD BOOK YEAR BOOK herewith offers significant new articles from the 1973 edition of THE WORLD BOOK ENCYCLOPEDIA. These articles should be indexed in THE WORLD BOOK ENCYCLOPEDIA by means of THE YEAR BOOK cross-reference tabs.

Mireille Vautier, A.A.A. photo

Rural Villages lie throughout the countryside of Bangladesh. A large majority of the nation's people live in rural areas. Boats provide their chief means of transportation. The boats travel along a network of waterways that flow through almost all parts of the country.

BANGLADESH

BANGLADESH, *BANG luh* DEHSH, is a South Asian nation that once formed part of Pakistan. Bangladesh gained independence in 1971 after a nine-month civil war between East Pakistan and West Pakistan. From 1947 to 1971, the region that is now Bangladesh was East Pakistan. More than half the people of Pakistan lived there.

The northeast part of India borders Bangladesh on three sides. Bangladesh shares many cultural and geographical features with neighboring West Bengal, a state of India. In fact, Bangladesh and West Bengal make up a region of Asia known as *Bengal.* Bangladesh is sometimes called *East Bengal.* The name *Bangladesh* means *Bengal nation.*

Bangladesh ranks eighth in population among the countries of the world. The nation's rapid population growth has led to serious overcrowding. Bangladesh covers about the same area as Wisconsin, but it has more than 17 times as many people as that state. The people of Bangladesh are called *Bangalees.*

Widespread poverty has long characterized the region. Most Bangalees are poor farmers who struggle to make a living on small plots of land. Many laborers in the cities work for a few cents a day. Only about 20 per cent of the population can read and write. About 85 per cent of the people are Moslems, and most of the rest are Hindus.

The contributor of this article is Robert I. Crane, Director of the South Asia Program and Ford-Maxwell Professor of South Asian History at Syracuse University.

Bangladesh has a lower percentage of city dwellers than do most South Asian nations. Only about 5 per cent of the people live in cities. Dacca, the capital and largest city of Bangladesh, has more than half a million persons. Chittagong is the only other city with a population of more than 200,000.

Plant life thrives in the warm, humid climate of Bangladesh. Most of the land consists of a flat, fertile flood plain, crisscrossed by innumerable rivers and streams. The rivers deposit fertile soil along their banks during periodic floods. But many of the floods also cause widespread destruction in rural villages.

The region that is now Bangladesh has been governed by Hindu, Moslem, and Buddhist rulers at various times in its history. It became part of the British empire when Great Britain took control of India in 1858. Bloody conflicts between Hindus and Moslems led to the division of India into two nations in 1947, when India gained independence. Pakistan—consisting of East Pakistan and West Pakistan—was created out of the northeastern and northwestern parts of India. Most of the people of both areas were Moslems.

Many differences, both cultural and economic, divided the peoples of East and West Pakistan. In 1971, these differences led to civil war and the establishment of East Pakistan as an independent nation—Bangladesh. For more detailed information on the events leading to the creation of Bangladesh, see the *History* section of this article.

BANGLADESH/*Government*

National Government. In January, 1972, government leaders issued a provisional constitution for Bangladesh that established the country as a republic. The provisional constitution provided for a parliamentary government headed by a prime minister. Cabinet ministers assist the prime minister and manage various government departments. A president acts as head of state, but he has little actual power.

In April, 1972, a constituent assembly was formed to write a permanent constitution for Bangladesh. The assembly consisted of legislators who had been elected as national and provincial representatives when Bangladesh was still part of Pakistan.

Local Government. Villages are the smallest units of local government in Bangladesh. They are grouped together to form *unions*, which, in turn, form administrative units called *thanas*. A group of thanas forms a *zilla*, the largest unit of local government. Governing councils at each level of local government consist of officials appointed by the central government.

Political Parties. The Awami League, the largest political party of Bangladesh, was founded in 1949. It led the campaign that established East Pakistan as the independent nation of Bangladesh in 1971. Opposition groups include the Bangladesh Communist Party and the National Awami Party.

Armed Forces. During the civil war of 1971, a guerrilla resistance army called the *Mukti Bahini* (Freedom Force) was formed in what was then East Pakistan. After the war, members of the Mukti Bahini became part of the regular army, navy, and air force of Bangladesh. The country also has a militia.

FACTS IN BRIEF

Capital: Dacca.

Official Language: Bengali.

Official Name: People's Republic of Bangladesh.

Form of Government: Republic.

Head of State: President.

Head of Government: Prime Minister.

Area: 55,126 square miles. *Greatest Distances*—(north-south) 464 miles; (east-west) 288 miles. *Coastline*—430 miles.

Elevation: *Highest*—Mount Keokradong, 4,034 feet above sea level. *Lowest*—sea level.

Population: *Estimated 1973 Population*—75,840,000; distribution, 95 per cent rural, 5 per cent urban; density, 1,376 persons to the square mile. *1961 Census*—50,853,721. *Estimated 1978 Population*—86,225,000.

Chief Products: *Agriculture*—hides and skins, jute, rice, sugar cane, tea, tobacco. *Manufacturing*—jute products, paper and paper products, textiles. *Mining*—natural gas.

National Anthem: "Amar Sonar Bangla" ("My Golden Bengal").

National Holidays: Shaheed Day (Martyrs Day), February 21; Birthday of the Father of the Nation, March 17; Independence Day, March 26; Victory Day, December 16.

Money: *Basic Unit*—taka. One hundred paisas equal one taka. For the value of the taka in dollars, see MONEY (table: Values).

Frederic Ohringer from Nancy Palmer

The National Assembly Building in Dacca, the capital of Bangladesh, is part of a complex of government buildings scheduled for completion in the 1970's.

The Bangladesh Flag was officially adopted in 1972. The red stands for the sun and the green for scenic beauty.

National Emblem. A water lily, the national flower of Bangladesh, appears in the center of the emblem.

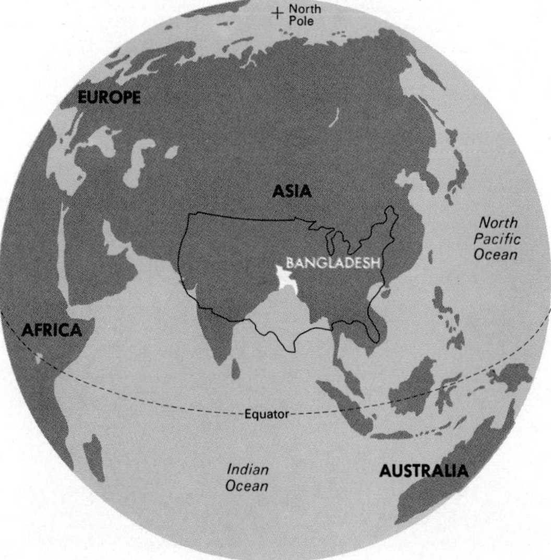

WORLD BOOK map

Bangladesh lies in South Asia. It is about 1½ per cent as large as the United States, not including Alaska and Hawaii.

J. Alex Langley, DPI

Traffic Jams occur frequently in the cities of Bangladesh. Bangladesh is one of the world's most densely populated nations, and overcrowding is a problem in both urban and rural areas.

Herta Newton, Van Cleve Photography

Rural Villagers live in simple one- or two-room homes with thatched roofs. The Bangalees shown above are building a brick home, but many rural dwellings are made of bamboo.

Population and Ancestry. Bangladesh is the eighth largest country in the world in population, with about 75,840,000 persons. Bangladesh is also one of the world's most densely populated countries. It has a population density of about 1,376 persons per square mile.

Most of the people of Bangladesh are probably descendants of tribal peoples who migrated thousands of years ago from what are now Burma, Tibet, and northern India. The term *Bangalee* refers to all the people of Bangladesh. More than 95 per cent of Bangladesh's population are *Bengalis*, a short, dark-skinned people who speak Bengali.

About 2 per cent of the people are *Biharis*. They closely resemble the Bengalis, but they speak a different language—Urdu. The Biharis originally migrated from Bihar, an area that is now a state of India. Other minority groups include various tribes that live mainly in the Chittagong Hills of southeastern Bangladesh. The largest tribes include the Chakmas, the Marmas, the Mros, and the Tipperas.

Way of Life. Most Bangalees farm the land with simple tools and ancient methods, much as their ancestors did hundreds of years ago. About 80 per cent of the people cannot read or write. They have not been exposed to modern ideas, and so they cling to traditional ways of life.

About 95 per cent of the people live in rural areas. Clusters of thatch-roofed houses dot the countryside. Most rural villagers build homes of bamboo. A typical home consists of only one or two rooms. Few rural homes have electricity or plumbing.

Most of the families in the cities and towns live crowded together in small wooden houses. Some wealthy city families have large brick or concrete homes. In urban slums, the houses are built of cardboard, scraps of wood, or sticks. Most Hindus and members of other minority groups live together in distinct neighborhoods.

Many of the people of Bangladesh do not have enough food to eat. The nation has a food shortage because it neither raises nor imports enough to feed its large population. Few Bangalees have much variety in their meals. Rice and fish are the two most important foods. They are usually served together in a spicy curry sauce. Tea sweetened with sugar is a popular beverage, though some people may drink only water most of the time.

People throughout Bangladesh wear loose, lightweight clothing because of the warm, humid climate. Most of the women wear a *sari*, a long piece of plain or printed cloth wrapped around the waist and draped over one shoulder. A short blouse is worn underneath. Many Moslem men wear a *lungi*, a tight skirtlike garment. The *dhoti*, worn by Hindu men, is a piece of cloth wrapped around the waist and between the legs. Men

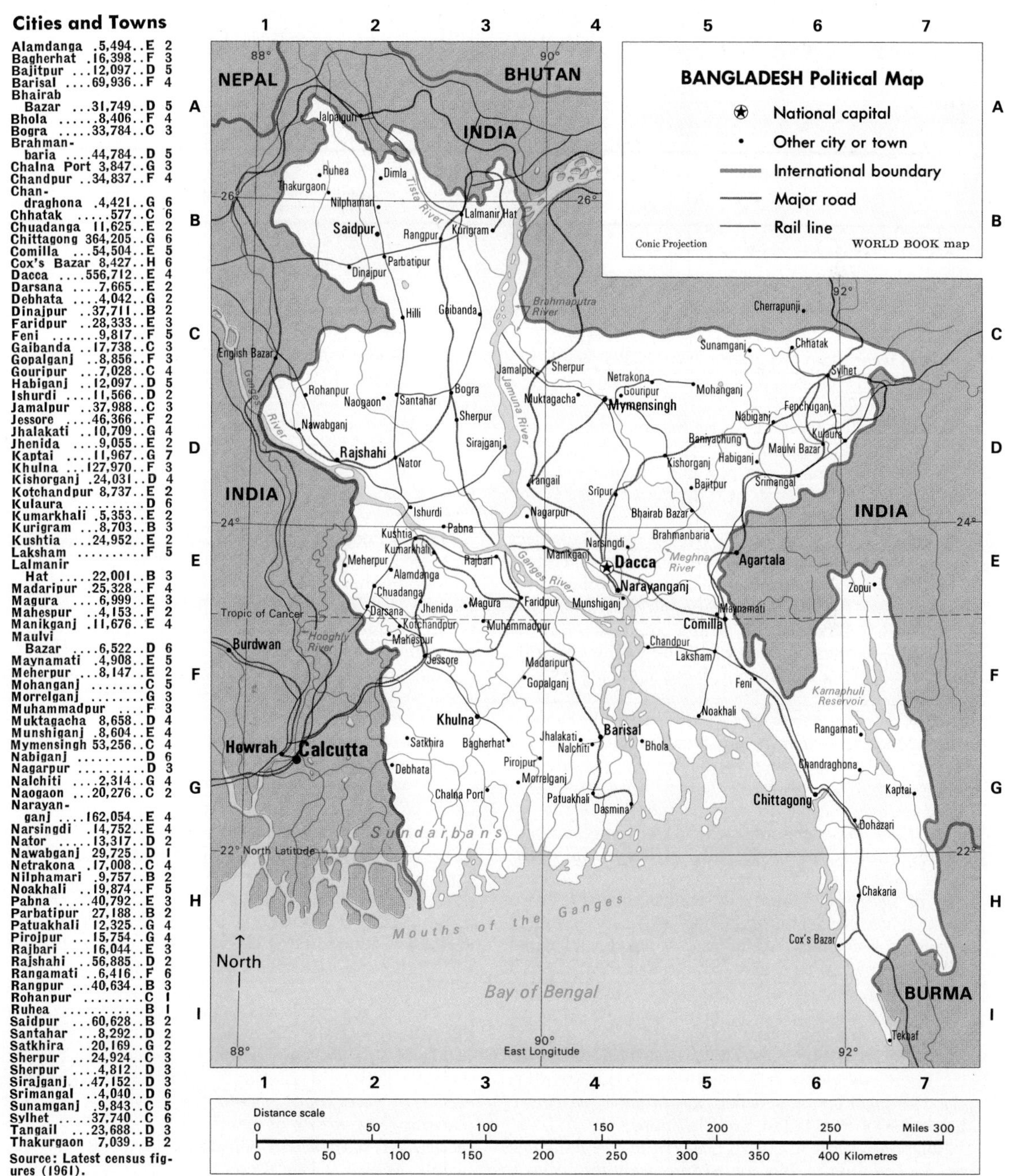

Cities and Towns

Alamdanga .5,494..E 2
Bagherhat .16,398..F 3
Bajitpur ...12,097..D 5
Barisal ....69,936..F 4
Bhairab Bazar ...31,749..D 5
Bhola ......8,406..F 4
Bogra .....33,784..C 3
Brahmanbaria ....44,784..D 5
Chalna Port 3,847..G 3
Chandpur ..34,837..F 4
Chandraghona .4,421..G 6
Chhatak .....577..C 6
Chuadanga 11,625..E 2
Chittagong 364,205..G 6
Comilla ...54,504..E 5
Cox's Bazar 8,427..H 6
Dacca ....556,712..E 4
Darsana ....7,665..E 2
Debhata ....4,042..G 2
Dinajpur ..37,711..B 2
Faridpur ..28,333..E 3
Feni ....9,817..F 5
Gaibanda ..17,738..C 3
Gopalganj ..8,856..F 3
Gouripur ...7,028..C 4
Habiganj ..12,097..D 5
Ishurdi ....11,566..D 2
Jamalpur ..37,988..C 3
Jessore ....46,366..F 2
Jhalakati ..10,709..G 4
Jhenida ....9,055..E 2
Kaptai ....11,967..G 7
Khulna ...127,970..F 3
Kishorganj .24,031..D 4
Kotchandpur 8,737..E 2
Kulaura ....D 6
Kumarkhali .5,353..E 2
Kurigram ...8,703..B 3
Kushtia ...24,952..E 2
Laksham ....F 5
Lalmanir Hat .....22,001..B 3
Madaripur .25,328..F 4
Magura ....6,999..E 3
Mahespur ..4,153..F 2
Manikganj .11,676..E 4
Maulvi Bazar ....6,522..D 6
Maynamati .4,908..E 5
Meherpur ...8,147..E 2
Mohanganj ....C 5
Morrelganj ....G 3
Muhammadpur ....F 3
Muktagacha 8,658..D 4
Munshiganj .8,604..E 4
Mymensingh 53,256..C 4
Nabiganj ....D 6
Nagarpur ....D 3
Nalchiti ....2,314..G 4
Naogaon ...20,276..C 2
Narayanganj ....162,054..E 4
Narsingdi .14,752..E 4
Nator .....13,317..D 2
Nawabganj 29,725..D 1
Netrakona .17,008..C 4
Nilphamari .9,757..B 2
Noakhali ..19,874..F 5
Pabna .....40,792..E 3
Parbatipur 27,188..B 2
Patuakhali 12,325..G 4
Pirojpur ...15,754..G 4
Rajbari ....16,044..E 3
Rajshahi ..56,885..D 2
Rangamati ..6,416..F 6
Rangpur ...40,634..B 3
Rohanpur ....C 1
Ruhea ....B 1
Saidpur ...60,628..B 2
Santahar ...8,292..D 2
Satkhira ..20,169..G 2
Sherpur ...24,924..C 3
Sherpur ....4,812..D 3
Sirajganj ..47,152..D 3
Srimangal ..4,040..D 6
Sunamganj .9,843..C 5
Sylhet .....37,740..C 6
Tangail ...23,688..D 3
Thakurgaon 7,039..B 2

Source: Latest census figures (1961).

Shoppers and Venders gather at open-air market places, such as this one in Dacca. In many families, the men do most of the shopping, and the women stay home doing household chores.

Alan Band Associates

may also wear plain or patterned shirts. People of rural areas generally go barefoot. City dwellers may wear shoes or sandals.

Bangalees like to spend their leisure time chatting with friends and relatives. The men usually gather in cafes, and the women visit one another at home. The people enjoy the festivities held during various Moslem and Hindu religious holidays.

Religion affects much in the lives of most Bangalees, including food, marriage customs, and family relationships. About 85 per cent of the people are Moslems. The laws of Islam, the Moslem religion, forbid the eating of pork. Most Moslem parents arrange marriages for their children. A Moslem man may have up to four wives at a time, but most Moslem men in Bangladesh are too poor to have more than one. The men in a Moslem family have far more authority and freedom than the women. Many Moslem women avoid social contact with men who do not belong to their family, and they participate in few activities outside the home. They cover their heads with veils in the presence of strangers. See ISLAM.

Less than 15 per cent of the people of Bangladesh are Hindus. Hindus are divided into various social classes called *castes*. Each caste observes its own customs and rules of behavior. Caste regulations limit the extent to which members of one caste may associate with members of another caste. Hindu parents also arrange their children's marriages. Intermarriage between castes is rare. Hindu women have more social freedom than Moslem women do, though Hindu women have few legal rights. See HINDUISM; CASTE.

Most of the tribes of the Chittagong Hills area practice Buddhism. Some tribes combine Buddhist principles with local religious beliefs. Less than 1 per cent of the people of Bangladesh are Christians.

Education. Only about 20 per cent of the Bangalees can read and write. No law requires children to go to school, and less than half the youngsters of school age do so. Bangladesh has about 31,700 elementary and high schools and about 170 colleges and technical schools.

The University of Dacca is the nation's largest university. Dacca is also the home of the Jahangirnagar Muslim University and the Bangladesh University of Engineering and Technology. Other universities are in Chittagong, Mymensingh, and Rajshahi.

Health. Food shortages and unsanitary living conditions in Bangladesh contribute to widespread cholera, leprosy, smallpox, tuberculosis, and other diseases. Mosquitoes that spread malaria thrive in the country's swampy regions, and the disease kills thousands of people annually.

Bangladesh has a serious shortage of doctors, nurses, hospitals, and medical supplies. The Red Cross and other organizations have sent medical teams and equipment to Bangladesh in an attempt to improve health conditions there.

The Arts. Bengali literature has flourished for hundreds of years in the form of stories and folk ballads. These stories and ballads tell romantic legends and tales of everyday life. Dramas based on religious stories are popular forms of entertainment in Bangladesh. Rabindranath Tagore, a Bengali poet born in India, became prominent in Bengali literature during the late 1800's and early 1900's. He still ranks as the most popular literary figure in Bangladesh. See TAGORE, SIR RABINDRANATH.

Much of the traditional architecture of Bangladesh developed under Moslem rule during the 1500's and 1600's. This style features domes, towers, and pointed arches. Traditional painting has the brilliant colors and elaborate decorations of Moslem religious art. Some contemporary artists of Bangladesh use techniques of modern Western art in painting everyday scenes and people, as well as in abstract designs.

BANGLADESH / *The Land*

Almost all of Bangladesh consists of a flat, low-lying *alluvial plain* (land formed from soil deposited by rivers). Most of the country lies less than 50 feet above sea level. The far northeast and southeast corners of Bangladesh have many hills. Mount Keokradong, the country's highest peak, rises 4,034 feet above sea level in the Chittagong Hills area in the southeast.

Rivers and Streams. Three major rivers—the Brahmaputra, the Ganges, and the Meghna—flow through the flat plains that cover most of Bangladesh. These rivers and their branches overflow during the rainy season and deposit fertile soil along their banks. The soil deposits that have built up at the mouths of the rivers form the broad Ganges Delta. Rice and jute, the most important crops of Bangladesh, thrive in the wet delta region.

Many small streams and canals also crisscross the country. Boats can reach almost every part of the Bangladesh interior.

Coastline of Bangladesh extends approximately 430 miles along the Bay of Bengal. Deep inlets mark the jagged coastline, and small islands dot the offshore delta area.

Forests. Bamboo, and such trees as mango, palm, and tamarind, grow throughout most of Bangladesh. But the most valuable forest resources are in the Chittagong Hills in southeastern Bangladesh, and in the Sundarbans in the southwest. Teak is an important product of the Chittagong Hills forests. The Sundarbans is a swampy region covered by mangrove trees and other tropical plants. Bengal tigers live in this area.

Emil Muench from Carl Östman

Countless Rivers and Streams flow through Bangladesh. The inland waterways provide an important source of fish, and they also serve as the country's chief transportation routes.

BANGLADESH / *Climate*

Bangladesh is generally warm and humid throughout the year. The temperature varies little from one part of the country to another, though the north may be slightly cooler than the south in winter. Temperatures in Bangladesh average about 82° F. (28° C.) in April, the hottest month in most parts of the country. January, the coldest month, has an average temperature of 64° F. (18° C.).

Bangladesh receives ample rain. The eastern part of the country has an average annual rainfall of about 100 inches, and the west has an average of about 65 inches. The far northeastern region gets the most rain—as much as 250 inches a year.

In most years, the rainy season in Bangladesh lasts from mid-March to the end of October. Afternoon thunderstorms occur frequently from mid-March to mid-May. The heaviest rain comes during the monsoon season, from mid-May to October. Many of the monsoon rains cause the rivers to overflow and flood the surrounding countryside.

Cyclones often strike Bangladesh at the end of the monsoon season. These violent storms may be accompanied by huge tidal waves that rise from the Bay of Bengal and sweep across the low-lying countryside. Some of the most severe cyclones and tidal waves have destroyed towns and villages and killed thousands of people.

R. T. W. from Carl Östman

The Warm, Humid Climate of Bangladesh is ideal for growing rice and other crops. Heavy rains water the flat, fertile plains that cover most of the country.

Bangladesh ranks as one of the poorest nations of the world. It has an average annual *per capita* (per person) income of less than $100 a year, compared with about $3,900 in the United States.

The economy of Bangladesh is underdeveloped and depends almost entirely on agriculture. The country has few natural resources, and it lacks the equipment and skilled labor necessary to develop heavy industries. The civil war of 1971 caused a serious breakdown of the economy. Farming activities were interrupted as millions of people fled their homes to escape the fighting. Factories and shops were destroyed, and transportation and communication lines were damaged.

Shortly after Bangladesh became independent, the government took control of the chief businesses and industries. Many of these establishments had been owned by West Pakistanis before the civil war.

Natural Resources. Fertile soil is probably the chief natural resource of Bangladesh. Farmers in almost all parts of the country grow jute, rice, sugar cane, and tobacco in the rich, wet soil.

Some natural gas and petroleum have been discovered in Bangladesh. The country also has small deposits of coal, limestone, and peat.

Agriculture is by far the most important economic activity in Bangladesh. About 80 per cent of the people farm the land. Even so, Bangladesh does not produce enough food for its large population. One of the main reasons for the low level of production is that most farmers in Bangladesh use outdated tools and methods. The nation's farms cover an average of only about $3\frac{1}{2}$ acres.

Rice, the chief crop, grows in almost all parts of Bangladesh. Farmers harvest three crops of rice in most years. Jute, a plant whose fibers are made into string or woven into cloth, is the chief export crop. Bangladesh produces more jute than any other country. Farmers also grow sugar cane, tea, and tobacco.

Many farmers in Bangladesh raise livestock. Most of the animals are undernourished, and the cattle do not produce much milk. But the large number of livestock make Bangladesh a leading supplier of animal hides and skins.

Manufacturing. Bangladesh has few large factories, and most of them process agricultural products. The nation is too poor to import the large quantities of raw materials needed for heavy industries.

The processing of jute ranks as the chief industry of Bangladesh. Factories spin the raw jute fibers into string and rope, which then may be woven into burlap or other materials. Bangladesh also has factories that manufacture matches, paper and paper products, and textiles.

Many Bangalees work in their homes making handicraft items that are sold in shops or exported. Some craftsmen weave cotton, jute, or silk into cloth. Others make embroidered items; leather goods; pottery; woodenware; and articles of brass, copper, gold, or silver.

Fishing Industry. Fish thrive in the many inland waterways of Bangladesh and in the coastal waters of the Bay of Bengal. The people catch large quantities of fish for their own use and for export.

Foreign Trade. Jute is the main export of Bangladesh. The country also exports animal hides and skins, fish, and tea. Leading imports include building materials, coal, electric appliances, food and food products, machinery, textiles, and transportation equipment.

Transportation. Waterways serve as the chief transportation routes in Bangladesh. The country has about 4,500 miles of navigable waterways. Passenger and cargo ships make regular trips on the major rivers between the largest cities and towns. The people also use canoes and small wooden boats for transportation. Chittagong is the nation's chief seaport. Major river ports include Barisal, Chalna Port, Chandpur, Dacca, and Narayanganj.

Roadbuilding is difficult and expensive in Bangladesh because of the need for bridges across numerous rivers and streams. Many of the country's roads and railroads become unusable during the monsoon season, when heavy flooding occurs. Bangladesh has about 3,600 miles of paved roads and about 1,800 miles of railroad track. An international airport handles flights to and from Dacca.

Communication. Bangladesh has both Bengali and English-language newspapers. The government owns the nation's six radio stations and one television station, and the telegraph and telephone systems. Few homes in rural areas have telephones or radios. Villagers may gather in cafes or other public places to listen to radio broadcasts. Only a small number of families can afford a TV set.

J. Alex Langley, DPI

The Processing of Jute ranks as the leading industry of Bangladesh. Workers in a jute mill spread the plant fibers outdoors to dry before spinning them into string or rope.

Early History. Ancient Hindu epics indicate that thousands of years ago, tribal people inhabited a kingdom called Vanga in the region that is now Bangladesh. Historians know little about the region before about the 200's B.C., when it formed part of the Maurya Empire. This empire broke up about 185 B.C., and local kings then ruled Bengal. From about A.D. 320 to 500, the region was part of the Gupta Empire. See MAURYA EMPIRE; GUPTA EMPIRE.

Buddhist rulers gained control of eastern Bengal in the mid-700's. Buddhist culture spread throughout the region. After about 300 years of Buddhist rule, Hindu kings came to power. Beginning in the 1200's, Turkish Moslems who had conquered northern India extended their control into eastern Bengal. Independent Moslem rulers governed parts of Bengal until 1576, when the Mogul emperor Akbar conquered the region.

Mogul Rule. Bengal became part of the Mogul Empire, which spread across most of what is now Afghanistan, India, and Pakistan. Moslem art and architecture flourished under Mogul rule. By about the 1600's, most of the people of eastern Bengal had converted to Islam.

The Mogul emperors appointed governors called *nawabs* to rule the provinces of the empire. In the early 1700's, the empire began to break up, partly because powerful Hindu groups in central and western India rebelled against Moslem rule. At the same time, Bengal and other provinces became increasingly independent as the nawabs took more power for themselves.

The Growth of European Influence. During the 1500's, British, Dutch, French, and Portuguese traders competed for control of the profitable trade between the East Indies and Europe. By the 1600's, European trade settlements had been established in Bengal. At first, the Europeans met strong resistance from the provincial nawabs, who demanded taxes in return for trade privileges. But after the Mogul Empire began to weaken in the 1700's, the Europeans increased their influence. Ambitious Mogul nawabs, nobles, and generals competed among themselves for power. The Europeans took sides in many of these conflicts, offering their support in return for monopoly trade privileges and other rewards.

The British East India Company was chartered by the British government in 1600 to develop trade with India and the Far East. By the mid-1700's, the company had become the strongest trade power in Bengal. In 1757, company forces led by Robert Clive defeated the nawab of Bengal in the Battle of Plassey. Clive put a puppet nawab in office, but the British East India Company actually ruled Bengal. See EAST INDIA COMPANY.

Corrupt company officials made huge profits on jute production in eastern Bengal, but they did little to improve the welfare of the people. Opposition to the company spread, not only in Bengal, but also in other areas of India that the firm controlled. The discontent led to the Sepoy Rebellion in 1857. The revolt failed, but it caused the British government to take over the company in 1858. All the Indian territory that the firm had governed became known as *British India.*

British India. Bengal became a province of British India. Under British rule, industrial development and educational reforms advanced rapidly in western Bengal, where most of the people were Hindus. Many Hindus gained economic and political power. But eastern Bengal, where most of the people were Moslems, remained backward and agricultural.

In 1905, the *viceroy* (governor) of British India divided Bengal into two sections—West Bengal and East Bengal. East Bengal became part of a new province. Many Hindu Bengalis objected to the division. They feared a loss of their economic and political power. But Moslems favored the division because they made up the majority of the population of the new province. The conflict led to bloody rioting between Hindus and Moslems in Bengal. The British reversed the division in 1911, and Bengal again became a single province. But the bitterness between Hindus and Moslems increased through the years.

Throughout British India, independence movements began to gain strength in the 1900's. The Moslem League, a political organization formed in 1906, became the spokesman for India's Moslem minority. By 1940, league leaders were demanding that a separate Moslem nation—to be called *Pakistan*—be created out of Indian territory. Riots between Hindus and Moslems during the 1940's convinced government leaders that India would have to be divided. In 1947, Great Britain granted independence to India and established Pakistan as an independent nation. The British divided Bengal between the two countries. Western Bengal became a state of India, and eastern Bengal became East Pakistan. See PAKISTAN (History).

East Pakistan was separated from West Pakistan by about 1,000 miles of Indian territory. The people of the two parts of Pakistan shared a common religion, but they had little else in common. They spoke different languages and had different cultures, traditions, and physical traits. East Pakistanis made up more than half the population of Pakistan, but West Pakistanis controlled the nation's government, economy, and armed forces. Only about a fourth of the money spent by the government went to East Pakistan. The per capita annual income of East Pakistan was less than three-fifths that of West Pakistan.

Through the years, East Pakistanis grew increasingly dissatisfied with the government of Pakistan. In November, 1970, a cyclone and tidal wave struck East Pakistan and killed about 200,000 persons. Many East Pakistanis accused the government of delaying shipments of relief supplies to the devastated areas.

In December, 1970, elections were held throughout Pakistan to choose an assembly that would serve as a legislature and write a new constitution. The Awami League, a party led by Sheik Mujibur Rahman of East Pakistan, won a majority of the seats. The party strongly supported the idea of increased self-government for East Pakistan.

On March 1, 1971, President Yahya Khan of Pakistan postponed the first meeting of the assembly. East Pakistanis demonstrated against his action, and Yahya Khan sent army troops to East Pakistan to put down the protests. Sheik Mujibur was imprisoned in West Pakistan.

Wide World

A Devastating Cyclone and Tidal Wave struck Bangladesh (then East Pakistan) in 1970. About 200,000 persons died in the disaster, and many rural villages were destroyed.

Wide World

Sheik Mujibur Rahman headed the movement that established East Pakistan as the independent nation of Bangladesh in 1971. Mujibur became the first prime minister of the new nation.

Civil War soon broke out. The fighting began in East Pakistan. Then, on March 26, 1971, the East Pakistanis declared East Pakistan an independent nation called Bangladesh. They formed a guerrilla army to fight the government troops. Thousands of civilians died in the bloody fighting that followed, and millions of refugees poured into India.

During the early months of the civil war, East Pakistani guerrillas also crossed into India. The government forces shelled Indian territory and followed the guerrillas across the border. Indian troops fought border clashes with the Pakistani government soldiers. In December, 1971, the Pakistani Air Force attacked several Indian air bases. The Indian Army then advanced into East Pakistan and joined the guerrillas. The combined forces of the Indians and guerrillas overpowered West Pakistan, which surrendered on Dec. 16, 1971.

The New Nation. Sheik Mujibur was released from prison in January, 1972. He returned to Bangladesh in triumph and became the new nation's first prime minister under a provisional constitution.

Bangladesh faced staggering problems as an independent country. Millions of its people were homeless. Many of the more than 9 million refugees who had fled to India returned to Bangladesh and found their villages destroyed. Trade, transportation routes, and communication lines had to be restored. Hospitals, factories, and schools had to be rebuilt.

Reconstruction of the devastated areas began almost immediately. The government of Bangladesh estimated that $3 billion would be needed to recover from the effects of the war. Foreign governments, international organizations, and private groups donated millions of dollars to aid the recovery effort.

ROBERT I. CRANE

BANGLADESH / *Study Aids*

Related Articles in WORLD BOOK include:

Bay of Bengal
Bengal
Brahmaputra River
Chittagong
Dacca
Ganges River
Islam
Jute
Moslem
Rice (graph)

Outline

I. Government

II. People
- A. Population and Ancestry
- B. Way of Life
- C. Religion
- D. Education
- E. Health
- F. The Arts

III. The Land
- A. Rivers and Streams
- B. Coastline
- C. Forests

IV. Climate

V. Economy
- A. Natural Resources
- B. Agriculture
- C. Manufacturing
- D. Fishing Industry
- E. Foreign Trade
- F. Transportation
- G. Communication

VI. History

Questions

What does the name *Bangladesh* mean?
Who was Rabindranath Tagore?
What is the Awami League?
When did the British East India Company gain control of Bengal?
What are the chief agricultural products of Bangladesh?
Who are the Bengalis?
What three major rivers flow through Bangladesh?
What percentage of the people of Bangladesh live in cities?
What is the Sundarbans?
What is the most important natural resource of Bangladesh?

EUROPEAN COMMUNITY is a group of Western European nations working to unite their economic resources into a single economy. The original members of the community are Belgium, France, Italy, Luxembourg, The Netherlands, and West Germany. In 1972, Denmark, Ireland, and Great Britain signed agreements for membership by Jan. 1, 1973.

The European Community imports and exports more than any one country in the world. The United States is the community's chief trade partner. The community has special agreements with more than 20 African countries and several nations in the Middle East. These agreements provide for mutual trade benefits.

The European Community is based on the treaties of three organizations: (1) the European Atomic Energy Community (Euratom), (2) the European Coal and Steel Community (ECSC), and (3) the European Economic Community (EEC). Both the European Community and the European Economic Community are sometimes called the *European Common Market.*

In 1968, the six original members of the European Community abolished all tariffs affecting trade among themselves. They also set up a common tariff on goods imported from other countries into any member of the community. The group hopes to eventually remove all barriers to the free movement among its members of capital, goods, services, and workers. These economic resources would move as freely among members of the community as they do among the 50 states of the United States. The community's long-range goal is to establish a political union—a United States of Europe.

The community adopts laws similar to U.S. federal regulations to govern such matters as agriculture, transportation, and antitrust policies. It coordinates member nations' legislation on health, food, and industrial standards; taxes; and other issues. The community protects the social security rights of workers of member countries who take jobs in other member countries. The group hopes to have a monetary union and a common currency for all its members by 1980.

Administrative System. The three organizations that form the basis of the European Community operate under a single administrative system. The system has three branches: executive (the Commission and the Council of Ministers), legislative (the European Parliament), and judicial (the Court of Justice).

The Commission carries out the provisions of the three treaties that created the European Community. This body has exclusive power to propose legislation for the community. The nine commissioners are chosen by unanimous agreement of the member nations. They serve four-year terms. The commissioners pledge to disregard national and personal interests in making their decisions. The commission has headquarters in Brussels, Belgium.

The Council of Ministers serves as the community's policymaking body. It cannot propose legislation, but it accepts or rejects proposals made by the commission. Each member nation has one minister on the council. The council meets in Brussels or Luxembourg.

The European Parliament is an advisory body. It debates proposals of the commission and advises both the commission and the council. It can expel the entire commission by a two-thirds vote. The 142 members of the European Parliament are appointed from and by the parliaments of the member nations. The group meets in Luxembourg or in Strasbourg, France.

The Court of Justice is the supreme court of the community. It decides whether actions of the commission, the council, member governments, and private organizations comply with the rules of the community. The court hears appeals on community matters brought by member countries, the commission, the council, or private citizens. The court's decisions are final and binding on all parties involved, including the member governments. Its seven judges are chosen by unanimous agreement of the member governments. The court meets in Luxembourg.

History. Philosophers and statesmen have supported the idea of a united Europe for hundreds of years. But lasting unity has never been achieved. After World War II ended in 1945, Jean Monnet, a French statesman, promoted the idea of gradually uniting the economic interests of democratic European nations. Monnet believed the most important result of such a move would be the prevention of future wars.

In 1950, at Monnet's suggestion, Foreign Minister Robert Schuman of France proposed the pooling of French and German coal and steel resources. Other democratic nations of Europe were invited to join the pool. In 1951, Belgium, France, Italy, Luxembourg, The Netherlands, and West Germany signed the Treaty of Paris, which established the European Coal and Steel Community. The ECSC, sometimes called the *Schuman Plan,* began operating in 1952.

The ECSC brought the six member nations together in a single, common market for the production and trade of coal, steel, iron ore, and scrap metal. It abolished all trade barriers among the members for these products. It allowed coal and steel workers from the member nations to work in any ECSC country.

Perhaps the most important achievement of the ECSC has been the creation of Europe's first international governing institutions. Member governments transferred limited, but significant, powers to these institutions, and members must obey ECSC laws.

The success of the ECSC led its six members to sign the Rome Treaties in 1957. These agreements established the European Atomic Energy Community and the European Economic Community. Both organizations began operating in 1958. They shared the ECSC's judicial and legislative bodies, but had separate executive agencies. In 1967, the executive agencies merged to form a unified administrative system.

Through Euratom, the nations pool their resources to develop atomic energy for power production and other peaceful uses. The EEC gradually combines the members' economic resources so that all capital goods, services, and workers can move freely among them.

The European Community has experienced rapid economic growth since the late 1950's. It has recorded large increases in *per capita* (per person) national income, total value of goods and services produced, and volume of trade. With the admission of Denmark, Ireland, and Great Britain in January, 1973, the community surpassed the United States in production of steel and motor vehicles.

LEONARD B. TENNYSON

Emil Muench

Many Rural Villages in Pakistan look much as they did hundreds of years ago. Most of the houses and other buildings are made of clay or sun-dried mud. The villagers use animals as their chief means of transportation.

Emil Muench from Carl Östman

Most Pakistani Cities and Towns have outdoor market places called *bazaars,* where shoppers can buy food, clothing, and other products. Some businessmen, such as the silk merchant shown above, display their goods on the ground.

PAKISTAN

PAKISTAN, *PAK ih* STAN, or *PAHK ih* STAHN, is a Moslem nation in South Asia. The country's official name is the Islamic Republic of Pakistan. About 97 per cent of its people practice Islam, the Moslem religion. Religion was the chief reason for the establishment of Pakistan as an independent nation.

During the 1800's and early 1900's, Great Britain ruled the region that is now Pakistan. The region formed part of India. When the British granted India independence in 1947, they divided the country according to the religion of its people. Pakistan was created out of northwestern and northeastern India. The two sections of the new nation lay more than 1,000 miles apart. The majority of the people of both regions of Pakistan were Moslems. Most of the people of the remaining territory of India were Hindus.

The two sections of Pakistan were called West Pakistan and East Pakistan. Although the people of both regions shared the same religion, many differences divided them. These differences led to civil war in 1971 and the establishment of East Pakistan as an independent nation called Bangladesh. For information on the region that was formerly East Pakistan, see the World Book article on Bangladesh.

Cultural differences remain a problem in Pakistan today. The population consists of a number of cultural groups, each with its own language. The official language of Pakistan is Urdu, but large parts of the population speak only Baluchi, Punjabi, Pushtu, or Sindhi. Such language barriers, plus other divisions among its people, have made it difficult for Pakistan to develop into a unified, progressive nation.

Most Pakistanis are farmers or herders with little or no education. Many of them live much as their ancestors did hundreds of years ago. Traditional attitudes and customs do not have so great an influence over everyday life among Pakistan's educated people. Most of these people live in the cities.

Pakistan covers an area about twice as large as California, and it has more than three times as many people as that state. Pakistan has towering snow-capped mountains, high plateaus, fertile plains, and sandy deserts. Most Pakistanis live in the irrigated plains region of eastern Pakistan. The greatest concentration of population is in the Punjab, a fertile plain in the northeast. Islamabad, the nation's capital, lies in this area. Much of the western part of the country is lightly settled because the area is too dry and barren for farming.

The history of the region that is now Pakistan started at least 4,500 years ago, when an advanced civilization developed in the Indus Valley. This civilization lasted about 800 years and then declined and disappeared. For the next several thousand years, a number of peoples invaded and settled in what became Pakistan. Arabs, Greeks, Persians, Turks, and other invaders ruled the region before it came under British control in the 1800's. Pakistan's complex history helps explain the variety among its population today.

Robert I. Crane, the contributor of this article, is Ford-Maxwell Professor of History and Director of the South Asia Program at Syracuse University.

The National Government of Pakistan is based on a provisional constitution adopted in April, 1972. This constitution was scheduled to remain in effect until August, 1973, when a permanent constitution was expected to replace it. Under the provisional constitution, a president heads the government and holds most of the power. A Council of Ministers assists the president. Pakistan has a one-house legislature, called the National Assembly, with 146 elected members.

Provincial Government. Pakistan is divided into four provinces—Baluchistan, North-West Frontier Province (NWFP), the Punjab, and Sind. An elected assembly governs each province. The provinces have some self-governing powers in such areas as education, public health and welfare, taxation, and transportation.

Local Government. Elected and appointed officials govern Pakistani cities, towns, and villages. Islamabad, the capital, is governed by the central government as a separate district called the Capital Territory of Islamabad. Certain parts of Pakistan that border Afghanistan are called *Tribal Territories.* The central government has limited authority over these areas, and tribal members handle most of their own governmental affairs.

Political Parties. The Pakistan People's Party is the country's largest and most powerful political organization. Its members support the idea of a strong central government. Leading opposition groups include the Jamiat-ul-Ulema-e-Islami, the National Awami Party, and the Muslim League. The opposition groups generally favor increased self-government for the provinces.

Court System of Pakistan is made up of civil, criminal, and appeals courts. A *High Court* heads the system in each province. The Supreme Court of Pakistan is the nation's highest court.

Armed Forces of Pakistan consist of an army, navy, and air force. Pakistan is a member of the Central Treaty Organization (CENTO). See CENTRAL TREATY ORGANIZATION.

J. Alex Langley, DPI

The Main Buildings of Pakistan's Government stand in Islamabad, the nation's capital. Construction began in 1961, and the city replaced Rawalpindi as capital in the mid-1960's.

Pakistan's Flag has a star and crescent, traditional symbols of Islam. Green stands for the nation's Moslem majority.

Coat of Arms. A wreath of narcissus, the national flower, encircles a shield on the Pakistani coat of arms.

FACTS IN BRIEF

Capital: Islamabad.

Official Name: The Islamic Republic of Pakistan.

Official Language: Urdu.

Form of Government: Republic.

Head of Government: President.

Area: 310,403 square miles. *Greatest Distances* (north-south) 935 miles; (east-west) 800 miles. *Coastline*—506 miles.

Elevation: *Highest*—Mount Godwin Austen (in Kashmir), 28,250 feet above sea level. *Lowest*—sea level.

Population: *Estimated 1973 Population*—64,604,000; distribution, 77 per cent rural, 23 per cent urban; density, 208 persons to the square mile. *1961 Census*—42,978,261; *Estimated 1978 Population*—73,451,000.

Chief Products: *Agriculture*—barley, cotton, fruits, oilseeds, rice, sugar cane, tobacco, wheat. *Manufacturing*—cement, cotton textiles, fertilizer. *Mining*—coal, limestone, natural gas, petroleum.

National Anthem: "Qaumi Tarana" ("National Anthem").

Money: *Basic Unit*—Pakistani rupee. One hundred paisas equal one rupee. For the value of the rupee in dollars, see MONEY (table: Values).

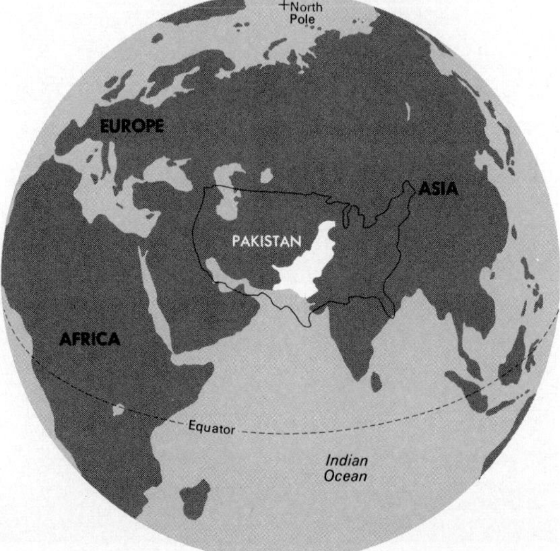

WORLD BOOK map

Pakistan lies in South Asia. It is about 10 per cent as large as the United States, not counting Alaska and Hawaii.

The earliest people of what is now Pakistan belonged to the same racial group as the people of northern India. Through the years, many invaders intermarried with the inhabitants. These invaders included Arabs, Afghans, Greeks, Persians, and Turks. All contributed to the mixed ancestry of present-day Pakistanis.

Cultural Groups and Languages. A number of cultural groups live in various parts of Pakistan. Each has its own customs and characteristics. Differences among the groups have caused problems throughout Pakistan's history. Some Pakistanis feel greater loyalty to their own cultural group than to the nation itself.

Language is the chief difference that divides the various cultural groups. Although Urdu is the official language of Pakistan, less than 10 per cent of the people speak it as their primary language. Each cultural group has its own language or *dialect* (local form of a language). Most Pakistanis who know Urdu use it only as a second language.

The Punjabis, who make up the largest cultural group, live mainly in the Punjab. They speak various dialects of the Punjabi language. Through the years, the Punjabis have controlled the government, economy, and armed forces of Pakistan.

Other leading cultural groups, in order of size, include the Sindhis, the Pathans, and the Baluchis. The Sindhis form most of the population of Sind Province. Their language is also called Sindhi. The Pathans are divided into various tribes that occupy the North-West Frontier Province. The Pathan language is called Pushtu. The Baluchis include many nomadic tribes that live near oases and along a few small streams in Baluchistan. They speak Baluchi, which has many dialects.

J. Alex Langley, DPI

Moslem Rituals, such as group prayer meetings, play an important part in the everyday lives of most Pakistanis. About 97 per cent of the nation's people are Moslems.

Emil Muench

Various Cultural and Language Groups make up Pakistan's population. Punjabis, such as the woman above, form the largest group. The man is a Pathan from the North-West Frontier Province.

Rural Life. More than three-fourths of the people of Pakistan live in rural villages. Most of the villagers are farmers or herders. Many others who live in rural areas have jobs in nearby cities or towns.

Traditional customs and beliefs have a strong influence on life in rural Pakistan. For example, men have far more social freedom than women do. Women avoid contact with men outside their family, and they cover their face with a veil in the presence of strangers. Women may help with farm work, but they do little else outside the home.

Housing and clothing vary from one region to another, depending on climate, local customs, and other factors. Most of the rural villages consist of clusters of two- or three-room houses made of clay or sun-dried mud. A typical home may have a few pieces of simple furniture, with straw mats covering the bare earth floors. Few rural homes have plumbing or electricity.

The most common garment of both men and women is the *shalwar-qamiz*, which consists of loose trousers and a long overblouse. Women may wear a *dupatta* (scarf) over their shoulders and head. Outside the home, women usually cover themselves with a tentlike garment called a *burqa*. In the Punjab, men may wear a skirtlike garment called a *lungi* instead of a shalwar-qamiz. Turbans or various types of woolen or fur caps are popular head coverings among Pakistani men.

City Life. Pakistan has seven cities with a population of more than 200,000. Karachi, the largest city, has almost 2 million people. See the separate articles on Pakistani cities listed in the *Related Articles* at the end of this article.

Most city people in Pakistan are factory workers, shopkeepers, or craftsmen. They have little or no education and live in small houses in old, crowded neighborhoods. Their customs resemble those of the rural villagers. Pakistan's urban population also includes educated middle- and upper-class people who have adopted many Western styles and ideas. A well-to-do Pakistani family may live in a large, modern home. Many middle- and upper-class women are active in politics, social work, and women's rights movements.

Religion. About 97 per cent of Pakistan's people are Moslems. Islam, the Moslem religion, is the chief link

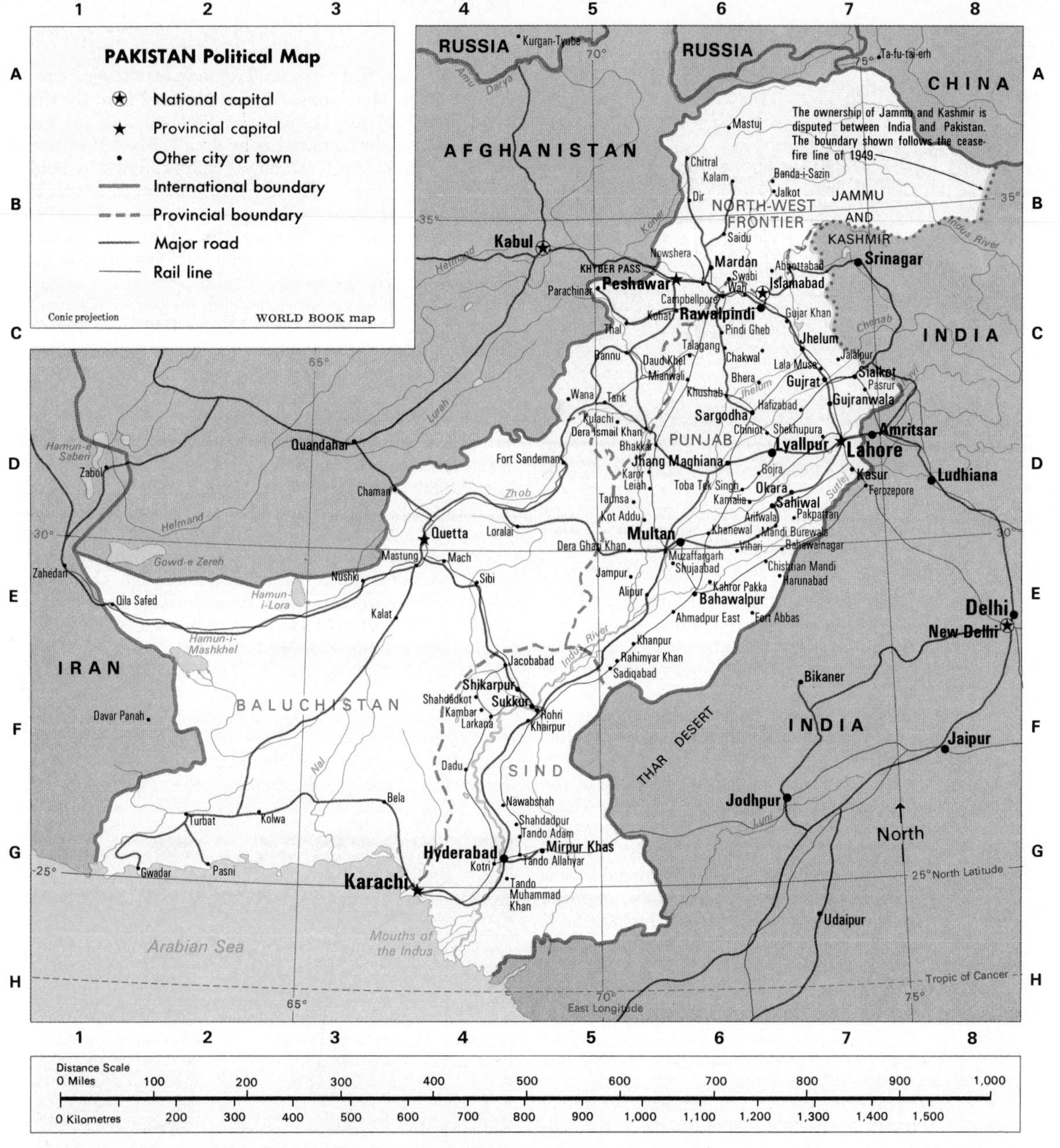

PAKISTAN MAP INDEX

Cities and Towns

Abbottabad 31,036..B 6
Ahmadpur East .....32,423..E 5
Arifwala ...18,558..D 6
Bahawalnagar ......36,290..E 6
Bahawalpur 84,377..E 6
Bannu .....31,623..C 5
Bhakkar ...21,749..D 5
Bhera .....17,992..C 6
Campbellpore .....19,041..C 6
Chakwal ...16,843..C 6
Charsadda* 37,396..B 6
Chichawatni* ...21,380..D 5
Chiniot ....47,099..D 6
Chishtian Mandi ...26,041..E 6
Dadu ......19,142..F 4
Daska* ....20,406..C 7
Daud Khel .17,524..C 6
Dera Ghazi Khan ...47,105..E 5
Dera Ismail Khan ...46,140..D 5
Gojra ......29,665..D 6
Gujranwala 196,154..C 7
Gujrat ....59,608..C 7
Hafizabad .34,576..C 7
Harunabad 22,575..E 6
Hyderabad 434,537..G 4
Islamabad .50,000..C 6
Jacobabad .35,278..E 4
Jalalpur ...16,988..C 7
Jampur ....13,161..E 5
Jaranwala* 26,953..D 6
Jhang Maghiana 94,971..D 6
Jhelum ....52,585..C 7
Kahror Pakka ...16,870..E 6
Kamalia ...35,248..D 6
Kamoke* ..25,124..D 7
Karachi .1,912,598..G 4
Kasur .....74,546..D 7
Khairpur ..34,144..F 4
Khanewal .49,093..D 6
Khanpur ...31,465..E 5
Khushab ...24,851..C 6
Kohat .....49,854..C 6
Kotri ......20,262..G 4
Kundian* .14,429..C 6
Lahore .1,296,477..D 7
Lala Musa .22,633..C 7
Larkana ...48,008..F 4
Leiah .....19,608..D 6
Lyallpur ..425,248..D 6
Mailsi* ....13,617..E 6
Mandi Bahauddin* .....22,295..C 7
Mandi Burewala 34,237..D 6
Mardan ....77,932..B 6
Mian Channun* 19,888..D 6
Mianwali ..31,398..C 6
Mirpur Khas 60,861..G 4
Mitha Tiwana* .16,046..C 6
Multan ...358,201..D 6
Muzaffargarh ..14,474..D 6
Nankana Sahib* ...17,140..D 7
Narowal* ..16,127..C 7
Nawabshah 45,651..G 4
Nowshera ..43,757..B 5
Okara .....68,299..D 7
Pakpattan .27,974..D 6
Parachinar 22,953..C 5
Peshawar .218,691..C 6
Quetta ....106,633..E 4
Rahimyar Khan ...43,548..F 5
Rawalpindi 340,175..C 6
Rohri .....19,072..F 5
Sadiqabad .16,007..F 5
Saidu .....15,920..B 6
Sahiwal ...75,180..D 6
Sangla* ....13,738..D 7
Sargodha .129,291..D 6
Shahdadkot 15,043..F 4
Shahdadpur 21,537..G 4
Shekhupura 41,635..D 7
Shikarpur .53,910..F 4
Shujaabad .16,815..E 6
Sialkot ...164,346..C 7
Sukkur ...103,216..F 5
Swabi .....17,542..B 6
Tando Adam ...31,246..G 4
Tando Allahyar .17,273..G 4
Tando Muhammad Khan 15,536..G 4
Tangi* ....14,706..B 6
Toba Tek Singh ...17,847..D 6
Vihari .....15,410..D 6
Wah ......37,035..C 6
Wazirabad* 29,399..C 7

*Does not appear on map; key shows general location.

Sources: Latest census figures (1961); official estimate (1967) for Islamabad.

Emil Muench from Carl Östman

Pakistani Schoolchildren attend classes outdoors in rural areas where classroom space is limited. Pakistan has a serious shortage of both schools and teachers.

among the various cultural groups that make up Pakistan's population. Most Pakistanis consider prayers and other religious rituals an important part of everyday life. Moslem holidays are national holidays throughout Pakistan. See ISLAM.

Christians make up about $1\frac{1}{2}$ per cent of the population. Pakistan also has a small number of Hindus, Buddhists, and Parsis.

Food. Wheat and other grains form the basis of the diet of almost all Pakistanis. Rural villagers use wheat flour to make flat loaves of bread called *chapatty*. *Pilau*, a dish served throughout Pakistan, consists of rice mixed with meat, vegetables, or nuts. Most Pakistanis like foods flavored with curry, ginger, onions, peppers, or other spicy seasonings. Popular meats include beef, chicken, goat, and lamb. Islam forbids its followers to eat pork. Fresh or dried fruit is a favorite dessert.

Education. Only about a fifth of the Pakistani people can read and write, and less than half the children of school age go to school. Pakistan has a shortage of schools, teachers, and teaching materials, and no law requires children to attend school.

The school system consists of elementary school (grades 1 through 5), middle school (grades 6 through 8), and high school (grades 9 and 10). After high school, a student may go on to intermediate college (grades 11 and 12), where he prepares for a college or university. Pakistan has about 325 colleges and 7 universities. Lahore is the home of the University of Punjab and the Pakistan University of Engineering and Technology. Other universities are in Hyderabad, Islamabad, Karachi, Lyallpur, and Peshawar.

The Arts. Each of Pakistan's cultural groups has its own folk literature, composed of stories and songs about legendary or historical figures. Rural Pakistanis enjoy plays based on myths and legends. In the cities, motion pictures are a favorite form of entertainment. Islam has influenced traditional architecture and painting throughout Pakistan (see ISLAMIC ART).

PAKISTAN/*The Land*

Pakistan has five main land regions: (1) the Northern and Western Highlands, (2) the Punjab Plain, (3) the Sind Plain, (4) the Baluchistan Plateau, and (5) the Thar Desert. The country has an area of 310,403 square miles, not including Kashmir, a region claimed by both Pakistan and India. The official name of Kashmir is Jammu and Kashmir.

The Northern and Western Highlands. Mountains cover much of northern and western Pakistan. Mount Godwin Austen, the second highest peak in the world, towers 28,250 feet above sea level in the part of Kashmir controlled by Pakistan. Only Mount Everest is higher. Mountain passes cut through the rugged peaks at several points. The most famous of these, the Khyber Pass, links Pakistan and Afghanistan (see KHYBER PASS).

The Punjab and Sind Plains occupy most of the eastern part of the country. These regions are *alluvial plains* (land formed of soil deposited by rivers). In the north, the Punjab is watered by the Indus River and four of its tributaries—the Chenab, Jhelum, Ravi, and Sutlej rivers. The combined waters of the tributaries join the Indus in east-central Pakistan. South of this meeting point, the broadened Indus flows through the Sind plain. Extensive irrigation systems have made the Punjab and Sind plains fertile agricultural regions.

The Baluchistan Plateau is located in southwestern Pakistan. Most of the plateau is dry and rocky and has little plant life.

The Thar Desert lies in southeastern Pakistan and extends into India. Much of the desert is a sandy wasteland. But irrigation projects have made parts near the Indus River suitable for farming. See THAR DESERT.

Kay Muldoon, Meyers Photo-Art

Irrigation Systems in the Punjab and Sind Plains have made these regions fertile for agriculture. Water from the Indus River and its tributaries irrigates millions of acres of farmland.

PAKISTAN Physical Map

This map shows the five land regions of Pakistan. The Northern and Western Highlands, which include peaks more than 25,000 feet high, are broken by the Khyber Pass and other mountain passes. The Indus River flows through the Punjab and Sind plains, which separate the Baluchistan Plateau from the hot, dry, Thar Desert.

- Land region boundary
- International boundary
- National capital
- Other city or town
- Mountain pass
- Elevation above sea level
- Desert
- Glacier
- Intermittent lake
- Swamp

Distance scale
0 100 200 300 Miles
0 100 200 300 400 Kilometres

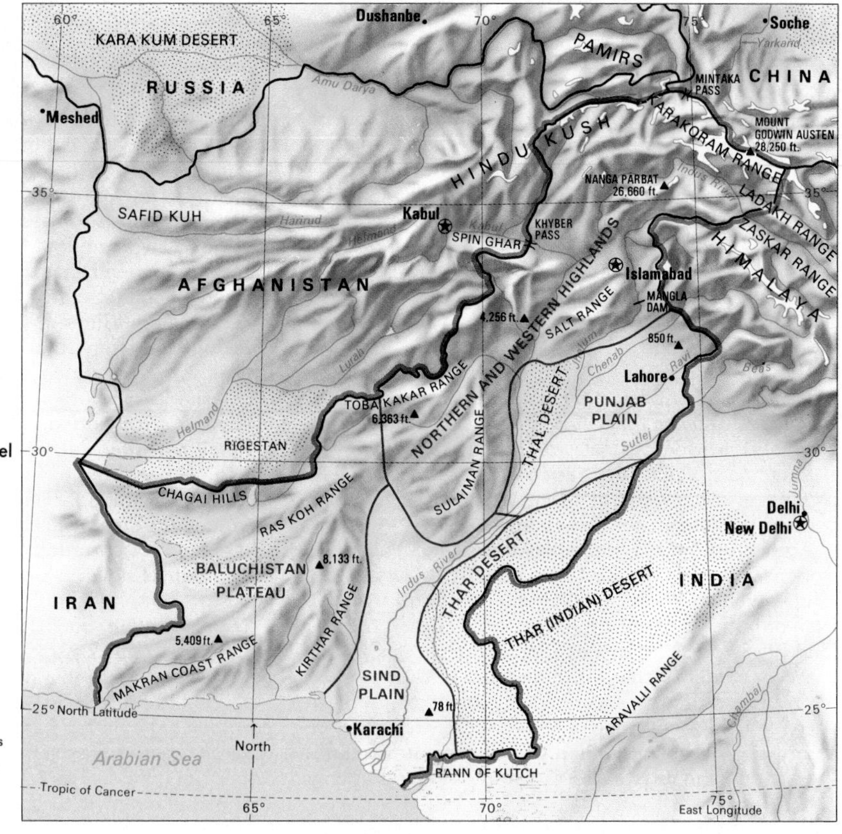

WORLD BOOK map

PAKISTAN/*Climate*

Most of Pakistan has a dry climate, with hot summers and cool winters. An average of only about 10 inches of rain falls throughout the country annually. But the amount of rainfall varies greatly from year to year. Long dry spells may be broken by severe rainstorms that cause rivers to overflow and flood the countryside.

In general, most of the rain falls from July to September, when the summer *monsoon* (seasonal wind) blows across Pakistan. The eastern part of the Punjab receives the most rain—more than 20 inches a year. Southwestern Pakistan is the driest area. Much of the Baluchistan Plateau receives less than 5 inches of rain a year.

Average temperatures vary from one part of Pakistan to another. The mountain regions have the coolest weather. Summer temperatures in the north and northwest average about 75° F. (24° C.), and winter temperatures frequently fall below the freezing point. In the Punjab, summer temperatures average more than 90° F. (32° C.), and winter temperatures average about 55° F. (13° C.). Summer temperatures in the Baluchistan Plateau average about 80° F. (27° C.). Winter temperatures average less than 40° F. (4° C.). The southern coastal region has mild, humid weather most of the year. Temperatures range from about 66° F. (19° C.) in winter to about 86° F. (30° C.) in summer.

J. Alex Langley, DPI

Cool, Sunny Weather is common in the mountainous regions of northern and western Pakistan. Most of the country has a dry climate, with an annual average rainfall of only about 10 inches.

Pakistan's economy is based largely on agriculture. Most Pakistanis make a living by farming the land or by raising goats or sheep. Pakistan had few factories when it gained independence in 1947. Since then, the country has worked to develop its manufacturing industries.

The government manages most of the nation's major heavy industries, such as oil refining and iron and steel production. The government has drawn up five-year plans that set production goals for agriculture and industry and establish programs for economic development. Many of Pakistan's development programs have been financed by aid from other countries and from international organizations.

Natural Resources. Pakistan's rivers are its most important natural resource. The rivers supply the water that irrigates more than 25 million acres of farmland. They also provide hydroelectric power.

Large natural gas fields lie in central Pakistan. The country also has deposits of chromite, coal, iron ore, gypsum, limestone, petroleum, and salt.

Agriculture employs about two-thirds of Pakistan's workers. Many of the farmers own only a few acres of land, which they work with simple tools and teams of oxen or buffalo. About two-fifths of the farmers own no land but work as tenants on large estates.

Since the 1950's, the government has worked to modernize agriculture by encouraging farmers to use fertilizer, pesticides, and new types of seeds. The government has also sponsored land reform programs to limit the size of large estates and distribute the land among poor farmers.

Wheat is the chief crop of Pakistan. The farmers also grow barley, cotton, fruits, oilseeds, rice, sugar cane, tobacco, and other crops. Cattle are raised mainly for use as work animals, but they also provide meat, milk, and leather. Many Pakistanis, especially in Baluchistan and the North-West Frontier Province, tend flocks of goats or sheep.

Manufacturing. About a tenth of the workers of Pakistan are employed in manufacturing industries. The manufacture of cotton textiles ranks as the nation's leading industry. Other manufactured products include cement, chemicals, drugs, fertilizer, leather goods, and steel. Pakistan also has oil refineries, silk and woolen mills, and sugar mills. Many craftsmen work in their homes or in small factories. They make carpets, embroidered goods, metalware, pottery, woodenware, and other handicraft items.

Fishing is an important industry in the coastal regions of Pakistan. Fishermen catch herring, mackerel, sardines, sharks, and other fish in the Arabian Sea. Most of the fish are exported.

Foreign Trade. Pakistan trades chiefly with China, Japan, Great Britain, the United States, and West Germany. Its imports include chemicals, electric equipment, food, iron and steel, machinery, petroleum products, and transportation equipment. Pakistan exports such products as carpets, cotton, hides and skins, leather goods, textiles, and wool.

Transportation and Communication. Pakistan has about 30,000 miles of roads, but only about a third are paved. Few Pakistanis own cars. In rural areas, the villagers use camels, cattle, donkeys, or horses for transportation. The nation has about 5,400 miles of railroad track. Karachi is Pakistan's only seaport. International airports operate in Karachi and Lahore.

Government-owned companies provide telephone and telegraph service. The government also owns and operates Pakistan's 3 television stations and 10 radio stations. About 75 daily newspapers are published in Pakistan.

Fred Ward, Black Star

Modern Farm Equipment simplifies the harvesting of wheat, Pakistan's chief crop. Government programs have helped modernize agriculture in Pakistan. But most of the nation's farmers still use simple tools to cultivate their small plots of land.

The Indus Valley Civilization. About 2500 B.C., one of the world's first great civilizations began to develop in the Indus Valley in what is now Pakistan. Ruins of Harappa and Mohenjo-daro, the two major cities of the civilization, show that both were large and well planned. By about 1700 B.C., the Indus Valley civilization had disappeared. Scholars do not know why it collapsed. See INDUS VALLEY CIVILIZATION.

Invasions and Conquests. During the next several thousand years, many peoples from southwest and central Asia came into the region that is now Pakistan. About 1500 B.C., a central Asian people called *Aryans* came through the mountain passes to the Punjab region. In time, they settled across almost all of India.

The Persians conquered the Punjab during the 500's B.C. and made it part of the huge Achaemenid Empire (see PERSIA, ANCIENT [The Achaemenid Empire]). In 326 B.C., Alexander the Great took control of most of what is now Pakistan. A few years later, the emperor Chandragupta Maurya made the region part of the Maurya Empire (see MAURYA EMPIRE).

The Maurya Empire began to break up about 230 B.C. Greeks from the independent state of Bactria in central Asia then invaded the Indus Valley. They established a kingdom with capitals near the present-day cities of Peshawar and Rawalpindi. About 100 B.C., Scythians from Afghanistan came into Baluchistan and Sind. In time, they conquered the Indus region. The Afghans were replaced by the Parthians, who, in turn, were conquered by the Kushans of central Asia.

The Kushans ruled what is now Afghanistan, Pakistan, and northwestern India from about A.D. 50 to the mid-200's. They controlled the trade routes from China to India and the Middle East. Peshawar, the Kushan capital, became a major commercial center. See KUSHAN EMPIRE.

During the mid-300's, the Indus Valley became part of the Gupta Empire, which had expanded westward from northeastern India. Huns from central Asia conquered the empire in the mid-400's.

The Coming of Islam. In A.D. 711, Arab Moslems sailed across the Arabian Sea and invaded Sind, bringing Islam to the region. Beginning about A.D. 1000, Turkish Moslems invaded northern Pakistan from Iran. The Turkish ruler Mahmud of Ghazni established a Moslem kingdom that in time included the entire Indus Valley. Lahore became the capital of the kingdom and developed into a major center of Moslem culture.

In 1206, most of what is now Pakistan became part of the Delhi Sultanate, a Moslem empire that included northern India. The Delhi Sultanate lasted until 1526, when Babar, a Moslem ruler from Afghanistan, invaded India and established the Mogul Empire.

The Mogul Empire included almost all of what is now Pakistan, India, and Bangladesh. Under Mogul rule, a culture developed that combined Middle Eastern and Indian elements. This culture included a new language, Urdu, which was influenced by both Hindi and Persian. It also included a new religion, Sikhism, which drew beliefs from both Hinduism and Islam.

The Mogul Empire began to decline in the 1700's. Several groups, including Persians and Afghans, then controlled the region that is now Pakistan. Sikh kingdoms gained strength in the Punjab during the early 1800's. See MOGUL EMPIRE.

The Rise of British Influence. Beginning in the 1500's, European traders competed for control of the profitable trade between Europe and the East Indies. A number of trade companies established settlements in India with the cooperation of the Mogul emperors. By the 1700's, the British East India Company had become the strongest trade power in India.

In the 1740's, after the Mogul Empire began to break up, the East India Company gained political control over much of India. The company fought a series of wars in the Punjab and Sind during the 1840's and added these territories to its holdings.

The British government took over control of the East India Company in 1858. All the company's territory then became known as *British India.* By 1900, as a result of wars and treaties with local rulers, British India included all of what is now Pakistan.

British Control. Britain introduced a number of reforms in India, including the establishment of a Western system of education. Many Hindus enrolled in the British schools, but most Moslems continued to attend their own schools, which stressed religious instruction. By the late 1800's, Western-educated Hindus far outnumbered Moslems in India. The Moslems had previously been outnumbered by the Hindus, who made up about three-fourths of the population. But the Moslems' lack of Western education reduced their power even further. Large numbers of Hindus gained positions in business and government, but the great majority of Moslems remained farmers and laborers.

In 1875, Syed Ahmad Khan, a Moslem leader, founded the Muhammadan Anglo-Oriental College (now Aligarh Muslim University) in Aligarh. This school combined Moslem and Western methods of education. Many of its graduates became leaders of India's Moslem community.

Moslem leaders were divided in their attitude about the Hindus. Some believed the Moslems should cooperate with the Indian National Congress, a political organization led by Hindus. But many Moslems thought that if the congress gained political power, it would never treat the Moslem minority fairly. In 1906, the Moslems formed a separate political organization called the Moslem League.

Independence Movements in India began to gain strength during the early 1900's. The Indian National Congress and the Moslem League both sought greater self-government for India. But at the same time, differences between the Hindus and Moslems increased. Almost all the Moslems believed the Hindus would have too much power over them if India gained independence from Britain. In the early 1930's, the Moslem League called for the creation of a separate Moslem nation. Such a nation would have been formed from the parts of India that had a Moslem majority. The president of the Moslem League, Mohammed Ali Jinnah, became a leading supporter of this proposal. The name *Pakistan*, which means *land of the pure* in Urdu, came to be used for the proposed nation.

In 1940, the Moslem League demanded *partition* (division) of India along religious lines. British and Hindu leaders rejected the idea, but the league refused any other settlement. Riots occurred between Hindus and Moslems during the mid-1940's. In 1947, Britain and the Hindu leaders finally agreed to the partition.

The New Nation. On Aug. 14, 1947, Pakistan became an independent dominion in the Commonwealth of Nations. India gained independence the next day. Pakistan was created from the northwestern and northeastern parts of India, where Moslems made up the majority of the population. More than 1,000 miles of Indian territory lay between the two sections, which were called West Pakistan and East Pakistan. Mohammed Ali Jinnah, considered the founder of Pakistan, became the new nation's first head of government.

Fighting between Hindus and Moslems continued even after the partition of India. Thousands died while migrating between India and Pakistan. About 6 million Hindus and Sikhs fled from Pakistan to India, and about 7 million Moslems left India to go to Pakistan.

In 1948, India and Pakistan went to war over Kashmir. That region had remained independent after the partition of India. But Pakistan claimed Kashmir because most of the people there were Moslems. After Pakistani troops invaded Kashmir, the region's Hindu ruler made it part of India. Indian and Pakistani troops fought until 1949, when the United Nations arranged a cease-fire. See KASHMIR.

The Republic. Pakistan became a republic in 1956, and the voters elected Major General Iskander Mirza their first president. Military leaders controlled the government throughout the late 1950's and 1960's.

In 1956, Pakistan began its first five-year plan for economic development. Most of the development projects took place in West Pakistan. In 1967, completion of the Mangla Dam on the Jhelum River provided West Pakistan with flood control, irrigation, and electric power. Construction of the world's largest dam, the Tarbela Dam on the Indus River, began in 1969.

The dispute over Kashmir led to renewed fighting between India and Pakistan in 1965. Once again, the United Nations arranged a cease-fire.

Civil War. The people of East and West Pakistan had been divided both geographically and culturally ever since the nation's creation in 1947. They shared only one major characteristic—their religion. Most of the people of East Pakistan had different physical traits, cultural backgrounds, and traditions than the people of West Pakistan. Many East Pakistanis objected to West Pakistani control over the nation's government, economy, and armed forces.

In 1970, a cyclone and tidal wave struck East Pakistan and killed about 200,000 persons. Many East Pakistanis accused the government of delaying shipments of food and relief supplies to the disaster area.

In 1971, the many differences and disagreements between East and West Pakistan erupted into civil war. The year before, Pakistanis had elected a National Assembly that was to draft a new constitution. East Pakistan had about 56 per cent of the nation's population, and so a majority of the assemblymen were East Pakistanis. The people of East Pakistan wanted a constitution that would give them some self-government.

In March, 1971, President Yahya Khan postponed the first meeting of the National Assembly. East Pakistanis staged demonstrations in protest against his action, and Yahya Khan ordered the Pakistani Army into East Pakistan. The East Pakistanis resisted, and civil war broke out. On March 26, 1971, East Pakistan declared itself an independent nation called Bangladesh.

In December, 1971, India joined Bangladesh against West Pakistan. The war then developed into a conflict between India and Pakistan, and the fighting spread into parts of West Pakistan and Kashmir. On Dec. 16, 1971, two weeks after India entered the war, Pakistan

Wide World

Millions of Moslems fled India in 1947 to settle in the newly created nation of Pakistan. Pakistan was carved out of regions of India that had a Moslem majority.

J. Alex Langley, DPI

Construction of the World's Largest Dam, the Tarbela Dam on the Indus River, began in 1969. The dam was designed to generate hydroelectric power and provide water for irrigation.

surrendered. More than a million persons had died in the bloody fighting. A few days later, Yahya Khan resigned. Zulfikar Ali Bhutto, head of the Pakistan People's Party, succeeded him. See also BANGLADESH.

Pakistan Today. As a result of the war, Pakistan lost about a seventh of its area and more than half its population. Its economy was badly disrupted. In January, 1972, Pakistan withdrew from the Commonwealth of Nations after Britain established diplomatic relations with Bangladesh.

During the first months of his presidency, Bhutto restored constitutional government and civilian rule to Pakistan. He announced programs for economic recovery and educational reform. In July, 1972, Bhutto met with Prime Minister Indira Gandhi of India. Mrs. Gandhi agreed to withdraw Indian troops from all Pakistani territory except in Kashmir, which remained a disputed region. The two leaders also agreed to work for the establishment of normal relations between India and Pakistan. ROBERT I. CRANE

PAKISTAN/*Study Aids*

Related Articles in WORLD BOOK include:

CITIES

Gujranwala, Hyderabad, Islamabad, Karachi, Lahore, Lyallpur, Multan, Rawalpindi, Sialkot

HISTORY

Ayub Khan, Mohammad
Central Treaty Organization
Colombo Plan
India
Iqbal, Sir Muhammad
Jinnah, Mohammed A.
United Nations (The India-Pakistan Conflict)

PHYSICAL FEATURES

Arabian Sea, Hindu Kush, Indus River, Khyber Pass, Sutlej River, Thar Desert

OTHER RELATED ARTICLES

Baluchistan, Cattle (graph), Cotton (graph), Kashmir, Moslems, Punjab, Shalimar Gardens, Sikhism, Sugar Cane (graph)

Outline

I. Government
II. People
A. Cultural Groups and Languages
B. Rural Life
C. City Life
D. Religion
E. Food
F. Education
G. The Arts
III. The Land
IV. Climate
V. Economy
A. Natural Resources
B. Agriculture
C. Manufacturing
D. Fishing
E. Foreign Trade
F. Transportation and Communication
VI. History

Questions

What is Pakistan's leading industry?
Who was Mohammed Ali Jinnah? Syed Ahmad Khan?
What was the main reason for the creation of Pakistan as an independent nation?
Why is Kashmir disputed between India and Pakistan?
What is a *shalwar-qamiz? Chapatty?*
How has Pakistan's government tried to modernize agriculture?
What are the chief cultural groups of Pakistan?
What has made the Punjab and Sind plains fertile farming regions?
Why did Moslems want a separate nation when India gained independence?
In what region do most Pakistanis live?

Tana Hoban, DPI

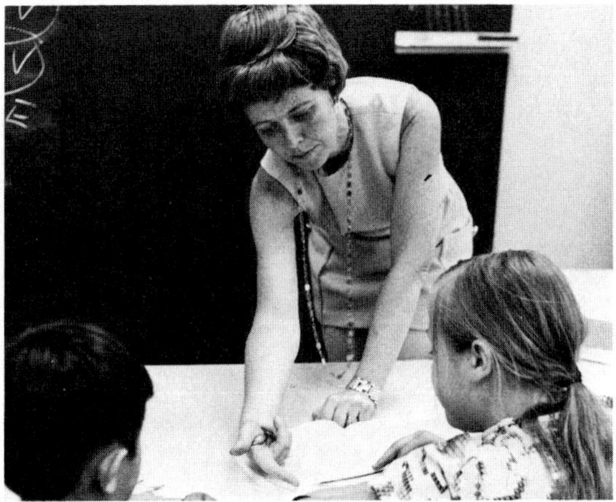

WORLD BOOK photo

WORLD BOOK photo

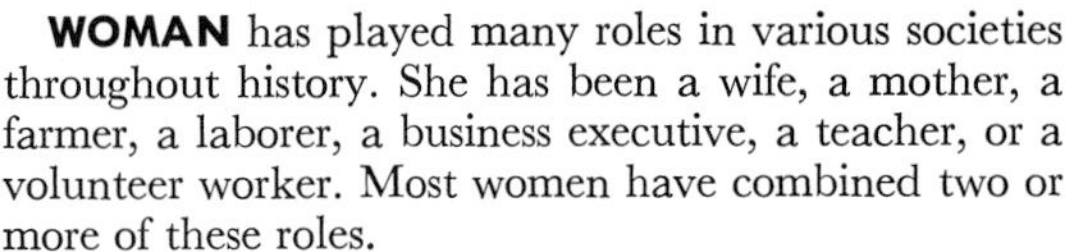

A Woman may devote herself to being a wife and mother, *above*. Or she may choose to work outside the home or combine these roles. Women have worked in such professions as teaching, *above right*, for over a hundred years. Other fields, including stockbroking, *right*, have been open to women for a much shorter time.

WOMAN has played many roles in various societies throughout history. She has been a wife, a mother, a farmer, a laborer, a business executive, a teacher, or a volunteer worker. Most women have combined two or more of these roles.

Through the centuries, almost every society has developed definite ideas of what activities are proper for women. Some societies have given women honor. Others have considered women less important than men. Some of these ideas have disappeared or have changed greatly, but others have changed little or not at all.

Today, women in many countries make at least some of the decisions about what they will do with their lives. In the United States, Canada, and most European nations, a woman can choose whether she wants a career, whether she wants to marry, and whether she wants to raise children. In many countries throughout the world, women are increasingly challenging society's traditional image of what a woman may choose to be.

Physical Characteristics and Woman's Roles

Most societies have related their ideas about women to beliefs about their physical characteristics. Some of these beliefs have little or no scientific basis. But they have been accepted for so many years that few people question them.

Cynthia Fuchs Epstein, the contributor of this article, is Associate Professor of Sociology at Queens College of the City University of New York. She is the author of Woman's Place: Options and Limits of Professional Careers.

Motherhood has played a major part in determining woman's place in society. In almost all societies, people have believed that woman's ability to bear children makes it every woman's duty to do so. Many women have chosen the job of caring for their family as a demanding and rewarding career. But there is no adequate scientific evidence that women have a *maternal instinct*—that is, a natural desire to bear and care for children. Many sociologists maintain that the so-called maternal instinct results from society's teaching girls that they should get married and raise children.

From earliest times, motherhood has helped bring about a division of tasks between men and women. In most societies, women remain home while pregnant or nursing their babies. This may be why they have traditionally done most of the jobs connected with the home. Men, on the other hand, have taken jobs near or far from home. In a primitive society, such a division of labor might not suggest inequality. But in a more advanced society, the tradition of women staying home and men going to work gives men economic superiority. A woman who stays home must depend on someone else to earn money for the necessities of life.

Size and Strength. Distinctions between the roles of men and women have also developed because most women are smaller and less powerful than most men. Such physical differences have led to men holding the most physically demanding and dangerous jobs. However, some differences in strength might result from society's traditional belief that boys should develop their muscles but girls should not.

Eventually, the division of tasks that may have been

determined by physical differences and motherhood became based almost exclusively on the sex of an individual. All societies have not classified male and female work in the same way, but most cultures have observed strict divisions between the two. Most societies have considered it improper for men to do women's work or for women to do men's work. In almost all societies, for example, women have the major responsibility for child rearing. In many societies, even unmarried women and older women who have stopped bearing children are given jobs close to the home.

Science and technology have eliminated many of the reasons for work differences between the sexes. For example, women can easily operate machines that do much of the heavy work once assigned only to men. Various methods of birth control enable women to limit the number of children they bear, to determine when to bear them, or to avoid bearing any. Many women practice birth control so they can take part in activities outside the home. Women in developed societies live about a third of their lives past their child-bearing years. Mothers may therefore enter—or resume—careers after raising their children.

Temperament and Emotions have traditionally been attributed to biological differences between men and women. In many societies, people believe that women are naturally more emotional than men, particularly during menstruation and the *menopause*, the time in life when menstruation ends. But scientists have found little evidence that woman's emotional makeup differs significantly from man's. Research shows that a woman's feelings depend strongly on what she has been taught. Many women are taught that they can expect to become emotionally upset during menstruation and the menopause. These women experience such upsets more frequently than do women who have been taught that menstruation and the menopause are normal parts of life.

Many people believe that a person's sex determines his or her intelligence, creativity, and ability to make decisions. But, though boys and girls may develop physically at different rates, no major differences in intelligence exist between men and women. Neither is there scientific evidence that a person's sex affects the ability to do creative work or make decisions. Many societies label women as naturally indecisive, one of the main reasons that men hold the majority of jobs requiring important decisions.

Western cultures consider gentleness, meekness, and motherliness as feminine traits, and aggressiveness and bravery as masculine characteristics. Some people believe that hormones create such definite masculine and feminine personality traits. These traits supposedly appear at *puberty*, a period that marks the end of childhood and the beginning of physical maturity. Scientists have tested this theory by injecting female rats with male hormones and male rats with female hormones. The females became aggressive, and the males became gentle. But male and female behavior varies so widely among different animal species that such tests cannot be considered proof of the effects of human hormones. For example, some female spiders and the female mantid eat their mates.

Margaret Mead, an American anthropologist, has indicated that culture, more than biological features, determines masculine and feminine personality traits. She studied three tribes that lived on islands in the Pacific Ocean. In one tribe, both men and women had a gentle, quiet nature. In the second tribe, both behaved aggressively. In the third tribe, the women took the dominant and impersonal role, and the men were gentle and tender.

Research shows that men and women have the same range of emotional characteristics. Social scientists believe that societies may harm individuals by insisting that they conform to a certain cultural pattern of masculine and feminine behavior. In Western societies, for example, a tender, sensitive boy may be mocked as a sissy, and a noisy, adventurous girl may be scolded for being unladylike. Such *stereotypes* (fixed images) of masculinity and femininity have barred many men and women from jobs and other activities that they enjoy and for which they are qualified.

Woman's Roles Through the Ages

In Ancient Societies, most women married and began raising children soon after reaching puberty. They remained at home, received no formal education, and had little economic or social power. Exceptions included the women judges who are mentioned in the Bible and the women of ancient Egypt and Sparta. Both Egyptian and Spartan women could own and inherit property. In addition, Egyptian women could work outside the home, and Spartan women could receive a formal education.

In ancient Rome, the law gave husbands control over their wives. But Roman women had more legal and social freedom than did most women in Europe for the next several centuries. They were highly respected, managed household affairs, and moved freely through the city to attend public functions.

In India, women owned property and took part in public debates thousands of years before the birth of Christ. But about 200 B.C., Hinduism developed laws that gave women an inferior status to men. Most Hindu parents arranged for their daughters to be married before reaching puberty and taught them to always obey their husbands. Later, other religions, including Christianity, adopted practices that gave men a status superior to that of women.

In Medieval and Early Modern Societies, religion remained an important factor in determining woman's position. As Christianity spread through Europe, women lost much of the freedom they had had under Roman law. The Roman Catholic Church followed Old Testament law and early German tradition regarding male domination. A European nobleman of the Middle Ages could end his marriage if his wife did not bear at least one son. Most women received no formal education. Noblewomen learned to sew, spin, weave, and direct household servants. Peasant men and women had fairly equal legal and social rights, though the men were dominant.

The Reformation, the religious movement of the 1500's that gave rise to Protestantism, removed some church restrictions on marriage and divorce. But Protestant leaders also regarded women as being completely under the control of their fathers or husbands.

Islam, the religion of the Moslems, spread through the Middle East, northern Africa, and parts of Europe and Asia from the 700's to the 1200's. Like Christianity and Hinduism, Islam taught women to obey their husbands. Men were allowed to have more than one wife. Moslem women began wearing veils over their face, and many men secluded their women in harems (see HAREM). But Moslem women did have the right to own property and to divorce their husbands.

Before the 1800's, most women worked only in and around the home. In England, a number of women worked in trade, and some were partners with their husbands. Men approved such work only if it did not take women out of the home. The few women who did work outside the home did not have the right to spend their own wages.

Until the 1800's, few women had any voice in politics or economics except through their husbands. Most European countries forbade wives to own property or to enter a profession. According to English common law, a husband controlled his wife and any property she had owned before their marriage (see COMMON LAW).

In Industrialized Societies. During the late 1700's and early 1800's, the Industrial Revolution brought great changes in the lives of people in many countries (see INDUSTRIAL REVOLUTION). A shortage of men resulted in large numbers of women beginning to work outside the home. English and American textile mills of the early 1800's were among the first factories to employ women. Later, other kinds of factories in industrialized nations started to hire women, partly because not enough men were available.

At first, the labor shortage assured women of fairly good working conditions—though they worked long hours and earned less than men. Unmarried working women gained some independence from their families because they could spend their earnings or save for an education. But many single women lived under strict supervision in dormitories operated by their employers. Married women had no legal right to do as they wished with their own earnings.

By the 1830's, many thousands of women worked in the textile mills of such industrialized regions as England and the New England States. In time, industry developed better machines, and large factories began to replace small shops. At the same time, more people left farming and sought factory work. As a result, working conditions became worse and wages dropped. But many unmarried women and widows continued to work in factories because they had little chance of finding other jobs.

Women's Rights Movements began to develop during the first half of the 1800's, when social and political revolutions were occurring in many nations. Various groups in Europe and the United States debated woman's role in business, the family, politics, and society.

Some of the first organized attempts to improve woman's status took place in the United States. These actions occurred in the areas of educational, social, and political reform. In 1835, Oberlin College in Oberlin, Ohio, became the first U.S. coeducational college. In 1841, Oberlin became the first college in the country to award degrees to women. During the next several decades, coeducation developed rapidly in the United States, with much support from state universities.

As women gained more education and greater opportunities to work outside the home, they began to demand other rights as well. During the 1840's, married women in New York led a campaign to revise state property laws. In 1848, the New York legislature passed a bill giving married women the right to own real estate in their own name.

In 1848, two reformers—Lucretia Mott and Elizabeth Cady Stanton—called a Woman's Rights Convention in Seneca Falls, N.Y. From then on, until the Civil War began in 1861, national women's rights conventions met almost every year. The delegates discussed the rights of women regarding divorce, guardianship of children, property control, voting, and other matters. During the Civil War, from 1861 to 1865, most women reformers, both North and South, abandoned the movement and gave their full support to war activities.

In 1868 and 1870, the 14th and 15th amendments to the U.S. Constitution guaranteed *suffrage* (the right to vote) to all men, but not to any women. Thereafter, the women's rights movement directed most of its efforts at gaining suffrage. Several groups split away from the movement because they thought other social and political reforms deserved equal effort. A constitutional amendment granting women full suffrage was introduced during every session of Congress from 1878 to 1920, when it passed as the 19th Amendment.

During the late 1800's and early 1900's, woman suffrage became an important issue in many countries. In 1893, New Zealand became the first nation to grant women the vote. Australia and the Scandinavian countries did so in the early 1900's. Russia gave women the vote in 1918 when the newly formed Soviet government declared equality of the sexes. That same year, Canada granted women the right to vote in national elections. British women campaigned more than 40 years before finally receiving voting rights in 1928. See WOMAN SUFFRAGE.

Educational and employment reforms slowly increased the rights of European and American women during the last half of the 1800's and in the early 1900's. British women fought for education and the right to choose a profession. In 1848, Queen's College for Women opened in London. Other women's colleges followed, but women could not go to college with men. In 1884, Oxford University began admitting women to examinations for a bachelor's degree. But Oxford did not admit women as full-time students until 1920.

In the late 1800's, British women began finding jobs outside the home and factory. In 1870, the government started to employ women for typing and other clerical work. But many positions remained closed to women. Women could study medicine but had to take their qualifying examinations outside England until 1875, when the Royal College of Surgeons began to admit women. Nor could women doctors work in British hospitals until 1877, when a London hospital opened to them. British women could not become lawyers until 1919.

In the United States, women had first graduated from medical school and started practicing medicine in 1849, though they met much opposition. In 1869, Iowa licensed the first woman lawyer in the United States. But not until 1920 did all the states allow women to practice law under the same provisions as men. In the United States, as in most other Western countries, women teachers did not become common before 1850.

In Great Britain before 1870, married women who worked could not spend their own earnings, though divorcees and unmarried women could. In 1881, French law gave married female factory workers the right to open a bank account without their husband's consent. Other French working wives received that right in 1907.

Wartime Changes. During World War I (1914-1918) and World War II (1939-1945), women in the warring countries took over many traditionally male jobs to free men for combat. Thousands of women served in the U.S., Canadian, and British armed forces. In the United States, about 18 million women worked in war plants during World War II. Many industries sponsored child-care centers so that mothers could be free to work. The U.S. government established a policy of equal pay for equal work in industries with government contracts. Many labor unions also adopted this policy. But little discussion took place about equal employment and advancement opportunities for men and women. After both world wars, most women returned to their old jobs or to their homes. Until the 1960's, few women campaigned actively to extend women's rights.

Woman's Roles Today

In the 1970's, more women went to college and held a wider variety of jobs than ever before. Women in many countries could, if they wished, live independently and control their own earnings and property. Women can vote and run for public office in almost all countries that have elections. In 1971, the male voters of Liechtenstein defeated a proposal to give women the vote. All other European nations have woman suffrage.

The United Nations has a Commission on the Status of Women. Many nations have agreed to follow the commission's policies on divorce, education, property rights, suffrage, and other issues related to women's rights. One commission document provides that no marriage should take place unless both the man and woman freely consent. This policy protects women from marriages arranged against their will. But the commission does not have the power to enforce its policies.

Mary Ellen Mark, Woodfin Camp, Inc.

Women's Liberation Demonstrations became common in the United States and Canada during the 1960's and 1970's. Women of all ages joined in a demand for equal rights.

In the United States and Canada. Women make up more than 40 per cent of the labor force in the United States. In Canada, about 34 per cent of the workers are women. In the United States, about 40 per cent of the college graduates are women. In Canada, the figure is about 35 per cent.

Despite the high percentage of working women in both the United States and Canada, few hold executive or managerial positions. In the early 1970's, more than a third of the U.S. working women held clerical jobs, such as secretary, file clerk, or telephone operator. Less than 7 per cent of the working men held similar jobs. In general, women received only about 60 per cent of the pay men received for the same job.

In both the United States and Canada, women make up only about 7 per cent of the physicians, 3 per cent of the lawyers, and less than 1 per cent of the engineers. These low figures result partly from the general attitude that such professions are unsuitable for women. But today, more women than ever before graduate from professional schools and go on to careers in traditionally male fields.

Although women in both countries may run for public office, no woman has been President of the United States or Prime Minister of Canada. The United States has had only three women governors. Neither nation has had many women in its national legislature.

Laws passed in the United States and Canada during the 1960's and early 1970's aimed at ensuring equal treatment of men and women. The Canadian Bill of Rights, passed in 1960, states that no individual may be denied any rights because of his or her sex. All of Canada's 10 provinces and the Northwest Territories passed laws in the 1950's and 1960's providing for equal pay for equal work by men and women.

In the United States, the Civil Rights Act of 1964 prohibits job discrimination on the basis of sex. In 1971, the Supreme Court ruled that unequal treatment based only on sex violates the 14th Amendment to the U.S. Constitution. This amendment provides all citizens with equal protection under the law.

In March, 1972, the Senate approved the so-called Women's Equal Rights Amendment. This amendment states that sex has no effect on equality of rights under the law. The House of Representatives had approved it in 1971.

The Equal Rights Amendment, as proposed, would make several state and local laws unconstitutional. For example, it outlaws limits on the types of jobs women may hold and on the number of hours a week they may work. The amendment also prohibits limitations on the right of women to start businesses or to handle property on an equal basis with men. It bans laws that treat women more harshly than men for certain crimes, such as adultery or repeated drunkenness. The amendment also ends the favorable treatment women had automatically received in alimony, child custody, and child support cases. For example, in most divorce proceedings, the mother has received custody of the children, and the father has been forced to provide money to support them. Under the amendment, each case would be decided individually without regard to sex.

Women's rights groups had demanded such an amendment for 49 years, but many people thought the 14th Amendment made it unnecessary. By late 1972, 20 states had ratified the Equal Rights Amendment. An amendment becomes law when 38 states approve it.

The Women's Liberation Movement. Many women's groups protest what they consider unequal treatment of men and women. Such groups became prominent in the United States and Canada during the 1960's and early 1970's. The activities of these groups came to be known as the Women's Liberation Movement.

In 1963, an American woman named Betty Friedan published *The Feminine Mystique.* In this book, she attacked society for having long treated women as second-class citizens. She formed the National Organization for Women (NOW) in 1966. By 1972, this organization had grown into the largest group in the women's movement, with about 18,000 members. NOW has been especially active in demanding reform of educational policies, which it claims teach girls to aim only for "women's jobs." Such jobs include nursing, office work, and teaching. Other women's liberation groups in the United States include the National Women's Political Caucus and the Women's Equity Action League. In Canada, the movement developed among female members of the Student Union for Peace Action. This group first organized for nuclear disarmament and later protested the Vietnam War.

Women's liberation groups work for strict enforcement of laws and regulations that promote women's equality. Most of these groups call for better child-care facilities that would free mothers for work outside the home. Some groups demand that abortion be legalized without restriction so that every woman can decide for herself whether to bear a child. Many women's liberation groups insist that the abbreviation "Ms.," rather than "Miss" or "Mrs.," should be used before women's names. They believe there is no reason to have different titles for married and unmarried women.

Some women's liberation groups think that women will achieve equality only through basic changes in society. These groups say men should help with housework and child care to free women for outside work. They believe such sharing of tasks would result in relationships between men and women based on mutual interests, respect, and affection, rather than on men's economic and physical dominance.

In Other Countries, changing laws and customs are giving women a greater voice in political and social matters. In 1960, Sirimavo Bandaranaike of Ceylon became the first female prime minister in the world. Golda Meir of Israel and Indira Gandhi of India also became prime ministers of their countries in the 1960's.

In Africa, more women are being educated than ever before. About 40 per cent of Kenya's high school pupils are women, and the number of educated women is rising in other African countries. Some women occupy important government positions, such as supreme court judge in Ghana and chief minister in the Congo.

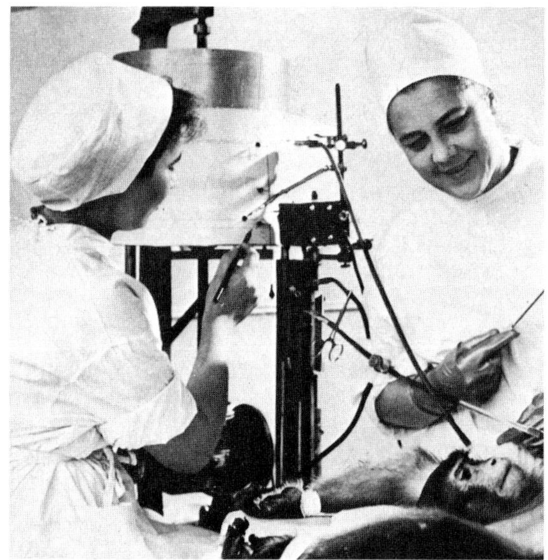

Pictorial Parade

Russian Women, such as this research doctor, make up about three-fourths of their nation's physicians. Women in Russia also have prominent roles in economics, engineering, and law.

During the 1960's and early 1970's, large numbers of women left their villages to seek education or work in the cities. But most African women still live in tribal villages and devote their lives to child raising and household work. Many men have more than one wife. In many areas, a man must pay a woman's parents a *bride price* before he can marry her.

In Western Europe, women make up a large portion of the labor force, but few hold high-paying jobs. Although almost half the women in Sweden work, they make up only about 6 per cent of their country's lawyers, a little more than 1 per cent of the physicians, and 1 per cent of the university teachers. In West Germany, about 40 per cent of the married women work, but they hold only 3 per cent of the best jobs. In Great Britain, only about 2 per cent of the top positions are held by women.

As elsewhere, many women in Western Europe are demanding increased rights. They have demonstrated for liberalized divorce laws, the widespread availability of birth control information, and enforcement of existing laws providing equal pay for equal work.

In South America, most women accept traditional roles of housekeeping and raising families. But many who live in the major cities or have had some high school education seek jobs outside the home. Most Latin-American nations recognize the principle of equal pay for equal work, and most have women's bureaus connected with their department of labor. These bureaus teach women about their rights as workers and provide technical training to help women get better jobs. The Organization of American States, an association of 23 Latin-American countries, has an Inter-American Commission of Women that aids the women's bureaus of member states.

In Russia, women and men receive equal pay for equal work. But men still hold most top government and management positions. Most Russian women work outside the home to supplement their husband's income and because their society encourages them to work. But they also do almost all the housework and shopping. The government provides nurseries where working mothers can leave preschool children.

Women make up about half the labor force of Russia. About 75 per cent of the nation's physicians, almost half its judges, and a third of its engineers and lawyers are women. Women make up about 70 per cent of the teachers and 60 per cent of the economists. About a third of the members of the Supreme Soviet, Russia's parliament, are women, but few women are on the Central Committee of the Communist Party. No woman has ever sat on the Politburo, Russia's highest ruling body.

In China, as in Russia and other Communist countries, society considers women equal to men and expects them to work just as hard. Women drive trucks and bulldozers, work on street construction crews, and fly military planes. Women make up more than half the labor force of China's textile industry and from 30 to 40 per cent of the farm and commune workers. Most of the nation's teachers are women. Working wives leave their children in child-care centers or with elderly relatives. Many Chinese women hold important positions on local government bodies, but few serve on the Central Committee of the Communist Party. Although two women have served on the Party's 21-member Politburo, none sits on the Politburo's 5-member standing committee, which rules China.

In Japan, a growing number of married women work outside the home. Women make up about a third of the nation's work force, but more than 60 per cent of this group work in family-owned businesses. Women earn an average of less than half as much pay as men.

Many Japanese women belong to organizations that work to improve the status of women. During the late 1960's and early 1970's, these women's groups often marched and picketed to protest high food prices, the lack of child-care facilities, and other conditions.

In India, women have equal rights, including the right to vote and to own property. Political parties encourage women to run for political office. During the 1960's and early 1970's, increasing numbers of educated working women emerged in India. More than 10 million women have professional or technical jobs. But most of this group came from the top levels of Indian society. About 19 per cent of all Indian women can read and write compared with 40 per cent of the men.

In Arab Lands, women's roles are changing slowly. Women in some areas of Bahrain, Kuwait, and Saudi Arabia see few men outside their immediate families. Some restaurants and hotels in these areas separate men and women. But many young husbands and wives attend social events together, and the tradition of keeping women in harems has almost disappeared.

For centuries, Arab custom required women to veil their faces. Turkey banned the veil in the 1920's, and Iran abolished it in 1935. Today, few women wear veils in Egypt, Iraq, Lebanon, Palestine, and Syria. Saudi Arabian law still requires veils, but many women choose veils of thin fabric that does not conceal the face.

Arab families arrange most marriages, and most girls marry in their teens. But many women attend high school and continue their education in college, a correspondence school, or a foreign institution. Women make up about a fourth of all students in Arab universities. A small but growing percentage of women work outside the home, especially in such professions as teaching.

CYNTHIA FUCHS EPSTEIN

Related Articles in WORLD BOOK include:

LEADERS IN WOMEN'S RIGHTS MOVEMENT

Anthony, Susan B.
Bloomer, Amelia J.
Catt, Carrie C.
Howe (Julia Ward)
Lockwood, Belva Ann Bennett
Morris, Esther Hobart
Mott, Lucretia C.
Pankhurst, Emmeline G.
Sanger, Margaret
Shaw, Anna H.
Spencer, Anna G.
Stanton, Elizabeth Cady
Stone, Lucy
Terrell, Mary C.
Truth, Sojourner
Walker, Mary E.
Willard, Emma H.
Willard, Frances E. C.

OTHER RELATED ARTICLES

Abortion
Alimony
Birth Control
Colonial Life in America
Divorce
Egypt, Ancient (Family Life)
Family
Homemaking
Labor (table: Men and Women in the United States Labor Force)
Life (table: Life Expectancy at Birth)
Marriage
Menstruation
Pioneer Life in America
Planned Parenthood
Sparta (Way of Life)
Vocations (table: Annual Income in the U.S.)
WAC
WAF
WAVES
Woman Suffrage
Woman's Club
Women's Bureau
Wyoming (Territorial Progress)

Outline

I. Physical Characteristics and Woman's Roles
A. Motherhood
B. Size and Strength
C. Temperament and Emotions

II. Woman's Roles Through the Ages
A. In Ancient Societies
B. In Medieval and Early Modern Societies
C. In Industrialized Societies

III. Woman's Roles Today
A. In the United States and Canada
B. In Other Countries

Questions

What subjects did the women's rights conventions of the 1800's discuss?

What special rights did ancient Egyptian and Spartan women have?

How did the two world wars change woman's position in society?

How did factory work change the lives of unmarried women?

What professions include large percentages of women in Russia?

How do cultural stereotypes harm both women and men?

What role has religion played in determining woman's status in society?

What helped cause the divisions between men's and women's work, dating back to earliest times?

How does the Civil Rights Act of 1964 affect women?

How is the role of Arab women changing?

Reading and Study Guide

For a *Reading and Study Guide on Women*, see the RESEARCH GUIDE/INDEX, Volume 22.

WORLD BOOK photos

Bicycle Riding in a park provides fun and exercise for the entire family, *left*. Increasing numbers of adults ride bikes to and from work, *right*. Some parks and city streets have special bicycle lanes.

BICYCLE is a vehicle with two wheels mounted one behind the other on a metal frame. The rider supplies the power to move a bicycle by pushing two pedals around in a circle with his feet. Both children and adults use bicycles for recreation and transportation.

Bicycles are a common sight in North America, in parts of South America, throughout Europe, and in many African and Asian countries. The United States ranks among the chief bicycle-producing nations, along with Austria, France, Germany, Great Britain, and Japan.

In the United States, boys and girls on bikes ride to school, run errands, and perform many tasks in less time than it would take to walk. Increasing numbers of men and women ride bicycles to and from work.

During World War II (1939-1945), many people in the United States, Canada, and other countries rode bicycles because of the shortage of automobiles, gasoline, and tires. During the 1950's, a concern for health and physical fitness brought a new interest in bike riding. This interest continued into the 1970's.

Kinds of Bicycles

Bicycles are manufactured in various sizes and styles. They range from small sidewalk models with removable training wheels to multispeed bikes for long-distance travel and racing. Bicycles come in six main sizes based on the wheel *diameter* (length across) measured in inches: 10-inch, 16-inch, 20-inch, 24-inch, 26-inch, and 27-inch. The various sizes suit riders of different ages. For example, most children 5 to 8 years old find 20-inch bicycles to be the proper size for them. Most adults ride 26- or 27-inch models. Manufacturers make three main styles of bicycles: (1) lightweight, (2) middleweight, and (3) specialty.

Lightweight Bicycles include both racing and touring models. These bikes are built for speed and easy handling. Most models have gear systems that enable the rider to pedal at different speeds. The most popular lightweight models have 5, 10, or 15 speeds. For touring, many riders prefer bikes with 15 speeds. Racing bikes weigh about 21 pounds. Touring bikes resemble racers, but they weigh from 25 to 30 pounds.

Middleweight Bicycles have heavier wheels and wider, softer tires than lightweights. Most middleweight bicycles weigh from 35 to 45 pounds. Some models have three or five speeds. They are not so fast as lightweights and are not well suited for long-distance riding.

Specialty Bicycles include the *high-riser*, popular with riders from 10 to 14 years old. It has high-rise handle bars and a seat shaped somewhat like a banana. Many high-risers have three- or five-speed gears. Another specialty bike, the *tandem*, carries two riders, one behind the other, operating separate sets of pedals.

How a Bicycle Works

Power and Speed. When the rider pushes the pedals of a bicycle, they turn a *sprocket* (toothed wheel) called the *chainwheel.* A chain fits over the metal teeth around the edge of the chainwheel. The chain extends to a smaller sprocket on the rear wheel of the bicycle and fits over the teeth of this sprocket. As the large sprocket turns, it moves the chain. The moving chain turns the small sprocket and the rear wheel.

Multispeed bicycles have gears that make pedaling easier for a rider at certain times. The gears enable the rider to choose the most efficient combination of pedaling effort and pedaling speed. For example, a rider shifts into a low gear when going up a hill or riding against the wind. This makes pedaling easier, but it also slows him down unless he pedals faster. The rider uses a high gear for maximum speed on level surfaces. This enables him to pedal slower, but it also makes pedaling more difficult.

The gears of a multispeed bike are sprockets of different sizes. The number of gears a bicycle has determines its range of speeds. For example, a 5-speed bicycle has five gears on its rear wheel. A 10-speed bicycle has five gears on its rear wheel and two gears that form the chainwheel. The combination of these front and rear gears gives the bike its 10 speeds.

The rider shifts gears on a 3-speed middleweight bicycle by moving a lever on the bike's handle bar. On 10- and 15-speed bicycles, a mechanism called a *derailleur* shifts or "derails" the chain from one gear to another. On most bicycles with derailleur gears, the rider shifts gears by squeezing two levers on the bike's down tube. Some bikes have gear controls in the handle bars.

Steering and Stopping. The rider uses the handle bars to guide and balance a bicycle. The handle bars turn the front wheel from side to side. A rider stops his bike by using the brakes. Some middleweight bicycles have a *coaster* brake on the rear wheel. The rider operates this brake by pushing backward on the pedals. Most lightweight bikes and some middleweights and high-risers have *caliper* brakes, which the rider operates by squeezing two levers on the handle bars. The levers operate rubber brake pads called *shoes* that press against the wheel rims to slow down or stop the bicycle.

Bicycle Care and Safety

Safety Rules require bicycle riders to obey all traffic laws. In addition, when slowing, stopping, or turning, a cyclist should signal with his left arm and left hand.

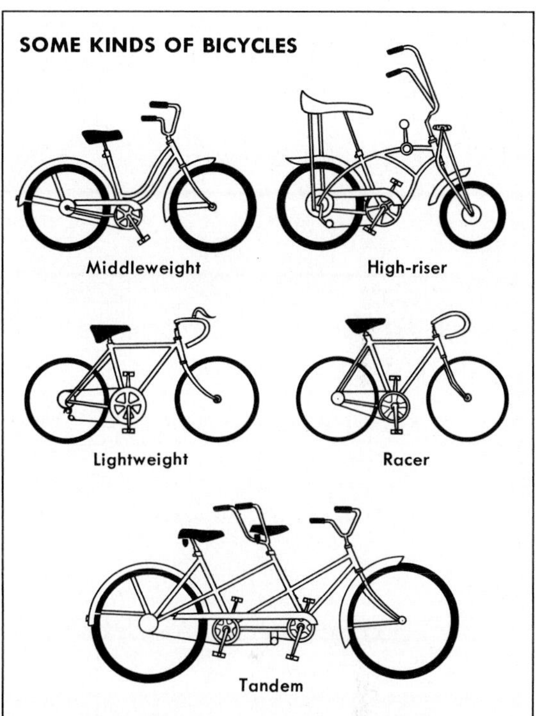

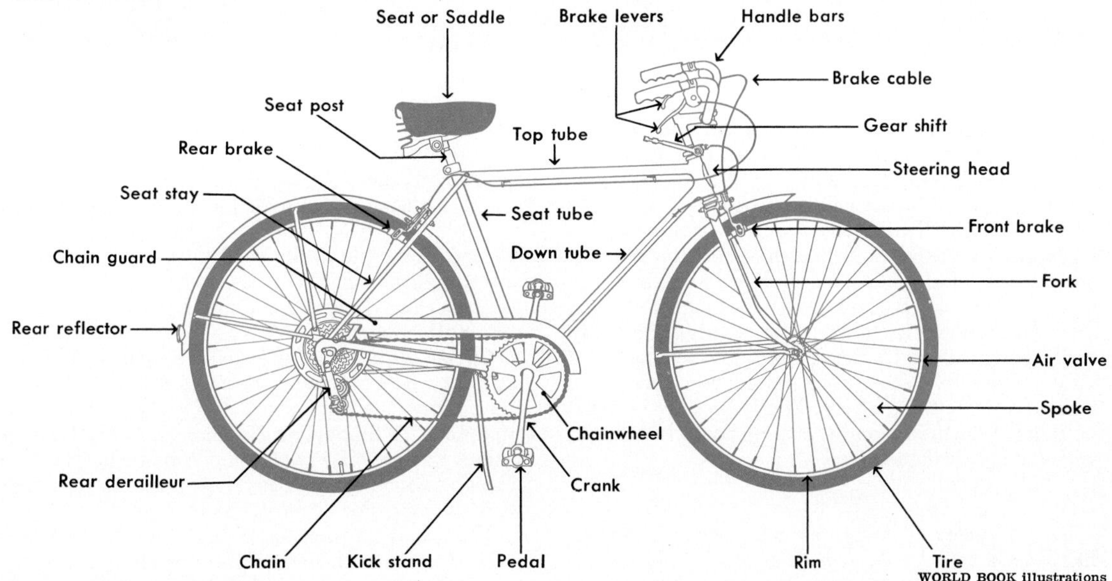

WORLD BOOK illustrations

WORLD BOOK illustration

When riding in the street, he should stay on the right side of the road. Wise cyclists never race, stunt, or hold on to another vehicle. Nor do they carry passengers on a bicycle built for one rider only.

Equipment and Care. Cyclists who ride at night should have protective lights. Safety experts recommend a white light on the front of a bike, a red light or reflector on the rear, and yellow reflectors on the sides and pedals. A horn or bell warns people of a bike's approach.

A cyclist should keep all the parts of his bike clean and properly oiled. The chain should be removed and oiled frequently. Wheel hubs should be cleaned and greased at least twice a year. The brakes must always be in good condition, and the tires should be inflated with the right volume of air.

History

Early Bicycles. The first bicycle, a wooden scooter-like vehicle called a *dandy horse* or *walk-along*, was invented about 1790 by Comte Mede de Sivrac of France. In 1816, Baron Karl von Drais of Germany invented an improved model called a *draisine*. It had a steering bar connected to the front wheel. A Scottish blacksmith, Kirkpatrick Macmillan, added foot pedals to the draisine in 1839. Pierre Lallement, a French carriage maker, developed a bicycle in the 1860's that more nearly resembled today's models.

The first bicycle with an all-metal frame was developed in England in 1872. This bike, called a *high-wheeler*, had a huge front wheel and a small rear wheel. The front wheel of some models was 5 feet high.

The *safety bicycle* appeared about 1885. It was invented by J. K. Starley, a foreman in an English sewing machine factory. The safety bicycle had wheels of the same size, which made it easier and safer to ride than a high-wheeler. Pedals drove the rear wheel by means of a chain and sprockets, as they do on today's bikes. By 1890, bikes had air-filled rubber tires. Other im-

Historical Pictures Service

The Draisine, 1816

Historical Pictures Service

Pierre Lallement's Pedal-Powered Bicycle, 1866

Historical Pictures Service

High-Wheeler, Late 1800's

Safety Bicycle, 1893 Culver

provements about this time included the coaster brake and adjustable handle bars. An early form of the modern bicycle gear shift was invented about 1900 by Paul de Vivie, a French bicycle shop owner.

By 1897, about 4 million Americans were riding bicycles regularly, more than at any previous time. Then, during the early 1900's, the rapid development of the automobile caused many people to lose interest in bikes.

Bicycle Riding Today. In the early 1970's, bicycle riding in the United States became more popular than ever before. By 1972, about 75 million Americans were riding bikes. Many cities across the country established special lanes called *bikeways* for cyclists in parks and on streets.

Several organizations work to promote long-distance bike trips. One of these groups, American Youth Hostels, Inc., plans bicycle trips for young people and provides inexpensive lodging for them throughout the United States. The International Youth Federation performs a similar service throughout Europe and in Africa, Asia, and Australia. EUGENE A. SLOANE

See also BICYCLE RACING; NETHERLANDS (picture: Bicycle Riding); JINRIKISHA; PEDICAB.

BICYCLE RACING became a sport in 1883 when G. M. Hendrie defeated W. G. Rowe in Massachusetts in the first contest on record. Pneumatic tires made road races popular in 1888.

Early races were held outdoors, but in the late 1880's, promoters began building arenas with saucerlike tracks. The first six-day bicycle race was held in Madison Square Garden in New York City in 1891. It soon became a popular spectator sport. Two-man teams traveled on a nationwide circuit, and earned as much as $15,000 a year. Interest in the sport declined in the late 1930's in the United States. It is still popular in Europe, and has been an official Olympic Games sport, called *cycling*, since 1896. RICHARD G. HACKENBERG

See also FRANCE (Sports).

Wide World

Racers in the Annual Paris-to-Brussels Bicycle Race pedal away from the starting point on the outskirts of Paris.

Dave Bartruff, Artstreet

Christina Kilander from Sven Samelius

Korea's Cities have grown rapidly since the early 1950's. Tall, modern buildings constructed during this period make parts of Seoul, *left,* and Pyongyang, *right,* look like American cities. Seoul is South Korea's capital and largest city. Pyongyang is the capital and largest city of North Korea.

KOREA

KOREA is a land in eastern Asia that consists of two nations. One of these nations is the Republic of Korea—usually called *South Korea.* The other is the Democratic People's Republic of Korea—commonly called *North Korea.* South Korea is a republic. Seoul is its capital and largest city. North Korea is a Communist state. Pyongyang is its capital and largest city.

The two nations lie on the Korean Peninsula, which extends south from northeastern China. The peninsula is about the same size as the state of Utah. North Korea covers the northern half of it, and South Korea occupies the southern half. North Korea is slightly larger than South Korea, but the South has more than twice as many people as the North.

Plains stretch along the western, northeastern, and southern coasts of Korea. Mountains cover most of the rest of the peninsula. Most of the Korean people by far live on the coastal plains or in river valleys.

William E. Henthorn, the contributor of this article, is Acting Director of the Center for Korean Studies at the University of Hawaii and author of A History of Korea.

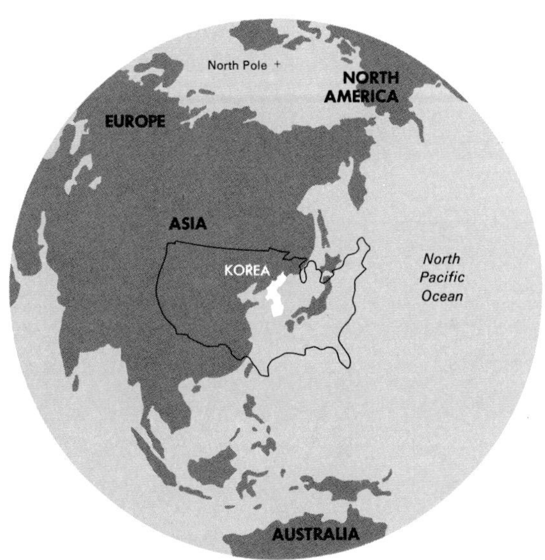

WORLD BOOK map

Korea has an area more than 2 per cent as large as that of the United States, not including Alaska and Hawaii. North Korea is larger than South Korea.

Until the 1950's, Korea's economy was based on agriculture, and the vast majority of the people worked as farmers. Since then, both South and North Korea have made special efforts to develop their industries. As a result, industry has become about as important as agriculture in South Korea and more important than agriculture in North Korea. Only about half the people in both nations now work on farms. Industrial development has helped give South and North Korea two of the world's fastest-growing economies.

Ancestors of the Korean people lived in what is now Korea at least 30,000 years ago. Since ancient times, other nations have often had strong influence on the peninsula. China, for example, controlled part of it from 108 B.C. until the early A.D. 300's, and Japan controlled it from 1910 until the end of World War II in 1945. Korea was a single nation before World War II. But Communists took over the north in 1945, and the present two nations were formed in 1948.

North Korean troops invaded South Korea in 1950. This action started the Korean War, which was part of the Cold War struggle between Communist and non-Communist nations. Non-Communist United Nations countries—chiefly the United States—supported South Korea. China and Russia, two Communist nations, aided North Korea. The war ended in 1953. But neither side won complete victory, and a permanent peace treaty has never been signed. For detailed information about the war, see the KOREAN WAR article in WORLD BOOK.

Korea has remained divided since the Korean War, and small-scale fighting between the South and North has taken place from time to time. In 1972, however, the two nations agreed to begin working together to make Korea one country again.

Ministry of Culture and Information, Seoul, Korea

Buddhism has long been important in Korea. But today, the Communist North Korean government discourages religion. The temple and the huge statue of Buddha above are in South Korea.

FACTS IN BRIEF

SOUTH KOREA

Capital: Seoul.

Official Language: Korean.

Official Name: *Taihan Minkuk* (Republic of Korea).

Form of Government: Republic.

Head of Government: President.

Area: 38,022 square miles, including islands and excluding the 487-square-mile demilitarized zone. *Greatest Distances*—(north-south) 300 miles; (east-west) 185 miles. *Coastline*—819 miles.

Elevation: *Highest*—Halla-san (Halla Peak), 6,398 feet above sea level; *Lowest*—sea level.

Population: *1970 Census*—31,469,132; distribution, 62 per cent rural, 38 per cent urban. *Estimated 1973 Population*—34,130,000; density, 898 persons to the square mile. *Estimated 1978 Population*—38,430,000.

Chief Products: *Agriculture*—barley, beans, potatoes, rice, wheat. *Manufacturing*—chemicals, machinery, processed foods, textiles. *Mining*—anthracite, fluorite, graphite, iron ore, salt, tungsten. *Fishing*—shellfish and many kinds of salt-water fish, including anchovy and herring.

National Anthem: "Aegug-ka" ("National Anthem").

Money: *Basic Unit*—won. For its value in dollars, see MONEY (table: Values).

NORTH KOREA

Capital: Pyongyang.

Official Language: Korean.

Official Name: *Choson Minju Chui Inmin Kong Hwa Kuk* (Democratic People's Republic of Korea).

Form of Government: Communist dictatorship.

Head of Government: Premier.

Area: 46,540 square miles, including islands and excluding the 487-square-mile demilitarized zone. *Greatest Distances*—(north-south) 370 miles; (east-west) 320 miles. *Coastline*—665 miles.

Elevation: *Highest*—Paektu-san (Paektu Peak), 9,003 feet above sea level; *Lowest*—sea level.

Population: No census figures available. *Estimated 1973 Population*—15,100,000; distribution, 62 per cent rural, 38 per cent urban; density, 324 persons to the square mile. *Estimated 1978 Population*—17,320,000.

Chief Products: *Agriculture*—barley, corn, millet, rice, wheat. *Manufacturing*—chemicals, iron and steel, machinery, processed foods, textiles. *Mining*—graphite, magnesium, tungsten. *Fishing*—shellfish and many kinds of salt-water fish, including anchovy and herring.

National Anthem: no official anthem. "Aegug-ka" ("National Anthem") used as unofficial national anthem.

Money: *Basic Unit*—won.

South Korea is a republic. Its Constitution, adopted in 1948, calls for the election of national government leaders by the people. The Constitution guarantees such rights as freedom of the press and religion. But the government has sometimes limited certain freedoms, such as freedom of the press, to prevent criticism of its policies. Government leaders have said that too much criticism might weaken the government and reduce its ability to guard against attack by North Korea.

National Government. The president of South Korea serves as both head of state and head of the government. The people elect him to a four-year term, and he may be re-elected twice. The president appoints the 10 to 20 members of the State Council. Council members serve as heads of the various government departments and as the president's chief advisers.

South Korea has a one-house legislature called the National Assembly. It must have between 150 and 250 members. Assemblymen are elected to four-year terms.

Local Government. South Korea has nine provinces and two special cities—Pusan and Seoul—that have the rank of province. Each province is divided into two kinds of smaller government units—(1) cities with more than 50,000 persons and (2) counties. The national government appoints the mayors, provincial governors, and other high-ranking local officials. These officials appoint all other local officials.

Courts. The Supreme Court, South Korea's highest court, consists of a chief justice and up to 15 other justices. The president appoints all members of the court. South Korea has 3 appeals courts and 10 district courts. The appeals courts rule on appeals of district court decisions.

Politics. The Democratic Republican Party (DRP) is by far the strongest political party in South Korea. DRP members hold most National Assembly seats and most other national government offices. As a result, the party controls the National Assembly and the appointment of national and local government officials. The main opposition party is the New Democratic Party.

Armed Forces. South Korea maintains one of the world's largest armies—about 540,000 men. The South built up this huge force during the 1950's and 1960's, because of the threat of conflict with North Korea. South Korea also has a navy of about 20,000 men and an air force of about 30,000. The government may draft men 18 to 31 years of age for $2\frac{1}{2}$ years of military service.

North Korea calls itself a republic, and its Constitution, adopted in 1948, gives political power to the people. But the country's Communist Party, called the Korean Workers' Party, holds the real political power. Only about 12 per cent of the people belong to it. Even so, the party makes the country's laws and chooses all candidates for elections. All persons appointed to public office must have the party's approval. The Constitution guarantees such rights as freedom of the press, religion, and speech. But the Communists limit these freedoms to ensure their control of the country.

National Government of North Korea is headed by a premier. The North's most powerful government body is the Presidium, which includes the premier. It varies in size, but usually has fewer than 30 members. North Korea's legislature, called the Supreme People's Assembly, goes through the steps of electing the Presidium members. But these officials, who are all high-ranking members of the Communist Party, really hold office because of their positions in the party.

The legislature has 457 members, elected by the people to four-year terms. According to the Constitution, it is North Korea's highest government authority. But the legislature has little power. It meets only one or two weeks a year and functions according to the wishes of the Communist Party.

Local Government. North Korea has nine provinces and one special city, Pyongyang, that has the rank of province. Smaller political divisions include cities, counties, towns, villages, and workers' settlements. The people of each division elect a people's assembly that directs the local government.

Courts. The Supreme Court is North Korea's highest court. Its justices are chosen by the Communist Party and elected by the Supreme People's Assembly. Other courts include provincial courts and people's courts.

Armed Forces of North Korea consist of a 360,000-member army, an air force of about 30,000 members, a navy of about 10,000, and local militia forces with about 1,000,000 members. Militia members serve part time. The government may draft men and women 20 to 25 years old for military service. The women serve as clerks, nurses, or telephone operators. Members of the army must serve $3\frac{1}{2}$ years. The air force and navy require 4 years of service.

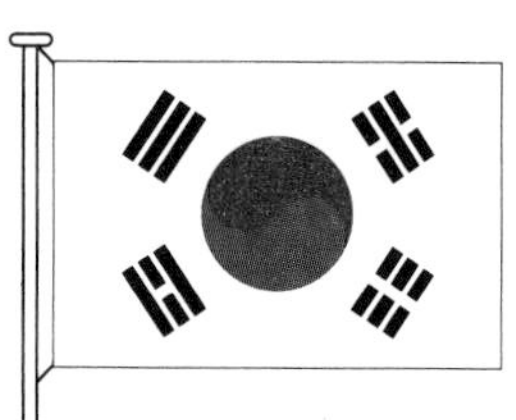

Symbols of South Korea. The South's flag and coat of arms feature a red and blue circle. This ancient Asian symbol represents the balance in the universe between opposites—such as night and day, and life and death. The flag was adopted in 1948.

Symbols of North Korea. The North's flag and coat of arms have a red star that represents Communism. Rice and an electric power plant on the coat of arms stand for the importance of agriculture and industry to the North. The flag was adopted in 1948.

The earliest ancestors of the Korean people settled in what is now Korea at least 30,000 years ago. They came from regions to the north and northwest, but no one knows exactly when this movement began.

The Koreans resemble the Chinese and the Japanese. Most Koreans have broad faces, straight black hair, olive-brown skin, and dark eyes that appear to be slanted because of an inner eyelid fold. These people make up almost the entire population of Korea. Even the largest minority group in Korea, the Chinese, includes fewer than 50,000 persons.

Population. In 1973, South Korea had a population of more than 34 million, and North Korea had more than 15 million persons. About a third of the people in both nations lived in cities or towns.

Nineteen South Korean cities have populations of more than 100,000. The largest city is Seoul, with about $5\frac{1}{2}$ million persons. Ten cities in North Korea have more than 100,000 persons. Pyongyang, with about $2\frac{1}{2}$ million persons, is the largest city. See the separate articles on Korean cities listed in the *Related Articles* at the end of this article.

Way of Life. Before the 1900's, Korea was an agricultural society built on strong family ties. Almost all the people lived in small villages and worked on farms. A person owed his loyalty to his family. The family's interest was more important than that of the individual or the nation. In many cases, grandparents, parents, their sons and unmarried daughters, and the sons' wives and children all lived together. This arrangement is called an *extended family*. The oldest male served as the head of the family, and all persons were expected to obey their elders without question.

The Korean way of life began to change after Japan seized control of the country in 1910. The Japanese brought industry to Korean cities and took much farmland away from the farmers. As a result, many young Koreans moved to the cities to work. This movement weakened Korea's strong family ties.

The Korean way of life changed more than ever following World War II. The Communists brought about great changes in North Korea. They taught many people to hold the interests of the nation above those of the family. They encouraged women to take jobs and work as the equals of men, and they established centers to care for children while their mothers worked. These developments further weakened family ties. In addition, the Communists took complete control of the economy, changing the North into an industrial society.

Life in South Korea has also changed since World War II. The South's economic and political ties with Western nations have brought South Koreans under the influence of Western customs. For example, Western clothing has become common in South Korea. Family ties in the South have weakened as young people continue to move to cities. But the South Korean government, unlike that of the North, has not tried to force changes, and so traditions remain stronger in the South than in the North.

Clothing. Western clothing styles have become popular in South Korea, especially in the cities. But most people in rural areas and some in the cities still wear traditional styles. Most traditional clothing is made of cotton material, which is quilted to make it warm. Traditional clothing for women consists of a long, full skirt that hangs to below the knees and a tight-fitting jacket worn under a looser, long-sleeved jacket. The men wear loose-fitting trousers and jackets.

Many North Koreans also still wear traditional styles. But most of them have plain, uniformlike clothing.

John Launois, Black Star

A Mealtime Scene in rural South Korea, *left*, illustrates Korean customs. One custom calls for people to remove their shoes before entering a home, as these people have done. Following another custom, the people sit on the floor while eating. This group, which includes three brothers, their mother, and their wives and children, has gathered for supper on the porch of the oldest brother's home.

Milt & Joan Mann, Van Cleve Photography

A South Korean Farm Village includes a cluster of small, simple houses between a rice field and the sea. Many Koreans who live near the sea earn a living from both farming and fishing.

Carl Purcell

Education in Korea is available to almost all children. Most Koreans today receive at least an elementary education. The boys shown above attend a South Korean elementary school.

These people either buy their clothes at state-owned stores or receive clothing free from the government. Many people in the cities wear Western styles.

Housing. Many high-rise apartment buildings and modern houses have been built in Seoul and other large South Korean cities. But most of the housing in the South, especially in rural areas, consists of traditional one-story houses made of stones or homemade bricks. Most of these houses have thatch roofs and stone floors and include a living room, a kitchen, and a bedroom. They are heated by a method called *ondol,* in which pipes under the floor carry hot air from an indoor fireplace. Most urban homes in South Korea have electricity. More than half of the rural homes do not. Most homes in both South and North Korea have little furniture. The people usually sit on cushions on the floor.

Before the division of Korea, most houses in the north were the same style as those in the south. The Communists claim that most such houses in rural areas have been replaced by brick houses with tile or slate roofs. Most North Koreans in cities live in one- or two-room apartments built since the division. Few city people other than high-ranking government officials have houses. Almost all homes in the North have electricity.

Food. Rice is the basic food of most Koreans. Other common foods include barley; fish; such fruits as apples, peaches, and pears; and such vegetables as beans and potatoes. One of the most popular dishes other than rice is *kimchi,* a highly spiced mixture of cabbage, onions, turnips, and several other vegetables. Meat and dairy products are scarce in Korea.

Language. Korean is the official language of South Korea and North Korea. About half of all Korean words come from Chinese. But the structure of Korean resembles that of Japanese. There are about seven major *dialects* (local forms) of Korean. Most Koreans can understand all the dialects except the one spoken on Cheju, a Korean island south of the peninsula.

The Korean alphabet, called *hangul,* has 24 letters. South Koreans use some Chinese symbols in addition to hangul in their writing. North Koreans use only hangul.

Education. Since the late 1940's, South Korea and North Korea have made special efforts to improve their educational systems. As a result, the percentage of Koreans who can read and write increased from less than 50 per cent in the mid-1940's to more than 90 per cent in the early 1970's.

South Korea. South Korean law requires that all children complete elementary school, which in that country goes through grade 6. Parents must pay some of the costs of their children's education. But in spite of this expense, more than 90 per cent of the children finish sixth grade.

After completing elementary school, a South Korean student may go on to middle school (grades 7 through 9) and then to high school (grades 10 through 12). The cost of education increases after elementary school, but about 70 per cent of the elementary school graduates continue their schooling. Technical training, which prepares students for industrial jobs, begins in the middle schools and continues through all higher levels of education.

Qualified high school graduates may enter one of South Korea's more than 200 college-level schools. These schools provide training in a wide variety of subjects. But the government limits the number of students enrolled in nontechnical courses after high school.

The South Korean government offers special classes

for adults who cannot read and write. In addition, student volunteers spend summer vacations in rural areas teaching villagers to read and write.

North Korea. The North Korean government requires children to attend school for at least nine years. The state pays all educational expenses. Students must work for the state two months each summer beginning after their fifth year of school.

In North Korea, elementary school consists of grades 1 through 4, and middle school consists of grades 5 through 9. Students must have the approval of the Communist Party to continue their education after middle school. Those who continue attend a two-year high school, a two-year general vocational school, or a three- or four-year technical school that provides training for engineering and scientific jobs. Students who complete high school or technical school may go on to college immediately. Vocational school graduates must complete a year of special study to prepare for college.

North Korea has one university—Ilsung Kim University in Pyongyang—and more than 100 specialized colleges. Each college offers training in one area of study, such as agriculture, engineering, medicine, or teaching. The government provides night schools for adults, training schools in factories, and courses for workers to take by mail.

Religion. The government of South Korea permits complete freedom of religion. The North Korean government discourages religion because it conflicts with the teachings of Communism.

Confucianism, which is more a philosophy than a religion, traditionally has been the most widely followed set of beliefs in Korea. It stresses the duties that people have toward one another. Today, most South Koreans —no matter which religion they follow—believe in at least some of the teachings of Confucianism. For example, most families in the South follow the Confucian practice of honoring their ancestors in special ceremonies. Of the South Koreans who follow a religion, about 7,100,000 are Buddhists, about 3,200,000 are Protestants, and about 800,000 are Roman Catholics. See BUDDHISM; CONFUCIANISM.

The Arts. Early Korean art developed under the influence of both Chinese art and the teachings of Buddhism and Confucianism. Popular themes included love of nature, respect for learning, and loyalty to the king. The most widely practiced art forms included music, poetry, pottery, sculpture, and wall painting.

In North Korea today, the government controls the work of artists. The government prohibits works of art that conflict with Communist principles. It encourages artists to show support in their work for the policies of the Communist Party.

South Korean artists enjoy greater freedom. But the government sometimes prohibits publication or display of art that criticizes its policies. In South Korea, artists work with both the traditional themes and such modern subjects as the Korean War and political and social changes since the war. Western art has influenced all forms of South Korean art. This influence appears especially in the rapid development of Western forms of drama and of motion pictures since 1945. Motion pictures now rank as the most popular form of entertainment in South Korea.

Ministry of Culture and Information, Seoul, Korea

Traditional Korean Music included special royal ceremonial music. Today, this music is performed for entertainment in South Korea by members of the National Classical Music Institute, shown above. These musicians play copies of instruments used hundreds of years ago.

Specially created for **World Book Encyclopedia** by Rand McNally and World Book editors

KOREA / *The Land*

The Korean Peninsula extends southward from northeastern China. It is about 670 miles long and, at its widest point, about 320 miles wide. Korea's coastline measures 1,484 miles. More than 3,000 islands, which are part of Korea, lie off the southern and western coasts of the peninsula. The peninsula and the islands cover a total area of 85,049 square miles. The Sea of Japan, east of the peninsula, separates Korea from Japan. The Yellow Sea lies west of Korea, and the Korea Strait lies to the south.

Korea has six main land regions. They are (1) the Northwestern Plain, (2) the Northern Mountains, (3) the Eastern Coastal Lowland, (4) the Central Mountains, (5) the Southern Plain, and (6) the Southwestern Plain.

The Northwestern Plain stretches along the entire western coast of North Korea. Rolling hills divide the region into a series of broad, level plains. The Northwestern Plain has most of North Korea's farmland. The nation's major industrial areas, including Pyongyang, are also there. About half the North Korean people live in the region.

The Northern Mountains region, east of the Northwestern Plain, covers almost all of central North Korea. Forested mountains make up most of the region. These mountains are an important source of valuable minerals and forest products.

Korea's highest mountain, Paektu-san (Paektu Peak), is in the Northern Mountains. It rises 9,003 feet on the border between North Korea and China. The 490-mile-long Yalu, North Korea's longest river, flows westward from this mountain along the border all the way to the

LAND REGIONS OF KOREA

The map below shows the six land regions of Korea: the Eastern Coastal Lowland; the Northern and Central mountains; and the Northwestern, Southwestern, and Southern plains.

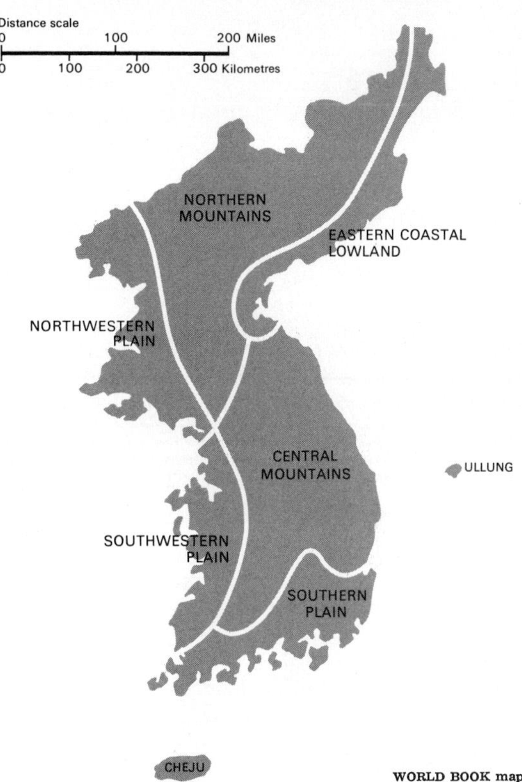

WORLD BOOK map

KOREA MAP INDEX

Cities of South Korea

Andong ....76,434..D 4
Angang* ...32,985..E 4
Ansong* ...25,788..D 3
Anyang ....91,876..D 3
Changhang* 25,547..D 3
Changhung .28,976..E 3
Changnyong* 23,302..E 4
Changsong 103,312..D 4
Changsong* 25,782..E 3
Chechon ...62,249..D 4
Cheju ....106,456..F 3
Chinhae ...91,947..E 4
Chinju ....121,622..E 4
Chochiwon .27,996..D 3
Chomchon ..37,366..D 4
Chonan ....78,316..D 3
Chongdo ...26,349..E 4
Chongju ...143,944..D 3
Chongup ...49,667..E 3
Chonju ...262,816..E 3
Chumunjin .35,734..D 4
Chunchon .122,672..D 3
Chungju ...87,727..D 3
Chungmu ..54,974..E 4
Chungpyong* 24,093..D 3
Haenan* ...24,756..E 3
Hallim* ...23,500..F 3
Hampyong* 22,830..E 3
Hamyang ..26,110..E 3
Hongsong* .23,814..D 3
Hwasun* ..23,592..E 3
Inchon ...646,013..D 3
Iri ....86,770..E 3
Kanggyong .25,683..D 3
Kangjin* ..23,852..E 3
Kangnung .74,489..D 4
Kimchon ...62,157..D 4
Kimhae ....45,863..E 4
Kimje .....35,023..E 3
Kochang ...36,766..E 3
Kochang* ..23,061..E 3
Kongju ....33,210..D 3
Kosong* ...25,652..E 4
Kumsan* ..26,014..D 3
Kunsan ...112,453..E 3
Kuryongpo .30,988..E 4
Kwangchon* 23,680..D 3
Kwangju .502,753..E 3
Kwangyang 27,565..E 3
Kyongju ...92,093..E 4
Kyongsan* .25,556..E 4
Masan ....190,992..E 4
Miryang ...42,165..E 4
Mokpo ....177,801..E 3
Mukho .....56,404..D 4
Naju ......29,615..E 3
Namwon ...46,532..E 3
Nonsan ....32,736..D 3
Okchon* ...23,090..D 3
Onyang ....31,829..D 3
Pohang ....79,451..D 4
Polgyo .....42,310..E 3
Puan ......26,552..E 3
Pukpyong ..37,796..D 4
Pusan ...1,880,710..E 4
Puyo* .....26,047..D 3
Pyongtaek ..41,697..D 3
Samchok ...38,815..D 4
Samchonpo .54,945..E 4
Samnye ....23,216..E 3
Sangju ....52,504..D 4
Seoul ...5,536,377..D 3
Sintaein ...22,038..E 3
Sogwi ......43,404..F 3
Sokcho ....73,096..C 4
Songjong ..37,770..E 3
Songtan ...51,595..D 3
Sosan .....32,428..D 3
Sunchon ...90,910..E 3
Suwon ....170,518..D 3
Taechon ...33,437..D 3
Taegu ..1,082,750..E 4
Taejon ...414,598..D 3
Togye ......38,883..D 4
Tongduchon 60,245..D 3
Uijongbu ..94,518..D 3
Uisong* ....24,827..D 4
Ulsan .....159,340..E 4
Waegwan ...30,871..E 4
Wissosa ....56,534..D 3
Wonju ....111,972..D 3
Yechon ....27,003..D 4
Yesan .....34,172..D 3
Yongchon ..49,630..E 4
Yongdong ..26,905..D 3
Yongju .....58,527..D 4
Yongsanpo .28,062..E 3
Yongwol* ..29,693..D 4
Yonmu ....36,194..D 3
Yosu .....113,651..E 3

Cities of North Korea

Anak ......35,000..C 2
Anju ......40,000..C 2
Aoji ....90,000..A 5
Chaeryong ..45,000..C 2
Chongjin ..400,000..B 4
Chongju ...50,000..C 2
Chongsong* 50,000..A 4
Haeju ....131,000..C 2
Hamhung .525,000..C 3
Hoeryong ..45,000..A 4
Hongwon ..45,000..B 3
Hwangju ...31,000..C 2
Hyesan ....65,000..B 4
Kaechon ...52,000..C 2
Kaesong ..400,000..D 3
Kanggye ...90,000..B 3
Kangso* ...30,000..C 2
Kilchu ....55,000..B 4
Kimchaek .281,000..B 4
Kowon* ...75,000..C 3
Kujang* ...30,000..C 3
Kumchon* .30,000..C 3
Kusong* ...35,000..C 2
Kyongsong .45,000..B 4
Maengsan* .30,000..C 3
Manpo ....85,000..B 3
Mundok* ..30,000..C 2
Musan .....60,000..A 4
Najin ......70,000..A 5
Nampo ...165,000..C 2
Ongjin .....45,000..D 2
Onsong* ...75,000..A 4
Oro* ....35,000..B 3
Pakchon ...34,000..C 2
Panmunjom ....D 3
Pukchang ..35,000..C 3
Pukchong ..45,000..B 4
Pyongsan* ..40,000..C 3
Pyong-
yang ..2,500,000..C 2
Sakchu* ...40,000..B 2
Sariwon ...130,000..C 2
Sinanju ....50,000..C 2
Sinpo ......85,000..B 4
Sinuiju ...500,000..B 2
Songnim ...96,000..C 2
Sunchon ...48,000..C 2
Taechon* ...50,000..C 2
Tanchon ...60,000..B 4
Tokchon ...35,000..C 3
Uiju ......35,000..B 2
Unggi .....35,000..A 5
Unsan* ....25,000..C 3
Wonsan ...350,000..C 3
Yomju* ....30,000..C 2
Yonan .....35,000..D 3
Yongampo ..35,000..C 2
Yongbyon* .30,000..C 2
Yonggang* .30,000..C 2
Yonghung ..46,000..C 3

Physical Features

Changjin River .....B 3
Cheju (Island) .....F 3
Chii-san (Peak) ....E 3
Halla-san (Peak) ..F 3
Han River ....D 3
Hong (Island) .....E 2
Kanghwa Bay ......D 2
Koje (Island) ......E 4
Korea Bay ....C 2
Korea Strait ....F 4
Kwanmo
(Mountain) ......B 4
Naktong River .....E 4
Oeyon (Island) ....D 2
Paengnyong
(Island) ....D 2
Puksubaek-san
(Peak) ....B 3
Sinmi (Island) ....C 2
Sohuksan (Island) ..E 2
Tokchok (Island) ..D 2
Tolsan (Island) ....E 3
Tongjoson Bay .....C 3
Tumen River ....A 4
Ullung (Island) ...D 5
Yalu River ....B 3
Yellow Sea ....D 2
Yongil Bay ....D 4

*Does not appear on map; key shows general location.

Sources: North Korea—contributor's estimates (1971).
South Korea—latest census figures (1970).

SE Hedin-Bild

The Southern Plain, which extends along the southern coast of South Korea, is an important agricultural region. It consists of a series of plains separated by low hills and has the mildest weather in Korea. Nearly a fourth of the South Korean people live in this region.

Yellow Sea. The 325-mile-long Tumen River forms the border eastward from Paektu-san to the Sea of Japan. Almost a fourth of North Korea's people live in the Northern Mountains region.

The Eastern Coastal Lowland covers almost all of North Korea's east coast. This strip of land between the Northern Mountains region and the Sea of Japan consists of a series of narrow plains separated by low hills. The plains provide much farmland, and the sea makes fishing important in the region. The Eastern Coastal Lowland also has some industrial areas. More than a fourth of North Korea's people live in this small but heavily populated region.

The Central Mountains region extends throughout most of central and eastern South Korea and into a small part of southern North Korea. Forested mountains cover most of this region, including much of the seacoast. River valleys, hillsides, and some land along the coast are used for farming. The coastal waters yield large amounts of fish. More than a fourth of the South Korean people live in the Central Mountains region.

The Southern Plain covers the entire southern coast of South Korea. This important agricultural region consists of a series of plains separated by low hills. Pusan, an important industrial center of South Korea, is located in the region. The 325-mile-long Naktong River, the longest river in South Korea, flows through the Southern Plain from mountains in the north to the Korea Strait. Almost a fourth of the South Korean people live in the region.

The Southwestern Plain extends along almost the entire western coast of South Korea. Like most of the rest of coastal Korea, this region consists of rolling hills and plains and is a farming center. It also includes the South's major industrial area, around Seoul. The 290-mile-long Han River flows through the region from mountains in the east to the Yellow Sea. About half of South Korea's people live in the region.

Islands. Korea has more than 3,000 islands. People live on the larger ones. Cheju Island, about 50 miles south of the peninsula, is the largest Korean island. It covers about 700 square miles. Cheju has its own provincial government. The other islands are governed by provinces on the mainland. South Korea's highest mountain, Halla-san (Halla Peak), rises 6,398 feet on Cheju Island.

KOREA / *Climate*

Seasonal winds called *monsoons* affect Korea's weather throughout the year. A monsoon blows in from the south and southeast during the summer, bringing hot, humid weather. A cold, dry monsoon blows in from the north and northwest during the winter, bringing cold weather to the peninsula.

Summer weather varies little throughout Korea. July temperatures average between 70° F. (21° C.) and 80° F. (27° C.). Korea's massive mountains protect the peninsula's east coast from the winter monsoon. As a result, the east coast generally has warmer winters than does the rest of Korea. Average January temperatures range from about 35° F. (2° C.) in southeastern Korea to about −5° F. (−21° C.) in parts of the Northern Mountains region.

Most of South Korea receives from 30 to 50 inches of *precipitation* (rain, melted snow, and other forms of moisture) yearly. Precipitation averages between 30 and 60 inches a year in most of North Korea. Heavy rainfall from June through August accounts for about half of Korea's yearly precipitation. In most years, one or two typhoons hit the peninsula during July and August.

Ever since the Korean War ended in 1953, the economies of South and North Korea have been among the fastest growing in the world. This growth has resulted chiefly from industrial development. Before the war, the economy of each country depended chiefly on agriculture. Today, agriculture and industry have about equal importance in South Korea, and the North is primarily an industrial nation.

South Korea

The value of goods and services produced each year in South Korea totals nearly $9 billion. This total value is the country's *gross national product* (GNP). Agricultural and industrial production each account for about 30 per cent of South Korea's GNP. The remaining 40 per cent comes from such service activities as communication, government, trade, and transportation. Agriculture employs about 50 per cent of all South Korean workers, industry about 20 per cent, and service activities about 30 per cent.

South Korea has only a small part of the peninsula's mineral resources—chiefly *anthracite* (hard coal), fluorite, graphite, iron ore, salt, and tungsten. In addition, the peninsula's best rivers for producing hydroelectric power are in North Korea. As a result, the South had few power plants and little industry when Korea was divided in 1948. Since then, South Korea has built more than 20 electric power plants and has made much progress in developing its industries.

Industry. Almost all South Korean industry is privately owned. Manufacturing accounts for more than 75 per cent of the South's industrial production. Construction accounts for about 20 per cent and mining for about $3\frac{1}{2}$ per cent. South Korea has more than 24,000 manufacturing firms. Most of them are in the Seoul and Pusan areas. The chief manufactured products are chemicals, machinery, processed foods, and textiles.

Agriculture. South Korea has about $2\frac{1}{2}$ million farms. They average about $2\frac{1}{4}$ acres in size. Almost all the farmland is privately owned, and the farmers do most of their work by hand. Rice is by far the country's chief crop. Other important farm products include barley, beans, potatoes, and wheat. The South's major agricultural areas lie along the western and southern coasts. Many people who live on the coasts are fishermen, and many farmers work part time as fishermen.

Foreign Trade. South Korea trades chiefly with the United States and Asian nations, especially Japan. The South's chief exports include clothing, electronic devices, fish, raw silk, textiles, and tungsten. Its main imports include chemicals, crude oil and other industrial raw materials, machinery, and motor vehicles.

Transportation. South Korea's rapidly growing highway system carries most of the country's passenger traffic. The South has more than 23,000 miles of roads. Most South Koreans do not own an automobile, but buses run between and within almost all cities. Many people use bicycles for short trips. The government-owned Korean National Railroad carries most of the freight transported in South Korea. The South has more than 3,200 miles of railroad track. Korean Air Lines, which is privately owned, connects major South Korean cities with Hong Kong, Japan, South Vietnam, Taiwan, Thailand, and the United States.

Communication. Four privately owned radio networks and one government-owned network serve South Korea. Most families own at least one radio. In rural areas that have no electricity, people use battery-powered transistor radios. Three television networks, one owned by the government and two privately owned, operate in South Korea. Television broadcasts reach most parts of the country, but there is only about one TV set for every 40 persons in the South. South Korean cities have public telephone service, but most rural areas

Ministry of Culture and Information, Seoul, Korea

Jan Lönn from Carl Östman

Industry has developed rapidly in both South and North Korea since the early 1950's. Production from industrial plants—such as the South Korean oil refinery, *left,* and the North Korean steel mill, *right*—has helped the economies of these two countries rank among the fastest growing in the world.

do not. About 40 daily newspapers are published in South Korea, about 15 of them in Seoul.

North Korea

North Korea's GNP totals between $3 billion and $4 billion yearly. Industrial production accounts for about 70 per cent of the GNP, agricultural production for about 20 per cent, and service activities for about 10 per cent. Industry employs about 35 per cent of North Korea's workers, agriculture about 50 per cent, and service activities about 15 per cent.

North Korea traditionally has been the chief industrial region of the peninsula. It has rivers suitable for producing electric power, as well as some of the richest mineral deposits in eastern Asia. North Korea ranks among the top five nations of the world in the production of graphite, magnesium, and tungsten.

Industry. Manufacturing accounts for about 80 per cent of North Korea's industrial production, construction for nearly 15 per cent, and mining for over 5 per cent. The North's chief manufactured products are chemicals, iron and steel, machinery, processed foods, and textiles. These and all other major products are made in government-owned factories. Some minor industries, such as handicrafts, may be privately owned. Most manufacturing takes place in the coastal regions.

Agriculture. The Communists have organized all farmland in North Korea into government-owned *collective farms*. The government operates the collectives, and the workers receive a share of the products and some cash payment. North Korea has about 3,700 collective farms. About 300 families live on each one. The North's major agricultural region is the Northwestern Plain.

Rice is by far North Korea's chief crop. Other important farm products include barley, corn, millet, and wheat. Many farmers use tractors and other farm equipment for most heavy work.

Foreign Trade. North Korea carries on about 90 per cent of its foreign trade with Communist nations, especially China and Russia. North Korea's leading exports are minerals, chiefly copper, iron ore, lead, tungsten, and zinc. The North also exports food products and machinery. North Korea's major imports are crude oil, fuels, machinery, rubber, and wheat.

Transportation. Railroads carry most of North Korea's freight and passenger traffic. The North has about 3,000 miles of railroad track and more than 12,000 miles of roads. Buses operate in the cities and for short distances in rural areas. Few North Koreans own an automobile. Many people in the cities ride bicycles. North Korea's airline is used chiefly for government business. The state controls the entire transportation system.

Communication. The government controls all broadcasting, publishing, and other means of communication in North Korea. It runs the nation's only radio network, which has stations in every province. Few families own a radio, but almost every home has a loudspeaker that receives radiobroadcasts. Limited television broadcasting has begun in Pyongyang, but nowhere else in the country. North Korean cities have public telephone service, but most rural areas do not. About 30 daily newspapers are published in North Korea.

KOREA / *History*

Early Years. Scientists have found evidence that people lived in the southwestern part of the Korean Peninsula about 30,000 years ago. But little is known about prehistoric times in what is now Korea. In 108 B.C., China conquered the northern half of the peninsula and established four territories there. Korean tribes won back three of the territories by 75 B.C. The other territory, called Lolang, remained under Chinese control.

Lolang covered the northwestern part of the peninsula. Through contact with Lolang, the Koreans adopted many Chinese arts and sciences and much of the Chinese system of government. This strong Chinese influence in Korea continued until the 1890's.

During the A.D. 100's, several Korean tribes united and formed the state of Koguryo in the northeastern part of the peninsula. Two other Korean states—Paekche in the southwest and Silla in the southeast—were formed during the late 200's. Historians call Koguryo, Paekche, and Silla the *Three Kingdoms*.

In 313, Koguryo conquered Lolang and took control of the northern half of Korea. Koguryo developed close relations with China. Buddhism, which the Koreans learned about from the Chinese, became the chief religion of the Three Kingdoms during the 300's and 400's.

Silla conquered Paekche and Koguryo in the 660's and thus took control of the entire peninsula. Korean art and learning flourished during the next 200 years. Silla's rulers had close ties with China. Confucianism was introduced into Silla from China and became a strong influence on Korean thought and behavior.

In the 800's, Silla broke apart as provincial warlords fought to control it. But by 936, a general named Wang Kon had reunited Silla. He renamed the country *Koryo*. The word *Korea* came from the word *Koryo*.

The government of Koryo worked to improve education in the country. It built schools and encouraged the development of printing to make books available to more people. The Koreans invented the first movable metal printing type in 1234.

Mongol tribes from the north repeatedly attacked Koryo from the early 1200's until they conquered it in 1259. Koryo regained its freedom in 1368. Two groups in the country then fought for control until 1388, when a general named Yi Songgye led one group to victory.

The Yi Dynasty. General Yi became king of Koryo in 1392 and renamed the country *Choson*. The Koreans

IMPORTANT DATES IN KOREA

108 B.C. China conquered the northern half of Korea.

A.D. 313 Korean forces drove the Chinese from Korea.

1259 Mongol armies conquered the Koreans.

1368 The Koreans freed themselves of Mongol rule.

1392 General Yi founded the Yi dynasty. It lasted until 1910.

1630's Manchu armies conquered Korea.

1910 Japan took control of Korea.

1945 Russian forces occupied northern Korea, and U.S. forces occupied southern Korea after World War II.

1948 Korea was divided into two nations.

1950-1953 South Korea fought North Korea in the Korean War.

1972 South Korea and North Korea agreed to begin working for the reunification of Korea.

used this name for their country until the 1940's.

Yi founded a *dynasty* (line of rulers of the same family) that lasted until the early 1900's. Yi ended the government's official support of Buddhism, which had existed since the 700's. Buddhism declined in importance and did not become popular in Korea again until the 1900's.

Yi and the rulers who followed him reunited Korea. But during the 1500's, government officials and wealthy landowners began to struggle for political power. This struggle weakened Korea's government.

Japanese forces invaded Korea in the 1590's but were driven out. Manchu armies from China conquered Korea in the 1630's. The Manchus received *tribute* (payments) from the Koreans until the late 1800's, but members of the Yi family continued as kings.

Beginning in the 1600's, Korea's rulers closed the country to all foreigners for almost 200 years. Roman Catholic missionaries from Europe first entered Korea during the 1830's. But the Korean authorities persecuted the missionaries and killed thousands of Koreans who had become Catholics. Korea was called the *Hermit Kingdom* during this period because it had little contact with any country except China.

In 1876, Japan forced Korea to open some ports to trade. The United States, Russia, and several European nations signed commercial treaties with Korea during the 1880's. Japan defeated China in the Chinese-Japanese War of 1894-1895, and Japan's influence in Korea became stronger than that of China.

Japanese Rule. In 1910, Japan took complete control of Korea. The Japanese governed Korea chiefly to benefit their own interests. They took over the management of Korean businesses. They also set up many new industries on the peninsula and put them under Japanese control. The Japanese government took much of the land in Korea and sold it to Japanese settlers.

A Divided Nation. Korea remained under Japanese control until 1945, when Japan was defeated in World War II. After Japan's defeat, U.S. troops occupied the

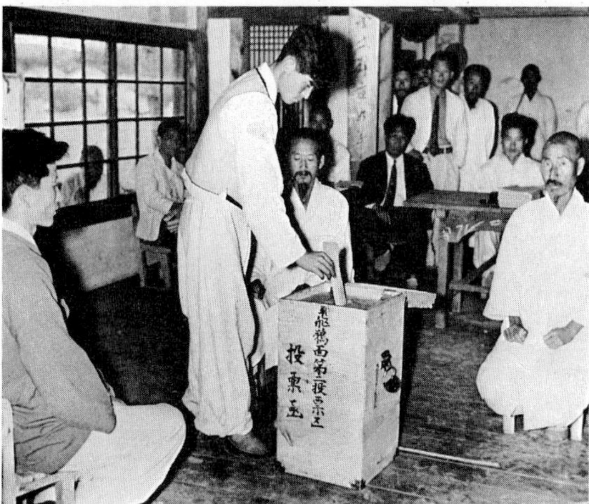

United Nations

The Formation of South and North Korea took place in 1948. A South Korean voter, *above,* casts his ballot during the election of his country's first government.

southern half of Korea, and Russian forces occupied the northern half. A separate Korean government was formed in each half of the country. For two years, the United States, Russia, the two Korean governments, and Britain tried to develop a plan for reuniting Korea. They failed, and the United States submitted the problem to the United Nations (UN) in 1947.

The UN wanted to supervise elections to choose one government for Korea. But the Russians refused to allow UN representatives into the north. In the south, in 1948, UN representatives supervised an election of representatives to a national assembly. The assembly drew up a constitution. In July, 1948, the assembly elected Syngman Rhee president of the Republic of Korea, which was formed on August 15. In northern Korea, the Communists announced formation of the Democratic People's Republic of Korea on September 9. Both governments claimed to represent all of Korea.

In December, 1948, Russia announced that all its troops had left North Korea. The United States withdrew its last troops from South Korea in mid-1949.

North Korean troops invaded the South in June, 1950, and the Korean War began. The fighting continued until a truce was signed in July, 1953. Neither side won complete victory. The war involved not only the two Koreas, but also the most powerful Communist and non-Communist nations. See Korean War.

South Korea. The division of Korea left the South with a weak economy. It had little industry and few electric power plants. The Korean War added to South Korea's economic problems. The fighting ruined farm crops and destroyed many factories.

During the early 1950's, members of the National Assembly became increasingly critical of Rhee for failing to solve the nation's economic problems. Rhee feared the legislators would not re-elect him in 1952. He pushed through the Assembly a constitutional amendment that turned over election of the president to the people. The voters re-elected Rhee by a wide margin, and re-elected him again in 1956. But during the late 1950's, Rhee lost the support of more and more South Koreans, and he began to use increasingly undemocratic methods to keep control of the government.

In March, 1960, Rhee ran for a fourth term. He was unopposed because his opponent died one month before the election. Rhee and his party won. But they had to fix the National Assembly elections to ensure victory in the legislature. During March and April, South Korean students led nationwide demonstrations against the government. Rhee saw that he was rapidly losing political and military support, and he resigned in April.

Elections were held in July, 1960, and a new government took office. South Korea's economic difficulties continued, and the new government weakened as rival groups fought for political power.

In May, 1961, a group of military officers led by General Toyon Chang and General Chung Hee Park overthrew the government. Chang headed the new government until July, 1961, when Park replaced him. In 1963, Park called for nationwide elections to restore democratic rule in South Korea. Park won the election for president, and his Democratic Republican Party won a majority of the seats in the National Assembly.

South Korea's economy developed rapidly under Park's leadership. His government concentrated on developing industries and increasing foreign trade. In 1967, Park and his party won re-election by a large margin. In 1969, the South Korean people approved a constitutional amendment permitting the president to serve three successive terms instead of only two. In 1971, Park again won re-election by a wide margin.

North Korea. At the end of World War II, Ilsung Kim became the chief government leader in northern Korea. He had led resistance to Japanese rule during the 1930's. Kim became premier of North Korea in 1948 and chairman of its Communist Party in 1949. He has headed the government and the party ever since.

In 1946, the North's Communist government took farmland from wealthy landowners and gave it to the farmworkers. It also took control of most banks, industries, and communication and transportation systems. Between 1953 and 1958, the government organized all the country's farmland into collective farms.

In 1954, the government announced the first of a series of plans for economic development. Until the mid-1960's, these plans emphasized industrial development. But agricultural production fell short of the country's needs, and the government had to turn more of its efforts toward increasing farm output.

North-South Relations. In 1967, North Korean forces began to make frequent attacks into the *demilitarized* (neutral) zone between the North and the South and into South Korea itself. In 1968, about 30 North Koreans raided Seoul. They tried to assassinate Park but failed. The amount of small-scale fighting between the North and South increased at about the same time.

North Korea's aggression involved the United States as well as South Korea. In January, 1968, North Korea seized the U.S. intelligence ship *Pueblo* in the Sea of Japan. North Korea claimed the ship had been operating in North Korean waters and accused the *Pueblo's* crew of spying. The United States denied the charges.

Wide World

Western Influence has brought great change to South Korea since the early 1950's. High-rise apartment buildings and Western clothing styles have become common in such cities as Seoul, *above.*

North Korea released the 82 survivors of the 83-man crew in December, 1968, but refused to return the *Pueblo.* In 1969, the North shot down a U.S. Navy plane almost 100 miles off the North Korean coast.

The tense Korean situation became a cause of worldwide concern. But in 1972, the South and North unexpectedly agreed to begin working for the peaceful reunification of Korea. As part of that effort, they agreed to establish friendlier and more cooperative relations with each other.

WILLIAM E. HENTHORN

KOREA / Study Aids

Related Articles in WORLD BOOK include:

Asia (picture: A Fish Market)	Inchon	Russo-Japanese War
	Kaesong	
Chinese-Japanese Wars	Korean War	Seoul
	Panmunjom	Sinuiju
Chongjin	Park, Chung Hee	Taegu
Clothing (picture: Traditional Costumes)	Pusan	Taejon
	Pyongyang	Wonsan
	Rhee, Syngman	Yalu River

Outline

I. Government

II. People
- A. Population
- B. Way of Life
- C. Clothing
- D. Housing
- E. Food
- F. Language
- G. Education
- H. Religion
- I. The Arts

III. The Land
- A. The Northwestern Plain
- B. The Northern Mountains
- C. The Eastern Coastal Lowland
- D. The Central Mountains
- E. The Southern Plain
- F. The Southwestern Plain
- G. Islands

IV. Climate

V. Economy

VI. History

Questions

When was Korea divided into two nations?

When did China control Korea? When did Japan?

What is the chief crop grown in Korea?

What percentage of the workers in Korea are farmers?

What percentage of Koreans can read and write?

Why was Korea once called the *Hermit Kingdom?*

What is the chief difference between the government of South Korea and that of North Korea?

How do monsoons affect the weather in Korea?

What economic disadvantages did the South have after Korea was divided?

How has the Korean way of life changed since 1900?

KOREA STRAIT. See KOREA (The Land); YELLOW SEA.

Section Five

Dictionary Supplement

This section lists important words to be included in the 1973 edition of THE WORLD BOOK DICTIONARY. This dictionary, first published by Field Enterprises Educational Corporation in 1963, keeps abreast of our living language with a program of continuous editorial revision. The following supplement has been prepared under the direction of the editors of THE WORLD BOOK ENCYCLOPEDIA and Clarence L. Barnhart, editor in chief of THE WORLD BOOK DICTIONARY. It is presented as a service to owners of the dictionary and as an informative feature to subscribers of THE WORLD BOOK YEAR BOOK.

A

al·pha·scope (al′fə skōp), *n.* a device connected to a computer on which letters, numerals, and symbols are displayed on a cathode ray tube screen. [< *alpha*numeric (using both letters and numbers) + *-scope*]

Am·trak (am′trak′), *n.* National Railroad Passenger Corporation, a corporation of the United States government created to manage long-distance passenger service of railroads in the United States. [< *Am*(erican) + *Trak* (a phonetic spelling of *track*)]

ap·o·ap·sis (ap′ō ap′sis), *n.* the point in the orbit of a satellite body farthest from the center of the heavenly body around which it is orbiting. [< *apo-* off, away + *apsis*]

B

behavior therapy, *Psychology.* therapy that conditions a patient to break old habits or patterns of behavior and build new ones in their place.

bike·way (bīk′wā′), *n.* a road or path reserved for bicycling.

bi·o·rhythm (bī′ō riᴛʜ′əm), *n.* the cycle of functions or activities of an organ or organism: *Symptoms of biorhythm upset ... are experienced by jet airplane travelers who fly through several time zones in 12 hours or less* (World Book Science Annual).

black hole, 1. a hypothetical hole in outer space into which energy and stars and other heavenly matter collapse and disappear: *If the theory can be believed, the final outcome of this process in nature is a "black hole" in space into which matter can be said to have vanished, leaving, however, all its gravitational effects behind* (Tom Alexander).

body language, the unconscious gestures of the body as a form of communication: *Body language, it's now believed, carries as much information as spoken or written speech—perhaps more* (Barbara Ford).

bum·mer (bum′ər), *n. Slang.* **2.** a bad experience.

C

catalytic converter, a device in automobiles which contains a chemical catalyst to oxidize exhaust gases, converting them into harmless products.

Chi·ca·no (chē kä′nō), *n.* a Mexican American. [< Mexican Spanish (Chihuahua) dialect *Chicano,* alteration of *Mexicano* Mexican]

➤ Some speakers and writers believe that *Chicano* is a derogatory term and avoid using it. However, Mexican Americans apply the name to themselves and do not regard it as unfriendly in any way.

class action, a legal action brought on behalf of all to whom the case applies: *... the right of citizens to bring "class actions" against polluters ...* (New Yorker).

clone (klōn), *n., v.,* **cloned, clon·ing.** —*v.t., v.i.* to reproduce asexually: *Cauliflowers have been cloned ... by cutting slices of cauliflowers ... a single plant can be made to yield many more plants* (New Scientist).

col·lap·sar (kə lap′sär), *n.* black hole.

contact inhibition, *Biology.* cessation of cell division when the surface of one cell comes into contact with the surface of another cell: *No one knows how contact inhibition works. Some investigators have suggested that as the cells touch each other the distribution of electric charge on their surface changes, and that the change serves as a signal and halts growth* (Scientific American).

core city, central city.

D

de·grad·a·ble (di grā′də bəl), *adj.* that can be decomposed or is subject to decomposition, especially by bacterial or chemical agents: *There has been a reduction of residual amounts of synthetic detergent material ... after the complete substitution ... of anionic detergents which are biologically degradable* (Nature).

E

ec·o·cide (ek′ə sīd), *n.* destruction of the suitability of the earth's environment for living things: *The irony of development is that to the extent that it succeeds, the world situation worsens and the dangers of ecocide are increased* (New Scientist).

eu·troph·i·cate (yů trof′ə kāt), *v.i.,* **-cated, -cat·ing.** to accumulate nutrients, especially in lake waters: *The increased growth of vegetation in the water and the proliferation of algae in huge blotches of green slime ... causes lakes to eutrophicate* (New York Times).

eye·wall (ī′wôl′), *n.* a layer of turbulent clouds around the eye, or calm center, of a storm: *Planes flew there to dump their crystals, in hopes of causing supercooled water droplets in the hurricane's eyewall to condense* (Science News).

F

firm·ware (ferm′wãr′), *n.* the components of a computer that are neither hardware nor software, such as devices for storing data used in a computer: *Efforts also were made to transfer some of the functions of software—the programs of instructions to computers—to small, high-speed memories which could operate as "assistants" to computer processing circuitry ... This function, which was given the new label "firmware" ...* (James A. Pearre).

free university, a college or university organized chiefly by students to study subjects of interest to them, usually without tuition or academic credit: *... the so-called "free university," which eliminates the traditional boundaries between students and faculty, one academic discipline and another, the cognitive (knowing) process and the affective (feeling) process* (Time).

G

growth center, a place where encounter groups meet and sensitivity training takes place: *One index of the rapid expansion of encounter groups has been the proliferation of "growth centers"* (Irvin D. Yalom and Samuel Moffat).

H

heat pipe, a pipe containing a fluid that transfers heat through the pipe by a difference in pressures requiring no external pumping.

hinc·ty (hingk′tē), *adj.,* **-ti·er, -ti·est.** *U.S. Slang.* snobbish; conceited: *None of these stores hire colored, but the help are the hinctiest* (Louise Meriwether). [origin unknown]

I

im·mu·no·as·sa y (i myü′nō as′ ā), *n.* analysis of a bodily substance by testing its immunological or antibody-producing reactions.

in·ca·pac·i·tant (in′kə pas′ə tənt), *n.* a chemical agent or drug that temporarily induces sleepiness, dizziness, disorientation, etc.: *One of the standard US incapacitants produces dizziness, heart palpitation, urinary retention and constipation* (New Scientist).

in·ter·mo·dal (in′tər mō′dəl), *adj.* **1.** combining road, rail, water, and air transportation or goods into an integrated system: *Both vessels are part of an intermodal system in which United States Freight uses railroads to "piggyback" trailers and container vans to ports for delivery* (New York Times). **2.** used in such a system of transportation: *intermodal containers.*

J

Jane Crow, *U.S.* discriminating against women: *Men hate an "uppity" woman; they also hate an "aggressive" woman. Ours has been a Jane Crow society for several thousands of years* (Time).

Jesus people, (in the United States) an evangelical, fundamentalist group of chiefly young people who emphasize an intense personal relationship with Jesus Christ: *"Jesus People," part of a nationwide movement of youths who are "turning on to Jesus" and dressing up the old-time religion in hippie garb* (New York Times).

K

knee-jerk (nē′jėrk′), *adj.* reacting in a predictable or automatic manner: *Erwin is hardly a knee-jerk reactionary. Like many a Texas Democrat, he is coldly conservative on some issues, warmly liberal on others* (Time). —*n.* a knee-jerk reactionary.

L

learning curve, a graphic representation showing the progress in acquiring a new skill: *In order to evaluate properly the cost estimates ... the Secretary would have needed a compilation of experience statistics,* *based largely on so-called learning curves* (Atlantic).

li·ku·ta (li kü′tə), *n., pl.* **ma·ku·ta** (mə kü′tə). one hundredth of a zaire, a unit of money in the Republic of Zaire, worth about 2½ cents.

linear-induction motor, an electric motor that produces thrust directly without torque by the movement of the magnetic field which creates a linear impelling force rather than a rotating force: *A linear induction motor is like a regular rotary motor that has been sliced open and laid out flat* (Lowell K. Bridwell).

M

male chauvinism, excessive male pride or exaggerated loyalty to members of the male sex: *Historically hampered by archaic laws and antique moral codes, European women . . . taking a cue from their more combative sisters across the Atlantic, have launched their attack on male chauvinism* (Time).

meth·yl·mer·cu·ry (meth′əl mėr′kyər ē), *n.* a highly toxic compound of mercury widely used in technology and as a pesticide: *Poisoning by methylmercury compounds . . . has been characterized by the permanence and irreversibility of the injury to the nervous system* (New York Times).

mi·cro·e·col·o·gy (mī′krō i kol′ə jē), *n.* the branch of ecology dealing with environmental conditions in very small areas.

mi·cro·pro·gram (mī′krō prō′gram), *n., v.,* **-gramed, -graming** or **-grammed, -gram·ming.** —*n.* special data in the memory of a computer, used as part of a more complex program or to control the operations of a subordinate computer. —*v.t.* to provide (a computer) with a microprogram: *A given microprogrammed machine may be easily adjusted to duplicate the characteristics of another machine, so that programs written in machine language for other computers can be handled without reprogramming* (Introduction to Programming).

min·i·state (min′ē stāt), *n.* a very small country, especially one of the recently established independent small states of Africa or Asia: *South Africa's economic predominance radiates from here to the three ministates of Botswana, Lesotho and Swaziland* (New York Times).

Ms. (miz), abbreviated title used instead of *Miss* or *Mrs.*: *Unliberated honorifics like "Mrs." and "Miss" are replaced by the noncommittal "Ms."* (Time).

my·o·e·lec·tric (mī′ō i lek′trik), *adj.* using electric currents produced by muscular contraction to actuate movement of an artificial limb, such as an arm or a hand. [< *myo-* + *electric*]

N

ngwee (əŋ gwē′), *n.* a monetary unit of Zambia, worth about 1½ cents.

nu·cle·o·syn·the·sis (nü′klē ō sin′thə sis, nyü′-), *n.* the process by which chemical elements are created: *Further points in favour of lunar water, free or combined, are that the universe consists practically entirely of hydrogen and helium—hydrogen being the starting material for nucleosynthesis in stars—and that oxygen is now known to be abundant in the Moon's crust* (Science Journal).

O

OD, *n., v.,* **OD'd, OD'ing.** *Slang.* —*n.* an overdose of a narcotic, especially in reference to a person who has taken an overdose: *"When I was shooting up . . . I liked to hear about the ODs, and I'd think I was brave for taking it"* (Time). —*v.i.* to become sick or die from an overdose of a narcotic.

o·lig·o·mer (ō lig′ə mər), *n.* a chemical compound with a few recurring subunits (in contrast with a polymer with many recurring subunits and a monomer with no recurring subunits). [< *oligo-* few + *-mer,* as in *polymer*]

P

pa'an·ga (pä äng′gə), *n.* the monetary unit of Tonga, worth about $1.10.

paper gold, a monetary reserve from which a nation may draw credit in proportion to its contribution to the International Monetary Fund. Its special drawing rights provide a supplement to real gold and currencies: *When it was first proposed that the world's reserves be supplemented by new drawing rights in the IMF—a matter of giving the fund the right to print "paper gold" in carefully controlled quantities . . .* (Manchester Guardian Weekly).

participatory democracy, active participation in public demonstration to achieve some right or protest an injustice: *But those who practice this "participatory democracy" can ultimately achieve their objectives only if they work through electoral processes and win control of Congress and the Presidency* (New York Times).

per·i·ap·sis (per′ē ap′sis), *n.* the point in the orbit of a satellite body closest to the center of the heavenly body around which it is orbiting. [< *peri-* near + *apsis* orbit]

phase·down (fāz′doun′), *n.* the gradual reduction of a program or operation: *I believe we should proceed with our phasedown forthwith and carry it through expeditiously to completion—that is, until all U.S. Army, Navy, Marine Corps and Air Force personnel, except Embassy guards, are out of Vietnam* (Matthew B. Ridgway).

phase-locked (fāz′lokt′), *adj.* operating in precise synchronization (with).

plat·form (plat′fôrm), *n.* **9.** a navigation system or radio-signal device to determine location.

po·le·mol·o·gy (pō lə mol′ə jē), *n.* the study of war: *Students of polemology will not find anything startlingly original . . . His thesis is that America should not disarm since "the war system" is necessary to preserve her social and political stability* (London Sunday Times). [< Greek *pólemos* war + *-logy* study]

pole position, an advantageous position: *The German company retained a pole position in hormone research which led to the Pill* (London Sunday Times).

power structure, 1. the institutions and groups that make up or control a society, especially as they determine the character or nature of a society: *You struggle to make it as a person—not a white or a Negro—in the white world, inside the white power structure, and then you go back to the ghetto when you're in a position to do something* (Maclean's). **2.** the ruling circle of any institution: *Massell countered with charges of antisemitism and claimed that his opponents were members of a business "power structure" trying to keep control of Atlanta* (Gene Stephens).

Q

quan·ta·some (kwän′tə sōm), *n.* one of the granules containing chlorophyll found inside the chloroplast of plant cells. [< *quanta* (plural of *quantum* smallest unit of energy) + *-some* body]

R

ra·di·o·e·col·o·gy (rā′dē ō i kol′ə jē), *n.* the study of radioactivity in the environment and its effect on plants and animals, especially in a particular locality.

re·jas·ing (rē jā′sing), *n. U.S. Slang.* the act or practice of putting rubbish or discarded items to useful purpose: *The biggest benefit of rejasing is that virtually indestructible objects never reach the garbage heap* (Time). [< *re*using *j*unk *as* something else]

remote sensing, observation or scanning, especially of natural features, from a great distance by means of radar, aerial infrared photography, seismography, and similar techniques: *A remote-sensing satellite could provide information on vegetation, soil, and water infinitely faster and often more accurately than ground observation* (Robert B. Rathbone).

ret·ro·re·flec·tor (ret′rō ri flek′tər), *n.* a prismlike device that reflects a laser beam, and is designed for placement on a distant object, such as a heavenly body, to calculate its distance from the earth by measuring the time elapsed to reflect a beam of light.

revenue sharing, *U.S.* the distribution among local governments, especially the State governments, of a part of the revenue from Federal taxes.

S

S.D.R., Special Drawing Rights.

sen·gi or **sen·ghi** (sen′gē), *n. pl.* or *sing.* a unit of money in the Republic of Zaire equal to 1/100 of a likuta.

shatter cone, a cone-shaped rock fragment with distinctive ridges, produced by intense shock forces.

sick-out (sik′out′), *n.* an organized absence of employees from their jobs on the pretext of being sick, to avoid the legal penalties that may result from a formal strike.

space shuttle, a space vehicle to transport men and material to a space station: *Unlike the cone-shaped Apollo vehicles, which are not maneuverable in the atmosphere, the space shuttle will be capable of controlling where and how it lands* (Science News).

Special Drawing Rights, a monetary reserve of the International Monetary Fund from which member nations may draw credit in proportion to their contribution to the Fund: *The new special drawing rights were intended to supplement, not supplant, gold and foreign exchange* (Manchester Guardian Weekly).

street Christian, *U.S.* one of the Jesus people: *Many prefer to be called street Christians . . . they are the latest incarnation of that oldest of Christian phenomena: footloose, passionate bearers of the Word* (Time).

street people, a term for hippies or others who have rejected traditional social values including homes, so that they are usually found congregating on streets, in parks, and other public places: *At Berkeley an angry confrontation erupted over the university's decision to fence in a two-block, off-campus area which radical elements and "street people" had turned into a people's park* (Fred M. Hechinger).

strong force, the force that causes neutrons and protons to bind in the nucleus of an atom. It is stronger than any other known force and is probably interactive in meson coupling. *Knowledge of the internal structures of the proton and the neutron may provide the key to understanding the "strong" force that holds the atomic nucleus together and endows the universe with its stability* (Scientific American).

structural gene, a gene that controls the sequence of amino acids and three-dimensional shape of proteins.

su·per·plas·tic (sü′pər plas′tik), *n.* a plastic material, especially a metal, that is unusually pliable at an elevated temperature. The grain is so fine that atoms slip easily along crystal planes without cleavage. *This metal, after treatment which reduces the grain size to about a micrometre, behaves like a superplastic at room temperature—it can be stretched by a factor of about 10 in one direction without breaking* (New Scientist). *—adj.* of or characteristic of a superplastic: *Some alloys, when deformed at certain rates and in certain temperature ranges, can stretch out like chewing gum and be tremendously deformed without breaking. This superplastic behavior is being studied . . . to put it to industrial use* (O. Cutler Shepard). *Superplastic cars should be quieter, and their scrap value far higher than that of steel cars* (London Times).

T

tel·e·di·ag·no·sis (tel′ə dī′əg nō′sis), *n.* a medical diagnosis by telemetry. The diagnosis is made from readings of instruments before a doctor, while the data is transmitted over radio or telephone circuits from sensors connected to a patient who may be many miles away.

thrust stage, a theatrical stage extending into the auditorium, with seats surrounding the stage on three sides.

time reversal, a principle in physics which postulates that if the time in which a sequence of operations occurs is reversed, the same sequence will occur again but in the reverse order: *Another symmetry consideration is that of "time reversal." This notion says in effect that a motion-picture film of any process should show the system appearing to obey the same laws of physics whether the film is run forward or backward* (Scientific American).

Tom[2], *U.S. —n.* an Uncle Tom (used in an unfriendly way). *—v.i.* to be or act like an Uncle Tom (used in an unfriendly way): *She was an absolutely direct black woman. No Tomming, not a shade of the phony to her* (New Yorker).

Tom·ism (tom′iz əm), *n. U.S.* Uncle Tomism: *One could always hustle the world, could con it, or adopt some form of Tomism, but was there a way of really making it without pretending that one was white?* (Harper's).

trans·earth (tranz ėrth′), *adj.* in or toward the earth, especially of a spacecraft returning to earth: *trans-earth trajectory.*

trans·plant·ate (trans plan′tāt), *n.* an organ or section of tissue that has been transplanted, especially from one person to another: *. . . for heart or kidney transplants . . . far more than the mere physical structure of the transplantate is required* (Science Journal).

tri·jet (trī′jet′), *n.* an aircraft with three jet engines.

U

Un·cle-Tom (ung′kəl tom′), *v.i.,* **-Tommed, -Tom·ming,** to act as an Uncle Tom (often used in an unfriendly way): *Married or not, for sexual reasons or social ones, most women still find it second nature to Uncle-Tom* (Time).

ur-, *prefix.* original or earliest, as in *ur- performance.* [< German *ur-* primitive, original]

urb (ėrb), *n.* a large urban area; megalopolis: *The growth of American suburbia, fed by the yearning for a home of one's own, raises problems for urb and suburb alike* (New York Times). [shortened for *urban*]

ur·text (ůr′tekst′), *n.* the original text: *This is the last word on Feuerfest, unless someone produces an urtext containing Strauss's own marginalia on the subject* (Saturday Review).

V

vir·i·on (vir′ē ən), *n.* a virus particle consisting of RNA enclosed in a protein shell and capable of controlling the form of a virus in replication: *. . . in certain tumour-producing viruses the first two steps may be reversed and it is RNA from the virus chromosome or virion which makes DNA* (Science Journal).

W

water bed, a bed with a mattress consisting of a vinyl bag filled with water and usually equipped with a temperature-control device.

weak force, the force that governs the interaction of neutrinos. It is probably interactive in fermion coupling and causes some radioactive decay. *The weak force is only a trillionth as strong as electromagnetism. But feeble as it is, the weak force is still a trillion trillion trillion times stronger than gravity* (Tom Alexander).

work·fare (wėrk′fãr′), *n.* a welfare program in which recipients of public welfare payments are required to work at assigned jobs: *One of Evers' programs is what he calls workfare; he has said that everybody ought to work for what he gets, that welfare ought to exist only for those who can't work or for whom no jobs can be made available* (Harper's).

Y

yen·ta (yen′tə), *n. U.S. Slang.* a female gossip or busybody. [< Yiddish *yente,* originally a woman's name]

Z

ze·ner diode (zē′nər), a silicon semiconductor used as a voltage stabilizer. [< Clarence *Zener,* an American physicist]

zero population growth, the condition in which a population ceases to grow and a balance is reached in the average number of births and death: *How attainable is zero population growth in the U.S.? That is, what would have to happen to bring the net reproduction rate to 1.0?* (Scientific American).

Section Six

Index

How to Use the Index

This index covers the contents of the 1971, 1972, and 1973 editions of THE WORLD BOOK YEAR BOOK.

Each index entry is followed by the edition year (in *italics*) and the page numbers, as:

BURMA, *73*–247, *72*–255, *71*–236

This means that information about Burma begins on the pages indicated for each of the editions.

An index entry that is the title of an article appearing in THE YEAR BOOK is printed in capital letters, as: **AUTOMOBILE.** An entry that is not an article title, but a subject discussed in an article of some other title, is printed: **Pollution.**

The various "See" and "See also" cross references in the index list are to other entries within the index. Clue words or phrases are used when two or more references to the same subject appear in the same edition of THE YEAR BOOK. These make it easy to locate the material on the page, since they refer to an article title or article subsection in which the reference appears, as:

Unemployment: Brazil, *73*–244; Canada, *73*–253

The indication "*il.*" means that the reference is to an illustration only. An index entry in capital letters followed by "*WBE*" refers to a new or revised WORLD BOOK ENCYCLOPEDIA article that is printed in the supplement section, as:

BICYCLE, *WBE, 73*–586

A

C

D

E

F

G

H

M

N

Q

R

S

T

U

V

Acknowledgments

The publishers acknowledge the following sources for illustrations. Credits read from left to right, top to bottom, on their respective pages. An asterisk (*) denotes illustrations created exclusively for THE YEAR BOOK. All maps, charts, and diagrams were prepared by THE YEAR BOOK staff unless otherwise noted.

3	Gilbert L. Meyers*
8	Pictorial Parade; Wide World; Wide World
9	Frederic Ohringer from Nancy Palmer; Wide World
10-11	Wide World
12	Wide World; Pictorial Parade; Pictorial Parade
13	Gerold Jung, Expression; Wide World; Fred Ward, Black Star
14	Wide World
16-17	David Hurn*; United Press Int.; WideWorld; G.Guillaume, Magnum; United Press Int.; Wide World; Wide World
18-19	Wide World
20	United Press Int.
21	Wide World
22-23	Robert Isear*; Jim Garrett, *New York Daily News;* Wide World; Wide World; Bernard Gotfryd, *Newsweek;* Wide World; Wide World; Bay Area Rapid Transit
24	Gilbert L. Meyers*
25	United Press Int.
26-27	Wide World
28	Robert Isear*
29	Bob Brigham, *Life* © Time Inc.; Charles McCormish, *Erie Times-News;* Jeff Lowenthal; Fred Sweets; Leviton-Atlanta
30	WORLD BOOK photo*
32	Pictorial Parade
34-35	Photoreporters; Gene Trindl*; Allis-Chalmers Corporation; Lee Balterman*; Dennis Brack, Black Star; National Coal Association
36	Baldev*
37	Universal Science News Service, Inc.
38	British Information Service
39	Gilbert L. Meyers*
40	Dan Budnik*; Ralph Crane, *Life* © Time Inc.; Dave Dedio, *Miami Herald;* Lynn McLaren, Rapho Guillumette; Boris Spremo, *Toronto Daily Star;* © 1972 *Instructor* Magazine. Used by permission.
42	Bob East
43	John R. Hamilton, Globe
44	The Johns Hopkins University
45	Direk Halsted, *Time* © Time Inc.
46-47	Jack Manning, *The New York Times;* Dan Budnik*; Wide World; Wide World; Rogers, Cowan & Brenner, Inc.; Boyd Lewis, Jr.; Steve Schapiro, Transworld Feature Syndicate Inc.; Wide World
48	Wide World
49	From Stanley Kubrick's *A Clockwork Orange.* Released by Warner Bros.
50	Copyright © 1972 by Paramount Pictures Corporation. All rights reserved.
52	Rich Clarkson; John Dominis, *Life* © Time Inc.; Micha Bar-Am; Wide World; John Zimmerman, *Life* © Time Inc.
53	J. R. Eyerman*
54-55	Wide World
56	Pictorial Parade
58	Franklin McMahon, Jr.
61-62	D. R. Baston, FIA†
65	Richard G. Rawlings, FIA†; Richard G. Rawlings, FIA†; D. R. Baston, FIA†
66	Franklin McMahon, Jr.
67	Franklin McMahon, Jr.; Franklin McMahon, Jr.; D. R. Baston, FIA†
68-71	Jay H. Matternes*
72	Franklin McMahon, Jr.
74	Richard G. Rawlings, FIA†; D. R. Baston, FIA†; Richard G. Rawlings, FIA†; D. R. Baston, FIA†; D. R. Baston, FIA†; Franklin McMahon, Jr.; D. R. Baston, FIA†; D. R. Baston, FIA†
79-86	Franz Altschuler*
88	Supreme Court of the United States
90-91	Franz Altschuler*
94-95	Marilyn Hammersley-Houlberg
96-97	Ken Heyman
98	Peter Turner; Georg Gerster, Rapho Guillumette
100-101	Anne Marie Picou, A.A.A. Photo
116	Kirk Breedlove, Photophile; Reine Turner, DPI
117	Marc & Evelyne Bernheim, Rapho Guillumette; James Pickerell, Black Star; R. Strange, Carl E. Östman; Victor Engelbert, Black Star
118-119	Ken Heyman
121-123	Marilyn Hammersley-Houlberg
124	Ken Heyman
125	Victor Engelbert, Black Star; Steve Heyneman
126-127	Abbas, Black Star; Donald McCullin, Magnum
128	Marc & Evelyne Bernheim, Woodfin Camp, Inc.; Victor Engelbert, Black Star; Marc & Evelyne Bernheim, Woodfin Camp, Inc.; Marc & Evelyne Bernheim, Woodfin Camp, Inc.; Ian Berry, Magnum
130-131	Burt Glinn, Magnum; Marc & Evelyne Bernheim, Woodfin Camp, Inc.
132	Marilyn Hammersley-Houlberg; Ian Berry, Magnum; Marc & Evelyne Bernheim, Woodfin Camp, Inc.
133	Ken Heyman; Marilyn Hammersley-Houlberg; Ian Berry, Magnum
134	Ken Heyman
135	Marilyn Hammersley-Houlberg; Marc & Evelyne Bernheim, Woodfin Camp, Inc.; Steve Heyneman
136	Ian Berry, Magnum
138	Gilbert L. Meyers*
141	Gilbert L. Meyers*; Illinois Secretary of State
143	Gilbert L. Meyers*; Science Research Associates, Inc.
144	Gilbert L. Meyers*
146	Science Research Associates, Inc.
147	Gilbert L. Meyers*
150	Mas Nakagawa*; Culver; LC††; Lawrence Fried, Magnum; Werner Wolff, Black Star; LC††; Bettmann Archive; Romaine Photography; Bettmann Archive; NOW†††; LC††; LC††; Wide World; Michael Ginsburg, Magnum
153	Mas Nakagawa*; Brown Bros.; Gilbert L. Meyers*
155	Mas Nakagawa*; NOW†††; NOW†††; Gilbert L. Meyers*; NOW†††; NOW†††
156	Mas Nakagawa*; Bettmann Archive; Wide World; Lawrence Fried, Magnum; LC††; Lawrence Fried, Magnum
158	Mas Nakagawa*; U.S. Dept. of Defense; U.S. Dept. of Defense; Wyoming State Archives and Historical Department; U.S. Dept. of Defense
159	Mas Nakagawa*; Werner Wolff, Black Star; LC††
161	Ken Regan, Camera 5
164-165	J. Allan Cash from Photri; Earl Keith from Nancy Palmer
166	Brown Bros.
167	Burt Glinn, Magnum; Steven Alman, Black Star
168	Culver
169	R. Välme from Carl Östman; D. Gorton, Woodfin Camp, Inc.; Curt Gunther, Camera 5
170	Leonard Freed, Magnum; Brown Bros.
171	R. Välme from Carl Östman
173	Charles Harbutt, Magnum; *Chicago Sun-Times;* Charles Gatewood, Magnum
174	Raghubir Singh, Woodfin Camp, Inc.
175	Hiroji Kubota, Magnum
176	*Chicago Sun-Times;* Earl Keith from Nancy Palmer; Richard Balagur from Nancy Palmer; *Chicago Sun-Times*
179	Steven Altman, Black Star; Peter Marteus from Nancy Palmer
181-191	Hogan Smith, Prescott College
195	The Advertising Council, Inc.
196	Wide World
201	Bob Brigham, *Life* © Time Inc.
204	Simonpietri, Gamma
207	University of Michigan Medical Center
208	University of Pennsylvania
209-210	Ezra Stoller, American Institute of Architects
211	Sovfoto
213	Wide World
214	Frederic Ohringer from Nancy Palmer
215	William Mauldin, © 1972 *Chicago Sun-Times*
219	NASA
220	Wide World
222	Gilbert L. Meyers*

†Foundation for Illinois Archaeology

††Library of Congress

†††National Organization for Women

225 Barton Silverman, *The New York Times*
226 Wide World
230 Penny Tweedie
234-235 Wide World
236 *Los Angeles Times*
239 Oak Ridge National Laboratories
240 United Press Int.
245 Gerold Jung, Expression
246 Intercontinental Hotels
249 Wide World
250 Progressive-Conservative Party Headquarters
253 Wide World
254 United Press Int.
257 Agencia-JB
261-263 Wide World
264-265 United Press Int.
266 Wide World
267 Office of Public Services, Boston
268 United Press Int.
270 Wide World
273 Bell Telephone Laboratories
274 James Pickerell
278 Wide World
279 Washington Star Syndicate, permission granted by King Features Syndicate
281 National Park Service
282 Wide World
284 Don Wright, *The Miami News*
285 Wide World
286 George Tames, *The New York Times*
287 Wide World
288 Simonpietri, Gamma
291 Martha Swope, *Time* © Time Inc.
292-295 Wide World
296 Wide World; United Press Int.; Wide World
297 Wide World; © National Geographic Society; Wide World
298 Wide World
299 Philippe Halsman; WORLD BOOK photo*; Wide World
300-301 Wide World
302 Pictorial Parade; Wide World
305 Ken Feil, *The Washington Post*
306 Enrique Ponce de Leon, *El Sol De Mexico*
307 Wide World
308 William Mauldin, © 1972 *Chicago Sun-Times*
311 Fred Sweets
312 Charles McCormish, *Erie Times News*
315 Wide World
317 Joe Clark
318 Declan Haun, Smithsonian Institution
320 Pat Oliphant, © *The Denver Post.* Reprinted with permission of Los Angeles Times Syndicate.
321 Steve Northup
322 Wide World
324 Ragen Precision Industries, Inc.
325 *The New York Times*
329 Photoreporters
330 Per-Olof Odman
332-333 A. S. Norsk Telegrambyra
334-338 Wide World
339 Robert R. McElroy, *Newsweek*
341 Wide World
342 YEAR BOOK photo*
343 William Mauldin, © 1972 *Chicago Sun-Times*
344 Fred Stein, *Chicago Daily News*
348 Gamma
349 Loomis Dean, *Time* © Time Inc.
351 American Museum of Natural History
352 United Press Int.
354-355 Wide World
356-357 Pictorial Parade
358 E. Hamilton-West, *The Guardian*
359 Pictorial Parade
360 The Klistron Agency
362 Wide World
363 Photo-Tanjug
364 Chuck Kirman, *Chicago Sun-Times*
365 Wide World
367 Lee Balterman, *Life* © Time Inc.
370 Wide World
371 Pictorial Parade
372 Wide World
375 Stendig Inc.
376 Sovfoto
378 Chapelle from Monkmeyer
379-383 Wide World
386 Salisbury/Lee, *The New York Times*
388 Merkle Press
391 Organization of American States
396 Jack Dykinga, *Chicago Sun-Times*
397 United Press Int.
399 Jill Krementz
401 Wide World
402 From Leonard Baskin's *Hosie's Alphabet.* Publisher: Viking Press
403 From N.M. Bodecker's *Miss Jaster's Garden.* Publisher: Western Publishing Co.
404 From Tana Hoban's *Count and See.* Publisher: The Macmillan Co.
408 Wide World
409 Pictorial Parade
411 Michael Mauney, *Life* © Time Inc.
413 Pennsylvania Hospital, Philadelphia, Pa.
414 Patricia N. Farnsworth
417 Wide World
418-419 *The New York Times*
421 *Israel Sun*
422 Jeff Lowenthal
424 Steve Schapiro, Transworld Feature Syndicate Inc.
425 Allied Artists-ABC Picture Presentation
426 © AMPAS
427 Wide World
428 Boyd Lewis, Jr.
430 Wide World; John White, *Chicago Daily News*
432 U.S. Army
433-436 Wide World
437 Dukes, *The New York Times*
439 Hubert le Campion, *Life* © Time Inc.; Wide World; Wide World
440 John Fischetti, © 1972 *Chicago Daily News*
441 Gilles Peress, Magnum
445 Wide World
446 Wide World; Rich Clarkson
447 Wide World; Wide World; Rich Clarkson; Wide World; Wide World
454 United Press Int.
455-461 Wide World
462 Eastman Kodak Company
463 Argonne National Laboratory
465 Bernard Gotfryd, *Newsweek*
470-471 Wide World
472 United Press, Int.
474 Wide World
476 Tony Rollo, *Newsweek*
478 United Press Int.
480 Wide World
482 United Press Int.
483 Wide World
484 Fred Ward, Black Star; Wide World
485 Leviton-Atlanta
486 Pictorial Parade
487 United Press Int.
489 Wide World
490 United Press Int.
491 Valtman, *Hartford Times*
494-499 Wide World
502-503 NASA
505 Wide World
506 NASA
507 Wide World
508 Barton Silverman, *The New York Times*
510 American Philatelic Research Library
511 Jesse Birnbaum, *Time* © Time Inc.
513 Wide World
515 United States Steel Corporation
518-520 Wide World
523 NBC-TV; © BBC
524-525 Pictorial Parade
526 Friedman-Abeles
528 Solters/Sabinson/Roskin Inc.
529 Wide World
531 Bay Area Rapid Transit
533 Robert Walker, *The New York Times*
534-537 Wide World
539 United Nations
546 Sovfoto
547 Wide World
548 United Press Int.
549 Gilbert L. Meyers*
551 Gary Gulliver, *The New York Times*
555 Wide World
557 Agencia-JB
558 Gilbert L. Meyers*

A Preview of 1973

January

S	M	T	W	T	F	S
	1	2	3	4	5	6
7	8	9	10	11	12	13
14	15	16	17	18	19	20
21	22	23	24	25	26	27
28	29	30	31			

1 **New Year's Day.**

3 **93rd Congress** convenes for first session.

6 **Epiphany,** 12th day after Christmas, celebrates visit of the Three Wise Men.

19 **Robert E. Lee's Birthday,** celebrated as a legal holiday in most Southern states.

21 **Jaycee Week** through January 27, marks founding of Jaycees.
World Religion Day, emphasizes need for world religious unity.

30 **Holiday of the Three Hierarchs.** Eastern Orthodox holy day, commemorating Saints Basil, Gregory, and John Chrysostom.

February

S	M	T	W	T	F	S
				1	2	3
4	5	6	7	8	9	10
11	12	13	14	15	16	17
18	19	20	21	22	23	24
25	26	27	28			

1 **National Freedom Day.**
American Heart Month through February 28.
Boy Scouts of America Anniversary Celebration through February 28.

2 **Ground-Hog Day.** Legend says six weeks of winter weather will follow if ground hog emerges to see its shadow.

3 **Chinese New Year,** begins year 4671 of the ancient Chinese calendar, the Year of the Ox.

12 **Abraham Lincoln's Birthday,** celebrated in 26 states.

14 **Saint Valentine's Day,** festival of romance and affection.

15 **Susan B. Anthony Day,** commemorates the birth of the suffragist leader.

17 **National FFA Week,** through February 23, publicizing the role of Future Farmers of America in U.S. agriculture.

18 **Brotherhood Week** to February 25.

19 **George Washington's Birthday,** according to law, is now legally celebrated by federal employees and the District of Columbia on the third Monday in February, not on the actual anniversary, the 22nd. Forty-two states also follow this practice.

March

S	M	T	W	T	F	S
				1	2	3
4	5	6	7	8	9	10
11	12	13	14	15	16	17
18	19	20	21	22	23	24
25	26	27	28	29	30	31

1 **Easter Seal Campaign** through April 22.
Red Cross Month through March 31.

2 **World Day of Prayer.**

4 **Save Your Vision Week** to March 10.

6 **Mardi Gras,** last celebration before Lent, observed in New Orleans and many Roman Catholic countries.

7 **Ash Wednesday,** first day of Lent, the penitential period that precedes Easter.
Volunteers of America Week through March 13.

11 **Girl Scout Week,** through March 17, marking 61st birthday of U.S. Girl Scouts.

17 **St. Patrick's Day,** honoring the patron saint of Ireland.

18 **Camp Fire Girls Birthday Week,** to March 24, marks 63rd birthday of the organization.
Purim, commemorates the saving of Jews through the death of the ancient Persian despot Haman.

20 **First Day of Spring,** 1:13 P.M., E.S.T.

April

S	M	T	W	T	F	S
1	2	3	4	5	6	7
8	9	10	11	12	13	14
15	16	17	18	19	20	21
22	23	24	25	26	27	28
29	30					

1 **April Fools' Day.**
Cancer Control Month through April 30.

8 **National Boys' Club Week** through April 14.
Pan American Week through April 14.
National Library Week through April 14.

15 **Palm Sunday,** marks Jesus' final entry into Jerusalem along streets festively covered with palm branches.
Holy Week, through April 21, commemorates the Crucifixion and Resurrection of Jesus Christ.

17 **Passover,** or Pesah, first day, starting the 15th day of the Hebrew month of Nisan. The eight-day festival celebrates the deliverance of the ancient Jews from bondage in Egypt.

19 **Maundy Thursday,** celebrates Christ's injunction to love each other.

20 **Good Friday,** marks the death of Jesus on the cross. It is observed as a public holiday in 17 states.

22 **Easter Sunday,** commemorating the Resurrection of Jesus Christ.

27 **National Arbor Day.**

29 **Daylight Saving Time Begins** at 2 A.M. in most of the United States.

30 **Walpurgis Night,** according to legend the night of the witches' Sabbath gathering in Germany's Harz Mountains.

May

S	M	T	W	T	F	S
		1	2	3	4	5
6	7	8	9	10	11	12
13	14	15	16	17	18	19
20	21	22	23	24	25	26
27	28	29	30	31		

1 **May Day,** observed as a festival of spring in many countries.
Law Day, U.S.A.
Mental Health Week through May 7.

6 **National Music Week** through May 12.

13 **Mother's Day.**

14 **Salvation Army Week** through May 20.

19 **Armed Forces Day.**

22 **National Maritime Day.**

28 **Indianapolis 500-Mile Race** in Indianapolis, Ind.
Memorial Day, according to law, is the last Monday in May.

31 **Ascension Day,** 40 days after Easter Sunday, commemorating the ascent of Jesus into heaven.

June

S	M	T	W	T	F	S
					1	2
3	4	5	6	7	8	9
10	11	12	13	14	15	16
17	18	19	20	21	22	23
24	25	26	27	28	29	30

1 **Stratford Festival,** drama and music, Ontario, Canada, through October 31.

2 **Queen's Official Birthday,** marked by trooping of the colors in London.

6 **D-Day,** commemorates the day the Allies landed to assault the German-held continent of Europe in 1944.
Shabuot, Jewish Feast of Weeks, marks the revealing of the Ten Commandments to Moses on Mt. Sinai.

10 **National Flag Week** through June 16.
Whitsunday, or Pentecost, the seventh Sunday after Easter, commemorating the descent of the Holy Spirit upon Jesus' 12 apostles.

14 **Flag Day,** commemorates adoption of the Stars and Stripes in 1777 as the official U.S. flag.

17 **Father's Day.**

21 **First Day of Summer,** 8:01 A.M., E.S.T.

27 **Freedom Week** through July 4.

A Preview of 1973

July

S	M	T	W	T	F	S
1	2	3	4	5	6	7
8	9	10	11	12	13	14
15	16	17	18	19	20	21
22	23	24	25	26	27	28
29	30	31				

1 **Dominion Day** (Canada), celebrates the confederation of the provinces in 1867.
Battle of Gettysburg commemorative ceremonies in Gettysburg, Pa., through July 7.

4 **Independence Day,** marks Continental Congress's adoption of Declaration of Independence in 1776.

14 **Bastille Day** (France), commemorates popular uprising against Louis XVI in 1789 and seizure of the Bastille, the infamous French prison.

15 **Saint Swithin's Day.** According to legend, if it rains on this day, it will rain for 40 days.
Captive Nations Week through July 21.

20 **Moon Day,** the anniversary of man's first landing on the moon in 1969.

26 **Salzburg International Music and Drama Festival,** Salzburg, Austria, through August 30.

August

S	M	T	W	T	F	S
			1	2	3	4
5	6	7	8	9	10	11
12	13	14	15	16	17	18
19	20	21	22	23	24	25
26	27	28	29	30	31	

1 **Boy Scouts of America National Jamboree** through August 9.

7 **Tishah B'ab,** Jewish fast day, on ninth day of Hebrew month of Ab, marking Babylonians' destruction of the First Temple in Jerusalem in 587 B.C.; Roman destruction of the Second Temple in A.D. 70; and Roman suppression of Jewish revolt in 135.

14 **V-J Day** (original), marks Allied victory over Japan in 1945.

15 **Feast of the Assumption,** Roman Catholic and Eastern Orthodox holy day celebrates the ascent of the Virgin Mary into heaven.

19 **National Aviation Day.**
Edinburgh International Festival, music, drama, and film, through September 8.

26 **Women's Liberation Day,** commemorating the ratification of the 19th Amendment, giving women the vote.

September

S	M	T	W	T	F	S
						1
2	3	4	5	6	7	8
9	10	11	12	13	14	15
16	17	18	19	20	21	22
23	24	25	26	27	28	29
30						

3 **Labor Day** in the United States and Canada.

12 **Harvest Moon,** the full moon nearest the autumnal equinox of the sun, shines with special brilliance for several days and helps farmers in the Northern Hemisphere to get more field work done after sunset.

16 **Constitution Week,** through September 22, commemorating signing of U.S. Constitution in Philadelphia, on Sept. 17, 1787.

17 **Citizenship Day.**

22 **First Day of Autumn,** 11:21 P.M., E.S.T.

27 **Rosh Hashanah,** or Jewish New Year, the year 5734 beginning at sunset. It falls on the first day of the Hebrew month of Tishri and lasts for two days.

28 **American Indian Day,** honoring native Americans.
Ramadan begins, the ninth month of the Moslem calendar, observed by fasting.

October

S	M	T	W	T	F	S
	1	2	3	4	5	6
7	8	9	10	11	12	13
14	15	16	17	18	19	20
21	22	23	24	25	26	27
28	29	30	31			

6 **Yom Kippur,** or Day of Atonement, most solemn day in the Jewish calendar, marking the end of the period of penitence.

7 **National Employ the Physically Handicapped Week** through October 13.
National 4-H Week through October 13.
Fire Prevention Week through October 13.

8 **Thanksgiving Day,** Canada.
Columbus Day commemorates Columbus' discovery of America in 1492. Previously celebrated on October 12.
Child Health Day.

9 **Leif Ericson Day,** honoring early Norse explorer of North America.

11 **Sukkot,** or Feast of Tabernacles, begins the nine-day Jewish observance, which originally celebrated the end of harvest season.

14 **National Y-Teen Week** through October 20.

15 **National Cleaner Air Week** through October 21.

21 **American Education Week** through October 27.

22 **Veterans Day,** observed on the fourth Monday in October.

28 **Daylight Saving Time Ends** and standard time resumes at 2 A.M.

31 **Halloween,** or All Hallows' Eve.
Reformation Day, celebrated by Protestants, marks the day in 1517 when Martin Luther nailed his Ninety-Five Theses of protest to the door of a church in Wittenberg, Germany.
United Nations Children's Fund (UNICEF) Day.

November

S	M	T	W	T	F	S
				1	2	3
4	5	6	7	8	9	10
11	12	13	14	15	16	17
18	19	20	21	22	23	24
25	26	27	28	29	30	

1 **All Saints' Day,** observed by the Roman Catholic Church.

5 **Guy Fawkes Day** (Great Britain) marks the failure of a plot to blow up King James I and Parliament in 1605 with ceremonial burning of Guy Fawkes in effigy.

6 **Election Day.**
Christmas Seal Campaign through December 31.

7 **Anniversary of 1917 Bolshevik Revolution,** Russia's national holiday, through November 8.

12 **National Children's Book Week** through November 18.

22 **Thanksgiving Day.**

December

S	M	T	W	T	F	S
						1
2	3	4	5	6	7	8
9	10	11	12	13	14	15
16	17	18	19	20	21	22
23	24	25	26	27	28	29
30	31					

2 **Pan American Health Day.**
Advent, first Sunday in the month-long Christian season preceding Christmas.

6 **Saint Nicholas Day,** observed in parts of Europe by the giving of gifts.

10 **Human Rights Week** through December 16.

11 **Nobel Peace Prize Presentation,** in Stockholm, Sweden.

15 **Bill of Rights Day,** marks the ratification of that document in 1791.

20 **Hanukkah,** or Feast of Lights, Jewish holiday beginning on the 25th day of the Hebrew month of Kislev and lasting eight days, celebrates the Jewish defeat of the Syrian tyrant Antiochus IV in 165 B.C. and the rededication of The Temple in Jerusalem.

21 **First Day of Winter,** 7:08 P.M., E.S.T.

25 **Christmas.**

31 **New Year's Eve.**